REAL AND PER CAPITA DATA

LESS	EQUALS	LESS: PERSONAL OUTLAYS			EQUALS	PERCENT OF DISPOSABLE PERSONAL INCOME			Gross national product		Disposable personal income		
						Personal outlays			Current prices	1958 prices	Current prices	1958 prices	
Personal tax and nontax payments	Disposable personal income	Total	Personal consumption expenditures	Interest paid by consumers	Personal saving	Total	Personal consumption expenditures	Personal saving	Per capita dollars	Billions of dollars	Per capita dollars	Billions of dollars	
Billions of dollars						Percent							
2.6	83.3	79.1	77.2	1.5	4.2	95.0	92.7	5.0	846	204	683	150	1929
2.5	74.5	71.1	69.9	.9	3.4	95.4	93.8	4.6	734	184	605	138	1930
1.9	64.0	61.4	60.5	.7	2.6	95.9	94.4	4.1	610	169	516	134	1931
1.5	48.7	49.3	48.6	.5	− .6	101.3	99.8	− 1.3	464	144	390	114	1932
1.5	45.5	46.5	45.8	.5	− .9	102.0	100.6	− 2.0	442	142	362	112	1933
1.6	52.4	52.0	51.3	.5	.4	99.3	98.0	.7	514	154	414	120	1934
1.9	58.5	56.4	55.7	.5	2.1	96.3	95.2	3.7	566	170	459	132	1935
2.3	66.3	62.7	61.9	.6	3.6	94.6	93.3	5.4	644	193	518	148	1936
2.9	71.2	67.4	66.5	.7	3.8	94.7	93.4	5.3	700	203	552	153	1937
2.9	65.5	64.8	63.9	.7	.7	98.9	97.6	1.1	652	192	504	144	1938
2.4	70.3	67.7	66.8	.7	2.6	96.3	95.0	3.7	690	209	537	156	1939
2.6	75.7	71.8	70.8	.8	3.8	94.9	93.6	5.1	754	227	573	166	1940
3.3	92.7	81.7	80.6	.9	11.0	88.2	86.9	11.8	933	264	695	190	1941
6.0	116.9	89.3	88.5	.7	27.6	76.4	75.7	23.6	1,170	298	867	213	1942
17.8	133.5	100.1	99.3	.5	33.4	75.0	74.4	25.0	1,402	337	976	223	1943
18.9	146.3	109.1	108.3	.5	37.3	74.5	74.0	25.5	1,518	361	1,057	232	1944
20.9	150.2	120.7	119.7	.5	29.6	80.3	79.7	19.7	1,514	355	1,074	230	1945
18.7	160.0	144.8	143.4	.8	15.2	90.5	89.6	9.5	1,474	312	1,132	227	1946
21.4	169.8	162.5	160.7	1.1	7.3	95.7	94.6	4.3	1,605	310	1,178	218	1947
21.1	189.1	175.8	173.6	1.5	13.4	92.9	91.8	7.1	1,757	324	1,290	230	1948
18.6	188.6	179.2	176.8	1.9	9.4	95.0	93.8	5.0	1,719	324	1,264	231	1949
20.7	206.9	193.9	191.0	2.4	13.1	93.7	92.3	6.3	1,877	355	1,364	250	1950
29.0	226.6	209.3	206.3	2.7	17.3	92.4	91.0	7.6	2,128	383	1,469	256	1951
34.1	238.3	220.2	216.7	3.0	18.1	92.4	90.9	7.6	2,200	395	1,518	263	1952
35.6	252.6	234.3	230.0	3.8	18.3	92.8	91.1	7.2	2,284	413	1,583	275	1953
32.7	257.4	241.0	236.5	4.0	16.4	93.6	91.9	6.4	2,246	407	1,585	278	1954
35.5	275.3	259.5	254.4	4.7	15.8	94.3	92.4	5.7	2,408	438	1,666	297	1955
39.8	293.2	272.6	266.7	5.4	20.6	93.0	91.0	7.0	2,492	446	1,743	309	1956
42.6	308.5	287.8	281.4	5.8	20.7	93.3	91.2	6.7	2,575	452	1,801	316	1957
42.3	318.8	296.6	290.1	5.9	22.3	93.0	91.0	7.0	2,569	447	1,831	319	1958
46.2	337.3	318.3	311.2	6.5	19.1	94.4	92.3	5.6	2,731	476	1,905	333	1959
50.9	350.0	333.0	325.2	7.3	17.0	95.1	92.9	4.9	2,788	488	1,937	340	1960
52.4	364.4	343.3	335.2	7.6	21.2	94.2	92.0	5.8	2,830	497	1,984	351	1961
57.4	385.3	363.7	355.1	8.1	21.6	94.4	92.2	5.6	3,001	530	2,065	367	1962
60.9	404.6	384.7	375.0	9.1	19.9	95.1	92.7	4.9	3,118	551	2,133	381	1963
59.4	438.1	411.9	401.2	10.1	26.2	94.0	91.6	6.0	3,292	581	2,283	408	1964
65.7	473.2	444.8	432.8	11.3	28.4	94.0	91.5	6.0	3,520	618	2,436	435	1965
75.4	511.9	479.3	466.3	12.4	32.5	93.6	91.1	6.4	3,806	658	2,604	459	1966
83.0	546.3	506.0	492.1	13.2	40.4	92.6	90.1	7.4	3,985	675	2,749	478	1967
97.9	591.0	551.2	536.2	14.3	39.8	93.3	90.7	6.7	4,295	707	2,945	499	1968
116.5	634.4	596.2	579.5	15.8	38.2	94.0	91.3	6.0	4,590	726	3,130	514	1969
116.6	691.7	635.5	617.6	16.8	56.2	91.9	89.3	8.1	4,769	723	3,376	535	1970
117.5	746.0	685.8	667.2	17.7	60.2	91.9	89.4	8.1	5,099	745	3,603	555	1971
142.2	797.0	747.2	726.5	19.7	49.7	93.8	91.2	6.2	5,533	790	3,816	578	1972
152.9	882.6	828.7	805.0	22.5	53.8	93.9	91.2	6.1	6,123	837	4,195	608	1973

CONTEMPORARY ECONOMICS

Second Edition

CONTEMPORARY ECONOMICS

SECOND EDITION

MILTON H. SPENCER

Professor of Economics

School of Business Administration

Wayne State University

WORTH PUBLISHERS, INC.

Contemporary Economics, Second Edition

Copyright © 1971, 1974 by Milton H. Spencer

All rights reserved. No part of this publication

may be reproduced, stored in a retrieval system,

or transmitted in any form or by any means,

electronic, mechanical, photocopying, recording,

or otherwise, without the prior written

permission of the copyright holder.

Printed in the United States of America

Library of Congress Catalog Card No. 73-89305

ISBN: 0-87901-031-2

Designed by Malcolm Grear Designers

Second printing, May 1974

Worth Publishers, Inc.

444 Park Avenue South

New York, New York 10016

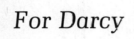

For Darcy

Preface

Economics is exciting and important. Anyone who thinks otherwise has failed to realize that economic ideas and practices have moved men to rebellion, and nations to war. All the great issues that confront us today—among them recessions, inflation, poverty, racial discrimination, urban blight, and ecological decay—have economic roots. In order to diagnose and cure these ailments, we must first understand their complex nature.

DISTINGUISHING FEATURES

In this book I have tried to convey a vivid sense of the pertinence and importance of economics by presenting a balanced treatment of theory, problems, and policies. A list of special features will best convey the ways in which this balance is achieved.

Organization

The sequence of topics is from macro to micro. Although the coverage is comprehensive, I have tried throughout to be concise. I believe that most instructors will find the book comfortable to teach from and easily adaptable to both long and short courses.

Exhibits, Boxed Essays, and Photographs

A great many charts, tables, and illustrations are employed—considerably more than are found in most texts. Short boxed essays are used to highlight important ideas and to provide pleasant but pertinent diversions. In addition, photographs, both historical and current, have been included where they are particularly useful in providing an appreciation of institutions, events, and situations.

Leaders in Economics—Historical and Contemporary

Essays on many of the great economists of the past and present are introduced at appropriate places (topically, not chronologically) throughout the book. These essays are primarily substantive, not biographical; they stress the individual's main ideas and contributions as they relate to the chapter in the text, thus providing brief but interesting side trips into the history of economic thought.

Issues and Cases

Optional issues and case problems involving topics of current interest are presented at the ends of selected chapters and parts. Each issue and case concludes with several questions. Some of the questions involve discussion; others require pencil-and-paper computation, graphing, and problem-solving. All provide excellent vehicles for oral or written analysis.

References and Reading Suggestions

The use of footnote commentaries and references has been avoided in order to maintain an informal style. In their place, a substantial bibliography with many annotations is provided at the end of the book. These sources have been carefully selected for their accessibility and readability. Instructors at both large and small institutions report that most of the books and articles are available in their college libraries and that students find the sources useful.

Dictionary

All technical terms and concepts are defined when they are first introduced. These expressions, and many others not mentioned in the text, are catalogued in a complete dictionary containing nearly 500 entries at the back of the book. The text can thus serve as a convenient and permanent source of reference—not only for this course, but for future courses that may be taken in economics, business administration, and the social sciences.

SUPPLEMENTS AND TEACHING AIDS

A complete set of additional materials is available with the text. The supplementary items include:

Student Study Guide

The second edition is completely rewritten to stress concepts. Each chapter corresponds to a chapter in the text and includes the following:

☐ A concise list of the concepts to be learned.

☐ Fill-in questions that focus on the definitions and key terms and concepts.

☐ Problems, many of which are analytical, requiring graphing or simple computation.

☐ Self-tests, both true-false and multiple-choice.

☐ Behavioral objectives—what the students should be able to do in each chapter.

☐ Questions for discussion.

☐ Answers to the fill-in questions, problems, and all self-test questions are provided at the end of each chapter.

Teaching Aids

A complete set of pedagogical aids is available to the instructor, including a *Teacher's Manual*, special examination materials, and *Transparency Masters* which are suitable for reproduction.

THE SECOND EDITION

Although the structure of the book remains the same, more than 50 percent of this edition is either entirely new or has been revised from the previous edition. Some topics which users felt were unnecessary were dropped, and much new material has been added. All of the figures have been redrawn, making more creative use of color. All in all, there is hardly a chapter that has gone without change—thanks to the suggestions of numerous instructors.

For example, large sections and entire chapters deal with such *new* or *substantially revised* topics as:

graphs—a complete unit on how to construct and interpret them, including straight lines and curves (Chapter 1).

the scientific method—a discussion with applications to economic reasoning (Chapter 1).

goals and resources of our economy—a fuller analysis of objectives, technical and institutional constraints, and a more comprehensive treatment of production-possibilities curves (Chapter 2).

capitalism and our mixed economy—a more extensive theoretical and critical analysis, plus two- and three-sector circular flow charts (Chapter 3).

supply and demand models—a more concise discussion, with welfare implications of a pure market system (Chapter 4).

income and wealth distribution—a new chapter, with many new facts and data, plus theories of distribution and a simple geometric method of measuring inequality (Chapter 5).

social responsibility of business—part of a new chapter, with arguments pro and con, and proposed reforms (Chapter 6).

public and social goods—part of a new chapter, with a survey of theoretical concepts in terms of supply and demand models and incremental analysis (Chapter 7).

taxation—a fuller treatment of theories, loopholes, and equity considerations (Chapter 7).

national income—a more complete discussion of both GNP and GNI, and implications for measuring social welfare (Chapter 8).

inflation—modern views on anticipated vs. unanticipated price changes, and the calculation of gains and losses for net debtors and creditors (Chapter 9).

Phillips curves—a more complete discussion of theoretical issues and long-run shifts (Chapters 9, 17).

income and employment theory—a substantially fuller treatment, with comprehensive new diagrams (Chapters 10, 11).

our monetary and banking system—all institutional material placed in one chapter (Chapter 13).

commercial banking—a new treatment of money creation and contraction, extensively illustrated with T-accounts (Chapter 14).

bank portfolio management—a new discussion of financial theory, problems, and goals of commercial banks, with implications for the economy (Chapters 14, 17).

monetary theory and interest rates—part of a new chapter on Fisher's and Keynes' theories, with modern interpretations for public policy, and the economic importance of real vs. market interest rates (Chapter 16).

macroeconomic equilibrium—a new chapter integrating macro theory with simple, diagrammatic illustrations (Chapter 16).

economic stabilization—a concluding macro chapter discussing recent monetarist and fiscalist viewpoints, with implications for public policy (Chapter 17).

perfect competition—a fuller treatment of partial and general equilibrium, and consequences in terms of social welfare (Chapter 24).

monopoly—a revised discussion with greater emphasis on pricing, discrimination, and social welfare considerations (Chapter 25).

marginal productivity and factor pricing—a more concise treatment with fewer and simpler diagrams (Chapters 27, 28).

equilibrium models—part of a new chapter on stability problems and on statics and dynamics, with illustrations in terms of supply and demand (Chapter 29).

general equilibrium and welfare economics—a new chapter integrating many micro concepts in a supply and demand framework, plus welfare criteria, Pareto optimality, and the meaning of economic efficiency (Chapter 29).

business and government; labor—a substantially shorter treatment with less description (Chapters 30, 31).

insecurity and poverty—a shorter and more analytical treatment, including both market and nonmarket approaches to overcoming poverty (Chapter 32).

urban problems—a more analytical discussion of housing problems and related issues (Chapter 33).

international economics—an updated discussion of world trade and financial problems, including international turmoil through the early 1970s (Chapters 34, 35, 36).

Russia and China—a review of their economic plans and progress through the early 1970s (Chapter 39).

In addition to this new and revised material, instructors will be interested to know that the book abounds with numerous new supplementary topics —including principles and analytical techniques— developed in the form of chapter-end questions, issues, and cases. Some of these supplementary topics require simple computation, graphing, and problem-solving. Students can thus become more deeply involved in the learning process by "practicing economics" and by putting ideas to work, rather than merely reading about them.

MILTON H. SPENCER
Detroit, Michigan
January, 1974

Acknowledgments

It is a pleasure to acknowledge the help and co-operation I have received in the preparation of this book.

A particularly grateful expression of thanks goes to Roger Beardwood, a distinguished economic commentator and Paris correspondent for *Time* magazine (formerly with the London *Financial Times* and *Fortune* magazine). He edited the entire manuscript and made numerous suggestions for improvement.

Luigina D'Onofrio typed a substantial portion of the material and was helpful in many other ways.

Over the life of this book, I have benefited greatly from the advice and criticisms of hundreds of dedicated teachers and scholars. Unfortunately, I cannot list them all. However, it is a privilege to mention the names of those who made substantial contributions to this edition, thank them for their comments, and absolve them of any shortcomings in the final product.

JOHN R. AIDEM, Miami-Dade Junior College
CARL J. AUSTERMILLER, Oakland Community College
CHARLES A. BENNETT, Gannon College
HAROLD BLACK, University of Florida
GEORGE S. BOHLER, Florida Junior College at Jacksonville
DENNIS L. BREEDEN, University of Tennessee
ROBERT C. BUSHNELL, Wayne State University
RALPH T. BYRNES, Clemson University
CHARLES C. COX, Ohio State University
J. RONNIE DAVIS, University of Florida
ABDEL MONEM FAREED, University of Tennessee at Nashville
JAMES P. FORD, Mt. San Antonio College
DAVID A. HUETTNER, Wayne State University
SOL D. KAUFLER, Los Angeles Pierce College
BRUCE KIMZEY, New Mexico State University
BARBARA KNEESHAW, Wayne County Community College
HOU-SHUN LIEU, SUNY Agricultural and Technical College

ALLAN MANDELSTAMM, Michigan State University
THOMAS MAYER, University of California, Davis
WALTHER P. MICHAEL, Ohio State University
HERBERT MILIKIEN, American River College
DWIGHT PERKINS, Harvard University
TODD SANDLER, Arizona State University
GENE R. SCHWAB, Mankato State University
RICHARD U. SHERMAN, JR., Ohio State University
WILLIAM O. SHROPSHIRE, Emory University
VIVIAN SMARGON, Wayne County Community College
ANTHONY H. STOCKS, Youngstown State University
MYRA H. STROBER, University of Maryland
GEORGE A. SPIVA, University of Tennessee at Knoxville
OBIE G. WHICHARD, University of Georgia

Contents in Brief

Contemporary Issues and Cases

Contents

xx   Contents

Suggested Outlines for One-semester Courses

These recommendations are flexible. Many other chapter combinations are possible.

Chapter topic	Macro-economic Emphasis	Micro-economic Emphasis	Balanced Macro/Micro Emphasis	Problems and Policy Emphasis
1. Economics: What Is It All About?	○	○	○	○
2. Resources and Goals of Our Economic System	○	○	○	○
3. Capitalism and Our Mixed Economy	○	○	○	○
4. The Laws of Supply and Demand	○	○	○	○
5. Households: Distribution of Income and Wealth		⊡		⊡
6. Businesses: Organization, Size, Social Responsibility		□		⊡
7. Government: Functions, Social Goods, Taxation	⊡		⊡	
8. National Income and Product	□		□	□
9. Economic Instability: Unemployment and Inflation	□		□	□
10. Consumption, Saving, Investment	□		□	□
11. Income and Employment Determination	□		□	□
12. Fiscal Policy and the Public Debt	□		□	□
13. Our Monetary and Banking System	□		□	□
14. Commercial Banking: Money Creation, Portfolio Management	□		□	□
15. Central Banking: Monetary Management and Policy	□		□	□
16. Money, Interest, and Macroeconomic Equilibrium	□			
17. Economic Stabilization: Coordination and Conflict	□		□	□
18. Explanations of Economic Growth	⊡		⊡	
19. Problems of Economic Growth				
20. Ecology and the Economics of Pollution				⊡
21. Supply, Demand, and Elasticity	○	○	○	○
(can follow Chapter 4 if desired)				
22. Utility and Consumer Demand				
23. Costs of Production		□	□	
24. Perfect Competition		□	□	
25. Monopoly Behavior		□	□	
26. Imperfect Competition		□	□	
27. Factor Markets: Marginal Productivity		⊡		
28. Determination of Factor Prices		⊡		
29. Stability, General Equilibrium, and Welfare Economics		□	□	
30. Business and Government		□		⊡
31. Labor Unions and Industrial Relations		□		⊡
32. Insecurity and Poverty		⊡		⊡
33. City and Suburb				⊡
34. International Trade	⊡			
35. International Finance	□			
36. International Policies	□			⊡
37. Less Developed Countries				⊡
38. Understanding Socialism and Communism		□		⊡
39. Command Economies: Russia and China				⊡

○ = Common core of chapters
□ = Chapters for kinds of emphasis desired
⊡ = Optional topic, time permitting

PART 1

The Problem and
Its Setting

CHAPTER 1

Economics: What Is It All About?

CHAPTER PREVIEW

What is economics? Why should you study it?

Is economics theoretical? Is it practical?

What kinds of errors must you watch for in reasoning about economic problems?

This is a book about a subject that has a long and curious history. The ideas of economics have swayed the minds of kings and presidents, statesmen and politicians, philosophers and laymen. Its principles and practices have shaped the domestic and foreign policies of nations as well as the everyday lives of their citizens. Over its hundreds of years of existence, the discipline of economics has attracted its fair share of brilliant minds, but has also experienced no shortage of crackpots and cranks. Perhaps most significant, economics is an activity in which nearly everyone is engaged but about which relatively few have any knowledge.

Today, such knowledge is more vitally needed than ever before. For economics is concerned with most of the complex issues of modern society—such things as inflation, unemployment, and poverty; pollution, urban decay, and shortages of raw materials; taxes, monopoly, and the role of government. Everyone is affected by these matters. Every day we are asked to express an opinion on them, sometimes by voting, but more often by taking part in a discussion or evaluating a current government proposal or news item. We are flooded with information and advice, some of it right and much of it wrong.

Economics helps us to form valid opinions about these crucial problems. It does not provide a fixed set of rules that guarantees solutions; no discipline or book can do that. Instead, economics provides a body of knowledge, a way of thinking, and some useful tools for understanding and coping with many of society's ills.

The Meaning of Economics

Experts in any area, from anthropology to zoology, are usually reluctant to define their field for fear of what their definition might omit. Nevertheless, students beginning the study of a subject like to have a concise description of its nature and content. Here is a modern definition of economics:

Economics is a social science concerned chiefly with the way society chooses to employ its limited resources, which have alternative uses, to produce goods and services for present and future consumption.

More specifically, economics describes and analyzes the nature and behavior of an economy. The word "economy" comes from the Greek *oikonomia*, which means the management of a household or state. We say that someone is economical when he is frugal in the expenditure of money or in the utilization of materials. When we speak of an economy (whether it be the American or the Russian economy, the economy of New England or of Chicago) we are referring to the ways in which a community manages its limited resources.

In economics we explore the ways in which economic systems of different types—whether capitalistic, communistic, or socialistic—organize their limited human and material resources to meet people's individual wants for such things as food, clothing, shelter, recreation, and the myriad other goods that people buy; and society's collective wants for such things as education, transportation, and sanitation. To put it in a nutshell, *economics is broadly concerned with the efficient production and delivery of a standard of living.*

To say that resources are limited means simply that people want more goods and services than there are means—human labor, machines, natural resources—to produce them. An economy's resources are therefore *scarce* relative to society's demands, and people must choose the most effective ways of utilizing those limited resources.

The forces that determine how those choices are made will occupy much of our attention. We shall learn how economic systems cope with the problems of what, how much, and for whom society's limited human and material resources should be used to produce the goods that are wanted.

What is an economic system? Every economy operates within a framework of rules and regulations. Public utilities must establish their rates with the approval of government agencies; restaurants have to be licensed in order to sell food; doctors must be graduates of approved medical schools if they are to practice medicine; sellers of commodities are legally forbidden to engage in false advertising. These are only a few of the many rules that exist in our economy. All of the laws, regulations, customs, and practices taken together, and their relationships to the components of an economy—its firms, households, and government—constitute an *economic system*.

ECONOMICS IS A SOCIAL SCIENCE

Is economics a science or an art? A dictionary will tell you that "science" involves the accumulation, classification, and systematization of knowledge for the purpose of discovering fundamental principles or the operation of general laws. "Art," in the sense used here, pertains to the skillful execution of a task or the application of a procedure. In the final analysis, economics is concerned with both the scientific development of economic principles and their artful application to the solution of real-world problems. Hence, economics is both a science and an art; it is a science in its methodology and an art in its application.

Since economics deals with the activities of society, it is a *social* science intimately related to other social or behavioral sciences—history, political science, psychology, and sociology. It deals with human behavior, with the ways in which people (consumers, workers, businessmen, and other economic decision makers) may be expected to react under given conditions. But conditions do not always remain constant for a long enough time to permit expected results to be realized. As a consequence, economic policies must often be revised as conditions—political and social as well as economic—change, and as new information becomes known.

WHY STUDY ECONOMICS?

Economics is for people who like to climb mountains. This book will guide you to the foothills, but the climb will be up to you. When you reach the peak and look back, you will see many intriguing and challenging questions. Here are a few examples:

☐ Why is the American standard of living among the highest in the world, while poverty exists in many areas of the country?

☐ What will business conditions be like next year, and what should the government do—if anything—to alter them?

☐ How do changes in tax rates, the supply of money in the economy, or the level of interest rates affect businessmen's decisions to produce commodities or to build new factories? Do these decisions also affect consumers? Lenders? Workers?

☐ Do capitalistic countries have to experience sharp changes in their levels of income and employment? Do socialistic countries avoid these problems and thereby experience stability in their economies?

☐ Within the framework of democratic free enterprise, is it possible to have the best of all economic worlds: a healthy rate of economic growth with continuous full employment, stable prices, and an equitable distribution of income and wealth?

In economics, asking good questions rates almost as high as answering them. Some of the questions may not mean very much to you now. However, the purpose of this book is to help you think about and discuss such problems intelligently.

The questions above indicate that, contrary to some people's beliefs, economics is not a study of how to get rich quick or a guide for becoming a success in business. Economics is concerned with the way in which the economy functions—and with the steps that can be taken to improve its performance. However, economics is also concerned with business behavior and government policy. Therefore, if you end up in the business world, or in government, or in one of the professions, you may come to feel that a familiarity with basic economics has made you better at your job than you would otherwise have been. But in any case, whatever career you pursue, a knowledge of economics will make you a more effective citizen, and this alone justifies the time devoted to its study.

Microeconomics and Macroeconomics

Economists traditionally divide the study of economics into two broad categories: microeconomics and macroeconomics.

Microeconomics is concerned with the specific economic units or parts that make up an economic system and the relationships between these parts. In microeconomics, emphasis is placed on understanding the behavior of individual firms and households and the ways in which such entities interact.

Macroeconomics is concerned with the economy as a whole or large segments of it. In macroeconomics, attention is focused on such problems as the level of unemployment, the rate of inflation, the nation's total output of goods and services, the ways in which government raises and spends money, and other matters of economy-wide significance.

In short, microeconomics examines the trees, whereas macroeconomics studies the forest. Both microeconomics and macroeconomics involve the construction of theories and formulation of policies. In view of this, a few words about the meaning of theory and policy are appropriate.

REASONING WITH THEORIES AND MODELS

Economics, like every science, deals with the study of relationships between variables and with the formulation of theories about those relationships. At one time it was popular to call a relationship a *hypothesis* if there was no evidence to support it, a *theory* if there was some evidence in its favor, and a *law* or *principle* if it was certain. But scientists no longer emphasize these distinctions. They know that a sensible hypothesis cannot be made about a subject of which one is completely ignorant, and that no scientific law is ever certain. As a result, it is now quite usual for "theory," "law," and "principle" to be used synonymously in scientific discussions.

The Elegance of Theory

One of the highest compliments you can pay an economist (or any scholar for that matter) is to say that his theory is "elegant" or "beautiful." The notion of what constitutes beauty may be as hard to define in a theory as it is in a pretty girl. All it really means is that the ideas which make up the theory are interesting, and they are woven together in a harmonious way.

However, the elegance of a theory is also affected by the quality of its structure—that is, the elements of which it is composed. Basically, every theory consists of three sets of elements:

1. Definitions, which state clearly the meaning of the various terms in the theory.

2. Assumptions, which define the conditions under which the theory holds.

3. Hypotheses, which serve as working guesses about the way things actually behave, or about relationships between things in the real world. (In economics, the "things" about which hypotheses might be formulated include consumers, workers, businessmen, investors, government, households, business firms, and other economic entities).

The quality and usefulness of a theory depend on the way its elements are structured. In a general sense:

A *theory* is a set of definitions, assumptions, and hypotheses put together in a manner that expresses apparent relationships or underlying principles of certain observed phenomena in a meaningful way. The construction of useful theories is one of the chief goals of all scientists.

A theory may be stated in the form of a model. A *model* is a representation of the essential features of a theory or of a real-world situation. It may be expressed in the form of words, diagrams, tables of data, graphs, mathematical equations, or any combinations of these. A model is easier to manipulate than the reality it represents, because only the *relevant* properties of reality are presented. A road map, for example, is a model of a portion of the earth's surface, but it does not show vegetation or climatic variations because these are not relevant to its purposes. A model of a business firm, when it is constructed by an accountant, is quite different in nature and purpose from one constructed by an economist.

A theory or model, since it is a simplification of reality, usually fits the observed facts approximately rather than exactly. Hence the theory may fail to incorporate newly discovered facts, in which case it may have to be revised or perhaps discarded. In physics, for example, Einstein's theory of relativity has revised and partly replaced Newton's model. Similarly, new economic theories have revised and replaced older ones.

POSITIVE AND NORMATIVE ECONOMICS

When an economist steps out of the realm of economic theory, he enters the world of economic policy. This means he has shifted his emphasis from *positive economics*, which concerns what *is*, to *normative economics*, which concerns what *ought to be*.

If you and I disagree over positive statements, we should be able to settle our controversy by logical thinking and an appeal to the facts. But if we disagree over normative statements, we are disagreeing over value judgments—statements about what is "good" and what is "bad," what is "right" and what is "wrong." We may not be able to reach an agreement because our views are based on a complex mixture of philosophical, social, and cultural factors.

The question, "How much should the government spend, holding tax rates constant, in order to keep unemployment from rising to more than 4 percent of the labor force?" is positive because the answer can be tested by empirical research. However, the statement, "Unemployment should be a problem of greater concern than inflation" is normative, and the question, "Should we have more economic freedom or more government regulation?" is a normative question.

Most of the questions and problems in economics deal with positive rather than normative matters. But many normative questions pertaining to economic policy are of enormous significance. Indeed, the normative issues are sometimes the most interesting and exciting parts of the discipline.

Reasoning and Logical Thinking

In economics, as in our daily lives, logical reasoning plays an important role. We draw conclusions about ourselves, about others, about important events that have happened or are expected to happen, and about the state of the world. Obviously we want our conclusions to be reliable, and we realize that they may not be if they are not based on a critical examination of available evidence and an exploration of alternative interpretations of the facts. Therefore, an examination of the reasoning process—especially the means of arriving at scientific conclusions—should be of interest, and it is particularly appropriate before launching into the study of economics.

FORMS OF LOGICAL REASONING

Reasoning is a highly complex mental process which has long occupied the attention of psychologists. What do we mean by reasoning? It may be regarded as a special kind of thinking—one in which conclusions or inferences are drawn from premises. The process may take two forms: one is called induction, the other, deduction.

Induction

Induction is a method of reasoning from specific facts to general conclusions. This form of thinking guides the choices we make in our daily lives. We "learn from experience" by classifying particular observations or events and then discovering how they lead to a generalization. Subsequent observations or experiences may tend to confirm the generalization, or they may show it to be false. If the latter occurs, the generalization will have to be modified in order to be "logical," that is, to be justified by all of the information that is known. In either case, the specific facts lead to the general conclusion. Here are some examples of inductive reasoning:

1. The sun rose today.
   The sun has risen every day for as long as anyone knows.
   Therefore the sun will rise tomorrow.

2. In a study of headache remedies, we conducted a random survey of 30 percent of the doctors practicing in Chicago.
   Seventy percent of the doctors surveyed said that they prefer our brand to plain aspirin.
   Therefore we may assume that about 70 percent of all doctors in Chicago prefer our brand to plain aspirin.

3. Tax increases take purchasing power away from consumers, thereby reducing their spending.
   Therefore tax increases are an effective means of curbing inflation.

These examples show that inductive reasoning develops patterns of reality by inferring facts from other facts. It sometimes happens, however, that patterns are broken, or what was thought to be a pattern turns out to be a coincidence of facts. In such cases, the inductive generalizations lead to false conclusions. To avoid such errors, we need to ask three basic questions:

1. Are the facts *representative*? Is the generalization based on typical cases or are there some significant exceptions?

2. Is the evidence *sufficient*? Are there enough facts or observations to permit a conclusion to be drawn with confidence?

3. Are there *alternative explanations*? Is the conclusion the only logical one, or can alternative generalizations be made with equal logic?

Deduction

Induction may be described as a process of "leading up." Deduction has the opposite meaning—"leading down." More precisely, *deduction* may be defined as reasoning from general premises to specific conclusions. The general premises are statements which are believed to be true and relevant to a particular problem. If the reasoning is correct, the premises will force a *valid* conclusion. Incorrect reasoning, on the other hand, will result in an *invalid* conclusion. Here are some examples of valid deductive reasoning:

1. All businessmen seek to maximize profits.
   Mr. X is a businessman.
   Therefore Mr. X seeks to maximize profits.

2. Measures that reduce unemployment are desirable.
   Military conscription reduces unemployment.
   Therefore military conscription is desirable.

3. Inflation and unemployment cannot rise simultaneously.
   The economy is experiencing a rise in inflation.
   Therefore unemployment is not rising.

It is interesting to note that a conclusion may be *valid* without being *true*. In the above examples, the conclusions are logically valid; but whether or not they are true depends on demonstrating that their premises are true. In all three examples at least one of the two premises is either doubtful or untrue; hence each of the conclusions is questionable.

We can now appreciate the basic difference between deductive and inductive reasoning. In the deductive method, if the premises are true, and we are sure that our reasoning is accurate, we can be certain that the conclusion is true. In the inductive method, if the facts are correct, and we are sure that our reasoning is accurate, the most we can say is that the conclusion is probably true.

Which of these forms of reasoning do economists use? The answer is both, depending on the kinds of problems with which they are dealing. There will be many examples in future chapters where these approaches are illustrated and evaluated in some detail.

THE SCIENTIFIC METHOD

Science must begin and end with facts, regardless of what theories it builds in between. This means that the scientist first observes the real world. Then by induction he proceeds from factual knowledge to the formation of theories which provide general descriptions of reality. Next he makes predictions by deducing particular conclusions from his general statements or theories. Then he verifies his predictions by checking them against the facts. Finally he decides whether to retain the theory, to revise it, or to abandon it in favor of a new one.

This technique is called the *scientific method*. It consists of induction, deduction, and verification, carried on in an unending cycle. The result is an expanding and self-correcting body of knowledge. The scientific method—which is employed not only in economics, but also in all of the social and physical sciences—can be outlined in six steps.

1. *Recognition and definition of a problem.* The world that the scientist observes consists of an infinite number of facts and events. When he encounters an obstacle, he tries to put it in a form in which he can deal with it intelligently. He does this by isolating and limiting the range of his inquiry. In this way he uses *reason* to identify the problem so that he can attempt to solve it. At this stage, therefore, the scientist's attention is focused on asking the right questions.

2. *Observation and collection of data.* All scientists need data—hard facts. Economists may obtain them from sources such as government agencies, research bureaus, trade associations, business firms, newspapers, magazines, and professional journals. The investigator may also obtain his own data, perhaps by conducting surveys or experiments.

3. *Organization or classification of data.* After the data are collected, they must be ordered and arranged into groups or classes in ways that allow analyses and comparisons to be made. The soundness of this procedure will have a major influence on the usefulness of the results. Description and classification are thus essential to science, because they provide the basis for *explanation*, which is the ultimate goal.

4. *Formulation of hypotheses.* The way in which something is explained depends upon the conceptual relationships that are attached to it. Thus when the facts have been organized and classified, the scientist formulates an *hypothesis*—a working guess or tentative statement about the behavior of things, usually stated in the form of an "if-then" proposition. For example: "*If* the price of bread falls while all other factors affecting the consumption of bread remain the same, *then* the amount of bread purchased will increase." This hypothesis offers a ten-

tative explanation of a possible relationship between the price of bread and the amount of bread that people will purchase. It also states the conditions that must prevail, and the observations that are needed in order to verify the original tentative statement.

5. *Deductions or predictions from hypotheses.* The fundamental characteristic of a science is the establishment of hypotheses from which relationships between the things being investigated can be deduced or inferred. When one can say, if A, then B, one has a statement of cause and effect—a scientific law. The advantage of a scientific law is that it permits prediction and, hopefully, control. For unless one knows what "causes" a particular phenomenon, one cannot influence its occurrence.

6. *Testing and verification of hypotheses.* The scientist is now ready to turn again to the facts and see whether his specific prediction is right. If it is not, he may formulate another hypothesis and repeat the process. Ultimately, his hypothesis, if it is to be scientifically acceptable, must not only meet the test of experience, it must also be *consistent* with hypotheses that have been established and verified by others.

Common Fallacies or Mistakes in Reasoning

"He who enlists a man's mind wields a power even greater than the sword." This familiar quotation, although centuries old, is particularly pertinent to economics. The ideas of economists, whether they are right or wrong, can sometimes shape and sway the world. Indeed the ideas of some economic philosophers have helped to undermine governments and to inspire revolutions—both intellectual and bloody. It follows that if the pen can in fact be mightier than the sword, the ability to reason correctly is necessary to avoid pitfalls in economic thinking.

You will encounter the word "fallacy" in at least two different ways. In everyday conversation, it designates any mistaken idea or false belief, like the "fallacy" of believing that all people are sincere. But in a stricter sense "fallacy" means an error in reasoning or argument. Of course, an argument may be so incorrect that it deceives no one. But for our purposes it seems more useful to reserve the term "fallacy" for certain types of arguments which, although incorrect, are nevertheless persuasive. By familiarizing yourself with the following typical fallacies in economic thinking you will be able to pinpoint the errors in other people's reasoning as well as your own.

Fallacy of False Cause (*Post Hoc Ergo Propter Hoc* **Fallacy**)

Every science tries to establish cause-and-effect relationships. The fallacy of false cause, or the so-called *post hoc* fallacy (after the Latin expression *post hoc ergo propter hoc*, which means "after this, therefore because of this"), is often encountered in such efforts. This fallacy is committed when a person mistakenly assumes that because one event follows another, or both events occur simultaneously, one is the cause and the other the effect.

The fallacy of false cause may be illustrated by the following "if-then" form of argument, or variation of it:

If A occurs, then B occurs.
Therefore A causes B.

Is this good grounds for concluding that A causes B? Not necessarily. There are other possible explanations:

B may occur by chance.

B may be caused by factors other than A (or by a third factor C which is a common cause of both A and B).

B may cause A.

Some possibilities are illustrated in the following examples:

EXAMPLE 1. Company X hired a new sales manager and the firm's sales soared during the ensuing year.

Therefore, the growth in sales was due to the new sales manager.

This argument is obviously a "false cause" or *post hoc* fallacy. It fails to point out that although some of the growth in sales may be due to the manager's efforts, much or even most of it may be the result of lower prices, higher incomes of buyers, a larger number of buyers in the market, or other factors that affect the demand for the company's product.

EXAMPLE 2. The severity of hay fever varies inversely with the price of corn. That is, the lower the price of corn, the greater the severity of hay fever and vice versa.

Therefore, the price of corn is the cause of hay fever.

It is indeed true that the price of corn and the severity of hay fever are inversely related. However, the fact is that ragweed is a cause of hay fever, and the summer conditions that will produce a bumper crop of ragweed—high temperatures and adequate rainfall—will also produce a bumper crop of corn and hence usually a lower price of corn. Thus it may *seem* as if corn prices affect hay fever; in reality these factors are independent of each other and there is a third factor which is a common cause of both.

Fallacious relationships such as these frequently occur in economics. Since they are not often apparent, a careful study of the subject is necessary before we can learn to recognize such errors and to avoid the fallacy of "false cause."

Fallacy of Criticizing the Man (*ad Hominem* **Fallacy**)

The *ad hominem* fallacy is committed when, instead of trying to disprove the truth of an assertion, one attacks the person who made the assertion. This amounts to criticizing the individual instead of his ideas. Hence the full Latin name of this fallacy is *argumentum ad hominem*, the literal translation of which is "argument directed to the man."

To argue in this way is fallacious because a man's personal character or circumstances are logically irrelevant to the truth or falsehood of his statements or the correctness or incorrectness of his views. Of course, such arguments may often persuade, but they will do so for emotional rather than logical reasons.

Thus, to argue that an economic policy is bad or wrong *solely* because it was proposed by a liberal or by a conservative, by a union leader or by a manager, by a white or by a black, by a Democrat or by a Republican, is to commit the *ad hominem* fallacy. A man's proposals should be judged on their own merits, independent of his political or social beliefs or his economic circumstances.

Fallacy of Appeal to the People (*ad Populum* Fallacy)

The *ad populum* fallacy, the complete Latin name of which is *argumentum ad populum*, is frequently employed as an emotional appeal "to the people" or "to the gallery" for the purpose of arousing the feelings and enthusiasm of the multitude. It is widely used by propagandists, demagogues, editorialists, and politicians to mobilize public sentiment for or against a particular measure—without presenting reliable evidence upon which to base a rational argument.

The *ad populum* fallacy is often encountered in advertising. If consumers buy a product because the maker advertises "10 million housewives can't be wrong," they are succumbing to the *ad populum* fallacy. General acceptance of an idea or widespread assent to a claim does not prove it to be true.

Fallacy of Appeal to Authority (*ad Verecundiam* Fallacy)

The fallacy of appeal to authority occurs when one attempts to support a conclusion by seeking the endorsement of a person who is *not* an authority on the subject. If a friend of yours supports his views on economics solely by saying that his uncle, a prominent businessman, agrees with them, he may be committing the fallacy of *argumentum ad verecundiam*. However, if your friend's uncle, aside from being a successful businessman, has investigated the issue carefully and objectively before coming to a conclusion, the argument may be correct.

The basic question, of course, is what makes a person an "authority" in a particular field. His education and experience are factors to consider; recognition and acceptance by other professionals in the field is another test. Despite these tangible criteria, students sometimes accept an economic conclusion simply because they "read it in the paper" or because some self-proclaimed "expert" said it was true.

The most valuable lesson you can learn from your first course in economics is the habit of thinking for yourself, analytically and critically, about economic issues.

Fallacy of Special Pleading

When someone gives only the reasons which support his views, he is committing the fallacy of special pleading. This fallacy is illustrated by the following paragraph from a newspaper editorial:

Gambling should be legalized in our state just as it is in Nevada. This would encourage more tourists to visit and spend their money here, and the state would benefit from a rich source of new revenue. Further, these increased revenues could be used to finance the construction of new schools and hospitals, thus providing some relief for citizens who are now paying for these items through various local and state taxes.

This argument fails to take into account the economic reasons for *not* legalizing gambling. For example, law-enforcement agencies might have to be expanded, and new administrative facilities established to supervise gambling. Further, undesirable moral implications might be attached to legalized gambling. All of these are costs to the community because of their adverse effects on society. Thus there are usually many sides to an argument, and all should be evaluated before a judgement is made.

Fallacies of Composition and Division

Two fallacies are involved here. The *fallacy of composition* is committed when one reasons that what is true of the parts of a whole is also true of the whole. An example would be to argue that since individuals A, B, C, D . . . are excellent ball players, a team composed of these individuals is sure to win the championship. The error in this reasoning, of course, is based on the fact that a successful team requires its members to be not only good players, but also able to work well together as a group.

The converse of the fallacy of composition is the fallacy of division. The *fallacy of division* is committed when one contends that something which is true only of the whole is also true of its parts taken separately. Thus you would be committing the fallacy of division if you inferred that because a certain book is difficult to understand, every paragraph or page is difficult to understand.

The following *true* statements illustrate some situations in economics that can seem contradictory if you are not wary of the fallacies of composition and division:

1. In a recession it may be desirable for a family to increase its savings by cutting down on its consumption expenditures. However, if all families do this, spending in the economy will decline, the level of total income will fall, and families will find themselves saving *less* rather than more.

2. If prices in a specific industry were to increase tomorrow by X percent, the firms in that industry

would probably experience an increase in profits. But if prices of everything throughout the economy were to increase tomorrow by X percent, no firms would experience an increase in profits.

3. There are periods when a *general* increase in taxes is beneficial for the economy as a whole. Yet an increase in taxes may at times be damaging to particular persons and businesses. On the other hand, a general decrease in taxes is always beneficial to individuals and businesses, but there are times when it may have strong adverse effects on the economy as a whole.

4. Economic policies that may be wise for a *nation* are not necessarily wise for an *individual*, and vice versa.

To repeat: Each of these four statements is true, despite the possibility that each may seem to be contradictory. One of the main objectives of this book is to clear up these and many other paradoxes by learning how to think clearly about economic problems and issues.

The fallacies of composition and division are particularly relevant to micro- and macroeconomics:

The fallacy of composition warns us that what is true of the parts is not necessarily true of the whole; hence generalizations of a microeconomic nature may not always be applicable to a macroeconomic situation. The fallacy of division warns us that what is true of the whole is not necessarily true of the parts; therefore, generalizations of a macroeconomic nature may not always be applicable to a microeconomic situation.

These ideas may seem obvious when they appear in a textbook, but they can be remarkably subtle in discussions of actual economic problems.

SUMMARY OF IMPORTANT IDEAS

1. There are many definitions of economics, but the most common one today would define it in terms of a question: How does society utilize its scarce human and material resources, which have alternative uses, to produce goods and services for present and future consumption? Economics is thus seen to be concerned in a broad sense with the efficient production and delivery of a standard of living.

2. Economics is both a science and an art. We study economics in order to gain a better understanding of national issues and policies. While a knowledge of economics may be of little direct help in running a business, it familiarizes us with the economic environment within which business operates.

3. Economic activity consists of people and institutions carrying on the processes of production, exchange, distribution, and consumption of goods and services. In economics we study these processes by induction, deduction, and verification.

  (a) The inductive method goes from actual observations of the real world to the formation of general principles based on this factual knowledge.

  (b) The deductive method proceeds by logical analysis of what these general principles indicate about the occurrences or predictions of particular events.

  (c) The verification process consists of returning to the facts and, through experiment and observation, checking both the occurrences and the accuracy of the predictions.

This cycle is the essence of the scientific method. The general principles derived are known as laws, and they are closely related to theories or models. These form the skeleton of economics.

4. Some economic laws are as exact as elementary principles of physics, chemistry, or engineering. But most economic laws express *tendencies* which hold on condition that many other things remain the same. Since in the real world, change is the rule rather than the exception, economic laws serve as approximations of reality. To the extent that they are good approximations, they serve as guides for economic prediction, policy formulation, and control.

5. Many types of fallacies can be committed in economic reasoning. Perhaps the most common are the fallacy of false cause and the fallacies of composition and division.

FOR DISCUSSION

1. *Terms and concepts to review:*

economics	hypothesis
economic system	positive economics
microeconomics	normative economics
macroeconomics	induction
theory	deduction
model	verification
principle	scientific method
law	

2. "Everyone knows that the United States is the richest country in the world. Therefore, the definition of economics given in the chapter may be correct for poor countries, but certainly not for America where the problem is one of abundance, not scarcity." True or false? Explain.

3. How would you evaluate the following statements?
   (a) "The American economic system is the best in the world."
   (b) "America is great because it is good, and when it ceases to be good it will cease to be great."

4. "One of the most fundamental requirements of a science is that it contain principles or laws which can serve as a basis for prediction. Therefore, economics (as opposed to physics) is not a science because you can find exceptions and even contradictions to virtually every economic principle." Evaluate.

5. Senator Jason is campaigning for a tax reduction. He argues that tax cuts in other major industrial nations have stimulated their rapid economic growth. Senator Blaine replies that what happens in nations thousands of miles away is no guide to what will happen here. Do you agree with Senator Blaine? Why or why not?

6. Economics, like all social sciences, deals with human behavior. Since human behavior is not predictable, economic principles cannot be used for making predictions. Why is this statement true or false?

7. Explain the meanings of economic description, economic theory, and economic policy, placing particular emphasis on their differences and interrelationships. Do you conclude from your answer that economics is "theoretical and impractical"?

8. (a) Are scientific laws created by man or are they discovered? (b) Why do we seek scientific laws?

9. What is "unscientific" about each of the following examples? (SUGGESTION: look up the meanings of such words as "analogy" and "extrapolate" in a good dictionary. Do you think that economists sometimes reason by analogy? Do they extrapolate? What about scholars in other sciences? Explain.)

The male has more teeth than the female in mankind, and sheep, and goats, and swine. This has not been observed in other animals. Those persons which have the greatest number of teeth are the longest lived; those which have them widely separated, smaller, and more scattered, are generally more short lived.

Aristotle, *History of Animals* (4th Century B.C.)

There are seven windows in the head: two nostrils, two eyes, two ears, and a mouth; so in the heavens there are two favorable stars, two unpropitious, two luminaries, and Mercury alone, undecided and indifferent. From which and many other similar phenomena of nature, such as the seven metals, etc., which it were tedious to enumerate, we gather that the number of planets is necessarily seven.

Francesco Sizzi

In the space of one hundred and seventy-six years the Lower Mississippi has shortened itself two hundred and forty-two miles. That is an average of a trifle over one mile and a third per year. Therefore, any calm person, who is not blind or idiotic, can see that in the old Oolitic Silurian Period, just a million years ago next November, the Lower Mississippi River was upward of one million three hundred thousand miles long, and stuck out over the Gulf of Mexico like a fishing-rod. And by the same token any person can see that seven hundred and forty-two years from now the Lower Mississippi will be only a mile and three-quarters long, and Cairo and New Orleans will have joined their streets together, and be plodding comfortably along under a single mayor and a mutual board of aldermen. There is something fascinating about science. One gets such wholesale returns of conjecture out of such trifling investment of fact.

Mark Twain, *Life on the Mississippi* (1875)

Identify at least one fallacy in each of the following:

10. All rich nations have steel industries, so the surest way for a poor nation to become rich is to develop its own steel industry.

11. "Last week Mr. George Jackson, president of American Steel Corp., made a strong plea before a Congressional committee for a tariff on steel. Since a tariff is a tax on imports, his arguments should be considered with suspicion. After all, his company has everything to gain from a tariff that would protect the nation's steel industry from foreign competition."

Detroit *Daily Tribune*

12. "Both the U.S. Department of Justice and the Federal Trade Commission are government agencies which enforce the antitrust laws. As such, their purpose is to prevent the monopolization of industry by encouraging free competition. Unfortunately, these agencies sometimes become overly zealous; they forget that America's greatness was built by

enterprise, ingenuity, and hard work. Hence if they are not careful in their enforcement activities, they will change us from a vigorous nation into one which lacks the drive and imagination that are needed for progress and growth."

St. Louis Sentinel

13. The students who do best in economics have some working experience, so the surest way to receive a good grade in this course is to go out and get a job.

14. Democratic socialism must indeed be better than capitalism, for even a great mathematician and physicist like the late Dr. Albert Einstein once said: "I am convinced there is only *one* way to eliminate these grave evils of capitalism, namely through the establishment of a socialist economy, accompanied by an educational system which would be oriented toward social goals."

Albert Einstein, "Why Socialism?"
Monthly Review, May, 1949

15. "To press forward with a properly ordered wage structure in each industry is the first condition for curbing competitive bargaining; but there is no reason why the process should stop there. What is good for each industry can hardly be bad for the economy as a whole."

Twentieth Century Socialism,
Penguin Books, 1956, p. 74.

16. "Each person's happiness is a good to that person, and the general happiness, therefore, a good to the aggregate of all persons."

John Stuart Mill, Utilitarianism

17. In a capitalist system, each manufacturer is free to set his own price on the product he produces, so there can't be anything wrong with all manufacturers getting together to agree on the prices of the products they produce.

18. All economics textbooks are long and dull, so we can't expect this one to be short and interesting.

19. "Roger Babson, who was best known for his predictions of the stock market, once became ill with tuberculosis. Against his doctor's advice, he chose to convalesce at his home in Massachusetts rather than remain in the West. During the freezing winter, he kept his windows open, wore a coat with an electric heating pad in the back, and had his secretary do her typing by wearing mittens and hitting the keys with rubber hammers. Babson recovered and remained a fresh-air fiend ever since. He believed that air from pine woods had chemical and/or electrical qualities of great medicinal value.

"On another occasion, Babson wrote an article in which he contended that gravity affects weather and crops, crops influence business, and business affects elections. He supported his thesis with an analysis of 27 presidential elections, from 1844 to 1948. In 75 percent of the cases, he said, the party in power remained in power when weather and business were good, and was voted out when weather and business were bad."

Martin Gardner, Fads and Fallacies in the Name
of Science, New York, Dover, 1957, p. 97.

20. "A number of years ago a team of Japanese mountainclimbers was given permission by a native government to climb one of the highest peaks of the Himalayas. When the team arrived in the village at the foot of the mountain, the members were stoned by the villagers. The reason, it turned out, was that an exploring party of Japanese had been there a year earlier to scout the climb, and had desecrated the holy mountain. Six months later the gods loosed their wrath in a great avalanche. Despite the time that had elapsed, none of the villagers doubted the connection between the two events."

Stuart Chase, Guides to Straight Thinking,
New York, Harper & Row, 1956, p. 76.

Exhibit 1

Working with Graphs

One of the most common ways of presenting a model is in the form of a line graph. Such a graph shows relationships between variables—that is, it shows how one quantity varies with another. The procedure for making line graphs is illustrated in the following paragraphs and in Charts (a)–(g).

In Chart (a), a common sheet of graph paper is shown. Two intersecting straight lines at right angles to each other are drawn on the graph paper. The horizontal line is called the X axis, the vertical line the Y axis, and the point of intersection the origin. The two lines divide the chart into four parts called quadrants. These quadrants are identified by starting with the upper right-hand corner and numbering them counterclockwise. Observe that

positive numbers on the X axis are to the right of the origin, and negative numbers are to the left. Positive numbers on the Y axis are above the origin, and negative numbers are below. These procedures for labeling and numbering are used in all branches of science.

You can now locate any point on the chart with two numbers—one for x and one for y—in much the same way as you would locate a ship at sea by its latitude and longitude. The two numbers are called the coordinates of the point. Thus in Chart (b), the coordinates of point A are (3,5), those of point B are (5,2), and those of point C are (4,0). Observe that the horizontal coordinate is always stated first and the vertical coordinate second. Can you give the coordinates of the remaining points?

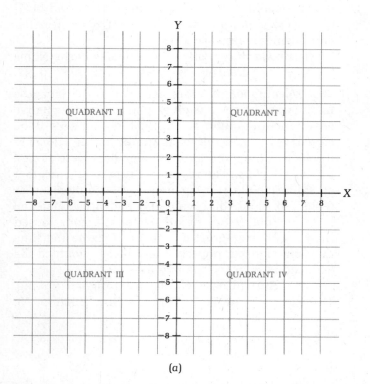

(a)

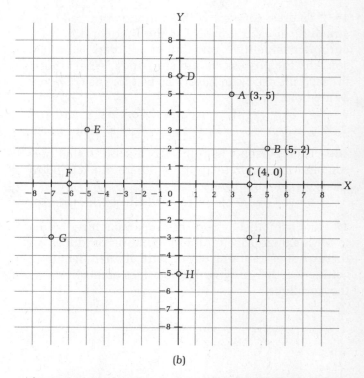

(b)

(a) The two intersecting straight lines divide the chart into four quadrants numbered counterclockwise. Positive values are measured to the right along the X axis and upward along the Y axis. Negative values are measured to the left along the X axis and downward along the Y axis.

(b) Any point on the chart can be located by its coordinates. For brevity, we write the coordinates of a point in the form (x,y), where x represents the value on the X axis, and y the value on the Y axis.

Charts such as these are used to show how one quantity varies with another. In Chart (c), for example, the values of x and y are plotted from the data in the accompanying table. First, the points representing each pair of x,y values are located and marked. The points are then connected with a smooth curve—in this case a straight line. Since the line slopes upward from left to right, the two variables are said to be directly related: as x increases, y increases; as x decreases, y decreases. In contrast, the line in Chart (d) slopes downward from left to right. Hence the two variables are said to be inversely related: as x increases, y decreases; as x decreases, y increases.

In economics, the lines plotted usually fall entirely in the first quadrant because the data on which they are based are positive, although there are important exceptions. Sometimes two or more lines are plotted on the same chart in order to examine the relationships between them, as in Chart (e). Can you read the coordinates of the points determining these lines? Different scales and labels are used on the horizontal and vertical axes in order to suit the particular purpose of the graph, as in Chart (f). The curve in this chart shows the purchase price, $P, of a $1,000, $5\frac{1}{2}$ percent bond redeemable in 20 years if the bond is purchased t years from now and the investment is to yield 4 percent. For example, at t = 0, P = $1,204; at t = 2 years, P = $1,190. Finally, Chart (g) shows the unit costs, $C, which a certain firm experiences as a result of producing different quantities, Q, of a commodity.

x	-3	-2	-1	0	1	2	3	4
y	-2	-1	0	1	2	3	4	5

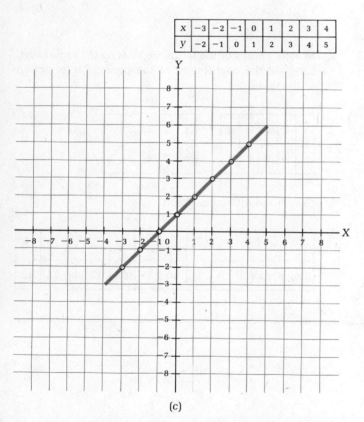

(c)

(c) A line which slopes upward from left to right exhibits a direct relation between the two variables. As one variable increases, so does the other; as one decreases, so does the other.

x	-3	-2	-1	0	1	2	3	4
y	5	4	3	2	1	0	-1	-2

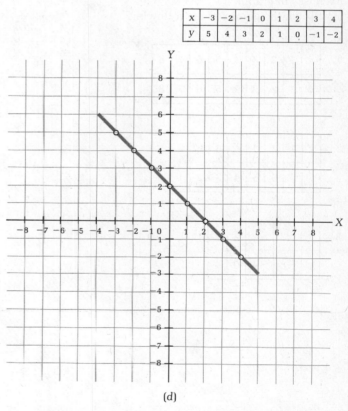

(d)

(d) A line which slopes downward from left to right exhibits an inverse relation between the two variables. As one variable increases, the other decreases; as one decreases, the other increases.

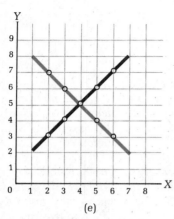

(e)

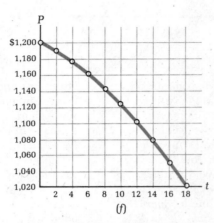

(f)

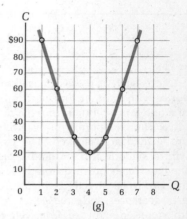

(g)

(e) *Two or more lines may be graphed on the same chart in order to study their interrelationships.*

(f) *Scales should be chosen and axes labeled in a manner which best suits a particular problem.*

(g) *The points should be connected with care since the resulting curve may be quite pronounced.*

Exercises in graphing

Sketch the graphs of the following:

1.

x	1	2	3	4	5	6	7	8
y	1	2	3	4	5	6	7	8

2.

x	1	2	3	4	5	6	7
y	7	6	5	4	3	2	1

3.

x	−2	0	2	4
y	−8	−4	0	4

4. Sketch graphs of the following data on the same chart. Estimate the coordinates of the point of intersection of the two lines.

x	1	2	3	4
y	2	3	4	5

x	1	2	3	4
y	5	4	3	2

5. Sketch the following graph:

time, t	0	1	2	3	4	5	6	7	8
hog prices, P	8	33	40	35	24	13	8	15	40

Too Many Sciences, Not Enough Principles?

Division of labor has conferred great benefits on society. In business, it has increased the productivity of labor and capital to levels that could not otherwise have been achieved. In the sciences, it has helped to extend the frontiers of knowledge by encouraging men to specialize. But whereas in manufacturing the components made by different specialists are eventually brought together to be assembled into a whole, in the sciences the different disciplines tend to stay separate. As a result there is fragmentation of knowledge. The tendency is particularly disturbing in the social sciences.

Speaking different jargons, and holding different views of society, sociologists, anthropologists, political scientists, psychologists, and economists find communication difficult—and sometimes downright impossible. Clearly, a synthesis of their disciplines is needed. But what university has a department of synthesis? What charitable foundation has paid for research into the methods of synthesis?

A Call for Communication

Fortunately, social scientists are increasingly aware of their need to speak to each other—to bring together into a meaningful whole the results of their research. The National Bureau of Economic Research, a prestigious nonprofit group, has recently called for more communication between economists and other social scientists. Without that communication, the Bureau fears, economists may be hampered in their attempts to see their discipline in its social perspective.

The need for synthesis is urgent. As society becomes more complex, and its balance more delicate, social scientists of every variety are in greater demand as advisers to government and business. Furthermore, each discipline increasingly relies on mathematical formulations—and often ignores what

it cannot measure. As management consultant Peter R. Drucker puts it: "We cannot put into the computer what we cannot quantify—and we cannot quantify what we cannot define."

Ignoring the Unmeasurable

In economics, as in other social sciences, there is a temptation to discount or even ignore what cannot be measured. Examine what happens, for example, when a study is made of alternative sites for an airport. The study will usually include a cost-benefit analysis—in plain English, a study of how much the builders and users will get for their money. That can be measured; and into the computer it will go. The study will also include estimates of future needs, based on projections of area population and patterns of air travel. These estimates can be quantified; and into the computer they will go.

But how can the objectors to an airport measure the loss of quiet that nearby residents will suffer? How can they measure the loss of green fields and wildlife? They cannot. All they can use to oppose the airport's supporters is their own common sense, and outrage at the proposed despoliation of the countryside. Those feelings might, to be sure, find their way into the computer in the form of opinion research studies; but they are pitifully weak barriers against the flood of apparently objective economic data.

"Apparently" is the right word, because even if the data are objective, their selection from the huge choice of facts available is not. Supporters and opponents of any project naturally emphasize the aspects that buttress their case, and even if they are rigorously honest, they are hardly likely to dwell on those data that will weaken it.

In one sense, at least, economics has not progressed. The great economists of the past were primarily social theorists;

they were more concerned with people than with things. Furthermore, most of them made no false distinctions between economy and society, which were correctly perceived as two aspects of the same phenomenon. Most of the classical economists saw very clearly indeed that a change in the mode of production and distribution implied changes in the structure and nature of society.

In those days—the eighteenth and nineteenth centuries—economists were known as political economists. The term expressed a truth frequently overlooked today: there is a vital nexus between politics and economics. Political and economic decisions are inextricably intertwined; together, those decisions shape the future of society. Thus, in most economic studies due attention must be paid to social results. As the late John Maynard Keynes, a noted economist, reminds us, the master economist "must study the present in the light of the past for the purposes of the future. No part of man's nature or his institutions must lie entirely outside his regard."

QUESTIONS

1. *How might economists be aided by other social scientists in studying the economic problems of the inner city?*

2. *"There are no 'principles' of economics, sociology, or political science. There are only principles of science which we may hope to discover and apply to social behavior." Do you agree?*

3. *A large part of advanced economic theory can be formulated rigorously and mathematically. Does this make economics more scientific?*

4. *"Economic theory is a science; economic policy is an art." What is the difference between theory and policy? Discuss.*

CHAPTER 2

Resources and Goals of Our Economic System

CHAPTER PREVIEW

What are the human and nonhuman resources of our economy?

What are the goals of our economic system? What do we want it to accomplish?

Are our resources scarce or plentiful? Should they be used economically or lavishly?

What goods should society produce—and how much of each? How should these goods be produced? For whom should they be produced?

This evening it would be nice if you could (1) read this chapter, (2) do all your homework, (3) earn some money, (4) engage in pleasant recreational activity, and (5) relax and enjoy a leisurely dinner at the best restaurant in town. But you cannot do all these things. You will have to give up one or more because you are faced with limitations of time, and possibly of money.

Every economic system also faces limitations—limitations of the human and nonhuman resources needed to produce the goods and services that society wants. This chapter describes the nature of those limitations and how an economy adjusts to them in the light of the objectives it tries to attain.

Resources of Our Economic System: What Do We Have?

Every economic system, whether advanced or underdeveloped, whether capitalistic, socialistic, or communistic, has various resources at its disposal to produce the goods and services that are wanted. These resources are of two broad types:

1. *Property resources*—including such things as natural resources, raw materials, machinery and equipment, buildings, and transportation and communication facilities

2. *Human resources*—consisting of the productive physical and mental abilities of the people who comprise an economy

This classification of resources is adequate for informal discussion, but is too general for most practical problems. Economists therefore divide property resources into two subcategories called "land" and "capital," and human resources into two subcategories called "labor" and "entrepreneurship." These four types of resources are known as the *factors of production.*

FACTORS OF PRODUCTION

The four factors of production—land, capital, labor, and entrepreneurship—are the basic ingredients or "inputs" which any society must use to obtain the "outputs" that it desires.

Land

Land includes all nonhuman or "natural" resources such as land itself, mineral deposits, timber, and water. In short, it includes all the basic and natural physical stuff on which any civilization must be built.

Capital

Capital may be defined as a produced means of further production. In this sense, capital means *capital goods* or *investment goods,* the things that are used by business. Examples are raw materials, tools, machinery and equipment, factory buildings, freight cars, and office furniture. Capital is thus an economic resource which is used to help produce consumer goods and services. *Consumer goods* are those bought and used by households—food, cars, appliances, clothing, health services, and so on.

An important distinction must be kept in mind— namely, the difference between *physical* capital (goods used in production) and *finance* capital (money). Businessmen, *but not economists,* generally use the term "capital" to mean money—the funds owned or borrowed to purchase capital goods and to finance the operation of a business. But for the economy as a whole, money is not a productive resource; if it were, nations could become rich by simply printing money. Instead, money's chief function is to facilitate exchange of goods and services. Hence it serves as a "lubricant," rather than as a factor of production, within the economic system.

Labor

Land and capital are of no use unless they can be worked. That requires *labor,* the hired workers whose efforts or activities are directed toward production.

In a broader sense, "labor" includes everyone who works for a living and refers to the labor force of a nation, that is, all the employable population above a certain age. The meaning of "labor force" and the notion of labor as a factor of production are different concepts in economics. Although they are sometimes related in economic discussions, the distinction between the two is always clear from the context in which the terms are used.

Entrepreneurship

The three factors of production described above must be organized and combined in order to produce. In other words, labor must be given a purpose if it is to work with land and capital to turn out goods and services. This is where the *entrepreneur* enters the picture. He recognizes a need and the opportunities to be gained from production. Accordingly, he generates new ideas and puts them into effect: he assembles the factors of production, raises the necessary money, organizes the management, makes the basic business policy decisions, and reaps the gains of success or the losses of failure. In some businesses the entrepreneur may double as a manager; in others he may not. But in any case, the *entrepreneurial function* is necessary in the economy.

FOR DISCUSSION

Is there such a thing as "human" capital? For instance, are scientists, engineers, teachers, doctors, lawyers, skilled workers, and so forth, part of a nation's capital? What criteria would you suggest in order to decide whether something is qualified to be called capital?

RETURNS TO RESOURCE OWNERS

In a capitalistic system the factors of production are privately owned, as opposed to other types of economic systems where one or more of the productive resources might be collectively owned.

Since there are not enough factors of production to satisfy everyone, their owners can command a price for them in the market. Those who supply land receive a payment called *rent*. The suppliers of capital —that is, the suppliers of the money which businessmen borrow in order to purchase capital goods—receive a return called *interest*. Workers who sell their labor receive a payment called *wages*, which includes salaries, commissions, and the like. Finally, those who perform the entrepreneurial function receive *profits* (or losses).

This classification of factors of production and their corresponding income payments is an outgrowth of the social structure which prevailed in England during most of the nineteenth century. At that time it was customary to distinguish between landowners, capitalists, and wage earners, representing the upper, middle, and lower classes. By the turn of the century, economists recognized a fourth factor of production, enterprise; profits then became the share of income attributed to entrepreneurship, and interest became the income received by suppliers of capital.

How is society's income divided among the four classes of resource owners? That is, what are the proportions of wages, rent, interest, and profit paid to the owners of the factors of production for supplying them? This question concerns what is known as *functional income distribution*. It differs from *personal income distribution*, which refers to the actual way in which income—such as that from labor, savings accounts, stocks and bonds, and other property—is distributed among individuals or families in the economy. Both types of income distribution are important and will be the subject of our attention in later chapters.

Four Facilitating Features

It is sometimes useful to think of an economic system as a machine. The inputs are the economy's factors of production—its land, capital, labor, and entrepreneurship. These are fed into the machine where they are *transformed* into outputs of goods and services—much the same as an electric motor, for example, transforms electrical inputs into energy outputs. If the economy's machine is to produce more and better products, it needs four "lubricants": (1) an adequate rate of technological progress and capital formation, (2) a high degree of specialization and exchange, (3) the availability of a suitable form of money, and (4) an environment conducive to economic advancement.

These features influence the productivity and efficiency of an economic system, and have been critically important in the development of modern industrialized economies.

TECHNOLOGICAL PROGRESS AND CAPITAL FORMATION

We live in an age of technology. Basically technology is a part of applied science; in the processes of production, technology is the application of new ideas —ideas which result in the development of new or different products, markets, production methods, and activities which raise the economy's average level of productivity. The use of society's productive resources to construct capital equipment—tools, machines, factories, and so forth—is known as capital formation. The growth of technology makes a greater amount of capital formation possible, and this in turn permits a much larger output of consumer goods.

Labor and capital, of course, are closely related in the overall scheme of production because they are combined in various ways to produce society's output. The process of capital formation within a nation may therefore proceed along two lines:

1. The stock of capital may increase at the same rate as the growth of the labor force and consist of the same types of machines, tools, and other productive instruments already in use. This serves to enlarge the economy while maintaining the same volume of capital per worker and hence the same average output per worker. It is therefore known as *capital widening*.

2. The stock of capital may increase at a faster rate than the growth of the labor force, resulting in more capital per worker. This increases average output per worker and is known as *capital deepening*.

Ordinarily, capital widening and capital deepening take place simultaneously, but we shall find the distinction between them useful for analyzing the economic development of nations.

SPECIALIZATION AND EXCHANGE

The birds do it. The bees do it. In most societies nearly everyone does it. What do they do? They *specialize*.

Specialization is the division of productive activities among individuals and regions so that no one person or area is self-sufficient. *Division of labor* refers to specialization by workers. The result of specialization is an enormous gain in productivity, because each individual or region is able to use to its best advantage any natural or acquired differences in abilities and resources. And even if there are no peculiar differences in a given situation, specialization may still pay because it is often the only way of getting a significant increase in total output. Adam Smith, the founder of modern economics, pointed this out as long ago as 1776 in what has become a classic quotation. (See Box 1.)

To generalize from Smith, specialization and division of labor increase production because they:

1. Allow the development and refinement of skills

2. Avoid the time that is wasted in going from one job to another

3. Simplify human tasks, thus permitting the introduction of labor-saving machines

Specialization also has its shortcomings. It leads to *interdependence*—indeed, specialization and interdependence go hand in hand. But specialization also alienates workers because many never see the completed product to which they have contributed only one small part. Their jobs become naked means of subsistence, offering little personal satisfaction. This poses such interesting questions as whether specialization is "good" or "bad," whether it is worth paying the price of specialization, and whether society as a whole would be "better off" if each of us were self-sufficient. These are normative questions which economics is not equipped to answer, because there is no universal agreement on the precise meanings of the words in quotation marks.

Specialization results in individuals, firms, and regions producing more of a product than they consume. This makes it necessary for them to engage in *exchange*—to give up something in return for something else. Exchange is thus a transfer of values between parties in which both parties expect to benefit—each placing a higher value on what is received than on what is given up. The basis for this valuation depends entirely on the *amount* of anything that each party possesses. This principle (which we shall study in a later chapter under the formal name of the "law of diminishing marginal utility") is one of the most fundamental axioms of economics. Stated in simplest terms:

The more we have of anything, the less we care for one more unit of it. The less we have of anything, the more we care for one more unit of it.

Thus, if you had an ample supply of bread and no meat, you would care very little for an additional slice of bread, but you would care a great deal for an additional ounce of meat. Hence you would be willing to exchange some bread for some meat. In this way, through specialization and exchange, you would be able to satisfy your wants better than if you tried to be self-sufficient by producing your own bread and your own meat. The same principle applies to nations and regions as well as to individuals. By engaging in specialization and exchange, societies can have more of all goods and services than if they try to be self-sufficient.

MONEY ENTERS THE PICTURE

It has been said that man's three greatest inventions are fire, the wheel, and money.

What is money? Is it gold, silver, or paper currency? Is it fishhooks, whale teeth, elephant-tail bristles, or wampum? The answer is yes. All of these things and many others have served as money. Money is indispensable in an organized economy.

Robinson Crusoe had no need for money when he was alone on a deserted island; he provided his own food, clothing, and shelter. Even in a small community it would be possible to get along without money if one family made clothes, another raised sheep for wool and meat, another baked bread, and so on, and they all traded with each other for the things they needed. This swapping of one good for another is called *barter*.

But, barter is obviously a cumbersome way of doing business. If you want to trade cows for a plow, you have to find a person who has a plow and is willing to exchange it for some cows. This basic principle of barter is sometimes called the "double coincidence of wants" because it correctly implies that if barter is to occur, each party must have what the other desires and be willing to make an exchange on terms that are suitable to both.

When an economy grows beyond the simplest stage, barter is no longer feasible. Money is developed because it is more convenient to exchange labor or goods for money than it is to find the person who has what is wanted and is willing to trade for what is offered.

Money has four functions:

1. *A medium of exchange.* Money is widely accepted and generally used in payment for goods and services; people want money for what it will buy.

2. *A measure of value.* Money enables us to keep business records and to express the prices of things that people and business firms buy and sell.

3. *A standard of deferred payment.* Money allows us to borrow or lend for future repayment with interest.

4. *A store of value.* Money can be saved so that it can be spent in the future.

These four functions of money have long been epitomized by a popular rhyme:

Money is a matter of functioning four,
A medium, a measure, a standard, a store.

Money, therefore, may be broadly described as a social convention. It is anything that the members of a society will accept as money—cattle, shells, stones, or what have you. (See Box 2.) Its effectiveness is directly dependent on the extent to which it fulfills

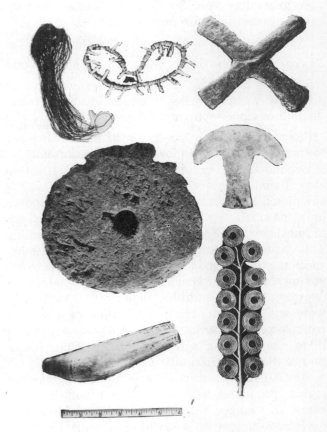
its four functions. In our modern society coins and currency serve as money, while checks and credit cards serve as instruments through which money is transferred or borrowed. In fact, you may be surprised to learn that over 90 percent of the *value* (not number) of all transactions in our economy is conducted by checks.

A FAVORABLE ECONOMIC ENVIRONMENT

The political, social, and cultural framework within which decisions are made influences the ways in which a society administers its scarce resources. It is no accident that countries like the United States, Great Britain, Japan, and the Soviet Union, despite their different political systems, are among the advanced economies of the world, while many nations in Africa, Asia, and Latin America remain poor and underdeveloped. In the advanced countries, favorable attitudes toward productive efficiency, technological progress, and capital formation have long been fostered, while in many of the less-developed countries these objectives have been discouraged and even been regarded as sinful.

The mechanisms for administering scarce resources have differed among nations. In the United States and other advanced capitalistic nations, primary reliance has been placed on the purchase and sale of resources in free markets. In some authoritarian socialistic countries, such as Cuba, Russia, and China, a different mechanism has been employed—one in which resources are largely allocated by the commands of central authorities. In still other countries and regions, "traditional" or primitive economies continue to exist, and most exchange is carried on by barter.

We may conclude:

The four facilitating factors—technology, specialization, money, and environment—serve to supplement and complement a nation's factors of production. When available in the proper combinations, they permit a society to accelerate its production of goods and services by making the best use of scarce resources.

Goals of Our Economic System: What Do We Want to Accomplish?

When we refer to the economy as a "system," we imply there is purpose or order in its structure. What do we want our economy to do? What do we want it to be?

Most economists agree in principle that the following objectives characterize our economic system, but many economists disagree over the interpretations and compromises that these goals entail.

1. *Continuous full employment.* Society should make maximum efficient utilization of all resources available for employment. This is the meaning of full employment. Of course, with respect to human resources, some unemployment will always exist because some people are temporarily out of work and others are unable to find a job in their line of work or in their community. As a general rule, a figure equal to about 4 percent of the labor force is widely accepted as the maximum unemployment level compatible with what is called a full-employment economy. The *labor force* is defined as all people sixteen years of age or older who are employed, plus all those who are unemployed, but actively seeking work.

2. *Strong and sustained economic growth.* The economic system must grow rapidly enough to absorb net additions to the labor force. Otherwise there will be mounting unemployment. The economy must also grow if it is to provide the goods and services needed for a rising standard of living.

3. *Clean environment.* Contamination of land, air, and water has been part of the cost which society has paid for economic growth. Therefore, methods must be found for achieving growth without defiling our natural environment.

4. *Stable prices.* The purchasing power of the dollar should be maintained at a level that encourages investment, production, and employment of the economy's resources. This does not mean that prices must remain at a constant level, but it does mean that substantial inflationary and deflationary price movements should be avoided because they disrupt the smooth flow of economic activity.

5. *Equitable distribution of income.* Wide differences among income groups are due to both controllable and uncontrollable factors, such as native ability and intelligence, education and training, the extent of property ownership, and market power. Since equitable means "fair" or "just" (*not* "equal"), this goal requires that society seek reasonable methods of altering the controllable factors that cause wide disparities in income.

6. *Economic security.* Society should provide reasonable assistance to people who cannot care for themselves, such as those whose income is cut off as a result of old age, loss of the breadwinner, unemployment, accidents, and illness. This is a humanitarian goal which involves significant economic decisions.

7. *Freedom of choice.* With the evolution of democracy has come a close connection between political

freedom and economic freedom. Citizens vote for legislators who influence government policy; consumers choose the goods they want; workers select their occupations; and holders of wealth employ their assets as they see fit. Although the government may impose certain restrictions for the protection of the public, and although social or racial discrimination may deprive some people of equal opportunities, the preservation and enhancement of freedom of choice are primary objectives of our political and economic system.

CAN WE ACHIEVE THE GOALS?

The goals listed above seem reasonable enough, but on closer examination it becomes evident that they are not sufficiently precise. To illustrate: How long should society tolerate a lapse from full employment before insisting that corrective action be taken? What annual rate of economic growth qualifies as "strong and sustained"? How clean an environment do we want—and are we willing to pay the costs of increased cleanliness? When do inflationary or deflationary price movements become sufficiently "substantial" to merit concern? What pattern of income distribution would be considered "equitable"? How can society distinguish between economic security and "big-brother" paternalism? Finally, to what extent are we willing to sacrifice personal freedom of choice for greater direction by centralized authority? Until such questions can be answered, implementing in a systematic way the goals outlined above will remain difficult for government policymakers.

Some of the goals also tend to conflict with each other. For example, full employment can conflict with the goal of stable prices by exerting inflationary pressures on the economy. Similarly, economic growth can conflict with the goal of a clean environment by causing land, air, and water pollution. Where such conflicts occur, government may exert efforts through legislation or regulation to promote the desirable goals while minimizing the undesirable consequences. However, such efforts are likely to entail some costs. For instance, legislation in the form of wage and price controls can curb inflation, but will also limit freedom of choice for consumers, workers, and businessmen. In view of this, would you recommend such legislation?

Every decision involves a choice between alternatives. If the choices are to be made rationally, a system of tradeoffs must be established so that the alternative cost or sacrifice of choosing one objective over another, or of formulating compromises between them, can be better understood. Thus, an overall problem faced by society is to establish a proper mix of goals.

The goals of nations vary according to their political as well as their economic philosophies. To achieve certain objectives such as full employment and rapid economic growth, autocratic (as distinct from democratic) socialistic countries like Russia, China, and Cuba have been willing to sacrifice much more economic freedom than have predominantly capitalistic countries like the United States, Canada, and most of the nations of Western Europe.

A Fundamental Economic Challenge

In economics, *scarcity* is the name of the game and *economizing* is the way it is played. Every society has to cope with a fundamental economic challenge: How can it best use its *limited resources* to satisfy its *unlimited wants*?

THE LAW OF SCARCITY

Some people think it paradoxical to be told that resources in the United States are scarce. After all, the country covers several million square miles and embraces untold billions of dollars' worth of real and untapped natural resources. The population is expanding and with it the civilian labor force. Science and technology are continually providing new and better types of capital equipment. Colleges and universities are turning out millions of educated men and women. In the face of these developments, can it be true that our resources are scarce?

Compared with many nations, our modern industrial society seems wealthy indeed. We have a substantially higher standard of living than our great-grandparents had. Nevertheless our economic system does not provide enough of all the things that people want—such as more and better homes, clothing, transportation systems, health and educational facilities, and longer vacations.

For some rich people scarcity of material things is no problem—although they may find their time is too scarce to accomplish everything they want to do. But for the majority of people scarcity is a fact of life because most of the things they want and need are *economic goods*—they have a price. In this sense, they differ from *free goods*—the market price of which is zero. But even "free goods" may be scarce in some circumstances. Sunshine and surf are free for residents of Hawaii, but not for tourists who must expend time, effort, and money to get there. Trout in a mountain stream are free goods, but in a city they are scarce.

Since scarcity pervades the economic life of all societies, we may formulate an important law:

Law of Scarcity. Economic resources are scarce. There are never enough at any given time to produce all the things that people want. Scarce resources can be increased, if at all, only through effort or sacrifice.

Thus, despite the fact that America is a so-called "affluent society," the law of scarcity still prevails. Our economic system does not satisfy everyone's wants.

ECONOMIZING—THE ANSWER TO SCARCITY

Scarcity creates the need to economize. What does it mean to "economize"? To tighten one's belt or to be stingy? These interpretations are correct in the narrow sense of the word, but for an economist the term has a broader meaning—*to economize is to do the most with what is available.*

To do the most it can with limited resources, society must make choices. A decision to produce one thing frequently implies a decision to produce less of other things. Therefore society often faces the basic problem of deciding what it is willing to *sacrifice* in order to get the things it wants. Sacrificing and economizing are thus closely related concepts.

In general:

Economics is fundamentally concerned with choice or decision in the use of resources. Problems of choice arise when there are alternative ways of achieving a given objective. Economics develops specific criteria which define the conditions for making the best use of society's resources, and employs these criteria as guidelines for formulating and evaluating public policy.

THE GREAT QUESTIONS: WHAT? HOW? FOR WHOM?

Economic life in every society is characterized by three features: a stock of scarce resources to provide the things that people desire; unlimited wants of different intensities for various products; a state of technology for converting resources into goods. It is the task of an economic system to combine efficiently these *resources, wants,* and *technologies.* In order to do so, it must answer three fundamental and interdependent questions.

WHAT Goods and Services Should Society Produce—and in What Quantities?

Resources are limited; there are not enough to produce all the goods and services that people want. How should these scarce resources be allocated? Should some of them be taken out of the production of consumer goods (food, clothing, automobiles, and appliances) and put into the production of capital goods (tools, machines, tractors, and factories), or would the reverse be better? By enlarging its proportion of capital goods now, the economy will be able to produce more consumer goods in the future. The problem, therefore, is to decide how much consumption should be sacrificed today in order to provide capital goods for increased output of consumer goods later.

A related question is, *How much of each good should society produce?* How many automobiles? How much food and clothing? How many tractors, factories, and so on? The values and priorities involved in such decisions are extremely complex. Nevertheless, in answering this question society is again choosing between present and future satisfactions—making a "tradeoff" between the amount of consumption to be sacrificed today in return for increased consumption at some later time.

HOW Should Resources Be Organized for Production?

Most goods can be produced in more than one way by using resources in different quantities and combinations. In the early days of America, for example, agricultural commodities were produced by farming larger quantities of land extensively, while using only small quantities of labor, because labor was relatively more scarce than land. In parts of the Far East, on the other hand, land is farmed intensively because it is relatively more scarce than labor. Similarly, in manufacturing it is often possible to vary the combinations of resources. Automobiles, for example, can be produced with different combinations of materials such as steel, aluminum, or fiberglass, as well as different combinations of labor and capital.

Any society must decide how it will *organize* its scarce resources in order to use them efficiently. Economic efficiency requires that the product be produced with the *least-cost* combination of resources. Economic efficiency thus affects the profitability of products and the nature of industrial processes. It helps determine whether resources should be shifted away from industries that are relatively less profitable and into industries that are relatively more profitable, and it influences the types of technologies that are employed.

FOR WHOM Shall the Goods Be Produced?

Who is to receive what share of the economic pie? This question is of enormous significance, because an economic system is often judged by the way in which it distributes its goods and services. It is also a question of direct concern to each of us, since the answer determines not only the nation's well-being but our individual standard of living as well.

The three great questions—WHAT, HOW, and FOR WHOM—are fundamental in all societies. Each society meets these challenges in different ways. At one extreme is the *command economy* in which an authoritarian government exercises primary control over decisions concerning what and how much to produce; it may also, but does not necessarily, decide for whom to produce. Countries such as Russia, China, and Cuba are among the best examples. At the other extreme is the *market economy* in which all three questions are decided in open markets through competitive forces of supply and demand. This is the ideal of "pure" capitalism, also called theoretical capitalism—an extremely useful model which cannot be represented by any real-world economies, but which is examined closely in some later chapters. Between the two extremes is the *mixed economy* in which the three great questions, or specific applications of them, are decided partially by the free market and partially by a central governmental authority. Most of the advanced nations fall into this category, but they vary in the degree of reliance they place on the market mechanism as opposed to government direction.

Society's Production Possibilities

For every society, the answers to the questions of WHAT, HOW, and FOR WHOM are intimately re-lated to the need for economizing. In reality the problem of economizing is a complex one; therefore we must simplify in order to focus on the basic concepts involved.

We may begin by constructing a model of the economizing process for a hypothetical society. The model is based on several assumptions:

1. *The economy produces only two types of goods: agricultural, such as crops and livestock, and capital, like machines and factories.* This assumption permits the derivation of principles for a simple two-good economy—principles which are also applicable to a complex economy producing many goods.

2. *The same resources can be used to produce either or both of the two classes of goods and can be shifted freely between them.* This means, for example, that labor as well as the other factors of production can be used to produce either food or machines, or different combinations of both.

3. *The supply of resources and the state of technological knowledge are fixed.* This is equivalent to assuming a short-run state of affairs, because in the long run the supply of resources and the level of technological knowledge are expandable rather than fixed.

4. *Society's resources are fully employed in the most efficient way.* This assumption enables us to measure the costs of shifting resources from one industry to the other; it also emphasizes the fact that in the short run the economy may be able to increase the production of one class of goods by taking resources away from the production of the other, but it cannot increase the production of *both* classes of goods.

Our model teaches us this fundamental point: Since resources are fully employed in the most efficient way, any increase in the production of capital goods will require the shifting of resources out of agriculture; conversely, any increase in the production of agricultural goods will require resources to be shifted out of the manufacture of capital goods.

This is illustrated by Exhibit 1. The table is called a *production-possibilities schedule*. If society chooses production alternative A, it will be devoting all of its resources to the production of agricultural goods and none of its resources to the production of capital goods; it will thus be producing 14 units of agricultural goods and zero units of capital goods. At the

Exhibit 1

Society's Production Possibilities

PRODUCTION-POSSIBILITIES SCHEDULE

Production alternatives	Capital goods production	Agricultural goods production	Sacrifice of agricultural goods for capital goods
A	0	14	
			−1
B	1	13	
			−2
C	2	11	
			−2
D	3	9	
			−2
E	4	7	
			−3
F	5	4	
			−4
G	6	0	

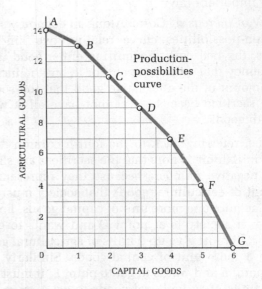

other extreme, if society chooses alternative *G*, it will be putting all its resources into the production of capital goods; it will thus be producing 6 units of capital goods and zero units of agricultural goods.

These two alternatives are extremes; realistically the society must seek some balance in between. However, as it tries to increase its capital goods production by choosing any of the alternatives, *B, C, D,* etc., it finds that it must *sacrifice* or give up some agricultural goods. The amount of sacrifice for each production alternative is shown in the fourth column of the table.

All the information in the production-possibilities schedule can be transferred directly to the accompanying chart. Note that the units of capital goods are scaled on the horizontal axis and those for agricultural goods on the vertical. The line which connects the various production alternatives *A* through *G* is called a *production-possibilities curve* because it reveals all possible combinations of total output for the society it represents.

LAW OF INCREASING COSTS

The production-possibilities curve raises two challenging questions:

1. *Is there an optimum or best combination of agricultural and capital goods?* The production-possi-

bilities curve alone cannot tell us what combination of the two goods to produce. For example, some countries, such as the Soviet Union and China, have sought rapid economic growth by emphasizing capital goods production at the expense of consumer goods. Other nations, such as New Zealand and Uruguay, have traditionally allocated larger proportions of their resources to agricultural than to capital goods production. Choices such as these are based on each society's value judgments and goals, and hence involve questions which economics per se cannot answer.

2. *Why does the sacrifice of agricultural products increase as society gets more capital goods?* Greater and greater sacrifices of agricultural output must be made to get more capital goods because the economy's factors of production differ and are not all equally suitable for producing the two types of goods. Fertile land, for example, is more suitable for crops than for factories, and unskilled farm workers are more adaptable to agriculture than to manufacturing. Therefore, even though an economy's resources may be substitutable within wide limits for given production purposes, they are relatively more efficient in some uses than in others. For this reason, society finds that as it tries to increase its production of capital goods, it must take increasing amounts of resources out of agriculture, where they are rela-

tively more productive, and put them into the manufacture of capital goods, where they are relatively less productive. This suggests the operation of an important law:

Law of Increasing Costs. Along an economy's production-possibilities curve relating two kinds of goods, the real cost of acquiring either good is not the money that must be spent for it, but the increasing amount of the alternative good that the society must sacrifice because it cannot have all it wants of both goods.

Thus, referring back to the fourth column of the table in Exhibit 1, note that the sacrifices are shown with negative numbers because they represent the amount of agricultural goods that society must *give up* to acquire one more unit of capital goods. For example, if society is at point D and wants to go to point E, it must give up 2 units of agricultural goods to get 1 more unit of capital goods. Similarly, if it is at point E and wants to get to point F, it must give up 3 units of agricultural goods to get 1 more unit of capital goods.

AN INTERESTING PROBLEM

You should be able to verify that the law of increasing costs also applies in going from G to A on the chart. That is, society must give up increasing amounts of capital goods to get successive one-unit increases in agricultural goods. The curve is "bowed out" or concave to the origin because of the law of increasing cost. What would it mean if the curve were a straight line? What if it were "bowed in" or convex to the origin? Would such curves make economic sense? Illustrate your answer graphically.

SOME USES OF THE PRODUCTION-POSSIBILITIES CURVE

The production-possibilities model discussed above is based on several assumptions: (1) a two-good economy, (2) substitutability of resources, (3) a fixed supply of resources and a given state of technology, and (4) a full and efficient employment of resources. When one or more of the assumptions is relaxed, as in the real world, several interesting situations result.

Exhibit 2

Effect of Resource Underutilization

An economy which underutilizes its resources is producing at some point such as U inside its production-possibilities curve. Three of the moves it can make to get back on the curve are to produce either more capital goods, more agricultural goods, or more of both.

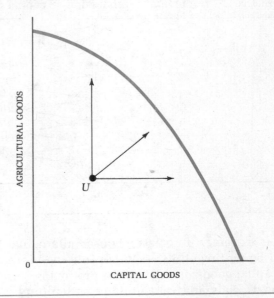

Depicting Resource Underutilization

Suppose some resources are unemployed or are used with less than maximum efficiency—as happens in an economic recession. In that case the economy will not be producing at its boundary of maximum potential as defined by its production-possibilities curve. Instead it will be producing a smaller volume of output such as that represented by point U in Exhibit 2. Since this point is inside the curve, you can readily infer that the economy is not fully utilizing its available resources.

How can society utilize its resources more fully? Three of the moves it can make to get back to the curve are shown in Exhibit 2. It may increase agricultural goods production without increasing capital goods production, as indicated by the vertical arrow. It may increase capital goods production without increasing agricultural goods production, as shown by the horizontal arrow. Or it may increase both agricultural and capital goods production in any one of various combinations, as suggested by the diagonal arrow.

Illustrating Economic Growth

A different aspect of a production-possibilities model can be demonstrated by assuming that the economy's supply of resources and level of technology is expandable rather than fixed. This situation would undoubtedly occur over the long run as the supply of the factors of production grew with a rising population, and more efficient machinery and equipment increased productivity.

In Exhibit 3, Chart (a), this increase is indicated by the shift to the right of the production-possibilities curve. At any point on the new curve, the economy would enjoy a larger total output than it would at any point on the old curve. For example, suppose the economy was initially at point A. The arrows indicate that if it moved to point B, it would produce the same amount of agricultural goods plus more capital goods. If it moved to point C, it would produce the same amount of capital goods plus more agricultural goods. If it moved to any point between B and C, such as D, it would produce more agricultural goods and more capital goods.

Any movement from a point on the inner curve to a point on the outer one represents economic growth. Of course there is no assurance that society will know how to make full enough utilization of its available resources to get itself onto the outer curve. In later chapters possible solutions to this basic problem are explored.

Exhibit 3

Economic Growth

Increases in resources or improvements in technology will shift the curve outward to the right. The resulting expansion in the quantities of goods available represents economic growth. As shown in Charts (b) and (c), the new curve need not necessarily be "parallel" to the old one. Changes in resources or technology may be such as to bring about a relatively greater shift in favor of one type of output as compared to the other.

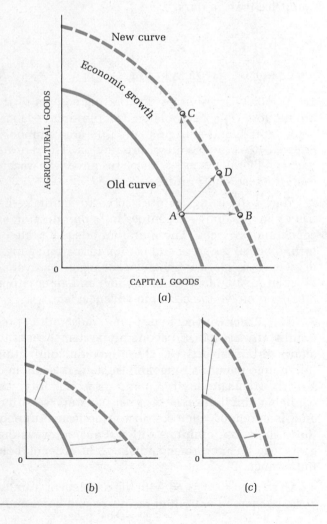

(a)

(b)   (c)

Choosing Between Present Goods and Future Goods

As a third illustration of the many uses of production-possibilities curves, we consider what would happen if the choice of producing agricultural goods were broadened to include a larger category which we call "consumption goods." In other words, society must now choose between current consumption goods (i.e., not just food but also automobiles, color television sets, and the like) and current capital goods (such as machines, education, research)—but the choice of capital goods will make it possible to have more of *both* classes of goods in the future.

The results are demonstrated in Exhibit 4. Chart (a) shows what would happen if society chose to live "high off the hog" by producing relatively more consumer goods than capital goods, as indicated by point A on the curve. Chart (b) shows what would happen if society chose to produce relatively more capital goods than consumer goods, as indicated by A'. The outcome is that, in Chart (b), the future production-possibilities curve will be farther to the right than in Chart (a). This evidences the fact that by doing with fewer consumer goods now and producing more capital goods instead, society will have the means of producing more consumer goods and capital goods in the future.

Exhibit 4

Present Goods vs. Future Goods

The more resources an economy allocates in the present to the production of capital goods relative to consumer goods, the more it can have of both kinds of goods in the future. These charts show how the degree of outward shift of an economy's future curve is affected by whether it chooses to be at point A or at point A' on its present curve.

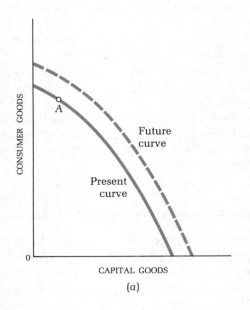

(a)

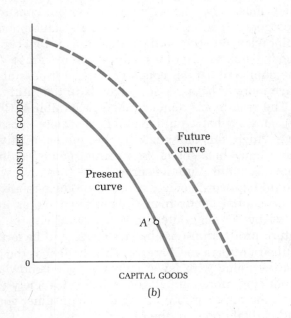

(b)

We can generalize these ideas in the form of a principle:

The degree of outward shift of an economy's production-possibilities curve is determined by its present allocation of resources between capital goods and consumer goods.

This principle has a number of real-world applications. Some countries such as Russia, China, and several African and Latin American nations have sought rapid industrialization and growth and have allocated relatively large proportions of their resources to the production of capital goods as opposed to consumer goods. As a result, their economies have at times grown faster than ours. The *real cost* of such a policy to the people of those countries can be measured in terms of the quantity, quality, and variety of consumer goods sacrificed—goods such as automobiles, clothing, housing, and modern conveniences—all of which are much scarcer in those countries than in ours.

SUMMARY OF IMPORTANT IDEAS

1. A society's resources are the ingredients of its production. The four classes of resources—labor, land, capital, and entrepreneurship—are commonly referred to as the factors of production. The returns received by the owners of these resources are wages, rent, interest, and profits.

2. Four supporting features serve to facilitate the use of an economy's resources in the production of goods and services. These are: an adequate rate of technological progress and capital formation; a high degree of specialization and exchange; the availability of a suitable form of money; and an environment conducive to economic advancement.

3. The American economy (and most other predominantly capitalistic economic systems) seeks to attain certain objectives. These include continuous full employment; strong and sustained economic growth; a clean environment; price stability; an equitable distribution of income; economic security; and freedom of choice. Most Americans support these goals, but opinions differ about the ways the goals may be interpreted and about the order of their importance.

4. All societies are faced with the problem of scarcity because they have limited resources and apparently

unlimited wants. Therefore, economizing is necessary if the best use is to be made of these scarce resources.

5. Most economic problems are aspects of the three big questions that every society must answer: WHAT to produce—and in what quantities? HOW to produce? FOR WHOM to produce? In the United States these questions are answered within the framework of the goals summarized above. In other economic systems, where the goals are different, the answers are also different.

6. In an economy characterized by full employment of resources, any increase in the output of goods and services in one sector causes a reduction of output elsewhere in the economy. With given resources and technology, the production choices open to an economy can be summarized by its production-possibilities curve.

7. A society's production-possibilities curve illustrates several basic economic concepts: any point inside the curve indicates some underutilization of resources; an outward shift of the curve represents an increase in the supply of resources or in technological capability; a choice between the present proportions of consumption goods and capital goods production will affect the degree of outward shift of the economy's future curve.

FOR DISCUSSION

1. *Terms and concepts to review:*

property resources	barter
human resources	money
factors of production	free good
land	economic good
capital	law of scarcity
labor	command economy
entrepreneurship	market economy
wages	mixed economy
rent	production-possibilities
interest	schedule
profit	production-possibilities
specialization	curve
division of labor	law of increasing costs

2. Would entrepreneurship exist in a pure communistic society, that is, one in which all citizens live and work by the motto: "From each according to his ability, to each according to his needs"?

3. What are the bases of distinction between functional and personal income distribution?

4. Which factor of production is relatively most important in each of the following lines of activity: (a) iron mining, (b) radio and TV repair, (c) electric power generation, (d) toys and games.

5. "No one in the United States has to starve or go naked. Therefore, it is incorrect to say that scarcity pervades our economy. Food and clothing are available to all and hence are not scarce." True or false? Explain.

6. It is sometimes contended that the act of exchange does not *create* wealth since it merely results in a redistribution of goods already in existence. Evaluate this argument.

7. Formulate at least three fundamental principles or propositions concerning specialization and exchange.

8. Denmark produces some of the world's best butter. Yet some Danish butter producers use margarine in their homes instead of butter. Does this make sense? Explain.

9. Money is a resource because a person who has it can put it to productive use. The same is true of a nation. Do you agree?

10. Examine the economic goals of our society as given in this chapter, and list at least three *pairs* of goals that are in conflict. What are the bases of these conflicts?

11. The question, FOR WHOM shall goods be produced? is concerned with distributing total output among the members of society. Can you suggest at least three different criteria or rules to decide who gets how much? Which criterion is best?

12. Illustrate a production-possibilities curve representing (a) constant costs and (b) decreasing costs. Define the meaning of each case.

13. Suppose an economy produces only agricultural goods and capital goods. Using production-possibilities curves, illustrate the effect of a new invention, assuming that the invention has *no impact* on agriculture. Describe the possible adjustment paths which society may take as a result of the invention.

CHAPTER 3

Capitalism and Our Mixed Economy

CHAPTER PREVIEW

What is the nature of capitalism? What are its fundamental institutions?

When did capitalism come into existence? How has it changed over its course of development?

What is wrong with capitalism? Does it have a future?

Can we construct a model which provides a broad overview of a capitalistic system?

"Capitalism," it has been said,

has created more massive and more colossal forces than have all preceding generations together. . . . It has accomplished wonders far surpassing Egyptian pyramids, Roman aqueducts, and Gothic cathedrals; it has conducted expeditions that put in the shade all former migrations of nations and crusades.

These words were not taken from a recent speech by the head of the National Association of Manufacturers or the United States Chamber of Commerce. They were written by none other than history's greatest enemy of capitalism and the founder of modern socialism—Karl Marx—in a pamphlet entitled *The Communist Manifesto*, published in 1848.

Modern capitalism had its origin in eighteenth-century Britain, and was later transplanted to northwestern Europe and North America. Scholars now agree that capitalism was a "revolution"—not always bloody as the American, French, and Russian Revolutions, but certainly more fundamental in the shaping of modern society. Today capitalism is more than an economic process; it is a *civilization* rooted in an ideology that reflects a way of life.

What Is Capitalism?

The economic system of the United States and many other countries of the Western world is commonly known as "capitalism," "free enterprise," or "private enterprise." These terms are generally regarded as synonymous. What do they mean?

Capitalism is a system of economic organization characterized by private ownership of the means of production and distribution (land, factories, railroads, etc.) and their operation for profit under predominantly competitive conditions.

On what foundations does the theory of capitalism rest? Is our economic system a prototype of theoretical, or pure, capitalism?

PILLARS OF CAPITALISM

Certain rights, traditions, and institutions are basic in a capitalistic system. The more important of these may be noted.

Private Property

The institution of *private property* is the most basic element of capitalism. It assures each person the right to acquire economic goods and resources by legitimate means, enter into contracts involving their use, and dispose of them as he wishes. This concept originated in the writings of the late seventeenth-century English philosopher John Locke, who justified private ownership and control of property as a "natural right" independent of the power of the state. This right, he maintained, provides maximum benefits for society as a whole. (In contrast, socialist views prevailing since the nineteenth century have held that private property is a means of exploiting the proletariat or working class.)

The granting of property rights fulfills three important economic functions: (1) it provides individuals with personal incentives to make the most productive use of their assets; (2) it strongly influences the distribution of wealth and income by allowing individuals to accumulate assets and pass them on to others at the time of death; and (3) it permits a high degree of exchange, since individuals must have property rights before they can transfer those rights. The social and economic consequences of these functions, as we shall see, have been instrumental in the development of capitalism.

Self-interest—The "Invisible Hand"

In 1776, a Scottish professor, Adam Smith, published *The Wealth of Nations*. This masterful exposition of economic ideas earned him the title "founder of economics." In this book he described his principle of the "Invisible Hand"—the idea that each individual, if left to pursue his self-interest without interference by government, would be led as if by an invisible hand to achieve the best good for society. In Smith's words:

An individual neither intends to promote the public interest, nor knows he is promoting it. . . . He intends only his own gain, and he is led by an invisible hand to promote an end which was no part of his intention. . . . It is not from the benevolence of the butcher, the brewer, or the baker that we expect our dinner, but from their regard to their self-interest. We address ourselves not to their humanity, but to their self-love, and never talk to them of our necessities, but of their advantages.

Self-interest drives men to action, but alone it is not enough. Men must also think rationally if they are to make the right decisions. This requirement ultimately led economists to introduce the concept of *economic man*—the notion that each individual in a capitalistic society, whether worker, businessman, consumer, or investor, is motivated by economic forces, and hence will always act in such a way as to obtain the greatest amount of satisfaction for the least amount of sacrifice or cost. To a businessman these satisfactions may take the form of profits; to a worker they may be leisure; to a consumer they may be the pleasure he gets from the goods he buys.

The modern economist knows these assumptions are not always realistic. People may be motivated by forces other than self-interest. The assumption of economic man, if pushed to its logical extreme, would require each individual to have the mind of a computer in order to solve the myriad of problems that he encounters in his economic activities. But the assumption does serve as a reasonable approximation of the way people tend to pattern their economic behavior in a capitalistic society. And in economics, just as in the other social sciences, reasonable approximations are often the most that can be made.

Economic Individualism—Laissez-faire

In the late seventeenth century, when Louis XIV reigned as King of France, his finance minister Jean Baptiste Colbert asked a manufacturer by the name of Legendre how the government might help business. Legendre's reply was *"laissez nous faire"* (leave us alone). The expression became a watchword and motto of capitalism.

Today we interpret *laissez-faire* to mean that absence of government intervention leads to economic individualism and economic freedom. An individual's economic activities are his private affair: as a consumer he is free to spend his income as he chooses; as a producer he is free to purchase the economic resources he desires and to organize them as he wishes for the purpose of producing the things that society wants. In reality, this concept of laissez-faire is significantly limited, because economic freedom is subject to restraints imposed by society for its protection and general welfare. Can you give some examples?

Competition and Free Markets

Capitalism operates under conditions of *competition*: rivalry among sellers of similar goods to attract customers; among buyers to secure the goods that they want; among workers to obtain jobs; among employers to obtain workers; among buyers

---

Leaders in Economics

ST. THOMAS AQUINAS

1225–1274

The Great Scholastic of Medieval Economic Thought

The period known as the Middle Ages covers approximately one thousand years—from the fall of the Roman Empire in A.D. 476 to about 1500.

In the last three of these ten centuries modern capitalism took root, as money and credit instruments gained wider acceptance in trade among European towns and cities, the ownership of the tools of production became separated from their use, and a wage system emerged with the growth of urbanization and more centralized production.

The outstanding intellectual achievement of the late Middle Ages was the system of thought known as Scholasticism; the participants in this system are referred to as Scholastics or Schoolmen. Essentially, Scholasticism was an attempt to harmonize reason with faith by integrating philosophy and theology primarily on the basis of rationalism or logic rather than science and experience.

The greatest of the Scholastic philosophers was Thomas Aquinas, and his most famous work was the *Summa Theologica*. The English translation runs to some twenty volumes. In his writings on economic problems, he applied the principles of Aristotelian philosophy and logic to biblical teaching and canonical dogma. He held that private property accords with natural law; production under private ownership is preferred to production under communal ownership; trade is to be condoned to the extent that it maintains the household and benefits the country; a seller is bound to be truthful with his buyers; fairness exists when goods are exchanged at equal values and at a "just" price which reflects the customary price; wealth is good if it leads to a virtuous life; among the most vulgar of trade practices is "usury."

Aquinas and the Schoolmen were not in sympathy with many of the economic practices of their time, but could do little to change them and hence proceeded to make them as respectable as possible by establishing moral and ethical rules of economic behavior. Many of these rules are now an integral part of American capitalistic philosophy.

Radio Times Hulton Picture Library.

For example, Aquinas decried usury, which he defined as a return for the use of a loan. But he permitted it if a lender had to forgo an alternative investment that would have yielded him an income. This was the principle of *lucrum cessans*—a concept similar to that of "opportunity cost" in modern economics. Similarly, he justified the idea that buyers on credit could pay more than the cash price, that discounts were allowed on promissory notes, and that many business transactions could involve special charges and payments.

Aquinas was canonized in 1323 and his teachings are held in the highest esteem by most Catholic as well as by many non-Catholic educators. He is perhaps the foremost authority among Catholics on social subjects, especially since his views were endorsed by Pope Leo XIII in an 1879 encyclical.

and sellers of resources to transact their business on the best terms that each can get from the other.

Theoretical capitalism is often described as a free-market system. Competition and free markets are closely related. In their most complete or pure form free markets are characterized by (1) a sufficiently large number of buyers and sellers, each with a small enough share of the total business that no one buyer or seller can affect the market price of the commodity in which he is dealing; and (2) the ability of buyers and sellers, unencumbered by economic or institutional restrictions, and possessing full knowledge of market prices and alternatives, to enter or leave markets as they see fit. Under such circumstances, the market price of a particular commodity is established by the interacting forces of demand and supply. Each buyer and each seller, acting in his own best interest as an economic man, decides whether or not he wants to transact business at the going price—a price over which he has no control because he exerts no perceptible influence in the market.

In the real world, competition does not exist in this pure form. The closest we get to a pure free market is in organized exchanges such as the Chicago grain market or the Boston wool market, which are open to all buyers and sellers and which deal in standardized commodities.

A free market (1) establishes competitive prices for both consumer goods and the factors of production and (2) encourages the efficient use of economic resources. Since free markets are at least partially destroyed by the growth of monopolistic practices, society frequently regulates such practices.

The Price System

Who tells workers where to work or what occupations to choose? Who decides that automobiles should be made in Detroit and steel in Pittsburgh? Who declares how many cars should be produced and how many homes should be built? Who specifies the predominant style of women's fall dresses or the color of men's suits?

The greater the degree of competition in an economy, the more these matters will be decided not by some individual or group of individuals, but impersonally and automatically by the *price system* or the *market system*. This essentially is a system of rewards and penalties—profits for firms and individuals who are able to survive, and losses or possibly bankruptcy for those who are not. The price system is fundamental to the traditional concept of capitalism.

How does the price system work? Basically, it operates on the principle that everything that is exchanged—every good, every service, and every resource—has its price. In a free market characterized by a great many buyers and sellers the prices of these things reflect the quantities that sellers make available and the quantities that buyers wish to purchase.

Thus if buyers want to purchase more of a certain good, its price will rise, which will encourage suppliers to produce and sell more of it. On the other hand, if buyers want to purchase less of a certain good this will cause a fall in its price, and suppliers will thereby find it to their advantage to produce and sell less of it.

This interaction between sellers and buyers in a competitive market, and the resulting changes in prices of the commodities in which they deal, are what most people refer to by the familiar phrase "supply and demand."

Government: Rule-maker; Protector; Umpire

The doctrine of laissez-faire, which came into prominence in the eighteenth century as a result of its popularization by Adam Smith in *The Wealth of Nations*, has strong political as well as economic implications. According to this doctrine, the functions of government in a capitalistic system should be confined to certain minimal traditional activities such as maintaining order, defining property rights, enforcing contracts, promoting competition, defending the realm, issuing money, prescribing standards of weights and measures, raising funds by taxation and other means to meet operating expenses, and adjudicating disputes concerning the interpretation of the rules.

Government is thus essential to the existence of capitalism. When society's economic, social, or political values are violated, they must be corrected. When personal freedoms conflict, one man's freedom must be limited so that another's may be preserved. In theoretical capitalism government fulfills the roles of rule-maker, protector, and umpire by imposing minimum restrictions on personal freedoms to protect the well-being of society and by reconciling conflicts of values resulting from the free exercise of property rights.

CONCLUSION: OUR MIXED ECONOMY

Is the doctrine of laissez-faire observed today? Does the invisible hand perform as smoothly as Adam Smith said it would, thereby resulting in the best of all possible economic worlds?

The answers to these questions are neither completely positive nor completely negative. Over the years our economy has become increasingly complicated, and the role of government has expanded. (See Box 1.)

Through the use of legislation of one type or another such as protective tariffs to curb imports, subsidies to stimulate production, and so forth, government has come to play a significant role as a protector and regulator of certain groups within the economy.

Leaders in Economics

ADAM SMITH

1723–1790

Founder of Economics

The year 1776 was marked by two great events in man's struggle for emancipation.

In North America, representatives of the British colonies adopted the *Declaration of Independence*—an eloquent statement setting forth a doctrine of political freedom. In Europe, a former Scottish professor of philosophy at the University of Glasgow published a monumental book entitled *An Inquiry into the Nature and Causes of the Wealth of Nations*—or simply *The Wealth of Nations*, as it is usually called. This was an equally eloquent statement expounding a doctrine of economic freedom. Both events, despite the geographic chasm that separated them, stand as milestones in the Age of Enlightenment and Liberalism that blossomed during the eighteenth century.

Born in Scotland and educated at Glasgow and Oxford, Adam Smith became a lecturer on literature and philosophy in his mid-twenties, and at twenty-eight was appointed professor of logic and moral philosophy at the University of Glasgow. His great book, *The Wealth of Nations*, took him ten years to write, and earned for him the title of "founder of economics" because it was the first complete and systematic study of the subject.

It is a masterful synthesis of centuries of accumulated but separate economic ideas. The book argues that labor, rather than land or money, is the basic source of a nation's wealth; that individuals know best what is good for them; and if unrestricted by government controls or private monopolies will be motivated by the quest for profit to turn out the goods and services that society wants most. Therefore, through free trade and free markets, self-interest will be harnessed to the common good.

Many of the topics Smith discussed in *The Wealth of Nations*—labor; value and price determination; the theory of income distribution involving wages, rent, and profit; the accumulation of capital; and the principles of public finance—appear today in economics textbooks. However,

Historical Pictures Service, Chicago.

Smith's view of "the economic problem" was somewhat narrower than the modern one.

Smith conceived the central task of economics as man's struggle to conquer nature in the production of material wealth. Hence his concern was with increasing the productivity of labor and expanding the size of the market. Today, on the other hand, the basic problem of economics is seen to be a broader one of allocating scarce resources among different uses so as to maximize consumers' satisfactions, and to achieve full employment and steady economic growth without inflation.

To cite a few examples, it has promoted the interests of agriculture, labor, and the consumer. It has controlled competition among the regulated industries, such as domestic transportation, communication, and power. It has sought to maintain effective competition in the unregulated industries that comprise the bulk of our business sector. It has assumed the responsibility of keeping the economy's total production and spending in balance in order to achieve the long-run objectives of economic growth and full employment. And it has become a large provider of many goods and services, among them education, highways, and national defense.

These historical trends suggest the following conclusion:

The American economy is neither a pure market economy nor a pure command economy; it is a mixed but capitalistically oriented economy in which both private individuals and government exercise their economic influence in the marketplace. *The same is true in all capitalistic countries today.*

Evaluation of Capitalism

At the National Weather Service in Washington, D.C., a sign reads: "When we are right, no one remembers; when we are wrong no one forgets."

The same may be said of many of the critics of capitalism. Few observers deny the system's great flexibility and adaptability to cataclysmic changes; nor do they question its ability to organize and stimulate the factors of production to the end of producing a growing stock of goods and services and continually rising standards of living. Criticism usually is directed toward the failure of capitalism to promote human welfare—economic as well as moral and cultural. Since these are attacks against the basic institutions of the system, they must be evaluated before any judgements can be made about the future of capitalism.

RESOURCE ALLOCATION AND EMPLOYMENT

In the traditional or theoretical model of capitalism —in a pure *market economy*—individuals are free to use their resources as they see fit, provided they do not violate one another's property rights. As a result, the factors of production are allocated efficiently and automatically through the free play of market forces.

The reason for this is not hard to understand. Since a market economy is characterized by large numbers of independent buyers and sellers who possess full knowledge of market conditions and are free to enter or leave particular markets as they wish, resources are highly mobile. Therefore, the allocation of these resources is guided by an inexorable law of fundamental importance:

Box 1

Capitalism and Freedom

In his provocative book entitled Capitalism and Freedom, *the distinguished University of Chicago economist and libertarian, Professor Milton Friedman, argues that competitive capitalism provides the strongest assurance of personal freedoms. He points out that an individual who is barred from entering an occupation of his own choosing because he is unable to obtain a license, or a consumer who cannot buy a foreign-made product because of an import restriction, or a farmer who is forbidden to plant wheat without a quota is being deprived of an essential part of his freedom. Further, Friedman contends, economic and political freedoms are not unrelated—as history bears out. "I know of no example," he says, "of a society that has been marked by a large measure of political freedom, and that has not also used something comparable to a free market to organize the bulk of economic activity."*

In general, it is Professor Friedman's position that competitive capitalism is a morally superior type of system because it recognizes the individual's "natural rights" and is noncoercive. Thus Friedman opposes legislation against discrimination in employment by arguing:

Such legislation clearly involves interference with the freedom of individuals to enter into voluntary contracts with one another. It subjects any such contract to approval or disapproval by the state. . . . [T]he appropriate recourse of those of us who believe that a particular criterion such as color is irrelevant is to persuade our fellows to be of like mind, not to use the coercive power of the state to force them to act in accordance with our principles.

Professor Friedman apparently believes that it is more moral to preserve the legal freedom of contract for the employer than to improve the effective bargaining freedom of the weaker employee. Is this a fair assessment of Friedman's position? How would you answer his argument?

Law of Equal Advantage. In a market economy, the owners of resources will always transfer productive factors from less advantageous to more advantageous uses. As this happens, the occupations *out* of which resources are transferred often tend to become more advantageous while the occupations *into* which resources are transferred tend to become less advantageous. This transfer process continues until all occupations are equally advantageous. At that point there is no gain to be made by further transfer of resources; hence the system may be said to be in balance or *equilibrium.*

NOTE: The term "advantageous" includes both monetary and nonmonetary considerations. The latter helps explain why permanent differences in monetary rewards may exist between various occupations.

For example, suppose there is an excess supply of a commodity. Producers will experience a drop in price and profit, causing them to shift their production to more profitable lines. Resources will be reallocated as labor, capital, and other factors of production move out of less advantageous activities where payments for them are declining into more advantageous ones where their services are in greater demand and their owners can command higher returns. In the long run, since productive factors are mobile and prices of goods and resources are free to respond smoothly and quickly to changing demands and supplies, the transfer of resources will bring about an adjustment to equilibrium—a state in which all the factors of production are fully and efficiently utilized.

Our economic system does not perform this smoothly in practice. Although there is a *tendency* for the law of equal advantage to operate, the adjustment to equilibrium is often slow and imperfect. Many obstacles prevent productive resources from responding quickly to advantageous differences among markets. For example, labor acquires specialized skills which are of value only to selected industries. Workers become attached to geographic areas for financial or social reasons. Wage rates in many industries are fixed by union-management contracts. And capital equipment, which is often designed for specific purposes, is likely to have few if any alternative uses. As a result of these and other rigidities, our economy may suffer from prolonged periods of resource misallocation and unemployment. This is a major shortcoming of the capitalistic system. The problem, therefore, occupies a large part of our attention throughout this book as we seek to develop methods for overcoming it.

ECONOMIC INEQUALITY

A second criticism of capitalism is that private property and inheritance are major causes of inequality in the distribution of income and wealth. Adam Smith and most later nineteenth-century classical economists who propagated the traditional doctrines of capitalism did not sanction economic inequality, but condoned it on the ground that it enabled society to finance capital formation with the savings of the rich. One of the great classicists, the eminent economist and philosopher John Stuart Mill (1806–1873), went so far as to say that inequality is "a repugnant evil of human society," but necessary for economic progress.

Modern economists recognize that wide differences in income and wealth can cause social discontent, unequal opportunities for education and employment, and a general loss of economic efficiency. While many concur that some economic inequality may be desirable because it provides incentives, they also agree that democratic societies should seek to reduce large disparities.

The chief method used to limit economic inequality is taxation—especially taxes on income and inheritance. But many loopholes exist in the tax laws, enabling high-income groups to decrease substantially by legal means the taxes they pay. As a result, a larger share of the total tax burden is borne by others—particularly those at the middle- and lower-income levels. We shall have more to say about this problem in later chapters.

CONCENTRATION OF ECONOMIC POWER

A third criticism of capitalism arises from the development of the modern corporation. In the classical view, each individual has the natural right to own and use property. Competition among buyers and sellers then ensures that efforts of individuals to pursue their own best interests enhance rather than impair the general welfare.

The growth of the corporation as the dominant form of business organization has greatly altered this traditional concept of capitalism. *Separation of ownership and control* has developed because the owners and the managers of many corporations constitute two distinct groups: passive stockholders whose shares of ownership are often widely dispersed; and managers who are usually hired, nonowning administrators, but who control the corporation's property and determine its use.

In addition, the emergence of giant corporations and strong unions has strengthened monopolistic powers throughout the economy, helping to undermine competitive markets and misallocate scarce resources. Through legislative and judicial means, government has tried to curb such concentrations of economic power, but often with only limited success. Society is thus faced with a profound problem:

Modern industrial capitalism (unlike classical capitalism) permits *power without property,* by virtue of office rather than of ownership. In view of this, how can a democratic society prevent an oligarchy of corporation managers from abusing its power, and how can it direct this power into channels that will best serve the general welfare?

There is no simple solution to this complex problem. Attempts to solve it, we shall find, involve many political as well as economic considerations.

SOCIAL BALANCE: PRIVATE VS. SOCIAL GOODS

A fourth criticism of capitalism is that it overallocates resources to the production of private goods such as automobiles, television sets, bowling alleys, and shopping centers, while underallocating them to the production of such social goods as schools, libraries, public hospitals, and parks. As a result, it causes an inefficient distribution of resources between private and social goods—a lack of *social balance.* The existence of social imbalance is said by critics to be due to two major factors:

First, a capitalistic system by its very nature tends to favor the production of private goods over social goods. This is because private goods are sold in the marketplace, where consumers can express their preferences by paying for the commodities they want and rejecting those they do not. Many social goods, on the other hand, come into existence only through the painful process of taxation. To the extent that they are made available "free," it is impossible to know what values consumers place upon them. Since political representatives are acutely aware of their constituents' reluctance to bear increased taxes in return for more social goods, there is a tendency for resources to be underallocated to the production of such goods.

Second, private goods are heavily advertised and promoted, whereas most social goods are not. Consumer choice is therefore biased toward private consumption. The result is that much private expenditure goes to satisfy superficial wants artificially created, while many fundamental public needs are neglected because they cannot compete successfully for the same resources.

In reply to these arguments, some people deny the significance of social imbalance, contending that in a democratic, competitive capitalistic society the problem is unimportant—for several reasons:

1. In their dual roles as consumers and taxpayers, citizens ultimately decide the proportion of the economy's resources to be allocated between private and social goods, by expressing their wishes in the marketplace in terms of the prices they bid for the goods they want, and at the polls in terms of the votes they cast for the candidates and issues they support.

2. People know better than the government how to spend their income.

3. Tax money spent for social goods does not necessarily yield greater satisfactions than the same money spent for private goods.

4. Social goods usually tend to be overproduced because they are "given away" rather than sold. Further, the increased production of various social goods over the years provides ample evidence that the growing desire for such goods is not being neglected.

Whether or not you agree that social imbalance exists, it is clear that in the short run an economy operating at full employment can expand its production of social goods only by reducing its production of private goods. This can be seen by expressing the alternatives in terms of a production-possibilities curve. Such a curve emphasizes that the *real costs* (sacrifices) to society of having more of one class of goods are the satisfactions it forgoes by doing with less of the other. In the long run, however, it can have more of both classes of goods if it experiences economic growth—that is, an outward shift of its production-possibilities curve.

OTHER CRITICISMS OF CAPITALISM

Capitalism has further been condemned for some of its other widely held beliefs and practices. For example, the goal of ever-increasing production is questioned on the basis that it is damaging to society and its environment. Other critics have concluded that rich, advanced capitalistic countries profit from exploiting poor, less developed ones. Still others argue that the United States—the world's leading exponent of capitalism—benefits economically from perpetuating a class structure which associates wealth with privilege, and poverty with oppression.

Many critics thus conclude that most of our economic and social disparities are the fault of capitalism per se. They believe that an advanced capitalistic society, because of its vested interests and its inherent emphasis upon monetary rather than human values, is neither able nor willing to solve these problems within the framework of its existing institutions. Therefore, they further conclude, the institutions themselves must be altered—or at least radical measures must be introduced—before any significant improvements in human welfare can be realized.

The Future of Capitalism

Criticisms such as these raise fundamental questions about the future of capitalism. Will the system survive? If it does not, what will replace it? If it does survive, what form will it take?

Since the nineteenth century, theorists and philosophers have predicted that tendencies inherent within the capitalistic system will destroy it, making way for some form of collectivism. In this new system there would be no institution of private property; instead there would be social ownership of the means of production and distribution. Self-interest, laissez-faire, and other pillars of capitalism, since they are closely tied to the tradition of private property, would also largely disappear.

Is this prediction likely to materialize? Probably not. Democratic capitalism has always demonstrated substantial adaptability to change. This is perhaps its greatest strength. Modern mixed capitalistic economies differ from the nineteenth-century ideal of pure capitalism precisely because politicians and businessmen have made efforts to overcome particular shortcomings while still preserving as much of the basic institutions as possible. Two post-World War II developments have been particularly responsible for shaping mixed capitalism as it exists in many countries today.

1. Neoliberalism underwent a renascence in Western Europe during the late 1940s and 1950s. Unhappy experiences with totalitarian regimes before World War II made most Europeans receptive to the election of social democratic parties of the liberal re-formist type. These political groups disavowed any connection with hard-line Marxism or communism and advocated social evolution rather than revolution. The United States encouraged this neoliberalist trend in Europe because the movement retained the basic premises of nineteenth-century classical liberalism—personal freedom, law, parliamentary institutions, and so on—while permitting the war-torn countries to hasten their economic recovery.

2. In all capitalistic countries, the state became increasingly involved in the regulation of economic affairs—a trend which has continued to the present time. During the Great Depression of the 1930s, much thought and effort were given to alleviating unemployment. John Maynard Keynes, a British economist whose ideas were responsible for a large part of modern economics, urged government to intervene in the economy to promote full employment by engaging in heavy deficit spending, financing public works projects, and controlling interest rates on money. These fiscal and monetary measures gained increasing acceptance in the United States and the United Kingdom after World War II. On the other hand, several other Western European countries chose a somewhat different kind of involvement with the state by implementing the concept of a *planned economy*. In this type of economic system, the government, through a preconceived plan, plays a primary role in directing economic resources for the purpose of deciding what to produce, how much, and possibly for whom. Such a system may or may not be a command economy, depending on whether the government operates within an authoritarian or a democratic framework. In Western Europe the countries which adopted planned economies remained democratic; as a matter of fact, in some of them the sponsoring political parties were later voted out of office in free elections. By that time, however, the greatly enhanced role of the state had become firmly established.

Based on these lessons of recent history we can state with reasonable confidence:

Modern capitalism, through government legislation and policies, will continue seeking to combine freedom, stability, and progress. Today's mixed capitalistic economies will therefore thrive only as long as they (1) remain adaptive to the changing needs of their societies and (2) preserve democratic mechanisms for correcting outdated institutions and laws.

The Circular Flow of Economic Activity

Some important features of a pure capitalistic system are illustrated by the diagram in Exhibit 1. This model assumes that the total economy is divided into two sectors: households and businesses; it also shows how these sectors meet one another in two sets of markets: the product markets and the resource markets.

In the *product markets*, households buy the goods and services that businesses sell. Their payments for these are represented by consumption expenditures which become the receipts of businesses. In the *resource markets*, businesses buy the factors of production that households sell. Their payments for these are costs which become the money incomes of households.

All these transactions are accomplished in free markets by a price system that registers the wishes of buyers and sellers. Through the price system, therefore, the product markets are the places where businesses decide WHAT to produce, whereas the

---

Exhibit 1

The Circular Flow of Economic Activity
or How Millions of Businesses and Households Take in
Each Other's Washing

Households and businesses are linked through the product markets, where goods and services are exchanged, and through the resource markets, where the factors of production are exchanged. The questions of WHAT and HOW to produce are answered in these markets. Households act as buyers in the product markets and as sellers in the resource markets, whereas the reverse is true of busi- *nesses. The outer loop shows physical flows in one direction, while the inner loop shows money flows in the opposite direction. (NOTE: The question, FOR WHOM? is not directly apparent in this chart because it depends not only on factor prices which are determined in the resource market, but also on the way in which the factors are distributed in the household sector.)*

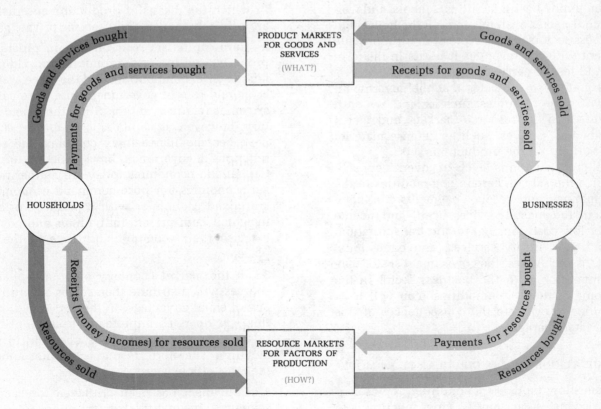

resource markets are the places where they decide HOW to produce.

One other feature of the diagram should be noted: the outer loop portrays the physical flow of goods and resources in one direction, while the inner loop shows the corresponding dollar flow in the opposite direction. In a barter economy, of course, only goods and resources would be exchanged and hence there would be no dollar flows.

ENLARGING THE FLOW: A MIXED-ECONOMY MODEL

The two-sector model can be expanded to include a third sector: government. This has been done in Exhibit 2. This enlarged model is a closer approximation of a modern mixed capitalistic system. The government sector, it should be noted, embraces all levels—federal, state, and local. Observe that the addition of government has greatly increased the complexity of the system by adding *twelve* new flows to the previous two-sector model.

Government buys the services of factors of production in the resource markets and pays for them at going rates. It then uses some of these resources to produce nonmarket or "free" social goods and services such as national defense, police and fire protection, public health facilities, schools, and welfare, which it makes available to both the household and business sectors. These sectors, in turn, provide government with the revenues it needs in the form of taxes and fees to carry on its operations.

The diagram also indicates that the government sector owns some resources, such as land, which it sells or leases in the resource markets, and that it buys goods and services, such as defense matériel and clerical help, in the product markets.

In addition, the various levels of government sell, or subsidize the sale of, certain commodities in the product markets and receive payments for them. Examples include postal services, health and income insurance, low-cost housing, public transportation, packaged liquor, utility services, and educational materials. In such cases, the government sector may be in competition with the business sector in the sale of some of these commodities. You will have opportunities to evaluate the consequences of this in several later chapters.

SOME LIMITATIONS OF THE CIRCULAR-FLOW MODEL

The circular-flow model is a simplified representation of an economic system. Its chief function is to illustrate important aggregate economic relationships. But, like any model, it is an abstraction from reality and therefore omits certain features. Among them:

1. The model says nothing about the behavior of individual buyers and sellers or about the ways in which they react to determine prices and quantities in the product and resource markets. Hence it is a *macroeconomic* rather than microeconomic model.

2. The model assumes a stable, rather than a fluctuating, circular flow. It does not disclose the effects of variations in the flow on the economy's production and employment. Therefore it overlooks the problems of recession and inflation, which are among the most critical economic issues of our time.

Despite these shortcomings, the circular-flow model provides many useful insights. They will become increasingly apparent as we amplify its underlying implications and ideas in subsequent chapters.

SUMMARY OF IMPORTANT IDEAS

1. The economic system of the United States and most other countries of the Western world is capitalistic. Capitalism is a type of economic organization in which the means of production and distribution are privately owned and used for private gain.

2. Pure capitalism rests on certain pillars: private property, self-interest, economic individualism or laissez-faire, competition, and the price system. The economic role of government in a pure capitalistic system is relatively minor. Since the nineteenth century, however, as capitalistic or market economies have become increasingly complex, the economic functions of government have gained in importance. Capitalistic economies today are neither pure market economies nor pure command economies; they are mixed economies with capitalistic orientations in which both private individuals and government exercise their economic influence in the marketplace.

3. In the market economy of pure capitalism, resources will distribute themselves according to the law of equal advantage. In the real world, however, this law operates imperfectly because of rigidities in the economy and various obstacles to resource mobility. Therefore, resources are not allocated in the most efficient way.

4. Capitalism has been criticized for encouraging economic inequality, concentrations of economic

Exhibit 2

The Circular Flow in a Mixed Capitalistic Economy

Inclusion of the government sphere permits a closer approximation of our mixed capitalistic economy. The resources that government buys are used to produce many nonmarket or "free" social commodities like national defense, public safety, and welfare as well as various market commodities (which may be partially subsidized) such as postal services, public transportation, and utility services. Most of the revenues which finance government activities come from taxes and fees (income taxes, property taxes, license fees, etc.). Government also sells or leases some of its resources, such as land, in the resource markets and buys goods and services, ranging from military equipment to clerical help, in the product markets. (NOTE: As explained in the previous exhibit, the question of FOR WHOM is not directly apparent in this chart.)

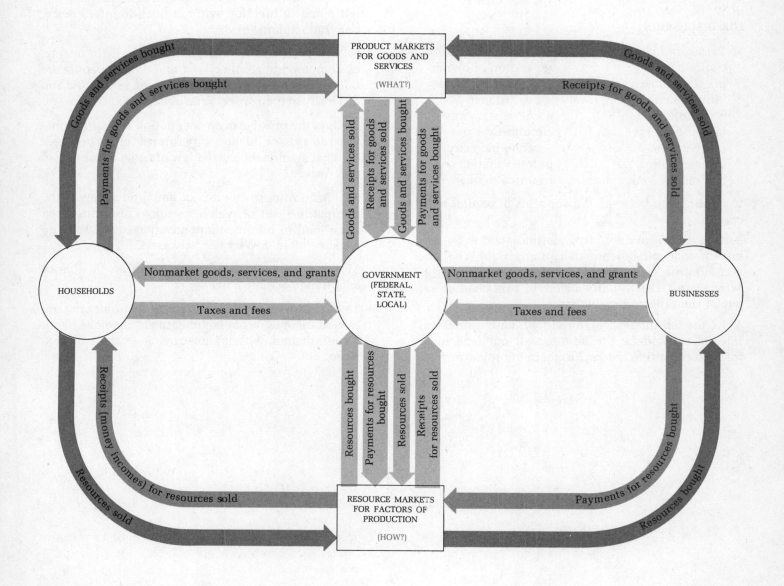

power, social imbalance between private and social goods, environmental destruction, imperialism and exploitation of poor countries, and class differences. Whether these charges are true or not, the future of today's mixed capitalistic economies depends on their remaining able to adapt to the changing needs of their societies while preserving democratic mechanisms for correcting existing shortcomings.

5. The circular-flow model is a simplified representation of our economy. It focuses on aggregate relationships by depicting the streams of money, goods, and resources that link major sectors and markets.

FOR DISCUSSION

1. *Terms and concepts to review:*

capitalism	separation of owner-
private property	ship and control
"invisible hand"	social balance
economic man	planned economy
laissez-faire	circular flow of
competition	economic activity
price system	product markets
law of equal advantage	resource markets

2. Distinguish between the concepts of *capital* and *capitalism*.

3. The "profit motive" is sometimes said to be the most fundamental feature of capitalism. (a) What do you suppose is meant by the "profit motive"? (b) Why wasn't it explicitly listed in this chapter as one of the pillars of capitalism?

4. Do the self-interests of individuals and businesses interact to produce the best overall outcome in a freely competitive market? Explain your answer.

5. (a) "In a free competitive economy, the consumer is king." What does this mean? (b) "The producer, not the consumer, is king. After all, the producer is the one who advertises; hence he is the one who creates wants and thereby influences what consumers will purchase." True or false? Explain.

6. Does the price system settle the three questions of WHAT, HOW, and FOR WHOM in some particular order? Explain. Can you give an illustration or example?

7. It is often said that the beauty of the price system is to be found in its self-regulating nature. As a result, the market is its own guardian—provided it is left alone to function without outside interference. Can you explain this?

8. One of the shortcomings of a capitalistic society, as compared to a collectivist one, is that people are not compensated in proportion to the usefulness and difficulty of their work. True or false? Explain.

9. Does the prestige of an occupation affect its monetary rewards, or do monetary rewards affect prestige? Of what significance is the law of equal advantage in this respect?

10. According to the law of equal advantage, "the occupations *out* of which resources are transferred often tend to become more advantageous." Why do we say "often"? Why not "always"?

11. In what ways has capitalism been flexible or adaptive to society's needs?

12. Capitalism is often criticized for producing unearned income. What is "unearned" income? Can it be eliminated without destroying capitalism? Explain.

Should We End Restrictive Licensing?

Would you like to operate a radio or TV station? All you have to do is persuade the Federal Communications Commission to grant you a license. The cost of the license would be nominal—if you could get it. And, if you waited a reasonable time, you could sell the license to a "reputable" buyer at an extraordinary profit—without the FCC so much as raising an eyebrow.

You don't want to operate a radio or TV station? Then how about a commercial airline instead? In that case you would have to persuade the Civil Aeronautics Board to grant you the necessary license. This too would be extremely difficult.

Perhaps you want to go into the oil business. If so, you can often purchase foreign oil for considerably less than domestic oil—provided you can first convince the Department of Interior to grant you a permit.

If you want to open a liquor store, set up a bank, own a taxi, run a barber shop or in some places even a bootblack stand, you must first acquire a license. In most cases the number of licenses granted is strictly limited, and for many activities they are simply unobtainable. Many economists believe that the licensing mechanism, instead of being a legitimate device which government can use to raise revenue and to protect the general welfare, has too often become a restrictive measure for controlling competition within an industry. No economist has expressed this view more forcefully than Professor Milton Friedman of the University of Chicago.

What Should Be Done?

In various books and articles, Professor Friedman has argued that most restrictive licensing should be abolished completely. (He even believes that medical doctors should not be licensed—that anyone who wants to practice medicine

should be free to do so.) For example: TV and radio should not be controlled by government. Oil import quotas should be eliminated permanently. Free competition should be permitted among the airlines, subject only to objective safety standards. Since 1938, when CAB control was introduced, not a single new line has been granted permission by the CAB to operate—and not for lack of applicants. Similarly, anyone who wants to set up a liquor store, or a commercial bank, or drive a cab should be free to do so, provided he can satisfy objective minimum standards of responsibility or competence. Freedom to sell a product or service should not, as now, depend also on a bureaucrat's judgement about whether additional units are "necessary" to serve the public. Let the market decide.

Auctioning Rights

Suppose, however, that the government decides to limit the number who may engage in any activity to a smaller number than wish to do so. The least government can do is to avoid giveaways. It can determine how many people it is going to permit in an activity, specify the terms and conditions, announce these publicly, and hold an open auction to decide which particular persons will engage in the activity.

This is a simple and direct way to end giveaways. TV licenses can be auctioned off. So can rights to import oil. Rights to particular air routes, to establish one of a limited number of liquor stores, to operate one of a limited number of cabs—each and every one of these can be auctioned off. The public will still suffer from governmentally created monopoly, but at least it will recover some of its loss in the form of revenue.

The general principle works both ways. The argument for selling limited

rights to the highest bidder rather than giving them away is precisely the same as the argument for buying resources that government needs rather than commandeering them—whether those resources be land for public buildings, the services of policemen, or the services of soldiers.

QUESTIONS

1. In his argument for free TV, how do you suppose Professor Friedman would reply to the question: "But the number of TV channels is limited to a fairly small number. Shouldn't the government, in all fairness, decide who is to use them?" Explain your answer.

2. If you were to ask Professor Friedman to describe the type of TV system that would emerge in a free and unrestricted market, what do you suppose would be his answer? (HINTS: Think of the different kinds of newspapers, magazines, books, and various other publications we have today, some supported all or in part by advertising, fees, subscriptions, etc. Would a similar situation develop with free TV? Would TV programs be better or worse?)

3. Professor Friedman contends that the auctioning of rights would provide "a simple and direct way to end giveaways." It would also eliminate the use of licensing as "a restrictive measure for controlling competition within an industry."

Unfortunately, however, Professor Friedman fails to point out that auctioning would result in an inequitable distribution of rights. Can you explain why this would happen?

CHAPTER 4

The Laws of Supply and Demand: The Price System in a Pure Market Economy

CHAPTER PREVIEW

What are the laws of supply and demand? How do they determine prices?

How does a market economy operate? What is a price system?

What can be said about the pros and cons of a market economy? How well does it answer the three fundamental questions: WHAT? HOW? FOR WHOM?

One unusual thing about economics is that even a parrot can answer many questions about economics with just three simple words, *supply and demand.* Here are a few examples.

QUESTION: Why are Rembrandts expensive while water is cheap—especially since everyone needs water more than he needs Rembrandts?

ANSWER: Supply and demand.

QUESTION: Why is the cost of medical care rising faster than prices generally?

ANSWER: Supply and demand.

QUESTION: Why are some luxurious apartments vacant, while there is a shortage of low-cost housing?

ANSWER: Supply and demand.

QUESTION: Why do the prices of some commodities fluctuate while the prices of others remain stable?

ANSWER: Supply and demand.

Such simplistic answers to complex problems are not very illuminating. Nevertheless, much of economics is concerned with supply and demand—and in this chapter you discover more about this apparently simple but actually complicated subject.

What Do We Mean by Demand?

If pizzas were $4 each, how many would you buy per month? What if the price were $3? $2? Would you buy twice as many at $1 as at $2?

These are typical of the questions that arise in the study of demand. What is demand? In economics it has a special meaning:

Demand is a relation showing the various amounts of a commodity that buyers would be willing and able to purchase at possible alternative prices during a given period of time, all other things remaining the same.

The commodity can be anything—pizzas, shoes, transistor radios, television sets, haircuts, books, houses, labor time, bulldozers, computers, or any other good or service bought by consumers, businesses, or government agencies. Further, the definition assumes that demand means both desire and ability to pay, and that either of these taken separately is of no economic significance in the marketplace.

Thus if you want a steak but cannot pay for it—or if you can pay but prefer hamburger—you exercise no economic influence in the market for steaks. But if you have both the desire and the ability to pay, these together will affect your demand for the product—that is, the number of pounds of steak you would be willing to purchase at various prices during a period of time.

THE DEMAND SCHEDULE

Suppose you were a grain merchant dealing in, for example, wheat, corn, barley, or oats. What is your demand for a specific commodity such as wheat?

According to the above definition of demand, you must first ask, "At what prices and for how long?" It seems likely that within a given period you would buy more wheat at a lower price than at a higher one, and at a given price you would probably buy more in a longer period than in a shorter one. In view of this you might prepare a hypothetical list of the number of bushels of wheat you would buy at different prices during a particular time interval, such as a day, assuming that your income and the prices of other commodities remain the same.

Such a list is what economists call a demand schedule, as shown in Exhibit 1. This schedule represents your individual demand for wheat over the price range shown. The schedule tells you that at $5 per bushel you would buy 5 bushels a day. At a price of $4 per bushel you would buy 10 bushels a day, and so on. Of course, the schedule can be made more detailed by extending the price scale from zero to "infinity" and by quoting the prices in dollars and

Exhibit 1

An Individual's Demand Schedule for Wheat

A demand schedule is a list showing the number of units of a product that would be purchased at various possible prices during a given period of time.

	Price per bushel	Quantity demanded per day
A	$5	5
B	4	10
C	3	20
D	2	35
E	1	60

cents instead of just dollars alone. But such detail is not necessary. As you will see, the schedule already gives you the highlights of your demand for wheat, which is all you need to draw a graph. (See also Box 1.)

SKETCHING A DEMAND CURVE

Most people prefer to look at a chart instead of a table of figures. This is easily done by converting the information in Exhibit 1 to the diagram in Exhibit 2. The graphing process is done in three steps.

Step 1. Draw the vertical and horizontal axes of the chart and put the labels on them as shown. It is customary in economics to label the vertical axis P for price and the horizontal axis Q for quantity. The starting point or origin of the chart is always at the lower left-hand corner labeled 0.

Step 2. Plot the corresponding prices and quantities with large dots, and label them with the appropriate letters A, B, C, D, E from the demand schedule in Exhibit 1. These letters help you to identify the points, as you will see below. After you gain some experience in graphing, the emphasized points and letters will no longer be necessary.

Step 3. Connect the points with a smooth curve.

What you now have is called a demand curve. It represents the graphic equivalent of the demand schedule in Exhibit 1. The advantage of the curve is that it enables you to "see" the relationship between price and quantity demanded, and to read off the values at a glance, much as you would use a map to locate a ship at sea by its latitude and longitude.

Box 1

Why Wheat?

Why are we using wheat as an example? Why not use a more familiar product like cars or television sets?

The answer is that we want to demonstrate how the price is established for a uniform or standardized product in a highly competitive market characterized by a great many buyers and sellers, each acting independently according to his best interests. This type of situation or model will result in a single market price for the product at any given time. Clearly, autos and television sets do not meet these requirements for several reasons: each is produced by a relatively small number of sellers; each is nonstandardized or differentiated by brand name, model, year, style, color, etc.; and each is characterized by different prices rather than by single prices. These conditions are true in varying degrees for nearly all the other products we buy every day.

On the other hand, products like wheat as well as the other commodities shown in the accompanying list approximate the requirements rather closely. Any one of them may be used in a model to illustrate the "pure" operation of supply and demand. Later you will see how this model may be modified in order to reflect the ways in which prices are determined in other industries of our mixed capitalistic system.

Commodities

Cash Prices

(quotations as of 4 P.M. Eastern Time)

FOODS	Mon.	Fri.	Yr. Ago
Flour, hard winter NY cwt	\$11.65	\$11.60	\$8.10
Coffee, Santos 4s NY lb...........	.70	.70	$.57\frac{1}{2}$
Cocoa, Accra NY lb	.77	$.77\frac{1}{4}$	$.37\frac{3}{8}$
Sugar, Raw NY lb	.1107	.1107	.0902
Butter, Fresh A-92 sc NY lb......	$.74\text{-}.74\frac{1}{2}$	$.74\text{-}.74\frac{1}{2}$	$.69\frac{3}{4}$
Eggs, Lge white, Chgo., doz	$.64\frac{1}{2}$	$.64\frac{1}{2}$	$.39\frac{1}{2}$
Broilers, Dressed "A" NY lb ...	.36	.36	$.28\frac{1}{2}$
GRAINS AND FEEDS			
Pepper, black NY lb.................	.59	.58	.45
Wheat, No. 2 ord hard KC bu......	$4.64\frac{1}{2}$	4.65	$2.21\frac{3}{8}$
Oats, No. 1 wh. hvy, Chgo., bu	$1.40\frac{1}{2}$	1.36	.85
Rye, No. 2 Minneapolis bu......	2.45	2.45	1.15
Barley, top qlty., Mpls., bu......	2.66	2.65	1.35
MISCELLANEOUS			
Cottonseed Oil, crd Miss Vly lb	.19	.19	$.10\frac{1}{2}$
Soybean Oil, crd Decatur, Ill. lb	.1982	.1918	.0976
Peanut Oil, crd Southeast lb ...	$.24\frac{1}{2}$	$.24\frac{1}{2}$	$.17\frac{3}{4}$
Cotton, 1 in. mid Memphis lb...	.7250	.7105	.2950
Print Cloth, 64x60 45-in. NY yd	.50	.50	$.23\frac{1}{2}$
Steel Scrap, 1 hvy melt Chg. ton	86.00	86.00	38.00
Lead, NY lb	$.16\frac{1}{2}$	$.16\frac{1}{2}$	$.14\frac{3}{4}$
Zinc, per lb	$.20\frac{1}{4}$	$.20\frac{1}{4}$	.18

SOURCE: Adapted from *The Wall Street Journal*.

Exhibit 2

An Individual's Demand Curve for Wheat

A demand curve is the graph of a demand schedule. Each point along the curve represents a different price-quantity combination. A demand curve slopes downward from left to right, reflecting the fact that the quantity demanded of a product varies inversely with the price. This is called the law of demand.

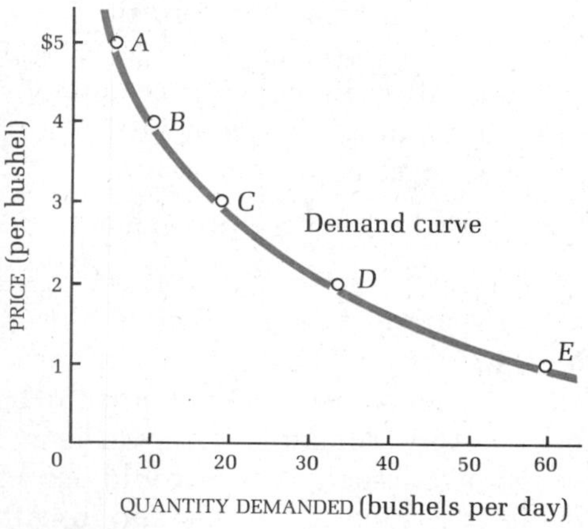

For instance, point C represents 20 bushels of wheat demanded per day at a price of \$3 per bushel. Would you agree that at \$1.50 per bushel the quantity demanded is 45 bushels per day? Can you verify from the chart that at a quantity demanded of 35 bushels per day, the *highest price* (called the *demand price*) you would be willing to pay is \$2 per bushel?

THE LAW OF DEMAND

A look at the demand curve in Exhibit 2 reveals its most fundamental property: *the curve slopes downward from left to right*—from northwest to southeast. This characteristic illustrates the law of demand, which applies to virtually all commodities: wheat, books, houses, automobiles, stereo records, clothing, or practically anything else you care to name. Here is a definition:

Law of Demand. The quantity demanded of a good varies inversely with its price, assuming that all other things which may affect demand—especially the buyer's income, tastes, and the prices of other commodities—remain the same. ("Inversely" means that as the price of a good decreases, the corresponding quantity demanded increases; as the price of a good increases, the corresponding quantity demanded decreases.)

Why does the law of demand operate as it does? This question can be answered in several ways.

1. If the price of a good decreases, you can *afford* to buy more of it if your income, tastes, and the prices of other goods remain the same. For instance, if you like pizza with all the trimmings, but find it too expensive to buy frequently, a lower price might induce you to purchase it more often.

2. When the price of a product is reduced, you may buy more of it because it becomes a better bargain than other goods are—assuming as before that your income, tastes, and the prices of other goods remain constant. Thus if the price of steak falls, you might buy more steak and fewer substitutes like hamburger or hot dogs. On the other hand, if the price of steak rises, you would tend to buy less steak and more substitutes.

3. Finally, the downward-sloping demand curve tells you that you would be willing to pay a relatively high price for a small amount of something; but the more you have of it—other things remaining the same—the less you would care to pay for one more unit. Why? Because *each extra unit gives you less additional satisfaction or "utility" than the previous unit.*

For example, however crazy you are about ice-cream sundaes, there is a limit to the number you can eat in any given period: after the first few you would probably get sick.

No matter how much you like a product, your demand curve will slope downward for the three sets of reasons given above. And businessmen, of course, often operate as if they believe a law of (downward-sloping) demand exists, for why else would they advertise bargains that encourage people to buy more goods at lower prices?

MARKET DEMAND IS THE SUM OF INDIVIDUAL DEMANDS

If you were the only buyer of wheat in the market, your individual demand schedule would also be the total market demand schedule. In reality, of course, there are many other buyers. Hence the total market demand schedule is obtained by simply adding up the quantities demanded by all buyers at each possible price.

Exhibit 3 shows how this is done. This assumes there are only three buyers in the market—Mr. X, Mr. Y, and Mr. Z—but the example can easily be expanded to include as many buyers as you wish. Note that the individual demand curves have all been labeled so that they can be referred to as needed.

TWO KINDS OF CHANGES INVOLVING DEMAND

Once you understand the notion of a demand curve, you can use it to distinguish between two basic types of variation: One is called a "change in the quantity demanded"; the other is a "change in demand."

Changes in the Quantity Demanded

Let us look again at Exhibit 2. According to the law of demand, a downhill movement along the same curve in the general direction A, B, C, etc.,—signifies an increase in the quantity demanded as the price is reduced; on the other hand, an upward movement along the curve in the general direction E, D, C, . . . signifies a decrease in the quantity demanded as the price is raised. Any such movement along the same curve, whether downward or upward, is called a *change in the quantity demanded.* Note that this expression refers to changes in the quantities purchased by buyers.

Changes in Demand

The law of demand says that the quantity demanded of a good varies inversely with its price, assuming that all other things remain the same. What are these "all other" things? What happens if they do not remain the same?

Among the "all other" factors that will influence the demand for a commodity are the following: (1) buyers' money incomes, (2) prices of related commodities, and (3) nonmonetary factors. Since these conditions are assumed to be constant when you draw a demand curve, a change in any one of them will cause a shift of the demand curve to a new position. When this happens, we say that there has been a *change in demand.*

Exhibit 3

Market Demand for Wheat, Three Buyers

The total market demand for wheat is obtained by summing all of the individual quantities demanded at each price.

Price per bushel	Quantity demanded by Mr. X		Quantity demanded by Mr. Y		Quantity demanded by Mr. Z		Total market demand per day
$5	0	+	15	+	20	=	35
4	9	+	20	+	26	=	55
3	22	+	27	+	33	=	82
2	42	+	38	+	43	=	123
1	80	+	65	+	60	=	205

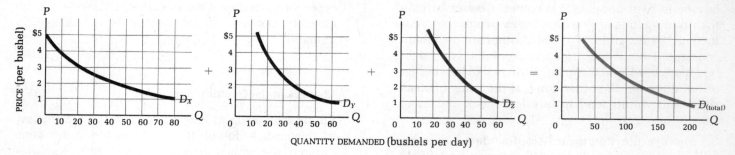

QUANTITY DEMANDED (bushels per day)

1. An increase in demand can be visualized on a chart as a shift of the demand curve to the right, as shown in Exhibit 4. The shift takes place from the old demand curve *D* to the new demand curve *D'*.

What does this increase in demand tell you? It shows that, *at any given price, buyers are now willing to purchase more than they were willing to purchase before.* For example, the dashed lines on the chart indicate that at a price of $30 per unit, buyers were previously willing to purchase 300 units per week. After the increase in demand, they are willing to buy 400 units a week at the same price of $30 per unit.

2. A decrease in demand, shown in Exhibit 5, can be visualized as a shift of the demand curve to the left. This time the chart illustrates that, *at any given price, buyers are now willing to purchase less than they were willing to purchase before.* Thus at $30 per unit, people were willing to buy 300 units a week. Now, after the decrease in demand, they are willing to buy only 200 units per week at the same price of $30 per unit.

TEST YOURSELF I

An increase in demand also means that for any given quantity demanded, buyers are now willing to pay a *higher price* per unit than they were willing to pay before.

1. Can you define a decrease in demand in a parallel way?

2. In Exhibit 4, what is your estimate of the highest price per unit that buyers were willing to pay for 300 units per week, before and after the increase in demand?

3. In Exhibit 5, what is your estimate of the highest price per unit that buyers were willing to pay for 200 units per week, before and after the decrease in demand?

How do changes in any of the three demand determinants listed above bring about a change in demand—that is, a shift of the demand curve either to the right or to the left?

1. *Buyers' incomes.* The demands for most goods vary directly with buyers' incomes. This means that demand curves shift to the right when incomes rise and to the left when incomes fall. Goods whose demand curves behave in this way are known as *superior goods,* or more popularly as *normal goods,* because they represent the "normal" situation. Examples include most food, clothing, appliances, and other nondurable and durable items that people typically buy.

For some goods, however, changes in consumption (prices remaining constant) vary inversely with changes in income over a certain range of income. Such goods are called *inferior goods.* Typical examples are bread, potatoes, beans, hamburger, and used clothing, bought by poor families. As the incomes of these families rise, they can afford to buy better qualities of goods. Thus they spend less on bread and potatoes and more on fresh fruits and vegetables, less on beans and hamburger and more on steaks and chops, less on used clothing and more on new suits and dresses.

2. *Prices of related goods (in consumption).* A second factor determining the demand for any good

is the price of related goods. The degree of relationship depends on the extent to which the products are competitive or complementary with each other. Thus if buyers' incomes remain constant, the commodities they purchase may be placed in one of two categories.

Some products are *substitute goods;* the more that people consume of one product, the less they consume of the other. Thus, an increase in the price of one leads to an increase in the demand for the other, and a decrease in the price of one leads to a decrease in the demand for the other. For example, if the price of Coke increases, people will probably buy less Coke and more Pepsi instead. The market demand curve for Pepsi will therefore shift to the right. On the other hand, if the price of Coke decreases, people will be inclined to buy more Coke and less Pepsi. Hence the market demand curve for Pepsi will shift to the left. What other substitute products can you think of?

Some products are *complementary goods;* the more that people consume of one, the more they consume of the other. An increase in the price of one leads to a decrease in the demand for the other,

---

Exhibit 4

Increase in Demand

An increase in demand can be represented by a shift of the demand curve to the right. At any given price, people are now willing to buy more than they were willing to buy before.

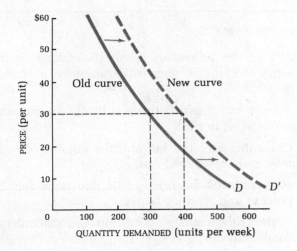

Exhibit 5

Decrease in Demand

A decrease in demand can be represented by a shift of the demand curve to the left. At any given price, people are now willing to buy less than they were willing to buy before.

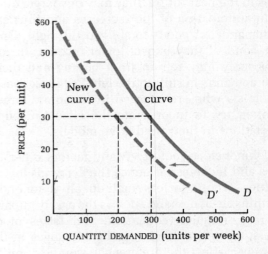

and a decrease in the price of one leads to an increase in the demand for the other. For example, if the price of cameras increases, people will buy fewer cameras—and less film. The market demand curve for film will shift to the left.

Products which are neither substitutes nor complements are unrelated; the consumption of one does not affect the consumption of the other. Therefore a change in the price of one does not cause a change in the demand for the other. Some examples are salt and pencils, chewing gum and paper clips, thumbtacks and mustard. Keep in mind, however, that expenditures on unrelated pairs of commodities must represent a relatively small percentage of the consumer's budget. Otherwise, if a buyer's expenditure on a good absorbs a relatively large proportion of his budget, a change in its price may affect the buyer's demand for another product even if the latter is neither competitive nor complementary with the former.

To generalize thus far:

If buyers' incomes remain constant, the market demand curve of any commodity will move in the same direction as a change in the price of its substitute and in the opposite direction from a change in the price of its complement. This means that for substitute products the relationship between a change in the price of one commodity and the resulting change in demand for the other is *direct*; for complementary products the relationship is *inverse*.

Of course, buyers' expectations of incomes and prices can also influence their demands for commodities. If buyers expect higher incomes or higher prices in the near future, they may buy larger quantities in anticipation of the increases and thus cause the demands for goods to shift to the right. On the other hand, if they expect lower incomes or lower prices, they may refrain from buying and thereby cause demands to shift to the left. For these reasons, economists who are engaged in economic forecasting often try to incorporate the effects of buyers' expectations in their predictive models.

3. *Nonmonetary factors.* Many factors other than prices and incomes influence the demands for commodities. These factors include all nonmonetary determinants of demand such as the age, occupation, sex, race, religion, education, and tastes of consumers, as well as their number. Changes in these factors can affect the preferences, composition, and

quantity of buyers. It is customary to assume, however, that for large numbers of consumers these nonmonetary factors are stable because they (a) vary widely among individuals so that their effects in the market tend to cancel out and (b) change slowly over the long run since they are primarily the result of demographic characteristics and cultural traditions. Therefore, short-run changes in demand caused by economic factors can be analyzed exclusively in terms of prices and incomes.

Thus, demand can be represented by a schedule or curve which reflects buyers' attitudes at the time. If the demand curve does not shift, a change in price leads to a *change in the quantity demanded*, not to a change in demand. This means that there has been either an increase in the quantity demanded, as represented by a movement downward along the curve, or a decrease in the quantity demanded, as represented by a movement upward along the curve. The change is due either to a decrease or an increase in the price of the product (while all other demand determinants remain the same).

A *change in demand* means that the schedule itself has changed, and hence that the demand curve has either shifted to the right, if there has been an increase in demand, or to the left, if there has been a decrease in demand. The shift is due to a change in any of the demand determinants that were assumed to remain constant when the curve was initially drawn.

It is easy to commit many errors in economic reasoning by failing to understand the important distinctions between a change in the quantity demanded and a change in demand.

TEST YOURSELF II

Which of the following involve a change in the quantity demanded and which involve a change in demand:

1. People buy more bathing suits in the summer than in the winter.

2. Consumer incomes fall and the number of automobiles purchased declines.

3. RCA reduces the price of its television sets by 10 percent and its sales increase.

4. State College raises its tuition and student enrollments fall off.

What Is Supply?

You now have a basic knowledge of demand. The other half of the picture involves supply. What do we mean by supply? Is there a law of supply?

Supply is a relation showing the various amounts of a commodity that sellers would be willing and able to make available for sale at possible alternative prices during a given period of time, all other things remaining the same.

How does this definition of supply compare with the definition of demand given near the beginning of this chapter? Are there any similarities? Any differences?

SUPPLY SCHEDULES AND SUPPLY CURVES

Each seller in the market has his own supply schedule for a product, just as each buyer has his own demand schedule. Thus if you were a wheat farmer, Exhibit 6 might represent your individual supply schedule for wheat. This schedule indicates that at a price of $1 per bushel you would not be willing to supply any wheat at all. At a price of $2 per bushel you would be willing to supply 21 bushels of wheat per day, and so on. Plotting these data on a chart gives the supply curve shown in Exhibit 7. What is your estimate of the quantity supplied at a price of $2.50 per unit? What is the *least price*, approximately, that will persuade you to supply 40 bushels per day?

Exhibit 6

An Individual's Supply Schedule for Wheat

A supply schedule is a list showing the number of units of a product that sellers would be willing and able to make available for sale at various prices during a given period of time.

Price per bushel	Quantity supplied per day (bushels)
A'	$5	50
B'	4	42
C'	3	33
D'	2	21
E'	1	0

Exhibit 7

An Individual's Supply Curve for Wheat

A supply curve is the graph of a supply schedule. Each point along the curve represents a different price-quantity combination. A supply curve slopes upward from left to right, reflecting the fact that the quantity supplied of a product varies directly with the price. This is called the law of supply.

REMARK. The "least price" is more often called the *supply price*, which is the price necessary to call forth a given quantity. What do you estimate the supply price to be for 25 bushels per day?

An example of the supply schedules for three individual producers, Mr. A, Mr. B, and Mr. C is presented in Exhibit 8. When you plot the data, you get the corresponding supply curves shown on the charts. Note that the total market supply schedule is obtained by adding up the quantities supplied by all sellers at each market price. How does this compare with the way in which the total market demand schedule was derived earlier?

THE LAW OF SUPPLY

The supply curve as drawn has a distinguishing feature: *the curve slopes upward from left to right*— from southwest to northeast. This feature reflects the law of supply:

Law of Supply. The quantity supplied of a commodity usually varies *directly* with its price, assuming that all other factors that may determine supply remain the same. ("Directly" means that the quantity of a product produced and offered for sale will

Exhibit 8

Market Supply of Wheat, Three Sellers

The total market supply of wheat is obtained by summing all of the individual quantities supplied at each price.

Price per bushel	Quantity supplied by Mr. A		Quantity supplied by Mr. B		Quantity supplied by Mr. C		Total market supply per day
$5	52	+	56	+	60	=	168
4	46	+	49	+	50	=	145
3	36	+	42	+	40	=	118
2	26	+	28	+	26	=	80
1	0	+	15	+	10	=	25

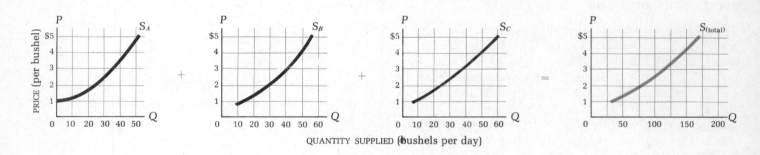

QUANTITY SUPPLIED (bushels per day)

increase as the price of the product rises, and decrease as the price falls.)

Note that the direct relation between quantity and price is "usually" true, but not always. There can be some supply curves where larger quantities are offered for sale at the same price or even at *lower* prices. You will learn more about this in later chapters.

If you were a producer—say a farmer cultivating both wheat and corn—the law of supply would prompt you to act in the following way: When the price of wheat in the market rose relative to the price of corn, you would make greater profits by shifting your limited resources—fertilizer, land, labor, machinery, etc.—out of corn and into wheat production. If the price of wheat rose high enough, you would even find it worthwhile to grow wheat on land where you previously grew nothing. Thus it seems that the law of supply does indeed make sense.

TWO KINDS OF CHANGES INVOLVING SUPPLY

Two types of change in supply may occur: one is called a "change in the quantity supplied"; the other is known as a "change in supply." On the basis of what you now know about the theory of demand, can you guess the meanings of these two concepts before we proceed to explain them?

Changes in the Quantity Supplied

Look again at Exhibit 7. According to the law of supply, an upward movement along the same curve signifies an increase in the quantity supplied as the price is raised; on the other hand, a downward movement along the curve signifies a decrease in the quantity supplied as the price is reduced. Any such movement along the same curve, whether upward or downward, is called a *change in the quantity supplied*.

Changes in Supply

The law of supply says that the quantity supplied of a product usually varies directly with its price, assuming that all other things remain the same. The "other things" that may have an influence in determining supply are the following: (1) resource prices or the costs of the factors of production, (2) prices of related goods (in production), and (3) nonmonetary factors. If any of these conditions change, a new relationship is established between price and quantity offered. In terms of a graph, this means a shift of the supply curve to a new position. When that happens, we get what is called a *change in supply*.

1. An increase in supply is a shift of the supply curve to the right, as shown in Exhibit 9. *At any given price sellers are now willing to supply more than they were willing to supply before.* For example, the dashed lines indicate that at a price of $30 per unit sellers were previously willing to supply a total of 300 units per week. Now, after the increase in supply, they are willing to sell a total of 400 units per week at the same price of $30 per unit.

2. A decrease in supply is represented by a shift of the supply curve to the left. *At any given price, sellers are now willing to supply less than they were willing to supply before.* Thus in Exhibit 10, they were previously willing to supply a total of 300 units per week at a price of $30 per unit. Now, after the decrease in supply, they are willing to sell a total of 200 units per week at the same price of $30 per unit.

How will a change in any of the supply determinants listed above bring about a change in supply —that is, a shift of the supply curve either to the right or to the left?

1. *Resource prices.* Ordinarily, a decrease in resource prices in a particular industry will reduce production costs and thus broaden the profit potentials. However, if there is vigorous competition among businessmen within the industry they will be prompted to increase their output at each possible price in order to capture some of these profits. This action will shift the total market supply curve to the right. Conversely, an increase in resource prices in a given industry would tend to have the opposite effect, since it raises production

---

Exhibit 9

Increase in Supply

An increase in supply can be represented by a shift of the supply curve to the right. At any given price, sellers are now willing to supply more than they were willing to supply before.

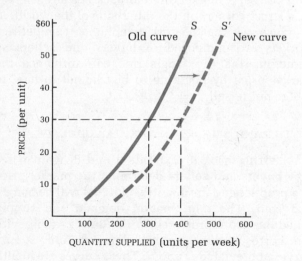

Exhibit 10

Decrease in Supply

A decrease in supply can be represented by a shift of the supply curve to the left. At any given price, sellers are now willing to supply less than they were willing to supply before.

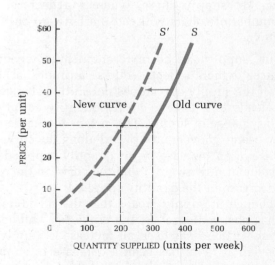

costs and decreases profits, thereby encouraging businessmen in that industry to reduce their output at each possible price. This action shifts the market supply curve to the left.

2. *Prices of related goods (in production).* Businessmen produce goods to make profits. Changes in the relative prices of goods which compete in production may change their relative profitabilities and thereby bring about changes in their respective supply curves. For instance, if the price of wheat increases relative to the price of corn, farmers may find it more profitable to transfer resources out of corn and into wheat, thereby shifting the market supply curve of corn to the left and the market supply curve of wheat to the right.

Of course, sellers' expectations of prices will also influence their supply decisions. Thus some producers may decide to hold back on their current output because they anticipate higher prices for their goods—and therefore higher profits; other producers may decide to increase their current output because they anticipate lower prices for their goods—and therefore lower profits or possibly losses.

3. *Nonmonetary factors.* Various factors other than prices can affect the supply of a commodity. The most important are the state of technology and the number of sellers in the market. The adoption of a new invention or a new production technique may improve efficiency and increase supply by shifting the market supply curve to the right, whereas a decline in efficiency can have the opposite effect. Similarly, an increase in the number of sellers in the market will result in a rightward shift of the market supply curve, whereas a decrease in the number of sellers will cause a leftward shift of the curve.

Thus, supply can be represented by a schedule or curve which reflects sellers' attitudes at the time. If the supply curve does not shift, a change in price leads to a *change in the quantity supplied,* not to a change in supply. This means that there has either been a movement upward along the curve in the case of an increase in the quantity supplied, or a movement downward along the curve in the case of a decrease in the quantity supplied.

A *change in supply* means that the schedule itself has changed—that is, the curve has shifted to the right if there has been an increase in supply or to the left if there has been a decrease in supply. The shift is due to a change in any of the supply-determining factors that were assumed to remain constant when the curve was initially drawn.

TEST YOURSELF III

An increase in supply also means that for any given quantity supplied sellers are now willing to accept a *lower price* per unit than they were willing to accept before.

1. Can you define a decrease in supply in a parallel way?

2. In Exhibit 9, what is your estimate of the lowest price per unit that sellers were willing to accept for a supply of 300 units per week, before and after the increase in supply?

3. In Exhibit 10, what is your estimate of the lowest price per unit that sellers were willing to accept for a supply of 200 units per week, before and after the decrease in supply?

Supply and Demand Together Make a Market

The concepts of supply and demand must be united to provide an explanation of how prices are determined in competitive markets.

A market exists whenever and wherever one or more buyers and sellers can negotiate for goods or services and thereby participate in determining their prices. A market, therefore, can be anywhere— on a street corner, on the other side of the world, or as close as the nearest telephone. *Competitive markets* are composed of buyers and sellers so numerous that no single one can influence the market price by deciding to buy or not to buy, to sell or not to sell.

BUYERS AND SELLERS IN THE MARKETPLACE

By referring back to Exhibits 3 and 8, we can see how buyers and sellers determine the market price of a product and the quantity of it that will be bought and sold. The *total* market demand and supply schedules are reproduced in Exhibit 11, along with the corresponding market demand and supply curves abbreviated *D* and *S*. These curves are identical with the total market curves that were graphed in Exhibits 3 and 8, but now they are both graphed on the same chart so that their interactions can be observed.

The most important thing to notice is that the supply and demand curves intersect at an *equilibrium point*. A dictionary will tell you that "equilibrium" is a state of balance between opposing forces. Let us see what this means in terms of Exhibit 11.

Exhibit 11

The Equilibrium Price and Quantity for Wheat

The intersection of the supply and demand curves determines the equilibrium price and the equilibrium quantity. At any price above the equilibrium price, the quantity supplied exceeds the quantity demanded and the price tends to fall. At any price below the equilibrium price, the quantity demanded exceeds the quantity supplied and the price tends to rise. At the equilibrium price, the quantity supplied precisely equals the quantity demanded and hence there is no tendency for the price to change.

Price per bushel	Total market supply per day (bushels)	Total market demand per day (bushels)
$5	168	35
4	145	55
3	118	82
2	80	123
1	25	205

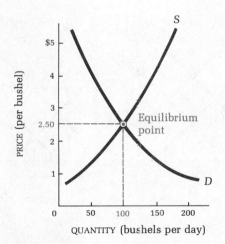

At any price above $2.50 per bushel, the quantity supplied exceeds the quantity demanded. For example, at a price of S5 per bushel, the quantity supplied is 168 bushels per day and the quantity demanded is 35 bushels per day. This means there is a *surplus* of 168 − 35 = 133 bushels per day. Since sellers thus have more wheat available than buyers want, sellers will compete with one another to dispose of their product and thereby drive the price down.

At any price below $2.50 per bushel, the quantity demanded exceeds the quantity supplied. Thus at $1 a bushel, for example, the quantity demanded is 205 bushels per day and the quantity supplied is 25 bushels per day. There is then a *shortage* at this price of 205 − 25 = 180 bushels per day. Since buyers want more wheat than sellers have available at this price, buyers will compete with one another to acquire the product and thereby drive the price up.

ARRIVING AT MARKET EQUILIBRIUM

At a price of $2.50 per bushel, the quantity demanded just equals the quantity supplied, namely 100 bushels per day. At this price there will be no surpluses or shortages. Hence we refer to this price as the *equilibrium price* and to the corresponding quantity as the *equilibrium quantity*.

Thus when the quantity demanded equals the quantity supplied, there is a state of *market equilibrium* because the price of the product and the corresponding quantities bought and sold are "in balance"—they have no tendency to change as a result of the opposing forces of demand and supply. On the other hand, when the quantities demanded and supplied at a given price are unequal or "out of balance," prices and quantities will be changing so that the market is then in a state of *disequilibrium*.

CHANGES IN DEMAND AND SUPPLY

Demand and supply curves rarely remain fixed for very long. This is because the factors determining them, such as buyers' incomes, resource costs, or prices of related products are continually changing, causing the curves to shift either rightward or leftward. Since we are interested in learning about the behavior of prices and quantities in competitive markets, we must be able to analyze such shifts in order to evaluate their effects.

What happens when a demand or supply curve moves to a new position? The answer is that there may also be a change in the equilibrium price, the equilibrium quantity, or both. Some examples are presented in Exhibit 12 with the arrows indicating the directions of change.

REMARK. Supply and demand curves may be drawn as straight lines rather than curved lines, because straight lines are often simpler to work with and are usually just as informative for most practical purposes. However, even when they are drawn as straight lines, we still refer to them as supply and demand *curves*.

What can you say about Exhibit 12?

In each of Charts (*a*) through (*d*), one of the curves shifted while the other remained unchanged. The effects on the equilibrium price and quantity in each case are depicted by the arrows. Thus in Chart (*a*), an increase in demand resulted in an increase in both the equilibrium price and the equilibrium quantity. The opposite situation occurred in Chart (*b*) as a result of a decrease in demand. In Chart (*c*) on the other hand, an increase in supply resulted in a decrease in the equilibrium price and an increase in the equilibrium quantity. The opposite situation occurred in Chart (*d*) as a result of a decrease in supply.

Can you explain what happened in Charts (*e*) and (*f*)?

The Market Economy: Is It "Good" or "Bad"?

In a competitive market, prices are determined solely by the free play of supply and demand. An economy characterized entirely by such markets would be a *pure market economy*, sometimes called a "competitive economy." The two expressions are often used interchangeably.

What are the desirable features of such an economy? Does it have shortcomings? Is it realistic as a description of the capitalistic system?

THE BENEFITS OF A PURE MARKET ECONOMY

Most economists agree that a pure market economy has several major points in its favor:

1. *Consumer sovereignty*. In a competitive economy the consumer is king (or queen). Consumers "vote" by offering relatively more dollars for products that are in greater demand and relatively fewer dollars for products in lesser demand. In this way con-

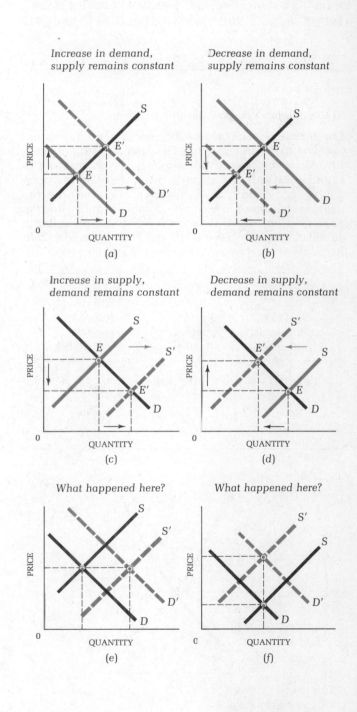

Exhibit 12

Changes in Demand and Supply

Shifts in the demand or supply curves will cause changes in equilibrium price, equilibrium quantity, or both.

Increase in demand, supply remains constant

(*a*)

Decrease in demand, supply remains constant

(*b*)

Increase in supply, demand remains constant

(*c*)

Decrease in supply, demand remains constant

(*d*)

What happened here?

(*e*)

What happened here?

(*f*)

sumers cause relative shifts in demand curves. Hence, in competing for consumers' dollars, producers find it profitable to produce more of a product at a higher price, and less of a product at a lower price, all other things being equal. In short, although producers decide WHAT shall be produced, their decisions are based on what they expect to sell to consumers.

2. *Maximum efficiency.* In a pure market economy resources will be used as efficiently as possible, provided that supply and demand reflect all costs and benefits of production and consumption. The efficient use of resources occurs because firms in each industry respond to the dollar "votes" of consumers by providing the largest volume of output at the lowest prices consistent with existing costs and technology. At the same time, the factors of production tend to move into their most remunerative employments, thereby ensuring that the entire income of production is distributed to the owners of resources in proportion to their contribution to the economy's total output.

3. *Economic freedom.* Freedom of enterprise is an extension of the institution of private property—the most fundamental pillar of a capitalistic system and, hence, of a pure market economy. Freedom of enterprise means that owners of resources are free to employ them where they see fit, subject only to the minimal governmental restraints needed to protect the welfare of society. Unlike a command economy, therefore, a pure market economy has no central authority that decides WHAT, HOW, and FOR WHOM economic resources should be used. Instead these decisions are made individually by producers as they seek to earn profits by allocating resources according to the ways in which consumers freely register their preferences through the price system.

4. *Dispersion of economic power.* Economic power exists when a buyer or seller can exert an influence on the market price of a good or resource. The fragmentation of economic power is an integral feature of a pure market economy and is closely related to economic freedom. Economic power does not exist in a highly competitive system because, as we have seen, the market price of a commodity is established by the bids and offers of numerous buyers and sellers. An individual buyer or seller can either accept or reject the going market price, but he cannot influence it. He is thus a passive participant whose presence or absence has no influence on the economic process.

THE SHORTCOMINGS OF A PURE MARKET ECONOMY

Critics of the pure market economy offer their own arguments against it. Among them:

1. *Economic inequality and inequity.* In a market economy, incomes are distributed in proportion to one's contribution to production. If Smith adds twice as much to the value of total output as Johnson does, then Smith's income will tend to be twice that of Johnson's. This difference is further magnified by the institution of inheritance, which permits the accumulation and concentration of wealth within families. Such disparities in income and wealth lead to economic and social inequities. As critics point out, in a market economy a rich man has more dollar votes than a poor man; hence the former can satisfy his whims while the latter may find it hard to satisfy his needs.

2. *Market imperfections and frictions.* The market does not always work as neatly in the real world as the theoretical models suggest. Imperfections and frictions such as imperfect knowledge, resource immobility, and barriers to entry impede the smooth functioning of the system. For example, buyers and sellers of goods and resources do not usually have complete market information about alternative prices, working conditions, and the like. Unemployed people frequently must be retrained before they can qualify for new jobs, and even then they may not be willing to bear the economic or psychic costs of moving long distances to accept employment. Entrepreneurs and workers are often prevented from entering new industries because they lack the large amount of capital or the specialized know-how required, or because they cannot overcome monopolistic barriers such as patent rights and apprenticeship requirements that protect various business firms and unions from increased competition. These and other obstacles retard the rate at which the factors of production shift out of declining industries and into expanding ones. As a result, shortages and surpluses arise in various product and resource markets—imbalances which would not ordinarily occur, or at best would be short-lived, if a real market-oriented economy functioned as smoothly as the theory assumes.

3. *Technology and large-scale production.* The model of a pure market economy makes the unrealistic assumption that industries are composed of numerous small firms, as envisioned by Adam Smith. Yet modern technology dictates that in many indus-

tries like automobiles, steel, and cement, firms must be very large if they are to make use of the most efficient means of production. In such industries a few large firms are dominant, and small firms just cannot survive. In fact, the massive scale of operations dictated by modern technology provides one of the chief explanations of why many major industries in all advanced industrial nations including our own are dominated by one or a few large firms.

4. *Social effects and "externalities."* A fourth criticism is that the market system fails to reflect all of the costs and benefits associated with production and consumption. As a result, there are "externalities." For example, production of some commodities such as steel, rubber, and chemicals pollutes the environment, and thus contributes to *social costs,* while production of other commodities such as education, sanitation services, and park facilities, adds to community satisfactions and thus contributes to *social benefits.* To the extent that these externalities are not fully reflected in the market prices of commodities, supply and demand curves fail to incorporate *all* of the costs and benefits of production. Hence either too large or too small a quantity of goods is produced, and resources are misallocated.

IS A PURE MARKET ECONOMY REALISTIC?

For these reasons, the model of a pure market economy does not convey a true picture of the way in which the price system operates in a modern capitalistic society. For example, in many markets we do not have large numbers of buyers and sellers in rivalry with one another, as envisioned by Adam Smith. Instead, we have big business, big unions, and big government. As a result, concentrations of market power influence commodity and factor prices, and distort the allocation of resources—hardly the type of economy that Adam Smith had in mind. Nevertheless, as we will see later, our pure market model provides a useful framework for evaluating the performance of a capitalistic system.

SUMMARY OF IMPORTANT IDEAS

1. The purpose of studying about supply and demand is to learn how a competitive or pure market economy answers the three great questions: WHAT to produce, HOW to produce, and FOR WHOM to produce.

2. Demand is a relationship between the price of a commodity and the quantity of it that buyers are willing and able to purchase at a given time, other things such as buyers' incomes, prices of related goods in consumption, and number of buyers or other nonmonetary determinants remaining the same. The law of demand states that this relationship is inverse. Hence demand curves slope downward from left to right.

3. Supply is a relationship between the price of a commodity and the quantity of it that sellers are willing and able to sell at a given time, other things such as resource costs, prices of related goods in production, and technology or other nonmonetary determinants remaining the same. The law of supply states that this relationship is usually direct. Hence supply curves slope upward from left to right.

4. The intersection of a market demand curve with a market supply curve determines the equilibrium price and quantity of a commodity. Demand or supply curves may shift either leftward or rightward as a result of changes in any of the determinants which were assumed to remain constant when the curves were drawn. When such shifts occur, we refer to them either as a change in demand or a change in supply, depending on which curve has shifted.

   In contrast, movements along the same curves, either upward or downward, may occur as a result of changes in the price of the commodity while the underlying determinants of demand and supply remain constant. Movements such as these are called either a change in the quantity demanded or a change in the quantity supplied, depending on the particular curve.

5. In dynamic markets, demand and supply curves are always shifting. A change in demand or a change in supply may result in either a new equilibrium price, a new equilibrium quantity, or both—depending on the relative shifts of the curves.

6. A market economy is highly competitive. Prices and quantities are determined by numerous buyers and sellers through the free operation of supply and demand. Organized markets for trading commodities typify this situation, but most of the markets in our economy differ from the competitive market in varying degrees.

FOR DISCUSSION

1. *Terms and concepts to review:*

demand	supply price
demand schedule	law of supply
demand curve	change in quantity
demand price	supplied
law of demand	change in supply
change in quantity	equilibrium
demanded	equilibrium price
change in demand	surplus
normal goods	shortage
inferior goods	equilibrium quantity
substitute goods	disequilibrium
complementary goods	pure market economy
supply	consumer sovereignty
supply schedule	social benefit
supply curve	social cost

In the following problems, use graphs whenever possible to verify your answer.

2. Do the numerical quantities of a demand schedule characterize buyers' behavior? If not, what is the fundamental property of a demand schedule?

3. Evaluate the following editorial comments on the basis of what you know about the meaning of demand and scarcity in economics. (HINT: How meaningful are the italicized words?)

"Our community *needs* more schools and better teachers; after all, what could be more critical than the education of our children as future citizens?"

Lynwood *Times*

"The health of our citizens is uppermost in our minds. Ever since the rate of garbage pick-up in our northwest suburbs deteriorated to its present deplorable levels, it has been evident that our *shortage* of collection facilities has reached *emergency* proportions."

Lexington *Daily Explicit*

4. Some people would buy more of a good (such as jewelry or furs) at a high price than at a low price. This results in an upward-sloping "demand" curve. Would such a curve be an exception to the law of demand? Explain.

5. What would happen to the market demand curve for steak as a result of each of the following: (a) an increase in the average level of income, (b) an increase in the number of families, (c) an increased

advertising campaign for veal and pork, (d) an increase in the prices of veal and pork, (e) a decrease in the prices of veal and pork.

6. What would happen to the demand for Pepsi-Cola if the price of Coca-Cola were doubled? Why would it happen?

7. What would be the effect on the supply of office buildings if each of the following things happened: (a) the price of land rose, (b) the price of steel fell, (c) the price of cement fell, (d) a new and faster method of construction were adopted, (e) the number of firms building offices declined, (f) rents for office buildings were expected to decline.

8. Analyze the following:
   (a) What would happen to the equilibrium price and quantity of butter if the price of margarine rose?
   (b) What would happen if there were an increase in the cost of producing butter?

9. "Wheat is wheat. Therefore, the price of wheat at any given time should be the same in Chicago as it is in Kansas City." Do you agree? Explain.

10. In organized commodity markets, buyers often become sellers and sellers often become buyers, depending on the price of the good. Consider the following schedule of five individuals, A, B, C, D, and E.

Price per unit	Quantities which individuals will buy (+) or sell (−) at each market price				
	A	B	C	D	E
$1	+6	+5	+3	+8	−2
2	+3	+4	+2	+7	−5
3	0	+3	+1	+6	−8
4	−2	+2	0	+5	−10
5	−2	−3	−1	+4	−10
6	−4	−5	−2	+3	−11
7	−5	−6	−3	+2	−12

   (a) Draw the market supply and demand curves, and estimate the equilibrium price and quantity.
   (b) Show the effects on the supply and demand curves if C drops out of the market.

The Consumer: Prince or Pawn?

The belief in consumer sovereignty is surprisingly durable. There is the marketplace, with a great many buyers milling around. At the end of the day some booths are empty of goods; their owners go home with bulging pocketbooks. But some booths are still stacked with goods; the consumer has used his right to reject them. It is an appealing picture and still useful as a simplified explanation of what happens in a free market.

But we don't happen to live in one. The bulk of private-sector economic activity in the United States is conducted by corporations. The 500 largest account for most of the goods produced in the United States. And whatever their other virtues, the giant corporations cannot be counted among supporters of a free-market system.

Managing Demand

Whereas the man selling wicker baskets from his booth in that hypothetical free market has invested a few hours of his time and a little money in raw materials, the giant corporation has spent several years and millions of dollars on designing, tooling-up for, and launching its product—a plastic basket perhaps. With all that and a reputation at stake, the large corporation seeks to turn a gamble into a sure thing by *managing demand*. It will advertise the plastic basket on television and in magazines; retailers may turn it into a special promotional item; it may even be offered as a gift in return for two cornflake box tops.

The plastic basket may still fail; business history is littered with the corpses of failed products. Supporters of the consumer-sovereignty theory are fond of pointing to them. But failed products do not prove that demand cannot be managed. *They only prove it cannot be managed all the time.*

Although manufacturers of similar products are clearly in competition for shares of the market, they are also in alliance. By their ceaseless promotion of a *class* of product—self-cleaning ovens, let us say—they are helping to create overall demand for it. The alternative would be to lose dollars to another class of product.

Because manufacturers of a class of product have a shared interest in promoting it, their products tend to be similar. The man who goes shopping for a car made in the United States is faced with a limited choice. In each price range the rival products are priced within a few dollars; their motors are of comparable size; and they feature similar gadgets. Detroit explains its lack of innovation by saying it provides what people want. But how can the consumer demand a car that is not offered?

Threat from Foreigners

The size of the four big automobile manufacturers makes the entry of a new competitor impractical; the only real competition Detroit faces is from foreign cars. But the range of foreign cars is also limited.

Much of the similarity of technology, models, and prices is inevitable: like most consumer durables, the car is mass produced. Certainly, mass production has benefited most consumers; goods are more readily available and cheaper than they would be under any other production system. But mass production is precisely what its name implies; it is incapable of meeting a particular demand. The person unfortunate enough to have a taste shared by relatively few people is doomed either never to satisfy it or to pay a very high price indeed for his eccentricity.

The Price of Size

The basic cause of sluggish response to changing consumer demands may be technological. But the very large corporations have sometimes abused their power. As consumer-crusader Ralph Nader has shown, some manufacturers have deliberately designed their products to cease functioning after a certain time, have willfully disregarded warnings that their products are dangerous, and have turned with fury on their critics. The major corporations have a more powerful voice in government than any consumer or group of consumers. Even the federal agencies that are supposed to regulate business frequently do so inadequately.

Fortunately, consumers are becoming aware of the pressures exerted by corporations. To be sure, consumers are still diffused and weak in comparison with the corporations they confront; but legislation being passed to protect consumers shows that important changes are taking place.

Unfortunately, it is unlikely that even in the long run the consumer will ever be sovereign in life as he is in theory. But at least consumers, organized into groups and willing to use their political power, will be able to prevent manufacturers from abusing their privileged position as the few suppliers of many customers.

QUESTIONS

1. Do you agree that large corporations are able to manage demand? What does this expression mean?

2. Does advertising create new demands or does it merely shift existing demands?

3. Why is it often assumed that creation of demand is bad? What is "bad" about it?

CHAPTER 5

Households: The Distribution of Income and Wealth

CHAPTER PREVIEW

How are income and wealth distributed in our mixed economy? Why are some people rich and some poor?

How do we measure inequalities in income and wealth? What has government done to reduce inequalities? Has it been successful?

How should income and wealth be distributed? Can ethical principles serve as standards of distribution?

In the United States, concern with the distribution of wealth is as old as the nation itself. Alexander Hamilton believed that liberty without inequality of property is impossible because the latter "would unavoidably result from that very liberty itself." Thomas Jefferson remarked that the perpetuation of wealth through inheritance "sometimes does injury to the morals of youth by rendering them independent of, and disobedient to, their parents." And James Madison supported legislation that "would reduce extreme wealth towards a state of mediocrity and raise extreme indigence toward a state of comfort."

The question of what constitutes an equitable or fair distribution of income and wealth among individuals has been debated for centuries—not only by economists but also by politicians and social critics. In this chapter, we shall be primarily concerned with the problem of economic equity among households. Households, together with businesses comprise the *private* sector of our mixed economy—as distinguished from the *public* sector, which embraces all levels of government. Problems of the business segment and of the public sector are discussed in later chapters.

A Look at the Facts

It is widely believed that income and wealth in our economy have been distributed inequitably and that this maldistribution is one of the most fundamental social problems of our time. This belief is not new; it has had cyclical upswings and downswings since the early nineteenth century. Whether it is correct is a question we try to answer in this and in later chapters.

To begin with, we have to examine the facts. This is not easy, because there are different concepts of income and wealth. To most of us, income is simply money that people receive from various sources; wealth is the value of the goods and property they own. But a significant part of many people's incomes consists of more than wages and salaries; it also consists of unearned incomes and nonmoney benefits which are never reported to the tax authorities or to census takers. A similar situation exists in the reporting of wealth holdings—especially by the rich. As a result, no government or private source provides complete and accurate information about the distribution of income and wealth. With these deficiencies in mind, let us turn our attention to the available facts. First, however, we need two definitions:

Income is the gain derived from the use of human or material resources; it is a flow of dollars per unit of time. *Wealth* is anything which has value because it is capable of producing income; it is a "stock" of value as distinct from a "flow" of income.

FUNCTIONAL INCOME DISTRIBUTION

The study of income distribution customarily is divided into two parts. One is called functional income distribution and the other personal income distribution.

Functional income distribution concerns the income payments made to owners of productive factors in return for their supplying the human and material resources that contribute to the production of the nation's output. The payments include wages, rent, interest, and profit. Today it is not unusual to find an individual receiving all four kinds of payments, for at the same time he may be a wage earner, landlord, creditor, and stockholder in a corporation. Thus our interest here is in the relative shares of income payments going to the various classes of resource suppliers—not in the people who receive those payments.

In our economy, two kinds of forces determine which factor of production will receive how much:

1. Economic or market forces, represented by demand and supply conditions for the human and material resources used in production

2. Noneconomic or nonmarket forces, such as laws, customs, and union agreements, which modify the income that a resource owner would have received based on market forces alone

Long-term Trends

Exhibit 1 shows the relative shares of national income going to each resource class. The proportions change very little from one year to the next; hence it is more instructive to convey the highlights of the information over intervals of years, as has been done in the exhibit. It should be noted that the classification "proprietors' income" is included here for statistical convenience; it combines both wages and the return on investment earned by self-employed professionals (doctors, lawyers, accountants, etc.) and individual proprietors of business establishments. In theoretical discussions in later chapters, this category is eliminated by allocating parts of it to two other classes of income payments—"compensation of employees" and "net interest"—leaving the four familiar groups of factor incomes: wages, profit, rent, and interest.

Three major long-term trends account for the historical changes in relative income shares—especially compensation of employees, which comprises the largest proportion (about 75 percent) of the total:

1. The shift of farm workers out of proprietary-type agriculture into the growing manufacturing and service industries

2. The growth of the corporate form of business organization relative to simpler types of enterprise such as the individual proprietorship or partnership

3. The expanding activities of government at all levels—federal, state, and local—tending to reduce unemployment

These factors have brought about a rising proportion of wage- and salary-earners relative to self-employed workers and business proprietors.

SOMETHING TO THINK ABOUT

Can you suggest some explanations for the changing patterns of the other shares of national income—especially the fluctuations in corporate profits and the trends of net interest and rental income? These questions are examined later in the book, but you may have some ideas of your own.

Exhibit 1

National Income by Type of Income

FUNCTIONAL DISTRIBUTION OF INCOME IN THE UNITED STATES
(in percent of national income)*

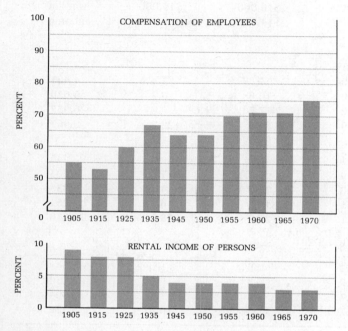

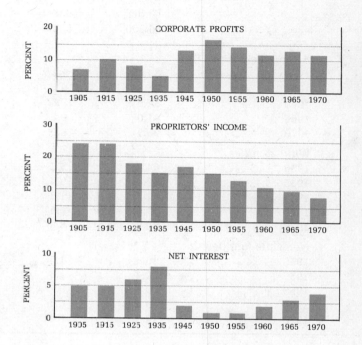

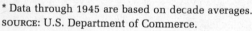

* Data through 1945 are based on decade averages.
SOURCE: U.S. Department of Commerce.

PERSONAL INCOME DISTRIBUTION

Personal income distribution—the relative allocation of income among people—is causing increasingly urgent problems. The American poor—black and white, Indian and Mexican—are no longer content merely to complain about their small slice of the economic pie. With growing militance, organized groups of poor people are challenging existing income distribution by demonstrating, by taking their case to Congress, and sometimes by rioting. Equitable distribution of income is an issue that has moved men and nations for centuries, bringing revolution and war in its wake. The lesson of history is that society is in peril when it disregards the plight of the poor.

How incomes are distributed in the United States—who is rich and who is poor, and what the gap is between them—is the problem of personal income distribution. Exhibit 2 shows that the percentage of all families in the lower-income groups—that is, below the $6,000 level—has been declining since World War II, while the percentage of families in the upper-income groups has been rising. Note too that the median income has been rising. (A *median* is a type of average that divides a distribution of numbers into two equal parts—one-half of the cases being equal to or less than this value and one-half being equal to or greater than it.) Can you interpret the median income for the most recent year? What important differences does the table reveal between white and nonwhite families?

Exhibit 3 shows the relative share of total money income before taxes received by each fifth and the top 5 percent of all families. This table reveals that since 1950:

1. The lowest fifth of families has consistently received less than 6 percent of total income; the highest fifth has received over 40 percent—or a long-run average of about 8 times as much.

Exhibit 2

Money Income—Percent Distribution of Families, by Income Level and by Color of Head of Family*

INCOME LEVEL (percent distribution)

Year	Under $6,000	$6,000–$6,999	$7,000–$9,999	$10,000–$14,999	$15,000 and over	Median income
All families						
1950	85.8%	5.2%	5.8%	3.3%		$3,319
1955	71.3	9.5	12.9	4.8%	1.4%	4,421
1960	54.9	10.8	20.0	10.6	3.7	5,620
1965	41.0	9.5	24.2	17.7	7.6	6,957
1970	25.1	6.0	19.9	26.8	22.3	9,867
White families						
1950	84.8	5.5	6.1	3.5		3,445
1955	69.4	9.9	13.9	5.3	1.5	4,605
1960	52.3	11.2	21.3	11.2	4.1	5,835
1965	37.8	9.8	25.5	18.8	8.3	7,251
1970	22.5	5.8	20.1	27.9	23.7	10,236
Nonwhite families						
1950	96.6	1.5	1.7	0.3		1,869
1955	91.4	4.8	3.1	0.6	(Z)	2,549
1960	79.6	6.7	8.7	4.3	0.6	3,233
1965	70.4	6.8	13.7	7.6	1.4	3,994
1970	46.1	7.4	18.2	17.3	10.9	6,516

* "Money income" is defined by the Census Bureau to include money factor income and transfer payments and to exclude all capital gains.
Z less than 0.05 percent.
SOURCE: U. S. Department of Commerce.

Exhibit 3

Percent of Aggregate Income (Total Money Income Before Taxes) Received by Each Fifth and Top 5 Percent of Families*

Income rank	1950	1955	1960	1965	1970
Lowest fifth	4.5	4.8	4.9	5.3	5.5
Second fifth	12.0	12.2	12.0	12.2	12.0
Middle fifth	17.4	17.7	17.6	17.6	17.4
Fourth fifth	23.5	23.7	23.6	23.7	23.5
Highest fifth	42.6	41.6	42.0	41.3	41.6
Top 5%	17.0	16.8	16.8	15.8	14.4
Ratio of top 5% to lowest 20%	3.8	3.5	3.4	3.0	2.6

* Columns may not add to 100 due to rounding.
SOURCE: U.S. Department of Commerce.

2. The ratio of the share received by the top 5 percent to the share received by the lowest 20 percent has declined substantially, but the former is still more than twice the latter.

3. The entire distribution has remained remarkably stable.

Of course, if incomes were divided equally among families, each fifth would receive 20 percent of the total. For 1970, this would have amounted to an average income of over $11,000 per family, or about 11 percent more than the median income of almost $9,900 shown in Exhibit 2.

How have incomes of both whites and nonwhites fluctuated in relation to each other over the years? Exhibit 4 shows that most of the gains in income of nonwhites relative to whites have occurred in years of prosperity when unemployment was low or declining. There are several reasons for this:

Exhibit 4

Ratio of Nonwhite* to White Median Family Income

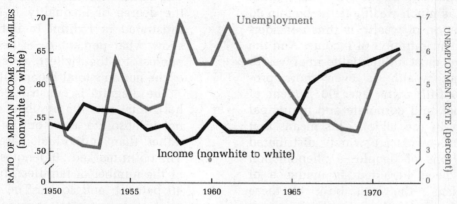

* Black families account for about 90 percent of all nonwhite families, the remainder being Indians, Asians, Mexican-Americans, and others.

SOURCE: U.S. Department of Commerce. Data through 1960 adapted by Thomas M. Humphrey.

First, a greater proportion of nonwhite than white workers are "marginal" because they lack skills and experience. Hence they are among the first to be let go when general economic conditions worsen. On the other hand, during prosperity the labor market tightens and the nonwhite unemployment rate declines more sharply than the white rate.

Second, during periods of prosperity and tight labor markets many employers are less discriminatory in their hiring practices. Nonwhites thus find it easier to compete with whites and to find better-paying jobs.

Third, the relative shortage of skilled and semi-skilled workers during periods of low unemployment encourages firms to expand their employee training. To the extent that nonwhites are included in these programs, their productive efficiency is increased, thereby helping to raise their relative income levels.

DISTRIBUTION OF WEALTH

The distribution of income is concerned with who *gets* how much. The distribution of wealth is concerned with who *has* how much. The same inequality that exists in the distribution of income also exists in the distribution of wealth—but in a more pronounced way; there is a much heavier concentration at the top and a considerably thinner scattering at the bottom.

Wealth consists of both income- and non-income-producing assets, such as stocks, bonds, savings accounts, land, houses, and automobiles. Holdings of both types are important. Unfortunately, the facts are not readily available. Data on the distribution of wealth are limited and are not published periodically. As a result, we must rely on infrequent studies.

Exhibit 5 shows that the wealthiest 1 percent of consumer units, defined as families and unrelated

Exhibit 5

Percent of Total Wealth Held by Each Fifth of Consumer Units (latest data)

Wealth rank of consumer units (families and unrelated individuals)	1970 (percent)
Lowest fifth	Less than 0.5
Second fifth	1
Third fifth	5
Fourth fifth	18
Highest fifth	76
Top 5 percent	40
Top 1 percent	25

SOURCE: Survey Research Center, University of Michigan.

individuals, owns one-fourth of the total wealth. In fact, this small proportion of people owns as much wealth as the lowest 80 percent of families. The wealthiest 20 percent, on the other hand, owns about three times as much wealth as the bottom 80 percent. Concentration of wealth is thus considerably greater than concentration of income. And the concentration of the most influential form of wealth —income-producing wealth—is even more pronounced. The top fifth owns over 90 percent of both corporate stock and corporate and municipal bonds (not shown in the table). This means that although stocks and bonds are widely distributed among many millions of people—a phenomenon which has often been heralded as evidence of "people's capitalism"—the vast bulk of these securities is owned by a relatively small percentage of the population.

Measuring Inequality and Explaining the Facts

The commonest method of depicting and measuring the degree of inequality is by a *Lorenz diagram*, illustrated in Exhibit 6. Both the table and chart show what percentage of people, ranked from the poorest to the richest, received what percentage of the nation's total income in a given year.

The diagram is constructed by laying off on the horizontal axis the numbers of income recipients— not in absolute terms but in percentages. Families, rather than individuals, are usually represented. The point marked 20 denotes the lowest 20 percent of the number of families; the point 40, the lowest 40 percent; and so on. The vertical axis measures percentages of total income. Both axes have the same length and equal scales, so by enclosing the

---

Exhibit 6

Illustrating Inequality with a Lorenz Diagram

PERCENT OF AGGREGATE INCOME RECEIVED BY EACH FIFTH OF FAMILIES

Income rank of families	1973
Lowest fifth	6
Second fifth	12
Middle fifth	17
Fourth fifth	23
Highest fifth	42

SOURCE: U.S. Department of Commerce.

You can use the data from the table to construct a Lorenz curve. This curve shows the extent of departure between an equal distribution of income and the actual distribution of income.

Can you estimate from the curved line showing actual distribution the percent of income received by the lowest 20 percent of families? The lowest 40 percent? 60 percent? 80 percent? 100 percent? Check your estimates against the results in the table to see if you are correct.

The axes in the lower half of the diagram represent the curve of absolute inequality. Thus, on the horizontal axis, a point near the right end of the scale can be designated, showing where 99 percent of the families receive no income, and the remaining 1 percent receive it all.

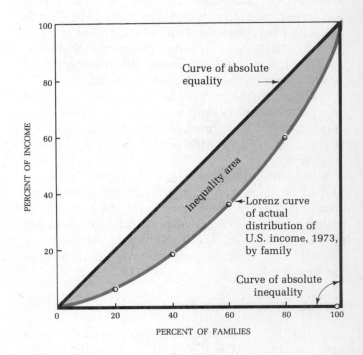

The Gini coefficient measures the degree of income inequality. It is equal to the inequality area divided by the entire triangular area under the diagonal.

diagram in a square, a diagonal line can be drawn representing a curve of absolute equality. You should be able to verify from the chart that along this line of equal distribution, the lowest 20 percent of the families would receive 20 percent of total income, the lowest 40 percent of the families would receive 40 percent of total income, and so on. This line is compared with the curve of actual distribution—called a *Lorenz curve*—derived from the data in the table. The area between the diagonal line of equal income distribution and the curved line of actual income distribution reflects the degree of income inequality. Thus the more that the curved line is bowed downward in a southeasterly direction, the greater is the inequality of income distribution.

THE GINI COEFFICIENT

We measure the precise degree of income inequality with the *Gini coefficient of inequality*. This may be defined in terms of a Lorenz diagram as the numerical value of the area between the Lorenz curve and the diagonal line, divided by the entire area beneath the diagonal line. In other words, as can be visualized from the diagram, it is the ratio of the inequality area to the entire triangular area, thus:

$$\text{Gini coefficient of inequality} = \frac{\text{inequality area}}{\text{triangular area}}$$

The value of the ratio may therefore vary from 0 to 1. For example, as incomes become more equal, the inequality area narrows relative to the triangular area and the Gini coefficient approaches zero (no inequality). On the other hand, as incomes become more unequal, the inequality area widens relative to the triangular area and the Gini coefficient approaches unity (absolute inequality). Exhibit 7 suggests a method of finding the value of the Gini coefficient.

WHY ARE SOME PEOPLE RICH? SOME POOR?

Why do some people make more money than others? There are four major reasons:

1. *Differences in wealth.* Since wealth is a significant source of income, it appears obvious that a widely distorted distribution of wealth is perhaps the most important cause of income inequality. (See Box 1.)

Exhibit 7

Estimating the Gini Coefficient of Inequality

You can calculate the Gini coefficient of inequality quite easily by connecting the successive points of the Lorenz curve with straight lines. The area under the Lorenz curve will then consist of a triangle and trapezoids. In a problem at the end of this chapter, a simple procedure for making the calculation is explained. Meanwhile, you may want to see if you can figure it out for yourself.

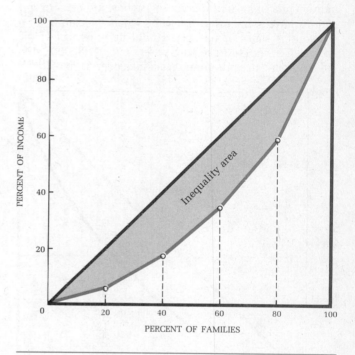

2. *Differences in earning ability and opportunity.* People differ widely in education, intelligence, skill, motivation, energy, and talent. Also, they face job barriers because of age, sex, race, religion, and nationality. Legislation has made some of these barriers less formidable, but they are still responsible for many of the inequalities in income distribution.

3. *Differences in resource mobility.* The factors responsible for differences in earning ability and opportunity also make for differences in resource mobility. Many people, for example, are prevented by lack of information or resources from moving into higher-paying occupations or locations. Consequently low incomes and even poverty may exist unchanged for years in the same regions, as in parts

Box 1

Lorenz Curves of Income and Wealth Distribution

(latest data)

The distribution of wealth is considerably more unequal than the distribution of income. However, it is not clear which is the cause and which the effect. High income leads to higher saving, which enables further accumulation of wealth; this begets still higher income. On the other hand, although only 5 percent of Americans inherited a significant part of their current wealth, inheritance is important among the richest groups. Several studies have shown that inherited wealth accounts for a substantial share of the assets held by one-third of the very rich—that is, those with assets over $500,000—and 50 to 60 percent with annual incomes over $100,000.

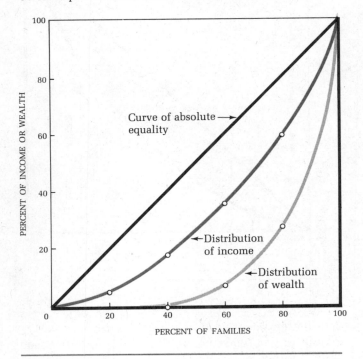

of the South where sharecroppers, migratory farm workers, and some factory laborers eke out a substandard living. (See Exhibit 8.)

4. Differences in luck. The individual who is born into the right environment and is provided with opportunities to develop his inherited talents stands a considerably greater chance of earning a higher income than one who is not so fortunate. Sociological studies of "vertical mobility"—the climb up the socioeconomic ladder—have borne this out. Unfortunately, what is not yet known is

how changes in vertical mobility are affected by changes in income distribution and in the degree of equality.

REDUCING INCOME INEQUALITY

From the mid-1930s to the present, the distribution of incomes in the United States has become somewhat more even—the inequality area on the Lorenz chart has narrowed. Most of the shift toward greater income equality occurred between 1935 and 1945 as the economy—especially its laborers and farmers—advanced from a depressed to a considerably more prosperous state. The Gini coefficient of inequality declined during that period from 0.44 to 0.38. Since 1945, the shift toward greater income equality has been less pronounced: the Gini coefficient has shown a slight downward trend, decreasing to where it now stands at about 0.35. This means that on a scale of equality like the following, ranging from 0 to 1.00, the degree of income equality in the United States is currently about 0.65.

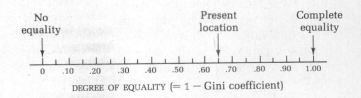

A number of factors have encouraged this gradual leveling process:

1. Reduction of the low-income farm population due to improvements in agricultural efficiency.

2. Greater opportunities for working women and racial minority groups.

3. Decline of earnings differentials between white-collar workers and manual workers.

4. Larger income provisions for the unemployed.

5. The federal income tax, which takes a larger percentage of higher incomes than of lower ones. Although the income redistribution effects of this tax are questionable, it nevertheless helps to keep incomes from becoming more unequal than they already are.

These income-leveling factors are, however, subject to various counterforces that may retard or even reverse long-term trends toward greater equality:

First, rigid patterns of wage and salary differentials have become deeply embedded in our economy.

Exhibit 8

Per Capita Personal Income, 1972–1973

For most of the years since 1950, aggregate personal income has been increasing fastest in the Southeast, Southwest, and Far West. In the South, historically an area with low per capita income, marginal (low wage) agriculture has been on the decline while job growth in nonfarm sectors has been strong. Continuing migration to the Far West, historically a high-income region, has stimulated—and has been stimulated by—expansion in economic activity there. In addition, the weight of defense spending has shifted from the Mideast and Great Lakes areas to the South and West.

Per capita incomes differ by region in part because of regional differences in the mix of industries and in the prevalence of large cities—where wage levels tend to be higher than in small towns and rural areas.

A small but significant share of personal income (as measured by the Department of Commerce) comprises items that are not direct payments to consumers.

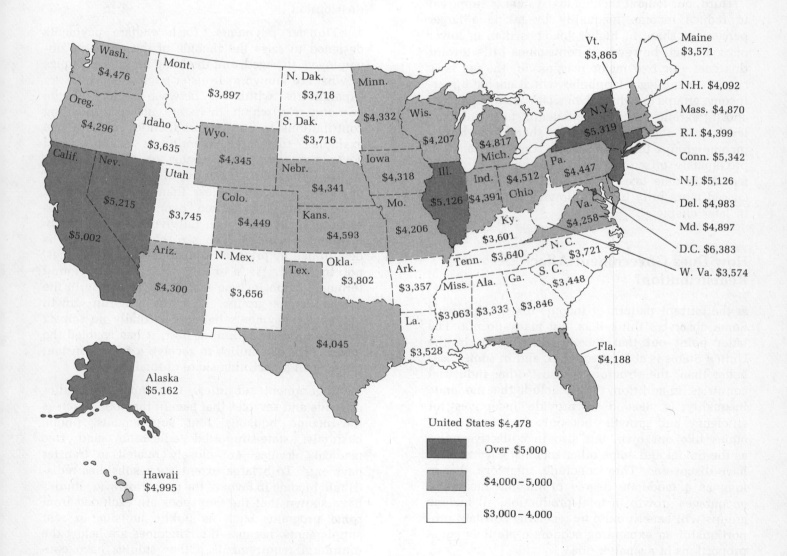

Wash. $4,476
Mont. $3,897
N. Dak. $3,718
Minn. $4,332
Vt. $3,865
Maine $3,571
N.H. $4,092
Mass. $4,870
R.I. $4,399
Conn. $5,342
N.J. $5,126
Del. $4,983
Md. $4,897
D.C. $6,383
W. Va. $3,574

Oreg. $4,296
Idaho $3,635
Wyo. $4,345
S. Dak. $3,716
Wis. $4,207
Mich. $4,817
N.Y. $5,319
Pa. $4,447

Calif. $5,002
Nev. $5,215
Utah $3,745
Colo. $4,449
Nebr. $4,341
Iowa $4,318
Ill. $5,126
Ind. $4,391
Ohio $4,512
Va. $4,258

Ariz. $4,300
N. Mex. $3,656
Kans. $4,593
Mo. $4,206
Ky. $3,601
Tenn. $3,640
N. C. $3,721
S. C. $3,448

Okla. $3,802
Ark. $3,357
Miss. $3,063
Ala. $3,333
Ga. $3,846

Tex. $4,045
La. $3,528
Fla. $4,188

Alaska $5,162

Hawaii $4,995

United States $4,478

Over $5,000
$4,000–5,000
$3,000–4,000

SOURCE: U.S. Department of Commerce.

Although individual workers may move up the scale from one type of job to another, groups within organized labor strongly resist changes in traditional patterns of job classification. Each class of worker strives to maintain its relative position in the pay structure, thereby impeding progress toward a more equal distribution of income.

Second, when the economy is booming, a larger proportion of young adults and elderly people set up housekeeping for themselves. These new uni-generation families usually have lower incomes than the multi-generation ones. As a consequence, income inequality among the total number of households is increased.

Third, our federal income tax system is supposed to reduce income inequality by taking a larger percentage share of higher incomes than of lower ones. In fact, however, it contributes little toward this goal—for two major reasons: (a) the tax laws contain many legal loopholes which enable upper-income groups to reduce their share of tax payments; and (b) various taxes at the federal, state, and local levels take a larger percentage share from lower-income groups than from higher ones, thereby approximately offsetting the graduated effect of the federal income tax. These considerations are discussed more fully in the following paragraphs and in later chapters.

How Does Government Affect Redistribution?

Is the current pattern of income distribution bad? Some observers think it is, but many do not. The latter point out that income distribution in the United States is at least equal to, and in some cases better than, the structure in most other industrial countries. In addition, they conclude that moderate inequality is needed to provide incentives for efficiency and growth—not only in mixed economies like our own, but also in collective ones, as the Soviet and some other socialist governments have discovered. They conclude, therefore, that as long as a moderate degree of income inequality encourages growth in total production, all income groups will benefit more by receiving constant proportions of an expanding economic pie than equal proportions of a smaller one.

The trouble with this conclusion, according to its critics, is that (1) the degree of income inequality is more extreme than moderate and (2) the benefits

(as well as sacrifices) among income groups have been outrageously disproportional. These shortcomings arise primarily from the distorted impact of certain government expenditure and taxation policies.

THE IMPACT OF GOVERNMENT ON INCOME

Government uses three major sets of measures to alter the distribution of income: (1) transfer payments, (2) subsidies for goods and services, and (3) income taxes. In addition, certain other taxes, such as social security payroll taxes and state and local taxes, have unintentional impacts on income distribution.

1. *Transfer payments.* Cash welfare payments designed to raise the income of the poor, the unemployed, the aged, and the blind provide examples of what are known as *transfer payments.* These are expenditures within or between sectors of the economy for which there are no corresponding contributions to current production. In the above examples, they are expenditures made by the government or public sector to the household sector. Contrary to much popular opinion, transfer payments account for less than 10 percent of all personal income; further, over half the total is social security (Old Age, Survivors, and Disability Insurance) benefits. The size of these benefits is determined by prior tax contributions and earnings, not by need. As a result, recipients are found throughout the income scale—*not* primarily in the lowest-income groups. Thus the long-run growth of transfer payments has had virtually no impact on income distribution; at best, it has enabled the lowest fifth of families to receive a fairly constant rather than a declining share of total income.

2. *Government subsidies.* Government subsidies of goods and services that benefit the poor—such as low-income housing, rent supplements, public hospitals, state-supported education, and free medical services—are closely related to transfer payments. To a large extent such subsidies redistribute income in favor of the poor. However, studies have shown that the very poor are excluded from some programs such as public housing or rent supplements, because their incomes are below the minimum requirements. Other studies have concluded that many state-supported public services like higher education, highways, and airports, though legally available to all, primarily benefit

the middle- and upper-income classes rather than the lower ones. In view of this, it cannot be *generally* assumed that government services benefit low-income families more than those with higher incomes.

3. *Income tax.* The federal personal income tax in theory is progressive. This means that it should take a larger share of income from higher-income groups than from lower ones. However, if your income is entirely from wages and salaries, you pay a higher tax than someone who earns the same amount of income from, for example, oil wells or state and municipal bonds. This is because the progressive effect of the tax has been weakened over the years by the introduction of "loopholes"—primarily percentage depletion allowances, depreciation allowances, exclusion of interest on state and local bonds, and favorable treatment of capital gains, expense accounts, and other types of income. The upper-income groups can take most advantage of these favorable tax provisions because they have income from sources other than wages and salaries. Hence, the loopholes have made the effective tax rates—the rates actually paid—far lower than the nominal rates. They have also distributed the burden of taxes unequally and unfairly. As a result, the impact of the federal individual income tax on income redistribution has been relatively minor. However, revisions in the tax laws may alter this conclusion as Washington places greater effort on reducing the tax burden in the lower-income levels and raising it in the higher. (See Box 2.)

4. *Other taxes.* Social security payroll taxes and state and local taxes—notably excise, sales, and property taxes—are regressive rather than progressive. This means that low-income families pay a larger percentage of their income in these taxes than do high-income families. With the growing needs of state and local governments to finance education, public welfare, highways, and other

---

Box 2
Revisions in the Tax Laws

Since 1969, the income tax burden has been reduced in the $0-to-$3,000 income class by 82 percent and has been reduced in gradually decreasing percentages in each

higher income class to the $50,000-to-$100,000 level. But in the income level above $100,000 the liability has been raised 7.4 percent.

EFFECT ON INDIVIDUAL INCOME TAX LIABILITY OF
TAX REFORM ACT OF 1969 AND REVENUE ACT OF 1971
(full-year effect at calendar year 1971 levels of income)

Adjusted gross income class	Tax under 1968 law* (in millions)	Tax under 1972 law (in millions)	Change under 1972 law from 1968 law	
			(in millions)	(percent)
$0–$3,000	$1,469	$265	− $1,240	− 82.0
$3,000–$5,000	3,488	1,995	− 1,493	− 42.8
$5,000–$7,000	5,543	4,025	− 1,518	− 27.4
$7,000–$10,000	12,263	10,112	− 2,151	− 17.5
$10,000–$15,000	22,065	19,202	− 2,863	− 13.0
$15,000–$20,000	15,287	13,891	− 1,396	− 9.1
$20,000–$50,000	19,375	18,377	− 998	− 5.2
$50,000–$100,000	7,344	7,217	− 127	− 1.7
$100,000 and over	7,131	7,658	+ 527	+ 7.4
Total	$93,965	$82,743	−$11,222	− 11.9

*Excluding surcharge.
SOURCE: Joint Economic Committee of the Congress, July 21, 1972.

social goods more reliance is being placed on regressive taxes. As a result, progressive taxes tend to have an overall canceling effect, leaving the country moving toward a proportional tax system that hits the rich and the poor with about equal impact.

These facts and trends suggest the following conclusion:

Taxes per se have done relatively little to alter the distribution of income. When combined with transfer payments and subsidies, the overall impact of the tax system is, at best, only moderately progressive and, at worst, approximately proportional.

THE IMPACT OF GOVERNMENT ON WEALTH

"The parent who leaves his son enormous wealth generally deadens the talents and energies of the son, and tempts him to lead a less useful and less worthy life." So wrote Andrew Carnegie, one of America's greatest industrialists and humanitarians, in 1889. Carnegie, a multimillionaire, advocated the taxation of wealth as a means of preventing the rich from passing on substantial inheritances to later generations. Today the taxes used for this purpose are death taxes and gift taxes.

Death taxes are levied on the transfer of property after death. They consist of two main types—the estate tax and the inheritance tax. The *estate tax* is a progressive tax imposed by the federal government on the transfer of all property owned by a person at the time of death. Property or wealth subject to tax includes stocks, bonds, mortgages, real estate, savings bonds, savings deposits, and the family home and car. The *inheritance tax* is imposed by most state governments on property received from the dead. This tax is primarily progressive in its rate structure. Of course, death taxes can be avoided by transferring property by gift between living persons. Therefore, associated with estate and inheritance taxes is the *gift tax*—a progressive tax imposed by the federal government and by some state governments. It is paid by the donor—the person who makes the gift—rather than the donee or recipient of it. Since death and gift taxes are levied by the federal and by most state governments, they vary in their rate structures and in the exemptions and deductions they provide.

What effect have death and gift taxes had on reducing economic inequality? Generous exemptions and deductions, and the use of elaborate trusts, have made it possible for the richest people to avoid the brunt of these taxes and to preserve much of their wealth within their families. Such loopholes explain why less than 4 percent of the estates of adults who die each year and about 25 percent of the total wealth of the decedents is subject to the tax. Further, estate and gift taxes account for less than 2 percent of annual federal revenues. For these reasons, many conservatives and liberals agree that death and gift taxes are in serious need of complete overhaul.

In general:

Death and gift taxes have had little effect on the distribution of wealth. Although the rate structures of these taxes are progressive, the impact of the graduated rates is virtually nullified by various escape clauses. As a result, the rich are able to avoid most of the taxes and to pass on the bulk of their wealth to their heirs.

CONCLUSION: NOT MUCH REDISTRIBUTION

Despite a general rise in living standards over the years, the *absolute* dollar gap between the rich and the poor has widened because their relative shares have remained fairly stable. The reason for this is not hard to see. If two individuals, A and B, receive 10 percent and 90 percent, respectively, of a joint $100 income, then A receives $10 and B receives $90. The absolute dollar gap between them is therefore $80. If their joint income rises to $1,000 while their *relative* shares remain the same, A receives $100 and B receives $900. The absolute dollar gap between them has thus widened to $800. This is essentially what has happened in the years since World War II. The rich have become richer while the poor have experienced a steady erosion of the income shares they derive from the private sector. As a result, the poor have had to receive increasing amounts of financial aid in the form of grants or transfer payments from the public sector (government) in order to maintain their relative income position.

Government action to reduce inequalities created by the private sector has weakened over the long run, and in some respects has even encouraged further inequality. Thus: (1) transfer payments have not been sufficient to improve the relative income share of the poor, (2) reliance of the public sector on progressive taxes to finance government has declined while reliance on regressive taxes has increased, and (3) legal loopholes have enabled those with higher income and greater wealth to reduce their effective taxes, thereby placing greater tax burdens on lower- and middle-income groups.

What is being done to correct these inequities? Legislative reforms adopted in Washington since the late 1960s have narrowed or reduced the number of tax loopholes. But the wheels of tax reform grind slowly—sometimes agonizingly so—since the issues involved are political as well as economic. This is because the exemptions, deductions, and special provisions that individuals and businesses enjoy were written into the tax code piecemeal by Congress over many years. Some were designed to achieve greater equality among taxpayers; others were intended to stimulate certain types of economic activity; and still others were introduced to offset a handicap. Whatever their initial purpose, the beneficiaries want them to be continued. Therefore, a legislator faced with a particular proposal for tax reform—such as the elimination of an exemption, or a deduction, or some other tax preference—finds it prudent to consider not only the ways in which the measure will influence both the nation's and his own economic well-being, but also how his vote will affect his political career.

Distributive Criteria—
The Ethics of Distribution

The seventeenth-century English philosopher and essayist Francis Bacon remarked that "Money is like muck [manure]; not good except it be spread." But what criteria can be used for spreading money? In other words, who should get *how much*? This is the age-old problem of economic justice to which there is no completely satisfactory solution because justice in any form is at best a tolerable accommodation of the conflicting interests of society. Nevertheless a number of distributive standards have been proposed over the long history of discussions on the subject. Most of these standards derive from three basic criteria: (1) distribution based on productive contribution, (2) distribution based on needs, and (3) distribution based on equality.

CONTRIBUTIVE STANDARD

It is generally agreed that an individual should be paid what he deserves. This criterion, which may be called a *merit standard*, represents one of the oldest concepts of justice known to man. Unfortunately, it is difficult to define and impossible to measure. How can we decide, in a manner acceptable to everyone, what each person deserves? Surely responsibility in a job is not the criterion, for aircraft mechanics earn less but have greater responsibility than heart surgeons; nor are years of formal education a criterion, for most plumbers are more highly paid than school teachers. These, as well as almost all other standards of merit, lead to similar contradictions. However, there is one standard that is unique to capitalism:

The criterion of distribution in a capitalist society can be expressed by the phrase, "To each according to what he produces." This may be called a *contributive standard* since it is based on the principle of payment according to contribution.

The contributive standard is a value judgement rooted in the capitalistic ethic. Even so, some of the severest critics of capitalism have implicitly accepted it as fair. Karl Marx (1818–1883), the founder of modern socialism, based his entire thesis on the premise that in capitalistic societies labor creates the whole of the nation's output but gets back only a fraction of it—enough to subsist and rear children. The rest is "surplus value" which is appropriated—literally stolen—from the workers by their capitalistic employers. Labor, according to Marx, is therefore exploited. Why? Because labor is entitled to get back all of what it produces—not just a part. We must infer from this that even if one accepts all of Marx's beliefs, his conclusion that labor is exploited can be true only if one also accepts the contributive standard as ethically just.

How is one's productive contribution measured? The most objective measure is the value placed upon it in a free market where the prices of the factors of production are established by the interactions of supply and demand. The contribution to the total product made by a particular factor and the payment received for it can then be measured by multiplying the price per unit of the factor by the number of units supplied. Thus under these conditions, if the market price of your labor is $6 an hour, and if you work 2,000 hours a year, your contribution to the total product and the payment you receive are both equal to $12,000. However, much more is involved in determining factor contributions and payments than is implied by this simple example. Nevertheless, the illustration emphasizes an important principle:

In a capitalistic or market economy the payment received for a factor of production is the measure of its merit. This payment, which reflects the value of the factor's contribution to total product, is determined by the impersonal pressure of market forces—not by the judgement of a central authority.

Of course, society also recognizes obligations to its nonproducers—the aged, the disabled, the very young, the involuntarily unemployed, and so on—as a result of which it employs some noncontributive criteria for apportioning income. Nevertheless, the contributive standard is the dominant one in our economy. This gives rise to what some people believe is considerable inequality of income and wealth. Can such inequality be attributed to the development and existence of capitalism? Does capitalism create greater inequality than alternative systems? The answers to these and related questions must await later chapters.

NEEDS STANDARD

The distributive principle of capitalism, as we have seen, is expressed by the phrase, "To each according to what he produces." In contrast, the distributive principle of pure communism may be described by the expression, "To each according to his needs." It is interesting to note, however, that the latter standard is not just an ethical principle of communist philosophy; it serves roughly as a criterion of distribution within most families, and in time of war or other emergency is adopted by all kinds of governments as a means of rationing a limited supply of goods.

Distribution according to need has wide appeal. But upon close examination its implementation poses two major difficulties.

First, no impersonal mechanism exists for measuring need. As a result, decisions to allocate goods according to need—whether such decisions are made within a family or within a nation—must be based on the subjective judgement of a central authority. Further, the problem cannot be avoided by distributing goods equally to everyone, because such a distribution would not be an allocation based on individual needs. No two individuals necessarily enjoy the same goods to the same degree; hence a commodity which may be a "luxury" to some people may be a "necessity" to others.

Second, even if individual needs could be measured, it is likely that the implementation of a needs standard would not precisely utilize the economy's entire output; there would be either shortages or surpluses, depending on whether the sum of needs was greater or less than the total product. This is less likely to occur when output is distributed according to the contributive criterion of capitalism, because under such a system there is a tendency for the market—depending on the degree of competition and the mobility of resources—to equate the incomes people receive with the values of what they contribute.

We must conclude, therefore, that individual needs are impossible to measure. As a result, if distribution of income according to needs were to be adopted, it would have to be based on some central authority's personal judgement of what constitutes "needs." In addition, peoples' diverse needs would somehow have to be matched up with available products if surpluses and shortages were to be avoided.

EQUALITY STANDARD

A third criterion of distribution, which was debated as far back as biblical times, is the *equality standard*. It is expressed most simply by the phrase, "To each, equally." It is a just standard only if we assume that all men are alike in the *added* satisfaction or utility they receive from an extra dollar of income. If, on the other hand, an additional dollar of income provides a greater gain in utility to some people than to others, then justice is more properly served by distributing most of any increase in society's income to those who will enjoy it more. In reality, there is no conclusive evidence that people are either alike or unlike in the satisfactions they derive from additional income. Therefore, the equalitarians argue, since we cannot prove that people are unlike, we should assume they are alike and distribute all incomes equally.

This conclusion, regardless of how plausible it may seem, illustrates a logical fallacy in reasoning—one which may be called "argument from ignorance." It is committed whenever one argues that a proposition is true simply because it has not been proved false, or that it is false because it has not been proved true. In terms of the present problem, this implies that we must go beyond the stage of theorizing about individual utilities and consider instead some of the realistic effects of an equality standard. Among the most important are the "motivational" ones:

An equal distribution of income would eliminate incentives of rewards. Hence it would provide no economic motivation for people to develop or apply their skills, or to use economic resources efficiently since there is no commensurate return. The result would be declining economic progress and probable stagnation.

This argument assumes, of course, that economic progress attributable to inequality is desirable in itself. Some critics think it is not. We shall have more to say about this issue in later chapters.

CONCLUSION: AN "OPTIMAL" DISTRIBUTION?

The foregoing arguments suggest the possibility that there is some "ideal" degree of income inequality—a distribution which is not too extreme either way. What can be said about this hypothesis?

In a society characterized by a very unequal distribution of income, the economic surplus or savings of the rich minority can finance investment in capital, and therefore material and cultural advancement. This helps to explain why such ancient civilizations as Egypt, Greece, and Rome, whose economies were based on slavery—the most unequal distributive system of all—were able to produce magnificent art, architecture, and other cultural achievements. On the other hand, in a society whose limited income is distributed equally among the masses, virtually all of its income is spent on needed consumption goods, leaving little if any savings with which to acquire capital goods. (This is the familiar production-possibilities concept of earlier chapters, involving the notion that every society must make choices between the proportions of consumption goods and capital goods it wishes to have.) Such a society, though equalitarian in income distribution would tend to remain poor because of its distributive policy.

Every society, of course, seeks the best compromise—the "optimum" distribution—between these two extremes. But each society's concept of optimum differs, depending on its goals and institutions. Therefore, it is impossible to state objectively whether a particular distribution of income is "good" or "bad."

SUMMARY OF IMPORTANT IDEAS

1. Income and wealth are among the measures of a society's economic well-being. Therefore, their dis-

tribution within society and the forces determining their distribution are of central concern.

2. Since 1950, the lowest fifth of families in the United States has consistently received less than 6 percent of total income, while the highest fifth has received over 40 percent—or a long-run average of about eight times as much. The lopsided distribution of wealth is even more pronounced: the lowest fifth of families owns less than $\frac{1}{2}$ percent of total wealth, while the highest fifth owns over 75 percent.

3. The personal distribution of income in the United States has become more equal since the 1930s, but there are still significant disparities between income levels. These are primarily due to differences among people with respect to (a) the distribution of wealth or income-producing assets, (b) their earning ability and opportunity, (c) their mobility, and (d) their luck or personal endowment—both inherited and acquired. Since 1950, the distribution of income and wealth has remained quite stable.

4. On the whole, governmental measures have not significantly reduced economic inequality, and in some respects they have even enhanced it. Transfer payments have merely enabled the poor to maintain their relative income position, while regressive taxes and legal loopholes have made it possible for the rich to decrease their effective taxes, thereby placing greater tax burdens on lower- and middle-income groups.

5. Ethical criteria exist for allocating income. Three major ones are (a) productive contribution, (b) needs, and (c) equality. The first is the primary standard of distribution in capitalistic economies; the second and third are philosophical goals of pure communistic and of equalitarian societies—neither of which exist anywhere on a national scale.

6. Economic history shows that the higher a nation's per capita real income, the more it tends to progress toward greater income equality. This is because a high-income economy enables people to save enough to provide for capital accumulation and hence for society's material advancement.

FOR DISCUSSION

1. *Terms and concepts to review:*

private sector	personal income
public sector	distribution
income	functional income
wealth	distribution

median   death taxes
Lorenz curve   estate tax
Gini coefficient of   inheritance tax
   inequality   gift tax
transfer payments

2. What factor of production receives the largest share of national income? Has this share tended to be stable or unstable over the long run? Why?

3. What are the chief causes of income inequality among households? Would it be better if all incomes were equal? Explain.

4. Is it a necessary condition of capitalism that some people be rich and some poor? Is it morally right for the government to tax the incomes of the rich and redistribute them to the poor? Defend your answer.

5. Suppose a society consists of only five families with a combined money income of $100,000. The distribution of income among the families is shown in the following table. Construct a Lorenz curve and calculate the Gini coefficient of inequality. Here are some helpful hints and suggestions:

(a) Fill in the table. Then derive the Lorenz curve from the last three columns. Note that the lowest 20 percent of the families receive 5 percent of the income; label this point B on the curve. The lowest 40 percent receive 15 percent of the income; label this point C on the curve. And so on.

(b) Connect the points with straight lines. If there had been many more income classes than five, the Lorenz curve would be a smooth, rounded line instead of a series of straight-line segments.

(c) The entire area under the Lorenz curve is equal to the sum of the separate triangular and trapezoidal areas beneath it. (A trapezoid is a quadrilateral plane figure having two parallel and two nonparallel sides.)

To perform the necessary calculations, make use of the fact that the area A in terms of the base b and height h is found as follows:

$$\text{for a triangle} \quad A = \tfrac{1}{2}bh$$
$$\text{for a trapezoid} \quad A = \tfrac{1}{2}b(h_1 + h_2),$$

where h_1 and h_2 represent, respectively, the heights of the left-hand and right-hand vertical sides.

6. We cannot distribute goods according to needs because we do not know how to determine peoples' needs. Therefore, why not solve the problem by (a) distributing incomes according to needs, and (b) permitting goods to be allocated through the price system, thereby preserving freedom of consumer's choice?

7. The principle of payment according to product (i.e., the contribution standard) assures that people get what they deserve; hence it is more democratic than payment based on needs or on equality. Do you agree? Explain.

8. "If payments to individuals are based on needs or on equality, some people are bound to be exploited for the benefit of others." What does "exploitation" mean? Explain.

9. In a democracy, we do not allocate political votes in proportion to one's intelligence and the ability to use it. Instead, everyone gets an equal vote. Therefore, the same should be true of dollar votes (income); everyone's should be equal. Do you agree? Explain.

10. "The value of a culture is measured by its peak accomplishments, not by its average level of achievement. Thus a society of mud huts and a great cathedral is better than a society of stone huts and no cathedral. To put it differently, it is by the quality of its saints and heroes, not its common men, and by its masterpieces and not its domestic utensils, that a culture should be judged." What implications does this have for income distribution?

Percent of families	Income received (thousands of $)	Percent income received	Cumulative percent of families	Cumulative percent of income received	Point on Lorenz curve
0	$ 0	0%			
Lowest fifth	5	5			
Second fifth	10	10			
Third fifth	15	15			
Fourth fifth	20	20			
Highest fifth	50	50			

Should Higher Education Be Tuition-free?

All civilized nations provide free education for children up to high-school level. But in the United States that's generally as far as it goes: many colleges charge, in one form or another, for education. That is very curious when one stops to think of it.

Provision of free schooling is rooted in the principle that both the individual and society as a whole benefit from the individual's being able to read, write, and do arithmetic. That view is demonstrably correct. It is no coincidence that the countries with the highest living standards also are the countries with the highest levels of literacy.

A generation ago the youth with a high-school diploma could get a job and, with energy, ability, and some luck, hope to get ahead. That is no longer true. As the economy has become increasingly dependent on the higher technologies and on sophisticated management techniques, the minimum educational level has risen. Today, the person without a college degree is handicapped from the day he or she starts work until the day of retirement.

Yet there is little or no hope that tuition-free colleges will soon become the rule rather than the exception in the United States. Higher education continues to be to some extent the province of an elite—an elite founded more on income than on ability. If their parents are rich enough, a stupid boy or girl will find some college ready to take them—and teachers willing to give extra tutoring in return for cash. In contrast, many bright children from poor families cannot afford to go to college; most are then doomed to take jobs below their real intellectual capacity.

Why Free Tuition?

Recently, the arguments for and against free college education have been particularly acute in New York City. One reason is that City College of New York —part of the City University of New York, CUNY—is bulging with students who pay no tuition fees, and the college is reeling under huge deficits. Seeking to reduce the overload, some politicians are proposing that CUNY should charge tuition for the first time in its long history. As one might expect, the voluble Albert Shanker, president of the United Federation of Teachers, is an outspoken opponent of that solution. Indeed, he advocates that tuition should be free not only at CUNY, but also at all public colleges and universities.

In his writings and speeches, Shanker tears into those who argue that CUNY should charge tuition to those who can afford it and continue free tuition for those who cannot afford it. "The weakness of this position can be readily seen if it is logically extended," Shanker wrote recently. "Thus, why not do the same in elementary and high schools? Why not impose additional charges for police, fire, sanitation and other public services on those able to pay?" Shanker believes that the voters will support the ideal of free higher education so long as both individual and social good are thereby advanced. Unfortunately, he adds, that belief has been severely shaken by some colleges in their lowering of educational standards and their capitulation to demands from extremist groups.

Opposing View: There Are No Free Lunches

Trenchant though the views of Shanker and many other professional educators are, they do not persuade everyone. Many influential legislators and business groups argue quite the opposite. Their arguments fall into three categories. First, higher education is a privilege, not a right—unlike high school. Second, tuition-free colleges benefit the middle classes proportionately more than the very poor, who cannot afford the "lost" income when a student goes to college instead of taking a job. Third, if virtually everyone had a college degree, an ordinary bachelor's or master's degree would become little more valuable in the job market than a high-school diploma is today, because many employers would raise the minimum educational requirement to doctorate level.

In a special report on the issue, First National City Bank of New York said flatly: "The problem is best expressed by the aphorism 'there are no free lunches'; in other words, the free-tuition policy ignores a fundamental economic fact of life. In a world of scarce resources, someone must bear the cost. And in many cases where goods and services are distributed free of direct user charges, the burden is borne by the very people the subsidization is designed to help." The report says that the free-tuition debate ignores the main point: "The cost of education to the poor consists not only of free tuition, which they must pay for through taxes, but also of lost income to the family while the children attend college. In fact, some analysts find that this cost—the opportunity cost of being educated—is the largest portion of a student's investment in his education. To be consistent, then, the proponents of free tuition must provide subsidies to lower-income families to make up for that lost income."

Economic and Noneconomic Issues

Well, why not? Most countries that conscript men into the armed forces provide allowances for dependents, for example, elderly or handicapped parents who cannot afford the loss of the son's income from his civilian job.

It's but a short step to saying that higher education is virtually analogous to service in the army: both are deemed by government and by most citizens to advance the well-being of the nation as a whole.

When one cuts through the mass of argument and counter-argument to the heart of the matter it seems that most people agree with free education in principle, but for some curious reason think it should stop at high school. In purely economic terms this is nonsense: if it can be shown that lower education benefits both individuals and society and that higher education is even more beneficial, then society is being contradictory by offering one form free but charging for the other. But, of course, the argument is not purely economic; it contains elements of snobbery and fear that universal higher education would reduce the earning power of certain occupational groups and generally wreak havoc with the hierarchical system that is so comfortable for those on the uppermost rungs—and so frustrating for those at the bottom.

QUESTIONS

1. Do you believe that higher education should be available free to everyone—rich and poor alike?

2. The distribution of intelligence may be more unequal than the distribution of income. In view of this, should colleges grant tuition-free scholarships on the basis of academic achievement or on the basis of income? Which criterion is fair?

3. In an article in Fortune magazine in 1970, Edmund K. Faltermayer wrote: "One way to motivate students is to make them responsible for financing their own education. Society, of course, should continue to bear the full costs of elementary and secondary education for all. But once that basic social investment is made, society's commitment to pay the costs of education should largely come to an end." Can you suggest a plan to enable students, regardless of current income, to pay for their education? What would be the advantages of such a plan?

CHAPTER 6

Businesses: Organization, Size, and Social Responsibility

CHAPTER PREVIEW

How are businesses organized? What are the major types of business organization, their advantages and disadvantages?

How "big" is big business? Why do firms become big?

Does business have any particular roles to perform in today's society? If so, how can these roles be implemented?

Business is a major institution. It is powerful, and its decisions and policies influence the nature, structure, and goals of American society. This makes business highly controversial, and its motives are the subject of ceaseless debate.

The traditional economic functions of business are the production of goods and services, and the consequent generation of wealth. Some people believe that business best serves the public by confining itself to doing these things as efficiently and profitably as possible. In this view, to ask business to do otherwise would be to subvert our free-enterprise system.

However, in the opinion of many thoughtful observers—including social scientists, political leaders, and businessmen themselves—the traditional *economic* functions are not sufficient in modern society. Business must also fulfill *social* responsibilities. Not that business is necessarily the cause of society's ills—such as poverty, urban blight, and ecological damage—but that large corporations have the resources and skills needed to help correct them.

These conflicting viewpoints deserve to be examined in detail. But first we must understand how businesses are organized, who owns them, who runs them, and how some of them get so big.

Businesses—Their Organization and Income

Between 80 and 90 percent of all productive activity in the American economy is carried on by 11 million firms, of which 5 million are manufacturers and retailers, $3\frac{1}{2}$ million are farms, and $2\frac{1}{2}$ million are professional firms in accounting, law, and the like. The remaining 10 to 20 percent of productive activity is accounted for by government.

Productive activity may be carried on in factory buildings, mines, mills, warehouses, stores, and so forth. Any such establishment is called a *plant*. A business organization which owns a plant is called a *firm*. Most firms own only one plant, but some firms, such as large steel or chemical companies, may own hundreds of plants.

One way in which firms may be classified is by the products they make. Firms that produce similar or identical products are in the same *industry*. Thus General Motors and Ford are in the automobile industry. But General Motors also produces trucks, buses, and diesel locomotives among other things, so it would be correct to say that it is also in the truck industry, the bus industry, and the diesel locomotive industry. Indeed most of the largest companies make more than one product. Can you name at least five industries in which General Electric is an important producer?

Another method of classifying firms is by their legal form of organization. Three types are particularly common: the individual proprietorship, the partnership, and the corporation.

THE INDIVIDUAL PROPRIETORSHIP

The simplest, oldest, and commonest form of business is the sole or *individual proprietorship*. There are more than 9 million of these one-man firms in the United States. You see them every day—restaurants, drugstores, gas stations, radio and TV repair shops, grocery stores, and so on. An individual proprietor may hire help and borrow money just as larger and more complex business organizations do. Unlike them, however, he does not have to pay special taxes to the state in order to get started or to remain in business, nor is he ordinarily subject to special government controls or regulations (except in a few businesses like restaurants, pharmacies, and liquor stores, where a license is necessary and certain standards of health and safety must be met).

If you were the sole owner of a business, the general credit of the business would be limited to your personal resources. Thus in the eyes of creditors, there would be a danger of your business lacking stability and continuity. They would regard you as a substantial risk, and you would find it difficult to borrow funds for long periods in order to finance expansion. Consequently the growth of the enterprise

would rest largely on your ability to reinvest its earnings. If the business failed, you could find yourself with debts greater than your assets. You would be held personally liable for those debts, and creditors would be able to take your savings, your house, your car, and most of your other property in order to help satisfy their claims.

The chief advantages of the individual proprietorship are the following:

1. Ease of formation and simplicity of control

2. Presence of a strong personal element in the business

3. Freedom from organizational taxes and government regulation

There are also some important disadvantages:

1. Difficulty of raising funds for expansion

2. Lack of stability or permanence

3. Unlimited liability of the owner for all unpaid debts of the business

THE PARTNERSHIP

Suppose you decide that your business needs more money—perhaps to expand or to move into a new and better location. You might decide to take in a partner. He would put up an agreed amount of money, and in the resulting partnership the profits and responsibilities of the business would be shared by both of you. Thus a *partnership* is an association of two or more individuals to carry on, as co-owners, a business for profit. There are about 1 million partnerships in the United States.

Of course, a partnership agreement should be in writing and should stipulate such things as the number of partners, the amounts contributed by each, the salaries of each, and the percentage of each partner's share in the profits or losses of the business.

A partnership is similar in many ways to an individual proprietorship. It has the same advantages listed in the preceding section and the additional advantages of (1) sharing of managerial talents and responsibilities among the partners and (2) the ability of the partners to combine their financial resources.

But there are disadvantages to a partnership as well:

1. Division of authority and disagreements among partners may lead to instability.

2. Withdrawal or death of a partner dissolves the partnership.

3. Ability to command resources is often inadequate.

4. The partners have unlimited liability for all unpaid debts of the firm.

THE CORPORATION

By this time the nature of your business may have become such that a partnership is no longer suitable. In that case you will want to consider forming a corporation.

What is a corporation? The most common definition that still stands was given by Chief Justice John Marshall of the United States Supreme Court in the famous Dartmouth College case of 1819:

> A corporation is an artificial being, invisible, intangible, and existing only in the contemplation of the law. Being the mere creature of law, it possesses only those properties which the charter of its creation confers upon it, either expressly or as incidental to its very existence. . . . Among the most important are immortality, and, if the expression may be allowed, individuality: properties by which a perpetual succession of many persons are considered as the same, and may act as a single individual.

This means, in short, that a *corporation* is an anonymous entity in which the identity of its owners is irrelevant for the purpose of conducting business.

How does a corporation get started? It comes into existence when interested parties file a certificate of incorporation with the state, authorizing their group to act as a legal entity for the purpose of carrying on a specific activity or business. Unlike an individual proprietorship or partnership, a corporation must pay an initial organizational tax and an annual franchise tax to the state, as well as federal income tax.

Managerial and Financial Features of the Corporation

The ownership of a corporation is divided into units represented by shares of *stock*. A stockholder who owns 100 shares of stock in a corporation has twice as much "ownership" as a stockholder with only 50 shares. Each stockholder participates in the profits of the corporation by receiving *dividends* in the form of a certain amount of dollars or cents per share. If there are no profits, there may be no dividends.

One of the distinguishing features of a corporation is the *limited liability* of its stockholders. Unlike the individual proprietorship or the partnership, where the owners can be held personally liable for the debts of the business, stockholders in corporations cannot be held liable for any of the firm's debts. For almost all practical purposes, the most that stockholders can lose if the business goes bankrupt is the money they paid for stock.

Stockholders elect a board of directors which is responsible for the management of the corporation. Each stockholder gets one vote for each share of stock he owns. A stockholder may thus elect himself to the board if he owns enough shares or if he can get enough of the other stockholders to vote their shares for him. In large corporations, the board employs officers—a president and vice-presidents—to manage day-to-day operations and report back to it the results of these operations. In smaller corporations it is common to find one or more members of the board serving as officers as well. (See Box 1.)

The corporation has durability. Stockholders may come and go, but the corporation itself lives on. Indeed, some corporations in existence today were originally chartered hundreds of years ago. This stability and permanence make the corporation highly flexible. It can raise large amounts of capital by selling stocks and *bonds* (promises to pay money plus interest in future years) to the public, and it can adapt itself to changing market needs and conditions.

The corporation has some important advantages:

1. Limited liability of stockholders

2. Ability to raise large amounts of funds for expansion through the sale of stocks and bonds

3. Stability and permanence

4. Flexibility in organization and management

It also has the following chief disadvantages:

1. Formation may be complicated, depending on the nature of the business.

2. Taxation is burdensome, since there are not only organizational and franchise taxes, but also "double" income taxes including (a) the income tax paid by the corporation on its profits and (b) the income tax paid by the stockholder on the dividends he receives out of the corporation's profits.

3. Some difficulties may arise because of the nonuniformity of corporation laws among the states.

4. Accounting methods and various financial practices are subject to strict government regulations.

Big Business in America

There are over 1 million corporations in the United States. More than half of them are "small," with assets (cash, buildings, equipment, inventories, etc.) totaling less than $100,000 each. At the other extreme are more than 100 giants in the "billion-dollar club"—companies whose total assets exceed $1 billion.

The names of the five largest United States companies in each of several fields are presented in Exhibit 1, along with some measures of size. Most

---

Box 1

Organization of A Typical Corporation

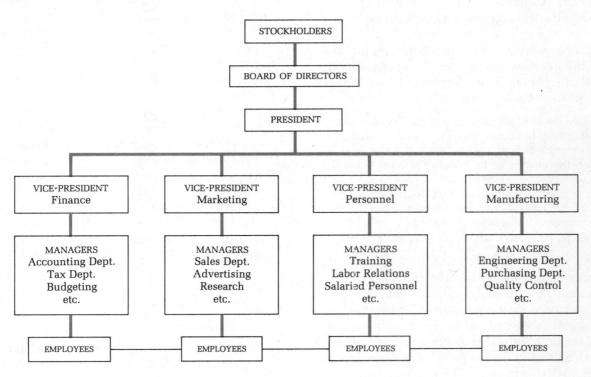

BOARDS OF DIRECTORS: ORNAMENTS ON THE CORPORATE CHRISTMAS TREE?

Do today's corporate boards set company objectives, strategies, and broad policies, or do they simply rubber stamp the edicts of management? The answer, in most medium- and large-sized publicly held firms, appears to be the latter—according to Harvard Business School Professor Myles L. Mace. In a study entitled Directors: Myth and Reality *(Cambridge, Mass., Harvard Business School, 1971), Mace points out that all too often, "management winds up electing directors who are congenial, sympathetic, understanding—and who don't make waves." There is thus a wide gulf between what boards are theoretically supposed to do and what they actually do.*

Why does this happen? Professor Mace's study suggests several reasons. Among them:

□ *Board members do not often have an intimate knowledge of the company's operations and are therefore reluctant to criticize its management.*

□ *Outside directors (those from other firms) frequently serve on numerous corporate boards; hence it is virtually impossible for them to devote the time necessary to running a large company.*

As a result, Mace says, the boards do not do much more than meet the statutory requirements. Besides, in the words of one chief executive interviewed by Mace: "You have got to have directors whose names look impressive in the annual report. They are, after all, nothing more or less than ornaments on the corporate Christmas tree."

---

of these companies are familiar to all of us. Not only their total assets, but also their annual sales and annual net profits after taxes are in excess of a billion dollars. Each employs hundreds of thousands of workers and distributes profits to hundreds of thousands or even millions of stockholders. Together these companies control a large share of the nation's income-producing wealth.

How big is big? By way of comparison, the annual value of the total production of General Motors often ranks with that of Argentina and Belgium, while exceeding by many billions of dollars the output of more than a dozen other countries. A number of other U.S. corporations also have total outputs larger than that of some nations.

These facts raise issues that are among the most fundamental of our time: How and why do firms become big? Is bigness "good" or "bad"?

Exhibit 1

Who's Who Among the Giants? America's Largest Corporations, 1972–1973

FIVE LARGEST INDUSTRIAL CORPORATIONS (ranked by sales)

	Sales (billions)	Assets (billions)
General Motors	$30.4	$18.3
Exxon (Standard Oil of New Jersey)	20.3	21.6
Ford Motor	20.2	11.6
General Electric	10.2	7.4
Chrysler	9.8	5.5

FIVE LARGEST COMMERCIAL BANKS (ranked by assets)

	Assets (billions)	Deposits (billions)
Bank America	$40.9	$35.1
First National City	34.4	27.7
Chase Manhattan	30.7	25.0
J. P. Morgan	16.5	12.8
Manufacturers Hanover	16.3	14.0

FIVE LARGEST LIFE INSURANCE COMPANIES (ranked by assets)

	Assets (billions)	Life insurance in force (billions)
Prudential	$34.0	$182.4
Metropolitan	30.8	185.6
Equitable Life Assurance	16.4	89.7
New York Life	11.9	58.5
John Hancock Mutual	11.2	69.9

FIVE LARGEST RETAILING COMPANIES (ranked by sales)

	Sales (billions)	Assets (billions)
Sears, Roebuck	$11.0	$9.3
Great Atlantic & Pacific Tea	6.4	1.0
Safeway Stores	6.1	1.2
J. C. Penny	5.5	2.2
S.S. Kresge	3.9	1.4

FIVE LARGEST TRANSPORTATION COMPANIES (ranked by operating revenues)

	Operating revenues (billions)	Assets (billions)
United Airlines	$1.8	$2.3
Penn Central Transportation	1.8	4.3
Southern Pacific	1.4	3.3
Trans World Airlines	1.4	1.6
American Airlines	1.4	1.7

FIVE LARGEST UTILITIES (ranked by assets)

	Assets (billions)	Operating revenues (billions)
American Tel. & Tel.	$60.6	$20.9
General Telephone and Electronics	9.5	4.4
Consolidated Edison	5.3	1.5
Pacific Gas & Electric	5.0	1.4
Southern Company	4.5	1.0

SOURCE: *Fortune Directory*, 1973.

HOW AND WHY DO FIRMS BECOME BIG?

A business may expand through internal growth by plowing most of its profits back into the business and/or selling securities such as stocks and bonds to the public. In this way it acquires the funds it needs to pay for new equipment, research, and product development. A classic example of this type of growth is the Ford Motor Company. For several decades after its formation, it remained a privately (mostly family) held corporation. After its stock became available to the public, it often paid out as little as 33 to 40 percent of its profits to stockholders while other major industrial firms were distributing between 50 and 65 percent.

A firm may also expand by combining or merging with others. This has been the most prevalent method of growth in American industry. As one of many classic examples, Exxon (formerly Standard Oil Company of New Jersey), under the aggressive leadership of John D. Rockefeller, reached a point in 1911 where it owned 65 companies and held a controlling interest in 49 more. As a result of a Supreme Court decision in that year, the corporation was broken up into 47 different companies. This dissolution permanently affected the basic structure of the petroleum industry. Today fewer than a dozen major oil companies dominate the production and marketing of crude and refined oil.

Why do some firms become large? Their ultimate objective is usually to strengthen their financial position. For instance, a firm may combine with other firms in the same or in related types of activity in order to gain economies in production or distribution, or to regularize its supplies, or to round out its product line. Thus some container manufacturers also make tin cans, glass jars, and plastics. Some automobile producers own rubber companies, iron mines, and steel mills. Many companies have also chosen to grow by combining with firms in totally unrelated activities. This may reflect a desire on the part of the acquiring company to spread risks, find investments for idle capital funds, add products which can be sold with the firm's merchandising knowledge and skills, or simply to gain greater economic power on a broader front.

IS BIGNESS A CURSE OR A BLESSING?

Is it "good" or "bad" to have an economy whose major industries are dominated by a few giant corporations—by companies like U.S. Steel in the steel industry, General Motors in the automobile industry, Exxon Corporation in the petroleum industry, AT&T in the electronic communications industry, and so on? Would we be better or worse off if we had an economy whose industries were composed of many small firms in active competition?

There is no simple answer. The best we can do is sketch the main aspects of the problem and leave you to think out some tentative conclusions. As you study later chapters, you may very well come to see some of these conclusions in a different light.

1. A striking feature of the modern corporation is its *separation of ownership and control*. Some of the largest corporations like General Motors and AT&T have millions of stockholders, and quite a few others have hundreds of thousands. Most of these stockholders, however, own relatively few shares—much less than even 100 shares each—but small minorities own enough shares to gain working control of their corporations.

Because stockholders are not usually sufficiently organized to do anything about correcting misuses and abuses of corporate powers, several undesirable consequences arise from the separation of ownership and management. The insiders of a corporation (the board of directors and officers) may be able to keep themselves in control even if they do not perform particularly well; they may also vote themselves high salaries, bonuses, pensions, and benefits at the stockholders' expense. To some extent these problems have been mitigated over the years—thanks to government regulations and laws to protect the interests of stockholders. But the difficulties continue to exist in varying degrees and will probably never be completely eliminated.

2. Many important industries are dominated by a few large companies. Examples include aluminum, automobiles, telephone equipment, steel, cigarettes, and breakfast foods—plus many others. The giants in these industries exercise varying degrees of monopoly power over the markets in which they deal. This means, among other things, that (a) they may charge prices higher than would occur if the industries were very competitive; (b) they may not improve their efficiency and productivity as much as they would do if they were subject to greater competition; and (c) they may have the power to influence the very legislators and federal agencies responsible for regulating them.

However, many of these giants—like General Electric, Boeing, IBM, General Motors, etc.—are the same companies whose massive productive resources and scientific know-how are vital to the country for peace as well as war. And as some qualified observers have contended, these are also firms which have been instrumental in no small way in providing us with the standard of living that we now possess.

Perhaps the problem for modern capitalism, therefore, is not one of choosing between large firms and small ones, but of finding improved ways of encouraging big business to employ more of its resources for the betterment of society. We will have more to say about this at a later point.

Does Business Have a Social Responsibility?

According to traditional philosophy, social progress under capitalism is a by-product of economic efficiency. As Adam Smith asserted in 1776, the businessman pursuing his own self-interest would be led by an invisible hand to do the most good for society—not out of duty or responsibility to his fellow man, but out of his own drive for personal gain. Businessmen have accepted this capitalistic credo for two centuries. By seeking to maximize their profits and efficiency—subject to such constraints as honest dealing with customers, fair dealing with workers, and no "dealing" with competitors—they have believed they would simultaneously be creating wealth for themselves as well as jobs, goods, and wealth for others.

Although this fundamental doctrine of capitalism has not been abrogated, it has undergone substantial modification since the 1960s. Prior to that time, it was generally believed that a corporation can only fulfill its obligations to society if it continues to be a profitable investment for its stockholders. Since then, many observers both in and out of the executive suite have argued in favor of a reversal of priorities: A corporation, they say, can only continue to be a profitable investment for its stockholders if it fulfills its obligations to society.

RESPONSIBILITIES BEYOND PROFIT

What are these obligations? Corporations, partly due to the failure of other institutions, have become increasingly involved in training and assisting poorly educated minorities, building and providing financing for ghetto housing, operating child-care centers, strengthening and improving urban school systems, cleaning up the environment—in short, taking on social problems that would have been inconceivable as recently as the mid-sixties. In fact, so pervasive has been this trend that the rare large corporation today is one which does not have some active social program.

It appears, however, that some of these activities are but straws in the wind. An economic recession, for instance, cuts deeply into many corporate social programs, throwing a large proportion of newly trained minority employees out of work. Further, there is a growing realization among businessmen that any type of social action involves costs. These costs need not always take the form of direct money outlays by the firm. Quite frequently they may consist of some short-term loss of profit in return for protecting long-term self-interests of the company. Thus many executives attribute improvements in their firms' recruiting and public relations activities to social action programs undertaken some years earlier.

A CRITICAL VIEW

Interestingly enough, not everyone agrees with the "social responsibility doctrine." Many critics claim that it is a euphemism for socialism, breeding conditions which will eventually undermine the basis of a free society. The best known modern exponent of this view is the noted economist and libertarian, Professor Milton Friedman of the University of Chicago. According to him, discussions which proclaim a "social consciousness" for business are ill-conceived and ill-defined, rooted more in emotion than in logic. The essence of his argument can be reduced to several fundamental propositions:

1. In a capitalistic system, a corporate executive is an employee of the owners (stockholders) of the business. His responsibility is to conduct the business in accordance with their wishes, which generally is to make as much money as possible without violating the laws or ethical customs of society.

2. A corporate executive, of course, is also an individual in his own right. As such, he may assume whatever social responsibilities he chooses—to his community, his church, his favorite charities, his country. However, any time or money he devotes to social causes, regardless of their worthiness, must be his own, not his employers'.

3. The corporate executive who fails to adhere to these rules and chooses instead to make his com-

pany more socially responsible by involving it, beyond the levels required by law, in such activities as pollution control and urban problems is spending money which rightfully belongs to others. Thus to the extent that his actions result in a reduction in corporate profits, he is spending stockholders' money; to the extent that his actions result in higher prices, he is spending consumers' money; and to the extent that his actions result in lower wages, he is spending employees' money.

4. The stockholders, customers, and employees could each spend their own money for social causes if they wished to do so. By exercising corporate social responsibility, the executive is acting in an unauthorized capacity for these groups. He is in effect taxing them and deciding how the tax proceeds are to be spent.

5. The executive, therefore, is usurping governmental functions pertaining to the imposition of taxes and the expenditure of tax proceeds. These are functions for which society has established elaborate legislative and judicial provisions to assure that taxes are imposed so far as possible in accordance with public preferences and desires. Indeed, "taxation without representation," was one of the contributing factors to the American Revolution.

Friedman concludes that:

In a capitalistic society, the acceptance by corporate executives of a social responsibility other than to make as much money for their stockholders as possible is fundamentally subversive of free enterprise. It involves the adoption of the socialist view that exhortations and policies of political leaders, rather than market forces of supply and demand, are better able to determine the allocation of society's scarce resources among alternative uses.

What do you think? Should self-appointed private individuals decide not only what the social interest is, but also how great a burden others should share in serving that interest? This problem will be with us for a long time to come. It has many social, political, and economic ramifications, thereby lending itself to interesting research investigations and provocative discussions.

The Need for Corporate Reform

Is the modern, large corporation an economic body in the classical market sense, or is it a social and political enterprise which can be properly managed only by giving the public a role in corporate decision making? This question is of fundamental importance, for corporate policies and decisions profoundly affect the general welfare of society, not merely the financial interests of stockholders. In view of this, we must examine the differences between the traditional and sociopolitical concepts of the corporation, in order to propose some steps for reforming its internal governance in the light of modern society's needs.

PRIVATE AND PUBLIC INSTITUTIONS

In the traditional view of capitalism, a distinct separation exists between the business and public sectors of the economy. The business sector is conceived of as consisting of numerous industries, each containing many small firms none of which possesses enough market power to influence the prices of commodities it sells or of resources it buys. The market rather than the state thus serves as the regulator of business behavior. Businessmen find that in order to survive in such a market—a market in which the consumer is king—they must respond to public wishes by producing to fulfill consumers' demands. Even if the market should sometimes fail by permitting the growth of monopolistic corporations, the solution need not consist of the state stepping in to regulate corporate power. Instead, government can restore competition by vigorously enforcing the nation's antitrust (antimonopoly) laws, breaking up large corporations into smaller ones and thereby reviving the market as a regulatory mechanism. In short, the traditional view holds that regulation of private enterprise by the state is not only unnecessary but unwise—except perhaps in some relatively extreme cases involving public utilities, strictly defined.

A more recent viewpoint concerning business-government relationships in modern capitalism differs sharply from the traditional one. It emphasizes the need for a "partnership" between large corporations and the public sector. According to its advocates—one of whom is Harvard's widely known economist, John Kenneth Galbraith—there comes a point in the development of a business firm when its size and market power no longer permit it to be considered "private." At that point the organization becomes both a political system and social enterprise—a "public institution." In the United States, firms that fall into this category include General Motors, Ford Motor Company, General Electric, International Business Machines, and several hundred other giant corporations whose annual sales, and in many cases assets, amount to billions of dollars. These organizations, it is held, possess sufficient market power to fix their prices, persuade—and sometimes bamboozle—their customers, control supplies and prices of many raw materials, and even influence government legislation. For such firms the traditional concept of a competitive market is a myth. Hence, according to Galbraith and other supporters of the "partnership" view, where there is a clash between corporate goals and the public interest —as in the areas of product safety, industrial effects on the environment, or the impact of price and wage settlements on the economy—the corporation has no natural right to be left alone.

To summarize:

According to Galbraith and some others, today's markets do not resemble the traditional competitive model. Instead, they are dominated by large firms which, because of their monopolistic power, misallocate economic resources and engage in practices that conflict with the public interest. Therefore, closer ties between big corporations and government are necessary if business is to meet society's needs.

SAVING CAPITALISM FROM ITSELF

Numerous industry leaders, not to mention social critics, concur in this belief. Fearing capitalism's death by its own hand, they view the doctrine of corporate social responsibility as an opportunity for the system to redeem itself. Accordingly, they implore executives to seek wider and more socially fulfilling goals for business. Failure to do so, they warn, will result in governmental controls, for the corporation cannot afford to disregard its impact on society, nor can the corporate manager measure his success solely in terms of profits maximized.

How can business get back into the "mainstream"? Evidently, corporate good intentions to deal with society's problems are not sufficient, because most executives do not know how best to allocate their firm's resources for both private and social purposes. Consequently, if they were to assume full responsibility for meeting society's needs, they might fail in both functions.

Nor does the answer lie entirely in government stepping in to protect society from the damage done by monopolistic market forces. Government's record

as a regulator of business practices and protector of special interests has not always been favorable, and in certain areas government intervention has even caused great social inequities—as you will see in later chapters. At present, it need only be mentioned that in some cases governmental regulatory policies have served to strengthen monopolistic power rather than weaken it; in others, government regulatory agencies have been influenced or even dominated by the organizations they were designed to regulate. This situation, of course, is not unique to our particular economic system. It is naive to believe that personal aggrandizement and political patronage exist only in capitalistic countries.

STEPS TOWARD CORPORATE REFORM

If corporate good intentions and government regulation are not enough to ensure business responsiveness to social needs, what other measures are desirable? Several may be suggested.

Revise Accounting Systems

Business should broaden its system of accounting to include not only the money outlay costs that are actually incurred in production, but the full social and economic costs as well. This would encourage resources to be allocated more in line with society's wishes. For example, if a firm discharges untreated wastes into the environment, the costs are borne by the community, not by the company responsible or by its customers. If these costs were included in the firm's accounting system, which they are not, they would be reflected in its prices. This would influence not only consumers' decisions to purchase the product but also the firm's method of producing it—and hence the manner in which it allocates its resources. Although considerable effort has been made by some firms to develop standards and techniques for measuring social performance, many corporate managements are still resisting the idea. As a result, unless legislation forces it, the day when social performance is integrated with financial performance may be a long way off.

Support Shareholder Participation

Most corporate managements tend to be self-perpetuating and to determine company goals as if they, rather than stockholders, owned the company. These practices are in serious need of revision. Managements should encourage shareholders to express at annual meetings their views on matters relating to social responsibility. In addition, legislation which reduces the opportunity for management to self-perpetuate itself would be desirable. One possibility suggested by some critics is that shareholder voting be revised to provide one man, one vote instead of one share, one vote. You will have an opportunity to evaluate the implications of this proposal in a question at the end of this chapter.

Institutionalize Self-criticism

Another improvement would be to establish mechanisms for independent self-criticism as part of institutional reform. This is to assure that critics of corporate policy are heard as a matter of right, rather than by management magnanimity. Some large corporations have moved in this direction by appointing representatives of minority groups to their boards, and others have created public policy review committees composed of independent directors. But further steps along these lines are needed if firms are to fulfill their obligations not only to stockholders, but to employees and the public as well.

Require Fuller Disclosure

Government regulations have long required corporations to furnish periodic accounting statements disclosing assets, liabilities, profits, and related information. One of the purposes of these reports is to provide financial protection for investors. These requirements should be broadened to include details pertaining to social questions as well. Full disclosure of a firm's practices in such areas as minority hiring, product safety, and pollution abatement can contribute as much to the protection of the public interest as can full disclosure of financial information to investors.

CONCLUSION: RESHAPE THE CORPORATION

A growing proportion of the public has come to realize that some corporate practices conflict with the welfare of society. To remedy the situation, many social critics and businessmen have contended that the twin goals of production and quality of life could best be met by some sort of business-government partnership. It is not clear, however, precisely what form this partnership might take. At one extreme it could involve virtual nationalization or government take-over of corporations; at the other, it could entail nothing more than cosmetic changes of a regulatory nature. Based on our own and on the experiences of other mixed economies (which are examined in later chapters), neither alternative is likely to provide an adequate solution. Therefore:

The most promising approach—and one which accords with our institutions and goals—is to make the corporate system work for society instead of against it. This can be done by reshaping the corporation around a system of social cost accounting and by adopting measures which give shareholders a greater degree of control over policies affecting the public interest. Adherence to this course would enable the free market, rather than a central authority, to serve as the vehicle for bringing about social and economic change.

SUMMARY OF IMPORTANT IDEAS

1. The business sector of the economy consists primarily of proprietorships, partnerships, and corporations. The number of proprietorships greatly exceeds the number of partnerships and corporations. However, corporations produce by far the largest proportion of the nation's goods and services. This is mainly because of their two principal advantages: (a) the possibility of accumulating large sums of money to finance expansion and (b) limited liability of stockholders.

2. There is a trend toward "big business" resulting primarily from firms merging with other firms and to a lesser extent from internal reinvestment of earnings. Firms seek to become large for various reasons. The chief one is perhaps to improve efficiency and financial strength through growth or expansion along different lines.

3. The consequences of bigness are mixed. On the one hand, it has created separation of ownership and control in the large corporation, and in many industries resulted in increased monopoly power for the largest firms. On the other hand, the largest firms have also been significantly responsible for some of the major advances in our standard of living and in our military preparedness.

4. Many corporate executives have accepted the doctrine of social responsibility—the notion that their firms should become involved in the solution of social problems. Those who oppose this view argue that the exercise of social responsibility by business results in corporate executives (a) acting

in an unauthorized capacity at the expense of their company's stockholders, employees, or consumers, (b) usurping the taxation and expenditure functions of government, and (c) substituting political exhortations and policies for the free market. The result, according to these critics, is the subversion of free enterprise and the encouragement of socialism.

5. It is in the interest of business to meet society's needs. Some critics contend that this should be done through a business-government partnership. But the concept is vague at best. An alternative view is to seek ways of revitalizing the corporation through the adoption of internal reform measures that permit self-critical evaluation. The latter approach preserves the framework of our existing institutions by enabling the free market to serve as a mechanism for advancing society's social as well as economic goals.

FOR DISCUSSION

1. *Terms and concepts to review:*

plant	stock
firm	bond
industry	dividend
proprietorship	limited liability
partnership	separation of owner-
corporation	ship and control

2. What are the two most important economic features of the corporate form of organization, as distinguished from the proprietorship or partnership form?

3. How and why do firms become big? Explain.

4. Is big business "good" or "bad"? Give some pros and cons of big business.

5. Some critics contend that the corporate search for "social responsibility" is more fundamentally a search for a stable standard of behavior resulting from the failure of the market to do its job. Can you explain what this means?

6. An eminent political scientist, Professor Robert A. Dahl of Yale University, has challenged the assumption that stockholders should control the direction of a company. "I can discover absolutely no moral or political basis," he says, "for such a special right. Why investors and not consumers, workers or, for that matter, the general public?" What implications does this statement have for the future of capitalism?

7. It has been suggested that one way to give shareholders more voice in the affairs of a corporation is to revise the voting procedure from one share, one vote to one man, one vote. Those who support this view point out that in political elections, people with unequal economic stakes in society nevertheless get one vote each; therefore, the same should be true in corporate elections. What do you think of this proposal? Explain.

Contemporary Issue

The Stock Market: Capital, Supermoney, and Random Walks

The stock market is different things to different people, and it performs many roles. To the investment banker it has the sacred economic function in the capitalistic system of allocating capital to businesses through its pricing and distribution systems. To the broker, the stock market is a place where the small and large owners of businesses can buy and sell shares of those businesses. To the individual investor, the pension fund, or the life insurance company, the stock market is the repository of individuals' and institutions' savings. To everyone it represents a continuing day-to-day valuation of the worth of the 3,000 or so of the largest businesses in the country and of the collective wealth of the nation.

All this is fine and high-faluting, but the stock market also surges up and down with apparently irrational violence. To many people it is more of a gambling casino than a true marketplace. Furthermore, at times the gyrations in prices seem totally mysterious as a stock's price declines horribly when an apparently favorable (to the untutored eye) earnings report is issued.

In its role as an allocator of capital, the stock market, by deciding (because of expectations of future earnings growth, for instance) that one company's stock will sell at forty times its annual earnings while another's will trade at only eight, is making it most attractive for the owners of the first business to raise additional equity capital, while the second company's owners are faced with severe dilution of their ownership, if indeed they can sell new stock at all. Assuming both companies are earning $2 per share, each of them has 5 million shares outstanding, and both need additional capital of $25 million, note the tremendous difference the stock market's judgement makes:

	Forty times earnings	Eight times earnings
Price per share	$80	$16
Shares to be sold by the company	312,500	1,562,500
Equity given up by present stockholders	6%	31%

Remembering the very simple but very basic fact that the shareholders are the owners of the company, the original shareholders of the first company will still own 94 percent of it after the $25 million has been raised, but the original shareholders of the second company retain only 69 percent ownership.

From Money to Supermoney

It also can be argued that the stock market provides the incentive, the pot of gold for the entrepreneur in our system. The stock market makes what has been called "supermoney." For example, suppose a man figures out how to organize and to run a new kind of chain of hamburger stores. He invests $10,000 and gets some friends to put up another $90,000. They agree he will get half the stock for his idea and for being the manager, and they will receive the other half of the stock for putting up most of the money. Incidentally, is that a fair deal? If not, why not? It's quite typical.

Anyway, the hamburger chain becomes another McDonald's and grows 40 percent a year for 15 years until it has profits of $5 million. At that point our entrepreneur and his friends decide their company needs more money to keep growing and they go to an investment banker. The investment banker studies what multiple of earnings other hamburger chains are selling at, thinks about the mood of the market, studies the company in detail as to its strengths and weaknesses, and finally decides

it's worth twenty times earnings (McDonald's shares may be selling at more or less) or, in other words, that the whole company is worth $100 million. Presto, our entrepreneur's 50 percent interest is worth $50 million. From $10,000 to $50 million. That's supermoney, and nowadays that's about the only way to get so rich in one lifetime.

However, there's another important aspect to the stock market—its role as the depository of the people's savings, as an investment media. Over the long term—like 30 years—the total return on common stocks (dividends plus appreciation) has been about 9 percent compounded annually. This is a superior return to that which can be obtained from most corporate bonds and far better than the return available from a savings account, life insurance, or a government bond. On the other hand, the stock market is a far riskier investment.

Over the short term, the stock market is volatile, emotional, and irrational. Its day-to-day and even month-to-month behavior is heavily influenced by crowd psychology and fads. When these are superimposed on the prospect of large monetary rewards for the winners (greed) and financial disaster for the losers (fear), the speculative, emotional atmosphere around the stock market can be appreciated. But remember that the term "speculate" comes from the Latin word that means to peer into the future, and the modern stock-market speculator quite literally is only trying to estimate which girl will win next week's beauty contest. Or, as a famous financier once put it, "a speculator is a man who observes the future and acts before it occurs."

Forecasting Stock Prices—Random Walks

Can stock-market prices be predicted? Security analysts like to think so. However, "random-walk" theory, which has been developed since the early 1960s, reflects the belief that future stock prices cannot be predicted.

An economist who has explored

these ideas is Princeton University professor, Burton Malkiel. In a fascinating book entitled *A Random Walk Down Wall Street* (Norton, 1973), Malkiel states that no scientific evidence exists to indicate that the investment performance of professionally managed portfolios as a group has been any better than that of randomly selected portfolios. Says Malkiel: "A random guess will enable you to predict the next market move with the same (or higher) degree of accuracy as the estimate provided through either technical or fundamental analysis. . . . Bluntly stated, the careful earnings estimates of security analysts (based on industry studies, plant visits, interviews with management, etc.) do little if any better than those that would be obtained by simple extrapolations of past trends, which . . . (as all random walkers know) are of no help at all."

Malkiel identifies himself as a random-walk theorist. He explains the theory in these words: "Random walk assumes that what is known about a stock is already reflected in the price. The next move cannot be predicted, because no one can predict what will come next to influence the price. Under these circumstances, public knowledge is just as effective as the use of charts and professional investment advice." Following the trends, therefore, is useless, according to Malkiel. If you toss a coin four times and guess correctly each time, it would show a nice uptrend on a chart. But in spite of four correct guesses, there is still a 50 percent chance that your next guess will be wrong.

Hold That Dart!

According to random-walk theory, if you blindfolded yourself and threw darts at the newspapers' financial pages, you could select a portfolio that would do just as well as one carefully selected by professional investment advisers. But before you begin throwing darts, consider the fact that the random-walk theorists don't necessarily advise throwing darts or throwing in the towel in trying to achieve above average investment performance. Professor Malkiel himself offers several rules for successful stock selection. And there are many, not persuaded by the random-walk theory, who hold that while the stock market may be irrational, emotional, and unpredictable in the short term, it is rational, and thus to some extent predictable, over the longer run. "Value will out" is the proverb. Unfortunately, it may take more time for the market to reflect the value of a stock than the impatient investor can tolerate.

Meanwhile, for those who like happy endings, a pretty reliable investment tactic is to buy the stocks of growing companies and never sell them. Presumably, the dividend paid on the shares will keep increasing with the rising earnings, and so, with good reason, stocks that grow rapidly and steadily are called "money trees."

For example, the magic of compounding is such that if you invested $100 in the stock of a company that was selling at ten times earnings and the company's profits grew 20 percent annually for ten years and, as a result, the stock sold at 30 times those profits, your $100 would then be worth $1,860. Furthermore, assume that the company paid out half of its earnings in dividends. By year ten, your annual dividend would be $31, or a return of 31 percent a year on your original investment. Money trees are nice.

One of the greatest stock-market men of all time was once asked what his philosophy of investing was. His reply: "Buy low, sell high." Only a very revered old man could have gotten away with such simplicity, but his answer about sums it up.

QUESTIONS

1. It is often said that the stock market is a forecaster of economic activity. Does the chart in Figure 1 confirm this belief? Discuss. (NOTE: The shaded bars marked "recession" denote periods of significant downturn in the economy.)

2. Draw a straight trend line through the graph in Figure 1 to represent the long-run "average" course of stock prices. What would be wrong with projecting this line into the future and using it as a means of forecasting stock prices?

3. Why do stock markets exist only in capitalistic countries, not in socialistic ones like Russia, China, Cuba, and eastern European nations?

Figure 1

STANDARD & POOR'S INDEX OF 500 COMMON STOCKS

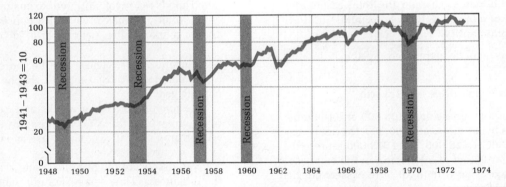

Supplement

The Financial Statements of Businesses: What They Tell You and How to Read Them

Business finance and accounting, like all other professions, have their own specialized vocabulary and ideas. After mastering a few technical terms and concepts, you will be in a good position to understand the two principal financial statements of businesses—the balance sheet and the income (or profit-and-loss) statement.

The Balance Sheet

A *balance sheet* represents the financial position of a firm on a particular day of the year. It shows what the firm owns (its assets), what it owes (its liabilities), and the residual or equity of the owners (net worth). Thus a balance sheet reveals three broad classes of items:

Assets. The resources or things of value that a business firm, household, individual, or other economic entity owns, such as cash, property, and the rights to property

Liabilities. The monetary debts that a business firm, household, individual, or other economic entity owes, as represented by the claims of creditors

Net worth. The difference between the total assets and the total liabilities of a business firm, household, individual, or other economic entity

These definitions can be expressed by the following equation:

$$\text{Assets} - \text{liabilities} = \text{net worth}$$

If the total assets of a business are $100,000 and the total liabilities or claims by creditors are $80,000, the net worth is $100,000 − $80,000 = $20,000. This $20,000 represents the owner's equity or extent of ownership in the business. The owner may have legal title to all of the assets but he owns only $20,000 of them.

The above equation may be transposed to the form in which it is more commonly written:

$$\text{Assets} = \text{liabilities} + \text{net worth}$$

This equation is a fundamental identity that underlies every balance sheet. It tells you that everything a business owns (its total assets) is precisely equal to or *balanced* by everything that it owes (its total liabilities and net worth). To illustrate this, look at the balance sheet of the XYZ Corporation in Exhibit 1. Note that the assets are recorded on the left, the liabilities and net worth on the right. Let us see how this statement is interpreted.

ASSETS

Current assets. These include cash and those other assets that will be turned into cash in the near future, usually within the coming year.

Cash is what you would expect—bills and silver on hand and money in the bank.

Marketable securities are stocks and bonds of other corporations, and government securities. The XYZ Corporation earns dividends and interest on these investments. However, they are only temporary investments, the intention being to sell them for cash if the need arises. Hence both their cost and market value are shown for information purposes, but only the lower of the two is customarily used in the calculation of assets.

Accounts receivable represents amounts due from XYZ's customers who purchased goods on credit. XYZ's experience has been that some of these customers will fail to pay their debts. Therefore the company deducts what it believes is a typical percentage of accounts receivable that will not be paid and calls this a provision for bad debts.

Inventories include raw materials to be used in production, goods that are in process of manufacture, and finished goods ready for shipment to customers. The accountant normally values inventories conservatively—at their cost or market value, whichever is lower.

Noncurrent assets. These are the more permanent assets of the business—those that will still be in use beyond the coming year.

Investments consist of stocks and bonds of other corporations which the XYZ Corporation intends to keep for a long time and, if necessary, use as collateral to borrow cash for current needs.

Fixed assets are the durable assets used to help carry on the business. They may include land, buildings, machinery, equipment, office furniture, automobiles, and trucks.

Depreciation is the decline in useful value of a fixed asset due to wear and tear. (A fixed asset may also decline in value due to obsolescence as new and better techniques are developed.) If a fixed asset is expected to last for more than a year, its cost should be spread over its anticipated useful life. The balance sheet will then record in each year that portion of the asset's original value which still remains.

Thus, suppose the company buys a machine for $1,000 which it expects to use for 5 years, after which time it will be discarded. One way to take depreciation is to assume the machine depreciates by an equal amount each year, in this case $200. At the end of the first year the balance sheet would show:

Exhibit 1

XYZ Corporation, Balance Sheet, December 31, 19--

Assets			Liabilities and Net Worth		
Assets			**Liabilities**		
Current assets			Current liabilities		
Cash		$ 475,000	Accounts payable	$ 500,000	
Marketable securities, at					
cost (market value:			Notes payable	425,000	
$800,000)		775,000	Accrued expenses payable	165,000	
Accounts receivable	$1,050,000		Federal and state taxes	270,000	
Less: provision for bad debts	50,000	1,000,000	Total current liabilities		$1,360,000
Inventories		750,000	Long-term liabilities		
Total current assets		$3,000,000	Bonds payable		1,350,000
			Total liabilities		$2,710,000
Noncurrent assets					
Investments (long-term)		150,000	**Net Worth**		
Fixed assets			Capital stock:		
Land	$ 75,000		Preferred stock	$ 200,000	
Buildings	1,900,000		Common stock	300,000	
Machinery	475,000				
Office equipment	50,000		Accumulated retained		
	$2,500,000		earnings	1,640,000	
Less: accumulated					
depreciation	900,000				
Total fixed assets		1,600,000	Total Net Worth		2,140,000
Prepayments and deferred charges		50,000			
Goodwill, patents, trademarks		50,000			
Total assets		$4,850,000	Total liabilities and Net Worth		$4,850,000

Machine (cost)	$1,000
Less: accumulated depreciation	200
Net depreciated value for balance sheet	$ 800

At the end of the second year the balance sheet would show:

Machine (cost)	$1,000
Less: accumulated depreciation	400
Net depreciated value for balance sheet	$ 600

Depreciation is thus a method of allocating the cost of a fixed asset by charging a portion of its cost to each year of its expected life. In Exhibit 1, the figure shown for accumulated depreciation represents buildings, machinery, and office furniture. Land is not subject to depreciation and is always shown on a balance sheet at its original cost.

Prepayments and deferred charges represent expenditures made in advance for items that will yield portions of their benefits in this and in future years. Examples include the advance premium paid on a 3-year fire insurance policy, expenses incurred in developing and marketing a new product, costs of moving to a new location, etc. The benefits from these expenditures will be received over a period, and hence their costs will be amortized (prorated) over that period instead of writing them off entirely in the year that they were incurred.

Goodwill, patents, trademarks are "intangible" assets: they exist and they have considerable value to the company that owns them, but no one really knows how much. (What value can you place on the reputation of a company? How much is the name "Coke" worth to Coca-Cola? The symbol ◁▬▷ to Chevrolet?) The value of these intangibles is decided almost arbitrarily by different companies. Many list them at the nominal value of $1. Other firms (e.g., General Motors) value them at millions of dollars.

LIABILITIES AND NET WORTH

These are, respectively, the claims of the creditors against the company and the equity of the owners. Creditors always have a prior claim over owners. Hence the net worth may also be regarded as a "residual" claim. What do you suppose this means?

Current liabilities. These include all debts due within the coming year. Generally speaking, the Current Assets classification is the counterpart to the Current Liabilities classification because current assets are the source from which current liabilities are paid.

Accounts payable are debts that the company owes to creditors from whom it has bought goods, supplies, or services, usually on a payment basis of 30 to 90 days.

Notes payable are promises to pay the holder, such as a bank, a sum of money at a certain time within a year at a stated rate of interest.

Accrued expenses payable are items like salaries and wages to employees, interest on borrowed funds, pensions, and similar obligations which accrue from day to day. The portions of these that are unpaid on the day the balance sheet is drawn up are included here.

Federal and state taxes include income taxes, social security taxes, and property taxes due to the federal, state, and local governments.

Long-term liabilities. These are obligations to creditors which will not be paid within one year, such as mortgages, long-term notes, and bonds.

Bonds payable are promises to pay the holder a sum of money at a certain time beyond one year at a stated rate of interest.

Net Worth. This is the difference between the total assets and the total liabilities. It represents the financial investment or equity of the owners.

Capital stock represents units of ownership in a corporation. Each owner of a share is called a stockholder. Capital stock thus represents the stockholders' proprietary interest in the company. Two typical classes of capital stock are preferred stock and common stock.

Preferred stock gets preference over common stock in the distribution of dividends, or in the distribution of assets if the company is liquidated, or both. If it is preferred as to dividends, the holders receive dividends at a certain rate or amount per share before dividends may be declared on the common stock. If it is preferred as to assets, the holders receive their capital contributions before the common stockholders in the event that the corporation is dissolved.

Common stock shares have no fixed rate of dividends. Hence they can receive better dividends than the fixed dividend rate that may exist on preferred stock if the corporation's earnings are high.

Accumulated retained earnings represent net profits earned since the company was organized, after deducting losses sustained and dividends paid to stockholders. In some balance sheets the terms "surplus" or "earned surplus" are used instead of accumulated retained earnings.

To conclude, here are two important points about the balance sheet:

1. The values of some of the assets shown on a balance sheet—especially the fixed assets—are *estimates;* they do not represent what the firm could actually get for them if they were sold. In fact most of the fixed assets would probably bring in much less than the values estimated for them. Their value to the company is a "going-concern" value, since the firm ordinarily expects to remain in business and use these assets, not sell them.

2. There is no *specific correspondence* between individual items on the two sides of a balance sheet. Therefore any attempt to link pairs of items will lead to confusion and error. Generally speaking, only the totals have meaning.

The Income Statement

Whereas a balance sheet reflects the financial position of a company as of a given date, an income (or profit-and-loss) statement shows the company's operating activities over a period, usually a year. A balance sheet is thus a financial "snapshot" of the company, whereas an income statement is somewhat like a financial "motion picture."

An *income statement* compares the revenues of a firm during a period with its costs during that period in order to arrive at a measure of profit for the period as a whole. An equation underlies every income statement, namely:

$$\text{Total profits} = \text{total revenue} - \text{total costs}$$

This equation is a fundamental identity of the income

statement. An illustration of such a statement for the XYZ Corporation appears in Exhibit 2. Can you find the items that comprise the terms in the above equation?

Note that this statement includes both income and expenses resulting directly from the operations of the business, as well as income and expenses from other sources. Can you tell which is which?

Relationships Between the Balance Sheet and the Income Statement

The two types of financial statements supplement and complement one another. For instance, income tends to increase net worth, while expenses and losses tend to decrease it. At the beginning of each period, the net profit from the income statement after dividends are paid to stockholders will be brought over to the balance sheet as part of "accumulated retained earnings." The net profit is also reflected in the increases or decreases of various assets and liabilities when compared to those at the beginning of the period. Thus the two statements should usually be examined and interpreted together, not separately.

Some Important Ratios

A fundamental economic question that is sometimes asked is, What is the earning power of a company, and how does its profitability compare with other firms in the same industry? The managers, stockholders, and creditors of an enterprise are obviously interested in this question because they are all involved in one way or another with its future success. Labor unions and government agencies are also concerned—the former when they seek wage increases for their members; the latter when they investigate a particular firm's degree of monopoly power in an industry.

There are four measures (or formulas) of profitability that are typically used to evaluate a firm's performance. Here is what they look like when the data are taken from the balance sheet and income statement of the XYZ Corporation.

1. *Operating profit ratio.* This is the ratio of the firm's operating profit to net sales, and it tells you the profit per dollar of sales—it indicates how well the company is performing on its selling operations.

$$\text{Operating profit ratio} = \frac{\text{operating profit}}{\text{net sales}}$$

$$= \frac{\$550,000}{\$3,250,000} = 0.169 = 16.9\%$$

2. *Net profit ratio.* This is the ratio of net profit after taxes to net sales, thus providing a more general performance picture of the year's activities.

$$\text{Net profit ratio} = \frac{\text{net profit after taxes}}{\text{net sales}}$$

$$= \frac{\$280,000}{\$3,250,000} = 0.087 = 8.7\%$$

3. *Return on total assets.* This is the ratio of net profits after taxes to total assets. It measures the rate of return on the total asset investment in the firm—that is, the productivity of the total assets.

$$\text{Return on total assets} = \frac{\text{net profit after taxes}}{\text{total assets}}$$

$$= \frac{\$280,000}{\$4,850,000} = 0.058 = 5.8\%$$

4. *Return on net worth.* This is the ratio of net profit after taxes to net worth. It measures the rate of return on stockholders' investment, thus telling you how well the owners' funds are being utilized.

$$\text{Return on net worth} = \frac{\text{net profit after taxes}}{\text{net worth}}$$

$$= \frac{\$280,000}{\$2,140,000} = 0.131 = 13.1\%$$

To be useful, these percentages must be compared with those of other firms in the same industry groups. Fortunately, such comparisons are readily available. One of the chief publishers of this information is Dun and Bradstreet whose periodic reports on the subject can be found in the business and economics section of many university and public libraries.

Exhibit 2

XYZ Corporation, Income Statement for the Year 19--

Net sales		$3,250,000
Cost of sales and operating expenses		
Cost of goods sold	$2,000,000	
Depreciation	450,000	
Selling and administrative expenses	250,000	2,700,000
Operating profit		$ 550,000
Other income		
Dividends and interest		50,000
Total income		$ 600,000
Less: interest paid out on bonds		50,000
Profit before provision for federal and state taxes		$ 550,000
Provision for federal and state taxes		270,000
Net profit after taxes		$ 280,000

SUMMARY OF IMPORTANT IDEAS

1. The balance sheet and the income statement are the two most important financial statements of businesses.

2. For purposes of financial evaluation and control, four convenient ratios are operating profit ratio, net profit ratio, return on total assets, return on net worth. The last two in particular are often used in labor-management wage negotiations, economic studies of monopoly power within an industry, pricing practices of business firms, and so on.

FOR DISCUSSION

1. *Terms and concepts to review:*

balance sheet	accounts receivable
assets	inventories
liabilities	fixed assets
net worth	depreciation
current assets	prepayments

goodwill	common stock
current liabilities	income statement
accounts payable	operating profit ratio
notes payable	net profit ratio
accrued expenses	return on total assets
capital stock	return on net worth
preferred stock	

2. Draw up a list of items that accountants would classify as assets. Do the same with liabilities.

3. How much would you pay for a business which yields a net profit of $20,000 a year after taxes? Assume that the business is secure, with little or no risk. (NOTE: Explain how you arrived at your answer.)

4. Calculate the operating profit ratio, the net profit ratio, the return on total assets, and the return on net worth of the ABC Corporation. Of what use are these ratios?

BALANCE SHEET, ABC CORPORATION, DECEMBER 31, 19--

Assets		Liabilities and Net Worth	
Cash	$ 50,000	Accounts payable	$ 39,000
Accounts receivable	60,000	Notes payable	50,000
Inventories	170,000	Other current liabilities	26,000
Total current assets	280,000	Total current liabilities	115,000
Net fixed assets	125,000	Long-term debt	50,000
		Net worth	240,000
Total assets	$405,000	Total liabilities and net worth	$405,000

INCOME STATEMENT, ABC CORPORATION, FOR YEAR ENDING DECEMBER 31, 19--

Net sales	$560,000
Cost of sales and operating expenses	415,000
Operating profit	145,000
Less: interest paid	5,000
Net profit before taxes	140,000
Less: taxes paid	85,000
Net profit	$ 55,000

CHAPTER 7

CHAPTER PREVIEW

What are the economic scope and functions of government? How do they influence our economy? Are there criteria for judging the appropriate size of government?

What is the nature and structure of the American tax system? What do we get for the taxes we pay?

Is the tax system fair? What guides can be used to judge the relative merits of a tax?

Government: Functions, Social Goods, and Taxation

One of the most remarkable trends in contemporary history has been the growing importance of government in economic life. In 1930, public-sector activity at all levels, as measured by government purchases of goods and services, was responsible for 10 percent of the nation's total output. By 1960 this figure had risen to 20 percent. Today it is close to 25 percent. These facts raise many problems concerning the economic functions of government in our mixed economy. This chapter examines a few of the more important ones and provides some basic concepts for understanding them.

Of course, any serious discussion of government is bound to raise questions of taxes. Yet taxes, as everyone knows, have also been the subject of many witticisms.

Benjamin Franklin is reputed to have said, "Only two things in life are certain—death and taxes—and I resent that they don't come in that order." But we shall see that things have changed somewhat since Franklin's time: Certain taxes today do indeed come in that order. Similarly, Lewis Carroll, author of *Alice's Adventures in Wonderland*, once remarked that the things he hated most were spiders, ghosts, gout, an umbrella for three—and the income tax. Today there are probably few who would disagree.

The list of adages and aphorisms could go on. But taxes, for those who recall their study of history, have also been the cause of wars and revolutions. Obviously anything that can have such widespread influences ought to be worth knowing something about.

When we speak of government, we ordinarily mean the federal government. But in this chapter we shall say some things about government at the state level and also at the local level, which includes counties, cities, villages, townships, school districts, and so on.

Economic Scope and Functions of Government

For centuries, political scholars have theorized about the purposes and functions of the state. Adam Smith asserted in *The Wealth of Nations* that government's role should be limited to national defense, the administration of justice, the facilitation of commerce, and the provision of certain public works. Many social scientists today would agree with Smith although some might add a few provisos of their own. For present purposes, the role of government can be discussed within a framework of four major areas: (1) promotion and regulation of the private sector, (2) provision of social goods, (3) redressing of spillover effects, and (4) trends in government expenditures.

PROMOTION AND REGULATION OF THE PRIVATE SECTOR

Government promotes and regulates the private sector in many ways—sometimes to the net advantage and sometimes to the net disadvantage of society as a whole. A complete listing of the public sector's economic activities is impossible, but six major areas can be identified.

1. Government *provides a stable environment* in which firms and households can engage in orderly exchange. It performs this basic function by defining property rights, upholding contracts, adjudicating disputes, setting standards for weights and measures, enforcing law and order, and maintaining a monetary system. These conditions are so fundamental to organized society that they have existed in even the most ancient civilizations. The Code of Hammurabi (circa 2100 B.C.), as well as the later laws of ancient Egypt and Rome, went into considerable detail in defining property rights and related matters pertaining to commerce.

2. Government *performs public welfare* activities. It establishes health and safety standards in industry, regulates minimum wages for certain classes of workers, and provides old-age, disability, sickness, and unemployment benefits for those who qualify.

Public welfare measures are enacted primarily for humanitarian reasons. Nevertheless, they may be a tacit admission that the private sector has failed to fulfill society's needs in an equitable and suitable manner.

3. Government *grants economic privileges* to specific groups. Through selective subsidies, tariffs, quotas, credit programs, price supports, legal provisions, and taxes, it favors particular consumers, industries, unions, and other segments of the economy. This elaborate network of privileges and controls results as much from political pressures as from economic logic. Hence to a large extent it causes higher prices, reduced efficiencies, and misallocations of society's resources.

4. Government is empowered *to maintain competition* within the economy. Specific laws forbid unregulated monopolies, and unfair trade and labor practices. If government enforces these laws vigorously, it ensures the perpetuation of a strong private sector.

5. Government seeks *to maintain high employment* through appropriate tax, expenditure, and monetary policies. At the same time it also seeks to encourage a steady rate of economic growth while curbing inflation and minimizing environmental decay. These activities are undertaken primarily by the federal government, but state and local governments also influence them through their own taxing, spending, and legislative policies.

6. Government *redistributes income and wealth* among firms and households through income taxes, inheritance taxes, property taxes, zoning ordinances, and other types of controls. Thus through taxation and regulation, all major levels of government reallocate within the private sector some of the income and wealth that is generated therein.

This brief sketch shows that the promotional and regulatory activities of government are complex and widespread. But do they achieve desired social and economic goals? This problem is explored at various points later in this book. In the meantime, other forms of government activity must be examined. (But first, see Box 1.)

PROVISION OF SOCIAL GOODS

All economic systems are concerned with the three fundamental questions of WHAT will be produced, HOW it will be produced, and WHO will receive the

Box 1

What Future for Free Enterprise?

Does the capitalistic system measure up to what its folklore suggests? Is America the land of free enterprise and the home of brave entrepreneurs? There was a time when many people would have answered both questions with a resounding yes, but today few would reply with such strong enthusiasm.

Throughout America's history, the government has served as a savior, subsidizer, owner, and regulator of special interests. It has financed roads and canals, subsidized firms and industries, sheltered workers, protected consumers and businesses, stabilized credit, refereed competition, and regulated markets. But although various groups in the private sector have frequently been partners with government in common-law marriages, historians a few decades hence will probably concur on at least two points: (1) the long process of government involvement was intensified during the last third of the present century and (2) conservatives, who are among the first to exalt the virtues of unfettered competition, are also the ones who often urge the government to step in.

Since the late 1960s, to an increasing degree, conservative business and political leaders have sought the protection of government in various ways. For example, they have strongly defended direct and indirect subsidies to airline, aerospace, news media, ship building, railroad, and other industries; they have welcomed increased governmental expenditures on irrigation and flood control, thereby raising the value of the land benefited; and they have staunchly opposed legislation which would limit or reduce farm subsidies in politically important congres-

sional districts. And, perhaps most significant, many of them enthusiastically embraced the imposition of price and wage controls by President Nixon in the early 1970s. This was the first time in the nation's history (outside of a military emergency) that any administration—much less a Republican one—made such a drastic incursion into the economy's private sector.

LOOKING FORWARD

Government influence in the private economy will increase. This does not mean that the nation will move toward socialism in the sense of government taking over basic industries—although some of that is a distinct possibility. It does mean that Washington will become further involved in setting economic goals and in defining the legal constraints within which business can operate. Within this framework, the solution of many national economic problems will still be left to the private market.

Numerous economists, businessmen, and union leaders agree that government standards and guidelines can greatly strengthen free enterprise. They concur that the real threat to a viable, competitive private sector does not come from rules set by government but from economic power concentrated in large corporations and large unions. One of the most challenging tasks confronting government, therefore, will be to find ways of reducing this power. Only in that way can free enterprise be preserved. And only then will the economy become more competitive and more responsive to the nation's needs.

---

final output. In mixed capitalistic economies such as ours, these questions are answered primarily by the market system. But certain types of commodities are not adequately provided by a free market. Their supply then becomes a function of government. We refer to such commodities as "social goods," of which there are several different types.

Public (Collective) Goods

Certain social products may be classified as public or collective goods. Examples are national defense, law and order, the administration of justice, air traffic control, and public safety. These products have three common characteristics:

1. *Inclusiveness.* The benefits of a public good are indivisible: they cannot be denied to anyone, re-

gardless of whether he pays for them or not. This is not the case with "nonpublic" goods—that is, a private good like food or clothing or certain social goods such as toll highways or national parks—since someone who does not pay can conceivably be excluded from their use. Hence, a nonpublic good is subject to what is technically known as the *exclusion principle*, whereas a public good is not. This method of distinguishing between a public and a nonpublic good is crucial. Can you formulate a definition of the principle in your own words? How does your definition compare with the one given in the Dictionary at the back of this book?

2. *Zero incremental or marginal costs.* There is no increase in the cost of a public good if it is provided to one more consumer. Hence we say that the additional or incremental cost—commonly called "mar-

ginal cost"—of the commodity is zero. Thus the cost of national defense, law and order, or any other commodity mentioned above does not increase with unitary gains in the population. However, this characteristic is also true of many private as well as other social goods. For example, there are no significant incremental or marginal costs to a movie theater or to a public library resulting from the admittance of one more patron.

3. *Spillover effects.* A public good creates *spillovers*—external benefits or costs resulting from activities for which no compensation is made. For example, air traffic control at busy airports reduces noise for some nearby residents while increasing it for others. This is an unpaid-for benefit to the former group and an uncompensated "cost" to the latter. Similarly, in the private sector of the economy a factory may provide income and employment benefits to a community while at the same time polluting its environment. Thus, spillover effects, like zero incremental costs, are not a unique property of public goods.

These characteristics provide the basis for a definition:

Public goods are those not subject to the exclusion principle—their benefits are indivisible and hence no one can be excluded from receiving them whether he pays or not. For this reason, public goods are commodities which the private sector is usually unable or unwilling to produce. (Radio and most television transmission are exceptions. Can you think of others?) Two further, but not unique, characteristics of public goods are (1) zero incremental or marginal costs and (2) spillover effects.

Other Social Goods

Public goods are not the only commodities supplied by government. Other social goods are also provided, each sharing in different degrees some of the properties of both public and private goods. Examples are highways, national parks, libraries, museums, elementary and secondary education, public housing, and public hospitals. These goods are subject to the exclusion principle—even though the principle may not always be invoked. Therefore they are not public goods; people could be charged for the use of these goods instead of receiving them "free" or at less than market value. This raises interesting problems about the effects of social goods on society's welfare—problems that will occupy much of our attention in this book.

REDRESSING SPILLOVER EFFECTS

Many economic activities create spillovers or "fallout" in the form of uncompensated benefits or costs; hence these effects are also frequently referred to as *externalities.*

Examples of externalities abound. Education, for instance, provides *social benefits* not only in the form of *private benefits* such as higher incomes and other satisfactions to its recipients, but also in the form of a more stable and enlightened citizenry. Likewise, the production of many commodities results in *social costs* which include not only *private costs* to the firms producing them, but also such costs as air and water pollution, land defilement, and other dissatisfactions. We shall have more to say about these matters in later chapters.

Some of the economic effects of spillovers can be analyzed in terms of a competitive free-market model as represented by the demand and supply curves of Exhibit 1. In Chart (a), any point on the normal market demand curve D expresses the *demand price*—the highest price that buyers are willing to pay for a given quantity of the commodity. The curve therefore reflects only private benefits to purchasers, not spillover benefits to nonpurchasers or to society. Similarly, any point on the normal supply curve S expresses the *supply price*—the least price necessary to bring forth a given output, or in other words, the lowest price that sellers are willing to accept in order to supply a given quantity of the commodity. The curve thus depicts only private costs to producers of the product while omitting spillover costs to everyone else. This suggests a fundamental shortcoming of the competitive free market:

The equilibrium quantity, determined by the intersection of the demand and supply curves, is 0Q. These curves reflect only direct private benefits and direct private costs while excluding spillover benefits and spillover costs. Therefore, to the extent that the omission of these spillover benefits and costs is significant, the equilibrium quantity will not be socially ideal—*the competitive free market will fail to provide an optimum allocation of society's resources.*

How can spillovers be incorporated in the model? In Chart (b), the inclusion of the commodity's spill-

Exhibit 1

Spillover Effects in a Competitive Market

Chart (a). No spillovers. In a competitive free market, the demand and supply curves reflect direct private benefits and direct private costs, not spillover benefits or spillover costs. To the extent that these social consequences or spillovers exist, the equilibrium quantity 0Q does not represent an optimum allocation of society's resources.

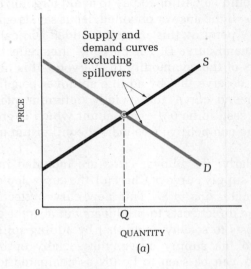

(a)

Chart (b). Spillover benefits. When spillover benefits of V per unit are added to the market demand curve, the new curve D' reflects this addition. The socially optimum output is 0M as compared to the free-market equilibrium quantity 0Q.

  Specific subsidy. In order to bring output to the socially optimum level, government can grant a specific subsidy to sellers equal to U per unit of output. This will reduce production costs and lower the supply curve to S', resulting in output 0M.

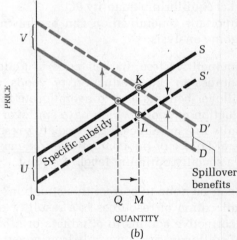

(b)

Chart (c). Spillover costs. When spillover costs are added to the market supply curve, the new curve S' reflects this addition. The socially optimum output is 0N as compared to the free-market equilibrium quantity 0Q.

  Specific tax. In order to bring output to the socially optimum level, government can impose a specific tax on sellers equal to T per unit of output. This will increase production costs and raise the supply curve to S', resulting in output 0N.

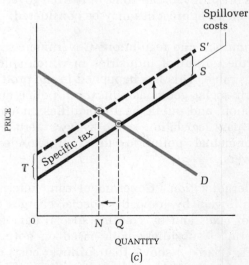

(c)

over benefits is depicted by the curve D'. This curve might be derived by asking people how much the spillover benefits are worth to them—how much they would be willing to pay to avoid forgoing those benefits. If the answer obtained, let us say, is equivalent to V per unit, this amount is added vertically to the demand curve D. The curve D' thus reflects the benefits of the commodity to everyone. It is important to observe that by adding spillover benefits to the demand curve, the socially optimum quantity can be seen to be OM—an amount which is greater than the competitive free-market equilibrium quantity OQ.

Similarly, if spillover costs are included in the market supply curve of Chart (c), the curve depicting these inclusions is S'. This new curve reflects not only the direct costs to producers but also the spillover costs to society. Note that by adding spillover costs to the supply curve, the socially optimum quantity can be seen to be ON as compared to the free-market equilibrium quantity OQ.

An important generalization can be drawn from the foregoing analysis:

The competitive free market tends to underallocate resources to the production of goods which have spillover benefits and to overallocate them to the production of goods which have spillover costs. This results in a misallocation of society's resources —a general failure of the competitive free market to provide a socially optimum level of output.

What can be done to correct this situation? Since the misallocation of resources is a result of market failure, corrective actions to eliminate or offset the effects of spillovers can come only from government. Three major approaches may be considered:

1. *Promotion and regulation.* Government can promote the output of industries in which spillovers are desirable. This has happened in the production of such social goods as education, police and fire protection, and public health facilities. In addition, it can pass legislation—such as laws pertaining to environmental pollution—to control undesirable spillovers.

2. *Internalization.* Government can "internalize" the spillovers by imposing special charges in the form of taxes and by granting special payments in the form of subsidies—both based on output. Exhibit 1, Chart (c) shows that spillover costs can be corrected by requiring sellers to pay a *specific tax*—a per unit tax on the commodity—equal to T per unit. This will increase their production costs by shifting the entire supply curve upward to S'. The resulting output will then be ON—which was seen to be the socially optimal output when spillover costs were added to the supply curve.

By similar reasoning, Chart (b) suggests that the socially optimal output can be achieved by granting a specific subsidy to sellers. A *subsidy* is a payment (usually by government) to businesses or households that enables them to produce or consume a product in larger quantities or at lower prices than they would otherwise. Hence a *specific subsidy* is a per unit subsidy on a commodity. In this case, a specific subsidy to sellers equal to U per unit of output will reduce their production costs and shift the entire supply curve downward to S' where it intersects the original demand curve D at L. The resulting equilibrium quantity will then be the socially optimal output OM.

REMARK. It may be noted that spillover benefits and costs can also be redressed by subsidizing and taxing buyers rather than sellers. In a problem at the end of this chapter, you will have an opportunity to demonstrate this idea graphically in terms of supply and demand curves. In the meantime, on the basis of the foregoing analysis, can you suggest how to go about it?

3. *Mitigation.* Government can seek to mitigate or reduce spillover costs resulting in environmental damage by undertaking clean-up campaigns, beautification programs, reclamation projects, and the like. Government has long engaged in these activities, and although such programs do not eliminate the causes of spillovers, they do serve to decrease many of their adverse effects.

TRENDS IN GOVERNMENT EXPENDITURES

In the past few decades the public sector has been characterized by a remarkable growth of expenditures at all levels of government—federal, state, and local. The historical record is shown in Exhibit 2. What are the chief reasons for these steep increases in government spending?

1. *War and national defense.* Most of the increase in federal spending can be attributed to expenditures on wars, national defense, and defense-related activities including international military assistance, space research and technology, veterans' services, and interest on the federal debt resulting mainly from the financing of our most recent major wars. Taken together these items constitute well over half

—and in some years more than two-thirds—of all federal expenditures.

2. *Increased demand for social goods and services.* The American people have come to expect federal, state, and local governments to provide more in the way of social goods and services. As a result, the public sector has increased its expenditures in numerous areas. These include education, public assistance and welfare, transportation, housing, sanitation, water supply, public safety, and consumer protection.

3. *Inflation and lagging productivity.* The costs of social benefits provided by government have been increasing for at least two reasons. First, inflation (i.e., rising prices) has been a long-run trend in our economy. This has made it necessary for government to pay more for the goods and services it provides. Second, most of the civilian benefits provided by government consist of services such as education, public safety, and health. Productivity in these fields has not risen as fast as in the private economy, whereas public employees' wages have risen at roughly the same pace as wages in the private sector. Hence, government finds that the salaries it pays out are growing faster than the volume or efficiency of the services it performs.

Government revenues for the most part have increased concurrently with government expenditures over the years. In Exhibit 3 on the next page, Chart (a) shows the federal government's budget. As the chart suggests, the government's total revenues and expenditures for any given year are rarely equal. When they are, the budget is said to be *balanced*. On the other hand, when total revenues exceed total expenditures in any given year, the budget is said to have a *surplus*; when total revenues are less than total expenditures, the budget has a *deficit*.

Budgeting: Where Does the Money Come From? Where Does It Go?

The budget of the United States, like the budget of a family, is a study in hopes, daydreams, and hard facts. A *budget* is an itemized estimate of expected revenues and expenditures for a given period in the future. The federal budget covers a fiscal year beginning July 1 and ending the following June 30.

THE FEDERAL BUDGET

Like every budget, the one for the federal government, illustrated in Exhibit 3(b), consists of two parts—one showing where the money comes from, the other showing where it goes.

On the receipts side *income taxes*, both individual and corporate, make up the largest source of revenue. The base of these taxes is net income, which is the difference between gross income for a given year and certain specific items that are subtracted from it. The great bulk of personal income tax revenues comes from people in the middle- and lower-income groups. *Employment taxes* (social insurance taxes

Exhibit 2

Growth of Government Expenditure

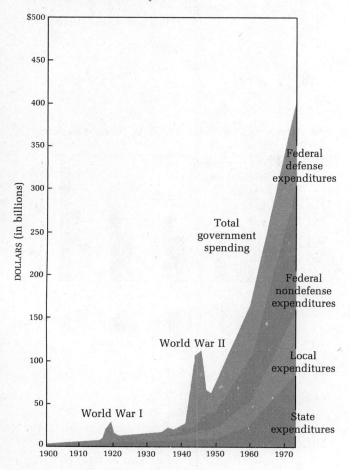

SOURCE: U.S. Department of Commerce.

Exhibit 3

Federal, State, and Local Budgets*

(a) FEDERAL BUDGET RECEIPTS AND OUTLAYS: 1960 to 1972

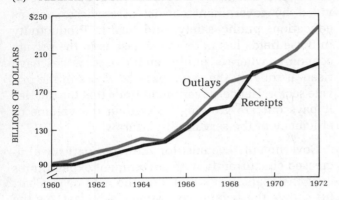

(b) ANNUAL FEDERAL BUDGET: AVERAGE, 1971–1973

WHERE IT COMES FROM . . .

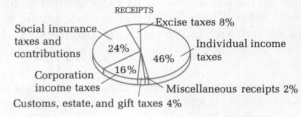

RECEIPTS

Social insurance taxes and contributions 24%

Excise taxes 8%

Individual income taxes 46%

Corporation income taxes 16%

Miscellaneous receipts 2%

Customs, estate, and gift taxes 4%

WHERE IT GOES . . .

OUTLAYS
(Expenditures and net lending)

Other 1%
Interest 9%
National defense 39%
Agriculture 3%
Education 4%
Commerce and transportation 5%
Space programs 2%
International affairs 2%
Income security 24%
Health 7%
Veterans 4%

(c) STATE AND LOCAL GOVERNMENT BUDGETS: AVERAGE, 1971–1973

WHERE IT COMES FROM . . .

RECEIPTS

Utilities and liquor stores 6%
Insurance trusts 7%
Property taxes 22%
Federal government 15%
Charges and miscellaneous 15%
Sales and gross receipts taxes 20%
Other taxes 15%

WHERE IT GOES . . .

OUTLAYS

Insurance trusts 5%
Utilities and liquor stores 6%
Education 35%
Other general expenditures 27%
Public welfare, hospitals, and health 16%
Highways 11%

(d) PER CAPITA TAX REVENUE, BY LEVEL OF GOVERNMENT

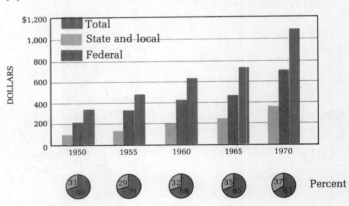

Total
State and local
Federal

1950 1955 1960 1965 1970

31 / 69   29 / 71   32 / 68   35 / 65   37 / 63   Percent

* For fiscal years ending June 30.
SOURCE: U.S. Department of Commerce.

and contributions), which are the next major source of revenue, are compulsory social security payments made by employers and employees as part of the nation's social security program. *Excise taxes*, which are levies imposed on the sales of goods like tobacco and alcohol products, and other income consisting of customs duties and interest on trust fund investments provide most of the remaining revenue.

On the expenditure side the chief categories are national defense and transfer payments (not labeled in the chart). *National defense* and defense-related activities include expenditures for the U.S. armed forces and those of America's allies, atomic energy programs, and the like. Most of the other expenditures can be classified as transfer payments. These were discussed in an earlier chapter; you can refresh your memory by looking up the term in the Dictionary at the back of the book. Examples are veterans' benefits, social security payments, unemployment compensation, and certain government subsidies. Transfer payments redistribute income from one group to another and thus tend to modify the composition of goods and services produced by the private sector in favor of the recipients of the payments.

STATE AND LOCAL BUDGETS

Exhibit 3(c) shows where the numerous state and local governments get their money and how they spend it.

Property taxes, the principal source of income, consist mainly of taxes on real property such as land and buildings. In some states they also include taxes on personal property like furniture, clothing, and jewelry, and on "intangibles" such as savings accounts and securities. *Sales taxes*, the second major source of revenue, consist of retail sales taxes, gross receipts taxes, processing taxes, and other similar taxes. They have been gaining in relative importance over the years as state and local governments seek new ways to meet their mounting expenses.

The remaining major sources of revenue include highway-user taxes such as vehicle license fees and gasoline taxes; income taxes on individuals and corporations; income from employee retirement and unemployment compensation trust funds; payments from the federal government to help meet the expenses of public welfare, education, highways, and social insurance; and income from the operation of

gas, electricity, and water utilities, and from liquor stores.

Education—mainly schools—is the largest single item on the expenditure side. The remaining expenditures are self-explanatory. Some of the specific items under the category of "Other general expenditures" include payments made for police and fire protection, the development and maintenance of natural resources and recreation facilities, and the administration of legislative and judicial functions.

Exhibit 3(d) shows the tax revenues received by the federal government and by state and local governments. Can you interpret this chart? Does there seem to be a trend? If so, what does it suggest?

INTERGOVERNMENTAL GRANTS-IN-AID

Certain types of financial aids that are becoming increasingly important are so-called intergovernmental *grants-in-aid*. They consist of (1) revenues received by local governments from their states and from the federal government and (2) revenues received by state governments from the federal government.

These revenues are used primarily to pay for public welfare assistance, highways, and education. They tend to reduce the effects of—but by no means eliminate—the great differences in income that exist between rich states and poor states, high-income regions and low-income regions. Thus, if you live in a wealthy state like California or New York, some of your federal income tax payments will go to poorer states like Alabama and Mississippi. If you live in a well-to-do suburb, some of your state income taxes will help to build schools and pave roads in rural areas and in the large cities. A portion of corporation income taxes is also used for these purposes.

In this way the federal and state governments serve as transfer agents, shifting some tax revenues from high-income areas to low-income areas according to social needs. This practice will become increasingly significant as states and localities find themselves faced with the growing financial strains imposed by an expanding population.

The American Tax System

A *tax* is a compulsory payment to government. The objectives of a tax may be to (1) reallocate resources so as to produce more of some commodities and less of others, (2) alter the distribution of income and wealth from that produced by the private sector, or (3) stabilize the economy by reducing fluctuations in economic activity. Taxes can be levied and classified in many ways. In the United States there are three main types of taxes:

1. Taxes on income
   (a) Personal income taxes
   (b) Corporation income taxes

2. Taxes on wealth (including its ownership and transfer)
   (a) Property taxes
   (b) Death (estate and inheritance) and gift taxes

3. Taxes on activities (consumption, production, employment, etc.)
   (a) Sales and excise taxes
   (b) Social security taxes

Dozens of other less important kinds of taxes exist, but nearly all can be placed in one of these three main categories.

TAXES ON INCOME

Income taxes are based on net income—what remains after certain items are subtracted from gross income. The items that can be subtracted and the tax rates that are applied are specified by law and differ between (1) the personal income tax and (2) the corporation income tax.

Personal Income Tax

In the spring a young man's fancy turns to thoughts of love. But for millions of American taxpayers, spring is the season when their thoughts turn to much more mundane and certainly less romantic activities as they begin to sort their previous year's income and expense records. As you can see from Exhibit 4, this is the first step that must be completed in order to determine the personal income tax.

In calculating this tax you would be allowed to make specific types of deductions and exemptions. For instance, some deductions that may be made (within limits) from your income are donations to the Red Cross, to your alma mater, and to various other nonprofit organizations; payments for doctors' bills, X-rays, and medicines; sales and other taxes paid to state and local governments; interest paid on loans; and various other outlays. In addition, tax

allowances or exemptions are permitted for support of yourself, your family, and your dependents. In this way the government acknowledges the fact that larger families require more funds than smaller ones to meet their living costs.

The amount of income tax you would have to pay at a given income level depends on several things. They include whether you are single or married and what the particular tax rates happen to be at the time. These rates usually change every few years. A hypothetical but fairly realistic tax rate schedule is illustrated in Exhibit 5.

Column (1) shows the different income levels, and column (2) tells you the amount of tax to be paid at each of these income levels. Note that the tax starts with $0 at the low income end and rises to $680,000 for an income of $1 million.

Exhibit 4

Logical Structure of the Federal Personal Income Tax

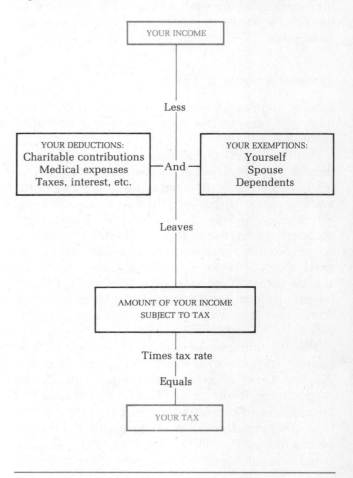

Exhibit 5

Personal Income Tax Schedule
(hypothetical data)

(1)	(2)	(3)	(4)	(5)	(6)
Total taxable income	Total personal income tax	Average tax rate* (percent) (2) ÷ (1)	Change in column (1)	Change in column (2)	Marginal tax rate† (percent) (5) ÷ (4)
Less than:					
$ 1,000	$ 0	0			
			$ 1,000	$ 100	10
2,000	100	5			
			1,000	110	11
3,000	210	7			
			1,000	130	13
4,000	340	8.5			
			1,000	160	16
5,000	500	10			
			5,000	1,000	20
10,000	1,500	15			
			10,000	3,500	35
20,000	5,000	25			
			30,000	15,000	50
50,000	20,000	40			
			50,000	30,000	60
100,000	50,000	50			
			100,000	70,000	70
200,000	120,000	60			
			200,000	140,000	70
400,000	260,000	65			
			600,000	420,000	70
1,000,000	680,000	68			

$$\text{* Average tax rate} = \frac{\text{total personal income tax}}{\text{total taxable income}}.$$

$$\text{† Marginal tax rate} = \frac{\text{change in total personal income tax}}{\text{change in total taxable income}}.$$

Column (3) reveals the percentage of tax at each income level. Since these percentages increase as income rises, the tax rate is said to be "graduated" or *progressive*: it takes a larger share of higher incomes than of lower ones.

Columns (4) and (5) are shown in order to calculate column (6). What does column (6) tell you? It reveals the *extra* tax rate on additional dollars of income earned. This rate starts at 10 percent for incomes over $1,000 and increases—at first slowly and then steeply—until it levels off at 70 percent for incomes over $100,000. The distinction between the *average tax rate* in column (3) and the *marginal tax rate* in column (6) is shown by the formulas beneath the table.

In comparing columns (3) and (6), note that the marginal tax rate is always higher than the average tax rate in going from one income level to the next. Observe also that you can never find yourself worse off by making an extra dollar. According to the marginal tax rate schedule, if your total taxable income were $1 million, you would still be able to keep 30 cents of every additional dollar you earned.

Two controversial aspects of the personal income tax should be noted.

1. Through legal methods of *tax avoidance*, taxpayers in the higher-income brackets often pay average rates of only 40 to 50 percent. This is because our tax system contains certain legal "loopholes" which permit relative tax advantages for the rich. Some millionaires pay no federal income taxes at all. (In contrast, illegal methods of escaping taxes, such as lying or cheating about income or expenses, come under the general heading of *tax evasion*.) Most economists agree that if the legal loopholes were closed the government could raise the same amount of revenue at significantly lower tax rates for everyone. As it is, the great bulk of tax revenues comes from the lower- and middle-income groups.

2. The steepness of the marginal tax rate schedule may have serious economic consequences. It must be high enough at all income levels to yield the desired amounts of revenues. However, rates that are too high at the upper-income levels may discourage investment and risk taking, whereas rates that are too high at the lower levels may reduce the incentive for taking on overtime work or second jobs. Is there a "best" or optimum schedule for the economy as a whole? There probably is, but it changes with different needs and conditions, reflecting political as well as economic circumstances. Some of the historical rates for the United States are shown in Exhibit 6 on the next page.

Corporation Income Tax

The federal government's second largest source of revenue is the corporate income tax. (Many states also tax corporate incomes, but at lower rates.) The corporation income tax is simple to calculate since it is based on the difference between a company's total income and its total expenses—its net profit.

Exhibit 6

Taxation of One Additional Dollar of Income As
Related to Net Income of an Individual

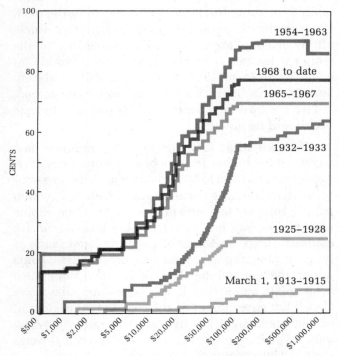

NET INCOME BRACKETS (logarithmic scale)

Exhibit 7

United States Corporate Income Tax Rates

*The rates shown are the standard rates on taxable cor-
porate income over $25,000 imposed by the federal gov-
ernment. Note that the tax rates are often changed by
Congress every few years. Since the late 1960s, the rate
has been 22 percent on the first $25,000 of taxable income,
plus 48 percent on income over the $25,000 level. No ac-
count is taken in this chart of excess profits taxes which
have been imposed at various times. The tax rate includes
a 10 percent surtax imposed in 1968 and removed in 1970.*

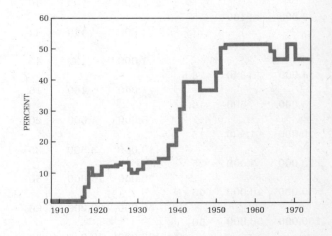

The tax rate has varied over the years, as illustrated
in Exhibit 7. Since 1950 it has averaged close to 50
percent.

The corporation income tax raises two major
issues:

1. Some experts argue that lower rates would leave
corporations with more profits to use for expanding
their operations, thereby creating more jobs. Other
authorities, however, contend that the rates should
be higher so that the government could then reduce
other taxes, especially personal income taxes.

2. The claim is widely made that the tax is actually
an unfair form of *double taxation*: the corporation
pays a tax on its profits, and the stockholder pays a
personal income tax on the dividends he receives
from those profits.

Neither argument is completely right nor wrong.
Each has valid aspects, and these are discussed in
subsequent chapters.

The remaining two categories which make up the
structure of the American tax system—taxes on
wealth and taxes on activities—can be sketched
briefly.

TAXES ON WEALTH

Property taxes, which are levied primarily on land
and buildings, vary from low rates in some rural
areas where services are minor to high rates in
localities with good streets, schools, and public
safety facilities.

Death taxes are levied on estates and inheritances,
depending on values and amounts. They are imposed by the federal government and by individual
states. Like income taxes, they exempt small estates
and inheritances but tax the unexempt portions at
progressive rates. Since many wealthy people would
try to avoid these taxes by distributing most of their
property before death, *gift taxes* are imposed on the
transfer of assets beyond certain values. However,

various legal devices such as trust funds and family foundations still enable many wealthy individuals to lighten the weight of these taxes.

TAXES ON ACTIVITIES

Sales taxes are flat percentage levies on the retail prices of items. In some states or cities certain commodities like food, medicine, and services are exempt, and in other places they are not. The federal government imposes no "general" sales tax on the final sale of goods, but it does impose special sales taxes called *excise taxes* on the manufacture, sale, or consumption of liquor, gasoline, and certain other products. (See, however, Box 2.)

Social security taxes are payroll taxes which finance our compulsory social insurance program covering old-age and unemployment benefits. The contributions come from both employees and employers and are based on the incomes of the former.

Box 2
The Value-added Tax
or
How to Pluck the Goose

> The art of taxation consists in so plucking the goose as to obtain the largest possible amount of feathers while provoking the smallest possible amount of hissing.
> Jean Baptiste Colbert (1619–1683)

Colbert, Louis XIV's famous finance minister, understood human nature—at least when it came to taxation. Most people dislike a sales tax, but they are not likely to complain very much if it is not too painful. This is one reason why many legislators and economists have long been advocating a value-added tax.

A value-added tax, VAT, is a type of national sales tax, paid by manufacturers and merchants on the value contributed to a product at each stage of its production and distribution. When a farmer, for example, sells his wheat for more than he paid for the seed, he pays a tax on the value he added. When a miller processes the wheat into flour, he pays a tax on the value he added. When a baker converts the flour into bread, and a grocer marks up the price of the bread to cover his own costs and profit, they each pay a tax on the value they added.

VAT is thus a special kind of sales tax. But unlike the sales tax, it is paid all through the manufacturing process, not as a separate tax at the point of final sale. Although VAT does not yet exist in the United States, there are strong political and economic pressures for its adoption. It is widely used throughout Europe, where the rates between countries vary widely, and in some nations it serves as a substitute for income or other taxes. Since the nature of VAT is controversial, it has staunch supporters as well as critics.

Proponents of VAT offer many arguments in its favor. Among them:

1. Broad base. It provides a large source of revenue even at a low rate because it encompasses the broadest conceivable tax base—the economy's total output of goods and services.

2. Nondiscriminatory. It is neutral in its application because unlike, for example, property taxes, payroll taxes, and corporate income taxes, it does not discriminate against specific resources in production or against specific forms of business organization.

3. Encourages efficiency and exports. It does not punish success, since less profitable firms pay almost as much tax as the more profitable ones, in contrast to the corporate income tax. Also, to the extent that the tax is imposed on imports and rebated on exports, it improves America's trade position relative to other countries.

4. Simple and flexible. It is relatively easy to administer if the tax rate is uniform, and the rate can be readily adjusted to meet changing fiscal needs.

These arguments are strong and persuasive. Nevertheless, those who oppose VAT give three major reasons:

1. Inflationary. It tends to be passed along at each stage of production, thereby raising prices and encouraging inflation.

2. Incidence. It is ultimately borne primarily by consumers in the form of higher prices for the goods they buy.

3. Regressiveness. It imposes a heavier burden on the poor than on the rich, because the former consume a larger percentage of their incomes than do the latter.

The effects of these criticisms—especially the last—can be mitigated by exempting necessities such as food, clothing, medicine, and shelter, by granting special deductions on personal income taxes, and in other ways. The tax can thus be designed to fit whatever specific objectives are desired. For these reasons, it is likely that the value-added tax, if adopted in the United States, will play a major role in the American tax system.

These taxes are actually a "reverse" form of income tax, since they exempt incomes above a certain level but not below it. This assures every income earner of being covered.

Some Theories of Taxation—Some Issues of Fairness

In his *Wealth of Nations*, Adam Smith advised governments to follow four guiding rules of taxation:

1. *Equality*. Each individual should pay taxes in proportion to his income—that is, he should pay the same percentage of his income as taxes.

2. *Certainty*. Every taxpayer should know precisely what his taxes are and when they should be paid.

3. *Convenience*. Taxes should be levied in a manner that is of greatest convenience to the taxpayer.

4. *Economy*. The cost of collecting a tax should be small in proportion to its yield.

Modern economists have revised and extended these rules to encompass three broad criteria for judging the relative merits of a tax:

☐ *Equity*. Tax burdens should be distributed justly among the people.

☐ *Efficiency*. A tax should not only be certain, convenient, and economical (as advised by Smith); it should also contribute toward improving resource allocation, income distribution, or economic stabilization.

☐ *Enforceability*. A tax should be adequate for its purpose and acceptable to the public, or else it will be impossible to enforce.

These criteria are simple and persuasive, but implementation—especially of the first—has caused a good deal of economic controversy. Let us see why.

TWO PRINCIPLES OF TAX EQUITY

A good tax system should be fair. If people generally believe it is unfair—that too many loopholes benefit some individuals and not others—taxpayers' morale and the effectiveness of the tax system itself will deteriorate. Hence, two fundamental principles have evolved over the years.

Benefit Principle

The so-called *benefit principle* holds that people should be taxed according to the benefits they receive. For example, the tax you pay on gasoline reflects the benefit you receive from driving on public roads. The more you drive, the more gasoline you use and the more taxes you pay. These tax revenues are typically earmarked (set aside) for financing highway construction and maintenance. Similarly, local governments pay for at least part of the construction of streets and sewers by assessing those residents who benefit directly from the services of these goods.

What is wrong with the benefit principle as a general guide for taxation? There are two major difficulties:

1. Relatively few publicly provided goods and services exist for which all benefits can be readily determined—and for many goods and services they would be impossible to determine. The entire nation benefits from public education, health and sanitation facilities, police and fire protection, and national defense. How can we decide which groups should pay the taxes for these things and which should not?

2. Those who receive certain benefits may not be able to pay for them. For instance, it would be impossible to finance public welfare assistance or unemployment compensation by taxing the recipients.

Ability-to-pay Principle

About 2,400 years ago, in his classic work *The Republic*, the philosopher Plato remarked: "When there is an income tax, the just man will pay more and the unjust less on the same amount of income."

Plato was speaking of an ideal world—a utopia in which all men strive to do what will be best for society. Unfortunately, with human nature as it is, most people are not inclined to pay any more taxes than the law requires of them.

However, the *ability-to-pay principle* is actually a modern and realistic restatement of Plato's ancient dictum, for it states that the fairest tax a government can impose is one that is based on the financial ability of the taxpayer—regardless of any benefit he may derive from the tax. This means that the more wealth a man has or the higher his income, the greater his taxes should be—on the assumption that each dollar of taxes paid by a rich man "hurts" less than each dollar paid by a poor man. The personal income tax in the United States is based on this principle.

There are two major difficulties in the use of this principle as a general guide for taxation:

1. Ability to pay is a debatable concept—difficult to determine and impossible to measure. How can we really know that an additional thousand dollars a year in income always means less to a rich man than to a poor man? If nothing else, a rich man who has all the material things he desires may derive as much or even more of an increase in satisfaction from earning an extra thousand dollars than a poor man gains from spending it. Hence, although we ordinarily *assume* that certain taxes should be based on ability to pay, the entire concept involves deep psychological and philosophical issues that economics is not equipped to explore.

2. Even if we could really be clear about what we mean by ability to pay, how could we distinguish between *degrees* of ability among different individuals? As with the benefit principle, the hardest problem is to develop a way of measuring the right concepts.

SOME PRACTICAL COMPROMISES

As a result of these philosophical difficulties, it has become necessary to adopt convenient methods of implementing the benefit and ability principles— even though the methods may not always be ideal. Accordingly, three major classes of tax rates have evolved over the years: proportional, progressive, and regressive. They differ from each other according to the way in which the amount of the tax is related to the *tax base*, that is, the item being taxed, such as the value of a taxpayer's property (in the case of a property tax), income (in the case of an income tax), or the value of goods sold (in the case of a sales tax). The resulting figure, expressed as a percentage, is called the *tax rate*. For example, a $10 tax on a tax base of $100 represents a tax rate of 10 percent. It follows that the tax base times the tax rate equals the tax yield to the government.

Proportional Tax

This is a tax whose percentage rate remains *constant* as the tax base increases. Hence the amount of the tax paid is proportional to the tax base. The property tax is an example. If the tax rate is constant at 5 percent,

a man who owns property valued at $10,000 pays $500 in taxes; a man who owns property valued at $100,000 pays $5,000 in taxes. Similarly, an income tax would be a proportional tax if it were applied at the same percentage rate to all people regardless of their level of income.

Progressive Tax

This type of tax is one whose percentage rate *increases* as the tax base increases. In the United States, the federal personal income tax is the best example. The tax is graduated so that theoretically a man with a higher income pays a greater percentage in tax than a man with a lower income. We say "theoretically" because in reality, large loopholes in the tax structure distort and sometimes even prevent the progressive principle from operating over the full range of income—especially for those in the high-income brackets.

Regressive Tax

This is a tax whose percentage rate *decreases* as the tax base increases. In this strict technical sense there is no regressive tax in the United States. However, if we compare the rate structure of the tax with the taxpayer's net income rather than with its actual base, the term "regressive" applies to any tax which takes a larger share of income from the low-income taxpayer than from the high-income taxpayer. Most proportional taxes, such as consumption taxes of various kinds, are thus seen to have regressive effects. For instance, a 4 percent sales tax is the same rate for everyone, rich and poor alike. But people with smaller incomes spend a larger percentage of their incomes and hence the sales taxes they pay are a greater proportion of their incomes.

In the narrow *technical* sense, definitions of proportional, progressive, and regressive taxes are expressed in terms of their actual tax bases such as income, property, or value of goods sold. But in the broad *equity* sense, the base chosen for reference is always income—regardless of the actual tax base. *In general, the equity interpretation is the one commonly employed by economists, legislators, and the public at large in evaluating the structure of a tax.*

How do the foregoing principles and compromises apply to the American tax system? Generally speaking, some of our taxes tend to lean more toward the

Exhibit 8

Proportional, Progressive, and Regressive Tax-rate Structures in Equity Terms

The structure of a tax is usually evaluated in equity terms by comparing the tax rate to the taxpayer's income—regardless of the actual tax base to which the tax is applied.

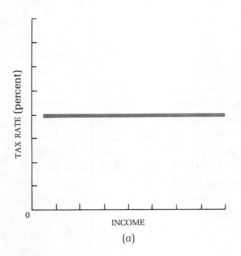

(a)

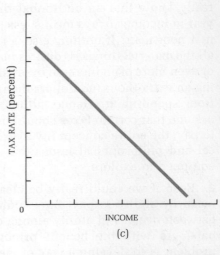

(b)

(c)

(a) **Proportional tax.** *The tax takes the same percentage of income from high-income taxpayers as from low-income taxpayers.*

(b) **Progressive tax.** *The tax takes a larger percentage of income from high-income taxpayers than from low-income taxpayers.*

(c) **Regressive tax.** *The tax takes a smaller percentage of income from high-income taxpayers than from low-income taxpayers.*

---

benefit principle and others toward ability to pay. Social security, license, and gasoline taxes are some typical examples of the former, whereas income and death (estate and inheritance) taxes are illustrative of the latter.

We can also find examples of progressive, regressive, and proportional taxes. Income and death taxes are progressive in both the technical and equity sense because their percentage rates increase with the tax base. Property taxes, general sales taxes, and excise taxes are proportional in their technical structure since their rates are a constant percentage of the tax base; however, they tend to have regressive effects from an equity standpoint when related to the *incomes* of the taxpayers. (See also Box 3.)

TAX SHIFTING AND INCIDENCE: DIRECT OR INDIRECT TAXES?

Surprisingly enough the person or business firm upon whom a tax is initially imposed does not al-ways bear its burden. For instance, a company may be able to *shift* all or part of a tax "forward" to its customers by charging them higher prices for its goods, or "backward" to the owners of its factors of production by paying them less for their materials and services. When a tax has been shifted, its burden or *incidence* is on someone else. It thus proves convenient to classify taxes into two categories: direct and indirect.

1. *Direct taxes.* These taxes are not shifted; their burden is borne by the persons or firms originally taxed. Typical examples are personal income taxes, social security taxes paid by employees, most property taxes (excluding rental and business property), and death taxes. Certain taxes, notably those on corporate income, are probably only partially direct. Can you suggest why?

2. *Indirect Taxes.* These include all taxes that can be shifted either partially or entirely to someone other than the individual or firm originally taxed.

Examples are sales taxes, excise taxes, taxes on business and rental property, social security taxes paid by employers, and most corporation income taxes.

In what direction will a tax be shifted—assuming it is shifted at all? This is a thorny problem in economic theory, and the experts do not always agree. In general, most taxes are like an increased cost to the taxpayer, and hence he will try to pass them on to someone else. As a result, once a tax is imposed, it tends—like lightning or water—to follow the path of "least resistance" through the markets in which the taxpayer deals, altering his prices, inputs, or outputs according to the least degree of opposition encountered. We shall examine this process more closely in a later chapter. Meanwhile, an interesting development which affects all of us is discussed in Exhibit 9 on the following page.

Box 3

Is Our "Progressive" Income Tax Regressive?

The personal income tax is presumably based on "ability to pay." This means it is supposed to allow for each individual's special circumstances and to tax the rich more heavily than the poor. There is widespread agreement, however, that the tax falls far short of this goal. Although on paper the rates are graduated, the tax laws contain so many loopholes and special provisions that the rates are hardly more than elaborate window dressing.

Many economists are strongly critical of the personal income tax, but none of them is more censorious than the University of Chicago's Professor Milton Friedman. This renowned economist points out that the tax would come closer to achieving its professed objectives if, simultaneously, it: (1) substituted a flat rate above personal exemptions for the present graduated rates; (2) eliminated present loopholes; and (3) disallowed all deductions except those related to occupational expenses strictly interpreted.

In Friedman's view, a revision of the personal income tax along these lines would yield several major benefits. It would permit the present exemptions—which are disgracefully low—to be greatly increased without the government's losing any revenue. It would provide a more equitable, vastly simpler, and much more efficient tax system. And it would eliminate the untold man-hours spent by accountants and lawyers advising their clients how to avoid taxes under the present law.

Even if it accomplished none of these things, however, it would at least release most people from the drudgery of unpaid bookkeeping they must now engage in to satisfy the Internal Revenue Service. That alone would make it a welcome blessing.

SUMMARY OF IMPORTANT IDEAS

1. The economic scope and functions of government may be viewed within a framework of four major areas: (a) promotion and regulation of the private sector; (b) provision of social goods; (c) efficiency in government activity; and (d) trends in government expenditures.

2. Government promotes and regulates the private sector in many ways. Among them, it (a) provides a stable environment, (b) performs social welfare activities, (c) grants economic privileges, (d) seeks to maintain competition, (e) promotes high employment, and (f) redistributes income.

3. Government provides social goods consisting of (a) public goods such as national defense, law and order, and fire protection, and (b) nonpublic goods such as libraries, museums, highways, and many other commodities. A unique feature of public goods is that they are not subject to the exclusion principle; other social goods are subject to this principle, even though it is not always invoked. All public goods as well as many other social goods have two further characteristics: zero incremental or marginal costs, and spillover effects.

4. Many economic actions create spillovers or externalities. To the extent that spillovers are significant, a free market fails to provide an optimum allocation of society's resources, and government action is needed to achieve the desired allocation.

5. The last several decades have witnessed a remarkable growth of expenditures at all levels of government. This has been due primarily to (a) war and national defense, (b) increased demand for collective goods and services, (c) inflation and lagging productivity. Government revenues have also increased with government expenditures at roughly the same rate over a period of years, but not usually within any one year.

6. In the federal budget, the chief sources of revenue are personal and corporate income taxes, and employment and excise taxes. The main expenditure items are national defense and transfer payments (such as veterans' benefits and social security).

7. In state and local budgets, the chief sources of revenue are property taxes and sales taxes, whereas

Exhibit 9

The Trend Toward Indirect Taxes

The United States, unlike most other countries, has long relied on direct taxes (namely, taxes on income and wealth) as distinct from indirect taxes (such as sales taxes) for the bulk of its revenue. But this trend may be coming to an end—for three major reasons:

1. The percentage contribution of corporate income taxes to federal revenues has been declining since the 1950s because liberalization of tax legislation has substantially reduced taxable corporate profits. On the other hand, employment taxes (including social security and unemployment insurance levies) are flat-rate, regressive taxes which, since 1967, have far outperformed the corporate income tax as a source of federal revenue.

2. The individual income tax, long extolled for its progressiveness, is now seen to be much less progressive than was once believed. The availability of legal loopholes for high-income taxpayers makes the effective average tax in the higher brackets about 40 percent. As a result, public confidence in the fairness of the individual income tax has been declining. Indeed, the tax would long ago have been subject to more vigorous attack if the withholding system did not conceal the full impact of the tax on wage earners, and if taxpayers' lobbies, unlike industry's, were better organized in Washington.

3. Indirect taxes, generally criticized because they fall hardest on people with low incomes who spend most of their incomes, need not continue to bear this stigma of regressiveness. Some studies show, for instance, that a sales tax which exempts food and medicine turns out to be approximately proportional—taking nearly the same share from all income groups. The tax can even be made progressive by graduating the rate—charging one rate on purchases under, say, $100 and a higher rate on more expensive items—and by providing rebates and deductions which vary inversely with taxpayers' income levels.

WHAT FUTURE?

Economists point out that one of the important functions of taxes is to help stabilize the economy. A major advantage of the individual income tax is its automatic stabilizing effect: in recession, federal revenues contract and the tax is not as much of a drag on the economy; in prosperity, they expand.

Even critics of the income tax agree that indirect taxes fall short of the stabilization ideal. Nevertheless, for the reasons given above, indirect taxes may well replace direct taxes as the dominant source of federal revenues. If that happens, the income tax will play a smaller role in redistributing income from rich to poor. However, since indirect taxes (such as a value-added tax) will yield larger revenues, they can provide the funds to finance more social programs for the poor, thus taking on the redistributive function previously performed by the income tax.

the main expenditure items are education (especially schools), public welfare and health, and highways. Intergovernmental grants-in-aid to state and local governments are becoming increasingly important.

8. The American tax structure consists of taxes on income, taxes on wealth, and taxes on activities. Taxes on income, both personal and corporate, are graduated or progressive.

9. A chief requirement of a good tax system is that it be fair. The benefit principle and the ability-to-pay principle are the two major criteria for judging the fairness of a tax. These principles are often difficult to determine and measure. Hence they are usually implemented in practice by the use of proportional, progressive, and regressive taxes.

10. Those upon whom a tax is levied may sometimes be able to shift it forward or backward through changes in prices, inputs, or outputs so that its burden or incidence is on someone else. Such taxes are therefore indirect, as contrasted with direct taxes, which cannot be shifted.

FOR DISCUSSION

1. *Terms and concepts to review:*

exclusion principle	private cost
spillovers	social cost
public goods	demand price
externalities	supply price
private benefit	subsidy
social benefit	specific subsidy

specific tax
budget
balanced budget
budget surplus
budget deficit
grants-in-aid
tax
income tax
average tax rate
marginal tax
  rate
tax avoidance
tax evasion
corporate income tax
double taxation
surtax
property tax

death tax
gift tax
sales tax
excise tax
value-added tax
social security tax
benefit principle
ability-to-pay principle
tax base
tax rate
proportional tax
progressive tax
regressive tax
tax shifting
tax incidence
direct tax
indirect tax

2. Since public goods are not subject to the exclusion principle, how do you explain the fact that some public goods are nevertheless provided by the private sector? Give some examples.

3. What are some of the economic effects on employment and prices of granting a specific subsidy to sellers as opposed to levying a specific tax on them?

4. "Spillover benefits and costs in a competitive market can be redressed by subsidizing and taxing *buyers* rather than sellers." Demonstrate this proposition graphically in terms of supply and demand curves.

5. (*a*) Suppose that the *additional* or *incremental* social cost of a unit of output is $50,000 and the *additional* or *incremental* social benefit is $80,000. Assuming you want *net* social benefit—the difference between social benefit and social cost—to be as large as possible, would you recommend that the unit be produced? Explain. (*b*) What if the above figures for additional social cost and social benefit were reversed?

6. Net social benefit represents the difference between social benefit and social cost. Can you use the concept of net social benefit to determine the optimum size of a government program in terms of *incremental* social benefit and *incremental* social cost?

7. How can the costs of benefits provided by government be reduced?

8. Some economists and legislators contend that the present federal income tax reaches too far down into low-income brackets. Assuming that you disagree with this contention, what arguments can you offer to defend your position?

9. If you were considering taking on an extra part-time job, would you base the decision on your average tax rate or on your marginal tax rate? Why?

10. The ability-to-pay principle of taxation may also be called the "equal-sacrifice principle." Can you explain why?

11. How can a market-oriented economy such as ours justify the large expenditures made by government on free public education?

12. Is the desire to maximize net social benefit a goal useful only to capitalistic economies, or does it apply to socialistic economies too?

13. If you were advising a legislator on whether the government should spend an additional $2 billion on space exploration as opposed to public transportation, what approach would you use? What difficulties would you expect to encounter?

14. When the private costs of a decision are equal to its social costs, *all* of the costs are borne by the decison maker. Do you agree? Explain.

15. What is wrong with using figures showing expenditures by government as a measure of the importance of government in our society?

The Tax Collector's Lottery

Organized crime in the United States has a powerful new rival for gambling revenues in several states. It is the state lottery, which raises money for state governments by draining off some of the cash that might otherwise have gone to the numbers game and other forms of legal and illegal betting. The innovation has respectable antecedents: most European and Latin American countries have for generations raised money by running lotteries of one kind or another.

At first glance the lottery is a good idea. It keeps taxes down by diverting to government some additional (gambling) money, and offers big prizes to the lucky—who are then taxed on their winnings. But even though state lotteries seem to be here to stay, their desirability is seriously challenged by some politicians and economists. One of the most thoughtful commentators is Ronald D. Watson, of the Federal Reserve Bank of Philadelphia. In a study of lotteries Watson asks—and answers—some hard questions.

Who Pays?

The first question is who really pays? Watson points out that an important objective of taxation policy is the redistribution of income from rich to poor. The chief instrument of taxation is the so-called progressive income tax, which theoretically burdens the rich relatively more than the poor. But, of course, the income tax is also a revenue-raising device, just as the lottery is. Is the lottery progressive or regressive in nature? That is, does it redistribute income from rich to poor? Many critics argue that it does not, because a disproportionate number of tickets are sold to poor people. Watson contends that the evidence fails to support that argument: surveys in both New York and New Jersey show that the typical ticket-buyer is middle class and middle income. Conclusion: "The poor certainly contribute to the state's lottery revenues, but probably not to the extent that they benefit as a group from state government income-redistribution programs."

Many people believe that government should not encourage gambling for moral or economic reasons because it diverts personal income from savings or from spending on goods and services. As Watson puts it: "Something has to give." But what gives may be spending on alcohol or drugs as well as more desirable things, such as food, clothing, furniture, books, and records. Watson's conclusion: "There is simply no information currently available to suggest which substitutes are most likely to occur in the absence of lottery purchases."

Those who contend that the states should not run lotteries because they thereby encourage gambling are in that tradition which assumes that a small group of determined people have the right to decide what a far larger group should or should not do. In America that tradition ushered in Prohibition—and with it unparalled opportunities for organized crime to provide and eventually monopolize the sale of alcohol. Quite clearly Prohibition was a failure, because it ran counter to most citizens' desires. Bans on gambling have had a similarly dismal result, enriching gangsters and encouraging the corruption of police and law officers. Recognizing this empirical and common-sense view of the limits of governmental ability to regulate behavior, Watson says: "The final factor to consider is the welfare of the consumer, before and after legalization of a lottery. To offer him the choice of buying or not buying lottery tickets may be more important to his welfare than whether the proceeds of the sales are subsequently used to promote egalitarian social goals. This is as true for the poor as for any other group of purchasers." Further, even if the poor purchase more than their fair share of lottery tickets, these purchases would be evidence that lottery tickets are preferred to other goods and services on which these people are equally free to spend their money. Thus, the gambler is better off (in his own estimation) as a result of making this purchase than he would otherwise have been.

Public or Private Lotteries?

If we grant that it is better for gambling to be legal and controlled rather than illegal and hence uncontrolled, who should actually operate the lottery: the state or private enterprise? Much confusion results from viewing the lottery as a kind of tax. Certainly, it costs far more to raise a dollar of revenue through the lottery than it does through taxation. Watson cites figures showing that for each 50-cent ticket sold in New Jersey about 24 cents is paid in prizes, $2\frac{1}{2}$ cents is paid as a commission to the seller, $4\frac{1}{2}$ cents goes to meet other expenses, and about 19 cents reaches the state treasury. No form of taxation costs as much to collect—the equivalent of 7 cents for each 19 cents of net revenue.

But, of course, the lottery is not purely a revenue-raising operation. It is also a service to consumers, and if the number of tickets they buy is any guide, it is a service they want. As a result, Watson observes, "It would be unfair to compare the costs of collecting lottery money with the cost of collecting an income or sales tax." Further, there is no evidence to show whether private enterprise could run lotteries more efficiently than states could. The closest analogy to a privately run lottery is in England, where millions of people "do the pools" each week—that is, forecast which football teams will win. Competition among the operators of football pools has forced them to offer larger and larger prizes over the years; none of the pools enjoys a net profit as a percentage of revenues as high as the "profit" made by New York and New Jersey on their lotteries. Fragmentary though that evidence is, it does suggest that if the states licenced a number of firms to run lotteries and received a fixed proportion of the revenues, the result would be a smaller take for the treasuries. The alternative would be, of course, for each state to franchise or licence only one lottery firm; but, in effect, that would be a mere transfer of monopoly from state to company.

Taxation without Pain

On balance it seems that the state lottery is a fairly efficient and painless way of raising revenues that would otherwise be raised through taxation. Because it is an alternative or complement to the illegal numbers game, the lottery does not violate the basic American principle that government should avoid competition with legitimate private enterprise. Indeed, the lottery appears to be a first step along a desirable road leading to recognition of the fact that people will gamble regardless of what the law says. That being so, the states might well consider opening or licensing casinos where people can gamble legally with the guarantee that the game is honest.

QUESTIONS

1. A secondary objective of some state lotteries has been to compete with organized crime for the profits of illegal gambling. Should states follow a similar policy with respect to other illegal but profitable activities, such as prostitution and narcotics?

2. The lottery has been subject to several major criticisms: (a) it is a poor bet because the odds against winning are inordinately high; (b) it has not been successful in competing against illegal gambling; (c) it may be tantamount to a regressive tax on the poor, although the evidence is not clear. In view of these shortcomings, should the lottery be retained?

PART 2

National Income,
Employment, and
Fiscal Policy

CHAPTER 8

National Income and Product: How Do We Measure the Economy's Performance?

CHAPTER PREVIEW

What are the basic measures of a nation's economic performance? What do these measures tell us? What do they fail to tell us?

How are the basic measures related to one another? What has been the nature of their historical pattern?

Americans like to take their own pulse, tirelessly searching for signs of normality, abnormality, and other statistical measurements of health—or illness.

Economic diagnoses and prognoses are as much a part of the daily news as football and baseball scores, and arouse similarly partisan feelings. That is unfortunate. The economic system is highly complicated, and more a subject for cool, rational analysis than hot, emotional debate.

The tools for analyzing the economy's performance, strengths, and weaknesses are the tables, charts, and data published by the federal government and some other public and private agencies. Since the early 1930s the U.S. Department of Commerce has been the nation's bookkeeper; its methods, terms, and concepts are the foundation on which economists have built what they call "national-income accounting."

Gross National Product—The Basic Measure of a Nation's Output

The most comprehensive measure of a nation's economic activity, and the one quoted most frequently in newspapers and magazines, is *gross national product* (GNP). It is always stated in money terms, representing the total value of a nation's annual final output. More precisely:

GNP is the total market value of all final goods and services produced by an economy during a year.

The items that comprise GNP range from apples and automobiles to zinc and zippers. However, since you cannot add these different things, you must first express these diverse items in terms of their monetary values. Then, when you add X dollars' worth of automobiles to Y dollars' worth of oranges to Z dollars' worth of doctors' services, and so on, you arrive at a total dollar figure. If you do this for all final goods and services produced in the economy during any given year, the result is GNP. And if you repeat this process for several years, the different GNPs can be compared to tell whether there has been a long-run growth or decline.

However, there are several pitfalls to avoid.

Watch Out for Price Changes

If the prices of goods and services change from one year to the next, the GNP may also change—even if there has been no change in physical output. For instance, if apples cost 10 cents each this year, five apples will have a market value of 50 cents. But next year if the price rises to 15 cents each, five apples will have a market value of 75 cents.

How can we tell whether the variations in GNP are due to differences in prices or to differences in *real* output—that is, output unaffected by price changes?

The answer is shown in Exhibit 1, where GNP is expressed in two ways: (*a*) in *current dollars*, reflecting actual prices as they existed each year; (*b*) in *constant dollars*, reflecting the actual prices of a previous year, or the average of actual prices in a previous period.

The use of constant dollars is thus a way of compensating for the distorting effects of inflation—the long-run upward trend of prices—by a reversing process of *deflation*. You can get an idea of how this is done by studying Exhibit 2.

Avoid Double Counting of Intermediate Goods

Note that the definition of GNP covers only *final* goods and services purchased for last use—as distinguished from *intermediate* goods and services which enter into production of final commodities. For example, if you purchase a new automobile this year, it is a final good; but the materials of which it is made, such as steel, engine, tires, and paint, are intermediate goods. Since the values of final goods include the values of all intermediate goods, only final goods are included in calculating GNP. If you allow intermediate goods to enter the picture you will commit the cardinal sin of *double counting*—or even triple and quadruple counting.

Exhibit 1

Gross National Product
(in current and in constant dollars)

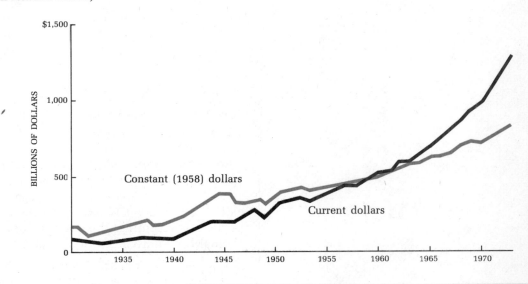

Exhibit 2

Deflating with a Price Index

HOW A VALUE SERIES IN *current dollars* IS CONVERTED
INTO A VALUE SERIES IN *constant dollars* OF ANOTHER
YEAR.

Index numbers—*percentages of a previous base period*
—are widely used by government and private sources in
reporting business and economic data. Column (4) expresses the prices of column (3) in the form of index numbers. Ordinarily, the base period chosen is assumed to be
fairly "normal." In this illustration, since the data are
hypothetical, Year 2 has been arbitrarily selected as the
base.

When the value series in current dollars [column (5)] is
divided by these index numbers, the result is a new value
series in constant dollars of the base year as shown in
column (6). The two value series are plotted for comparison in the accompanying chart.

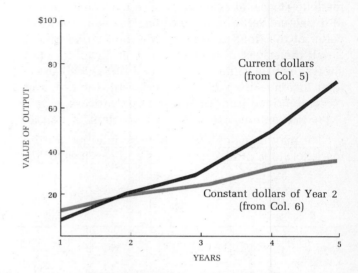

(1)	(2)	(3)	(4)	(5)	(6)
Year	Units of output	Price per unit of output	Price index; data in col. (3) as percent of price in Year 2	Value of output in *current dollars* of each year (2) × (3)	Value of output in *constant dollars* of Year 2 (5) ÷ (4)
1	3	$2	2/4 = 0.50 or 50%	$ 6	6/0.50 = $12
2 = base period	5	4	4/4 = 1.00 or 100%	20	20/1.00 = 20
3	6	5	5/4 = 1.25 or 125%	30	30/1.25 = 24
4	8	6	6/4 = 1.50 or 150%	48	48/1.50 = 32
5	9	8	8/4 = 2.00 or 200%	72	72/2.00 = 36

*Is deflation important? This chart shows percentage
changes in GNP from one year to the next—with and without a correction for inflation. (When you finish reading
this chapter, you will know how to update this chart.)*

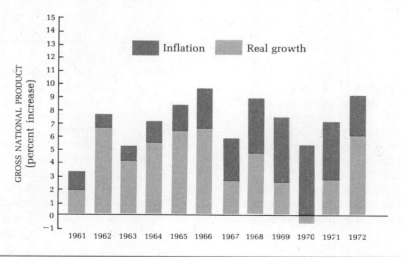

Exhibit 3 shows why, in terms of producing a loaf of bread. As you can see in column (2), the "total sales values" of 72 cents includes all the intermediate stages, and hence is an incorrect statement of the actual value of the product. However, the sales value of the final product or the total *value added* for all the stages of production, given in column (3), shows the true value of the total output as well as the total income—the sum of wages, rent, interest, and profit—derived from the production process.

We can summarize with an important principle:

GNP may be calculated either by totaling: (*a*) the market values of all final goods and services, or (*b*) the values added at all stages of production, which is equal to the sum of all incomes—wages, rent, interest, and profit—generated from production.

Include Productive Activities; Exclude Nonproductive Ones

The purpose of deriving GNP is to develop a measure of the economy's total output, based on the market values of final goods and services produced. However, even if all these market values are estimated, some *productive* activities still do not show up in the market but should nevertheless be included in GNP. In addition, there are *nonproductive*

Exhibit 3

Sales Values and Value Added at Each Stage of Producing a Loaf of Bread

(1) Stages of production	(2) Sales values (cents per loaf)	(3) Value added (income payments: wages, rent, interest, profit) (cents per loaf)
Stage 1: Fertilizer, seed, etc.	$.01	$.01
Stage 2: Wheat growing	.07	.06
Stage 3: Flour milling	.12	.05
Stage 4: Bread baking, final	.22	.10
Stage 5: Bread retailer, value	.30	.08
Total sales values	$.72	
Total value added (= total income)		$.30

Stage 1: A farmer purchases 1 cent worth of seed and fertilizer which he applies to his land.

Stage 2: The farmer grows wheat, harvests it, and sells it to a miller for 7 cents. The farmer has thereby added 6 cents worth of value. His factors of production receive this 6 cents in the form of income: wages, rent, interest, and profit.

Stage 3: The miller, after purchasing the wheat for 7 cents, adds 5 cents worth of value by milling it into flour. The miller's factors of production receive this 5 cents as income: wages, rent, interest, and profit.

Stage 4: The baking company buys the flour from the miller for 12 cents, then adds 10 cents worth of value to it by baking it into bread. This 10 cents becomes factor incomes in the form of wages, rent, interest, and profit.

Stage 5: The retailer buys the bread from the baker for 22 cents and sells it to you, the final user, for 30 cents. The retailer has thus added 8 cents in value, which shows up as factor incomes in the form of wages, rent, interest, and profit.

Note that the value of the final product, 30 cents, equals the sum of the values added.

activities which do appear in the market but should be excluded from GNP.

Here are some examples of productive nonmarket activities:

1. *Rent of owner-occupied homes.* The rent which people pay to landlords enters into GNP. However, more than half the dwellings in the United States are owner-occupied. Therefore the rental value of this housing—the rent which people "save" by living in their own homes—may be thought of as the value of shelter produced. This value is assumed to be the same amount that homeowners would receive if they became landlords and rented out their homes to others. Hence this amount is included in GNP.

2. *Farm consumption of home-grown food.* The value of food which people buy is included in GNP. But the value of food that farmers grow and consume themselves also is a part of the nation's productive output and is therefore included in GNP.

Some productive nonmarket activities never enter into GNP because their values are either too difficult to estimate, or involve complex definitional issues. These include such things as the labor time of a do-it-yourselfer who performs his own repairs and maintenance around the house, and the productive services of a housewife in her capacity as a cook, housekeeper, and governess for which she does not receive a salary. No wonder a famous British economist once remarked that a man who marries his housekeeper reduces the nation's output and income. Can you see why? (See Box 1.)

Here are some examples of nonproductive market activities:

1. *Transfer payments.* As you recall, these are shifts in funds within or between sectors of the economy with no corresponding contribution to current production. Hence they are excluded from GNP. Some examples of transfer payments are social security benefits, unemployment insurance, and welfare payments.

2. *Securities transactions.* When you buy or sell stocks or bonds, you exchange one form of asset for another—either money for securities or securities for money. These financial transfers add nothing to current production, and therefore are excluded from GNP. (However, broker commissions on security transactions are included in GNP, since brokers perform a productive service by bringing buyers and sellers together.)

3. *Used-goods sales.* Billions of dollars are paid each year for used automobiles, houses, machines, factory buildings, and so on. But these goods are omitted from the calculation of current GNP because they were already counted as part of GNPs in the years in which they were sold new. (As with brokers, however, the value added by dealers in used-merchandise transactions is included in current GNP.)

IS GNP A MEASURE OF SOCIETY'S WELL-BEING?

GNP is a comprehensive indicator of the economy's output. However, it is an imperfect measure of society's "well-being" because it fails to tell anything about:

1. The growth of leisure time, that is, the substantial reduction in the workweek that has taken place during the past several decades (See Exhibit 4.)

2. The composition of the nation's total output in terms of the quality and variety of goods and services

3. The growth and distribution of total output among the members of society

On the basis of the first two factors, the long-run trend of our economy is better than the GNP figures indicate. As for the third, you will often see GNP quoted on a per capita basis over the years, thereby reflecting the share that each person would have in the nation's total output if it were distributed equally to every man, woman, and child. What does it mean in terms of the economy's growth if the trend of GNP per capita increases over the years? Decreases? Remains the same?

WHAT ABOUT GROSS NATIONAL "DISPRODUCT"?

The gross national product—our standard index of economic output—measures everything from the cost of hospital care to the wages of belly dancers. But it is only an index of dollar values—not social benefits.

Exhibit 4

The Shrinking Workweek

The average workweek has declined from 53 hours in 1890 to about 37 hours today (not counting the time spent commuting to work—anywhere from 2 to 4 hours daily in metropolitan areas). Not everybody, of course, works the "average" week. Many white-collar workers, professionals, and farmers put in as much as 50 or 60 hours a week, or even more.

The major determinant of reductions in the workweek is the size of gains in productivity, or output per man-hour. The long-run trend of these gains has been upward. If the trend continues, workers may prefer to take the benefits of improved productivity in the form of higher pay, shorter hours, longer weekends or vacations, or sabbatical leaves every few years. If they choose any of the nonmonetary alternatives, the benefits to society resulting from increased productivity will not be reflected in the calculation of GNP.

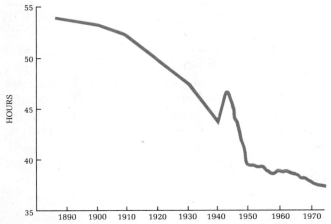

SOURCE: National Bureau of Economic Research 1890–1942; U.S. Bureau of Labor Statistics.

THE TIMES,
THEY HAVE CHANGED

Rules for store clerks, circa 1822, included the following admonishments to the staff:

● This store must be opened at Sunrise. No mistake. Open 6 o'clock A.M. Summer and Winter. Close about 8:30 or 9 P.M. the year around.

● After the 14 hours in the store the leisure hours should be spent mostly in reading.

● Men clerks are given one evening a week off for courting and two if they go to prayer meeting.

● Each clerk must pay not less than $5.00 per year to the Church and must attend Sunday School regularly.

● The clerk who is in the habit of smoking Spanish Cigars, being shaved at the barbers, going to dancing parties and other places of amusement, and being out late at night will assuredly give his employer reason to be ever suspicious of his integrity and honesty.

SOURCE: Courtesy, Morgan Guaranty Trust Co.

In other words, GNP makes no distinction between the useful and the frivolous—regardless of the price that has been paid. For example, GNP includes cloth coats for people as well as mink coats for dogs, life-saving antibiotics as well as useless patent medicines. Further, there is no measure of the amount of "disproduct" or *social cost* that results from producing the "regular" GNP. Thus, to society:

☐ The cost of air and water pollution is the disproduct of the nation's factories.

☐ The cost of treating lung cancer victims is the disproduct of cigarette production.

☐ The cost of geriatric medicine is the disproduct of good medical care in the earlier years which results in increased longevity.

☐ The cost of commuter transportation is the disproduct of suburbia.

☐ The cost of aspirin for headaches resulting from TV commercials is the disproduct of advertising.

Can you suggest some more examples?

If this process were carried through our whole product list, the aggregate would be *gross national disproduct*. And if the total were then set against the aggregate of production as measured by GNP, it would indicate our degree of progress toward (or departure from) social welfare. In fact, if we could discover a true "net" between disproduct and product, we would have our first great "social" indicator of what the country has accomplished.

The results would be disillusioning. We would find that while satisfying human wants from today's productivity, we were simultaneously generating present and future wants and needs to repair the damage and waste created by current production.

CONCLUSION: GNP AND SOCIAL WELFARE

Since GNP measures the market value of final goods and services, it can only reflect the amount of money that society exchanges for commodities. As a result, many important activities that affect our level of living are excluded from the calculation of GNP. For example, some activities which are excluded— and corresponding ones which are included—are:

☐ The nonpaid value of housewives' services—but not the salaries paid to housekeepers

☐ The benefits received from the public sector—but not the costs of providing them

☐ The environmental pollution that results from production—but not the money spent to clean it up

☐ The social value of education—but not the expenditures incurred to acquire it

☐ The rising level of crime—but not the funds allocated to fight it

Some economists are trying to devise a better measure of the economy's true output by incorporating the negative as well as positive contributions of production. If this can be done, GNP will come closer to measuring *social welfare* rather than just the market value of final commodities.

However, many economists disagree with the idea that GNP should serve as an indicator of society's well-being. They point out that "social welfare" is a multidimensional concept with too many deep psychological as well as economic implications to permit precise definition, let alone measurement. Hence, the conversion of GNP from a measure of output to a one-dimensional summary measure of society's satisfaction is, they believe, fraught with danger: it can mislead the nation into believing that GNP is at last measuring social welfare when in fact it is not. This misunderstanding might impede progress toward urgently needed social legislation.

SOMETHING TO THINK ABOUT

1. Would it be better to produce wool suits and vaccines instead of mink coats and patent medicines, so that the nation moves closer to "worthwhile" national goals?

2. Does the GNP of an advanced, interdependent economy necessarily contain a considerable amount of disproduct in comparison to a relatively simple type of economic system?

3. Are the costs of the disproducts of our economy borne in the present or in the future?

Two Ways of Looking at GNP

Since GNP is the market value of the nation's output of final goods and services, it can be expressed conceptually by the simple diagram in Exhibit 5 or equivalently by the following fundamental identity

Exhibit 5

Gross National Product = Gross National Income

A Two-sector Model

(Without a Government or Foreign Sector)

A simplified circular-flow model can be used to illustrate the fundamental principle that gross national product and gross national income are actually two sides of the same coin. The nation's flow of output in the upper pipeline equals the nation's flow of income in the lower pipeline. Profit is the residual or "balancing item" that brings this equality about. Can you explain why? How is the model affected if profits are positive? Zero? Negative (i.e., losses)?

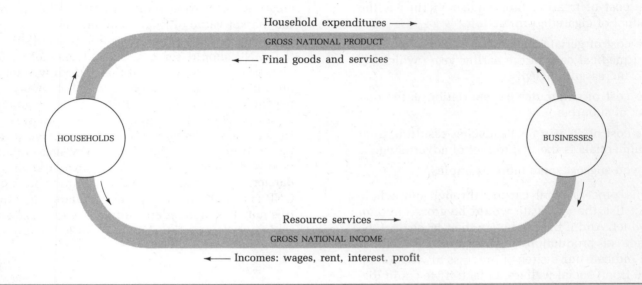

which says that the *total amount spent equals the total amount received.*

$$\left.\begin{array}{l}\text{Total flow of}\\\text{expenditures}\\\text{on final output}\end{array}\right\} \text{GNP} = \text{GNI} \left\{\begin{array}{l}\text{Total flow of}\\\text{income from}\\\text{final output}\end{array}\right.$$

The left side of the identity or upper pipeline of Exhibit 5 views GNP as a sum of expenditures or flow of product; the right side or lower pipeline views it as a sum of incomes or values added at each stage of production. This lower pipeline thus represents *gross national income* (GNI), which is the sum of wages, rent, interest, and profit earned in the production of GNP, and is always equal to GNP. It is to be emphasized that this diagram illustrates a *simple* circular-flow system. It provides a "first look" at the relation between an economy's output and income, but a more elaborate model is necessary for understanding the underlying forces at work. Such a model is presented in Exhibit 6.

GNP FROM THE EXPENDITURE VIEWPOINT: A FLOW-OF-PRODUCT APPROACH

On the left side of the diagram in Exhibit 6, the economy is divided into four major sectors: households, government, business, and foreign. These are the major markets for the output of the economy. In any one year, the total expenditures of these sectors comprise the nation's GNP. The historical record of these expenditures is presented in the first four columns of the front endpapers of this book—along with GNP in the fifth column. What major trends can you discern from the table over the past 10 years? In particular:

1. What have been the trends of personal consumption expenditures, government purchases of goods and services, and gross private domestic investment?

2. What has been the trend of net exports?

You can answer these questions by referring directly to the front endpapers. However, you will also find it useful to prepare a chart showing the

Exhibit 6

Gross National Product = Gross National Income

A Four-sector Model

The data for measuring the nation's total output can be estimated from two points of view:

☐ *The product side—showing the value of goods and services produced*

☐ *The income side—showing the costs incurred and payments received in producing those goods and services*

The product side is divided into four sectors representing the major markets for the output of the economy: households, government, business, and foreign. The sum of their expenditures on final products comprises GNP. The income side summarizes the payments or costs incurred by business firms to produce final products—wages, rent, interest, profit, indirect business taxes, and capital consumption allowances or depreciation—the sum of which comprises GNI.

Can you explain why it must be true that for any given period, GNP = GNI? What is the meaning of the expression "national income at factor cost"? Why is profit listed as a "cost"?

EXPENDITURE VIEWPOINT: FLOW OF PRODUCT	INCOME VIEWPOINT: FLOW OF COSTS
HOUSEHOLD SECTOR Personal consumption expenditures	NATIONAL INCOME (AT FACTOR COST) Wages Rent Interest Profit
+	
GOVERNMENT SECTOR Government purchases of goods and services	+
+	NONINCOME (EXPENSE) ITEMS Indirect business taxes Capital consumption allowance (Depreciation)
BUSINESS SECTOR Gross private domestic investment	
+	
FOREIGN SECTOR Net exports of goods and services	

GNP = GNI

graphs of the four classes of expenditures over the past decade. Meanwhile, what can be said about the meaning of these four categories?

Personal Consumption Expenditures

Frequently referred to as "consumption expenditures" or simply "consumption," this category includes household expenditures on such consumer nondurable goods as food and clothing, consumer durable goods such as automobiles and major appliances, and services such as those of doctors, lawyers, and repairmen.

Government Purchases of Goods and Services

The items in this category are purchased by all levels of government. They include guided missiles, school buildings, fire engines, pencils, paper clips, and the services of accountants, economists, statisticians, and all other government employees. However, recall that a significant part of government expenditures—transfer payments—is omitted because it does not represent current output or purchases of goods and services.

Gross Private Domestic Investment

This category includes total investment spending by business firms. The term "investment" has two meanings: (1) In everyday language, a person makes an investment when he buys stocks, bonds, or other properties with the intention of receiving an income or making a profit. (2) In economics, *investment* means additions to or replacement of real productive assets; hence it represents spending by business firms on new job-creating and income-producing goods which thereby add to GNP. This concept of investment is the one that concerns us in this book.

Investment goods fall into two broad classes:

1. New capital goods, such as machines, factories, offices, and residences including apartment houses and owner-occupied homes—the last on the assumption that they could just as well be rented out and thereby yield incomes to their owners, as do apartment houses. Recall that when a firm buys a used machine or existing factory, it merely exchanges money assets for physical assets; the purchase itself creates no additional GNP. But when it buys *new* machines or *new* buildings the firm creates jobs and incomes for steelworkers, carpenters, bricklayers, and other workers, thereby contributing to the nation's GNP.

2. Increases in *inventories* (including raw materials, supplies, and finished goods on hand) are as much a part of business firms' physical capital as are plant and equipment. Therefore, the market values of any additions to inventories are part of the current flow-of-product that makes up GNP; conversely, any declines in inventories are reductions from the flow of product that makes up GNP.

In the process of producing goods during any given year some existing plant and equipment is used up or *depreciated*. Therefore, a part of the year's gross private domestic investment goes to replace it. Any amount left over is called *net private domestic investment* because it represents a net addition to the total stock of capital. For example, if

gross private domestic investment   = $50 billion
and replacement for depreciation   =   30 billion
then net private domestic investment = $20 billion

An economy will tend to grow, remain static, or decline according to whether:

1. Gross investment exceeds depreciation, in which case net investment is positive. The economy is thus adding to its capital stock and expanding its productive base.

2. Gross investment equals depreciation, in which case net investment is zero. The economy is merely replacing its capital stock and is neither expanding nor contracting its productive base.

3. Gross investment is less than depreciation, in which case net investment is negative. The economy is diminishing or *disinvesting* its capital stock and is thereby contracting its productive base.

To summarize:

Investment is spending by business firms on job-creating and income-producing goods. It consists of replacements or additions to the nation's stock of capital including its plant, equipment, and inventories, that is, its nonhuman productive assets.

Net Exports

Some American expenditures purchase foreign goods—imports. Some foreign expenditures purchase American goods—exports. To measure GNP in terms of total expenditures we have to (1) add the value of *exported goods and services* to our total expenditures, since this represents the amount that foreigners spent on purchasing some of our total output; and (2) subtract the value of *imported goods and services* from our total expenditures, since we are interested only in measuring the value of domestic output. In performing these adjustments it is simpler to combine the separate figures for exports and imports into a single figure called net exports, according to the formula:

$$\text{Net exports} = \text{total exports} - \text{total imports}$$

Thus, if a nation's total exports in any given year amount to $20 billion, and its total imports are $15 billion, its net exports of $5 billion are part of that year's GNP. Of course, its imports may exceed its exports in any particular year, in which case its net exports will be negative and will reduce its GNP. If you have any doubts about this, just look back at Exhibit 6 and note what the effect would be on GNP if net exports were negative.

As a result of the breakdown shown in Exhibit 6, economists sometimes use the term *gross national expenditure* (GNE) to represent the total amount spent by the four sector accounts of the economy (i.e., household, government, business, and foreign) on the nation's output of goods and services. Evidently, GNE = GNP = GNI.

GNP FROM THE INCOME VIEWPOINT: A FLOW-OF-COSTS APPROACH

Now turn your attention to the right side of the diagram in Exhibit 6. This shows a second method of calculating GNP—in terms of the flow of costs or payments which businesses incur as a result of production. The sum of these payments comprises *gross national income*, GNI. However, only the first four items—wages, rent, interest, and profit—represent incomes paid to the owners of the factors of production for their contribution to the nation's output; the remaining two types of payments—indirect business taxes and capital consumption allowance (depreciation)—do not. Let us see why.

Wages

The broad category of *wages* embraces all forms of remuneration for work. It thus includes not only wages, but also executive salaries and bonuses, commissions, payments in kind, incentive payments, tips, and fringe benefits.

Rent

Income earned by persons for the use of their real property, such as a house, store, or farm, is rent. This category also includes the estimated rental value of owner-occupied nonfarm dwellings, and royalties received by persons from patents, copyrights, and rights to natural resources.

Interest

Interest is expressed in net rather than gross terms; it represents the excess of interest paid by the domestic business sector over its interest receipts from all other sectors, plus net interest received from abroad. Interest payments within a sector, such as interest paid by one individual to another, or by one business firm to another, or by one government agency to another, have no net effect on the sector and are excluded from this category. Interest payments by government and by consumers, even when they flow between sectors as in the case of interest paid on government debt or on consumer loans, are considered unproductive and are also excluded here. Instead they are counted as transfer payments.

Profit

Profit, in our model, combines proprietors' income and corporate profits before taxes. (These items are treated separately, however, by Commerce Department statisticians.) The former represents the earnings of unincorporated businesses—proprietorships, partnerships, and producers' cooperatives. The latter measures the profits of corporations before payments of corporate income taxes or disbursements of dividends to stockholders. Proprietors' income and corporate profits both include an "inventory valuation adjustment" which attempts to remove the distorting effect on profits that rising or falling prices exert via the value of business inventories.

To generalize:

National income (at factor cost) is part of gross national income. It represents the sum of wages, rent, interest, and profit—the payments that business firms must make to the owners of the factors of production in return for the services provided by those factors.

The two remaining components of gross national income are indirect business taxes and capital consumption allowances (depreciation). Since they are not payments to the owners of productive resources, their inclusion in GNI requires some explanation.

Indirect Business Taxes

Indirect business taxes consist primarily of sales, excise, and real property taxes incurred by businesses. (Direct taxes on factor payments, such as employer contributions for social insurance or corporate income taxes, are not counted here because they were already included in wages, profits, and other specific items comprising national income at factor cost.) For accounting purposes, an indirect business tax is actually "paid"—that is, turned over to the government—by a business firm. Therefore the tax is regarded as a business expense, even though the real burden of the tax is likely to be borne by the firm's customers in the form of a higher price. As a result, the tax is included in GNI as a cost item.

To put it somewhat differently, indirect business taxes tend to be passed on or shifted forward by business firms to buyers. Sales taxes are typical. If you live in a state or city that has a 4 percent general sales tax and you buy a product whose price is $1, your total *expenditure* is actually $1.04. Of this, $1 goes to pay incomes—the wages, rent, interest, and profit—earned for making the product, and 4 cents goes to city hall, which has not contributed directly to production. It follows, therefore, that indirect business taxes cause the expenditure side of GNP to be greater than the income side. In view of this, indirect business taxes must be added to total incomes (or subtracted from GNP) if the two sides are to be brought closer together.

Capital Consumption Allowance (Depreciation)

In the process of producing GNP, some decline in the value of existing physical capital occurs due to wear and tear, obsolescence, destruction, and accidental loss. To reflect this decline, firms charge a *capital consumption allowance*—or simply "depreciation." The allowance consists primarily of depreciation on business plant and equipment and on owner-occupied dwellings. For purposes of national-income accounting depreciation may be thought of as the portion of the current year's GNP that goes to replace the physical capital "consumed" or used up in the process of production.

Depreciation is thus the difference between gross and net private domestic investment, as already explained. From the standpoint of national-income accounting, if there were no such thing as depreciation, and if the government returned all indirect business taxes to households, the nation's income from production as well as its output would be identical *in fact* as well as conceptually. However, since depreciation does exist, it causes the income side of GNP to be less than the expenditure side, and therefore must be added to incomes (or subtracted from GNP) in order to bring the two sides closer together.

To conclude:

Business firms view indirect business taxes and depreciation as part of their *costs*, and hence charge higher prices for their goods in order to cover these costs. Therefore, these nonincome expense items must be added to the other income payments or expense items (wages, rent, interest, and profit) in order for the total expenditures on GNP to equal the total payments or expenses incurred in producing it.

A comparison of the major components of GNP and GNI is presented in Exhibit 7.

Four Other Concepts—All Related

What relationship exists between the value of the nation's output and the money that households actually have available for spending? We may proceed by examining the items listed in the national-income accounts of Exhibit 8.

From Gross National Product to Net National Product

GNP is the total market value of the nation's annual output of final goods and services. But, as you know, this figure does not equal the actual dollar incomes available to households. To arrive at a closer measure of the dollars received by society we must subtract the proportion that was spent to replace used up capital goods—the so-called capital consumption allowance or depreciation figure. The number that results is net national product or simply NNP.

From Net National Product to National Income

Net national product measures the total sales value of goods and services available for society's con-

---

Exhibit 7

Gross National Product and Gross National Income, 1972*
(in billions of dollars)

EXPENDITURE VIEWPOINT: FLOW OF PRODUCT		INCOME VIEWPOINT: FLOW OF COSTS		
EXPENDITURES BY SECTORS		**NATIONAL INCOME (AT FACTOR COST)**		$ 942
Household Sector		*Wages*		
Personal consumption expenditures	$ 727	Compensation of employees: wages and supplements	$707	
Government Sector		*Rent*		
Government purchases of goods and services	255	Rental income of persons	24	
		Interest		
		Net interest	45	
Business Sector		*Profit*		
Gross private domestic investment	178	Proprietors' income (business, professional, farm)	74	
		Corporate profits before taxes (adjusted)	92	
Foreign Sector				
Net exports of goods and services	— 5	**NONINCOME (EXPENSE) ITEMS**		$ 213
		Indirect business taxes	$109	
		Capital consumption allowance (Depreciation)	104	
GROSS NATIONAL PRODUCT	$1,155	GROSS NATIONAL INCOME		$1,155

* Preliminary data.
SOURCE: U.S. Department of Commerce.

Exhibit 8

Gross National Product and Related Accounts*
(in billions of dollars)

	1955	1960	1965	1970
Gross national product (GNP)	$398	S504	$685	$974
Minus:				
Capital consumption allowance (Depreciation)	32	43	60	88
Equals: Net national product (NNP)	367	460	625	887
Minus:				
Indirect business taxes	32	45	63	93
Equals: National income (NI)	331	415	564	796
Minus: Income earned but not received				
Corporate income taxes	22	23	31	34
Undistributed corporate profits	17	13	27	16
Social insurance contributions	11	21	30	58
Plus: Income received but not earned				
Transfer payments	26	42	58	112
Equals: Personal income (PI)	311	401	539	804
Minus:				
Personal taxes	36	51	66	116
Equals: Disposable personal income (DPI)	275	350	473	688
Out of which:				
Personal consumption expenditures	260	333	445	616
Personal saving	15	17	28	54

* Discrepancies in totals are due to the omission of minor items.

sumption and for adding to its stock of capital equipment. As such, it may be thought of as "national income at market prices." But it still does not represent the dollars people actually had available to spend because NNP is overstated by the amount of indirect business taxes—such as sales taxes—which are shifted forward by sellers to consumers in the form of higher prices. These indirect business taxes must be deducted from NNP in order to arrive at a closer estimate of the dollars available to people for actual spending. This deduction results in national income at factor cost, usually abbreviated simply as *NI*.

From National Income to Personal Income

National income (at factor cost) is the total of all incomes earned by the factors of production—the sum of wages, rent, interest, and profit earned by the suppliers of labor, land, capital, and entrepreneurship. Does *NI* represent the dollars that people actually had available for spending? Once again the answer is *no*. Some people earned income they did not receive; others received income they did not earn.

The stockholders in a corporation are its owners

SIMON SMITH KUZNETS

1901–

Father of National-income Accounting

Wide World Photos.

Few scholars in any field are capable of deciding, by their mid-twenties, the precise type of work they want to do for the remainder of their professional careers. One person who made that decision, and has earned lasting fame for his accomplishments, is Simon Kuznets.

Born in Russia, Kuznets migrated to the United States as a young man. After receiving his doctorate from Columbia University, he joined the staff of one of the nation's major research organizations, the National Bureau of Economic Research, and also served as a consultant to the Commerce Department. In addition, he taught for many years at the University of Pennsylvania, Johns Hopkins, and Harvard.

More than anyone else, Kuznets pioneered the development of national-income data. When the nation plunged into the Great Depression of the early 1930s, the amount of factual information available was, said Kuznets, "a scandal. No one knew what was happening. The data available then were neither fish nor flesh nor even red herring."

It remained for Kuznets to point out the kind of information that was needed. When the Senate ordered official income estimates, the Commerce Department turned to the National Bureau of Economic Research for assistance. Kuznets went to Washington as a consultant, lecturing government economists and statisticians on his concepts. On January 4, 1934, a Senate document was published containing the country's first national-income figures, for 1929 to 1932. This was the beginning of one of the most significant advances in the history of economics. Although the measurement of GNP and related concepts was not fully developed by the Commerce Department until the 1940s, and the technical structure is quite different from Kuznets' original conceptual scheme, he is nevertheless recognized as the person most responsible for its statistical formulation.

Kuznets was well aware that national income served as an imperfect measure of society's well-being. He gave two reasons:

First, nonmarket activities, such as the services of housewives, amateur gardeners, and others engaged in productive pursuits, do not enter the national-income accounts. As a result of these omissions, our national-income data are less than they otherwise would be.

Second, certain "occupational expenses" such as the costs of commuting to work, buying banking services because we live in a money economy, and other necessary "costs" of carrying out our daily activities are included in national-income accounts, even though they may not all yield positive returns to us from the economic system. Hence the accounts tend to be higher than they otherwise would be.

These and other shortcomings, Kuznets pointed out, introduce biases in national-income accounts which make it difficult to compare one economy with another. For example, in 1953 he wrote: "That such [errors] are hardly in the nature of minutiae may be illustrated by a tentative calculation made in attempting a comparison of per capita income in the United States and China and purifying the former for what may be called inflated costs of urban civilization: the inflation in question amounted to from 20 to 30 percent of all consumers' outlay . . . as estimated by the Department of Commerce."

Kuznets' whole career has been devoted to closely related tasks. Sifting through mountains of historical data, he has estimated the changing significance of capital, labor, income distribution, productivity, and other variables on the economic growth of this and other countries. To a degree rarely equaled by any other economist, he has the rare ability to generate and analyze large masses of data from which he draws many provocative socioeconomic hypotheses about long-term economic development.

Kuznets' lifework has been crowned with honors. In 1971, when he was 70, the Swedish Royal Academy of Science awarded him the Alfred Nobel Memorial Prize in Economic Science.

and hence receive its profits. However, they do not receive all its profits, for two reasons. Some profits are paid to the government in the form of corporation income taxes, and some are plowed back into the business for future expansion instead of being distributed to stockholders as dividends. Likewise, social security contributions are taken out of workers' current earnings, and hence are also part of income earned but not received.

As for income received but not earned, the major items are transfer payments, which have already been defined. These are merely shifts of funds within the economy, primarily from the government sector to households—for reasons other than current production.

To measure the dollars people actually had available for spending, we therefore adjust the NI by *subtracting* income earned but not received and *adding* income received but not earned. This results in a figure called personal income, or *PI*.

From Personal Income to Disposable Personal Income

Personal income is the total received by persons from all sources—the dollars that you and I receive for performing our jobs and thereby contributing to GNP. Does it measure the dollars actually available to people for spending? The answer is still *no*, because out of personal income people must first pay their personal taxes. This amount must therefore be deducted from *PI*, leaving a figure called *disposable personal income*, or *DPI*. It is this amount that people actually had available for spending. As you can see from the front endpapers of this book, the great bulk of it went for personal consumption, while the rest of it was saved.

There are thus five measures of income and output for the economy:

1. Gross national product
2. Net national product
3. National income
4. Personal income
5. Disposable personal income—or simply, disposable income

All five measures are closely interrelated, can be derived from one another, and tend approximately to parallel one another over the years. (See Exhibit 9.) In many economic discussions (except those involving specific accounting practices as described in this

Exhibit 9

Five Measures of Income and Output

GNP and its components tend roughly to parallel one another. In recent years, personal income has exceeded national income. Can you explain why? Note that the vertical axis of the figure is a logarithmic scale. This permits comparisons of relative changes.

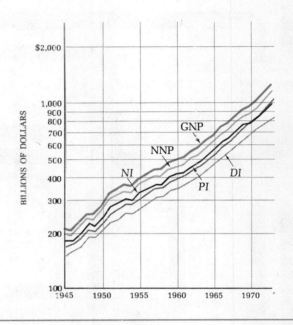

chapter) *economists frequently use the term "national income" or simply "income" to represent all five terms.* A complete circular-flow model is shown in Exhibit 10 on the next page.

SUMMARY OF IMPORTANT IDEAS

1. GNP, the basic and most comprehensive measure of a nation's output, represents the total market value of all final goods and services produced during a year.

Three pitfalls to avoid in calculating GNP include: (a) the effects of price changes; (b) the possibility of double (actually multiple) counting; (c) the inclusion of nonproductive transactions.

2. From the expenditure standpoint GNP is the sum of personal consumption expenditures, government purchases of goods and services, investment,

Exhibit 10

The Flow of National Income and Related Concepts

Can you fill in the data for the most recent years? See front endpaper.

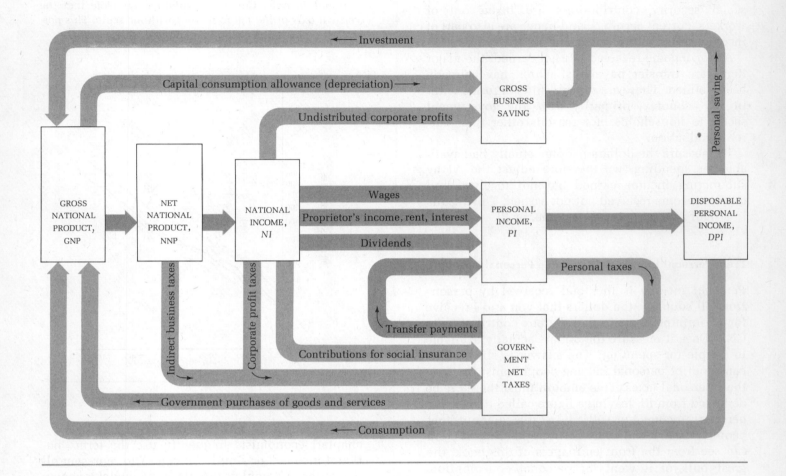

and net exports. GNP can be viewed from the income standpoint as gross national income (GNI) or the sum of wages, rent, interest, and profit, plus two nonincome business expense items: indirect business taxes and depreciation.

3. The items which make up the nation's income accounts are: GNP, NNP, *NI, PI,* and *DPI.* All five measures are closely related and can be derived from one another. They are among the most important measures of our economy's performance. In economic discussions (except those involving actual accounting practices) we often refer to all five measures as "national income" or simply "income."

FOR DISCUSSION

1. *Terms and concepts to review:*

gross national product	gross national income
current dollars	investment
constant dollars	inventory
deflation	disinvestment
index numbers	depreciation
value added	gross national
transfer payments	expenditure
social cost	capital consumption
real output	allowance
gross national	net national product
disproduct	personal income

national income
(at factor cost)

disposable personal
income

2. Suppose a nation's GNP increased from $100 billion to $200 billion. What has happened to its *real* GNP during that period if:
   (a) prices remained the same
   (b) prices doubled
   (c) prices tripled from their constant level in (a)
   (d) prices fell by 50 percent of their constant level in (a)

3. When you "deflate" a *rising* current-dollar series, as in Exhibit 1, the constant-dollar series lies below the current-dollar series for all years after the base year, and above it for all years prior to the base year. What would happen if you deflated a current-dollar series that was *declining* rather than rising? Explain.

4. Why is "value added" a logically correct method of measuring the nation's output?

5. The level of inventories serves as a "balancing" item between sales to final users and current production. True or false? Can sales to final users exceed current production? Can they be less than current production? Explain, in terms of changes in inventories and their effects on GNP.

6. How is the growth or decline of an economy related to its net investment? Do you think an economy's percentage growth or decline is related to its percentage change in net investment? Explain.

7. What is the effect on national income if a man (a) marries his housekeeper, (b) takes an unpaid vacation? Is there any effect on social welfare from either act?

8. Which of the following is included, and which is not included, in calculating GNP:
   (a) one hundred shares of General Motors stock purchased this week on the New York Stock Exchange
   (b) wages paid to teachers
   (c) a student's income from a part-time job
   (d) a student's income from a full-time summer job
   (e) value of a bookcase built by a do-it-yourselfer
   (f) purchase of a used car
   (g) a monthly rent of $250 which a homeowner "saves" by living in his own home instead of renting it out to a tenant

9. Each year the total amount of dollar payments by checks and cash far exceeds—by many billions of

dollars—the GNP. If GNP is the market value of the economy's final output, how can this huge difference exist?

10. Gross business saving represents that part of business income available for various forms of investment. Examine the following hypothetical data (in billions of dollars):

Corporate profits	$90
Corporate income taxes	43
Dividends to stockholders	25
Retained profits	22
Depreciation	75

   (a) How much is gross business saving? Show your method of calculation.
   (b) Of what significance is depreciation in your calculation?
   (c) Can gross business saving be larger than corporate profits *before* taxes and dividends? Can it be smaller? Explain.

11. Examine the following hypothetical data (all in billions of dollars) and answer the questions below.

(1)	Gross private domestic investment	$ 59
(2)	Contributions for social insurance	8
(3)	Interest paid by consumers	3
(4)	Personal consumption expenditures	206
(5)	Transfer payments	20
(6)	Undistributed corporate profits	13
(7)	Indirect business taxes	25
(8)	Net exports of goods and services	4
(9)	Capital consumption allowances	21
(10)	Government purchases of goods and services	59
(11)	Corporate income taxes	22
(12)	Personal tax and nontax payments	29

On the basis of these data, calculate (a) gross national product, (b) net national product, (c) national income, (d) personal income, (e) disposable income.

12. Examine the following hypothetical data (all in billions of dollars) and do the problem below.

(1)	Indirect business taxes	$ 32
(2)	Corporate profits before taxes	47
(3)	Capital consumption allowances	32
(4)	Compensation of employees	225
(5)	Undistributed corporate profits	17
(6)	Proprietors' income	42
(7)	Contributions for social insurance	11
(8)	Corporate income taxes	22
(9)	Net interest	4
(10)	Transfer payments	27

(11) Personal tax and nontax payments   36
(12) Rental incomes   14
(13) Personal consumption expenditures   254

On the basis of these data, calculate the five types of national income discussed in this chapter? (HINT: Do not try to calculate GNP first.)

13. Gross national product rose from $285 billion in 1950 to $504 billion in 1960. During the same period the Consumer Price Index (1967 = 100) rose from 72.1 to 88.7.

(a) What was the percentage increase of GNP over the decade?

(b) By how much have average prices, measured by the Consumer Price Index, risen over the decade?

(c) How would you calculate GNP for 1950 and for 1960, expressed in 1967 dollars?

(d) Is the percentage change of GNP in constant dollars greater or less than the percentage change in current dollars? Show your calculations.

14. Convert personal consumption expenditures into 1967 dollars for the years shown in the following table. What is the economic significance of your calculations? Have you "deflated" or "inflated"? Explain.

Year	Personal Consumption Expenditures (billions)	Consumer Price Index (1967 = 100)
1950	$191.0	72.1
1955	254.4	80.2
1960	325.2	88.7
1965	432.8	94.5

15. Which measure of national income best tells you:

(a) the amount by which the economy's production exceeds the capital equipment used up in producing it

(b) the amount of income available to consumers for spending

(c) the market value of commodities produced for final use

(d) the amount of income available to people for government taxation

(e) the incomes earned by resource owners engaged in production

Which measure of national income is best?

Contemporary Issue

Wisdom or GIGO?

In the late eighteenth century, many English observers were convinced that their population was declining, and a prime minister of the day, the younger Pitt, recommended paying the poor to have more children. Remarkably, in view of their anxiety, the English preferred speculation to measurement: not until 1801 did they take their first census. Predictably, it showed Britain to be more populous than the doomsayers thought it was.

Since then statistics has become a growth industry in every nation that is civilized—and in some that are not. Everything that can be measured is, however trivial. Undoubtedly, some statistician could pull out of the files figures showing that consumption of hot dogs at National League baseball games has risen in the past decade, although consumption of mustard has fallen. Whereas the eighteenth-century English erred by preferring fears to figures, many people today are too prone to accept statistics uncritically. That tendency is understandable; many figures come cloaked in authoritarian mystique. What, for example, is more apparently authoritative and factual than the statement, "U.S. gross national product per capita was $4,756 in 1970"?

Errors of Omission and Commission

For a start—and this is obvious—the figure is an average, obtained by dividing the total population in 1970 into the total GNP as defined. But do we really know how many Americans were living in the United States in 1970? We do—but only within the limits of statistical error, which may be as large as 10 percent, or roughly 21 million people. This may seem to be a staggeringly large number; but it gains credence when we recall two facts. First, the Bureau of the Census itself warns that its accounting of black males may understate the total by as much as 10 percent. Second, after the 1970 census a number of cities and localities successfully challenged the Bureau's figures, demonstrating that their population had been substantially undercounted.

As for the GNP figures, they are probably as accurate as human ingenuity can make them; but they are still open to question. First, they depend on the cooperation of the people who supply the basic data—households, businesses, banks, and so on. Some of these respondents may lie; others may make honest errors in their answers. Second, and more important, the GNP figures deliberately exclude some activities that are economic in nature (for example, illegal gambling, sales of heroin and other drugs, prostitution), merely estimate others (the value of food consumed by farm families, for example), and totally ignore so-called "nonmarket" activities (homemade clothing, the work of housewives, etc). All right and proper, perhaps. But the inclusions and exclusions are the result of subjective judgements. In a warning that is too often overlooked, Professor Simon Kuznets of Harvard wrote in 1941 in a pioneering work on national-income accounting: "The statistician who supposes that he can make a purely objective estimate of national income, not influenced by preconceptions concerning the 'facts,' is deluding himself; for whenever he includes one item or excludes another he is implicitly accepting some standard of judgement, his own or that of the compiler of his data. There is no escaping this subjective element in the work, or freeing the results from its effects. In consequence, all national-income estimates are appraisals of the economic system rather than colorless statements of fact; and, like all appraisals, they are predetermined by criteria that are at worst a matter of chance, at best a matter of deliberate choice."

GIGO

Computer experts put it more succinctly and rudely: "GIGO," acronym for "garbage in, garbage out." Both Kuznets and the irreverent computerologists are making the same point, however: always treat statistics skeptically, asking on what definitions they rest, who compiled them, and how the figures were collected. The computer is a wondrous tool: it can store and collate data, it can spew out calculations faster than any human being can, and if programmed correctly it is inhumanly accurate. But its output is only as good as its input.

As with national-income figures, so with another vital measure of economic performance, the unemployment rate. "Jobless rate at 5 percent" and "Unemployment up in 3rd quarter" have become staple headlines on front pages. Most people accept the figures as being "objective," in the sense of measuring down to the last decimal point the number of workers without jobs. But the U.S. Department of Labor is candid in offering the figures as estimates—and that is what they are, being based on interviews conducted in sample households and on the number of workers who register as unemployed. Furthermore, to be "unemployed" officially a worker must be "actively seeking work"—a definition that excludes those many people who have ceased to look for jobs, having decided that their race, or age, or lack of skills, or all three factors, have made them unemployable.

Faced with the unreliability of apparently objective data some intellectuals despair; a few fear that their tidy, measurable universe is collapsing around them. We must accept most statistics for what they are: better than guesses, but less than precise counts. And when propagandists for statistics protest that the figures have been stored and processed by computers we should choose one of two rebuttals. The first and more polite is *argumentum ad verecundiam*. The second is a brusque "and GIGO to you too."

QUESTIONS

1. *If national-income accounting is inaccurate, why do we bother to use it? Discuss.*

2. *Even if the unemployment figures are inaccurate by a percentage point or two, does it really make much difference? Explain.*

3. *"There are lies, there are damned lies, and there are statistics." Does this famous quotation mean that statistics should never be believed?*

CHAPTER 9

Economic Instability: Unemployment and Inflation

CHAPTER PREVIEW

What are business cycles? What causes them? Can they be predicted and controlled?

How significant is unemployment in our economy? What are the "costs" of unemployment? Who pays these costs?

What is inflation? Who benefits from it? Who suffers from it? Can inflation be avoided?

Fluctuations in economic activity—or "business cycles" as they are often called—have been an unending plague for capitalistic nations. Inflation and unemployment are the costs of that plague—costs we have paid throughout much of our history.

This chapter examines the nature of business cycles, unemployment, and inflation, and their interrelationship. Once we understand their characteristics we can start to do something about the problems themselves, which are among the most potent challenges confronting affluent Western nations.

Essentially, as you will learn, the United States government tries to keep all three ailments at bay simultaneously; but it is not consistently successful because both the ailments themselves and their cure are still subjects of debate and experiment.

Business Cycles—The "Dance of the Dollar"

Although we no longer have the extreme booms and busts that characterized the economy in the decades prior to World War II, we do have fluctuations in business activity. The following modern definition of business cycles is appropriate:

Business cycles are recurrent but nonperiodic fluctuations in general business and economic activity that take place over a period of years. These fluctuations occur in aggregate variables like income, output, employment, and prices, most of which move at about the same time in the same direction, but at *different rates*.

Business cycles, therefore, are not just cumulative fluctuations in the absolute level of important economic variables, but are accelerations and retardations—speeding up and slowing down—in their rates of growth. Note that the definition is important for what it excludes:

1. Business cycles are not *seasonal fluctuations*, such as the upswing in retail sales that occurs each year during the Christmas and Easter periods.

2. Business cycles are not secular *trends*, such as the long-run growth or decline—or the sweeping upward or downward "drift"—that characterizes practically all economic data over a long period of years.

HOW DO BUSINESS CYCLES LOOK?

We can visualize business cycles as deviations around a long-term trend, like the deviations of

---

Exhibit 1

Gross National Product—Actual and Trend

The vertical axis of this chart is a "ratio" or logarithmic scale on which equal distances are represented by equal percentage changes. For example, the changes from 100 to 200, 200 to 400, 300 to 600, etc., all equal 100 percent, and hence are presented by equal distances on the chart.

This type of scale permits the trend of GNP to be plotted as a straight line; it would have appeared as a line curving upward if an ordinary (nonratio) scale had been used.

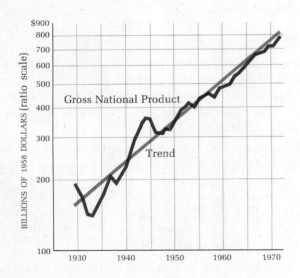

GNP around its trend as shown in Exhibit 1. In this and in all other instances when data such as GNP, sales, prices, employment, or any other figures are arranged chronologically, they are referred to as *time series*. The measurement of "time" may be in years, months, weeks, days, or other units, and is usually scaled on the horizontal axis when depicted graphically.

According to the definition of business cycles, the fluctuations may occur in production, prices, income, employment, or in any other time series of economic data. In order to measure business cycles for the economy as a whole, therefore, it is necessary to combine many different time series into a single index of business activity. Then, if the value of the index for each year is expressed as a percentage of the long-term trend, the resulting data when graphed might look like the fluctuations in Exhibit 2. No wonder a famous American economist, Irving Fisher (1867–1947), once described business cycles as the "dance of the dollar."

PHASES OF THE CYCLE

The ups and downs which occurred before World War II, as shown in Exhibit 2, prompted speculation on whether these fluctuations were actually "cycles" —that is, whether the peaks and troughs occurred at regular time intervals as shown by the idealized cycle in Exhibit 3. If this were actually the case, the cycle would resemble a sine or cosine curve in trigonometry, or perhaps an alternating electric current, and would therefore be highly predictable.

However, as more data and improved methods of measurement became available, it was found that business cycles are *recurrent but not periodic*. Hence the terms "business cycles" and "business fluctuations" are used synonymously in economics, with the understanding that the word "cycles" in no sense implies periodicity.

The names of the four phases of the business cycle shown in Exhibit 3 are probably familiar to you since you often encounter them in the news media. But since they may mean different things to different people, the following brief explanations will help to avoid ambiguity:

1. *Prosperity.* The upper phase of a business cycle in which the economy is operating at or near full employment, and a high degree of business and consumer optimism is reflected by a vigorous rate of capital investment and consumption.

Exhibit 2

An Historical Picture of American Business Cycles

Recurrent but not periodic.

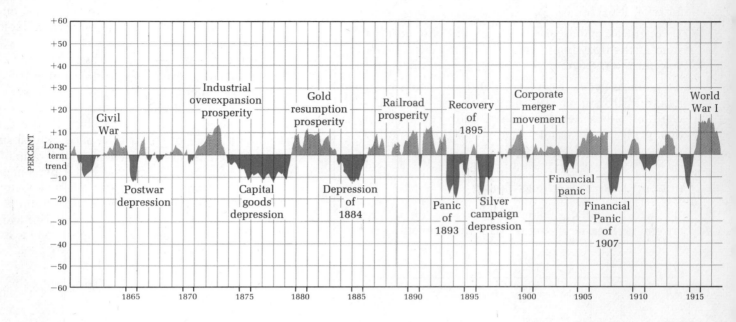

SOURCE: Cleveland Trust Company. Adapted with changes.

2. *Recession.* The downward phase, in which the economy's income, output, and employment are decreasing; and declining business and consumer optimism is reflected by a falling rate of capital investment and consumption.

3. *Depression.* The lower phase, in which the economy is operating with substantial unemployment of its resources, and there is very little business and consumer optimism, as reflected by a sluggish rate of capital investment and consumption.

4. *Recovery.* The upward phase, in which the economy's income, output, and employment are rising; there is a growing degree of business and consumer optimism as reflected by an expanding rate of capital investment and consumption.

The four phases of the cycle are by no means equal in scope or intensity, and do not always come in the order shown. For example, an economy may fluctuate between contractions and expansions for many years without experiencing either high prosperity or deep depression. Further, the transition from one phase of a cycle into the next is occasionally imper-

ceptible; it may be almost impossible to distinguish between the end of one phase and the beginning of another. For these reasons, the names of the four phases should be viewed only as convenient descriptions, and the diagram in Exhibit 3 as a highly simplified picture.

SOME FACTS ABOUT BUSINESS CYCLES

Economists who specialize in business cycles have learned a great deal about them from studies going back as far as the early nineteenth century. Business cycles have certain economic characteristics which must be understood. For instance:

Over the course of a business cycle, the durable goods industries tend to experience relatively wide fluctuations in output and employment and relatively small fluctuations in prices; the nondurable goods industries tend to experience relatively wide fluctuations in prices and relatively small fluctuations in output and employment.

The reasons for this are based primarily on two sets of factors: durability and competition.

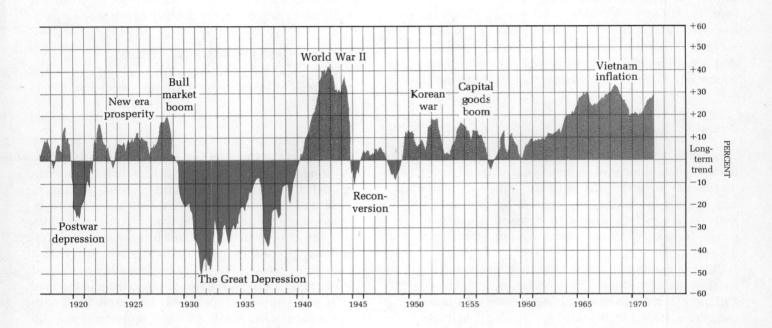

World War II

New era prosperity

Bull market boom

Korean war

Capital goods boom

Vietnam inflation

Long-term trend

Postwar depression

Recon-version

The Great Depression

1920 1925 1930 1935 1940 1945 1950 1955 1960 1965 1970

+60
+50
+40
+30
+20
+10
-10
-20
-30
-40
-50
-60

PERCENT

Exhibit 3

Idealized Business Cycles

Recurrent and periodic . . . like a sine or cosine curve in trigonometry, or an alternating electric current.

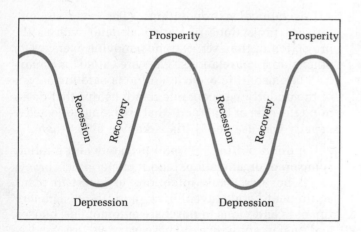

Prosperity   Prosperity

Recession   Recovery   Recession   Recovery

Depression   Depression

Durability

Durable goods—precisely because they are durable—do not have to be replaced at a particular time; they can be repaired and thereby made to last longer if necessary. What effect does this have on businessmen who buy capital goods like iron and steel, cement, and machine tools, and on consumers who purchase durable goods like automobiles, refrigerators, and television sets?

In a recession or depression, when aggregate demand (total value of output that all sectors of the economy are willing to purchase) is low, businessmen find themselves with excess production capacity, and therefore see little prospect of profiting from investment in capital goods. Likewise, consumers find they can get along with their existing cars and other durable goods rather than purchase new ones. Hence the "hard goods" industries experience sharp decreases in demand.

During recovery and prosperity, on the other hand, the reverse situation occurs. Aggregate demand is high, and businessmen and consumers are ready to replace as well as add to their existing stocks of capital and durable goods. The hard goods industries therefore experience sharp increases in demand.

Purchase of capital goods and consumer durables can be postponed to a later date. The contrary, however, is true of nondurables and semidurables—the so-called "soft goods" like food, clothing, and some services. Their purchase is not readily postponable, and hence the change in demand for them over the course of a business cycle is much less pronounced.

Competition

The degree of competition in an industry, as determined by the number of sellers, usually has a bearing on the way in which the industry adjusts its prices and outputs to changes in demand. In view of this, how does a fall in aggregate demand affect hard goods producers as compared to soft goods producers?

Durable goods industries tend to be characterized by fewness of sellers. The aluminum, locomotive, automobile, electric lamp, and telephone equipment industries, among others, are typical. The "big three" or "big four" producers in these industries dominate the markets for their products and control such a large proportion of the total output of their commodity that they can influence the prices they charge and can formulate stable pricing policies despite fluctuations in sales. As a result, when they are confronted with a decline in aggregate demand, they try to reduce costs and maintain profit margins by cutting back production and employment. Eventually, if market sluggishness continues, some hardpressed firms may seek to reduce their inventories by cutting prices. But even then, price decreases are likely to be small relative to the declines in output and employment.

The opposite situation tends to occur in industries producing nondurable and semidurable goods—such as ladies' dresses, men's suits, millinery, furniture, and lumber. In these industries, unlike most durable goods industries, a considerable number of sellers are usually competing in the same market. Each firm, therefore, is likely to have too small a share of the market to ignore the importance of price reduction as a means of countering a decrease in demand. Consequently, when aggregate demand falls, firms in such industries tend to reduce their prices while holding output and employment relatively steady.

These factors explain why, in a recession, we first hear about production cutbacks and layoffs in industries like automobiles and steel—not in food processing or textiles. These latter industries may also reduce their output and employment, but for them the percentage decreases are usually much smaller.

CAN WE FORECAST BUSINESS CYCLES?

If we could first know where we are and whither we are tending, we could better judge what to do and how to do it.

Abraham Lincoln

These words are more than a century old, but they explain as well as any the necessity of forecasting. As long as we live in a world in which no one can predict the future with certainty, virtually all business and economic decisions rest upon forecasts. If you were a businessman, would you invest without knowing something about future economic conditions in your industry or in the economy? As a consumer, would you delay buying a house or a car if you thought the price was going to drop in the near future? If you were a speculator in commodities or in common stocks, would you buy and sell if you did not expect to make a profit? If you were a congressman, would you vote for a tax increase to help curb inflation if you thought that prices throughout the economy were going to leap upward next year?

Each of these questions involves a prediction of the future. Forecasting is a means of reducing uncertainty that surrounds the making of business and economic decisions.

How are the forecasts made? Several methods are employed by economic forecasters working in industry, government, and universities:

1. *Mechanical extrapolations.* These are straightforward projections of statistical data, such as the projection of time-series trends, moving averages, or other statistical relations. They are called "mechanical" because little or no attention is paid to analysis of the underlying economic relationships that determine the data or the trends that are being projected—usually because very little is known about them.

2. *Opinion polling.* Several privately and publicly sponsored organizations conduct periodic surveys of (a) businessmen's intentions to invest in plant, equipment, and inventories; and (b) consumers' finances and plans to purchase automobiles, houses, and major appliances. These surveys are used as bases for predictions about the economy as a whole.

3. *Econometric models.* These are economic relationships expressed in mathematical terms and verified by statistical methods. They may be constructed for firms, industries, regions, or the entire economy, and may serve not only as a basis for prediction, but also as a guide for policy-making. A large-scale econometric model may contain hundreds of equations and require a staff of economists and statisticians to keep it up to date.

4. *Economic indicators.* Literally thousands of time series cover economic and business activity. Many of them may be classified into one of three categories:

(a) *Coincident indicators.* These time series move approximately in phase with the aggregate economy, and hence are measures of current economic activity.

(b) *Leading indicators.* These time series tend to

Leaders in Economics

WESLEY CLAIR MITCHELL

1874–1948

Wesley C. Mitchell was born in Illinois, educated at the University of Chicago, and served for many years as a professor of economics at Columbia University in New York. He was a founder of the National Bureau of Economic Research, which is one of the world's major centers for quantitative research in aggregate economic activity, and a recipient of honorary degrees for distinguished research and scholarship from the Universities of Paris, Chicago, California, Columbia, Harvard, Pennsylvania, and Princeton, and the New School for Social Research. In 1947 the American Economic Association—the major organization of economists in the United States—bestowed upon him its highest honor, the Francis A. Walker Medal (named after the Association's first president, 1885–1892), which is awarded once every five years to an American who "in the course of his life made a contribution of the highest distinction to economics."

Although many of Mitchell's writings were in the history of money and prices, his lifework and greatest research appeared in several editions of his book *Business Cycles,* first published in 1913. This was a monumental work. Mitchell studied, sifted, and analyzed data on commodity prices, wages, bond yields, bond prices, and money for the United States, Great Britain, Germany, and France, covering the period of 1890 to 1911. He then presented, as he said, "an analytic description of the complicated process by which seasons of business prosperity, crisis, depression, and revival come about in the modern world."

In later years, as research director of the National Bureau of Economic Research, Mitchell inspired original investigations into many aspects of capitalism. In 1927 he published *Business Cycles, The Problem and Its Setting,* a revised edition of his earlier book. This served as a standard textbook in economics courses for many years. Finally, in 1946 he coauthored his last volume on the subject, *Measuring Business Cycles,* in which his thesis was carried to its conclusion.

Culver Pictures.

Broadly, Mitchell viewed business cycles as self-generating processes based on mutual interdependencies of causes and effects. Perhaps his greatest contribution was the impetus he gave to the use of empirical data and quantitative model-building, which have characterized much of macroeconomics and business cycle research since the early 1950s.

Modern business cycle models are not intended to give detailed accounts of economic phenomena. However, if we make meaningful assumptions about the data and about the relationships between such variables as income, consumption, saving, and investment, we can construct models that convey many of the essential workings of an economy. Such models help to explain past economic changes, to predict future changes, and to serve as guides for policy-makers. But they can never give results with certainty because they represent the "highlights" of reality rather than the complete picture.

move ahead of aggregate economic activity, thus reaching peaks and troughs before the economy as a whole.

(c) *Lagging indicators.* These time series follow or trail behind aggregate economic activity.

Which forecasting method is best? All four have been used with varying success. However, the last three incorporate the most scientific and reliable means we have for predicting future economic activity.

Unemployment

You will often hear it said that one of our primary national objectives is to maintain the economy's resources at a "full" or "high" level of employment. What do these terms mean?

Before this question can be answered, it is necessary to understand some basic terms and concepts that are part of the modern language of economics. The first is the *labor force*. It may be defined as all people 16 years of age or older who are employed, plus all those unemployed who are actively seeking work. The total labor force includes those in the armed services plus the civilian labor force. However, only the *civilian labor force* is of interest to us here, since this is the segment that experiences unemployment.

TYPES OF UNEMPLOYMENT

The U.S. Department of Labor encounters certain difficulties when it tries to measure unemployment. It finds that the circumstances and conditions of unemployment vary widely among individuals. Accordingly, economists distinguish three different kinds of unemployment.

1. *Frictional unemployment.* A certain amount of unemployment, which is of a short-run nature and is characteristic of a dynamic economy may be called *frictional unemployment.* It exists because of "frictions" in the economic system resulting from imperfect labor mobility, imperfect knowledge of job opportunities, and the economy's inability to match people with jobs instantly and smoothly. Typically, it consists of people temporarily out of work because they are between jobs or in the process of changing jobs. Frictional unemployment can be reduced by improving labor mobility and knowledge, but cannot—and in a democratic society should not —be completely eliminated. In view of its nature, an equally suitable and more descriptive name for it might be *transitional unemployment.*

2. *Cyclical unemployment.* In mixed economies such as ours, the major kind of unemployment has been *cyclical*—resulting from business recessions and depressions when aggregate demand is below the full-employment level of aggregate output and income. Obviously, society would like to reduce cyclical unemployment as much as possible, but this can be done only by conquering the business cycle. Substantial progress has been made in this direction since the depression of the 1930s. As we shall find in later chapters, cyclical unemployment can virtually be eliminated through proper policies designed to maintain a high level of economic activity.

3. *Structural unemployment.* Unlike cyclical unemployment, which responds to stimulative measures, *structural unemployment* is more stubborn because it arises from basic changes or "structural" alterations in the economy. Two major groups of people make up structural unemployment. The first group, which has become increasingly apparent since the 1950s, consists of the *hard-core unemployed* who lack the education and skills needed in today's complex economy. (Discrimination is also a contributing factor.) It is a class composed mainly of minorities: blacks, Puerto Ricans, Mexicans, the "too young," the "too old," the high-school dropouts, and the permanently displaced victims of technological change. The second group has gained significance since around 1970. It consists of skilled workers and professionals whose talents have been made obsolete by changes in technology, markets, or national priorities. Because the existence of both groups constitutes one of America's major economic challenges, we will examine the problems posed by structural unemployment and the means of coping with those problems in later chapters.

FULL EMPLOYMENT AND THE COST OF UNEMPLOYMENT

Ideally the economy should maintain *full employment*—maximum efficient utilization of all resources available for employment. In terms of human resources, this means that the entire civilian labor force should be working, except for the proportion which is frictionally unemployed—typically about 3 percent. This is equivalent to saying there should be no *involuntary unemployment*—a condition in which people who want to work are unable to find jobs at going wage rates for the skills and experiences they have to offer.

The goal of full employment is generally expressed in terms of a percentage of the labor force. What minimum percentage unemployment constitutes full employment? There is always some disagreement on this question, and the figure chosen is likely to be revised upward from time to time. Until 1962, for instance, it was widely accepted that full employment existed when the "normal" unemployment rate was no more than 3 percent of the labor force. Since then the figure has been raised to 4 percent, partly to reflect the growing significance of structural unemployment and partly for other reasons explained in the following paragraphs. If you think such relatively small differences in percentages are unimportant, remember that even a difference of only 1 percent can involve the employment or unemployment of hundreds of thousands of people—depending on the size of the labor force. Take a look at the recent labor-force figures in the back endpapers of this book and estimate the consequences for yourself.

How much higher is the "normal" unemployment level likely to go? Some pessimists predict that before the end of this century 10 or perhaps 15 percent unemployed will constitute "full employment." They base their beliefs on three major trends:

1. *Changing composition of the labor force.* The proportion of secondary income earners in the labor force—teenagers, women, and part-time jobholders —has been increasing relative to the proportion of primary breadwinners. Since the percentage of unemployed within these groups is usually relatively high—in some instances as much as 20 or 30 percent—their growing importance in the labor force helps to boost the overall unemployment rate.

2. *Rising minimum-wage rate.* According to some observers, continued increases in the minimum-wage rate will intensify unemployment by eliminating jobs that cannot be done productively at the required wage rate. They point out that many unskilled, low-paying occupations that could be held by teenagers will not be available because employers will find it unprofitable to pay the minimum wage. Various studies done by economists in universities and in the Labor Department support this view, showing that teenage unemployment rates are remarkably low or virtually nonexistent in many industrial countries which have no minimum-wage laws.

3. *Advances in technology.* Accelerations in science and technology have been occurring at particularly rapid rates since the early 1960s. As a result, increasing proportions of unskilled and untrained workers have been permanently displaced, thereby aggravating the problem of structural unemployment. This trend will continue unless methods are developed—through manpower-training programs, subsidies, tax incentives, and other devices—to absorb the displaced workers in new jobs. We shall have more to say about this problem in later chapters.

These are among the major factors contributing to a rising level of "normal" unemployment. But what are the costs to society of unemployment beyond this level—that is, of involuntary unemployment? There are two—an economic cost and a social cost:

1. The economic cost is the output that society forgoes and never gets back. It consists of all the consumer goods and capital goods that would be produced if there were full employment of all resources, as well as the deterioration of human capital resulting from loss of skills. Even at very low unemployment rates, the value of forgone output may amount to many billions of dollars.

2. The social cost includes not only the economic cost, but also the human misery, deprivation, and social and political unrest brought on by large-scale unemployment. Social cost is usually more difficult to measure than economic cost, but it is nevertheless a matter of deep and general concern. Further, it is a cost which is higher for some groups than for others — see Exhibit 4 on the next page.

Inflation

What is it that hits the consumer's pocketbook by eroding the purchasing power of the dollar, sometimes acts as a hidden tax, reduces a nation's competitiveness in world markets, and can have a general debilitating effect on almost all types of economic activity? The answer is, inflation.

Inflation is a rise in the general price level (or average level of prices) of all goods and services. The general price level thus varies inversely with the purchasing power of a unit of money (such as the dollar). For example, if prices double, purchasing power decreases by one-half; if prices halve, purchasing power doubles. Therefore, inflation is also a reduction in the purchasing power of a unit of money.

Exhibit 4

How meaningful is it to talk about an "average" unemployment rate? Equally important is the distribution of unemployment rates by age, sex, race, and occupational *categories. A desirable "average" of 3 to 4 percent for all workers may actually be hiding much higher rates among some groups.*

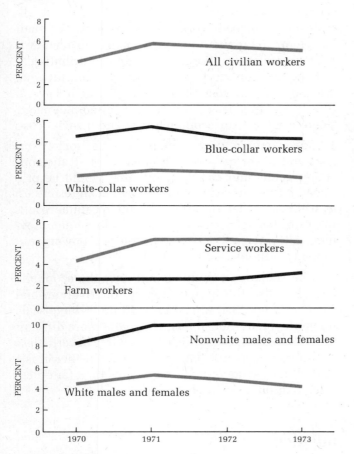

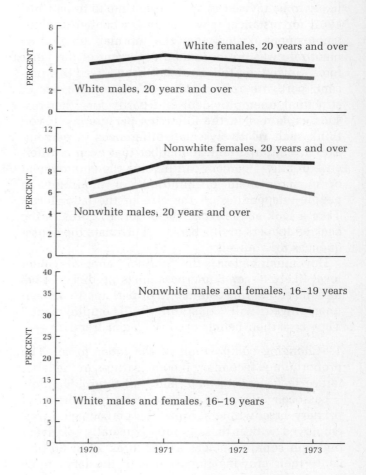

SOURCE: U.S. Department of Labor.

The opposite of inflation is *deflation*. Can you formulate your own definition? (Be careful not to confuse its meaning here with that of deflating a time series, as described in a previous chapter.)

Does inflation mean that all prices rise? Clearly not. In almost any inflation some prices rise, some are fairly constant, and some even fall. However, the "average" level of prices—the so-called *general price level*—rises.

TYPES OF INFLATION: IS THE UNITED STATES INFLATION-PRONE?

Different explanations for inflation have been given from time to time—both in this country and abroad. Here are the more common types you are likely to encounter in the news media and should know something about. Note that some of them may be overlapping in their causes and effects.

Demand-pull Inflation

The traditional type of inflation, known as *demand-pull inflation*, takes place when aggregate demand is rising while the available supply of goods is becoming increasingly limited. Goods may be in short supply because resources are fully utilized or because production cannot be increased rapidly enough to meet the growing demand. As a result, the general level of prices begins to rise in response to a situation sometimes described as "too much money chasing too few goods."

This is the meaning behind the model in Exhibit 5. It assumes a time period in which the stock of resources and their productivity are constant. Consequently, so long as there are excess resources, as total demand rises from a depressed level, producers can increase the output of goods without raising prices. This is the noninflationary phase. As the economy comes closer to utilizing all its available labor and other productive factors, the inflationary phase begins. Less efficient resources are brought

---

Exhibit 5

The General Price Level and Inflation

Increases in aggregate demand or total spending may result in moderate increases in the general price level as full employment is approached. Thereafter further increases in total spending result in pure or hyperinflation as the general price level rises without any increases in output. (NOTE: *This does not mean that hyperinflation is synonymous with full employment. The underlying conditions of each are vastly different—as explained in the text.*)

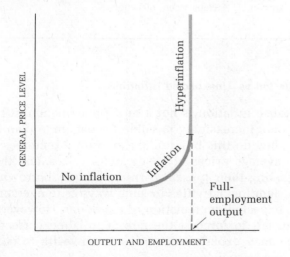

---

into use, some inputs become substantially scarcer than others, labor markets become tighter thereby strengthening the bargaining position of unions and exerting upward pressure on wages, and business firms find it easier to raise prices and also to pass on wage increases to buyers. Output and employment thus reach a point where further increases in aggregate demand cause more than proportional increases in the general price level. Once the full-employment level of labor and other resources is attained, additional increases in output are no longer possible during the given period. Any further rise in aggregate demand, therefore, drives the economy into a hyperinflationary phase characterized by spiraling prices as producers bid against each other for the same fixed supply of resources.

Cost-push (Market-power) Inflation

A second type of inflation, *cost-push inflation*, occurs when prices increase because factor payments to one or more groups of resource owners rise faster than productivity or efficiency. There are two typical forms of cost-push inflation: "wage-push" and "profit-push." The former occurs when strong labor unions manage to force wage increases in excess of productivity gains. This raises unit costs of production and exerts pressure on sellers to increase prices in order to maintain profit margins. Profit-push inflation occurs when sellers try to increase their profit margins by raising prices—rather than by reducing costs through improved efficiency. Rising prices prompt workers and other factor owners to "catch up" by seeking higher resource payments, thereby increasing unit costs of production and giving inflation a further push.

Cost-push inflation is usually attributed to monopolistic market power. For example, it is often contended that some unions are strong enough to impose wage increases on employers, and some business firms are large enough to "administer" the prices they charge. "Market power" thus refers to the effective degree of discretion which unions and firms have to set wages and prices. This power depends to some extent on the general level of unemployment. In periods of prosperity when unemployment is low, both unions and businesses have wider discretionary power—unions because of their stronger bargaining position and businesses because of the greater insensitivity of buyers to price increases. On the other hand, in periods of recession when unemployment is high, the opposite situation tends to prevail. Discretionary powers of unions and businesses are weaker because there is a larger pool of unemployed labor and because buyers are likely to be more price-conscious. Of course, the extent of market power is influenced by other conditions—institutional, social, and psychological—as a result of which there can be inflationary price rises in recession periods when unemployment is substantial. In later chapters we try to disentangle these contributing factors.

Structural Inflation, Creeping Inflation, and Hyperinflation

Demand-pull and cost-push inflation are the fundamental types of inflation. Any other kinds of inflation that you may read or hear about in the news media are simply different aspects of these basic forms. The ones that are most often mentioned are structural inflation, creeping inflation, and hyperinflation. On the basis of what you have already learned, can you formulate definitions of these terms? An explanation is given in the Dictionary at the back of the book.

The rate of inflation in the United States has varied, due at one time or another to both demand-pull and cost-push factors. These forces have been at work in different degrees—especially in a high-employment economy—thus suggesting that the United States is inflation-prone or that it has a built-in inflationary bias. Some of the implications of this will be examined shortly.

WHO SUFFERS FROM INFLATION? WHO BENEFITS?

As you can see from Exhibit 6, the long-run trend of prices has been upward. Should we conclude from this that inflation is a burden on all of us? Not necessarily. The effects of inflation are not distributed equally; some people may suffer from it, but others actually benefit.

To see why this is so, we must understand the difference between two kinds of income: *money income*, which is the amount of money received for work done, and *real income*, the purchasing power of money income as measured by the quantity of goods and services that it can buy. Clearly, your money income may be quite different from your real income, since the latter is determined not only by your money income, but also by the prices of the commodities you buy.

Exhibit 6

Price Indexes
1967 = 100

The Consumer Price Index and the Wholesale Price Index, prepared by the U.S. Department of Labor, are the most widely used measures of inflationary price trends in our economy.

SOURCE: U.S. Department of Labor.

Expected vs. Unexpected Inflation

Because inflation is not a new phenomenon, it has become increasingly possible for people to plan for it. They do this by *anticipating* future increases in the average prices of goods and services, and then adjusting their *present* earning, buying, borrowing, and lending activities in such ways as to overcome the expected depreciation of the dollar. However, if they fail to forecast the rate of inflation correctly, they may experience a transfer of wealth to other groups in society.

As an illustration, suppose you lend a friend $100 for one year. If you expected the general price level to remain stable, and if you wanted to earn a real return (in terms of constant purchasing power) of 5 percent, you would charge him 5 percent interest on the loan. Assume, however, that you expect the average level of prices to rise by 10 percent. In that case, you should charge him about 15 percent interest on the loan—of which 5 percent represents a real return, and 10 percent represents compensation for your loss in purchasing power.

Suppose a year elapses and your friend pays you what he owes you, but the rise in prices has been greater than you anticipated. Are you better or worse off? Obviously, the repaid loan plus interest has not provided full compensation for your decreased purchasing power. Hence your change in real wealth is less than you anticipated—a loss from inflation. Your friend, on the other hand, has repaid the loan in terms of less purchasing power than he originally borrowed. Hence he has experienced an increase in wealth—a gain from inflation. On the whole, therefore, there has been a redistribution of wealth—in this case from you to your friend—because of your failure to make a full adjustment to inflation. In general:

People who do not predict inflation correctly are unable to adjust their economic behavior to compensate for it. As a result, some people experience gains while others experience losses. The net outcome is a redistribution of wealth between debtors and creditors.

See Box 1 for an example of calculating gains and losses from unanticipated inflation.

Redistributive Effects

What, then, is wrong with unanticipated inflation? One of the chief criticisms is that it redistributes wealth arbitrarily—that is, in a manner which may not always accord with society's goals. This can be explained in terms of the net monetary financial position of the economy's three major sectors.

1. The public sector—in particular the federal government—has had a rising public debt since World War II (as you can see from the back endpapers of this book). It is by far the largest net monetary debtor in our economy and, therefore, benefits from unanticipated inflation. Since government belongs to all of us, the gains that accrue to it are passed along

to everyone. *But the distributions are not equal.* As an earlier chapter showed, your income, wealth, age, occupation, or certain other factors can affect the various forms of benefits you receive from government—including subsidies, financial aids, and even the "benefit" of reducing your taxes through legal loopholes.

2. The nonfinancial business sector of the economy (i.e., the business sector, excluding banks, insurance companies, etc.) is also a net monetary debtor, but on a much smaller scale than the public sector. Therefore, the owners (stockholders) of those firms that are net monetary debtors are the ultimate beneficiaries of unanticipated inflation.

3. The household sector is the economy's largest net monetary creditor, because it is the ultimate source of most of the funds borrowed by the public and private sectors. Consequently, those households which are net monetary creditors suffer from unanticipated inflation.

In general, therefore:

Both the business and household sectors contain net monetary debtor and creditor units. As a result, unexpected price-level changes cause a redistribution of wealth among these units by taking from some and giving to others—not on the basis of income levels, number of dependents, or other socially accepted economic criteria—but haphazardly and inequitably in a manner unrelated to society's objectives.

It should be noted that inflation may also have adverse consequences in the foreign sector of the economy. If prices and costs rise faster in this country than abroad, our productive capacity and ability to compete in world markets are impaired. This may cause a decrease in exports, an increase in imports, and a decline in the levels of production and employment. It may also create international economic problems of major significance—as it has for a number of countries. These problems are somewhat complex and are examined at later points in the book.

Conclusion: The Need for Price Stability

Economists today place great emphasis on the distinction between anticipated and unanticipated inflation. This is because unanticipated inflation has two major effects:

Box 1

Calculating Gains and Losses

The *ways in which an unanticipated inflation redistributes wealth can best be illustrated in terms of the changes it produces in assets, liabilities, and net worth. For any economic entity such as an individual, household, or firm,* assets *are things of value which it owns—cash, property, and the rights to property;* liabilities *are monetary debts or things of value which it owes to creditors; and* net worth *is the difference between its assets and liabilities. The financial statement on which these three classes of data are grouped together for analysis and interpretation is called a* balance sheet.

Take your own balance sheet as an example. Assume your assets consist of $100 in cash and a used car worth $1,000 which you just acquired by incurring a debt, that is, signing a promissory note, for that amount. Since you owe more money than is owed to you, you are a net debtor. Your balance sheet before an unanticipated inflation looks like this:

DEBTOR'S BALANCE SHEET 1
Market Value Before an Unanticipated Inflation

Assets		Liabilities and Net Worth	
Cash	$ 100	Note payable	$1,000
Car	1,000	Net Worth	100
	$1,100		$1,100

If a 10 percent inflation occurs, other things remaining the same, your cash holdings and note payable do not change, but the market value of your car increases to $1,100, that is proportionately with the price level. Therefore your net worth in current dollars rises to $200:

DEBTOR'S BALANCE SHEET 2
Market Value After a 10 Percent Unanticipated Inflation

Assets		Liabilities and Net Worth	
Cash	$ 100	Note payable	$1,000
Car	1,100	Net Worth	200
	$1,200		$1,200

To find your new net worth in terms of preinflation or constant dollars, simply divide net worth in current dollars by the appropriate price index, which is the ratio of the new price level to the old one:

$$\text{Net Worth in preinflation dollars} = \frac{\$200}{1.10} = \$181.82$$

The gain in your net worth, in terms of constant purchasing power, is $81.82. Where did the gain come from? It came from the wealth of the creditor who lent you $1,000 to finance the purchase of your car, but who failed to anticipate that prices would rise by 10 percent. If the creditor had correctly foreseen the increase in prices at the time of granting the loan, he would have required you to repay the loan more quickly or to pay him a higher interest rate in order to offset his loss from inflation.

Losses experienced by the creditor can be seen most clearly by comparing his balance sheets before and after the unanticipated inflation. To begin with, assume he possesses $100 in cash, has no debt, and holds your promissory note for $1,000. His net worth, therefore, is $1,100:

---

1. It creates general economic instability.
2. It results in individual inequities and costs—inequities in terms of the distribution of wealth, and costs in terms of the efforts that people must put forth to anticipate and adjust their asset and liability holdings to it.

Hence a major goal of society is to achieve price stability—that is, the avoidance of substantial inflationary or deflationary price movements—in order to encourage continuous full employment and a steady high level of economic activity.

The term "price stability" has much deeper meanings than this brief statement suggests. Some later chapters are devoted to analyzing its implications and to discussing the problems of achieving it.

HOW MUCH INFLATION? HOW MUCH UNEMPLOYMENT?

Can mixed economies maintain full employment *without* inflation? Many economists, political leaders, and other informed observers have been

CREDITOR'S BALANCE SHEET 1

Market Value Before an Unanticipated Inflation

Assets		Liabilities and Net Worth	
Cash	$ 100	Debt	$ 0
Note receivable	1,000	Net Worth	1,100
	$1,100		$1,100

After a 10 percent inflation, his balance sheet remains unchanged:

CREDITOR'S BALANCE SHEET 2

Market Value After a 10 Percent Unanticipated Inflation

Assets		Liabilities and Net Worth	
Cash	$ 100	Debt	$ 0
Note receivable	1,000	Net Worth	1,100
	$1,100		$1,100

The balance sheet remained the same because the creditor's assets consisted entirely of monetary assets or fixed-money claims which are unaffected by inflation or deflation. (Examples of monetary assets are bonds, accounts receivable, savings deposits, promissory notes, and cash.) These claims are distinguished from real assets (houses, cars, and most other commodities) whose money values are influenced by changes in the price level. Monetary liabilities and real liabilities can be defined in precisely analogous ways. Since the creditor held no real assets, his net worth or equity did not increase. Moreover, in terms of preinflation dollars, his net worth of $1,100 declined in purchasing power to $1,000 as a result of the 10 percent rise in prices:

$$\text{Net Worth in preinflation dollars} = \frac{\$1,100}{1.10} = \$1,000$$

The creditor has thus lost $100 to you, the borrower. But this is not all. He has also lost an additional $10 in purchasing power as a result of holding $100 in cash.

Can we infer from these examples that you will always benefit from unexpected price increases? Not necessarily. The chances of gaining or losing depend on whether you are a net monetary debtor or a net monetary creditor. If the former, your monetary liabilities exceed your monetary assets—you owe more money to others than is owed to you; hence you benefit from unanticipated inflation. If the latter, the reverse is true: your monetary assets exceed your monetary liabilities; therefore, you suffer from unanticipated inflation. As a result:

It cannot be stated categorically, as is often done, that people (such as government employees, white-collar workers, or teachers) whose money incomes do not rise as fast as prices, suffer from inflation because their real incomes decline. Most families hold both monetary and real assets as well as monetary and real liabilities—and it is the relative composition of these holdings that determines whether their real wealth (wealth in terms of constant purchasing power) expands or contracts during an unanticipated inflation.

In short, you must know the net monetary status of an economic group, not just its income, before you can tell how inflation will affect it. Interestingly enough, studies done since the 1960s have concluded that no single occupational group—farmers, workers, professionals, and so on—suffers a change in net monetary status because of rising prices. Only the elderly retired, living on fixed incomes such as old-age benefits and pensions, are hurt by unanticipated inflations. And even the significance of this finding is declining in relative importance as government continues to raise social security payments and other benefits in an effort to compensate for rising living costs.

concerned with this question since the late 1950s. In that period, an economist at the University of London—Professor A. W. Phillips—derived a relationship between unemployment and inflation of the type shown in Exhibit 7 on the next page.

A *Phillips* curve represents a tradeoff between unemployment and inflation. Every point along the curve denotes a different combination of unemployment and inflation, and a movement along the curve measures the reduction in one of these at the expense of a gain in the other.

Economists have confirmed the existence of a tradeoff between unemployment and inflation in virtually all advanced capitalistic economies. They agree it is possible to reduce unemployment through increased government spending, if necessary, as is shown in later chapters. But the consequences are likely to be inflationary, as evidenced by some Western European countries that have often maintained lower rates of unemployment—but higher rates of inflation—than has the United States.

For example, in the United States until the late

Exhibit 7

A Curve Named Phillips

The tradeoff between unemployment and inflation for the U.S. economy is reflected by the fact that along a given curve, a reduction in the unemployment rate involves an increase in the inflation rate. Particularly disturbing is the shift of the curve to a higher level—thus increasing the tradeoff and posing serious problems of public policy. (NOTE: These curves represent average relationships for the periods shown. Therefore, they may not express the actual relationship for any specific year.)

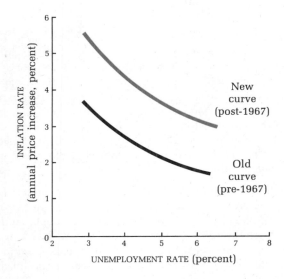

under more competitive conditions. If that is the case, one nonmarket solution would be the imposition of a permanent system of wage and price controls. (What is meant by a "nonmarket" solution? Can you suggest any "market" solutions?)

A second explanation is that the Phillips curve has shifted outward because of the changed composition of the labor force: the proportion of teenagers and women has increased, and "structural unemployment" among the unskilled and those whose skills are obsolete has risen. Both of these factors have been responsible for enlarging the pool of unemployed.

A number of measures have been proposed—and some have been adopted—to shift the Phillips curve inward toward its older position, thereby reducing the unemployment-inflation tradeoff. Among the measures are retraining programs, counseling services, subsidies to finance employee-relocation expenses, and tax credits to businesses that hire the hard-core unemployed. But the difficulties of achieving the desired objectives are considerable, as the next several chapters show.

1960s, according to Exhibit 7, an unemployment rate of 5 percent corresponded to an inflation rate of 2 percent. But the curve has shifted dramatically outward since then, as a result of which an unemployment rate of 5 percent now entails a higher inflation rate. (How much?) Similar comparisons can be made for other rates of unemployment and inflation. In all cases, the inflation rate corresponding to a given unemployment rate is greater on the new curve than the old.

Why has the curve shifted outward? Two explanations may be given:

First, some scholars argue that the economy has become more monopolistic. As a result, big business and big labor have the market power to raise prices and wages to a greater extent than if they operated

SUMMARY OF IMPORTANT IDEAS

1. Capitalistic economies suffer from recurrent but nonperiodic fluctuations in economic activity known as business cycles. The four phases of cycles are prosperity, recession, depression, and recovery.

2. Industries in the economy react to business cycles in different ways. Durable goods industries tend to be less competitive than nondurable goods industries, and therefore experience relatively wide fluctuations in output. The opposite situation tends to occur in nondurable goods industries: prices fluctuate relatively more than output and employment.

3. If economists can learn how to forecast business cycles, they will be in a better position to recommend government policies for avoiding downturns in economic activity. Today the most scientific methods of business-cycle forecasting involve the use of surveys and opinion polling, econometric models, and economic indicators.

4. The rate of unemployment is expressed as a percentage of the labor force. Until 1962, a jobless rate of 3 percent was generally regarded as constituting "full" employment. Since then the figure has been raised to 4 percent. It may continue to rise in future

years due to (a) the changing composition of the labor force, (b) a rising level of minimum-wage rates, and (c) advances in technology.

5. Inflation is a rise in the general price level or a reduction in the purchasing power of a unit of money. Inflations are commonly attributed to demand-pull or cost-push forces. Although there is widespread agreement on the former as a cause of inflation, there is much disagreement over the latter. In general, inflation tends to redistribute wealth haphazardly without regard to social goals. It may also impair a nation's efficiency and competitiveness in world markets.

6. There is considerable evidence that virtually all mixed economies, including our own, have an "inflationary bias"—that is, they are inflation-prone. A desirable social objective, therefore, is to maintain a constant rather than erratic rate of inflation. This enables people to anticipate and adjust to rising prices by altering their asset and liability holdings, thereby minimizing adverse redistributive effects.

7. A Phillips curve expresses a tradeoff between unemployment and inflation. The curve has shifted outward to the right over the long run, thus increasing the tradeoff. Among the reasons advanced for this are (a) increased monopolistic power by some large firms and unions and (b) changed composition of the labor force. In view of its implications, some of today's most important government policies are concerned with shifting the curve inward to the left.

FOR DISCUSSION

1. *Terms and concepts to review:*

business cycles	cyclical unemploy-
seasonal fluctuations	ment
trend	structural unemploy-
time series	ment
prosperity	hard-core unemployed
recession	involuntary unemploy-
depression	ment
recovery	inflation
econometrics	general price level
economic indicators	demand-pull inflation
leading indicators	cost-push inflation
labor force	money income
frictional unemploy-	real income
ment	Phillips curve

2. If business cycles were recurrent and periodic, would they be easily predictable? Why? What, precisely, would you be able to predict about them?

3. If you were to compare two industries, automobiles and agricultural products, over the course of a business cycle, which would be more stable with respect to (a) output and employment; (b) prices? Explain why.

4. Economists prefer to remove both the seasonal and long-term trend influences from their data before undertaking an analysis of cyclical forces. Although there are no unusual controversies concerning removal of the seasonal factor, there is considerable disagreement over removal of the trend. Can you suggest why?

5. Can you suggest how the interaction of changes in consumption and investment may cause business cycles?

6. What do you suppose are some of the chief difficulties in using leading indicators for forecasting purposes?

7. Is an increasing level of aggregate demand likely to cure the problems of cyclical unemployment and structural unemployment—without inflation? Explain.

8. Is it better to have full employment with mild inflation or moderate unemployment with no inflation? Explain.

9. "Because of the changing composition of the labor force, a single measure of full employment proves to be an inadequate goal." In view of this statement, what alternatives can you suggest? Discuss.

10. It is often said that our economy has a built-in inflationary bias and is inflation-prone. Can you give reasons to account for this statement?

11. Minimum-wage legislation, despite its good intention, has been called "the most anti-Negro law on the books"? Can you explain why? Can you show, with supply and demand curves, how minimum-wage legislation results in unemployment? What market solution can you suggest to increase employment among low-skilled members of the labor force?

12. Examine the following financial data for Mr. Johnson:

Wages	$20,000 per year
Savings deposit	500

Interest income, monthly   20
House   40,000
Annual property taxes   300
Mortgage   40,000
Insurance payments   200 per month

(a) Construct a balance sheet based on current market values. How much is his net worth?
(b) Is he a net monetary debtor or a net monetary creditor? Explain.
(c) What is the effect on his balance sheet if the price level doubles? Illustrate.
(d) How much is his new net worth in preinflation dollars? Has he had a real change in net worth? Explain.

13. Examine the following financial data for Mr. Smith:

Cash $ 500
Charitable contributions   1,000 per year
Monthly salary   2,000
Mortgage held   40,000
Commissions, annual
  average   800
Interest received   500 per month
Property taxes   400 per year

(a) Construct a balance sheet based on current market values.

(b) Is he a net monetary debtor or creditor? Explain.
(c) What is the effect on his balance sheet if the price level doubles? Illustrate.
(d) How much is his new net worth in pre-inflation dollars? Has he had a real change in net worth? Explain.

14. A bond is a claim to a fixed amount of money at some future date. In view of this, why do the selling prices of most bonds fluctuate?

15. Identify each of the following as a monetary asset, monetary liability, real asset, or real liability *to its owner*: (a) corporation bond, (b) share of stock, (c) washing machine, (d) inventory, (e) savings deposit, (f) life insurance, (g) mortgage (to the homeowner), (h) apartment lease (to the tenant).

16. Look up the meanings of such terms as balance sheet, assets, liabilities, and net worth in the Dictionary at the back of the book. Then answer the questions below based on the following balance sheet.

(a) Will the corporation benefit or suffer from an unanticipated inflation? Explain.
(b) The common stock is valued in the balance sheet at $10 per share. Its current market value is $25 per share. If you buy the stock, what will be your net monetary status per share for the shares purchased?

XYZ CORPORATION
Balance Sheet, Dec. 31, 19—

Assets		Liabilities and Net Worth		
Cash	$ 75,000	Liabilities		
Bonds	125,000	Accounts payable	$100,000	
Accounts receivable	300,000	Notes payable	50,000	
Inventory	150,000	Accrued expenses		
Plant and equipment	200,000	payable	25,000	
Land	50,000	Bonds payable	25,000	
Goodwill, patents, trademarks	100,000	Taxes	100,000	
				$300,000
		Net Worth		
		Common stock	$400,000	
		Retained earnings	300,000	
				$700,000
	$1,000,000			$1,000,000

Borrow Cheap; Lend Dear

The Irish have a story about inflation, borrowing, and lending, as they have about most things. One Monday morning, on a construction site in Dublin, Mike asks Pat for the loan of two quid until payday. "Ah sure," says Pat handing over two creased and dirty pound notes, "but I'll be needing it on Friday, with a little bit on top." Mike looks at him and shakes his head sadly. "Pat, Pat, you were never like this before, charging interest to an old friend." Pat sticks his spade in the ground and says scornfully: "Oh, ye're an ignorant divil, you are. Interest be damned. The price of beer is going up twopence a pint on Thursday, and here you are proposing to pay me back on Friday. On Friday I'll be thirsty, and I want the same number of pints I could have bought tonight for two quid."

It's very doubtful that Pat had ever studied the complex interaction between interest rates and the rate of inflation; but he had a feel for it, measured in pints of Guinness. In short, he was telling Mike that he wanted his money back with enough on top to ensure that he could buy on Friday the satisfactions he had forgone on Monday by making the loan. That is also the view of every sophisticated lender of money. But, except in the case of a personal private loan, such as the one made by Pat to Mike, the calculations are complicated by taxes. In the United States, the lender must pay taxes on the interest he receives from a borrower; whereas the borrower can deduct interest payments from his taxable income.

An Illustrative Case

The best way to look at the impact of inflation on returns to lenders and costs to borrowers is to focus on a hypothetical case.

Dr. L. is a psychiatrist and like many of his colleagues and neighbors, he has money to spare. Dr. L. lends a friend $1,000 and charges interest at the rate

of 10 percent, payable annually. "A fine friend," snorts the borrower, Mr. B. But what Mr. B forgets are Dr. L's tax bracket and the current rate of inflation. At the end of the year, to be sure, Dr. L. receives his $1,000 back plus $100 in interest from Mr. B. But Dr. L. pays taxes at the rate of 40 percent. This means that his $100 of interest income from Mr. B. immediately dwindles to $60. Further, the annual rate of inflation is 5 percent. This means that at the end of the year it takes $1,050 to purchase what $1,000 bought at the time the loan was made. Result: Table 1 shows that a combination of taxation and inflation has reduced Dr. L's true rate of return from a theoretical 10 percent to 0.95 percent. (Remember the $10 left over after taxes and inflation is also worth only 95 percent of what it was a year ago.) If Dr. L's real rate of return after taxes and inflation is only 0.95%, what are the real costs to Mr. B. of the loan?

Table 1
LENDER'S REAL RETURNS FOR VARIOUS INFLATION, LENDING, AND TAX RATES*

Tax rate (%)	Inflation rate					
	3 percent			5 percent		
	Lending rate (%)			Lending rate (%)		
	6	8	10	6	8	10
0	2.91	4.85	6.80	0.95	2.86	4.76
20	1.75	3.30	4.85	−0.19	1.33	2.86
30	1.17	2.52	3.88	−0.76	0.57	1.90
40	0.58	1.75	2.91	−1.33	−0.19	0.95
50	0.00	0.97	1.94	−1.90	−0.95	0.00
60	−0.58	0.19	0.97	−2.48	−1.71	−0.95
70	−1.17	−0.58	0.00	−3.05	−2.48	−1.90

* Assumes interest paid annually.

Inflation and U.S. tax laws have worked to Mr. B's advantage. He has, in effect, borrowed $1,050 for a year for only $50—equivalent to a true interest rate of only 4.76 percent. (See Table 2.) This hypothetical case assumes a single inflation rate, single interest rate, and

Table 2
BORROWER'S REAL COSTS FOR VARIOUS INFLATION AND LENDING RATES

Lending rate (%)	Inflation rate	
	3 (%)	5 (%)
6	2.92	0.95
8	4.86	2.86
10	6.80	4.76

single tax rate. But similar effects on lenders and borrowers occur even if the rates vary. Table 1 provides some permutations. The general conclusion is that *reduction of the borrower's real cost by inflation is less drastic than reduction of the lender's real return.* That conclusion can be supported by looking at recent inflation, interest, and tax rates. With inflation running at 5 percent, the owner of a bond providing 8 percent interest returns *less than nothing* net to a taxpayer in the 40 percent bracket. For a taxpayer in the 20 percent bracket, 6 percent from a savings and loan account is also less than nothing—that is, a reduction in net assets—in an era of 5 percent inflation.

Why Save?

Strangely, people continue to put their money into "investments" that actually depreciate over a period, thanks to a combination of inflation and tax rates. Why do they? Why, indeed, do people persist in believing that savings equal thrift when all the evidence shows that the policy is spendthrift? No single answer covers all people. But various studies show that an overwhelming majority of people—unlike Irish Pat— are unwilling or unable to make the complicated calculations that would prove the foolishness of their monetary policies. Other studies show that some savers and investors who are aware of the eroding effects of inflation and taxation still prefer to build a cushion of cash—even if it diminishes in buying power. An economist who specializes in behavioral studies puts it this way: "Some people have a psychological need for money in reserve. They would rather have 90 percent of something saved than 100 percent of nothing. Reason might dictate their borrowing instead of saving; their desire for security dictates the opposite."

Coping with Inflation

But what should the sophisticated personal investor do? Precisely what most of them are doing now—putting part of their surplus cash into so-called tax and inflation shelters. These are investments such as land, antiques, and paintings, that appreciate in value about as fast as the buying power of money falls—and if the laws of demand and supply are any guide, may appreciate a good deal faster, for the simple reason that supply is limited or even fixed. To be sure, the person who buys land or art needs a knowledgeable eye; but so does the buyer of corporate stocks. In fact, however, the people who have lost $1 million on Wall Street in the past decade probably could not be accommodated in the Houston Astrodome. Those who have lost $1 million or more in land and art investments on the other hand, almost certainly would not overcrowd a Boeing 747.

QUESTIONS

1. Why do individuals persist in making funds available (through savings accounts, saving bonds, life insurance, and other instruments) at rates that yield negative real after-tax returns?

2. What would be the probable reaction of banks, insurance companies, savings and loan associations and labor unions if inflation continued at a high rate?

CHAPTER 10

Consumption, Saving, and Investment: Elements of the Theory of Income and Employment

CHAPTER PREVIEW

Can a predominantly market or capitalistic economy such as ours achieve and maintain *full employment* of its resources?

How did the classical theory of the pre-1930s answer this question?

The modern theory of income and employment is built on such fundamental concepts as consumption, saving, and investment. What do these terms mean? What relationships do they involve?

In every era there is often a tendency for one economic question to dominate all others. In the 1930s it was the overcoming of depression. In the late 1940s and early 1950s it was the prevention of a new depression as the economy converted from war to peace. Since the mid-1950s the dominant question has been whether America's mixed economy can achieve and maintain full employment of all its resources without suffering inflation.

Now that we have examined the record of business cycles in the United States and the associated problems of unemployment and inflation, we must turn to a body of principles known as "the theory of income and employment." This theory is built on the associated phenomena of consumption, saving, and investment. Each plays a distinctive role in the economy; acting in combination they help to determine the social and economic course of history.

In this and following chapters we shall examine each phenomenon separately, and then show how they interact, how they can be controlled—and how economists rightly identify them as the foundations on which much of modern economic policy is built.

The Classical Theory of Income and Employment

You have probably heard about the "old" mathematics and the "new" mathematics, but did you know that there is an "old" economics and a "new" economics?

The "old" economics—or classical economics—started mainly with Adam Smith and grew until by the 1930s it was the predominant body of economic theory in the non-Communist world. The *New Economics*—or modern economics—started with a British scholar, John Maynard Keynes (pronounced "canes"), in the late 1930s. Since then it has been refined and modified, and its basic analytical tools and methods are now widely used by practically all economists.

But in the social sciences, great theories, like the phenomena they try to describe, rarely remain constant. Today's modern economic ideas represent a broad synthesis of the best thinking from the "old" and the "new" economics, as the following pages and chapters point out.

SAY'S LAW: "SUPPLY CREATES ITS OWN DEMAND"

In the early nineteenth century, a French economist, Jean Baptiste Say, wrote:

> . . . a product is no sooner created than it, from that instant, offers a market for other products to the full extent of its own value. . . . Thus, the mere circumstance of the creation of one product immediately opens a market for other products.

This conclusion has come to be known as *Say's Law*. But the idea has been expressed more pointedly by David Ricardo, a British contemporary of Say and one of the great pioneers in economic thought:

> No man produces but with a view to consume or sell, and he never sells but with an intention to purchase some other commodity which may be immediately useful to him or which may contribute to future production. By producing, then, he necessarily becomes either the consumer of his own goods, or the purchaser and consumer of the goods of some other person.

Say's Law—whether expressed in its original form by Say or in its more precise form by Ricardo—amounts to saying that *supply creates its own demand*. This occurs because in a specialized or exchange economy, as distinct from a self-sufficient, "Robinson Crusoe" economy, each person works at the occupation in which he is relatively most efficient and exchanges the surplus of what he produces above his own needs for the products of others. Thus the shoemaker, the butcher, and the baker acquire one another's wares by exchanging the portions of their outputs which they do not consume themselves. Expressed in monetary rather than barter terms, this means that the income a person receives from production is spent to purchase goods produced by others. For the economy as a whole, it means that aggregate demand equals aggregate supply, and any addition to output generates an equal addition to income.

It follows from Say's Law that:

Firms will always find it profitable to hire unemployed resources up to the point of full employment, provided the owners of unemployed resources are willing to be paid no more than their physical productivities justify. If this condition is granted, there can be no prolonged period of unemployment because workers and other resource suppliers will be receiving what they are "worth," and because the additional income earned from increased production will be spent on purchasing the additional output.

This viewpoint was central to classical economic thought of the nineteenth and early twentieth centuries, and is still held with varying degrees of conviction by some people today. In view of this, what does the classical model really tell us? What are its implications for our economic system?

ESSENTIALS OF THE CLASSICAL THEORY

The classical model assumes the operation of a free-enterprise, highly competitive economic system in which there are many buyers and sellers in both the product and resource markets, and in which all prices are flexible so that they can quickly adjust upward or downward to changing supplies and demands in the marketplace. In this type of economic system the output and resource markets will *automatically* adjust to full-employment levels as if guided by an "invisible hand" because:

Aggregate Demand = Aggregate Income or Output

We have learned that an economy's aggregate output equals its aggregate income. But the classicists argued that the purpose of earning income is to spend it on output. Hence the level of *aggregate demand*—which is the total value of output that all sectors of the economy are willing to purchase—always equals the level of aggregate income or output. This does not mean that oversupply of some particular items cannot occur. Overproduction of specific commodities can and does occur when businessmen misjudge the markets for their goods. But these errors are temporary and are corrected as entrepreneurs shift resources out of production of less profitable commodities into production of more profitable ones. Only *general* overproduction, or a deficiency in aggregate demand, is impossible according to the classical view.

But what if households choose to *save*—that is, not spend a certain proportion of their income on goods and services? Will these savings represent a withdrawal or "leakage" of funds from the income stream? Will aggregate demand then fall below ag-

Leaders in Economics

DAVID RICARDO

1772–1823

David Ricardo was born in England, the son of a broker on the London Stock Exchange. He received an early training in finance and prospered rapidly after going into business as a loan broker. While he was in his late twenties, Smith's book *The Wealth of Nations* stimulated his interest in economics and led him to become one of the great pioneers in economic thought.

In 1814 he retired from active business and turned his attention to research and scholarly contemplation. The result of this effort was the publication in 1817 of his famous *Principles of Political Economy and Taxation*. The book was an immediate success, and a school of Ricardian disciples formed within a few years. Ricardo's influence was pervasive and lasting: Ricardian economics became a synonym for classical political economy (or "classical economics" as we call it today). Fifty years were to pass before that influence waned.

Ricardo, like most other economists, was mainly concerned with the central problem of economics: the forces that determine the production of an economy's wealth and its distribution among the various classes of society. But he was not only a "pure" theorist, as were some of the other classical economists; he also made major policy recommendations concerning the dominant social and economic problems of his day.

For instance, in his writings on international trade, he demonstrated how England would be better off to import the food it needs from foreign countries and pay for those imports by exporting its manufactured goods. This provided the supporters of free trade with an admirable rationale for arguing in favor of repealing the English Corn Laws (tariffs) in order to lower the price of corn.

To Ricardo's analytical mind, the economy was like an elaborate watch with many interrelated parts. His task was to study this mechanism and to lay bare the laws that determine its behavior. Thus he formulated theories of value, rent, and wages which, though not entirely original, were for the first time stated completely, authoritatively, and systematically. Portions of these theories became the bases of many subsequent writings by later scholars, including Marx and Keynes.

Ricardo's scientific view of economics—or political

Historical Pictures Service, Chicago.

economy as it was known until the late nineteenth century—was expressed on October 9, 1820, in a letter addressed to his friend and colleague, the Reverend Thomas R. Malthus:

Political Economy you think is an enquiry into the nature and causes of wealth—I think it should be called an enquiry into the laws which determine the division of the produce of industry amongst the classes which occur in its formation. No law can be laid down respecting quantity, but a tolerably correct one can be laid down respecting proportions. Every day I am more satisfied that the former enquiry is vain and delusive, but the latter only the true objects of the science.

It is generally acknowledged by scholars that David Ricardo ranks not only as the greatest of the classical economists, but also as one of the most distinguished economists of all time.

gregate output or supply, resulting in excess production, increasing unemployment, and decreasing incomes? The classical economists' answer is no, because:

All Savings Are Invested

Say's Law tells us that total spending will always be high enough to maintain full employment. This means that even if some people save part of their income, there will always be other people—namely, businessmen—who will borrow those savings and pay a price for them called *interest*. They will then invest this borrowed money in capital goods in order to carry on profitable production. In classical theory, therefore, saving leads directly to spending—spending on capital or investment goods. And since aggregate income is always spent, a given level of aggregate income is spent partly for consumption and partly for investment.

What mechanism ensures equality between saving and investment at full employment? The classicist's answer was the interest rate, which they viewed as a reward for saving—a price which businesses pay households to persuade the latter to consume less in the present so that they can consume more at a later date. The equilibrium rate of interest is determined in a competitive money market where households' supply of savings interacts with businesses' demand for them as illustrated in Chart (a) of Exhibit 1. This model is based on the classical assumption that no household will save (and thereby forgo the pleasure of spending) unless it is offered interest in return, and no businessman will borrow (and thereby pay interest) unless he plans to invest. Therefore a flexible interest rate assures that every dollar saved by households will be borrowed and invested by businesses, thus *automatically* maintaining a full-employment level of aggregate spending.

But suppose some unemployment *did* develop, thus causing a decline in aggregate income or purchasing power. Would such a situation be more than temporary? The classicists answered no, because:

Prices and Wages Are Flexible

In classical theory, prices in *all* markets—the money market, the product markets, and the resource

---

Exhibit 1

Markets in the Classical Theory of Income and Employment

In the classical model, all markets are assumed to be competitive and all resources mobile. Hence, prices and quantities are flexible and adjust automatically to their full- *employment equilibrium levels through the free play of market forces.*

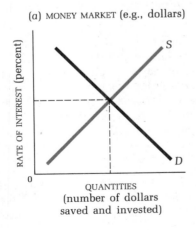

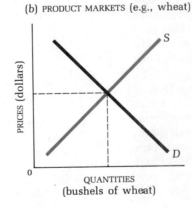

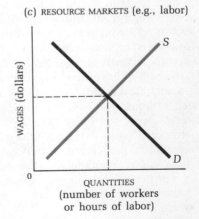

markets—are assumed to be flexible. Therefore, they *automatically* adjust to their individual full-employment equilibrium levels, as shown in Exhibit 1. Thus if the price in any market is below its particular equilibrium level, the quantity demanded will exceed the quantity supplied. Competition among buyers (demanders) in that market will therefore drive the price up. If the price in any market is above its equilibrium level, the quantity supplied will exceed the quantity demanded. Competition between sellers (suppliers) in that market will therefore drive the price down. At the equilibrium price in each market, the quantity that sellers want to sell is equal to the quantity that buyers want to buy. At these prices there are *no shortages* and *no surpluses* in any of the product, resource, or money markets; hence there must be full employment and full production throughout the economy.

Therefore, Capitalism Is a Self-regulating Economic System

In the classical economists' view it follows that a capitalistic economic system will tend *automatically* toward full employment through the free operation of the price system. Therefore the functions of government, as Adam Smith emphasized, should be limited to national defense, the administration of justice, the facilitation of commerce, and the provision of certain public works. Adherence to such a policy would establish laissez-faire as the watchword of capitalism. It would place government in an economically neutral position, leaving the economy to allocate its resources optimally as if guided by an "invisible hand."

To summarize:

Classical economics dominated the Western world from the late eighteenth century until the late 1930s. Among its chief proponents were Adam Smith (1723–1790), Jean Baptiste Say (1767–1832), and David Ricardo (1772–1823). It emphasized man's self-interest and the operation of universal economic laws which tend automatically to guide the economy toward full-employment equilibrium if the government adheres to a policy of laissez-faire or non-interventionism.

It would be a mistake to infer from the foregoing discussion that all economists of the pre-1930s presented a united classical front. In fact, many economists differed substantially, both philosophically and pragmatically. Some adhered to the classical tradition but advocated government spending programs as short-term measures to reduce unemployment. Others departed from the classical tradition by adopting socialistic ideologies. And still others turned to descriptive studies of the economy based on sociological and legal institutions. However, despite these dissentions from strict orthodox theory, the basic ideas of classicism represented the mainstream of economic thinking prior to the birth of the New Economics.

The Modern Theory of Income and Employment

The Great Depression of the 1930s was long and painful. At the bottom of the business cycle in 1933, unemployment in the United States reached almost 13 million, approximately 25 percent of the labor force. For the remainder of the decade it never recovered beyond 8 million, or 14 percent of the labor force. Comparable rates of unemployment existed in the United Kingdom during this period. Since such a prolonged and deep depression was contrary to classical thinking, many economists were inclined to explain the situation away by saying it was the "world" and not the theory that was at fault. One of the most distinguished classicists of that era, Professor Arthur C. Pigou of England's Cambridge University, in a famous book entitled *The Theory of Unemployment* (1933), wrote:

> With perfectly free competition . . . there will always be a strong tendency toward full employment. The implication is that such unemployment as exists at any time is due wholly to the fact that frictional resistances [caused by monopolistic unions and firms maintaining rigid wages and prices] prevent the appropriate wage [and price] adjustments from being made instantaneously.

A flexible wage and price policy, Pigou and other classical economists contended, would "abolish fluctuations of employment" entirely. In America, many orthodox economists added the proviso that the government under President Roosevelt's administration should also stop interfering with the free operation of the markets through its extensive regulatory legislation and activities.

Thus the classicists strongly adhered to the position that the system *automatically* tends toward full-employment equilibrium, and that frictional maladjustments alone are responsible for temporary short-run fluctuations. In response to this general view—and to Professor Pigou's book in particular—the eminent British scholar John Maynard Keynes published in 1936 his monumental treatise, *The General Theory of Employment, Interest and Money*, in which he undermined the classical theory and founded what has come to be called the New Economics.

KEYNES AND THE MODERN THEORY

The modern theory of income and employment (i.e., modern macroeconomic theory) is rooted in the work done by Keynes—but the theory has been greatly refined and extended since then. Today most of the major controversial economic issues you read and hear about—taxes, inflation, national debt, employment, balance of payments, interest rates, and so on—are analyzed within the framework of modern income and employment theory. The remainder of this chapter deals with the elements of this theory; subsequent chapters will build on these elements.

How does the modern theory of income and employment contrast with the classical theory?

Aggregate Demand May Not Equal
Full-employment Aggregate Income

Modern theory rejects the notion that aggregate demand always equals full-employment aggregate income, and that the economic system automatically tends toward its full-employment equilibrium level. Modern theory demonstrates that the economic system may be in equilibrium at less than full employment, and may remain so indefinitely.

Changes in aggregate demand play a critical role in the modern theory. An economy may be operating at a level equal to or below full employment, and may experience a drop in aggregate demand and a consequent decline in real output and resource use. On the other hand, an economy may be operating at a level below full employment and may experience an increase in aggregate demand and a consequent rise in real output and resource use. Further, if aggregate demand continues to increase above full-employ-

ment levels the result will be rising prices and inflation—a situation sometimes described as "too many dollars chasing too few goods."

Prolonged periods of unemployment, full employment, or inflation may occur because of the failure of the two classical adjustment mechanisms—the interest rate and flexible wages and prices.

Savers and Investors Are Different People
with Different Motivations

In a primitive economy, saving and investing are undertaken largely by the same groups for the same reasons. But in an advanced economy, saving and investing are undertaken by different groups for different reasons. In our own economy, for example, households like yours and mine may save for several reasons: to purchase a new car, finance an education, make a down payment on a house, or pay for a vacation; to provide for future security and loss of income resulting from illness, old age, or retirement; to amass an estate which can be passed on to future generations; to buy stocks and bonds for income or future profit; or simply to accumulate funds without any specific purposes in mind.

Business firms save when they retain some of their profits instead of distributing them to stockholders. Their reasons for saving, however, are different from those of households. Businesses usually save in order to invest in plant, equipment, and inventories; they may also borrow for the same purposes. In any case, they invest primarily on the basis of the rate of profit they anticipate. Thus:

Savers and investors are different people with different motivations. Much of the economy's saving is done by households, whereas its investment and net capital formation are done primarily by businesses on the basis of profit expectations. The amount businessmen want to invest fluctuates widely from year to year and is not likely to equal the amount households want to save. Consequently, fluctuations in income, output, and employment are characteristic of an advanced capitalistic economy.

Prices and Wages Are Not Flexible

Do prices and wages exhibit the flexibility the classicists assumed? The answer is no. Our economy is characterized by big unions and big businesses, and there is great resistance to reductions in prices and

JOHN MAYNARD KEYNES

1883–1946

Founder of the New Economics

John Maynard Keynes was among the most brilliant and influential economists of all time. As one who helped shape the thinking of future generations of scholars he ranks with Adam Smith and Karl Marx.

Keynes was born in Cambridge, England, the son of a noted economist, John Neville Keynes. He was educated at Eton and Cambridge, where he first majored in mathematics but later turned his attention to philosophy and economics. After college he took a civil service post in the India Office. Later, he returned to England and served as a teaching fellow at Cambridge, where his talents were quickly recognized. He became editor of the *Economic Journal*, Britain's most distinguished economic publication—a position which he held for 33 years.

To say that Keynes was brilliant is an understatement; he was a genius with diverse talents who combined teaching at Cambridge with an active and highly successful business life in the fields of insurance, investments, and publishing. In addition to his many publications in economics, he wrote a remarkable book on the philosophical foundations of probability which is required reading by graduate students in mathematical logic and philosophy; and he amassed a fortune of over $2 million by speculating in the international currency and commodity markets. Perhaps most impressive, however, is the fact that he accomplished these feats in his "spare time"; he wrote his mathematics book while employed in government service, and accumulated his fortune by analyzing financial reports and phoning orders to his broker for a half-hour each morning before breakfast.

Keynes' most celebrated work, *The General Theory of Employment, Interest and Money* (1936), was one of the most influential books ever written in economics. Here he made it clear that he was departing significantly from traditional economic theory which held that there is a natural tendency for the economy to reach equilibrium at full employment. Indeed, Keynes showed that equilibrium can

Wild World Photos.

be reached and maintained at a level of output less than full employment. He thus advocated reduction in the bank interest rate in order to stimulate investment, progressive income taxation in order to make incomes more equal and thereby increase the percentage of aggregate income that people spend on consumption, and government investment through public works and other means as a "pump-priming" process when private investment expenditures fall off. Today, these and related policy suggestions are part of a larger family of concepts which make up what we call the New Economics.

Nowadays, practically all economists are "Keynesians." That is, they use the fundamental theoretical tools and concepts which Keynes developed. However, they may not always agree on the ways in which those ideas should be implemented in matters of public policy.

---

wages. We almost always hear of prices and wages going up, but we rarely hear of them going down.

Nevertheless, let us assume for the moment that wages and prices are flexible, and that the fall in wages during a period of unemployment is greater than the fall in prices—which is what the classical economists postulated. If such decreases are experienced by one firm only, its profits will increase and

it will be encouraged to expand its production and employment. But if the decreases are experienced by all firms in the economy, *real wages* and general purchasing power will decline. The result is likely to be a further reduction in output and employment instead of the reverse. And if the interest rate should happen to be "sticky" rather than flexible, as is often the case, its failure to adjust downward will help to perpetuate, if not worsen, an already depressed situation.

We must conclude, therefore, that although a reduction in real wages (i.e., money wages relative to the general price level) within a single firm is not likely to affect the overall demand for that firm's product, it cannot be assumed that a general reduction in real wages of *all* workers throughout the economy will have no effect on aggregate demand. The classical economists failed to recognize this distinction between the "particular" and the "general," and thereby committed a logical fallacy in their thinking. Can you name the fallacy?

Therefore, Laissez-faire Capitalism Cannot Ensure Full Employment

Modern theory concludes there is *no automatic tendency* toward full employment in a capitalistic economy. The levels of aggregate output and employment are determined by the level of aggregate demand, and there is no assurance that aggregate demand will always equal full-employment aggre-

gate income. As aggregate demand increases, so do aggregate output and employment—up to the level of full employment. In view of this, let us see what modern theory says about the concept of *aggregate demand*, which consists of consumption demand, private investment demand, government demand for goods and services, and net export demand.

Consumption Demand

Which factors determine *consumption* demand or personal expenditures on goods and services in our economy?

Take your own case. What determines the amount spent by *your* family on goods and services? You can probably think of several factors, but first and foremost is your family's disposable income—the amount it has left after paying personal taxes.

The situation is much the same with other families. *Disposable income is usually the single most important factor affecting a family's consumption expenditures.* Other conditions such as the size of

---

Exhibit 2

A Family's Consumption and Saving Schedule

(hypothetical data, annual)

HOW DO CONSUMPTION AND SAVING RELATE TO INCOME?

(1) Disposable income, DI	(2) Consumption, C	(3) Saving, S (1) − (2)	(4) Average propensity to consume, APC (2) ÷ (1)	(5) Average propensity to save, APS (3) ÷ (1)	(6) Marginal propensity to consume, MPC Change in (2) / Change in (1)	(7) Marginal propensity to save, MPS Change in (3) / Change in (1)
$ 4,000	$ 4,600	−$ 600	1.15	−0.15		
					0.70	0.30
5,000	5,300	− 300	1.06	−0.06		
					0.70	0.30
6,000	6,000	0	1.00	0.00		
					0.70	0.30
7,000	6,700	300	0.96	0.04		
					0.70	0.30
8,000	7,400	600	0.93	0.07		
					0.70	0.30
9,000	8,100	900	0.90	0.10		
					0.70	0.30
10,000	8,800	1,200	0.88	0.12		
					0.70	0.30
11,000	9,500	1,500	0.86	0.14		
					0.70	0.30
12,000	10,200	1,800	0.85	0.15		

the family, the ages of its members, its past income, and its expectations of future income will also have an effect.

Although no two families spend their incomes in the same way, some generalizations about family expenditure patterns can be made. These generalizations are known as *Engel's Laws*, derived from the work of a German statistician, Ernst Engel, who first conducted such research in 1857. Here is a modernized version of Engel's Laws, based on budgetary studies of family expenditures.

As a family's income increases:

1. The percentage spent on food decreases.

2. The percentage spent on housing and household operations remains approximately constant (except for fuel, light, and refrigeration, which decrease).

3. The percentage spent on all other categories and the amount saved increases (except for medical care and personal care items, which remain fairly constant).

Note that the *total amount spent increases as a family's income increases*. The decreases occur only as a percentage of the total.

THE PROPENSITY TO CONSUME

The relationship between a family's income and its consumption expenditures is illustrated by the schedule in the first two columns of Exhibit 2. The difference between income and consumption is saving, shown in column (3). The first thing to notice is that as income increases consumption increases and so does saving.

The consumption and savings data are graphed in Exhibit 3. Let us consider the upper chart first.

Note that consumption expenditures are measured on the vertical axis and disposable income on the horizontal, and that both axes are drawn to the same scale. Therefore, the 45-degree diagonal is a line along which consumption C is 100 percent of disposable income, DI—that is, the ratio $C/DI = 1$.

The consumption curve C is the graph of the data in columns (1) and (2) of the table. The intersection of this curve with the diagonal line is the family's "break-even point"—the point where consumption is exactly equal to income. At this level the family is just getting by, neither borrowing nor saving.

To the right of the break-even point the vertical distance representing consumption is less than the horizontal distance denoting income. The differ-

Exhibit 3

A Family's Consumption and Saving in Relation to Its Income
(hypothetical data, annual)

The vertical distances show you how much will be consumed and saved at each income level. For example, at an income of $11,000 the amount spent on consumption is $9,500 and the amount saved is $1,500.

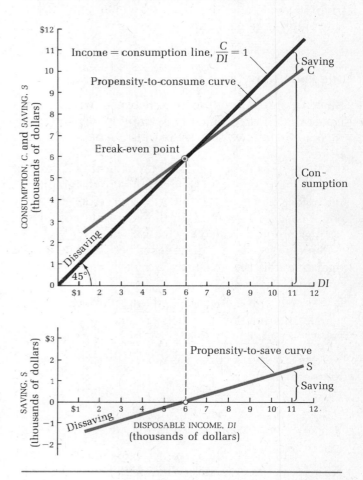

ence, saving, is represented by the vertical distance between the consumption line and the diagonal.

To the left of the break-even point the family is consuming more than its income. The difference is called *dissaving*. How does a family dissave or live beyond its means? Either by spending its previous savings, by borrowing, or by being subsidized.

Here are some important ideas to remember:

The level of consumption depends on the level of income in a manner such that as income increases, consumption increases, but not as fast as income. This relation between consumption and income is called the *propensity to consume* or the *consumption function*. The word "function" is thus used here in its mathematical sense to mean a quantity whose value depends on the value of another quantity, e.g., the value of consumption *depends on* the value of income.

Note that the consumption curve C is the family's propensity-to-consume curve. It assumes that, apart from income, all other factors which may affect consumption remain constant.

THE PROPENSITY TO SAVE

Since saving is the difference between income and consumption, and since consumption depends on income, it follows that saving also depends on income.

The savings data in column (3) of Exhibit 2, taken together with column (1), are shown in the graph in the lower panel of Exhibit 3. Here, disposable income is again measured on the horizontal axis, but savings are now scaled vertically. The saving curve S depicts the vertical differences between the diagonal line and the consumption curve in the upper chart.

The level of saving depends on the level of income. This relation between saving and income is called the *propensity to save* or the *saving function*.

Thus the saving curve S is the family's propensity-to-save curve.

AVERAGE PROPENSITIES TO CONSUME AND TO SAVE

What will the family's *average* consumption be in relation to its income? What will be its *average* amount of saving? The answers are given in columns (4) and (5) of Exhibit 2.

The *average propensity to consume*, APC, is simply the ratio of consumption to income:

$$APC = \frac{consumption}{income}$$

The APC tells you the proportion of each income level that the family will spend on consumption. Similarly, the *average propensity to save*, APS, is the ratio of saving to income and tells you the proportion of each income level that the family will save— i.e., not spend on consumption:

$$APS = \frac{saving}{income}$$

For example, at an income level of $10,000, the family will spend 88 cents of each dollar or a total of $8,800, and it will save 12 cents of each dollar or a total of $1,200. In other words, it will spend 88 percent of its income and save 12 percent.

Note that as income increases, APC decreases; therefore APS increases since both must total to 1 (or 100 percent) at each income level. What can you learn from the fact that APC declines with rising incomes? Basically, this tendency confirms the everyday observation that the rich save a larger proportion of their incomes than the poor. You probably would have guessed this without looking at the figures in the table; but they help to fix this important notion more firmly in your mind.

MARGINAL PROPENSITIES TO CONSUME AND TO SAVE

It is important to know the amount of each *extra* dollar of income that the family will spend on consumption, and the amount it will save. These amounts are shown in columns (6) and (7) of Exhibit 2.

The *marginal propensity to consume*, MPC, is the change in consumption resulting from a unit change in income. As you can see from the table, the formula for calculating MPC is

$$MPC = \frac{change\ in\ consumption}{change\ in\ income}$$

The MPC tells you the *fraction of each extra dollar of income that goes into consumption*. An MPC of 0.70, for instance, means that 70 percent of any increase in income will be spent on consumption.

The *marginal propensity to save*, MPS, is the change in saving resulting from a unit change in income:

$$MPS = \frac{change\ in\ saving}{change\ in\ income}$$

The MPS tells you the *fraction of each extra dollar of income that goes into saving*. An MPS of 0.30, for example, means that 30 percent of any increase in income will be saved.

What is the difference between *APC* and *MPC*? Between *APS* and *MPS*? At any given level of income, the *APC* relates total consumption to income, whereas the *MPC* relates a *change* in the amount of consumption to a *change* in income. The "average" may thus be quite different from the "marginal," as you can see from the table. The same kind of reasoning applies to *APS* and *MPS*. The "average" and the "marginal" tell you two distinctly different things. Note from the table, however, that just as *APC* and *APS* must always total 1 (or 100 percent) at any income *level*, *MPC* and *MPS* must always total 1 (or 100 percent) for each *change* in income.

The *MPC* and *MPS* are of great practical value, especially when applied at the macroeconomic level. Suppose the nation is in recession and the *MPC* for the economy as a whole is 0.70. This means that to increase the volume of consumption by $700 million in order to move the system closer to full employment, the level of aggregate disposable income must be raised by $1 billion. As shown in later chapters, legislators and the administration can adopt various economic measures to achieve such a goal.

By now you have probably recognized an important idea: Since the *MPC* is the change in total consumption resulting from a unit change in income, it measures the *slope* (steepness) of the consumption function or line. The slope of any straight line is defined as the number of units it changes vertically for each unit of change horizontally. Thus in the following diagram, the line rises 4 units on the vertical axis for a run of 6 units on the horizontal; hence the slope, which is measured by the rise over the run, is 2/3.

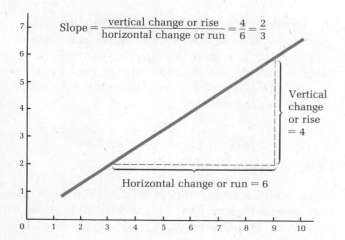

$$\text{Slope} = \frac{\text{vertical change or rise}}{\text{horizontal change or run}} = \frac{4}{6} = \frac{2}{3}$$

Vertical change or rise = 4

Horizontal change or run = 6

Similarly, the *MPS* measures the slope of the saving line. You should be able to verify that the slope of a straight line is the same at every point. This is why the table shows all values of *MPC* as equal and all values of *MPS* as equal: the consumption curve and the saving curve in this example are each straight lines.

TWO KINDS OF CHANGES INVOLVING CONSUMPTION

The consumption function or propensity-to-consume curve expresses a relation between consumption expenditures and income. Your understanding of this concept can serve as a basis for distinguishing between two kinds of variations in consumption: one of these is called a change in the amount consumed; the other is a change in consumption.

Change in the Amount Consumed

Examine the diagrams in Exhibit 4 on the next page. In the upper chart any movement along the consumption curve represents a *change in the amount consumed*—specifically, an increase in the amount consumed if income rises and a decrease in the amount consumed if income falls. This is indicated by the vertical dashed lines. A movement to the right always signifies an increase in income and hence a movement upward along the *C* curve; a movement to the left indicates a decrease in income and therefore a movement downward along the *C* curve. Note also in the lower chart that saving, like consumption, varies directly with income. Hence a change in the amount saved—either an increase or decrease—occurs for the same reason as a change in the amount consumed, namely, a change in income.

Change in Consumption

A second type of movement, shown in Exhibit 5 on the next page, is a *change in consumption*—an increase in consumption, whereby the curve shifts to a higher level, or a decrease in consumption, shown by a shift of the curve to a lower level. An increase in consumption from curve *C* to curve *C'* means that at any given level of income people are now willing to consume more and save less than they were willing to consume and save before. What does a decrease from curve *C* to curve *C''* mean?

The consumption curve—the consumption function or propensity to consume—may shift as a result

Exhibit 4

Changes in the Amounts Consumed and Saved

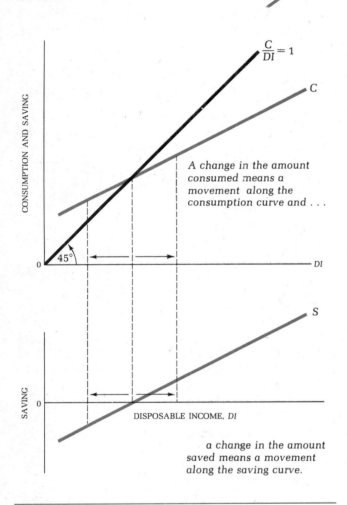

A change in the amount consumed means a movement along the consumption curve and . . .

a change in the amount saved means a movement along the saving curve.

Exhibit 5

Changes in Consumption and Saving

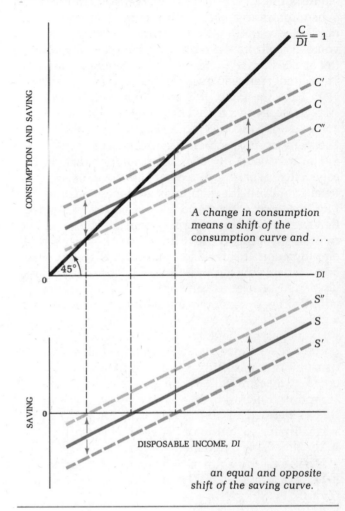

A change in consumption means a shift of the consumption curve and . . .

an equal and opposite shift of the saving curve.

of a change in any one of the "all other" things that were assumed to remain constant when the curve was initially drawn. What are these factors? Some of the more important ones are:

1. The volume of liquid assets (e.g., currency, stocks, bonds, etc.) owned by households

2. Expectations of future prices and incomes

3. Anticipations of product shortages (resulting, for example, from wars, strikes, etc.)

4. Credit conditions

An increase in any one of these factors (as well as several others you may be able to think of) can cause an increase in consumption and shift the curve upward; a decrease in any one can cause a decrease in consumption and shift the curve downward. Since these factors do not remain constant over the long run, the *true* consumption function for the economy is likely to vary.

A Closer Look at the Consumption Function

What would a consumption function for the economy as a whole look like? This is difficult to answer. Until now the consumption function has been inferred from the relationship expressed by the *propensity to consume*. This fundamental law states, as we learned above, that as income increases, consumption increases, but not as fast as income. When a consumption function is derived from actual data, however, it may not turn out exactly as expected. This is because various theoretical and statistical problems are encountered along the way.

FORM OF THE CURVE

One of the first problems concerns the *form* of the curve—its *slope* and *height*. The slope shows the *rate* at which consumption increases as income rises. This, as we know, is expressed by the marginal propensity to consume, *MPC*. Given the slope, the height of the curve above the horizontal axis must be established since this determines the *amount* of consumption out of any given income—or what

happens to the average propensity to consume, *APC*, as income rises.

All three curves in Exhibit 6 (as well as some others that can be drawn) represent possible consumption functions—they all fit the definition of the propensity to consume given above. In view of this, which curve is the "true" consumption function? Before answering this question, we must understand what happens to both the *MPC* and *APC* of each curve as income rises.

Exhibit 6(a) shows a consumption function of the form we have been dealing with until now. Since the *C* curve is a straight line, we know that the *MPC* (= slope) remains constant as income increases. What about the *APC*? Here the height of curve *C* is such that it intersects the 45° line. As a result, the amount of consumption out of any given income— the ratio of consumption to income (*APC*)—declines as income increases. You can verify this from the table accompanying the chart.

Exhibit 6

Three Forms of Consumption Functions

(hypothetical data, in billions of dollars)

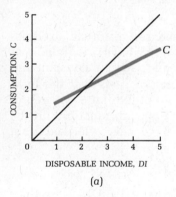

(a)

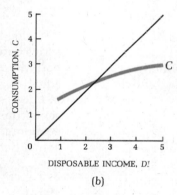

(b)

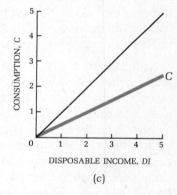

(c)

As income increases:	
MPC remains constant	
APC decreases	

DI	C	MPC	APC = C/DI
1	1.5		1.5
2	2.0	0.5	1.0
3	2.5	0.5	0.8
4	3.0	0.5	0.8
5	3.5	0.5	0.7

As income increases:	
MPC decreases	
APC decreases	

DI	C	MPC	APC = C/DI
1	1.5		1.5
2	2.0	0.5	1.0
3	2.4	0.4	0.8
4	2.7	0.3	0.7
5	2.9	0.2	0.6

As income increases:	
MPC and APC remain constant	
MPC = APC	

DI	C	MPC	APC = C/DI
1	0.5		0.5
2	1.0	0.5	0.5
3	1.5	0.5	0.5
4	2.0	0.5	0.5
5	2.5	0.5	0.5

Chart (b) illustrates a consumption function which increases at a decreasing rate. This means that the curve C gets flatter at higher levels of income. Consequently, the MPC decreases as income increases. Likewise the APC also declines as income rises because consumption does not increase as fast as income.

Chart (c) presents a consumption function in the form of a straight line emanating from the origin. In this case, not only do the MPC and APC remain constant as income increases, but they are also equal at all income levels. In other words, the ratio of the change in consumption to the change in income, which measures the MPC, is always equal to the ratio of consumption to income, which measures the APC. You should verify this from the accompanying table.

WHAT DOES THE EVIDENCE SHOW?

Which of these curves depicts the "actual" form of consumption function for the economy? The answer is influenced by a number of conditions such as the length of time covered by the analysis, the stage of the business cycle in which the data fall, and the statistical methods employed to obtain the needed information. Despite such complicating factors, empirical consumption functions derived by economists from actual data have been informative:

1. Short-run analyses, known as family-budget studies, have been done. The data are collected by recording the values of consumption and income for a large sample or cross section of households within a given year. By selecting households that are similar in all respects other than income, and by observing their consumption expenditures during the same time period, the overall influence of nonincome factors on consumption is minimized. The conclusions of such studies have been that (a) saving tends to be negative at low levels of income; (b) the APC decreases as income increases; and (c) the MPC probably decreases as income increases, although the decline may be relatively slight depending on other factors, especially the distribution of income among households. This suggests that the short-run consumption function of the economy is best represented by the forms shown in Charts (a) and (b) of Exhibit 6. Therefore, whenever we have to deal with a consumption function, we shall use these curves, especially the straight-line type in Chart (a) because of its greater simplicity.

Exhibit 7

Consumer Expenditures and Disposable Personal Income

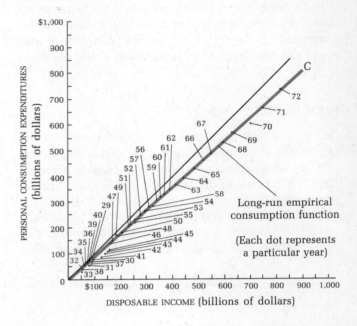

2. Long-run studies based on historical or time-series data covering many years have concluded that both the APC and MPC tend to remain constant and equal as income rises. This suggests that the form of curve shown in Chart (c) of Exhibit 6 best represents the long-run consumption function of the economy, as illustrated by a curve derived from actual data in Exhibit 7.

Private Investment Demand

Having studied consumption, we must now turn to the second component of aggregate demand—investment. Private *investment* demand consists of additions to plant, equipment, inventories, and so on.

If you were a businessman, what would determine your decision to invest? The fundamental answer, of course, is your profit expectation. If you think a new machine would add to your profit, you will try to purchase it; if you believe that an additional wing on your factory would yield greater profits, you will try to build it.

The profit from an addition to capital is usually expressed as a percent or rate of return on the investment. Economists call the expected rate of return on an investment the *marginal efficiency of investment, MEI.* More precisely, it is the expected rate of return over cost of an additional unit of a capital good. Thus you might have an *MEI* or expected rate of return of 25 percent for one type of investment, 15 percent for another, and so on.

THE "MEI" AND THE INTEREST RATE

For an individual firm, the relationships between the *MEI* and the interest rate are illustrated in Chart (a) of Exhibit 8. At any given time a firm is faced with alternative investment possibilities—such as renovating its existing plant, adding a wing to a factory,

purchasing new machines, acquiring additional power facilities, or installing a computer system. Each project competes for a firm's limited funds, but some are expected to be more profitable than others. Hence we may imagine that the managers of a firm rank alternative investment projects in decreasing order of their *MEIs.* Thus in the diagram, each project's cost and corresponding *MEI* are shown. As you can see, the most attractive investment open to the firm is the renovation of its plant at a cost of $2 million, for which it anticipates a rate of return or *MEI* of 27 percent. The next most profitable investment is the addition of a new wing to its factory at a cost of $1 million, for which the *MEI* is 20 percent. Each remaining investment project is interpreted similarly. If we assume that the risks of loss associated with these investments are the same, the descending order of *MEIs* indicates two things: (1) fewer in-

Exhibit 8

Private Investment Demand

The solid stepped line is the firm's MEI curve. It shows the amount of investment the firm will undertake at various interest rates. It is the firm's demand curve for investment.

The MEI curve for all firms is a smooth continuous line obtained by summing the individual MEI curves. It shows the total amount of private investment that will be undertaken at various interest rates. Thus it is the aggregate demand curve for private investment.

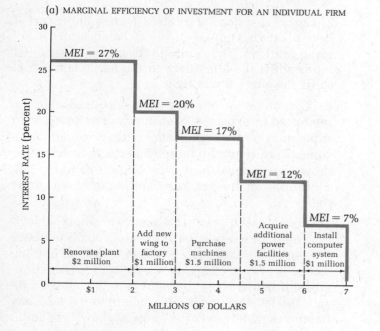

(a) MARGINAL EFFICIENCY OF INVESTMENT FOR AN INDIVIDUAL FIRM

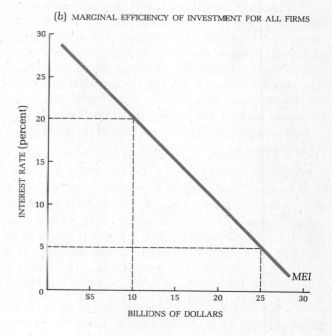

(b) MARGINAL EFFICIENCY OF INVESTMENT FOR ALL FIRMS

vestment opportunities are available to a firm at relatively higher, than at lower, rates of return, and therefore (2) the total volume of investment a firm can undertake varies inversely with its expected rate of return.

In view of this, how much investment will the firm undertake? To answer this question, we must understand that at any given time there is an interest rate in the market which represents the current cost of borrowed funds. If the interest rate is the *cost of (money) capital* to the firm, then a higher interest cost will mean a smaller expected return after allowance for interest cost, and hence a lower volume of investment. Conversely, a lower interest cost will mean a greater expected return after allowance for interest cost, and therefore a higher level of investment. We may conclude that in general terms:

Investment by a firm occurs when the *MEI* or expected rate of return on an addition to investment exceeds the rate of interest or cost of capital that is incurred in making the investment.

For example, look again at Chart (a) of Exhibit 8. The graph shows that at an interest cost of, say, 13 percent, this particular firm would demand $4.5 million for investment. Of this amount, $2 million would be spent on renovating its plant in anticipation of a return or *MEI* of 27 percent, $1 million would be allocated to a new wing for its factory for an expected *MEI* of 20 percent, and $1.5 million would be used to buy new machines in anticipation of an *MEI* of 17 percent. If the interest cost should fall to 6 percent, the firm will demand an *additional* $2.5 million or a *total* of $7 million, in order to invest in the next two projects—namely, power facilities and a computer system. In general, therefore, the firm's total demand for investment funds depends on its *MEI* relative to the interest rate.

This analysis leads to two important principles. *At any given time:*

1. A demand curve relates the quantities of a commodity that buyers would be willing and able to purchase at various prices. In this case the prices are interest rates. Hence the *MEI* curve shows the amounts of investment that a firm would be willing and able to undertake at various interest rates. This is illustrated by the solid irregular line in Exhibit 8, Chart (a). It follows that *a firm's MEI curve is its demand curve for investment.*

2. Each firm's own *MEI* curve is based on its particular investment needs and expectations. If the individual *MEI* curves are summed horizontally, we get the *MEI* curve for all firms in the economy. As a result, the irregularities disappear, giving a smooth continuous line like the one in Exhibit 8, Chart (b). *The aggregate MEI curve depicts total private investment demand at different rates of interest.* For example, at an interest rate of 20 percent, the amount of private investment would be $10 billion; if the interest rate fell to 5 percent, the amount of private investment would increase to $25 billion.

DETERMINANTS OF THE "MEI": SHIFTS OF THE CURVE

Since the *MEI* curve is an investment demand curve, it may, like any demand curve, shift to the right or left due to a change in one or more of the factors which determine it. At least four are particularly important:

1. *Expected product demand.* To an individual businessman, the *expected* net return on his investment will depend to a large extent on the demand that he anticipates for his product. For the economy as a whole, the expected return on new investment will be influenced by total consumer spending on the products of businesses.

2. *Technology and innovation.* Advances in technology and the introduction of new products generally require the construction of new plants or the installation of new equipment. This stimulates the demand for additional capital.

3. *Cost of new capital goods.* Changes in the cost of new plant or equipment affect businessmen's demand for them. Thus a rise in the cost of new capital goods shifts the *MEI* curve to the left; a fall in cost shifts the curve to the right.

4. *Corporate income tax rates.* Businessmen are interested in expected rates of return on investment expenditures *after* allowances for corporation income taxes. Hence an increase in the tax rates, other things being equal, shifts the *MEI* curve to the left; a decrease in the tax rates shifts the curve to the right.

These, as well as other economic and psychological conditions, affect businessmen's expected rates of return on investment. Since one or more of these factors is always changing, the *MEI* curve is continually shifting either to the right or to the left. As a result, the level of private investment in the economy fluctuates widely over the years, as shown in Exhibit 9. Indeed:

Fluctuation in private investment is the single most important cause of fluctuations in income and employment—the major reason for prosperities and recessions.

Exhibit 9

The Instability of Private Investment

The MEI curve is continually shifting due to changes in the factors determining it.

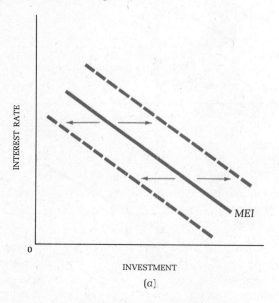

(a)

As a result, private investment spending fluctuates widely over the years.

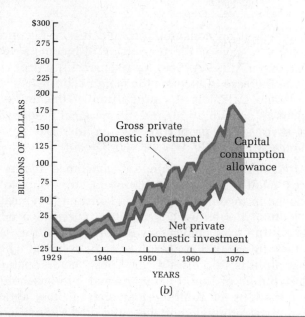

(b)

Government Demand and Net Foreign Demand

The remaining components of aggregate demand stem from government and from international sources. Government demand depends to a large extent on public needs (such as highways, schools, and welfare) and on defense requirements. The volume of government demand is independent of profit expectations and, beyond the minimum levels required by society, is determined at will by government. No scientific law or guiding set of principles exists to predict changes in the level of public investment.

Net foreign demand plays a relatively passive and fortuitous role in our economy. Since it represents the difference between our exports and our imports, it depends on such things as tariff and quota policies, the relative prices and incomes of nations, foreign exchange rates and restrictions, and the level of economic activity here and abroad. As with public investment, there are no guiding principles for predicting foreign investment. Moreover, foreign investment constitutes for our economy a very small proportion of expenditure of GNP (typically less than 1 percent) and hence we may neglect it for purposes of income and employment analysis.

Conclusion: Reviewing the Basic Relationships

We now have the basic building blocks that are needed for understanding the elementary theory of income and employment. The further development of this theory awaits us in the next chapter. In the meantime, you can test your understanding of the basic relationships learned thus far by verifying the truth of the equations presented in Exhibit 10 on the next page.

SUMMARY OF IMPORTANT IDEAS

1. The *classical theory* of income and employment holds that in a competitive capitalistic system, supply creates its own demand: aggregate demand equals aggregate income or output. Therefore the economy automatically tends toward full employment through the free operation of the market system in which prices, wages, and interest rates are free to adjust to their full-employment levels.

2. The *modern theory* of income and employment argues that aggregate demand may be greater than,

Exhibit 10

Some Key Relationships in the Theory of Income and Employment

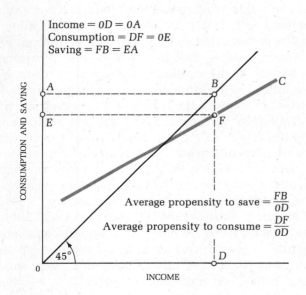

Income = 0D = 0A
Consumption = DF = 0E
Saving = FB = EA

Average propensity to save = $\dfrac{FB}{0D}$

Average propensity to consume = $\dfrac{DF}{0D}$

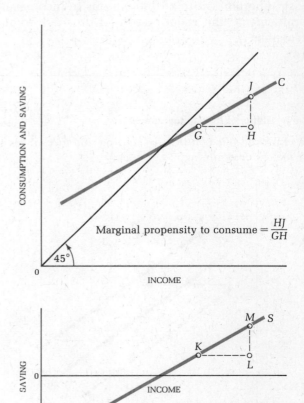

Marginal propensity to consume = $\dfrac{HJ}{GH}$

Marginal propensity to save = $\dfrac{LM}{KL}$

equal to, or less than full-employment aggregate income; that the interest rate need not equate intended saving and intended investment because these are done by different people for different purposes; and that prices and wages are not flexible—especially on the downside—due to resistance by business monopolies, unions, minimum-wage legislation, and other institutional forces. Hence the economy may not necessarily adjust itself to full-employment equilibrium.

3. The propensity to consume, or consumption function, expresses a relationship between consumption and income. The relationship, based on observation and experience, is such that as income increases, consumption increases, but not as fast as income.

4. At any given level of income, the average propensity to consume (APC) is the proportion of in-

come spent on consumption, and the average propensity to save is the proportion of income saved. Therefore: $APC + APS = 1$ (or 100 percent). Out of any given increase in income, the marginal propensity to consume (MPC) is the proportion of the increase spent on consumption, and the marginal propensity to save is the proportion of the increase saved. Hence: $MPC + MPS = 1$ (or 100 percent).

5. A *change in the amount consumed* means a movement along the consumption curve due to a change in income. A *change in consumption* means a shift of the entire consumption curve to a new level, due to a change in one or more of the "all other" things that are assumed to be constant when the curve is initially drawn. These factors include the volume of liquid assets owned by households; expectations of future prices and income; anticipations of product shortages; and credit conditions.

6. Investment demand, like consumption and saving, is a major variable in income and employment theory. The expected rate of return on an investment is called the marginal efficiency of investment, *MEI*. Investment occurs when the *MEI* exceeds the rate of interest or cost of (money) capital that is incurred in making the investment. In general, private investment spending depends on the profit expectations of businessmen, which in turn are determined by such factors as expected product demand, the rate of technology and innovation, cost of new capital goods, and corporate income tax rates. For these reasons, private investment tends to be highly volatile over the years and is the major cause of fluctuations in economic activity.

FOR DISCUSSION

1. *Terms and concepts to review:*

New Economics	average propensity to
Say's Law	consume
aggregate demand	average propensity to
aggregate supply	save
saving	marginal propensity to
interest	consume
classical economics	marginal propensity to
consumption	save
investment	slope
Engel's Laws	change in amount
dissaving	consumed
propensity to	change in consumption
consume	marginal efficiency of
consumption function	investment
propensity to save	

2. Of what significance are interest rates and prices in the classical model?

3. Does Say's Law apply to *individual* goods? Explain.

4. Why do people save? Why do businessmen invest?

5. During a recession, a firm will probably increase its sales if it cuts its prices, and it will reduce its costs if it cuts its wages. It follows that the whole economy will be better off if all firms do this. True or false? Comment.

6. Express Engel's Laws in terms of the average propensity to consume, *APC*.

7. Why does the *APC* differ from the *MPC*? *APS* from *MPS*?

8. What factors other than income are likely to be most important in determining consumption?

9. Complete the following table on the assumption that 50 percent of any increase in income is spent on consumption. Sketch the graphs of consumption and saving. Label all curves.

DI	C	S	APC	APS	MPC	MPS
$100	$150	−50			0	0
200	200				100	
300	250					
400	300					
500						
600						

10. Would you expect expenditures on consumer durable goods to fluctuate more widely than expenditures on consumer nondurable goods? Explain your answer.

11. What would be the effect on aggregate consumption if social welfare expenditures on public hospitals, parks, medical care, and so on, were financed entirely by our progressive income tax system? Does it make any difference if (a) the consumption function is a straight line or a curved line or (b) there are tax loopholes?

12. How would you distinguish between a "change in the amount invested" and a "change in investment"? Explain.

CHAPTER 11

Income and Employment Determination

CHAPTER PREVIEW

How do consumption and investment combine to determine an equilibrium level of income and employment?

What influences do changes in net investment have on the level of income? Is it possible for income to change by some multiple of the change in investment?

How do changes in saving, when not offset by changes in investment, affect the level of income and output?

What pressures, either inflationary or deflationary, are created in the economy when total spending on consumption and investment fails to correspond with full-employment levels?

In the previous chapter it was emphasized that the crucial factor in determining whether we live in a state of full employment or a state of unemployment is the level of investment. The reasons will become increasingly evident in the following pages as the level of investment is discussed in conjunction with the levels of consumption and saving in order to show how the three variables interact to bring about equilibrium in the economy as a whole.

After completing this chapter we shall be able better to analyze the way in which economic fluctuations arise, and to propose government policies designed to minimize them. Those policies are of great importance; upon their success depends the achievement of stable economic growth and full employment with minimal inflation.

The Basic Model of Income and Employment

The time has come to join together the concepts of consumption, saving, and investment in a model which shows how these variables interact to determine the level of income and employment in an economy.

The model to be constructed is "basic"—it focuses on the barest essentials. It covers only the household and private sectors while neglecting for the time being the public and foreign sectors. In this way, just as in earlier chapters, you can learn how the simplest system works before introducing additional factors to make the model more representative of the real world. However, despite its simplicity, the model is by no means an oversimplification of reality. Indeed, it sheds considerable light on some fundamental and rather complex economic problems.

STRUCTURE OF THE MODEL

We begin by examining the components of the model as shown in Exhibit 1 on the next two pages.

Columns (1) and (2) of the table show that for every level of aggregate supply or output there is a corresponding level of employment. Further, these variables are directly related: as aggregate supply decreases, employment decreases; as aggregate supply increases, employment increases. In reality, changes in aggregate supply may sometimes be achieved without changes in employment—for reasons explained in later chapters. However, the assumption that there is a close relationship between the two is both plausible and useful for our present model. Note that the graph of aggregate supply is the 45° line in Chart (a), since it shows the amount of total output, measured on the vertical axis, that will be made available for sale at each level of net national product (NNP), shown on the horizontal axis.

Columns (3) and (4) of the table illustrate the fact that consumption and saving vary directly with income, column (1). So too do their graphs, of course, in Charts (a) and (b). This is what you would expect from your knowledge of the propensities to consume and save. For present purposes it is useful to think of consumption and saving as the amounts which households *plan* or *intend* to consume and save at each income level.

Now look at column (5) of the table. Notice from the footnote to that column that net investment rather than gross investment is the appropriate concept because our basic model uses NNP rather than GNP as a measure of the economy's output. Why is net investment, including its graph in Chart (b), the same at all levels of aggregate supply? As emphasized in the previous chapter:

Businessmen's investment plans depend on the marginal efficiency of investment (*MEI*) relative to the interest rate. The *MEI* is determined by such factors as expected product demand, the rate of technology and innovation, the cost of new capital goods, and corporate income tax rates. Therefore, the level of investment—the amount which businessmen *plan* or *intend* to invest—is assumed to remain constant in relation to output (although it varies widely over time as we have already seen).

This assumption of a constant level of investment with respect to output plays a fundamental role in modern economics. Later it will be modified to permit the introduction of more complex considerations.

Aggregate demand, given in column (6) of the table, is simply the sum of consumption and investment at each level of income. It thus denotes total spending on output, or, in other words, the total amount of consumption and investment that all sectors of the economy *plan* or *intend* to undertake at each income level. Its graph is shown in Chart (a).

THE EQUILIBRIUM LEVEL OF INCOME AND EMPLOYMENT

We now have the information needed to interpret the model. The question we want to answer is: *What will be the equilibrium levels of income and employment—and why?* In other words, where will the level of output and the corresponding level of employment finally settle?

Columns (7) and (8) of the table point out that, at the *equilibrium* level of output, businessmen are holding the precise level of inventory they desire—they are neither accumulating nor depleting their stock. This is because the factor determining the inventory level, namely, the difference between aggregate supply and aggregate demand, or between saving and investment, is zero. The equilibrium point E in the charts depicts these notions graphically. Running your eye along the vertical line, you will see that in our hypothetical economy equilibrium occurs at an output level of $500 billion and an employment level of 50 million persons. We have thus answered the *what* part of the above question. Now let us answer the *why.*

The best way to understand why income and employment tend toward equilibrium is to ask yourself what happens when they are not in equilibrium. For example, suppose NNP or *DI* is greater than $500 billion—say, $600 billion. This means that businesses are paying $600 billion in the form of wages, rent, interest, and profit. At the same time, the corresponding level of total spending or aggregate demand, *C + I*, which is the amount that business firms are taking in, is $580 billion. As you can see from both the table and charts, aggregate supply exceeds aggregate demand, and the amount that households intend to save exceeds the amount that businessmen intend to invest. Therefore, businessmen find their sales to be less than they anticipated. This imbalance causes them to accumulate inventories beyond de-

Exhibit 1

Determination of Income and Employment Equilibrium
(hypothetical economy—all dollars in billions)

(1)	(2)	(3)	(4)	(5)	(6)	(7)	(8)
Aggregate supply (output = income),* NNP = DI	Level of employment (millions)	Consumption, C	Saving, S (1) − (3)	Net investment†, I	Aggregate demand, AD (3) + (5)	Inventory accumulation (+) or depletion (−) (1) − (6) or (4) − (5)	Direction of income and employment
$900	70	$780	$120	$40	$820	+$80	decrease
800	65	700	100	40	740	+ 60	decrease
700	60	620	80	40	660	+ 40	decrease
600	55	540	60	40	580	+ 20	decrease ↓
500	50	460	40	40	500	0	equilibrium
400	45	380	20	40	420	− 20	increase ↑
300	40	300	0	40	340	− 40	increase
200	35	220	−20	40	260	− 60	increase
100	30	140	−40	40	180	− 80	increase

* Includes only the private sector (households and firms), not the public sector (government) or the foreign sector. Also, households are assumed to be the sole source of savings. Therefore, NNP as a measure of aggregate supply equals *NI, PI,* and *DI* because there are no taxes, transfer payments, etc., that is, there is no government activity. Thus, the total income received by households (*DI*) equals the net value of the economy's output (NNP).

† Net investment is used rather than gross investment because we are dealing with NNP in column (1) rather than GNP. Net investment equals gross private domestic investment minus capital consumption allowance.

sired levels, so they cut back on production and lay off workers. As a result, output, income, and employment decrease toward their equilibrium levels as shown by the arrows in both the table and charts.

Conversely, at any output less than the equilibrium level, say, $400 billion, the reverse occurs. In Chart (*a*), aggregate demand exceeds aggregate supply, and in Chart (*b*), businessmen's intended investment exceeds households' intended saving. Households are consuming goods at a faster rate than firms are producing them. As a result, business inventories are being depleted—they are falling below desired levels. Businessmen then seek to expand their production and to hire more workers. This causes output, income, and employment to increase

toward their equilibrium levels as indicated by the arrows.

Thus three fundamental conclusions may be drawn from this model:

1. Income and employment tend toward an equilibrium level at which aggregate supply equals aggregate demand and intended saving equals intended investment.

2. The movement toward equilibrium takes place as businessmen seek to eliminate unplanned inventory changes.

3. Equilibrium can occur at *any* level of employment—not necessarily at full employment.

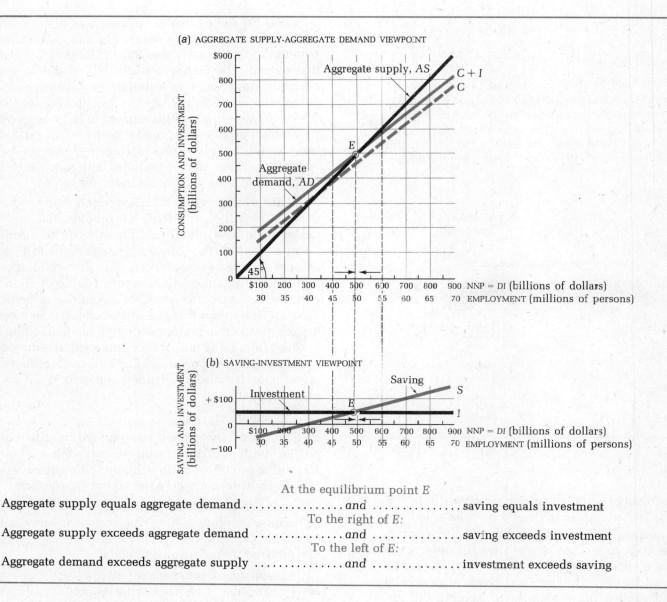

(a) AGGREGATE SUPPLY-AGGREGATE DEMAND VIEWPOINT

CONSUMPTION AND INVESTMENT (billions of dollars)

Aggregate supply, AS

C + I

C

E

Aggregate demand, AD

45°

$100 200 300 400 500 600 700 800 900 NNP = DI (billions of dollars)

30   35   40   45   50   55   60   65   70 EMPLOYMENT (millions of persons)

(b) SAVING-INVESTMENT VIEWPOINT

SAVING AND INVESTMENT (billions of dollars)

Saving

S

Investment

+ $100

E

I

0

−100

$100 200 300 400 500 600 700 800 900 NNP = DI (billions of dollars)

30   35   40   45   50   55   60   65   70 EMPLOYMENT (millions of persons)

At the equilibrium point E

Aggregate supply equals aggregate demand . . . . *and* . . . . saving equals investment

To the right of E:

Aggregate supply exceeds aggregate demand . . . . *and* . . . . saving exceeds investment

To the left of E:

Aggregate demand exceeds aggregate supply . . . . *and* . . . . investment exceeds saving

---

These ideas can also be illustrated pictorially by the "bathtub theorem" in Exhibit 2.

Planned and Realized Saving and Investment

What is meant by saying that in equilibrium, intended saving equals intended investment? How do adjustments in inventory levels bring about equilibrium?

When we studied the operation of supply and demand in an earlier chapter, we saw that buyers and sellers are each influenced by different factors. Consequently, their plans or intentions as reflected by market schedules or curves do not coincide. Although the number of units of a commodity actually purchased and sold is always equal, the quantities which buyers plan to buy and sellers plan to offer over the full range of their curves will always differ—except in equilibrium where the scheduled amounts intersect.

A similar idea exists with respect to saving and investment. As we have seen, *savers and investors are different people with different motivations,* and their plans to save and invest are not identical at all levels of output. Although saving always equals actual or realized investment, it never equals planned investment—except at the equilibrium level of output.

Exhibit 2

The "Bathtub Theorem"

Investment may be thought of as an injection into the income stream; saving may be thought of as a withdrawal. Hence the water in the bathtub can be in equilibrium at any level as long as the inflow equals the outflow. If the inflow exceeds the outflow, the level in the tub will rise. If the outflow exceeds the inflow, the level in the tub will fall.

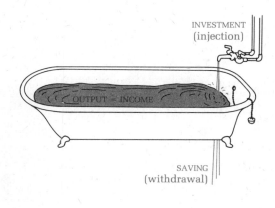

INVESTMENT (injection)

OUTPUT — INCOME

SAVING (withdrawal)

These concepts are illustrated graphically in Exhibit 3. The model is the same as before, but the scales of the charts have been magnified so you can see the important details more readily. Since the charts are virtually self-explanatory, you should be able to verify the following facts (which can also be checked against the schedules in Exhibit 1 if desired).

1. It is clear from Chart (*a*) that if businessmen plan to sell an output of $500 billion this is also the amount of *C* + *I* which the household and business sectors plan to purchase at that output. Therefore, aggregate supply equals aggregate demand and there is no inventory accumulation or depletion. Likewise in Chart (*b*), the amount which households plan to save at that output equals the amount which businessmen plan to invest. Hence there is no unplanned or unintended investment in inventories. (Remember from our study of national-income accounting that investment consists not only of expenditures on new plant and equipment, but also of *changes in inventory*.)

2. Chart (*a*) shows that if businessmen plan to sell $600 billion of NNP, households and businesses combined plan to purchase $580 billion of *C* + *I* at that output. The business sector will therefore experience unplanned investment or inventory accumulation of +$20 billion. In Chart (*b*), household saving exceeds planned investment of businesses by the amount of this unplanned investment. Nevertheless, saving equals actual or *realized* investment because the latter always includes both planned and unplanned (inventory) investment.

3. Chart (*a*) shows that if businessmen plan to produce $400 billion of NNP, households and businesses combined plan to purchase $420 billion of *C* + *I* at that output. Since aggregate demand thus exceeds aggregate supply, the algebraic difference represents unplanned *disinvestment* or negative investment because the stock of inventory is being used up faster than it is being replaced. In this case it amounts to an inventory depletion of −$20 billion. In Chart (*b*), saving falls short of planned investment by that amount. However, saving still equals *realized* investment because unplanned (inventory) investment is negative.

To summarize:

☐ Saving and investment are planned by different people with different motivations. Hence their schedules or curves are not likely to be equal—except in equilibrium where the amounts intersect.

☐ Saving (like consumption) depends on the level of income or output. It is that part of income not spent for consumption. Therefore, planned saving and realized saving are always equal.

☐ Investment is independent of income. Once a level of income is incurred, the amount of realized investment from that income includes both planned and unplanned (inventory) investment.

Hence:

Out of any *realized* level of income, it is always true that

Income = consumption + saving

and it is also true that

Income = consumption + realized investment

Therefore,

Saving = realized investment

These are actually fundamental identities of national-income accounting. You can verify them for

Exhibit 3

Planned and Realized Saving and Investment

Unplanned investment (and disinvestment), reflected by changes in inventory, occurs at output levels where aggregate demand differs from aggregate supply.

Saving and investment, as shown by the S and I curves, are planned by different people with different motivations. Hence they are not equal—except in equilibrium where the curves intersect. But for any realized level of income, saving always equals realized investment.

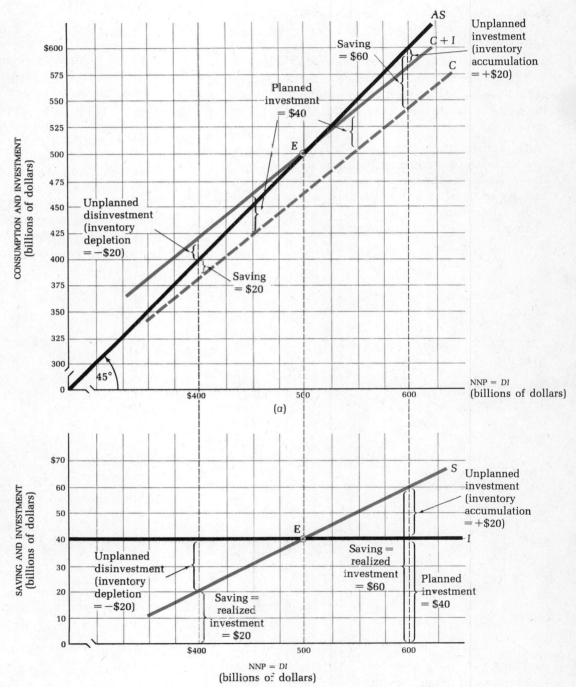

any given year from the front endpapers of this book —provided you make the proper calculations to reflect the fact that government and the foreign sector are excluded from this basic model.

The Multiplier Principle

One of the most critical problems of macroeconomics concerns the question of how changes in net investment affect the level of income. You already know that an increase in net investment will cause an increase in income; a decrease in net investment will cause a decrease in income. But what you may not know is that *investment spending has an amplifying effect on economic activity:*

An increase in net investment will cause a magnified increase in income and output, and a decrease in net investment will cause a magnified decrease in income and output. The amount by which a change in investment is multiplied to produce an ultimate change in income and output is called the *multiplier.*

For instance, if a permanent increase in investment of $5 billion per year causes an increase in income and output of $10 billion, the multiplier is 2. If instead the increase in income and output is $15 billion, the multiplier is 3. How does the multiplier work? It can be illustrated in three ways: numerically by a table, graphically by a chart, and algebraically by a formula.

NUMERICAL ILLUSTRATION

Suppose businessmen decide to spend $5 billion more per year on construction of new plant and equipment. If the owners of the unemployed factors of production hired to perform the construction— the workers, materials suppliers, etc.—are assumed to have an MPC of $\frac{4}{5}$ and hence an MPS of $\frac{1}{5}$, they will tend to spend four-fifths and save one-fifth of any additional income they receive.

The ultimate effect on income is illustrated in Exhibit 4. In the first round of expenditures the increase in investment of $5 billion becomes increased income to the owners of the hired resources. Since their MPC is $\frac{4}{5}$ and their MPS is $\frac{1}{5}$, they utilize 80 per-

Exhibit 4

The Multiplier Illustrated Numerically
(all data in billions)

$MPC = \frac{4}{5}$
$MPS = \frac{1}{5}$
Multiplier = 5

Expenditure rounds	Increase in income	Increase in consumption, $MPC = \frac{4}{5}$	Increase in saving, $MPS = \frac{1}{5}$
1 Increase in investment = $5 billion	$ 5.00	$ 4.00	$1.00
2	4.00	3.20	0.80
3	3.20	2.56	0.64
4	2.56	2.05	0.51
5	2.05	1.64	0.41
6	1.64	1.31	0.33
All other rounds	6.55	5.24	1.31
Totals	$25.00	$20.00	$5.00

cent or $4 billion for increased consumption and 20 percent or $1 billion for increased saving.

In Round 2, when the four-fifths is spent on consumption, firms find their sales increasing and their inventories decreasing; they therefore hire more resources in order to increase their production, thereby creating $4 billion of income for the owners of these resources. These income recipients then utilize four-fifths or $3.2 billion for increased consumption and one-fifth or $0.8 billion for increased saving.

In Round 3 and in all subsequent rounds, the process is repeated as four-fifths of each increase in income is spent in the following round and is thereby added to the income stream.

Thus, a permanent increase in investment of $5 billion in Round 1 has brought about an ultimate increase in income of $25 billion. The multiplier is therefore 5. This overall increase in income consists of a $20 billion increase in consumption plus a $5 billion increase in saving. The saving increase is always the amount of the original investment, as you can verify from the table.

Note from the table that the greatest increases in income occur during the first few rounds. After that the income effects tend to fade away—much like the ripples caused by a stone dropped into a pond.

GRAPHIC ILLUSTRATION

Exhibit 5 on the next page represents the same ideas graphically. It shows how an increase in investment, represented by an upward shift of the $C + I$ curve in the upper chart, or by an upward shift of the I curve in the lower one, causes a magnified increase in output. As before, the model is based on the assumption that the MPC is $\frac{4}{5}$ and the MPS is $\frac{1}{5}$. The point E in both charts represents the initial equilibrium level at which aggregate demand equals aggregate supply and saving equals investment. The point E' defines a new equilibrium resulting from an increase in investment. Note from the description accompanying the charts that the increase in income is a *multiple* of the increase in investment.

Can you see that the multiplier also works in reverse? What happens to income if investment falls back to its initial level? What happens if it falls below its initial level?

FORMULA ILLUSTRATION

The tabular and graphic illustrations of the multiplier demonstrate that the increase in income is

related to the marginal propensities to consume and to save. For example, it has already been established from the study of the consumption function that

$$MPC + MPS = 1$$

Therefore by transposing:

$$MPS = 1 - MPC$$

Further, you can readily verify from the information given in the numerical and graphic illustrations that

$$\text{Multiplier} = \frac{1}{MPS} = \frac{1}{1 - MPC}$$

This means that if you know either the MPC or the MPS, you can determine the multiplier immediately. Do this for the MPC and MPS figures given in the previous examples. Then, once you know the value of the multiplier, you can predict the ultimate change in income resulting from a change in investment by the formula:

Multiplier $\times$ change in investment = change in income

The same formula applies to a decrease as well as an increase in investment. Go back and check it out in the above illustrations, just to make sure that you see how it works.

Notice that *the multiplier is the reciprocal of the MPS.* (The reciprocal of a number is 1 divided by that number.) Thus the lower the MPS, the less withdrawal or "leakage" into extra saving that occurs at each round of income, and the greater the MPC; therefore the greater the value of the multiplier. Conversely, the greater the MPS, the lower the MPC, and hence the lower the value of the multiplier.

To summarize:

The *multiplier* principle states that changes in investment bring about magnified changes in income, as expressed by the equation: multiplier $\times$ change in investment = change in income. The formula for the multiplier coefficient is thus:

$$\text{Multiplier} = \frac{\text{change in income}}{\text{change in investment}}$$
$$= \frac{1}{MPS} = \frac{1}{1 - MPC}$$

Exhibit 5

The Multiplier Illustrated Graphically

$$MPC = \tfrac{4}{5}$$
$$MPS = \tfrac{1}{5}$$
Multiplier = 5

An increase in the level of investment by $5 billion causes an increase in the level of income by $25 billion. Hence the multiplier is 5.

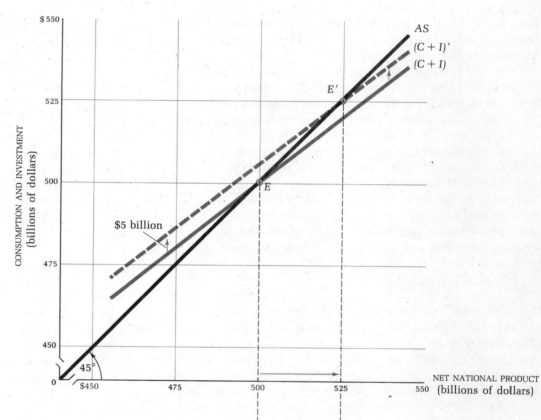

What happens to income if investment falls back to $40 billion? To $35 billion?

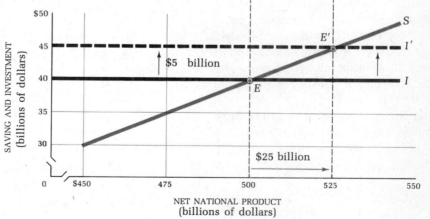

where *MPS* stands for the marginal propensity to save, and *MPC* the marginal propensity to consume. (NOTE: This multiplier is also sometimes called the *simple multiplier* or the *investment multiplier* to distinguish it from other types of multipliers in economics.)

The Paradox of Thrift

The multiplier principle states that any increase (or decrease) in investment sets in motion a multiple expansion (or contraction) of income. But do changes in saving or consumption also bring about a multiplied effect on income? The answer is yes—as your intuition would probably lead you to believe. But you can sharpen that intuition with some diagrams.

Take a look at Chart (*a*) in Exhibit 6. It illustrates the effect of an increase in saving (or equivalently, the effect of a decrease in consumption) on income and output. An increase in saving, such as from S to S′ means that at any given level of income households now plan to save more than they planned to save before. This might occur if they expect a recession and want to be better prepared for future contingencies.

Chart (*b*) in Exhibit 6 reflects the same idea as Chart (*a*), but now the investment curve is drawn with a moderate upward tilt. This indicates the more realistic fact that investment is not completely *autonomous*—that is, independent of income, output, and general economic activity—as we have assumed until now for the sake of simplicity. More likely, investment in the economy will tend to grow somewhat with expanding income and output, because businessmen become more optimistic and are willing to spend more on investment goods as economic activity increases. We are thus relaxing the assumption of a horizontal investment curve, as was promised earlier.

This tendency of rising economic activity to stimulate higher levels of investment is called *induced investment*. Note in Chart (*b*) that as a result of a rising I curve, the multiplier effect on output resulting from an increase in saving is even greater than in Chart (*a*).

What does the new equilibrium at E′ as compared to E tell us? As both charts illustrate: *A small upward shift of the saving curve (or downward shift of the consumption curve) when not offset by an up-*

Exhibit 6

Effect of an Increase in Saving: The Paradox of Thrift

An increase in saving causes a multiplied decrease in NNP, but at the new equilibrium point E′, saving is the same as it was previously at E.

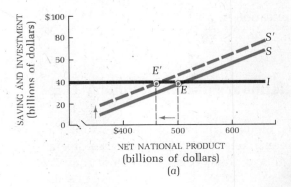

(a)

If investment depends on income so that the I curve slopes upward, the shift from S to S′ reduces income and therefore causes investment to fall. Note that at E′, saving is less than it was at E. People have tried to save more, and society has ended up saving less!

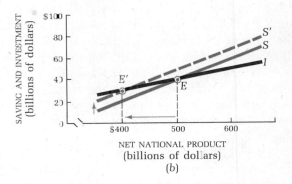

(b)

ward shift of the investment curve will cause a multiplied decrease in income and output. This results in an interesting paradox:

An increase in thrift may be desirable for an individual family because it can lead to greater saving and wealth. However, it may be undesirable for all of society because it leads to reductions in income, output, and employment, and where the investment curve is upward-sloping, will lead to a *reduction in society's rate of saving*. This is the *paradox of thrift*. Thus what is good for an individual is not necessarily good for everyone. (What logical fallacy is demonstrated by this paradox?)

The paradox of thrift leads to a remarkable economic implication. If, in a recession, there is an upward shift of the savings curve because households in general save more (consume less), they should be doing exactly the opposite if they want to improve their own and society's economic well-being—unless their actions can be offset by an upward shift in the investment curve. We shall learn more about this implication in a later chapter.

Inflationary and Deflationary Gaps

The modern theory of income and employment demonstrates that the level of aggregate demand may be greater than, equal to, or less than the level of aggregate supply. These three possibilities are shown in Exhibit 7.

The amount by which aggregate demand AD (equal to $C + I$) exceeds aggregate supply AS at full employment is called the *inflationary gap*, as shown in Chart (a), because the excess volume of total spending when resources are already fully employed creates inflationary pressures that pull up prices and hence the *money* rather than *real* value of NNP. When aggregate demand equals aggregate supply at full employment, as shown in Chart (b), there is no gap. The amount by which aggregate demand falls short of full-employment aggregate supply is called the *deflationary gap*, as shown in Chart (c), because the deficiency of total spending pulls down the *real* value of NNP.

In general, the economy does not move automatically toward full-employment equilibrium. Indeed, an inflationary gap, for instance, could create an upward spiral of further price inflation as businessmen grant union demands for wage increases, and then proceed to compensate for these demands with price increases.

Obviously, therefore,

In order to close an inflationary gap, we have to find ways of reducing aggregate demand: in order to close a deflationary gap, we have to find ways of increasing aggregate demand.

As you will soon see, although the modern theory of income and employment was born in the depression of the 1930s, it can be used to study "inflation economics" as well as "recession economics."

SUMMARY OF IMPORTANT IDEAS

1. The equilibrium level of NNP occurs where aggregate supply = aggregate demand, which is also where saving = investment. At this output, businessmen are holding the level of inventories they desire.

2. If aggregate supply exceeds aggregate demand, or planned saving exceeds planned investment, unwanted inventories accumulate. Businessmen seek to reduce these surpluses by cutting back production. As a result, output, income, and employment fall. Conversely, if aggregate supply is less than aggregate demand, or planned saving is less than planned investment, inventories are depleted. Businessmen try to replenish these shortages by expanding production. The result is an increase in employment as output and income rise.

3. Saving and investment are planned by different people with different motivations, and hence are not likely to be equal—except in equilibrium where the amounts intersect. By definition, saving is that part of income not spent on consumption. Therefore, out of any realized level of income, saving always equals the amount of realized investment because the latter consists of both planned and unplanned investment.

4. Any increase (or decrease) in investment causes a multiple expansion (or contraction) of income. Any changes in consumption, or saving, similarly produce multiple effects on income. All such effects are called *multiplier effects*. The simple multiplier, also called the investment multiplier, which shows how changes in investment cause magnified changes in income, is equal to the reciprocal of the marginal propensity to save.

5. The *paradox of thrift* tells us that although an increase in saving may be desirable for an individual, a general increase in saving by society can actually reduce income and employment. Therefore, what is good for an individual is not necessarily good for society.

6. The amount by which aggregate demand exceeds the full-employment aggregate supply is called the inflationary gap; the amount by which it falls short is called the deflationary gap. There is no automatic tendency for aggregate demand to equal the full-employment aggregate supply. Hence methods must be found to close inflationary and deflationary gaps if a capitalistic economy is to maintain full employment without inflation.

Exhibit 7

Inflationary and Deflationary Gaps

Inflationary and deflationary gaps are always measured at the full-employment level and are shown by the vertical distances. This model assumes for simplicity that prices are constant up to the level of full employment, and thereafter turn up sharply. In reality, they would tend to turn up before the economy reached full employment and continue to rise at steeper and steeper rates.

Chart (a). Inflationary gap. *Aggregate demand AD exceeds aggregate supply AS at full employment.*

Chart (b). No gap. *Aggregate demand AD equals aggregate supply AS at full employment.*

Chart (c). Deflationary gap. *Aggregate demand AD is less than aggregate supply AS at full employment.*

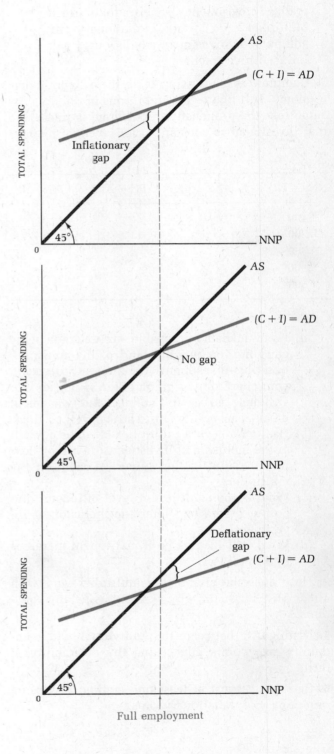

FOR DISCUSSION

1. *Terms and concepts to review:*

   realized investment   paradox of thrift
   multiplier   inflationary gap
   autonomous investment   deflationary gap
   induced investment

2. Complete the following table for a hypothetical economy. (All figures are in billions of dollars.) Assume that the propensity to consume is linear and that investment is constant at all levels of income.

NNP = DI	C	S	I	APC	APS	MPC	MPS
$100	$125		$25				
200	200						
300							
400							
500							

   (a) From the data in the table, draw a graph of the consumption function and of the consumption-plus-investment function. Underneath your chart, draw a graph of the saving and investment curves and connect the two sets of break-even points with vertical dashed lines.

   (b) Has there been a multiplier effect as a result of the inclusion of investment? If yes, by how much? What is the numerical value of the multiplier?

   (c) What is the equilibrium level of income and output before and after the inclusion of investment?

   (d) What will income be if investment increases by $10 billion?

3. How does the size of the multiplier vary with MPC? MPS? Explain why, without using any equations.

4. Distinguish between the individual and community viewpoints concerning the desirability of thrift.

5. Can you suggest at least one method of closing inflationary or deflationary gaps?

6. A student remarked to his instructor: "First you say that saving and investment are never really equal. Then you say they are always really equal. Why don't you economists make up your minds?" Can you help the student out of his muddle?

7. Suppose a consumption function is given by the equation:

$$C = 120 + 0.60 \; DI$$

   (a) What will be the amount of consumption at an income level of 100?

   (b) How much income is required to support a consumption level of 420?

   (c) What will be the amount of consumption if income is taxed 100 percent? How can consumption be financed under such circumstances?

   (d) What is the value of the MPC? The MPS?

   (e) Prepare a consumption and saving schedule, and graph the consumption and saving functions for income levels from DI = 100 to DI = 500. What is the equilibrium level of income?

8. If planned investment in Problem 7 were 50, what would be the equation for aggregate demand? Draw the aggregate demand curve and investment curve on your charts. Can you estimate the equilibrium level of income from your charts?

9. Referring to your charts in Problem 8:

   (a) At a realized income of 500, how much is unplanned investment? Realized investment? Is this an equilibrium situation? Explain.

   (b) At a realized income of 400, how much is unplanned investment? Realized investment? Is this an equilibrium situation? Explain.

   (c) At the realized income levels in (a) and (b), does saving equal investment? Explain.

10. How does the size of the MPC and of the MPS, or the steepness of the consumption curve and of the saving curve, affect the size of the multiplier? Explain.

11. Adam Smith wrote that a spendthrift is an enemy of society, but a frugal person is its benefactor. Benjamin Franklin advised that "a penny saved is a penny earned." Evaluate these statements in light of the paradox of thrift.

CHAPTER 12

Fiscal Policy and the Public Debt

CHAPTER PREVIEW

How do changes in government spending and taxes affect aggregate demand and hence the level of income and employment?

What are the basic principles of fiscal policy? How can they be made to work in order to achieve the goals of continuous full employment and price stability?

Is our public debt too large? What are the real burdens of the debt? How large should the debt be?

At the end of World War II, most economists and politicians feared that the United States would face widespread unemployment as servicemen returned to civilian life and many industries converted from wartime to peacetime production. Accordingly, Congress passed the *Employment Act of 1946* in which it said:

> The Congress hereby declares that it is the continuing policy and responsibility of the Federal Government to . . . create and maintain, in a manner calculated to foster and promote free competitive enterprise and the general welfare . . . maximum employment, production, and purchasing power.

This law is interpreted to mean that the government should use its fiscal powers of taxing and spending to stimulate full employment and economic growth. Since the early 1960s, increasing emphasis has been placed on achieving these objectives without causing inflationary pressures.

The noun "fisc" (from Latin *fiscus*, translated as basket, money basket, treasury) means a state or royal treasury. We use the adjective "fiscal" to refer to all matters pertaining to the public treasury, particularly its revenues and expenditures. Thus modern fiscal policy deals with the deliberate exercise of the government's power to tax and spend for the purpose of bringing the nation's output and employment to desired levels.

Introducing Government: Enlarging the Model

In our basic model of income and employment we assumed that net national product consists of two components, consumption expenditures C, and private net investment I. We concluded that in order to close an inflationary or deflationary gap, methods must be found to alter aggregate demand. Our objective now is to show how government fiscal policy can do this.

The proper economic role of government is always controversial. Should taxes be raised or lowered? Should government spending be increased or reduced? These are among the fundamental issues of fiscal policy. They are also typical of the questions you read and hear about almost every day in the news media.

GOVERNMENT EXPENDITURES INCREASE AGGREGATE DEMAND

Government fiscal policy affects our basic model of income and employment through two major variables—taxes and spending. Let us assume for the moment that *taxes are held constant*; then government spending on goods and services G becomes a net addition to total spending or aggregate demand—that is, a net addition to household consumption expenditures C, and business investment expenditures I, as illustrated in the hypothetical case of Exhibit 1, Chart (a).

The C + I + G curve shows total spending at each level of net national product. The new equilibrium point at which aggregate demand AD equals aggregate supply AS occurs at E. The corresponding information in terms of saving and investment is given in Chart (b). Note that the upward-sloping line now represents saving plus taxes (S + T) because taxes, like saving, denote a portion of income not spent on consumption.

REMARK. Since the basic model is now enlarged to include the public sector instead of just the household and business sectors, the existence of taxes must be recognized. Therefore, NNP in the enlarged model stands by itself—it does not equal DI as in the basic model. (Do you remember why—in terms of national-income accounting?)

In Chart (a) it is interesting to observe that even though the AD curve includes a certain amount of government spending, the equilibrium NNP of $600 billion is still short of the $700 billion needed to reach the full-employment level of output in our hypothetical economy. This means that in order to achieve full employment, the aggregate demand curve must be raised high enough to close the deflationary gap. This can be done by increasing any of

the components of AD—namely, C or I or G. If we assume that the C and I curves remain constant, an increase in G by the amount G' will be sufficient to close the deflationary gap by raising the aggregate demand curve from AD to AD'.

Note that an increase in government expenditure, with taxes held constant, has a multiplier effect on NNP just as does an increase in private investment expenditure. In the diagram, an increase in aggregate demand of $20 billion, from C + I + G to C + I + G', increases NNP by $100 billion. We can infer from this that a rise in government demand has the same multiplier effect on NNP as a rise in consumer demand and in business or investment demand; it increases the sales and profits of firms that sell to the government, and in turn causes further increases in output throughout the economy. Thus:

Increased government spending may be used to raise the level of aggregate demand from an unemployment to a full-employment level. However, any additional spending which raises aggregate demand above full-employment levels will be inflationary.

Observe how the multiplier principle actually comes into play. In Exhibit 1 we know from the constant slope of the consumption curve that MPC is $\frac{4}{5}$ at every point, and hence the multiplier is 5. Given this information, and knowing that the increase in NNP must be $100 billion in order to reach full employment, we can deduce that the increase in government spending must be $20 billion in order to achieve the desired goal, since 5 × $20 billion = $100 billion.

INCREASED TAXES REDUCE AGGREGATE DEMAND

What happens to the equilibrium level of NNP when government spending is constant and taxes vary? Your intuition tells you that an increase in taxes will reduce disposable income and hence consumption expenditures, and this in turn will decrease output and employment. Of course, the many different kinds of taxes—direct or indirect, progressive or regressive, personal or business—may all have different effects on income and employment. For simplicity's sake, however, let us assume that an increase in personal income taxes of $20 billion is imposed on consumers in our hypothetical economy.

In Exhibit 2, the consumption curve C, whose MPC is $\frac{4}{5}$, is shifted downward and parallel until it becomes C' as a result of the tax T. But has the con-

Exhibit 1

Effect of Increased Government Spending on Net National Product

Assumption: MPC $= \frac{4}{5}$; therefore, multiplier $= \dfrac{1}{1 - \frac{4}{5}} = \dfrac{1}{\frac{1}{5}} = 5$

Increased government spending raises aggregate demand from AD to AD′ and produces a multiplier effect on net national product. Since the multiplier is 5, increased government spending of $20 billion increases NNP by 5 × $20 billion = $100 billion—from $600 billion to $700 billion—thereby closing the deflationary gap.

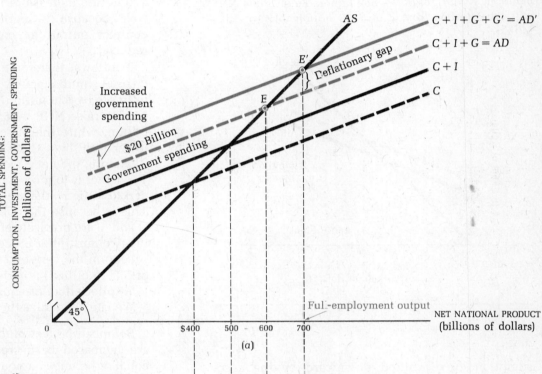

(a)

The multiplier effect of increased government spending can also be seen in terms of a saving-investment diagram. A $20-billion increase in government spending raises the equilibrium NNP from $600 billion to $700 billion.

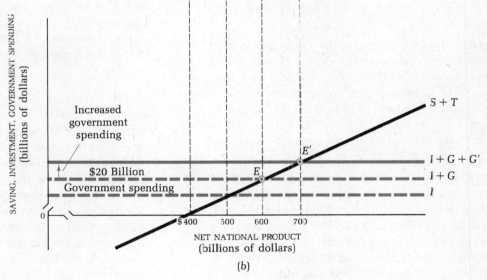

(b)

Exhibit 2

**Effect of Increased Taxes on Consumption
and on Net National Product**

Assumption: $MPC = \frac{4}{5}$; therefore, multiplier = 5

*The C curve will shift downward by an amount equal to
MPC × T. Thus since MPC = $\frac{4}{5}$ and the tax is $20 billion,
the C curve will shift downward by $\frac{4}{5}$ × $20 billion = $16
billion. However, since the multiplier is 5, NNP will decrease by 5 × $16 billion = $80 billion. Equilibrium NNP
will thus decline from E at $400 billion to E' at $320
billion.*

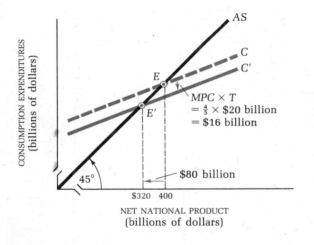

NET NATIONAL PRODUCT
(billions of dollars)

sumption curve shifted downward by the exact
amount of the tax? The answer is no:

After the tax the decrease in consumption, as
represented by the drop in the curve, means that at
any given level of NNP people will now consume
less than they consumed before because their disposable income is lower. Since the *MPC* is $\frac{4}{5}$, consumption will decrease by $\frac{4}{5}$ of $20 billion or $16
billion at every level of NNP, and saving will decline
by $\frac{1}{5}$ or $4 billion at every level of NNP.

The tax, therefore, causes a downward shift of the
C curve according to the value of the *MPC*. *The
amount of the downward shift equals MPC × T.*
What will be the effect of *T* on NNP? Since we know
that the multiplier is 5, it follows that a decrease in
consumption expenditures of $16 billion will re-
duce NNP by 5 × $16 billion = $80 billion. This is
shown in Exhibit 2, where the equilibrium NNP
changes from *E* at $400 billion to *E'* at $320 billion.

VARYING "G" AND "T" TOGETHER:
THE BALANCED-BUDGET MULTIPLIER

Suppose that we now allow government spending
G, and taxes *T*, to vary simultaneously. As you saw
in Exhibit 1, the effect of a $20 billion increase in *G*
is a $100 billion increase in NNP, because the added
expenditure goes through the rounds of consumption and saving according to the multiplier principle. In Exhibit 2, on the other hand, the effect of a
$20 billion increase in *T* is an $80 billion decrease in
NNP, because the multiplier operates in reverse to
contract output as consumption and saving are
reduced.

It follows, therefore, that if *G* and *T* are both increased simultaneously by the same amount—in our
example by $20 billion—the effect of the increase in
G is to raise NNP by 5 times that amount, or $100
billion, while the effect of the increase in *T* is to
lower NNP by 4 times that amount, or $80 billion.
Therefore, the *net* effect of equal increases in *G* and
T together is to increase NNP by 1 times that amount
or $20 billion—the amount of the initial increment.
This is because the effects of balanced increases in
G and *T* are precisely equal but opposite, and hence
the two multiplier processes cancel each other out—
except on the very first round when the full amount
of *G* ($20 billion) is added to NNP. Therefore, the net
multiplier effect of equal increases in *G* and *T* is 1.

We can generalize the foregoing ideas in this way:

Balanced-budget multiplier principle: If *G* and *T*
are increased or decreased simultaneously by an
equal or *balanced* amount, NNP will be increased or
decreased by the same amount. For example, a balanced increase of *G* and *T* by $1 will raise NNP by
$1, and a balanced decrease by $1 will lower NNP
by $1.

The balanced-budget multiplier principle has two
intensely practical implications. First, in a full-
employment economy an increase in government
spending for any purpose (e.g., defense spending)
will cause an inflationary gap unless taxes are increased by *more than the increase in spending*—
that is, by *more than enough to balance the budget.*
Second, in an economy operating at less than full
employment a general tax reduction will result in
an increase in consumption and aggregate demand.
This may be almost as effective in raising the equilibrium level of NNP as an increase in government
spending, but it might have the further advantage—
in the opinion of many—of expanding the private

(business) sector of the economy rather than the public (government) sector.

Several countries including our own have successfully applied this tax-cutting concept in order to increase their levels of output and employment. It is possible that these modern notions of fiscal policy may gain increasing use as time goes on.

Essentials of Fiscal Policy

The foregoing analyses suggest some guides for discretionary *fiscal policy*—that is, deliberate actions by the government in its spending and taxing activities to achieve price stability, help dampen the swings of business cycles, and bring the nation's output and employment to desired levels.

During recession when it is desired to raise aggregate demand to a full-employment noninflationary level, an *expansionary* fiscal policy is needed to close the deflationary gap. This may involve either an increase in G, a decrease in T, or some combination of both. If the federal budget is balanced to begin with, an expansionary fiscal policy of this type will require a budget *deficit*, since the government's expenditures will exceed its revenues.

During inflation when aggregate demand must be reduced, a *contractionary* fiscal policy is needed to close the inflationary gap. This may entail either a decrease in G, an increase in T, or some combination of both. If the federal budget is already in balance, a contractionary fiscal policy would require a budget *surplus*, since the government's revenues will exceed its expenditures.

REMARK. Strictly speaking, since a balanced increase in the budget is actually inflationary due to the balanced-budget multiplier principle, an increased budget that results in a relatively small surplus might also be slightly inflationary rather than deflationary. Therefore, the budget surplus must be large enough to induce deflationary effects if a contractionary fiscal policy is to operate effectively.

Not all fiscal activity is discretionary. Much is *nondiscretionary*, reflecting the fact that significant changes in government spending and taxes occur automatically over the business cycle without any explicit decisions by the President or Congress. Let us examine these changes.

AUTOMATIC OR BUILT-IN STABILIZERS

The U.S. economy has certain "built-in" stabilizers which go to work automatically, cushioning a reces-

sion by retarding a decline in disposable income and curbing an inflation by retarding an increase. They thus help to keep the economic system in balance without human intervention or control, much as a thermostat balances the temperature in a house.

Four of these stabilizers are particularly important:

1. *Tax receipts.* The federal government's chief sources of revenue are personal and corporation income taxes. Since the rates on these taxes—especially the former—are progressive, rising national income results in more than proportional increases in government tax receipts, thereby tending to dampen an economic boom; declining national income results in more than proportional decreases in government tax receipts, thereby tending to soften an economic recession.

2. *Unemployment taxes and benefits.* During prosperity and high employment total tax receipts to finance the unemployment insurance program exceed total benefits paid out, thus creating a surplus; during recession and unemployment, the reverse occurs, thereby creating a deficit.

3. *Agricultural price supports.* "Parity prices" for farmers have automatic stabilizing effects on agricultural prices and farm incomes. The Department of Agriculture buys and stores farm surpluses in order to put a "floor" under falling agricultural prices, and releases these goods (when it has them in stock) to impose a "ceiling" on rising agricultural prices.

4. *Corporate dividend policy.* Corporations maintain fairly stable dividends in the short run; that is, their dividend payouts to stockholders do not fluctuate with each reported increase or decrease in profits. As a result, corporate retained earnings or undistributed profits, to the extent that they are saved and not invested, tend to have a stabilizing influence in both inflationary and deflationary times.

On the whole, these automatic stabilizers tend to reduce the severity of business cycles. Some studies suggest that all of the automatic stabilizers acting together may reduce the amplitudes of cyclical swings by about one-third. But if we want to control the spread of economic booms or declines rather than merely reduce their highs and lows, we must turn to discretionary methods of fiscal policy.

DISCRETIONARY FISCAL POLICY IN ACTION

The prescriptions of discretionary fiscal policy seem to be simple and straightforward: to expand the economy, cut taxes and raise government expenditures; to contract the economy, raise taxes and cut government expenditures. The principal concerns of discretionary fiscal policy thus involve ways in which the federal government (represented by the Treasury) raises and spends money, and the economic consequences of these actions. Let us examine these activities carefully.

Raising Money

First, there is the problem of how the government chooses to raise money. Basically, it has three sources of revenue: taxation, borrowing, and printing new money.

1. *Taxation.* All increases in taxes tend to be contractionary because they take some purchasing power from those who are taxed. However, certain taxes such as the sales and excise taxes are regressive, while others such as the personal and corporation income taxes are progressive. Some economists believe that regressive taxes tend to be more contractionary because they depress total consumer spending; others think that progressive taxes may be more contractionary because they cause a decline in both consumption and corporate investment. Similar difficulties arise in assessing the results of tax decreases. Economists are not always sure whether reductions in progressive or regressive taxes have the greater expansionary effects in terms of production and employment.

The level of taxes is not the only factor to consider. Changes in the composition and rate structure may also affect government revenues and the pace of economic activity, *depending on the MPCs of the income groups involved.* For instance, a change in tax rates which puts a greater burden on higher-income groups and a lesser burden on lower-income groups may have the net effect of stimulating total consumer demand and raising the general level of economic activity. (Can you explain why?) Such a change may also reduce government tax revenues in the short run since the great bulk of revenues comes from the lower- and middle-income groups, but raise it in the long run as national income rises.

2. *Borrowing.* The government can also raise money by borrowing—that is, by selling Treasury bonds to the public, namely households and businesses. (It can also borrow from commercial banks, but we shall ignore the effects of such actions at this time.) If the public buys the bonds with income that it would otherwise have spent on consumption or investment, then the overall economic effect will be approximately neutral. But experience indicates that except in periods of full-scale war when patriotism runs high, neither households nor businesses are inclined to reduce significantly their consumption or investment in order to buy government bonds. Therefore this form of borrowing often has expansionary effects. Can you suggest conditions under which the effects will be contractionary?

3. *Printing new money.* Instead of taxing or borrowing, some governments—the United States is an exception—may simply decide to print money. (Printing money is a monetary rather than fiscal action—as you will see in a later chapter—but it is appropriate to say a few words about it at this time.) By printing money, a government can pay for the resources it wants without depressing private consumption and investment spending. This seems like a delightful and painless way to finance public expenditures. In fact, a number of governments—notably in some Latin American countries—turn frequently to the printing presses to pay for armies, build highways, and meet other obligations and expenses. But the results are not always painless, for two related reasons: (a) during high employment the effects will be inflationary unless private spending is reduced by raising taxes enough to offset the increase in government spending; (b) if private spending is not reduced, the resulting inflation will act as a "tax" by raising prices throughout the economy and thereby shrinking real incomes. These effects, however, would not necessarily occur during recession. That is, printing money to pay for public goods may not be inflationary if the increased government spending raises aggregate demand, thereby expanding real incomes as output and employment rise.

Spending Money

The second aspect of discretionary fiscal policy concerns the ways in which the government spends money. Two types of government spending are of chief concern: transfer payments and public works expenditures. How does each affect income and employment?

1. *Transfer payments.* As pointed out earlier, certain types of transfer expenditures such as unemployment compensation and old-age retirement benefits act as automatic stabilizers, rising and falling in a somewhat inverse relationship with national income. On the other hand, certain transfer expenditures such as veterans' bonuses and interest payments on the public debt are independent of national income and do not have this automatic stabilizing characteristic. But the *net* effect of transfer payments is expansionary to the extent that people spend them for goods and services instead of withholding them from the income-expenditure stream; otherwise, they tend to be neutral.

2. *Public works expenditures.* Highways, parks, public buildings, rural electrification, slum clearance, and regional development are examples of *public works*—government-sponsored construction or development projects which would not ordinarily be undertaken by the private sector of the economy. As an instrument of fiscal policy public works have at least three desirable features: (*a*) they stimulate the capital goods and construction industries, in which unemployment is usually greatest during a recession; (*b*) they provide society with socially useful goods like schools, parks, and highways; and (*c*) they provide jobs which help to maintain workers' morale and self-respect.

But public works also have certain fundamental disadvantages: (*a*) They pose a difficult timing problem because they are hard to start when the need for them is greatest and hard to stop when the need for them is past. For example, it takes several years for the design, engineering, and legal work to be approved before construction of a major bridge or freeway can begin. By that time the economy may be well on its way to prosperity. (*b*) Certain types of investment cannot be classified as either strictly public or strictly private. As a result, some public works such as low-cost housing and perhaps power and reclamation projects may compete with private investment and thereby discourage the development and expansion of the economy's private (business) sector.

DOES DISCRETIONARY FISCAL POLICY REALLY WORK?

How well do these principles of discretionary fiscal policy actually operate? Since they require implementation by Washington, many knotty economic and political issues arise. Four broad classes of difficulties may be identified.

First, there is the technical problem of cyclical forecasting and fiscal timing. Although substantial advances have taken place in economic model building over the years, business-cycle forecasting is still far from being an exact science. The proper timing of appropriate fiscal measures to ward off an inflation or recession is extremely difficult. In fact the fiscal measures are often applied after the inflation or recession has already occurred, instead of before.

A second problem is to gain political and public acceptance of fiscal measures. Even if business-cycle turning points are reasonably predictable, there is still the need to persuade a President or Congress to risk—and the public to accept—unpopular fiscal measures. Among these are increased taxes and reduced government spending. Further, there is the apparently insurmountable problem of overcoming the inherent sluggishness of the democratic process itself: it may take a year or more for Congress to hammer out a budget that incorporates the desired expenditures and taxes. By that time the fiscal needs themselves may have changed fundamentally or may no longer exist.

Third, there is a problem of federal vs. state and local fiscal policies. Ideally, federal fiscal policies should mesh with those of state and local governments, so that all three levels of government may launch a unified countercyclical attack against inflations and recessions. In reality, however, the reverse frequently happens. During prosperity, state and local governments often run deficits in their budgets in order to build highways, schools, and public libraries; in recession they frequently reduce expenditures so as to balance their budgets or even incur surpluses. The chief reason is that state and local governments are much more restricted than the federal government in their sources of funds: they cannot print money, and their opportunities for taxing and borrowing, which are considerably more limited, tend to vary directly with general economic conditions. In view of this, it becomes necessary to rely much more heavily on federal fiscal policy as compared to state and local fiscal policies in order to achieve and maintain economic stability.

A fourth problem is to dovetail government and private investment. As was pointed out earlier, government investment should supplement private investment and even stimulate it, but certainly not depress it. Yet government investment may clearly have depressive effects if it is competitive with private investment. To avoid this, public expenditures should be concentrated on projects that are clearly noncompetitive with private enterprise. Highway construction, slum clearance, and urban redevelopment are possibilities.

Does fiscal policy actually work in practice? Experience since the 1930s indicates that it does. Under different presidential administrations we learned that:

1. A tax cut may stimulate business activity so that in the long run, as national income rises, the government through our progressive tax system will collect larger revenues.

2. A cut in taxes will tend to stimulate both consumption and investment spending so as to produce a gradual rise in consumption and a magnified increase in income—just as the theories of the consumption function and the multiplier predict.

3. Too high a level of government spending, without any offsetting tax increases, will cause a demand-pull inflationary gap. This has been demonstrated since the latter part of the 1960s during periods of heavy government expenditures for military and other purposes.

THE FULL-EMPLOYMENT BUDGET; FISCAL DRAG AND FISCAL DIVIDENDS

As we have just seen, the surpluses and deficits which occur from year to year in the federal budget are not entirely *discretionary*; to some extent they are *automatic* as a result of our progressive tax structure. Thus, as national income increases, the rising tax revenues of the federal government automatically push the budget toward a surplus; as national income decreases, the falling tax revenues automatically push the budget toward a deficit.

Therefore, given the government's existing tax rates and spending policies, the actual budget surplus or deficit that occurs in any particular year is not necessarily the same as the surplus or deficit that would occur in a year of full employment. For instance, in a specific year when the economy is operating at less than full employment the government may incur a budgetary deficit of several billion dollars. Yet with the same tax rates and the same

amount of federal spending the government might instead have incurred a budgetary surplus of several billion dollars if the economy had been operating at full or close to full employment. Why? Because the greater level of national income during a period of high employment would have produced a larger volume of tax revenues for the government.

This prompts us to introduce a new concept called the *full-employment budget*. It may be defined as an estimate of annual government expenditures and revenues that would occur if the economy were operating at full employment. Any resulting surplus (or deficit) in this budget is called a *full-employment surplus* (or *deficit*). The calculation of the government's full-employment budget is usually based on the national-income accounts, and hence reflects more accurately the impact of budget surpluses and deficits on the economy's current levels of output and employment.

Like any other surplus, the effect of a full- or even high-employment surplus is deflationary: the government has taken more purchasing power out of the income stream through taxes than it has put back through spending. Under inflationary conditions this situation serves to dampen price increases; under expansionary conditions it tends to retard the economy's growth. In view of this, how can we assure a proper utilization of our full- or high-employment surpluses? There are two points that should be noted:

1. The automatic and more rapid increases in tax revenues relative to expenditures which a growing economy experiences will tend to impede the economy's growth. This phenomenon is called *fiscal drag*.

2. The federal government can offset the effect of fiscal drag by declaring a "fiscal dividend" in any one or combination of several ways:
   (a) Increased federal spending on important public goods like education, regional development, and health
   (b) Reduced taxes on the private sector in order to increase consumption and investment
   (c) Larger unrestricted revenue grants to the state and local governments which they can use to meet their expenditure needs

Over the long run the full-employment budget may gain increasing use by economic policy-makers in Washington, because it combines the principles of discretionary fiscal policy with the concept of fiscal dividends.

Budget Policies and the Public Debt

Modern fiscal theory calls for budget deficits to ward off recessions and budget surpluses to combat inflations. This is the essence of countercyclical fiscal policy. What does it mean as far as balancing the budget is concerned? How does the government debt, resulting from unbalanced budgets, affect our economy?

FOUR BUDGET POLICIES

Since the early 1930s, the question has often arisen whether the federal budget should be balanced frequently, occasionally, or not at all. Four distinctly different policies have been proposed: an annually balanced budget; a cyclically balanced budget; "functional finance"; and a full-employment balanced budget. Let us see what these policies involve.

Annually Balanced Budget

Those who argue that the budget should be balanced every twelve months claim that this policy would place the government in an economically "neutral" position by providing a constraint on runaway spending and fiscal disorder, and by assuring that annual revenues and expenditures are equal. Political leaders and businessmen often make such statements. Are they true?

If the federal government balanced the budget each year without regard to fluctuations in the private sector its actions would not be neutral; in fact, they would accentuate cyclical swings. The reasons for this are clear. In recession periods, when tax revenues are falling, tax rates would have to be increased and spending would have to be reduced in order to balance the budget. Conversely, during inflationary periods, when tax revenues are rising, tax rates would have to be reduced and spending would have to be increased in order to achieve budgetary balance.

Obviously, therefore, if the budget is to be used as a tool for countercyclical fiscal policy, adherence to annually balanced budgets is impossible.

Cyclically Balanced Budget

Another philosophy holds that the budget should be balanced over the course of the business cycle. This requires the government to incur budget deficits during depression in order to stimulate the economy, but to offset those deficits with budget surpluses during prosperity in order to curb inflationary pressures and help pay off the public debt. Some economists have argued that such a policy would turn the budget into a countercyclical fiscal tool, while still preserving the long-term objective of budgetary balance. In theory this is true.

In practice, unfortunately, business cycles are recurrent but not periodic, and their peaks and troughs are not ordinarily equal. Hence it would be virtually impossible for the government to forecast its revenues and expenditures over the length of a business cycle, and it would be very unlikely for the surplus in any given prosperity to equal or even approximate the deficit of a previous recession.

"Functional Finance"

Proponents of the "functional-finance" philosophy contend that the government should pursue whatever fiscal measures are needed to achieve noninflationary full employment and economic growth—without regard to budget balancing per se. The federal budget is thus viewed functionally as a flexible fiscal tool for achieving economic objectives, rather than as an accounting statement to be balanced periodically.

Functional finance is the logical consequence of the New Economics. However, it has not gone without criticism—especially by conservative economists and political leaders. In their opinion, a balanced budget serves as a rough fiscal guide that should be applied with discretion. They argue that by accepting functional finance as a budget policy, the long-run goal of a balanced budget is consigned to oblivion, and with it go both the means and criteria for preventing runaway spending and inflation.

Full-employment Balanced Budget

Can a budget policy incorporate the best features of the foregoing proposals? The Committee for Economic Development, an organization composed of some of the nation's most prominent business leaders, thinks that it can. The plan is simple. First, determine a level of expenditures based on long-term merits without regard to stabilization considerations. Then, set tax rates to cover those expenditures at full or high employment, and perhaps yield a moderate surplus besides.

This plan, in the opinion of the CED, has two major advantages: (1) it produces a balanced budget over the full course of a business cycle; and (2) it rejects the use of discretionary fiscal policy, which is often difficult to apply for both political and economic reasons, and relies instead on the use of automatic stabilizers to keep the economy at a high level of employment. The result is a long-run cyclically balanced budget with automatic built-in flexibility.

Unfortunately, however, the plan has some disadvantages. For example: Reliance on automatic stabilizers may not be enough to keep small swings from developing into big ones; and there are times when the private sector is either too weak or too strong, so that stabilization may require more substantial and intentional federal deficits or surpluses than this plan would permit.

As a general rule, therefore, a full-employment balanced budget would not necessarily assure full or high employment. Nevertheless, many economists believe that this plan would have worked quite well for the years since World War II—probably better than actual budget policies for most of those years. That alone is a major factor in its behalf.

THE PUBLIC DEBT: IS IT TOO LARGE?

Since the start of World War II, the number of general budget deficits has far exceeded the number of surpluses. As a result, the government has accumulated a substantial public debt, the size of which

Exhibit 3

The Public Debt and Interest Payments

Most of our public debt was not incurred as a result of countercyclical fiscal policy, but to help pay for World War II.

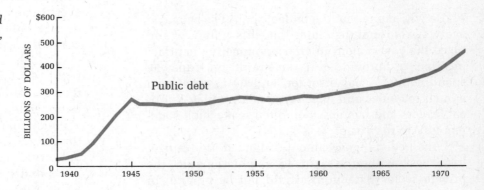

The growth of a nation's debt relative to its real income or GNP is the best indicator of its ability to carry that debt.

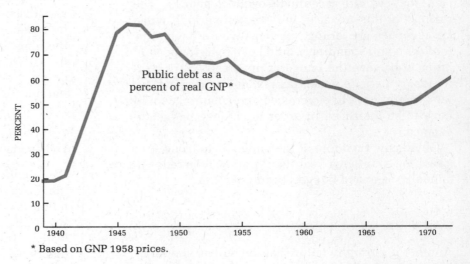

* Based on GNP 1958 prices.

has been the subject of a good deal of controversy and criticism. Before exploring the issues that are involved, you should examine the facts by studying the charts and statements in Exhibit 3.

Is our present public debt too large? Many people think it is, and they fear that the debt will (1) endanger the nation's credit standing and possibly lead to bankruptcy or (2) burden future generations unfairly. Are these dire predictions justified? Let us examine them and see.

Endangers National Credit and May Lead to Bankruptcy

The credit standing of the United States government is determined, as it is for any borrower, by those who lend it money—the banks, insurance companies, corporations, and households that buy the bonds and other securities sold by the Treasury. Despite its large debt, the government is able to borrow (i.e., sell securities) in competitive markets at the lowest interest rates.

Bankruptcy is a term applied to a borrower who is unable to pay his debts. But the federal government need never go bankrupt, for even if it is unable to borrow new funds to pay off old debts, it can always raise taxes or even print money if it wishes. In the final analysis, *the economic consequences of these actions will depend on the nation's productive output, such as its real GNP, and not on the size of the public debt per se.*

Thus objections that a large public debt may endanger the nation's credit rating, or lead to bankruptcy should be recognized for what they are:

The chief burdens of a public debt are the annual interest payments. The long-run trend of these payments has been upward since the forties.

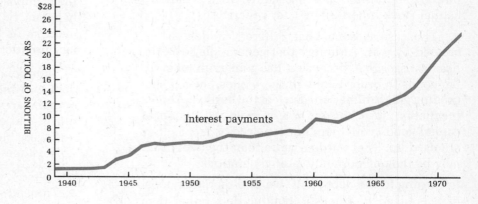

Interest payments

The long-run trend of interest payments as a percent of real GNP has been rising. Note, however, that the percentage is still relatively low.

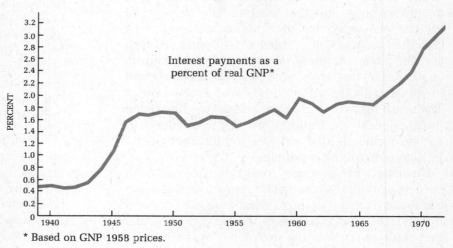

Interest payments as a percent of real GNP*

* Based on GNP 1958 prices.

criticisms based on the speaker's psychological fears rather than on economic facts.

Burdens Future Generations

Many people argue that when the government incurs long-term debt it burdens future generations with the cost of today's policies. There is some merit to this argument; but several aspects of it need to be examined. First, keep in mind that the basic idea of cost involves sacrifice; the real cost of anything is not the dollars you spend for it, but the value of the alternative to it that you renounce. In view of this, what are the real costs of public debt? The answer depends on the circumstances under which it is incurred:

1. If the debt is increased by deficit spending during a period of unemployment, resources are put to work that would otherwise have remained idle. Hence the increase in debt levies no real cost on either the generation that incurs it, or on future generations. Society has benefited from the greater output, and some of it has added to the nation's capital stock inherited by later generations.

2. The case is somewhat different if debt is increased by war. Although that generation bears the heaviest sacrifice, because it has gone without civilian goods in order to buy military ones, several succeeding generations can also feel the burden. Almost inevitably, spending on war starves the nation of capital goods which are not replaced as fast as they are used up. That burden, more than the debt itself, may be the one borne by later generations.

Turning to the debt itself, we find that, first, most of it is owed to domestic bondholders rather than to foreign ones; and that, second, the payment of interest and repayment of capital must therefore be classified as transfer payments. Of course, like all transfer payments these are made by one group to another; the taxpayers who finance them are not identical with the bondholders who receive them. The result may be a tendency to make the rich richer (because most bondholders are in the middle- and upper-income groups) unless offset by taxation and income redistribution policies.

However, in charging past generations with burdening the future, we must remember that *every* economic decision helps to determine the course of history. The world we live in was largely fashioned by people now dead; the decisions we make today will affect people not yet born. Society thus has an awesome responsibility and should not be too quick to incur large debts before considering both the burdens and the benefits.

WHAT ARE THE REAL BURDENS AND BENEFITS?

To conclude, these are the main burdens:

1. *External-debt burden.* A debt owed to foreigners does impose a burden on future generations, for it means they must pay interest and principal without necessarily receiving corresponding benefits in return. The foreign bondholders may well spend their incomes in their own country, rather than here. However, an exception occurs to the extent that the original borrowing was spent here to buy capital goods and create jobs, so that the resulting current output is at least large enough to cover the interest and principal payments on the debt.

2. *Capital-consumption burden.* As we learned earlier, any increase in public debt which uses up some of the nation's capital goods without replacing them imposes a burden on future generations. This happens typically during wars, when the government shifts resources out of civilian and into military production.

3. *Inflationary burden.* An increase in the public debt will impose inflationary burdens on the economy if, barring any offsetting measures, it is incurred during full employment, or if it makes bondholders feel wealthier and thereby raises their propensity-to-consume curve above the level that would otherwise exist.

4. *Transfer-payments burden.* Although each generation as a whole both bears the monetary costs and receives the benefits of the public debt, transfer payments will be a burden on it and on future generations to the extent that the taxpayers are not the same people as the bondholders. As we have seen, bondholders are predominantly in the middle- and upper-income groups, whereas total tax revenues are drawn from all income groups.

5. *Debt-management burden.* A large public debt may pose a conflict between fiscal and monetary policy. For example, the Treasury will normally desire low interest rates in the economy in order to keep down the costs of refunding or selling new bonds, whereas there are times when the monetary (i.e., Federal Reserve) authorities will desire high interest rates in order to help choke off inflationary

tendencies. The task of debt management thus raises significant problems. You will read more about them in later chapters.

In contrast, there are important benefits of a public debt:

1. Negotiable treasury bonds and other securities are a desirable investment for many families and large institutions, because these securities provide assured safety of principal, interest payments, and a high degree of liquidity.

2. Changes in the public debt, as already pointed out, can have desirable effects when used as a tool for discretionary fiscal policy. Indeed modern countercyclical fiscal theory relies heavily on debt manipulation to achieve and maintain full employment without inflation.

HOW LARGE SHOULD THE DEBT BE?

In view of these arguments, should the public debt be allowed to grow without limit? There is no simple answer. However, certain principles of debt management are illustrated by the facts presented earlier in Exhibit 3. They suggest that the government's ability to pay its debt interest and refundings is determined by the taxable capacity of the nation, and this in turn depends on the growth of its real GNP. Therefore, there need be no adverse consequences of an indefinitely large public debt— even a debt running into the trillions of dollars— provided that:

☐ The public debt does not, over the long run, grow faster than real GNP—that is, public debt as a percent of real GNP does not rise for a prolonged period.

☐ Taxes are used to curb inflationary pressures resulting from increases in debt.

☐ Interest payments on the debt are a relatively small percentage of real GNP.

The fact that some countries are always suffering from serious inflation due to an expanding public debt is often a result of their government's failure to adhere to these basic principles of debt management.

SUMMARY OF IMPORTANT IDEAS

1. The Employment Act of 1946 requires the government to strive for the achievement of continuous full employment. Modern fiscal policy would add to this the further objective of price stability.

2. Through government spending and tax policies, aggregate demand can be altered to close inflationary or deflationary gaps. For example, an increase in government spending, with taxes held constant, will raise aggregate demand; an increase in taxes, with government spending held constant, will reduce aggregate demand. A simultaneous and equal change in government spending and taxes will alter national income by the amount of the change because of the operation of the balanced-budget multiplier principle.

3. Fiscal policy may be discretionary or nondiscretionary. The former is "active" in that it involves conscious changes in government spending and taxation to create expansionary or contractionary effects; the latter is "passive" in that it relies on automatic or built-in stabilizers to keep the economy on course. Modern fiscal policy embraces some degree of both, but there are differences of opinion as to the proper combination. The controversy among economists hinges on the extent to which government should be involved in economic activity.

4. In carrying out its discretionary fiscal activities, the government's sources of funds may include taxation, borrowing, or printing of money, and its spending may include transfer and public works expenditures. In brief and general terms, taxation tends to be more contractionary than borrowing, whereas printing is ordinarily expansionary; transfer payments are expansionary if they are spent, but public works expenditures are even more expansionary because they stimulate the capital goods and construction industries directly.

5. Those who administer fiscal policy must grapple with problems of business-cycle forecasting and timing, political and public acceptance of fiscal measures, the meshing of federal with state and local fiscal policies, and the avoidance of government investment which may interfere with or discourage private investment.

6. The full-employment budget is usually based on the national-income accounts, and hence reflects the impact of budget surpluses and deficits on the economy's current levels of income and employment. The full-employment budget permits integration of the principles of discretionary fiscal policy with the concept of "fiscal dividends" in order to overcome the undesirable effects of "fiscal drag."

7. There is an erroneous tendency to associate some of the dangers of private debt with those of public

debt. Thus it is often mistakenly argued that a large public debt can endanger the nation's credit standing, lead to bankruptcy, and inevitably shift a burden of principal and interest payments to future generations. In fact, the real burdens of a debt depend on whether it (a) is externally held, (b) results in using up capital which is unreplaced, (c) induces inflationary effects, (d) imposes a transfer-payments burden due to its distribution among bondholders, and (e) creates a debt-management conflict between the fiscal and monetary authorities.

8. Although a large public debt may have adverse psychological consequences, its principal and interest must be assessed in relation to real GNP and to the growth of the economy as a whole before a meaningful evaluation can be made.

FOR DISCUSSION

1. *Terms and concepts to review:*

Employment Act of 1946
balanced-budget multiplier
fiscal policy
automatic fiscal stabilizers
public works
full-employment budget
fiscal drag
annually balanced budget
cyclically balanced budget
"functional finance"
refunding

2. Assume the economy is in recession, that the *MPC* is ½, and that an increase of $100 billion in output is needed in order to reach full employment. Then, using diagrams if necessary, and assuming that private investment is constant:

   (a) How much should government spending be increased in order to achieve full employment?

   (b) What would happen if taxes were reduced by $10 billion? Is this enough to restore full employment? If not, how much of a tax reduction is needed?

   (c) What would be the effect of a simultaneous increase in government spending and taxes of $50 billion? A simultaneous decrease of $50 billion? Explain why. Would the situation be different in the case of a simultaneous increase in G and T under full employment? Explain.

3. What are our chief automatic stabilizers, and how do they operate?

4. What are the government's sources of revenue and its outlets for expenditures? Which are expansionary? Contractionary?

5. In view of the difficulties of applying fiscal policies, it has been suggested that a law involving an automatic tax rate formula be enacted. In this way tax rates could be tied to GNP and perhaps other measures, and would vary automatically when these other measures changed by given percentages. What are some of the chief advantages of such a proposal?

6. What fiscal-policy advantages do you see in the concept of a full-employment budget?

7. "Some increases in government expenditures like those for health, education, and welfare are inflationary, while other government expenditures like those incurred for national defense and public works are not." Do you agree? What central questions must be considered to determine whether some government expenditures are more inflationary than others?

8. Evaluate the following argument about the public debt:

   No individual or family would be wise to continue accumulating indebtedness indefinitely, for eventually all debts must either be paid or repudiated. It follows that this fundamental principle applies equally well to nations, for as Adam Smith himself said, "What is prudence in the conduct of every private family can scarce be folly in that of a great kingdom."

9. Prepare a "checklist" of questions covering the chief factors to be considered in evaluating the consequences of a public debt.

Is Defense Spending Needed to Maintain Prosperity?

War has been closely linked with prosperity and inflation in the United States. As the accompanying charts show, heavy defense spending and its aftermath have caused significant episodes of inflation.

Figure 1 shows that during the Civil War, consumer prices rose at an average annual rate of 15 percent. In World War I, the existence of unused capacity in the early stages of the war helped keep consumer prices down, but from mid-1914 to mid-1920 they rose at an average rate of 13 percent a year. During World War II, government controls helped retard the increase in prices, but consumers paid an average of 7 percent more each year from late 1939 to late 1948. In the Korean War which was relatively short, speculative forces pushed consumer prices up by a phenomenal 12 percent between June 1950 and February 1951. In the Vietnam War, consumer prices increased by an average of about 4 percent per year between 1965 and 1970.

Gross national product increased at a 9.1 percent rate annually during the Korean War versus an average 8.1 percent annual rate through the four peak years of the Vietnam War. Personal income grew at almost identical rates of 8.6 percent per year and 8.7 percent per year, respectively, during the two periods. Corporate profits before taxes increased rapidly after hostilities com-

Figure 1

WAR AND PRICES

1851 = 100*

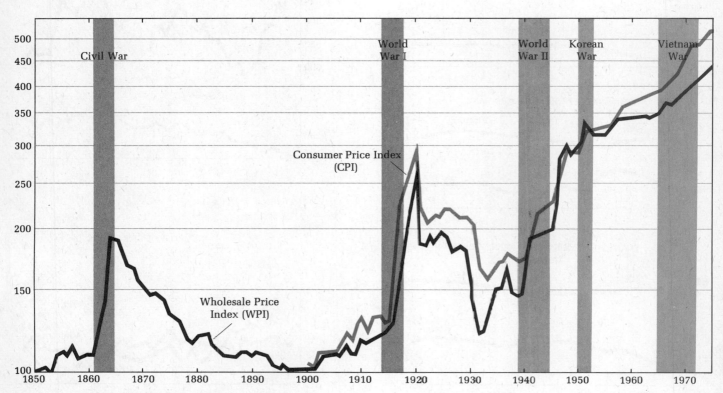

* Ratio scale to show proportionate changes. Annual data.
SOURCE: "Retail Prices After 1850," chapter by Ethel D. Hoover, in *Trends in the American Economy in the Ninteenth Century* (Princeton University Press for the National Bureau of Economic Research, 1960); U.S. Bureau of Labor Statistics, adjusted to 1851 = 100 basis. Adapted by First National City Bank of New York.

menced in Korea, quickly reached a peak, and then declined. They remained at a lower level, probably reflecting the imposition of price and wage controls.

Plant and equipment expenditures rose at a rate of 11.7 percent per year under the influence of Korea, and 8.0 percent per year during the four years of Vietnam. Outlays had increased substantially in 1964 and 1965 as a result of the 7 percent investment tax credit and the accelerated depreciation schedule. The GNP implicit price deflator increased about the same in both periods. The industrial production index increased more under the impact of Korea, accounting for the higher rate of growth in GNP during that period. (See Figure 2.)

War and inflation tend to go hand in hand for several reasons. The government sector bids away needed resources; the flow of consumer goods does not match the higher incomes generated by defense production; and fiscal or monetary policies are not usually restrictive enough to curb inflationary pressures.

Adjusting to Defense Cuts*

How successful have political administrations been in adjusting to

* Adapted from Emile Benoit, "Cutting Back Military Spending: The Vietnam Withdrawal and the Recession," *The Annals of the American Academy of Political and Social Science*, March, 1973.

Figure 2

ECONOMIC CHANGES DURING TWO
CONFLICTS: KOREA AND VIETNAM

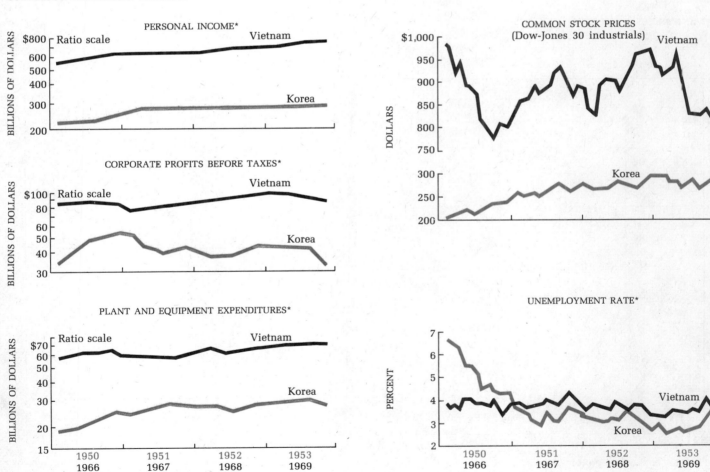

* Seasonally adjusted, annual rate.
SOURCE: The Conference Board, Inc.

Table 1

DEFENSE CUTS AND GNP LOSSES

	Truman 1945–1947 (percent)	Eisenhower 1953–1955 (percent)	Nixon 1969–1971 (percent)
1. Size of defense cuts (as percent of GNP)	30.75	3.66	1.6
2. Loss of GNP as percentage points of achievable (4.5 percent per annum) real growth	22.2	2.9	7.0
3. Transfer cost index (line 2 divided by line 1)	0.72	0.79	4.4

defense cuts? Each of the three two-year periods shown in Table 1 is from the peak year of defense expenditure to the year of temporary low after which an upturn occurred. The magnitude of the cuts is measured by the reduction in defense expenditures on goods and services as a percent of GNP. The loss of GNP during the period of the cuts is measured by the extent to which growth in real GNP over the two-year period fell below 4.5 percent per year. (Various studies show that real growth of 4.5 percent in GNP is possible in the U.S. economy even after full employment has been reached.)

The defense cuts from 1969 to 1971 involved a shift of only 1.6 percent of GNP out of defense, but were associated with a loss of 7 out of the 9 percent of achievable growth over this two-year period. The index of transfer costs—the losses in GNP in relation to the share of GNP shifted out of defense—was far higher than in past episodes of major defense cuts after wars.

Whereas in 1945–1947 and 1953–1955 the lost growth rates were only 0.72 and 0.79 percent per annum, respectively, for each percent of GNP shifted out of defense, in the defense cuts associated with the Vietnam withdrawal, the lost growth was 4.4 percent per annum for each percent of GNP shifted out of defense.

Many people believe that *a buoyant and growing capitalistic economy is dependent on high and rising defense expenditures.* Indeed, most students of the Left have adopted the dogma (which originated with V. I. Lenin, the founder of Soviet Russia) that the nature of capitalistic countries is to be aggressive and warlike in order to sustain economic expansion. Many other people of more moderate persuasion have also subscribed to this so-called "defense-economy thesis"—an hypothesis which holds that *heavy defense spending is vital to the growth of the economy.*

QUESTIONS

1. *From your previous study of America's business cycles during peacetime periods since the Civil War, does the defense-economy thesis appear warranted? Explain your answer.* (SUGGESTION: *Refer back to the historical chart of business cycles in Chapter 9.*)

2. *The defense-economy thesis first became popular at the beginning of World War I, and again during the early part of World War II. Can you suggest why?* HINT: *What economic conditions at the outset of these two wars prompted these views?*

3. *From your understanding of macroeconomic theory and policy, what basic assumptions underlie the defense-economy thesis?*

4. *Carefully examine Figure 2 and Table 1. In Table 1, applying the transfer-cost index of the post-Korean (1953–1955) defense cuts as a standard, evaluate the achievements of President Nixon, as compared with those of President Eisenhower, in shifting resources from defense to other uses.*

5. *Do you conclude from your analysis that a high level of defense spending is necessary to maintain prosperity? Discuss.*

PART 3

Money, Banking, and
Monetary Policy: The
Fiscal-Monetary Mix

CHAPTER 13

Our Monetary and Banking System

CHAPTER PREVIEW

What is the nature of money and of our monetary system?

Is credit the same as money? How important is credit in our economy?

What types of markets and financial institutions exist for facilitating the flow of money and credit?

What is a central bank? How is the central bank of the United States organized? What are its functions?

Most people want *money*. Few can define it. The average man will probably say: "It's cash, and whatever you've got in the bank." An economist may describe it in terms of the four functions of money you learned about in an earlier chapter:

1. A *medium of exchange*—money used to conduct transactions.

2. A *measure of value*—money used to express the prices of current and future transactions.

3. A *standard of deferred payments*—money borrowed or loaned, earning interest until it is repaid.

4. A *store of value*—money saved so that it can be spent in the future.

But money and credit—which is an "extension" of money—are even more important than these functions indicate. For money and credit have a direct influence on the level of economic activity, and some economists argue that the supply of money is the chief determinant of the economy's health.

Money and Our Monetary System

A monetary system's primary task is to provide society with money that is widely acceptable and flexible enough in supply to meet the needs of economic activity.

The long history of money shows this is no easy task. As a result there has been a continuous evolution of monetary systems designed to achieve these two objectives.

What does it mean to say that the supply of money must be flexible? Interestingly enough, this question can only be answered in terms of the demand for money. Indeed, the demand for money, as this and the following chapters show, poses the most fundamental problem faced by our monetary and banking system.

MONEY AND NEAR-MONIES

In the United States three main types of money are in use—coins, paper money or *currency*, and demand deposits or checking-account money.

Coins comprise about 1 percent of the total money supply. Coins are *token money*, which means that their value as money is significantly greater than the market value of the metals from which they are made. If this were not so, it would pay to melt the coins down for their metallic content.

Paper money—$1 bills, $5 bills, and so on—makes up roughly 20 percent of the money supply. Any paper money you have will almost certainly say "Federal Reserve Note" across the top, signifying that it is issued by the Federal Reserve Banks, about which you will read more later. Federal Reserve Notes represent more than 99 percent of the total value of paper money in circulation. The rest consists of other types of paper money—some dating back to Civil War days—which are collectors' items.

Demand deposits constitute the largest proportion of the money supply—almost 80 percent. Why are demand deposits regarded as money? Because a *demand deposit* is a promise on the part of a bank to pay immediately an amount of money specified by the customer who owns the deposit. Thus a demand deposit is sometimes called "checkbook money" because it permits transactions to be paid for by check rather than with currency. In contrast, money in a bank account for which the bank can require advance notice of withdrawal is called a *time deposit*. Such deposits are held in commercial banks and savings banks.

Since currency and demand deposits are freely convertible into one another, economists ordinarily regard money as consisting of both currency (and coin) and demand deposits; briefly, *money = currency + demand deposits*. But broader definitions which include savings deposits might be preferable for certain purposes. (See Exhibit 1.)

Some other assets are almost, but not quite, money. These are called *near-monies* because their values are known in terms of money and they can easily be converted into money if desired. The most important examples are (1) time deposits, (2) U.S. government short-term securities held by individuals and businesses, and (3) cash values of insurance policies. The concept of near-monies is important, because people who possess near-monies may feel wealthier and hence will have a higher propensity-to-consume curve.

MONETARY STANDARDS

Every nation has a *monetary standard*—a set of laws and practices which determines the quantity and quality of its money and establishes the conditions, if any, under which currency is ultimately redeemable. For instance, if a nation's money supply were based on the quantity of gold that it had, and if its currency were redeemable in gold, the country would be said to be on a gold standard.

Historically, certain metals have usually been used as monetary bases by most nations, but gold and silver—especially the former—have been preferred since the early Christian era. However, in principle, platinum, copper, diamonds, or any commodity—even skunks or pigs—could be used as a monetary base if the public were willing to accept it. Gold and silver are used because they are widely accepted, limited in supply, durable, and easily divided into monetary units. Diamonds and skunks, in contrast, do not meet all these qualifications. Historically, five major monetary standards have been used in various countries at one time or another.

Gold Coin Standard

The essentials of a *gold coin standard*, or simply a gold standard, are that (1) the national unit of currency (such as the dollar, pound, franc, mark) is defined by law in terms of a fixed weight of gold; (2) there is a free and unrestricted legal flow of the metal in any form into and out of the country; (3) gold coins are full legal tender for all debts; (4) there is free convertibility between the national currency and gold coins at the defined rate; and (5) there are no restrictions on the coinage of gold. This standard reigned supreme for the United States and about fifty other countries from the late 1800s to 1914, and then prevailed on a somewhat modified basis from 1914 to the early 1930s. Since then, no country has been on the gold standard.

Gold is said to be the disciplinarian *par excellence*, because under a gold standard the domestic money

Exhibit 1

Trying to Define Money

If you think you know exactly what money is, you are way ahead of most economists. For economists now are in the midst of a painstaking search for M_x—an ideal measure of the quantity of money available in the United States.

Right now, three basic definitions of the quantity of money are in use:

1. M_1—currency in circulation plus demand or check-book deposits. This is the narrowest definition of the money supply, covering only portions of the liquid wealth that are instantly acceptable in exchange. Most economists prefer this definition.

2. M_2—this includes not only currency and demand deposits, but also time deposits in commercial banks. This definition is preferred by some economists who believe that changes in the nation's total money stock are the most crucial factor in shaping the course of the economy.

3. M_3—this includes M_2 plus deposits at noncommercial-bank thrift institutions such as accounts at savings banks and at savings and loan associations. It is thus the broadest of the three measures of money.

The answer to the money enigma apparently lies in a blending of these definitions—with greatest weight given to the first two. Some monetary economists are working to develop a more precise definition, one which can be used to determine the influence of money on the levels of income, employment, and prices.

THE NATION'S MONEY SUPPLY

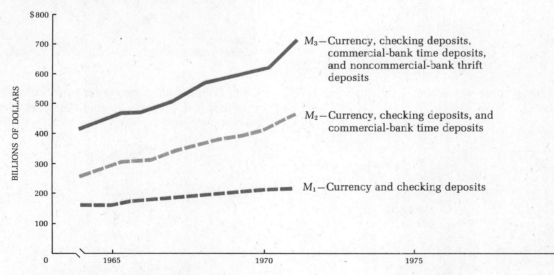

M_3—Currency, checking deposits, commercial-bank time deposits, and noncommercial-bank thrift deposits

M_2—Currency, checking deposits, and commercial-bank time deposits

M_1—Currency and checking deposits

SOURCE: Board of Governors of the Federal Reserve System.

Box 1

Paper Money—A Long and Interesting History

The oldest known paper money dates from China, Ming Dynasty, between the years 1368 to 1399. This piece bears a stern warning to counterfeiters.

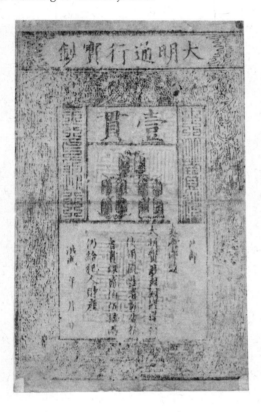

Obverse and reverse of three-pence note, Pennsylvania, 1764.

$1 BANK NOTE—1854

This note typifies the imaginative designs used on bank notes from 1837 to 1863. During this period, the government of the United States had little control over paper money issues, and state and city banks throughout the country printed hundreds of notes for circulation in their locales.

$2 SILVER CERTIFICATE—*Series of 1896*

One of a series considered among the most artistic and interesting ever issued by the U.S. government. The design shows science presenting steam and electricity to commerce and industry.

A $55 Continental Congress currency note, 1779, typical of issues to finance the Revolution. After 1781, the currency depreciated and was "Not worth a Continental."

Obverse and reverse of penny note issued by first United States chartered bank, 1789.

Dix or $10 note, Louisiana, 1856.

United States fractional currency note worth 50 cents, 1875.

Hungarian inflation currency, a 100 quintillion pengo note, 1946, highest denomination note issued in the history of currency. (100,000,000,000,000,000,000)

A 1,000 franc assignat note of the French Revolution. The republic issued these bills for a time, on the security of appropriated lands.

SOURCE: The Chase Manhattan Bank Museum of Moneys of the World, New York. Published by special permission of the United States Secret Service. Further reproduction, in whole or in part, is strictly prohibited.

supply is regulated by, and tied directly to, the amount of gold that a country has. When a nation adhered to this standard, it found that an outflow of gold for business or speculative reasons would reduce the domestic money supply, and this in turn could induce contractions in investment, income, and employment within the economy; an inflow of gold, on the other hand, would increase the domestic money supply and this could have expansionary or even inflationary effects at home. Thus the gold coin standard assured automatic contractions and expansions of the money supply. But it did not always provide such changes at the most appropriate times or in the most desirable ways. Indeed, in the early 1930s those changes were strongly adverse, prompting nations to abandon the gold coin standard during the Great Depression.

Gold Bullion Standard

A *gold bullion standard* defines the national unit of currency in terms of a fixed weight of gold, but the gold is held in bars rather than coin. Gold does not circulate within the economy, and it is available solely to meet the needs of industry (e.g., jewelers and dentists) and to settle international transactions. The United States and most of the other advanced nations adopted this monetary standard when they went off the gold coin standard in the 1930s. By switching from a gold *coin* to a gold *bullion* standard these countries felt that they would be able to "manage" their money rather than be subservient to it, while continuing to preserve confidence in their currencies both at home and abroad. However, the United States abandoned the gold bullion standard in 1971—for reasons explained below.

Gold Exchange Standard

Under a *gold exchange standard* a nation's unit of currency is defined in terms of another nation's unit of currency, which in turn is defined in terms of, and convertible into, gold. This standard was particularly popular among nations which lacked gold or were politically dependent on other nations (e.g., British Commonwealth countries) after World War I. But with the worldwide abandonment of the gold coin standard in the early 1930s, this standard ceased to exist.

However, to encourage orderly international trade and economic growth, a modified version of the gold exchange standard was reinstituted by noncommunist nations near the end of World War II. It prevailed from 1944 to 1971, and had two distinctive features:

1. By the end of World War II, the United States owned most of the free world's gold. Therefore, the U.S. Treasury, by international agreement, made gold and dollars mutually convertible to foreign central (government-operated) banks at the rate of $35 an ounce of gold. The dollar was thus legally defined as equal to 1/35 of an ounce of gold.

2. Most other noncommunist countries owned relatively little or no gold. Hence, by international agreement, the central banks of these nations maintained a fixed par value for their currencies in terms of the dollar by buying and selling their currencies in the open market when others were selling and buying.

The gold exchange standard accomplished what it was designed to do—stimulate international trade and development after World War II. But in the 1960s the system began to fall apart as foreign confidence in the inflated American dollar waned, and the U.S. gold stock diminished in the face of repeated "gold rushes" by foreign central banks seeking to exchange their green paper for the yellow metal. Hence, the gold bullion standard for the United States—and therefore the gold exchange standard for all other countries—came to an end when President Nixon announced on August 15, 1971, that the Treasury would no longer convert dollars into gold to meet the claims of foreign central banks. In addition, the dollar has been redefined by Washington in terms of gold several times since then—most recently at $42.22 an ounce. But this is only an accounting measure used by government and is unrelated to the price of gold on world markets.

It is clear from this brief historical sketch that the gold exchange standard is primarily of international significance. Therefore, we shall have more to say about it in a later chapter dealing with international commercial and financial policies.

Bimetallic Standard

Under a *bimetallic standard*, the national currency is defined in terms of a fixed weight of two metals, usually gold and silver. The results, for the most part, have been unsatisfactory, largely because of the operation of an interesting phenomenon first described by Sir Thomas Gresham, a sixteenth-century financier and Master of the Mint under Queen Elizabeth I:

Gresham's Law. When two kinds of metals of differing market values circulate with equal legal-tender powers, the cheaper metal will become the chief circulating medium while the more costly metal is hoarded, melted down, or exported, thereby disappearing from circulation. Thus, cheap money tends to drive out dear money.

Gresham's Law operates in the following way. Suppose the government fixes the official *mint ratio* of two metals, say silver and gold, at 15:1. This means that $1 can be converted into 15 grains of silver or 1 grain of gold—a situation that actually existed in the United States during part of the nineteenth century. It follows that any change in the world market value (as distinguished from the fixed official mint value) of one metal in relation to the other will cause the metal with the higher value to disappear from circulation. This is because the metal which is relatively cheaper in the market will be taken to the mint, coined, and put into circulation, while coins made of the metal that is relatively dearer in the market will be taken out of circulation and hoarded, or else melted down and sold as bullion. In other words, a fixed mint ratio and a variable market ratio allow people to hold the more valuable money and pass on the less valuable.

This happened during the nineteenth century when the United States was on a *de jure* (according to law) bimetallic standard. Either gold or silver was always disappearing from circulation. Thus, during the first period of bimetallism, from 1792 to 1834, gold went out of circulation, and the country was on a *de facto* (in fact) silver standard. During the second period, from 1834 to 1873, silver went out, and the nation was on a *de facto* gold standard. After 1873, the political power of the silver producers was strong enough to persuade Congress to overvalue silver at the mint, thereby benefiting the western silver-mining states. As a result, gold disappeared from circulation, and the country returned to a *de facto* silver standard.

In 1900 a Republican Congress passed the Gold Standard Act, placing the country for the first time on a legal gold standard. After that, nothing particularly significant was heard of silver for several decades. Evidently it had taken Congress more than a century to comprehend the workings of Gresham's Law and to adopt a monetary standard that overcame the inconsistencies of bimetallism.

Inconvertible Paper Standard

Under an *inconvertible paper standard*, the nation's unit of money cannot be freely converted into precious metals, although its value may be expressed in metallic terms. This standard has typically arisen during wars or economic emergencies when governments needed more freedom to control their money supplies than permitted by metallic standards.

During the 1930s inconvertible paper standards became universal as nations sought to manage their currencies in order to hasten economic recovery. The United States and some other advanced countries went on a gold bullion standard for international purposes and on an inconvertible paper standard for domestic purposes. Gold was used to settle international monetary claims, but removed from circulation at home by not allowing currencies to be exchanged for gold and by not making gold available for domestic monetary use (although it has been available for purchase and sale in many countries by private citizens). From a domestic standpoint, all countries have been on an inconvertible paper standard since the late 1930s.

WHAT IS THE VALUE OF MONEY?

If you cannot get gold for your money, what good is money? The answer is that the real value of money depends on its purchasing power—the quantity of goods or services that can be bought with a dollar.

You have probably heard it said that the dollar today is worth only 60 cents, or 50 cents—or perhaps even less. Such statements try to convey the idea that today's dollar buys only a fraction of what a dollar bought during some period in the past. Which period? It depends on the one you choose. The decline in the purchasing power of the dollar was much greater during some recent inflationary years than it was in the depressed 1930s. In general:

The value of a unit of money such as the dollar is defined in terms of its purchasing power and is measured as the reciprocal or inverse of the general price level. Thus the higher the level of prices, the lower the value or purchasing power of a unit of money, and vice versa.

These ideas are illustrated in Exhibit 2 on the next page.

Exhibit 2

The Value of Money and Consumer Prices

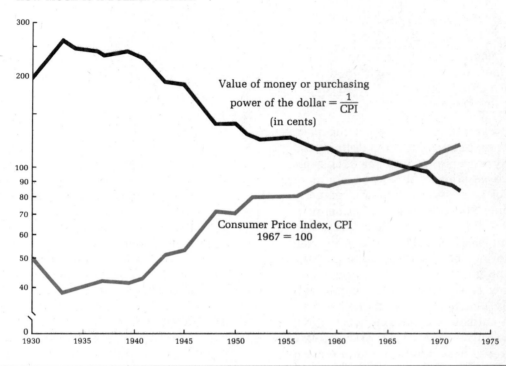

HOW MUCH IS A DOLLAR WORTH?

Value of money or purchasing power of the dollar $= \dfrac{1}{CPI}$ (in cents)

Consumer Price Index, CPI
1967 = 100

The Role of Credit

The term *credit* always implies a promise by one party to pay another for money borrowed or for goods or services received. Credit may therefore be regarded as an extension of money.

Credit and debt are really the same thing looked at from two different sides. If a friend lends you money, his credit to you is the same as your debt to him. The functions of credit and debt are intertwined with those of money, since credit replaces money, supplements money, and in the final analysis serves as the base of the money supply.

WHAT ARE THE FUNCTIONS OF CREDIT?

Credit, like money, serves at least two major functions:

1. It *facilitates trade.* The production and distribution of goods is a complex process involving exchanges of property and property rights on a credit basis. Imagine the effect on business if all credit were suddenly eliminated—if everyone in the economy had to pay cash for everything purchased.

2. It *channels savings* into productive investment, thereby encouraging technological progress and economic growth. A credit system means that businessmen can borrow savings and return them to the income stream through investment in plant, equipment, and research.

You may be able to think of other functions of credit. For example, credit could affect the time distribution of consumption expenditures. Can you see how, if no lending were possible, a person with a large income today might have to hoard part of it for consumption later, while a person with a low income would have to do without some possible present consumption?

CREDIT INSTRUMENTS

Some credit is negotiated informally by verbal agreement between the borrower and lender, and some is handled on an open-book-account basis between business firms. For our purposes, however, the most significant part of credit is that represented by *credit instruments*—written or printed financial documents serving as either promises to pay or orders to pay by means of which funds are transferred from one person to another.

The principal classes of credit instruments are notes, bonds, and drafts. A *promissory note,* or simply a *note,* is one person's promise to pay another a specified sum of money by a given date, usually within a year. Such notes are issued by individuals, corporations, and government agencies. Firms make heavy use of notes in order to borrow working capital from banks at certain busy times of the year. The interest (or discount) on such loans is a chief source of income for commercial banks.

A *bond* is an agreement to pay a specified sum of money (called the *principal*) either at a future date or periodically over the course of a loan, during which time a fixed rate of interest may be paid on certain dates. Bonds are issued by corporations (corporate bonds), state and local governments (municipal bonds), and the federal government (government bonds). Bonds are used for long-term financing.

A *draft* is an unconditional written order by one party (the creditor or drawer) on a second party (the debtor or drawee) directing him to pay a third party (the bearer or payee) a specified sum of money. An ordinary check is an example. When you write a check, you are drawing a draft against your bank, ordering it to pay someone a certain amount of money.

The above definition of a draft applies equally well to a *bill of exchange,* which is used in international trade. An exporter, for instance, draws up a bill of exchange against his customer, an importer, and discounts it—that is, sells it to his local bank at a little less than its face value. The bank then sends the bill to its correspondent bank in the city of the importer, which presents it to the importer for collection or acceptance at face value. If the bill of exchange were drawn on or accepted by a bank instead of an individual or firm, it would be called a *banker's acceptance.* This is a promise by a bank to pay specific bills for one of its customers.

THE MONEY MARKET

Markets exist for many types of credit instruments, just as they do for commodities. A *money market* is a center where short-term credit instruments such as Treasury bills and certificates, short-term promissory notes of businesses, and bankers' acceptances are bought and sold. It is thus distinguished from the *capital market,* which deals with long-term instruments such as bonds, stocks, and mortgages. The money market is closely related to the capital market and to the foreign exchange, commodity, insurance, and bullion markets, all of which rely on the money market for credit.

In the money market the supply of short-term funds made available by lenders meets borrowers' demands for funds. It is here that holders of short-term credit instruments convert these assets into cash. Lenders consist mainly of the Federal Reserve Banks, which are the primary source of credit for most other banks; large commercial banks which place their funds in various kinds of credit instruments; and financial institutions like insurance and trust companies which invest in short-term "paper." Borrowers are chiefly the United States government, which sells 90-day Treasury bills and other short-term certificates in order to meet its current expenses; brokerage houses and dealers in government securities, which borrow chiefly for the accounts of their customers; and investment banking houses, commodity dealers, importers, exporters, and business firms, all of whom sell future claims against money in order to obtain cash for current operations.

The New York money market is the largest in the United States. It attracts funds from the entire country and performs a vital function in financing the short-term needs of the federal government as well as the requirements of the business community.

THE CAPITAL MARKET

In contrast to the money market, the *capital market* deals in long-term credit instruments maturing in more than one year or having no maturity date at all. Examples of the latter are corporate stocks and consoles (a type of bond issued in perpetuity). Together, the money and capital markets constitute the *financial market.*

Five types of instruments are bought and sold in the capital market: (1) U.S. government bonds, (2) municipal (including state and local government) bonds, (3) corporate bonds, (4) mortgages, and (5) corporate stock. The yields on these securities differ from one another at any given time, reflecting such features as maturity dates, coupon rates, risk of default, tax treatment, and other factors. (See Exhibit 3.) In general, municipal bonds tend to have the lowest yields because the interest received by purchasers of such bonds is exempt from federal income taxes, so these bonds can be sold at lower yields than comparable Treasury and corporate taxable bonds. Treasury long-term bonds generally have a lower yield than comparable corporate bonds because Treasury bonds carry no risk of default. Yields on high-quality corporate bonds are, in turn, lower than those on mortgages, which cost more to service and are not so easily marketed.

Financial Intermediaries

The institutions that serve the money and capital markets are known as *financial intermediaries*. They act as middlemen between lenders and borrowers, creating and issuing financial obligations or claims against themselves in order to acquire profitable financial claims against others. A chief function of financial intermediaries, therefore, is providing liquidity. For our purposes, financial intermediaries may be divided into two broad classes: (1) commercial banks and (2) all other financial institutions, in-

---

Exhibit 3

Capital Market Yields

Yields on securities tend to differ from one another at any given time, depending on risk of default, maturity dates, tax advantages, and many other factors. Note that the various yields tend to rise and fall at about the same time.

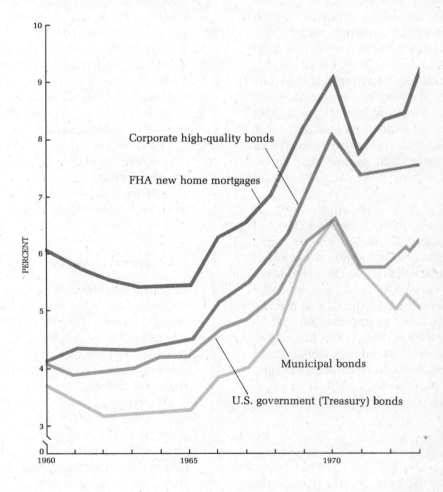

cluding mutual savings banks, savings and loan associations, credit unions, insurance companies, private pension funds, finance companies, mortgage companies, and so on. As indicated above, all financial intermediaries serve as wholesalers or retailers of funds.

COMMERCIAL BANKS

All banks deal in money and credit instruments. But a *commercial bank* is the only type of bank primarily engaged in making short-term commercial and industrial loans by creating demand deposits, and retiring loans by canceling demand deposits. (Remember that a demand deposit is the technical term for a checking account.) In addition, a commercial bank may also engage in some of the same activities carried on by other financial institutions, such as taking savings accounts or time deposits, and providing life insurance, but its major business is handling demand deposits.

When a commercial bank provides you with a demand deposit, it creates and issues a financial obligation or claim against itself, by agreeing to honor your checks on demand up to the amount of the deposit. When a bank accepts your savings or time deposit, it creates a claim against itself which is legally payable after a specified time. That is, the bank, if it wishes, can require notice of intended withdrawal—usually 30 days or more. Hence a time deposit may be thought of as a claim which possesses a stipulated maturity date. Other instruments representing time-deposit claims are savings bonds, saving certificates, and *certificates of deposit* (CDs), which are a special type of time deposit that a purchaser agrees to keep in a bank for a specified period, usually 90 days or more. Commercial banks sell CDs at rates competitive with other money-market instruments, in order to discourage corporations from withdrawing money for the purpose of investing in securities. Many CDs are negotiable and can be sold in a secondary market because they offer both liquidity (convertibility into cash) and a yield. However, they are not as liquid as demand deposits. In fact:

Commercial-bank demand deposits are the most liquid of all claims created and issued by financial intermediaries. Because checks written against them are instantly acceptable in exchange, demand deposits are included with currency as part of the money supply.

The role played by commercial banks in expanding and contracting demand deposits is of enormous importance in understanding how the economy works and will occupy a considerable part of our attention in this and in subsequent chapters.

OTHER FINANCIAL INTERMEDIARIES

Like commercial banks, other kinds of financial intermediaries seek to accommodate the particular needs and preferences of borrowers by creating and issuing claims against themselves. For example, mutual savings banks and savings and loan associations issue time-deposit claims which are very much like those provided by commercial banks—except in some cases for differences with respect to maturities and yields. The assets or claims against others that they acquire with the funds consist primarily of real-estate mortgages, corporate bonds, and government securities. Likewise, credit unions issue savings-deposit claims to their members and acquire claims against others primarily in the form of consumer loans; insurance companies issue claims in the form of policies against themselves and use most of the funds collected in premiums to purchase real-estate mortgages, corporate securities, and government bonds. In a similar manner, other financial intermediaries generate obligations against themselves in order to acquire funds with which to purchase profitable, but often less liquid, obligations against others.

CONCLUSION: MAINTAINING LIQUIDITY

It seems plausible, therefore, that since the claims acquired by financial intermediaries are frequently less liquid than the claims they issue, these intermediaries may sometimes find themselves temporarily illiquid by being unable to meet unexpected demands for payment out of their own assets. This situation has occurred frequently in American history and was especially serious during the depression of the 1930s, giving rise to financial crises or panics.

To help remedy this problem, legislation to protect the public was passed providing insurance for bank deposits and setting minimum financial requirements for banks, insurance companies, and some other financial intermediaries. In addition, federally sponsored institutions have been created to provide liquidity to some financial intermediaries by lending to them or by purchasing assets from them. Notable among these have been special federal banks which supply funds to savings and loan associations and which make intermediate-term loans to farmers. But most important for our purposes have been the Federal Reserve Banks, which supply funds to the commercial banks that are members of the Federal Reserve System.

The Federal Reserve System

On December 23, 1913, President Woodrow Wilson signed the Federal Reserve Act. It was, according to its preamble, "An Act to provide for the establishment of Federal Reserve Banks, to furnish an elastic currency, to afford means of rediscounting commercial paper, to establish a more effective supervision of banking in the United States, and for other purposes." Section 4 of the new statute charged the Federal Reserve Banks with making ". . . such discounts, advancements, and accommodations as may be safely and reasonably made with due regard for . . . the maintenance of sound credit conditions, and the accommodations of commerce, industry, and agriculture."

The act marked a new era in American banking. Periodic money panics, highlighted by the Panic of 1907, had plagued the country for many years. Basically, the act was designed to end extreme variations in the money supply and to end panics, and thus to contribute to economic stability.

MONEY PANICS AND THE BANKING SYSTEM

American banking history records a series of attempts to provide a currency which could expand or contract according to the demands of business.

Theoretically, the ability of commercial banks, through the lending process, to expand or contract the amount of money available should have provided for the demands occasioned by changes in business activity.

Commercial banks, however, while they could expand credit, could not add to the amount of available currency. Inasmuch as bank depositors had a legal right to withdraw their money in the form of currency and coin, banks provided for ordinary withdrawals by retaining a part of their total deposits in the form of reserves. These reserves usually consisted of currency, coin, and deposits in other banks.

A general increase in demand by depositors for their money, therefore, at a time when demand deposits created by loans were already high could create a situation where the available amount of currency and coin might not cover the percentage of reserves which the banks had set up. An unusual demand by depositors forced banks to exchange their assets for currency. An attempt by one bank to supply itself with currency by withdrawing its reserve balance from another all too frequently set up a "chain reaction" which resulted in a widespread shortage of currency among many banks.

Some banks were forced to close, although their assets could have been converted into currency if sufficient time had been allowed. A widespread closing of banks resulting from unusual demands by depositors invariably brought on a period of economic depression. These unusual demands were called "money panics," and one which occurred in 1907 set into motion a thorough study of the money system.

The congressional commission charged with this study found that almost all countries which had a money supply that could be expanded or contracted to meet the needs of the depositors also had some form of central bank. This bank had the power to issue a currency which depositors would accept. As a result of this and other studies, Congress in 1913 passed a law which created the Federal Reserve System. (See Box 2.)

OBJECTIVES, ORGANIZATION, AND FUNCTIONS OF THE FEDERAL RESERVE SYSTEM

The *Federal Reserve System* is the nation's central bank. Like other central banks throughout the world, its chief responsibility is to regulate the flow of money and credit in order to promote economic stability and growth. It also performs many service functions for commercial banks, the Treasury, and the public. In specific terms, the Federal Reserve System seeks to provide monetary conditions favorable to the realization of four national objectives: high employment, stable prices, economic growth, and a sound international financial position.

The Federal Reserve System is organized essentially like a pyramid, as illustrated in Exhibit 4. It is composed of (1) member banks, (2) Federal Reserve Banks, (3) Board of Governors, (4) Federal Open Market Committee, and (5) other committees.

Box 2

"When We All Get Wise": The Stock Market Titans

Before the establishment of the Federal Reserve System in 1913, the United States experienced a number of financial panics. Reckless speculation produced stock market booms and busts, with consequent large-scale unemploy- *ment. Labor and agrarian interests attributed the cause directly to the giant Wall Street "manipulators," as this 1911 cartoon indicates.*

Library of Congress, from *Life*, Oct. 26, 1911.

Member Banks

At the base of the Federal Reserve pyramid are the System's *member banks*. All national banks (chartered by the federal government) must be members, and state banks may join if they meet certain requirements. Of about 14,000 commercial banks, rather less than half are members. However these member banks are for the most part the larger banks in the country, holding about 80 percent of all commercial-bank deposits.

Each member bank has both obligations and privileges. The obligations include holding specified reserves at its district Federal Reserve Bank against the demand deposits of its depositors, subscribing to the captial stock (and thus being a part owner) of its district Federal Reserve Bank, and complying with the laws and regulations of membership. The privileges include prestige of membership, ability to borrow under certain conditions from its district Federal Reserve Bank, and the opportunity to use the many facilities and services provided by the System.

Federal Reserve Banks

The country is divided into 12 Federal Reserve districts, each with a *Federal Reserve Bank*. There are also 24 Federal Reserve Bank branches serving areas within the districts. (See map in Exhibit 4.)

Technically, each Federal Reserve Bank is owned by its member banks, which are the stockholders. However, unlike most private institutions, the Reserve Banks are operated in the public interest rather than for profit—even though they are in fact highly profitable. Thus, after meeting their expenses, they pay a relatively small part of their earnings to the member banks as dividends, and the major portion goes to the U.S. Treasury as "interest" on Federal Reserve Notes issued by the Reserve Banks. Note

Exhibit 4

Organization and Map of the Federal Reserve System

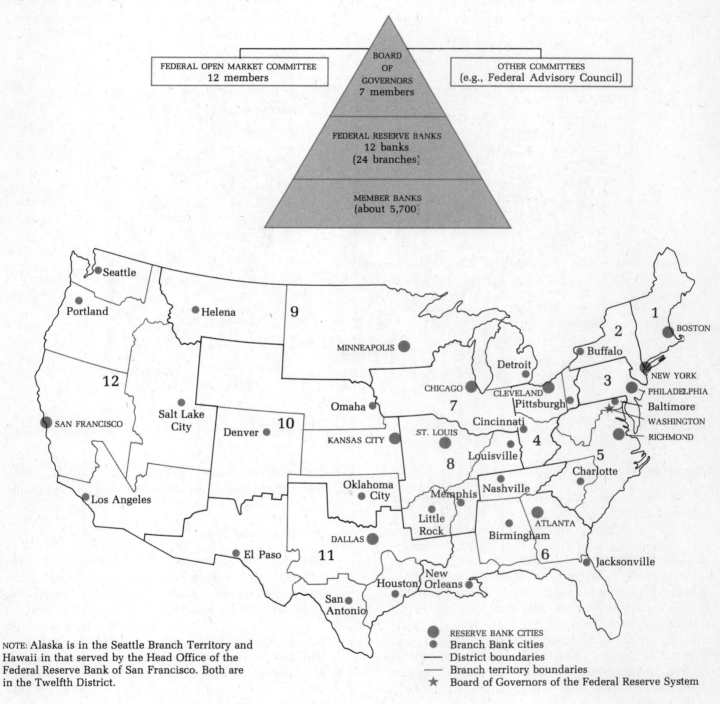

NOTE: Alaska is in the Seattle Branch Territory and Hawaii in that served by the Head Office of the Federal Reserve Bank of San Francisco. Both are in the Twelfth District.

● RESERVE BANK CITIES
● Branch Bank cities
— District boundaries
— Branch territory boundaries
★ Board of Governors of the Federal Reserve System

that the district Federal Reserve Banks (and branches) constitute the second level of the pyramid.

Board of Governors

At the peak of the pyramid is the *Board of Governors* in Washington. It consists of seven members appointed by the President and confirmed by the Senate. Members are appointed for 14 years, one term expiring every 2 years, thereby minimizing political influence.

The Board supervises the Federal Reserve System, and sees that it performs effectively. But its prime function is to influence the amount of money and credit within the economy by altering the reserve requirements of member banks, changing discount (or interest) rates which member banks incur when they borrow from their Reserve Banks, authorizing the purchase or sale of government securities by the Federal Reserve Banks, setting margin (or down payment) requirements on the purchases of securities by the public, and establishing maximum interest rates payable on member banks' time deposits.

Federal Open Market Committee

The most important policy-making body within the System, the *Federal Open Market Committee*, consists of 12 members—the 7 Governors plus 5 Presidents of the Federal Reserve Banks. Its chief function is to make policy for the System's purchase and sale of government and other securities in the open market in New York. Actual transactions are carried on by the so-called "Trading Desk" of the Federal Reserve Bank of New York. Government securities bought outright are then prorated among the 12 Reserve Banks according to a formula based upon the reserve ratios of the various Reserve Banks.

Other Committees

Several other committees play a significant role in the System's operations. One of these is the *Federal Advisory Council*, which advises the Board on important current developments.

Like the central banks of many other countries, the Federal Reserve System also provides a number of important services to the Treasury, the public, and commercial banks. These are described briefly in Exhibit 5.

Exhibit 5

Service Functions of the Federal Reserve System

1. Fiscal-agency functions. *The Reserve Banks service the Treasury's checking accounts; assist in the sale, transfer, and redemption of government securities; pay interest coupons; and assist the Treasury and other government agencies in many other ways.*

2. Collection of checks and noncash items. *The System operates a nationwide "clearing house" for checks, drafts, and similar items. Member banks route these items to Reserve Banks, which in turn send them to the proper places for collection. Settlement is accomplished by means of entries to the accounts which member banks maintain with the Reserve Banks.*

3. Wire transfer of funds. *The System transfers funds by wire from one part of the country to another. For example, if a national concern headquartered in New York wishes to transfer funds to its Chicago office it can have its bank request the transfer through the System's wire transfer facilities. The New York Reserve Bank will deduct the funds from the balance of the New York commercial bank, and the Chicago Reserve Bank will add the funds to the reserve balance of the firm's bank in Chicago, which will credit the account of the firm. The Reserve Banks will then settle by means of an entry on the books of the Interdistrict Settlement Fund—a Federal Reserve System clearing agency in Washington.*

4. Supplying coin and currency. *The Federal Reserve Banks provide a vital part of the machinery through which most coin and currency moves into and out of circulation. As the public demands more cash from commercial banks, the banks draw down their balances at the Federal Reserve in exchange for additional cash. Similarly, when cash flows in from the public, the banks deposit the funds in their accounts with the Reserve Banks.*

5. Note issue. *Look in your billfold and chances are that you will find a bill bearing a green seal. This is a Federal Reserve Note—the most common type of currency in circulation today. These notes, which are issued by the 12 Reserve Banks, are fully collateralized by government securities and certain other types of assets. When a Reserve Bank needs more currency to meet the demands of commercial banks, it can easily obtain the additional Federal Reserve Notes by pledging the proper collateral.*

SOURCE: Adapted from the Federal Reserve Bank of Richmond.

SUMMARY OF IMPORTANT IDEAS

1. Money is a medium of exchange, a measure of value, a standard of deferred payments, and a store of value. The demand for money is the most fundamental problem of our monetary and banking system.

2. The supply of money consists of both currency and demand deposits. Near-monies consist of highly liquid assets such as time and savings deposits, U.S. government short-term securities and the cash value of insurance policies.

3. Historically, the chief monetary standards of nations have been the gold coin standard, gold bullion standard, gold exchange standard, bimetallic standard, and inconvertible paper standard. Nations today are on an inconvertible paper standard.

4. In varying degrees, credit serves the same functions as money. The chief instruments of credit are notes, drafts, and bonds. Various types of short-term credit instruments are bought and sold in the money market, whereas long-term instruments are bought and sold in the capital market.

5. Financial intermediaries, such as banks, insurance companies, credit unions, and other financial institutions act as middlemen between lenders and borrowers. They create and issue financial claims against themselves in order to acquire proceeds with which to purchase profitable financial claims against others. In general, they serve as wholesalers or retailers of funds.

6. The Federal Reserve System is the central bank of the United States. It consists essentially of over 5,000 member (commercial) banks scattered throughout the nation, 12 Federal Reserve Banks (plus branches) located in various cities, and a 7-member Board of Governors appointed by the President and confirmed by the Senate. The function of the System is to foster a flow of credit that provides for stable prices, orderly economic growth, and strong international financial relationships.

FOR DISCUSSION

1. *Terms and concepts to review:*

money	near-monies
currency	monetary standard
token money	gold (coin) standard
demand deposit	gold bullion standard
time deposit	gold exchange standard
bimetallic standard	financial
Gresham's Law	intermediaries
mint ratio	commercial bank
inconvertible paper	certificate of deposit
standard	Federal Reserve
credit instrument	System
promissory note	member bank
bond	Federal Reserve Bank
draft	Board of Governors
bill of exchange	Federal Open Market
banker's acceptance	Committee
money market	Federal Advisory
capital market	Council
financial markets	

2. Which function of money is most important in today's society? Explain.

3. Which function does money perform least efficiently? Discuss.

4. How would the functions of money be affected if the value of the dollar increased from year to year?

5. The more money you have, the richer you are. Likewise, the more money a nation has, the richer it is. Therefore, nations can become rich simply by printing more money. Do you agree? Discuss.

6. If a nation is on a gold coin standard, as many nations were before World War I, what is its government supposed to do if prices rise? If prices fall?

7. Some of our money is legal tender, but most of it is not. How can this be? Explain.

8. During much of the nineteenth century, the notes (i.e., paper money) issued by state banks circulated at a discount from their face value, and the rate of discount usually varied directly with the distance from the issuing bank. For example, a $1 note issued by a bank in New York might have circulated at a 15 percent discount (or at 85 cents) in Chicago and a 30 percent discount (or at 70 cents) in San Francisco. Can you explain why?

9. Few people today would advocate the return to a gold coin standard. Can you suggest why?

10. Financial intermediaries play a much more important role in today's economy than they did several decades ago. They are also more significant in the United States than, say, African, Asian, or Latin American countries. Why?

11. Every nation has its own central bank. Why? What minimum functions does a central bank perform that a commercial bank does not?

CHAPTER 14

Commercial Banking: Money Creation and Portfolio Management

CHAPTER PREVIEW

How do commercial banks create money? How do they "destroy" it?

How does the process of credit creation by a single bank differ from that of the banking system as a whole?

What is a bank's portfolio? Of what does it consist? What goals and compromises are involved in managing a bank's portfolio?

The average person probably thinks of a bank as a place in which to deposit money against which he can write checks as the need arises. But banks are much more than mere depositories for people's funds. They play a fundamental role in the financial and monetary structure of our economy.

In a more specific sense, banks deal in money and credit instruments. A commercial bank, as we learned earlier, is a financial institution chartered by federal or state governments and primarily engaged in making short-term commercial and industrial loans by creating demand or checking deposits, and retiring loans by canceling demand deposits. In addition, it may or may not carry on functions performed by other financial institutions (e.g., insurance companies, savings and loan associations, etc.), such as providing life insurance, holding time or savings deposits, making long-term mortgage loans, renting safe-deposit boxes, operating a trust department, and so on.

The present chapter is concerned with surveying the basic economic functions of commercial banking.

The Fundamental Principle of Deposit Banking

We have already learned that money is usually defined to include both currency (and coin) and demand deposits. Briefly:

$$\text{Money} = \text{currency} + \text{demand deposits}$$

This formula states at a glance what economists ordinarily mean by money. (Coin is omitted from the equation because it is a negligible proportion of the total supply of money.) But most of us are more familiar with currency than with demand deposits. In view of this it seems appropriate to ask: Who determines the amount of currency in circulation?

The answer is "the public"—you and I and everyone else. Since currency and demand deposits are interchangeable, you will generally cash a check when you need currency, and deposit currency in your checking account when you have more cash than you need.

Everyone behaves in much the same way. As a result, the public always holds the exact amount of cash that it wants, shifting its holdings back and forth between currency and demand deposits. On an average in a year, the economy holds about 20 percent of its money in currency and 80 percent in demand deposits. But at certain times of the year, such as Christmas and Easter, the proportion of currency in circulation increases because people desire more cash for spending; after the holidays, the proportion of currency in circulation decreases as businessmen deposit their cash receipts in their checking accounts.

THE GOLDSMITHS' PRINCIPLE

Since demand deposits are by far the largest part of our money supply, it is important for us to know how they come into existence and the role they play.

The credit creation process of deposit banking is based on the following fundamental principle:

All of the customers of a bank will not withdraw their funds at one time. On any given day, some customers will decrease their deposits by withdrawing funds in the form of cash and checks drawn on the bank, while others will increase their deposits by depositing funds in the form of cash and checks drawn on other banks. Under normal conditions, the volume of deposits and withdrawals will tend to be equal over a period of time.

This is a modernized version of what may conveniently be called the goldsmiths' principle— because it was discovered centuries ago by the English goldsmiths. They found that when people deposited gold with them for safekeeping, it was not usually necessary to store all of the gold away; only a portion of it needed to be kept in reserve, for those individuals who might want to withdraw their gold, and the rest could be "put to work" earning interest by being loaned to others with the promise of repayment.

In a bank, of course, there is always the possibility that during some periods withdrawals will exceed deposits. To meet such contingencies, reserves equal to less than 5 percent of deposits are usually more than adequate. However, the percentage of reserves which banks actually keep on hand is considerably higher than this, for reasons of monetary control which will be explained.

THE GOLDSMITHS' PRINCIPLE AND FRACTIONAL BANK RESERVES

The ways in which demand deposits are expanded and contracted can best be illustrated in terms of changes in a bank's assets, liabilities, and net worth. What do these terms mean? For any economic entity such as an individual, household, or firm *assets* are things of value which it owns—cash, property, and the rights to property; *liabilities* are monetary debts or things of value which it owes to creditors; and *net worth* or equity is the difference between its assets and liabilities. When these three classes of data are grouped together for analysis and interpretation, the financial statement on which they appear is called a *balance sheet*. For example, on a bank's balance sheet, the principal assets are government securities and loans; the principal liabilities are demand deposits.

As stated above, the English goldsmiths discovered by experience that they could run a banking business by maintaining a fractional—rather than 100 percent—reserve in gold against their loans. Although U.S. banks today do not hold gold, the law requires them to maintain fractional reserves of liquid assets against their deposit liabilities. There are three types of reserves: legal, required, and excess.

1. *Legal reserves* are those assets that a bank may lawfully use as reserves against its deposit liabilities. For a bank that belongs to the Federal Reserve System, legal reserves consist of deposits held with the district Federal Reserve Bank plus currency held in the vaults of the bank—called "vault cash." Any other financial claims, such as government securities, are classified as "nonlegal reserves." For a nonmember bank of the Federal Reserve System, the laws vary by state, but they commonly permit

vault cash, demand deposits with other banks, and in some cases state and federal securities to count as legal reserves.

2. *Required reserves* denote the minimum amount of legal reserves that a bank is required by law to keep behind its deposit liabilities. For example, if the reserve requirement is 20 percent, a bank with demand deposits of $1 million must hold at least $200,000 of required legal reserves.

3. *Excess reserves* are the quantity of a bank's legal reserves over and above its required reserves.

As you can see from these definitions:

Legal reserves = required reserves + excess reserves

and therefore

Excess reserves = legal reserves − required reserves

It follows that anything which changes either a bank's legal reserves or its required reserves will change its excess reserves. But excess reserves, as we shall see, are the determinants of a bank's lending power, so you should keep the above simple equations in mind as you study the processes by which banks expand and contract demand deposits.

Deposit Expansion by a Single Bank

The easiest way to understand the deposit-banking process is to examine the transactions of a single bank over successive stages.

Stage 1. Let us begin by assuming the reserve requirement against demand deposits is 20 percent and that Bank A has the following simplified balance sheet:

BANK A: BALANCE SHEET

Stage 1: Initial position

Assets		Liabilities and Net Worth	
Legal reserves	$ 5,000	Demand deposits	$20,000
Loans	16,000	Net Worth	1,000
	$21,000		$21,000

Note from the right side of the balance sheet that demand deposits are a liability because the bank is obligated to honor checks drawn by its depositors upon it up to the amount shown. On the left side,

legal reserves (which consist of vault cash plus demand deposits with the district Federal Reserve bank) are an asset. Loans are also classified as an asset since they represent financial claims held by the bank against others. Returning to the right side of the balance sheet, net worth is the difference between total assets and total liabilities; it is a "balancing item" representing stockholders' (owners') equity in the bank. Note that with $20,000 of demand deposits and a reserve requirement of 20 percent, required reserves (not shown) are $4,000 and therefore excess reserves are $1,000. This makes legal reserves (on the left side) equal to $5,000.

Stage 2. Since the bank has $1,000 in excess reserves, it can make loans equal to this amount. Suppose you, a businessman, borrow the funds, and give the bank your promissory note in exchange. The bank then credits your account for $1,000. *Before you write any checks, how does the bank's balance sheet look?* As shown below, demand deposits have risen to $21,000 reflecting the bank's commitment (liability) to honor your checks up to $1,000; and loans have increased to $17,000 reflecting the promissory note (asset) you gave the bank for $1,000. As a result of this transaction, *the bank has created $1,000 of new money.*

BANK A: BALANCE SHEET

Stage 2: After the bank grants a loan of $1,000 but before checks are written against it

Assets		Liabilities and Net Worth	
Legal reserves	$ 5,000	Demand deposits	$21,000
Loans	17,000	Net Worth	1,000
	$22,000		$22,000

Stage 3. Of course, you can take your $1,000 out in currency if you wish, but since you are a businessman you will probably find it more convenient to write checks in order to pay your bills. Suppose you write a check for the full $1,000 and give it to a supplier from whom you purchased materials. The supplier then deposits the check in his own bank, Bank B, which in turn presents it to Bank A for payment. The effect on Bank A, as shown in the following balance sheet, is to reduce its demand deposits to $20,000 and its legal reserves to $4,000. Note that now required reserves are 20 percent of demand deposits, or $4,000—which equals the bank's legal reserves. The bank, in other words, no longer has excess reserves.

BANK A: BALANCE SHEET

Stage 3: Final position

Assets		Liabilities and Net Worth	
Legal reserves	$ 4,000	Demand deposits	$20,000
Loans	17,000	Net Worth	1,000
	$21,000		$21,000

The foregoing analysis leads to an important conclusion:

No individual bank in a banking system can lend more than its excess reserves. In other words, when a bank's excess reserves are zero, it has no unused lending power; the bank, therefore, is in "equilibrium" or *fully loaned up.*

Of course, the supplier to whom you gave your $1,000 check might have had an account in Bank A instead of Bank B. In that case the *total* demand deposits of Bank A would have been unaffected. The bank, when processing the check, would simply have reduced your account by $1,000 and increased the supplier's by the same amount. In the great majority of cases, however, this situation does not exist. Instead:

As a borrower writes checks against his deposit, his bank is likely to lose reserves and deposits to other banks within the banking system. Hence a bank cannot afford to make loans in an amount greater than its excess reserves.

Deposit Expansion by the Banking System

Although a single bank cannot make loans for more than its excess reserves, the banking system can lend several times the amount. This provides another interesting example of the familiar fallacy of composition: what is true of the individual is not necessarily true of the whole. Let us see why, by continuing with the above illustration. To keep matters simple, we will focus attention on relevant balance-sheet *changes* while disregarding all other items. As before, the reserve requirement is assumed to be 20 percent.

Stage 4. The $1,000 check you paid your supplier is deposited by him to his account in Bank B. The bank's demand deposits increase by $1,000 and its legal reserves (after the check clears) increase by $1,000.

BANK B

Stage 4: Bank B receives $1,000 deposit lost by Bank A

Assets		Liabilities	
Legal reserves	+$1,000	Demand deposits	+$1,000
	+$1,000		+$1,000

Assuming that prior to this transaction Bank B was fully loaned up, it sets aside 20 percent or $200 in required reserves, and hence has 80 percent or $800 in excess reserves.

Stage 5. Bank B, of course, will try to lend $800—an amount equal to its excess reserves. Assuming it grants such a loan, its balance sheet *before* any checks are written will show that demand deposits have risen from $1,000 to $1,800 and, therefore, loans have increased by a corresponding amount. Thus:

BANK B

Stage 5: After Bank B grants a loan for $800 but before checks are written against it

Assets		Liabilities	
Legal reserves	+$1,000	Demand deposits	+$1,800
Loans	+ 800		
	+$1,800		+$1,800

Stage 6. If we assume that the borrower writes a check for the entire amount of his loan, the check will be deposited by its recipient in Bank C. This will cause Bank B to lose $800 in deposits and (after the check clears) $800 of legal reserves to Bank C, leaving Bank B with the following net changes:

BANK B

Stage 6: After checks for $800 are written against Bank B

Assets		Liabilities	
Legal reserves (net change = +$1,000 − 800)	+$ 200	Demand deposits (net change = +$1,800 − 800)	+$1,000
Loans	+ 800		
	+$1,000		+$1,000

Notice that the increase in Bank B's legal reserves is equal to 20 percent of the increase in its demand deposits; therefore its excess reserves are zero. Hence it is in "equilibrium" or fully loaned up.

Stage 7. Bank C receives the $800 deposit which was lost by Bank B in Stage 6, and thus (after the check clears) gains $800 in legal reserves.

BANK C

Stage 7: Bank C receives $800 deposit lost by Bank B

Assets		Liabilities	
Legal reserves	+$800	Demand deposits	+$800
	+$800		+$800

Assuming Bank C had been fully loaned up, it sets aside 20 percent or $160 as required reserves, and therefore has 80 percent or $640 in excess reserves.

Stage 8. Suppose Bank C now grants a loan equal to the amount of its excess reserves. *Before* any checks are written, both its demand deposits and loans will have risen by $640.

BANK C

Stage 8: After Bank C grants a loan for $640 but before checks are written against it

Assets		Liabilities	
Legal reserves	+$ 800	Demand deposits	+$1,440
Loans	+ 640		
	+$1,440		+$1,440

Stage 9. After the borrower writes a check against the loan which is deposited in Bank D, demand deposits and (after the check clears) legal reserves in Bank C go down by $640, leaving it with the following net changes:

BANK C

Stage 9: After checks for $640 are written against Bank C

Assets		Liabilities	
Legal reserves (net change = +$800 − 640)	+$160	Demand deposits (net change = +$1,440 − 640)	+$800
Loans	+ 640		
	+$800		+$800

Since the increase in Bank C's legal reserves is equal to 20 percent of the increase in its demand deposits, its excess reserves are zero. The bank, therefore, is in equilibrium or fully loaned up.

Stage 10 and beyond. You can see by now that a logical expansionary process is taking place. It is sufficient, therefore, to illustrate a few further steps in the sequence by noting the changes experienced by each bank on its partial balance sheet, assuming that each bank is initially fully loaned up. (All data are rounded to the nearest dollar.)

BANK D

Assets		Liabilities	
Legal reserves	+$128	Demand deposits	+$640
Loans	+ 512		
	+$640		+$640

BANK E

Assets		Liabilities	
Legal reserves	+$102	Demand deposits	+$512
Loans	+ 410		
	+$512		+$512

BANK F

Assets		Liabilities	
Legal reserves	+$ 82	Demand deposits	+$410
Loans	+ 328		
	+$410		+$410

And so on.

The deposit-creation process thus continues until all excess reserves in the system are "used up"—that is, until no bank in the system has legal reserves greater than its required reserves.

The entire process of deposit expansion is illustrated in Exhibit 1 on the next page. Note that the *total* expansion of deposits created by the banking system as a whole is a multiple of the initial deposit or increase in excess reserves—in this case $5,000 for $1,000, or a ratio of 5:1.

This is the same process that was illustrated above in terms of changes in the bank's balance sheets. Either approach can be used to illustrate what may be called the principle of *multiple expansion of bank deposits.* Can you express this principle in your own words? (You may want to check your definition against that in the Dictionary at the back of the book.)

THE DEPOSIT-EXPANSION MULTIPLIER

You may have noticed that the expansion in demand deposits by the banking system as a whole is determined by two factors:

1. The required reserve ratio
2. The initial amount of excess reserves

You can verify this from Exhibit 1 by demonstrating that the reciprocal of the required reserve ratio—

Exhibit 1

Multiple Expansion of Bank Deposits through the Banking System (data are rounded to nearest dollar)

Cumulative expansion in deposits by the banking system as a whole, assuming a $1,000 initial deposit or increase in legal reserves and a required reserve ratio of 20 percent.

Banks	New deposits created	Required reserves @ 20%	New loans (= excess reserves)	Cumulative deposits
A	$1,000	$ 200	$ 800	$1,000
B	800	160	640	1,800
C	640	128	512	2,440
D	512	102	410	2,952
E	410	82	328	3,362
F	328	66	262	3,690
G	262	52	210	3,952
H	210	42	168	4,162
I	168	34	134	4,330
J	134	27	107	4,464
All other banks	536	107	429	5,000
Totals	$5,000	$1,000	$4,000	

If all banks in the system are aligned in decreasing order of new deposits created, the multiple expansionary process can be expressed in the form of a chart.

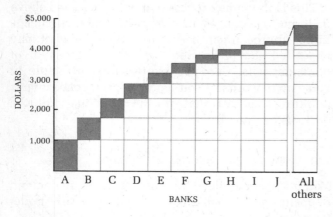

that is, the number 1 divided by the required reserve ratio—gives what may be called the "deposit-expansion multiplier." Thus, letting R represent the required reserve ratio:

Deposit-expansion multiplier =
$$\frac{1}{\text{required reserve ratio}} = \frac{1}{R}$$

Hence if you know the required reserve ratio, you can determine the deposit-expansion multiplier immediately. For instance, the required reserve ratio was assumed to be 20 percent or $\frac{1}{5}$. Therefore:

$$\text{Deposit-expansion multiplier} = \frac{1}{\frac{1}{5}} = 5$$

This means that an increase in the banking system's excess reserves by $1,000 may result in as much as a $5 \times \$1,000 = \$5,000$ total expansion of new deposits for the banking system as a whole. The same formula also applies in a downward direction: a $1,000 contraction in the banking system's *legal* reserves can cause as much as a $5,000 reduction in deposits for the entire system.

These ideas can be generalized and incorporated in a simple formula. Letting D represent the change in demand deposits for the banking system as a whole, E the amount of excess reserves, and R the required reserve ratio:

$$D = E \times \text{deposit-expansion multiplier}$$
or
$$D = E \times \frac{1}{R}$$

To illustrate, if $R = 10$ percent or $\frac{1}{10}$, the deposit-expansion multiplier is 10, and therefore excess reserves E of $1,000 can result in as much as a $\$1,000 \times 10 = \$10,000$ increase in the banking system's demand deposits, D.

You can use the above formula to answer practical questions involving deposit expansion and contraction. For the latter, E would represent deficient reserves and have a negative sign.

The following definition helps summarize the basic ideas:

Deposit-expansion multiplier. An increase in *excess* reserves of the banking system may cause a larger or magnified increase in total deposits; similarly, a decrease in the banking system's *legal* reserves may cause a larger or magnified decrease in total deposits. The total cumulative expansion (or contraction) will at most be some multiple of the required reserve ratio.

How does this multiplier principle compare with the simple multiplier pertaining to investment and income that you studied in an earlier chapter? Do you see any analogy between the required reserve ratio and the marginal propensity to save? Now is a good time to turn back and refresh your knowledge of the simple multiplier, but keep in mind as you compare the two multiplier concepts that income and money are not the same thing.

A "MONOPOLY BANK" AND THE BANKING SYSTEM

It is interesting to observe how the principle of multiple expansion of bank deposits would operate if there were just one bank—a monopoly bank—instead of many independently owned banks.

A monopoly bank would behave exactly as the banking system as a whole behaves. It would receive all deposits and grant all loans, and since it would be the only bank in the system, there would be no other banks to which it could lose reserves when checks that were drawn upon it were presented for payment. Thus, assuming a reserve requirement of 20 percent, the monopoly bank would simply continue to lend its excess reserves until it produced a 5:1 expansion of bank deposits. It would therefore be able to do what each individual bank in a system of many banks could not do.

THREE QUALIFICATIONS

The principle of multiple expansion of bank deposits assumes that the banking system will produce a magnified expansion in deposits, such as 5:1 or some other ratio, depending on the reserve requirement and the assumption that banks always make loans equal to their full amount of new excess reserves. Actually, this principle is modified in practice by at least three factors.

1. *Leakage of cash into circulation.* A businessman borrowing money from a bank may take part of it in cash. Or, someone who is paid a debt by check may "cash" some or all of it, rather than deposit the entire amount. For these reasons, some money that would otherwise serve as excess reserves will tend to leak out of the banking system, thereby leaving fewer new reserves available for banks to lend.

2. *Additional excess reserves.* Banks do not always lend out every dollar of their excess reserves. They may desire a "safety margin" or be unable to find good investments. Thus, if the reserve requirement were 20 percent, banks might have available an average reserve of 25 percent. This, of course, would reduce the deposit-creating ability of the banking system from 5:1 to 4:1.

3. *Willingness to borrow and lend.* The principle of multiple expansion of bank deposits that we have shown assumes, of course, that businessmen are willing to borrow and banks are willing to lend. This may not always be so. During a recession or depression, for example, when businessmen are gloomy about the future, they may not borrow all that banks have available for lending; and banks, on the other hand, may prefer the safety of liquidity and hence decide to maintain a higher level of excess reserves rather than risk heavy withdrawals by the public or possible default on loans. Banks could, however, buy government securities at these times. If they chose to do so, an expansion would still take place. (Can you explain why?)

As a result of these three factors:

The multiple expansion of deposits actually created by the banking system is always somewhat less than the theoretical amount determined from the formula. The formula establishes the upper limit of deposit expansion—not the amount actually realized in all cases.

DEPOSIT CONTRACTION

Does the multiple expansion of bank deposits work in a downward direction? If a bank loses a deposit when all banks are fully loaned up, would this cause a cumulative contraction of demand deposits throughout the system? The answer is yes—for reasons that are essentially the reverse of those given for deposit expansion.

For example, the most obvious way for a bank to lose a deposit is for a depositor to withdraw his money in currency instead of by check. (A less obvious but more significant way which will be examined subsequently is for the Federal Reserve System to sell government securities.) Suppose, for instance, that you withdraw $1,000 in currency from Bank A. The bank's balance sheet will show a reduction in demand deposits and in legal reserves (vault cash) by that amount. Thus:

BANK A
After depositor's withdrawal of $1,000 in currency

Assets	Liabilities
Legal reserves (vault cash) −$1,000	Demand deposits −$1,000

If the reserve requirement is 20 percent, the decrease in demand deposits of $1,000 reduces Bank A's required reserves by $200. But Bank A still has a reserve deficiency of $800 against its remaining deposits. The most likely way for it to correct this deficiency is to sell some of its earning assets—primarily government securities. If the buyer of the securities pays for them with a check written against his deposit in Bank B, the latter institution experiences a deposit decrease of $800. Of this, 20 percent or $160 represents a decrease in required reserves, and 80 percent or $640 is a reserve deficiency against its remaining deposits. Bank B, like Bank A, makes up this deficiency by selling some of its earning assets. The deposit contraction process thus continues in this way as indicated by the following table:

Banks	Demand deposits	Required reserves	Earning assets
A	−$1,000	−$ 200	−$ 800
B	− 800	− 160	− 640
C	− 640	− 128	− 512
D	− 512	− 102	− 410
E	− 410	− 82	− 328
All other banks	− 1,638	− 328	− 1,310
Totals	−$5,000	−$1,000	−$4,000

Note that the same end result—a reduction in deposits by $5,000 for the banking system as a whole—could have been reached by using the deposit-expansion multiplier. To illustrate, since the reserve requirement is assumed to be 20 percent, the multiplier is 5. Therefore, an initial change (decrease) in demand deposits—and hence in legal reserves—of −$1,000 results in a 5 × −$1,000 = −$5,000 change in demand deposits for the entire banking system.

To conclude:

The multiple contraction of bank deposits is essentially the reverse of the multiple-expansion principle. It assumes initially that all banks in the system are fully loaned up. To the extent that they are not, reductions in deposits can be met out of excess reserves, thereby reducing the multiplier effect of the contraction process.

Managing a Bank's Portfolio

As a bank expands and contracts its demand deposits it also acquires and disposes of income-earning assets. These assets, plus the bank's cash, make up what is known as its "portfolio." Income-earning assets—or simply earning assets—consist of securities issued by federal and municipal governments and quasi-governmental institutions, and of financial obligations, such as promissory notes issued by businesses. Taken together, earning assets typically comprise between one-fourth and one-third of a commercial bank's total assets. The remaining portion of its total assets consists primarily of other loans, and to a lesser extent of demand deposits with other banks (including Federal Reserve Banks) and vault cash.

A bank's earning assets are thus an important source of its income. The manner in which banks as a whole manage their portfolios, acquiring and disposing of earning assets as the need arises, can have important impacts throughout the financial markets and on the borrowing and expenditure practices of households and businesses. It is desirable, therefore, that we look into some implications of bank portfolio management as a prelude to examining its economic effects in subsequent chapters.

OBJECTIVES: LIQUIDITY, PROFITABILITY, AND SAFETY

Imagine yourself responsible for managing a bank's portfolio. Since one of your major tasks is to acquire earning assets, the problem you continually face is to achieve a proper balance between liquidity, profitability, and safety. What do these terms mean?

Liquidity is a complex concept, the precise meaning of which sometimes differs among economists and financial managers. For our purposes, however, it may be defined as the ease with which an asset can be converted into cash quickly without loss of value in terms of money. Liquidity is thus a matter of degree. Money is an asset which is perfectly liquid because it can be used as a medium of exchange, and it always retains the same value in terms of itself. A short-term government obligation is an asset which is almost as liquid as money, because it can be readily sold for cash with little or no loss of value. On the other hand, a bank building is a relatively illiquid asset; it cannot easily be sold and may yield a loss to its owners when it is. In general, the relative liquidity of an asset is associated with three interrelated factors:

☐ *Marketability.* An asset which is bought and sold in an organized market—such as a security traded on the New York Stock Exchange—is highly salable and hence more liquid than one which is not.

☐ *Collateral value.* An asset is likely to be more liquid if it is easy to borrow upon. In many cases the converse of this statement is also true.

☐ *Contractual terms.* An asset's liquidity is affected by the contractual conditions under which it is issued. The liquidity of a bond, for example, is greater if it has an earlier maturity date than a later one, or if it is paid off (amortized) in installments over its life instead of in a lump sum at maturity.

Profitability, a second goal of a bank's portfolio, is measured by the difference between what you pay for an asset and what you realize when you redeem or sell it, plus any returns you receive in the interim. In the case of government (including federal and municipal) bonds, which are a major form of earning assets for banks, these variables are reflected by a single percentage figure called *yield to maturity.* A bond's yield to maturity may be 5 percent, 6 percent, or some other amount—and it will fluctuate according to market conditions. Portfolio managers, therefore, are continually changing the compositions of their earning assets, selling bonds and other securities which have lower yields in order to purchase those which have higher ones.

Safety, a third goal in bank portfolio management, refers to the probability that the contractual terms of an investment—such as the interest and principal payments on a bond—will be fulfilled by the borrower. Safety is thus a matter of degree. The safest of all financial obligations are Treasury bills, Treasury notes, and Treasury bonds, since they are all backed by the good faith and taxing power of the federal government. Bonds issued by many municipal governments also rank very high on the safety scale. Interestingly enough, however, safety and liquidity do not always go together. Market prices of U.S. Treasury bonds, for example, may fluctuate

substantially, thereby impairing their liquidity, but their safety—that is, payment of interest and principal—is never in doubt.

THE CONFLICT BETWEEN LIQUIDITY AND PROFITABILITY

The ideal commercial-bank portfolio is liquid, profitable, and safe. But it is impossible to maximize all three objectives—for two reasons.

First, a bank's most immediate obligation is to pay cash upon demand. The moment it is unable to convert demand deposits into cash, it must close its doors. Hence the holding of a certain portion of its assets in the form of vault cash helps a bank to meet its liquidity needs.

Second, a bank is in business to make a profit for its owners (stockholders). The holding of earning assets is an important means of attaining this goal. Therefore:

Since a bank's vault cash yields no return, a conflict exists between liquidity and profitability: too large a proportion of the bank's assets in the form of cash provides greater liquidity but an unnecessary loss of income; too small a proportion in cash permits higher income from investment in earning assets, but at the risk of illiquidity and failure.

Evidently a compromise between these two extremes is needed. Moreover, the compromise must be achieved with a relatively high degree of safety because banks are subject to a variety of legal and conventional constraints which limit the types of earning assets they can acquire.

The nature of the conflict between liquidity and profitability is illustrated in Exhibit 2 on the next page. The axes of the chart denote the two alternatives available to a bank at any given time. For example, if you are a portfolio manager, you can keep all of the bank's funds in cash, in which case the amount is represented by the vertical distance *0M.* Alternatively, you can invest all of the bank's funds in earning assets, in which case the amount is shown by the horizontal distance *0N.* However, neither one of these extreme choices is acceptable, since the former would leave the bank in too liquid a position to earn income, whereas the latter would leave it completely illiquid and hence unable to pay cash on demand.

Exhibit 2

Investment-possibilities Line

Each point along the line MN denotes a different combination of cash and earning assets. Thus, point A denotes 0G dollars of cash and 0H dollars of earning assets; point B denotes 0J dollars of cash and 0K dollars of earning assets. The portfolio manager of a bank seeks to obtain an optimum combination of cash and earning assets, subject to various legal constraints designed to assure a high degree of safety.

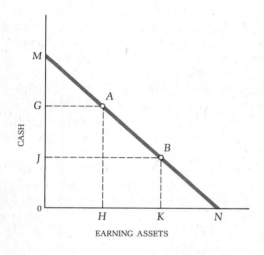

If we connect the two points, the resulting line *MN* shows all of the combinations of cash and earning assets in which you can invest the bank's funds. Therefore, it may be called an "investment-possibilities line." Of course, there is some point along the line—some combination of cash and earning assets —which is optimum for a particular bank. The challenge faced by every bank's portfolio manager, therefore, is to find that point—thereby achieving the highest possible level of earnings consistent with liquidity and safety.

PRIORITIES FOR ALLOCATING BANK FUNDS

Since the fundamental goals of a bank portfolio are liquidity, profitability, and safety, and since these goals are in conflict, priorities for allocating a bank's funds must be established. Four classes of uses for such funds may be distinguished:

1. *Primary reserves.* This category of assets receives the highest priority. It is comprised of a bank's legal reserves (consisting of vault cash and demand deposits with the Federal Reserve Bank if it belongs to the Federal Reserve System) and demand deposits with other banks.

2. *Secondary reserves.* This category of assets, which receives the second highest priority, provides "protective investment." It is made up of earning assets that are readily convertible into cash on short notice without substantial loss. Thus it consists of such short-term financial obligations as U.S. Treasury bills, high-grade commercial paper (such as promissory notes issued by large corporations), banker's acceptances, and call loans on stock market purchases. The main purpose of this application of a bank's funds is to meet expected and more or less regular seasonal demands for liquidity such as occur during the peak business periods of Christmas and Easter.

3. *Customer loan demands.* The third priority in allocating a bank's funds is meeting customer credit needs. This is the fundamental purpose for which a bank is created. By fulfilling this objective, a bank enhances its profits because interest rates on loans are usually higher than on securities.

4. *Investments for income.* The fourth priority concerns the use of a bank's funds after the three previous priorities have been satisfied. Thus any funds which a bank has available after fulfilling the above requirements are invested in long-term securities aimed at providing additional income. Since these investments are also subject to constraints of safety, they consist primarily of (a) government securities, namely, notes and bonds issued by the Treasury and by other federal agencies, and (b) municipal securities, namely, bonds and certain other obligations issued by state and local governments.

This order of priorities applies to all commercial banks. However, the relative distributions of funds for these four purposes differ somewhat among individual banks. In general:

The proportions of its funds which a bank allocates to cash and earning assets, and the proportions which it allocates among different types of earning assets, depend on (1) legal requirements, (2) local business needs, and (3) its ability to compromise the conflicting goals of liquidity and profitability at the required level of safety.

TYPES OF BANK INVESTMENTS

Since the types of investment a commercial bank can make are regulated by law, three classes of securities are likely to be found in a typical portfolio:

1. U.S. government securities consisting of *Treasury bills*, *Treasury notes*, and *Treasury bonds*, all of which are readily marketable and differ from each other by their periods of maturity. They also contribute greatly to satisfying the liquidity requirements of commercial banks.

2. *Municipals*—marketable financial obligations issued by state and local governments. Interest income received by holders of these securities is exempt from all federal income taxes—a major reason banks purchase them.

3. "Quasi-governmental" securities consisting of notes and bonds issued by various agencies of the federal government.

Since the 1940s, the holdings of municipals in commercial-bank portfolios have increased substantially relative to the other two—due largely to the tax-exempt features of municipals.

SUMMARY OF IMPORTANT IDEAS

1. Commercial banking rests on the goldsmiths' principle, which enables banks to maintain a fractional—rather than 100 percent—reserve against deposits, because customers will not withdraw their funds at the same time. Hence the banks can earn interest by lending out their unused or excess reserves.

2. A single bank in a banking system cannot lend more than its excess reserves. When a bank's excess reserves are zero, it is in equilibrium or fully loaned up.

3. The banking system as a whole can expand deposits by a multiple of its excess reserves. This process is known as the principle of multiple expansion of bank deposits—one of the most fundamental concepts in banking.

4. The amount by which the banking system as a whole can expand or contract demand deposits depends on the required reserve ratio and the initial amount of excess reserves. The required reserve ratio determines the deposit-expansion multiplier which, when multiplied by initial excess reserves, tells the maximum amount of expansion or contraction that can take place.

5. The objectives of a commercial-bank portfolio are liquidity, profitability, and safety. The portfolio manager seeks an optimum combination of cash and earning assets consistent with a high level of safety. Hence he is limited to three major classes of investments: U.S. government securities, municipal government securities, and quasi-government securities.

FOR DISCUSSION

1. *Terms and concepts to review:*

goldsmiths' principle	deposit-expansion
assets	multiplier
liabilities	liquidity
net worth	yield to maturity
balance sheet	primary reserves
legal reserves	secondary reserves
required reserves	Treasury bills
excess reserves	Treasury notes
multiple expansion of	Treasury bonds
bank deposits	municipals

2. What is meant by "fractional-reserve banking"? How did it come into existence? Is it relevant today?

3. An individual bank cannot lend more than its excess reserves. Let us see why—by observing what would happen if it tried to do so.

Suppose the reserve requirement is 20 percent, and Bank Z is holding:

Assets		Liabilities	
Vault cash	$ 50,000	Demand deposits	$200,000
Loans and			
other assets	160,000	Net Worth	10,000
	$210,000		$210,000

(a) How much are Bank Z's excess reserves?

(b) Since the reserve requirement is 20 percent or 1/5, show the effect on Bank Z's balance sheet after it expands its loans in a 5:1 ratio—that is, by 5 times its excess reserves—but before borrowers spend their new deposits. What is the percentage of reserves to demand deposits?

(c) Suppose borrowers write checks against their new deposits and the checks are deposited in other banks. Show the effect on Bank Z's balance sheet after all the checks are presented to it for payment. What has happened to the bank's reserves against deposits?

(d) What can Bank Z do to correct the situation? If it succeeds, how would its balance sheet look?

(e) What do you conclude from this exercise?

4. Suppose you borrow $1,000 in currency from Midwest Bank, and give the bank your promissory note in return.

(a) Show the effects on the following balance sheets:

YOUR BALANCE SHEET

Change in Assets	Change in Liabilities and Net Worth
+1,000	+1,000

BALANCE SHEET—MIDWEST BANK

Change in Assets	Change in Liabilities and Net Worth
OD +1,000	-1,000

(b) Complete Balance Sheet 2 below.

BALANCE SHEET 1—MIDWEST BANK

Before making $1,000 loan

Assets		Liabilities and Net Worth	
Cash	$ 3,000	Demand deposits	$20,000
Reserves	4,000	Other liabilities	25,000
Loans	15,000		
Other assets	50,000	Net Worth	27,000
	$72,000		$72,000

BALANCE SHEET 2—MIDWEST BANK

After $1,000 in cash is withdrawn by borrower

Assets		Liabilities and Net Worth	
Cash	2,000	Demand deposits	19,000
Reserves	4,000	Other liabilities	25,000
Loans	15,000		
Other assets	5,000	Net Worth	27,000
	71,000		71,000

(c) How would Balance Sheet 2 be affected if you had written $1,000 in checks against your deposit instead of withdrawing the money in cash?

5. Some people argue that "loans create deposits," while others contend that "deposits permit loans." Which statement is correct? Which is likely to be defended by economists? By bankers? Explain.

6. Assume the reserve requirement is 10 percent. There are no currency withdrawals. Bank A's partial balance sheet is as follows:

BANK A

Assets		Liabilities	
Legal reserves	$ 16	Demand deposits	$100
Loans	84		
	$100		$100

(a) How much can Bank A expand demand deposits? Explain.

(b) If all other banks are in equilibrium, how much can Bank B lend? Bank C? What is the maximum for the whole banking system? Explain.

7. What is the deposit-expansion multiplier when (a) required reserves are 1 percent; (b) required reserves are 10 percent; (c) required reserves are 100 percent?

8. For Bank A, legal reserves are $1,000, required reserves are $800, demand deposits are $8,000. All other banks are in equilibrium. By how much can the banking system expand its demand deposits?

9. Will the *actual* amount of deposit expansion by the banking system equal the *predicted* amount? Why or why not? Explain.

10. Fill in the gaps for the omitted banks in the following table, assuming a 15 percent reserve requirement against demand deposits. What fundamental principle does the table illustrate?

	Amount added to checking accounts	Amount lent	Amount set aside as reserves
Bank 1	—	$10,000	—
Bank 2	$10,000	8,500	$_____
. . .	. . .	. . .	. . .
Bank 11	2,315	1,968	347
. . .	. . .	. . .	. . .
. . .	. . .	. . .	. . .
. . .	. . .	. . .	. . .
. . .	. . .	. . .	. . .
Bank 20	537	457	80
All other banks	_____	_____	_____
Total—all banks	$ _____	$ _____	$_____

CHAPTER 15

Central Banking: Monetary Management and Policy

CHAPTER PREVIEW

What types of controls are available to the Federal Reserve for influencing the supply of money and the level of economic activity?

How well do these controls work? What are their favorable and unfavorable features? What sorts of difficulties arise in implementing them?

FEDERAL RESERVE RAISES RESERVE REQUIREMENTS

DISCOUNT RATE INCREASED BY FED

FED ENTERS MARKET TO SELL U.S. SECURITIES

Headlines like these often appear in the financial press and emphasize that the *Federal Reserve System* plays not one role, but two. It is a "banker's bank," performing for member banks much the same services that member banks perform for the public. But it is also an important influence on the nation's economic and monetary policy. In the preceding chapter we concentrated on the Fed's banking role. In this chapter we shall look at the part it plays in making and implementing economic decisions.

Essentially the Fed relies on five instruments to modify or even reverse the direction of the economy. They are (1) reserve ratios, (2) discount rate, (3) open-market operations, (4) margin regulations, and (5) moral suasion. The first three are general controls because they influence the nation's money supply and the availability of credit. The fourth is a selective tool aimed specifically at the stock market. The fifth is a psychological device which relies on personal talk and public opinion. It is convenient, however, to classify the first three as "quantitative controls" and the remaining two as "qualitative controls"—for reasons that will soon become apparent.

Before we begin, it helps to have a precise idea of what is meant by monetary policy, since that topic is the central concern of this chapter:

Monetary policy is the deliberate exercise of the monetary authority's (i.e., Federal Reserve's) power to induce expansions or contractions in the money supply in order to help dampen the swings of business cycles and bring the nation's output and employment to desired levels.

Quantitative Controls

The quantitative or general controls available to the Federal Reserve for influencing the level of economic activity consist primarily of (1) changes in member-bank reserve ratios, (2) changes in the discount rate, and (3) open-market operations. Let us examine these tools to learn how each helps to shape the nation's monetary policy.

RESERVE RATIOS

You already know that a member bank of the Federal Reserve System is required to maintain legal reserves against its demand-deposit liabilities. Why? Primarily to provide the monetary authorities—those who govern the central banking system—with one of several mechanisms for controlling the money supply.

As we have seen, commercial banks must maintain reserves equal to a minimum percentage of their deposits. Members of the Federal Reserve System may hold this minimum reserve as a deposit in a Reserve Bank and as cash in their own vaults. What economic effects are likely to occur as a result of changes in required reserve ratios?

The rules governing required reserves have varied. For some years prior to 1972, for example, banks were classified as either reserve city or as "country" banks, depending on the location and character of their business. The Board of Governors could change reserve ratios within the limits of 10 to 22 percent for reserve city banks, and 7 to 14 percent for country banks. In 1972, this distinction between banks was dropped. However, the minimum and maximum reserve limits of 7 to 22 percent were retained. Member banks, therefore, must maintain reserve ratios within these limits, but the exact percentages are graduated according to the size of their demand deposits, not according to their location or character of business.

You can readily see from the following partial balance sheets, that if the average required reserve ratio for member banks is 15 percent, $15 million of reserves would be needed to support $100 million of demand deposits:

MEMBER BANKS

Assets		Liabilities	
Required reserves	$15	Demand deposits	$100
Excess reserves	0		
Legal reserves	$15		

But if the average required reserve ratio for member banks is reduced to 10 percent, the amount of required reserves declines from $15 million to $10 million. This makes $5 million of excess reserves available for lending:

MEMBER BANKS

Assets		Liabilities	
Required reserves	$10	Demand deposits	$100
Excess reserves	5		
Legal reserves	$15		

The existence of excess reserves, as you already know, can lead to a multiple expansion of demand deposits for the banking system as a whole.

The reverse of this process is also true. For example, an increase in the average required reserve ratio from 10 percent to 15 percent would absorb the $5 million of excess reserves. If banks were fully loaned up and had no excess reserves, an increase in the average required reserve ratio would force them to sell some of their earning assets such as Treasury bills and commercial paper in order to raise the necessary funds to cover their reserve deficiency. This, as we have seen, causes a multiple contraction of demand deposits for the banking system as a whole.

Thus, changes in the required reserve ratio affect the economy as a whole in the following way:

A *decrease* in the required reserve ratio tends to be expansionary because it permits member banks to enlarge the money supply. An *increase* is contractionary because it requires member banks to reduce the money supply—depending on the degree to which they have excess reserves. The Federal Reserve System can thus affect the supply of money and the availability of bank credit through its control over reserve ratios and the volume of bank reserves.

The ability to alter the required reserve ratio is

the Federal Reserve System's most powerful monetary tool. But it is a somewhat blunt tool and is employed relatively seldom because other instruments of control can be applied with greater flexibility and more refinement.

CHANGING THE DISCOUNT RATE

Federal Reserve Banks lend money at interest to their member banks just as the member banks lend money at interest to the public. Thus it may be said that the Federal Reserve Banks are wholesalers of credit, while the member banks are retailers. No Federal Reserve policy tool is as well known or as poorly understood as the *discount rate*—the interest rate charged member banks on their loans from the Reserve Banks. (It is called a "discount rate" because the interest on the loans is discounted when the loan is made, rather than collected when the loan is repaid.)

Member banks can borrow from the Federal Reserve Banks in two ways: by giving their own secured promissory notes or by "rediscounting" drafts, bills of exchange, or notes which they have already discounted for their customers. Since the late 1930s, it has been the typical practice of borrowing banks to use their own notes secured by government obligations rather than their customers' promissory notes. Hence we use the expression "discount rate" rather than "rediscount rate," the latter term being an old-fashioned one which continues to hang on.

When a member bank borrows, the Federal Reserve Bank simply increases the member bank's reserves. Why would a member bank want to borrow from the Fed? Usually, it wants to replenish its reserves which may have "run down" for one or more reasons. (See Exhibit 1.) It follows that the Federal Reserve's policy at the "discount window" (an expression widely used in banking circles) can be quite significant for the economy as a whole.

Changes in the discount rate may be a significant tool for fighting inflationary and recessionary tendencies because (1) they directly affect the cost of borrowing by member banks, and (2) they indirectly affect interest rates and credit conditions in the economy.

Thus the direct effect of changes in the discount rate is to raise or lower the price of admission to the

Exhibit 1

Why Do Bank Reserves Fluctuate?

1. *Seasonal (or short-term) forces may increase reserves in one season and be a persistent drain on them in another. In agricultural areas, banks tend to experience an inflow of funds during the crop-marketing season, when farmers deposit the checks they receive from the sale of their crops, and an outflow of funds during the rest of the year, when farmers draw on their deposit balances to meet living expenses and the cost of producing next year's crop. In resort areas, banks gain funds during the vacation season and lose funds during the off season.*

2. *Trend (or long-term) forces due to a bank's own policies may cause it to gain or lose reserves. If a bank is expanding its loans and investments less rapidly than other banks in its market area, it will find its reserves increasing; if it is expanding more rapidly, it will suffer a persistent loss of reserves.*

3. *Irregular forces of one or a few days' duration may cause a bank to have a reserve deficiency one day, an excess the next. There are many possible reasons for this. For example, a corporation may authorize its bank to transfer a large portion of its deposit to a bank in another city where additional funds are needed to meet expenses; or a crop failure, flood, or similar disaster may put local banks under severe reserve pressure. Obviously, it is impossible for banks to anticipate these and other sudden changes with reasonable accuracy.*

discount window. An increase in the discount rate makes it more expensive for member banks to borrow; a reduction has the opposite effect. Indirectly, increases in the discount rate exert pressure to bring about a rise in interest rates and a general tightening of credit; decreases in the discount rate tend to reduce the level of interest rates and encourage an easing of credit. See also the effects described in Exhibit 2 on the next page.

The discount rate, although not the preeminent tool of monetary policy that it was during the early years of the Federal Reserve System, is nevertheless an important instrument. It is usually coordinated with open-market operations because each helps to make the other more effective.

Exhibit 2

Bond Prices and Bond Yields Vary Inversely

If you buy a debt security such as a bond, the effective or going market rate of interest on it is called the yield to maturity, or simply the yield.

The accompanying chart shows the relationship between the market price and effective yield of a $100 bond maturing one year hence with a nominal interest rate of 3.5 percent (paying its holder an interest of $3.50 per annum). The chart shows that if you could buy the bond in the market today for around $99, you would receive $100 upon maturity plus $3.50 in interest, which is an effective yield of about 4.5 percent. On the other hand, if you bought the bond today at a market price of $101, you would still get $100 back at maturity (thereby losing $1 from your purchase price) plus $3.50 in interest, making an effective yield of about 2.5 percent. Thus:

The price of a bond varies inversely with its yield.

What bearing does this inverse relationship have on the discount rate?

1. When the discount rate is increased, banks find it more costly to borrow from the Federal Reserve, and hence prefer to replenish their reserves by selling some of their debt securities instead. The increased sale of securities tends to lower security prices and raise their yields. These higher market yields in turn tend to push up longer-term interest rates.

2. On the other hand when the discount rate is lowered, banks are likely to maintain their borrowings at the Federal Reserve's discount window at a higher level than would otherwise be the case. This has effects on interest rates opposite to those given above. (Can you explain why?)

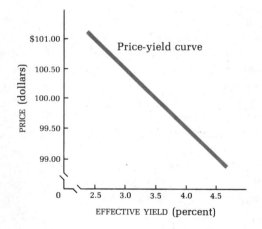

Price-yield curve

PRICE (dollars)

EFFECTIVE YIELD (percent)

OPEN-MARKET OPERATIONS: "THE FED IS IN THE MARKET"

"The Fed is in." This expression is heard frequently on Wall Street when the Federal Reserve Bank of New York buys or sells government securities such as Treasury bills and Treasury bonds—sometimes as agent for the Federal Open Market Committee and sometimes as agent for the U.S. Treasury, foreign central banks, and some of the member banks (as part of the services rendered by the Federal Reserve System).

Such transactions are commonly referred to as *open-market operations.* They directly affect the volume of member-bank reserves and hence the overall cost and availability of credit. They are the Fed's most important monetary tool for economic stabilization.

Here, essentially, is the way open-market operations work.

When the Fed *buys* government securities in the open market, commercial banks' reserves are increased:

1. If the Fed buys securities from member banks, it pays by increasing member banks' reserves with the Federal Reserve Banks by the amount of the purchase.

2. If the Fed buys securities from nonbanks (such as individuals or corporations), it pays with checks drawn on itself. The sellers then deposit these checks in their own commercial banks, which in turn send the checks to the Federal Reserve Banks for collection. The Reserve Banks pay by increasing the reserves of the commercial banks.

When the Fed *sells* government securities in the open market, commercial banks' reserves are thereby decreased:

1. If the Fed sells securities to member banks, they pay by reducing their reserves with the Federal Reserve Banks by the amount of the purchase.

2. If the Fed sells securities to nonbanks, they pay with checks drawn on commercial banks. The Federal Reserve Banks collect on these checks by reducing the reserves of the commercial banks. The commercial banks return the canceled checks to their depositors and reduce their deposit accounts accordingly.

Illustrations with Balance Sheets

You can gain a firmer grasp of these ideas by seeing them conveyed in terms of partial balance sheets. Here are some examples. (All data are in millions of dollars.)

Case 1. Suppose the Federal Reserve Bank purchases $1 million worth of government securities in the open market. If the seller of the securities is a member bank, the Reserve Bank pays the member bank by increasing its reserve deposit:

RESERVE BANK

Assets		Liabilities	
Government securities	+$1	Member-bank reserve deposits	+$1

MEMBER BANK

Assets		Liabilities
Government securities	−$1	
Reserves with Federal Reserve Bank	+$1	

Case 2. If the seller of the securities is a nonbank—such as an individual or corporation—the check received in payment from the Federal Reserve Bank will most likely be deposited in a short time at the seller's member bank. The member bank, in turn, sends the check to the Reserve Bank for credit to its reserve account:

RESERVE BANK

Assets		Liabilities	
Government securities	+$1	Member-bank reserve deposits	+$1

MEMBER BANK

Assets		Liabilities	
Reserves with Federal Reserve Bank	+$1	Demand deposits	+$1

Note that the effect on reserves is the same in both cases. That is:

Whether the seller of securities is a bank or a non-bank, the legal reserves of the member bank—its reserves with the Federal Reserve Bank—are increased by the value of the securities purchased by the Federal Reserve authorities.

Case 3. The opposite situation occurs when the Federal Reserve Bank sells $1 million of government securities in the open market. If the buyer is a member bank, it acquires $1 million in government securities and loses $1 million of reserves:

RESERVE BANK

Assets		Liabilities	
Government securities	−$1	Member-bank reserve deposits	−$1

MEMBER BANK

Assets		Liabilities
Government securities	+$1	
Reserves with Federal Reserve Bank	−$1	

Case 4. If the buyer of the security is a nonbank, the Federal Reserve Bank receives payment with a check drawn on a member bank. After the check "clears," the member bank's deposit at the Reserve Bank and the buyer's deposit at the member bank are both reduced by the value of the securities transacted:

RESERVE BANK

Assets		Liabilities	
Government securities	−$1	Member-bank reserve deposits	−$1

MEMBER BANK

Assets		Liabilities	
Reserves with Federal Reserve Bank	−$1	Demand deposits	−$1

Note in Cases 3 and 4 that the ultimate effect is the same:

The legal reserves of the member bank have been reduced by the value of the securities sold by the Federal Reserve Bank.

Although these open-market operations have been illustrated for only one member bank, the same ideas apply to all member banks within the Federal Reserve System. The overall economic effects of such transactions can be summarized briefly:

Open-market purchases of government securities are expansionary because they increase bank reserves and therefore permit a multiple growth of deposits; conversely, open-market sales of government securities are contractionary because they reduce bank reserves and hence force a multiple decline of deposits.

Qualitative Controls

In addition to its quantitative controls, the Federal Reserve can make use of certain qualitative tools for influencing the supply of money and the general level of economic activity. The principal qualitative controls available to it involve (1) margin regulations and (2) moral suasion.

MARGIN REGULATIONS

The Federal Reserve Board is empowered to set *margin requirements*: the percentage down payment required when borrowing to finance purchases of stock. This power was granted by Congress because the excessive use of credit was a significant factor that led to the stock market crash of 1929. The higher the margin requirement, the larger the proportion of a stock purchase that must be paid for in cash. Therefore:

An increase in margin requirements discourages speculation on borrowed credit; a decrease may encourage security purchases.

The margin requirement is thus a device for dampening or stimulating activity in the securities market.

MORAL SUASION

Of course, Reserve officials can always exert pressure on bankers by using oral and written appeals to expand or restrict credit without compelling compliance. This process, called *moral suasion*, has been successful on a number of occasions: in recessions, to stimulate the expansion of credit by encouraging banks to lend more; in inflations, to discourage lending and to restrict the expansion of credit. In a more general sense, the Federal Reserve exercises moral suasion every day when it advises individual member banks on ordinary loan policy.

The Board also has the power to establish interest ceilings on member-bank time and savings deposits. In the past, it has also exercised control over installment terms for the purchase of consumer goods and mortgage terms for the purchase of houses.

Of course, all the above instruments of monetary control are coordinated by the Federal Reserve in order to achieve its overall objective of promoting economic growth and stability through the money supply. (See Exhibit 3.)

Impact of the Treasury on Monetary Management

One of the interesting aspects of our financial system is that the Federal Reserve is not the only organization that can influence monetary management.

Exhibit 3

Flow of Federal Reserve Influence

FEDERAL RESERVE AUTHORITIES

regulate

VOLUME OF MEMBER-BANK RESERVES

which strongly influence

BANK LOANS AND INVESTMENTS

BANK DEPOSITS (AND MONEY SUPPLY)

which are a factor in

which are a factor in

CREDIT AVAILABILITY AND INTEREST COST

GENERAL LIQUIDITY

which influence

PRIVATE SPENDING FOR CONSUMPTION AND INVESTMENT (AND SAVING)

which largely determine

PRODUCTION, EMPLOYMENT, AND PRICES

SOURCE: Board of Governors of the Federal Reserve System.

The U.S. Treasury can, too. You can appreciate this when you realize that the Treasury raises and spends hundreds of billions of dollars annually, conducting its activities through commercial and Federal Reserve Banks. Ordinarily, such huge financial operations would wreak havoc with the banking system. To avoid this possibility, the Treasury plans its decisions very carefully so as to minimize the impact of its actions on Federal Reserve monetary management. Occasionally, however, it deliberately synchronizes its activities with the Fed's in order to supplement the latter's monetary policies.

To understand the Treasury's influence in monetary matters we will examine its practices with respect to deposit banking. The ways in which its actions can be used for contractionary or expansionary purposes will then become clear.

TREASURY DEPOSITS IN THE BANKING SYSTEM

The Treasury maintains demand deposits with almost every commercial bank in the country as well as with the Federal Reserve Banks. If you send a check to the Treasury in payment of your income tax, the Treasury deposits the check in one of its approximately 12,000 commercial-bank accounts. On the other hand, if the Treasury sends you an income tax refund, its check will almost certainly be drawn on one of its deposits at a Federal Reserve Bank. This practice is adhered to by the Treasury for virtually all its receipts and expenditures. In general:

The great bulk of the Treasury's deposits are with the nation's commercial banks, whereas almost all of its checks are drawn against the Federal Reserve Banks. This is because the money which the Treasury receives—say, from tax collections or from the sale of bonds—is deposited to its accounts in commercial banks; however, the money it disburses —say, for tax refunds or veteran's bonuses—is first transferred to its accounts at the Federal Reserve Banks and then checks are issued against those Federal Reserve deposits.

This seems like a strange way for the Treasury to conduct its transactions, but it adheres to this policy in order to create the least disruption within the banks and the money market. Periodically, the Treasury makes what are technically known as "calls" on the banks, informing them that on a certain date it intends to transfer a specified amount of funds from its commercial accounts to its Federal Reserve accounts. When the transfers are made, the reserves of commercial banks are reduced; however, when the Treasury disburses the funds with checks written against its Federal Reserve Bank accounts, the recipients deposit the checks in commercial banks, thereby increasing their reserves. On the whole, the Treasury is able to maintain fairly constant balances with the Reserve Banks because it can plan with reasonable accuracy the amount and timing of its disbursements. Consequently, the reductions in reserves created by the Treasury's transfers are approximately offset by the increases in reserves resulting from its outlays.

CONTRACTIONARY AND EXPANSIONARY ACTIONS

The ways in which the Treasury manages its cash balances can therefore exercise important influences on monetary policy. For example:

1. If the Treasury wishes to contract the availability of commercial-bank credit, it can increase its average balance at the Federal Reserve Banks by transferring from its commercial accounts to its Federal Reserve accounts more funds than it intends to disburse. The effect is to reduce the volume of commercial-bank reserves and hence create a multiple contraction of demand deposits.

2. If the Treasury wishes to expand the availability of commercial-bank credit, it can follow the reverse procedure—that is, decrease its average balance by transferring deposits from the Federal Reserve to the commercial banks. This action is not as flexible as the contractionary process because the Treasury always maintains some minimum level of Federal Reserve balances sufficient to carry on its operations. Nevertheless, the shifting of funds into commercial accounts provides the banking system with increased reserves. This may, of course, produce a multiple expansion of bank deposits.

There are other ways in which the Treasury can manage its cash balances with the intention of influencing monetary policy. In practice, however, it rarely uses any of them for that purpose. Instead it tries to perform its fiscal operations without disrupting the banks and the money market, and leaves matters of monetary management to the Federal Reserve authorities.

Is Monetary Policy Really Useful?

How effective is monetary policy in influencing economic activity? As with all policy areas of economics, this question is the subject of continuous debate. The chief pros and cons can be outlined briefly.

ADVANTAGES OF MONETARY POLICY

In evaluating the usefulness of monetary policy, it is often instructive to make comparisons with fiscal policy—an alternative and sometimes complementary method of fighting inflation and unemployment.

1. *Nondiscriminatory.* Monetary controls are ordinarily employed in a general way to influence the total volume of credit. The Fed is nondiscriminatory with respect to the borrowers or activities that are to be encouraged or curtailed, and leaves it to the market to be "discriminatory" instead. Thus the home construction industry, for example, feels the effects of tight credit more quickly than most other industries because of its dependence on the mortgage market. Fiscal policy, on the other hand, involves changes in taxation and government spending, and these changes can directly alter the composition of total production as well as its overall level.

2. *Flexible.* Since the Board of Governors controls monetary policy, changes can be made quickly and smoothly without getting snarled in administrative red tape. In contrast, fiscal policy involves budgetary considerations of taxation and spending; Congress usually deliberates for many months before arriving at a decision.

3. *Nonpolitical.* Congress gave the Federal Reserve System political independence to assure its effective performance. Thus, it provided 14-year terms of office for appointed Board members, made them ineligible for reappointment, staggered their terms of office, and provided for the election of Reserve Bank presidents by their own boards of directors subject to the approval of the Federal Reserve Board. As a result, the institution can base its day-to-day decisions on economic rather than political grounds. In contrast, fiscal policy is always partly influenced by politics.

LIMITATIONS OF MONETARY POLICY

Whereas the advantages of monetary policy are fairly general, most of its limitations arise out of specific situations and circumstances.

1. *Incomplete countercyclical effectiveness.* During an inflation the Federal Reserve can use its instruments of control to choke off borrowing and to establish an effective tight money policy. But during a recession even the easiest money policy cannot ensure that businessmen will want to borrow. If they regard the business outlook as poor, the desired increase in loans and spending will not be realized. Further, there is the possibility that commercial bankers may be unwilling to lend when they have excess reserves. For these reasons, monetary policy is far more effective as an anti-inflationary, rather than an antirecessionary, device.

2. *Cost-push or profit-push inflation.* Some observers contend that inflation often results from upward pressure on wages and prices. This pressure arises because of the monopolistic power which large unions and business firms are able to exert in the market. If this argument is true, monetary policy can do little to correct the situation. At most, actions taken by the Federal Reserve may help dampen either a cost-push or profit-push inflation, but will not eliminate either.

3. *Conflict with treasury objectives.* Every debtor likes low interest rates, especially the U.S. Treasury, which is the biggest debtor of all. Since the Treasury is continually refunding or selling new bonds, it wants to keep the interest cost as low as possible. Indeed, a difference of 1 percent in the interest rate on government securities can cost the Treasury several billion dollars. Reserve officials, on the other hand, regard high interest rates as an important anti-inflationary weapon. In the past these two distinctly different goals have at times resulted in a policy conflict between the Treasury and the Federal Reserve. Although compromises or "accords" were eventually worked out, they tended to reduce somewhat the full effectiveness of anti-inflationary monetary policies.

4. *Changes in the velocity of money.* Discretionary monetary policy, as we have seen, requires that the Federal Reserve authorities decrease the money supply in prosperity in order to avoid inflation and increase it in recession in order to stimulate re-

covery. However, the effectiveness of these actions may sometimes be at least partially reduced by opposite changes in the velocity of money—as measured, for example, by the number of times per year that a dollar is spent. This is because the velocity of money is affected by the public's confidence in the future course of the economy. In prosperity when people are optimistic they tend to spend more freely; hence velocity increases. In recession when people are pessimistic they tend to reduce their spending; hence velocity decreases. Significant changes in the velocity can exert a direct influence on the price level, causing prices to rise when velocity increases and to decline when velocity decreases. Since, over the business cycle, velocity tends to vary inversely with the quantity of money, changes in velocity may somewhat offset the efforts of the monetary authorities to contract the money supply in inflationary periods and to expand it during recessions. We shall examine these concepts more fully in the next chapter.

5. *Lack of complete control.* During the past several decades, two types of situations have made it more difficult for the Reserve authorities to exercise as much control over the total volume of lending as they would like. First, there has been a substantial growth of *financial intermediaries*—such nonbank lenders as savings and loan associations, insurance companies, personal finance companies, and credit unions. These institutions do not create demand deposits, but hold large volumes of savings which they are continually trying to "put to work" by investing or lending to the public. This helps to offset restrictive monetary policies of the Reserve officials. Second, large holdings of government securities are in the hands of commercial banks and business corporations, which can sell them off as needed. Thus a bank which is short of reserves or a company which is unable to obtain additional bank credit can sell securities in order to get the needed cash. Because both of these situations are outside the Fed's control, they tend to increase the velocity of money and weaken the effectiveness of monetary policies.

6. *Forecasting and timing.* Although monetary policies may be implemented more quickly than fiscal policies, they nevertheless suffer from similar kinds of forecasting and timing problems. As a result, the Federal Reserve has sometimes applied the brakes "too soon," thereby stopping economic expansions short of full employment.

The fact that there are more limitations than advantages should not lead you to believe that monetary policy is useless. It is a powerful force for stabilization and will continue to play an important role in the economy.

SUMMARY OF IMPORTANT IDEAS

1. The chief responsibility of the central banking system—the Federal Reserve System—is to regulate the supply of money and credit in order to promote economic stability and growth. The ways in which this responsibility is fulfilled determine our monetary policy.

2. The chief instruments of monetary policy available to the Federal Reserve System are reserve requirements, the discount rate, open-market operations, margin regulations, and moral suasion. These tools are usually coordinated by the Reserve officials in order to achieve the System's overall objectives of promoting stable economic growth through the money supply.

3. The U.S. Treasury, like the Federal Reserve, can also influence monetary management. However, it usually carries on its operations in a manner that creates minimum disruption within the banking system and the money market.

4. Monetary policy has advantages and limitations as a method of economic stabilization. Its chief advantages are that it is (a) nondiscriminatory; (b) flexible; (c) nonpolitical. Its main limitations are that it (a) may serve as an incomplete countercyclical weapon; (b) is relatively ineffective in combating inflationary forces caused by cost-push pressures; (c) sometimes conflicts with Treasury goals; (d) may be offset by changes in the velocity of circulation of money; (e) lacks control of nonbank lending and credit operations; (f) suffers from lack of precision due to imperfect forecasting and timing. Despite these shortcomings, monetary control will probably continue to play an integral role in our general stabilization policy.

FOR DISCUSSION

1. *Terms and concepts to review:*

   monetary policy
   open-market
      operations
   yield to maturity

   yield
   margin requirements
   moral suasion

2. How do changes in reserve requirements, the discount rate, and margin requirements affect economic activity? Explain.

3. How do open-market operations work? When might they tend to be expansionary? Contractionary?

4. Suppose the reserve requirement is 15 percent. If the Federal Reserve Bank purchases $1 million of government securities in the open market, a member bank increases both its legal reserves and demand deposits by that amount. (Do you remember why?) Using the axes below, construct a bar chart showing the initial net new deposit and the *potential* cumulative expansion of bank deposits that may take place at each "round" of deposit creation. (SUGGESTION: You may find it helpful to construct a table showing the multiple expansion of bank deposits. The table can then be used to sketch the chart.)

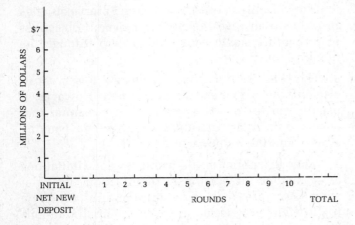

5. Suppose the Treasury issues more paper currency than people want. (a) What will happen to bank reserves? (b) What can the Federal Reserve authorities do to offset the consequences?

6. Using two long T-accounts arranged side by side as shown, depict the positive (+) or negative (−) changes represented by each of the following transactions.

FEDERAL RESERVE BANKS		COMMERCIAL BANKS	
Assets	Liabilities	Assets	Liabilities

(a) The Federal Reserve buys $100 of government securities from a dealer. The Fed pays the dealer with a check drawn on itself, which the dealer deposits in his bank.

(b) The bank sends the $100 check to the Federal Reserve, which credits the bank's reserve deposit.

(c) The Federal Reserve buys $100 of government securities from a member bank and pays with a check on itself.

(d) The bank sends the $100 check to the Federal Reserve for credit to its account.

(e) The Federal Reserve lends $100 to a member bank by discounting the latter's note.

(f) A depositor writes a check for $100 against his demand deposit and cashes it at his bank.

(g) A depositor adds $100 in currency to his demand deposit.

(h) The Treasury sells $100 of securities to the nonbanking public and deposits the checks it receives in commercial banks.

(i) The Treasury transfers $100 of deposits from member banks to Federal Reserve Banks.

(j) The Treasury pays $100 for services by writing a check against its deposit at the Federal Reserve; the person to whom the check is paid deposits it to his account.

(k) The bank sends the $100 check to the Federal Reserve for collection.

CHAPTER 16

Money, Interest, and Macroeconomic Equilibrium

CHAPTER PREVIEW

The monetary authorities (central bank) have the power to expand and contract the money supply. How do such decisions affect the general price level? What implications does this have for monetary policy?

How is the rate of interest determined? Of what significance is the rate of interest in the theory of income determination?

How do the strategic variables determining income or GNP fit together? Can they be integrated into a coherent whole—a model of macroeconomic equilibrium?

The importance of money essentially flows from its being a link between the present and the future.

So wrote J. M. Keynes in his important book, *The General Theory of Employment, Interest and Money* in 1936. The following year he went on to say: "The possession of actual money lulls our disquietude; and the premium which we require to make us part with money is the measure of the degree of our disquietude."

The "link between the present and the future"—the "premium" to which Lord Keynes referred—is the rate of interest. This variable plays a strategic role in the modern theory of income determination—a fact which was pointed out in an earlier chapter but which must now be examined in closer detail.

It is important to understand the relationship between money and interest. The rate of interest may be directly influenced by changes in the money supply. Therefore once the relationship between money and interest is established, the modern theory of income determination will be complete, and we will see how the strategic variables in the theory interrelate within the system as a whole.

Money Affects Output and Prices

We have seen that the Federal Reserve can influence the level of economic activity by its discretionary actions. For example, to encourage economic expansion, it can increase the supply of money by engaging in open-market purchases of government bonds; to initiate economic contraction, it can decrease the supply of money by undertaking open-market sales of government bonds. Thus, there is a direct relationship between the money supply and the level of economic activity: changes in the former can produce changes in the latter in the same direction.

The idea that changes in the money supply lead to changes in the price level was fundamental to classical economic thinking. But it was not stated with precision until the early 1900s. At that time a distinguished American economist at Yale University—Professor Irving Fisher (1867-1947)—expressed the link between money and prices by means of an equation that soon became famous. A modernized version of that equation can be developed in the following way.

EQUATION OF EXCHANGE

You may not be able to see how fast individual dollars are spent, but you can measure the average speed of money movements as a whole rather easily. Let V stand for the *income velocity of money*, that is, the average number of times per year a dollar is spent on purchasing the economy's annual flow of final goods and services—its GNP. Then, if M denotes the nation's money supply as measured by the amount of money including currency and demand deposits in the hands of the public, the income velocity of money is measured by the formula:

$$V = \frac{GNP}{M}$$

For example, if in a certain year the GNP was $800 billion and the stock of money was $200 billion, V = ($800/$200) = 4 per year for that year. In other words, each dollar must have been used an average of four times to purchase the economy's GNP.

The letter M in the above equation, of course, can be transposed to the left side so that the equation becomes

$$MV = GNP$$

Suppose, however, that we make the equation more refined by expressing GNP in terms of its components—prices and quantities. Let P stand for the average price of final goods and services produced during the year and let Q represent the physical quantity of those goods and services. The *value*

of final output is then price times quantity; that is, GNP = P × Q, since, for example, GNP = price of apples times number of apples, plus price of haircuts times number of haircuts, plus . . . and so on for all final goods and services produced. The above equation can therefore be written

$$MV = PQ$$

This is known as the "equation of exchange." To illustrate it, consider a highly simplified case in which the students in your class compose an economy whose total supply of money M is $80; the class produces a quantity of output Q, equal to 60 units of a good; and the average price P of this output is $4 per unit. Then the equation of exchange tells us that V must equal 3, since

$$MV = PQ$$

or

$$(\$80)(3) = (\$4)(60)$$

Each dollar is thus spent an average of three times per year on the class's output.

The equation of exchange is actually an identity because it states that the total amount of money *spent* on final goods and services, MV, is equal to the total amount of money *received* for final goods and services, PQ.

To summarize:

Equation of exchange. During any given period, the quantity of money (M), multiplied by the average number of times each unit of money is spent on purchasing the economy's final output of goods and services (V), is equal to the quantity of final output (Q), multiplied by its average price (P). Thus: MV = PQ.

The equation tells us that the given flow of money can be looked at either from the buyers' or the sellers' points of view. The aggregate flow is the same in either case. As in demand and supply analysis, the quantity of a commodity purchased is equal to the quantity sold.

THE QUANTITY THEORY OF MONEY

To understand what the equation of exchange tells us about the role of money in influencing national income and expenditure we have to examine some of its components.

1. Suppose we assume that V *remains constant.* This means that by controlling M we could control GNP. For instance, if M is increased, either P, or Q, or both will have to increase in order to maintain equality between the right and left side of the equation. The changes in P or Q will depend on the state of the economy. In a period of recession, Q will tend to rise relatively more than P as unemployed resources are put to work; in a period of high employment, P will tend to rise relatively more than Q as full utilization of resources is approached. What do you suppose would happen in a period of full employment?

2. Suppose we assume that *both V and Q remain constant.* This, in fact, is what the classical economists believed. They assumed that V was constant because it was determined by the long-run money-holding habits of households and business firms which, they argued, were fairly stable; and they assumed that Q was constant because the economy always tended toward full employment. They concluded that P depends directly on M. As a result, their theory has come to be known as the "quantity theory of money."

Quantity theory of money. The level of prices in the economy is directly proportional to the quantity of money in circulation, such that a given percentage change in the stock of money will cause an equal percentage change in the price level in the same direction.

The quantity theory thus states, for example, that a 10 percent increase in M will cause a 10 percent increase in P; a 5 percent decrease in M will cause a 5 percent decrease in P; and so on.

WHAT DOES THE EVIDENCE SHOW?

How well does the quantity theory of money correspond with the facts? Can changes in M be used to predict changes in P?

In evaluating the theory, it is necessary to distinguish between long- and short-term changes. The evidence suggests two major classes of findings.

1. During a number of long-run periods, changes in P have appeared to be closely tied to changes in M. For example, in the late sixteenth century, the Spanish importation of gold and silver from the New World caused major price increases in Europe; the discovery of gold in the United States, Canada, and South Africa during the latter half of the nineteenth century brought sudden expansions in the money supply and rapidly rising prices; and the excessive borrowing and printing of money by certain countries during and after World Wars I and II resulted in a continuous upward spiraling of prices. In these and various other cases prices rose with increases in the quantity of money and without corresponding increases in output, while the long-run income velocity of money was fairly stable.

2. In the short run, V varies a good deal, even though its long-run trend has been steadily rising—as shown in Exhibit 1. And output, of course, may also vary substantially from year to year. In addition, even if P increases as a result of an increase in M, the rise in prices might encourage an increase in V as people spend money more quickly for fear of future price increases. If this happens, P is no longer merely a passive variable dependent on M, but a *causal* variable contributing to changes in other factors.

As a result of complexities such as these, the quantity theory of money has not yet proved very suitable for predicting short-run changes in P on the basis of changes in M. However, as pointed out above, it provides a useful guide for judging the influence of monetary forces on long-run changes in the price level.

Exhibit 1

Income Velocity of Money—GNP/Money Stock

The income velocity of money usually fluctuates considerably within any given year. Its long-run trend, however, has been steadily upward.

MODERNIZING THE QUANTITY THEORY

The quantity theory of money played a critical role in classical economic thinking. Since the 1950s, it has undergone substantial revision by some economists—particularly by Professor Milton Friedman of the University of Chicago. The revised or "modern" quantity theory retains much of the traditional doctrine, but reorients it toward the importance of V. For example, V is not assumed to remain constant as in the old theory, but is believed instead to be influenced by many factors. One of these is *public confidence in the economy*—or *stage of the business cycle*. If people fear unemployment or are pessimistic about the future, they will tend to refrain from spending by increasing their percentage of income saved. The larger the proportion of saving that occurs without a corresponding increase in investment, the more slowly money turns over and hence the lower its velocity.

Modern quantity theorists believe that although V fluctuates over time, its range of short-run variation is limited and, with sufficient knowledge, *predictable*. Therefore, the underlying determinant of GNP (or *PQ* in the equation of exchange) is still the quantity of money. This conclusion has important policy implications. It suggests that:

The central bank, that is, Federal Reserve, should use its monetary instruments—such as open-market operations and control over the discount rate and reserve requirements—to provide a continuous expansion in the money supply at a rate sufficient to assure steady economic growth and full employment. Failure to follow this "rule," say the modern quantity theorists, leads inevitably to economic instability.

Does this mean that fiscal and monetary measures should be discarded in favor of a policy which provides for steady growth in the money supply at an established rate? Many informed observers would answer yes. But the majority of economists believe that an optimum fiscal-monetary mix must be found which will assure economic stability at a high level of income and employment. However, the difficulties of attaining such a mix are considerable—for reasons that will be pointed out subsequently.

Determination of the Interest Rate

Any study of money must inevitably lead to a discussion of the rate of interest and to an analysis of the forces determining it. This is a matter of great importance. As you will recall from the study of investment in an earlier chapter, businessmen invest in capital goods only as long as their anticipated rate of return over cost on an additional unit of investment—called the *marginal efficiency of investment*—exceeds the cost of money capital or rate of interest. In view of this, what determines the rate of interest? The answer, as you will see, provides the final link in a model of the macroeconomy.

What do we mean by *interest*? Simply stated, it is the price paid for the use of money or loanable funds over a period. Interest is expressed as a rate—that is, as a percentage of the amount of money borrowed. Thus an interest rate of 5 percent means that the borrower pays 5 cents per $1 borrowed per year.

As we learned in a previous chapter dealing with the monetary and banking system, there is no such thing as "the" interest rate—in the sense of a single rate on all financial instruments traded in the money and capital markets. Instead there are many different rates on specific types of notes, bonds, etc., depending on risk of default, maturity dates, tax advantages, and numerous other factors. Despite such differences, however, interest rates are interrelated in that they tend to increase or decrease together, although differentials between them often vary. Hence it proves convenient for present purposes to talk about "the" interest rate, thinking in terms of the whole structure of rates as rising or declining.

CLASSICAL EXPLANATION: FISHER'S THEORY

The arithmetic books tell us that interest is a payment for the use of money. This concept is adequate for most purposes, but to the classical economists interest had a special and quite different meaning.

You recall that in the classical circular-flow model, the total economy is divided into two parts—a household sector and a business sector. The household sector supplies the saving which the business sector borrows and invests in capital goods in order to carry on profitable production. Interest, therefore, is a price which businesses pay households to persuade the latter to consume less in the present so that they can consume more at a later date. Interest is a payment for "saving," for "abstinence" from consumption, or for overcoming a "time preference" for present as opposed to future consumption.

Why is interest necessary? The classicists believed that no household will save, and thereby forgo the

IRVING FISHER

1867-1947

Irving Fisher, a Professor of Economics at Yale University, was one of America's foremost economists prior to World War II. A mathematician as well as economist, he was a profound scholar and prolific writer—author of 28 published books as well as dozens of articles in professional journals. Of his books, 18 covered diverse areas of economics and statistics; the remainder consisted of some highly successful mathematics textbooks, plus several popular volumes on diet and health—subjects which interested him because he suffered from tuberculosis as a young man. In addition to engaging in research and writing, Fisher invented many mechanical devices. The only one to achieve commercial success was a card index system mounted on a rotary stand. Fisher received about $1 million for this, which he subsequently parlayed into $9 million in the stock market. He lost it all in the crash of 1929.

Among Fisher's major interests was the study of money and prices. In a book entitled *The Purchasing Power of Money* (1911), he stated the *equation of exchange*—which also subsequently became known as the *Fisher equation*:

$$MV + M'V' = PT$$

where M is the quantity of currency, V is its velocity of circulation, M' is the quantity of demand deposits, V' is their velocity of circulation, P is the average price level of all goods sold, and T is the volume of transactions or total quantity of all goods sold. The equation has often been shortened by economists to

$$MV = PT$$

by redefining M to include "money"—currency plus demand deposits—and V its velocity of circulation.

The equation, formulated long before national-income data were available, is theoretically interesting but of little practical use because it encompasses *all* transactions involving payment in money. It therefore covers not only the sale of final goods but also the sale of raw materials, partly finished goods, securities, real estate, and used goods. Hence it may be called the "transactions-velocity" formulation in order to distinguish it from the modern and much more practical "income-velocity" formulation, $MV = PQ$, which encompasses only transactions for *final* goods and uses readily available GNP data. Both equations, however, have similar structural properties and permit similar interpretations.

Culver Pictures, Inc.

Fisher employed his equation to explain a cause-and-effect relationship between the quantity of money and the price level. He assumed that the velocity of circulation (V) and the volume of transactions (T) were constant—or at least that they always tended toward equilibrium. Therefore, he concluded, if there is "a doubling in the quantity of money, . . . it follows necessarily and mathematically that the level of prices must double." Or in general, "one of the normal effects of an increase in the quantity of money is an exactly proportional increase in the general level of prices." From this it is evident, according to Fisher, that business cycles are not inherent in the economy, but are due almost entirely to excessive expansions and contractions in the money supply—"especially in the form of bank loans."

Fisher made important contributions to the study of business cycles, capital, and interest. He also did pioneering work in the fields of mathematical economics and statistics, the integration of which is known as *econometrics*. He was honored for his many achievements by being elected president of each of the three major professional organizations concerned with the advancement of economic science—the American Economic Association, the American Statistical Association, and the Econometric Society.

pleasure of spending, unless it is offered interest in return, and no businessman will borrow, and thereby pay interest, unless he intends to invest in profitable production. Saving, in classical theory, therefore, leads automatically to spending on capital or investment goods. And a flexible interest rate in the competitive money market, determined by the free play of supply and demand, assures that every dollar saved by households will be borrowed and invested by businesses—as illustrated in Exhibit 2.

The Real Rate and the Market Rate

These ideas of classical economics were further developed in the early part of this century by Irving Fisher. Hence the classical explanation of

interest is also sometimes called the Fisher theory of interest. It rests fundamentally on a distinction between two kinds of interest: (1) the real rate and (2) the market rate.

The *real rate of interest* is the interest rate measured in terms of goods. It is the rate which would prevail in the market if the general price level remained stable. Under such circumstances, if you lend a friend $100 today with the understanding that he will repay you $105 a year from today, you give up $100 worth of goods now for what you expect will be $105 worth of goods a year from now. The real rate of interest is therefore 5 percent. According to the classicists, this rate is established by real economic forces of demand and supply. The "real demand" for funds by businesses is determined by

---

Exhibit 2

The Market Rate of Interest in Classical Theory

The classicists theorized that the equilibrium rate of interest r is determined in the competitive money market where the supply of funds saved by households equals the demand for funds invested by businesses. They also

believed that if the investment-demand curve shifts from D to D', the intersection with the existing saving-supply curve would determine the new rate of interest r'.

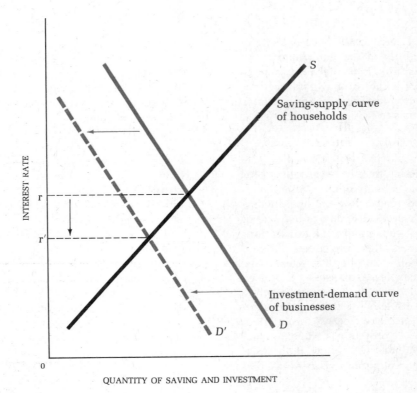

INTEREST RATE

r

r'

S

Saving-supply curve of households

Investment-demand curve of businesses

D'

D

0

QUANTITY OF SAVING AND INVESTMENT

the productivity of borrowed capital and the "real supply" of funds by households is determined by the willingness of consumers to abstain from present consumption.

The *market rate of interest* is the actual or money rate which prevails in the market at any given time. Unlike the real rate, which is not directly observable, the market rate is the one we see in the markets because it reflects the quantity of loans measured in units of money, not goods. Hence it is the rate which people ordinarily have in mind when they talk about "the" interest rate.

A crucial point in classical theory is that the real rate and the market rate usually are not equal. Only if borrowers and lenders expect the general price level, that is, the value of a unit of money, to remain constant will both rates be the same. This does not ordinarily happen. People are always expecting prices either to rise or fall. Therefore, the market rate of interest will depart from the real rate according to the following conditions:

1. If people believe prices will rise—and hence the purchasing power of a unit of money will decline—the market rate of interest will be higher than the real rate. For example, if lenders and borrowers expect the price level to rise 5 percent per year, the market rate of interest will be the real rate plus 5 percent. This "inflation premium" is necessary to compensate lenders for their loss in purchasing power. At the same time, borrowers will be willing to pay the premium because they will be repaying their loans with money worth 5 percent less per year than the money they borrowed.

2. If people believe prices will fall—and therefore the purchasing power of a unit of money will rise—the market rate of interest will be below the real rate. The difference is a "deflation discount" (or negative inflation premium) which is necessary to compensate borrowers for their loss in purchasing power. At the same time, lenders will be willing to grant the discount since they will be repaid with money worth 5 percent more per year than the money they initially lent.

These ideas can be summarized briefly:

In classical theory, the market rate of interest will be greater than, equal to, or less than the real rate depending on whether households and businesses expect the general price level to rise, remain constant, or decline. Any differential between the market rate and the real rate represents the amount necessary to compensate lenders or borrowers for adverse changes in purchasing power resulting from anticipated inflation or deflation.

Deriving the Real Rate

Many modern economists are sympathetic to this classical view. They contend that the inflation premium in interest rates reflects the rise in prices over the years, thereby indicating that market interest rates and prices tend to move together—just as the classicists theorized. Therefore, you can calculate the real rate of interest quite easily by subtracting the change in the general price level from the market interest rate, thus:

Real interest rate = market interest rate − change in general price level

For example, one of the most commonly used measures of the market interest rate is the yield on high-grade corporate bonds—such as Moody's Aaa bond yields shown in the back endpapers of this book. (Moody's is a large private firm which sells many financial services, including ratings and yields on various types of bonds.) The most comprehensive measure of the general price level is the *Implicit Price Index,* IPI, more popularly known as the GNP price deflator. As described in an earlier chapter, this index is a weighted average of the various price indexes used to deflate the components of GNP. The IPI is also shown in the endpapers at the back of this book. It follows from the above formula, therefore, that if, in a given period, Moody's Aaa yields are, say, 7 percent, and the IPI has increased from the previous period by 4 percent, the real rate of interest for that period is 3 percent. (See Exhibit 3 on the next page.)

Conclusion: Prices and Interest Rates Move Together

Is the connection between prices and interest rates valid? Today's classical economists believe it is. They point out that, historically, interest rates in the United States have risen when prices increased and have declined when they decreased. Admittedly, the response of interest rates to sustained price changes has sometimes lagged by several years, but that is because high market rates reflect expected as well as actual inflation. Evidence of this can be seen in many nations. Argentina, Brazil, and Chile, for example, traditionally experience steep inflations; hence interest rates are high. Australia and Switzerland, on the other hand, have historically

Exhibit 3

The "Real Cost" of Money

The real interest rate can be derived by subtracting the change in the general price level from the market rate of interest. A high market rate of interest reflects not only inflation itself, but the expectation that it will continue. However, expectations are psychological, and there may sometimes be a time delay, a lag, of several years before the market interest rate reacts to a substantial change in the general price level.

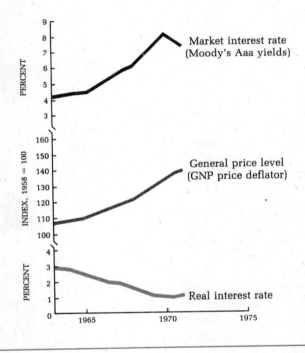

had reasonably stable price levels; as a result, interest rates are relatively low.

To conclude:

According to the classicists, increases in the quantity of money result in "too much money chasing too few goods." Consequently, prices and interest rates rise. By reducing the rate of growth in the money supply, the monetary authority (the central banking system) can retard inflation and bring about reductions in the market rate of interest.

LIQUIDITY-PREFERENCE EXPLANATION—THE KEYNESIAN THEORY

As we learned in earlier chapters, much of traditional economic thinking underwent major changes in the Great Depression of the 1930s. The person initially responsible for this restructuring of ideas was the eminent British economist, John Maynard Keynes. The revised theory, which Keynes called a "general theory," resulted in the birth of the *New Economics.* You will find it helpful to refresh your understanding of this expression by looking up its meaning in the Dictionary at the end of this book.

What did Keynes have to say about the role of the interest rate and the factors determining it? We already know part of the answer:

Capital spending or investment by businessmen is the strategic determinant of the level of income and employment. Such spending is undertaken as long as the marginal efficiency of investment exceeds the rate of interest. Therefore, the rate of interest is crucial in relation to investment.

As for the factors determining the rate of interest, Keynes argued that the classical theory is correct for an economy that tends automatically toward full employment. His own theory, on the other hand, is more general because it applies to an economic system that may be in equilibrium at *any* level of employment.

For example, the investment-demand curve in Exhibit 2 shows the amount of capital spending that businessmen are willing to undertake at each rate of interest. It is the same as the marginal-efficiency-of-investment curve in Keynesian income and employment theory. According to Keynes, the classicists erred by assuming that this curve could shift *without causing a change in income and a simultaneous shift in the saving-supply curve.* We know from Keynes and from modern income and employment theory that a decrease in the marginal efficiency of investment will cause aggregate investment to decline. Aggregate income, therefore, will also drop, and so will saving, which depends on income. The classical economists did not recognize this. As a result, they simply viewed interest as a "price" which equates the demand for investment with the supply of saving at the fixed full-employment level of income. Keynes argued that since the saving-supply curve must shift if the investment-demand curve shifts, the rate of interest in the classical scheme cannot be determined nor can the equilibrium quantity of saving and investment, because the information provided is insufficient.

In view of this, let us see how Keynes restructured the theory of interest.

Statement of the Theory

In classical theory, interest is a reward for "waiting" —for "abstinence" from consumption. In Keynes' theory, the rate of interest is determined entirely by the demand for and supply of money. But two factors underlying demand and supply must be considered: (1) liquidity preference and (2) the quantity of money.

On the demand side, in Keynes' view, money is wanted because it is the only perfectly liquid asset. People would rather hold some of their assets in money than in any other form. Therefore, if an individual is to be persuaded to give up some of his perfectly liquid assets, he must be paid a reward. *Interest is the price that must be paid to overcome liquidity preference.* To put it slightly differently, *interest is the reward for not hoarding money.*

On the supply side, according to Keynes, the quantity of money is the important factor. As we have said, the quantity of money is determined by the monetary authority (central bank) through its control over open-market operations, reserve requirements, and other factors. The monetary authority can use these mechanisms to increase the money supply if the public wants to hold a larger proportion of its assets in the form of money. If the public desires to hold a smaller proportion, the monetary authority can decrease the money supply. Expansions and contractions in the quantity of money can thus play a strategic role in the determination of the interest rate.

Determinants of Demand and Supply

The demand for money is a demand for liquidity. Why should you and I and everyone else prefer to hold assets in liquid form? Keynes provided three reasons which he called the transactions, precautionary, and speculative motives.

1. *Transactions motive.* Households and businesses must hold some of their assets in the form of money (currency and demand deposits) because they purchase goods and services more or less continuously from day to day, whereas they receive income only at intervals such as weekly or monthly. Therefore, a certain amount of money must be held to bridge the gap. The amount required—the transactions demand for money—does not depend on the interest rate. Instead, it is directly related to the level of economic activity. Thus as national income

rises, so too does the need for money for transactions purposes.

2. *Precautionary motive.* Households and businesses also want to hold part of their assets in liquid form to meet unforeseen developments such as illnesses, accidents, losses of employment, strikes, or market fluctuations. Although individuals and firms may be able to convert other assets into money at such times, the possibility of loss due to forced liquidation under unfavorable market conditions prompts them to prefer money for reserve contingencies. The precautionary demand for money is influenced primarily by national-income levels rather than by changes in the interest rate. Hence most precautionary demand may be combined with the transactions demand for money since both depend mainly on income. (See Exhibit 4.)

3. *Speculative motive.* Households and businesses also may prefer to hold part of their assets in the form of money to enable them to take advantage of changes in interest rates. Individuals and firms tend to hold more securities—especially long-term bonds—and less money when the interest rate is

---

Exhibit 4

Transactions and Precautionary Demands for Money

Households and businesses want to hold some of their assets in the form of money in order to carry on day-to-day transactions—the transactions motive—and also to meet unforeseen contingencies—the precautionary motive. Both demands for money depend primarily on the total level of money payments or national income. The straight line in this chart means that money demanded for transactions and precautionary purposes rises by some constant proportion of national income.

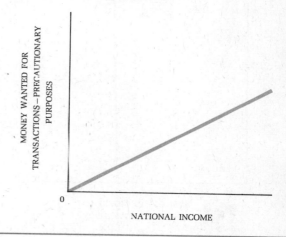

high, in order to take advantage of higher returns. Conversely, they also tend to hold more money and fewer securities when the interest rate is low because the risk of holding bonds—the possible fall in their prices—more than offsets the interest returns. Thus, as Exhibit 5 demonstrates, the interest rate is inversely related to the quantity of money wanted for speculative purposes.

The transactions, precautionary, and speculative motives determine the demand for money. What factors determine supply? As you know, the supply of money is simply the stock of money available to satisfy the demand, and is determined by the monetary authority through its control over open-market operations, reserve requirements, and discount-rate policy. Hence at any given time the supply or stock of money is fixed. This means that it can be represented by a vertical—or in the language of economics, a "perfectly inelastic"—supply curve as shown in Exhibit 6.

The reason for this terminology is not hard to see. Unlike most supply curves, which are upward sloping, this one is vertical, showing that increases or decreases in the interest rate ("price" of money) do not cause changes in the stock of money. Therefore, we may say that the quantity supplied of money is unresponsive to—or *perfectly inelastic* with respect to—changes in the interest rate.

Determining the Interest Rate

Of course, as in any demand and supply problem, either variable by itself cannot determine the price. The two must be combined in order for a price to be established. This is shown in Exhibit 7. As you can see, the equilibrium rate of interest r is determined by the intersection of the liquidity-preference curve L, representing the demand for money, with the money supply curve M, representing the stock of money. If the interest rate is higher

---

Exhibit 5

Speculative Demand for Money

Households and businesses desire to hold some of their assets in the form of money to take advantage of changes in interest rates. Their speculative demand for money varies inversely with the interest rate. At a high interest rate, they will hold less money and more securities; at a low interest rate, they will hold more money and fewer securities. Note that the line is curved rather than straight and that it tends to flatten out at its lower right end—for reasons explained later.

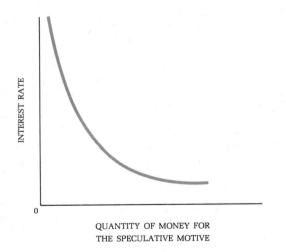

QUANTITY OF MONEY FOR
THE SPECULATIVE MOTIVE

Exhibit 6

Supply of Money

At any given time, there is a quantity or stock of money available to satisfy the public's demand. This quantity is determined by the monetary authority through its open-market operations, discount-rate policy, and reserve requirements. Hence the supply curve is a vertical line, indicating that the quantity supplied of money is unresponsive to changes in the interest rate.

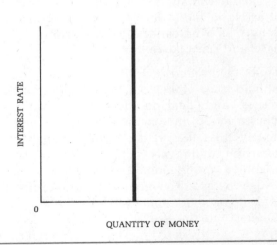

QUANTITY OF MONEY

---

than the equilibrium level, the quantity supplied exceeds the quantity demanded, thus driving the rate down; if the rate is below the equilibrium level, the quantity demanded exceeds the quantity supplied, thus driving the rate up. Note that the demand curve for money includes all three components of demand—as explained in the exhibit.

Like all demand and supply curves, those in Exhibit 7 are drawn on the assumption that all other things besides the interest rate that may affect demand and supply remain constant. If one of the factors changes, the relevant demand or supply curve will shift, bringing about a new equilibrium rate of interest. For example:

1. If national income rises, the quantity of money demanded for transactions and precautionary purposes also rises, causing an increase in liquidity preference or the demand for money at all interest rates. The L curve, in other words, shifts to the right,

as in Exhibit 8. The same result might be obtained if there were a decline in business expectations, because spending units might attempt to increase their holdings of money for precautionary purposes.

2. If the monetary authority increases the supply of money, the M curve will shift to the right. This is also explained in Exhibit 8.

To summarize:

The _liquidity-preference theory of interest_, formulated by J. M. Keynes, contends that households and businesses want to hold some of their assets in the most liquid form, namely, cash or checking accounts, in order to satisfy three motives: (1) the transactions motive, (2) the precautionary motive, and (3) the speculative motive. These motives determine the demand for money, whereas the monetary authority determines its supply. The demand for, and supply of, money together determine the equilibrium rate of interest.

Exhibit 7

Determination of the Interest Rate by Demand for and Supply of Money

At a given level of national income, the equilibrium rate of interest r is determined by the intersection of the L curve representing the total demand for money with the M curve representing total supply. Note that the L curve consists of the transactions and precautionary demands which are assumed to be dependent on the level of national income (but not on the interest rate), plus the speculative demand which depends on the interest rate.

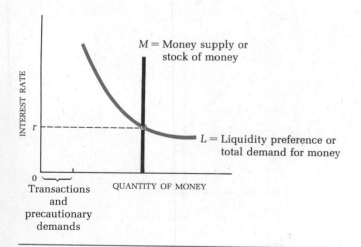

Exhibit 8

Changes in the Interest Rate Resulting from Shifts in the L and M Curves

If the M curve remains fixed, an increase in income will shift the liquidity-preference or total demand-for-money curve rightward from L to L', causing the equilibrium rate of interest to rise from r to r'. If the L curve remains fixed, an increase in the stock of money will shift the money supply curve rightward from M to M', causing the equilibrium rate of interest to decline from r to r''.

Of course, a decrease in income or a decrease in the money supply will correspondingly shift the L and M curves leftward. Can you show what happens to the equilibrium rate of interest under such circumstances? What may happen if the L and M curves shift simultaneously in the same direction? In opposite directions?

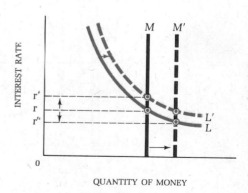

Practical Implications of the Liquidity-preference Theory

The liquidity-preference theory of interest is the final link in the entire Keynesian system. Without it there would be no determinate solution to our general economic model. You will gain a better appreciation of this fact later in the chapter when we construct an outline of macroeconomic theory based on the explanations of employment, interest, and money developed in this and in earlier chapters. First, however, it is useful to point out the practical implications of the theory of interest within the framework of what we have already learned.

MARGINAL EFFICIENCY OF INVESTMENT AND THE INTEREST RATE

You recall from the study of income and employment that the marginal efficiency of investment (MEI) is the expected rate of return on an investment. More precisely, it is the expected rate of return over the cost of an additional unit of a capital good. Each business firm has its own MEI curve showing the amount of investment it will undertake at various market rates of interest or costs of money capital. Hence a firm's MEI curve is its demand curve for investment. It follows that at any given time the sum of all firms' MEI curves yields an aggregate MEI curve showing the total amount of private investment that will be undertaken at various rates of interest. Therefore the aggregate MEI curve is the business sector's demand curve for investment.

This idea is illustrated in Exhibit 9. In Chart (a) the equilibrium rate of interest r is determined by the intersection of the demand and supply curves of money—the L and M curves—as we have already learned. This rate is the cost of money capital to firms. Hence in Chart (b) the amount of investment undertaken by the business sector at this rate of interest, shown by the aggregate MEI curve, is I. If

---

Exhibit 9

The Interest Rate and Investment

In Chart (a), an increase in the money-supply curve from M to M' increases the quantity of money from Q to Q' and decreases the rate of interest from r to r'. This increases the amount of investment from I to I' in Chart (b), since businessmen invest to the point where the MEI equals the interest rate (or cost of money capital).

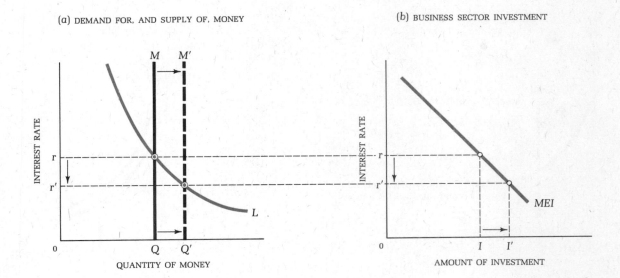

(a) DEMAND FOR, AND SUPPLY OF, MONEY

(b) BUSINESS SECTOR INVESTMENT

this volume of investment is insufficient to achieve full employment, the monetary authorities can lower the rate of interest by increasing the money supply—say, from Q to Q'. Assuming the L curve remains fixed, the equilibrium rate of interest will decline from r to r', causing the amount of investment to increase from I to I'. This increase in investment, as you know, will have a magnified effect on income due to the operation of the multiplier. Further, since the liquidity-preference (L) curve depends on income, it will shift to the right when income rises—as we have already learned.

You can see, therefore, that the effectiveness of monetary policy for stimulating economic activity poses some challenging questions. For example:

1. To what extent will the interest rate fall as a result of an increase in the money supply?

2. To what extent will the amount of investment increase as a result of a decline in the interest rate?

3. To what extent will income rise as a result of an increase in investment?

The answer to the first question depends on the relative steepness (technically, the elasticity) of the L curve; to the second, on the relative steepness of the MEI curve; and to the third, on the size of the multiplier. For instance, referring back to Exhibit 9, what would be the effect on the change in the interest rate and on the change in the amount of investment if both the L curve and the MEI curve were relatively flatter? Steeper? You can answer these questions by sketching some curves yourself and comparing the differences. As for the size of the multiplier, you recall that it depends on the marginal propensities to consume or to save, since it equals 1/(1-MPC) or 1/MPS.

THE LIQUIDITY TRAP

Should we infer from Exhibit 9 that increases in the quantity of money will always lower the rate of interest—and therefore increase the amount of investment? The answer is not a simple yes or no. As pointed out above, other factors must be considered. One of them is the shape of the L curve, which, as we saw in previous diagrams, is assumed to flatten out at its right end. As a result, the lower the rate of interest, the more resistant it becomes to further reductions, until a point is reached where the L curve becomes perfectly horizontal. From then on,

it is impossible to reduce the interest rate further merely by increasing the supply of money.

This concept is illustrated in Exhibit 10. The flat portion of the curve signifies that at some low rate of interest (say, 2 percent), everyone prefers to hold money rather than risk any loss from holding long-term securities yielding poor returns. Hence this horizontal segment of the curve is called the *liquidity trap*. It has been used by some economists to explain why monetary policy may not be effective in inducing recovery from a deep recession if the rate of interest, though low absolutely, is still too high relative to the marginal efficiency of investment. Under such circumstances, they contend, there is no stimulus for businessmen to increase the amount of their investment, despite low interest rates. It should be emphasized, however, that this is an hypothesis; there is no concrete evidence to support it.

Exhibit 10

The Liquidity Trap

Since the L curve "flattens out" at its right end, there is some low rate of interest, say 2 percent, beyond which an increase in the supply of money cannot reduce the rate further. Hence the total demand for money at this low interest rate is infinite, because everyone would prefer to hold money in idle balances rather than risk the loss of holding long-term securities offering such poor yields.

In geometric terms, the liquidity trap exists at that rate of interest where the liquidity-preference curve becomes perfectly horizontal.

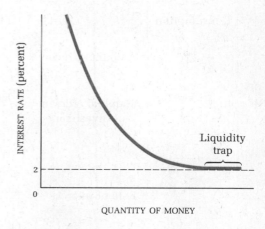

CONCLUSION: IMPORTANCE OF THE INTEREST RATE

The preceding analysis is based on a *given level of national income*. If national income is allowed to change, the problem becomes more complicated, because a change in national income will affect the rate of interest as well as the volume of saving and investment. To the extent that the amount of investment is responsive to a change in the interest rate, aggregate demand and hence the overall level of employment will also be affected. Further, a change in national income will influence the transactions and precautionary demands for money—which in turn influence the total demand for money for liquidity purposes.

This suggests an important conclusion:

The rate of interest is of strategic importance in income and employment analysis. It is the mechanism which establishes equilibrium between the supply of money in the economy and the amounts which people wish to hold as cash balances. Since the rate of interest is affected by the money supply, which in turn is controlled by the monetary authority, expansionary or contractionary monetary policies can influence the level of economic activity.

How does the rate of interest fit into the overall picture of income determination? It is one of several strategic variables that are instrumental in establishing macroeconomic equilibrium.

Macroeconomic Equilibrium: Putting the Pieces Together

The modern theory of income determination which we set out to study at the beginning of Part 2 is now completed. (You will find it helpful to refer to the table of contents to get an overview of the ground covered thus far.) We shall now bring together the major components of the theory. This will permit certain fundamental relationships between key variables to be integrated into a meaningful whole.

OUTLINE OF THE THEORY

A summary of the theory of income determination is outlined in Exhibit 11. The relationships may be stated briefly in the form of several propositions:

1. The level of income depends on consumption expenditure and investment expenditure.

2. Consumption expenditure depends on the pro-

Exhibit 11

Outline of the Theory of Income Determination

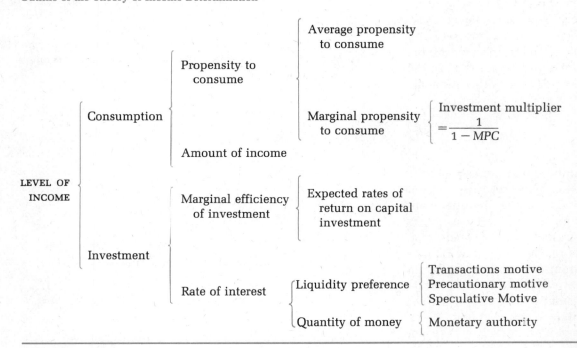

pensity to consume in relation to income, whereas investment expenditure depends on the marginal efficiency of investment relative to the rate of interest.

3. The propensity to consume (or consumption function) expresses a relationship between consumption and income: as income increases, consumption increases, but not as fast as income. In geometric terms the propensity to consume involves (a) the average propensity to consume, or ratio of consumption to income, and (b) the marginal propensity to consume, or change in consumption relative to the change in income.

4. The marginal efficiency of investment depends on expected rates of return on capital investment, whereas the rate of interest depends on liquidity preference and the quantity of money.

5. The marginal propensity to consume affects the size of the investment multiplier, and hence affects the amount by which an increase in investment causes a multiple increase in income.

6. Liquidity preference is determined by the transactions, precautionary, and speculative motives, whereas the quantity of money is controlled by the monetary authority.

These propositions contain only the main features of the theory. They do not express all the interrelations between the variables, many of which were discussed in this and earlier chapters.

SOME BASIC RELATIONSHIPS

Exhibit 12 shows an integration of important relationships. This highly simplified model conveys

---

Exhibit 12

Simplified Model of Income Determination

This model emphasizes the interrelationships among key variables by showing the four basic determinants of income or GNP:

1. Liquidity preference, L

2. Money supply, M

3. Marginal efficiency of investment, MEI

4. Consumption function, C

In Chart (a) the equilibrium rate of interest is determined by the intersection of the liquidity-preference (L) and quantity of money (M) curves. In Chart (b), the

amount of investment (I) is determined by the interest rate and the marginal efficiency of investment (MEI) curve. In Chart (c) the volume of investment is superimposed on the consumption function to give the C + I or aggregate demand (AD) curve, whose intersection with the 45° line or aggregate supply (AS) curve determines the equilibrium level of income.

As you can see from the charts, there can be no change in income or GNP without a change in—shift in the curve of—one or more of the four basic factors L, M, MEI, C, determining it.

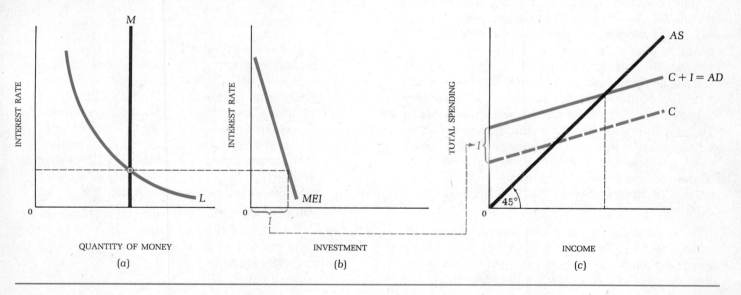

many of the essential ideas of macroeconomic equilibrium. In Chart (*a*), the equilibrium rate of interest is determined by the intersection of the demand or liquidity-preference curve for money *L* with the supply of money *M*. In Chart (*b*) this interest rate is brought together with the marginal efficiency of investment *MEI* to determine the amount of investment *I*. In Chart (*c*), this volume of investment is superimposed on the consumption function *C*. Hence the intersection of the *C* + *I* or aggregate demand (*AD*) curve with the 45° aggregate supply (*AS*) curve determines the equilibrium level of income.

If this level of income is either too low or too high to correspond to full employment, the result, as we learned in an earlier chapter, is either a deflationary or inflationary gap. To close the gap some combination of fiscal and monetary policy is needed. But government faces problems of considerable difficulty when it tries to choose a proper blend of policies, as we shall see in the next chapter.

SUMMARY OF IMPORTANT IDEAS

1. The equation of exchange, $MV = PQ$, states that the quantity of money (*M*), multiplied by the average number of times each unit of money is spent on purchasing the economy's final output of goods and services (*V*), is equal to the quantity of final output (*Q*), multiplied by its average price (*P*). The equation is thus a truism or identity because it tells us that the same flow of money can be looked at either from buyers' or sellers' points of view.

2. The quantity theory of money, as originally formulated by Irving Fisher, assumes that the velocity of money and the volume of output are constant; hence, in terms of the equation of exchange, changes in the general price level are directly proportional to changes in the quantity of money. Modern quantity theorists have extended Fisher's ideas. They believe that the income velocity of money fluctuates over time, but its range of short-run variation is limited and, with sufficient knowledge, predictable. Therefore, their attention is focused on the factors influencing velocity and on the role of the money supply as a determinant of GNP.

3. In classical theory, the market rate of interest will depart from the real rate if households and businesses expect the general price level to rise or decline. Any differential between the market rate and the real rate represents the amount necessary to compensate lenders or borrowers for adverse changes in purchasing power resulting from anticipated inflation or deflation.

4. In the classical view, interest is the reward which businesses pay households for abstaining from consumption. The equilibrium rate of interest is determined in a competitive money market where the supply of funds saved by households equals the demand for funds invested by businesses.

5. In the Keynesian view, interest is the payment made to households and businesses to overcome liquidity preference. The equilibrium rate of interest is determined by the intersection of the liquidity-preference or demand curve for money with the money stock or supply curve of money.

6. In modern theory, four basic factors determine income or GNP: the state of liquidity preference, the money supply, the marginal efficiency of investment, and the consumption function. No change in GNP can occur without a change in one or more of these factors. In macroeconomic equilibrium all four variables are synchronized or integrated; hence a change in one creates economic instability until a new equilibrium is reached.

7. An economic system may be in macroeconomic equilibrium at any level of income—not necessarily at the full-employment level. At any level of income other than the full-employment level, there will be either a deflationary or inflationary gap. Hence some combination of fiscal and monetary policy will be needed to close the gap.

FOR DISCUSSION

1. *Terms and concepts to review:*

income velocity of money	market rate of interest
equation of exchange	Implicit Price Index
quantity theory of money	New Economics
	transactions motive
	precautionary motive
marginal efficiency of investment	speculative motive
interest	liquidity-preference theory of interest
real rate of interest	liquidity trap

2. What basic differences are there between the equation of exchange as Fisher formulated it and the modern equation as it is used today? Is there any advantage to the modern equation as compared to Fisher's equation?

3. What has been the long-run trend of the income velocity of money (i.e., V in the equation of exchange) since the 1950s? Can you give the reasons for this trend?

4. Suppose the Federal Reserve buys securities in the open market and that the securities are sold by a nonbank (i.e., individual or corporation). As a result of this transaction alone, what will be the directions of change, if any, of M, P, Q, V (in that order), and MV in the equation $MV = PQ$? Explain.

5. In terms of the equation $MV = PQ$, what are likely to be the effects on P, Q, and PQ if there is a large increase in the money supply under conditions of (a) substantial unemployment, (b) high or full employment. Explain your answer.

6. If the rate on short-term loans is the same as on long-term loans, what are the advantages and disadvantages to lenders of being in short-term as opposed to long-term investments? Discuss.

7. If the yield on long-term securities is greater than on short-term securities, why would anyone want to invest in the latter?

8. "The classical theory holds that the equilibrium rate of interest equates the supply of, and demand for, savings in a competitive money market. The Keynesian theory holds that the equilibrium rate of interest equates the demand for money with its supply. Therefore, there is no essential difference between the two theories." Do you agree? Explain.

9. Do the transactions and precautionary demands for holding money depend entirely on income? If not, what else do they depend on? Explain.

10. If a reduction in the interest rate does not result in an expansion of investment, what might this suggest in terms of the Keynesian theory of interest?

11. If the economy is in a liquidity trap, would an increase in the quantity of money stimulate investment? Explain.

12. Assume the economy is in macroeconomic equilibrium. What effect would each of the changes below, considered separately and without regard to secondary results, have on income? Explain why.
   (a) Increase in the money supply
   (b) Increase in liquidity preference
   (c) Increase in the marginal efficiency of investment
   (d) Decrease in consumption

In general terms, how would secondary effects have influenced your answers?

Contemporary Issue

A Ceiling on Interest Rates?

Until near the end of the last decade, the United States was traditionally regarded as a low-interest economy. Credit was cheap and plentiful, and three decades of a rising trend of interest rates was tolerable as long as the level was not too high (see Figure 1). But since the late 1960s the level during some periods was well over 7 percent, causing considerable distress for consumers, home buyers, farmers, and some businessmen.

According to traditional doctrine, interest rates are the price of funds. Therefore, like any price, interest rates perform an allocative function: they ration the supply of scarce funds— the flow of savings—to the ultimate users. Those borrowers with the most promising investment opportunities pay the highest interest by bidding away funds from other competing users. In this way the interest-rate structure allocates funds among households, businesses, and government, and between private and public uses.

The Pros and Cons of Controls

Of course, when interest rates rise too high, the painful effects are felt in a widening circle of individuals, industries, states and localities, and the federal government itself. Pressures are placed on political leaders to control lending charges by legislating interest ceilings. Two major reasons for imposing controls are usually advanced:

1. Interest payments are a significant cost to business firms. Like other costs, an increase in interest rates is passed along in the form of higher prices, thereby furthering cost-push inflation.

2. Interest payments are incomes to people and institutions who grant loans. Therefore, increases in interest rates unjustly benefit lenders—especially banks—at the expense of borrowers.

Most economists do not find these arguments convincing. They believe that interest rates are a reflection of inflation rather than a cause. As a result, they oppose interest ceilings, for several reasons.

Figure 1

PRIME RATE: INTEREST PAID BY TOP FIRMS ON SHORT-TERM LOANS

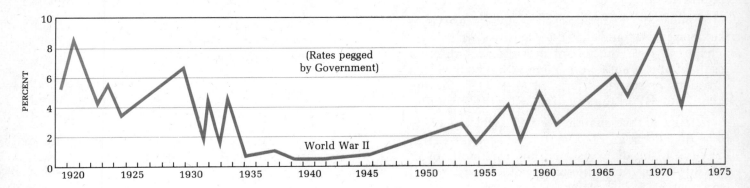

First, despite the trend of rising rates, interest charges play a minor role in cost-push inflation. Net interest charges average less than 3 percent of total production costs of nonfinancial corporations. In contrast, labor costs average 66 percent.

Second, an increase in interest rates may be necessary to help choke off inflation. Although a rise in borrowing costs need not immediately deter spending, it sooner or later deters some consumers from buying houses, automobiles, and major appliances, and some businessmen from buying new plants and equipment.

But regardless of the pros and cons, the really fundamental issue rests on the basic advantage of free over controlled markets. What the United States must decide is whether it prefers a government-controlled economy or an economy in which supply and demand forces are dominant in every field — including money.

QUESTIONS

1. Market controls of any kind are likely to create distortions. But wage and price controls probably cause less damage, at least initially, than interest-rate controls. Why?

2. All of the nation's 50 states have usury statutes of one sort or another. But the laws, which set general interest-rate ceilings on various kinds of loans, are usually riddled with exemptions. As a result, in recent years when interest rates reached their highest levels in decades, construction of owner-occupied homes in some states practically ceased, while construction of rental houses and commercial buildings continued at high levels. Can you explain why?

3. Is it possible for society to ease the burden of high interest rates on low-income families and still preserve free capital markets? Discuss.

CHAPTER 17

Economic Stabilization: Problems of Conflict and Coordination

CHAPTER PREVIEW

What is the nature of the conflict between full employment and price stability? Can policy-makers use practical guidelines to minimize the conflict?

Is there a conflict between economic growth and price stability? Can we select a "best" combination of fiscal and monetary policies—one which provides sustained economic growth without significant inflation?

How do fiscal and monetary policies affect our position in the world economy? Is one combination of policies desirable for domestic purposes and another for international purposes?

Can fiscal and monetary policies be coordinated to achieve full employment and price stability?

How can monetary and fiscal policy be used to bring about a high level of employment and steady economic growth without inflation? Responsibility for achieving these goals of economic stabilization has been given to various policy-making authorities.

Thus, the major responsibility for monetary management rests with the Federal Reserve System. Fiscal actions, on the other hand, consist of spending and taxing by the federal government, for which the Congress and the administration—including the Treasury, the Bureau of the Budget, and the President—are responsible.

The purpose of this chapter is to synthesize the two policy approaches by pointing out the need for their coordination and by illustrating the types of conflicts that arise in attempting to use monetary and fiscal tools for achieving the goals stated above.

Conflicts Between Full Employment and Price Stability

We have emphasized fiscal and monetary policy as means of maintaining the level of spending needed to assure full employment. To review briefly: in Exhibit 1 on the next page, the line $(C + I + G)$ represents the objective of a well-coordinated fiscal and monetary policy. It expresses the full-employment level of *total* spending by households, businesses, and government. A lower level of total spending such as $(C + I + G)'$ will produce a deflationary gap; a higher level will produce an inflationary gap.

Exhibit 1

Full Employment and Price Stability through Fiscal and Monetary Policy

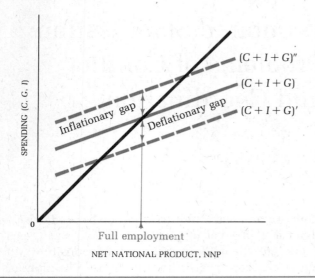

GUIDELINES FOR POLICY COORDINATION

What kinds of fiscal and monetary policies should be employed to close a deflationary or an inflationary gap?

Since fiscal policy alters government spending, its direct impact is felt through changes in G. And since it also varies taxes on both consumers and businesses, it may well have a direct impact on C and I. On the other hand, since monetary policy involves changes in demand deposits and the money supply, its direct impact is on businessmen and hence is first felt through modifications in I. Therefore, we can suggest several guidelines for coordinating fiscal and monetary policies.

If a deflationary gap exists, as represented by the aggregate demand schedule $(C + I + G)'$, then:

1. An appropriate fiscal policy would increase government expenditures and reduce taxes, thereby increasing G and probably C and I as well. (Why do we say "probably" C and I? Why not "surely"?)

2. An appropriate monetary policy would increase the money supply by easing credit, thereby further encouraging businessmen to increase I.

The result of these combined policies would be to shift the aggregate demand schedule back up toward the full-employment level represented by the $(C + I + G)$ line.

On the other hand, an inflationary gap as represented by the aggregate demand schedule $(C+I+G)''$ requires a different approach to fiscal and monetary policy. Can you suggest the proper guidelines?

This analysis emphasizes that different combinations of fiscal and monetary policy can be used to bring about full employment. In the real world, of course, political and administrative factors will also play a powerful part in determining the proper mix, and so the final choice may not always be the one suggested by economic considerations alone.

OBJECTIVES TEND TO CONFLICT

Unfortunately, the situation is not as simple as the above guidelines suggest. We have learned since the 1950s that *there is a conflict between maintaining price stability and achieving full employment; the general price level begins to rise before full employment is reached.*

This situation occurs for several reasons. As the economy approaches full employment:

1. Shortages of specific resources develop in some markets even though there are surpluses in others, thereby tending to raise production costs.

2. The overall reduction in unemployment strengthens the bargaining position of unions, enabling them to press more effectively for wage increases. Nonunion wages also tend to rise, sometimes more rapidly than union wages.

3. Rising profit margins and fuller utilization of capacity make it easier for businessmen to grant wage increases and to "pass on" part or all of these increases by raising prices.

Prices will remain stable only if aggregate spending is sufficiently below the full-employment level. What should fiscal and monetary policy do—feed inflation by raising aggregate demand to the full-employment level, or permit price stability with excess unemployment?

USING PHILLIPS CURVES

You will recall from an earlier chapter that the relationship between inflation and unemployment can be expressed by a Phillips curve. The concept is illustrated in Exhibit 2. Each point along a particular curve designates a specific combination of un-employment and inflation. The point labeled A, for instance, represents a 3 percent unemployment rate and a zero percent inflationary rate. At any given time an economy can be represented by only one Phillips curve.

On any higher curve—that is, on any curve located in a more northeasterly direction—a given point de-notes at least as much of one variable plus more of the other, when compared to a point directly below or to the left on the lower curve. Thus point B repre-sents the same 3 percent unemployment rate as point A, but denotes a 4 percent inflationary rate; point C, on the other hand, denotes the same zero percent in-flationary rate as point A, but a 6 percent unemploy-ment rate. The same idea applies to any other point you may choose. Any point on the curve between B and C, however, represents a higher rate of both unemployment and inflation as compared to point A.

Because of its importance, the earlier definition of the Phillips curve should be repeated:

A *Phillips curve* represents a tradeoff between unemployment and inflation. Every point along the curve denotes a different combination of unemploy-ment and inflation, and a movement along the curve measures the reduction in one of these at the ex-pense of a gain in the other.

FACTORS AFFECTING THE HEIGHT OF THE PHILLIPS CURVE

Since Exhibit 2 suggests that lower curves are "better" and higher curves are "poorer," what de-termines the height of a particular curve? The chief factor is the *overall competitive structure of the economy*. The evidence of this—and the elements contributing to the problem of inflation along with high unemployment—can be seen in at least four ways.

1. *Downward price rigidity*. At any given time some industries are expanding while others are contract-ing. This is to be expected in a dynamic economy. If industries are competitive, prices will adjust freely either upward or downward to changing market con-ditions. But if industries are dominated by a few large firms—as are the automobile, steel, electrical equipment, and many other major industries in our economy—they tend to raise prices in periods when markets are strong and to resist reducing them at times when markets are weak. As a result, since some prices are always rising regardless of the stage of the business cycle, the overall price index tends to rise even when business conditions are sluggish, thus creating an inflationary bias in the economy.

2. *Downward wage rigidity*. Just as a large segment of the product markets is dominated by concentrated (monopolistic) industries which do not respond to downward price pressures, so too a large segment of the resource markets is dominated by monopolistic labor unions which do not respond to downward wage pressures. This, combined with the inflation-ary bias described above, tends to create a familiar wage-price spiral. The reason is easy to see. When

Exhibit 2

Phillips Curves Showing the Tradeoff Between Inflation and Unemployment
(hypothetical data)

On any given curve, a movement from one point to the other measures the change in inflation corresponding to a change in unemployment. The lower the curve, the "better" it is for the economy as a whole.

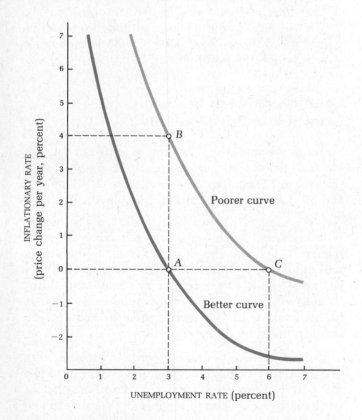

unions renegotiate contracts with manufacturers, they base their new wage demands both on economic changes in the past year or so and on what they think will happen in the coming year. In doing this, they use the most recent corporate earnings reports and the latest government cost-of-living (or consumer price) indexes covering the past several quarters as a basis for negotiation. Further, an increasing number of unions have incorporated cost-of-living escalator clauses into their contracts, thereby assuring that wage increases automatically follow cost-of-living increases. For both reasons, therefore, long-term union contracts negotiated during periods of economic overheating are likely to result in further wage and price increases even when inflationary pressures subside and even if unemployment increases.

3. *Changing composition of the labor force.* The proportion of inexperienced, secondary-income earners—consisting mainly of unskilled teenagers, women, and part-time job holders—in the labor force has been gaining relative to the proportion of experienced primary breadwinners. At the same time, accelerations in science and technology have been displacing large numbers of unskilled workers, thereby aggravating the problem of structural unemployment. Therefore, unless better methods are developed—through manpower-training programs, subsidies, tax incentives, and other devices—to absorb larger numbers of workers into new jobs, the task of achieving full employment without substantial inflation becomes increasingly difficult.

4. *Government price-fixing policies.* The federal government contributes to the inflationary bias through its price-fixing regulations. By raising minimum wages, discouraging transportation rate reductions, encouraging farm price supports and import quotas, and subsidizing inefficient industries, it puts a floor under prices and dampens rather than stimulates competition.

CONCLUSION: LONG-RUN AND
SHORT-RUN MEASURES NEEDED

An analysis of the problem of inflation with high unemployment focuses attention on two challenging tasks confronting policy-makers and legislators: (1) attaining a better (lower) Phillips curve and (2) selecting a particular point on the economy's existing Phillips curve. The first objective can be achieved

mainly by long-run measures; the second involves primarily short-run considerations.

1. *Lowering the Phillips curve: long-run measures.* Both legislative and fiscal actions can shift a Phillips curve in a southwesterly direction over the long run. In the legislative area, antitrust laws should be extended and vigorously enforced so as to make both the product and resource markets more competitive. In the fiscal area, government expenditures on such things as agriculture, housing, and medical care should supplement competition rather than replace it. Government investment in manpower development and training should seek to reduce structural unemployment by providing the hard-core unemployed with marketable skills. Government tax policies, on the other hand, should stimulate industrial growth and capacity so as to minimize upward pressures on prices.

2. *Choosing a point: short-run changes.* In the short run our economy has a given Phillips curve; hence, changes in fiscal or monetary policies can be used to select a particular point on that curve. But each point represents a different combination of unemployment and inflation, and value judgements must be used to decide which combination or tradeoff rate is best for the economy. No precise point may be "right" in any absolute sense, although most of us would probably agree on a fairly well-defined range within which the point should fall.

Conflicts Between Economic Growth and Price Stability

Suppose we want the economy to grow fast enough to raise real output per capita. To accomplish this, the rate of investment must be increased. What role should fiscal and monetary policy play?

Easy Money—Tight Fiscal Policy. Easy money with low interest rates encourages maximum investment. To achieve the desired level of investment without causing inflation, a tight fiscal policy consisting of higher taxes or lower government spending is needed to generate a full-employment level of saving equal to the full-employment level of investment induced by monetary policy.

Thus, if we want economic growth together with price stability through easy money, we have to pay the cost by refraining from consumption—that is, we have to save enough to provide the investment needed.

Conflicts Between Full Employment and the Balance of Payments

We have learned how fiscal and monetary policies affect full employment and price stability in our own country. But since the United States is a major trading nation, what international repercussions do our domestic fiscal and monetary policies have?

To answer this question, we must first explain the meaning of an important economic term—the *balance of payments*. This refers to the money value of all transactions that take place between a nation and the rest of the world during a year. The transactions consist of imports and exports of goods and services as well as the movements of short- and long-term investments, gifts, currency, and gold. Some transactions result in an inflow of funds to a country, while others result in an outflow. A nation has a balance-of-payments deficit when its payments to foreigners for the year exceed receipts; it has a balance-of-payments surplus when annual receipts from foreigners exceed payments to them.

THE AMERICAN EXPERIENCE

The United States has had a balance-of-payments deficit in most years since World War II—for several reasons:

1. Although the value of merchandise exports has, over the long run, tended to exceed the value of merchandise imports, our percentage share of world exports of manufactured goods has declined. This is particularly true of products like cars, steel, and machinery, in which there is growing competition from Western Europe and Japan. Hence our relative share of incoming receipts is not as large as we would like.

2. U.S. military and foreign-aid expenditures in other countries have been large, resulting in a heavy outflow of payments.

3. American business firms have built plants abroad; American citizens have invested in (purchased securities of) foreign corporations; and American lenders, during long periods of relatively lower interest rates in the United States, have tended to become a significant source of credit for foreign borrowers.

One of the approaches that may be taken to cut the deficit is to impose a tight monetary policy. This helps to reduce the United States outflow of funds relative to its inflows in three ways. First, it exerts an overall contractionary effect, thereby tending to dampen not only domestic demand for goods, but also import demand. Second, it reduces inflationary price pressures, thus making the prices of our goods relatively more attractive to foreigners and the prices of their goods relatively less attractive to us. Third, it raises our interest rates, thereby making it less advantageous for foreigners to borrow from us and more advantageous for them to invest here; in addition, it makes the yields on our own securities relatively more attractive than those of foreign securities.

THE CONFLICT AND SOME PROPOSED SOLUTIONS

Is there a connection between our country's level of employment and its balance of payments? If so, what role, if any, should monetary and fiscal policy play in influencing this relationship?

Evidence suggests that a rise in our national income tends to worsen our balance-of-payments situation. As our income and employment increase, we tend to import more goods from foreign countries; American tourists take more trips abroad; American corporations open more subsidiaries around the world. These conditions cause an outflow of dollars from the United States which may not be compensated by the inflow of dollars resulting from other offsetting factors such as higher returns on foreign investment for American firms, increased exports to the countries from which we import, and so on.

In view of this apparent conflict between full employment and the balance of payments, should we always seek to attain a high level of employment through an expansionary fiscal and monetary policy? Perhaps not. Some economists and legislators have suggested the following approach instead:

Tight Money—Easy Fiscal Policy. A restrictive monetary policy drives up interest rates, making it less attractive for foreigners to borrow here and making foreign securities less attractive to Americans. However, since a restrictive monetary policy tends to dampen national income and employment, its effects in this area could be offset by an easy fiscal policy consisting of lower taxes or increased government spending.

Do you agree with this policy? If so, keep in mind the price to be paid: a restrictive monetary policy with high interest rates tends to discourage investment and thus reduce the long-term expansion of output. This is in direct opposition to the previous objective of achieving long-run economic growth. Note, too, that this policy is inherently in conflict with the previous one of achieving economic growth, namely, "easy money—tight fiscal policy."

In view of the difficulty of reconciling these differences, the government has adopted an alternative approach to solving the conflict between domestic and foreign objectives—one which employs "selective" measures rather than the more general tools of fiscal and monetary policy. These selective measures which Washington has used with limited success at one time or another include efforts to attract tourists from abroad, increase exports to foreign countries, require that American loans and grants to foreign countries be spent on American goods, raise short-term interest rates to discourage American lending abroad while keeping the lid on long-term interest rates in order to stimulate domestic capital investment, encourage voluntary restraint on investment overseas by American corporations, and in other ways curb, if not reduce, the deficit in our balance of payments. In the meantime, fiscal and monetary policies have been used to cope mainly with domestic rather than international problems.

Conflicts Between Free and Controlled Markets

In mid-August, 1971, President Nixon stunned the world by imposing a system of wage, price, and international financial controls on the nation's economy. The purpose was to retard the rate of inflation and reduce a growing deficit in the U.S. balance of payments. This was the first time in American history (outside of a military emergency) that any administration—much less a Republican one—had made such a drastic incursion into the economy's private sector. (See Box 1.)

Mr. Nixon's controls were subsequently revised to meet changing economic circumstances. However, a lively debate has since existed among economists, businessmen, and political leaders over the desirability of wage and price controls as a tool of economic stabilization. Since such controls may become a permanent, or at least recurrent, feature of the economic system, the controversy surrounding them must be understood.

Box 1

Mr. Nixon's Eight Commandments—
Or, The Gospel According to Herbert Stein

In August, 1971, when President Nixon announced, without prior warning, his system of economic controls, officials in his own administration were as mystified as outsiders. According to Newsweek magazine, Dr. Herbert Stein, chairman of the Council of Economic Advisers, chose to enlighten everyone by issuing his own irreverent version of the new economic commandments:

On the fifteenth day of the eighth month the President came down from the mountain and spoke to the people on all networks, saying:

I bring you a comprehensive Eight Point Program, as follows:

First, thou shalt raise no price, neither any wage, rent, interest, fee or dividend.

Second, thou shalt pay out no gold, neither metallic nor paper.

Third, thou shalt drive no Japanese car, wear no Italian shoe, nor drink any French wine, neither red nor white.

Fourth, thou shalt pay to whomsoever buys any equipment 10 per cent of the value thereof in the first year, but only 5 per cent thereafter.

Fifth, thou shalt share no revenue and assist no family—not yet.

Sixth, whosoever buyeth an American automobile, thou shalt honor him and charge him no tax.

Seventh, thou shalt enjoy in 1972 what the Democrats promised thee in 1973.

Eighth, thou shalt appoint a Council of Elders to consider what to do for an encore.

ARGUMENTS AGAINST WAGE-PRICE CONTROLS

Those who oppose government wage and price controls as a means of curbing inflationary pressures believe that such controls have undesirable effects:

1. *Misallocate resources.* Under a system of controls, resource and product prices are determined, not by free-market processes, but by specific rules or orders of a governmentally appointed board of overseers. Buyers' and sellers' responses to the forces of supply and demand are replaced by governmental edicts. The wage-price structure is thereby rigidified, preventing producers from responding to dynamic changes in tastes and technology as they would if markets were unregulated. As a result, resources are misallocated and economic efficiency is impaired.

2. *Decrease productivity.* Controls put a lid on wages and prices—that is, keep them from rising to their free-market levels. This diminishes productivity in three ways:

(a) Millions of man-hours in government and industry are wasted on administering controls.

(b) To the extent that wage increases are restrained, workers' incentives are reduced and employers are prevented from paying for the high quality workers they want.

(c) If ceilings are imposed on profit margins, as they were during previous periods of control, businesses lose much of their incentive to improve efficiency since profits above the ceiling are taxed at prohibitive rates. As a consequence, firms look for frivolous ways to increase costs—by spending lavishly on advertising and promotion, buying corporate jets, providing generous expense accounts

for executives, etc.—all for the purpose of cutting down profits. (See Box 2.)

3. *Institutionalize inflation.* Wage and price controls provide at best only a temporary palliative rather than a permanent cure for inflation. They lull society into accepting inflation as a way of life instead of encouraging the public to press for eradication of the root causes. Those causes are found in the monopoly power wielded by large firms and trade unions, and in government legislation that establishes minimum wages, agricultural price supports, subsidies, tariffs, and import quotas. Since these monopolistic elements interfere with the effective functioning of a free market, public policy should be directed toward eliminating them in order to achieve price stability.

THE CASE FOR CONTROLS

On the other side of the fence, most advocates of wage and price controls—including many econ-

Box 2

How Companies Try to Beat the Profit Ceiling

There is ample evidence to show that when the government imposes profit ceilings, as it did from late 1971 to early 1973, companies set a course that would turn Adam Smith in his grave: rather than cut prices, they go out of their way to increase costs in order to hold profits down.

Interviews with leading businessmen have borne this out. "People look for ways to get inefficient," said a top auto executive. "I have some executives who, instead of looking for ways to maximize everything, which they have been trained for, are saying, 'Well, what would you want to get that efficient for? The government will just take it

away.' What am I supposed to tell them?" In a similar vein, a mobile home producer who was planning a company meeting in the Bahamas justified it with the statement: "If we've got to spend to stay legal, we might as well enjoy it."

Comments such as these are neither new nor unique. They were common during World War II and the Korean War, when executives were under pressure to find ways of reducing profits in order to avoid paying excess-profits taxes.

In a lush year, Deuce Manufacturing is earning too much profit. If it goes through the ceiling, Deuce may have to cut prices.

1	2	3	4	5	6
Buy a corporate jet	Step up spending on R & D	Give executives a free hand with expense accounts	Promote people to justify pay increases	Increase the budget for advertising and promotion	Merge with a company that's having a temporary profit slowdown

Adapted from a cartoon by R. Doty.

omists, businessmen, and political leaders—are in general sympathy with the competitive market philosophy. However, they believe that the inflationary bias in the economy has become too entrenched to be contained without a system of controls. In other words, they contend that inflation has already become institutionalized by our failure to eliminate monopolistic elements within the economy, and that it is unrealistic to assume that these elements, which are now deeply embedded, will ever be significantly reduced. Therefore, the choice is not between free markets or public controls; it is between free markets and some degree of public controls.

Perhaps the most notable advocate of this point of view is Harvard University's well-known economist, John Kenneth Galbraith. The popular 6 ft 8 inch professor, who served as Ambassador to India (1961-1963) under President Kennedy, argues that less than half the economy's private sector is responsive to reasonably competitive market forces; within the remainder, prices are essentially set by the great corporations in conjunction with the unions. It follows that public controls can be confined to the less competitive segment where market power is greatest, and that they are not needed in the more competitive segment where the market still functions.

CONCLUSION: STILL UNANSWERED QUESTIONS

U.S. policy-makers can achieve full employment with appropriate fiscal and monetary policies. However, they face a constraint of inflation resulting from monopolistic elements in the economy. In principle, the elimination of these market imperfections would solve the policy dilemma; in reality, there is no evidence that political leaders are willing to pursue this risky alternative to any great extent—because of the political costs it may entail. As a result, the problem narrows down to whether inflation can be fought effectively with wage and price controls. Assuming that it can—which in itself is debatable—there is the further question of whether such controls create even greater social costs resulting from resource misallocation, impairment of productivity, curtailment of economic freedoms, and other difficulties, than the cost of inflation itself. If they do, then anything beyond a temporary application of controls to counter a sudden flare-up of inflation is clearly undesirable.

Can We Coordinate Fiscal and Monetary Policy?

At the Federal Reserve Bank of St. Louis, a motto and symbol which appear on many memo pads reads:

$$MV = PT$$

The motto, in case you are unfamiliar with Latin, translates: "Under this sign we conquer." The equation, which is familiar to you from the previous chapter, is the shortened version of Irving Fisher's original equation of exchange—a modernized restatement of which is $MV = PQ$.

This "coat of arms" is significant because the St. Louis Fed is one of the nation's centers of research in an area broadly referred to as "monetarism." What does this term mean? Of what importance is it? To answer these questions, it helps to go back to a period in recent history.

During most of the 1960s, when the New Economists were riding high in Washington under Presidents Kennedy and Johnson, certain so-called "monetary" economists were looked upon as highly eccentric. That day has gone. Under the leadership of Professor Milton Friedman of the University of Chicago, the Monetarists have become what a leading New Economist has called "that small, but influential, brilliant, and growing circle of true believers."

True believers in what? The answer to this question opens the door to a great controversy that continues to rage among many economists and political leaders:

Is it the rate at which the Federal Reserve adds to the nation's money supply that chiefly determines the levels of output, employment, and prices, as the Monetarists hold?

Or is it mainly changes in the federal budget that make the difference, as the New Economists of the fiscal school contend?

Or, as a third possibility, does the answer lie somewhere in between?

These are the fundamental issues in today's great economic debate—a debate which may appropriately be called the "money-supply controversy."

HISTORY OF THE MONEY-SUPPLY CONTROVERSY

Today's great debate over the importance of money and the money supply has had a long and interesting history. Although it is rooted in some of the monetary debates that took place in Congress prior to the establishment of the Federal Reserve System, it is sufficient for our purposes to go back to the period just before the Great Depression.

The Classical or Pre-Keynesian View

If you had studied economics before the 1930s, you probably would have been taught that the quantity of money (currency plus private demand deposits) had a strong influence on prices, but very little if any influence on jobs, production, or general economic activity. This, in essence, was the crude *quantity theory of money* and prices that we studied in the previous chapter. You will recall that it could be interpreted in terms of the modern *equation of exchange:*

$$MV = PQ$$

where M stands for the quantity of money, V for the income velocity of circulation, P for the average price of final goods and services, and Q for the quantity of final goods and services.

According to this theory—both in its simple and more refined versions—the quantity of goods and the income velocity of circulation are important determinants of the price level. But they were believed to be stable and independent of changes in the quantity of money; hence, increases or decreases in prices within the economy as a whole were attributed primarily to increases or decreases in the quantity of money, and little else.

Thus, a simple version of the quantity theory would predict that a 10 percent increase in the money supply would bring about a 10 percent increase in the price level, assuming there was no increase in the quantity of final goods and services. This assumption of a stable quantity of output (and hence a stable volume of employment) accords with the classical theory of income and employment, because the classical model assumes that all production and all productive resources are guided to their full-employment levels by the "invisible hand" of market forces—independently of changes in the quantity of money.

Of course, not every economist saw the world in precisely this way. But these generalizations provide a reasonably accurate description of typical pre-Depression views—views which assumed an automatic tendency toward full employment, together with a price level determined by the quantity of money.

The Beginnings of a New View

The validity of prevailing economic doctrines was questioned long and seriously during and after the Great Depression. With millions of people out of work and the economy stagnating at levels far below its capacity, how could it be argued that the economic system "automatically" tends toward full employment? Something obviously was wrong, and classical theory was unable to explain what it was.

The British economist J. M. Keynes offered an answer. According to Keynes, the level of aggregate demand—or the amount of goods demanded by consumers, businessmen, and the government—was not high enough to keep the economy operating at full employment. After all, how could businessmen be expected to produce what they did not expect to sell? The Keynesian prescription was clear and straightforward: If private demand proved insufficient to pull the economy out of depression, then government should stimulate enough spending to provide buyers for the nation's full-capacity output. This prescription, as we have seen, later came to mean that the federal government was responsible for maintaining full employment. This responsibility was subsequently expressed in the form of the Employment Act of 1946.

THE FISCALIST VIEW AND THE NEW ECONOMICS

With the groundwork laid, the next question was how government could best fulfill its responsibility. It soon became clear to most Keynesians that fiscal policy—the use of the government's taxing and spending powers—offered the logical means of filling the gap between insufficient aggregate demand and the level needed to achieve and maintain full employment. The federal government could, for example, reduce taxes, thereby leaving the private sector with more disposable income to spend, or it could increase its own spending and thereby add directly to the total demand for goods and services. Although Keynesian economists did not always agree on the exact amount of change needed in taxation or spending, they agreed remarkably closely on the use of fiscal policy to achieve full employment.

"You Can't Push on a String"

This did not mean that Keynesians neglected the use of monetary policy. To them, however, monetary policy had a secondary and relatively passive role to play in most instances.

Keynesian economists tended to believe that monetary policy could ordinarily do little by itself to stimulate economic activity. In their view, the Federal Reserve System could adopt an easy-money policy which would result in lower interest rates, and this *might* induce businessmen to borrow funds for the purpose of spending on plant and equipment. However, low interest rates by themselves provided no assurance that businessmen would borrow, and, if they did not, the unused funds would simply pile up in the banks as excess reserves.

"You can't push on a string" was therefore a favorite homily of the 1940s and 1950s; it meant the same thing as the older and more familiar saying, "You can lead a horse to water but you can't make him drink." This attitude reflected the prevailing skepticism about the effectiveness of monetary policy.

When President Kennedy took office in 1961, he made a significant attempt to implement the New Economics propounded by the Keynesians. Through his efforts, Congress in 1964 enacted a tax cut for the express purpose of stimulating the economy, and in 1968, under similar economic policies pursued by President Johnson, Congress passed a tax increase designed to curb economic activity. There has been much dispute over whether these fiscal actions accomplished what they set out to do, but they nevertheless demonstrate that the philosophy of the New Economists was widely accepted—*a philosophy which held that the economy could be "fine-tuned" through fiscal and monetary action.*

Monetary Policy Catches On

Although fiscal policy reigned supreme during most of the 1960s, two facts prompted economists to reconsider the supposed superiority of fiscal over monetary policy as a tool for economic stabilization:

1. *Time lag in fiscal legislation.* Fiscal actions take much longer to implement than monetary actions, because the former require Congressional approval whereas the latter are decided at frequent periodic meetings of the Federal Reserve System's Board of Governors. This fact was driven home in 1967-1968, when it took Congress 18 months to enact a tax increase for the purpose of curbing inflationary pressures. Monetary policy could, of course, have been implemented much more quickly.

2. *Changed economic environment.* In the 1930s and 1940s, the main challenge (except during World War II) was to keep the economy buoyed up; therefore, attention tended to center on methods of economic stimulation. During the 1950s, a new problem —inflation—came to the forefront, and in the 1960s the United States experienced unprecedented difficulties with its balance of payments, as we have already learned.

"You Can Pull on a String"

These problems called for restrictive rather than expansionary policies. Consequently, many New Economists began to take the position that if "you can't push on a string," then perhaps "you can pull on a string." In other words, even if monetary policy cannot *push* total spending up, there is a good chance that it can *pull* it down. They have come to believe, therefore, that monetary policy is flexible and easy to implement, even if it happens to be more effective in restricting total spending than in stimulating it.

Conclusion: The New Economics—A Policy Mix

As a result of these and other developments, most New Economists today believe that an appropriate "mix" of fiscal and monetary actions should be used to achieve a stable rate of economic growth. They do not all agree on the proportions of the mix, but they tend to prefer a policy which combines occasional shifts in fiscal policy with flexible and frequent monetary actions by the Federal Reserve.

The New Economics thus provides political leaders with a clear guide for action: if unemployment rises, Washington should cut taxes in order to stimulate spending; if prices rise, Washington should "temporarily" raise taxes in order to soak up purchasing power. Monetary policy should also be used to supplement and complement the major shifts in economic activity brought about by changes in fiscal policy. By thus adhering to an appropriate blend of fiscal and monetary policy, it is not only possible, but also feasible, in the opinion of the New Economists, to "fine-tune" the economy.

A definition of the New Economics ties the foregoing ideas together:

The *New Economics* emerged in the 1930s from the ideas of John Maynard Keynes. In contrast with classical economic theory, it holds that a capitalistic economy does not tend automatically toward full employment. Therefore, the government should pursue active fiscal policies, supported by appropriate monetary policies, to achieve and maintain full employment and steady economic growth.

THE MONETARIST VIEW

Unlike the New Economists, who acknowledge the importance of both fiscal and monetary policy, the Monetarists argue that changes in the money supply are the chief determinants not only of prices, but also of production, employment, and spending. They do not believe that fiscal policy is an effective stabilizing device, and they object to the whole concept of fine-tuning the economy.

Who are the Monetarists? Just as the New Economists (or Keynesians) are linked with the late J. M. Keynes, the Monetarists are associated primarily with Professor Milton Friedman of the University of Chicago. The money-supply controversy which you can read about in prominent newspapers such as the *New York Times* and the *Wall Street Journal*, and in leading news and business magazines like *Time*, *Newsweek*, *Business Week*, and *Fortune*, is fundamentally a debate between the New Economists and the Monetarists.

Money and Economic Activity

Monetarists do not always agree on all points, but they are unanimous in their belief that money exercises a major influence on economic activity.

According to Monetarist theory, the amount of money people wish to hold is closely related to their level of income. Hence if the supply of money in-creases faster than income—that is, faster than the amount people want to have on hand—they will spend away the unwanted portion, thereby causing inflation. On the other hand, if the supply of money increases more slowly than income—that is, not fast enough to provide people with the amount of money they want to have on hand—the opposite effect will occur: people will try to build up their money balances by cutting back on their spending, thereby causing unemployment. Therefore, Monetarists conclude, there is a cause-and-effect relationship between the supply of money and the changes that occur in income, economic activity, and prices. They believe that changes in the money supply *cause* swings in the business cycle.

However, Monetarists do not claim that business cycles result exclusively from changes in the money supply. Like the New Economists, they recognize that the economy is always in the process of adjusting to the varying expectations of businessmen and to underlying structural changes in such things as population, consumer habits, and competition within industries. But they believe that changes in the supply of money are the dominant cause of business cycles.

Conclusion: Policy Recommendations and the Money-supply Rule

Monetarists contend that the economy is inherently stable and tends toward full employment and sustained growth. They cite detailed studies analyzing the behavior of money and prices going as far back as the Civil War. They believe these studies show that changes in the money supply have larger, more predictable, and quicker effects on GNP than do fiscal-policy changes in tax rates, government expenditures, and the federal deficit. In the Monetarists' opinion, therefore, the government should help the economy achieve its full-employment potential by adhering to a simple and well-defined guide:

The Federal Reserve should expand the nation's money supply at the economy's growth rate or capacity to produce, namely about 3 to 5 percent a year. More than this would lead to strong inflationary pressures; less would tend to be stagnating if not deflationary. This guide for economic expansion advanced by Monetarists is often called the *money-supply rule*.

Monetarists, in other words, believe that the Federal Reserve has the power to stabilize the economy

—or at least to permit the economy to stabilize it-self—through its ability to control bank reserves and therefore the supply of money. Monetarists contend that the New Economists—in their well-meant efforts to employ fiscal policy for purposes of economic stabilization—have misused monetary policy, and thereby magnified rather than mitigated business cycles. Thus the Monetarists believe that the growth of the money supply, as a result of discretionary efforts by the New Economists to "manage" the economy, has fluctuated; with the help of various charts and models, they allege that increases in the money supply have resulted in economic expansions while decreases have caused economic contractions.

Monetarists conclude, therefore, that even though the Federal Reserve's influence over the money supply may not be perfect, adherence to the money-supply rule would nevertheless produce better results for economic stabilization and growth than the flexible policy mix followed by the New Economists.

What about interest rates? Do they influence total spending and business activity as the New Economists contend? Monetarists think not. In line with the rest of their theory, they believe that spending and interest rates are a *result* of changes in the money supply.

SOME UNRESOLVED CONSIDERATIONS

The Monetarists' views are strong and persuasive. They have been the subject of congressional hearings and are among the most hotly debated economic topics of our time. Yet many economists are skeptical about the Monetarist position—as indicated by the following types of questions.

Is Money All-important?

The Monetarists, as we have seen, believe that the money supply is the dominant influence on economic activity and that other considerations may be neglected.

Many economists, however, feel that to neglect other factors would be a serious mistake. They argue that significant changes in total spending may result from a number of causes. For example: Businessmen may alter their expenditure decisions on plant and equipment because their expectation of profits changes; consumers may buy less for reasons unrelated to the money supply—such as an increase in

taxes; the government may alter its spending policy; strikes in important industries may reduce business activity. Any of these factors, they point out, can influence total spending and economic activity just as much as a change in the money supply.

Is Money a Cause or an Effect?

Monetarists believe that changes in the money supply *cause* changes in income and production. Is this contention correct? The answer is probably yes. But a reverse type of relation may also be true.

Thus, if spending and production increase, the expansion in business may increase the demand for money. If the Federal Reserve then enlarges the supply of money the increase in spending will be the cause of bringing more money into circulation. In such a case, the change in the money supply is an effect rather than a cause of total spending.

Is Velocity Significant?

It may be recalled that according to the familiar equation of exchange:

$$MV = PQ \qquad \text{and hence} \qquad V = \frac{PQ}{M}$$

The equation thus tells us that velocity is the ratio of income (or final output) to money; that is, velocity measures the average number of times each dollar is used to purchase the economy's final output, since PQ is the same as GNP.

The Monetarists believe that V tends to remain relatively stable in the short run. Whether they are correct in this belief, however, is still an unsettled question. If V does not remain stable, a decrease in M will not reduce total spending as the Monetarists contend; instead it may increase total spending if people decide to spend the smaller supply of money more quickly—that is, if the decrease in M is substantially offset by an increase in V. Some economists are investigating the possibility of this happening and the conditions that may lead to it.

What Is Money?

We have already learned that it is hard to define money precisely. The Monetarists prefer to include not only currency and private demand deposits in their definition, but also time deposits in savings accounts.

MILTON FRIEDMAN

1912–

Relatively few economists advocate the abolition of welfare, social security, graduated income taxes, and professional licensure—including the licensing of medical doctors. Milton Friedman is one who does. A professor of economics at the University of Chicago, he is not only one of America's leading economists, but also the foremost exponent of what is known as the "Chicago School" of economic thought. Like his distinguished predecessors at that renowned institution, he has an abiding faith in free enterprise and an unshakable conviction that the free market is the best device ever conceived for allocating society's resources and for ordering human affairs.

Friedman is more than a maverick economist. He has been called the most original economic thinker since John Maynard Keynes—a reputation earned largely because of his exhaustive criticisms of Keynesian ideas—and he is believed by many to equal if not outrank Keynes as the most influential economist of the twentieth century.

This belief is based primarily on Friedman's approach to money. Using carefully documented research going back to the late nineteenth century, he argues that the crucial factor affecting economic trends has been the quantity of money, not government fiscal policy. Accordingly, he opposes the use of discretionary monetary policy by the Federal Reserve to achieve economic stability, and advocates instead a *money-supply rule*—an expansion of the nation's money supply at a steady rate in accordance with the economy's growth and capacity to produce. Friedman gives four major reasons for this view.

1. *Past performance of the Fed.* Throughout its history, the Fed has proclaimed that it was using its monetary powers to promote economic stability. But the record often shows the opposite. Despite the Fed's well-intentioned efforts, it has been a major cause of instability by permitting the quantity of money to expand and contract erratically. Therefore, the urgent need is to prevent the Fed from being a source of economic disturbance.

2. *Limitations of our knowledge.* Economic research has established two propositions:
   (a) There is a close, regular, and predictable relation between the quantity of money, national income, and prices over a number of years. Therefore, a stable price level over the long run requires that the quantity of money grow at a fairly steady rate roughly equal to the average rate of growth of output.
   (b) The relation between the quantity of money and economic activity is much looser from month to

month, quarter to quarter, or even year to year than it is over a number of years. Therefore, any attempt to use monetary policy for "fine-tuning" the economy is bound to create economic instability.

3. *Promotion of confidence.* An announced, and adhered to, policy of steady monetary growth would provide the business sector with a firm basis for confidence in monetary stability that no discretionary policy could provide even if it happened to produce roughly steady monetary growth.

4. *Neutralization of the Fed.* An independent Fed is at times too removed from political pressures and at other times unduly affected by them. Hence a money-supply rule would insulate monetary policy both from the arbitrary power of a small group of men not subject to control by the electorate and from the short-run pressures of partisan politics.

Is the adoption of a money-supply rule technically feasible? Professor Friedman claims it is. Although he admits that the Fed could not achieve a precise rate of growth in the money supply from day to day or week to week, it could come very close from month to month and quarter to quarter. If and when it does, he says, it would provide a monetary climate favorable to economic stability and orderly growth. And that, Professor Friedman concludes, is the most we can ask from monetary policy at our present state of knowledge.

But what about the growing importance of other types of interest-bearing financial assets that have become increasingly important since the 1950s and which possess varying degrees of "moneyness"? Should these be included in a definition of money? The Monetarists agree that perhaps some of them should, because they recognize that their own measure of money is not an ideal one. However, they are not sure of just what to put into their definition and what to leave out. There is an entire spectrum of financial assets differing as to liquidity, dates of maturity, degrees of risk, and other considerations, all of which may serve as "money" for certain purposes.

For example, if time deposits which are an interest-bearing asset are included in a definition of money, why not also include Treasury bills or other highly marketable securities which investors often substitute for time deposits? The answer to this question, which is a definitional one, is as yet unresolved.

Is the Monetarist View Too Aggregated?

A final difficulty to be considered is the "aggregation" problem.

The Monetarists take an aggregate view of the economy and of the impact of changes in the money supply, while neglecting the disproportionate effects which monetary actions may have on certain segments of the economy. As pointed out in an earlier chapter, for example, the home-building industry is heavily dependent on the availability of mortgage money, and hence is among the first to feel the effects of changes in the flow of funds through savings institutions.

Monetarists, because of their aggregate outlook, prefer to let the distribution of money and income—that is, the impact of monetary changes—be determined by competitive forces in the market. Many other economists, however, feel that the market operates too imperfectly and too inequitably to be relied upon completely as a mechanism for allocating funds, and that a sound monetary policy is one which recognizes and adapts to special situations.

What Conclusion?

The New Economists have tended to practice curative medicine by prescribing a combined dose of fiscal and monetary remedies if the economy gets sick; the Monetarists have opted for preventive medicine by prescribing steady growth in the money supply and the counsel of patience.

It remains for future research and experience to test the effectiveness of those two approaches. In the meantime, you can expect to read and hear a great deal about this issue in the news media.

IS THERE A FUTURE FOR THE NEW ECONOMICS?

But what will happen to the New Economics? Will our children read about it as belonging to the past in their history books, or will it remain with us in varying degrees as a viable philosophy to be studied by present and future generations of students?

These are not idle questions. The American economy is one in which high employment, rising output of goods and services, stable prices, and a satisfactory balance of payments are among the accepted national economic goals. The voting population, like that in the other mixed economies of the world, will not tolerate for very long the adverse consequences of wide departures from these goals. It is appropriate to ask, therefore, what the New Economics achieved during its eight years under Presidents Kennedy and Johnson.

LET'S LOOK AT THE RECORD

The Bourbons, it has been said, never forgot anything because they never learned anything. The same may be said of those diehards who have never studied—or have refused to acknowledge—the economic accomplishments of the 1960s. During most of this period the fiscal policies of the New Economics—and the monetary policies of the Federal Reserve, which were often adapted to accommodate the immediate credit needs of the Treasury—produced high employment and unprecedented economic growth. True, the Vietnam War was responsible for a substantial rate of government spending, but this merely corroborates a fundamental lesson of the New Economics: If war can bring about high employment, so can peace; what war dollars can do, *any* dollars can do.

However, the economic achievements of the 1960s have levied substantial costs. During the latter part of the decade—with the help of hot-war Vietnam spending—we did indeed bring unemployment down to a 15-year low of less than $3\frac{1}{2}$ percent, but inflationary price increases took their toll at a rate of over 5 percent per year. In addition, heavy deficits in the balance of payments reduced our gold stock from $18 billion to less than $11 billion, resulting in the imposition of direct controls on foreign lending and investment; the surplus in our balance of trade essentially disappeared for the first time in many years; and a 10 percent surtax coupled with expenditure reductions legislated by Congress failed to eliminate budget deficits.

The effects of these events carried over into the 1970s, creating international economic repercussions on a wide scale. The consequences are examined in some detail in a later chapter.

THE CHOICE THAT CONFRONTS US

These results, some favorable and some unfavorable, suggest that two extreme policy questions face any administration, Democratic or Republican:

Should we adopt positive fiscal and monetary action to assure high employment and a strong, steady rate of growth, while taking our chances on coping with inflations and balance-of-payments deficits as they arise?

OR

Should we accept less employment and slower rates of growth, while paying the price in terms of losses of potential output and possible social unrest?

Most people would prefer a position somewhere between these two limits. Thus there is a growing awareness among the New Economists and the Monetarists that a synthesis of views must emerge. Indeed, there are already some signs of such a synthesis, indicating that a proper combination of both fiscal and monetary policy is needed to keep the economy on a chosen path. The choice of the precise combination is one of the great issues in economics today.

SUMMARY OF IMPORTANT IDEAS

1. A conflict between unemployment and price stability exists primarily because increases in the general price level occur before full employment is reached. Since there is a competitive relation between unemployment and inflation, the tradeoff between them can be represented by a Phillips curve.

2. A conflict between economic growth and price stability may occur if an easy-money policy which stimulates too rapid a rate of investment is not offset by a tight fiscal policy consisting of higher taxes and lower government spending.

3. A conflict between full employment and the balance of payments exists because as our levels of national income and employment increase, we tend to import more goods from abroad, open more branch companies and subsidiaries in foreign countries, and send more capital and tourists overseas. A tight money and easy fiscal policy might offer an appropriate solution, but it would be in direct opposition to the type of easy money and tight fiscal policy advocated for economic growth.

4. A conflict between free and controlled markets arises when government imposes wage and price controls to curb inflation. Although a major effect of controls is to misallocate resources, controls are defended by their supporters as necessary to counteract the inflationary pressures created by monopolistic elements in the economy.

5. "Fiscalists" or New Economists believe it is possible to maintain continuous full employment through proper coordination of fiscal and monetary policies. "Monetarists" disagree, contending that not enough is known about the economic impact of fiscal and monetary variables and that attempts to coordinate them lead to cyclical swings. They advocate, therefore, a steady expansion in the money supply at the economy's growth rate or capacity to produce.

6. Fundamental questions that remain to be answered are how to choose the proper tradeoff between inflation and unemployment, and what role fiscal and monetary policy should play in our economy. There is evidence that a synthesis of ideas is emerging, but the proper combination of fiscal and monetary policies continues to be one of the most hotly debated issues of our time.

FOR DISCUSSION

1. *Terms and concepts to review:*

Phillips curve	equation of exchange
balance of payments	New Economics
quantity theory of money	money-supply rule

2. What are the underlying reasons for the conflict between full employment and inflation?

3. (a) What is the difference between "good" and "bad" Phillips curves? Explain. (b) Explain the factors determining the height of a particular Phillips curve. (c) What actions would you recommend in order to improve an economy's Phillips curve?

4. Distinguish between (a) the conflict between economic growth and inflation, and (b) the conflict between full employment and the balance of payments. How do monetary and fiscal policies conflict in trying to achieve the goals of full employment, economic growth, and balance-of-payments equilibrium without significant inflation?

5. Do you see any connection between the Monetarists and the classical economists as far as basic philosophy is concerned?

6. How would the position or location of our economy's Phillips curve be affected by each of the following. Explain your answer. (a) A reduction in tariffs. (b) A decrease in import quotas. (c) A new law making labor unions illegal. (d) A merger of the largest firm in each major industry (e.g., automobiles, steel, etc.) with the second largest firm in its industry. (e) A new law prohibiting any firm's sales from exceeding 50 percent of its industry's. (f) Significant advances in automation throughout most of industry.

7. Some economists and political leaders contend: "Inflation promotes growth and diminishes unemployment. We must recognize that the costs of inflation are much less than the costs of avoiding it. Therefore, we should accept inflation and learn to live with it. This can be done by recognizing that it is easier to compensate the victims of inflation than the casualties of recession." What specific compensatory measures can you propose to make inflation less painful and inequitable? Discuss.

Forecasting with an Econometric Model

In your study of macroeconomics, emphasis was placed on the idea that economic activity could be explained by a set of relationships between economic variables. Based on this idea, a branch of applied science has developed known as *econometrics*. Breaking the word into its two parts, "econo" and "metrics," it is evident that the subject matter deals with the science of economic measurement. Indeed, econometrics may be defined as an integration of economic theory, mathematics, and statistics; econometric science expresses economic relationships in the form of mathematical equations and verifies the resulting models by statistical methods.

The economic variables of an econometric model may include consumption, saving, net investment, disposable income, and so on. By combining the relevant variables into what seems to be the best mathematical arrangement, econometricians predict the future course of one or more of these variables on the basis of the established relationships. The "best mathematical arrangement" is thus a model which takes the form of an equation or system of equations that seems best to describe the past set of relationships according to economic theory and statistical analysis. The model, in other words, is a simplified abstraction of a real situation, expressed in equation form, and employed as a prediction system that will yield numerical results.

An Illustrative Model

You can gain some appreciation of an econometric model by examining a simplified version of actual models. Note in the following paragraphs that in order to construct an econometric model, we must make specific the various hypotheses which are thought to explain the phenomena under investigation. These hypotheses are based on previous studies, empirical findings, or a priori reasoning. The hypotheses are then translated into a form that is suitable for empirical verification and testing, usually into mathematical equations.

(1) Consumption in the current period, C, depends on the current period's national income, Y, and on consumption in the previous period, C_{-1}:

$$C = a_0 + a_1Y + a_2C_{-1}$$

where a_0, a_1, and a_2 are constants, or fixed numerical values determined by statistical procedures. (You need not worry about these constants or about those provided in the following equations. The numerical values of the constants will be given in the problem below.)

(2) Net investment in the current period, I, is determined by nonwage income (rent, interest, profit) earned in the current period, N, and by the net capital stock available at the end of previous period, K_{-1}:

$$I = b_0 + b_1N + b_2K_{-1}$$

where b_0, b_1, and b_2 are constants.

(3) Wages in the current period, W, depend on national income in the current period, Y, and on time t. ("Time" is used as a catch-all substitute variable for all other variables which are unspecified, but which nevertheless exert an influence on wages.)

$$W = c_0 + c_1Y + c_2t$$

where c_0, c_1, and c_2 are constants.

(4) National income in the current period, Y, is the sum of consumption in the current period, C; net investment in the current period, I; and government expenditures in the current period, G. (This model assumes for simplicity that national income and net national product are the same. In reality, as you know, there are some accounting differences between them.)

$$Y = C + I + G$$

(5) Nonwage income (rent, interest, profit) in the current period, N, is the difference between national income in the current period, Y, and wage income in the current period, W:

$$N = Y - W$$

(6) Net capital stock at the end of the current period, K, is equal to the last period's net capital stock, K_{-1}, plus current net investment, I:

$$K = K_{-1} + I$$

This completes the set of hypotheses which we have expressed both in words and in equations for the purpose of explaining the phenomena being investigated. For convenience, the six equations which comprise the model may now be grouped together as a system of equations:

$$C = a_0 + a_1Y + a_2C_{-1} \qquad (1)$$
$$I = b_0 + b_1N + b_2K_{-1} \qquad (2)$$
$$W = c_0 + c_1Y + c_2t \qquad (3)$$
$$Y = C + I + G \qquad (4)$$
$$N = Y - W \qquad (5)$$
$$K = K_{-1} + I \qquad (6)$$

Comments About the Equations

A few words may be said about the nature of these equations.

The first three equations should be regarded as "approximate" rather than exact. This is because the independent variables (shown on the right side) in each equation do not account completely for the variations in the dependent variable (shown on the left side). For example, in Equation (1), consumption in the current period is, in reality, determined by other factors in addition to income in the current period and consumption in the previous period. Some of these other factors may be both economic and psychological. Further, there may be errors in the data employed to represent the relevant variables. All of these factors create "disturbances" in the equation. If we assume that no significant independent variables have been omitted, then the disturbances may be thought of as reflecting all of the unknown and unpredictable factors. Ideally, the variations in these "all other" factors will be small and random in nature, and will tend to cancel each other out, so that their overall net effect on the dependent variable is zero. To the extent that this assumption is realized in practice, the remaining explicit variables in the equation will account for the systematic or "causal" movements in the dependent variable—which is what we want.

The last three equations in the model are simply definitions expressed as mathematical identities. For example, Equation (4) says that national income (which in this simplified model is assumed to equal net national product) is the sum of consumption, investment, and government expenditures. This equation thus summarizes a familiar concept which you learned in national-income accounting. Similarly, Equations (5) and (6) are also symbolic expressions of definitions. These three definitional equations serve to fill in or complete the model.

An Application

Let us now see how an econometric model might be constructed in a given situation.

General Steel Corporation is a major manufacturer of iron and steel. For the past ten years the company has been working with several foreign governments in the planning of heavy industrialization programs. As a result, General Steel now has subsidiary iron and steel manufacturing corporations in three foreign countries.

Two years ago, the management of the company began exploring the possibility of opening a subsidiary corporation in Arcadia, a major industrial nation. Since the economic future of Arcadia is of obvious interest to the parent firm, General Steel's economists have been actively engaged in collecting data for the purpose of constructing an econometric model of that country.

Thus, according to recent studies by General Steel's economic research department, last year's corporate profits in Arcadia were about $42 billion. Although there is no way of being certain how much Arcadia's federal, state, and local governments will spend next year, General Steel's economists estimate from present budget information that the amount should be around $75 billion. Also, an analysis of the most recent business cycle in Arcadia covering a number of years indicates that annual consumption expenditures have averaged $40 billion plus 70 percent of national income; investment expenditures have averaged about $20 billion plus 90 percent of the preceding year's profits; and tax receipts have averaged about 20 percent of gross national product. GNP, of course, is composed of consumption, investment, and government expenditures, while national income is assumed, for simplicity, to equal the difference between gross national product and tax receipts.

QUESTIONS

1. Let C = *next year's consumption,* Y = *next year's national income,* I = *next year's investment,* P_{-1} = *preceding year's profits,* T = *next year's tax receipts by government,* G = *next year's gross national product,* E = *next year's government expenditures.*

(a) *Construct an econometric model of Arcadia.* (SUGGESTION: *You should construct a five-equation model on the basis of the facts in the problem. Do not use the equations of the illustrative model; simply take the relationships given in words above about General Steel's studies and put them into equation form. Thus, your first equation should be an equation for consumption, the second for investment, the third for tax receipts, the fourth for gross national product, and the fifth for national income. For instance, the study mentions that "consumption expenditures have averaged $40 billion plus 70 percent of national income." This can be expressed as* $C = \$40 + 0.7Y$. *Note that in this instance $40 and 0.7 are the values of constants, such as* a_0 *and* a_1 *referred to in the illustrative model. For convenience, you may find it helpful to construct the model first by using small letters such as a, b, c, d, e to represent the constants, and then substituting the correct numbers for the constants.*)

(b) *When you have written out all five equations, solve the system.* (HINT: *You want values of C, I, T, G, Y. The equations are not to be solved in chronological order. First, solve Equation* [2]. *Then, in solving* [1] *and the remaining equations, look for substitutions that can be made.*) *Here are the correct answers. See if yours check. For next year:* $C = \$259.9$ *billion;* $I = \$57.8$ *billion;* $T = \$78.5$ *billion;* $G = \$392.7$ *billion,* $Y = \$314.2$ *billion.*

2. It sometimes happens that econometric models fail to provide better predictions for the following year than less complex models such as simple trend projections. Does this mean that econometric methods should be abandoned?

PART 4   Economic Growth
              and Ecology

CHAPTER 18

Explanations of Economic Growth

CHAPTER PREVIEW

How do we define economic growth? What is the basis of the definition? How is economic growth measured?

Did the classical economists have anything to say about economic growth? Is their theory of use to us in explaining modern economic growth?

What types of specific factors determine a nation's economic growth? How are these factors "measured"?

Can a simple model be constructed to illustrate some of the basic concepts of growth? What do we mean by a full-employment growth rate? Can it be measured with a simple formula?

Since the late 1940s economic growth has been regarded as one of our fundamental economic problems. It has been a significant issue in political campaigns and will undoubtedly remain a major national concern for a long time to come.

Why this interest in growth? At least two reasons are already somewhat obvious: Our population and labor force are expanding rapidly, making it necessary for the economy to take care of millions more people and to provide them with jobs; living standards must rise if social tensions are to be reduced without government intervention.

Our purpose in this chapter is to sketch the meaning and implications of economic growth, thus providing a theoretical basis for judging the actual growth of various economies. We shall find that there is no single "theory" of economic growth in the sense of a unified body of propositions. Instead, certain elements are common ingredients to almost all theories, and when taken together constitute the basis for most modern discussions of the subject.

What Is Economic Growth?

There is often confusion about the meaning of economic growth, because politicians and economists are fond of hurling statistics at each other showing growth rates of various countries or regions over different periods of time. Hence an accurate definition is called for:

Economic growth is the rate of increase in an economy's real output or income over time—that is, the rise in its full-employment output in constant prices. Economic growth may be expressed in either of two ways: (1) as the increase in total real GNP or NNP over time; or (2) as the increase in per capita real GNP or NNP over time.

The first of these measures is usually employed to describe the expansion of a nation's economic output. The second is used to express the development of its material standard of living and to compare it with that of other nations.

In the most fundamental sense, economic growth is concerned with policy measures aimed at expanding a nation's *capacity* to produce. It thus contrasts with monetary and fiscal policies which seek to make full and efficient use of a nation's *existing* capacity.

The concept of economic growth can be illustrated in terms of the familiar production-possibilities curves in Exhibit 1. Since each curve represents an economy's capacity to produce, an outward shift of the curve is a measure of a nation's economic growth.

Exhibit 1

Economic Growth Can Be Seen as an Outward Shift of an Economy's Production-possibilities Curve

Economic growth is not a movement along a given curve such as from S to T, since this is merely a change in the composition of total output, nor is it a movement from a point of unemployment such as U to the production-possibilities curve. It is an outward shift of the curve.

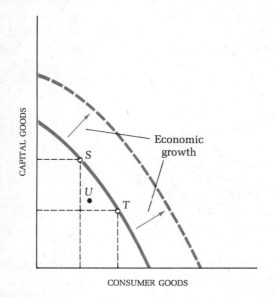

CONSUMER GOODS

MEASURING ECONOMIC GROWTH

Is the U.S. economy growing, declining, or stagnating? How does its growth compare with that of the Russian economy? The Japanese economy? The answers are determined by the way in which we measure growth. Although the definition seems clear-cut, economists do not always agree on the results, because the methods of calculation can involve some slippery procedures.

Part of the trouble is that the concept of growth, like so many concepts in economics, is derived from the natural sciences—in this case from biology. The classic definition of growth was given by the biologist D'arcy Thompson. Growth, Thompson said, is "a process, indirectly resulting from chemical, osmotic, and other forces, by which material is introduced into the organism and transferred from one part of it to another." In general terms, therefore, *growth is an organic process.*

Conceptually, economic growth should involve similar processes of expansion in economic organisms—in the firms, households, and governmental units that compose our economy. These organisms are responsible for producing and consuming the economy's stream of goods and services, and their complex interactions with one another determine the rate of economic growth.

In practice, the biological definition of growth makes it quite clear that we cannot measure the fundamental *organic* growth of an economy. Economists, therefore, have adopted an alternative approach: they use past measures of output or income, as suggested by the definition of economic growth given earlier, and they derive long-term growth trends from these historical records. Frequently, these trends are projected into the future at various assumed compound rates of growth—like money growing at compound interest in a savings account.

The "Classical" Theory of Growth

In the late eighteenth and early nineteenth centuries, certain classical British economists—notably Adam Smith, David Ricardo, and Thomas Malthus—formulated economic concepts and theories which dealt in large part with economic development. The conclusions of Ricardo and Malthus were basically pessimistic; they argued that a country's economic growth must end in decline and stagnation. The ideas of these men compose what may appropriately

Exhibit 2

The Subsistence Theory and Diminishing Returns

In the classical model of Ricardo and Malthus, the actual level-of-living curve L depends on the size of the population (or number of workers) applied to a fixed amount of land. The population tends toward an equilibrium size of 0M, corresponding to the subsistence level MR. Even an upward shift of the actual level-of-living curve from L to L', due to the development of new resources or new production techniques, is of short-run duration. The population simply expands to the size 0K, leaving the average output per person KT at the same subsistence level as before.

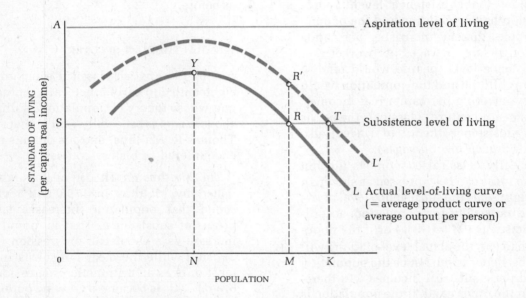

be called the "classical" theory of economic growth. Their views are interesting, and can help us to understand modern economic problems of growth.

THE SUBSISTENCE THEORY AND DIMINISHING RETURNS

The classical model of economic growth is based on a so-called *subsistence theory*. In its simplest form the classical model can be expressed in terms of two basic propositions:

1. The population of a country tends to adjust to a subsistence level of living.

2. Increases in population, with techniques and natural resources (land) held constant, result in *eventually* decreasing per capita incomes due to the operation of the "law of diminishing returns."

These concepts are illustrated in Exhibit 2. The population of a country is scaled on the horizontal axis, and its material standard of living as measured by per capita real income is scaled on the vertical. The curve labeled *L* shows the actual level of living that the society can maintain for each amount of population applied to the fixed quantity of other resources. It may therefore be thought of as an *average product curve* representing the average output per person (or per worker) which results from adding more and more people to a given amount of land while production techniques are held constant.

The average product or actual level-of-living curve, *L*, rises to a maximum and then declines, thereby evidencing the eventual tendency for "diminishing returns" to set in as a growing population is applied to a fixed amount of resources. The ideal or *optimum population* is therefore *0N*, since this yields a level of living equal to *NY*, which is the highest level attainable on the curve. Any other combination of population and fixed resources is not optimal because it yields a lower output per person.

The classical economists contended that there was some standard of living at which the population—especially the working population—would just maintain itself with no tendency to increase or decrease. They called this the "subsistence level." Although primarily a physical or biological level, this level is also determined by social and customary needs which in turn influence the rearing of children. Thus the classicists argued that if wages per worker fell below the subsistence level, people would tend to stop having children and the population would decline, thereby increasing per capita real incomes; conversely, if wages per worker rose above the subsistence level, people would tend to start having more children and the population would increase, thereby lowering per capita real incomes. This early-nineteenth-century classical theory is known as the *subsistence theory of wages* (also called the *iron* or *brazen law of wages*).

Although the early classical economists did not use graphs, these ideas can be expressed as shown in Exhibit 2. If OS represents the subsistence level of living, the equilibrium size of the population, according to the classicists, is OM ($= SR$). For if the population is larger than OM, the actual level of living will be below the subsistence level; hence the population will decline and per capita real incomes will therefore increase. On the other hand, if the population is less than OM, the actual level of living will be above the subsistence level; hence the population will increase and per capita real incomes will therefore decrease. Thus it is apparent that the "subsistence level" in the classical model is a long-run equilibrium level of living for the population as a whole.

Economics—The "Dismal Science"

Because of this pessimistic theory, economics (or political economy as it used to be called) came to be known as the "dismal science." For if the subsistence level of living is a long-run equilibrium toward which society is always tending, there is no hope of ever improving the lot of mankind. Even the discovery of new natural resources or the development of new techniques would at best provide only temporary benefits until the population had time to adjust to these new developments. Then a larger number of people would be left living in the same minimal circumstances as before.

For example, suppose that new natural resources

are discovered, or more land becomes available, or new production techniques are developed. The effect, as shown in Exhibit 2, is to raise the average product curve from L to L', for now the same population has more or better fixed resources with which to work. However, this increase in benefits per person from MR to MR' will be of limited duration. Since average product is now above the subsistence level, the population will increase until it reaches a new equilibrium, namely OK. At this point more people will be living at the same subsistence level OS ($= KT$) as before.

THE MALTHUSIAN SPECTER

Among the English classical economists of the late eighteenth and early nineteenth centuries, there was one whose theory of population as illustrated by the above model is especially well known. His name was Thomas R. Malthus, and his famous theory is often encountered in history courses.

The Malthusian Theory of Population (first published by Malthus in 1798 and revised in 1803) stated that population increases faster than the means of subsistence. That is, population tends to increase as a geometric progression (1, 2, 4, 8, 16, 32, etc.) while the means of subsistence increase at most only as an arithmetic progression (1, 2, 3, 4, 5, 6, etc.). This is because a growing population applied to a fixed amount of land results in eventually diminishing returns to workers. Human beings are therefore destined to misery and poverty unless the rate of population growth is retarded. This may be accomplished either by (a) preventive checks such as moral restraint, late marriages, and celibacy, or if these fail then by (b) positive checks such as wars, famines, and disease.

Has the prediction of Malthus been realized? There is no doubt that it has in certain crowded underdeveloped areas of Asia, Africa, and South America where the Malthusian specter hangs like a dark cloud. In these countries, industrialization and economic growth are impeded because agriculture is inefficient and unable to feed both the people on farms and those who live and work in the cities. In many of these countries wars, famines, and disease are the main curbs on population, although major efforts are now being made to encourage use of contraception.

Critics of colonialism point out, of course, that many of the poor countries' problems result from

Leaders in Economics

THOMAS ROBERT MALTHUS

1766–1834

In the last third of the eighteenth century two great problems occupied the attention of most thinking people in England: one was widespread poverty; the other was how many Englishmen there were. Socialists called attention to the poverty problem with a promise of a Utopian world—a paradise—in which all would be well. The population problem had prompted Adam Smith to remark in his *Wealth of Nations* (1776) that "No society can surely be flourishing and happy, of which the far greater part of the members are poor and miserable."

Were England's resources adequate to bring about a fulfillment of the socialists' dreams? A hitherto unknown English clergyman, Thomas Robert Malthus, thought not. In 1798 he published a treatise of fifty thousand words entitled *An Essay on the Principle of Population, as it Affects the Future Improvement of Society*. The essay was based on his observations and travels in various countries. From these he expounded his famous rule that "population, when unchecked, goes on doubling every twenty-five years or increases in a geometric ratio," but the means of subsistence can only increase in an arithmetic ratio.

Malthus became a professor of history and published a revision of his essay in 1803. In this he moderated his rigid "formula" and spoke more of a tendency of population to outrun the supply of food. Human beings, he concluded, were destined to misery and poverty unless the rate of population growth is retarded either by (a) preventive checks such as moral restraint, late marriages, and celibacy, or if these fail then by (b) positive checks such as wars, famine, and disease.

Malthus and his population theory were severely criticized by people in nearly every walk of life—politicians, clergymen, philosophers, and journalists—all of whom raised cries of heresy. Some, like the *Quarterly Review* (July, 1817), admitted that it was easier simply "to disbelieve Mr. Malthus than to refute him." And some, notably Ricardo and other classical economists, made Malthus' theory the basis of their own theories of wages and rent.

The generalizations expressed by Malthus have been recognized by governments throughout the world, and by the United Nations in its efforts to assist the overpopulated, underdeveloped countries. Although there may be a tendency to dismiss the gloomy forebodings of the Malthusian theory, its warnings cannot be pushed aside. They are a stark reality for millions of people in many nations today.

The Bettmann Archive.

In addition to his population theory, Malthus made outstanding contributions to economics, notably in his *Principles of Political Economy* (1820). He was an intimate friend of David Ricardo, and it is impossible to disassociate their economic views, even though the two men were often in substantial disagreement. For one thing, Ricardo was as incapable of grasping the pragmatic and empirical approach of Malthus as Malthus was incapable of appreciating the rigor and subtle deductive reasoning of Ricardo.

Among the notable contributions that Malthus made to economic thought was the concept of "effective demand," which he defined as the level of aggregate demand necessary to maintain continuous production. More than a century was to pass before the problem of effective demand would rise again to public notice: In his *General Theory*, John Maynard Keynes paid tribute to the pioneering work of Malthus on this subject.

foreign interference. For example, foreign exploitation of their natural resources has drawn workers away from the farms, while doing little to raise agriculture above subsistence levels. Well-meaning medical missionaries have contributed to the shortage of food by reducing infant mortality and death rates, thereby increasing population. In short, the poor countries' economies have been distorted by the rich countries' use of them as sources of raw material and cheap labor. Furthermore, the critics add, the rich nations have usually propped up regimes that defend foreign interests at the expense of local well-being.

Some Proposed Solutions

Can the underdeveloped, overpopulated countries escape from the "Malthusian trap"? Three ways out may be suggested.

One solution would be to shift millions of people from overpopulated to underpopulated regions—from the small farms in southeast Asia, for example, to the vast jungles of South America which await development. But the many obvious political and social obstacles make this policy unrealistic for the foreseeable future.

A second possibility would be to develop new resources and production techniques at a sufficiently rapid rate so that the upward shifts of the average product curve more than offset the growth in population. In this way the population would never catch up with the rising level of output per person, and the level of living would continually increase.

A third approach would be to seek ways of raising the "subsistence level" to the point at which it becomes an *aspiration level* or target for which to strive. In Exhibit 2, for example, the standard of living might be raised from $0S$ to $0A$. Since this new level is above the maximum possible actual level of living that is attainable with any present combination of population and resources, there would be continual pressure to: (*a*) reduce the existing population in order to rise higher on the average product curve; or (*b*) discover and develop new resources and production techniques so as to shift the entire average product curve upward.

The "Hot-baths" Hypothesis

The second and third solutions, in varying degrees, have occurred and are continuing to occur in the economic development of some of today's advanced nations. The third approach, that of raising the subsistence level to an aspiration level, is based on a fascinating assumption—one which suggests a connection between population growth and living standards that may be applicable to the overpopulated, underdeveloped countries. It can be called—facetiously—the *hot-baths hypothesis:*

There may be a significant relationship between fecundity and "hot baths." That is, once a society reaches a certain minimum level of living at which it has reasonable creature comforts of life—adequate food, clothing, housing, sanitation, etc.—its desire for more and better material things as measured by its aspiration level continually rises. If this is true, the society's population will tend automatically to seek its economically optimum size, provided its living conditions can first be brought (probably with outside help from other nations) to this minimum threshold level.

To repeat, this is only an hypothesis—a tentative proposition which has yet to be explored and tested in different nations under varying environmental (especially cultural and social) conditions. Nevertheless, it is an interesting and important concept. For as we shall see in a later chapter, foreign aid to poor, overpopulated nations since World War II has sought, at least in part, to raise living conditions in those countries to some minimum level at which their economies can break out of their stationary states and enter a new phase of more self-sustaining and self-propelling economic growth.

CAPITAL DEEPENING AND DIMINISHING RETURNS

The subsistence theory of wages in the classical model of a stationary state implies the existence of a *subsistence theory* of profits as well.

For example, the model of population growth which was developed in Exhibit 2 may be adapted to serve as a model of the growth of nonhuman capital including buildings, machines, inventories, and so on. This can be done by measuring the rate of interest along the vertical axis and the total stock of capital along the horizontal. For simplicity, we may ignore the existence of risk, so that the rate of interest is the same as the rate of profit. (Can you suggest why?) The curve L is then the profit curve of capital which results from applying different amounts of capital to a fixed quantity of other resources.

When looked at in this way, the model indicates that capital is accumulated in anticipation of future interest returns or profits. Thus when the stock of capital in the economy is relatively low, the anticipated return on capital is high, thereby encouraging further accumulation. As capital is accumulated, however, the law of diminishing returns eventually sets in. If we suppose that OS represents the "subsistence rate" of profits, capital accumulation will proceed to OM. Improvements in any of the fixed resources or in production techniques will, of course, shift the profit curve upward from L to L', thereby bringing about a further accumulation of capital to OK.

An increase in the stock of capital relative to other resources, especially labor, is called *capital deepening*. What are the effects of such a deepening, assuming that there are no changes in techniques? Clearly, with the operation of the inexorable law of diminishing returns, the interest or profit rate on capital must *decline*, while the real wages of labor must *rise* as this resource becomes more and more scarce relative to the growing stock of capital.

The Wages-fund Theory

These ideas gradually led to a reformulation of the subsistence theory of wages in the classical model. The reformulation, known as the "wages-fund" theory, existed or was implied in the writings of Smith (1776) and Ricardo (1817), but it was best articulated several decades later in 1848 by John Stuart Mill—not only the greatest economist of his time, but also one of history's most distinguished intellectuals.

The *wages-fund theory* was a mid-nineteenth-century classical theory of wages which held that the producer sets aside, from his capital, funds with which to hire the workers needed for production. The producer does this because of the indirect or "roundabout" nature of the production process: it takes time for goods to be produced, sold, and paid for. Therefore, workers must be given advanced payments—out of the producer's "wages fund"—in order to meet their basic needs. The amount of the wages fund, and hence the real wage of labor, depends directly on the size of the capital stock relative to the number of workers. But in the long run, as we have seen in the classical model, the accumulation of capital tends to be determined by the minimum subsistence rate of profits. Hence the only

effective way to raise real wages is to reduce the number of workers or the size of the population.

CONCLUSION: THE CLASSICAL VIEW OF GROWTH

These ideas led the English classical economists—especially Ricardo—to the conclusion that the development of an economy depends on the relative growth of two critical variables: *population* and *capital*. If population grows faster than capital, wages fall and profits rise; conversely, if capital grows faster than population, profits fall and wages rise. From time to time, one of these variables may grow faster than the other, thereby causing an upward shift in the level-of-living curve of population or in the profit curve of capital, but eventually both wages per worker and profits per unit of capital must tend toward a long-run level of subsistence. Land, on the other hand, remains fixed in supply; therefore, landlords stand to benefit over the long run as rents continue to rise with increases in population and in output per worker.

What Are the Long-run Trends?

Have these predictions been vindicated by history? For most of the advanced or developed economies of the Western world the answer is no. Since the nineteenth century in the United States, for example, three very long-run patterns have been evident:

First, the trends of real wages and of output per man-hour have been sharply upward, not downward. These trends result mainly from: (a) rapid expansion in technology; and (b) growth of the capital stock at a faster rate than the population, thus resulting in a deepening of capital.

Second, interest rates or profit have fluctuated in the business cycle with no particular upward or downward trend.

Third, land rents have moved upward only slightly, while actually declining in relation to other factor prices.

In general terms, the average product curve of the economy has shifted upward over time at a pace rapid enough to more than offset tendencies toward diminishing returns and Malthusian subsistence equilibrium. This upward shift can be attributed to changes in the conditions that are assumed to remain "fixed" when the curve is drawn. In broad terms

JOHN STUART MILL

1806–1873

John Stuart Mill was an eminent philosopher and social scientist, and the leading economist of the mid-nineteenth century. In many ways, he was one of the most unusual men who ever lived.

Any discussion of Mill must make mention of his remarkable education, based on the experiences reported in his famous *Autobiography*. He was the son of James Mill, a noted philosopher, historian, and economist. James Mill was also an intimate friend of David Ricardo and of the great utilitarian philosopher Jeremy Bentham. This intellectual background exercised a profound influence on the younger Mill, who was educated at home by his father.

Thus, at the age of three, before most children can even recite the alphabet, John Stuart was reading English fluently and beginning the study of Greek. By the time he was seven, he had read the dialogues of Plato; the great books of the ancient Greek historians Herodotus and Xenophon; the philosophical writings of Diogenes; and most of the nearly eighty works of the second century Greek prose writer, Lucian. At the age of eight he took up the study of Latin. Before he was twelve years old, he had already digested, among other things, the major writings of Aristotle, Aristophanes, Horace, Lucretius, Sallust, and Socrates; made a comprehensive survey of algebra, calculus, and geometry; embarked on a serious study of logic through the writings of the early seventeenth-century British philosopher Thomas Hobbes; and written, in addition to some verses, a "History of Rome," a "History of Holland," and the "Abridged Ancient Universal History."

At the age of thirteen, John Stuart was introduced by his father to the books of Smith, Ricardo, and Malthus. Thus began his education in political economy—an education that eventually established him as one of the abler critics of classical economic liberalism. For although Mill as an economist is considered a member of the classical school, he actually repudiated some of its most basic premises. In contrast to Smith, for example, he did not believe that laissez-faire led to the best of all possible worlds. Instead he advocated social reforms. These included the taxation and redistribution of wealth, a shorter working day, abolition of the wage system, and the establishment of democratic producers' cooperatives in which the workers would own the factories and elect the managers to run them. It should be emphasized, however, that Mill believed too strongly in individual freedom ever to go far as a socialist. He distrusted the power of the state, and his reason for favoring producers' cooperatives was not to exalt the laboring class, but to assure the individual worker the fruits of his labor.

Culver Pictures, Inc.

Mill's chief contribution to economics was his collection and systemization of its literature. His major two-volume work, the *Principles of Political Economy*, published in 1848, was considered to be a masterful synthesis of post-Ricardian economic writings. The book offered a calm prescription for peaceful progress and served as a standard text in economics for several decades. It is a noteworthy coincidence that in the same year, an incendiary pamphlet entitled the *Communist Manifesto* was published by a then relatively unknown prophet of socialism, Karl Marx, whose ideas ultimately shook the world.

As for Mill himself, few individuals were ever held in higher esteem. Like the great and beloved Greek philosopher Plato of some 2,200 years earlier, Mill was a selfless man with a gentle, kind, and reasonable manner that endeared him to everyone. He was regarded with the deepest affection and respect—indeed, he was almost worshiped—by his contemporaries throughout the world. And like Plato, when he died an entire nation mourned his passing.

these include (a) improvements in the quality of labor, (b) discoveries of new and better natural resources, and (c) technological advances in production. We shall see shortly that these are actually the kinds of factors that determine a nation's economic growth. As a result, the classical or "Ricardian" model is useful not only for what it includes, but also for what it excludes in explaining many of the dynamic processes of economic history.

What Factors Determine Economic Growth?

The classical theory of economic growth presents only a partial explanation of economic development. As yet, no unified body of principles provides what might be called a *general theory* of economic growth. However, certain factors will undoubtedly play a significant role in the development of such a theory. Our purpose at this time is to see what they are.

Let us assume that aggregate demand is sufficient to maintain full employment, and that government will take the necessary monetary and fiscal measures to assure this. The growth of real GNP will then be determined by improvements in the nation's resources and the "environment" in which they are used. These major growth-determining factors include (1) quantity and quality of human resources, (2) quantity and quality of "natural" resources, (3) accumulation of capital, (4) specialization and scale of production, (5) rate of technological progress, and (6) environmental factors. Since these are also the kinds of factors that influence an economy's production-possibilities curve, we shall examine the importance of each of them.

QUANTITY AND QUALITY OF HUMAN RESOURCES

On the basis of our earlier definition of economic growth, the following simple formula is a convenient guide for discussion:

$$\text{Real GNP per capita} = \frac{\text{total real GNP}}{\text{population}}$$

The rate of economic growth is measured by the rate at which the left side of this equation increases over time. This in turn will depend, in terms of the right side of the equation, on the rate at which the numerator of the ratio increases relative to the denominator.

The faster the rate of increase in total real GNP as compared to the rate of increase in population, the greater the rise in real GNP per capita and hence in the rate of economic growth.

The above formula uses population only in quantitative terms. But there are both quantitative and qualitative considerations that should be taken into account. For instance, increases in population will bring about increases in the size of the labor force— that is, in the number of people working or looking for work. The productivity of the labor force will influence the rate of economic growth. The chief factors determining labor productivity include: (a) the time spent at work, such as the average length of the workweek; (b) the education, health, and skills of workers; and (c) the quantity and quality of the tools and capital equipment with which they work. Over the past several decades, modern industrial nations have experienced a steady decline in the first of these factors along with a continuous increase in the last two.

Thus the *quality* as well as the *quantity* of a country's human resources influence its economic growth.

QUANTITY AND QUALITY OF "NATURAL" RESOURCES

An economy's output and economic growth also depend on the quantity and quality of its soil, minerals, water, timber and so on—its natural resources.

Some economists contend that there is no such thing as a "natural" resource. They argue that resources provided by nature are of no value to society unless man is able to put them to use. When that happens, the resources are not natural but manmade. Thus a nation may be rich in resources, but its material well-being or rate of economic growth will not be influenced in the slightest if these resources remain "neutral" or untapped. Consequently, demand and cost conditions must be favorable if a resource is to be converted from a neutral to a positive state. This means that there must be: (a) a high enough level of demand for the product which the resource will help to produce; and (b) an adequate supply of capital, labor, and technical skills to transform the resource to profitable use.

Of course, the quantity and quality of a nation's natural resources are not necessarily fixed. By diverting some of its *existing* labor and capital into research, a society may be able to discover or develop *new* natural resources within its own borders which will enhance its future rate of economic growth. In terms of the production-possibilities curve, this means that some consumer goods must be sacrificed in the present to enable the economy to reach a higher curve in the future.

ACCUMULATION OF CAPITAL

A society must also forgo some current consumption in order to build capital goods such as factories, machines, transportation facilities, dams, and educational institutions. The rate at which a nation can add to its stock of capital will influence its economic growth.

Why is the rate of capital accumulation greater in some countries than in others? We have already learned in the study of macroeconomic theory that many considerations may influence investment, but two are fundamental: (1) profit expectations of businessmen and (2) government policies toward investment. Although the influence of these conditions differs among nations, one aspect of the process of capital accumulation is relevant to all—the necessity for sacrifice.

Thus, capital accumulation is closely related to the volume of savings—the proportion of a society's income that is not spent for consumption. In order to add to their long-run stock of capital goods, the people of a country must refrain from consuming a portion of their current output so that a part of the flow can be diverted into investment. This principle helps to explain why poor countries, like poor families, are ordinarily unable to save as much as rich ones, and hence experience little or no economic growth. In general:

The *cost* of economic growth to a society is the consumption it must sacrifice in order to save for the purpose of accumulating capital.

SPECIALIZATION AND SCALE OF PRODUCTION

Adam Smith observed in his *Wealth of Nations* that "The greatest improvement in the productive powers of labor and the greater part of the skill, dexterity, and judgment with which it is anywhere directed, or applied, seem to have been the effects of the division of labour." He then gave the celebrated example of a pin factory: "One man draws out the wire, another straights it, a third cuts it, a fourth points it, a fifth grinds it. . . ." and as a result there is a far greater output than if each man were to make the entire pin himself.

Smith also made the interesting point that the division of labor is limited by the "extent of the market." He observed that in a small isolated economy there will be less division of labor and a smaller scale of operations to satisfy local needs than in a large exchange economy like Glasgow or a still larger one like London.

These comments on specialization and scale of production provide significant insights into the process of economic growth. In the early stages of a nation's economic development, production is relatively nonspecialized and the scale of operations is small; "manufacturers" produce only to supply the needs of the surrounding community. In a number of localities more extensive industries grow up without advancing to the factory stage of production. This situation prevailed in the United States until the end of the eighteenth century. But with the expansion of the market and advances in the technology of production, greater specialization and scale of operations became possible, thereby bringing about larger volumes of output at the same, if not lower, unit costs. This is a continuing process in the economic growth of nations and regions.

Modern economic growth is not just an increase in the quantity of the factors of production; it involves fundamental changes in the organization and techniques of production—that is, changes in the structure of production as represented by the input-output relationships that characterize an economy's firms and industries.

A nation's economic growth, therefore, will be determined in part by the potential it has for increasing the specialization of its resources and the scale of its production. There are thus qualitative as well as quantitative considerations that determine economic growth.

RATE OF TECHNOLOGICAL PROGRESS

One of the most important qualitative factors influencing economic growth is the rate of technological progress—the speed at which new knowledge is both developed and applied to raising the standard of living.

A remarkable series of events that took place in the United States within the short space of 13 years, between 1790 and 1803, provides an interesting example of how the rate of technological progress can influence the evolution of a national economy.

In 1790, a brilliant young Englishman, Samuel Slater, employed by a merchant firm in Rhode Island, began spinning cotton thread by machine, thus marking the first effective introduction of the factory system in this country. In the same year, John Fitch constructed and operated successfully the world's first regularly scheduled steamboat; when later employed on western waters, it cut the costs of transportation remarkably and enabled the West to become part of the national economy. In 1793, Eli Whitney invented the cotton gin, which made possible the extensive cultivation of cotton and subsequently transformed the economy of the South. In 1800 this same young graduate of Yale College contracted to manufacture 10,000 rifles for the government, and succeeded in producing them with precisely made interchangeable parts—the first step toward assembly-line production. By 1803, a Philadelphia inventor named Oliver Evans achieved almost complete automation in the milling of wheat into flour by an ingenious system of machines that weighed, cleaned, ground, and packed the flour with virtually no human assistance. (See Box 1.)

These technological advances were accompanied by legal and economic innovations which had important consequences for the nation's development. Two particularly spectacular advances were: (1) the sudden growth of banking, including the creation of the Bank of the United States as well as more than two dozen state-chartered banks, which provided new and important sources of credit for business transactions; and (2) the rapid adoption of the corporate form of business organization, which provided opportunities for accumulating large amounts of financial capital (money) with limited liability on the part of owners. In an expanding economy where risk-taking was a vital element of growth, these features made possible the financing and adoption of the technical innovations mentioned above. Clearly, therefore:

Technological progress involves more than just invention; it embraces an effort on the part of society as a whole to get the most out of existing resources and to discover new and better resources through continuous improvements in education, engineering, management, and marketing.

Box 1

Technological Progress

FIRST TRIP OF JOHN FITCH'S STEAMBOAT, PHILADELPHIA, 1790

ELI WHITNEY'S FIRST COTTON GIN, 1793

The Bettmann Archive.

The Bettmann Archive.

The steamboat and the cotton gin were two strategic inventions introduced in the early years after American

independence. These inventions played a key role in the nation's economic growth during the nineteenth century.

ENVIRONMENTAL FACTORS

All of the points considered thus far lead to the conclusion that the political, social, cultural, and economic environment must be favorable if significant growth is to occur. This means, among other things, that there must be a banking and credit system capable of financing growth, a legal system that establishes the ground rules of business behavior, a tax system that does not discourage new investment and risk-taking, and a stable government that is sympathetic to economic expansion. It is no accident that countries like the United States, Canada, Great Britain, Japan, and the Soviet Union have experienced periods of rapid economic growth despite their different political systems, whereas some Latin American and Asian countries have had little or no significant economic growth for many years—and in some cases even for many decades.

CONCLUSION: THE PROBLEM OF MEASUREMENT

How important is each of the above factors in determining a country's economic growth? Can we measure their separate influences? These questions are extremely difficult to answer because some causes of growth are qualitative rather than quantitative. Consequently, there is a tendency among economists to reduce the determinants of growth to three sets of "measurable" factors:

1. Growth of the labor force
2. Growth of capital
3. Technical progress (including "all other things")

The first two factors can be measured quite precisely, whereas the third cannot. Therefore, in measuring the causes of an economy's growth, once the contributions of the first two factors to total economic growth have been quantitatively estimated, the contribution of the third factor may be viewed as a "residual" or catch-all for all determinants other than labor and capital.

As a simple example, if an economy grows at the rate of 6 percent annually over a period, and 4 percent of that growth is estimated to have been due to the growth of labor and capital combined, then the remaining 2 percent might be attributed to technical progress. For purposes of measurement, therefore, "technical progress" includes such things as better machinery and technology, better management, and greater labor skills. It has been estimated that in the United States more than 80 percent of the increase in output per capita since the early part of the century has been due to this technical-progress factor, leaving less than 20 percent to be explained by the other two factors. In terms of *total* output (as distinct from output per capita), technical progress has accounted for almost 50 percent of the growth of production in the United States and various other industrial nations. This suggests that economic growth is best envisioned as a continuous development and discovery of new and better ways of doing things, rather than just a quantitative expansion of existing inputs.

A Simple Growth Model

Modern approaches to the theory of economic growth are closely tied to analysis of business cycles. The reasons are obvious. When we studied business cycles in an earlier chapter, we learned that an economy's rate of growth will vary in different stages of the cycle. We also learned that if the consumption function is assumed to be stable, the level of income and employment is determined by net investment.

But in the study of economic growth net investment has yet another function: It *adds to the economy's capacity.* Therefore, the more the net investment undertaken in any one period, the greater will be the productive capacity of the economy in the next period, and hence the higher the level of investment needed to sustain aggregate demand and full employment at capacity output.

THE CAPITAL-OUTPUT RATIO

This point is illustrated by the familiar consumption-function diagram in the upper chart of Exhibit 3. For simplicity, only the private sector is represented; the influence of the public sector (government) is excluded. Let us suppose that output ON_1 represents the economy's full-employment NNP in Year 1. Hence the corresponding level of consumption is N_1C_1 and the corresponding level of saving is C_1S_1. We assume that this volume of saving flows into new investment, that is, that planned saving equals planned investment, so that the output ON_1 is maintained.

As a result of this new investment, the economy's capacity to produce is enlarged in Year 2 to the out-

Exhibit 3

Investment and the Growth of Capacity at Full Employment

In the upper chart, let $0N_1$ be the full-employment NNP in Year 1. Then savings in that year will be C_1S_1 which, when invested in plant and equipment, will increase productive capacity in Year 2 by N_1N_2. Saving and investment must then rise to C_2S_2, and this in turn will increase productive capacity in Year 3 by N_2N_3. Investment must thus rise by increasing amounts, as emphasized in the lower chart, in order to sustain full employment of a growing productive capacity.

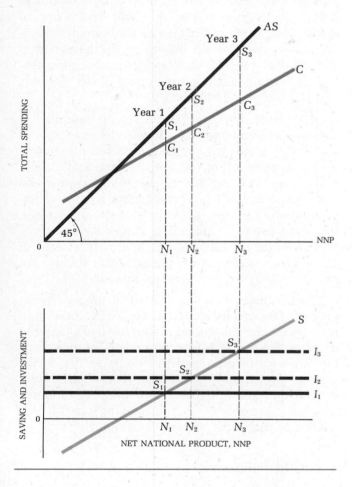

put $0N_2$. In order to produce this output, the volume of planned saving C_2S_2 must flow into new investment. If it does, the capacity of the economy will be further enlarged in Year 3 to the output $0N_3$.

If this process continues, the economy's ability to produce will expand by increasing amounts, requiring *increasing levels of investment* in order to sustain full employment of a *growing productive*

capacity. This is further emphasized by the lower chart in Exhibit 3, where the level of investment each year shifts upward by larger and larger amounts.

How much will the economy's productive capacity rise each year? The answer depends on the *capital-output ratio*, which is the relationship between the economy's stock of real capital and the resulting output or productive capacity. A ratio of 3:1, for instance, which has been the approximate long-run trend in the United States, means that 3 units of capital produce 1 unit of output per period.

FULL-EMPLOYMENT GROWTH RATE

We can extend the foregoing ideas to develop an important formula that is widely used as an expression of economic growth at full employment.

In addition to assuming full employment, let us also assume that *saving* equals *investment* and that all investment results in an increase in *capital*. Therefore, if we know the *average propensity to save*, that is, the proportion of the economy's income or output that is not spent on consumption, we can tell how much saving will flow into investment and hence into the creation of additional capital. Then, if we also know the capital-output ratio, we can calculate the expected full-employment growth of NNP.

The procedure is illustrated in Exhibit 4 on the next page. Columns (1) and (2) show the full-employment output for each year represented by NNP. For convenience, we begin with an arbitrary NNP of $100 in Year 1. In column (3) of the table, saving equals investment or the increase in capital, and the average propensity to save *APS* is assumed to be 10 percent. This is equivalent, of course, to saying that the average propensity to consume is 90 percent. If we assume that the capital-output ratio is also 3:1, the resulting increase in output will be $\frac{1}{3}$ of the increase in capital as shown in column (4). This increase in output then becomes the next year's addition to NNP in column (2), as emphasized by the arrows. The table can thus be extended very easily by simply continuing the pattern; that is, take 10 percent of NNP, than calculate $\frac{1}{3}$ of that, and add the result to the current year's NNP to get next year's NNP.

You may be able to estimate from the table that the full-employment output of NNP is growing at a rate of something over 3 percent per year. However, a closer estimate can be made in terms of the variables in the model by applying the simple formula:

Exhibit 4

The Full-employment Rate of Economic Growth

What will be the full-employment NNP for Year 5? To find out, take 10 percent of Year 4's NNP, then calculate ⅓ of that, and add the result to the NNP for Year 4. The arrows illustrate the pattern to be followed.

Year	(1)	(2) Full-employment output, NNP	(3) Saving = investment = increase in capital (APS = 0.10) [10% of col. (2)]	(4) Resulting increase in output (capital-output ratio = 3:1) [⅓ of col. (3)]
1		$100.00	$10.00	
				3.33
2		103.33	10.33	
				3.44
3		106.77	10.68	
				3.56
4		110.33		

Full-employment growth rate

$$= \frac{\text{average propensity to save}}{\text{capital-output ratio}}$$

This basic formula is widely used in modern theories of economic growth. It can be applied for any average propensity to consume and for any capital-output ratio. In the above model, for example, we assumed a long-run APS of 0.10 and a capital-output ratio of 3; hence the full-employment growth rate is 0.10/3 = 0.033 or 3.3 percent a year. Of course, a larger or smaller growth rate can be obtained, depending on the values of the APS and the capital-output ratio used in the formula.

The growth-rate formula and the simple model on which it is based are useful primarily because they illustrate important relationships. But it should be kept in mind that they assume a number of simplifying conditions, not the least of which are (a) a fixed capital-output ratio, (b) a fixed average propensity to save, and (c) a neglect of such real-world factors as business taxes, government monetary and fiscal policies, and changes in technology. These assumptions are the subject of much debate among economists.

SUMMARY OF IMPORTANT IDEAS

1. The study of economic growth is concerned with the rate of increase in an economy's actual and potential real output or income over time. Economic growth may be viewed as an outward shift of an economy's production-possibilities curve.

2. The classical theory of economic growth, developed in the early nineteenth century, was a subsistence theory, based on the operation of the law of diminishing returns. It held that the development of an economy depended on the relative rates of growth of population and capital, but the returns to both in the form of wages and profit tended toward subsistence levels in the long run. Although the evidence has not borne out this theory for the advanced nations of the world, the classical model, nevertheless, is useful for explaining many of the dynamic processes of economic history.

3. The more important factors that determine a nation's economic growth include the quantity and quality of its human and natural resources, rate of capital accumulation, degree of specialization and scale of production, rate of technological progress, and the nature of its socioeconomic-political environment. For measurement purposes, however, these are usually reduced to three sets of factors: (a) growth of the labor force; (b) growth of capital; and (c) technical progress (or "all other things" not represented by the previous two measurable factors).

4. The full-employment growth of an economy's productive capacity depends on its capital-output ratio which, for the United States, has had a long-run trend of about 3:1. A basic approach for measuring the full-employment growth rate is to divide the average propensity to save by the capital-output ratio. This formula is based, however, on a number of simplifying conditions, thus making it useful only for illustrating some important relationships.

FOR DISCUSSION

1. *Terms and concepts to review:*

economic growth	capital deepening
subsistence theory of wages	wages-fund theory
Malthusian theory of population	capital-output ratio

2. Is our economic definition of growth "better" than the biological definition? Explain.

3. What are the shortcomings of the economic defi-

nition of growth? That is, what sort of "amenities" does the definition omit as far as the growth of a society is concerned?

4. If Ricardo and Malthus had been living in the United States rather than England during the early nineteenth century, do you think they would have developed the same theory of economic growth? Explain your answer. (HINT: Think in terms of the subsistence theory and the supply of scarce resources as compared to plentiful ones.)

5. What is meant by an "optimum population"? Do you believe there really is such a thing? Is it as applicable to the United States as it is to India? Why or why not?

6. The factors that determine an economy's growth are both quantitative and qualitative. The quantitative factors are susceptible to measurement and can be incorporated in a growth model. Does this mean that such models are incomplete to the extent that qualitative factors are omitted? What can be done about correcting the situation? Explain your answer.

7. How is the full-employment growth rate of an economy influenced by the size of its APS relative to its capital-output ratio? Can you suggest some general policies that the government can adopt through the tax system to reduce the capital-output ratio and thus stimulate economic growth?

8. (a) It has been suggested that the income tax system, which provides equal deductions for each dependent, might be revised with the objective of regulating family size by taxation. How might this be done? Develop a specific example. (b) What do you think of a population-control plan which parallels several decades of American agricultural policy, giving subsidies for "fallow acres" and penalties for "overcropping"?

CHAPTER 19

Problems of Economic Growth

CHAPTER PREVIEW

What has been the record of American economic growth? How does it compare with that of other advanced nations? What are the sources of growth?

How fast should we grow? Are there some simple guides for understanding and measuring rates of growth?

Is economic growth "free," or does it have costs?

What obstacles must be overcome if a given rate of growth is to be sustained?

How do problems of taxation and inflation affect the rate of growth?

Until recently, the "goodness" of economic growth has, for most people, been an article of faith. After all, economic growth brings more goods, more services, and high employment. What could possibly be wrong with such objectives?

As it turns out, quite a lot. More goods include more chemicals, petroleum products, automobiles, and other items which defile the environment and upset the ecological balance. And, in an unplanned economy like ours, economic growth disrupts the lives of millions of people whose skills are made obsolete by changing technology—sometimes impoverishing whole regions of the country which lose their economic base when the demand for their traditional products or raw materials declines.

These problems are not new. But since the 1960s society's awareness of them has increased. Some economists have been questioning the wisdom of growth for its own sake, and many others have been asking what *kind* of growth is beneficial—in other words, which mix of goods and services will help to make America a better place.

We shall examine these issues in this and the following chapter. But first we must compare the historical record of growth in the United States with the experience of other advanced economies. Then we shall consider the costs of growth, both financial and social.

American Economic Growth: A Look at the Record

By summarizing some of the main trends, we shall understand better the pattern of economic growth in the United States. Before the Civil War "modern"

America was being born. The country was developing a *national* economy marked by increased specialization, interdependence of regions, and growing economies in the scale of production. In regional terms, however, economic growth was not "balanced." The South, for example, changed less than any other section of the country as cotton remained "king" and slavery became the region's most important economic institution.

When the Civil War broke out, the United States was still primarily an agricultural country; its industrial output, though important and increasing, was nowhere near that of major European nations. But the wave of industrialization after the Civil War had a profound effect on America's economic development, and the nation entered a period of sustained growth that has lasted until the present time.

By 1900, the United States was the world's leading manufacturing nation, far ahead of such major producing countries as Great Britain and Germany. In 1859, the value of American manufactured goods stood at $1.8 billion; in 1869 it was $3.3 billion; and in 1899 it was over $13 billion. In terms of the rate of economic growth, the period from 1875 to 1900 was one in which total real GNP is estimated to have increased at an average annual compound rate of 5 to 6 percent, and per capita real GNP at 2 to 3 percent.

MAJOR TRENDS SINCE 1900

During the twentieth century, the *long-run trend* of total real GNP has been rising at an average annual rate of more than 3 percent, while the *upward trend* of real GNP per capita has averaged a little less than 2 percent annually.

We may examine some of the implications of these trends by looking at several of the variables that play a key role in the theory of economic growth. These variables are presented in Exhibit 1. The charts reveal three important sets of features:

1. The top chart shows that NNP increased at about the same rate as the net capital stock, but the latter increased much faster than the population (as well as the labor force). Hence there has been a substantial amount of capital deepening, that is, more capital per worker.

2. The second chart shows that the trend of real wages has been steadily upward and that their rate of growth has approximately equaled the increase in per capita output. The rise in the latter, of course, is

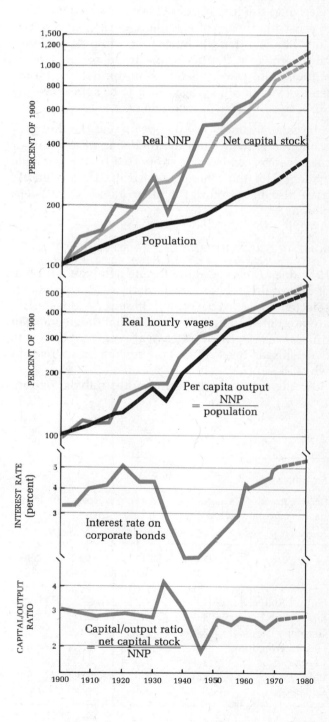

Exhibit 1

The Anatomy of U.S. Economic Development—with Projections to 1980 Based on Recent Trends

a reflection of capital deepening and advancements in technology. Thus, labor has continued to earn approximately the same *proportion* of total output over the years.

3. The three lower charts show that along with the process of capital deepening, real wages have risen relative to the interest rate or return on capital. This is what the theory of economic growth would predict. The fact that the long-run trend of the interest rate is roughly flat, as is the trend of the capital-output ratio, can probably be accounted for by the tendency of diminishing returns to be approximately offset by advances in technology.

In general, therefore, it appears that the theory of economic growth, with the inclusion of technological advance, tends to be supported by the available evidence for the United States. Similar tendencies have also been found for other advanced Western nations.

SOME INTERNATIONAL COMPARISONS

How does America's growth rate compare with that of other relatively advanced nations? Some data for selected countries covering different periods of time are presented in Exhibit 2. Note that there are fewer differences in growth rates over longer periods than over shorter ones. (Can you suggest some reasons why?)

As the data indicate, some industrialized nations have experienced faster rates of growth in recent decades than has the United States. Japan and West Germany, in particular, had very high growth rates after World War II, thus prompting many economists to believe that this was a temporary phenomenon of postwar recovery. But the high rates have persisted, so that the phenomenon has long since been regarded as anything but temporary.

THE SOURCES OF UNITED STATES GROWTH

In our discussion of the theory of growth we learned about the chief factors that determine a nation's economic development. For our present purposes, these may be summarized broadly in terms of the five factors listed in the table in Exhibit 3, which provides rough estimates of the contribution each factor makes to the nation's total economic growth. Note that before 1929 increases in the *quantitative* factors, namely, the supplies of labor and capital, accounted for about two-thirds of the economy's expansion, while the remaining one-third was due to increases in such qualitative factors as improvements in education and training, technology, and "all other things." Since 1929, the situation has almost reversed itself, with the *qualitative* factors playing a major role in economic growth and the quantitative factors a minor one. This influence is reflected in the chart.

Exhibit 2

Growth Rates of Gross National Product—Selected Countries
(latest comparative data)

GROWTH RATES OF REAL GROSS NATIONAL PRODUCT

	1870–1964	1929–1964	1950–1960	1960–1970
United States	3.6%	3.0%	3.2%	4.4%
Japan	3.8	4.2	8.2	11.1
Germany	2.8	3.9	8.6	4.7
United Kingdom	1.9	2.2	2.7	2.8
France	1.7	1.9	4.9	5.8
Italy	2.0	2.9	5.6	5.6
Canada	3.5	3.6	4.0	5.2

GROWTH RATES OF REAL GROSS NATIONAL PRODUCT PER CAPITA

	1870–1964	1929–1964	1950–1960	1960–1970
United States	1.9%	1.7%	1.4%	3.2%
Japan	—	—	7.0	9.9
Germany	1.7	2.8	7.1	3.7
United Kingdom	1.3	1.7	2.3	2.1
France	1.5	1.4	3.9	4.7
Italy	1.4	2.2	4.8	4.7
Canada	1.7	1.8	1.3	3.3

SOURCE: U.S. Department of Commerce.

Investment in Human Capital

The trends suggest that improvements in education and training have become the single most important factor contributing to economic growth. In other words, the scarcest resource for our society is not land or muscle power, but brainpower. The advances of modern science and technology are making this increasingly evident. Hence our investment in human capital, reflecting a rising long-run trend in the number of high-school and college graduates and in expenditures on public elementary and secondary education, as shown in Exhibit 4 on the next page, will continue to expand in the years to come. This is all the more likely in view of mounting evidence to suggest that society's returns from investment in human capital are higher than its returns from investment in capital goods.

Exhibit 3

Sources of U.S. Economic Growth

According to the table, the main factor contributing to economic growth since 1929 has been a "qualitative" one, namely, improved education and training of human resources. This results in a rising trend of GNP per worker, as shown in the chart. The projections assume that the rate of growth of real GNP will average 4.2 percent annually, based on assumed rates of increase in the labor force and productivity.

Contributions to total growth	1909– 1929	1929– 1957
Quantitative factors		
Increase in quantity of labor*	39%	27%
Increase in quantity of capital	26	15
Qualitative factors†		
Improved education and training	13	27
Improved technology	12	20
All other things‡	10	11
Total growth in real national income	100	100

* Adjusted for decreases in the workweek.
† Some qualitative factors are at least partially quantitative. Improvements in education, for example, depend on the number of years of schooling as well as on the quality of schooling.
‡ Consists primarily of increased economies of large-scale production resulting from the expanding size of the market.
SOURCE: Adapted from Edward Denison, *The Sources of Economic Growth in the United States*, New York, Committee for Economic Development, 1962.

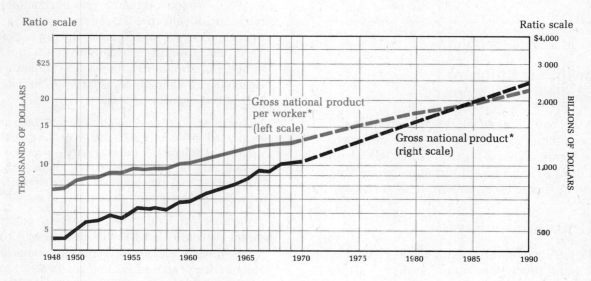

* Dashed lines are projections in 1971 dollars.

Exhibit 4

Educational Attainment and Expenditures on Public
Elementary and Secondary Education

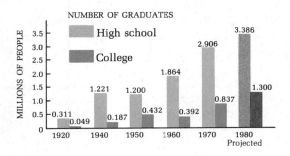

NUMBER OF GRADUATES

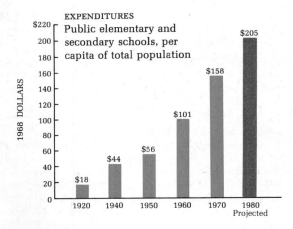

EXPENDITURES

SOURCE: U.S. Department of Commerce; U.S. Department of
Health, Education and Welfare.

The Growth-rate Problem:
How Fast Should We Grow?

Now that we have looked at the background and
history of economic growth, we may turn our attention to the future. What does it mean to talk about
growth rates of 3, 4, 5 percent, or more? Should we
try to set some desirable or target rate of growth?

GROWING AT COMPOUND INTEREST

First of all, we have to understand what is meant by
the term *annual percentage rate of growth*. This expression is based on what is known as *compound
interest*—interest which is computed on a principal
sum and also on all the interest earned by that prin-

cipal sum as of a given date. A convenient table
which conveys this type of information is presented
in Exhibit 5. This table shows the future values of $1
compounded annually at various rates of interest,
and can be employed to study several types of
growth problems.

EXAMPLE 1. If you deposit $1 in a savings account which
pays 5 percent interest compounded annually, how much
will your deposit be worth at the end of 1 year? 2 years?
10 years? 50 years? •

Solution. Looking at the table in the 5 percent column, we find that a deposit of $1 will be worth:
$1.050 at the end of the first year; $1.103 at the end
of the second year; $1.628 at the end of the tenth
year; and $11.467 at the end of the fiftieth year. (For
a deposit of $100, simply move the decimal point
two places to the right; for a deposit of $1,000, three
places to the right, and so on.)

EXAMPLE 2. Real GNP (in 1958 prices) increased from
$323.7 billion in 1948 to $487.7 billion in 1960. What was
the rate of growth at compound interest?

Solution. An increase from $323.7 billion to $487.7
billion is proportional to an increase from $1 to
$1.507:

$$\frac{\$487.7}{\$323.7} = \$1.507$$

Since this increase occurred over 12 years (from 1948
to 1960), we look at the 12-year horizontal line of the
table and locate the closest number to $1.507; then
read the interest-rate figure at the top of that column.
Thus the growth rate was between 3 and 4 percent
annually—apparently about 3.5 percent. (A closer
estimate can be made by interpolation if desired, but
this is not usually necessary.)

EXAMPLE 3. (a) If an economy's real income as measured
by its GNP per capita is $3,000, how long would it take to
double that income if the economy grows at a compound
annual rate of 6 percent? (b) If, in fact, the economy
doubled its real income or GNP per capita in 18 years,
what was its compound annual rate of growth?

Solution. (a) Under the 6 percent column in the
table, we note that $1 will double to $2 within 12
years (i.e., it will exactly double sometime during
the twelfth year, and will be worth $2.012 at the end
of the twelfth year). Hence, $3,000 will double to
$6,000 in the same amount of time. (b) On the 18-
year horizontal line, we find that $1 will double to

Exhibit 5

Growth-rate Table

THE GROWTH OF $1 COMPOUNDED ANNUALLY AT VARIOUS RATES OF INTEREST

End of year	1%	2%	3%	4%	5%	Future value of $1 at 6%	7%	8%	9%	10%	12%	15%
1	1.010	1.020	1.030	1.040	1.050	1.060	1.070	1.080	1.090	1.100	1.120	1.150
2	1.020	1.040	1.061	1.082	1.103	1.124	1.145	1.166	1.188	1.210	1.254	1.322
3	1.030	1.061	1.093	1.125	1.158	1.191	1.225	1.260	1.295	1.331	1.405	1.521
4	1.041	1.082	1.126	1.170	1.216	1.262	1.311	1.360	1.412	1.464	1.574	1.749
5	1.051	1.104	1.159	1.217	1.276	1.338	1.403	1.469	1.539	1.611	1.762	2.011
6	1.062	1.126	1.194	1.265	1.340	1.419	1.501	1.587	1.677	1.772	1.974	2.313
7	1.072	1.149	1.230	1.316	1.407	1.504	1.606	1.714	1.828	1.949	2.211	2.660
8	1.083	1.172	1.267	1.369	1.477	1.594	1.718	1.851	1.993	2.144	2.476	3.059
9	1.094	1.195	1.305	1.423	1.551	1.689	1.838	1.999	2.172	2.358	2.773	3.518
10	1.105	1.219	1.344	1.480	1.628	1.792	1.967	2.159	2.367	2.593	3.106	4.046
11	1.116	1.243	1.384	1.539	1.710	1.898	2.105	2.332	2.580	2.853	3.479	4.652
12	1.127	1.268	1.426	1.601	1.796	2.012	2.252	2.518	2.813	3.138	3.896	5.350
13	1.138	1.294	1.469	1.665	1.886	2.133	2.410	2.720	3.066	3.452	4.363	6.153
14	1.149	1.319	1.513	1.732	1.980	2.261	2.579	2.937	3.342	3.797	4.887	7.076
15	1.161	1.346	1.558	1.801	2.079	2.397	2.759	3.172	3.642	4.177	5.474	8.137
16	1.173	1.373	1.605	1.873	2.183	2.540	2.952	3.426	3.970	4.595	6.130	9.358
17	1.184	1.400	1.653	1.948	2.292	2.693	3.159	3.700	4.328	5.054	6.866	10.761
18	1.196	1.428	1.702	2.026	2.407	2.854	3.380	3.996	4.717	5.560	7.690	12.375
19	1.208	1.457	1.754	2.107	2.527	3.026	3.617	4.316	5.142	6.116	8.613	14.232
20	1.220	1.486	1.806	2.191	2.652	3.206	3.870	4.661	5.604	6.728	9.646	16.367
21	1.232	1.516	1.860	2.279	2.786	3.400	4.141	5.034	6.109	7.400	10.804	18.821
22	1.245	1.546	1.916	2.370	2.925	3.604	4.430	5.437	6.659	8.140	12.100	21.645
23	1.257	1.577	1.974	2.465	3.072	3.820	4.741	5.781	7.258	8.954	13.552	24.891
24	1.270	1.608	2.033	2.563	3.225	4.049	5.072	6.341	7.911	9.850	15.179	28.625
25	1.282	1.641	2.094	2.666	3.386	4.292	5.427	6.848	8.623	10.835	17.000	32.919
26	1.295	1.673	2.157	2.772	3.556	4.549	5.807	7.396	9.399	11.918	19.040	37.857
27	1.308	1.707	2.221	2.883	3.733	4.822	6.214	7.988	10.245	13.110	21.325	43.535
28	1.321	1.741	2.288	2.999	3.920	5.112	6.649	8.627	11.167	14.421	23.884	50.066
29	1.335	1.776	2.357	3.119	4.116	5.418	7.114	9.317	12.172	15.863	26.750	57.575
30	1.348	1.811	2.427	3.243	4.322	5.743	7.612	10.063	13.268	17.449	29.960	66.212
31	1.361	1.848	2.500	3.373	4.538	6.088	8.145	10.868	14.462	19.194	33.555	76.143
32	1.375	1.885	2.575	3.508	4.765	6.453	8.715	11.737	15.763	21.114	37.582	87.565
33	1.391	1.922	2.652	3.648	5.003	6.841	9.325	12.676	17.182	23.225	42.091	100.700
34	1.403	1.961	2.732	3.794	5.253	7.251	9.978	13.690	18.728	25.548	47.142	115.805
35	1.417	2.000	2.814	3.946	5.516	7.686	10.677	14.785	20.414	28.102	52.800	133.176
40	1.489	2.208	3.262	4.801	7.040	10.286	14.974	21.725	31.409	45.259	93.051	267.863
45	1.565	2.438	3.782	5.841	8.985	13.765	21.002	31.920	48.327	72.890	163.988	538.769
50	1.645	2.692	4.384	7.107	11.467	18.420	29.457	46.902	74.358	117.391	289.002	1083.657
55	1.729	2.972	5.082	8.646	14.636	24.650	41.315	68.914	114.408	189.059		
60	1.817	3.281	5.892	10.520	18.679	32.988	57.946	101.257	176.031	304.482		
65	1.909	3.623	6.830	12.799	23.840	44.145	81.273	148.780	270.846	490.371		
70	2.007	4.000	7.918	15.572	30.426	59.076	113.989	218.606	416.730	789.747		
75	2.109	4.416	9.179	18.945	38.833	79.057	159.876	321.205	641.191	1271.895		
80	2.217	4.875	10.641	23.050	49.561	105.796	224.234	471.955	986.552	2048.400		
85	2.330	5.383	12.336	28.044	63.254	141.579	314.500	693.456	1517.948	3298.969		
90	2.449	5.943	14.300	34.119	80.730	189.465	441.103	1018.915	2335.501	5313.023		
95	2.574	6.562	16.578	41.511	103.035	253.546	618.670	1497.121	3593.513	8556.676		
100	2.705	7.245	19.219	50.505	131.501	339.302	867.716	2199.761	5529.089	13780.612		

$2 at an interest rate between 3 and 4 percent as shown at the top of the columns—but at a rate somewhat closer to 4 percent. We can thus conclude that the economy grew at a compound annual rate of about 4 percent—or actually a little less than that if we wish to interpolate for a closer estimate.

THE "RULE OF 72"

The third example above, which involves the general problem of how long it takes for a number to double when it grows at compound interest, is an extremely practical one. Businessmen who borrow money, bankers who lend it, and people who buy bonds or other fixed income-yielding securities are often concerned with this question. For convenience, when a table is not readily available we can employ a quick way of getting good approximate answers to the problem. It may be called the *Rule of 72*:

The *Rule of 72* is a simple growth formula which states: Given the annual rate of compound interest, divide this rate into 72 to obtain the approximate number of years it takes for a quantity to double; conversely, given the number of years it takes for a quantity to double, divide this amount into 72 to obtain the approximate annual rate of compound interest.

EXAMPLE. If an economy's real GNP per capita grows at 6 percent, it will double its real income in 72/6 = 12 years; conversely, if it takes 12 years for an economy to double its real GNP per capita, its growth rate is 72/12 = 6 percent.

The Rule of 72, as well as the principles underlying compound interest, apply to any growing quantity, whether it be the growth of GNP, the growth of money in a savings account, or the growth of a tree.

IS THERE A TARGET RATE OF GROWTH?

Should we set a desired growth rate for the economy —a so-called "target rate" for which to shoot? If so, what should the rate be? The Japanese economy, for example, has gone through periods when its growth rate has been 10 percent or more. At this rate, an economy doubles its GNP in slightly more than seven years.

Consider what a 10 percent growth rate would mean over a period, say, of 30 years. If your income in 1970 was only $5,000 a year—which is approximately what GNP per capita was in the United States in 1970—it would expand to about $88,000 a year during the next 30 years. Can you imagine a per capita GNP of that amount by the year 2000? Even with our present rate of inflation it would be an astounding figure.

In real terms, our long-run growth record has been more like 3 percent rather than 10 percent. At this rate it takes about 24 years for per capita GNP to double. If we want to grow faster than this, we have to decide how much faster, and we have to know the costs that are involved. Keep in mind that an increase in growth from 3 to 4 percent amounts to a $33\frac{1}{3}$ percent increase in the annual rate. Looked at in this way, the difference is considerable. No wonder a country ordinarily finds it extremely difficult to raise its growth rate by an additional percentage point. Some of these difficulties are pointed out in detail below.

The Costs of Economic Growth

What are the costs of increased growth? The answer should be thought of in terms of society's *sacrifices* —the pleasures it must postpone today for greater future satisfactions. From this standpoint, the basic costs of economic growth are five in number: (1) the sacrifice of leisure for employment, (2) the sacrifice of consumption for investment, (3) the sacrifice of the present for the future, (4) the sacrifice of environmental quality for more goods, and (5) the sacrifice of security for progress. Let us see what each of these involves.

LEISURE VERSUS EMPLOYMENT

The rate of economic growth can be raised by using society's resources more fully. If this is done permanently rather than temporarily (for example, by increasing the size of the labor force or the length of the workweek), the result will be a larger economic pie to be divided at any given time.

The cost of this increased growth, however, must be measured in terms of a sacrifice of leisure. What do we mean by leisure? Is it the same as idleness? Emphatically not! Leisure is a matter of choice. Some people may choose to use their leisure by pursuing a hobby; others will prefer "civilized loafing." But in any case the value of leisure can be expressed in terms of (a) the income that can be obtained from alternative work-uses of time and (b) the contribution to the supply of goods and services that some leisure activities produce and which the man of leisure would otherwise have purchased in the market. Examples include the products of woodworking, photography, or needlework. Since these values are never actually recorded in the marketplace, they are omitted from estimates of GNP.

In contrast, idleness is not a matter of choice; it tends to have no uses and to yield no income. Consequently, if we consider leisure as one of the goals of society, or part of the real income for which we work, then who is to say that a 5 percent rate of growth in real GNP is better than a 3 percent rate of growth? Indeed, the latter rate of growth may include more leisure and may in fact be preferable to the former. Therefore, the loss of value of leisure for the sake of more rapid growth must be recognized as one of the costs of growth, even though that cost can at best be only roughly estimated rather than precisely measured.

CONSUMPTION VERSUS INVESTMENT

If an economy cannot use its resources more fully, can it still increase its output per capita or rate of growth? It probably can, provided it is able to reduce its consumption in the present so as to achieve higher investment that will increase production in the future. The consumption that is forgone (or in fact postponed) becomes the measure of society's real cost of growth. It is somewhat easier to determine than the cost of leisure forgone, because the prices of consumer goods and services can be obtained from the market, whereas the price of leisure cannot be estimated as readily.

The amount of investment is not the only thing that matters in increasing a nation's production; the type of investment is also important. This point is significant because in most theoretical discussions it is convenient to assume a rigid relationship between investment in capital and the resulting rate of output or economic growth. This relationship is typically expressed in terms of the familiar capital-output ratio. Thus if the ratio equals 3, an investment of $300 should increase the output rate per period by $100. In reality, however, the relationship between investment and economic growth (i.e., the productivity of investment) is not rigid, for several reasons:

1. Investment is not restricted to the production of tangible assets such as plant and equipment; it also includes expenditures on the "production" of in-tangible assets such as human resources and new skills, and on research and development. The returns to society of investment in intangibles are variable and are extremely difficult to estimate with close accuracy.

2. It is not always sufficient to think in terms of capital-output ratios. Some kinds of investment, such as investment in education, yield cultural and social benefits to a nation which are not reflected by its measures of GNP.

3. Certain types of investment may contribute to GNP, but do not enhance society's material welfare if the resulting output is not wanted by consumers. For example, investment that results in the creation of large agricultural surpluses for which there are no markets at existing prices detracts from society's welfare and even wastes resources that might better be used in other ways.

For these reasons, the nature and types of investment that an economy undertakes are at least as important as the amount of its investment as far as the costs to society are concerned.

PRESENT COSTS VERSUS FUTURE BENEFITS

The greater the rate of growth, the greater the sacrifice or postponement that must be made in leisure, in consumption, or in both. This does not necessarily mean, however, that any gain in economic growth (defined as an increase in real output per capita) is better than none. Future income or future consumption is never worth as much as present income or present consumption. Therefore, the value or cost of the sacrifices that must be made today and tomorrow in order to achieve a given rate of growth must be compared with the value of the benefits that will be received in the future.

In comparing these costs and benefits, three basic questions must be answered. First, what will be the increment in benefits as compared with the increment in costs? That is, how much will the economy's future income and consumption increase as a result of present and future sacrifices of consumption and leisure? Second, how long will it take before the increased benefits are realized? Third, is the increment in benefits and the time required to receive them worth the sacrifice? In other words, since present income and present consumption are worth more than the same amount of future income and future consumption, how does the *present value* of the future benefits compare with the *present value* of the costs?

The third question provides a guide for decision making and policy formulation. It asks us to express the future values of costs and benefits in equivalent terms of *today's* dollars, so that a correct comparison can be made in the present between the costs and benefits involved. (In more technical language, this entails a process in financial mathematics known as "discounting.")

ENVIRONMENTAL QUALITY VERSUS MORE GOODS

Ill fares the land, to hast'ning ill a prey,
Where wealth accumulates, and men decay.
Oliver Goldsmith

Writers, poets, and artists have long warned against the headlong pursuit of riches. But their voices were seldom heeded until as recently as the 1960s. Since then, it has become uncomfortably clear that they may have been right all along.

In America, the richest nation in the world, wealth continuously accumulates while men, the environment, the cities, and the quality of life itself decay. Much of this decay must be counted as a cost of growth, even though precise measurement is difficult, if not impossible.

Does this mean that economic growth is necessarily bad? Not at all. But it does mean that the pursuit of growth for its own sake is bad. Indeed, the thought of a nation with a per capita gross income of $88,000—as envisioned earlier—is horrifying, if the $88,000 is to be made and spent as it would be today.

The result would inevitably be larger traffic jams, sprawling airports, air and water pollution at lethal levels, lakes, rivers, and yacht marinas congested with pleasure craft—in short, a nation of rich people living in extreme discomfort and almost certainly racked by associated mental ailments.

Clearly, the composition of GNP may be even more important than its rate of growth. Hence a primary task for a free society is to determine what that composition should be. (In an authoritarian society, the decision would be made by a central agency.) This and related problems pertaining to environmental quality are as much a part of ecology as of economics. In view of the great significance today of ecological issues, we shall devote the following chapter to an analysis of their economic implications.

SECURITY VERSUS PROGRESS

The costs of growth described above are applicable to all types of economic systems. But in a capitalistic system there is still another cost. It takes such forms as fluctuations in economic activity, frictional and technological unemployment, and obsolescence of capital and skills. This is because economic growth tends to occur in spurts rather than as a smooth and continuous process. As a result, the eminent economist, Joseph Schumpeter (1853–1950), was led to conclude that a capitalistic economy by its very nature grows by replacing old methods of production, old sources of supply, and old skills and resources with new ones; to use his famous phrase, it grows by engaging in a continual *"process of creative destruction."*

The fundamental message in the above paragraph is that economic growth in a capitalistic economy entails a clash between security and progress. The basic question is whether this clash is really necessary—that is, whether some economic insecurity is inevitable in a dynamic economy, or whether we must turn to some form of command economy in order to achieve maximum security (and probable loss of some personal freedoms). As with most issues in economics, the approach to a solution is a matter of degree, a problem of achieving what society regards as a desirable "tradeoff" between the two extremes.

CONCLUSION: INCREASED COSTS VERSUS INCREASED BENEFITS

It is sometimes said that the best things in life are free, but economic growth certainly is not one of them. Costs must be paid and sacrifices must be made in order to sustain any rate of growth. It is not correct to assume, therefore, that the more we grow or the faster we grow, the better off we are. Instead, alternatives must be weighed:

It is necessary to balance the corresponding costs and benefits of alternative growth rates. In general, *the optimum rate of growth is determined where the increased costs of more growth are just offset by the increased benefits.* (It is assumed that these increased costs and benefits are expressed in terms of their present values.) The optimum rate may be "high" or "low," depending upon the value that society places on the advantages of growth.

Thus if an economy is growing, say, at 3 percent, it should compare the incremental or "marginal" costs and benefits involved if it wishes to increase its growth rate to 4 or 5 percent. Clearly, the optimum rate of growth need not be the maximum rate. An economy may increase its growth rate by putting its population on an austerity level of living and channeling all savings thus obtained into investment. This, in varying degrees, is a policy that has been followed at one time or another by the Soviet Union, China, and some other countries.

Barriers to Economic Growth

In any society there are obstacles to economic growth. These obstacles differ according to whether the particular society is "traditional" or "advanced."

In traditional societies, the obstacles to growth are primarily cultural, consisting of social and religious attitudes toward business practices, money and interest, new productive techniques, and new institutions. In such societies, the barriers to growth are mainly the result of conflicts of values rather than conflicts of interest.

In advanced societies such as our own the obstacles to growth are chiefly economic. They take such forms as (1) labor immobility, (2) capital immobility, and (3) limitations on the proportion of resources that can be committed to capital goods production. As we examine these barriers more closely, we find that they are primarily the result of conflicts of interest rather than conflicts of values.

LABOR IMMOBILITY

We have learned in a number of places in this book that labor immobility has been an important factor contributing to depressed conditions in certain industries and regions. Two typical examples are agriculture and sawmilling in several low-income areas of the South. The fundamental causes of labor immobility are ignorance of alternative employment opportunities and the costs of movement, which include such noneconomic factors as families' reluctance to leave their home towns. Although these obstacles to growth will never be entirely eliminated, their reduction helps significantly to clear the path for sustained economic development.

Ignorance of employment opportunities has decreased substantially over the past several decades.

This has been accomplished through the development of free government employment services, improved communication and information facilities pertaining to job openings—such as newspaper classified ads, trade publications, and school placement services—and a shift of population from rural to urban areas where job opportunities and the knowledge of such opportunities are more readily available.

Reductions in the cost of movement, on the other hand, are more difficult to achieve. The cost of moving from one city to another, for example, has been greatly reduced over the years, at least in relation to income. But this is only one aspect of the problem. The cost of transferring from one occupation to another, or even from one job to another, may involve a temporary decline in income while new skills are being acquired, and may also involve a permanent loss of pension rights, seniority privileges, job security, and other fringe benefits. In addition, there may be costs of entry into new jobs in the form of high license fees or union initiation fees, long periods of apprenticeship at low pay, or restrictions on the number of people admitted to an occupation.

To some extent, the costs of movement have been absorbed by federal and state governments through the provision of training programs, unemployment benefits, and the like, thereby reducing the costs of labor mobility as an obstacle to growth. But care must be taken not to shift too much of the cost from workers to the government, for this could result in excessive labor mobility. The result might be a waste of resources as reflected in high transfer costs resulting from frequent retraining, breaking into new jobs, and so on. These are activities which can be undertaken more productively if the workers who benefit are made to bear some of the costs.

CAPITAL IMMOBILITY

The factors that make for immobility of capital including money and capital goods are fundamentally the same as those that cause immobility of labor—namely, ignorance and the costs of movement.

Ignorance, where capital immobility is involved, may consist of inadequate information in such areas as new markets, changes in technology, or new methods of production, distribution, and finance. In general, the significance of ignorance as a barrier to capital movement has been reduced in recent decades as a result of the growing amount of diversified information and services provided by both government and private agencies such as the Departments of Agriculture and Commerce, trade associations, business publishing houses, and consulting firms. On the other hand, it is readily apparent that specialized plants and equipment are not easily adaptable to alternative uses (which is one type of capital immobility), as a result of which there are significant cost barriers to the movement of capital. But cost barriers can also arise in less obvious ways, as when government policies "protect" and thereby immobilize capital. Examples of such policies are discriminatory taxes, tariffs, quotas, subsidies, and price supports, which are given to particular industries and sectors of the economy in order to shelter them from the adverse effects they would experience under unrestricted competition.

The reduced mobility of capital which results from such policies can be overcome—but only at a price. The problem is whether society, and its elected representatives in Washington, can be made sufficiently aware of the price to decide whether it is worth paying.

LIMITATIONS ON THE PROPORTION OF RESOURCES THAT CAN BE COMMITTED TO CAPITAL GOODS PRODUCTION

The U.S. economy is already so highly capitalized that a substantial share of present resources must be devoted merely to replacing existing plant and equipment as it wears out. A fundamental problem, therefore, is to find ways of increasing the proportion of resources that can be applied to the production of capital goods, over and above the proportion needed to keep the existing stock of capital intact.

The problem is further compounded by the fact that our "standard" or *goal* of living seems to increase about as fast as our actual level of living so that the more we have, the more we want. As a result, the proportion of income saved does not appear to be rising over the long run, and may even be declining.

REMARK. Be careful to observe that this statement refers to a *long-run period* during which all factors in addition to income which may affect consumption and saving are allowed to vary. Hence it does not contradict the concept of the "consumption function," which is a principle that applies only at a *given* time when all factors other than income which may affect consumption and saving are assumed to remain constant.

Is the overall percentage of income saved likely to decline in the future? There is good reason to believe that it will. Reduced savings are encouraged by such factors as: (a) the increasing availability of easy credit and the growth in real assets per capita; (b) the expanding social welfare activities of government in providing for such contingencies as unemployment and old age; and (c) the possible shift in the economic attitudes of society toward a more high-consumption, "live-it-up" philosophy. In addition, there is probably a greater chance that income and inheritance tax rates will be raised in future years rather than lowered. If this happens, it will tend to make the distribution of income less unequal, and thereby reduce still further the proportion that is saved.

For all of these reasons:

The savings ratio of the economy—the average propensity to save—will probably decline gradually over the years. This means that corporate and government saving and investment will have to become increasingly important, as is already the trend, if a steady rate of economic growth is to be sustained.

Problems of Taxation, Inflation, and Economic Growth

In previous chapters dealing with fiscal and monetary policies we talked about the effects of taxation and inflation on economic growth. A few additional comments are appropriate at this time. In general terms, the questions we want to answer are: What role might government tax policies play in contributing to the rate of economic growth? How does inflation, which we have seen is closely tied to the problems of full employment and economic growth, fit into the picture?

TAXATION AND THE INVESTMENT DECISION

We have learned that increases in investment bring about increases in productivity which help to sustain economic growth. We have also learned from macroeconomic theory that the *expectation of profit* is the most important factor motivating businessmen to invest. This means that the volume of investment can be increased by improving the expectation of profit, or by reducing the risk of loss, or both. Taxes can be a critical factor in this respect.

For instance, when the executives of a corporation contemplate making *any* investment, they consider, among other things, three important variables:

1. The corporation income tax rate

2. The minimum accepted rate of return on the investment after taxes

3. The expected rate of return on the investment before taxes

The first of these factors is written into law by Congress and is therefore known. The second is predetermined in each firm as a matter of top-level corporate financial policy; it is based on the different returns and risks that are available to a firm from its alternative investment opportunities. (If you should ever take a course in business or corporate finance, you will find that determining the minimum acceptable rate is the single most critical economic task facing the top management of a corporation.) The third factor, which the firm compares with other investment alternatives before deciding on the one it wants, is determined directly from the previous two by the simple formula:

Expected rate of return before taxes

$$= \frac{\text{minimum accepted rate of return after taxes}}{1 - \text{tax rate}}$$

Thus if the management of a corporation believes that a minimum rate of return of 15 percent after taxes is necessary in order to persuade it to invest in a project (such as a machine or a plant), and if the corporation income tax rate is 48 percent, the denominator in the above formula will be $1 - 0.48 = 0.52$. Hence the expected rate of return before taxes must be *at least* $0.15/0.52 = 28.8$ percent in order for the investment to be considered. On the other hand, if the tax rate were, say, 55 percent, the expected rate of return before taxes would have to be at least $0.15/0.45 = 33.3$ percent in order for the investment to be eligible for consideration. Evidently, the higher the tax rate, the higher will be the expected rate of return before taxes, as is apparent from the above formula.

NOTE: The formula should not be taken as a rigid guide, since factors besides the tax rate influence investment and expected returns. It is merely intended to convey some basic tendencies within reasonable tax ranges.

TAX IMPLICATIONS

We learned in macroeconomic theory that at a given level of risk there are fewer investment opportunities available at higher rates of return than at lower ones. Therefore, it follows from the above formula that the volume of investment in plant and equipment will be influenced by the steepness of the corporation income tax in the following way:

Other things being equal, higher corporation income tax rates tend to raise the minimum required rate of return before taxes, thereby closing out many investment opportunities and reducing the total volume of investment; conversely, lower corporation income tax rates tend to reduce the minimum required rate of return before taxes, thereby opening up many investment opportunities and increasing the total volume of investment.

Does this mean that corporation income taxes should be abolished? The answer is no, for considerations other than growth must be taken into account. What it does mean, however, is that in order to finance a given level of government expenditures, alternative methods of raising revenue should be considered. Other forms of taxes such as higher sales taxes or higher personal income taxes may be less injurious to investment and economic growth than the corporation income tax.

How much less injurious? The answer is not yet known. But we do know that the *marginal* tax rate on personal income plays a significant role. Thus if the marginal tax rate—that is, the tax paid on an additional dollar of income—is high, the rate of economic growth may be retarded. Why? Because, other things being equal, high marginal tax rates tend to reduce the amount of personal savings and the incentive to invest among people in the higher income brackets. To some extent, however, this tendency may be offset by the capital-gains provisions in our income tax laws, which permit long-term profits on investment to be taxed at special lower rates.

Income Taxes or Sales Taxes?

The possibility that steep income tax rates may stifle economic growth has prompted many economists to advocate higher sales taxes as a partial substitute for higher income taxes. Most foreign governments, in fact, obtain the bulk of their revenues from sales taxes, as contrasted with the United States, which derives most of its revenues from taxes on income and wealth. Various tax studies indicate that a sales tax which exempts food and medicine is approximately proportional—taking about the same share from all income groups. It may be, therefore, that a partial reduction in income taxes and an increase in sales taxes with selected exemptions would perhaps be a desirable step to take in seeking to sustain a target of economic growth.

INFLATION AND FORCED SAVING

The relation between inflation and economic growth has been the subject of much discussion. Too rapid a rate of inflation discourages saving and thereby sets a limit on the volume of investment. This, in turn, can inhibit economic growth.

It has long been known that one way in which an economy can finance its investment in order to encourage economic growth is by *forced saving*—a situation in which consumers are prevented from spending part of their income. Forced saving may take place in different situations, as when (a) prices rise faster than money wages, causing a decrease in real consumption and hence an increase in real (forced) saving; (b) a corporation plows back some or all of its profit for investment instead of distributing it as dividend income to stockholders, thereby keeping stockholders from spending part of this income on consumption; and (c) a government taxes its citizens and uses the funds for investment, thus preventing the public from utilizing a portion of its income for the purchase of consumer goods.

In the United States, all three forms of forced saving, especially the second, have helped to finance economic growth. Other nations, by contrast, have leaned more toward the first or the third. For example, most Latin American countries have depended heavily on the printing press to run off the money they need to pay for investment. The outcome has been prolonged and severe inflation, resulting in the first of the above forms of forced saving. At the other extreme, Russia and China have placed heavy reliance on taxation to accumulate the funds needed for capital formation, thus placing greater dependence on the third form of forced saving.

CONCLUSION: "BALANCED" GROWTH

There is general agreement that a certain amount of inflation is probably inevitable in a dynamic economy such as ours, given its institutions and rigidities, its tendency to generate obsolescence, and its citizens' desire to raise their general standard of living at a rate at least as fast as the system's productive capacity. The problem, of course, is to hold back in-

flation to a rate that is compatible with sound economic growth. Too much inflation will impede economic growth, while excessive unsound growth will tend to promote inflation.

Assuming, therefore, that we must live with inflation—and anyone who is naive enough to deny this is simply ignoring the facts of history—is there some rate of inflation that can be regarded as "proper"? From what we have learned in previous chapters, an average annual rate not exceeding 2 percent would be compatible with the maintenance of full employment and would permit our economy to maintain a long-run real growth trend of 3 to 4 percent a year. If we allow inflation to proceed for a while at much higher rates than this, we run the risk of distorting the internal structure of the economy—that is, the relationships among firms, industries, and resources within the system. The result is that the economy achieves a type of unbalanced or disproportional growth—analogous, for example, to a biological situation in which a man's nose or ears grow too fast or too slow in relation to each other and to the rest of his head. What we seek, of course, is a healthy or "balanced" form of growth.

SUMMARY OF IMPORTANT IDEAS

1. For the United States, the long-run trend of total real GNP has been upward at an average annual rate of over 3 percent, while the growth trend of real GNP per capita has averaged a little less than 2 percent annually. In general, the theory of economic growth, with the inclusion of technological advance, tends to be supported by the available evidence for the United States and for other advanced Western nations.

2. International comparisons of long-term growth rates show that the United States has grown more slowly than a number of other advanced nations. Since 1929, the expansion of qualitative factors such as education and technology has been relatively more important in influencing U.S. economic growth than the increase in such quantitative factors as the amount of labor and capital; prior to 1929, the reverse was true.

3. "Growth" is a technical notion, which for measurement purposes involves the concept of compound interest. Compound interest tables can be used to estimate growth, and a simple growth formula like the "Rule of 72" can be employed when tables are not readily available.

4. The real costs of economic growth are expressed in terms of the sacrifices which society must bear in order to achieve growth. These include such sacrifices as leisure for employment, consumption for investment, present for the future, environmental quality for more goods, and to some extent, security for progress. The optimum rate of growth equates the increased costs of more growth with the increased benefits.

5. The chief barriers to economic growth in advanced societies are conflicts of interest rather than conflicts of values. They consist of labor immobility, capital immobility, and limitations on the proportion of resources that can be committed to capital goods production.

6. In addition to the foregoing challenges to economic growth, there are problems of taxation and inflation. Increases in corporation income taxes tend to reduce the number of investment opportunities, while decreases in taxes tend to expand them. This and other considerations suggest that a partial substitution of increased sales taxes for increased income taxes, with special exemptions for food and medicine, would be more conducive to economic growth. As for inflation, it appears that an average annual rate of 2 percent or less would be compatible with full employment and with a sustained "balanced" real growth of 3 to 4 percent annually.

FOR DISCUSSION

1. *Terms and concepts to review:*

compound interest	"process of creative
"Rule of 72"	destruction"
	forced saving

2. Outline briefly the major features of U.S. economic growth from the pre-Civil War period to the present.

3. From the standpoint of economic growth, is it better for our economy to invest relatively more of its resources in machines and factories, or should it concentrate instead on education and training? What are the "costs" of choosing either one? Discuss.

4. Can you develop a rule, analogous to the "Rule of 72," which tells you how long it takes for an investment to increase by 50 percent? (SUGGESTION: Use the growth-rate table in this chapter as a guide, and some trial-and-error experiments.) Using your newly derived "rule," how much better off will your children (i.e., the next generation) be if we merely grow at 2 percent? In view of your answer, do you think that an increase in growth is worth the extra costs and sacrifices that must be incurred to attain it?

5. Evaluate the statement: "The more we grow or the faster we grow, the better off we are."

6. Would industrial progress, or economic development in general, be faster or slower in a perfectly certain, as compared with an uncertain, economy? (NOTE: A perfectly certain economy is one in which the nature and time of occurrence of all future events can be predicted with certainty.) Of what significance is your answer to a welfare-oriented economy which seeks to eliminate the risks of unemployment, bankruptcy, etc.?

7. Evaluate the following suggestions that have been made by various people:

(a) "Labor mobility, and therefore economic growth, would be increased if the government simply absorbed all costs of moving, retraining, and the like."

(b) "The government should 'protect' important industries through tariffs, subsidies, price supports, etc., in order to encourage their development to the point where they can fend for themselves. This sort of policy would also encourage general economic growth."

8. "The government should reduce income taxes, thereby leaving more savings available for investment and economic growth." If the government followed this suggestion, how would it get the revenues it needs to finance its expenditures?

CHAPTER 20

Ecology and the Economics of Pollution

CHAPTER PREVIEW

What is ecology? How does it relate to economics?

How can we distinguish between the economic fallacies and realities of pollution?

Are there economic principles that can serve as guidelines for formulating policies pertaining to pollution control?

The Walrus and the Carpenter
Were walking close at hand;
They wept like anything to see
Such quantities of sand:
"If this were only cleared away,"
They said, "it would be grand!"

"If seven maids with seven mops
Swept it for half a year,
Do you suppose," the Walrus said,
"That they could get it clear?"
"I doubt it," said the Carpenter,
And shed a bitter tear.

Lewis Carroll, *Through the Looking Glass* (1872)

If the Carpenter were alive today, he would probably shed much more than a bitter tear. For while Americans are enjoying the benefits of the world's highest gross national product, their environment is seriously threatened by GNP's mirror image: gross national pollution. As the nation's production of goods has soared, so have dangerous doses of chemicals, garbage, sewage, fumes, and noise. Thus for each American, environmental decay is now a personal experience: the water he drinks may be bitter with impurities, the scenes he views may be obscured by haze, the air he breathes may be acrid with automobile exhaust and industrial smoke, and the piercing sounds he hears from trucks, jackhammers, and jets may cause permanent damage to his ears. This, in broad scope, is the problem of pollution. And, since it is an environmental problem, it involves ecological as well as economic considerations.

Economics and Ecology

The words "ecology" and "economics" stem from the same Greek root—*oikos*, meaning "house." Despite this common origin, these sciences had little contact with one another until the late 1960s. At that time, with concern mounting over problems of environmental quality, ecologists and economists began to recognize that they might have much to learn from one another, and that a new science of "econology" might someday be forged from a blending of their separate disciplines. To appreciate the implications of these possibilities, two fundamental questions must be explored: What is ecology? What basic similarities are there between ecology and economics?

WHAT IS ECOLOGY?

Ecology is a study of the relationships or interdependencies between living organisms and their environment, both at a micro and macro level, in order to see how they function together in their so-called "ecosystems." Ecology is thus a systems approach to nature—a science which attempts to describe and analyze the "web of life." Hence, according to its Greek root, ecology deals with the "household of nature," while economics deals with the "household of man."

An ecosystem, like any other system, is a collection of related elements. The collection may be small—a pond and the life within it; or large—the planet Earth and the life upon it. Every ecosystem, whether large or small, has four major elements, as shown in Exhibit 1:

1. *Nonliving or inorganic matter.* Sunlight, carbon dioxide, water, and minerals used by green plants for their growth

2. *Producer organisms.* Green plants, ranging from microscopic size through shrubs and trees, which convert sunlight, oxygen, water, and minerals into carbohydrates or food used by themselves and other organisms in the ecosystem

3. *Consumer organisms.* Primary consumers, such as cows, pigs, and sheep that feed upon the plant producers, and secondary consumers, such as man, the lion, the tiger, and the wolf that feed upon the primary consumers

4. *Decomposer organisms.* Simple nongreen organisms such as bacteria and fungi that complete the

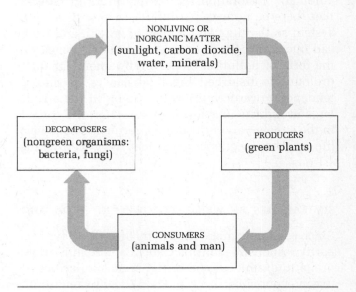

Exhibit 1

Elements of an Ecosystem: The Web of Life

circle of the ecosystem by breaking down the dead producers and consumers and returning their chemical compounds to the ecosystem for reuse by the producer plants

An ecosystem is governed by distinct laws of growth and decay; these laws operate simultaneously, tending to move the system toward a state of balance or equilibrium. For example, there is a law of "adaptation" which permits each species to find its own place in the particular ecosystem that will provide it with the food, water, and shelter it needs for survival. There is a law of "balance" between predator and prey which enables the former to keep a hold on the population of the latter. Hence the spider that devours the fly, or the cheetah that preys upon the gazelle, is performing a needed function. Still another law is the law of "diversity" which permits many different species to live in an ecosystem, thereby reducing the chance of any particular species proliferating and dominating the community. In this sense, even the rarest species is part of nature's grand design for a stable and viable ecosystem.

The problem is that man, as a result of careless efforts to raise his material level of living, has violated the laws of ecology—thereby endangering nature as well as himself. Ecologists have observed, for example, that many nonhuman species such as certain fish or rodent populations have remarkable resiliencies; as much as 50 percent or more of their populations in a particular ecosystem may be destroyed by disease or disaster, yet they will restore their original numbers within a year or two. But the automatic restoration of this equilibrium requires that there be no external interference with the ecosystem so that its natural laws of growth and decay can operate freely. It is man-made interference—in the form of pollution of the environment—that has profoundly disturbed the total ecosystem and its tendency toward equilibrium. Smog in the air, detergents, oil, and chemicals in the water, and garbage in the streets—all of these are altering the balance of life, with consequences that may very well be disastrous.

SIMILARITIES BETWEEN ECOLOGY AND ECONOMICS

Since economic motivations and attitudes have been partly responsible for this state of affairs, it is appropriate to examine some of the basic similarities between economics and ecology. We may then be able to recognize concepts and relationships which blend economic and ecological principles for the purpose of solving environmental problems.

At least five basic similarities may be identified.

Populations

Both ecology and economics are concerned with the study of "populations." In ecology the populations are classified by species, that is, groups of organisms which have certain common characteristics or qualities that distinguish them as a group from all other organisms. In economics the populations may be living, nonliving, or social, and they may also be classified by species. For example, economic species of living populations include consumers, workers, and businessmen; economic species of nonliving populations consist of commodities such as automobiles, machine tools, and refrigerators; economic species of social populations include households, steel firms, and labor unions. Each of these economic species, like populations in ecology, is born, grows, and often dies. It can therefore be said that commodities, firms, and even governments (which may be viewed as an economic species of social populations along with households, businesses, farms, etc.) are subject to their own laws of growth, survival, and decay according to the particular economic forces and environmental conditions that exist within the system.

Equilibrium

A second important feature which ecology and economics have in common is the tendency to move toward equilibrium. In ecology, as we have seen, the ecosystem will respond to its own natural laws to bring about a state of general balance between its four sets of elements: nonliving matter, producer plants, animal consumers, and decomposers. This requires that the birth and death rates of all species in the system be equated. In economics, the economic system is also conceived as having its own birth rates and death rates—the former being represented, for example, by the rate of production of commodities, and the latter by the rate of consumption of commodities. As we learned in earlier chapters, the stock of commodities in the economy (like the water in a bathtub) may be in equilibrium at any level, but the level itself will rise or fall according to the relative rates of production and consumption (or the rates of inflow and outflow) in the system as a whole.

Exchange

A third basic similarity between ecology and economics is the existence of a system of exchange. In ecology, exchange takes place between the four sectors that comprise the ecosystem. For example, the nonliving sector gives up sunlight, water, carbon dioxide, organic compounds, and other nutrients to the producer sector, which in turn gives up carbohydrates to the consumer sector, and so on. Eventually the circle of exchange is completed within the ecosystem as a whole. In economics, similar and perhaps more complex circles of exchange occur. Thus we find that exchange takes place between economic organisms such as consumers and producers, between workers and employers, and between sectors of the economy such as households, businesses, and government.

Development

A fourth feature that is common to ecology and economics is development. Neither an ecosystem nor an economic system ordinarily remains at the same level or stage of development. In ecology, the ecological process itself may bring about long-run growth or decline. Thus a lake may, through a gradual process of change among its four ecological sectors, eventually turn into a desert, a swamp, a prairie, or a forest. In economics, internal and external processes are at work which also make for changes in development. An economic system, for example, may experience growth or decline, depending on relative changes in its population, capital, technology, knowledge, and other fundamental variables.

Policy

A fifth similarity between ecology and economics concerns the role of man as an agent of change in the establishment of policy. In order to achieve particular objectives, man adopts policies which, sometimes intentionally and sometimes unintentionally, change the natural processes of the ecosystem. A farmer, for example, applies seed, chemicals, machines, and human effort to his land in order to produce marketable commodities like corn and hogs. If the farmer left the land alone, the ecosystem would produce its own natural but unmarketable products consisting of prairie grass, trees, and gophers. In economics, as in other social sciences, man establishes policies in the form of customs and laws for the purpose of adjusting the economic or social system in which he lives to his own values and ideals.

NEEDED: AN ECOLOGICAL OUTLOOK

Men in general, and economists in particular, have traditionally assumed that the reservoirs of land, air, and water provided by nature are infinite, that they can be drawn upon indefinitely, and that they can be polluted with impunity. This means, in effect, that the economy has been viewed as a closed system, drawing from nature the inputs it needs and returning to it the effluent wastes of its expanding output. This attitude has been less pronounced in the case of land, where soil conservation policies have existed for decades in many countries, but it is clearly noticeable where timberlands have been stripped and where soil mining has been practiced.

In contrast, ecology looks upon the earth—and perhaps even the universe—as a total ecosystem of which man's activities are only a small part. From this viewpoint the resources of nature are not infinite. Indeed, it may be possible for man, through imprudent actions, to deplete and to change the composition of these resources in a manner that can prove fatal. With the growth of population, the likelihood of this happening becomes greater.

Clearly, therefore, there is a great need for serious thinking about the relationships between economics and ecology. For unless we can derive unifying principles from these disciplines, and unless we can adopt an ecological outlook which views society as a great interacting network of coexisting populations, many of our social and economic policies will be doomed to failure.

Environmental Destruction: Fallacies and Realities

Any discussion of economics and ecology must come to grips with the very real problems of pollution. Critics and social reformers have had much to say on this subject. As a result, there has emerged a widespread belief that pollution can be attributed to one or more of three fundamental causes: (1) society's preoccupation with economic growth, (2) the trend toward overpopulation, and (3) too much private relative to public spending. All three explanations contain important elements of truth.

"GROWTHMANIA"

The penultimate Western man, stalled in the ultimate traffic jam and slowly succumbing to carbon monoxide, will not be cheered to hear from the last survivor that the gross national product went up by a record amount.
John K. Galbraith

As the carpet of increased choice is being unrolled before us by the foot, it is simultaneously being rolled up behind us by the yard.

E. J. Mishan

Those who attribute environmental defilement to economic growth contend that there is a direct relationship between GNP and the level of pollution: as the GNP increases, so does pollution, and both of them grow at compound (although not necessarily equal) rates. This has led certain critics of our society to contend that we should go back to a simpler life in which there is less concern with economic growth. Some have even argued that we should adopt measures which will cut our rate of economic growth from approximately 4 percent to about 1 or 2 percent—or perhaps even to zero—and that we should focus attention on improving the material well-being of society not by expanding total output but by redistributing output in a more equitable manner.

These critics, like Don Quixote, are seeking the impossible dream. The rising standard of living which Americans have experienced since the nineteenth century has been due to gains in productivity resulting from improved technology, better methods of management, and the development of a more skilled labor force. It is possible that further improvements would be realized through income redistribution, but it is folly to assume that this could be employed as a main solution. Even if as much as one-fourth of the money income received by the top 20 percent of America's families was distributed equally to the remaining 80 percent, it would increase the incomes of the latter by less than $2,000 each.

It appears, therefore, that we must look to increases in productivity as the chief means of fulfilling society's economic desires. This is especially true as long as the population continues to grow. Further, there is every indication that the great majority of people want more material things rather than fewer. Hence a return to the simpler life of the carriage and the spinning wheel would, *in a free society,* be impossible if not undesirable: it would not only be contrary to what most people want, it would also be a return to a life in which a much larger proportion of the population was poor. (On the other hand, a low or zero growth rate might stimulate significant debate and action with respect to income distribution—a sorely neglected topic in economics.)

In addition, it is most unlikely that any advanced economic system would eliminate economic growth entirely. This is as true in communistic and socialistic systems as in capitalistic ones. As long as resources are scarce, they must be used efficiently, and managers will seek to improve efficiency by introducing new and better methods of production. This can only result in greater productivity and a rising standard of living. It is no accident that the association between economic growth and pollution is as pronounced in Russia, for example, as in the United States. The desire for improved efficiency and for material advancement is not limited to particular political ideologies. (See Box 1.)

The "Iron Law" of Compound Interest

If the level of pollution is a consequence of economic growth, its rate of increase is a direct outcome of the law of compound interest. Pollution, to be sure, is not a new phenomenon; it existed in medieval and in ancient Europe. What is new, however, is its recognition as a critical problem of modern societies.

It was not until the late 1960s that the outcry against pollution reached widespread proportions. For a decade or so before then, concerned citizens had voiced occasional warnings, but these were looked on as hardly more than admonitions.

Why had pollution been such a minor consideration? Because, relatively speaking, it was of minor importance. In 1950 our GNP in constant dollars stood at $355 billion; corresponding to this was an inestimable but apparently tolerable level of smog, tin cans, and bottles. By 1968 our GNP practically doubled to $708 billion, which amounts to an average annual compound rate of growth of almost 4 percent. Associated with this larger GNP was a correspondingly higher level of pollution—one which also grew at some compound rate—although the exact percentage is impossible to determine.

The frightening thing is this:

If our GNP continues to expand at a rate of 4 percent compounded annually, it will double in 18 years. If the level of pollution should grow at the same rate, we will then be inundated with twice as much rubbish and refuse as we are at present; and even if the level should rise at only half that rate—at 2 percent rather than 4 percent—we would be 43 percent worse off in 18 years than we are now.

The Effluence of Affluence

There is no doubt that pollution is due in part to a rising GNP. Does this mean there is no escape from the inexorable law of growth at compound interest, and that Americans as well as other advanced societies are doomed to drown in the effluence of their affluence? At first glance it may seem so. But closer analysis indicates that to attack pollution in terms of this "iron law" is to wage a major part of the war on the wrong battlefield.

By focusing attention on economic growth, we are overlooking a critical consideration: *One of the fundamental causes of pollution is that society has made it profitable to pollute.* By not understanding that there is a "cost" of contaminating land, air, and water, governments at all levels (through market mechanisms) have failed to assess appropriate prices for the use of these natural resources, and hence have encouraged the development of industries whose production processes use relatively large

Pollution: Is There Less Under Socialism?

Protesters against environmental havoc disrupted scores of corporate annual meetings as the decade of the 1970s started. Many of them argued that pollution is an integral part of the capitalist system, because its control adds to cost, but not to value, and is therefore unprofitable. Some of the protesters concluded that the only cure for pollution was a change in the system itself. Oscar Lange, a Polish economist, added weight to their argument by asserting that socialism is environmentally superior to capitalism because it encompasses social values and costs.

Certainly, the command economies of eastern Europe have the power to eliminate pollution. But do they have the will? It seems they do not. Pollution became a big, emotional issue in the Soviet Union at about the time it became a popular cause in the United States and other capitalist nations. Soviet newspapers carried reports of wildlife being destroyed by the thoughtless use of pesticides and insecticides; of smog blanketing industrial cities; and of other environmental ailments familiar in the West. At the turn of the decade the Soviet government passed legislation designed to reduce pollution—and was promptly accused by some critics of not doing enough (their criticism was indirect and took the form of more prominent display of stories about pollution problems).

MASSIVE LURCHES
Dr. Marshall I. Goldman, an economist at Harvard University's Russian Research Center, believes that communism's record is no better than capitalism's when it comes to controlling pollution. The Soviet economy "often lurches suddenly and massively into new and sometimes unexpected directions," without regard for environmental effects, he writes. The labor theory of value, which teaches that all value derives from the labor used to produce a good, until recently encouraged Soviet economists to regard natural resources as "free goods." Dr. Goldman concludes: "The Russians have been no more successful than the rest of us in making explicit the social costs arising from an enterprise's activities and including them in the cost of production."

The lessons are clear. Whatever their underlying socioeconomic systems, all industrial countries are bound to pollute—unless the people in charge of their well-being have both the power and the will to enforce environmental standards. The American executive is under pressure to produce profits and believes antipollution laws will reduce them. The Soviet executive is under pressure to produce as cheaply as possible and believes that antipollution laws will add to costs. Each subscribes to what he thinks are the popular values of his society; and as it turns out each has a virtually identical allegiance to the cult of efficiency, narrowly defined as obtaining the maximum possible output from a given amount of input.

Pollution will continue without great check until industrial managers in both the socialist and capitalist countries are forced to redefine their objectives—and that redefinition will occur only when their respective governments give the lead.

---

amounts of these "free" inputs. Thus by not charging for the use of rivers and lakes, society has made it cheaper for individuals and manufacturing plants to discharge their residues into these waters than to develop more costly methods of waste disposal on land. And by not understanding the cost of utilizing air and land, society has given households and business firms an incentive to defile these environmental resources with smoke, smog, strip mines, and garbage dumps.

The problem of pollution, therefore, cannot be blamed entirely on economic growth. If an economic solution is to be found, it will have to be through an economic system which evaluates the costs to society of using air, land, and water, and assigns appropriate prices to these resources. Of course, this may well affect the rate of economic growth significantly. Nevertheless, since the physical and biological laws of the environment remain fixed, it is economics that must be adjusted to the needs of society. This helps to explain the growing interest which economists are showing in the field of ecology.

THE OVERPOPULATION ARGUMENT

A second factor that is frequently mentioned as a cause of pollution is overpopulation. The contention is made, for example, that since there are far fewer Americans than Asians, the former exert less of a drain on the earth's resources. Moreover, this difference is becoming increasingly pronounced as the gap between the population of the United States and that of the rest of the world rapidly widens, as shown in Exhibit 2. At these growth rates, the earth will not be able to support the billions of people that are projected for the coming decades. Therefore, either

Exhibit 2

Population Growth Trends

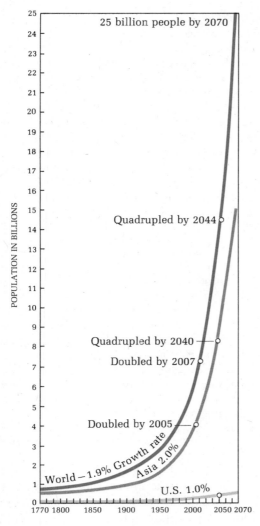

25 billion people by 2070

POPULATION IN BILLIONS

Quadrupled by 2044

Quadrupled by 2040

Doubled by 2007

Doubled by 2005

World — 1.9% Growth rate

Asia 2.0%

U.S. 1.0%

1770 1800   1850   1900   1950   2000   2050 2070

NOTE: Projection to 2070 based on growth rates in 1970.

family-planning practices must be adopted on a broad scale—especially in the poorer nations of Asia and Latin America where the pressures of over-crowding are severe—or else there will be war, pestilence, and famine to reduce the swarm of humanity. This, of course, is the familiar Malthusian thesis.

From an ecological standpoint, it is not enough to view the problem of population solely in terms of growth. The geographic distribution of population densities (such as population per square mile in spe-cific regional areas) and the volume of pollution per person are far more critical variables. On these bases, the United States is one of the most *overpopulated* countries of the world. More than half its people live in urban areas, and by the year 2000 over 80 percent of them will be living in cities occupying only 2 percent of the land.

The strains and massive filth that will be created within the urban ecosystem by this sheer density of people can only be imagined. Even now, the volume of pollution per person in the United States far sur-passes anything found in the most crowded coun-tries of Africa and Asia. For example, the average American uses more electric power (the generation of which is a prime cause of pollution) than 55 Afri-cans and Asians; he disposes of more detergents, pesticides, and fertilizers in water and on land than 1,000 Indonesians; he is responsible for contaminat-ing the air with more toxic gases such as carbon monoxide and sulfur dioxide than 200 Pakistanis or Indians; and he generates 2,500 pounds of waste a year—far more for the country as a whole than the rest of the world combined! In fact, the United States, with about 6 percent of the world's population, pro-duces one-third of all of the poisons discharged in the skies and seas, and half the world's total indus-trial pollution.

There is no doubt that the growth of population adds to pollution. This can perhaps best be appre-ciated from an engineering standpoint: just as an engine is not 100 percent efficient and hence creates waste as it transforms fuel inputs into energy out-puts, so too a population creates some waste as it transforms resource inputs into commodity outputs. The larger the population, the greater the volume of waste that it will create—all other things being equal.

However, in the real world all other things are not equal. Ecologists have estimated that a child born in the United States is 50 times more of a burden on the environment than a child born in India—even though India's population per square mile is almost ten times that of the United States. Therefore, it is a fallacy that Americans, because they are fewer in number, are less of a drain on the earth's resources than Asians or Africans. The problem is much more complex than population figures alone would indi-cate. The fact is that in the United States and other advanced countries, where millions of cars and bil-lions of bottles and cans are junked annually, ef-fluence is rising with affluence and population. Hence the task, as we shall see later, is to suggest some economic measures to deal with this relationship.

PRIVATE VERSUS PUBLIC SPENDING

A third approach that has been widely proposed as a solution to the pollution problem—especially by many college students and by members of the New Left—is for society to utilize less of its resources for the production of consumer gadgetry with its resulting by-products of waste and filth, and more of its resources for the production of those goods that will improve the fundamental quality of life. This amounts to the contention that the composition of GNP should be changed so as to include a larger proportion of social goods and a smaller proportion of private goods.

The argument sounds plausible but on closer examination is seen to be specious. This is because government spending is of three types:

1. Purchase of goods (military goods, school buildings, office equipment)

2. Transfer payments (social security payments, welfare, veterans' benefits)

3. Provision of services (police and fire protection, education, sanitation)

How would a shift from private to public spending affect the level of pollution? To the extent that the increase in public spending is funneled into the first two of the above categories, there would be just as much production of goods as before and therefore no improvement in environmental quality. On the other hand, to the extent that the higher level of public spending is directed into the third category, there would perhaps be some reduction in pollution levels because of the greater production of services as opposed to goods. But it is doubtful that very much could be accomplished by this approach because (a) the larger numbers of policemen, teachers, and other service workers on government payrolls would still want to spend their incomes on consumer goods just like everyone else, and (b) there are very real (but admittedly unknown) limits to the quantity of consumer goods that an advanced society would be willing to "trade off" in return for more services. Concerning the latter point, there is ample evidence that all advanced societies, capitalistic as well as socialistic, want more private as well as more social goods —not more of one type at the expense of less of the other.

CONCLUSION: ZERO POPULATION GROWTH OR ZERO ECONOMIC GROWTH?

United States population growth has been slowing down since about 1960. This has led many demographers to conclude that as birth control and abortion reform spread, America will reach a stage of zero population growth sometime in the 1970s. If this trend of population growth could be accompanied by a redistribution of people away from the overcrowded east and west coasts toward the more sparsely populated inner regions, it would help immeasurably to reduce the problems of congestion and ecological imbalance which are currently plaguing large sections of the country. Such a redistribution could be greatly encouraged through a new and enlarged type of "Homestead Act"—a comprehensive program of tax incentives and subsidies to businesses and individuals as an inducement to relocate.

On the other hand, there are some zealots who are advocating zero economic growth. Their arguments seem to make no sense whatsoever. If the economy does not grow, the millions of people currently trapped in the quagmire of poverty will never earn enough to extricate themselves. Further, the nation will not be able to obtain the resources to solve its social ills—to provide the schools, medical care, hospitals, and other things it needs. The results of a no-growth economy can only be lower per capita income and more unemployment. In 1969–1970, for example, there was almost no real growth, and unemployment rose to over 5.5 percent; some 4 million people were out of work. With a larger population and labor force, even a relatively low rate of economic growth will cause considerably higher levels of unemployment.

Three conclusions seem apparent. First, a movement toward zero population growth is compatible with environmental improvement and the eventual solution to the problem of poverty. Second, a short-run prescription of zero economic growth may sometimes be a painful but necessary antidote to curb inflationary excesses, but it cannot be sustained as a long-run goal of economic or social policy. Third, some redistribution of both population and the composition of output would be desirable from an ecological standpoint, but in a free society every effort should first be made to attain these objectives by the use of economic incentives or market-oriented mechanisms before resorting to direct regulations. We shall have more to say about this at a later point in the chapter.

Economic Analysis for Environmental Improvement

One major challenge of pollution stems from the widespread difference between private costs and social costs. According to classical economic theory, the operation of a free market assures that the price system will automatically allocate resources to their socially most efficient uses. But it appears that the price system is not always effective in dealing with environmental factors. For as firms seek to maximize profits, they generate adverse side effects in the form of polluted environments which become the real costs that are borne by society. The problem, therefore, is to develop modified market as well as nonmarket mechanisms for allocating resources when the internal or private costs of firms differ substantially from their social costs. Three analytical approaches are useful for this purpose: (1) marginal or incremental analysis; (2) benefit-cost analysis; and (3) cost-effectiveness analysis.

Box 2

Environmental Pollution

Give me your . . . huddled masses yearning
*   to breathe free,*
The wretched refuse of your teeming shore.
        Emma Lazarus, *The New Colossus* (1903)

Aero Service Corporation, Division of Litton Industries.

Magnum Photos, Bruce Davidson.

Photo by Max and Kit Hunn, from National Audubon Society.

As we shall see, the ideas underlying these methods of analysis are applicable not only to pollution control, but also to a wide variety of other socioeconomic problems as well.

MARGINAL OR INCREMENTAL ANALYSIS

One of the most fundamental rules of economics which serves as a guide for making rational decisions is the so-called "marginal" or "incremental" principle:

The net gain of any activity is maximized at the point where the incremental (added or "marginal") cost of that activity is equal to its incremental benefit. Thus, expenditures on pollution abatement will result in added costs as well as added benefits. But the degree of pollution will be at an optimum level from *society's* point of view when the incremental cost of reducing it further is equal to the incremental benefits derived therefrom.

This means that if an upstream steel mill discharges its wastes into a river, and if by spending a dollar it can save downstream fisheries at least a dollar, it should do so—from the standpoint of society's well-being.

As was pointed out above, a problem arises because of the fundamental distinction between private costs and social costs. The upstream steel mill, for example, disposes of its wastes in a manner that affects others, but does not pay for this disposal; it treats the stream as a free good, and hence its costs of production are artificially lower than they would otherwise be. The downstream fisheries, on the other hand, incur higher private costs because they must absorb the pollutants of the upstream mill. Therefore, to the extent that prices tend to reflect production costs, the upstream mill's prices are understated and the downstream fisheries' prices are overstated. The result is a net loss to society because of a failure of all firms concerned to equate their private and social costs. The general consequences are therefore undesirable: society gets too much steel and not enough fish; consumers of fish, by paying higher prices, subsidize consumers of steel; and economic resources are not allocated in the most efficient way.

Most private decisions produce side effects of one type or another, some of which may be favorable and some unfavorable. Social scientists refer to such consequences as *externalities*. In the case of pollution, the undesirable externalities can be reduced by special taxes, charges, subsidies, or laws. A fundamental challenge, of course, is to develop methods for evaluating each type of action.

BENEFIT-COST ANALYSIS

One method that has been developed for such purposes is known as *benefit-cost analysis*. It is a technique of evaluating alternative programs by comparing, for each program, the (discounted) present value of all expected benefits with all expected costs. The discount factor that is used to arrive at an estimate is a percentage figure representing the "opportunity cost" of capital—that is, a rate equal to what the funds would have earned in their best alternative use of equal risk.

EXAMPLE. Suppose the present value of expected benefits to be derived from a particular pollution-abatement program is estimated to be $1 million, and the present cost is $0.9 million. Then the ratio of benefit to cost is 1 to 1.1. This suggests that the program may be worth undertaking, depending on how it ranks with alternative investment projects, because the benefit/cost ratio is greater than 1; i.e., the incremental benefit exceeds the incremental cost, since each $1 of investment stands to return $1.11 in benefits. On the other hand, if the ratio turned out to be less than 1, the incremental cost would exceed the incremental benefit, and hence the program would not be warranted.

Benefit-cost analysis has been used since the 1930s, primarily in government investment projects for flood control and river valley development. It has also been employed to evaluate pollution-abatement projects as well as other socioeconomic programs such as manpower training, family planning, vocational rehabilitation, and disease control. Despite its extraordinary success in some of these areas, two major limitations prevent its widespread application:

1. *Benefits are difficult to define and measure.* In the case of a smog-abatement program, for instance, certain benefits are relatively easy to establish, such as the savings in painting and cleaning expenses that will result from purer air. But how do we define the effects on human life? If the program reduces the death rate from respiratory diseases, the benefit/cost ratio will rise. But if people live longer, the benefit/cost ratio will decline because older people become ill more often and require more medical care. Similarly, in a program to reduce the pollution of a lake or river, it may be possible to forecast the probable

financial benefits to fisheries in terms of the higher earnings they are likely to receive, but how do we establish the nonmonetary benefits of the program to the community?

2. *Priorities may conflict with benefits.* Even if all the monetary benefits of a program could be established, the resulting benefit/cost ratio would not always reflect the relative need for the program from society's overall standpoint. Thus a particular pollution-abatement project may yield an expected benefit/cost ratio of 1.2 to 1, whereas a program for training the hard-core unemployed may produce an expected benefit/cost ratio of 1.1 to 1. Does this mean that society's limited supply of funds should be taken from the latter and put into the former? Not necessarily. An attack on hard-core unemployment may have nonmonetary but socially desirable consequences that simply cannot be precisely identified for purposes of benefit-cost analysis.

COST-EFFECTIVENESS ANALYSIS

The difficulty of defining and measuring benefits led to the introduction in 1961 of another method of efficiency planning known as *cost-effectiveness analysis.* This is a technique of selecting from alternative programs the one that will attain a given objective at the lowest cost. It is most useful where benefits cannot be measured in money. Thus, cost-effectiveness analysis is of no use in deciding whether it would be better to develop a program for abating pollution or for reducing the number of deaths from traffic accidents, but given the decision to spend on one of these, cost-effectiveness analysis may be used to select the alternative that will cost least.

As a hypothetical example, a cost-effectiveness analysis of deaths resulting from smog might conclude that on the average, a reduction of one death could be achieved for each expenditure of $90,000 on the development of clean-burning fuels, or $60,000 on the installation of furnace and engine filtering devices, or $45,000 on the provision of improved medical treatment, or $18,000 on the vigorous enforcement of existing smog-abatement laws, or $150 on the production of special "gas masks" or breathing devices for all citizens. If the only factor to be considered were the cost, it follows that the last choice is the one to be adopted since it achieves the given objective at the lowest cost.

Unfortunately, there are many types of environmental problems—as well as urban and social welfare problems—where cost-effectiveness analysis has not yet demonstrated its usefulness. For example, should the limited funds available for general pollution abatement be spent for smog control, water purification, or waste disposal? This question is critical. Yet it may not be specific enough for cost-effectiveness analysis to answer, unless a common objective can be defined and measured, and the costs of alternative actions for achieving that objective can be identified, as in the hypothetical example above. These, of course, are the fundamental difficulties. However, as more and better information becomes available, cost-effectiveness analysis will continue to gain in importance as a powerful tool for program evaluation.

Some Guidelines for Public Policy

How much does it cost to undertake antipollution programs? Who pays? Some interesting facts are presented in Exhibit 3. They indicate that the federal government's cost of checking pollution on a national scale will continue to rise rapidly with the growth of the economy. What about the annual expenditure needed to reverse the course of pollution? This figure is not known, but estimates by various sources place it as high as 20 percent of GNP.

The trouble with statements and figures such as these is that they reflect our ignorance of the facts that are really important. We do not know very much about the damages caused by pollution, nor do we always know the value of eliminating a particular waste. Hence we may spend too much money reducing some wastes that are not very damaging, and not enough reducing those wastes that are. Clearly, some specific guidelines are needed for helping to formulate correct judgements. Four proposals may be considered: (1) levy emission fees on polluters, (2) sell pollution "rights," (3) subsidize pollution-abatement efforts, and (4) impose direct regulations. An analysis of these alternatives will suggest some conclusions for public policy.

LEVY EMISSION FEES ON POLLUTERS

Many economists and legislators have increasingly emphasized the idea that the costs of pollution should be built into the price-profit system as an

Exhibit 3

Pollution Control

THE ANNUAL COST OF POLLUTION CONTROL
(billions of dollars)*

Air pollution:		
Automobile afterburners	$2.6	
Sulfur dioxide removal from stack gases	1.4	
Industrial control equipment	0.3	
Total		$ 4.3
Water pollution:		
Reservoirs for seasonal equalization of river flows for waste oxidation	$0.4	
Municipal sewage collection and treatment	1.6	
Industrial effluent treatment	1.7	
Separation of combined sewers and storage of storm waters	0.5	
Electric utility cooling towers	0.7	
Total		$ 4.9
Solid waste disposal:		
Collection of municipal wastes	$2.8	
Incineration of municipal wastes	0.7	
Land fill of municipal wastes	0.3	
Junk auto disposal	0.2	
Demolition waste disposal	1.0	
Total		$ 5.0
Total		$14.2

* Includes capital and operating expenses.
SOURCE: Harvard Center for Population Studies. Adapted with changes to reflect price variations.

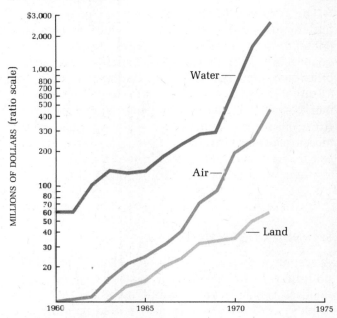

FEDERAL FUNDS FOR POLLUTION CONTROL AND ABATEMENT
(millions of dollars)

SOURCE: U.S. Department of Commerce

incentive feature. In simplest terms, this approach involves the use of metering devices to measure the amount of pollution emitted by factories and then charging fees for every unit of pollutant discharged. A pollution-control board—a state or federal agency —could determine safe limits of emission, and the fees it charges could be varied not only by the amount of waste emitted, but by the hour of the day, by the day of the week, and by geographic location. By setting its own multiple fee schedules on these bases, the board could exert a strong influence on *how much*, *when*, and *where* pollutants are discharged. And since the emission fees would become part of a firm's costs of operation, the board would be using the price mechanism as a carrot as well as a stick.

Several arguments are offered in favor of this approach:

1. It would permit the imposition of variable charges on the generation of wastes. Historically, governmental systems for controlling waste have usually been on a yes-or-no basis. However, as indicated above, we do not yet know enough about the different kinds of waste to permit them in terms of "all or none." By levying emission fees, it would be possible to impose degrees of control as the needs arose.

2. It would enable government to distribute pollution more evenly throughout the country. By charging lower emission fees in sparsely populated areas and higher fees in the more densely populated re-

gions, factories would be encouraged to locate away from the cities where they could pollute with less social damage.

3. It would cause firms to calculate the costs of waste, as well as the costs and benefits of abatement, and to consider these alternatives in their production and pricing decisions. They would thus be stimulated to seek methods of reducing waste—perhaps by "recycling" it into production, or by developing socially harmless methods of disposal.

The rebuttals to these arguments can be readily anticipated. Essentially, opponents of emission fees contend that: (a) only certain types of pollution can be measured with metering devices; (b) many factors other than emission fees, such as the availability of a suitable labor supply, access to raw materials and markets, etc., influence the geographic location of firms; and (c) benefits and costs are impossible to measure and use precisely. Therefore, those who object to the levying of emission fees argue that such a system would at best have only limited advantages.

SELL POLLUTION "RIGHTS"

A second proposal for dealing with the problem of pollution is to establish a system of marketable licenses. Each license would give its owner the "right" to pollute—up to a specified amount in a given place during a particular period of time. These licenses or rights could be bought and sold in an organized market—not unlike the stock market or the commodities market. Their prices would fluctuate according to the forces of supply and demand, reflecting the general desire of polluters to dispose of waste. The basic economic features of the proposal are explained in Exhibit 4.

At a very low price, those who wanted to pollute could do so at relatively little cost. If the price were very high, some form of supplementary rights would have to be issued to financially weaker firms in order to enable them to pollute, while limiting the opportunities for financially stronger firms through the market system. A similar type of scheme might also be developed for households.

This approach to waste control would not be adaptable to all forms of pollution. But to those for which it was suited, its fundamental advantage would be its operation through the free market and use of the price system as a mechanism for coping with pollution problems. (See Box 3.)

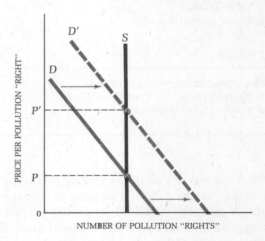
SUBSIDIZE POLLUTION-ABATEMENT EFFORTS

A third approach to curbing pollution is through government subsidization schemes for firms. This system could take various direct and indirect forms: outright payments for the reduction of pollution levels; subsidies for particular control devices; exemptions from local property taxes on pollution-

Box 3

The Market System and Property Rights

"EVERYONE'S PROPERTY IS NO ONE'S PROPERTY."[1]

Pollution most frequently occurs or is conveyed through such public goods as air, rivers, lakes, oceans, and commonly owned lands, such as public parks and streets. In most cases, rights to use these resources (public goods) are held by all of us in common or are simply unspecified by law. When rights to resources (goods) are vague or held in common, the rule is "first come, first served." A person has less incentive to maintain the purity of a lake or stream when he does not have the right to capture the value from doing so. Water in a private lake tends to be put to its highest valued uses (including those in the future) when the owner stands to gain. If the owner can capture that value by selling the lake, he has an incentive to protect the quality of the water. Unfortunately, no such incentive exists for our commonly owned air, water, and land. As a result, these resources are not being put to uses most highly valued by society—they are "overconsumed" (polluted), while other goods are "overproduced." One means of coping with this problem is to specify salable property rights in our commonly owned resources (or public goods).

PRIVATIZING PUBLIC GOODS[2]

Public goods are goods which cannot be provided for some without being provided for others. The normal market mechanism for achieving consumer sovereignty is therefore inapplicable. Those who would benefit from the provision of such goods will not pay for the benefits because they can enjoy them without paying if they are provided for anybody else. Everybody will wait for somebody else to buy them and hope to enjoy a free ride.

This is not a new problem. Indeed, in the beginning, before the invention of property rights, all goods were public. It did not pay anyone to improve on traditional procedures because any resulting increase in output would be free to everyone in the tribe. It did not pay anyone to build a house if he could instead find someone who had built one and then move in with him (or kick him out). Only with the establishment of privatization, or property,

was the decentralization of decisions necessary for efficient production made possible. Our problem now is that the invention and application of the special devices needed to privatize the public goods have lagged behind the great increase in production of goods of all kinds. Privatizing is nothing more than establishing the institutional arrangements by which the individual or group who pays for the benefit gets it and the one who does not pay for it does not get it.

However, not all public goods can be privatized. There will still be services which, if provided for some, are inevitably made available for all. The market mechanism cannot work. Everybody will refrain from buying them in the hope someone else will. And nobody will be willing to pay the total cost of a benefit to all.

NEED FOR AGREEMENT

Where this is the case, agreement is necessary for combined action. This is what government is for. A citizen will agree to be compelled to contribute to the cost of a project, provided enough others also are compelled, so that his benefit exceeds his contribution (or tax). I see no reason for expecting such nonprivatizable services—such inherently public goods—to become more important in the future. It is our failure to privatize where privatization is possible, and even our ideological deprivatization where it has already been achieved, that is responsible for most of these ills.

There will nevertheless remain public services that are not amenable to this type of decentralization and the refinements of market adjustment to individual preferences just cannot be achieved. Decisions have to be made in the large by legislative or administrative bodies and we are back in the realm of politics. Majorities will override minorities unless the minorities are able to impose their will on the majorities. Attempts will, of course, be made to avoid dissatisfactions, especially if they could lead to revolts. But we cannot have the nice adjustments by which each can get what he wants without this affecting what others get. We will not have solved the political problem by converting it into an economic problem.

---

[1] W. Lee Hopkins, "An Economic Solution to Pollution," *Business Review*, Federal Reserve Bank of Philadelphia, Sept., 1970. Adapted.

[2] Abba P. Lerner, "The Economics and Politics of Consumer Sovereignty," *The American Economic Review*, Papers and Proceedings, May, 1972.

abatement equipment; and special fast depreciation allowances and tax credits for the purchase of pollution-control equipment.

If subsidization of any type were to be employed in a pollution-control scheme, several considerations would have to be kept in mind:

1. It would be better to give firms outright payments for the reduction of pollution levels than to offer them tax credits for investing in abatement equipment. Outright payments would leave them free to adopt the least costly means of reducing the discharge of pollutants; tax credits would discourage them from seeking alternative methods of pollution abatement, including the possibility of burning non-polluting fuels.

2. If firms are to be subsidized for investing in pollution controls, the subsidies should be given for equipment that is likely to enhance their net profits by either adding to revenues or reducing costs. A pollution-control device which was not expected to increase profits would leave firms with very little incentive to acquire it—even if the government offered to pay part of the cost.

3. Subsidy payments should be tied to the amounts by which pollutants were reduced below "normal" —that is, below the levels that would have prevailed without the payments. Such standards are extremely difficult if not impossible to estimate, especially for new firms. Yet, failure to establish guidelines of this type would make any subsidization scheme largely ineffective.

4. Subsidy payments would violate the "benefit principle" of equity if, as is most likely, the subsidies were financed out of general tax revenues. According to the benefit principle—which has strong support on moral and ethical grounds—pollution-control measures should be part of the costs of production, and the consumers who buy products ought to pay the antipollution costs just as they pay for labor, capital, and other inputs. In other words, even though all of society benefits from subsidies to control pollution, it can be argued that consumers who buy the products which are responsible for pollution should pay the costs of reducing it.

5. Moral and ethical principles of fairness would be violated if indirect subsidies were given in the form of tax credits to firms that invest in pollution-abatement equipment. Such credits would mean that some taxpayers would have to pay higher taxes than otherwise. This would introduce further biases into the tax system, resulting in resource misallocation.

These considerations make it clear that subsidy schemes, though frequently proposed, are not necessarily the best approach for public policy.

IMPOSE DIRECT REGULATIONS

A fourth method for pollution control is to invoke the legislative powers of government at all levels. This would involve the use of licenses, permits, zoning regulations, registration, the maintenance of compulsory standards, and other controls, with violations subject to civil and criminal proceedings. Direct regulations such as these are wholly within the province of federal and state governments, which, under the "general welfare" and so-called "police power" clauses of the Constitution, have the authority to pass laws promoting the health and safety of citizens.

The general objection to direct regulation is the same for pollution abatement as for anything else. It leads to rigidities and, in many cases, unwieldy and inefficient forms of control. A law which sets a limit on pollution levels will cause a greater misallocation of resources than, say, a system of emission fees, since the latter can accomplish the same overall reductions in pollution while leaving firms free to adjust to their own particular production situations as they think best. This does not mean that direct regulations should be avoided at all costs. In a capitalistic economy they may very well be needed, but they should be adopted only after all other market-oriented mechanisms have been found unsuitable.

Which Policy?

It is impossible to say which of the four approaches to pollution control—emission fees, pollution "rights," subsidization, or direct regulations— would be best. There are different kinds and sources of pollution, many of which are not well understood. Hence a method of control that might work effectively for curbing air or water contamination might not be suitable for reducing noise levels or land exploitation. Each class of pollution problems must be analyzed separately and a specific control system designed for it. If such a procedure were followed, it might very well be found that different combinations of policies were needed for various kinds of pollution. In the meantime, almost all present pollution controls are in the form of direct regulation, leaving few or no bases for judging the effectiveness of alternative control schemes.

What about technology as a solution? To many environmentalists, including ecologists and economists, technology is the culprit that has been responsible for the mess. Cans and bottles, though they broaden consumer satisfactions (by providing "time" and "place" utility in the consumption of food), accumulate because they cannot be burned. The automobile, though it overcomes the distance barrier between people, turns cities into parking lots and greeneries into paved highways, thereby eliminating over 1 million acres of oxygen-producing trees each year. Environmentalists now fear that people will again turn to technology—perhaps to the dream of building air-conditioned geodesic domes over the cities, or to visions of inhabiting outer space—as an answer. But these are as yet only fantasies. Although technology will no doubt play a vital short-run role in rescuing society from its own effluence, man's most fundamental need if he is to survive on this planet is to *create a value system that will enable him to assess the various parts of the environment.* As philosopher Lewis Mumford once stated: "Any square mile of inhabited earth has more significance for man's future than all of the planets in the solar system."

SUMMARY OF IMPORTANT IDEAS

1. Ecology is concerned with the management of the household of nature, whereas economics deals with the management of the household of man. Both disciplines have certain features in common including concepts of populations, equilibrium, exchange, development, and policy.

2. Economic growth has given us a rising standard of living, but it has also caused pollution. However, it is not likely that a planned reduction in the rate of growth would be an acceptable weapon in the war against pollution. A much more effective method would be for society to evaluate the costs of using various parts of the environment and to assign appropriate prices for these resources instead of making them available "free."

3. The growth of population has also been a cause of pollution. However, the problem is much more complex than population figures alone would indicate.

Many ecologists point out that the level and growth rate of population in Asia and Latin America are far higher than in the United States, yet the average American as a consumer is a much greater burden on the total environment than the average Asian or Latin American.

4. Some people contend that the composition of GNP is a third cause of pollution because too few social goods and too many private goods are produced. It is doubtful, however, that very much can be accomplished by changing the composition of the GNP, because: (a) a large proportion of social goods consists of material goods rather than just services; and (b) there is ample evidence that a free society is not willing to sacrifice very much in the way of private goods in order to get more social goods. This is not to say that society does not *want* more social goods. But what it is willing to give up to get them is another matter—as emphasized by the production-possibilities curve.

5. Marginal or incremental analysis forces us to recognize both the costs and benefits of pollution. Thus the optimum level of pollution occurs where the incremental cost of reducing it further is equal to the incremental benefits derived therefrom. Two rough but practical analytical tools which are gaining increasing use for implementing this concept are benefit-cost analysis and cost-effectiveness analysis.

6. Several approaches to pollution control are possible: (a) levy emission fees on polluters; (b) sell pollution "rights"; (c) subsidize pollution-abatement efforts; and (d) impose direct regulations. Since relatively little is known about the many causes and effects of pollution, it is virtually certain that no one of these policies would be suitable in all cases. Instead, various combinations would be desirable. At present, however, most policies are in the form of direct regulations.

FOR DISCUSSION

1. *Terms and concepts to review:*
   benefit-cost analysis
   cost-effectiveness analysis

2. The four components of an ecosystem have been given in this chapter as (a) nonliving or inorganic matter, (b) producer plants, (c) animal consumers, and (d) decomposers. Can you suggest four sets of counterparts to these that exist in an economic system? Explain your answer.

3. The dictionary defines a system as "an ordered assemblage or combination of parts forming a complex or unitary whole." Is this a suitable definition of an ecosystem? An economic system? Explain.

4. "There is a 'tradeoff' between pollution and poverty: if we reduce pollution, we must increase poverty." What is the basis of this statement? Do you agree? Explain.

5. "If all land and inland waters were privately owned, this would be a first step in controlling pollution." Can you explain the justification for this statement?

6. One way of reducing pollution is to charge higher taxes of all kinds in urban areas and lower taxes in rural areas. Do you agree? Explain.

7. Ecologists and economists have expressed an interest in developing an ideal "index of pollution" —a single number which measures the degree of pollution at a given time. What sort of difficulties exist in developing such a measure?

8. A state agency recently submitted to its legislature two alternative 25-year investment programs for the abatement of river pollution. The relevant economic data for the two programs are as follows:

	Program A	Program B
(a) Initial investment costs	$15,000,000	$16,000,000
(b) Annual operating costs	5,000,000	8,000,000
(c) Annual benefits	8,000,000	10,000,000
(d) Present value of discounted total costs	54,200,000	63,040,000
(e) Present value of discounted total benefits	62,720,000	78,400,000

Other things being equal, which program would you vote for if you were a member of the state legislature? What are some of the significant implications of this type of problem?

9. Of the various policy alternatives suggested in this chapter, which one would probably be the most practical and least costly to administer, other things being equal? Explain your answer.

Projection for Disaster: Doomsyear 2075 ± 25

When Thomas R. Malthus, the early nineteenth-century economist, predicted eventual disaster because population would outrun the food supply, many people branded him a crackpot. More than a hundred years elapsed before the Malthusian specter was widely recognized as a grim reality in many parts of the world. And even then, it took several decades before some nations began to do anything about it.

Now, however, the deadline for making the necessary corrections is almost upon us—according to Dennis L. Meadows (currently at Dartmouth College) and his 16-member team of computer scientists. In a book entitled *The Limits to Growth* (New York, Universe Books, 1972), the Meadows group—which was at M.I.T.'s Sloan School of Industrial Management when the study was done—uses "systems dynamics" to construct a computer model that simulates the conflict between economic growth and human survival. Their conclusion is that further progress must take man over the edge of the abyss and result in the end of civilization sometime during the last half of the next century.

The study, which has aroused worldwide interest, rests on two basic propositions:

1. Five controlling variables—population, food production, industrialization, pollution, and consumption of nonrenewable natural resources—determine the course of economic growth. These variables are all interconnected; in the language of servomechanics, they interact on one another through "feedback loops."

2. The annual increase of the five controlling variables follows a pattern that mathematicians call exponential growth. This means that the variables expand at an accelerating rate, sometimes even geometrically, thereby doubling within certain time intervals.

The M.I.T. researchers show that under different sets of assumptions, interactions among the five controlling variables trace out different growth paths; however, they always lead to the same end result: the eventual collapse of civilization around the year 2075, give or take as much as 25 years.

For example, what would happen if worldwide birth control measures were introduced? A lowered birth rate would effectively increase per capita food production and capital investment. According to the computer model, population would then expand to take advantage of the larger food supply, while increased industrialization would accelerate the pollution crisis. Even a cut in the birth rate by as much as one-third (which is highly improbable) would, according to the M.I.T. team, delay the impending disaster by only 20 years at best.

Similar dire results are projected when other conditions of the model are

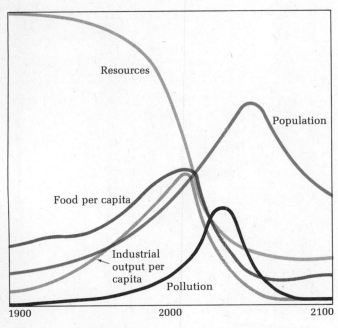

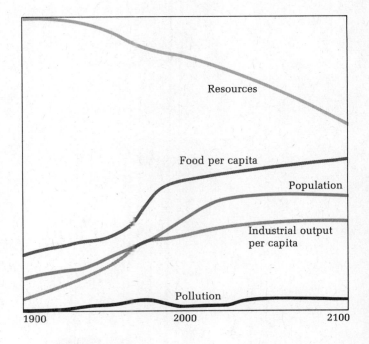

SOURCE: Potomac Associates.

allowed to vary. For instance, if new natural resources are developed, capital investment and industrialization will be encouraged; this will stimulate population growth—and eventual collapse from pollution. Alternatively, if pollution levels are reduced, population will grow and will absorb land that would otherwise be available for agriculture; hence, if pollution doesn't put an end to civilization, starvation will.

And so it goes, with each possible scenario leading to eventual disaster as typified by Figure 1 showing what would happen if present trends continue. Figure 2, on the other hand, illustrates a stabilized world model approaching a "steady state" or "equilibrium" condition. This is possible, according to the M.I.T. team, *only* if: (*a*) average family size is limited to two children, (*b*) capital investment is limited to replacing worn-out equipment, (*c*) technological innovations such as recycling and the development of longer-lasting machinery succeed in retarding the rate of resource depletion.

QUESTIONS

1. The solution to the problem, according to the M.I.T. group, is to achieve world equilibrium. Is this possible without a great deal of inequality?

2. A hundred years ago, a model such as this would quite literally have concluded that the cities of today would be asphyxiated beneath mountains of horse manure. (a) Why has this not happened? (b) What does your answer suggest about the shortcomings of the model?

3. Do you see any subtle assumptions in this model that are similar to the Malthusian model? Explain.

4. The M.I.T. model omits prices of resources. Of what significance is this?

PART 5

Using Supply and Demand. The Laws of Production and Cost

CHAPTER 21

Working with Supply, Demand, and Elasticity: Some Interesting Applications

CHAPTER PREVIEW

To what extent do changes in the price of a good affect changes in the quantities demanded or supplied? Can these changes be measured, compared, and interpreted?

The government has influenced market prices and quantities of certain commodities by imposing price controls, price supports, commodity taxes, and subsidies. How can supply and demand models analyze the effects of these actions?

What are some of the assumptions that underlie the use of supply and demand models?

How does the price system of a market economy "filter" out buyers and sellers in the marketplace?

Asked to defend the distinction between pure and applied science, the nineteenth-century French scientist Louis Pasteur replied, "No, a thousand times no; there does not exist a category of science to which one can give the name applied science. There are science and the applications of science, bound together as the fruit to the tree which bears it."

Supply and demand can be viewed in much the same way. You are already familiar with the "pure" side of the subject from an earlier chapter and can brush up on the basic concepts very quickly by studying the brief review in Exhibit 1 on the facing page. In this chapter we explore the "applied" aspects of supply and demand by solving some interesting problems. When you complete this chapter you will probably agree with Pasteur that the principles and applications of supply and demand, like those of any science, are indeed "bound together as the fruit to the tree."

The Concept of Elasticity— A Measure of Responsiveness to Changes in Price

You already know from Exhibit 1 that the relationship between the price and quantity of a good is causal. For instance, a rise in price will cause a decrease in the quantity demanded and an increase in the quantity supplied. A fall in price will produce the opposite effects—an increase in the quantity demanded and a decrease in the quantity supplied.

Exhibit 1

Brief Review of Supply and Demand

Chart (a). *The law of demand states that the quantity demanded of a good varies inversely with its price. This means that people will buy more of a good at a lower price than at a higher price.*

Chart (b). *The law of supply states that the quantity supplied of a good usually varies directly with its price. Thus sellers are willing to supply larger quantities at higher prices than at lower prices.*

Chart (c). *When demand and supply curves are graphed,* their intersection determines the equilibrium market price and quantity. Any price above this equilibrium level results in the quantity supplied exceeding the quantity demanded, thereby driving the price down; any price below the equilibrium level results in the quantity demanded exceeding the quantity supplied, thereby driving the price up. At the equilibrium level there are no product surpluses or shortages; the market is precisely cleared.

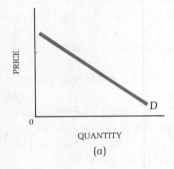

(a)

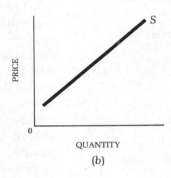

(b)

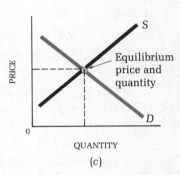

(c)

Charts (d) and (e). *A change in demand or a change in supply is represented by a shift of the given curve to a new position. Such shifts may occur as a result of changes in any of the factors that are assumed to remain constant when the curves are initially drawn. In the case of demand these factors include buyer incomes, tastes, expectations, the prices of related goods, and the number of buyers in the market. In the case of supply they are resource costs, technology, sellers' expectations, the prices* of other goods, and the number of sellers in the market. Changes or shifts in demand or supply may bring about new equilibrium prices and quantities.

Charts (f) and (g). *If the demand curve remains fixed, a movement along the curve from one point to another denotes a change in the quantity demanded; likewise, if the supply curve remains fixed, a movement along the curve denotes a change in the quantity supplied. Such changes are always associated with changes in price.*

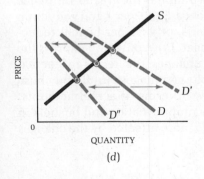

(d)

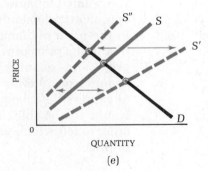

(e)

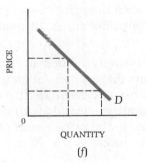

(f)

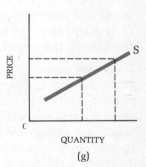

(g)

But by *how much* will a change in price affect the quantities supplied or demanded? There is a big difference, for example, between a commodity like salt, for which the quantity demanded varies relatively little with changes in price, and a commodity like vacation trips, for which changes in price may cause relatively large changes in the quantity demanded.

How can we measure these changes? One way is to use a concept called "elasticity" to reflect the responsiveness of a change in one variable due to a change in another.

The following interpretive definition of "elasticity" can be used to understand and explain its meaning:

Elasticity is the percentage change in quantity (demanded or supplied) resulting from a 1 percent change in price.

The following mathematical definition of "elasticity" can be used to calculate elasticities of supply or demand, as illustrated later:

Elasticity is the ratio of the percentage change in quantity (demanded or supplied) to the percentage change in price:

$$\text{Elasticity} = \frac{\text{percentage change in quantity}}{\text{percentage change in price}}$$

Since the law of supply expresses a *direct* relationship between price and quantity supplied, the coefficient you get when you calculate supply elasticity will be positive. On the other hand, since the law of demand expresses an *inverse* relationship between price and quantity demanded, the coefficient of demand elasticity will be negative. In practice, however, we often disregard the negative sign and express all elasticities as if they were either positive or zero, as you will see shortly.

VISUALIZING ELASTICITIES FROM GRAPHS

Since elasticity measures the responsiveness of changes in quantity to changes in price, it is helpful to distinguish among the different degrees of responsiveness. This is done in Exhibit 2, where five types of elasticity are defined and illustrated. Study these diagrams and definitions carefully, and notice from the statement near the top of the exhibit that the elasticity coefficients are expressed *numerically* without regard to algebraic sign. As mentioned above, this practice is common in economic discussions.

Here is an easy way to remember the charts in Exhibit 2: Think of them as the frames of a motion picture. The first "frames" start off with their curves in horizontal positions; in successive frames the demand curve gradually tilts downward while the supply curve tilts upward until both curves end up in a vertical position.

Do the five different definitions of elasticity in Exhibit 2 sound intuitively reasonable? They should. After all, elasticity is nothing more than the "stretch" in quantity compared to the "stretch" in price, with both stretches measured in percentages.

TEST YOURSELF

1. If you calculate the elasticity of supply for a given commodity as 2.8, this means that a 1 percent increase in the price of the product will result in a 2.8 percent increase in the quantity supplied. (a) What would a 1 percent decrease in the price mean? (b) A 10 percent increase in the price? (c) A 10 percent decrease in the price?

2. If you estimate the elasticity of demand for a product as −0.5, this means that a 1 percent increase in the price of the commodity will result in a 0.5 of 1 percent *decrease* in the quantity demanded. (a) What would a 1 percent decrease in the price mean? (b) A 10 percent increase in the price? (c) A 10 percent decrease in the price?

3. Instead of measuring elasticity in terms of relative amounts or percentages, why not measure it in terms of actual amounts instead? For example, suppose you wanted to know which has the greater influence on quantity demanded—a $100 per carat reduction in the price of diamonds, or a $1 per bushel reduction in the price of wheat: (a) Would you express the price and quantity changes in terms of actual amounts or in terms of percentages? (b) If you chose to express the changes in terms of actual amounts, would you be able to compare carats and bushels in order to tell which was more affected by the changes in price?

Exhibit 2

Five Different Kinds of Elasticity

E = numerical elasticity (i.e., algebraic signs are disregarded). The symbol < means "less than"; the symbol > means "greater than."

Case (a): Perfectly elastic. An infinitesimally small percentage change in price results in an infinitely large percentage change in the quantity demanded or supplied. The numerically elasticity is infinite. Thus a change in price from 0P to 0P' produces a change in quantity demanded or supplied from zero to a positive amount. In terms of percentages, this is an infinite change.

Case (b): Relatively elastic. A given percentage change in price results in a larger percentage change in quantity. The numerical elasticity is greater than unity. For example, a change in price from 0P to 0P' causes a more than proportionate change in quantity from 0Q to 0Q'.

Case (c): Unit elastic. A given percentage change in price results in an equal percentage change in quantity. The numerical elasticity is unity. Thus a change in price from 0P to 0P' causes an equal proportionate change in quantity from 0Q to 0Q'.

Case (d): Relatively inelastic. A given percentage change in price results in a smaller percentage change in quantity. The numerical elasticity is less than unity (but greater than zero). For example, a change in price from 0P to 0P' causes a less than proportionate change in quantity from 0Q to 0Q'.

Case (e): Perfectly inelastic. A given percentage change in price results in no change in quantity. The numerical elasticity is zero. Thus a change in price from 0P to 0P' causes a zero change in quantity.

REMARK. The slope of a curve at any point is its steepness (or flatness) at that point. A straight line has the same slope at every point, but not necessarily the same elasticity. Therefore you cannot always infer the elasticity of a curve from its slope alone. These charts are designed to help you visualize the five different kinds of elasticity.*

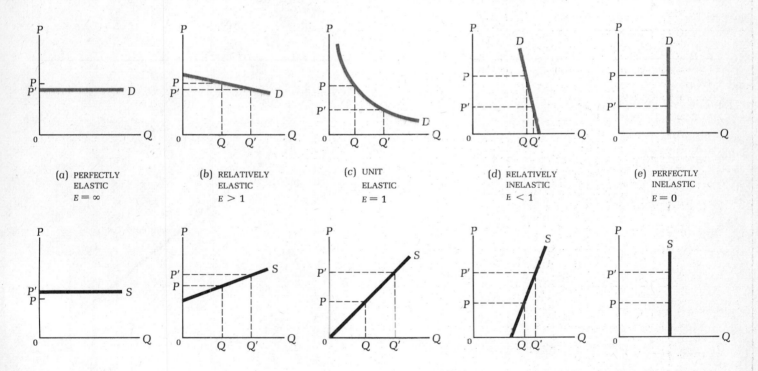

(a) PERFECTLY ELASTIC
$E = \infty$

(b) RELATIVELY ELASTIC
$E > 1$

(c) UNIT ELASTIC
$E = 1$

(d) RELATIVELY INELASTIC
$E < 1$

(e) PERFECTLY INELASTIC
$E = 0$

* TECHNICAL NOTE (optional). If you are mathematically inclined, you may be able to see that the slope and elasticity of a curve would be the same if the *logarithms* of price and quantity were plotted in the above charts, or, what is the same thing, if the demand and supply curves were plotted on a special type of graph paper whose vertical and horizontal axes were both scaled in logarithms. The reason for this is that on a logarithmic scale, equal distances are represented by equal proportional or *relative* changes. Since elasticity is nothing more than a measure of relative change, the slope of a straight line on logarithmic scales is the same as its elasticity. It is an interesting exercise to prove these ideas algebraically.

MEASURING ELASTICITY

A hypothetical demand curve is shown in Exhibit 3. Our objective is to estimate the elasticity of demand for this curve. We may choose two points near the ends of the line, such as the points A and B, because they are conveniently located on at least one of the grids, and calculate the elasticity for the segment AB.

How does the change in quantity demanded compare with the change in price over this segment? Disregarding for the time being the calculations shown beneath the chart, we observe from the chart alone that a movement along the curve from A to B is measured by two changes: an increase in quantity from 20 bushels to 80 bushels, and a corresponding decrease in price from about $52 to $17. A change or increase in quantity of 60 bushels is thus associated with an opposite change or decrease in price of $35. The change in quantity per unit change in price, therefore, is 60/−35 = −1.72, or simply 1.72 if the sign is disregarded.

Is this the elasticity of demand? *The answer is no*, because the result is obviously affected by the units in which the quantities and prices are measured. The solution would have been different, for example, if quantities had been expressed in millions of bushels or if prices had been expressed in British pounds or in French francs. Since a chief purpose of calculating elasticity is to permit relative comparisons to be made between products, we need a measure of elasticity that is unaffected by the units in which the data are quoted—that is, we need a *coefficient of elasticity*.

The Coefficient of Elasticity

You will recall from the definition of elasticity that its measurement is simply the percentage change in quantity divided by the percentage change in price. The most common method of measuring these percentage changes is to divide the observed change in quantity by the average of the two quantities, and the observed change in price by the average of the two prices. This enables us to express the definition by the formula:

Exhibit 3

Estimating the Elasticity of Demand for the Segment *AB*

Change from A to B:
  At A: $Q_1 = 20$, $P_1 = 52$
  At B: $Q_2 = 80$, $P_2 = 17$

$$E_D = \frac{\dfrac{(Q_2 - Q_1)}{(Q_2 + Q_1)}}{\dfrac{(P_2 - P_1)}{(P_2 + P_1)}} = \frac{\dfrac{(80 - 20)}{(80 + 20)}}{\dfrac{(17 - 52)}{(17 + 52)}} = \frac{0.60}{-0.51} = -1.2, \text{ or } 1.2 \text{ numerically}$$

Change from B to A:
  At B: $Q_1 = 80$, $P_1 = 17$
  At A: $Q_2 = 20$, $P_2 = 52$

$$E_D = \frac{\dfrac{(Q_2 - Q_1)}{(Q_2 + Q_1)}}{\dfrac{(P_2 - P_1)}{(P_2 + P_1)}} = \frac{\dfrac{(20 - 80)}{(20 + 80)}}{\dfrac{(52 - 17)}{(52 + 17)}} = \frac{-0.60}{0.51} = -1.2, \text{ or } 1.2 \text{ numerically}$$

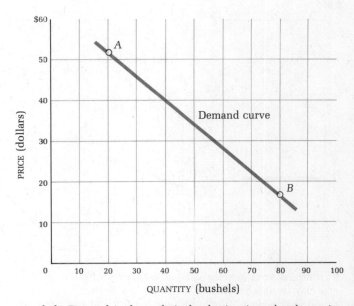

INTERPRETATION. A 1 percent change in price results in a 1.2 percent change in quantity demanded. (Similarly, a 10 percent change in price results in a 12 percent change in quantity demanded.) Demand is thus relatively elastic, since the change in quantity demanded is more than proportional to the change in price.

$$\text{Elasticity} = \frac{\begin{array}{c}\text{percentage change}\\\text{in quantity}\end{array}}{\begin{array}{c}\text{percentage change}\\\text{in price}\end{array}} = \frac{\dfrac{\text{change in quantity}}{\text{average quantity}}}{\dfrac{\text{change in price}}{\text{average price}}}$$

You can use this formula to calculate the elasticity of demand in Exhibit 3. In doing so, however, substitute the letters P for price and Q for quantity in the formula, and attach subscripts to the letters so that you do not mix up your Ps and Qs. Thus let:

Q_1 = old quantity, or quantity before change
Q_2 = new quantity, or quantity after change
P_1 = old price, or price before change
P_2 = new price, or price after change

The formula for elasticity of demand E_D is then

$$E_D = \frac{\dfrac{Q_2 - Q_1}{(Q_2 + Q_1)/2}}{\dfrac{P_2 - P_1}{(P_2 + P_1)/2}} = \frac{\dfrac{Q_2 - Q_1}{Q_2 + Q_1}}{\dfrac{P_2 - P_1}{P_2 + P_1}}$$

Notice from the middle part of the equation that the average quantity is the sum of the two quantities divided by 2, and the average price is the sum of the two prices divided by 2. These 2s then cancel out, leaving the complex fraction at the end.

An application of this formula is illustrated by the equations in Exhibit 3. Observe that the same result is obtained whether the change is from A to B or from B to A. This is an important advantage, since many practical situations arise in which we know only two prices and two quantities, and we wish to find the elasticity of demand.

EXAMPLE. The Savemore Paint Company sold an average of 300 gallons of paint per week at $5 per gallon, and 500 gallons of paint per week at $4 per gallon. What is the elasticity of demand?

The answer is -2.25, or 2.25 numerically, regardless of the values you choose for your initial price and quantity. Work it out both ways and see for yourself. How do you interpret this answer? What would you expect the percentage change in quantity to be if the price changed by 10 percent? (HINT: Refer back to Exhibit 3.)

What about elasticity of supply E_S? Do we measure it in the same way? The answer is yes, and the formula is exactly the same, except that Q_1 and Q_2 stand for the quantities supplied before and after the change, and P_1 and P_2 are the corresponding prices.

ELASTICITY OF DEMAND AND TOTAL REVENUE

In many practical situations involving the study of demand, it is convenient to have a simple guide for judging whether demand is elastic or inelastic. An easy method that can be used for this purpose is to compare the change in the price of the commodity with the corresponding change in the seller's gross receipts or, as it is customarily called in economics, his total revenue. It is important to keep in mind that a seller's total revenue (abbreviated TR) is equal to his price (P) per unit times the quantity (Q) of units that he sells; that is, $TR = P \times Q$. Thus if a shirt manufacturer charges $6 per shirt and sells 50 shirts, his total revenue is $300.

Exhibit 4 on the next page provides convenient visual illustrations of the connection between demand elasticity and total revenue. These charts are similar to three of the five types of demand elasticities described in Exhibit 2.

Relatively Elastic Demand

Exhibit 4, Chart (a) illustrates a relatively elastic demand curve. If the price is assumed to be $0P$, the corresponding quantity demanded is $0M$ and the seller's total revenue is simply price times quantity or $0P \times 0M$. This is also the area of the rectangle $0PSM$, since the area of any rectangle is the product of its base and height.

Suppose the seller lowers his price to $0T$. The quantity demanded then increases to $0N$, and the seller's new total revenue is again equal to price times quantity, or the area of the rectangle $0TVN$. This new rectangle is larger in area than the old one; that is, as a result of a price reduction the seller has lost a relatively small amount of total revenue represented by the rectangle $TPSU$, but has gained a larger amount of total revenue, represented by the rectangle $MUVN$. Since the gain more than offsets the loss, the seller's final total revenue is larger after the price reduction than before.

What happens if price increases, say from $0T$ to $0P$? The result is exactly the opposite: total revenue declines from $0TVN$ to $0PSM$. In other words, the large loss more than offsets the small gain.

This relationship between changes in price and changes in total revenue can be readily explained in terms of elasticity. When demand is relatively elastic, a given percentage decrease in price is more than offset by a corresponding percentage increase in

Exhibit 4

Demand Elasticity and Total Revenue

A seller's total revenue is equal to his price per unit multiplied by the number of units that he sells, and therefore can be measured by the rectangular area under the demand curve. Thus at a price of 0P, quantity demanded is 0M, and total revenue is the area of the rectangle 0PSM. At a price of 0T, quantity demanded is 0N, and total revenue is the area of the rectangle 0TVN. Hence we see that:

Chart (a): Relatively elastic. When demand is relatively elastic, a decrease in price results in an increase in total revenue, and an increase in price results in a decrease in total revenue.

Chart (b): Unit elastic. When demand is unit elastic, a decrease or increase in price results in the same total revenue.

Chart (c): Relatively inelastic. When demand is relatively inelastic, a decrease in price results in a decrease in total revenue, and an increase in price results in an increase in total revenue.

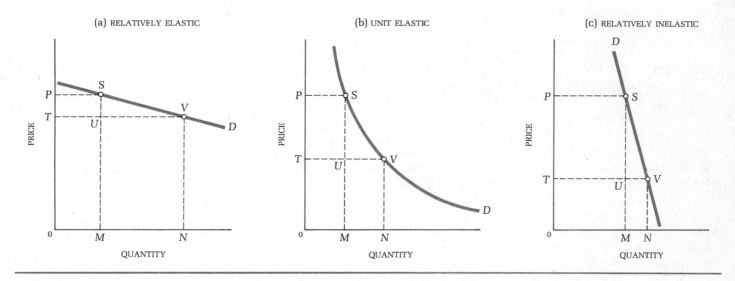

(a) RELATIVELY ELASTIC   (b) UNIT ELASTIC   (c) RELATIVELY INELASTIC

quantity demanded, so total revenue rises; conversely, a given percentage increase in price is more than offset by a corresponding percentage decrease in quantity demanded, so total revenue falls.

Unit Elastic Demand

A second type of situation is illustrated in Exhibit 4, Chart (b), where demand is unit elastic. At a price of 0P the quantity demanded is 0M; hence the seller's total revenue is the area of the rectangle 0PSM. On the other hand, at a price of 0T the quantity demanded is 0N; therefore the seller's total revenue is the area of the rectangle 0TVN. In both these cases—and in any others involving a unit elastic demand curve—the rectangular areas associated with each corresponding price and quantity are always equal. This means that a given percentage

decrease (or increase) in price is exactly offset by an equal percentage increase (or decrease) in quantity demanded, so that the total revenues remain the same. These principles help to explain why a unit elastic demand curve has such a special shape. It is the only type of mathematical curve (called a "rectangular hyperbola") that permits percentage changes in price to be exactly offset by equal percentage changes in quantity demanded so that the elasticity remains equal to 1 and hence the total revenue stays constant.

Relatively Inelastic Demand

What happens in the case of a relatively inelastic demand, as in Exhibit 4, Chart (c)? The relationships are obvious. When price is reduced from 0P to 0T, total revenue decreases from *0PSM* to *0TVN*. Clearly, the percentage decrease in price more than offsets the percentage increase in quantity demanded, causing total revenue to fall. The opposite occurs in the case of a price increase, say from *0T* to *0P*. Total revenue rises because the percentage increase in price more than offsets the percentage decrease in quantity demanded.

The foregoing ideas are helpful for analyzing and predicting the effects of price changes on sellers' total revenues. We shall encounter many practical situations in later chapters where such predictions are a useful guide to policy formulation. A brief summary of these basic concepts is appropriate.

The relationship between price and total revenue depends on whether the elasticity of demand is greater than, equal to, or less than unity. Thus:

1. If demand is relatively elastic, a change in price causes a change in total revenue in the *opposite* direction.

2. If demand is unit elastic, a change in price causes *no* change in total revenue.

3. If demand is relatively inelastic, a change in price causes a change in total revenue in the *same* direction.

How well do you understand these basic ideas? You can judge for yourself by answering the following practical questions.

FOR DISCUSSION

1. Public transit systems have often raised their rates to offset increased costs. Many of these systems found that their gross incomes declined in the first few weeks or months after the rate increase, and then rose. What does this suggest about the elasticity of demand for their services?

2. When a country devalues its unit of currency (makes its currency cheaper for foreigners to buy), it may experience both (a) an increase in exports and (b) an influx of tourists. How would you interpret these occurrences?

3. If your college football stadium is drawing less than capacity crowds, under what conditions might a price increase be desirable? A price decrease? No change in price?

WHAT DETERMINES ELASTICITY?

Once you have learned how to calculate elasticity you have mastered only half the job; the other half is to understand the factors that determine elasticity so that this important concept can be put to use. For example, what makes some demand or supply curves elastic and others inelastic? The answers involve three key words—"substitutes," "inexpensiveness," and "time."

1. The most important determinant of both demand and supply elasticity is the number and closeness of available substitutes.

This means that the elasticity of demand for a product depends on the ease of substitution in consumption. If a commodity has good substitutes, and if the prices of these substitutes remain the same, a rise in the price of the commodity will divert consumer expenditures away from the product and over to the substitutes. A fall in the commodity's price will swing consumer expenditures away from the substitutes and back to the product. The demand therefore tends to be elastic. On the other hand, if a commodity has poor substitutes, consumers will not respond significantly to changes in its price and hence the demand for the product will tend to be inelastic.

The elasticity of supply depends on the ease of substitution in production. For example, suppose the resources used in the production of a certain commodity can easily be supplemented by resources employed in other occupations. If the price of the commodity rises relative to its costs of production, while the prices of other products remain the same, many resources will tend to shift out of the other occupations and into the production of the higher-priced and more profitable product, thereby significantly increasing its output. Conversely, a fall in the price of the product relative to its costs will cause many resources engaged in the production of the less profitable commodity to shift into other occupations, thus significantly decreasing its output. In both instances, supply tends to be elastic. On the other hand, if it is difficult for resources to enter or leave a particular occupation the supply curve will tend to be inelastic.

2. The more *inexpensive* a good—that is, the smaller the fraction of their total expenditures that consumers allocate for a good—the more inelastic in demand it is likely to be.

Thus the demand for such commodities as salt, matches, toothpicks, and soft drinks tends to be relatively inelastic; each is such a relatively small part of consumers' total expenditures that changes in their prices result in less than proportional changes in the quantities demanded.

3. Elasticities of demand and supply for a given product tend to increase over *time*—that is, to be greater in the long run than in the short run—because buyers and sellers have more time to adjust to changes in price.

This principle is based on the observation that the longer the time that elapses after a change in price, the easier it may become for buyers and sellers to use substitutes. Demands for specific products may therefore tend to become more elastic as buyers develop new tastes and habits of consumption. Supplies of specific products may tend to become more elastic as sellers find alternative resources for production of their outputs.

You may think of exceptions to one or more of these principles—as you can with almost any principle in the social sciences. But there is ample evidence to indicate that the principles work in most cases.

Models of Supply and Demand

Many people do not enjoy learning about a subject unless they can see how it works in the world around them. After studying supply and demand we can apply its principles to the solution of practical problems. Fortunately, supply and demand analysis lends itself to a wide variety of concrete applications. Some are illustrated here in the form of real-world models.

PRICE FIXING BY LAW

Government may interfere with the normal operation of supply and demand because it wants to establish a price that is either lower or higher than that which would rule in an unregulated market. For example, price ceilings have been placed on many consumer goods during war or other critical inflationary periods to keep their prices from going "too" high; price floors keep the hourly wages of many workers from going "too" low. What are some of the economic effects of these legally established prices?

Price Ceilings Cause Shortages

The nature of a price ceiling is illustrated by the normal supply and demand curves in Exhibit 5. The equilibrium price that would be established in the market if there were no outside interference would be OP (= NP'), and the equilibrium quantity would be ON.

What happens if the government regards the equilibrium price as too high and establishes a ceiling price making it illegal to sell the product at a price above OH? The result will be a *shortage* equal to the amount RL, since this represents the excess of quantity demanded over quantity supplied at the ceiling price.

When this situation occurs, the limited supplies of the commodity OR will be snatched up by the early buyers, leaving nothing for later customers who want the remaining RL units of the product at the ceiling price. The government, therefore, may introduce *rationing* as an equitable method of restricting purchases. This happened during World War II, for example, when there were shortages of such price-controlled items as sugar, butter, meat, and gasoline. The government distributed ration

---

Exhibit 5

Price Ceilings Result in Product Shortages

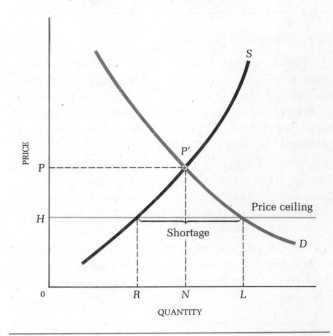

coupons to consumers permitting them to purchase limited quantities each week.

REMARK. The ration coupons were in the form of "points" which entitled consumers to purchase a wide variety of price-controlled commodities at "point prices." For example, a housewife buying hamburger might pay 25 cents per pound *plus* 3 points in ration coupons. The point prices were changed from time to time by the government in an attempt to minimize the imbalances between consumption and production. Thus the ration coupons became a supplementary form of money, and *the ration-coupon price combined with the dollar price performed the market function of adjusting consumption to available supplies!*

Price Floors Cause Surpluses

Price floors are the opposite of price ceilings; they are designed to prevent a price from falling below a specified level. Although price ceilings have typically but not exclusively been a wartime phenomenon in the United States (but not in some other countries), price floors play a continuing role in our daily lives. Two types are particularly common: agricultural price supports and minimum wage legislation.

In the general model of Exhibit 6 the equilibrium price and quantity that would emerge from an un-

regulated market are 0P and 0N, respectively. But now 0H represents a government-imposed price floor. At this price the quantity supplied will exceed the quantity demanded, resulting in a *surplus* of the amount RL.

What can be done about this surplus? In agriculture, where surpluses have been a recurrent phenomenon for decades, the government has sought to cope with the situation in three major ways:

1. *Restrict supply* by imposing acreage allotments on farmers, thereby limiting the amount of land they can use to grow certain agricultural commodities

2. *Stimulate demand* by encouraging research in order to find new uses for agricultural products

3. *Buy up surpluses* of certain agricultural commodities and store them for future sale or disposal

With respect to price floors, Exhibit 6 may be thought of as a model of the supply and demand for labor. The horizontal axis measures the quantity of labor in terms of hours of labor time; the vertical axis measures the price of labor in terms of wages per hour. The surplus is then the volume of unemployment RL occurring at the minimum-wage level 0H. Therefore, one way to reduce this labor surplus is to lower the hourly wage rate. What would this do to total payrolls if the demand for labor were relatively elastic? Relatively inelastic? Can you suggest other possible methods of reducing the unemployment surplus?

EFFECTS OF SPECIFIC TAXES AND SUBSIDIES

Supply and demand analysis can be helpful in solving problems involving certain kinds of commodity taxes and subsidies. Different degrees of elasticities affect in surprising ways the prices and quantities of some of the things we buy every day.

Specific Taxes

Suppose a *specific tax* is imposed on the sale of a commodity. That is, for each unit of a commodity sold a fixed amount of money must be paid to the government. A specific tax is thus a *per unit* tax independent of the price of the product. Some of the taxes on cigarettes and gasoline are of this kind.

How does a specific tax on a product affect its market prices and quantities? Is the *incidence* or burden of such a tax borne by those upon whom it is initially imposed, or is it *shifted* to others? These are the practical questions which our analysis answers.

Exhibit 6

Price Floors Result in Product Surpluses

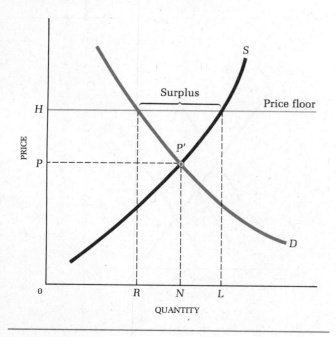

We can proceed by first examining the model in Exhibit 7, Chart (a). The curves D and S are the market demand and supply curves before the tax is imposed. The equilibrium quantity is therefore ON; the equilibrium price is NP.

Suppose that sellers are required to pay a tax of T per unit. The results of such a tax can be analyzed in two steps:

1. The supply curve shifts leftward to the parallel position S′, showing that less will be supplied at any given price. This is because the tax is an added cost to the producer at all levels of output. Hence the *supply price*—the price necessary to call forth a given output—will be higher by the amount of the tax. For example, before the tax consumers paid a price of NP in order to obtain the quantity ON. After

---

Exhibit 7

Effects of Specific Taxes and Subsidies

Taxes will affect the equilibrium prices and quantities of commodities, depending on the relative elasticities of demand and supply. Subsidies have the opposite effects of *taxes, but their influence is also determined by the relative elasticities of demand and supply.*

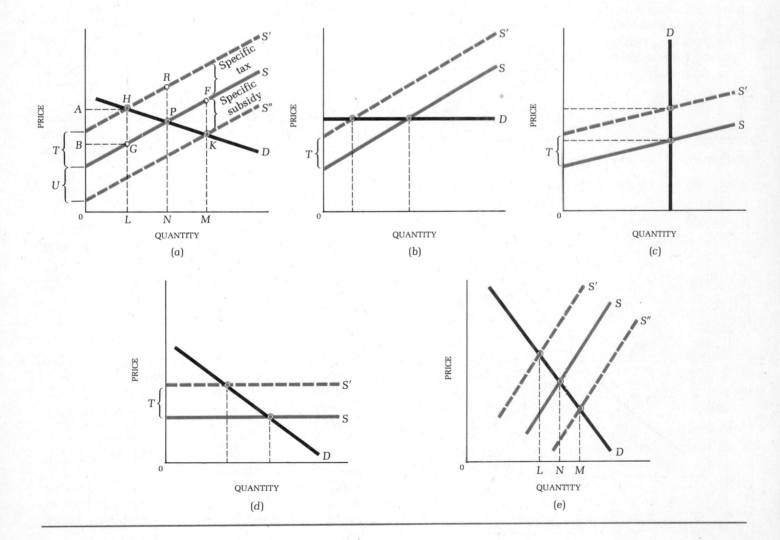

(a) (b) (c)

(d) (e)

the tax they must pay a price of NR in order to call forth the same quantity ON. When the seller receives NR, he will pay a tax of PR (= T) to the government, leaving himself with a net price of NP.

2. The tax will therefore cause the equilibrium point to shift from P to H. This movement will be associated with a decrease in quantity from ON to OL and an increase in price from NP to LH, where GH is the amount of the tax.

Are there any general principles that can tell us the extent to which prices and quantities will be altered as a result of the tax? The next three charts in Exhibit 7 will help answer this question.

In Chart (b), since demand is perfectly elastic, any increase in price will cause sales to drop to zero. Therefore the same price is maintained after the tax as before, but sellers compensate for the added cost of the tax by reducing their quantity. Consumers thus get fewer units of the good even though they continue to pay the same price per unit.

In Chart (c) the demand curve is perfectly inelastic. Therefore the entire burden of the tax is shifted forward from sellers to buyers in the form of a higher price, with no reduction in the equilibrium quantity.

In Chart (d) both price and quantity are affected as a result of a perfectly elastic supply curve: the burden of the tax is shifted entirely to buyers and the equilibrium quantity is reduced. Note how this compares with the case in Chart (c), where only price is affected, and not quantity. What would have happened in Chart (d) if the demand curve had been perfectly inelastic?

We can now establish two important principles:

1. The more inelastic the demand and the supply of a commodity, the smaller will be the decline in output resulting from a given tax. (This is illustrated in Chart (e), where the letters have the same meaning as before.)

2. The relative burden of a tax among buyers and sellers tends to follow the path of least resistance, being shifted in proportion to where the inelasticity is greatest.

The first principle leads to the conclusion that if we want to minimize disruptions in production, industries whose commodities are inelastic in demand and supply are better suited to commodity taxation because they suffer smaller contractions in output and hence in employment.

The second principle results in the conclusion that in most supply and demand situations (except the extreme ones involving perfect elasticity or inelasticity) the tax will be shared by both consumers and producers according to the relative elasticities of demand and supply. Thus the consumer's price will rise, but by less than the amount of the tax; the producer's net price will fall, but by less than the amount of the tax.

REMARK. Exhibit 7 does not demonstrate the effect of a tax in the case of a perfectly inelastic supply curve. Can you illustrate such a case and explain it? Be careful; this is a tricky question. (HINT: Since the supply curve is perfectly inelastic, can it shift as a result of the tax?) You will learn more about this problem in a later chapter when you encounter a concept known as the "single tax." In the meantime, see if you can deduce the answer yourself.

Subsidies

A subsidy is a payment a government makes to businesses or households that enables them to produce or consume a product in larger quantities or at lower prices than they would do otherwise. Government subsidies are granted to agriculture, airlines, railroads, shipping and shipbuilding, low-income households, and to certain other groups in the economy.

A specific subsidy is a per unit subsidy on a commodity; it is the opposite of a specific tax—in fact, it can be thought of as a "negative" specific tax since the government is giving money to the seller or to the consumer rather than taking it away.

The effects of a specific subsidy to sellers are illustrated in Exhibit 7, Chart (a). As a result of a subsidy equal to the amount U, the supply curve shifts downward from its normal position S to the new position S". This is because the subsidy is like a reduction in cost to the producer at all levels of output. Therefore his supply price will be lower by the amount of the subsidy.

For instance, the subsidy causes the equilibrium point to shift from P to K, and hence the equilibrium price to decrease from NP to MK and the equilibrium output to increase from ON to OM. At this new and larger output, buyers will pay the price MK but sellers will receive the additional amount KF (= U), which is the amount of the subsidy per unit of output.

This analysis leads us to an important principle:

The more elastic the supply and demand curves, the greater will be the expansion in output and the less will be the reduction in price resulting from a subsidy.

This can be verified by comparing Charts (a) and (e) in Exhibit 7.

Although the economic purposes of a subsidy are to reduce price or to increase output, the latter objective is usually the primary one when the product is to be used wholly for domestic consumption. The above principle thus leads to the conclusion that *if we want to increase production through the use of a subsidy, industries whose commodities are elastic in demand and supply are better suited to subsidies because they experience larger expansions in output and hence in employment.*

Subsidies are also quite common in international trade, as, for example, when a government subsidizes a firm or even an entire industry in order to help it penetrate foreign markets at lower prices. For example, at various times Japan has been accused by its trading partners of subsidizing the production of automobiles, electronic products, and cameras in order to encourage their export to the United States and other countries.

AD VALOREM TAXES OR SUBSIDIES

The foregoing analyses can also be applied to ad valorem taxes and subsidies. An *ad valorem* (at value) *tax* is a fixed percentage of the price or value of a commodity. Therefore, unlike a specific tax, which yields eroding revenues to the government in times of inflation, an ad valorem tax is affected only by changes in the price of the product itself; hence it tends to yield tax revenues increasing at approximately the rate of inflation. Examples of ad valorem taxes are general sales taxes, property taxes, and most import duties.

A model of an ad valorem tax is presented in Exhibit 8. We can analyze its effect in four basic steps:

1. The original supply and demand curves are S and D. Their intersection at P determines the equilibrium output 0N and the equilibrium price NP.

2. When an ad valorem tax is imposed, sellers' costs increase as a result of the tax, thereby shifting the supply curve to S'. The equilibrium point thus changes from P to H, signifying a decrease in the equilibrium level of output from 0N to 0L and an increase in the equilibrium price from NP to LH. This means that in order to call forth the output 0L consumers will pay and sellers will receive the price LH, but sellers will turn the tax GH over to the government, leaving them with a *net* price of LG.

So far the effects of an ad valorem tax do not seem to vary significantly from those of a specific tax as described previously. However, there is this essential difference:

3. Although an ad valorem tax is a *constant percentage* of the selling price, the *amount* of the tax, as measured by the vertical distance between the old supply curve S and the new supply curve S', becomes larger with increases in output and price. (Verify this analysis by substituting your own numbers for the letters in the diagram. Once this is done, you can analyze the effects of an *ad valorem subsidy* in the same way.)

4. How much total revenue does the government get from the tax? You can find out by drawing the rectangle AHGB. The area of the rectangle is the number of units sold *times* the amount of the tax per unit, and this equals the government's total revenue. Note that the same kind of rectangle has been drawn in Exhibit 7, Chart (a).

Exhibit 8

Effect of an Ad Valorem Tax or Subsidy

The vertical distance between the old and the new supply curve must get larger with increases in output and price, in order for the amount of the ad valorem tax (or subsidy) to remain a constant percentage of the selling price. Thus the amounts of the tax T and subsidy U at zero quantity are relatively small, but get larger as quantity and price increase.

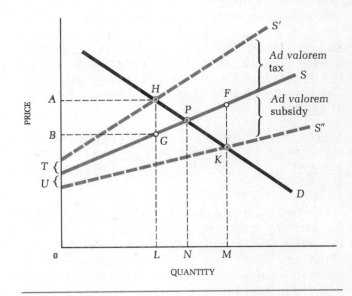

Some Assumptions and Conclusions

Before concluding this elementary study of supply and demand, we must emphasize certain key assumptions that underlie the previous models and some of the implications about the overall role of supply and demand in a market economy.

TWO UNDERLYING ASSUMPTIONS

In addition to the general assumptions about the law of supply and the law of demand, two special assumptions are relevant to the kinds of models developed in this chapter. These serve as warnings about the limitations of the analysis.

First, theoretical models of supply and demand assume that a particular economic action—such as the imposition of price ceilings, price floors, taxes, or subsidies—can be analyzed in terms of simple economic considerations alone, rather than in terms of multiple considerations involving both economic and noneconomic factors. In reality, of course, both forces are usually at work. For example, a tax on cigarettes may prompt some people to give up smoking for psychological reasons because they associate the unpleasant task of paying taxes with the act of smoking. This will cause the demand curve to shift to the left, resulting in a different equilibrium situation from the one in our model. Likewise, in analyzing the effects of taxes, subsidies, and so on, it must be remembered that supply and demand curves are always changing over time due to changes in technology, tastes, and the other underlying economic as well as psychological factors that we ordinarily assume to be constant. Hence, although our models have purposely been kept simple, it should be apparent that complexities such as these must be introduced if the models are to be made more realistic.

Second, another important limitation of supply and demand models is that they are *static* rather than *dynamic*. In a dynamic model the influence of expectations by buyers or sellers would be recognized, because the process of moving toward an equilibrium position might itself cause changes in the supply and demand curves. As an example, a fall in price might prompt consumers to postpone their purchases in anticipation of further price decreases. This would cause a fall (shift to the left) of the demand curve. Similarly, the supply curve might rise (shift to the right) as suppliers sought to offset the future effects of the expected price drop by producing and selling more now at the higher price. Situations such as these continually occur in the stock and commodities markets.

Such limitations do not, however, make our models too simple to be useful. They merely remind us that any model is a simplification of reality, and we should be careful not to claim more for it than it really is.

MARKET PRICE AND NORMAL PRICE

Having learned how prices and quantities are determined under competitive market circumstances, it is useful at this point to summarize:

1. Central to supply and demand is the idea that competition among many buyers and sellers will cause market prices and quantities to move toward equilibrium.

2. Prices in a market reflect the eagerness of people to buy or sell. In competitive markets there will be a tendency for equilibrium prices to establish themselves automatically through the free operation of supply and demand.

3. Once equilibrium prices are established, they will have no tendency to change unless there are changes in the factors that determine supply and demand.

The third point requires some amplification. In reality, the equilibrium price is rarely if ever the actual price that exists at any given instant of time. The forces that are at work to determine an equilibrium price are always changing, thereby causing the equilibrium price to change. In view of this, it helps to distinguish between two kinds of price: *market price* and *normal price*.

The *market price* is the actual price that prevails in a market at any particular moment. The *normal price* is the equilibrium price toward which the market price is always tending but may never reach. (Normal price may thus be viewed as a dynamic equilibrium price.)

You can think of the market price as pursuing the normal price in much the same way as a missile pursues a moving target. The missile may never reach the target, just as the market price may never reach the dynamic equilibrium price. Yet the target is necessary in order to explain where the missile is heading, just as the concept of a normal price is necessary in order to explain where the market price is heading.

THE PRICE SYSTEM AS A RATIONING MECHANISM

We now come to one of the most significant conclusions in our study of economics—an explanation of the way in which the market system allocates scarce goods among competing buyers.

You already know that scarcity—the inability of limited resources to produce all the goods and services that people want—is an economic fact of life. In a command economy some central authority—perhaps a king, a commissar, or a committee—decides the alternative uses to which these limited resources will be put, and to a large extent may also ration the fruits among the members of society. The central authority thus answers the three big questions: WHAT to produce, HOW to produce, and FOR WHOM.

In a pure market economy, on the other hand, these questions are answered by a competitive price system through the free operation of supply and demand. The concept is described in Exhibit 9. Thus for any given commodity or resource which may be represented by a pair of supply and demand curves, the equilibrium price automatically admits certain buyers and sellers to the marketplace while simultaneously excluding others. The cost of admission to the market is the *demand prices* of buyers and the *supply prices* of sellers—two terms that are already familiar to you. The diagram and its accompanying description thus lead to the following conclusion:

A *price system* is a mechanism that allocates scarce goods or resources among competing uses by rationing them among those buyers and sellers in the marketplace who are willing and able to deal at the going price.

A price system in a competitive market, as we have seen, allocates and rations goods or resources through the free play of supply and demand resulting from the interaction of many sellers and buyers. But what about "noncompetitive" price systems, where buyers or sellers are relatively few? As is shown in later chapters, this results in pricing situations quite different from the familiar supply and demand models we have studied so far.

Exhibit 9

How a Market Economy Rations Goods or Resources Among Buyers and Sellers

The equilibrium price serves as a highly selective filter. It admits to the market only those buyers whose demand price is greater than or equal to the equilibrium price, and those sellers whose supply price is less than or equal to the equilibrium price. All other buyers and sellers who are not able and willing to deal at the going price are excluded.

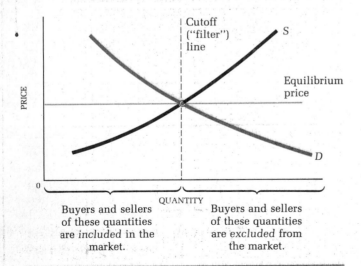

SUMMARY OF IMPORTANT IDEAS

1. Elasticity is a basic concept in supply and demand analysis. It may be defined interpretatively as the percentage change in quantity (demanded or supplied) resulting from a 1 percent change in price; or it may be defined mathematically by the ratio: Elasticity = (percentage change in quantity)/(percentage change in price).

2. The coefficient of elasticity is commonly expressed in its absolute-value or numerical form; in other words, the minus signs are disregarded. There are five types of elasticity ranging from zero to infinity:

perfect elasticity	$(E = \infty)$
relative elasticity	$(E > 1)$
unit elasticity	$(E = 1)$
relative inelasticity	$(E < 1)$
perfect inelasticity	$(E = 0)$

These five types apply both to supply and to demand.

3. Since elasticity is a measure of relative changes, it may vary for each segment along a curve. Our formula for elasticity gives a type of "average" elasticity over an entire segment.

4. Elasticity is *not* the same as slope. Therefore, the elasticity of a curve cannot always be judged from its slope alone. An exception occurs in the case of vertical and horizontal curves. In most other cases the exact elasticity must be calculated.

5. You can tell whether demand elasticity is greater or less than unity by observing the effect of a price change on total revenue. If price and total revenue change in opposite directions, demand elasticity is greater than unity. If price and total revenue change in the same direction, demand elasticity is less than unity.

6. The availability of good commodity substitutes tends to make demand more elastic; likewise, the availability of good resource substitutes tends to make supply more elastic. Goods which are relatively inexpensive tend to be more inelastic in demand because they are a small part of the consumer's total expenditures. Elasticities of both demand and supply tend to be greater over longer periods because buyers and sellers can adjust to the use of substitutes or to changes in price.

7. Price ceilings are imposed to keep the market price of a commodity below its normal (free market) equilibrium price. Price floors, on the other hand, are imposed to keep the market price of a commodity above its normal (free market) equilibrium price. Price ceilings cause product shortages and the need for rationing. Price floors cause product surpluses, which may require government action to absorb them.

8. Specific taxes tend to be shifted between buyers and sellers according to where the inelasticity is greatest. Industries whose commodities are inelastic in demand are better suited to commodity taxation because they suffer smaller contractions in output and hence in employment. On the other hand, industries whose commodities are elastic in demand are better suited to subsidies because they experience larger expansions in output and hence in employment.

9. Some important lessons are to be learned from supply and demand concepts:
   (a) Our simple supply and demand models do not take into account complex economic and noneconomic considerations, and are static rather than dynamic.

(b) The competitive market is always tending toward the equilibrium price, but may never reach it because the underlying forces are always changing.
(c) In a market economy, the price system allocates goods or resources by rationing them among those buyers and sellers whose demand and supply prices are sufficient to admit them to the market.

FOR DISCUSSION

1. *Terms and concepts to review:*

elasticity	subsidy
shortage	specific subsidy
rationing	ad valorem tax
surplus	ad valorem subsidy
specific tax	market price
incidence	normal price
supply price	price system

2. Several studies have found that the overall demand for automobiles has an elasticity of about 1.3. (a) How do you interpret this coefficient? (b) After hearing about these studies, a Ford dealer in Chicago cut his prices by 10 percent and sold 22 percent more cars. What is the elasticity of demand in this case? Does it mean that the estimate of 1.3 is incorrect? Explain.

3. Suppose we are given the following demand schedule for a commodity.

	Price (cents)	Quantity demanded
A	20	50
B	15	100
C	10	200
D	5	400

(a) Calculate the elasticity between points A and B, B and C, C and D. (SUGGESTION: Sketch the demand curve and label it with the points A, B, C, D in order to help you "see" what you are doing.)
(b) How will your results compare if you calculate the elasticity in reverse directions, i.e., from B to A, C to B, and D to C? Explain.

4. Fill in the blank cell in each of the following rows:

Price	Total revenue	Elasticity
increases		> 1
decreases	decreases	
decreases	no change	
	increases	< 1
	decreases	> 1
increases		1

5. "At a given price ceiling or price floor, the size of a shortage or surplus varies directly with the elasticity of the demand and supply curves." Demonstrate this proposition graphically.

6. Use a supply and demand diagram to answer the following questions about specific and ad valorem taxes:

(a) Assuming that both types of taxes imposed on sellers are the same at zero output, which type will yield a higher revenue per unit to the government: a 10-cent specific tax or a 10 percent ad valorem tax? (HINT: Draw all the relevant curves on one diagram.)

(b) Which will cause less disruption of output?

(c) How would you compare the total revenues received by the government from the two types of taxes?

7. Many people criticize public transit systems (subways, buses, etc.) for being too crowded during rush hours. From what you know about the price system as a rationing mechanism, how would you correct the situation?

8. The R. H. Lacy Co., a department store, conducted a study of the demand for men's ties. It found that the average daily demand D in terms of price P is given by the equation $D = 60 - 5P$.

(a) How many ties per day can the store expect to sell at a price of $3 per tie?

(b) If the store wants to sell 20 ties per day, what price should it charge?

(c) What would be the demand if the store offered to give the ties away free?

(d) What is the highest price that anyone would be willing to pay for these ties?

(e) Plot the demand curve.

9. The demand D for sugar in the United States in terms of its price P was once estimated to be $D = 135 - 8P$. If this equation were valid today:

(a) How much would be demanded at a price of 10?

(b) What price would correspond to a demand of 95?

(c) How much would be demanded if sugar were free?

(d) What is the highest price anyone would pay?

10. The demand D for a certain product in terms of its price P is given by the equation $3D = 3a - 3bP$, where a and b are positive constants.

(a) Find the price if the quantity demanded is $a/2$.

(b) Find the quantity demanded at a price of $a/3b$.

(c) How much will be demanded if the product is free?

(d) What is the highest price anyone will pay for the good?

11. *Principles or proverbs?* Many statements of an economic nature often parade as principles when in reality such statements are hardly more than proverbs. The differences between the two are by no means trivial. For one thing, principles are never contradictory whereas proverbs often are. (EXAMPLE: *"Look before you leap"*; however, *"He who hesitates is lost."*) Statements like the following are often heard. Are they principles or proverbs? Explain. Rephrase if necessary to improve the statement. Use examples.

(a) "Inexpensive products tend to have inelastic demands."

(b) "The demands of rich consumers are less elastic than the demands of poor consumers."

(c) "Products whose purchases are closely correlated with income are elastic in demand."

12. "Demand elasticity measures percentage changes in quantity demanded relative to percentage changes in price. It follows that with ten equal demanders for a product, the elasticity will be ten times as great as it is for one." True or false? Explain.

13. "The elasticity of demand for a product usually increases with the length of time over which a price change persists. Thus, a 1 percent decrease in price may result at first in a less than 1 percent increase in quantity demanded, but eventually the quantity may increase by 2 percent, 5 percent, or even more." True or false? Explain why.

Contemporary Issue

The Free Market: Myth or Goal?

Even the phrase itself has an appealing ring: the *free* market. How often newspapers publish editorials lauding the desirability of freedom and competition; how often politicians and speakers at Chamber of Commerce meetings hold forth on the evils of government intervention in the workings of the market. Yet the question has to be asked: How many of those who support the free market in theory would enjoy it in practice? Do they really understand what a free market would entail?

Shattering the Giants

There would, for a start, be no labor unions. In a free market, each worker would receive a wage determined by the impersonal play of supply and demand forces. When labor was scarce relative to demand, wages would rise. When the reverse was true, wages would fall. For employers, that situation might appear to be desirable; but they, too, would be the playthings of market forces. A government dedicated to the institution of a free market would have to break down corporate giants into smaller companies. The objective would be to ensure that in no industry could a handful of very large companies have sufficient power to interfere with the free-market system—in which, by definition, neither buyers nor sellers have any individual influence over prices.

The government would also have to abandon some of its current activities. At present, for example, federal funds encourage farmers to reduce their output by offering them guaranteed prices for some of the commodities they produce. In a free-market system, each farmer would have to decide for himself what and how much to grow. If his appraisal of market conditions were accurate, he would survive. If it were not, he would go bankrupt. Similarly, a government dedicated to the free-market system would have to end subsidies to shipowners, aerospace companies, and scientific research organizations.

Paradoxically, some people in these groups inveigh against what they conceive to be government interference in their business. But they also resist vigorously any attempts to lessen the financial benefits they receive from government. Like most other supporters of the free-market ideal, they recognize that an equitable economic system allows government to intervene when the alternative would be hardship for a group or sector.

Theory and Practice

When we strip the rhetoric from the speeches, we find that most people really want a mixture of competitive and regulated markets. Indeed, the person who believes that competition in consumer goods provides greater choice and keeps prices keen, will frequently support regulation of electricity supply, telephones, and transportation. In those activities, he believes, regulation keeps prices low.

In the traditional theory of a competitive market, of course, regulation does not exist. But economic policy in the real world strays far from theory, impelled there by such noneconomic forces as popular pressures on politicians, the persuasive power of special-interest groups, and considerations of national security.

A Case for Freedom?

The result of such departures from economic theory is sometimes detrimental both to the consumer and to industry. One example is natural gas. Since the start of the 1970s there has been a widely proclaimed shortage of natural gas. The producers argue that the shortage is caused by regulation of prices, which has two harmful results: First, natural gas at the regulated price is cheap in relation to other fuels, and consequently has risen in popularity. Second, the low price makes natural gas an unattractive investment for producers in comparison with other investments available; the consequence is a failure to explore for and develop sufficient natural gas supplies. Some producers contend that natural gas should no longer be regulated, but should be allowed to find its own price in the marketplace.

There is certainly some merit in those (and similar) arguments for a free market in fuels. Unfortunately, the structure of the energy industry and the pattern of production and consumption have been formed by the mixture of freedom and regulation evolved over the years. It is always difficult to unscramble such a situation—and the task is always unwelcome to politicians.

QUESTIONS

1. Can you think of any industries for which competitive free markets would not work at all or be inefficient?

2. Can you think of any publicly supplied services that could be supplied efficiently by competitive free markets?

3. Do you think that production would be greater, and prices lower, if large firms like those in the automobile and steel industries were regulated by government as though they were public utilities?

CHAPTER 22

Looking Behind the Demand Curve: Utility and Consumer Demand*

CHAPTER PREVIEW

What is the basis for the law of (downward-sloping) demand? What are the underlying assumptions and principles of consumer behavior on which the law rests?

In economics, the term "demand," with reference to market demand, has a specific meaning: it is a dependent relationship revealing the quantity that will be purchased of a particular commodity at various prices—other things remaining the same. This relationship, as we have seen, can be portrayed arithmetically in the form of a demand schedule or graphically in the form of a demand curve. (It can also be represented algebraically in the form of an equation, but this is not usually necessary for understanding the basic ideas.)

What are the underlying factors that account for the law of (downward-sloping) demand? This is a question we have not yet considered. To answer it, we must turn our attention to the study of consumer behavior—a topic that draws partially on psychology and one which has played an interesting and important role in the history of economics.

Theory of Utility and Consumer Demand

Economists have long been interested in the factors that account for the shape of demand curves. Until now we have taken it pretty much for granted that such curves slope downward from left to right. Upon closer examination we find several reasons for their negative inclination.

One explanation is simply "common sense"—by

---

*NOTE TO INSTRUCTOR: This chapter is optional. It may be omitted without affecting continuity.

which we mean observation and intuition. On the basis of our experiences it seems reasonable to expect that a reduction in the price of a product will enable a buyer to purchase more of it; an increase in its price will reduce that ability.

A second and more formal explanation can be given in terms of what economists call "income effects" and "substitution effects." The income effect tells us that a decrease in the price of a product, while the prices of other goods and the consumer's money income and tastes remain the same, enables the consumer to buy more of the commodity and perhaps more of other commodities as well; hence this results in an increase in the consumer's real income. The substitution effect says that a reduction in the price of a product, with the consumer's income, tastes, and other prices remaining constant, makes the cheaper good relatively more attractive and thus enables the consumer to substitute more of it for other products.

These concepts can be expressed in more formal terms:

1. The *income effect* is the change in quantity demanded by a buyer due to the change in his real income resulting from a change in the price of a commodity. It assumes that the buyer's money income, tastes, and the prices of all other goods remain the same.

2. The *substitution effect* is the change in quantity demanded by a buyer resulting from a change in the price of a commodity while his real income, tastes, and the prices of other goods remain the same.

These ideas can be summarized as follows:

The total effect of a price change may be divided into two parts: an income effect and a substitution effect. The income effect is the change in quantity demanded due exclusively to a change in real income. The substitution effect is the change in quantity demanded due exclusively to a change in the price of a good relative to the prices of other goods.

The concepts of income and substitution effects thus provide somewhat deeper insights into the shape of a consumer's demand curve. They tell us that the demand curve slopes downward because a reduction in the price of a commodity relative to the prices of other goods enables a consumer to increase his quantity demanded of the product for two reasons: (1) his higher real income and (2) his improved ability to substitute the cheaper good for other commodities in his total expenditure plan. Taken to-

gether, therefore, the income and substitution effects explain how a price change affects a consumer's *willingness* and *ability* to buy—two terms which were emphasized when we first studied the nature of demand.

THE MEANING OF UTILITY

A third and in many ways much more fundamental explanation of the downward-sloping demand curve can be given in terms of utility. By *utility* is meant the ability or power of a good to satisfy a want as determined by the satisfaction that one receives from consuming something—whether it be pizzas, vacation trips, or textbooks.

The concept of utility was employed by the classical economists of the eighteenth and early nineteenth centuries, but the theory of utility as such did not come into full flower until the late nineteenth century, when it was crystallized by certain neoclassical economists. As you study the theory in the following paragraphs be careful not to confuse "utility" with "usefulness." At any given time, water may be much more useful than diamonds, but the utility of either one may be quite different for various individuals.

Total Utility and Marginal Utility

Although no one knows how to measure utility, it is interesting to *assume* that it can be measured. Suppose for example, that a "utility meter" could be strapped to your arm to measure the units of satisfaction, called *utils*, that you get from consuming a product—much as a doctor could strap a meter to your arm to measure your blood pressure. What would such a utility meter reveal?

The answer is suggested by the data and curves in Exhibit 1, showing the utils or units of satisfaction that you might experience from consuming a hypothetical product. This model assumes that your consumption is taking place at a *given period of time during which your tastes are constant*. Otherwise, it would make no sense to talk about the utility of different quantities of a product, as will become evident shortly.

The exhibit illustrates that one unit of the commodity yields a certain amount of total utility, two units yield a larger amount, three units still more, and so on. Eventually, a level of intake is reached at which total utility is a maximum; thereafter, the con-

Exhibit 1

Total and Marginal Utility

The table and charts convey the same fundamental relations: As consumption of the product is increased, both total utility and marginal utility rise to a maximum and then decline. The marginal utility curve is most important, for it reveals the operation of the law of diminishing marginal utility. *The vertical dashed line emphasizes the fact that marginal utility equals zero when total utility is at a maximum.* (NOTE: The marginal utility curve is plotted to the *midpoints* of the integers on the horizontal axis, since it reflects the *change* in utils from one unit of product to the next.)

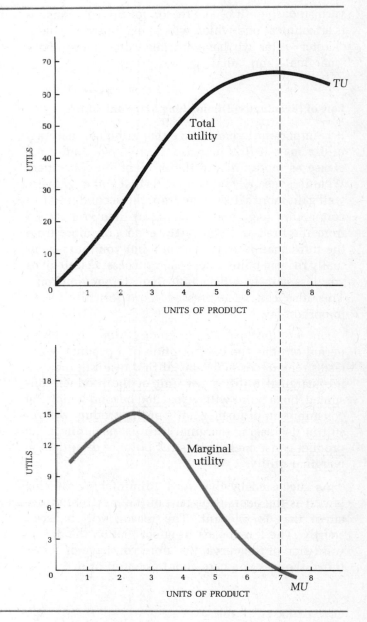

(1) Units consumed of product	(2) Total utility, TU	(3) Marginal utility, MU $\dfrac{\text{Change in (2)}}{\text{Change in (1)}}$
0	0	
		10
1	10	
		14
2	24	
		15
3	39	
		13
4	52	
		9
5	61	
		3
6	64	
		1
7	65	
		−1
8	64	

sumption of further units results in total utility declining. This is clearly seen from the graph of total utility in the exhibit.

Much more important than total utility is *marginal utility*, which is defined as the change in total utility resulting from a unit change in the quantity of the product consumed. As you can see from column (3) of the table, it may be measured by the formula

$$\text{Marginal utility} = \frac{\text{change in total utility}}{\text{change in quantity consumed}}$$

Marginal utility thus measures the *ratio of change* in the two variables. This is emphasized by the way its values are recorded in column (3) of the table—a half-space "between" those shown for columns (1) and (2). Note that its graph is plotted in the same way—to the *midpoints* of the integers on the horizontal axis—as explained in the exhibit.

Observe from the charts that the marginal utility curve reaches a maximum and begins to turn downward while the total utility curve is still rising. When the total utility curve reaches its maximum height the marginal utility curve is at zero height, that is, it intersects the horizontal axis, as emphasized by the vertical dashed line. The reason for this relationship is a technical one which will be explained in a later chapter—after we have learned some more about "marginal" and "total" curves.

Law of (Eventually) Diminishing Marginal Utility

It is important to emphasize that although marginal utility may at first increase, it must *eventually* decrease as more units of the product are consumed. What this means, for example, is that you might very well gain more satisfaction from the second unit of a commodity (e.g., a slice of pizza) than you gained from the first, and you might even gain more from the third than from the second, but you must eventually reach a point where each successive unit gives you less gain in satisfaction than the previous one. This idea can be expressed more formally by an important law:

Law of Diminishing Marginal Utility. In a given period of time, the consumption of a product while tastes remain constant may at first result in increasing marginal utilities per unit of the product consumed, but a point will be reached beyond which the consumption of further units of the product will result in decreasing marginal utilities per unit of the product consumed. This is the point of diminishing marginal utility.

As suggested by the word "diminishing" in this law, it is the *decreasing* part of the marginal utility curve that is relevant. The reason will be seen shortly. The law means in effect that on the downward side of the curve, the more you have of something, the less you care about *one* unit of it.

CONSUMER EQUILIBRIUM

How can these concepts be used to describe the economic theory of consumer behavior and the existence of negatively inclined demand curves?

Consider the case of a consumer with a given amount of money to spend on two commodities, A and B. Let us designate his marginal utility for product A as MU_A, and the price of product A as P_A; similarly, let his marginal utility for product B be represented by MU_B, and the price of product B by P_B.

Now, keeping in mind that it is the *downward* side of a product's marginal utility curve that is relevant, how should the consumer distribute his expenditures on these two products so as to maximize his

total satisfaction or utility? The answer is that he must allocate his expenditures so that the marginal utility *per dollar* spent on the two commodities is equal; that is,

$$\frac{MU_A}{P_A} = \frac{MU_B}{P_B}$$

In other words, the consumer will adjust the quantities he buys to achieve this result. If this is not the case—if, for example, he has a combination of A and B such that the left-hand ratio is greater than the right-hand ratio—he can increase his total utility by giving up some of product B (thereby moving up on his MU curve of B) and buying more of product A (thereby moving down on his MU curve of A). It can be demonstrated that the gain will more than offset the loss.

For example, suppose the consumer has a combination of products A and B such that

$$\frac{MU_A}{P_A} = 30 \text{ utils per dollar} \qquad \frac{MU_B}{P_B} = 10 \text{ utils per dollar}$$

If he spends a dollar less on B, he will lose 10 utils, and if he spends a dollar more on A he will gain 30 utils. The transfer of a dollar from B to A will result in a net gain of 20 utils, and therefore he will make the transfer. As the transfer proceeds, the marginal utility per dollar of B rises as the amount purchased decreases, and the marginal utility per dollar of A falls as the amount purchased increases. When the two ratios are equal—say, at 20 utils per dollar—there is no further gain by transferring expenditures from B to A. At this point the consumer's total utility is at a maximum.

But what about the consumer's *money* which is being exchanged for these products? We can think of money like any other commodity, with its marginal utility to the consumer represented by MU_m and its price by P_m. The above equation, in order to be complete, should then be extended to read:

$$\frac{MU_A}{P_A} = \frac{MU_B}{P_B} = \frac{MU_m}{P_m}$$

But since the price of a dollar is $1, the denominator in the last ratio may be omitted and the equation becomes

$$\frac{MU_A}{P_A} = \frac{MU_B}{P_B} = MU_m$$

This last equation expresses the consumer's equilibrium—the conditions which exist when he has allocated his money and commodities in the face of market prices in such a way as to maximize his total utility. This equation is also equivalent to the following statement:

<u>For the consumer to be in equilibrium the last dollar spent on A must yield the same marginal utility per dollar's worth of A as the last dollar spent on B, which in turn must equal the marginal utility of money (per dollar of expenditure).</u>

This principle can be extended to any number of commodities. The point is that in order for the consumer to be in equilibrium his marginal utility per dollar of expenditure must be equal for all commodities, which in turn must equal his marginal utility for money. Otherwise he will be able to increase his total utility by reshuffling his expenditures.

MARGINAL UTILITY AND DEMAND CURVES

We now wish to derive the consumer's demand curve for a specific commodity based on his utility data. The above equation tells us that for any particular commodity, say commodity A,

$$\frac{MU_A}{P_A} = MU_m$$

If we "transpose" and solve for P_A, we get

$$P_A = \frac{MU_A}{MU_m}$$

Suppose we now simplify by assuming that in the short run the consumer's marginal utility for money is a constant positive amount. For example, let us assume that MU_m is any positive number, say 3. (The number itself makes no difference for our present purposes; any positive number can be chosen, as will be seen momentarily.) The consumer's individual demand curve for commodity A can then be derived if his marginal utility schedule is known.

This is illustrated in Exhibit 2, where the price data in column (4) are obtained from the given information in the other columns. As you can see from the explanation accompanying the diagram, the demand curve represents the demand schedule from columns (1) and (4) of the table. This curve is negatively sloped, a fact which is uninfluenced by the constant positive value chosen for MU_m.

Exhibit 2

Deriving a Consumer's Demand Curve for a Commodity, Based on Utility Data

The demand curve is graphed from columns (1) and (4) of the table. The curve will be negatively inclined regardless of the constant positive value chosen for MU_m.

(1) Units of product A (given)	(2) Marginal utility of money, MU_m (given)	(3) Marginal utility of product, MU_A (given)	(4) Price of product, P_A (3) ÷ (2)
1	3	15	5
2	3	12	4
3	3	9	3
4	3	6	2
5	3	3	1

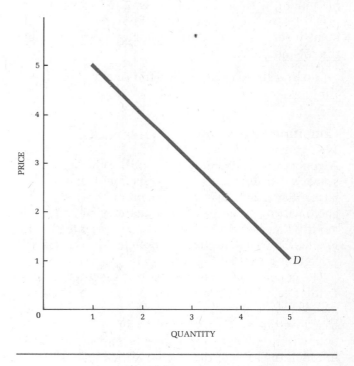

SOME APPLICATIONS OF UTILITY THEORY

The development of utility theory in general, and the concept of marginal utility in particular, permit us to interpret more precisely problems that would otherwise be handled in relatively crude ways.

For example, a question asked earlier was: Why is the price of water low and the price of diamonds high, especially since everyone needs water but no one really needs diamonds? If we knew nothing about utility theory the answer would be given simply in terms of "supply and demand." But now we can go a step further. Thus, to most of us the marginal utility of water is ordinarily low because it is usually available in ample amounts, that is, the more we have of something, the less we care about *one* unit of it; hence, we do not usually hesitate to use the extra water we need to sprinkle our lawns and wash our cars. The marginal utility of diamonds, on the other hand, is relatively high and their supply is scarce, so a single unit has considerable value. In a desert or on a battlefield, however, the circumstances might be quite reversed: we might be quite willing to trade a diamond for a pint of water, or perhaps a "kingdom" for a "horse."

This suggests an interesting point:

For some products, total utility may be high while marginal utility is low or even zero (for example, an urban freeway during off-peak hours, a fire department when there is no fire, a doctor's service when there is no need for it).

Can you think of other illustrations?

Consumer's Surplus

A concept directly relevant to utility theory is *consumer's surplus*. This is any payment made by a buyer that is less than the maximum he would have been willing to pay for the quantity of the commodity that he purchases; thus it represents the difference between the buyer's *demand price* and the price that he actually pays.

The concept of consumer's surplus is illustrated in Exhibit 3, where it is measured from a buyer's demand curve and from his marginal utility curve, both based on the data given previously in Exhibit 2. In both cases, however, the curves have been extended to touch the axes of the charts. Notice that although the curves seem to look alike, the scales on the vertical axes of the charts are measured in different units.

In Chart (a), the demand curve tells us that the consumer would be just willing to pay $2 for the fourth unit of the commodity, and that he would have been willing to pay more, if necessary, for the first, second, and third units. He therefore gets a consumer's surplus—a net amount of "pure" satisfac-

tion—by paying only $2 each for all four units. His total expenditure is therefore $8, which is the rectangular area (equal to base × height) shown in the diagram. His consumer's surplus, which is the right-triangular area (equal to ½ base × height), also happens to be $8 in this case. These two amounts, of course, need not always be the same, depending on the slope of the demand curve.

In Chart (b) we can calculate the same information

Exhibit 3

Measuring Consumer's Surplus from a Demand Curve and from a Marginal Utility Curve

The rectangular and triangular areas, respectively, measure total expenditure and consumer's surplus, whether in dollars as in Chart (a) or in utils as in Chart (b).

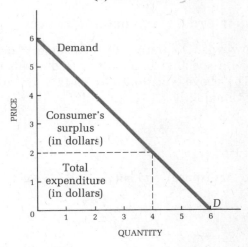

(a) DEMAND CURVE

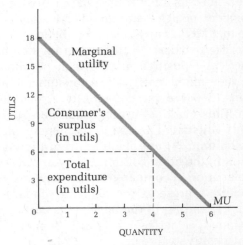

(b) MARGINAL UTILITY CURVE

in utils. Thus the total expenditure *in utils* equals $4 \times 6 = 24$ utils; likewise consumer's surplus *in utils* equals $(4 \times 12)/2 = 24$ utils. If we invoke our earlier assumption that the marginal utility of money is equal to 3 utils per dollar, the total expenditure in dollars comes to $8, and the consumer's surplus in dollars also comes to $8. These amounts, of course, are the same as those calculated previously from the demand curve in Chart (a).

The concept of consumer's surplus has a long and interesting history. For our present purposes it poses two important questions:

1. Since consumer's surplus represents the "extra" value of satisfaction to a buyer, could the government tax it away without affecting either the quantity purchased or its price?

2. If a seller could measure a buyer's demand curve, would the seller be able to capture the consumer's surplus for himself by charging the highest price he can get for the first unit, the next highest price he can get for the second unit, and so on—instead of charging the *same* price per unit for *all* units?

The answer to both questions is yes, but there are limitations and conditions. Some of these are spelled out below; the rest must wait until we have covered more ground in a later chapter.

Conclusion: Two Major Shortcomings of Utility Theory

As mentioned earlier, the theory of utility provides one of the more fundamental explanations of why a demand curve is downward-sloping. However, the theory suffers from serious shortcomings, at least two of which are especially important.

1. *Indivisibility of products.* The theory assumes that commodities are sufficiently divisible to be consumed in small units—like ice-cream cones, candy bars, or cups of coffee. To the ordinary consumer who may buy one house or one piano in a lifetime, or a new and different type of car every several years, the idea of marginal utility has little or no application, since it is a concept which by definition refers to the consumption of increasing units of the *same commodity within a given period of time while tastes remain constant.* The theory of utility is thus weakened by the fact that many products bought by consumers are indivisible and cannot be consumed in small, successive doses.

2. *Immeasurability of utility.* A more fundamental difficulty is that no method has yet been devised for measuring a consumer's intensity of satisfaction (utility) in the same way as we might measure the weight of an object in ounces or pounds, or the distance between two points in inches, feet, or miles. In other words, we cannot measure utility in terms of *cardinal* numbers like 10, 23, 32.7, and so on, as the theory of utility assumes.

In view of the theory's rather tenuous assumptions, must we conclude that one of its most fundamental features—namely the law of diminishing marginal utility—is invalid? Most economists think not:

Despite the shortcomings of utility theory, the law of diminishing marginal utility is valid because if the ratio of the marginal utility of commodity A to the price of A were greater than the ratios of the marginal utilities of all other commodities to their respective prices, and if the marginal utilities of all other commodities remained constant as the consumption of them increased, the consumer would spend his entire income on commodity A and nothing on the other commodities. In reality, of course, we know that consumers do not behave in this way.

In other words, if it were not for the law of diminishing marginal utility, we would spend all of our money on the one commodity that gave us the greatest gain in satisfaction. Since this does not happen in reality, the above argument suggests the conclusion that even though there is no absolute measure of utility, the theory nevertheless permits the development of meaningful principles pertaining to consumer demand and equilibrium.

SUMMARY OF IMPORTANT IDEAS

1. An explanation of the law of (downward-sloping) demand can be given on the bases of observation and experience, substitution and income effects, or the theory of utility. The last assumes that utility can be measured in cardinal numbers, thus giving rise to the law of diminishing marginal utility—one of the most famous laws in economics.

2. The theory of utility shows how consumer equilibrium is obtained when the marginal utility per dollar of expenditure is equal for all commodities including money. On the basis of this principle, a consumer's demand curve for a commodity can be derived and the concept of consumer's surplus can be demonstrated.

WILLIAM STANLEY JEVONS

1835–1882

Marginal Utility Theorist—Mathematical Economist

"Repeated reflections and inquiry have led me to the somewhat novel opinion that *value depends entirely upon utility*. Prevailing opinions make labor rather than utility the origins of value; and there are even those who distinctly assert that labor is the *cause* of value. I show, on the contrary, that we have only to trace out carefully the natural laws of the variation of utility, as depending on the quantity of commodity in our possession, in order to arrive at a satisfactory theory of exchange, of which the ordinary laws of supply and demand are a necessary consequence."

These were the words with which the great English economist Jevons introduced his major work in economics, a book entitled *Theory of Political Economy* (first published in 1871, with three subsequent editions appearing in later years).

Jevons is one of the towering figures in the development of economic thought. He made many significant contributions to value and distribution theory, capital theory, and to statistical research in economics. But he is perhaps best known as a leading contributor to marginal utility analysis. In one of the key passages of his book, he points out that exchange between two individuals will cease when "the ratio of exchange of any two commodities is . . . the reciprocal of the ratio of the final degrees of utility of the quantities of commodity available for consumption," which is just a clumsy way of saying that in equilibrium marginal utilities will be proportionate to prices.

Jevons was educated in England; he majored in chemistry and the natural sciences, but maintained a strong interest in philosophy, science, logic, mathematics, and political economy (i.e., economics). He served as Professor of Political Economy at Owens College, Manchester, and at University College, London. In addition to a famous study called *The Coal Question* (1865), which gained him recognition as an economist, Jevons wrote a distinguished text entitled *Elementary Lessons in Logic and Principles of Science* (1870). His main work, however, was *Theory of Political Economy,* mentioned above, in which he made clear his desire to develop economics as a mathematical science. In his own words:

"It is clear that Economics, if it is to be a science at all, must be a mathematical science. There exists much prejudice against attempts to introduce the methods and language of mathematics into any branch of the moral sciences. Many persons seem to think that the physical

Radio Times Hulton Picture Library.

sciences form the proper sphere of mathematical method, and that the moral sciences demand some other method— I know not what. My theory of Economics, however, is purely mathematical in character. Nay, believing that the quantities with which we deal must be subject to continuous variation, I do not hesitate to use the appropriate branch of mathematical science, involving though it does the fearless consideration of infinitely small quantities. The theory consists in applying the differential calculus to the familiar notions of wealth, utility, value, demand, supply, capital, interest labour, and all the other quantitative notions belonging to the daily operations of industry. As the complete theory of almost every other science involves the use of that calculus, so we cannot have a true theory of Economics without its aid."

Jevons also did pioneering work in statistics and business forecasting. He formulated statistical correlations and forecasts of business and economic data which he sold to businessmen—an idea that was at least 50 years ahead of its time.

Jevons' productive efforts were brought to an untimely end. In his late thirties he began to suffer ill health, and at the age of 47 he drowned while visiting a health resort.

THORSTEIN BUNDE VEBLEN

1857–1929

The Great Iconoclast—Institutionalist—"Antimarginalist"

Theories in economics are not always accepted without reservation; throughout their development, economic doctrines have been challenged and criticized. But no one has ever been more challenging and more critical than Thorstein Veblen—philosopher, anthropologist, sociologist, economist, "compleat" social scientist, and prophet extraordinary. Indeed, Veblen ranks as one of the most creative and original thinkers in the history of economics, and he influenced an entire generation of brilliant economic scholars who succeeded him.

Veblen was born on a backwoods farm in Wisconsin, of Norwegian immigrant parents. His life was unusual; in fact, there is no question that in material terms he was a failure. After his undergraduate education at Carleton College, he spent a checkered career in which he pursued some graduate work at Johns Hopkins University and eventually ended up at Yale where he received a Ph.D. degree in philosophy in 1884.

Despite his brilliant mind, Veblen was quite eccentric, found it difficult to get along with people, and earned a reputation for being an extremely dull and uninteresting teacher of undergraduate students. As a result he stumbled from one precarious teaching position to another, never reaching a rank higher than associate professor, which he held at Stanford University from 1906 to 1909. In later years he taught at the University of Missouri and at the New School for Social Research in New York City.

Veblen was part of what is known as the "institutionalist" school of economic thought. He believed that human behavior could best be understood in terms of the practices and customs of society, its methods of doing things, and its ways of thinking about things, all of which compose "settled habits of thought common to the generality of men." These habits become institutions—deeply ingrained patterns of thought and action on which all material civilization is built.

Institutions, however, are not permanent. They unfold and grow into new patterns of change. In this sense, socioeconomic behavior is more evolutionary and dynamic than it is mechanistic—more like biology than physics—because it is devoid of the "natural," "normal," "controlling principles" that are found in the writings of marginal utility theorists and other neoclassical economists.

This is the type of argument that Veblen used in hammering away at the accepted economic doctrines of his time. He wrote more than a dozen books, all of them interesting and controversial. His first and most well-known

Historical Pictures Service, Chicago.

book, *The Theory of the Leisure Class* (1899; new ed., 1918), is often required reading even today for students taking courses in sociology. In this book he coined a famous phrase, *conspicuous consumption*, by which he meant the tendency of those above the subsistence level, i.e., the "leisure class," to be mainly concerned with impressing others through standards of living, taste, and dress—that is, through what he called "pecuniary emulation"—which is the hallmark of society. This, Veblen argued, was a "commonly observed pattern of behavior" which was contrary to marginal utility theory, for it clearly could imply that people may sometimes buy more of a good at higher prices than at lower prices in order to impress others.

Thorstein Veblen, more perhaps than any other social scientist, criticized practically every phase of social life. Throughout his writings there are prophecies about the changing structure of society, many of which have materialized with astounding accuracy. History may someday record that Veblen was one of the greatest prophets of social and economic change who ever lived.

1. *Terms and concepts to review:*

income effect	consumer's surplus
substitution effect	demand price
utility	conspicuous
marginal utility	consumption
law of diminishing marginal utility	

2. Assume that Mr. R is rich and Mr. P is poor, and that both have the same marginal utility of money curve (MU_m), as shown in the figure below. Let Mr. R's income be OR and Mr. P's income be OP.

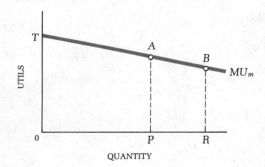

(a) What is Mr. R's marginal utility for money? Mr. P's?

(b) What is Mr. R's total utility for money? Mr. P's?

(c) If you could reallocate the total incomes of these two individuals, how would you do it so as to maximize their *combined* total utility for money? Illustrate on the diagram.

(d) Which individual would experience a loss in total utility for money as a result of this income reallocation? Which individual would experience a gain?

(e) Is the *net* effect of income reallocation a gain or a loss in the total utility for money?

(f) Does this problem suggest any implications for society as a whole? Discuss.

3. "A progressive income tax is a fair tax because, other things being the same, people with equal incomes pay equal taxes, and therefore make equal sacrifices." On the basis of this chapter, do you agree? Discuss. (NOTE: Look up the meaning of *progressive taxes* in the Dictionary at the back of this book.)

4. Suppose that after some minimum level of income is attained, each person's marginal utility of income (a) decreases at a rate *equal* to the percentage increase in his income; or (b) decreases at a rate *faster* than the percentage increase in his income; or (c) decreases at a rate *slower* than the percentage increase in his income.

On one chart, sketch the three curves depicting the above conditions. Which type of taxation—progressive, proportional, or regressive—would you suggest in order to assure equal subjective sacrifice by taxpayers. Explain your answer. (NOTE: Look up the meanings of *progressive, proportional,* and *regressive tax* in the Dictionary at the back of this book.)

5. Fill in the empty cells in the following table:

Total utility	Marginal utility
increasing at a constant rate	
	increasing
increasing at a decreasing rate	
	zero
decreasing	

Supplement: Indifference Curves

The law of diminishing marginal utility has long been used to explain the existence of downward-sloping demand curves. The chief difficulty with this explanation, however, lies in our *inability to measure utility*. Unlike the weight of an object or the distance between two points, utility cannot be ascertained in terms of cardinal numbers. It was largely because of this shortcoming that economists devised an alternative approach for explaining demand phenomena—an approach that makes use of a concept known as *indifference curves*.

The Price Line or Budget Line

Imagine a consumer possessing, say, $2, entering the market to spend his money on goods. He is confronted with two commodities, X and Y. The price of X is $2; the price of Y is $1. In other words, the price of X is twice the price of Y. Algebraically, if P denotes price, then $P_X = 2P_Y$.

Now the consumer could spend his entire $2 on X, in which case he could buy only one unit and have nothing left to spend on Y; or he could spend his whole $2 on Y and have nothing left to spend on X. The table in Exhibit 1 shows some of the combinations of X and Y that he could purchase with his $2. Thus, for $2, with P_X equal to $2 and P_Y equal to $1, our individual can buy any of the combinations shown in the table as well as any other combinations that will total $2.

The diagram in Exhibit 1 illustrates the same situation graphically. In this chart, the vertical axis $0Y$ represents the different quantities of commodity Y that the consumer can purchase, whereas the horizontal axis $0X$ shows the amounts of X that can be had.

Thus if our consumer spends his entire $2 on Y, he can purchase two units or an amount equal to $0M$. If he spends his $2 on X, he can purchase one unit or an amount equal to $0N$. If we connect these two points with a line, the resulting MN is called a "price line" or "budget line."

Just what does this price line tell us? It indicates all the possible combinations of X and Y that could be purchased for a total of $2, assuming that $P_X = $2 and $P_Y = $1. Thus, point Q shows that the consumer could purchase one unit of Y and one-half unit of X for a total of $2. Likewise, with any other point on MN. Notice, however, that as we move along the line from M to N, more of X can be purchased and less of Y. This is just as we should expect: out of any given money income, the more we spend on one commodity the less we have to spend on other things.

By definition, therefore, a *price line* (or *budget line*) represents all the possible combinations of two commodities that a consumer can purchase at a particular time, given the market prices of the commodities and the consumer's money budget or income.

Exhibit 1

A Consumer's Alternative Purchase Combinations

Assumptions: *consumption budget = $2; price of X = $2; price of Y = $1.*

Purchase combinations	Units of X	Units of Y	Total amount spent
N	1	0	$2 + $0 = $2
Q	$\frac{1}{2}$	1	$1 + $1 = $2
M	0	2	$0 + $2 = $2

The price line represents all the possible combinations of commodities X and Y that the consumer can purchase at a particular time, given the market prices of the commodities and the consumer's budget.

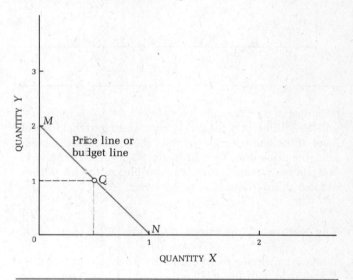

MANY POSSIBLE PRICE LINES

Suppose now that our individual, instead of possessing only $2, had, say, $4. Since he has twice as much money, he can buy twice as much of each commodity, provided that their prices do not change. Thus, for $2, he was able to buy as much as $2Y$ or $1X$, or any combination in between. Now he can buy as much as $4Y$ or $2X$, or any combination in between. This fact is shown in Exhibit 2, where $M'N'$ represents the new price line at a higher income or budget of $4, and MN the old price line at a lower income

Exhibit 2

An Increase in the Price Line

An increase in the consumer's income results in the price line being shifted outward, thus enabling him to buy more of X and Y at the given market prices.

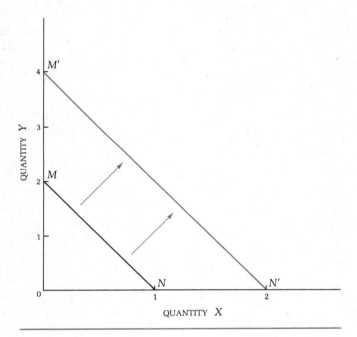

or budget of $2. Obviously, for every level of income there will be a different price line corresponding to that income level. If income rises, so too does the price line; if income falls, the price line falls. Thus, since an infinite number of budgets or income levels are possible, so too an infinite number of price lines are possible.

The Nature of Indifference Curves

When a consumer is confronted with two commodities, X and Y, he will probably not spend his entire income on only one of these commodities. Instead, he will probably purchase some combination of the two. Since there are many possible combinations of X and Y that can be bought, the question is: Just which combination of the many possible combinations will he purchase?

Let us disregard the price relationships that were made in the previous section and pay attention solely to the satisfaction our consumer would derive from possessing commodities X and Y. That is, let us forget for the moment that $P_X = \$2$ and $P_Y = \$1$ and that the consumer has a given income.

We start by constructing what is called an *indifference schedule*. This is a list showing the various combinations

of two commodities that would be equally satisfactory to the consumer at a given time. Column (1) of the table in Exhibit 3 is an example of a possible indifference schedule for two commodities X and Y.

In this column, each combination of X and Y is equally satisfactory to the consumer. Thus, the consumer would just as soon have combination 1, that is, 60Y and 1X, as he would combination 2, that is, 50Y and 2X, or combination 3, 41Y and 3X, and so on. This is true because each combination yields him the same total satisfaction or utility. Hence, he is completely *indifferent* as to which combination he prefers, for he prefers no one combination; they are all equally desirable because they *all yield the same total utility.*

Now there is this important thing to notice about an indifference schedule: Since each combination yields the same total utility, it follows that if the consumer were to increase his X intake by one unit at a time, he would have to decrease his Y holdings by some amount in order that each successive combination continue to yield the same total utility. For example, when he possesses combination 1 of 60Y and 1X, he derives a certain amount of total utility. If now he were to have 60Y and 2X, his total utility would be greater than the total utility of 60Y and 1X, for he would have the same amount of Y plus more of X. Therefore, in order to keep his total utility the same, he must give up a certain amount of Y for each unit increase in X. Column (1) shows this relationship.

MARGINAL RATE OF SUBSTITUTION

Next, we should notice that as the consumer increases his X intake, the amount of Y that he is willing to give up *decreases*. Thus, when he possesses combination 1 of 60Y and 1X, he is willing to give up 10 units of Y for 1 unit of X, leaving him with 50Y and 2X, or combination 2. At this point, he is willing to give up only 9 units of Y for 1 more unit of X, which would leave him at combination 3. Column (2) indicates this relationship. It shows us the amount of Y he is willing to surrender for every unit increase in his X holdings in order that the new combination yield him the same satisfaction as the previous one, that is, the same total utility.

The rate at which the consumer is willing to substitute commodity X for commodity Y is called the *marginal rate of substitution (MRS)*. It may be defined as the change in the amount of one commodity which will just offset a unit change in the holdings of another commodity so that the consumer's total utility remains the same. Since the ratio of the change in Y to the change in X is negative (because the amount of one commodity decreases when the other increases), we may express the marginal rate of substitution by the formula:

$$MRS = -\frac{\text{change in } Y}{\text{change in } X}$$

Exhibit 3

**A Consumer's Indifference Schedule, Indifference Curve,
and Marginal Rate of Substitution**

*Each combination in column (1) yields the consumer the
same total utility. Hence he is indifferent as to which
combination he prefers.*

*In column (2), the marginal rate of substitution mea-
sures the amount of commodity Y the consumer must give
up to get one unit of commodity X, while maintaining the
same total utility. The numerical value of this ratio decreases as additional units of X are acquired.*

*An indifference curve is a graph of an indifference sched-
ule. Any point on the curve denotes a particular combination of commodities X and Y that yields the same total
utility.*

*Note that as X increases one unit at a time, the amount
of Y that the consumer is willing to give up decreases. This
reflects a decreasing marginal rate of substitution of X
for Y.*

Combina-tions	(1) Indifference schedule	(2) Marginal rate of substitution of X for Y
1	60Y and 1X	
2	50Y and 2X	10/1
3	41Y and 3X	9/1
4	33Y and 4X	8/1
5	26Y and 5X	7/1
6	20Y and 6X	6/1
7	15Y and 7X	5/1
8	11Y and 8X	4/1
9	8Y and 9X	3/1
10	6Y and 10X	2/1
11	5Y and 11X	1/1

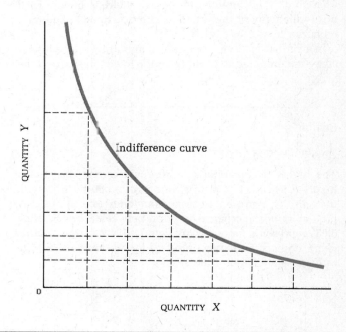

As a general rule the minus sign is understood; hence it
may be omitted in written and oral discussions.

Why does the *MRS*, as shown in column (2) of the table,
decrease? You will remember that the reason a demand
curve sloped downward from left to right was that the
marginal utility of the commodity decreased as more of the
commodity was consumed. (The more we have of something, the less we care for one unit of it.)

The concept of a decreasing *MRS* is similar to that of
decreasing marginal utility. As *X increases* (one unit at a
time), the marginal utility of *X decreases*. As *Y decreases*,
the marginal utility of *Y increases*. Thus, the more we
have of *X*, the less we want more of it, and the less we have
of *Y*, the less we are willing to give up more of it. That is,
as we give up *Y* for *X*, the less of *Y* we are willing to give
up for further units of *X*.

For example, when the consumer possessed 60Y and
1X, he was willing to give up a relatively large amount of
Y, namely 10Y, for 1 unit of X. After that, he was willing
to give up only 9 units of Y, then 8Y and so forth, for
further units of X. This is because he cares less and less
for additional units of X, and hence is willing to give up
less and less of Y. (Or conversely, he cares more and more
for his smaller holdings of Y and is willing to give them up
at a slower and slower rate.)

MANY POSSIBLE INDIFFERENCE CURVES

Suppose now that we were to extend our indifference
schedule far enough and then plot the various combinations on a chart. We would get a curve similar to the one

in Exhibit 3. This curve is called an *indifference curve* because every point on it represents a particular combination of the two commodities X and Y that is equally satisfactory to the consumer, that is, yields him the same total utility.

Just as it is possible to have an infinite number of price lines, so too it is possible to have an infinite number of indifference curves. This is suggested in Exhibit 4, where point Q represents a combination of $0M$ of X and $0N$ of Y. This combination yields the same total utility as any other combination on the same curve. On the higher curve at point R, however, the consumer possesses the same amount of Y, namely $0N$, plus more of X, namely $0M'$. Therefore, this combination must yield a higher total utility than any of the previous combinations to be found on curve 1.

In a similar fashion we note that at point S on the higher curve as compared to point Q on the lower one there is the same amount of X plus more of Y. Finally, at any point between S and R on the higher curve, say at T, there is more of *both X and Y as compared to the combination denoted by point Q on the lower curve.*

These ideas suggest three important conclusions about indifference curves:

1. The higher an indifference curve—that is, the farther it lies to the right—the greater the consumer's total utility, for any point on a higher curve will always denote *at least* the same amount of one commodity plus more of the other.

2. A consumer will always try to be on his highest possible indifference curve, since it is assumed that he will always try to maximize his total utility.

3. Each indifference curve represents a *different* level of total utility; therefore, indifference curves can never intersect at any point.

The Equilibrium Combination

Now let us combine the concepts of price lines and indifference curves. Superimposing one diagram upon the other, we get a result such as that depicted in Exhibit 5.

The price line MN shows us the possible combinations of X and Y that could be purchased with given prices of X and Y at a given income. The indifference curves 1, 2, and 3 show various combinations of X and Y that yield the same total utility. The higher the indifference curve, the greater the total utility; therefore, the consumer will always try to be on the highest possible indifference curve.

Given these price lines and indifference curves, precisely what combination of X and Y will be purchased? The answer is based on the following fundamental notions:

1. The indifference curves represent the consumer's *subjective* valuations of X and Y and have no relationship to the *objective* facts that X and Y have certain prices and that the consumer has a certain money income to spend. These objective facts are shown by the price line.

2. Subjectively, the consumer will try to be on the highest possible indifference curve; objectively, he is limited in doing so by the price line. The problem, therefore, is to reconcile this difference.

Since the price line shows all the possible combinations of X and Y that can be purchased for a given money income, it follows that there will be only one point on the price line that will also be on the highest possible indifference curve. This is point Q, where the price line is tangent to curve 2. Point Q, therefore, shows the combination of X and Y that will be purchased, namely $0L$ of Y and $0P$ of X.

Thus the consumer would not want to be on curve 1, where he would purchase a combination determined by D

Exhibit 4

Two Indifference Curves

The higher a consumer's indifference curve, the greater his total utility. *The points S and R, in comparison with the point Q, represent at least as much of one commodity plus more of the other. Any point between S and R, such as T, represents more of* both *commodities. Although this chart depicts only two indifference curves, an infinite number of such curves exists.*

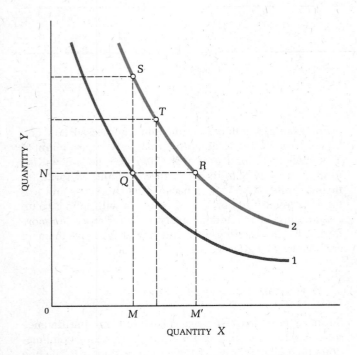

or E, because his purchasing power as determined by the price line permits him to be on a higher indifference curve. The highest curve that he can be on and yet remain within his income as determined by the price line is curve 2, and the only place where the price line touches the highest indifference curve within the consumer's means is point Q. This point, therefore, indicates the combination of X and Y that will be purchased at the prevailing prices and income.

The consumer is thus in a position not unlike that of the legendary Buridan's ass. The ass, it will be remembered, stood equidistant between two equal bundles of hay, and starved to death because it could not choose between them. Likewise:

All combinations on any one indifference curve are equally desirable; it is the point of tangency of an indifference curve with a price line that determines the equilibrium purchase combination.

What Happens When Income Changes?

Suppose now that the consumer's income increases while the prices of X and Y remain the same. The consumer could now purchase more of both X and Y. This condition is shown in Exhibit 6, where the price line shifts to the right from MN to M'N' to M"N", indicating that a greater combination of both commodities can be purchased. At each new level of income there is a tangency with a new and higher indifference curve. Connecting these points of tangency, we get the line QRS, and extending vertical and horizontal lines from each of these points to the X and Y axes shows us by how much the consumer increases his purchases of both X and Y as his income rises.

The line QRS may be called an *income-consumption curve (ICC)*; it connects the tangency points of price lines and indifference curves by showing the amounts of

---

Exhibit 5

The Equilibrium-purchase Combination

The tangency of the price line with an indifference curve determines the equilibrium-purchase combination. Thus, since the tangency is at point Q, the consumer will buy 0P units of X and 0L units of Y.

A given price line may intersect any number of indifference curves, but it can be tangent to only one indifference curve.

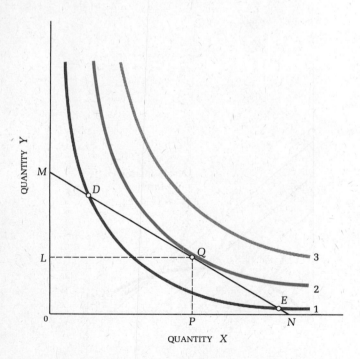

Exhibit 6

Income-consumption Curve

An increase in income may increase the consumer's purchases of both X and Y. The line QRS connects the tangency points of price lines and indifference curves as the consumer's income increases. It is called an income-consumption curve (ICC).

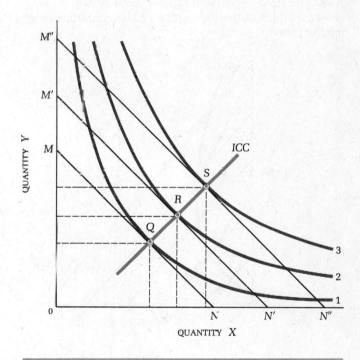

two commodities that a consumer will purchase if his income changes while their prices remain constant.

It is possible, however, that as income increases, the consumption of one commodity may increase while the consumption of the other commodity decreases. This is shown in Exhibit 7. In Chart (a), as income rises, the consumption of Y also rises, and though X at first increases, it gradually falls off. The opposite is seen in Chart (b); as income rises, the consumption of both X and Y increases, but Y soon decreases.

A good whose consumption varies inversely with money income (prices remaining constant) over a certain range of income is called an *inferior good*. Some classic examples are potatoes, used clothing, and other "cheap" commodities bought by low-income families. The consumption of these commodities by low-income families declines in favor of more nutritious foods, new clothing, and so on, as their incomes rise. It should be noted, however, that in a larger sense almost any good may become "inferior" at some income level. Thus when a family "steps up" from a Chevrolet to an Oldsmobile because of an increase in its income, the Chevrolet becomes an inferior good.

On the other hand, a good whose consumption varies directly with money income (prices remaining constant) is called a *superior good*. Most consumer goods are of this type. Superior goods are also sometimes called *normal goods* because they represent the "normal" situation. Examples include most food, clothing, appliances, and other nondurable and durable items that people typically buy.

What Happens When Price Changes?

The previous case assumed that the consumer's income increased while the prices of X and Y remained constant. Let us now allow both the consumer's income and the price of Y to remain constant, but the price of X to decrease. What happens?

The result is seen in Exhibit 8. The lower end of the price line shifts to the right from MN to MN' to MN", indicating that as P_X falls, more of it can be purchased. The price line thus fans outward as a result of decreases in P_X.

We can work the same idea in the other direction by permitting the lower end of the price line to shift left. For instance, let us assume that the price line to begin with is MN". Then suppose that the price of X gradually rises while the price of Y and the consumer's income remain the same. As P_X rises, less of X can be bought, until finally the price of X is so high that it is not purchased at all, and the price line becomes the vertical line 0M, indicating that the consumer spends his entire income on Y.

Exhibit 7

Superior and Inferior Goods

As a consumer's income increases, he may buy more of one commodity (superior good) and less of another commodity (inferior good).

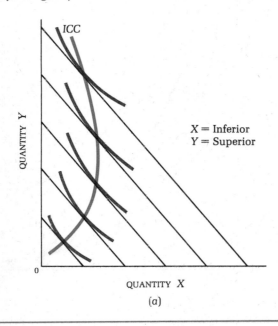

(a)

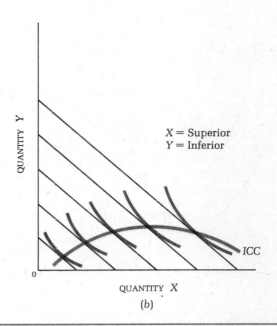

(b)

Exhibit 8

Price-consumption Curve

With the consumer's income and the price of Y constant, decreases in the price of X result in the consumer buying more of it. The line QRS connects the tangency points of price lines and indifference curves under these circumstances. It is called a price-consumption curve (PCC).

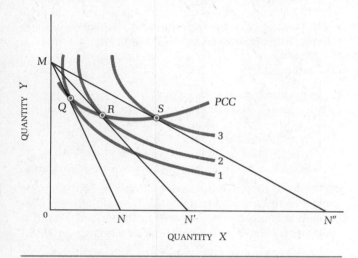

The line QRS in the diagram is thus a *price-consumption curve (PCC)*. It connects the tangency points of price lines and indifference curves and shows the amounts of two commodities that a consumer will purchase when his income and the price of one commodity remain constant while the price of the other commodity varies.

Deriving a Demand Curve

How do the principles of indifference curves and price lines relate to the law of demand? As you recall, this is the problem we started out to solve.

The answer is that we can now combine the foregoing concepts to derive a *demand curve*. This is illustrated in Exhibit 9, where numbers are used with letters so that the computations can be followed easily.

In Chart (a), the price line MN signifies that with a consumer income of $10, and with $P_Y = \$1$ and $P_X = \$2$, the buyer can purchase either 10 units of Y, or 5 units of X, or various combinations in between. The tangency of this price line with the consumer's indifference curve, however, shows that the buyer will maximize his total utility by purchasing 4 units of Y and 3 units of X.

Suppose now that the price of X falls to $1, while the consumer's income and the price of Y remain constant. The tangency of the new price line MN' with the higher

indifference curve indicates that the consumer will be in equilibrium by purchasing 3 units of Y and 7 units of X.

We need this kind of information to derive a demand curve. For example, in Chart (b) we see the relationship between the price of X and the quantity demanded of X

Exhibit 9

Derivation of a Demand Curve from Indifference Curves

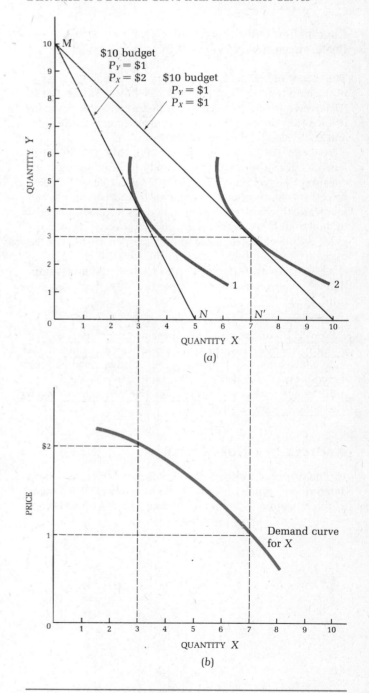

while all other things—namely, the buyer's income and the price of Y—remain the same. Thus the dashed lines emphasize the fact that the buyer will purchase 3 units of X at a price of \$2 per unit, and 7 units of X at a price of \$1 per unit. Connecting these two points (as well as all the in-between points that may be similarly derived) we get the demand curve for X. As you can see, this curve obeys the law of demand: the lower the price, the greater the quantity demanded.

Conclusion: Only Consumer's Preferences Are Needed

The theory of indifference curves had its origins in the late nineteenth century and reached full flower in the 1930s. It marked a major advance in the history of economics, for it freed the concept of demand from a reliance on the older and controversial concept of utility.

You can easily see the reason for this. In the indifference-curve approach, it need only be assumed that the consumer knows his preferences. He must know whether he prefers one combination of goods to another, or whether he regards them as equivalent. He does not have to know by *how much* he prefers one good to another. Hence the older approach to demand theory, which rested on the unrealistic assumption of a cardinal utility relationship (1, 2, 3, etc.), is replaced by the more realistic assumption of an ordinal preference relationship (first, second, third, etc.).

The significance is clear:

From the standpoint of indifference-curve analysis, the inability to measure utility is no longer a problem, for such a measure is no longer needed: A downward-sloping demand curve can be derived directly from a consumer's indifference curves and price lines without using or even assuming a "law" of utility.

SUMMARY OF IMPORTANT IDEAS

1. The theory of indifference curves relates *objective* facts determined by market prices and the consumer's income to the consumer's *subjective* valuations of commodities.

The key mechanisms employed in the theory are price lines and indifference curves.

2. Through indifference-curve analysis, we can show how the consumption of goods changes when a buyer's income increases while prices are held constant; we can also illustrate how a buyer's consumption of a good changes when its price varies, while his income and all other prices remain the same.

3. A consumer's demand curve can be derived directly from the tangency points of indifference curves and price lines. The law of demand can thus be established without relying on the controversial theory of utility.

FOR DISCUSSION

1. *Terms and concepts to review:*

price line (budget line)	income-consumption
indifference schedule	curve
marginal rate of	inferior good
substitution	superior good
indifference curve	price-consumption curve

2. We have drawn indifference curves so that they are *convex* to the origin. What would it mean to draw an indifference curve that is *concave* to the origin? Would it make sense? Explain. (HINT: Think in terms of the *MRS*.)

3. Draw a consumer's indifference curve which represents each of the following situations:
   (a) two commodities that are perfect complements, i.e., used in 1:1 proportions, such as left shoes and right shoes
   (b) two commodities that are perfect substitutes, such as nickels and dimes in the ratio of 2:1

4. Commodities such as diamonds and furs are sometimes cited as an exception to the law of demand because some people will buy more of these at a higher price than at a lower price. Does this mean that the "demand" curve for these products is upward-sloping? Explain. (Be careful in your thinking. This is a much deeper question than is immediately apparent.)

5. In terms of indifference-curve analysis, what might be the effects of each of the following: (a) an increase in taxes; (b) an increase in the cost of living; (c) expectation of inflation.

CHAPTER 23

Costs of Production

CHAPTER PREVIEW

What does the word "cost" mean? Is the term employed in different senses? Can we establish some definitions of costs that can be useful in analyzing and interpreting production problems?

How are costs related to production? Can this information help us to understand the economic behavior of business firms?

According to a familiar saying, you have to spend money in order to make money. In the business world this can be translated to mean that a company must be willing to incur costs if it is to receive revenues.

What do we mean by costs? The term is by no means as simple as most people think. Engineers, accountants, and economists are all concerned with the nature and behavior of costs, but all deal with different cost concepts in solving different problems.

For example, if you were the president of a corporation and were interested in constructing a new manufacturing plant, you might employ an industrial engineer to study the cost of designing the plant, and a cost accountant to classify and analyze production costs after the plant was in operation. You might also hire an economist to advise you on the ways in which the plant's costs of production would be affected by changes in its volume of output, and how these costs could be used as a guide to helping you achieve the volume of production that would bring maximum profits.

Thus, the analysis of costs by engineers, accountants, and economists may be undertaken for quite different purposes. This chapter explains the basic cost concepts and relationships that are of interest in economics.

What Do We Mean by "Cost"?

As long ago as 1923, a famous economist, Professor J. M. Clark, wrote, "A class in economics would be a success if the students gained from it an understanding of the meaning of cost in all its many aspects." Clark was prompted to make this statement by the fact that although the general idea of cost can cover a wide variety of meanings, one meaning is common to all types of cost:

Cost is a sacrifice that must be made in order to do or to acquire something. The nature of the sacrifice—that is, what is given up—may be tangible or intangible, objective or subjective, and may take one or more of many forms such as money, goods, leisure time, income, security, prestige, power, or pleasure.

Let us amplify this definition by describing and illustrating the notion of cost.

OUTLAY COSTS VERSUS OPPORTUNITY (ALTERNATIVE) COSTS

To most of us, the concept of cost that readily comes to mind is what we may call *outlay costs*. These are the moneys expended in order to carry on a particular activity. Some examples of outlay costs to a business are wages and salaries of its employees; expenditures on plant and equipment; payments for raw materials, power, light, and transportation; disbursements for rents, advertising, and insurance; and taxes paid to the government. Such costs are also frequently called *explicit costs*, *historical costs*, or *accounting costs* because they are the objective and tangible expenses that an accountant records in the company's books.

Economists use a more basic concept of cost: *opportunity cost*, defined as the value of the benefit that is forgone by choosing one alternative rather than another. This is an extremely important concept because the "real" cost of any activity is measured by its opportunity cost, not by its outlay cost. How do you identify opportunity costs? By making a comparison between the alternative that was chosen and the one that was rejected. Here are some examples:

1. To a student, the cost of getting a full-time college education includes not only his outlay costs on tuition and books, but also his opportunity costs, that is, the income he forgoes by not working full time.

2. To a business firm, the cost of allocating more money for advertising includes not only its outlay costs for magazine space or TV time, but also its opportunity costs, that is, the earnings it forgoes by not putting these funds to some other use—perhaps into the purchase of new equipment or the training of more salesmen.

3. To a city, the cost of a public park includes not only its outlay costs for construction and maintenance, but also its opportunity costs, that is, the tax income that it forgoes by not zoning the land for residential, commercial, or industrial use.

You can probably think of other examples, and it should be evident why opportunity costs are often called "alternative costs."

The concept of opportunity cost arises whenever the inputs of any activity are scarce and have alternative uses. The real cost or sacrifice is then measured by the value of the forgone alternative. This principle applies at all levels of economic activity—macro as well as micro. Thus:

For any economic organism such as a society, a business, a household, or an individual, it is incorrect to confine the cost of an activity or a decision to what the organism is doing. *It is what the organism is not doing but could be doing that is the correct cost consideration.*

What About Nonmonetary Alternatives?

The principle of opportunity cost raises an important question: Is it not true that the alternative cost of a given action may often involve nonmonetary considerations such as riskiness, working conditions, prestige, and similar factors? The answer is yes. This helps to explain why window washers in skyscrapers earn more than dishwashers in restaurants; why college professors on the average earn less—but probably have fewer headaches—than corporation executives; why the prices of "glamor" securities in the stock market fluctuate much more widely than the prices of public utility shares; and why a man may be willing to work for a smaller return in his own business where he can be his own boss, rather than for a higher return in someone else's.

Of course, the nonmonetary elements that help make for differences in resource allocation are often difficult to measure. But *in principle* the monetary returns plus or minus the various nonmonetary advantages and disadvantages determine the ways in which the owners of the factors of production put their human and material resources to use.

ECONOMIC COST INCLUDES NORMAL PROFIT

Once we recognize the existence of opportunity costs, it becomes apparent that there is a sharp distinction between costs in accounting and costs in economics. *Economic costs* are payments that must be made to persuade the owners of the factors of production to supply them for a particular activity. This definition emphasizes the fact that economic costs are supply prices or "bids" that buyers of resources must offer to attract the factor inputs they want.

Thus a firm buys its resources such as capital, land, and labor in the open market. Expenditures for these resources are part of its economic costs, and these money outlays are the *explicit costs* that an accountant records in the company's books. But there are other types of economic costs, called *implicit costs* because they are the costs of self-owned or self-employed resources that are not entered in a company's books of account. For example, if an individual owns a business, including the building and its real estate, and if he manages this business himself, part of his cost includes these implicit items:

1. The *interest* return on his investment that he is forgoing by not putting his money into an alternative investment of equal risk

2. The *rental* receipts that he is passing up by not renting the land and building to another firm

3. The *wages* (including the return for entrepreneurship) that he would earn if he could be hired to manage the same kind of business for someone else

These implicit costs of ownership comprise what may be called *normal profit*—that is, the least payment the owner of an enterprise would be willing to accept for performing the entrepreneurial function, including risk taking, management, and the like. Normal profit is thus part of a firm's total economic costs, since it is a payment which the owner must receive in order to keep him from withdrawing his capital and managerial effort and putting them into some other alternative. Further, since economic costs include both explicit costs and implicit costs, and since implicit costs include normal profit, any receipts which a firm may get over and above its economic costs represent *economic* or *pure profit*.

SHORT RUN AND LONG RUN

Any discussion of costs must include an explanation of two useful concepts—the short run and the long run. These do not refer to clock or calendar time, but to the time necessary for resources to adapt fully to new conditions—regardless of how many weeks, months, or even years this may take. At any given time a firm has available a certain *capacity* to produce as determined by the quantity or scale of its plant and equipment. If it experiences unexpected increases or decreases in the demand for its products, it can change its level of output by using existing plant and equipment either more or less intensively, but it cannot alter plant scale or production capacity with equal speed. Business firms do not put up new factories or discard old ones with every increase or decrease in demand, any more than colleges and universities erect new classroom buildings or abandon old ones with every rise or fall in enrollment.

This leads to an important distinction between the short run and the long run. The *short run* is a period in which a firm can vary its output through a more or less intensive use of its resources, but cannot vary its capacity because it has a fixed plant scale. The *long run* is a period long enough for a firm to enter or leave an industry, and to vary its output by varying all its factors of production, including plant scale.

These concepts of the short run and the long run suggest an appropriate passage from Henry Wadsworth Longfellow's famous poem, *The Day Is Done:*

> And the night shall be filled with music,
>   And the cares that infest the day,
> Shall fold their tents, like the Arabs,
>   And as silently steal away.

In economics as in poetry, business firms, like the Arabs to whom Longfellow referred, can also come and go by unfolding or folding their tents—but by our definition they can do this only in the long run, not in the short run.

The Production Function

Every businessman is well aware that his costs of production depend on two things: the quantity of resources he buys and the prices he pays for them. At this point our concern is with the quantity. Therefore, it will be useful to analyze a concept known as the *production function*—a relationship between the number of units of inputs that a firm employs and the corresponding units of output that result.

THE LAW OF (EVENTUALLY) DIMINISHING RETURNS

You have probably heard of the *law of diminishing returns*—a law that is as famous in economics as the law of gravity in physics. But you are not likely to have a precise understanding of this law without a prior course in elementary economics, any more than you would have a clear understanding of the law of gravity if you had never taken a basic course in physics. Hence Exhibit 1, which displays a production function based on only one variable input, enables you to "see" the operation of the law of diminishing returns as well as to understand it in terms of the following definition:

Law of (eventually) Diminishing Returns. In a given state of technology, the addition of a variable factor of production, keeping the other factors of produc-

tion fixed, will yield increasing marginal returns per unit of the variable factor added until an input point is reached beyond which further additions of the variable factor will yield diminishing marginal returns per unit of the variable factor added. (NOTE: This law is also known by the more general name of the *law of variable proportions.*)

The law of diminishing returns was first discovered (by the great English classical economist, David Ricardo) in agriculture in 1815, and marked an heroic advance in the history of economics. Indeed, it is one of the most widely held and best-developed principles in all of economics, for it is a law that encompasses many kinds of production functions ranging from agriculture and automobiles through retailing and textiles to zinc and zippers. It thus has enormous significance as well as generality.

First, note that columns (1) and (2) of Exhibit 1 are in general terms. In order to put them into specific terms, the variable input in column (1) of the table might represent pounds of fertilizer applied to an acre of land, whereas the corresponding output in column (2) could be bushels or pounds of an agricultural product. Or the variable input might be the number of workers on an assembly line in a factory and the output could be the number of units of the finished good produced. Practically any simple type of "input-output" relationship or production process could be used to illustrate the basic concepts that are involved.

Second, the curves in the chart are actually "idealized" or smoothed-out versions of the data given in the table. This enables us to focus most of our attention on the graphs rather than the numbers. Thus, the horizontal axis of the chart shows the variable factor from column (1) of the table, and the vertical axis represents the corresponding output from the remaining columns.

Exhibit 1

Production Function

	(1)	(2)	(3)	(4)
			Average product,	Marginal product, *MP*
	Units of variable factor, *F*	Total product, *TP*	*AP* (2) ÷ (1)	Change in (2) / Change in (1)
A	1	6	6	
B	2	14	7	8
C	3	26	8.7	12
D	4	37	9.3	11
E	5	46	9.2	9
F	6	52	8.7	6
G	7	57	8.1	5
H	8	60	7.5	3
I	9	61	6.8	1
J	10	58	5.8	−3

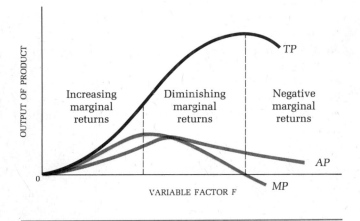

HOW IS THE LAW INTERPRETED?

The first thing you probably noticed in the chart in Exhibit 1 is the shape of the total product or *TP* curve. As the variable input increases from zero, the *TP* curve goes through three phases—first rising rapidly, then tapering off until it reaches a maximum, and then declining. These three phases are reflected by the *marginal product, MP,* which is defined as the change in total product resulting from a unit change in a variable input. For measurement purposes, however, the expression "resulting from" in this definition means the same thing as "divided by"; hence marginal product is given by the formula:

$$MP = \frac{\text{change in total product}}{\text{change in variable input}}$$

You can verify these changes in MP from the table. *Average product, AP,* on the other hand, is simply the ratio of total product to the amount of variable input needed to produce that product:

$$AP = \frac{\text{total product}}{\text{variable input}}$$

For example, if Exhibit 1 is taken to represent the number of men working on a given parcel of land in order to produce tomatoes, the results could be interpreted in the following way:

When the first man, call him *A*, is applied to the fixed amount of land, he has to spread his efforts too thinly by covering all the land, and so the total output is only 6 boxes of tomatoes. If a second man, *B*, is added who is *equally as efficient* as *A*, they can work the same amount of land and thereby increase total output to 14 boxes of tomatoes. The average output is then 7 boxes of tomatoes per man, but the marginal product or gain in output is 8 boxes of tomatoes. Adding further men increases the total output, but a point is eventually reached where there are so many men that they get in each other's way and even trample the tomatoes—the *TP* curve passes its maximum point and turns downward. The gain in output or marginal product then becomes negative.

Note, therefore, that the *MP* curve at first rises and eventually begins to fall even though *all the men are equally efficient.* This is an extremely important point. The reason the *MP* curve declines is not that the last man hired is less efficient than the previous one. It declines solely for quantitative reasons; that is, it declines because of the changing proportions of variable to fixed factors employed, while all qualitative considerations are assumed to remain equal. This is why the term "law of variable proportions" is more often employed than "law of diminishing returns."

Mathematically, of course, the *MP* curve is derived from changes in the *TP* curve. Indeed, the *MP* curve represents the *slope* of the *TP* curve, since the slope of any curve is the change in its vertical distance per unit of change in its horizontal distance. Thus the fact that the *TP* curve first increases at an increasing

rate and then at a decreasing rate is what causes the *MP* curve to rise to a maximum point and then fall. The resulting three phases—*increasing marginal returns, diminishing marginal returns,* and *negative marginal returns*—are labeled on the chart. It is to these phases—especially the first two—that the definition of the law of diminishing returns refers.

Since all three curves rise to a maximum and then decline, it can be said that *a law of diminishing returns applies to the total product, the average product, and the marginal product curves.* Indeed, from the time the law was initially formulated in 1815 until the early part of this century, it was often stated in general terms without distinguishing between total, average, and marginal returns. But it then came to be realized that *marginal* returns are of key importance for decisions involving changes in either input or output, as will become increasingly apparent in subsequent chapters.

It is clear from Exhibit 1 that the point of diminishing marginal returns occurs at the input level where the *MP* curve is a maximum. Where is the point of diminishing average returns? Diminishing total returns?

Short-run Costs

We have seen that in the short run some resource inputs for a firm are variable while others are fixed. This is because it may be possible in a given production process, for example, to vary the number of unskilled workers or to draw down larger or smaller quantities of raw materials available in inventory, but it may take considerable time to construct a new wing on a plant or have machines built to specification.

In view of this, what is the nature and behavior of a firm's costs in the short run? We shall answer this question by analyzing three families of cost concepts: *total cost, average cost,* and *marginal cost.*

COST SCHEDULES AND CURVES

The table in Exhibit 2 presents a company's cost schedule, illustrating the relationship between quantities of output produced per day, as shown in column (1), and the various costs per day of producing these outputs, as shown in the remaining columns. The accompanying charts present the graphs of the various cost data in the table. Note that, as usual, output

Exhibit 2

Short-run Cost Schedules and Curves for a Firm

(1) Quantity of output per day, Q	(2) Total fixed cost, TFC	(3) Total variable cost, TVC	(4) Total cost, TC (2) + (3)	(5) Average fixed cost, AFC (2) ÷ (1)	(6) Average variable cost, AVC (3) ÷ (1)	(7) Average total cost, ATC (4) ÷ (1) or (5) + (6)	(8) Marginal cost, MC Change in (4) / Change in (1)
0	$25	$ 0	$ 25	$ —	$ —	$ —	
1	25	10	35	25.00	10.00	35.00	$10
2	25	16	41	12.50	8.00	20.50	6
3	25	20	45	8.33	6.67	15.00	4
4	25	22	47	6.25	5.50	11.75	2
5	25	24	49	5.00	4.80	9.80	2
6	25	27	52	4.17	4.50	8.67	3
7	25	32	57	3.57	4.57	8.14	5
8	25	40	65	3.13	5.00	8.13	8
9	25	54	79	2.78	6.00	8.78	14
10	25	75	100	2.50	7.50	10.00	21

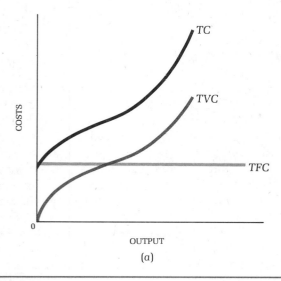

(a)

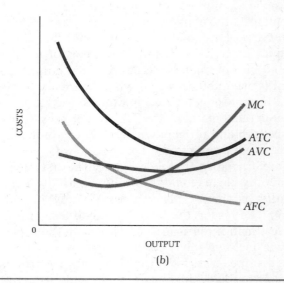

(b)

is measured on the horizontal axes of the charts and dollars on the vertical axes.

Our objective is to see how the different costs in Exhibit 2 are related to output—how they do or do not vary with changes in output. Since the cost curves have a number of important properties, it is important to examine them closely. Remember that we are assuming that *a firm's total costs are its economic costs and hence include normal profit.*

The Family of Total Costs

The first class of costs to be considered is the "total" group shown in columns (2), (3), and (4) of the table.

Total fixed costs. TFC in column (2) represents those costs that do not vary with output. Examples are rental payments, interest payments on debt, property taxes, depreciation of plant and equipment, and the wages and salaries of a skeleton staff that the firm would employ as long as it stayed in business—even if it produced nothing. The TFC figure is $25 at all levels of output in the table and hence appears as a horizontal line on the chart.

Total variable costs. TVC in column (3) consists of those costs that vary directly with output, rising as output increases over the full range of production. Examples are payments for materials, labor, fuel, and power. Note from the chart that as output increases TVC increases first at a decreasing rate and then at an increasing rate, thus reflecting the operation of the law of diminishing (total) returns as explained earlier.

Total costs. TC in column (4) represents the sum of total fixed cost and total variable cost. Thus we have the following equation:

$$TC = TFC + TVC$$

By transposing, you can get for TFC

$$TFC = TC - TVC$$

and for TVC

$$TVC = TC - TFC$$

You should also note from the table and chart that TC equals TFC at zero output; this is because there are no variable costs when there is no production. Observe too that the shape of the TC curve is the same as—or "parallel" to—the shape of the TVC curve, the only difference between them being the constant vertical distance represented by TFC. In other words, since total fixed cost is constant, changes in total cost are due to changes in total variable cost.

The Family of Average Costs

Columns (5), (6), and (7) give us three different types of average costs. These are also represented by the chart which accompanies the table.

Average fixed cost. AFC is the ratio of total fixed cost to quantity produced:

$$AFC = \frac{TFC}{Q}$$

Note from the chart that AFC continually decreases as output increases. This is because TFC in the above equation is constant; therefore increases in Q will always reduce the value of the ratio.

Average variable cost. AVC is the ratio of total variable cost to quantity produced:

$$AVC = \frac{TVC}{Q}$$

Notice that as output increases, the AVC curve falls to a minimum point and then rises. The AVC curve thus reflects the operation of the law of diminishing (average) returns described earlier.

Average total cost. ATC is the ratio of total cost to quantity:

$$ATC = \frac{TC}{Q}$$

Hence it is also equal to the sum of AFC and AVC:

$$ATC = AFC + AVC$$

Of course, you can also transpose either AFC or AVC in order to express the equation in terms of the other variables.

REMARK. Businessmen often use the terms "unit cost" or "cost per unit" when they mean average *variable* cost. If you were a shirt manufacturer, for example, you might figure your cost per shirt to be $3.50 based on the cost of labor, materials, and other variable resources used. You would then set a "markup" price of perhaps $6 per shirt to cover "overhead" or fixed costs. Economists, on the other hand, include fixed costs with total costs right from the outset, and hence use unit cost or cost per unit to mean average *total* cost.

Notice that the vertical distance between ATC and AVC diminishes as output increases; that is, ATC and AVC come progressively closer together. This is because the difference between them, AFC, continually decreases as output expands.

Marginal Cost

There is an important lesson to be learned from the table and graph of Exhibit 2: *Total cost always increases as output increases.* That is, the more a firm produces, the greater its total costs of production, since increased production always requires the use of more materials, labor, power, and other variable resources. Only average costs—in particular ATC and AVC—decrease as output increases until some "optimum" or best level of production is reached.

Thus when you hear a businessman say that he needs to increase production in order to lower costs, he is talking about his unit costs—either his *ATC* or his *AVC*—not his *TC* or *TVC*.

The fact that total cost changes with variations in production gives rise to an important cost concept called *marginal cost, MC*, which is defined as the change in total cost resulting from a unit change in output. As you know from your previous acquaintance with marginal concepts in economics, the expression "resulting from" is used for interpretive purposes, and it means the same thing as "divided by" for mathematical purposes. Therefore, marginal cost may be measured by the formula:

$$MC = \frac{\text{change in } TC}{\text{change in } Q}$$

Of course, changes in *TC* are due to changes in *TVC*, since *TFC* remains constant as production varies; hence, marginal cost can also be measured by dividing the change in *TVC* by the change in *Q*.

What does marginal cost really mean?

Mathematically, marginal cost represents the *slope* of the total cost curve (just as we saw earlier that marginal product represents the slope of the total product curve). Economically, it tells you, for any given output, the *additional* amount of cost a business firm would incur by increasing its output by one unit.

We shall see later that *for economic decisions involving changes in output, marginal cost is the single most important cost concept.*

THE AVERAGE-MARGINAL RELATIONSHIP

By this time you may have noticed an interesting geometric principle that characterizes all average and marginal curves. For convenience, Exhibit 3 groups the foregoing production curves and cost curves together so that they may be examined simultaneously. However, we are interested for the moment only in the average and marginal curves, so these curves are shown in separate charts below their corresponding total curves.

Referring to these lower charts, we note an important relationship:

When an average curve is rising, its corresponding marginal curve is above it; when an average curve is falling, its corresponding marginal curve is below it; and when an average curve is neither rising nor falling, that is, is either at a maximum or at a minimum, its corresponding marginal curve intersects (is equal to) it. This may be called the *average-marginal relationship.*

Does this relationship hold true for the production-function curves as well as for the cost curves? The diagrams indicate that it does, but in the production diagram the marginal curve intersects the average curve at its maximum point, whereas in the cost diagram the marginal curve intersects the two average curves at their minimum points.

The sense behind the average-marginal relationship can be appreciated by a simple example. If to a class of students we add an extra or "marginal" student whose age is above the average age of the class, the average will increase; if we add a student whose age is below the average, the average will decrease; and if we add a student whose age is equal to the average, the average will remain the same.

In later chapters we will encounter other types of average and marginal curves, but the underlying principle stated above characterizes all of them.

THE TOTAL-MARGINAL RELATIONSHIP

A geometric principle is also common to all total and marginal curves; hence it is generally called the "total-marginal relationship." It is based on the fact that every marginal curve is a graph of the *slope* of its corresponding total curve, as we have already seen.

Referring again to Exhibit 3, this time to both the upper and lower charts, we see an interesting relationship which is emphasized by the vertical dashed lines:

When a total curve is increasing at an increasing rate, its corresponding marginal curve is rising; when a total curve is increasing at a decreasing rate, its corresponding marginal curve is falling; and when a total curve is increasing at a zero rate, as occurs when it is at its maximum, its corresponding marginal curve is zero. This is the *total-marginal relationship.*

Observe from the diagrams that the point at which the rate of change of the total curve changes is called the *point of inflection* and that this point corresponds to either a peak or trough of the marginal curve as shown by the vertical dashed lines.

Exhibit 3

Illustration of the Average-marginal Relationship (*lower charts*) **and Total-marginal Relationship** (*upper and lower charts*)

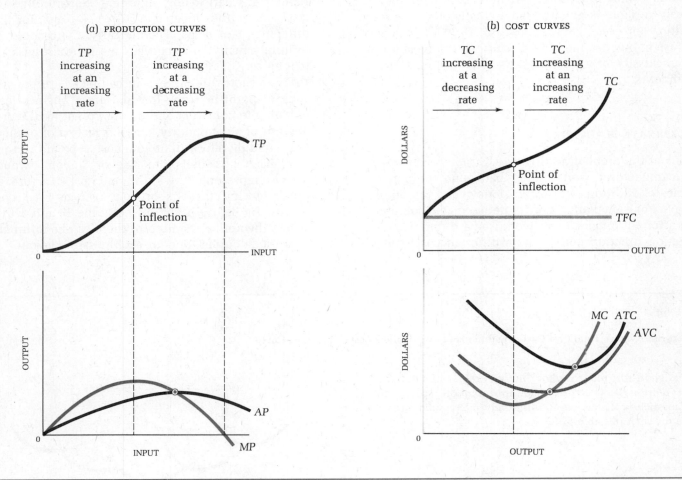

(a) PRODUCTION CURVES

(b) COST CURVES

Note that in the above statement of the total-marginal relationship, it is not necessary to include the fact that when the total curve is falling—as in the case of the *TP* curve at its right end—the corresponding *MP* curve is negative. Although negative marginal curves may exist from a theoretical standpoint, they do not ordinarily have any economic significance. An employer, for example, will not knowingly hire so many units of an input as to yield him a negative marginal product. (Of course, an exception might occur if the input happens to be the boss's son-in-law.)

As with the average-marginal relationship, there are several total-marginal relationships that we shall be encountering in later chapters, but the above statement of the principle characterizes all of them.

Long-run Costs

It was emphasized earlier that a chief distinction between the short run and the long run is this: In the *short run* a firm can vary its output but not its plant capacity, and hence will have some variable costs and some fixed costs; in the *long run* a firm can vary not only its output but also its plant capacity, and therefore has no fixed costs. *In the long run all costs are variable.*

Of what practical value is this in the study of costs? We can answer this question by noting that the previous analysis of short-run costs reveals how a firm's costs will vary in response to output changes within a period short enough for the size of the plant to remain fixed. If we now extend the logic one step further, we can develop a firm's *long-run cost curve*, which, correspondingly, shows the variation of cost with output in a period long enough for all its resource inputs, including plant and equipment, to be freely variable in amount. Once this is done, the resulting knowledge of the long-run cost curve can be of use to businessmen in determining the most economical size of a plant and its general operational standards.

ALTERNATE PLANT SIZES

Look at the problem in this way. Suppose you were a manufacturer whose plant had gone through a series of additions and expansions over a period of years. For each plant size with its associated complement of equipment there would be a different production function and hence a different cost struc-

ture. Each of these cost structures would be represented by a different set of short-run cost curves of the type we have already studied. To illustrate, Exhibit 4, Chart (a) presents five short-run average total cost curves labeled ATC_1, ATC_2, etc., for five different plant sizes. Theoretically, there could be infinitely many such curves, one for each possible plant size.

These short-run curves can be looked at from still another point of view. If you were a businessman planning to construct and equip a plant for the production of a commodity, all your factors of production—and therefore all of your costs—would be variable. Each possible plant size or "layout" would then be represented by a different cost structure, as illustrated by these short-run average total cost curves. As before it should be borne in mind that from a theoretical standpoint there can be infinitely many such curves, one for each possible layout.

Exhibit 4

Short-run Average Total Cost Curves and the Long-run Average Cost or Planning Curve

Each short-run plant size or "layout" represents a different plant-cost structure. The optimum output is ON. Theoretically, there may be infinitely many such curves, one for each possible plant size.

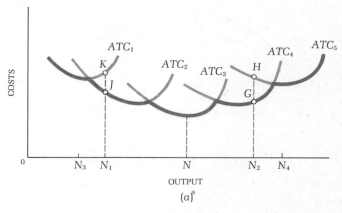

(a)

The planning curve or long-run average cost curve is tangent to all the short-run curves. But it can only be tangent to the minimum point of the lowest short-run curve. For all other short-run curves the tangency occurs on either their declining or rising sides.

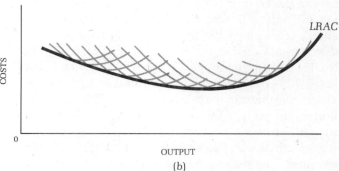

(b)

Some important lessons may be learned from this diagram. On the basis of the information presented it seems intuitively clear that the "optimum" output level is ON, and the lowest-cost plant for producing this output is represented by ATC_3. However, for all other levels of output two interesting principles exist —based on the assumption of infinitely many ATC curves:

1. At any output less than the optimum output ON, it pays better to "underuse" a larger plant than to "overuse" a smaller one. For example, in order to produce output ON_1, it is cheaper to use the larger-scale plant ATC_2 at an average production cost of N_1J per unit than to use the smaller-scale plant ATC_1 at an average cost of N_1K per unit.

2. At any output greater than the optimum output ON, it pays better to "overuse" a smaller plant than to "underuse" a larger one. Thus in order to produce output ON_2, it is cheaper to use the smaller-scale plant ATC_4 at an average cost of N_2G per unit than to use the larger-scale plant ATC_5 at an average cost of N_2H per unit.

It should be noted that these principles are true for *all* outputs—even for outputs like ON_3 and ON_4. Why? Because of the assumption that infinitely many ATC curves may be drawn. Hence you can sketch in the possible ATC curves for ON_3 and ON_4 to demonstrate the validity of these concepts.

THE PLANNING CURVE

These principles suggest that the lower portions of the short-run average total cost curves are the only ones economically relevant to the selection of a particular plant. What would happen to these lower portions if, instead of having just five short-run curves, there were an infinitely large number of them, as we have theoretically assumed? To find out look to Chart (b). The heavy line, which is called a *planning curve,* is a long-run average cost curve ($LRAC$) that is tangent to each of the short-run average total cost curves from which it is derived. The reason for calling it a "planning curve" has already been indicated: When the plant is still in the blueprint stage and all costs are variable, the $LRAC$ curve tells you the average total cost of producing a given level of output. Thus it can be thought of as a curve that shows what costs would be like at the present time for alternative outputs if different-sized plants were built.

THE BEHAVIOR OF LONG-RUN AVERAGE COST: ECONOMIES AND DISECONOMIES OF SCALE

We now come to an important question: What causes the $LRAC$ curve (or the successive ATC curves of which it is composed) to decrease to a minimum and then rise? Or, to put the question in terms of real-world examples: Why are steel mills larger than machine shops? Why do some firms remain small while others become large?

The answers are based on what may be called *economies and diseconomies of scale*—the decreases or increases in a firm's long-run average costs as the size of its plant is increased.

Economies of Scale

Several factors may give rise to economies of scale— that is, to decreasing long-run average costs of production.

1. *Greater specialization of resources.* As a firm's scale of operation increases, its opportunities for specialization—whether performed by men or by machines—are greatly enhanced because a large-scale firm can often divide the tasks and work to be done more readily than a small-scale firm.

2. *More efficient utilization of equipment.* In many industries, the technology of production is such that large units of expensive equipment must be used. The production of automobiles, steel, and refined petroleum are notable examples. In such industries, companies must be able to afford whatever equipment is necessary and must be able to use it efficiently by spreading the cost per unit over a sufficiently large volume of output. A small-scale firm cannot ordinarily do these things.

3. *Reduced unit costs of inputs.* A large-scale firm can often buy its inputs—such as its raw materials— at a cheaper price per unit, thus incurring quantity discounts resulting from larger transactions. And for certain types of equipment, the price per unit of capacity is often much less when larger sizes are purchased. Thus, the construction cost per square foot for a large factory is usually less than for a small one. The price per horsepower of electric induction motors varies inversely with the amount of horsepower.

4. *Utilization of by-products.* In certain industries, large-scale firms can make effective use of many by-products that would be wasted by a small firm. A

typical example is in the meat-packing industry, where companies like Swift and Armour make glue from cattle hoofs, as well as pharmaceuticals, fertilizer, and other products from the remains of livestock.

5. *Growth of auxiliary facilities.* In some places, an expanding firm may often benefit from, or encourage other firms to develop, ancillary facilities such as warehousing, marketing, and transportation systems, thus saving the growing firm considerable costs. For example, urban colleges and universities benefit from nearby public libraries; individual farms benefit from common irrigation and drainage ditches; commercial and industrial establishments often encourage the development of, and receive the benefit from, improved transportation facilities.

Diseconomies of Scale

At the same time that economies of scale are being realized, a point may be reached where diseconomies of scale begin to exercise a more than offsetting effect. As a result, the long-run average cost curve starts to rise primarily for two reasons.

1. *Decision-making role of management.* As a firm becomes larger, heavier burdens are placed on management so that eventually this resource input is overworked relative to others, and "diminishing returns" to management set in. Of course, management may be able to delegate authority to others, but ultimately decisions must emanate from a final center if there is to be uniformity in performance and policy. Even the modern principles of scientific management do not eliminate these diseconomies; at most they may only postpone them or perhaps lessen their seriousness.

2. *Competition for resources.* Rising long-run average costs can occur as a growing firm increasingly bids labor or other resources away from other industries. This may raise the prices it pays for its factors and cause increases in its per unit production costs.

A CLASSIFICATION OF ECONOMIES AND DISECONOMIES

These causes of increasing and decreasing returns to scale are often classified according to whether they are internal or external to the firm. The distinction is important, since the internal factors may be subject to a certain amount of managerial control, whereas the external factors are not.

☐ *Internal economies and diseconomies* are those conditions that bring about decreases or increases in a firm's long-run average costs or scale of operations as a result of size adjustments within the firm as a producing unit. They occur regardless of adjustments within the industry and are due mainly to physical economies or diseconomies. Thus, reductions in long-run average costs occur largely because the indivisibility of productive factors is overcome when size and output are increased; on the other hand, increases in long-run average costs occur because of adverse factor interaction between management and other resources.

☐ *External economies and diseconomies* are those conditions that bring about decreases or increases in a firm's long-run average costs or scale of operations as a result of factors that are entirely outside the firm as a producing unit. They depend on adjustments of the industry and are related to the firm only to the extent that it is part of the industry.

On the basis of this distinction, you should be able to classify each of the various economies and diseconomies of scale listed above as either internal or external.

CONCLUSION: WHAT DOES THE EVIDENCE SHOW?

How have business firms adjusted to the existence of economies of scale? Do the long-run average cost curves of firms actually look like the ones shown earlier or do their shapes vary according to the economics of the industry in which they operate?

Relatively few studies have been done on this question, and no conclusive statements can be made. Nevertheless, the limited evidence that exists, coupled with what economists know about the theory of production and costs, suggests that there may be three basic variations of curves. These are illustrated and described in Exhibit 5.

SUMMARY OF IMPORTANT IDEAS

1. Cost is a sacrifice that must be made in order to acquire something. The sacrifice may include monetary and nonmonetary elements.

2. Opportunity costs are critical in economics because they measure the value of a forgone alternative. Opportunity costs arise because resources are limited and have alternative uses.

3. Economic costs are payments that must be made to attract resources. Such costs include not only explicit costs or money expenditures for resources, but also the implicit costs of self-owned or self-employed resources.

4. The law of diminishing returns—a more general name is the law of variable proportions—states what happens to output when a variable input is combined with fixed inputs. Although the law covers total, average, and marginal returns, the last is

---

Exhibit 5

Three Typical Long-run Average Cost Curves

The shapes of different firms' long-run average costs vary in different industries.

Chart (a) *shows the situation in which economies of scale outweigh the diseconomies over a wide range of output. Examples are the aluminum, automobile, cement, and steel industries.*

Chart (b) *shows the situation in which diseconomies of scale set in quickly and many small firms exist side by side. Examples are the retailing, textiles, metal fabrication, and publishing industries.*

Chart (c) *shows the situation in which economies of scale are either quickly exhausted and diseconomies take a long time coming, or else the economies and diseconomies tend to cancel each other out. Examples are the chemicals, food processing, furniture, and appliance industries.*

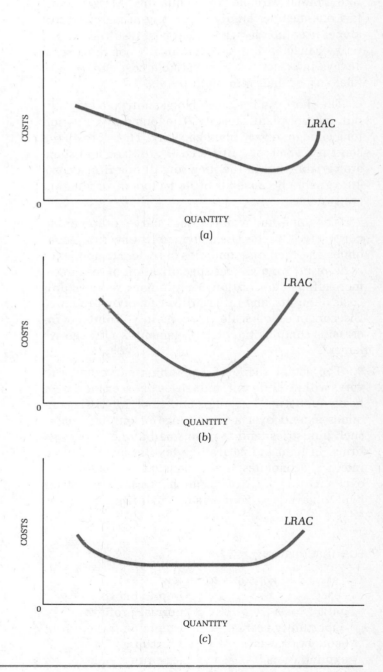

most important where output changes are involved. Graphically, marginal product always intersects average product at its maximum point.

5. There are three families of costs: total, average, and marginal. The family of total costs consists of total fixed costs, which do not vary with output, and total variable costs, which increase as output increases. The family of average costs consists of average fixed cost, which is the ratio of total fixed cost to quantity, and average variable cost, which is the ratio of total variable cost to quantity. Marginal cost is a one-member family consisting of marginal cost alone: it is the change in total cost resulting from a unit change in output. Graphically, marginal cost always intersects average variable cost and average total cost at their minimum points.

6. The short run is a period long enough to vary output, but not plant capacity. The long run is a period long enough to vary plant capacity. Therefore, in the short run some of a firm's costs are fixed and some are variable, but in the long run all of a firm's costs are variable because all of its factors of production are variable.

7. The long-run average cost curve or planning curve tends to be U-shaped, reflecting first economies and then diseconomies of scale. Economies of scale result from greater specialization of resources, more efficient utilization of equipment, reduced unit costs of inputs, and fuller utilization of by-products. Diseconomies of scale arise mainly from the increasing complexities of management as a firm grows larger.

8. The actual shape of a planning curve tends to vary within different industries. For example, in heavy industries like autos and steel, internal economies extend over a wide range of output; hence, such industries tend to have small numbers of large firms. In light industries like textiles and retailing, internal economies are exhausted rather quickly over a narrow range of output; hence such industries tend to have large numbers of small firms.

FOR DISCUSSION

1. *Terms and concepts to review:*

cost	implicit costs
outlay costs	normal profit
opportunity cost	economic (pure) profit
economic costs	short run
explicit costs	long run
production function	total-marginal relationship
law of diminishing returns (law of variable proportions)	long-run average cost curve (planning curve)
marginal product	economies and diseconomies of scale
average product	
total fixed costs	internal economies and diseconomies of scale
total variable costs	
total cost	external economies and diseconomies of scale
average fixed cost	
average variable cost	
average total cost	
marginal cost	
average-marginal relationship	

2. Complete the table on the next page showing the cost schedule of a firm; then graph the family of total costs on one chart and all of the remaining costs on another. (NOTE: When you graph the marginal-cost curve, plot each MC figure to the midpoint between successive outputs. Thus on your chart, the first MC figure corresponds to an output of 0.5, the second to 1.5, the third to 2.5, and so on.)

Discuss the various curves in terms of their shape as influenced by the law of diminishing returns. (HINT: Sketch the family of total costs on one chart, and the family of average and marginal costs on another chart directly beneath it. Then see if you can draw a vertical dashed line through both charts such that the stage of increasing marginal returns is on the left side of the vertical line, and the stage of decreasing marginal returns is on the right.) In your answer, account for the relative distances between ATC and AVC at different levels of output, and the reason for the intersection of MC with ATC and AVC at their minimum points.

3. Are opportunity costs entered in the accounting records of a firm? If so, what are they used for? If not, of what good are they?

4. In estimating the annual cost of owning a fully paid-up $3,000 automobile, you might show the following cost entry on your books: "Interest on investment at 5 percent: $150." What would this mean? Explain.

5. Why do you suppose that some teachers, who could earn considerably more by working in industry, continue to accept a lower salary by remaining in education?

COST SCHEDULE OF A FIRM

(1) Quantity of output	(2) Total fixed cost	(3) Total variable cost	(4) Total cost	(5) Average fixed cost	(6) Average variable cost	(7) Average total cost	(8) Marginal cost
0	$100	$ 0	$_____	$_____	$_____	$_____	$_____
1	____	40	____	____	____	____	____
2	____	64	____	____	____	____	____
3	____	80	____	____	____	____	____
4	____	88	____	____	____	____	____
5	____	96	____	____	____	____	____
6	____	108	____	____	____	____	____
7	____	128	____	____	____	____	____
8	____	160	____	____	____	____	____
9	____	216	____	____	____	____	____
10	____	300	____	____	____	____	____

6. Do you agree with the theory that as a firm becomes larger and decision-making more complex, the long-run average cost curve turns upward because the burden of administration becomes disproportionately greater and "diminishing returns" to management set in? Would this be true of such well-managed firms as Proctor & Gamble or General Motors? Of what significance is technology, organizational structure, managerial ability, etc.?

7. The law of diminishing returns was originally intended to serve as an explanation of an historical process. In England, for example, as the population grew during the eighteenth and nineteenth centuries, it was predicted (by David Ricardo) that the marginal productivity of labor on land would decline. If this were true:

(a) What would happen to aggregate values of agricultural land?

(b) What would happen to total land rent as a percentage share of national income?

(c) What would happen to the price of food relative to nonfood goods?

(d) How would you answer these questions with respect to the United States during most of the nineteenth century?

8. What is the effect of a technological improvement on a company's production function?

9. "If it were not for the law of diminishing returns, it would be possible to grow all of the world's food in a flowerpot." Do you agree? Explain.

10. The most common type of production function is one which is characterized by "constant returns to scale." This means that if *all* inputs to a production process are increased in the same proportion, output is increased in that proportion. For example, if *all* inputs are expanded by 10 percent, output is expanded by 10 percent; if *all* inputs are doubled, output is doubled; etc. In view of this, how do you account for the following situation?

(a) A men's suit manufacturer doubled the size of his factory, the number of machines in it, the number of workers, and the quantity of materials employed. As a result his output increased from 200 to 420 suits per day. Is this an example of *increasing returns to scale*, that is, economies of large-scale production?

(b) The manufacturer then doubled the quantity of managers and found that his output fell to 370 suits per day. What do you suppose might have happened?

11. BIOLOGICAL GROWTH ANALOGIES OF RETURNS TO SCALE

(a) There is a relationship between the volume V and the surface area A of regular physical bodies. This relationship may be approximated by the "square-cube" law:

$$V = A^{3/2} = \sqrt{A^3}$$

For example, if the surface area of an object increases 4 times, its volume should increase about $\sqrt{4^3} = 8$ times. Can you use this notion to explain why there are no small warm-blooded animals in the Antarctic or in the ocean, and why the largest insect is about as large as the smallest warm-blooded animal?

(b) There is often a tendency to think that constant returns to scale should be common in economic life, yet variable returns (i.e., both increasing and decreasing) are frequently encountered. For example, we should expect that by doubling *all* inputs to a production process, the output ought to double. Yet there are examples from nature to illustrate why this is not so. Thus, if a house were scaled down so that it stood in the same proportion to a flea as it now stands to a man, the flea would be able to jump over the house. However, if a flea were scaled up to the size of a man, the flea would not be able to jump over the house. In fact, it couldn't jump at all because its legs would break. Can you explain why?

(c) What conclusions relevant to the size and growth of organizations can you draw from these notions? (HINT: It has been said that prehistoric monsters became extinct because they could not adjust to their changing environment. Why not?)

(d) Do you see any connection between questions (a) through (c) and the following quotation:

There is a story of a man who thought of getting the economy of large-scale production in plowing, and built a plow three times as long, three times as wide, and three times as deep as the ordinary plow and harnessed six horses to pull it, instead of two. To his surprise, the plow refused to budge, and to his greater surprise it finally took fifty horses to move the refractory machine. In this case, the resistance, which is the thing he did not want, increased faster than the surface area of the earth plowed, which was the thing he did want. Furthermore, when he increased his power to overcome this resistance, he multiplied the number of his power units instead of their size, which eliminated all chance of saving there, and since his units were horses, the fifty could not pull together as well as two.

J. M. Clark, *Studies in the Economics of Overhead Costs*, Chicago, University of Chicago Press, 1923, p. 116.

Case

Sunshine Dairy Products Corporation: Constructing New Plants

Sunshine Dairy Products Corporation is a leading producer of milk, ice cream, cheese, and various other dairy products. Recently, after many years of research, the company succeeded in developing a very low-calorie ice cream. Extensive taste tests have indicated that this new ice cream is every bit as delicious as any of the leading brands. Accordingly, the management of the company has decided to produce and market the new ice cream on a "test" basis within one region of the country and to construct the necessary production facilities for this purpose.

The Sunshine Corporation conducted a market survey of the three largest population areas of the region. The results indicated that the company could expect to sell 10,000, 5,000, and 2,500 gallons per week in each area, respectively. An economic consultant for the company has suggested either of two alternatives with respect to the construction of ice cream plants: (1) to construct a single plant equidistant between the three population areas, with a production capacity of 20,000 gallons per week at a fixed cost of $5,000 per week and a variable cost of 70 cents per gallon; or (2) to construct three plants (one in each market area) with weekly capacities of 12,000, 6,000, and 3,000 gallons, respectively, with weekly fixed costs of $4,000, $3,000, and $2,000 respectively, and a variable cost of only 60 cents per gallon due to the reduction of shipping costs.

QUESTIONS

1. Assuming that the market survey is correct, which alternative should management select? At a price of $1.99 per gallon, what would be the profit (or loss) per gallon and in total?

2. If demand were to increase to production capacity, which alternative would be better?

3. Suppose that management selects the second alternative rather than the first, and that demand is at the level of production capacity in all three markets. If the company wanted to make a profit of $1 per gallon in each of the three markets, what price per gallon would it have to charge in each of these markets? Can management be sure of realizing its expected profit? Explain why.

4. Instead of constructing a new plant, the management of Sunshine is contemplating the purchase of an existing plant. An economic consultant has provided the following cost estimates for the plant under consideration:

(a) The ATC of 5,000 gallons is $12,600.
(b) AVC for 4,000 gallons is $10,000.
(c) TC rises by $13,000 when production rises from 5,000 to 6,000 gallons.
(d) AFC of 5,000 gallons is $2,000.
(e) The increase in TC from producing nothing to producing 1,000 gallons is $15,000.
(f) TC of 8,000 gallons is $170,000.
(g) TVC increases by $25,000 when production rises from 6,000 to 7,000 gallons.
(h) AFC plus AVC for 3,000 gallons is $16,000.
(i) ATC falls by $6,000 when production increases from 1,000 to 2,000 gallons.

On the basis of this information, complete the following cost schedule. [HINT: First fill in all the data given in (a) through (i).]

COST SCHEDULE OF AN ICE CREAM PLANT
(thousands of dollars per week)

Output (thousand gallons per week)	TFC	TVC	TC	AFC	AVC	ATC	MC
0	$__	$__	$__	$__	$__	$__	$__
1	__	__	__	__	__	__	__
2	__	__	__	__	__	__	__
3	__	__	__	__	__	__	__
4	__	__	__	__	__	__	__
5	__	__	__	__	__	__	__
6	__	__	__	__	__	__	__
7	__	__	__	__	__	__	__
8	__	__	__	__	__	__	__

PART 6

The Economics of the Firm: How Are Prices and Outputs Determined?

CHAPTER 24

Perfect Competition: Criteria for Evaluating Competitive Behavior

CHAPTER PREVIEW

What do we mean by perfect competition? Is it a fantasy or is it real?

How do business firms operate under perfect competition? Do they receive profits? Do they incur losses? How much do they produce?

What are the consequences of perfect competition? Does it have both favorable and unfavorable features? What would it be like to live in a world of perfect competition?

Early in this book we learned that economics is concerned with how society allocates its limited resources, which have alternative uses, to the production of goods and services. Economists have always wanted to see this task accomplished with the least amount of waste. Hence they have developed a theory which yields certain ideal results as far as the attainment of this goal is concerned.

This is the theory of "perfect competition" or "pure competition." (The two terms are used synonymously for most purposes, although a technical distinction that is sometimes made between them will be explained subsequently.) The theory underlies the operation of supply and demand that we studied in previous chapters. It attempts to explain how a "perfect" market economy or "pure" free-enterprise system tends to operate.

What Is Perfect Competition?

When a scientist seeks to describe a complicated problem, he starts by constructing a simplified picture of the situation, or a *model*. In this chapter we shall develop a model or theory of perfect competition.

Let us begin with a definition.

Perfect (or *pure*) *competition* is the name given to an industry or market structure characterized by a large number of buyers and sellers all engaged in the purchase and sale of a homogeneous commodity, with perfect knowledge of market prices and quantities, no discrimination, and perfect mobility of resources.

This definition contains five essential conditions which require further examination.

PERFECT COMPETITION: EXPLAINING THE DEFINITION

The expression "perfect competition" can be used in discussing either an industry or a market. The distinction is always clear from the context in which the term is used, and the above definition is applicable to both categories—industries as well as markets. Now let us analyze the rest of the definition.

1. *Large number of buyers and sellers.* What do we mean by a "large" number of buyers and sellers? Is 1,000 large and 999 small? To answer yes would be silly since the words "large" or "small" are relative rather than absolute terms. Hence our definition does not establish the size of a perfectly competitive market in terms of numbers. Instead, it uses the word "large," as we have discussed in earlier chapters, to mean *large enough so that no one buyer or seller can affect the market price by offering to buy or not to buy, to sell or not to sell.* Therefore, whether it takes 1,000 or 1 million buyers or sellers is of no relevance. The only requirement is that the market price for any buyer or seller is *given.* He can take it or leave it, but he cannot alter it by going into or out of the market.

2. *Homogeneous commodity.* This means that all units which sellers make available must be identical in the minds of buyers. The reason for this requirement, as will be shown later, is that buyers must be indifferent as to which seller they deal with; they must be willing to purchase from the seller who offers the good at the lowest price.

Notice, therefore, that we are referring to *economic homogeneity,* not physical homogeneity. Two sellers may be selling the same physical product, but buyers may be willing to pay more to seller A than to seller B because seller A provides service with a smile, or a more attractive package, or perhaps a brand name.

In that case the two products are *not* economically homogeneous.

We can illustrate this point with a concrete example. Beet sugar and cane sugar are physically the same for all practical purposes: they look and taste the same. Yet in most regions of the country beet sugar sells for less than cane. Why? Because buyers do not regard them as the same; instead, they believe that beet is somehow inferior to cane, and since a package of sugar must be labeled either "beet" or "cane," there tends to be a price difference between them. In this case the two products are physically homogeneous but *economically heterogeneous;* that is, they are similar but not identical. How about butter and margarine? Two nickels and a dime? Are they homogeneous? Heterogeneous?

3. *Perfect knowledge of market prices and quantities.* The third condition—"perfect knowledge"—means that all buyers and sellers are completely aware of the prices and quantities at which transactions are taking place in the market and that all have the opportunity to participate in those transactions. For example, perfect knowledge does not exist if buyers do not know that sellers across the street are charging a lower price for a certain commodity. Likewise, perfect knowledge does not exist if sellers do not know that buyers across the street are offering a higher price for a certain product. In both instances the buyers and sellers on one side of the street are not competing with the buyers and sellers on the other side, and hence are not even in the same market.

4. *No discrimination.* This condition tells us that buyers and sellers must be willing to deal openly with one another—to buy and sell at the market price with any and all that may wish to do so—without offering any special deals, discounts, or favors to selected individuals. Discrimination thus has an economic meaning, not just a social one.

5. *Perfect mobility of resources.* The condition of perfect resource mobility requires that there be no obstacles—economic, legal, technological, or others —to prevent firms or resources from entering or leaving the particular market or industry, and there be no impediments to the purchase or sale of commodities. This means that firms, resources, and commodities can be shifted about swiftly and smoothly without friction. For example, the land, labor, capital, and entrepreneurship used in wheat production can be moved quickly into corn production if it

is more profitable. Potatoes stored in Idaho can be sold instantly in New York or in San Francisco if the price is right. And, in general, owners of resources and commodities are free and able to take advantage of the best market opportunities as they arise.

IS PERFECT COMPETITION REALISTIC?

Is the concept of perfect competition realistic or a fantasy? After all, no market or industry anywhere in the world exactly meets all five requirements described above. Should you infer, therefore, that the notion of perfect competition is "theoretical and impractical"?

The answer is no. As we shall see shortly, the concept of perfect competition is a *theoretical extreme*—like the concept of a perfect vacuum or the assumption of a frictionless state in physics. For example, in elementary physics it is expressly assumed in many problems of motion that there is *no friction*, although everyone knows that friction always exists in the real world. The assumption creates an idealized situation which permits simplification of a problem in order to analyze it. Similarly, in the theory of perfect competition in this chapter, you will be studying a "frictionless" economic system in which the movement of goods and resources is unobstructed. In this way, as in physics, you are using an idealized model in order to simplify and analyze the problems involved.

But our model will not be completely unreal. Some markets do approach the conditions of perfect competition at least roughly, although none meets all the conditions precisely. The examples that come closest to the ideal are the organized commodity and stock exchanges in New York, Chicago, and many other cities, and to a lesser extent some industries producing standard raw materials. In these markets the approximation to perfect competition varies, but is close enough to make the theory and conclusions of this chapter both meaningful and useful.

REMARK. As you will see below, the conditions of perfect knowledge and perfect resource mobility are not absolutely essential to our theory. They are desirable, however, because they serve as "lubricating" features which tend to make a perfectly competitive system operate more quickly and smoothly than it would if these two conditions did not exist.

Costs, Revenues, and Profit Maximization in the Short Run

It follows from our explanation of perfect competition that the market price of a commodity under such circumstances would be established independently through the free operation of total supply and total demand. We have already seen in previous chapters how this happens: No individual buyer or seller can influence the price, yet the price emerges automatically as a reflection of the interaction of numerous buyers and sellers.

This leads us to ask a vital question: How does a firm in perfect competition, faced with a market price over which it has no influence, decide how much of a commodity it will produce? The answer to this question is one of the most fundamental principles of economics.

TOTAL COSTS AND TOTAL REVENUES

Let us begin by turning our attention to the table in Exhibit 1 on the next page, which gives the costs and revenues of a firm in perfect competition. The only costs shown are those needed for our analysis.

Columns (1) and (2) are already familiar concepts, since they represent quantities produced and the corresponding levels of total cost. As always, total cost increases as quantity increases.

Column (3) denotes *average revenue (AR)*, the price per unit of output or, as we shall see momentarily, the ratio of total revenue to quantity. In this case the average revenue is $10 per unit. Thus we are assuming that the price established in the market through the free interaction of supply and demand is $10, and hence this is the price with which the firm is faced and over which it has no control. Or, to put it somewhat differently, the firm finds that it can sell all the units it wants to at the market price P of $10.

Column (4), called *total revenue (TR)*, is simply the price per unit times the number of units sold. Looking at the headings of columns (3) and (4) together, we need only the simplest arithmetic to see the connection between average revenue, total revenue, and price:

$$AR = \frac{TR}{Q} = \frac{P \times Q}{Q} = P$$

Finally, we can skip temporarily to column (8) of the table and note that *net revenue* or net profit—the difference between total revenue and total cost—is at first negative, but it rises to a peak of $15 at 8 units of output and then falls.

Exhibit 1

Cost and Revenue Schedules of a Firm Under Perfect Competition

(1) Quantity per day, Q (given)	(2) Total cost, TC (given)	(3) Price per unit, or average revenue, $P = AR$ (given)	(4) Total revenue, TR (3) × (1)	(5) Average total cost, ATC (2) ÷ (1)	(6) Marginal cost, MC Change in (2) / Change in (1)	(7) Marginal revenue, MR Change in (4) / Change in (1)	(8) Net revenue, NR (4) − (2)
0	$ 25	$10	$ 0	$ —			−$25
					$10	$10	
1	35	10	10	35.00			− 25
					6	10	
2	41	10	20	20.50			− 21
					4	10	
3	45	10	30	15.00			− 15
					2	10	
4	47	10	40	11.75			− 7
					2	10	
5	49	10	50	9.80			1
					3	10	
6	52	10	60	8.67			8
					5	10	
7	57	10	70	8.14			13
					8	10	
8	65	10	80	8.13			15
					14	10	
9	79	10	90	8.78			11
					21	10	
10	100	10	100	10.00			0

Graphic Illustration

The TC and TR figures are graphed in the upper chart of Exhibit 2. The TC curve has a familiar shape, but note that the TR curve is a straight line. This reflects the fact, as stated above, that the firm receives the same price per unit for all the units it sells.

The points labeled B_1 and B_2 are called *break-even points* because they designate levels of output at which a firm's revenue equals its cost: the firm is incurring neither an economic profit nor an economic loss. At any output between these two points, the firm's profit or net revenue is positive, and at any output beyond the break-even points it has a net loss (or negative net revenue) because its costs exceed its revenues.

Finally, it should be pointed out that net revenue, as represented by the vertical distance GH, is a maximum at 8 units of output. At this output the *slope* of the total cost curve as measured by the slope of the tangent at H is equal to the *slope* of the total revenue curve. This suggests an important fundamental concept:

The *slope* (steepness) of a line is the change in its vertical distance per unit of change in its horizontal distance. The slope of a straight line (such as the

TR curve) is the same at every point, but the slope of a curved line (like the TC curve) differs at every point. Geometrically, you can find the slope of a curve at a point by drawing a straight-line tangent to the curve at that point. The slope of the tangent will then be the slope of the curve at the point of tangency. As you will recall from high school geometry, parallel lines have equal slopes. Thus the tangent at H is parallel to the TR curve.

This important concept is amplified further in the paragraphs below and in the descriptions in Exhibit 2.

MARGINAL COST AND MARGINAL REVENUE

The use of total revenue and total cost is a valid way to determine the most profitable level of output for a firm. However, it is not the method that economists usually employ. They prefer to use an approach which at first may seem a bit strange, but is actually much more useful for understanding and interpreting changes in production and costs.

Referring back to the table in Exhibit 1, note that column (5) gives average total cost, and column (6) presents marginal cost. Column (7), however, has a new term called *marginal revenue (MR)*, which is

Exhibit 2

Cost and Revenue Curves of a Firm Under Perfect Competition

PROFIT MAXIMIZATION: THREE VIEWPOINTS

1. Total curves. The most profitable level of output is determined where the difference between the curves TR and TC, as represented by the distance GH, is a maximum. This occurs at an output of 8 units. At this output, a tangent to the TC curve, such as the tangent at H, is parallel to the straight-line TR curve. At smaller or larger outputs such as 6, 7, or 9 units, a tangent to the TC curve would not be parallel to the TR curve.

The break-even points are at B_1 and B_2, where TC = TR. The break-even outputs are thus 5 units and 10 units.

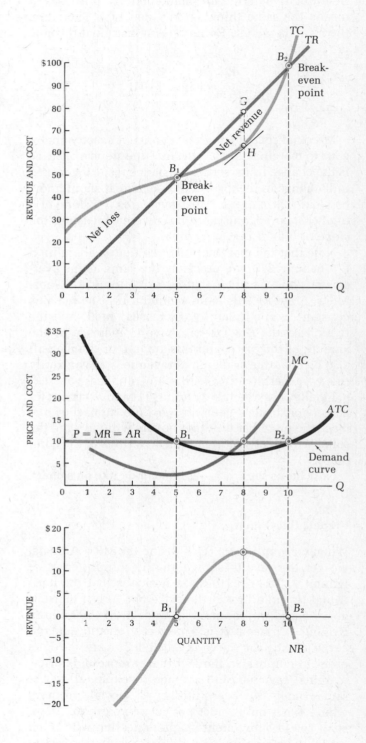

2. Marginal curves. The most profitable level of output is determined where MC = MR, as explained in the text. This is also evident by following the vertical dashed line downward at 8 units of output.

The break-even points are at B_1 and B_2, where ATC = AR.

3. Net revenue curve. The most profitable level of output is determined where the net revenue curve NR (= TR − TC) is a maximum. The vertical dashed line at 8 units of output emphasizes these profit-maximizing principles in all three charts.

TECHNICAL NOTE (OPTIONAL). If you are geometrically inclined, you may note that since parallel lines have equal slopes, the most profitable output in the top chart is the one at which the *slope* (steepness) of the *TC* curve equals the *slope* (steepness) of the *TR* curve. In the middle chart, marginal cost is the graph of the *slope* of total cost, and marginal revenue is the graph of the *slope* of total revenue. Hence at the level of maximum profit:

$$MC = MR$$

which is the same as saying that:

$$\text{Slope of } TC = \text{slope of } TR$$

defined as the change in total revenue resulting from a unit change in output. As in previous cases, the expression "resulting from" in the definition is an interpretative term; for mathematical purposes it means the same thing as "divided by." Therefore, the formula we use for measuring marginal revenue is

$$MR = \frac{\text{change in } TR}{\text{change in } Q}$$

Marginal revenue is thus a concept exactly analogous to marginal cost. And, since the slope of a curve is the change in its vertical distance resulting from a unit change in its horizontal distance, it should now be clear that *marginal cost measures the slope of a total cost curve, and marginal revenue measures the slope of a total revenue curve.*

Note that the marginal revenue figures in column (7), namely $10, are precisely the same as the average revenue or price figures in column (3). Thus, $MR = AR = P$. This is no accident. If price remains constant while quantity increases, total revenue (which equals $P \times Q$) will have to increase by the amount of the price, and this amount of change will also be the same as marginal revenue. You can verify this by experimenting with a few numbers yourself.

Finally, observe that columns (1) and (3) taken together constitute a *demand schedule,* since they disclose the price per unit that buyers will pay (and the seller will receive) for various quantities of the commodity.

Now let us see what these data look like on a chart.

Graphic Illustration

When we graph the ATC, MC, and the $MR = AR$ data, we get the results shown in the middle chart of Exhibit 2. The first thing to notice is that the horizontal revenue line at the price of $10 is a demand curve based on columns (1) and (3) of the table in Exhibit 1; indeed, it is a *perfectly elastic demand curve.* Hence the curve is labeled $P = MR = AR$ in order to emphasize the fact that it represents price, marginal revenue, and average revenue—all at the same time. However, this is a special property which exists only under perfect competition. As we shall see in subsequent chapters dealing with other types of competition, a different situation arises when the demand curve slopes downward instead of being horizontal.

REMARK. For graphing purposes, you should recall from previous chapters that marginal values, in this case MC and MR, are plotted to the *midpoints* of the integers on the horizontal axis, since they reflect, respectively, the change in total cost and in total revenue resulting from a unit change in quantity.

What is the firm's most profitable level of output? We already know that the answer is 8. But we can verify it further by extending the vertical dashed line at 8 units of output from the top chart in Exhibit 2, down to the middle chart, and then to the bottom chart which shows the graph of net revenue NR from column (8) of the table. When we do this, the middle chart, along with the other two supporting charts, reveals the operation of one of the most important principles in all of economics:

The most profitable level of output for a firm occurs where its $MC = MR$. This is a general principle which applies under all types of competition. But under the special case of perfect competition it is also true that the most profitable level of output occurs where $MC = MR = P = AR$, since the last three terms are one and the same. It is only at $MC = MR$ output that a firm's net revenue, as measured by the difference between its total revenue and total cost, is at a maximum.

This $MC = MR$ rule is of such great importance that it may appropriately be called the *fundamental principle of profit maximization.* You may also verify that in the table of Exhibit 1 the demarcated section at 8 units of output shows that when NR reaches a maximum of 15, MC rises from 8 to 14, while MR remains constant at 10. The charts in Exhibit 2, of course, reveal the relationships more clearly; hence you should study them and their accompanying explanations carefully.

INTERPRETING THE $MC = MR$ RULE

The $MC = MR$ rule must be elaborated more fully. In particular, we need to ask: Why does the rule "work" as a guide for profit maximization, and how does a firm react to the rule within the setting of a competitive market?

Part of the answer is given in Exhibit 3. In Chart (a), the market price OP and market output ON are determined by the intersection of *total* demand and *total* supply, representing the interactions of many buyers and many sellers. In Chart (b) any individual seller finds that by producing to where his $MC = MR$ he maximizes his net revenue or profit, and his out-

Exhibit 3

An Industry and Firm in a Perfectly Competitive Market

A perfectly competitive market with many buyers and sellers. *The market price 0P and market output 0N are determined by the intersection of the total market demand and supply curves. The total market demand curve is downward-sloping, because the quantity demanded will be greater at lower prices.*

A typical firm in a perfectly competitive market. *Each seller is confronted with a perfectly elastic demand curve at the market price. By producing to where his MC = MR, his most profitable output 0J is an infinitesimal fraction of the industry's output 0N.*

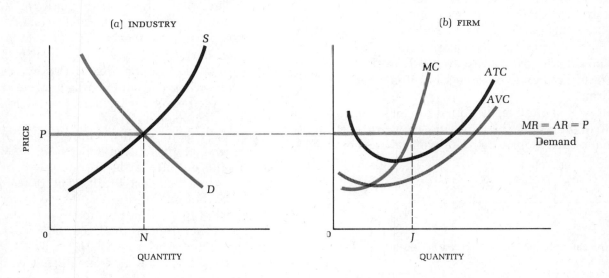

put *0J* is an infinitesimal proportion of the industry's output *0N*. Note this important principle:

Under perfect competition, each seller faces a perfectly elastic demand curve at the market price—for two reasons:

1. Since the product is homogeneous, buyers will purchase the commodity from the seller who offers it at the lowest price.

2. Since each seller supplies only an infinitesimal part of the total market, he can sell *all* his output at the going market price. He cannot sell any of his output for more than that price, and he has no reason to sell any of it for less.

Thus at any output less than *0J*, each one-unit increase in output adds more to total revenue than it adds to total cost—that is, *MR* exceeds *MC*—so it pays to expand production. Conversely at any output greater than *0J*, each one-unit decrease in output reduces total cost more than it reduces total revenue—that is, *MC* is greater than *MR*—so it pays to cut

back production. Only at the point where *MC = MR* do we find the most profitable output *0J*; hence we call this *MC = MR* point the seller's *equilibrium position* because it determines the profit-maximizing output that his firm will seek to achieve and maintain under the given market conditions and the company's existing cost curves.

We can illustrate this concept with a simple example. Suppose you were a manufacturer of some commodity, and knew that by increasing your production by a specific amount you would raise your total revenue by $10 and your total cost by $8. In that case you would try to expand output and thereby increase net profit by $2. On the other hand, if you knew that by decreasing production by a given amount you would cut total cost by $15 and total revenue by $10, you would try to reduce output in order to increase net profit by $5. As a general rule, the only time you would not want to alter the production rate is when profits were already at a maximum. In that case the *changes* in *TC* and *TR* would be the same—that is *MC* would equal *MR*.

ANALYZING SHORT-RUN EQUILIBRIUM

What is the nature of the profit-maximizing or equilibrium position which the firm is trying to attain? Some of its important properties are illustrated by the diagram in Exhibit 4.

First, note from the title that the diagram depicts the firm in short-run equilibrium. This means that under the existing market conditions for the inputs that the firm buys and the output that it sells, and the given set of cost curves with which it operates, the most profitable output is OJ because it is here that $MC = MR$ for this particular firm. We shall see later that in the long run certain market conditions, as well as the seller's cost curves, are likely to change, thereby resulting in a different equilibrium position for the firm.

Second, you should verify that at the most profitable level of output OJ, the following geometric cost and revenue conditions exist. The average total cost

of producing output OJ is represented by the distance $JK (= OT)$, and the average revenue received from the sale of this output is $JL (= OU)$. The difference between these two amounts, of course, is the net revenue per unit—that is, average net revenue—as represented by $KL (= TU)$. Therefore, the total net revenue can be found by multiplying the net revenue per unit by the number of units, thereby obtaining the area of the rectangle $TULK$.

The same result can also be arrived at in a different way. The average revenue per unit (JL) times the number of units (OJ) equals total revenue, which is the area of the large rectangle $OULJ$. Similarly, average total cost (JK) times the number of units (OJ) equals total cost or the area of the rectangle $OTKJ$. Therefore, when you subtract the total cost rectangle from the total revenue rectangle, the difference is the net revenue rectangle $TULK$.

Finally, it is important to observe that profits are maximized at the output where $MC = MR$, even though this output may be beyond the point of minimum average total cost. Profit, in other words, is *not* maximized at output OR, despite the lower average total cost of that output, namely RS. For by increasing his output from OR to OJ, the seller's net revenue rectangle increases from $GUHS$ to $TULK$. The rectangle thus gains the larger area $EHLK$ while losing the smaller area $GTES$. In general, the output at which the largest net profit rectangle can be drawn is determined by the point L where $MC = MR$ and by the corresponding point K on the ATC curve. Or, to put it differently, it can be proved mathematically that any other net profit rectangle must of necessity be smaller than the one determined by points K and L. But this is equivalent to saying that the net revenue curve reaches a maximum at the output where $MC = MR$, which is a fact you already know.

Exhibit 4

Profit Maximization in the Short Run for a Perfectly Competitive Firm

At the output where a firm's MC = MR, the area of its net revenue rectangle TULK is a maximum. This is the largest net profit rectangle that can be drawn.

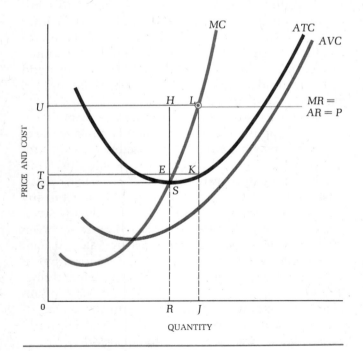

DERIVING SUPPLY CURVES FROM MARGINAL COST CURVES

When we first studied the operation of supply and demand we learned that a supply curve expresses a relation between the price of a product and the amount that sellers would be willing and able to produce at each price. We are now in a position to show how a perfectly competitive firm's supply curve is actually derived, based on what we know about the $MC = MR$ rule.

Suppose we represent a firm in perfect competition by the cost curves shown in Exhibit 5. If the market price of the product is OP_1, the firm will produce an output ON_1 since this is where its MC is equal to MR_1. If the price falls to OP_2, it will reduce its output to ON_2 following its marginal cost curve. At a price of OP_3 it will produce the amount ON_3, but since this price is tangent to its minimum average total cost, it will not be earning a positive net revenue; its net revenue will be zero. This means, as we learned earlier, that the firm is only normally profitable, since average total cost includes normal profit.

We conclude from this that a perfectly competitive firm maximizes its profit by always adjusting its output so as to follow its marginal cost curve.

MINIMIZING SHORT-RUN LOSSES

What will the firm do if the price falls below OP_3, say to OP_4? The answer is the same as before: It will decrease its output following its marginal cost curve, thus producing the amount ON_4. At this output the

firm's net revenue will be negative, but it will be *minimizing its losses* for the following reason.

In the short run, the firm has certain fixed costs such as rent, property taxes, and utilities. It must continue to pay these expenses as long as it remains in business, regardless of how much it produces. Therefore, as long as it can get a price that is at least high enough to cover its average variable (or "out-of-pocket") costs, anything that it earns over and above this amount will go toward paying its fixed costs, which it is "stuck" with in any case. Hence, even at a price of OP_4, the firm will lose less by operating and producing ON_4 than by temporarily shutting down. In the long run, on the other hand, it must receive a price at least high enough to cover all its costs including a normal profit if it is to stay in business, that is, it must cover its ATC.

We can now summarize with an important principle:

A perfectly competitive firm will increase or decrease its output by following its marginal cost curve, thereby maximizing its profit or minimizing its losses. Therefore, *a perfectly competitive firm's supply curve is its marginal cost curve above its average variable cost.*

Exhibit 5

In Perfect Competition, a Firm's Supply Curve Is Its MC **Curve Above Its** AVC

The firm will always produce to where its MC = MR. *Therefore, as the market price falls from* OP_1 *to* OP_4, *the firm reduces its output from* ON_1 *to* ON_4 *following its marginal cost curve. At* OP_4 *it is just covering its average variable (out-of-pocket) costs.*

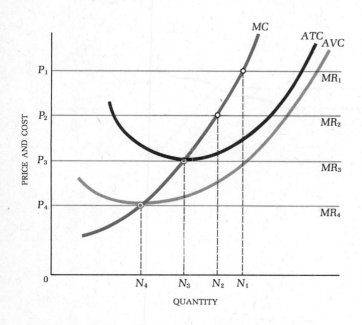

DERIVING THE INDUSTRY'S SHORT-RUN SUPPLY CURVE

The principle given above can easily be extended to include all firms in a perfectly competitive industry. The industry's supply curve is then derived from all of the firm's marginal cost curves.

The idea is illustrated in Exhibit 6 on the next page. Although only four firms are included for illustrative purposes, it is a simple matter to generalize the conclusions to any number of firms.

At the market price of OP_1 Firm A produces the output OR_1. At the price OP_2 it will produce the larger output OS_1, while Firm B will produce the output OS_2. Similarly, at higher and higher prices firms that are already in the market find it profitable to increase their production by following their marginal cost curve, while firms that were previously not in the market because their costs were too high now find it profitable to enter.

The overall effect on the industry supply curve is shown in the bottom diagram. As the market price rises because of a rightward shift of the total demand curve, the aggregate supply curve also rises, thereby reflecting the increasing outputs of the various firms.

Exhibit 6

**The Derivation of an Industry Supply Curve
from Marginal Cost Curves**

As the market price rises due to a rightward shift of the demand curve, each firm increases its output following its marginal cost curve. Each firm's supply curve is the same as its marginal cost curve above its average variable cost. The industry's short-run supply curve is the sum of these marginal cost (supply) curves. Thus:

Industry's $0R_1$ = Firm A's $0R_1$
Industry's $0S_1$ = Firm A's $0R_1 + R_1S_1$

Industry's $0S_2$ = Firm A's $0R_1 + R_1S_1$ + Firm B's $0S_2$ *and so on.*

(NOTE: Since we are assuming only four firms, the industry supply curve is discontinuous in its horizontal portions. Therefore, the horizontal segments are drawn as dashed lines. If there were many firms in the industry, the industry supply curve would be a smooth, upward-sloping line.)

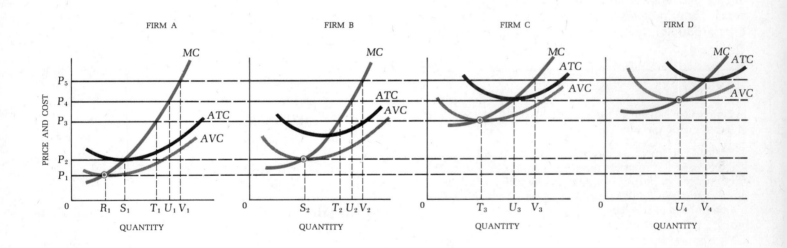

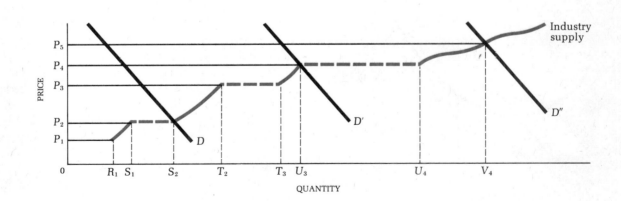

The industry's short-run supply curve is thus the sum of all the individual firm's marginal cost curves above their average variable costs.

Long-run Equilibrium of a Firm and an Industry

We have seen that in the short run a firm in a perfectly competitive industry may earn profits in excess of its normal profits. Can this also happen in the long run? The answer is no, because the conditions that are assumed in our definition of perfect competition prevent it from occurring. Let us see why.

THE ADJUSTMENT PROCESS

An industry is said to be in *equilibrium*—that is, in a state of "balance"—when there is no tendency for it to expand or to contract. This means that the least-profitable or borderline firm in the industry—usually called the "marginal" firm—is only normally profitable.

For instance, if any firms in the industry are earning less than their normal profit in the long run, then by definition of normal profit their owners are receiving less than the least return they are willing to accept on the basis of their opportunity costs. They will therefore leave the industry, causing the industry supply curve to shift to the left and the market price to rise. The remaining firms will then become more profitable. This exodus of firms will continue until the least-profitable firm is just normally profitable, at which point the industry will have no further tendency to contract.

The opposite situation occurs when the least-profitable firm is earning more than normal profits. New firms will then be tempted to enter the industry in order to get a share of those profits. The industry will thus expand, its total output will increase as the industry supply curve shifts to the right, and the market price will fall, thereby making existing firms less profitable. This entry of new firms will continue until the least-profitable firm is just normally profitable, at which point the industry will have no further tendency to expand.

GRAPHIC ILLUSTRATION OF LONG-RUN EQUILIBRIUM

The final adjustment to long-run equilibrium for a typical firm is illustrated in Exhibit 7. The firm will

have an average total cost curve and a corresponding marginal cost curve for each possible scale of plant. It follows that if some firms in the industry operate with optimum-size plants when the price is higher than the long-run equilibrium level, they will earn above-normal profits, which in turn will attract new firms into the industry. Market supply will increase, market price will fall, and supernormal profits will disappear. Firms with plants that are larger or smaller than the optimum size will thus suffer losses, whereas those with optimum-size plants will earn normal profits. Therefore:

Firms in perfectly competitive industries have no choice of whether they want to build large-scale or small-scale plants; they must eventually build optimum-size plants if they are to survive in the long run.

The firm's optimum-size plant is thus ATC_3, the long-run equilibrium price is OP, and the firm's rate of output is ON. Exhibit 7 represents a typical single firm, and a diagram similar to this could be made for each firm in the industry.

Exhibit 7

Long-run Equilibrium for a Typical Firm in Perfect Competition

At any given time, a firm may be represented by an ATC curve and a corresponding MC curve.

In the long run, competition will force each firm in the industry to end up with an optimum-size plant such as ATC_3. At the optimum level of output for each firm, such as ON for this particular firm,

$$MC = P = MR = AR = ATC = LRAC$$

This equation defines the long-run conditions of equilibrium for the firm.

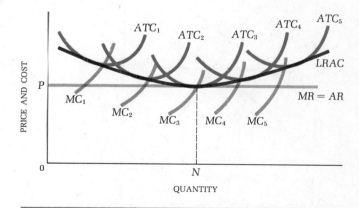

THE LONG-RUN INDUSTRY SUPPLY CURVE

We now know enough about the operation of supply and demand in competitive markets to introduce a new concept pertaining to the long-run supply price of an industry.

Each of the diagrams in Exhibit 8 represents the supply and demand situation for a different industry. We assume in each case that the industry is in equilibrium and that the point E, representing the intersection of the industry's supply and demand curves, defines its equilibrium price and output. Remember that an industry supply curve is made up of the individual supply curves of all its sellers. Our purpose is to examine the nature of each industry's long-run supply curve or supply price.

Suppose there is an increase (shift) in demand from D to D'. If the costs of the firms in the industry remain the same, the equilibrium point shifts from E to E', representing a higher market price and a larger market output than before. This expanded output occurs because firms that are already in the industry find it profitable to increase their production in response to the higher market price.

The equilibrium at E', however, is likely to be of relatively short duration because the higher and more profitable price will soon attract new firms into the industry. As this happens, the supply curve of the industry will shift to the right and the market price will be driven down along the D' curve until it is no longer profitable for new firms to enter the industry. The supply curve will ultimately settle at S', and the final equilibrium will be at E'', where the new supply and demand curves intersect. The point E'' represents the *long-run equilibrium* position of the industry.

This analysis suggests the following principle:

If we connect the industry's two long-run equilibrium points E and E''—the equilibrium points that existed before and after the changes in both demand and supply—we get the *long-run industry supply curve* labeled S_L. This curve may be either horizontal, rising, or falling, depending on whether the industry is one of constant, increasing, or decreasing costs.

This principle requires an explanation of constant-cost, increasing-cost, and decreasing-cost industries.

Exhibit 8

Long-run Supply Curves for Constant-, Increasing-, and Decreasing-cost Industries

The immediate effect of an increase in demand from D to D' is to change the industry's equilibrium from the long-run point E to the short-run point E'. At this higher price, new firms will find it profitable to enter the industry, and the supply curve will shift to the right until it reaches S'.

The industry's final equilibrium will thus settle at the long-run point E''. The long-run industry supply curve S_L is therefore defined as the locus or "path" of the industry's long-run equilibrium points.

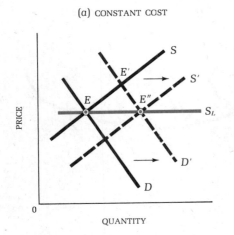

(a) CONSTANT COST

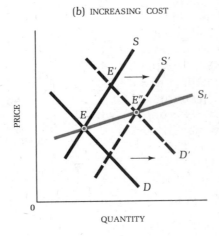

(b) INCREASING COST

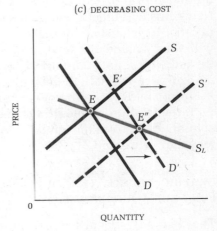

(c) DECREASING COST

Constant-cost Industries

A *constant-cost industry* experiences no increases in resource prices or costs of production as new firms enter the industry. This tends to happen when an industry's demand for the resources it employs is an insignificant proportion of the total demand for those resources. In that case, new firms will be able to enter the industry and buy the labor, capital, and other inputs they need without bidding up the prices of these factors of production. The long-run industry supply curve will thus be perfectly elastic. Unspecialized resources (such as unskilled workers) which are in wide use by many industries are examples of such inputs.

Increasing-cost Industries

An *increasing-cost industry* experiences rising resource prices and therefore increasing costs of production as new firms enter the industry. This happens because the industry's demand for resources is a significant enough proportion of the total demand that any new firms must bid up the prices of the factors of production in order to acquire them from other firms. Specialized resources (such as skilled workers) whose supplies are not readily expanded as the demand for them increases provide examples of such inputs. In general, increasing-cost industries are more common than constant-cost industries. This is especially true in our expanding scientific and technological age, when firms must make growing use of highly specialized resources. The computer, electronic, and aircraft industries are a few prominent examples of increasing-cost industries.

Decreasing-cost Industries

A *decreasing-cost industry* experiences declining resource prices and therefore falling costs of production as new firms enter the industry and the industry expands. This, of course, is not as common as the two previous cases, but it could exist for a while as a result of substantial external economies of scale, as we have already learned. Can you give some examples?

Partial and General Equilibrium

What are the achievements of perfect competition? Are they "good" or "bad"? What would it be like to live in a world of perfectly competitive industries?

These questions require that we evaluate the social consequences of perfect competition—its effects on society as a whole. We shall see that it has many favorable features, but also some unfavorable ones.

THE EQUILIBRIUM CONDITIONS

Look back at Exhibit 7 and note carefully the properties that characterize a perfectly competitive firm in long-run equilibrium. As you can see, these properties may be described succinctly by the equations:

$$MC = P = MR = AR = ATC = LRAC$$

These equations are called *equilibrium conditions*. They constitute a set of relationships that define the equilibrium position of an economic organism—in this case a firm in perfect competition. In certain advanced courses in economic theory, other sets of equilibrium conditions are studied—not only for firms, but also for households, and even for entire economies.

Our purpose is to analyze and interpret the meaning of the above equations, and in so doing we will see what perfect competition actually accomplishes. You may find it helpful to refer back to Exhibit 7 while reading the following explanation. Keep in mind that these characteristics apply to *each* firm in the industry.

☐ $MC = P$ means that the additional cost of the resources used by the firm to produce the last unit of the product is just covered by the price it receives. In other words, the value of the last unit of the good to the consumer (measured by the price he pays for the last unit, which is equal to the price he pays for any unit) is equal to the value of the resources used to produce that unit.

☐ $MC = MR$ means that the firm is maximizing its profits and there is no incentive for it to alter its output; the firm is thus in short-run (as well as long-run) equilibrium.

☐ $MR = AR \, (= P)$ means that the firm is selling in a perfectly competitive market, for as we shall see in the following chapters, any other type of market situation results in a firm's marginal revenue always being less than its average revenue or demand price.

☐ $ATC = AR$ means that the firm is earning only normal profits and there is no incentive for other firms to enter or leave the industry.

□ $MC = ATC$ means that the firm is operating at the minimum point on its average total cost curve and hence is combining the variable resources available to it with its given plant so as to produce at the least cost per unit.

□ $MC = ATC = LRAC$ means that the firm is producing the optimum output with the optimum-size plant, and therefore is allocating *all* its resources in an optimum manner.

These equilibrium conditions are at the heart of microeconomics. Their implications and importance will become increasingly evident in the following chapters.

PARTIAL AND GENERAL EQUILIBRIUM THEORY

The set of properties enumerated above and the entire analysis on which it is based prompt us to distinguish between two viewpoints of equilibrium theory, called "partial" and "general."

Partial equilibrium theory analyzes and develops an economic model of a particular market on the assumption that other markets are in balance. It thus ignores the mutual interrelationships of prices and outputs that may exist between markets. The familiar supply and demand analysis is a typical example of partial equilibrium theory. Although the supply and demand curves in previous chapters were extremely helpful in analyzing the economic effects of such things as price control, rationing, minimum wages, and commodity taxes, they always focused on a particular market, ignoring the ramifications and repercussions of price and output changes which may have occurred in other markets and which could in turn affect the market we were studying.

General equilibrium theory analyzes the interrelations between prices and outputs of goods and resources in different markets and demonstrates the possibility of simultaneous equilibrium between all markets. It is based on the assumption that if, for each market, we are given such information as consumer demand schedules, resource supply schedules, production functions, and the demand for money, equilibrium forces will cause resource and commodity prices to adjust themselves in a mutually consistent manner. The entire system can then settle down in a stable equilibrium of supply and demand. Any change in the determinants affecting one good can, however, upset the entire system and have widespread repercussions on the equilibrium prices and outputs of all other goods. Although general equilibrium analysis is primarily of theoretical interest, it nevertheless forces us to keep in mind the fact that in the real world there is often a significant degree of interdependence among various markets.

FAVORABLE FEATURES OF A PERFECTLY COMPETITIVE PRICE SYSTEM

The equilibrium conditions listed above can serve as a basis for describing the favorable features of an economic system composed entirely of perfectly competitive markets. Such a system would yield certain beneficial consequences in long-run equilibrium:

1. Consumer preferences as reflected in the marketplace would be fulfilled with the largest amount of goods consistent with the minimum (average cost) prices and known production techniques of business firms.

2. Society's resources would be allocated in the most efficient way, both within and between industries.

3. Flexible factor and product prices would assure full employment of all resources.

4. Competition among employers for inputs and among factors for jobs would cause factor owners to be paid their opportunity costs; these would be determined by the respective contributions to total output of each factor, as measured by its marginal productivity.

5. With consumer incomes and tastes given, aggregate consumer satisfaction would be maximized because goods would be distributed among consumers according to their demands.

These desirable features of a perfectly competitive price system in long-run equilibrium, and other characteristics which we have not mentioned, can be formulated as theorems which are actually proved in more advanced theoretical discussions. For our purposes, it is sufficient that the favorable consequences be described as above so that they can be compared with the following shortcomings.

SOME UNFAVORABLE FEATURES

Several undesirable consequences of a perfectly competitive price system were pointed out when we first studied the laws of supply and demand earlier in the book. At that time we did not have a formal knowledge of the theory of perfect competition, nor did we know that it is the basis for supply and de-

ALFRED MARSHALL

1842–1924

Partial Equilibrium Analysis

In the last quarter of the nineteenth century there arose in Europe and America a system of economic thought known as the *neoclassical* school. One of the leaders of this school was Alfred Marshall, a British scholar whose landmark treatise, the *Principles of Economics* (1890), will forever be regarded as a masterwork.

Marshall was born in London and educated at Cambridge University where he majored in the classics and mathematics. "My acquaintance with economics," he once wrote, started in 1867–1868 and "commenced with reading [John Stuart Mill and David Ricardo] while I was still earning my living by teaching mathematics at Cambridge; and translating the doctrines into differential equations as far as they would go; and, as a rule, rejecting those which would not go."

Several decades later, John Maynard Keynes, himself a leading scholar and at one time a student of Marshall's at Cambridge, referred to his former teacher "as a scientist . . . who, within his own field, was the greatest in the world in a hundred years."

Alfred Marshall was, indeed, one of the great economic thinkers of all time. His *Principles,* which went through eight editions, was a leading text in economics for several decades. Among the major contributions of this and other works by Marshall were the distinction between the short run and the long run, the extensive use of partial equilibrium models to describe economic behavior, the equilibrium of price and output resulting from the interaction of supply and demand, the concept of elasticity, the distinction between money cost and real cost, and many other ideas. In short, almost everything we read today pertaining to supply and demand analysis, equilibrium, and related notions was originally formulated precisely and definitively by Marshall. Few students today realize or appreciate the significant role that Marshall's ideas play in their economics education.

Although he was acquainted with the general equilibrium theory of Continental economists and was an adept mathematician, Marshall chose the less vigorous method of partial equilibrium analysis because it served to make economic science a better "engine for discovery" in the investigation of specific problems. His approach to his predecessors was unusually conciliatory, and throughout his career he tended to phrase his own doctrines so as to minimize the change from the classical tradition. In contrast to the earlier utility theorists, he did not take supply for granted but considered it as "the other blade of a pair

Historical Pictures Service, Chicago.

of scissors." Underlying demand was marginal utility as reflected in the price offers of buyers. Underlying supply was marginal effort, reflected in the supply prices of sellers.

Marshall's partial equilibrium method is illustrated in typical fashion by his discussion of demand. Since the demand schedule relates solely to the relationship between price and quantity demanded, other things must be held constant, or, as Marshall has it, "impounded in *ceteris paribus.*" Thus, the taste of consumers, their money incomes, the number of buyers, and the prices of other commodities are held constant in the discussion of the equilibrium determination of supply and demand. This procedure is still the accepted method of analyzing changes in demand.

By the time he retired from his professorship at Cambridge, Marshall had trained several generations of England's greatest economists, and these disciples went on to assume major positions in universities and government service. Although much has changed in economics since the eighth edition of *Principles of Economics* was published in 1920, these changes have for the most part been gradual, and Marshall's neoclassical structure is still clearly identifiable today throughout the whole body of economic literature.

mand analysis. Now, however, we are in a better position to enrich our understanding of the various shortcomings. Since the paramount concern of economics is to study the way in which society allocates its scarce resources, we shall evaluate the shortcomings of a perfectly competitive price system against this objective.

Incomplete Reflection of Consumer Desires

In a perfectly competitive system, sellers react only to those preferences that consumers register through their "dollar votes" in the marketplace. Consequently, this type of system does not measure the desires of consumers for "collective" or public goods like national defense, highways, parks, and unpolluted air and water. Further, to the extent that incomes are unequally distributed, the competitive price system will reflect the dollar votes of the rich more than the poor. Hence as Charles Dickens might have portrayed it, Ebenezer Scrooge could buy the milk for his cat that poor Bob Cratchit could not afford for his frail, crippled son, Tiny Tim.

Inadequate Reflection of Social Welfare

A chemical company disposes of its waste products in a nearby lake; a steel mill's smoke permeates the air of a neighboring city; a drive-in theater discharges its patrons onto a highway at the end of a movie. In each of these and many other situations, two types of costs are involved: *private costs*, which are the economic costs to a firm for performing a particular act; and *social costs*, which are the reductions in incomes or benefits that accrue to society as a result of a particular act. In the above examples, the social costs would include the displeasures suffered by the community due to water pollution, destruction of recreational areas, and congested highways.

A similar distinction can be made in terms of benefits. If you get a good education, this act will lead to *private benefits* for you in the form of higher income, but society will also incur *social benefits* because you will (hopefully) become a more enlightened and informed citizen. Likewise, if you maintain an attractive lawn, your neighbors will be pleased; bathing regularly will help keep you from becoming a social outcast.

Of what significance are these distinctions between private and social benefits and costs? Since economics is a social science, a perfectly competitive price system must be evaluated in terms of its effects on society. As we know, competitive prices tend to reflect private costs and private benefits and may exclude some social costs and social benefits. Therefore, the equilibrium condition $MC = MR$ only guarantees maximum profit for a firm; it does not guarantee maximum welfare for society. To achieve the latter, the costs and benefits of production to *society* must be incorporated in firms' activities. To the extent that they are not, the $MC = MR$ condition fails to reflect the full effect of production on social welfare.

This distinction between the private and social consequences of economic activities is important. It is discussed more fully in a number of other places in this book.

Insufficient Incentives for Progress

A third major criticism frequently leveled against a perfectly competitive system is that it dampens incentives to innovate and therefore retards economic progress. This happens because the typical firm in perfect competition is relatively small and is not likely to have access to the considerable financial resources needed to support the substantial research and development projects that often lead to major innovations. Further, even if a firm had the money to finance large-scale research, it would probably refrain from undertaking the needed capital investment because the innovation, if successful, would be adopted quickly by competing firms.

LIFE UNDER PERFECT COMPETITION— DISMAL AND DULL?

What would it be like to live in a perfectly competitive world? Most of us might find it monotonous. Goods would be standardized in each industry and the range of consumer choices severely limited. At the grocery store, bread would be bread and ketchup would be ketchup, and the modern supermarket with its endless and colorful varieties of goods would cease to exist. The choice of an automobile, like eggs in the dairy case, might be confined to "small," "medium," and "large," and would be alike except for size. There would clearly be no need for advertising (except perhaps for industry-wide or institutional advertising like "Eat more bread" or "Drink more milk") or even for trademarks or brand names, and the excitement of New York's Madison Avenue, where most of these creations are born, would—for good or evil—be lost. There would be no commercial television as we now know it, and newspapers and magazines (could they possibly be homogeneous?) would cost more. For in a world of perfect competition, where it would be assumed that consumers knew their alternatives, the only type of advertising needed would inform rather than persuade. This means that there would be no need for anything other than, perhaps, classified advertising and the Sears, Roebuck catalog.

CONCLUSION—AND A LOOK FORWARD

Is this the kind of world we want? Each individual must answer for himself, for in economics the most we can do is identify the alternatives and their consequences, and leave it up to each person to make his choice. As we have already seen, although a perfectly competitive economy would have various beneficial consequences, it would also have what many people would undoubtedly regard as undesirable features.

Since the imaginary world of perfect competition is so unreal, why do we study it? Does it have any practical value? The answer is simple: We do not necessarily learn about perfect competition in the vain hope of making it a reality; instead, we study it because it provides us with a guide for evaluating and improving the real world of imperfect competition, which we shall be analyzing later on.

REMARK. The terms "perfect competition" and "pure competition" are ordinarily used synonymously for most purposes. However, when a distinction is made, pure competition is defined simply as a large number of buyers and sellers dealing in a homogeneous commodity, without discrimination. Pure competition thus tends to operate in essentially the same way and to attain the same long-run equilibrium conditions as perfect competition. However, it may not achieve these results as quickly or smoothly because the two "lubricating" features of perfect competition—namely perfect knowledge and perfect resource mobility, which eliminate any frictions in the system—are left out of the definition.

SUMMARY OF IMPORTANT IDEAS

1. A perfectly competitive industry or market is characterized by many buyers and sellers engaged in the purchase and sale of a homogeneous commodity, with perfect knowledge of market prices and quantities, no discrimination, and perfect mobility of resources. Perfect competition is thus a theoretical extreme rather than real-world phenomenon, although some of its features are roughly approximated in the organized commodity and stock markets.

2. In perfect competition, prices are established in the market through the interaction of many buyers and sellers. Each firm thus finds itself faced with a market price over which it has no influence. It cannot sell any of its output at a price which is the slightest bit above the market price; it can sell its entire output at the market price, and hence there is no inducement for it to sell at any lower price.

3. In terms of costs and revenues, each firm's most profitable level of output occurs where its marginal cost equals its marginal revenue. This is the output at which its total revenue minus total cost is a maximum.

4. In perfect competition, a firm's supply curve is its marginal cost curve above its average variable cost. The industry's short-run supply curve is thus derived by summing all the firms' marginal cost curves at each price above average variable cost. In the short run, a firm will operate as long as the market price is at least equal to its average variable (out-of-pocket) costs, since any price it gets over and above that will go to pay at least part of its fixed costs. In the long run, the firm will have to receive a price high enough to cover all costs, including a normal profit, if it is to remain in business.

5. In the long run, competition will force all firms to earn only normal profits and to operate with optimum-size plants. When this occurs, the industry as well as all firms in it will be in long-run equilibrium, with no tendency to expand or contract.

6. The industry's long-run supply curve connects all of its long-run supply-and-demand equilibrium points. The long-run supply curve may be constant (or perfectly elastic), increasing, or decreasing.

7. Partial equilibrium theory deals with prices and outputs in a particular market without regard to the influence of other markets, as in the familiar supply and demand analysis. General equilibrium theory deals with the interrelations of prices and outputs in all markets simultaneously. In view of its much greater complexity, general equilibrium analysis is primarily of theoretical interest.

8. In long-run equilibrium, a perfectly competitive economy will have allocated its resources in the most efficient way so as to maximize consumer satisfactions. This is assured by the equations

$$MC = P = MR = AR = ATC = LRAC$$

which if analyzed separately tell us that firms are maximizing their profits and making the most efficient use of their resources, given the distribution of consumers' incomes and tastes.

9. Among the favorable features of a perfectly competitive price system are (a) it fulfills consumer preferences with the largest amount of goods in the most efficient way; (b) it allocates resources optimally and, as a result of flexible product and factor prices, tends to encourage full employment of all resources; (c) it provides for factor payments at their opportunity costs as determined by their respective marginal productivities. Among the unfavorable features are (a) it reflects consumer desires incompletely; (b) it does not always measure social costs and social benefits; (c) it provides insufficient incentives for economic progress.

FOR DISCUSSION

1. *Terms and concepts to review:*

perfect competition	equilibrium conditions
average revenue	partial equilibrium
total revenue	theory
net revenue	general equilibrium
break-even point	theory
marginal revenue	neoclassical economics
long-run industry	private costs
supply curve	social costs
constant-cost industry	private benefits
increasing-cost	social benefits
industry	pure competition
decreasing-cost	
industry	

2. What is the "fundamental principle of profit maximization"? Explain. What special application of this rule applies to perfect competition? Why?

3. Is the price of a product determined by its cost of production, or is the cost of production determined by the price?

4. If new firms enter an industry, they will compete for factors of production and thereby raise the prices of those factors. How will this affect the cost curves of firms in the industry? Discuss.

5. "The farmer must receive a living price for milk." Discuss in terms of this chapter.

6. If you owned a shoe store and the shoes you carried cost you $10 a pair, would you stay in business if the highest price you could get for them was $10 a pair? Explain your answer in terms of this chapter.

7. The long-run history of the automobile industry reveals an enormous growth of output and a substantial reduction in prices. How do you account for this, since we have usually assumed that larger outputs come only from higher prices?

8. Insert words in the following sentences to make them true. Do not delete any words. Underline your inserted words.
   (a) A firm is in equilibrium when its costs and revenues are equal.
   (b) A perfectly competitive firm is in equilibrium when it is producing at its minimum average cost.
   (c) A perfectly competitive firm cannot earn supernormal profits.
   (d) A perfectly competitive firm's supply curve is its marginal curve.

9. What are the "equilibrium conditions" for a perfectly competitive industry in long-run equilibrium? Explain.

10. "It is an indictment of our economic system that our country can spend more on such unimportant things as cosmetics or liquor than it spends on education." Evaluate this statement.

Meat Prices: Competition or "Consumer Gouging"?

In this decade of rising prices, the price of meat has been one of the fastest-rising. Americans, who had been accustomed to plentiful supplies of meat at relatively stable prices, were both perplexed and furious as first beef and then other meats became costly rarities. Questions about profiteering and conspiracy were raised, and politicians promised solemnly to hunt down and punish the conspirators and restore steak to the American freezer. Was there a conspiracy behind the price rise? Should the federal government control meat prices? Or would control banish beef from the American diet?

Market Factors

A thoughtful report, recently published by the Federal Reserve Bank of St. Louis, dispels notions of a conspiracy to raise meat prices. Rather, they say, the rise is due to the interplay of market forces. "Behind retail price increases is often found greater consumer demand. When the demand for a commodity increases, the first change one typically observes is a higher sales volume which results initially in a reduction of inventories. In order to restore depleted inventories, retail grocers increase their meat orders from packers hoping to continue selling a larger volume at the prevailing price. Upon receiving increased orders for meat the packers in turn increase their rate of meat slaughter and seek to restore meat animal inventories by purchases from farmers. Since the prevailing price only provides sufficient incentive for producing the current number of animals, additional animals are not available for immediate delivery at current prices."

In the short run, meat is highly inelastic on the supply side: only a small increase in the quantity supplied will result from a far larger increase in price. However, over the longer run a rise in demand makes it profitable for farmers and ranchers to increase production. Conversely, declines in demand for meat or improvements in technology that increase supply tend to lower prices; when that happens, farmers will reduce output. If demand then rises relative to supply, prices will increase and, if the demand is sustained, output will eventually increase also. As a result of recent increases in per capita incomes, in population, and in food subsidies for low-income groups and for institutions there has been a greater demand for meat. In the normal operation of a competitive market, the long-run effect of these increases would have been a rise in output. But in 1973, a new element entered the equation: in the face of inflationary price increases, President Nixon froze many prices, among them, those for beef. As a result, some farmers found it unprofitable to sell animals for slaughter and this created a shortage. At the same time, the freeze on beef prices kept demand high. The inevitable effect: a nationwide shortage of beef. As consumers switched to other kinds of meat, including chicken, they too became scarce.

Conspiracy or Competition?

Did ranchers and slaughterhouses further conspire to hold beef off the market until the date given by Nixon to remove controls? The study by the St. Louis bank indicates that such a conspiracy was both unlikely and unnecessary because the meat industry generally operates in a competitive, free-enterprise atmosphere where there are many producers, many processors, and many retailers. In this atmosphere, prices are determined largely by basic supply and demand conditions. Almost certainly many producers did hold supplies back until the price freeze thawed; but in doing so they behaved only as prudent businessmen, willing to sacrifice a given income today for the sake of a larger one tomorrow. Further, it is perfectly possible that some producers would have lost money or merely broken even at the controlled price; for them, the higher future price was not only preferable, but vital.

The Federal Reserve Bank of St. Louis concludes: "If people want more meat they will bid up the price and the higher prices . . . will provide the incentive for increased production. Productive resources will flow freely into this sector when anticipated returns are attractive. The higher meat prices in recent years have been necessary to attract the additional resources used in producing the larger volume of meat demanded by consumers. If prices had been set arbitrarily at a lower level, a smaller volume would have been produced and some consumers would have had less meat."

In retrospect, many experts agree that the meat shortage of 1973, rather than being a conspiracy, was more the result of misguided economic decisions flowing from Washington.

QUESTIONS

1. Some critics contend that the long-run upward trend of meat prices shows that the consumer is being exploited or that the meat industry is callous, or inefficient, or both. Do you agree?

2. How would production have been affected if the government had not allowed meat prices to rise since the mid-1960s? Discuss.

CHAPTER 25

Monopoly Behavior:
The Other End
of the Spectrum

CHAPTER PREVIEW

What do we mean by monopoly? Are there different types of monopolies?

How are price and output determined under monopoly?

Are monopolies "good" or "bad"? Should something be done about them?

Can monopolies "discriminate" in price in order to earn larger profits?

How can the theory of monopoly pricing be used to help explain the pricing practices of public utilities?

Competitive systems are usually classified into several categories. Each of these categories may be regarded as occupying a position along a spectrum. Up to now we have studied only the system called perfect competition, which may be visualized at the left end of the competitive spectrum:

Perfect competition	?	Pure monopoly

In this chapter we turn our attention to the extreme opposite of perfect competition—pure monopoly. We shall find that this type of market structure is, like perfect competition, a theoretical limiting case, and that it is virtually nonexistent in its pure (unregulated) form.

Does this mean that the study of monopoly is theoretical and impractical? The answer is no. The theory of monopoly provides many useful tools and concepts for understanding the behavior of actual business firms. Against this background, the next chapter will combine the features of perfect competition and monopoly in order to help explain the competitive behavior of firms in the real world. For the time being, we represent this "real" world by a question mark in the spectrum above.

The Meaning and Types of Monopoly

What do we mean by monopoly? How do monopolies come into existence? What conditions must prevail in order for monopolies to survive? How does a monopolist determine his price and output? What is wrong with monopoly and what can be done about it?

The answers to these questions comprise the basic aspects of the theory of monopoly to which we now turn our attention.

WHAT IS A MONOPOLY?

A *monopoly* is defined as a single firm producing a product for which there are no close substitutes. This means that no other firms produce a similar product. Hence the monopoly firm constitutes the entire industry and is thus a "pure" monopoly. A buyer who wants this particular product must either buy it from the monopolist or do without it.

REMARK. According to Webster, the derivation of the word "monopoly" is from the Greek *monopolion*, which means a right of exclusive sale. The dictionary, however, will also tell you that *mono* means "one" and *poly* means "many," which implies that a monopoly is one seller facing many buyers. This is the way in which we ordinarily think of monopoly. But in a later chapter relationships are studied in which one seller faces either one or several buyers. A number of interesting models will be constructed from such situations.

Pure monopolies are relatively rare, but they do exist. The electric, gas, and water companies in your locality are good examples, since each produces a product for which there are no close substitutes. But notice that a firm's degree of monopoly may vary among markets. For instance, the electric company has a monopoly in the production of electricity for lighting purposes, but for heating purposes its electricity may compete with gas, coal, and fuel oil sold by other producers. An electric company may thus be a pure monopoly in the lighting market, but a "partial" monopoly in the heating market in the sense that it faces some degree of competition from reasonably adequate substitute goods. Similarly, railroads, buses, taxis, and airlines are not pure monopolies, but they are certainly partial monopolies depending on the extent to which buyers can substitute the products of these industries in meeting their transportation needs.

In view of this, most firms in our economy, as we shall see, may be characterized as "partial monopolies." In this chapter we shall develop a theory of pure monopoly; many of its principles and conclusions, however, are applicable to partial monopolies as well.

SOURCES AND TYPES OF MONOPOLY

What are the origins of monopoly, and why do monopolies continue to exist? There are several possible explanations, all of which amount in one form or another to "obstacles to entry"—that is, economic, legal, or technical barriers that permit a firm to monopolize an industry and prevent new firms from entering. These obstacles give rise to several common types of monopolies.

Natural Monopoly

A *natural monopoly* is a firm which experiences increasing economies of scale—long-run decreasing average costs of production—over a wide range of output, enabling it to supply the entire market at a lower unit cost than two or more firms could do. Electric companies, gas companies, and railroads are classic examples of natural monopolies. The technology of these public utilities is such that once the heavy fixed-cost facilities are established (such as power generators, gas transmission lines, or railroad tracks and terminals), additional customer service will reduce average total costs over a wide range of output and also permit the construction of more optimum-size plants so as to lower long-run average costs.

Legal and Government Monopolies

In some industries, unrestricted competition among firms may be deemed undesirable by society. In such cases government grants one firm in an industry an exclusive right to operate—a status of *legal monopoly*—in return for which government may also impose standards and requirements pertaining to the quantity and quality of output, geographic areas of operation, and the prices or rates that are charged. Privately (as distinguished from governmentally) owned public utilities are typical examples of legal monopolies.

The justification of legal monopoly is based on judicial opinions handed down for many decades by the courts that a "business affected with a public interest" may qualify as a public utility (and therefore a legal monopoly) because the welfare of the entire community is directly dependent on the manner in which the business is operated. In some states the result of this vague definition has been the establishment of the following as public utilities: common carriers of all kinds, water, gas, electricity, telephones, telegraphs, bridges, warehouses, cemeteries, gristmills, sawmills, grain elevators, stockyards, hotels, docks, cotton gins, refrigeration plants, markets, and news services.

Whereas legal monopolies are privately owned but governmentally regulated, there are other monopolies, called *government monopolies*, that are both owned and regulated by the federal or local government. Examples are the U.S. Postal Service, the water and sewer systems of almost all local municipalities, the electric power plants of many cities, and the central banks of most countries.

Strategic-resource Monopoly

A firm might achieve a monopoly by gaining control of an essential input to a production process. The classic example of this is the Aluminum Company of America (ALCOA), which, prior to World War II, had a monopoly in aluminum production because it controlled all the bauxite-ore deposits from which aluminum is made. Similarly, at one time International Nickel Company of Canada owned almost the entire world's supply of nickel reserves, and the De Beers Company of South Africa today owns most of the world's diamond mines.

Patent Monopoly

A *patent monopoly* is a firm upon which government has conferred the exclusive right—through issuance of a patent—to make, use, or vend its own invention or discovery. A patent therefore enables a firm to profit from its invention while preventing its adoption by competitors. The National Cash Register Company and the United Shoe Machinery Company each held a series of patents on their line of products which for many years enabled them to monopolize their respective industries. Today, IBM, Xerox, Polaroid, and others have varying degrees of monopoly power through patent protection.

It is interesting to note that although a patent gives one an exclusive right to produce a specifically defined product, it does not preclude others from producing a closely related substitute good. Xerox Corporation, for example, has the exclusive right to produce copiers which function in a particular way, as described in the patents they hold, but a number of other firms produce competing copying machines. Although patents sometimes enable firms to establish pure monopolies, more often they only provide partial monopolies.

Price and Output Determination

We learned that in the theory of perfect competition, a perfectly competitive seller has no influence over the price at which he can sell his output; he is faced with a perfectly elastic demand curve at the market price, and he maximizes his profit by producing the output at which his $MC = MR \ (= P)$.

A pure monopolist is in a different situation. Since he comprises the *entire* industry, instead of just a small part of it, he can exercise complete control over the price at which he sells his output. He will thus find that he can sell more of his product at a lower price than at a higher one. This means that the market demand curve for his product will be less than perfectly elastic: *it will slope downward instead of being horizontal.* On the other hand, we may assume that the *shapes* (curvatures) of his production function and cost curves are similar to those studied in previous chapters since he must purchase both his variable and fixed factors in the input markets and then combine these factors in order to produce a product. These activities are subject to the same laws of production and cost as any other seller's.

COST AND REVENUE SCHEDULES

The cost and revenue data of a monopolist, illustrating the ideas discussed above, are shown in Exhibit 1. It should be apparent from this table that columns (1) and (2) actually compose the demand schedule facing the monopolist. Note that his average revenue (= price) is inversely related to the quantity. This means that *for the monopolist to sell more units of his product he must charge a lower price per unit for all units that he sells.*

Since the average revenue or price varies inversely with quantity, total revenue rises to a maximum and then begins to fall. The changes in total revenue, as always, are reflected by marginal revenue [column (7)], which now turns out to be different from average revenue because of the changes in price.

The cost schedules in the table are those we used in the previous chapter for a perfectly competitive firm, since, as stated above, we are assuming that the *shapes* or curvatures of the monopolist's cost curves are similar to those of any other seller's. Besides, by using the same cost data, we shall be able to see more clearly that the chief differences between the two firms originate in the output market where

Exhibit 1

Cost and Revenue Schedules of a Monopolist

(1) Quantity per day, Q (given)	(2) Average revenue or price, AR = P (given)	(3) Total revenue, TR (1) × (2)	(4) Total cost, TC	(5) Average total cost, ATC (4) ÷ (1)	(6) Marginal cost, MC Change in (4) / Change in (1)	(7) Marginal revenue, MR Change in (3) / Change in (1)	(8) Net revenue, NR (3) − (4)
0	$16	$ 0	$ 25	$ −			−$25
					$10	$15	
1	15	15	35	35.00			− 20
					6	13	
2	14	28	41	20.50			− 13
					4	11	
3	13	39	45	15.00			− 6
					2	9	
4	12	48	47	11.75			1
					2	7	
5	11	55	49	9.80			6
					3	5	
6	10	60	52	8.67			8
					5	3	
7	9	63	57	8.14			6
					8	1	
8	8	64	65	8.13			− 1
					14	−1	
9	7	63	79	8.78			− 16
					21	−3	
10	6	60	100	10.00			− 40

goods are sold, rather than in the input market where factors are bought.

A look at the table shows quite clearly that the fundamental principle of profit maximization still holds: the monopolist's most profitable level of output—the output at which his net revenue [column (8)] is a maximum—is at six units, which is also where his MC is equal to MR. Why is this so? Because as we learned in the previous chapter, at any output less than this the added cost of an additional unit is less than the added revenue, so it pays to increase production. At any output greater than this the opposite is true. Only where MC = MR is the firm's output at its most profitable level.

LOOKING AT THE GRAPHS

You can visualize these ideas more easily by examining the graphs of the cost and revenue schedules rather than the data. In Exhibit 2 on the next page, the monopolist's total revenue and total cost curves are shown in the top chart, his appropriate average and marginal curves in the middle chart, and his net revenue curve in the bottom chart. The vertical dashed line that passes through all three charts emphasizes the fact that at the most profitable level of output:

1. TR − TC is a maximum.

2. MC = MR, since the tangents to TC and TR are parallel.

3. NR is a maximum.

Note also in the middle chart that the average revenue or demand curve facing the monopolist slopes downward, which was not the case for a perfectly competitive seller. This means, as explained above, that for the monopolist to sell more units of his product he must charge a lower price per unit for *all* units that he sells. Since the AR curve is downward sloping, the MR curve lies below the AR curve due to the *average-marginal relationship*, as learned in a previous chapter. You can verify this for yourself by experimenting with a few prices and quantities on your own and then sketching their graphs.

REMARK. For graphing purposes, you should recall from previous chapters that the MC and MR curves are plotted to the *midpoints* of the integers on the horizontal axis, since they reflect, respectively, the change in total cost and in total revenue resulting from a unit change in output.

USING THE MC = MR PRINCIPLE

We must examine the profit-maximizing behavior of a monopolist more closely so that we are in a better position to evaluate the consequences of his actions.

Exhibit 2

Cost and Revenue Curves of a Monopolist

PROFIT MAXIMIZATION: THREE VIEWPOINTS

1. *Total curves. The most profitable level of output is determined where the difference between the curves TR and TC, as represented by the distance GH, is a maximum. This occurs at an output of 6 units. At this output, a tangent to the TR curve is parallel to a tangent to the TC curve, as at G and H. At smaller or larger outputs such as 5 or 7 units, the tangents would not be parallel.*

2. *Marginal curves. The most profitable level of output is determined where MC = MR, as explained in the text. You can verify this by simply following the vertical dashed line downward at 6 units of output.*

3. *Net revenue curve. The most profitable level of output is determined where the net revenue curve NR (= TR − TC) is a maximum. The vertical dashed line emphasizes these profit-maximizing principles in all three charts.*

TECHNICAL NOTE (OPTIONAL). If you like to think in geometric terms, remember that parallel lines have equal slopes or steepness. Hence the most profitable output in the top chart is determined where the *slopes* of the *TC* and *TR* curves are equal, which is where the tangents are parallel. In the middle chart, since marginal cost is the graph of the *slope* of total cost, and marginal revenue is the graph of the *slope* of total revenue, it is true that at the level of maximum profit:

$$MC = MR$$

or, equivalently,

$$\text{Slope of } TC = \text{slope of } TR$$

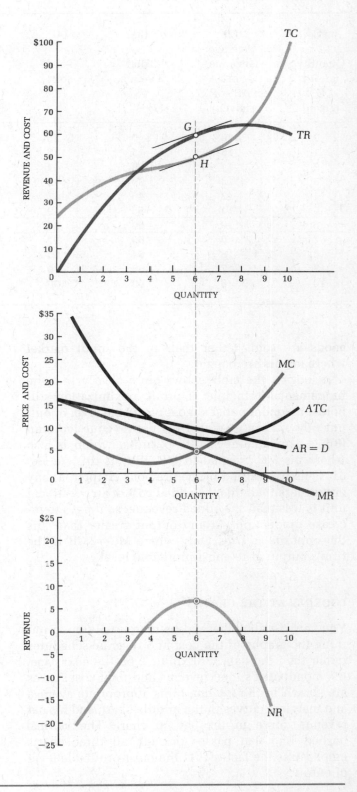

Let us therefore analyze his performance in terms of the fundamental $MC = MR$ principle illustrated by the diagrams in Exhibit 3.

In Chart (a), the monopolist finds that the $MC = MR$ rule leads him to produce the output ON. At this output, the demand curve facing him indicates that the highest price he can charge is NG ($= 0P$). His total profit, or net revenue, is thus the area of the rectangle shown in the chart, as explained in the accompanying description.

In Chart (b), the monopolist's costs are relatively high compared to his revenues. This is due either to an increase in the prices of his factors of production which causes his cost curves to shift upward, or a decrease in demand for his output which causes his revenue curves to shift downward, or both. He finds that at the $MC = MR$ output, namely ON, the corresponding price NG is just high enough to yield a normal profit. Since the ATC curve is tangent to the AR curve at this output, he knows that any other level of production would yield losses because his ATC would be greater than his AR.

In Chart (c), the monopolist's ATC curve is everywhere higher than his AR curve, which, as before, can be the result of an increase in costs or a decrease in demand, or both. He finds that, at least for the short run, the $MC = MR$ rule still prevails because the output ON and the corresponding price NG will *minimize his loss*; that is, any other price and output will yield a larger loss area than the rectangle in the diagram.

You can see from these types of problems that it is essential to sketch correctly both average revenue and marginal revenue curves. Therefore, here is a convenient geometric rule to remember when the curves are straight lines (as they usually are):

<u>An MR curve always bisects any horizontal line drawn from the vertical axis to the AR curve. Thus in Chart (a), the distance $PW = WG$, and similarly for any other horizontal line that may be drawn.</u>

This rule is based on a theorem which we shall not prove here, but you can easily verify it for yourself by constructing your own tables and plotting the graphs. Actually, all that this rule means is that at any given price, an MR curve is twice as steep as (or has twice the slope of) its corresponding AR curve.

MARGINAL REVENUE IS NOT PRICE;
MARGINAL COST IS NOT SUPPLY

We are now in a position to discover an important distinction between a monopoly firm and a perfectly

Exhibit 3

Three Possible Profit Positions for a Monopolist

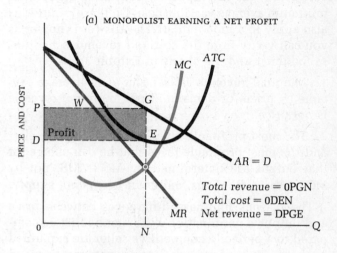

(a) MONOPOLIST EARNING A NET PROFIT

Total revenue = 0PGN
Total cost = 0DEN
Net revenue = DPGE

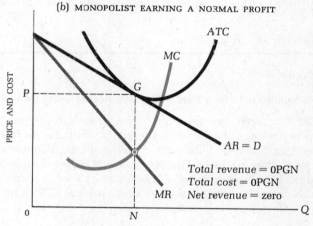

(b) MONOPOLIST EARNING A NORMAL PROFIT

Total revenue = 0PGN
Total cost = 0PGN
Net revenue = zero

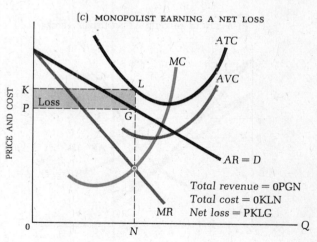

(c) MONOPOLIST EARNING A NET LOSS

Total revenue = 0PGN
Total cost = 0KLN
Net loss = PKLG

competitive firm. When we studied the theory of perfect competition, we learned that the seller's marginal revenue curve was the same as his average revenue (= price) or demand curve, and his marginal cost curve was his supply curve above the level of minimum average variable cost. Do these conditions also apply to a monopolist? The answer is *no*, for as you can verify from the cost and revenue schedules in Exhibit 1 and the charts in Exhibit 3:

1. Marginal revenue falls faster than average revenue (= price) or demand. Thus, *marginal revenue is not price.*

2. The most profitable level of output for the seller and the most profitable price that he can charge for that output are determined by $MC = MR$, not by $MC = AR (= P)$. Thus, *marginal cost is not supply.*

The reasons for these differences between price and output determination by a monopolist as compared to a perfectly competitive seller are explained further in Exhibit 4. Each diagram compares a given MC curve of a monopolist with two arbitrarily different demand or AR curves and their corresponding MR curves. A study of these diagrams and the accompanying analysis leads to the conclusion that *a less than perfectly competitive firm has no supply curve.*

In view of this, can we conclude that only under perfect competition are prices determined by supply and demand? You will have an opportunity to discuss this important question in a problem at the end of this chapter.

DO MONOPOLIES EARN "LARGE" PROFITS?

We now know enough about the behavior of a monopolist to draw three important conclusions about monopoly pricing:

1. The price charged by an unregulated monopolist is not, as Adam Smith once remarked, "the highest which can be got"—a fact that may surprise many

---

Exhibit 4

No Supply Curve for a Firm with a Downward-sloping Demand Curve

For any given marginal cost curve, the most profitable price and output depend on the firm's particular average revenue curve and its corresponding marginal revenue curve. Thus in Chart (a) the single output at N corresponds to the two prices at P and at S. In Chart (b), the two outputs at N and at L correspond to the single price at K. This suggests the following principle:

A firm faced with a downward-sloping (or less than perfectly elastic) demand curve has no supply curve, since there is no single quantity that the firm will necessarily supply at a given price, and no single price at which the firm will necessarily supply a given quantity.

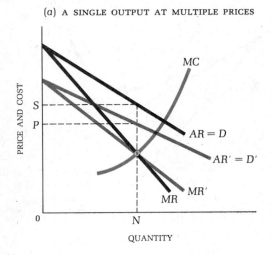

(a) A SINGLE OUTPUT AT MULTIPLE PRICES

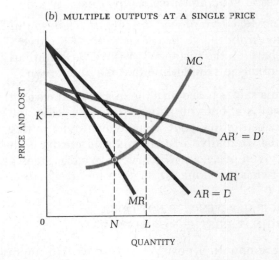

(b) MULTIPLE OUTPUTS AT A SINGLE PRICE

people. Instead it is the highest that is consistent with maximizing profits. For instance, the monopolist of Exhibit 3, Chart (a), could produce somewhat less than ON and charge a price higher than NG; then, as long as his ATC did not exceed his AR he would still make a profit, but he obviously would not make the maximum possible profit.

2. A pure monopolist does not necessarily receive "high" profits just because he is a monopolist. In fact, if his profits are relatively high, he may find that the owners of some of his factors of production, such as workers or landlords, will absorb part of the surplus by demanding larger payments. This will cause the monopolist's ATC curve to rise, possibly to the point where he is earning a "small" profit or perhaps only a normal profit, as in Exhibit 3, Chart (b).

3. In the short run a monopolist may earn less than a normal profit and still remain in business, as in Exhibit 3, Chart (c). But in the long run he would have to earn at least a normal profit to continue in operation.

Thus, having a pure monopoly does not in itself assure extraordinary profit, although a monopoly is likely to be more profitable than a perfectly competitive firm. A monopolist is faced with certain market restraints that affect his price and output decisions, and his ability to cope with these restraints will affect the profitability of his firm. By adhering to the MC = MR principle, the monopolist will always maximize his profits (or minimize his losses), but this principle in itself does not guarantee whether those profits will be large or small.

Evaluating Monopoly: What's Wrong with It?

You have probably heard that monopoly is "bad," but may not know exactly why. Now, however, on the basis of what you have learned from economic theory, you can give three significant reasons.

It Misallocates Resources

The basic economic criticism of pure monopoly is this:

By adhering to the MC = MR principle of profit maximization, a monopoly misallocates society's resources by restricting output and charging a higher price than if it followed the MC = P standard of competitive industry.

This basic criticism embodies three fundamental ideas, all of which are best understood in terms of Exhibit 5.

First, in seeking to maximize profit, the monopolist produces the equilibrium output 0Q and charges the equilibrium price QS. The latter is called the *monopoly price* because it is determined by the intersection of the MC and MR curves. Note that this price is greater than the monopolist's marginal cost at that output. This means that the value of the last unit to the marginal user (measured by the price he pays for the last unit, which is equal to the price he pays for any other unit) is greater than the value of

---

Exhibit 5

Price and Output Effects of Monopoly Behavior

At the monopoly price—the price determined by MC = MR—the monopolist maximizes his profit. But his price is higher, and his corresponding output is less, than if he adhered to the marginal cost price MC = P of competitive industry.

Note too that by adhering to the MC = MR principle, the monopolist underuses his plant by operating on the declining side of his ATC curve. This condition can continue indefinitely—in contrast to perfectly competitive firms which, in the long run, operate at the minimum point of their ATC curves.

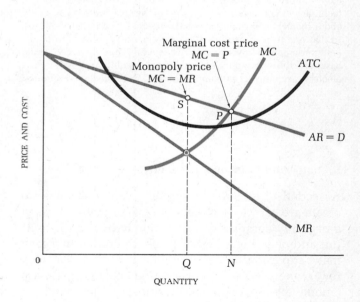

the resources used to produce that unit. In other words, society is not getting as much of the good that it wants in terms of what that good costs society to produce.

Second, if the monopolist followed the $MC = P$ rule of perfect competition, he would produce the larger output ON and charge the lower price NP. The latter is called the *marginal cost price*. It is the optimum price for society because at this price, the value of the last unit to the marginal user is equivalent to the value of the resources used to produce that unit. Therefore, society is getting as much of the good that it wants in terms of what that good costs society to produce.

Third, by adhering to the $MC = MR$ principle of profit maximization, the monopolist typically "underuses" his plant by producing on the declining side of his ATC curve. Since the entry of other firms into the industry is blocked, the monopolist can remain in this equilibrium position indefinitely. In contrast, you will recall that firms in perfect competition operate in the long run at the minimum point of their ATC curves. Thus, in a sense to be described more fully in a later chapter, society's resources are ordinarily used relatively less efficiently in monopoly markets than in perfectly competitive markets. (See also Box 1.)

REMARK. The above criticisms should *not* be interpreted to mean that a monopoly necessarily produces less, and charges more, than a perfectly competitive industry with the same total demand curve. In fact, the opposite may often be true. In some industries, technology may widen the "spread" of the cost curves by bringing about increasing economies of scale over a broad range of output, so that one firm can supply the entire market at a lower unit cost (and perhaps at a lower price) than several. This, you recall, is the basis of natural monopolies, for example, public utilities such as electric companies, gas companies, and railroads, as mentioned earlier.

It Contributes to Income Inequality

A second criticism of monopoly is that it tends to create greater income inequality than would exist in a perfectly competitive economy. By restricting output and charging a higher price, the monopoly may make supernormal profits. These go to its relatively few owners who, as corporation stockholders, are among the upper-income groups in the economy. This class thus benefits at the expense of the many consumers and resource owners who make up the rest of society.

Box 1

Pricing Under Monopoly

"A monopoly granted either to an individual or to a trading company has the same effect as a secret in trade or manufactures. The monopolists, by keeping the market constantly understocked, by never fully supplying the effectual demand, sell their commodities much above the natural price, and raise their emoluments, whether they consist in wages or profit, greatly above their natural rate.

"The price of monopoly is upon every occasion the highest which can be got. The natural price, or the price of free competition, on the contrary, is the lowest which can be taken, not upon every occasion indeed, but for any considerable time together. The one is upon every occasion the highest which can be squeezed out of the buyers, or which, it is supposed, they will consent to give: the other is the lowest which the sellers can commonly afford to take, and at the same time continue their business.

"The exclusive privileges of corporations, statutes of apprenticeship, and all those laws which restrain, in particular employments, the competition to a smaller number than might otherwise go into them, have the same tendency, though in a less degree. They are a sort of enlarged monopolies, and may frequently, for ages together, and in whole classes of employments, keep up the market price of particular commodities above the natural price, and maintain both the wages of the labor and the profits of the stock employed about them somewhat above their natural rate."

Adam Smith, Wealth of Nations, 1776, Book I, chap. 7

The concept of a downward-sloping demand or AR curve did not exist in Smith's time. As a result, he made an error in his evaluation of monopoly. Can you find the error and correct it?

It Lacks Incentives for Efficiency, Innovation, and Progress

A third major criticism is that a monopoly, unlike a perfectly competitive firm, is not under constant pressure to meet consumer needs and to seek maximum productive efficiency. In addition, it need not be sufficiently inspired to develop better methods of production, and hence may retard economic progress. This is because the obstacles to entry make the monopolist relatively secure in his position; he does not face competitive pressures which would otherwise stimulate him to innovate. Public utilities—especially the railroads and telephone companies—

are often used as illustrations of monopolies that have intentionally retarded the development of new and improved products to avoid an increase in the obsolescence rate of their existing equipment.

WHAT CAN BE DONE ABOUT MONOPOLY?

The general criticisms of monopoly are rooted in the fundamental notion of resource misallocation resulting from the restriction of output and higher prices. In view of this, what can be done about monopolies in our society? There are three major possibilities, all of which require government action:

1. Tax away all the profits of monopolies above their normal profits and distribute these revenues to the public through more or improved government services. This would not drive monopolies out of business, since they would still be normally profitable, but it would reduce the tendency for monopolies to contribute to income inequality.

2. Treat all monopolies as public utilities by regulating their outputs and prices, requiring them to produce more and charge less than they would if they were completely free and unregulated.

3. Break monopolies up into competing firms.

No one of these approaches, nor any combination of them, would overcome completely the fundamental problem of resource misallocation, but each would tend to reduce somewhat the adverse effects of misallocation. Some of the important problems that arise from these suggestions are discussed in a later chapter dealing with antitrust problems involving government regulation of business.

Price Discrimination

Until now we have assumed that when a monopolist decides on his most profitable volume of output, he sells the required number of units at the *same* price per unit. However, a monopolist may sometimes find it more profitable to charge different prices instead of a single price for the units he sells. He is then engaging in what is known as "price discrimination"—one of the most interesting problems in the theory of monopoly.

Price discrimination may be defined as the practice of charging different prices to the same or to different buyers for the same good. Hence it is also sometimes called *differential pricing*. In general terms, price discrimination or differential pricing is a method that some sellers may use to tailor their prices to the specific purchasing situations or circumstances of the buyer.

"TAPPING" THE DEMAND CURVE

An example of price discrimination occurs when a monopolist "taps" the demand curve of the buyer by charging lower prices for larger quantities instead of a single price per unit for all units purchased. This approach may also be combined with charging different prices to different classes of buyers.

For example, an electric company does not usually charge the same price per unit of electricity to all buyers for all units. Instead it *segments* the total market—that is, divides it into homogeneous submarkets consisting, say, of residential users, commercial users, and industrial users—and charges a different price to each class of user. In this way it earns more money than it would if all users paid the same price.

A simplified version of this concept is illustrated in Exhibit 6 on the next page. Assuming the AR curve to be the demand curve of a single buyer or of a single homogeneous class of buyers, the seller may simply charge a price of OP_4 per unit and sell ON_4 units. In this case there is no discrimination, and the seller's total revenue is his price times quantity, or the area of the rectangle $OP_4M_4N_4$.

However, he can enlarge his total receipts considerably if he discriminates in price. Thus, he may charge a price of OP_1 for the first ON_1 units, giving him a total revenue of $OP_1M_1N_1$. Then he may lower his price to OP_2 per unit and sell an additional N_1N_2 units. After that, he can lower the price to OP_3 and sell an additional N_2N_3 units, and finally he can lower it to OP_4, where he sells a further N_3N_4 units. Although he still ends up selling the same total number of units, namely ON_4, his total revenue is now the entire shaded area instead of the area $OP_4M_4N_4$ when he charged a price of OP_4 per unit without discrimination. Evidently, the smaller the reductions in his price, the narrower the steps under the demand curve become and hence the larger his total revenue. Theoretically, the limit would be a total revenue equal to the entire area under the curve, but this would require price reductions in infinitesimal amounts. In practice, the reductions are in finite amounts for blocks of units, and the sales are made simultaneously to different classes of buyers at different price scales.

Exhibit 6

Price Discrimination Based on Quantity

By charging a different price to the same buyer (or to the same homogeneous class of buyers) according to the quantity purchased, the seller earns a larger total revenue (shown by the shaded areas) than if he charges the same price per unit for all units purchased.

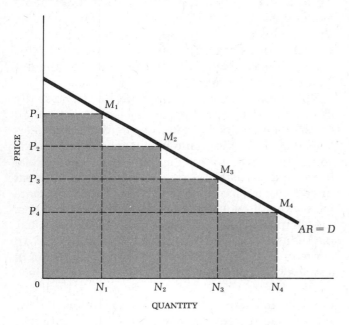

DUMPING

Another form of price discrimination occurs when a monopolist sells the same product in different markets at different prices. This practice is known in international trade as *dumping*, but its underlying principles are equally applicable to domestic trade.

The basic concept is illustrated by the diagrams in Exhibit 7. A firm which has a monopoly in the domestic market, for example, will probably find that the demand for its product at home is more inelastic than the demand abroad because foreign buyers have more alternative sources from which to purchase the product, which makes their demand for the monopolist's product more elastic.

Exhibit 7, therefore, shows the demand curve in the domestic market to be more inelastic than that in the foreign market. The total demand in both markets may be obtained by simply summing the horizontal ordinates in the domestic and foreign markets —that is, the quantities demanded in both markets at

each price—thus yielding the curve $AR_1 + AR_2$. The total marginal revenue of both markets, namely $MR_1 + MR_2$, is derived in a similar way by summing the horizontal ordinates to the MR_1 curve and the MR_2 curve in the domestic and foreign markets, or in other words the quantities in both markets at each marginal revenue.

The MC curve in the total market is the monopolist's marginal cost curve. His most profitable total output is O_3N_3 because this is where the marginal cost of his output equals the total marginal revenue. It should be emphasized that only one marginal cost curve is assumed to exist in this case, since it makes no difference to costs whether the product is sold at home or abroad; the product is still the same, and the marginal cost is determined by the total output. Hence at the output O_3N_3, the monopolist's marginal cost is N_3L_3, and this is equal to N_1L_1 in the domestic market and N_2L_2 in the foreign market.

Equilibrium in the Submarkets

How will the monopolist divide his total output among the two submarkets? What price will he charge in each market? The answers to these questions follow from the $MC = MR$ principle we have already learned. In order to maximize profit, the monopolist will sell O_1N_1 units in the domestic market at the price N_1P_1 because this is where the marginal revenue in that market is equal to his marginal cost N_1L_1. Likewise, he will sell the remaining O_2N_2 units in the foreign market at the price N_2P_2 because this is where the marginal revenue in that market equals his marginal cost N_2L_2.

There are many illustrations of dumping at both the domestic and international level. For example, some manufacturers of appliances and various other products sell part of their output to mail-order firms and department stores (e.g., Sears and Montgomery Ward) at lower prices under different brand names. Milk cooperatives frequently sell milk at a high price to consumers and at a low price to butter and cheese manufacturers. Tire manufacturers have sold under their own brand names in the domestic market and under different brand names through other marketing channels in both domestic and foreign markets. In each case, the seller earns a higher profit by making fuller utilization of his excess capacity—provided that the extra or marginal cost of the additional output does not exceed the extra or marginal revenue.

Exhibit 7

Illustration of Dumping

By adhering to the MC = MR principle, the monopolist maximizes profit by allocating his total equilibrium output O_3N_3 among the two submarkets, and charging a higher price in the submarket where the demand elasticity is less.

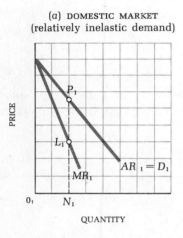

(a) DOMESTIC MARKET
(relatively inelastic demand)

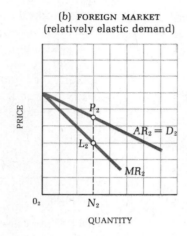

(b) FOREIGN MARKET
(relatively elastic demand)

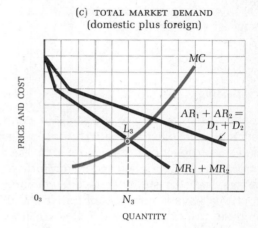

(c) TOTAL MARKET DEMAND
(domestic plus foreign)

THE CONDITIONS FOR PRICE DISCRIMINATION

Price discrimination is thus a practice of charging different prices to different *segments* of a market for the same good, where each segment defines a distinct market or submarket for the product. If you were a seller, what practical conditions would have to exist in order to enable you to practice price discrimination effectively? There are three: (1) multiple demand elasticities, (2) market segmentation, and (3) market sealing.

Multiple Demand Elasticities

There must be differences in demand elasticity among buyers due to differences in income, location, available alternatives, tastes, or other factors. Otherwise, if the underlying conditions that normally determine demand elasticity are the same for all purchasers, the separate demand elasticities for each buyer or group of buyers will be approximately equal, and a single rather than multiple price structure may be warranted.

Market Segmentation

The seller must be able to partition (segment) the total market by segregating buyers into groups or submarkets according to elasticity. Profits can then be enhanced by charging a different price in each submarket. There are many ways in which a total market can be effectively segmented into submarkets. For example:

☐ *Segmentation by income*—as when a doctor charges a rich patient more than a poor patient for the same operation

☐ *Segmentation by quantity of purchase*—as when a manufacturer offers quantity discounts to large buyers

☐ *Segmentation by geographic location*—as when a state university charges out-of-state students a higher tuition than in-state residents

☐ *Segmentation by time (including clock time and calendar time)*—as when a theater, tennis club, or telephone company charges more at certain hours than at others, or when a resort hotel, restaurant, or clothing store charges higher prices during certain seasons of the year

☐ *Segmentation by brand name*—as when the same product is sold under different brand names at different prices

☐ *Segmentation by age*—as when an airline charges less for children than for adults, despite equal time and space costs of serving them

Segmentation by race, religion, sex, and education provide still further opportunities for partitioning a market into relatively homogeneous subgroups. Can you suggest some examples?

Market Sealing

The seller must be able to prevent—or natural circumstances must exist which will prevent—any significant resale of goods from the lower- to the higher-priced submarket. Any leakage in the form of resale by buyers between submarkets will, beyond minimum critical levels, tend to neutralize the effect of differential prices and narrow the effective price structure to where it approaches that of a single price to all buyers. For example, a movie theater may use tickets of different color for matinees and for evenings, or for children and for adults. In this way it seals the segmented markets and prevents buyers from purchasing at the lower price and selling or using the product at the higher price. Similarly, some publishers of magazines, newspapers, and professional journals sell subscriptions to students at special rates. Of course, market sealing cannot always be accomplished with 100 percent perfection. When it is not, a certain amount of leakage will occur between submarkets, thereby reducing the effectiveness of price discrimination.

Public Utility Rates

Public utilities provide an interesting application of monopoly pricing. As we have seen, these firms are industries characterized by substantial economies of scale, so that one large firm may be able to produce a given quantity more cheaply than several small firms could. Legislatures have therefore protected these firms from competition by granting them franchises to operate, in return for which utility rates are controlled by state or federal regulatory commissions.

THREE ALTERNATIVE PRICING POLICIES

Three types of pricing policies for public utilities may be identified: monopoly (or profit-maximizing) pricing; full cost pricing; and marginal cost pricing. Each of these is illustrated in Exhibit 8.

Monopoly (Profit-maximizing) Pricing

The *monopoly price* N_1P_1 maximizes the firm's profit since it is determined by the intersection of marginal cost with marginal revenue. This $MC = MR$ price, if charged by a public utility, would probably not be socially acceptable. Why? Because as we have already learned, it results in a monopoly profit at society's expense. That is, it brings about output

---

Exhibit 8

Public Utility Rates: Three Alternatives

The monopoly price maximizes profit, but is socially undesirable because it results in a misallocation of society's resources.

The full cost price is the one regulatory commissions try to establish because it represents a "fair rate of return" on the utility's investment.

The marginal cost price is the socially optimum price for the welfare of society, but in this particular case it leaves the utility suffering a loss because it results in a price below average total cost. This may not always happen, however, as you saw earlier in the evaluation of monopoly.

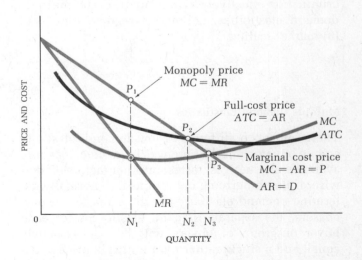

---

restriction and a misallocation of resources because the value to consumers of additional output exceeds the value of the resources used to produce that additional output. (Remember the criticisms of monopoly given earlier.)

Full Cost Pricing

The price N_2P_2 represents what economists call the *full cost* (or *average cost*) *price*. It is the price at which the firm covers all of its costs, both fixed and variable, and earns a normal profit. Regulatory commissions usually try to set this price because it provides a fair rate of return on investment for the utility.

The history of utility rate-making, however, is long and controversial, involving such questions as what to include in the "rate base" and what constitutes a "fair" return. For example, should the original cost of the utility's assets be used, or should the current replacement costs serve as a base? The choice is important because during periods of inflation the cost of replacing assets is usually greater than the original cost. Similarly, what rate of return does the utility need to earn in order to attract stockholder investments and yet not cause the price of its product to be so high as to exploit consumers? These are among the basic issues raised in the study of public utility rate regulation.

Marginal Cost Pricing—Some Welfare Implications

The price N_3P_3 illustrates the *marginal cost price*—the price at which a firm's marginal cost equals its average revenue or demand. There is a branch of economic theory called "welfare economics" which has much to say about the importance of this price. Thus, if you recall what was learned earlier when we examined the shortcomings of monopoly, as we move down the demand curve toward the marginal cost price, the welfare of society is increased because the added value of the extra output exceeds the added cost of providing it. Below this price, the welfare of society is decreased for the opposite reason. The marginal cost price is therefore the socially optimum price—the price that maximizes society's welfare—because at this price the value of the last unit to the marginal user (measured by the price he pays for the last unit, which is equal to the price he pays for any other unit) is equivalent to the value of the resources used to produce that unit.

The marginal cost price, however, has a disadvantage in this case: as you can see from Exhibit 8, it lies below the utility's ATC curve and hence if the regulatory commission required that the utility charge this price the result would be financial loss and eventual bankruptcy. In such cases, some economists who favor marginal cost pricing have argued that the government should pay a subsidy to the utility so that it can cover all its costs, or that the government should simply own the utility itself, in which case it would not have to be concerned with covering all costs out of revenues. What do you think of these proposals?

PRICE DISCRIMINATION BY UTILITIES

All three of the alternative pricing possibilities outlined above have assumed, for simplicity, a single price policy. In reality, public utilities often segment their total market into homogeneous subgroups and set different price structures for each segment. This, as we know, results in multiple prices or *price discrimination*—the opposite of single prices. Thus, telephone companies have different rates for different classes of users (such as residential and business), as well as different rates based on time and distance. Similarly, public utilities such as railroads, electric companies, and gas companies, also have complex rate structures.

In general, all regulatory commissions in the United States and in most European countries adhere to the full cost approach for setting overall rate structures, but they allow modifications and exceptions for discriminating in special segments of the market. In France and Sweden, on the other hand, there has been a growing interest in applying marginal cost pricing to public utilities—particularly in those cases where the firm's marginal cost is above its average total cost at the desired output.

SUMMARY OF IMPORTANT IDEAS

1. A monopoly is a single firm producing a product for which there are no close substitutes. Major types are natural monopolies, legal monopolies, government monopolies, strategic-resource monopolies, and patent monopolies.

2. The most profitable output of a monopoly is determined where its $MC = MR$. Unlike a firm in perfect competition, any firm faced with a downward-sloping demand curve is a partial monopoly. It thus

finds that its marginal revenue curve is not a demand curve, and its marginal cost curve is not a supply curve.

3. The basic economic criticism of monopoly is this: by adhering to the $MC = MR$ principle of profit maximization resources are misallocated by restricting output and charging a correspondingly higher price than if the $MC = P$ standard of competitive industry were followed. In addition, monopolies contribute to income inequality and they may lack incentives to be efficient, innovative, and progressive. Three possible "solutions" are to tax away their supernormal profits, regulate them as public utilities, or break them up into competing firms.

4. Price discrimination enlarges revenues by segmenting the market into submarkets and charging different prices in each according to relative demand elasticities. Markets may be segmented by income, brand names of products, location of buyer, and various other criteria. Dumping is a typical form of price discrimination.

5. Public utilities are regulated monopolies. Their rates tend to accord with principles of full cost pricing, rather than monopoly pricing or marginal cost pricing.

FOR DISCUSSION

1. *Terms and concepts to review:*

monopoly	price discrimination
natural monopoly	dumping
government monopoly	monopoly price
strategic-resource monopoly	full cost (average cost) price
patent monopoly	marginal cost price
average-marginal relationship	

2. Evaluate the judicial definition that a monopoly is "a business affected with a public interest."

3. Answer true or false, and explain why:
   (a) A monopolist is secure since, by controlling his price and output, he can guarantee himself a profit.
   (b) A perfect monopoly is almost as unlikely as perfect competition.
   (c) A monopolist's price is higher than a perfect competitor's price in the long run.

(d) A monopolist maximizes his profit by charging the highest price he can get.

4. "A monopolist is most likely to be successful when the demand for his product is relatively inelastic." True or false? (HINT: Prove that a monopolist will never produce at an output at which the elasticity of demand is numerically less than 1. You can do this by first proving that when marginal revenue is positive, the elasticity of demand is numerically greater than 1.)

5. What is the most profitable output for a monopolist who is faced with a unit elastic demand curve throughout its entire length? (HINT: What is marginal revenue when demand is unit elastic?) Explain.

6. If the government wanted to extract the maximum revenue from a monopolist without driving him out of business, should it tax his profits, or tax each unit of output? Explain.

7. "The prices of automobiles, TV sets, and cornflakes are each determined by supply and demand." Evaluate this statement in light of the fact that a less than perfectly competitive firm has no supply curve. What do "supply" and "demand" actually mean in this case?

8. Complete the table on the next page showing cost and revenue data of a monopolist. Sketch the following curves on three separate charts, one beneath the other, as was done in this chapter: (a) total revenue and total cost; (b) marginal cost, average total cost, average revenue, and marginal revenue; (c) net revenue.

Draw vertical dashed lines showing the most profitable level of output and the two break-even points. (NOTE: You will have to "project" the curves in order to obtain the second break-even point.) Label all the curves and explain their significance. Remember that marginal curves are plotted to the midpoints of the integers on the horizontal axis.

9. Suppose you were an economic advisor to a monopolist. Can you suggest ways in which he could engage in price discrimination by segmenting his market on the basis of (a) quantity, (b) geographic location, and (c) "time"?

10. What do you think of the suggestion that public utilities should be subsidized, or even governmentally owned, in order to have them adhere to a socially desirable policy of marginal cost pricing?

COST AND REVENUE SCHEDULES OF A MONOPOLIST

Quantity per day, Q	Average revenue or price, AR = P	Total revenue, TR	Marginal revenue, MR	Total cost, TC	Average total cost, ATC	Marginal cost, MC	Net revenue, NR
0	$21	$ 0		$22			
1	20	20		37			
2	19	38		42			
3	18	54		45			
4	17	68		47			
5	16	80		50			
6	15	90		54			
7	14	98		59			
8	13	104		65			
9	12	108		72			
10	11	110		80			
11	10	110		89			
12	9	108		99			

CHAPTER 26

The Real World of Imperfect Competition

CHAPTER PREVIEW

Can some features of monopoly and perfect competition be combined to develop new and more realistic models of market behavior?

What is the theory of monopolistic competition? Of oligopoly? How well do these theories serve to describe the behavior of industries in our economy?

Do imperfectly competitive firms compete in the same way as competitive firms? What are the similarities? The differences?

If the world of perfect competition is largely imaginary, and the world of monopoly is relatively limited and regulated, what does the *real* world look like? In this chapter we answer that question by constructing models that come closer to approximating the kinds of markets in which most firms and industries in our economy tend to operate. We shall find that our knowledge of perfect competition and monopoly provides a basis for comparing and evaluating the consequences of these more realistic situations.

To give yourself a bird's-eye view of where you are at the present time and where you will be heading in this chapter, simply examine the following spectrum of market structures:

Perfect competition	Varying degrees of imperfect competition—monopolistic competition and oligopoly	Pure monopoly

We have already analyzed the cases of perfect competition and monopoly at the extreme ends of the spectrum. Now we turn our attention to the broad middle range in order to examine situations encompassing what is known as "imperfect competition"—market structures which are classified as "monopolistic competition" and "oligopoly." These names arise from the fact that *imperfect competition* consists of various "mixtures" of perfect competition and pure monopoly. We shall find that these mixed structures characterize most of the markets in our economy.

Theory of Monopolistic Competition

We have seen that perfect competition consists of many firms producing a homogeneous product, and monopoly consists of one firm producing a unique product for which there are no close substitutes.

Both are important for economic analysis. Some industries—for example, the producers of standard raw materials, and the organized commodity and stock exchanges—operate under conditions that exhibit many characteristics of perfect competition. Other industries, such as the public utilities, have features similar to those of monopoly.

In reality, most of our economic activity is carried on under conditions of imperfect competition—that is, in industries and markets that fall between the two extremes of perfect competition and pure monopoly. One in-between case which exists in a large portion of the American economy is called *monopolistic competition*; it may be defined as an industry characterized by a large number of firms of different sizes producing heterogeneous (similar but not identical) products, with relatively easy entry into the industry. We will study this type of competition first. The other subcategory of imperfect competition, known as "oligopoly," is examined later in this chapter.

PRODUCT DIFFERENTIATION IS A KEY FACTOR

Does the term "monopolistic competition" contradict itself? How can a market be both monopolistic and competitive at the same time?

The answer is based on the fact that in an industry characterized by monopolistic competition the products of the firms in the industry are *differentiated*. But product differentiation, like beauty, is in the eye of the beholder—and in economics the beholder is always the buyer. This means that products may be differentiated by brand name, color of package, location of the seller, customer service, credit conditions, or the smile of the salesman—even if the products themselves are physically the same. As a result, each firm has a partial monopoly of its own differentiated product.

Monopolistic competition is found in many industries. Retailing provides a good general illustration. Some more specific examples include the manufacture of clothing, household goods, shoes, and furniture; and, in some areas, the services provided by most barbers, doctors, and dentists. In each of these industries the products sold are usually only moderately differentiated. This helps to explain why similar kinds of goods in monopolistic competition tend to have similar prices—as is usually the case in certain regions with haircuts, appendectomies, and teeth fillings. The less the degree of product differentiation in the minds of buyers, the less the disparity in prices.

PRICE AND OUTPUT DETERMINATION

When we apply these ideas to the construction of a model, we find that the theory of monopolistic competition is as much a *theory of the firm* as it is of market or industry behavior. Thus:

1. Since each seller has a partial monopoly due to product differentiation, there will be a separate *AR* or demand curve for each firm. These curves will be downward-sloping, indicating that a seller can raise his prices to some degree without losing all of his sales.

2. We learned in the study of monopoly that a firm with a negatively inclined demand curve has no supply curve, since a given price may be associated with multiple outputs and a given output may be associated with multiple prices, depending on the position of the *AR* curve. Hence there can be no industry supply curve; indeed, the whole concept of an industry becomes somewhat cloudy and vague in monopolistic competition because of the existence of product differentiation.

3. Since the products of competitors are close but not perfect substitutes, we may assume that their elasticity of demand is relatively high. Indeed, the coefficient of elasticity will vary inversely with the degree of product differentiation. And of course, the less the degree of product differentiation and the greater the number of sellers, the closer the model will be to pure competition.

The $MC = MR$ Principle Again

As always, each firm will seek to produce to where $MC = MR$ in order to maximize its profit. But since many firms are in the industry, and entry is relatively easy, some firms will, in the short run, earn modest supernormal profits.

In the long run, however, there will be a *tendency* for surviving firms to be only normally profitable, but not necessarily precisely so, depending on the degree of product differentiation and the number of firms. For example, a small retail store might continue to be somewhat more than normally profitable because it happens to be in a particularly good location. On the other hand, a similar kind of store in a different location may continue to be less than normally profitable, because the seller would prefer to be his "own boss"—even if he has to incur an economic loss in doing so—rather than hire himself out to do the same job at a higher salary for someone else. Hence, although most firms in a monopolistically competitive industry *tend* to earn normal profits in the long run, some firms do not. These possibilities are illustrated by the firms in Exhibit 1.

THE IMPORTANCE OF SELLING COSTS

Since product differentiation plays such a key role in monopolistic competition, many firms spend money on advertising, merchandising, sales promotion, public relations, and the like in order to increase their profits. Marketing expenditures of this type, which are aimed at adapting the buyer to the product, are termed *selling costs*. This distinguishes them from production costs, which are designed to adapt the product to the buyer. For purposes of analysis, economists generally view all sales outlays or selling costs as synonymous with advertising.

The seller in monopolistic competition who engages in advertising seeks to attain a delicate balance between commodity homogeneity and heterogeneity. To attract customers away from his competitors he must convey two ideas:

1. His product is not sharply differentiated from the competing products, so that buyers will find it feasible to purchase his product instead of his competitors'.

2. His product is somehow superior to those of his competitors', so that buyers believe there is greater heterogeneity than exists in fact.

These objectives of advertising account for the erroneous statement sometimes made about it as explained in Exhibit 2. As you can see from the explanation accompanying the diagram, the purpose of advertising is to *shift* the demand curve to a higher position.

IS ADVERTISING "GOOD" OR "BAD"?

Advertising has been a subject of much debate among economists. The arguments have revolved around three major issues:

1. *Information versus persuasion.* Those in favor of advertising argue that it educates and informs buyers about firms, products, and prices, and thereby tends to make markets more perfect than they otherwise would be. Those who oppose advertising reply that it seeks to persuade buyers rather than inform them, thereby creating wants that result in a distortion of "natural" preference patterns.

2. *Efficiency versus waste.* Proponents of advertising contend that it familiarizes consumers with products and thereby broadens the market for goods; this not only encourages further capital investment and employment, but also large-scale operations that result in low-cost mass production. Critics of adver-

---

Exhibit 1

Firms in Monopolistic Competition

Firm A is earning above-normal profits, Firm B is receiving only normal profits, and Firm C is earning below-normal profits. In the long run most firms in monopolistic competition will tend to be normally profitable, but there may be some exceptions due to locational factors or other special circumstances.

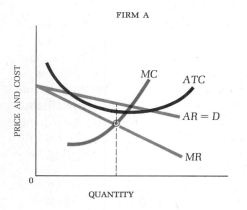

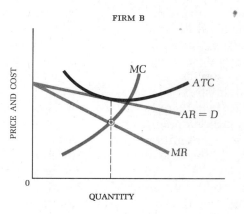

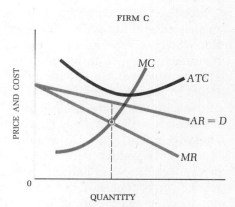

---

tising reply that it encourages artificial product differentiation among goods that are physically similar and that advertising among competing firms tends to have a canceling effect; this duplication of effort results in a waste of resources, higher product costs, and higher prices, so that any real economies of scale—even if they exist—are lost through inefficiencies. This argument of efficiency versus waste is amplified in Exhibit 3.

Exhibit 2

Advertising and Demand

It is often said that the seller's purpose in advertising is to make the demand curve more inelastic, thus allowing a higher price to be charged for each unit sold. If this statement were true, it would mean that the seller would prefer to be confronted with the demand curve D_1 rather than D_2. Yet if his most profitable output is beyond ON_1, say at ON_2, then D_2 is clearly preferable to D_1 because it allows for sales at a higher price even though D_2 is more elastic than D_1. On the other hand, if his most profitable output were ON_3, then he would prefer D_1 to D_2. Therefore, the argument that advertising is desirable for the seller because it results in a more inelastic demand curve may be only partially true and in many instances may be completely false.

The statement can be correctly reformulated by noting that what the seller really wants is not necessarily a more inelastic demand curve, but rather a new and higher curve level. This is illustrated by D_3. With this demand curve he can charge a higher price per unit relative to either D_1 or D_2, regardless of the most profitable output volume indicated on the chart.

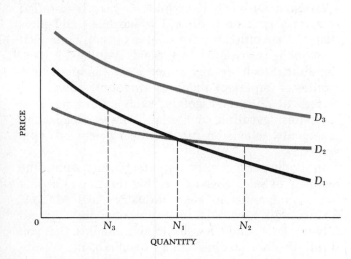

Exhibit 3

Advertising and Economies of Scale

Chart (a). *In the short run, advertising raises a firm's average total cost curve by the advertising cost per unit. Thus, at output 0M, if the advertising cost per unit is DC, total advertising expenditures are equal to the area of the rectangle ABCD.*

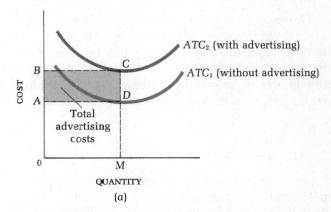

(a)

Chart (b). *Advertising may also shift a firm's demand curve to the right and raise its long-run average costs, thereby influencing its economies of scale. For example, suppose that without advertising the firm would have produced the output 0J at a unit cost of JE. Then, as a result of advertising, there may be several possible effects:*

1. *Advertising may give the firm economies of scale, enabling it to produce the larger output 0K at the lower unit cost KG, even though point G is on a higher LRAC curve than point E.*

2. *Advertising may have a canceling effect, leaving output unchanged at 0J and simply increasing unit costs from JE to JF.*

3. *Advertising may cause diseconomies of scale, causing the firm to produce the output 0L at unit costs of LH. This case is not very likely, however, since monopolistic competition results in firms of less than optimum size, as will be pointed out in the text.*

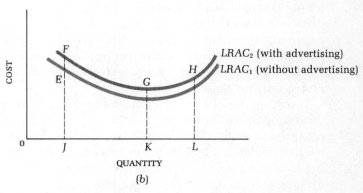

(b)

3. *Competition versus concentration.* Defenders of advertising argue that it encourages competition by exposing consumers to competing products, and enabling firms to gain market acceptance for new products more rapidly than they could without advertising. Critics of advertising contend that it facilitates the concentration of monopoly power because large firms can usually afford continuous heavy advertising, whereas new and small firms cannot.

These arguments indicate the fundamental nature of the controversy. Many students find the economics of advertising an interesting topic for a term paper. You can obtain a great deal of information on the subject in your college library, since numerous books and articles have been written about it.

EVALUATING MONOPOLISTIC COMPETITION

From what we already know about the results of perfect competition and monopoly, the more relevant social effects of monopolistic competition may be stated briefly.

First, monopolistically competitive firms determine their production volumes and prices by the $MC = MR$ rule of profit maximization. They therefore misallocate resources by restricting outputs and charging higher prices than if they adhered to the $MC = P$ standard of perfect competition. Note that *this is the same basic criticism that was given for monopoly.* However, in the case of monopolistic competition, the extent of resource misallocation with its associated output restriction and higher prices will depend, in each industry, on the degree of product differentiation and the number of sellers.

Second, monopolistic competition encourages *nonprice competition*—that is, methods of competition that do not involve changes in selling price. Examples include advertising, sales promotion, customer services, and product differentiation. Nonprice activities that result in greater innovation and product improvement may be desirable; but to the extent that they result in higher production costs due to duplication of resources, excessive style changes, and so on, they tend to be undesirable.

Third, monopolistically competitive firms create what economists have called the *"wastes" of monopolistic competition*—the existence of "sick" industries characterized by chronic excess capacity resulting from too many sellers of differentiated products dividing up markets, operating inefficiently at outputs less than their minimum average costs, and

charging higher prices. Examples abound in the retail trades, such as grocery stores, clothing shops, and restaurants, as well as in the light manufacturing industries like textiles, shoes, and plastics.

Why do the chronically sick industries of monopolistic competition continue to exist? There are several reasons: low initial capital requirements, not much need for technical know-how, and the desire to own a business and "be your own boss." As a result, new firms enter the industry as fast or even faster than the unprofitable ones leave it.

Theory of Oligopoly

When you drive a car, open a can of tuna fish, replace a light bulb, buy cigarettes, wash your hands with soap, play a phonograph record, type a term paper, or talk on a telephone, you are using products manufactured by oligopolistic industries. An *oligopoly* is an industry composed of a few firms producing either: (1) a homogeneous product, in which case it is called *perfect oligopoly;* or (2) heterogeneous products, in which case it is called *imperfect oligopoly.* Oligopolistic industries are typically characterized by high obstacles to entry, usually in the form of substantial capital requirements, technical know-how, patent rights, and the like.

Examples of perfect oligopoly are found primarily among producers of industrial goods like aluminum, cement, copper, steel, and zinc. These goods are bought by other manufacturers who usually order them by specification—that is, in a particular form such as sheet steel, structural steel, or cold-rolled steel of a specific temper (i.e., hardness and plasticity). A specified type of steel is virtually identical whether it is made by U.S. Steel, Bethlehem Steel, Republic Steel, or any other steel company. Examples of imperfect oligopoly are found among producers of consumer goods, such as automobiles, cigarettes, gasoline, major appliances, soaps and detergents, television tubes, rubber tires, and typewriters.

In both perfect and imperfect oligopolies, the majority of sales goes to the "big three" or the "big four" companies in each industry—like ALCOA, Kaiser, and Reynolds in aluminum, and General Motors, Ford, and Chrysler in automobiles. Can you think of other leading firms in some of the oligopolistic industries mentioned above?

EDWARD HASTINGS CHAMBERLIN

1899–1967

JOAN ROBINSON

1903–

The theory of monopolistic competition had its origin in the early 1930s. Prior to that time there was only a theory of perfect competition and a theory of monopoly.

In the United States, the person responsible for the development of the theory was a professor at Harvard University, Edward Chamberlin. His distinguished treatise, *The Theory of Monopolistic Competition,* was published in 1933. As Chamberlin put it, the theory was needed because:

> . . . With differentiation appears monopoly, and as it proceeds further the element of monopoly becomes greater. Where there is any degree of differentiation whatever, each seller has an absolute monopoly of his own product, but is subject to the competition of more or less imperfect substitutes. Since each is a monopolist and yet has competitors, we may speak of them as 'competing monopolists,' and of the forces at work as those of 'monopolistic competition.'
>
> It is this latter problem which is of especial interest and importance. In all of the fields where individual products have even the slightest element of uniqueness, competition bears but faint resemblance to the pure competition of a highly organized market for a homogeneous product.

In the same year, quite independently (the two were unknown to each other), an eminent economist at Cambridge University in England, Mrs. Joan Robinson, published a volume entitled *The Economics of Imperfect Competition.* These two books by Chamberlin and Robinson formed the basis of what we know today about economic behavior in monopolistically competitive markets.

Both authors stressed the joint influence of competitive and monopolistic elements in the determination of equilibrium. They pointed out that the distinguishing characteristics in imperfect markets are product differentiation and consumer preferences, rather than the absence of a large number of sellers. This makes each seller a "partial" monopolist, regardless of the number of competitors in his industry.

Although there were some differences in their views, both used the critical concepts of marginal cost and marginal revenue, and both showed how the firm maximizes profits by equating these two variables. They also discussed short- and long-run equilibrium, barriers to entry into an industry, and the role of normal profits. Chamber-

Harvard University News Office.

Ramsey and Muspratt, Cambridge.

lin, in addition, provided a substantial analysis of the role of advertising.

One year later, in 1934, a German economist named Heinrich Von Stackelberg published a book entitled *Marktform und Gleichgewicht (Market Structure and Equilibrium),* which emphasized the interdependence of firms and the problems of oligopoly. One of Stackelberg's chief conclusions was that a democratic state cannot eliminate market structures that fail to achieve a socially desirable equilibrium, whereas authoritarian states can. He thus developed a defense of government intervention in the economy in order to bring about the results deemed best by society.

SOME CHARACTERISTICS OF OLIGOPOLIES

In addition to fewness of sellers, high obstacles to entry, and similar if not identical products, most oligopolistic industries tend to have several other characteristics in common.

1. *Substantial economies of scale.* Firms in oligopolies typically require large-scale production in order to obtain low unit costs. If total market demand is sufficient only to support a few large firms of optimum size, then competition will ensure that only a few such firms survive.

2. *Growth through merger.* Many of the oligopolies that exist today have resulted from mergers of competing firms—in some cases as long ago as the late nineteenth or early twentieth centuries. In 1901, for example, the U.S. Steel Corporation was formed from a merger of 11 independent steel producers. The purpose, as in most mergers, was to gain a substantial increase in market share, greater economies of scale, larger buying power in the purchase of its inputs, and various other advantages which smaller firms did not possess to the same extent.

3. *Mutual dependence.* The fewness of sellers in an oligopolistic industry makes it necessary for each seller to consider the reactions of his competitors when he sets his own price. In this sense the behavior of oligopolists in the marketplace may be somewhat similar to the behavior of players in games of skill like chess, checkers, and bridge; in such games, the participants try to win by formulating strategies that recognize the possible counterreactions of their opponents.

4. *Price rigidity and nonprice competition.* These features, and others that are mentioned below, give rise to a "live and let live" policy in most oligopolistic industries. Firms find it more comfortable to maintain constant prices and to engage in various forms of nonprice competition such as advertising and customer service in order to hold if not increase their market shares. Price reductions, when they occur, tend to be sporadic, and ordinarily come about only under severe pressures resulting from weakened demands or excessive inventories.

PRICE AND OUTPUT DETERMINATION

With these characteristics as a background, how do oligopolistic firms determine their prices and outputs?

A number of different models may be used to portray various types of oligopoly situations. One of the more interesting possibilities is demonstrated in Exhibit 4. This model illustrates what is known as the *kinked demand curve*—a "bent" demand curve and a corresponding discontinuous marginal revenue curve, facing an oligopolistic seller.

Thus, suppose the oligopolist's current price is 0P and his output is 0N. When contemplating a change in price either up or down he must consider how his rivals will react. Hence, he might visualize his firm's demand curve by reasoning in the following way:

Exhibit 4

A Kinked Demand Curve Facing an Oligopolist

Given the kink at K, any price reduction below 0P will increase sales slowly along KD because other firms will probably match any price cuts. A price increase above 0P will reduce sales rapidly along LK because other firms will probably not match the price rise. Since marginal cost can fluctuate widely between G and H, the equilibrium price 0P and output 0N tend to be stable. However, this model leaves some price uncertainty because it does not explain why the kink happens to occur at K rather than at some other point.

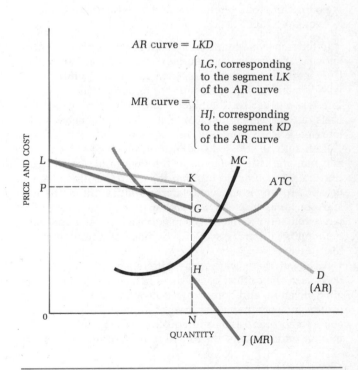

If I reduce my price below OP, my competitors will lose some of their customers to me and this will probably prompt them to match my price cut. Therefore, my sales will increase relatively little following the curve KD. On the other hand, if I increase my price above OP, my competitors probably won't match the increase and I'll lose some of my customers to them. Therefore, my sales will fall off rapidly along the curve KL.

In other words, the kinked demand curve reflects the greater tendency of competitors to follow price reductions than price increases. Price reductions take sales away from other firms, and prompt them to cut prices in retaliation; price increases do not usually invite such responses because other firms will take sales from the firm that raises its price. It follows that the more homogeneous or standardized the product, the sharper the kink, since customers will shift more readily and sellers will therefore react more quickly to changes in prices.

As you can see, the large discontinuity in the MR curve between G and H permits the MC curve to fluctuate widely within this range. This helps to explain why oligopolies exhibit a high degree of price stability. But there is also this seeming paradox:

The kinked demand curve model leaves oligopolists with a considerable degree of price uncertainty. The model demonstrates that once the kink is given, the price at that point will tend to be stable; however, it does not say anything about why the kink happens to occur where it does instead of at some other point.

Some oligopolies have tried in various ways to reduce the state of uncertainty in which they operate. Two such methods have been collusion and price leadership.

OLIGOPOLIES IN COLLUSION

Oligopolists in some industries have occasionally colluded—"gotten together" and agreed on a single industry-wide price which they would all charge. This situation is most probable when the firms in the industry are faced with similar demands and either the same or different cost curves, as might occur in a case of perfect oligopoly. The result may then be much the same as in monopoly, except that there is more than one firm. Two interesting models can be employed to illustrate these possibilities.

Duopoly with Identical Costs

In Exhibit 5 for simplicity we assume a case of perfect oligopoly, in which the industry consists of only two firms producing a standardized product. An industry composed of two sellers is also called a

---

Exhibit 5

Price and Output Determination: Two Oligopolists

In Chart (a) each firm maximizes its profits by adhering to the MC = MR rule, thereby producing ON units and charging OP per unit. Both firms may also agree to stick to this rule at all times, thereby always charging a single, industry-wide price.

In Chart (b) if each firm followed the MC = MR rule, Firm X represented by MC_X would prefer price OP, whereas Firm Y represented by MC_Y would prefer price OP'. By colluding, both firms might agree on a price within this range. But through price leadership by the larger firm, Firm Y may be willing to follow a price of OP established by Firm X.

(a) IDENTICAL DEMANDS AND COSTS

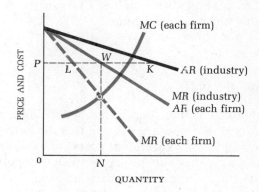

(b) IDENTICAL DEMANDS AND DIFFERENT COSTS

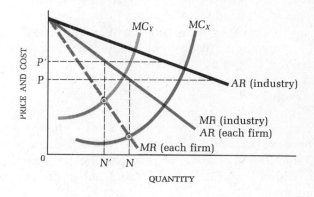

duopoly. It may be either a perfect or an imperfect duopoly, depending on whether the product is standardized or differentiated.

In Chart (a), we further suppose that if the products and the prices of the two firms are identical, each firm will have a 50 percent chance of selling to any buyer, and hence the market will be divided equally between them. Therefore, the AR curve of the industry will be downward-sloping. At any given price such as OP, the quantity sold by each firm will be one-half the industry's total. Also, as we learned earlier in the study of monopoly, it is mathematically true for all straight-line MR and AR curves that the *marginal revenue curve must bisect any horizontal line drawn from the vertical axis to the average revenue curve*. Hence the AR curve of each firm corresponds to the MR curve of the industry, and so the distance $PW = WK$. Similarly, the MR curve of each firm is such that $PL = LW$.

If we assume that the two firms have identical marginal cost curves, it follows that each will maximize its profits by following the $MC = MR$ rule, producing ON units of output and charging OP per unit. They might also collude by agreeing not to deviate from the $MC = MR$ rule even temporarily and to maintain a single-price policy even in the face of changing business conditions.

Duopoly with Different Costs

The identical demand conditions are also illustrated in Chart (b), but now we assume that the two duopolists X and Y have different costs. Thus duopolist X is a larger-capacity producer than duopolist Y because the marginal cost curve of Firm X as represented by MC_X is farther to the right than the marginal cost curve of Firm Y as represented by MC_Y. This means that for any given marginal cost, Firm X can produce more than Firm Y.

In this case, by following the $MC = MR$ rule, Firm X will maximize its profit by producing ON units and charging OP per unit, whereas Firm Y will maximize its profit by producing ON' units and charging OP' per unit.

The two firms are thus in conflict. If Firm X charges its preferred lower price, Firm Y *must* charge the same price or else lose sales. If Firm Y charges its preferred higher price, Firm X need not do the same, in which case Firm Y will again suffer the consequences.

What will the two firms do? They might collude by agreeing on a single price for both. This price may be OP, or OP', or some price in between, and it may be a price that is profitable for both firms as long as each is earning at least normal profits.

In practice, there are a number of real-world obstacles to collusion. They include: (a) the antitrust laws (to be studied in a later chapter) that make such behavior illegal; (b) the number of firms in the industry—since the larger the number, the harder it may be for sellers to "get together"; and (c) the degree of product differentiation—since greater differentiation makes collusion more difficult. Despite these obstacles, cases of collusion are sometimes uncovered by the government.

PRICE LEADERSHIP

Instead of formally agreeing on a mutually satisfactory price as in Exhibit 5, Chart (b), it is possible that Firm Y would adhere to a policy of *price leadership*—a situation in which all firms in an oligopolistic industry adhere, often tacitly and without formal agreement, to the pricing policies of one of its members. Usually, but not always, the price leader will be the largest firm in the industry, and other firms in the industry will simply go along with the leader.

Thus in the diagram, Firm X is the largest, and would probably be the price leader; it could therefore set a price of OP to maximize its own profit, and Firm Y would follow the leader by charging the same price. This policy avoids uncomfortable price wars, it is not regarded as illegal by the courts (unless it is proven to be the result of collusion or other monopolistic practices), and it leaves the price followers earning at least normal, although not maximum, profits. This explains why price leadership has at one time or another been a widespread practice in most oligopolistic industries including cigarettes, steel, anthracite coal, farm equipment, newsprint, tin cans, lead, sulfur, sugar, and many others.

EVALUATING OLIGOPOLY

Oligopoly is a major form of market structure in our economy. What can be said about its social consequences? Unfortunately, the issues are extremely complex and the conclusions are by no means clearcut. Nevertheless, three aspects of oligopoly are worth noting.

1. The basic criticism of oligopoly is the same as that of monopoly and monopolistic competition: It misallocates resources by restricting output short of the point where $MC = P$. But this criticism does not necessarily mean that an oligopoly produces less, or has higher unit costs, than a perfectly competitive industry. In oligopolistic industries where technology is such that economies of scale are important (e.g., automobiles or steel), larger outputs and lower long-run unit costs may be achieved than if these industries were perfectly competitive. An automobile manufacturer, for example, could not gain significant reductions in unit costs without the technology and economies of assembly-line mass production.

2. Oligopolistic industries tend to be more progressive in research and development than perfectly competitive industries, but evidence suggests that they are considerably less progressive in research than in development, as explained in Exhibit 6.

3. The economic influence of oligopoly (and also monopoly) may be somewhat offset by the growth of *countervailing power*. This term means that the growth of market power by one group may stimulate the growth of a counterreaction and somewhat offsetting influence by another group on the other side of the market. For instance, powerful labor unions have grown up to face oligopolistic industries across the bargaining table; chain stores have emerged to deal with large processing and manufacturing firms; and even government has grown larger, partly in response to the growth of big business and big labor. Countervailing power therefore has some favorable competitive effects within the economy, but it does not exist with equal effectiveness in all oligopolistic industries.

To conclude:

Although oligopolies are subject to the same basic criticism as monopolies and monopolistic competi-

---

Exhibit 6

Are Oligopolies Progressive in Research and Development?

Economists have long believed that since oligopolistic firms may earn substantial pure profits over the long run, it is to their advantage to use some of these profits to finance research on new and better products in order to ensure their market position. Indeed, this type of research and development (R & D) is a significant and often necessary form of nonprice competition. Yet, various analyses of patent statistics as well as several studies of inventions and innovations have come up with the following findings:

1. Approximately two-thirds of the major inventions since 1900, including air-conditioning, automatic transmissions, power steering, cellophane, the cotton picker, the helicopter, the gyro-compass, the jet engine, quick-freezing, insulin, the continuous casting of steel, and the catalytic cracking of petroleum are the products of independent inventors working alone or in universities and small research firms—rather than in the laboratories of large oligopolies. Only a relatively small proportion of the major inventions, including nylon, tetraethyl lead, the diesel electric locomotive, and transistors were developed by large private firms such as DuPont, General Motors, and Bell Telephone laboratories.

2. Although basic research is done mainly in academic institutions and private research firms, the development part of R & D is the specialty of large industrial corpora-

tions. In fact, the great bulk of their R & D outlays is for this purpose. Some of the leading oligopolistic industries in terms of development are aircraft and missiles, electrical equipment, and communication. Although a substantial share of development expenditures has been financed by the federal government for defense reasons, the proportion paid by Washington has declined from more than half in 1960 to less than one-third today.

3. In many oligopolistic industries such as agricultural machinery, basic metals, and food products, relatively little has been spent on research.

In contrast, research and development in agriculture, which serves as a rough approximation of perfect competition, has been accomplished mainly by government support in federal research laboratories, experiment stations, and land grant colleges and universities.

SOURCE: U.S. Congress, Hearings before the Joint Economic Committee, Employment, Growth and Price Levels, Washington, 1959, pp. 2337–57; Daniel Hamberg, "Invention in the Industrial Research Laboratory," Journal of Political Economy, April, 1963; John Jewkes, David Sawers, and Richard Stillerman, The Sources of Invention, New York, St. Martin's Press, 1958; National Science Foundation; Science News, April 22, 1972.

tion—namely, resource misallocation, resulting from output restriction and higher prices—they may mitigate these shortcomings to the extent that they seek to realize known economies of scale, and develop and innovate with new products and techniques.

Do Firms Really Maximize Profits?

Now that we have completed our introduction to the theory of business behavior under imperfect competition, it is appropriate to ask: Do firms really strive to maximize profits as economic theory assumes? In other words, do businessmen actually behave the way we have said they do, equating their MC and MR?

This problem often comes up in discussions of politics, labor-management relations, and other areas of current social and economic interest. Hence we should look closely at three dimensions of the profit-maximization problem. These dimensions involve (1) definitional, (2) mensurational, and (3) environmental considerations.

DEFINITIONAL PROBLEMS:
WHICH CONCEPT OF PROFIT?

It is easy to define profit as total revenue minus total cost. But is this all there is to the concept of profit? The answer is not as simple as it may seem because (a) businessmen do not always know whether they are seeking to maximize short-run profit or long-run profit, and (b) they do not always view the approach to profit management in the same way. As a result of these *definitional* problems, it becomes extremely difficult to state unequivocally that firms in the real world either do or do not strive to maximize their profits.

For example, firms often adopt policies which may reduce short-run profits but which are designed to establish a better long-run situation. Illustrations of such policies include (a) costly research and development programs for creating new products and new markets, and (b) fringe benefits to employees aimed at developing long-run loyalties. At the same time, these firms may exploit short-run market situations to the fullest advantage at the risk of adversely affecting their corporate image in the long run.

Likewise, firms often view the profit problem in discordant ways. Many studies conducted by business economists and management researchers have found that corporations tend to approach the formulation of profit policies differently. A policy that may seem wise to one firm may seem folly to another. A typical illustration of this is found in the field of employee relations. One firm may regard pension programs, health and accident plans, or even coffee breaks as means of raising labor morale and productivity. Another firm may consider them at best a necessary evil.

MENSURATIONAL PROBLEMS:
WHICH INDICATOR OF PROFIT?

The problems of defining a concept of profit are closely tied to the problems of measuring it. Our elementary theory of the firm has assumed that businessmen know their marginal costs and marginal revenues and can simply adjust their outputs to the most profitable levels—the levels at which $MC = MR$.

But in a dynamic economic environment, where changes in technology, tastes, and other underlying forces constantly influence costs and demands, businessmen cannot possibly have a precise understanding of how changes in their output will affect their costs and revenues. At best they may be able to gain a rough idea of their costs at a few "typical" or standard volumes of output, but even this would be of relatively limited value as a guide to profit maximization in the manner described by economic theory.

As a result of these and other difficulties, business firms in imperfect competition do not, as economic theory assumes, set prices with full knowledge of their marginal costs and marginal revenues. Instead, they establish their prices on the basis of experience, trial-and-error, and the customs and practices of the industry of which they are a part. And their prices are not usually set with the direct objective of maximizing profits, but rather to achieve other objectives, including the following ones, which may (or may not) indirectly maximize profits:

1. Pricing to achieve a certain target or percentage return on investment

2. Pricing to stabilize a firm's prices and outputs over the business cycle

3. Pricing to achieve a certain target or percentage share of the market

4. Pricing to meet or match the prices of competitors

None of these measures is a substitute for profit maximization. All, however, influence a firm's net revenue and are usually easier for executives to use as a practical guide for profit management and control. Hence they serve as *indicators* of profit rather than measures of profit. In studies of pricing practices of large corporations, it has been found that the first of the above goals is dominant, but the others also play important roles.

ENVIRONMENTAL CONDITIONS: PROFIT-LIMITING FACTORS

From a different point of view, conditions may exist in the economic environment which encourage a firm to avoid—purposely and consciously—the maximization of (short-run) profits, although the execution of these policies may be argued to be best in the long run. Four such motives for limiting profit may be noted.

1. *Discourage competitive entry.* If profits could be large due to higher prices rather than lower costs and superior efficiency, or if the company has a weak monopoly position in the industry, management may prefer lower profits in order to discourage potential competitors from entering the industry. In this case a long-run price policy that is in line with the rest of the industry will be more advantageous to the firm than one which exploits current market conditions for immediate profit.

2. *Discourage antitrust investigation.* Certain monopolistic practices are illegal. (We shall be reading about them in a later chapter dealing with the antitrust laws.) Profits are one of a number of criteria used by the government as evidence of firms' monopolistic market control. This can seem somewhat paradoxical when contrasted with the previous consideration. On the one hand, management may maintain lower profits in order to exclude competitors and thereby strengthen its monopoly control. Yet the federal government's antitrusters may consider high profits, not low profits, as one of several indexes of monopoly power.

3. *Restrain union demands.* Reducing the possibility of having to pay higher wages is another factor prompting management to restrain profits. This is particularly applicable in industries with strong labor unions. As long as the economy is prosperous and profits are rising, unions can more easily demand higher wages without inflicting damage on the firm. But if, in a recession, prices are falling faster than wages, the profit margin is squeezed at both ends. Those companies that curbed wage increases in the beginning would then have a better opportunity to cope with changing market conditions.

4. *Maintain consumer goodwill.* Management may choose to limit profits in order to preserve good customer relations. Consumers frequently have their own ideas of a "fair" price, whether such ideas are based on "what used to be in the old days," or whether they are the results of "comparison shopping."

CONCLUSION: MAXIMIZE OR "SATISFICE"?

The profit problem is complex, making it extremely difficult to state unequivocally that firms in imperfect competition do or do not seek to maximize profits. Perhaps in reality they do not seek to maximize but to "*satisfice*"—that is, to attain targets of satisfactory performance such as a specific rate of return on investment, a particular share of the market, or a defined average annual growth of sales—as some scholars have suggested. In economic theory, however, we *assume* that the underlying objective is to maximize profit because, as already shown, this assumption enables us to evaluate the social performance of the firm as a resource allocator.

SUMMARY OF IMPORTANT IDEAS

1. Monopolistic competition exists in industries characterized by many firms producing heterogeneous products. Product differentiation, which is a matter for buyers to decide, is thus a key factor among firms in such industries. Monopolistically competitive industries are a major segment of our economy.

2. The $MC = MR$ principle serves as a guide for profit maximization in monopolistic competition. Since there is reasonable freedom of entry, firms will *tend* to earn normal profits in the long run, but there may be exceptions.

3. Advertising plays a major role in monopolistic competition because of the importance of product differentiation. The pros and cons of advertising have centered around three major issues: information versus persuasion; efficiency versus waste; competition versus concentration.

4. Monopolistic competition is subject to the same basic criticism as monopoly—namely, resource mis-

allocation resulting from output restriction and higher prices as a result of following the $MC = MR$ instead of the competitive $MC = P$ standard of production and pricing. In addition, it encourages nonprice competition which may or may not be undesirable, and it results in the "wastes" of monopolistic competition or the perpetuation of "sick" industries that are overcrowded and inefficient.

5. Oligopolistic industries consist of several firms producing either homogeneous products (perfect oligopoly) or heterogeneous products (imperfect oligopoly). These industries play a major role in our economy. Oligopolistic firms usually tend to be characterized by substantial economies of scale, a history of growth through merger, mutual dependence, price rigidity, and nonprice competition.

6. The $MC = MR$ principle applies to oligopolistic firms that seek to maximize profit. In addition, each firm tends to see itself as being faced with a kinked demand curve, indicating that competitors will follow a price decrease by any one seller, but not a price increase.

7. The kinked demand curve results in a stable price, but it leaves the seller uncertain about the determination of the price itself. This has prompted oligopolists to reduce price uncertainty either by colluding with competitors or by accepting one of the competitors as a price leader and matching his price.

8. Oligopolies are subject to the same basic criticism as monopolies—namely, resource misallocation resulting from output restriction and higher prices. This is due to their adherence to the $MC = MR$ rather than $MC = P$ standard of production and pricing. (However, like natural monopolies, the cost structures of oligopolistic firms may be subject to more substantial economies of scale than those of perfectly competitive firms.) In addition, oligopolies have not exhibited as much progress in basic research as might be expected. On the other hand, their market power has in some cases been mitigated by the growth of countervailing power.

9. It is difficult to state unequivocally that firms in imperfect competition either do or do not seek to maximize profits. In reality, it is quite likely that they strive to "satisfice" rather than maximize. Nevertheless, the assumption of profit maximization is fundamental in microeconomic theory because it permits an evaluation of the social function of the firm as a resource allocator.

FOR DISCUSSION

1. *Terms and concepts to review:*

imperfect competition	oligopoly
monopolistic competition	kinked demand curve
	duopoly
selling costs	price leadership
nonprice competition	countervailing power
"wastes" of monopolistic competition	"satisfice"

2. Firms in monopolistic competition tend to be only normally profitable in the long run. The same is true of firms in perfect competition. Therefore, why criticize monopolistic competition?

3. Why should firms in monopolistic competition spend so much money on advertising if much of it has canceling effects?

4. Is the kinked demand curve an objective fact of the marketplace, or is it a subjective phenomenon in the mind of each oligopolist? Explain.

5. Why is there a tendency toward some type of externally imposed price decision in oligopoly? What are some examples?

6. The need for self-protection is one reason often given for the rise of labor unions, consumer cooperatives, and agricultural cooperatives. Can you explain in the light of this chapter?

7. One could easily argue that it is more *ethical* for people to cooperate than to compete. Do you agree?

8. "Economic theory is unrealistic because it assumes that firms seek to maximize profits. Yet we know that in reality this assumption is not a valid one." Evaluate.

9. Are prices determined by costs of production or are costs of production determined by prices? Discuss. (SUGGESTION: Think in terms of perfect competition as well as imperfect competition.)

10. Saturn Publishing Co. publishes two monthly magazines called *Action* and *Brisk*. The company charges the same price for both magazines, but the sales of *Brisk* are about twice those of *Action*. Both magazines are among the leaders in their field, with combined sales of 5 to 6 million copies a month. In this sales range, therefore, the marginal cost of producing the two magazines is practically constant. Further, it has been established on the basis of previous pricing experiments in various markets that the elasticity of demand is equal for the two magazines at the present price.

Recently, the president of the company posed the question of whether it is consistent with profit maximization for the two magazines to carry the same price. The sales manager replied that in order for Saturn to maximize its profits, it ought to charge a higher price for *Brisk* than for *Action*, since demand is greater for the former.

The president has called you in as a consulting economist to settle the question. Both the president and sales manager studied a considerable amount of economics while in college and are fairly familiar with such concepts as average revenue, marginal revenue, and marginal cost. Can you provide them with an analytical (graphic) solution to the problem?

11. In the book publishing business, it is inherent in the royalty arrangement that the publisher's pricing policy results in an economic conflict between the author and the publisher. Thus, in the great majority of cases, the author's royalty is a percentage of the total revenue which the publisher receives on the sale of the book. The publisher, however, determines the price of the book (and also incurs all costs of manufacturing, promotion, and distribution). It follows that *the price which maximizes profit for the publisher is higher, and the output lower, than the price and output which maximizes royalty payments for the author!* Why? Demonstrate this proposition graphically, using marginal analysis.

12. Scrumptious Pizza Co. operates a national chain of pizza parlors on a franchise basis. The company maintains a closely controlled, uniform set of production standards and selling prices as a condition for granting franchises. One of the unique features of Scrumptious pizzas is that they are made with a special blend of imported exotic cheeses.

Recent cost increases of cheeses, dough, and other ingredients have made it necessary for the company to consider a revision of its pricing and product policies for all its franchises. Three alternatives have been proposed: (A) increase price by some specified percentage, but maintain quantity and quality; (B) reduce quantity by some specified percentage, but maintain price and quality; (C) reduce quality, but maintain price and quantity.

The company hired an economic consulting firm to estimate the effects on profits of each of these choices. In its report, the consulting firm submitted the following *payoff matrix*—a table showing the probable level of profit that will result from each alternative and its associated sales level.

Alternatives, profits, and probabilities	Average daily national pizza sales			
	6,000	7,000	8,000	9,000
Alternative A				
Profit	$2,000	$2,800	$4,000	$4,200
Probability*	0.15	0.25	0.30	0.30
Alternative B				
Profit	$1,500	$3,000	$5,000	$5,100
Probability*	0.25	0.25	0.40	0.10
Alternative C				
Profit	$1,200	$2,500	$4,500	$4,800
Probability*	0.05	0.05	0.40	0.50

* The probability of an outcome is the likelihood of its occurrence. It can be expressed as a percentage by multiplying by 100.

For example, suppose the company chooses alternative A, and its average daily national sales are 6,000 pizzas. Then its *expected profit* on those sales will be 15 percent of $2,000 or $300. On the other hand, if its sales are 7,000, its expected profit will be 25 percent of $2,800 or $700. By extending this idea, you can see that the total expected profit of any alternative is simply the *sum* of the separate expected profits which comprise it. (Notice that for each alternative, the probabilities must add to 1.0 or 100 percent.)

(a) Which alternative should the company choose, assuming it wants to maximize its profit?

(b) Which alternative should the company choose in order to maximize its sales?

(c) Is it possible to have a situation in which one alternative would maximize profit and another would maximize sales, or must the same alternative do both? Explain.

This Message Could Change Your Life

Dozens of advertising slogans have become part of American folklore, the subject of countless jokes and of almost as many solemn academic investigations, theories, and theses. In all capitalistic industrial nations advertising is pervasive, often accounts for a surprisingly high proportion of a firm's costs, and passes its messages into the language.

Advertising provokes passionate polemics from proponents and opponents. Is it a vital source of information about available products, processes, and services? Or is it a dishonest form of promotion that either misinforms or—creates a legend about a company's offerings without saying much about the reality? Those are the main lines of the debate.

Some Important Issues

Social critics generally view advertising as wasteful. They argue that it does not increase aggregate demand, but is primarily a means of one company's holding or gaining a certain share of the market. In this view, advertising of, say, refrigerators is a cost passed on to consumers, who are unwittingly paying for the battle for market shares waged by General Electric, Westinghouse, Frigidaire, and so on. But is that view really correct? Certainly, each of those companies wants to increase its market share; but an important and intentional side effect of advertising a *class* of product is that total sales rise. Bombarded by promotion of the *idea* of a refrigerator, and of the regular product improvements claimed by the industry, many consumers come to regard the refrigerator as a necessity.

But what happens when virtually every household has a refrigerator? At that point, aggregate refrigerator sales are determined chiefly by population growth, by family incomes, and by the frequency with which households replace refrigerators. At this stage it's probably true to say that advertising has only a small effect on aggregate sales.

What about advertising a product whose market is not saturated, such as color television or pocket calculators? This may be beneficial because it raises aggregate demand. By so doing, advertising helps to amortize development costs over a larger number of units, to raise production toward the optimum level of efficiency, and thereby to keep prices down. Unfortunately, nobody knows what proportion of advertising expenditures goes to increasing aggregate sales and what to maintaining or increasing individual firms' market shares. As an eminent English businessman once said: "I know that half my advertising expenditures are wasted, but I don't know which half."

For most products, advertising helps to reduce distribution as well as production costs because products which have rapid turnover produce more revenue per square foot of shelf space.

Advertising, Competition, and Truth

The need to advertise greatly increases the "cost of entry" for small firms seeking to break into markets dominated by large firms. In some industries, notably cosmetics and nonprescription pharmaceuticals, advertising and packaging costs are a high proportion of total costs. In those industries only large firms can afford the heavy cost of advertising, and small firms are barred, whatever the virtues of their products. However, advertising expenditures are only one cost of entry. The costs of entry are also high in certain businesses that advertise rather little, notably steel, aluminum, and other industries that require heavy capital investment and large-scale production.

A further charge against advertising is more ethical than economic in nature. Too much advertising is untruthful—despite recent federal and state laws requiring truth in advertising. Critics point out that the laws have discouraged specific claims that cannot be proved, and have encouraged "mood" advertising: the "Pepsi Generation" or "Coke: It's the Real Thing" are examples, telling us nothing about the product but a great deal about the people at whom the campaign is directed. Some critics of advertising charge that such slogans are even more dishonest than the old hard-sell, because they can be neither proved nor disproved.

Although the trend is disturbing, there are those who maintain that advertising can only persuade a consumer to make the first purchase, and no amount of advertising can sell a product a second time if the product is unsatisfactory.

QUESTIONS

1. "Advertising serves to protect existing products. It is therefore a barrier to competition and a means of monopolizing markets." Evaluate.

2. The Federal Trade Commission has charged some oligopolistic firms with (a) conspiring to share markets and (b) maintaining market shares through advertising. Are these charges logically consistent?

3. Do you agree with those critics who contend that advertising should inform rather than persuade? Do you believe that advertising bamboozles consumers into buying unwanted things? Discuss.

CHAPTER 27

The Firm in the Factor Markets: Marginal Productivity and Income Distribution

CHAPTER PREVIEW

We have already learned that the $MC = MR$ rule determines the most profitable level of *output* for a firm. Can a similar rule be developed for determining the most profitable level of *input* for a firm?

What conditions determine a firm's demand for inputs or factors of production?

Can any social implications be drawn from the principles pertaining to the hiring of factors of production?

Until now we have focused on the behavior of firms in the *output* markets by examining the principles of product pricing and production under the three classes of market conditions—perfect competition, monopoly, and imperfect competition.

But to manufacture products, firms have to buy factors of production. In this chapter we concentrate on the behavior of firms in the *input* markets in order to see how principles of resource employment can be developed. This chapter thus counterbalances some of the previous chapters by establishing microeconomic principles pertaining to the input rather than output side of the market. As you will soon see, the most interesting aspect of input principles is the way in which they parallel the ones that we learned about earlier, so that the various pieces fit together like a large jigsaw puzzle.

The Marginal Productivity Theory: How the Firm Buys Factors of Production

If you were a businessman, what principles would guide you in deciding how much of a resource you should purchase? After all, buying too little can be just as unprofitable as buying too much. A major problem facing a firm that wishes to maximize its profits is to utilize precisely the right combination of inputs. In order to do this, management must understand the nature of its demand for resources.

The demand for any resource is a *derived demand* —one based on what a particular factor of production contributes to the product for which it is used. For example, the demand for steel is derived in part from the demand for automobiles; the demand for land in the heart of a city is derived from the demand for office space and stores that will be built upon it; the demand for college professors is derived mostly from the demand for education as measured by college enrollments. As a general rule, and as we shall see shortly, the concept of derived demand embraces the following principles:

Other things being equal, the quantity of a factor of production which a firm demands will depend on three things: (1) the productivity of the factor; (2) the value or price of the product which the factor is used to make; and (3) the price of the factor relative to the prices of other factors.

These principles make a good deal of practical sense. For instance, they tell us that, other things remaining constant:

1. An increase in the output of a factor of production relative to its input will result in a greater demand for that factor by the firms that use it.

2. If improvements in a product or reductions in its price create a greater demand for it, the need for the factors which produce or use that commodity will also increase (for example, electronic computers and computer programmers).

3. If the price of a factor of production becomes cheaper relative to other factors, the demand for the lower-priced factor will increase if producers begin to substitute it for the more expensive inputs (for example, labor-saving machinery relative to high-cost labor).

PHYSICAL INPUTS, OUTPUTS, AND REVENUES

Exhibit 1 gives us a more precise understanding of a firm's demand for an input. The first three columns show how, through the law of diminishing returns, the total and marginal physical products change when a variable input such as labor is applied to fixed inputs like land and capital. The remaining columns of the table convert these physical data into revenues on the assumption that the firm is a perfect competitor in the sale of the product to which the variable factor is contributing. The price [column (4)], therefore, is assumed to be constant at $10 per unit.

Exhibit 1

The Demand for a Resource by a Firm

PERFECT COMPETITION IN THE OUTPUT MARKET; PERFECT COMPETITION IN THE INPUT MARKET

(1) Units of variable factor, F (labor)*	(2) Total physical product, TPP	(3) Marginal physical product, MPP Change in (2) / Change in (1)	(4) Product price, P	(5) Total revenue, TR (2) × (4)	(6) Marginal revenue product, MRP Change in (5) / Change in (1)	(7) Average revenue product, ARP (5) ÷ (1)
0	0		$10	$ 0		$?
1	4	4	10	40	$40	40.0
2	12	8	10	120	80	60.0
3	17	5	10	170	50	56.7
4	20	3	10	200	30	50.0
5	21	1	10	210	10	42.0
6	20	−1	10	200	− 10	33.3

* Labor is assumed to be the only variable input. All other inputs are fixed and are available free. Therefore, total (labor) cost equals total variable cost.

Based upon the total revenue figures [column (5)], the last two columns of the table introduce two new terms: *marginal revenue product (MRP)*, defined as the change in total revenue resulting from a unit change in input, and *average revenue product (ARP)*, which is the ratio of total revenue to the quantity of the variable input employed.

Since the firm is operating under perfect competition in the input market, the supply of labor resources is so large that the firm cannot influence the price by buying or not buying. The firm can purchase as many units as it wants at the given price. Hence *the marginal cost of the resource will be the same as its price.*

THE MOST PROFITABLE LEVEL OF INPUT

When the revenue data from the table in Exhibit 1 are graphed, we get the curves shown in the charts. In this case since we want to relate the firm's revenues to the labor that it hires, it is easier to plot the revenue curves against input rather than output on the horizontal axis. It also helps simplify matters a bit to assume, as stated in the footnote to column (1) of the table, that there are no fixed costs—that the firm's fixed factors of production are available free. This means that the firm's total variable costs are the same as its total costs, and therefore the TC curve emanates from the origin of the chart instead of from a point higher up on the vertical axis.

Exhibit 1

Chart (a). *The most profitable input level occurs where the distance between the TR and TC curves is a maximum—that is, where a tangent to the TR curve is parallel to the TC curve. (For example, at $20 per man, the most profitable input is 4 men, because this is the input at which the tangent at D is parallel to the straight-line TC₁ curve.)*

Chart (b). *By following the vertical dashed lines downward, it can be seen that the most profitable input also occurs where the marginal cost of the factor (MCF) or its price (P_F) equals its marginal revenue product (MRP). Therefore, given the marginal costs or prices of the factors of production, the firm will maximize its profits by hiring each factor of production up to the point where its MCF = P_F = MRP. The firm's demand curve for an input is thus the MRP curve up to the maximum point on the ARP curve. As the price of the input falls, the firm hires more of it by following its MRP curve. (NOTE: The MRP curve, like the marginal curves in previous chapters, is plotted to the midpoints of the integers on the horizontal axis, since it reflects the change in total revenue from one unit of input to the next.)*

TECHNICAL NOTE (OPTIONAL). Here is a simple explanation in geometric terms. Each *MCF* curve in the lower chart is a graph of the *slope* of its corresponding *TC* curve in the upper chart. Likewise, the *MRP* curve in the lower chart is a graph of the *slope* of the *TR* curve in the upper chart. The input at which the slopes are equal (or at which a tangent in the upper chart is parallel to a *TC* curve) is the one at which net profit is maximized. You can verify these profit-maximizing principles by following the vertical dashed lines downward at each level of input.

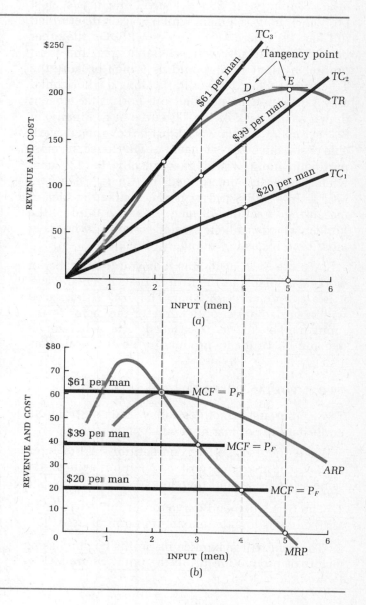

We now ask: What is the most profitable level of input for the firm? The answer depends on the *marginal cost of the input* as compared to its *marginal revenue product*—or in other words the amount that each additional unit of the input adds to the firm's total cost as compared to the amount that it adds to total revenue.

For example, Chart (a) shows that when the marginal cost or price of labor is $20 per man, the most profitable input level is 4 men; at this input the TC_1 curve in the chart is parallel to a tangent drawn to the TR curve at D. At the same time, Chart (b) shows that at this level of input the marginal cost of the factor MCF, which is the same as the price of the factor P_F, is equal to its marginal revenue product MRP. Similarly, at $39 per man, the firm's most profitable input is 3 men, which is again determined in Chart (b) where $MCF = P_F = MRP$. On the other hand, if the factor were available free, the most profitable input level would be 5 men because the TC curve in Chart (a) would lie along the horizontal axis and would be parallel to a horizontal tangent drawn at the peak of the TR curve at E. Finally, at $61 per man the firm would just be covering its variable costs, since TC_3 is tangent to TR. Hence the most profitable input would, theoretically, be 2.2 men, which is again determined in Chart (b) where $MCF = P_F = MRP$. (NOTE: If you dislike the idea of measuring "fractions of men," you can think of the horizontal axis as being scaled in terms of hours of labor time instead of numbers of men.)

Since the MCF or P_F line tells you the number of workers available to the firm at the particular wage, it is a *supply* curve of labor. The firm is thus faced with a horizontal supply curve of the factor in the input market just as it is faced with a horizontal demand curve for its product in the output market.

TWO IMPORTANT PRINCIPLES

Two important principles follow directly from our understanding of marginal concepts.

When there is perfect competition in the input market, the marginal cost of an input will be the same as its price, and therefore:

1. The firm's demand curve for an input will be its MRP curve below the maximum point of its ARP.

2. The firm will maximize its profits by purchasing factors of production up to the point where $MCF = P_F = MRP$.

By this time you may have noticed a certain symmetry between the theory of input and the theory of output. For example, these two principles are analogous to the notion that in the output market a perfectly competitive firm finds that: (a) its MC curve is its supply curve above the minimum point on its AVC; (b) it maximizes its profit by producing to where its $MC = P = MR$. In fact, if you flip Chart (b) in Exhibit 1 upside down on its horizontal axis (or if you turn the book upside down and look through the back of the page while holding it up to the light), the ARP and MRP curves will resemble the AVC and MC curves of a firm in perfect competition. This is evidence of the fact that there is indeed a symmetry between the theory of perfect competition in the input and output markets, in that the curves in one market are the reciprocals of the corresponding curves in the other market.

In economic terms, why does the firm maximize its profit at the input level where $MCF = P_F = MRP$? Because at any input less than this the added cost of an additional unit is less than the added revenue, so it pays to hire another unit. At any input greater than this the opposite is true. Hence the fundamental principle of profit maximization—the $MC = MR$ rule which we learned in previous chapters—applies here as well. In addition, we can now state a conclusion of fundamental importance:

The principle which holds that in competitive input markets, the price paid to a factor of production will equal its marginal productivity, and therefore that each factor will be paid the value of what it contributes, is called the *marginal productivity theory of income distribution*.

Demand for Inputs

We learned in our study of the theory of supply and demand that the market demand curve for a product is derived by summing the individual demand curves of all buyers in the market. A parallel situation exists in the market for input: Other things remaining the same, the market demand curve for a factor is derived by summing the individual demands or MRP curves of all firms in the market. Like any other demand curve, this aggregate MRP curve for a factor of production will be subject to two kinds of changes: (1) changes in demand and (2) changes in the quantity demanded.

CHANGES IN DEMAND

The market *MRP* curve for a given factor may shift from one position to another for several reasons:

1. *A change in demand for the final product.* For example, a change in demand for houses will affect the price of houses and may also change the demand for lumber, bricks, carpenters, and other resources.

2. *A change in productivity.* Improvements in the quantity and quality of the fixed factors of production will increase the productivity of the variable factor. Thus, workers who have more and better machines and land are more productive than those who do not.

3. *A change in the prices of substitute or complementary factors.* Some resources may be substitutable, some may be complementary, and some may be neither. Labor and machines provide typical examples of all three possibilities; changes in the price of one relative to the other may encourage firms to use more or less of either or both, depending on the proportions in which they must be used—such as the number of workers needed to operate a machine.

CHANGES IN THE QUANTITY DEMANDED: ELASTICITY OF DEMAND FOR FACTOR SERVICES

There are also conditions that will determine changes in the quantity demanded for a given factor. As you recall, these changes represent movements along the curve due to a change in price. Hence these movements reflect the sensitivity or elasticity of demand for the resource. What determines this elasticity?

1. *The rate of decline of marginal physical product.* The rate at which the *MPP* curve declines as the variable factor is added to the fixed factors depends on the technological nature of the production process. The faster it declines, the more inelastic the resulting *MRP* curve will be and hence the less will be the change in the quantity of input demanded relative to a change in its price.

2. *The elasticity of demand for the final product.* The greater the elasticity of demand for the final product, the more elastic the demand for the factors used in making it. For instance, if the demand for a final product is relatively elastic, a small increase in its price will result in a more than proportional decrease in the purchase of it and hence a relatively

large drop in the quantity demanded of the resources that are used to produce it.

3. *The proportion of the factor's cost relative to total production cost.* The larger the cost of a factor of production relative to the total cost of the product, the more elastic the demand for the factor. For example, if labor costs are only 10 percent of the cost of a product, a 10 percent wage increase will raise production costs by 1 percent; hence the effect on the final price of the product should be small, and the quantity demanded of the factor should be relatively little affected. On the other hand, if labor costs are 90 percent of production costs, a 10 percent wage increase will have a more substantial impact on production costs as well as on final prices and sales. Therefore the decrease in the quantity demanded of the factor is likely to be relatively large.

4. *The ease of factor substitutability.* The greater the number of different factors that can be substituted for one another in a given production process, the larger will be the elasticity of demand for any one of these factors. Thus if copper, aluminum, and other light metals had equal conductive properties, the demand for each of them by the electrical industry would be highly elastic; but the fact is that copper is a superior conductor and hence the demand for it is relatively inelastic within its typical price ranges.

THE OPTIMUM ALLOCATION OF INPUTS

The foregoing principles apply to all factors of production that the firm may purchase. Let us assume, therefore, that the firm is buying two factors of production, labor and capital, and that these factors are substitutable for one another. There are two questions to be answered:

1. What is the least-cost combination of factors needed to produce a given output?

2. Which combination of factors yields the largest profits to the firm?

The first question is concerned with cost minimization; the second, with profit maximization.

Cost Minimization

If you were a manufacturer interested in producing a certain volume of output, in what proportion would you use the various inputs? The question is important because many different combinations will produce a given level of output, but only one combination is cheapest. Clearly, the cheapest combination depends on the relative prices of the inputs. As a businessman, therefore, you would adhere to the following fundamental principle:

Least-cost principle. The least-cost combination of inputs is achieved when a dollar's worth of any input adds as much to total physical output as a dollar's worth of any other input.

To illustrate, suppose you are buying only two factors of production, A and B, in a perfectly competitive market. Letting MPP_A represent the marginal physical product of A, and P_A the price of A, and similarly for factor B, the equation of minimum cost is

$$\frac{MPP_A}{P_A} = \frac{MPP_B}{P_B} \qquad (1)$$

This indicates that if the price of an input rises, less of it should be used, thereby increasing its marginal product, and more of the other input should be used, thereby decreasing its marginal product. As an example, suppose P_A and P_B are each $1, and at some given volume of output

$$MPP_A = 10 \text{ units}$$
$$MPP_B = 8 \text{ units}$$

Assuming you want to minimize costs at the prescribed output level, you should proceed as follows:

1. Buy $1.00 less of B, thereby reducing production by 8 units.

2. Buy $.80 more of A, thereby increasing production by 8 units ($= \frac{4}{5}$ of the marginal product of a dollar's worth of A).

3. Save $.20.

This example shows how you would go about minimizing total costs for a given volume of output. Equation (1), of course, can be extended to include any number of inputs and corresponding prices. When all of the ratios are equal, total costs are minimized at the established output volume. If a change should then occur in the price of one of the factors, the equality will no longer hold. This means that the cheaper factor will have to be substituted for more expensive ones until equality is restored.

Profit Maximization

The second problem concerns the question: Of all possible factor combinations, which one yields the largest profits for the firm? The answer has already been indicated in previous pages and may now be expressed as a general principle:

Maximum-profit principle. The most profitable combination of inputs is achieved by employing each factor of production up to the point where the marginal cost of the factor is equal to its marginal revenue product.

This principle was demonstrated in the charts in Exhibit 1. When the firm is hiring a resource in a perfectly competitive market, it will employ further units of the resource as long as the MRP of the factor is greater than its price (or marginal cost). Why? Because each additional unit adds more to the firm's total revenue than to its total cost. Conversely, the firm will release some units of the resource if the MRP of the factor is less than its price, because each reduction of one unit of the input lowers the firm's total cost by more than it lowers total revenue.

These ideas can be summarized with a formula. We know that the firm will maximize profits by hiring units of factor A up to the point where the marginal revenue product of that factor, MRP_A, is equal to its price, P_A:

$$MRP_A = P_A$$

If both sides of this equation are divided by P_A (or in other words, if P_A is "transposed" to the left side), then

$$\frac{MRP_A}{P_A} = 1 \qquad (a)$$

Similarly, the firm will buy units of factor B up to the point where the marginal revenue product of that factor, MRP_B, is equal to its price P_B,

$$MRP_B = P_B$$

or equivalently

$$\frac{MRP_B}{P_B} = 1 \qquad (b)$$

Since the two ratios are each equal to 1, equations (a) and (b) can be expressed as a single equation for maximum-profit equilibrium:

$$\frac{MRP_A}{P_A} = \frac{MRP_B}{P_B} = 1 \qquad (2)$$

Equation (2), like equation (1) for least cost, can be extended to include any number of inputs and their corresponding prices. In general, equation (2) defines the profit-maximizing or equilibrium conditions of a firm in a perfectly competitive input market and shows that:

The most profitable level of input for a firm in a perfectly competitive input market occurs where it earns the same increment in revenue *per dollar of outlay* from each of the factors that it hires, with each ratio equal to 1. That is, the firm hires each factor up to the point where the marginal revenue product of the factor equals its price.

It helps to translate these ideas into concrete terms. For example, if a firm were hiring two factors of production, labor L and capital C, and if these factors were substitutable for one another, equation (2) says that the company will maximize profits in a perfectly competitive input market by hiring to the point where

$$\frac{MRP_L}{P_L} = \frac{MRP_C}{P_C} = 1$$

If this equality did not occur—that is, if the first ratio in this equation were greater than the second, and if the employment of capital were already in equilibrium at the point where $MRP_C/P_C = 1$, the firm would be earning more of an increment in revenue on its labor relative to the price of labor than it would be earning on its capital relative to the price of capital. Graphically, this means that the firm would be to the *left* of its optimum input point for labor. Hence it would pay for the company to hire more workers, thereby reducing MRP_L until the ratios were equal. Conversely, if the first ratio were less than the second, the firm would be to the *right* of its optimum input point for labor. Therefore it would pay for the company to reduce its number of workers, thereby raising MRP_L until the ratios were again equal.

In a more general sense, neither factor need be in equilibrium to start. You can think of the firm as juggling all its factors of production simultaneously until it achieves the desired equilibrium ratio noted above.

Marginal Productivity, Income Distribution, and Social Justice

We have seen that when there is perfect competition in the input market, each firm will purchase factors of production up to the point where the price or marginal cost of the factor is equal to its marginal revenue productivity. Expressed in real terms, this means that each factor will be paid a value equal to what it contributes to the national output—it will be paid what it is "worth." This concept, as we have learned, is known as the *marginal productivity theory of income distribution*.

The theory itself was first introduced near the turn of the present century by the distinguished American economist, John Bates Clark, and was widely supported because it showed that a competitive (capitalistic) system distributed the national output in a socially "just" and "equitable" manner. But over the years economists and social critics have pointed out three fundamental criticisms of this interpretation.

1. A large part of the market for input is imperfect rather than perfect. Thus, certain factors of production tend to be relatively immobile, and in some markets there may be only one or a few firms buying inputs instead of a large number of firms. In addition, union restrictions, patent controls, tariff barriers, and other limitations also create obstacles to a smoothly functioning market for inputs as envisioned in the competitive model.

2. Many production processes are complex. When a variety of factors are employed it is usually impossible to divide the total output into the amounts contributed by each class of factors such as labor and capital, much less by each "subfactor" such as each type of worker.

3. Terms like "just" and "equitable" involve normative rather than positive concepts, and their meanings may vary from time to time and from place to place according to the customs and beliefs of society. Thus, it is not necessarily "just" that a man who is twice as productive as another should be paid twice as much. It might equally well be argued, for example, that it is "just" for a family of six to receive twice as much as a family of three—regardless of

JOHN BATES CLARK

1847–1938

Marginal Productivity Theory

It is the purpose of this work to show that the distribution of the income of society is controlled by a natural law, and that this law, if it worked without friction, would give to every agent of production the amount of wealth which that agent creates.

In these words, J. B. Clark outlined the general plan for his book, *The Distribution of Wealth,* which was published in 1899. This was the first American work in pure economic theory. Prior to that time, American economists were generally interested in the socioeconomic problems of their period and with the achievement of social reforms. Clark's book still stands as one of the greatest works in economic theory published in any language.

Clark began by asking: "Is there a natural law according to which the income of society is divided . . . ? If so, what is that law? This is the problem which demands solution."

As he proceeded to answer this question, he developed a distinction between static and dynamic forces in the economy. The static forces, he said, are the result of "universal economic laws" which are always applicable to the economy, such as the law of diminishing returns, the law of diminishing utility, and so on. But the dynamic forces that exist in society, namely changes in population, capital, production techniques, and forms of industrial organization, are constantly causing fluctuations in production, prices, and the like. In Clark's words, "Static forces set the standards, dynamic forces produce the variations." He then went on to say:

> Each unit of labor . . . is worth to its employer what the last unit produces. When the force is complete, no one body of a thousand men can withdraw without lessening the product of the whole society by the same amount that we have attributed to the one that we last set working. The effective value of any unit of labor is always what the whole society with all its capital produces, minus what it would produce if that unit were to be taken away. This sets the universal standard of pay. A unit of labor consists, in the supposed case, of a thousand men, and the product of it is the natural pay of a thousand men. If the men are equal, a thousandth part of this amount is the natural pay of any one of them.

Actually, Clark had much in common with his great British contemporary, Alfred Marshall. Each used the so-

Historical Pictures Service, Chicago.

called static analysis, but Marshall was more realistic and analyzed many problems of dynamics and change. Clark, however, raised marginal utility analysis to its highest standard of perfection, and in so doing he founded a "marginalist school" of thought which established a pattern for teaching and research in economics that exists to this day.

The modern version of the marginal productivity theory is essentially due to Clark's treatment. His theory of wages is a demand theory which assumes a given quantity of labor in its analysis of the marginal product of labor. It was this theory, with its impeccable logic, that was widely employed by others to support the contention that a (perfectly competitive) capitalistic system distributes incomes in a "just" manner according to what each factor contributes.

In later decades, the development of the theory of imperfect competition and the growing power of labor unions made some of the unreal assumptions of Clark's theory more apparent.

their relative productivities. In other words, the normative question of what constitutes a just distribution of income is quite different from the positive question of what specific steps should be taken to alter the distribution of income. The former is a philosophical question; the latter is an economic one.

We can therefore conclude with an important generalization:

The central idea of the marginal productivity principle is that an employer will not pay more for a unit of input—whether it be a man, or an acre of land, or a dollar's worth of borrowed capital—than it is worth to him. He will continue to acquire an input as long as each unit he purchases adds more to his total revenue than it adds to his total cost. Since we assume in theory that the units can be infinitesimally small, the net result is that the employer's profit is maximized where the added (or marginal) cost of the input equals its added (or marginal) revenue product.

In short, although the marginal productivity principle is correct in the sense that it can be deduced logically from given assumptions, it should be understood for what it is: *a guide for maximizing a firm's profits in the input market under prescribed market conditions.*

SUMMARY OF IMPORTANT IDEAS

1. The marginal productivity theory explains how a firm purchases its inputs in the factor market. In general, a firm's demand for any factor of production is a derived demand based on the productivity of the factor, the price of the final product, and the price of the factor relative to the prices of other factors.

2. If a firm's production function and the market prices of the resources it purchases are given (i.e., if it is hiring factors in a perfectly competitive market for inputs), it can seek the factor combination which assures (a) least cost and (b) maximum profit. The least-cost combination requires that the marginal physical product per dollar spent on every factor be equal; the maximum-profit combination requires that the marginal revenue product per dollar spent on all factors be equal to 1. Both equilibrium conditions can be achieved simultaneously.

3. The aggregate *MRP* curve for a factor of production is determined by summing the individual *MRP* curves. Like any demand curve, the *MRP* curve is subject to changes in demand for a factor and to changes in the quantity demanded. The latter reflects the elasticity of demand for a factor.

4. The marginal productivity theory of income distribution is a guide for profit maximization in the input market. It does not purport to say what pattern of income distribution is "just" or "equitable," for this is a normative question based on philosophical rather than economic considerations.

FOR DISCUSSION

1. *Terms and concepts to review:*

derived demand	marginal productivity
marginal revenue	theory of income
product	distribution
average revenue	
product	

2. What analogies do you see between a firm in the output market and a firm in the input market with respect to each of the following: (a) the profit-maximizing rule; (b) marginal cost and average variable cost, and marginal revenue product and average revenue product.

3. Distinguish between a change in demand for an input and a change in the quantity demanded. What are the causes of each?

4. "The way to eliminate poverty and unemployment is through minimum-wage legislation. By raising the minimum wage, workers are given more purchasing power. This creates a greater demand for goods and services, thereby putting unemployed people to work."

Evaluate this argument using the graphic tools employed in this chapter. (HINT: There are *two* issues involved here. Can you identify them?)

5. "The marginal productivity theory of income distribution is a *fair* theory because it demonstrates that each worker gets what he earns." Evaluate.

6. "It is meaningless to say that the equilibrium factor price will equal the marginal revenue product, since the latter varies with the number of factor units employed." Comment. Rephrase if necessary.

CHAPTER 28

Determination of Factor Prices

CHAPTER PREVIEW

Are there wage-determination models that can explain why workers in some occupations earn less than workers in others, and why some industries establish wage levels by collective bargaining between management and labor?

Is there any connection between the rent paid for land and the prices received for the products of land?

What is interest? Why does it exist?

What are the sources of profit? How are profits determined?

Most of the national income consists of wages and salaries paid to workers. The rest of the economic pie is sliced into rent, interest, and profit. These incomes, we have learned, are the payments made to resource owners who sell their factors of production —labor, land, capital, and entrepreneurship—in the economy's markets.

What forces determine the levels of wages, rent, interest, and profit? In this chapter we seek answers to these questions by deriving basic principles. We shall find that many of the ideas from previous chapters dealing with supply and demand, competition, market structures, cost and demand curves, and the like play an integral role in determining factor prices.

What will not be so apparent, however, is that although the theory of wages, and to a somewhat lesser extent the theory of rent, are fairly well established in modern economics, the theories of interest and profit involve various unsettled questions that are the subject of more advanced discussions. We shall not delve into these issues in much detail, since our purpose at this time is to concentrate on the main features of the various theories rather than on the controversies which surround them.

Theory of Wages

Wages constitute about three-fourths of the national income. But what determines their level? Let us begin with some definitions.

Wages are the price paid for the use of labor and are usually expressed as time rates, such as so much per hour, day, or week, or, less frequently, as piece rates of so much per unit of work performed.

Labor, as defined in economics, means all personal services including the activities of wageworkers, professional people, and independent businessmen. "Laborers" are thus workers who may receive compensation not only in the form of wages, but also in the form of salaries, bonuses, commissions, and the like. Our interest in this chapter is with wages as defined above, especially wages expressed as time rates.

Money wages are the amount of money received per unit of time, such as cash wages received on an hourly, weekly, or monthly basis. In contrast, *real wages* are the quantity of goods that can be bought with money wages; real wages thus depend on money wages and on the prices of the goods that are purchased with money wages. For instance, it is quite possible for your money wages to increase while your real wages rise, remain the same, or fall, depending on what happens to prices.

THE TRENDS OF WAGES AND PRODUCTIVITY

Most of us know that wages differ between occupations and individuals. Nevertheless, there tends to be a close long-run relationship between the wages of workers and their productivity. Over the years both have increased at roughly the same rate, although wages have tended to outstrip productivity since the late 1960s, as shown in Exhibit 1. These gains in productivity are due partly to improvements in the quality of labor, which result from better education, training, and health, and partly to the remarkable growth in the quantity and quality of the other factors of production with which labor works. Since an economy's real income is the same as its real output, its income per worker is likely to keep pace with its output per worker over the long run if its markets are reasonably free and competitive.

SOME WAGE-DETERMINATION MODELS

How are wages determined in the market at any given time? The answer depends on the type of market model that is assumed to exist in a particular situation. There are several interesting possibilities.

Competitive Model: Many Buyers, Many Sellers

Suppose there is such a large number of employers hiring a certain type of labor and such a large num-

Exhibit 1

Output and Earnings in the Private Sector

Wages and productivity have tended to increase at about the same rate over the years. But the gap has widened considerably since the late 1960s.

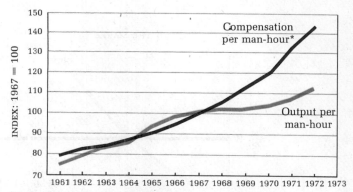

* Includes wages and fringe benefits.
SOURCE: U.S. Department of Labor.

ber of employees selling it that no single employer or employee can influence the wage rate. We would then have a competitive model of wages as illustrated in Exhibit 2 on the next page.

In Chart (a), the downward-sloping aggregate demand curve for this type of labor represents the sum of the individual *MRP*s of the buyers; the upward-sloping aggregate supply curve reflects the fact that if these workers are already employed, the firms buying labor will have to offer higher wages to attract workers from other occupations and localities. The equilibrium wage *OW* and equilibrium quantity *OM* are determined by the intersection of the labor supply and labor demand curves.

In Chart (b), the buying firm is faced with a perfectly elastic supply curve of labor at the market wage. The horizontal supply curve represents the marginal cost or price of the factor, as we learned earlier in the study of marginal productivity analysis. Since the firm's most profitable input is obtained by following the *MCF = MRP* rule, it will hire *ON* units of labor at the market wage of *OW*.

What analogies do you see between this model and that of a perfectly competitive seller in the output market?

Exhibit 2

A Competitive Model of Wage Determination

In the competitive model, the wage 0W and the quantity 0M for a particular type of labor are determined in the market through the free interaction of supply and demand. Each firm can buy all the labor it wants at the market wage; therefore the supply curve of this factor to any individual firm is perfectly elastic and is the same as the marginal cost of the factor. The firm's most profitable input 0N at the wage 0W is determined where its MCF = MRP.

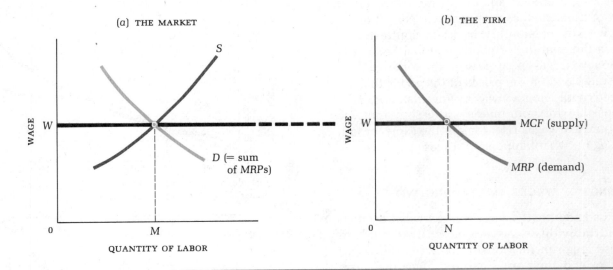

(a) THE MARKET (b) THE FIRM

Monopsony Model: One Buyer, Many Sellers

A *monopsony* is a market structure consisting of a single buyer and many sellers of a good or service. Hence it may be thought of as a "buyer's monopoly." An example would be a firm which is the sole employer in a company town, as has been the case in many mining communities. Similarly, in some farm areas a single food-processing plant dominates employment for many miles around.

A monopsony wage model is shown in Exhibit 3. As you can see from his cost schedule, the monopsonist must offer a higher wage rate or price per unit for *all* units in order to acquire more labor (just as a monopolist in the output market must charge a lower price per unit for *all* units in order to sell more products). The result is that the marginal cost of labor will be greater than its average cost at each input, as shown in the chart.

The monopsonist's most profitable input level is determined, as always, where his *MCF = MRP*. Thus he will employ 0L units of labor and pay the lowest price he can for that quantity of labor, namely LT per unit. In so doing, he will restrict his input as compared to the amount 0N and pay a lower price per unit as compared to the wage NW that he would have paid if he were a perfectly competitive buyer in the input market.

What analogies do you see between this model and that of a pure monopolist in the output market?

Monopoly Model: One Seller, Many Buyers

Suppose that a labor monopoly, such as a craft union whose members include all skilled workers in a particular trade like printing or plumbing, faces a market composed of many buyers of that particular skill. What level of wages and what corresponding volume of labor output will result?

The model is illustrated in Exhibit 4. The curves S and D represent the normal supply and demand curves for labor in a free market. The equilibrium quantity of labor will be 0N and the equilibrium wage 0W. A monopoly union, however, will seek to restrict the supply of its labor in order to attain a higher wage for its members; it will shift the supply curve to the left from S to S'. This will reduce the

Exhibit 3

A Monopsony Model of Wage Determination

In order to acquire more labor, the monopsonist must offer a higher price per unit for all units that he wants to hire. His average cost of labor will thus rise, and his marginal cost of labor will be different from his average cost.

COST SCHEDULE OF LABOR FACTOR

Units of labor factor, F	Average cost of labor factor (= wage rate or supply price of labor), ACF or S	Total cost of labor factor, TCF	Marginal cost of labor factor, MCF
1	$5	$ 5	$ 7
2	6	12	9
3	7	21	11
4	8	32	13
5	9	45	

The MCF curve lies above the average cost curve ACF, which is also the labor supply curve S. By hiring to the point where MCF = MRP, the monopsonist employs 0L units and pays the lowest price per unit consistent with that volume of input, namely LT.

The monopsonist thus restricts his employment of resources and pays a lower price per unit of input than he would if he were a perfectly competitive buyer in the factor market.

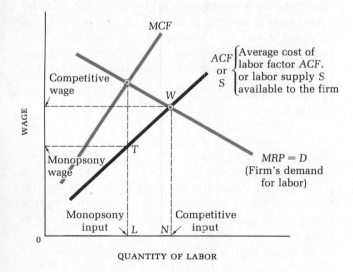

Exhibit 4

A Monopoly Model of Wage Determination

A monopoly union, such as a craft union composed of skilled workers like plumbers or electricians, will behave like any monopolist: it will restrict the supply of labor in order to command a higher price or wage rate as compared to the competitive case.

The curves S and D represent the free-market or unrestricted supply and demand curves. By restricting the supply of labor from S to S', the monopoly union reduces the equilibrium output from 0N to 0N', and raises the equilibrium wage from 0W to 0W'.

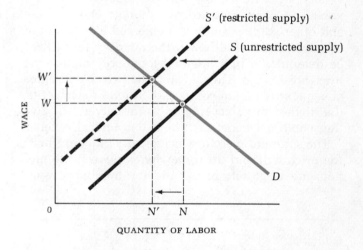

QUANTITY OF LABOR

equilibrium quantity of labor to 0N' and raise the equilibrium wage to 0W'.

This analysis helps to explain why some labor unions, especially certain craft unions, have established long apprenticeship requirements, high initiation fees, and similar obstacles to entry. Their motives, at least partly, have been to curb the supply of labor in the market and to boost wage rates. Of course, there are also unions that do not seek to maximize wages; they may try to maximize membership instead so that they can wield more market power. In such cases, the model in Exhibit 4 must be modified to reflect these objectives. This will be done in a later chapter.

Bilateral Monopoly Model: One Buyer, One Seller

A *bilateral monopoly* is a market structure in which a monopsonist buys from a monopolist. The simplest version, which *combines the main features of the previous monopsony and monopoly models*, is shown in Exhibit 5. Both the buyer and the seller are seeking to maximize their net benefits from the transaction. Therefore, if the two parties can agree on a given quantity to be exchanged, say *0M*, the monopsonist will wish to purchase that quantity at the lower price of *0U*, while the monopolist will want to sell that quantity at the higher price of *0V*. What will be the transaction price?

Economists have been trying to solve this problem for decades. Some years ago a remarkable series of controlled experiments was conducted by an economist and a psychologist at Pennsylvania State University, in which many pairs of students were involved in bargaining for real money. Out of these and other studies, there has emerged a fair amount of agreement that although the quantity figure may be determinate in a bilateral monopoly model, the price level is not. Thus, even if the two traders agree on a quantity that maximizes their *joint* net benefits, the highest price acceptable to the buyer will give the whole net benefit to the seller, and vice versa.

The solution, therefore, is logically indeterminate; the price will end up somewhere between the monopsony wage rate of *0U* and the monopoly wage rate of *0V*, but the theory does not predict the precise level within this range.

Which Model Exists Today?

All of these models are applicable to the modern economy. In the input markets, just as in the output markets, there are *degrees* of competition and monopoly. Hence these models, or mixtures and modifications of them, can be useful in describing fundamental patterns of wage determination.

About three-fourths of the American labor force is not organized in any labor union. Among agricultural and white-collar workers, for example, union membership is relatively slight and the situation conforms roughly to the competitive model. On the other hand, in some of the service industries and in parts of the South and Midwest where significant segments of the labor force are unorganized and relatively immobile for long periods, the monopsony model provides a good approximation—with an allowance, of course, for the legal minimum wage (although the minimum does not apply to many farmworkers).

Within the one-fourth of the labor force that is organized into unions there are some segments, such as those in the garment and building trades, coal mining, and stevedoring, where the balance of power is with the unions rather than the employers. The situation in those segments approximates that of monopoly. In most of manufacturing, transportation, and related sectors, strong unions face strong employers or employers' associations and the bilateral monopoly model applies. In these cases, collective bargaining between unions and management is the chief means of settling issues. Thus a wide variety of situations exists in American labor markets. These models or modifications of them can go a long way toward explaining and predicting the consequences of various outcomes.

Theory of Rent

In the early nineteenth century, a political controversy arose that was responsible for producing one of the great theoretical advances in the history of economics.

The place: England. The period: 1814–1816.

For most of the previous century, from 1711 to 1794, the price of "corn" (the generic name for all

---

Exhibit 5

A Bilateral Monopoly Model of Wage Determination

In a bilateral monopoly, both parties may agree on some quantity such as 0M, but the theory does not predict the exact price. At best, we can only say that the price of labor will be somewhere between the monopsonist's preferred wage of 0U and the monopolist's preferred wage of 0V.

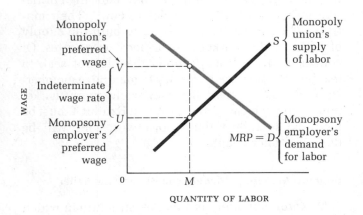

grains) had been extremely stable. But between 1795 and 1800 the price tripled, and it continued to rise over most of the following two decades. Since grain was a primary source of food, the rise in price created considerable political unrest. Many workers starved, and employers reluctantly raised wages because of soaring food prices.

One group argued that the landlords were in a "conspiracy" to keep up corn prices by charging high rents to farmers. Another group, including the great English classical economist David Ricardo, argued exactly the opposite: Corn prices are high, said the "Ricardians," because of shortages resulting from the Napoleonic Wars. The high price of corn makes corn cultivation more profitable; this increases the demand for land and hence the price paid for the use of the land—namely, rent. If the price of corn fell, corn cultivation would become less profitable, and this would bring decreased rents. In Ricardo's own words:

"Corn is not high because a rent is paid, but a rent is paid because corn is high." Ricardo meant that the price of land is determined by demand and supply, and that *rent is price-determined, not price-determining.*

Ricardo and his followers carried on a vigorous battle for the repeal of the English Corn Laws (tariffs) of 1815 in order to bring more corn into the country, thereby increasing its supply and lowering its price.

ECONOMIC RENT IS A SURPLUS

Ricardo's argument was based on the assumptions that the amount of land available is unchangeable; that land used for growing corn has no alternative uses; and that a landlord would prefer to receive *any* payment for his land rather than leave it idle and receive nothing. In the language of modern economics, this is equivalent to saying that the *supply of land is perfectly inelastic,* as illustrated in Exhibit 6, Chart (a).

The intersection of the supply curve (S) with the demand curve (D) establishes the equilibrium quantity ON and the equilibrium price OP. It follows that this price (or rent) per unit of land must be a *surplus* to the landlord since he would be willing to supply the same amount of land at a lower price, even down to a price of zero, depending on where the demand curve intersects the supply curve. We call this surplus "economic rent" and define it as follows:

Economic rent is any payment made to a factor of production, in an industry in equilibrium, in excess of the factor's supply price or opportunity cost—that is, in excess of the minimum amount necessary to keep that factor in its present occupation.

Exhibit 6

The Determination of Rent

Chart (a). *The landlord's opportunity cost is zero. Hence the total amount he receives, namely the area 0PRN, represents economic rent, since he would be willing to supply the same amount of land at zero rent.*

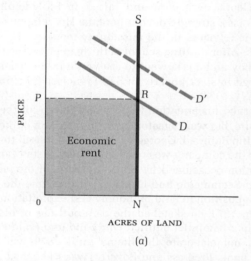

(a)

Chart (b). *The total amount received by the bus drivers is the area 0PRN. However, only the "Nth" driver is getting his opportunity cost; those to the left of him are getting more than their opportunity costs as represented by their total economic rent, namely the triangular area KPR.*

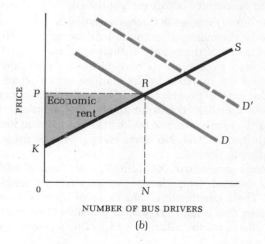

(b)

Note that this definition restricts the concept of economic rent to an *equilibrium* surplus. This is because some factors may receive surpluses while they are in a transitory stage from one equilibrium position to another and because such surpluses may exist even in long-run equilibrium. It follows that the en-tire rectangular area in Chart (*a*), namely *OPRN*, represents the total economic rent received by the landlord.

Originally, "rent" meant the payment made for the use of land. But economists eventually realized that any factor of production, not just land, may re-

---

Leaders in Economics

HENRY GEORGE

1839–1897

The Single Tax

Henry George was born and raised in Philadelphia by middle-class, strongly devout parents. His religious background is reflected in the missionary tendency in all his writings. After quitting school at thirteen he worked as an errand boy and clerk, went to sea while in his teens, and then lived in stark poverty in San Francisco for a number of years.

He turned his attention to politics and ran for the state legislature, but was defeated by the opposition of the Central Pacific Railroad. George vehemently opposed the land subsidy the company was receiving from the state, and the speculation occasioned by the completion of the railroad between Sacramento and Oakland. At this time the seeds of his opposition to land monopoly and exploitation were sown. In 1871 he sketched the bare outlines of his later theory in a pamphlet entitled *Our Land and Land Policy*, but did not elaborate the theme until 1879, when his famous book, *Progress and Poverty*, was published.

Ironically, George had difficulty in finding a publisher. But the book turned out to be a work that brought him great fame, for it was an immediate success both at home and abroad. Many millions of copies have been sold throughout the world, and it is undoubtedly the most successful popular economics book ever published.

The central concept in George's writing is that poverty is caused by the monopolization of land by the few, who deprive the rest of the people of their birthright. Since land is endowed by nature, all rent on land is unearned surplus, and the injustice to the landless grows when, as a result of natural progress, the value of land is augmented and rent increases correspondingly. The solution, therefore, is the confiscation of rent by the government through a *single tax* on land. No other taxes would be necessary, according to George.

Famous economists, including Alfred Marshall and J. B. Clark, debated with Henry George over the single-tax issue. Their conclusions, and those of later economists, suggested that a land tax would probably have fewer adverse effects on the allocation of society's resources than

Culver Pictures, Inc.

other taxes. However, it would have three major shortcomings: (1) a *single* tax on land alone would not produce enough revenue to meet governments' needs; (2) the tax would be unjust because surpluses or economic rent may accrue to other resource owners besides landlords if the owners can gain monopolistic control over the sale of their resources in the marketplace; (3) the tax might be impossible to administer because it does not distinguish between land and capital—that is, between the proportion of rent that represents a surplus and the proportion that results from improvements made on the land.

George entered politics again in 1886 as a candidate of the Labor and Socialist parties for mayor of New York City. By this time he was enormously popular, and it took the maximum efforts of a coalition of parties to defeat him at the polls. He became a candidate again in 1897, but the strain was too much for him, and he died during the campaign at the age of 58.

---

ceive a surplus above its opportunity cost. Hence they coined the expression "economic rent" to represent all such differentials.

Exhibit 6, Chart (b) is a hypothetical model of the supply and demand for bus drivers under perfect competition. According to the chart, a quantity of bus drivers equal to ON would each receive a wage of OP. But only for the Nth bus driver is this wage his supply price or opportunity cost: each of the others that make up the amount ON would have been willing to work for less as determined by the height of the segment KR of the supply curve. Therefore all of the other drivers are receiving a total economic rent equal to the triangle KPR. You should be able to see from the dashed lines in both diagrams in Exhibit 6 that if the supply curve remains the same, an increase in demand from D to D' will enlarge the amount of economic rent, whereas a decrease in demand will reduce it.

This leads to the important conclusion that economic rent arises because the owners of the various units of a particular factor of production differ in the eagerness with which they are willing to supply those units; that is, the owners differ in their supply price. If all owners had equal supply prices, the supply curve would be perfectly elastic and there would be no economic rent. Thus in Exhibit 6, Chart (b), the area of economic rent would diminish to zero if the supply curve were to pivot on point R so as to approach the horizontal.

Economic rent is a concept similar to that of net revenue, since both represent surpluses. The difference between them is merely a matter of reference: When the surplus is received by a factor of production it is called economic rent; when the surplus is incurred by a firm it is referred to as net revenue.

IS RENT A COST OR A SURPLUS?
WHICH VIEWPOINT?

Contrary to Ricardo's assumptions, units of land often have alternative uses and are of different quality. This explains why the demand for an acre of real estate in the heart of a city's business district may be quite different from the demand for an acre of farm land or an acre of desert land elsewhere in the country. These differences in demand also account for the differences in rent that are paid by their users.

Are these rents a cost or a surplus? The answer depends on the point of view you take. From the firm's viewpoint, rent is the price it must pay to attract land from its alternative uses. Hence rent is a cost. From the economy's viewpoint, rent is the value which society receives for making available the land provided free by nature, regardless of the alternative uses to which the land is put and the rents that are paid. Hence rent is a surplus. The fallacy of composition thus plays a role in the interpretation of rent from the individual versus social viewpoint.

Theory of Interest

If you borrow money to buy a car, a house, or a washing machine, you must pay interest to the lender for the money that you borrow. Hence interest is defined as the price paid for the use of money or loanable funds over a period of time.

What forces determine the rate of interest? The answer was spelled out in considerable detail in an earlier chapter dealing with macroeconomic equilibrium. We can now broaden these ideas to include some microeconomic concepts as well, thus providing a more comprehensive explanation of interest-rate determination.

Since interest is the price paid for the use of money or loanable funds, it is always expressed as a percentage of the amount of the loan. Thus an interest rate of 5 percent means that the borrower pays 5 cents per $1 borrowed per year, or $5 per $100 borrowed per year, and so on. Although interest is paid for the use of money, and money in turn is used to buy productive resources or capital goods, you will often hear reference made to the interest on capital. What this really means, of course, is the interest on the money represented by capital invested.

In our economy there are many different interest rates on debt instruments of all types—notes, bonds, mortgages, and so on. The rates vary according to several factors:

☐ Risk—the chance of the borrower's defaulting on the loan

☐ Maturity—the length of time over which the money is borrowed

☐ Liquidity—the ease with which the creditor can convert the debt instrument into cash quickly without loss of value in terms of money

☐ Competition—the extent to which lenders compete for borrowers in particular money markets

Other things being equal, interest rates will tend to vary directly with the first two factors and inversely with the second two. If you are not sure of the reasons for this, ask yourself how these factors would affect the interest rate that you would charge if you were a banker making loans.

As a result of the wide structure of interest rates, economists find it convenient to talk about "the" rate of interest. By this they mean the theoretical pure interest rate on a long-term riskless loan. This rate is best approximated by the interest on long-term negotiable government bonds.

Since the interest rate is the price of money or loanable funds, we shall see shortly that it is determined by the interaction of demand and supply forces. But first, what are the sources of demand and supply?

DEMAND FOR LOANABLE FUNDS

You and I and everyone else want money, but from the economy's viewpoint we fall into three major groups: businesses, households, and government.

1. *Businesses.* Businesses are the largest source of demand for loanable funds. Corporations borrow money because they want to invest the funds in new capital goods, including the building up of inventories. A firm undertakes such investments as long as it expects to receive a yield which exceeds the cost of its funds. The expected yield or rate of return on investment projects can be depicted by the marginal revenue product (*MRP*) curve of capital expressed in terms of percentages—as illustrated in Exhibit 7. You can see from the diagram that the *MRP* curve should be viewed as a cumulative investment demand curve. It tells you, for example, that the firm can earn 18 percent on the first $200,000 of investment and 16 percent on the next $100,000. Therefore it can earn *at least* 16 percent on the first $300,000. Similarly it can earn *at least* 14 percent on the first $400,000 invested. Interpreted in this way, we see that since the rate of interest on borrowed funds is also expressed in percentage terms, *any point on the curve shows the amount of investment the firm will undertake at various interest rates.* For example, at a 10 percent interest rate on borrowed funds, the firm will demand $600,000 for investment. If the rate is lowered to 8 percent, the firm will increase the amount of funds demanded for investment to $700,000.

Exhibit 7

A Firm's Demand Curve for Capital

In a competitive market, the firm will demand loanable funds up to the point where the MRP of capital equals the interest rate or price. Thus a decrease in the interest rate from 10 percent to 8 percent will increase the quantity of capital demanded from $600,000 to $700,000. (NOTE: In macroeconomics, a firm's MRP curve of capital is called its marginal efficiency of investment, MEI.)

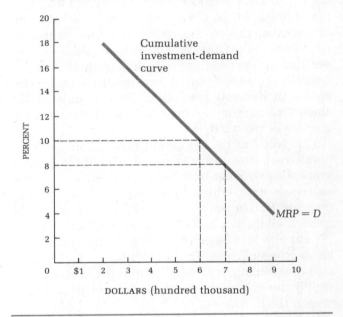

The diagram thus suggests a familiar marginal principle:

Under competitive conditions, a firm will demand loanable funds up to the point where the capital purchased with those funds is such that its marginal revenue productivity is equal to the interest rate (or price) that must be paid for the loan. *The MRP curve of capital is therefore the firm's demand curve for capital.*

2. *Households.* Households are the second major source of demand for loanable funds. Households borrow to buy automobiles, washing machines, vacation trips, homes, and so forth. There is some limited evidence to suggest that the household demand curve for funds is downward-sloping, indicating that households will tend to borrow larger amounts of money at lower interest rates.

3. *Government.* The public sector is the third major source of demand for loanable funds. Governments

at all levels—national, state, and local—borrow money to finance national defense, highways, schools, welfare, and so forth. The federal government often borrows to finance a budget deficit, and therefore we cannot assume that its demand for loanable funds depends on the interest rate. However, there is ample evidence that this is not true for state and local governments; they tend to borrow more when interest rates are low than when they are high.

In general, as indicated by many studies:

For all three sources—businesses, households, and government—taken together, the total market demand curve for loanable funds is downward-sloping. In addition, the demand curve is probably relatively inelastic. Therefore, changes in the interest rate are likely to result in less than proportional changes in the quantity demanded of loanable funds.

SUPPLY OF LOANABLE FUNDS

We must now turn our attention to the supply side of the picture and ask: What are the sources of loanable funds? There are two:

1. *The central banking system* of a country (the Federal Reserve System in the United States) exercises a great deal of influence over the supply of money and hence the supply of loanable funds. This influence is intertwined with government monetary and fiscal policies for combating recessions and inflations.

2. *Households and businesses* supply some loanable funds to the money market out of their past or present savings. Household savings are that part of household income not spent on consumption. Business savings are mainly undistributed (plowed back) profits and depreciation reserves. Most businesses reinvest their savings in new plant and equipment, but some savings find their way into the money market. In general, very little is known about the effects of interest rates on household and business saving, but the influences are believed to be relatively slight.

DETERMINATION OF THE INTEREST RATE

The demand and supply forces generated by government, businesses, and households combine to determine the equilibrium interest rate in the market, as shown by the familiar supply and demand diagram in Exhibit 8. As mentioned above, the downward-

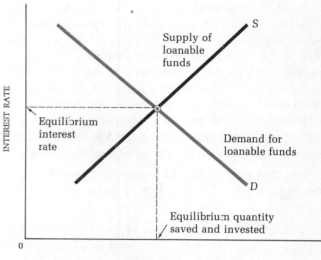

Exhibit 8

Determination of the Interest Rate

sloping aggregate demand curve at any *given level of national income* reflects the willingness on the part of businessmen to demand more funds for investment at a low interest rate than at a high interest rate. The upward-sloping supply curve, though it is based on much more complex and uncertain factors, *assumes* that household and business savers will make available somewhat larger quantities of loanable funds at a high interest rate than at a low one.

Actually, the determination of the interest rate has much deeper implications than is apparent from this simple supply and demand diagram. Further, government monetary and fiscal policies, as learned in macroeconomics, exercise a powerful influence on the forces that help determine the interest rate. As a result, the interest rate tends to be more stable and does not fluctuate as freely as do the prices of commodities that are determined by supply and demand in perfectly competitive markets.

THE RATIONING OR ALLOCATING FUNCTION OF INTEREST

Since the interest rate is a price, it performs the same rationing function as any other price by allocating the economy's scarce supply of funds among those who are willing to pay for them. Thus in a free market, only the most profitable investment projects—those projects whose expected return or productivity is equal to or greater than the rate of interest—are undertaken. Any project whose prospective yield is below the interest rate is dropped from consideration. In this way the interest rate decides the critical question of *who* shall participate in the limited supply of capital, and in so doing directs the growth of productive capacity in a capital-using economy.

Does the interest rate actually perform this function in our economic system? For the most part the answer is yes, but there are some qualifications:

The interest rate in our economy is not the sole mechanism for allocating scarce funds for two reasons:

1. The government allocates some of the available capital to projects which it believes to be in the public interest, regardless of their financial profitability.

2. The unequal distribution of bargaining power among borrowers may enable many large firms to borrow on more favorable terms (at lower interest rates) than most small firms—even when the latter have relatively greater prospects for growth.

LOANABLE-FUNDS AND LIQUIDITY-PREFERENCE THEORIES

Two main theories of interest have been an integral part of economics since the 1930s: the loanable-funds theory and the liquidity-preference theory.

The *loanable-funds theory of interest* holds that the interest rate is determined by the demand for, and supply of, loanable funds only, as distinguished from *all* money. The sources of demand for loanable funds are businesses that want to invest, households that want to finance consumer purchases, and government agencies that want to finance deficits. The sources of supply of loanable funds are the central banking system which influences the supply of money (and hence loanable funds) in the economy, and households and businesses that make loanable funds available out of their past or present savings.

The *liquidity-preference theory of interest* (formulated by J. M. Keynes) contends that people would rather hold their assets or wealth in the most liquid form, namely cash, in order to satisfy three motives: the "transactions motive" to carry out everyday purchasing needs; the "precautionary motive" to meet

possible unforeseen conditions; and the "speculative motive" to take advantage of a rise in interest rates. Accordingly, interest is the price or reward that must be paid to overcome liquidity preference. The equilibrium rate of interest is determined by the demand for, and supply of, money.

These two approaches should not be regarded as alternative theories of interest. Although they involve many complexities which are treated in greater detail in more advanced courses, they tend to supplement and complement each other rather than compete.

Theory of Profit

We have learned that *profit* or net revenue represents the difference between total revenue and total cost. Profit is thus a *residual* or *surplus* over and above normal profit, and it accrues to the entrepreneur after all costs including explicit costs and implicit costs have been deducted from total revenue. What does economic theory tell us about the determinants of profit? What functions does profit perform?

The history of economics reveals a number of theories of how profits are derived. Today, three are generally recognized as being particularly relevant: (1) friction and monopoly theory; (2) uncertainty theory; (3) innovation theory. This system of classification is not all-inclusive and any one of the theories may contain elements of the others. The system merely emphasizes the main lines that have been followed in the course of thinking on the subject.

FRICTION AND MONOPOLY THEORY

By the end of the nineteenth century, the theory of a perfectly competitive economy was well on its way toward becoming a unified body of thought. Against this setting the noted American economist J. B. Clark constructed a model of the economy that was intended to reconcile the static laws of theory with the dynamic world of fact.

According to Clark's "stationary" model (or the theory of perfect competition as it is called today), the economy is characterized by a smooth and frictionless flow of resources, with the system automatically clicking into equilibrium through the free play of market forces. Changes may occur that cause a departure from equilibrium, but so long as resources are mobile and opportunities equally accessible (i.e., knowledge is perfect) to all economic entities, the adjustment to change and a new equilibrium will be accomplished quickly and smoothly. In this type of economic equilibrium all factors of production would receive their opportunity costs; the revenues of each enterprise would exactly equal its costs (including the implicit wages and interest of the owner), and no economic surplus or profit residual could result.

In the real world, however, surpluses do occur. According to the theory, they can be attributed only to the frictions (or obstacles to resource mobility) and monopoly elements that actually characterize a dynamic economy. In the long run, according to theory, the forces of competition would eliminate any surpluses, but the surpluses in reality recur because new frictions and new monopoly elements continually arise. Therefore:

Profits are the result of institutional rigidities in the social and economic system that prevent the working-out of competitive forces, and are to the temporary advantage of the surplus recipient.

Many illustrations from real life substantiate the existence of friction and monopoly as a cause of economic surplus. The construction of military posts during a war brings profit bonanzas to neighboring cities; cold-war crises have often rescued domestic industries from threatening oversupplies of their products; the existence of patents and franchises enables many firms to reap profits by legally excluding competitors from the field; a favorable location for a business may result in the value of the site exceeding the rental payment for it. In general, the control of any resource whose supply is scarce relative to its demand provides a basis for pure or windfall profits. A surplus would not arise if resources were sufficiently mobile to enter the market, or if the economy were frictionless (perfect) in its competitive structure. At best, any surpluses that did arise would be short-lived and vanish entirely when the adjustments had time to exert their full effect in the market. But social processes—customs, laws, and traditions—make such rapid adjustments impossible.

UNCERTAINTY THEORY

The uncertainty theory of profit was introduced by Professor Frank Knight of the University of Chicago in a remarkable doctoral thesis entitled *Risk, Uncertainty, and Profit* published in 1921. The theory is rooted in a distinction between "risk" and "uncertainty."

The Meaning of Risk

Risk is defined as the quantitative measurement of an outcome, such as a gain or a loss, in a manner such that the mathematical probability (or "odds") of the outcome can be predicted. Since the distinguishing feature of risk is predictability, the firm can "insure" itself against expected losses by incorporating them in advance into its cost structure. This is true whether the risk is of an intrafirm or interfirm nature.

1. *Intrafirm risk.* Such risk occurs when management can establish the probability of loss because the number of occurrences within the firm is large enough to be predicted with known error. For example, a factory may experience a loss of about 2 machine-hours out of every 100 machine-hours due to equipment breakdown. In this case, the cost of the production lost can be added to the cost of the production resulting from the remaining 98 machine-hours, and the profit rate altered by the revision in the cost structure. In other words, where the average expected loss for the company can be predicted for the coming period, the loss can be "self-insured" by treating it as a cost of doing business, and hence no insurance from outside sources is necessary. Thus, small-loan companies expect a certain percentage of defaults; banks regularly charge off as bad debts a portion of their loans; and many companies institute self-insurance programs against risks for which they can prepare themselves through proper reserve accounting.

2. *Interfirm risk.* For some risks the number of observations or experiences is not large enough within any one firm for management to feel that it can predict the loss with reasonable confidence. However, when many firms are considered, the observations become numerous enough to exhibit the necessary stability for prediction. Examples of such risks are losses caused by floods, storms, fires, or deaths. Since managers are unable to predict such losses for themselves, they are able to shift the burden of the risk to insurance companies whose function is to establish the probability of such losses based on a large number of cases. Although insurance companies cannot establish that a particular individual will die or that a particular building will burn, they

can predict with small error how many people will die next year or how many buildings out of a given number will burn. It follows that since a firm pays a risk premium for insurance, it can and does treat this risk premium as a cost of doing business.

The Meaning of Uncertainty

Uncertainty is defined as a state of knowledge in which the probabilities of outcomes resulting from specific actions are not known and cannot be predicted. Unlike risk, therefore, uncertainty is a subjective (rather than objective) phenomenon: no two individuals who view the same event will necessarily formulate the same quantitative opinion about it because there is not enough information on which to base a definite probability estimate.

Under uncertainty conditions, decision makers must make choices based on incomplete knowledge. They may do this by forming mental images of future outcomes that cannot be verified quantitatively. It follows from this that uncertainty is not insurable and cannot be integrated within the firm's cost structure, as can risk. At best, each businessman may harbor his own subjective probability about a future outcome, but it is nothing more than a strong hunch. According to this theory:

The great majority of events in our society are unpredictable—they are uncertainties. Therefore, *profits are the rewards, and losses are the penalties, of bearing uncertainty.*

The uncertainty theory concludes that in a market economy entrepreneurs undertake an activity because they *expect* but do not necessarily *receive* profits. Like a dog chasing a rabbit, the expectation of profit is the incentive that keeps entrepreneurs running.

INNOVATION THEORY

In the 1930s, one of the most distinguished economists of this century, Joseph Schumpeter, introduced a theory of business cycles based on innovations. This theory has often been extended to include the notion of innovation as a cause of profits.

An *innovation*, as economists define it, is "the setting up of a new production function"—that is, a new relation between the output and the various inputs (capital, land, labor, etc.) in a production process. Innovations may thus embrace such wide varieties of activities as the discovery of new markets, differentiation of products, or, in short, new ways of doing old things or different combinations of existing methods to accomplish new things. There is an important distinction between invention and innovation: Invention is the creation of something new; innovation is the adaptation of an invention to use. Many inventions never become innovations.

Schumpeter's original purpose in propounding the innovation theory was to show how business cycles result from these disturbances and from successive adaptations to them by the business system. His procedure was to assume a stationary (perfectly competitive) system in equilibrium—in which all economic life is repetitive and goes on smoothly, without disturbance. Into this system a shock—an innovation—is introduced by an entrepreneur who foresees the possibility of extra profit. The quietude and intricate balance of the system is then shattered as if the system had been invaded by a Hollywood-staged cattle stampede. The successful innovation causes a herd of businessmen (followers rather than leaders) to plunge into the new field by adopting the innovation, and these mass rushes create and stir up secondary waves of business activity. When the disturbance has finally ironed itself out, the system settles into equilibrium once again, only to be disturbed later on by another innovation. Profits and economic activity are thus experienced as a series of fits and starts (cycles) rather than progressing smoothly and continuously.

FUNCTIONS OF PROFITS

As mentioned earlier, there is no single "correct" theory of profit; all three theories contribute significantly to explaining the causes of profit. They also help us to understand the two major functions of profits in our economy:

1. Profits stimulate innovation by inducing businessmen to undertake new ventures and to improve production methods.

2. To the extent that markets are free and competitive, the desire for profits induces businessmen to allocate their resources efficiently in accordance with consumer preferences.

These functions are important because the role of profits and the profit system account for a fundamental distinction between our capitalistic system and the socialistic systems of countries like the Soviet Union and China, which we will be studying later on.

JOSEPH ALOIS SCHUMPETER

1883–1950

The "Crumbling Walls" of Capitalism

One of the most famous economists of the twentieth century was Joseph Schumpeter. Indeed, in the opinion of some scholars he was one of the great economic thinkers of all time. His claim to this title rests as much on his total achievements as a social scientist as on his contributions to the advancement of economics. Although many scholars have excelled in special fields, Schumpeter was one of the few who was extraordinarily well versed in many, including economics, mathematics, philosophy, sociology, and history.

Schumpeter was born in Moravia (now part of Czechoslovakia) and educated in law and economics at the University of Vienna. After a varied and successful career as a professor, cabinet minister, banker, and jurist, he accepted a teaching position at the University of Bonn in 1925. When Hitler came to power, he immigrated to the United States, and was a professor of economics at Harvard University until his death.

Schumpeter's output of books, essays, articles, and monographs was enormous, but his most important works fell broadly in the field of business-cycle theory. Perhaps his greatest theoretical contribution was the model he developed to describe how business cycles result from *innovations* by a business system under capitalism. This innovation theory was subsequently adopted by many economists as a partial explanation of how profits (surpluses) arise in a capitalistic system.

In one of his classic works Schumpeter discussed the "crumbling walls" of capitalism—that is, the eventual decay of the system due to the obsolescence of the entrepreneurial function. In his own words:

> . . . The economic wants of humanity might some day be so completely satisfied that little motive would be left to push productive effort still further ahead. Such a state of satiety is no doubt very far off even if we keep within the present scheme of wants; and if we take account of the fact that, as higher standards of life are attained, these wants automatically expand and new wants emerge or are created, satiety becomes a flying goal, particularly if we include leisure among consumers' goods. However, let us glance at that possibility, assuming, still more unrealistically, that methods of production have reached a state of perfection which does not admit of further improvement.
>
> A more or less stationary state would ensue. Capitalism, being essentially an evolutionary process, would become atrophic. There would be nothing left for entre-

The Bettmann Archive.

preneurs to do. They would find themselves in much the same situation as generals would in a society perfectly sure of permanent peace. Profits and along with profits the rate of interest would converge toward zero. The bourgeois strata that live on profits and interest would tend to disappear. The management of industry and trade would become a matter of current administration, and the personnel would unavoidably acquire the characteristics of a bureaucracy. Socialism of a very sober type would almost automatically come into being. Human energy would turn away from business. Other than economic pursuits would attract the brains and provide the adventure.

Although Schumpeter was widely respected, and his many pioneering works were studied by scholars throughout the world, he never founded a "school" of economic thought or gathered a following which could eventually assume the status of a school. In other words, no "Schumpeterians" ever emerged, as did, for example, Marshallians or Keynesians. Various reasons may be advanced for this. Perhaps the most significant is that his theory contained no *cause célèbre*—no fundamental challenge that could offer a rallying point. Although his innovation theory of business cycles was developed on a high theoretical plane, it offered no concrete solutions to the world's economic problems.

SUMMARY OF IMPORTANT IDEAS

1. The long-run trend of real wages in our economy has been upward, based fundamentally on the increased productivity of labor resulting from improvements in the quality and quantity of the factors of production.

2. Wages are determined in the market under different competitive conditions. Four models which explain most of the situations that exist in our economy are the competitive model, monopsony model, monopoly model, and bilateral monopoly model. The bilateral monopoly model may yield a determinate solution on quantity, but it yields an indeterminate solution on price.

3. Economic rent is a surplus which is price-determined, not price-determining. To an individual firm, rent is a cost of production just like any other cost; but to society rent is a surplus which is received for making available nature's free land.

4. Interest is the price paid for the use of money or loanable funds over a period of time. Although the interest rate is determined by the supply of, and demand for, loanable funds, it is administered by the government and is not freely fluctuating. The chief function of the interest rate is to allocate scarce funds for alternative uses, thus directing the flow of capital.

5. Profit is a residual or surplus over and above all costs including normal profit. It may result from frictions and monopoly elements in our economy, from uncertainty, and from innovations. The chief functions of profit are (a) to stimulate economic progress by inducing businessmen to invest in plant and equipment, and (b) to the extent that markets are competitive, to allocate resources in accordance with consumer preferences.

FOR DISCUSSION

1. *Terms and concepts to review:*

wages	real wages
labor	monopsony
money wages	bilateral monopoly
economic rent	liquidity-preference
single tax	theory of interest
interest	profit
pure interest rate	risk
loanable-funds theory	uncertainty
of interest	innovation

2. Why has the long-run trend of real wages been upward, especially since the supply of labor today is so much larger than it was years ago?

3. Which wage-determination model best explains each of the following? Illustrate and explain each with an actual model. (a) The wages of file clerks and secretaries, (b) the wages of unskilled farm workers, (c) the wages of typographers and longshoremen.

4. A union official once advised the men in an industry to ask for a 10 percent wage cut. Was he crazy? What economic factors might have prompted him to offer such advice?

5. "Wages are determined by the marginal productivity of labor just as prices are determined by costs of production." True or false? Explain.

6. Do you see any similarity between the concept of economic rent received by a factor of production and net revenue received by a firm? Explain.

7. Henry George ran for mayor of New York in 1886. If you had been a voter at that time, how would you have reacted to his single-tax idea?

8. Money itself is not a resource and is unproductive. Why, then, should people be willing to pay a price in the form of interest in order to acquire it? What determines the interest rate that is paid? What functions does interest perform?

9. Classify each of the following as an interfirm or intrafirm risk: (a) glassware and china breakage in a restaurant, (b) egg breakage on a chicken farm, (c) absenteeism in a factory, (d) "acts of God" (cite examples).

10. (a) From a chicken farmer's standpoint, is the price of eggs a risk or an uncertainty? (b) How about the sale of next year's Plymouths by Chrysler? Why?

11. "Economic profits should be taxed away since they result from frictions and monopolistic influences." Evaluate.

CHAPTER 29

Stability, General Equilibrium, and Welfare Economics

CHAPTER PREVIEW

What is the deeper meaning of equilibrium? Why is it important in economics (and in all other sciences)?

In what sense is our economy a "system"—a complex network in which "everything depends on everything else"?

Does the study of economics provide us with a norm for judging whether actions should or should not be undertaken to improve society's welfare?

Equilibrium is one of the fundamental concepts of economics, and we have already made considerable use of it. But what does "equilibrium" really mean? How important is it in economic analysis?

Equilibrium was defined in earlier chapters as a state of balance between opposing forces. An object is in equilibrium when it is at rest; it has no tendency to change its position because the forces acting upon it are canceling each other. In economics, as we have seen, the "objects" may be prices, quantities, incomes, or other variables. You cannot consider a problem solved if, at the point you terminate your analysis, the variables which are germane to the particular problem are still changing. Only when the variables settle down to steady levels, or only when their future equilibrium positions can be predicted, can you consider the solution complete.

However, the study of equilibrium is not an end in itself. We must also understand the forces which can disturb an equilibrium, and the measures that may have to be undertaken to restore it. These ideas will become more meaningful as we explore the ramifications of equilibrium in this chapter.

Stability of Equilibrium

An object at rest may or may not have the ability to reestablish its position if the forces acting upon it suddenly change. If it does, the equilibrium is stable; if it does not, the equilibrium may be either unstable or neutral. Let us examine these ideas in both a physical and economic context.

STABLE, UNSTABLE, AND NEUTRAL EQUILIBRIUM

Exhibit 1 provides some interesting examples of the stability of equilibrium in terms of supply and demand curves.

Chart (a) illustrates a case of stable equilibrium. This represents the normal situation. In physical terms, it may be depicted by a cone resting on its base. In economic terms, it can be represented by the interaction of ordinary supply and demand curves. If the system is subjected to an external "shock" or disturbance sufficient to dislodge it from equilibrium, self-corrective forces will cause it to return to its initial position. If the price, for example, should for some reason rise above its equilibrium level at P, quantity supplied of the product will exceed quantity demanded, thereby driving the price down. If the price should fall below P, quantity demanded will exceed quantity supplied, thereby driving the price up.

Although Charts (b)–(d) do not depict typical situations, they are useful for providing deeper insights into the concept of equilibrium.

Chart (b) presents a case of unstable equilibrium. A physical example is a cone balanced on its vertex. An economic example is one in which price is determined by the intersection of supply and demand, but the supply curve is downward-sloping and cuts the demand curve from below. As you can see from the chart, the system is in a delicate state of balance; if the equilibrium is disturbed, the object will be forced away from its initial state. For example, if for some reason the price should rise above its equilibrium level, quantity demanded will exceed quantity supplied and the price will continue to rise; conversely, if the price should fall below its equilibrium level, quantity supplied will exceed quantity demanded and the price will continue to fall. Note, however, that these conclusions would not hold if the downward-sloping supply curve cut the demand curve from above instead of from below. In that case the equilibrium would be stable. You should be able to demonstrate this by sketching the curves.

Charts (c) and (d) provide illustrations of neutral equilibrium. The physical situation can be depicted by a cone lying on its side; if the cone's equilibrium is disturbed it simply "rolls" to some other neutral position. The analogous economic situation occurs in those ranges of price and quantity where the supply and demand curves happen to coincide. Thus in Chart (c) any price between the points P and P' is in neutral equilibrium—the price is "rolling" or indeterminate within this range. Similarly in Chart (d),

any quantity between the points Q and Q' is in neutral equilibrium—and therefore the quantity is indeterminate within this range.

STATICS AND DYNAMICS

The concepts of stable, unstable, and neutral equilibrium can also be depicted by the charts in Exhibit 2. Note from the titles of Exhibits 1 and 2 that Exhibit 1 consists of static models whereas Exhibit 2 is composed of dynamic ones. Let us examine these concepts more closely.

A *static model* is one in which economic phenomena are studied without reference to time—without reference to preceding or succeeding events. In a static model, time is not permitted to enter into the analysis in any manner that will affect the results. When we construct a static model, therefore, we are taking a "snapshot" and analyzing its essential features. Each of the diagrams in Exhibit 1, and most of the other theoretical situations and charts studied in this book, are static models.

Of course, in many practical situations you want to analyze the effects of a change in one or more of the determining conditions in a static model. This method is known as *comparative statics*. It consists of comparing two "snapshots"—one taken before the change and one after. For example, when you analyzed supply and demand situations in previous chapters by comparing equilibrium prices and quantities before and after a shift in one or both of the curves, you were using comparative statics. Statics and comparative statics encompass most of the theory in this book—and by far the larger part of economic theory in general.

A *dynamic model* is one in which economic phenomena are studied by relating them to preceding or succeeding events. The influence of time is taken explicitly into account. Illustrations of the results of dynamic models are shown in Exhibit 2. Each chart depicts a possible way in which price may behave in relation to its equilibrium level over a period of time. Each of these dynamic models, therefore, is like a "motion picture" as distinguished from the "snapshot" of Exhibit 1.

Fluctuations in prices like those shown in Exhibit 2 do not continue in the same pattern indefinitely. Why? Because the underlying supply and demand curves which determine prices tend to change fairly frequently, so that different patterns are generated which at any given moment may be tending toward stable, unstable, or neutral equilibrium. However,

Exhibit 1
Stable, Unstable, and Neutral Equilibrium: Static Models

Chart (a). Stable equilibrium. *The equilibrium at P is stable—like a cone resting on its base. A "shock" sufficient to disturb the equilibrium brings self-corrective forces into play which automatically restore the initial position.*

Chart (b). Unstable equilibrium. *The equilibrium at P is unstable—like a cone balanced on its vertex. If the equilibrium is disturbed, the system is forced away from its initial state. Thus at any price higher than 0P, quantity demanded exceeds quantity supplied so the price continues to rise; at any price below 0P the reverse is true. Note, however, that the equilibrium at P would be stable if the downward-sloping supply curve cut the demand curve from above instead of from below.*

Charts (c) and (d). Neutral equilibrium. *In Chart (c), any equilibrium between P and P′ is neutral; in Chart (d) any equilibrium between Q and Q′ is neutral. Within their neutral ranges, price and quantity are indeterminate; they may take on any values. Hence the situation is analogous to a cone rolling on its side.*

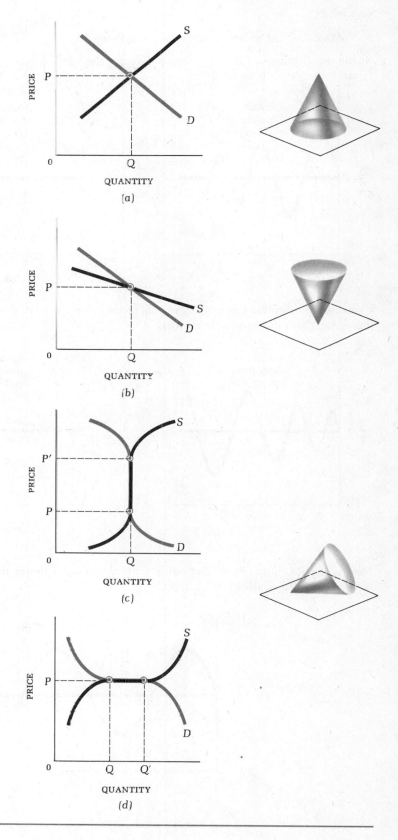

Exhibit 2

Stable equilibrium. *Price converges toward the equilibrium level at P. Price may oscillate or it may approach equilibrium from above or below.*

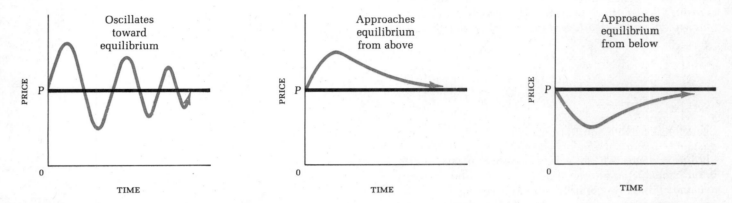

Unstable equilibrium. *Price diverges from the equilibrium at P. Price may oscillate or it may "explode" upward or downward from the equilibrium level.*

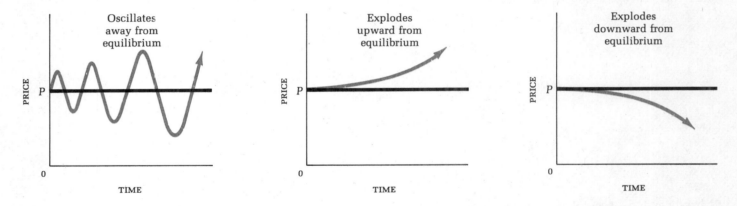

Neutral equilibrium. *Price fluctuates around the equilibrium level at P. Price has no permanent tendency to converge toward equilibrium or diverge from it.*

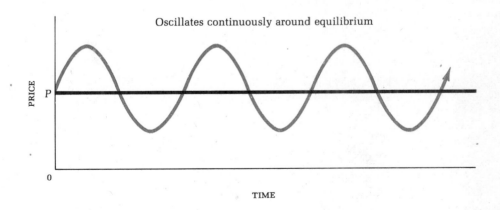

over a period of time, prices in most markets tend toward some stable equilibrium level.

This suggests the following definition:

Stable equilibrium is a condition in which an object or system (such as a price, firm, industry, market, etc.) in equilibrium, when subjected to a shock sufficient to disturb its position, returns toward its initial equilibrium as a result of self-restoring forces. (In contrast, an equilibrium which is not stable may be either unstable or neutral.)

As you can see from this discussion, the concept of stable equilibrium is of fundamental importance. Indeed, it has occupied the interest of a number of scholars—among them Professor Paul Samuelson, whose pioneering work on stability analysis contributed significantly to his being the first American to receive the Nobel prize in economics.

General Equilibrium: "Everything Depends on Everything Else"

In the early part of this century, a famous American economist, Henry J. Davenport, investigated relationships between the prices of corn, pork, and land. He noted part of his conclusions in a poem:

> The price of pig
> Is something big;
> Because its corn, you'll understand
> Is high-priced, too;
> Because it grew
> Upon the high-priced farming land.
>
> If you'd know why
> That land is high
> Consider this: its price is big
> Because it pays
> Thereon to raise
> The costly corn, the high-priced pig.

Long before Davenport observed connections between these three variables, a prominent mid-nineteenth-century French economist, Frederic Bastiat, expressed wonderment about the Paris of his day. Hundreds of thousands of people, he remarked, live in the city, yet each day a wide variety of goods and services are provided in approximately correct quantities without coordination or planning by any single agency. "Imagination," Bastiat wrote, "is baffled when it tries to appreciate the vast multiplicity of commodities which must enter tomorrow

to preserve the inhabitants from famine. Yet all sleep and their slumbers are not disturbed for a single minute by the prospects of such a frightful catastrophe."

What Davenport and Bastiat (and many other observers as well) were commenting upon is the notion that a complex economy is a vast system of interrelated components—a system in which "everything depends on everything else." We can gain a better appreciation of this idea by examining some of the features of what is known as general equilibrium theory.

PARTIAL AND GENERAL EQUILIBRIUM THEORY

Until now, almost all of our attention in microeconomics has been focused on "partial" as distinguished from "general" equilibrium theory. What do these terms mean?

Partial equilibrium theory analyzes and develops models of a particular market on the assumption that other markets are in balance. It thus ignores the interrelationships of prices and quantities that may exist between markets.

For example, ordinary supply and demand analysis is normally of a partial equilibrium nature since it focuses on a single market while neglecting others. This method of investigation can be extremely useful for gaining a better understanding of how a market works and for analyzing the effects of such things as price control, rationing, minimum wages, and commodity taxes as was done in earlier chapters. However, by ignoring the ramifications and repercussions of price and quantity changes which may occur in other markets, we are overlooking the fact that such changes could have a significant influence on the market we are studying.

In view of this, it is necessary to think of the price system as an interrelated whole, and to recognize that partial analyses can provide only approximations to full explanation. This being the case, a "general" approach which simultaneously takes into account all product and resource markets in the economy, is needed.

General equilibrium theory analyzes the interrelationships between prices and quantities of goods and resources in different markets, and demonstrates the possibility of simultaneous equilibrium between all markets. It thus views the economy as a system composed of interdependent parts.

PAUL ANTHONY SAMUELSON

1915–

America's First Nobel Laureate in Economics

In 1935, an extraordinary young man born in Gary, Indiana, received his B.A. degree from the University of Chicago. He went on to pursue graduate work at Harvard University, from which he received a Ph.D. in economics in 1941. During that six-year period he published eleven major professional journal articles—most of which became classics in their own time—plus a path-breaking doctoral dissertation which later appeared as a book, *Foundations of Economic Analysis* (Harvard University Press, 1947). The impact of this treatise, which was largely conceived and written in 1937 by the then twenty-three-year-old author, was noted in 1970 by the Swedish Royal Academy of Science when it bestowed upon Samuelson the Alfred Nobel Memorial Prize in Economic Science.

Paul Samuelson is probably the world's most widely known economist. Several generations of college students in the United States and abroad took their first course in economics from his introductory textbook. Millions of readers of American and foreign newspapers and magazines have been exposed to his articles on current economic policies. And professional economists throughout the world have studied and been stimulated toward further research by the extraordinary range of his scientific work: hundreds of profound papers and several books dealing with theoretical topics in consumer behavior, business cycles, public finance, international trade, linear programming, and other technical subjects. In all these fields, Samuelson's originality has been evidenced by his ability to develop sophisticated applications of economic concepts through the use of advanced mathematics.

For example, among his many classic publications is a mathematical essay on the interaction of the multiplier and the accelerator—an important topic of macroeconomic theory. Samuelson wrote this celebrated article when he was a graduate student; it was initially prepared as a term paper for a seminar course in business cycles under Professor Alvin Hansen. The article reflected Samuelson's early interest in the important concept of stability.

In the *Foundations*, which immediately established his reputation as a highly creative mathematical economist, he presented a systematic analysis of static and dynamic economic theory describing (in terms of systems of mathematical equations) the "state" of an economic system in equilibrium, and the process or path of adjustment from one state to another. He then linked statics and dynamics by what he called the *correspondence principle*—a proposition which demonstrates that in order for comparative statics (the comparison of equilibrium positions in static states) to be meaningful, it is first necessary to develop a dynamic analysis of stability.

In general, Paul Samuelson's scientific contributions—developed in precise mathematical rather than literary form—have greatly deepened our understanding of how the economic system works. He has shown the general applicability of the concept of maximization, subject to constraints, to many branches of economics. For example, the consumer tries to maximize his satisfactions, subject to such constraints as his income and the prices of the goods he buys; the business firm tries to maximize its profit, subject to the constraints of technology, resource limitations, and costs; and government tries to maximize net social benefits, subject to various economic (not to mention political) constraints. These and many other ideas had long been part of economics, but Samuelson revealed them in new and provocative ways. As a result, he has provided a storehouse of theoretical insights which have both stimulated and facilitated important research by others.

An Institute Professor at the Massachusetts Institute of Technology, Paul Samuelson has been on the faculty of that renowned institution since 1941. Among those who know him, it is generally acknowledged that his scholarship and wit are exceeded only by his personal helpfulness and capacity for friendship.

General equilibrium theory is based on the assumption that if, for each particular market, all participants are given such information as consumer demand schedules, resource supply schedules, production functions, and the demand for money, equilibrium forces will cause commodity and resource prices to adjust themselves in a mutually consistent manner. The entire system can then settle down in a stable equilibrium of supply and demand. Any change in the determinants affecting the price and quantity of a good or resource can, however, upset the entire system and have widespread repercussions on the equilibrium prices and quantities of all other goods and resources. These ideas empha-size the fact that in the real world there is often a significant degree of interdependence among various markets.

A GENERAL EQUILIBRIUM MODEL: TWO COMMODITIES

A full explanation of general equilibrium requires the use of mathematics. However, many of the basic notions can be conveyed without mathematics by a simple supply and demand analysis involving only two commodities—say, meat and fish.

In Exhibit 3, Chart (a), the intersection of the market demand curve for meat D_M and supply curve

---

Exhibit 3

General Equilibrium—A Two-commodity Model

DEMAND AND SUPPLY CURVES FOR MEAT AND FISH

In Chart (a), the demand curve for meat D_M is drawn on the assumption that the equilibrium price of fish P_F in Chart (b) is given. Similarly, in Chart (b) the demand curve for fish D_F is drawn on the assumption that the equilibrium price of meat P_M in Chart (a) is given. The supply curves of meat S_M and of fish S_F are drawn under the same assumptions.

In Chart (a), if a specific tax of T per unit is imposed on meat sellers, the supply curve shifts from S_M to S'_M to reflect the cost increase. The equilibrium price of meat

rises to P'_M and the equilibrium quantity falls to Q'_M. Consumers, therefore, substitute fish for meat, causing the demand curve for fish in Chart (b) to shift to the right from D_F to D'_F. As a result, the equilibrium price of fish increases to P'_F and the equilibrium quantity to Q'_F.

In addition to these changes, some resources (not shown in the diagrams) will move out of meat production and into fish production, causing the supply curves in both industries to shift. This process will continue until a new state of general equilibrium is reached.

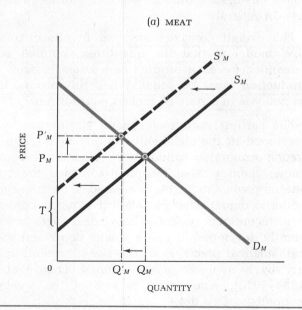

(a) MEAT

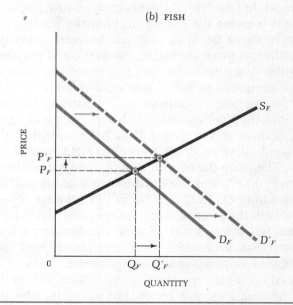

(b) FISH

---

for meat S_M determines the equilibrium price of meat P_M and equilibrium quantity of meat Q_M. Similarly in Chart (b), the intersection of the market demand and supply curves of fish, D_F and S_F, determines the equilibrium price of fish P_F and equilibrium quantity of fish Q_F.

Before considering any change, it is important to note some of the assumptions underlying the curves. Basically, each curve in any one market is drawn on the assumption that the equilibrium price of the commodity in the other market remains constant. For example, in Chart (a) the demand curve for meat assumes that the price of fish in Chart (b) is at its equilibrium level P_F. Similarly in Chart (b) the demand curve for fish assumes that the equilibrium price of meat in Chart (a) is at its equilibrium level P_M. Other assumptions not evident from the charts are also made. In particular, it is assumed that (a) consumer preferences for commodities are given, (b) the stock of resources available for production is fixed, and (c) the techniques of production (the production functions for commodities) are given. These conditions are among the basic determinants of the system we are describing. Therefore a change in any one of them will disturb the existing equilibrium pattern.

Effect of a Specific Tax

Now suppose that a *specific tax*—a tax per unit of commodity—is imposed by government on sellers of meat. In Chart (a), if the tax is equal to T per unit, it will increase the cost to suppliers by shifting the supply curve from S_M to S'_M. This will cause the equilibrium price of meat to rise to P'_M and the equilibrium quantity to fall to Q'_M. Since the price of meat compared to fish is now *relatively* higher than before the tax, consumers will substitute fish for meat in their consumption patterns. This will cause an increase in the demand for fish—a shift of the demand curve in Chart (b) to the right from D_F to D'_F. Therefore the equilibrium price of fish will rise from P_F to P'_F and the equilibrium quantity will increase from Q_F to Q'_F. As a result of the tax, therefore, both the price of meat and the price of fish have risen, but the quantity of meat produced and consumed has decreased while the quantity of fish produced and consumed has increased.

Various other repercussions which are not shown in the diagrams may occur. For example, after the tax fewer resources are needed to produce the smaller quantity of meat, while more resources are needed to produce the larger quantity of fish. Therefore the price of resources and their employment in meat production will decline, while the price of resources and their employment in fish production will rise. As a result, some resources will move out of meat production and into fish production. As this happens, the supply curves in the two industries will shift, causing market prices and quantities to change. In addition, the change in relative resource prices will cause shifts in the pattern of income distribution, and this will have further repercussions on the demands for the two commodities. This adjustment process continues until the system is once again in general equilibrium.

INTERDEPENDENCE AND THE CIRCULAR FLOW

The interdependence that exists between markets in the economy can be extended beyond what is shown in the simple model of Exhibit 3. However, the model would then be considerably more complicated. It is sufficient, therefore, to convey the overall nature of the interrelationships by means of a familiar circular-flow diagram. This is done in Exhibit 4.

The model is self-explanatory. Note that it lists the conditions that are assumed to be given or fixed in the household and business sectors, and that it emphasizes the interdependence between households, businesses, product markets, and factor markets. In general:

The overall concept conveyed by the circular-flow model is that the quantities supplied and demanded for each product and for each factor of production must be equal. When this occurs, the economy is in a state of general equilibrium.

The earliest notion of general equilibrium was developed in the eighteenth century by a group of French economists called the physiocrats. Foremost among them was an economist named Francois Quesnay who, in 1758, presented a circular-flow model to depict what he called the "natural order" of an economic system. These ideas were subsequently developed in much greater depth and with mathematical precision in the late nineteenth century by a Swiss-French economist, Leon Walras (1834–1910), who ranks as one of the greatest economists of all time.

Exhibit 4

**Economic Interdependence—General Equilibrium
and the Circular Flow**

Households and businesses are linked through the product markets where goods and services are exchanged and through the resource markets where the factors of production are exchanged. The economy is in a state of general equilibrium when the quantities supplied and demanded for goods and services and for factors of production are equal.

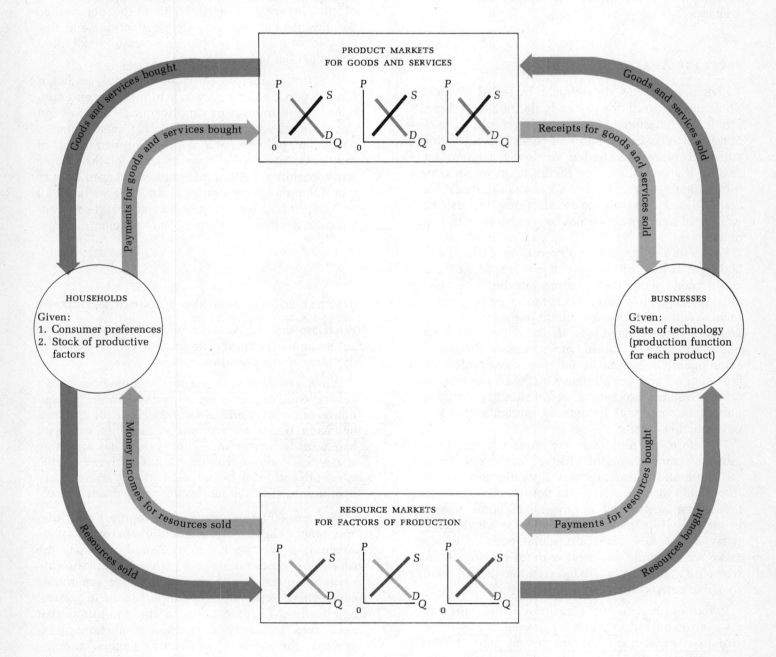

Welfare Economics

The concept of general equilibrium provides us with an overview of a perfectly competitive economy. But what are the main characteristics of such an economy? Is perfect competition "good" or "bad"? In answering these questions, we will gain some insights into what is known as *welfare economics*—a branch of economic theory concerned with the development of principles for maximizing social welfare.

PARETO OPTIMALITY

To begin with, what do we mean by social welfare? The concept cannot be precisely defined, and therefore it is impossible to measure. As a result, we cannot assert objectively that any particular economic situation represents higher or lower welfare for society than another. One of the main reasons for this difficulty is that *we cannot make interpersonal comparisons of utility* or satisfactions; that is, the welfare of one person cannot be compared with that of another.

For example, as a rational consumer, I would feel better off if I could keep all of my income so that I could spend more for consumption; but as a good citizen I might feel better off if I gave up part of my income (through taxes and charitable contributions) and thereby consumed less, so that others who were not as fortunate as I could consume more. Similarly, some people argue that as a nation of consumers we are better off keeping all of our income for ourselves; others contend, however, that we should contribute part of our national income as foreign aid to less developed countries.

Therefore, even though we cannot make interpersonal comparisons of utility, such comparisons are made all the time. Indeed, it would be virtually impossible to have any social policy without them, for almost any social policy makes some people better off while making others worse off. Ideally, what we usually want are social policies which make some people better off without making others worse off. This involves what economists and other social scientists call "Pareto optimality."

Pareto optimality is a condition which exists in a social organization when no change can be made which will make at least one person better off (in his own estimation) without making someone else worse off.

This concept, named after a famous Italian-Swiss sociologist and economist, Vilfredo Pareto (1848–1923), leads to two important principles:

1. Any social action which benefits at least one person without harming someone else will clearly increase social welfare, and therefore should be undertaken.

2. The effect on social welfare of any action which benefits some while harming others—the *numbers* of people are immaterial—cannot be determined because we cannot compare satisfactions and dissatisfactions among people—we cannot make interpersonal comparisons of utility.

The first principle provides a useful guide for formulating public policies, while the second contains some interesting implications. The second principle tells us, for example, that even though a particular policy—such as the imprisonment of criminals—benefits a large majority of the people while harming a small minority, we cannot be sure that adherence to it results in an increase in social welfare. At best we can only assume that it does, but we cannot prove it in any objective, scientific way.

GENERAL EQUILIBRIUM AND ECONOMIC EFFICIENCY

What are the implications of Pareto optimality for an economic system? The answer can be stated in the form of a proposition:

When a perfectly competitive economy achieves a general equilibrium of prices and quantities, no economic organism (individual, household, or firm) can be made better off without some other organism being made worse off. The system has therefore attained a Pareto optimum—it has achieved an *efficient* allocation of resources. (NOTE: Certain qualifications to this statement are pointed out below.)

The proof of this proposition requires considerably more advanced economic theory than is covered in this book, but you can appreciate the sense of it on the basis of what was learned in previous chapters. For example, suppose a perfectly competitive economy has settled down in general equilibrium. Keeping in mind the conditions that are "given"—namely, the pattern of consumer preferences, the stock of productive factors, and the state of technology—what are the main characteristics of the resulting state of balance?

Efficiency in Consumption

In the household sector, each consuming unit spends its income on the goods and services it wants most, given the prices it must pay. It therefore allocates its income so as to maximize total utility or satisfactions. In terms of Pareto optimality, this means that society has achieved efficiency in consumption because no transfer of commodities can be made between any two consuming units which will make one consuming unit better off without making the other worse off.

Efficiency in Production

In the business sector, as you learned in the study of perfect competition, each firm in the long run ends up producing in the output market at the level of production where the following conditions apply:

1. $MC = P$. This means that the value of the last unit of the good to the consumer (measured by the price he pays for the last unit, which is equal to the price he pays for any unit) is equal to the value of the resources used to produce that unit.

2. $MC = ATC = LRAC$. This means that the firm is producing the optimum output with the optimum-size plant, and therefore is allocating all its resources in an optimum manner.

At the same time, the firm also achieves equilibrium in the input market by hiring each factor of production up to the point where the price paid to the factor is equal to the value of what it contributes (the price of the factor being equal to its marginal revenue product).

What do these equilibrium conditions mean in terms of Pareto optimality? Fundamentally they tell us that society has achieved efficiency in production by producing the largest possible volume of output for its given collection of resources. Therefore, no transfer of resources can be made between any two commodities which will increase the production of one commodity without decreasing the production of the other. In other words, the economy is on its production-possibilities curve instead of at some point inside it.

Overall Efficiency and Full Employment

When a perfectly competitive economy is in general equilibrium, it has achieved not only efficiency in consumption and in production, but overall effi-

ciency as well. As reflected by the $MC = P$ condition described above, the value which consumers place on any unit of a commodity is equal to the value of society's resources used to produce that unit. Further, in the product and in the resource markets the amount of a commodity or of a factor of production supplied is equal to the amount demanded at the existing price. Therefore there are no surpluses or shortages in any market, and since the economy is on its production-possibilities curve there is full employment of all resources.

General equilibrium and economic efficiency thus go hand in hand. It is particularly interesting, however, to realize the remarkable way in which these end results come about:

All participants in the economy—consumers, businessmen, resource owners—acting *independently* in their own self-interest and without direction from government, make millions of market decisions daily which determine what, how, and for whom goods shall be produced. Yet the economic system, because it is perfectly competitive, is guided by Adam Smith's "invisible hand" toward general equilibrium and economic efficiency—an end result which, as Smith pointed out, is "no part of anyone's intention."

IMPLICATIONS FOR SOCIAL WELFARE

Should we conclude from this that perfect competition leads to the best of all possible worlds? As pointed out above, when a perfectly competitive economy is in general equilibrium, it has attained a Pareto optimum—a situation in which no person can be made better off (in his own estimation) without someone else being made worse off. However, there are some qualifications. The more important ones have already been discussed in several earlier chapters. Therefore, it is sufficient to summarize them briefly at this time.

1. *Social costs and social benefits.* Competitive prices tend to reflect private costs and private benefits while they may exclude some social costs and social benefits. Environmental pollution arising from production is a typical example of a cost to society which may not be included in a manufacturer's private costs. Likewise, flood control and conservation practices undertaken by a seller provide illustrations of benefits that accrue to many people other than those who buy the producer's product. Therefore:

To the extent that *all* social costs and benefits are not incorporated in firms' activities, general equilibrium will not provide an optimum allocation of society's resources.

2. *Income distribution and equity.* In a system of perfect competition, each factor of production is paid according to the "contributive standard." That is, each factor is paid what it is "worth" as measured by what it contributes to total output. This is known as the *marginal productivity theory of income distribution.* According to this principle, a man who is twice as productive as another is paid twice as much. But whether or not this is a just or equitable standard of income distribution is a normative rather than positive question which each society

---

Leaders in Economics

MARIE ESPRIT LEON WALRAS

1834–1910

VILFREDO PARETO

1848–1923

The "Lausanne School"

Walras ranks as one of the most significant figures in the history of economic thought. His fame rests on his formulation of the theory of general equilibrium, which he developed rigorously by the use of mathematics. He thus became one of the founders of an approach to economics known as mathematical economics which has flourished to this day.

Born and educated in France, Walras studied to be a mining engineer but left engineering school before his training was completed to become a free-lance journalist. In this capacity he wrote many articles advocating economic, especially agrarian, reform. In 1870 he was appointed to the chair of political economy at the University of Lausanne, Switzerland, where he remained until 1892.

A few years after his arrival at Lausanne, Walras published his great work, *Elements of Pure Economics.* In this book he showed how, given the mathematical equations of demand and supply at equilibrium, and the *numéraire* (the accounting unit) derived from them, the solution of the problem of general equilibrium is determinate; that is, there is a set of simultaneous equations the number of which equals the number of unknowns, with the number of prices to be ascertained. The problem, however, is determinate in a formal sense only. The necessary data cannot be obtained, and the number of simultaneous equations which would have to be solved is virtually infinite. Nevertheless, this does not destroy the value of general equilibrium theory, for the virtue of the concept lies in the precise way in which it demonstrates the mutual interdependence of economic phenomena.

Walras was succeeded at Lausanne by Vilfredo Pareto, an Italian scholar who abandoned a career as an engineer

Charles Phelps Cushing.   Historical Pictures Service—Chicago.

to devote time to scholarly pursuits. Heavily influenced by Walras, Pareto contributed significantly to the literature of pure economics, and his expositions in mathematical economics are even today considered among the most elegant and erudite available. In his major work, *Manual of Political Economy,* he presented economic theory in an aridly pure, static, and general way in the sense that it can be applied to any economic system. Like that of Walras, Pareto's formulation of theory is one of general equilibrium under static conditions. However, Pareto was also concerned with the problem of how to maximize total satisfactions in an economy. He developed the concept now commonly referred to as Pareto optimality—a notion which is fundamental to modern welfare economics. In passing, it should be noted that Pareto also made notable contributions to sociology. In fact, his reputation in that field is as strong as it is in economics.

Together, Walras and Pareto comprise what is known as the "Lausanne School" of economic thought. The influence of this school on subsequent writers—especially in mathematical economics, general equilibrium theory, and welfare economics, has been enormous. Indeed, modern microeconomic theory owes much of its present content to the pioneering scientific work first done at Lausanne.

---

must answer for itself. Some might argue, for example, that it is "just" for a family of six to be paid twice as much as a family of three—regardless of their productivities. Therefore:

<u>To the extent that society regards the contributive standard as unjust, general equilibrium will not provide an equitable distribution of the economy's income.</u>

CONCLUSION: NORMS OF ECONOMIC EFFICIENCY

You can now appreciate more fully the role played by modern welfare economics. In broad terms, welfare economics deals with the normative aspects of microeconomics. Welfare economics is not concerned with what the perfect world would look like, but with the changes that may be undertaken to improve the well-being of consumers and producers. It does this by providing us with a norm expressed in terms of economic efficiency, thus enabling us to state unambiguously whether one equilibrium position is better or worse than another.

From what we now know about microeconomics, it is clear that perfect competition, by means of Smith's "invisible hand," leads (with some qualifications) to an optimum allocation of society's resources. Other types of market structures—such as unregulated monopoly, monopolistic competition, and oligopoly—do not. This suggests that the norm provided by welfare economics can serve as a guide for government intervention in markets—either through taxes, subsidies, direct regulation, or other means—to correct for costs and gains which result when the norm is violated. In other words, in markets where supply and demand forces serve efficiently as mechanisms for allocating society's resources, no intervention by government is needed. But when markets fail to perform efficiently, certain types of intervention may be called for. The nature and effects of various kinds of intervention pose many interesting problems that will occupy our attention in the following chapters.

SUMMARY OF IMPORTANT IDEAS

1. The concept of equilibrium is of fundamental importance in economics. An equilibrium position may be stable, unstable, or neutral—in a static or in a dynamic sense.

2. A static model provides a "snapshot" of the essential features of an economic phenomenon at an instant of time, whereas a dynamic model provides a "motion picture" over a period of time. Although static analysis encompasses most of economic theory, many important problems cannot be analyzed without the use of dynamics.

3. General equilibrium, as distinguished from partial equilibrium, emphasizes the interdependence that exists between markets and sectors of the economy. The notion of general equilibrium can be depicted by a circular-flow diagram.

4. The concept of general equilibrium goes hand in hand with the science of welfare economics. The latter is concerned with the development of principles for maximizing social welfare. Thus when a perfectly competitive economy achieves a general equilibrium of prices and quantities, it has attained a Pareto optimum—an efficient allocation of resources—and therefore has maximized social welfare. Some qualifications to this conclusion may exist, however, depending on such factors as the inclusion of social costs and social benefits in firms' activities, and the extent to which society regards the contributive standard of income distribution as inequitable.

FOR DISCUSSION

1. *Terms and concepts to review:*

equilibrium	general equilibrium
static model	theory
comparative statics	welfare economics
dynamic model	Pareto optimum
stable equilibrium	marginal productivity
partial equilibrium	theory of income
theory	distribution

2. Which is more important—the stability of an equilibrium position or its location? Explain.

3. You have already learned the concepts of *demand price* and *supply price* in previous chapters. (To refresh your memory, look up their meanings in the Dictionary at the back of the book.) Using these notions, and thinking in terms of supply and demand curves, formulate definitions of stable and unstable *quantity* equilibrium. (HINT: You may find it helpful first to formulate definitions of stable and unstable *price* equilibrium in terms of quantity supplied and quantity demanded. Then use a parallel procedure to define stable and unstable quantity equilibrium in terms of demand price and supply price.)

4. In terms of supply and demand curves, can a price equilibrium be stable for an upward movement and unstable or neutral for a downward movement, and vice versa? Is the same true for a quantity equilibrium in terms of a leftward or rightward movement? Explain.

5. If the world economy were perfectly competitive, a tariff (tax on imports) would result in a misallocation of resources and a reduction in net social welfare for the world community. Do you agree? Why?

6. Nations sometimes employ rationing as a means of distributing scarce goods. Usually, consumers are given ration coupons entitling them to purchase, say, 1 pound of meat and 1 pound of fish per week. In this way, an equal amount of each good is assigned to each consumer. Is this "fair"? Can you propose an alternative method of rationing which is more equitable?

7. A famous economist, Professor Abba Lerner, has argued that since we do not know the actual distribution of income which will maximize satisfaction, it must be assumed that an equal distribution of income out of any given level of national income would most likely maximize satisfaction. Evaluate this argument.

Case

The Automobile Industry: Demand Elasticity and Price Reduction

Union leaders, government economists, and various other people have contended from time to time that since the overall demand for automobiles is relatively elastic, an across-the-board price cut of, say, 10 percent, would increase the sale of automobiles and therefore the profits of the companies. These arguments are particularly prominent during periods of recession, since an increase in the sale of a product like automobiles would have significant beneficial effects on other industries, for example, steel, rubber, and so forth, and would thereby help boost the level of employment, national income, and economic activity in general.

On the face of it, this argument may seem plausible. Upon further analysis, however, it becomes apparent that there are actually two sets of elasticities to be considered:

1. *Demand elasticity*, since there is a question of the effect which the price reduction will have on demand and thus on revenues.

2. *Cost elasticity*, since there is a question of the effect which the increased sales volume will have on production and thus on costs.

Obviously, both questions would have to be considered by automobile manufacturers if they were contemplating a general price reduction. However, those who have suggested such price reductions have usually considered only the first question and have completely neglected the second question.

Economists who have conducted demand analyses for new automobiles have estimated price elasticities of demand ranging from 0.5 to 1.5. Obviously, the higher the coefficient of elasticity, the greater the percentage increase in quantity demanded which will result from a given percentage decrease in price. Thus, if we assume an elasticity as high as 1.5, this means that a 1 percent decrease in price would produce a 1.5 percent increase in quantity demanded, and hence a larger total revenue for the seller than he would obtain with a lower elasticity coefficient. Therefore, let us agree on this liberal elasticity measure of 1.5, and proceed to explore the question of whether it pays, even with such a high elasticity, for an automobile manufacturer to reduce the list price of a line of cars by, say, $100.

We must assume because of the nature of the automobile industry that a price reduction by one producer will be met by his competitors. (Why?) Therefore, we are not considering a relative price advantage but rather the effect of a general price change by all sellers. In addition, the following conditions may also be specified:

Average price of the line of cars	$2,500 per car
Expected sales volume @ $2,500 per car	1,000,000 cars
Average total cost of the line of cars	$2,300 per car
Total variable cost	$1,840,000,000

QUESTIONS

1. *What is the change in total revenue, if any, resulting from a price reduction of $100?*

2. *What will profit be before the price reduction?*

3. *Find total fixed cost, average fixed cost, and average variable cost before the price reduction.*

4. *What will profit be after the price reduction?*

5. The price reduction of $100 has reduced revenues per car by $100. How much did it change the cost per car? What will average total cost be at the new sales volume?

6. What do you conclude from your calculations?

7. What is the proportion of total variable cost to total cost? Total fixed cost to total cost? Are these proportions realistic?

8. "In general, the higher the level of total fixed cost relative to total cost (or the lower the level of total variable cost relative to total cost), the lower the price elasticity of demand must be in order to justify a price reduction, and vice versa." True or false? Why?

9. The following special formula (based on certain assumed straight-line relationships) may be used to determine the price elasticity of demand that is needed for a given price reduction, leaving profits unimpaired, when the respective ratios of fixed and variable cost to total cost within the expected volume range are known.

Q = Percentage increase of output quantity required

P = Price decrease in dollars

$\overline{N}$ = Net profit per unit at the old price (read: "N-bar")

$\overline{C}$ = Cost per unit (i.e., average total cost) at the old price (read: "C-bar")

V/C = Ratio of total variable cost to total cost

$$Q = \frac{P}{\overline{N} - P + [1 - (V/C)]\,\overline{C}}$$

The elasticity coefficient is then

$$\text{Elasticity} = \frac{Q(\overline{N} + \overline{C})}{P}$$

How much would the elasticity have to be in order to justify a price reduction? How does your answer compare with measures of demand elasticity for automobiles that have been estimated by various scholars? Interpret your result.

10. What conclusion do you draw as to the advisability of a price reduction in order to increase the sale of automobiles?

PART 7

Domestic Economic
Problems

CHAPTER 30

Business and Government

CHAPTER PREVIEW

What is the nature of the "monopoly problem" in the United States?

What are the major laws that seek to prevent monopoly and to maintain competition in our economy? How zealously are these laws enforced?

What methods have firms used to monopolize markets? What have been the major court cases dealing with monopolization and related activities?

Is our economy "monopolized" at the present time? If so, what is the extent of monopolization, and what should be done about it?

Adam Smith remarked in a famous passage in the *Wealth of Nations*:

> People of the same trade seldom meet together, even for merriment and diversion, but the conversation ends in a conspiracy against the public, or in some contrivance to raise prices. It is impossible indeed to prevent such meetings, by any law which either could be executed, or would be consistent with liberty and justice. But though the law cannot hinder people of the same trade from sometimes assembling together, it ought to do nothing to facilitate such assemblies; much less to render them necessary.

According to Smith, competition among businessmen is not a "natural" form of behavior; given the opportunity, businessmen would prefer to seek ways of avoiding competition if they could strengthen their market positions by doing so.

The history of American business suggests that this is indeed the case. As a result, the American government has, since the late nineteenth century, been engaged in constructing a body of laws and policies to assure that competition in our economy is at least maintained if not enhanced. This chapter sketches the main features of these laws, notes the interesting ways in which they have been applied in some exciting court cases, and evaluates the chief economic issues pertaining to problems of competition and monopoly in our society.

Big Business and the Monopoly Problem

In economic theory, a market is said to be monopolized when it consists of a single firm producing a product for which there are no close substitutes.

This narrow definition is usually adequate for analyzing market structures, but when it comes to matters of public policy, economists, government officials, and judges in courts of law take a much broader view: They regard a market as being monopolized if it is dominated by one or a few firms—that is, if it is "oligopolized." The automobile, aluminum, chemical, and steel industries, as well as many others in the American economy, are notable examples. In each of these industries the sales of two, three, or four large firms account for a major share of the total market, leaving a relatively minor share for smaller competitors to divide among themselves. According to this interpretation, big businesses like General Motors, Alcoa, du Pont, and U.S. Steel, as well as their chief competitors, qualify as "monopolies."

SOME PROS AND CONS OF MONOPOLY

The charges against big-business monopolies and the arguments in defense of them have been debated for decades. Among the chief objections are that: (a) they maximize profit by restricting output and charging higher prices than they would if they were more competitive, thereby misallocating society's resources and contributing to inequality in income distribution; (b) they retard economic progress and technological advance because they are protected from the pressures of competition; and (c) they exert disproportionate influences at all levels of government, giving rise to an "industrial-political complex" which favors big business at the expense of the rest of society.

Arguments in defense of big-business monopolies assert that: (a) they are more effectively competitive than the numbers of firms alone indicate, since there is rivalry among particular products in specific markets (e.g., aluminum versus copper, steel, plastics), as well as countervailing power on the opposite side of the market exerted by monopolistic sellers of resources; (b) they permit mass-production economies at lower unit costs and prices than would be possible with large numbers of small firms; (c) they have the financial ability to support extensive research and development; and (d) they have the ethical and moral sense not to exploit their monopoly power.

There are varying degrees of truth and falsity in all of these statements, and one must analyze the facts in each case before judging the relative merits of the arguments.

Reactions to Monopoly: The Antitrust Laws

The period 1879–1904 saw the first great *merger movement* in American history. During these years, an unprecedented number of firms expanded by combining or merging with others, thereby forming new single business units with huge investments, capacities, and outputs. These new business organizations were called monopolies or "trusts" and in reaction to them and to subsequent economic developments Congress has passed a body of legislation known as the "antitrust laws."

The *antitrust laws* passed since 1890 commit the government to preventing monopoly and maintaining competition. There are also antitrust laws in almost every state in the country, but these are largely ineffectual and spasmodically enforced, because states are powerless to control agreements or combinations in major industries whose activities extend into interstate commerce. This weakness, coupled with inadequate funds, has left the task of maintaining competition via antitrust law enforcement almost entirely to the federal government. Thus it is the federal antitrust laws that will be of concern to us here. These laws include the Sherman Antitrust Act, the Clayton Antitrust Act, the Federal Trade Commission Act, the Robinson-Patman Act, the Wheeler-Lea Act, and the Celler Antimerger Act.

THE SHERMAN ACT (1890)

The *Sherman Antitrust Act* was the first attempt by the federal government to regulate the growth of monopoly. The provisions of the law were concise (probably too concise) and to the point. The act declared as illegal:

1. Every contract, combination, or conspiracy in restraint of trade which occurs in interstate or foreign commerce

2. Any monopolization or attempts to monopolize, or conspiracy with others in an attempt to monopolize, any portion of trade in interstate or foreign commerce

Violations of the act were made punishable by fines and/or imprisonment and persons injured by violations could sue for triple damages. (See Box 1.)

The act was surrounded by a cloud of uncertainty by failing to state precisely which kinds of actions were prohibited. Also, no special agency existed to

Box 1

"The Bosses of the Senate"

This classic 1889 sketch by Joseph Keppler depicts the public's attitude toward the Senate on the trust problem.

Shortly thereafter, as a result of mounting pressure, hearings began on the Sherman Antitrust Act.

THE BOSSES OF THE SENATE

Library of Congress, from *Puck,* 1889.

enforce the law until 1903, when the Antitrust Division of the U.S. Department of Justice was established under an Assistant Attorney General.

THE CLAYTON AND FEDERAL TRADE COMMISSION ACTS (1914)

In 1914, in order to put some teeth into the Sherman Act, Congress passed the Clayton Act and the Federal Trade Commission Act. Aimed at practices of *unfair competition*—deceptive, dishonest, and injurious methods of competition—the *Clayton Antitrust Act* was concerned with four specific areas: price discrimination, exclusive and tying contracts, intercorporate stockholdings, and interlocking directorates.

1. *Price discrimination.* For sellers to discriminate in prices by charging different prices to different buyers for the same good is *illegal*. However, such discrimination is permissible where there are differences in the grade, quality, or quantity of the commodity sold; where the lower prices make due allowances for cost differences in selling or transportation; and where the lower prices are offered in good faith to meet competition. Illegality exists where, according to the law, the effect is "to substantially lessen competition or tend to create a monopoly."

2. *Exclusive and tying contracts.* For sellers to lease, sell, or contract for the sale of commodities on condition that the lessee or purchaser not use or deal in the commodity of a competitor is *illegal* if such exclusive or tying contracts "substantially lessen competition or tend to create a monopoly."

3. *Intercorporate stockholdings.* For corporations engaged in commerce to acquire the shares of a competing corporation, or the stocks of two or more

corporations competing with each other, is *illegal* if such intercorporate stockholdings "substantially lessen competition or tend to create a monopoly."

4. *Interlocking directorates.* For corporations engaged in commerce to have the same individual on two or more boards of directors is an interlocking directorate, and such directorships are *illegal* if the corporations are competitive and if any one has capital, surplus, and undivided profits in excess of $1 million.

Thus:

Price discrimination, exclusive and tying contracts, and intercorporate stockholdings were not declared by the Clayton Act to be absolutely illegal, but rather, in the words of the law, only when their effects "may be to substantially lessen competition or tend to create a monopoly." On interlocking directorates, however, the law made no such qualification: The fact of the interlock itself is illegal, and the government need not find that the arrangement results in a reduction in competition.

The *Federal Trade Commission Act* served primarily as a general supplement to the Clayton Act by stating broadly and simply that "unfair methods of competition in commerce are hereby declared unlawful." But what significant contribution to monopoly control was made by these laws?

Essentially, both the Clayton Act and the Federal Trade Commission Act were directed toward the prevention of abuses, whereas the Sherman Act emphasized the punishment of abusers. To be sure, the practices that were prohibited in the two later laws could well have been attacked under the Sherman Act as conspiracies in restraint of trade or as attempts to monopolize, but now the nature of the problem was brought more sharply into focus. Moreover, under the Federal Trade Commission Act, the *Federal Trade Commission* (FTC) was established as a government antitrust agency with federal funds appropriated to it for the purpose of attacking unfair competitive practices in commerce.

The FTC is also authorized under the act to safeguard the public by preventing the dissemination of false and misleading advertising of foods, drugs, cosmetics, and therapeutic devices used in the diagnosis, prevention, or treatment of disease. It thus supplements in many ways the activities of the Food and Drug Administration which, under the Food, Drug, and Cosmetic Act (1938), outlaws adulteration and misbranding of foods, drugs, devices, and cosmetics moving in interstate commerce.

THE ROBINSON-PATMAN ACT (1936)

Frequently referred to as the "Chain Store Act," the *Robinson-Patman Act* was passed for the purpose of providing economic protection to independent retailers and wholesalers, such as grocers and druggists, from "unfair discriminations" by large sellers attained "because of their tremendous purchasing power." The law was an outgrowth of the increasing competition faced by independents when chain stores and mass distributors developed after World War I. Supporters of the bill contended that the lower prices charged by large organizations were attributable less to lower costs than to sheer weight of bargaining power, which enabled the large organizations to obtain unfair and unjustified concessions from their suppliers. The act was thus a response to the cries of independents who demanded that the freedom of suppliers to discriminate be more strictly limited.

The act, which amended Section 2 of the Clayton Act relating to price discrimination, contained the following essential provisions:

1. The payment of brokerage fees where no independent broker is employed is *illegal*. This was intended to eliminate the practice of some chains of demanding the regular brokerage fee as a discount when they purchased direct from manufacturers. The argument posed was that such chains obtained the discount by their sheer bargaining power and thereby gained an unfair advantage over smaller independents that had to use and pay for brokerage services.

2. The making of concessions by sellers, such as manufacturers, to buyers, such as wholesalers and retailers, is *illegal* unless such concessions are made to all buyers on proportionally equal terms. This provision was aimed at preventing advertising and promotional allowances from being granted to large-scale buyers without allowances being made to small competing buyers on proportionally equal terms.

3. Other forms of discrimination, such as quantity discounts, are *illegal* where they substantially lessen competition or tend to create a monopoly, either among sellers or among buyers. However, price discrimination is not illegal if the differences in prices make "due allowances" for differences in cost or if offered "in good faith to meet an equally low price of a competitor." But even where discounts can be justified by lower costs, the FTC is empowered to fix quantity limits beyond which discounts may not be

granted, if it believes that such discounts would be "unjustly discriminatory or promotive of monopoly in any line of commerce."

4. It is *illegal* to give or to receive a larger discount than that made available to competitors purchasing the same goods in equal quantities. Also, it is *illegal* to charge lower prices in one locality than in another for the same goods, or to sell at "unreasonably low prices," where either of these practices is aimed at "destroying competition or eliminating a competitor."

THE WHEELER-LEA ACT (1938)

An amendment to part of the Federal Trade Commission Act, the *Wheeler-Lea Act* was passed for the purpose of providing consumers, rather than just business competitors, with protection against unfair practices. The act makes *illegal* "unfair or deceptive acts or practices" in interstate commerce. Thus, a consumer who may be injured by an unfair trade practice is, before the law, of equal concern with the merchant who may be injured by an unfair competitive practice. The act also defines "false advertising" as "an advertisement other than labeling which is misleading in a material respect," and it makes the definition applicable to advertisement of foods, drugs, curative devices, and cosmetics.

THE CELLER ANTIMERGER ACT (1950)

The *Celler Antimerger Act* is an extension of Section 7 of the Clayton Act relating to intercorporate stockholdings. The Clayton Act, as stated earlier, made it illegal for corporations to acquire the stock of competing corporations. But that law, the FTC argued, left a loophole through which monopolistic mergers could be effected by a corporation acquiring the *assets* of a competing corporation, or by first acquiring the stock and, by voting or granting of proxies, acquiring the assets. Moreover, the Supreme Court in several cases held that such mergers were not illegal under the Clayton Act if a corporation used its stock purchases to acquire the assets before the FTC's complaint was issued or before the Commission had issued its final order banning the stock acquisition.

The Antimerger Act plugged the loophole in the Clayton Act by making it illegal for a corporation to acquire the stock *or assets* of a competing corporation where the effect may be "substantially to lessen competition, or to tend to create a monopoly." The

Celler Act thus bans all types of mergers—*horizontal* (plants producing similar products under one ownership, such as steel mills), *vertical* (plants in different stages of production, integrated under one ownership), and *conglomerate* or *circular* (dissimilar plants and unrelated product lines)—provided the Commission can show that the effects *may* substantially lessen competition or tend toward monopoly.

It should be noted, however, that the intent of Congress in passing the Celler Act was that there be a maintenance of competition. Accordingly, the act was intended to apply to mergers between large firms or of large with small firms, but not to mergers among small firms which may be undertaken to strengthen their competitive position.

ENFORCEMENT OF THE ANTITRUST LAWS

In general, the antitrust laws are applied on a *case-by-case* basis. That is, an order or decision resulting from an action is not applicable to all of industry, but only to the defendants in the particular case. Cases may originate in the complaints of injured businessmen, suggestions made by other government agencies, or in the research of the Antitrust Division of the Department of Justice, since it is this organization which may bring into the federal courts criminal or civil suits against violators of the law. About 90 percent of the cases, it has been estimated, arise from complaints issued by injured parties, and at present most of the ensuing investigations are conducted by the Federal Bureau of Investigation (FBI). The Federal Trade Commission Act, on the other hand, is enforced by the FTC and, when their orders become final, through suits brought by the Department of Justice. Finally, with respect to the Clayton Act, both the FTC and the Justice Department have concurrent jurisdiction in its enforcement, and in practice it is usually a matter of which agency gets there first.

Section 14 of the Clayton Act fixes the responsibility for the behavior of a corporation on its officers and directors and makes them subject to the penalties of fine or imprisonment for violating the laws. Under the Sherman Act, the fine is limited to $50,000, but fines have actually been pyramided into several hundred thousand dollars in a single case by exacting the $50,000 on each count of an indictment (e.g., monopolizing, attempting to monopolize, conspiring, and restraining trade) and by imposing the fine on each of the defendants in a suit (e.g., a trade association, each member of the association, and each of the directors and officers of the member firms). Other penalties are also possible as provided in other acts.

Businessmen who want to avoid risking violation of the law may consult with the Justice Department by presenting their proposed plans for combination or other particular practices. If the plans appear to be legal, the department may commit itself not to institute future criminal proceedings, but it will reserve the right to institute civil action if competition is later restrained. The purpose of a civil suit is not to punish, but to restore competition by providing remedies. Typically, three classes of remedies are employed:

1. *Dissolution, divestiture,* or *divorcement* provisions may be used. Examples include an order to dissolve a trade association or combination, to sell intercorporate stockholdings, or to dispose of ownership in other assets. The purpose of these actions is to break up a monopolistic organization into smaller but more competitors.

2. An *injunction* may be issued. This is a court order requiring that the defendant refrain from certain business practices, or perhaps take a particular action that will increase rather than reduce competition.

3. A *consent decree* may be employed. This is usually worked out between the defendant and the Justice Department without a court trial. The defendant in this instance does not admit guilt, but agrees nevertheless to abide by the rules of business behavior set down in the decree. This device is now one of the chief instruments employed in the enforcement of the Sherman and Clayton Acts.

Finally, the laws are also enforced through private suits. Under the Sherman Act, injured parties (individuals, corporations, or states) may sue for treble damages including court costs. Under the Clayton Act, a private plaintiff may also sue for an injunction—a restraining order—whenever he is threatened by loss or damage resulting from some firm's violation of the antitrust laws. Under the Federal Trade Commission Act, the FTC is authorized to prevent unfair business practices as well as to exercise, concurrently with the Justice Department, enforcement of the prohibited provisions of the Clayton Act as amended by the Robinson-Patman Act. Accordingly, the FTC has taken action against agreements that have tended to curtail output, fix prices, and divide markets among firms.

EXEMPTIONS AND INTERPRETATIONS

A compact summary of the antitrust laws is presented in Exhibit 1. A few industries and economic groups are exempt from these laws. The most important ones are (a) the transport industries, including railroads, trucks, ships, and barges, which are largely subject to the control of regulatory agencies such as the Interstate Commerce Commission, and (b) labor unions. The exemption of labor unions was originally justified on the basis that they do not normally seek to monopolize markets or engage in methods of unfair competition, but seek instead to protect and enhance the position of labor. However, unions may be subjected to antitrust prosecution if

---

Exhibit 1

The Antitrust Laws in a Nutshell

1. *It is flatly illegal, without any qualification, to:*
   (a) *Enter a contract, combination, or conspiracy in restraint of trade (Sherman Act, Sec. 1)*
   (b) *Monopolize, attempt to monopolize, or combine or conspire to monopolize trade (Sherman Act, Sec. 3)*

2. *When and if the effect may be substantially to lessen competition or tend to create a monopoly, it is illegal to:*
   (a) *Acquire the stock of competing corporations (Clayton Act, Sec. 7)*
   (b) *Acquire the assets of competing corporations (Clayton Act, Sec. 7, as amended by the Antimerger Act in 1950)*
   (c) *Enter exclusive and tying contracts (Clayton Act, Sec. 3)*
   (d) *Discriminate unjustifiably among purchasers (Clayton Act, Sec. 2, as amended by Robinson-Patman Act, Sec. 1)*

3. *In general, it is also illegal to:*
   (a) *Engage in particular forms of price discrimination (Robinson-Patman Act, Sec. 1 and 3)*
   (b) *Serve as a director of competing corporations of a certain minimum size (Clayton Act, Sec. 8)*
   (c) *Use unfair methods of competition (Federal Trade Commission Act, Sec. 5)*
   (d) *Use unfair or deceptive acts or practices (Federal Trade Commission Act, Sec. 5, as amended by Wheeler-Lea Act, Sec. 3)*

Thus the laws taken as a whole are designed not only to prevent the growth of monopoly, but to maintain competition as well.

they combine with management to violate the antitrust laws.

Thus:

The Sherman Act forbade restraints of trade, monopoly, and attempts to monopolize; the Clayton Act forbade practices whose effects may be to lessen substantially the degree of competition or tend to create a monopoly; and the Federal Trade Commission Act forbade unfair methods of competition.

But though Congress succeeded in passing these laws, it failed to define, and left up to the courts to interpret in their own way, the meaning of such terms as "monopoly," "restraint of trade," "substantial lessening of competition," and "unfair competition." As a result, judicial interpretations have been crucial in determining the applications and effects of the antitrust laws. In view of this, we shall attempt to sketch briefly some of the major issues, court decisions, and leading trends that have emerged in the past few decades—confining ourselves for the most part to the years since World War II.

Restrictive Agreements—Conspiracies

The state of the law as to restrictive agreements or conspiracies of virtually any type among competitors is reasonably clear, and the courts have almost always upheld the government in such cases. In general, a *restrictive agreement* is regarded by the government as a conspiracy of firms that results in a restraint of trade among separate companies. It is usually understood to involve a direct or indirect, overt or implied, form of price fixing, output control, market sharing, or exclusion of competitors by boycotts or other coercive practices. It makes no difference whether the agreement was accomplished through a formal organization such as a trade association, informally, or even by habitual identity of behavior frequently referred to as *conscious parallel action*—identical price behavior among competitors. The effect, more than the means, is judged.

For instance, in a major case against the American Tobacco Company in 1946, the government charged that the "big three" cigarette producers exhibited striking uniformity in the prices they paid for tobacco and in the prices they charged for cigarettes, as well as in other practices. Despite the fact that not a shred of evidence was produced to indicate that a common plan had even so much as been proposed,

the Supreme Court declared that conspiracy "may be found in a course of dealings or other circumstances as well as in an exchange of words"; hence the companies were held in violation of the law.

Thus:

No secret meetings in a smoke-filled room and no signatures in blood are needed to prove the conspiracy provisions of the Sherman Act. Any type of agreement, explicit or implicit, any practice, direct or indirect, or even any action with the knowledge that others will act likewise to their mutual self-interest, is likely to be interpreted as illegal if it results in exclusion of competitors from the market, restriction of output or of purchases, division of markets, price fixing, elimination of the opportunity or incentive to compete, or coercion.

The doctrine of conscious parallel action was partially repudiated by judges in some subsequent cases. However, it still remains as a fairly significant antitrust barometer, although the doctrine has not often been employed since the American Tobacco case of 1946.

THE GREAT ELECTRICAL CONSPIRACY

In February, 1961, one of the most significant antitrust cases in the history of the United States was concluded. More than $2 million in fines were levied on the electrical equipment industry, and seven executives were jailed for terms of 30 days. Several dozen companies, including General Electric and Westinghouse, and a number of corporate officials were charged with unlawful price-fixing and dividing the market.

Though the fines were huge, it was the jail sentences that were more remarkable. For, although sending men to jail is not unheard of in antitrust cases, it is unusual—especially when the individuals are "pillars of the community."

NOTE: From 1890 to 1959 a total of about 200 people had received prison sentences for violating the Sherman Act. Most of these were union members and petty racketeers, and a few were wartime spies. Only seven were businessmen, all of whom received suspended prison sentences. Thus, until 1959, no important businessman ever spent a day in jail for violating the Sherman Act.

In 1959, however, a Federal District Court in Columbus, Ohio, decided that four officials of garden tool companies who pleaded *nolo contendere* (no contest or no defense) to price-fixing charges should not, as was typically the case, get off merely with fines and lectures. Accordingly, even though the government (Department of Justice) had not sought jail terms, the judge gave 90-day sentences to each of the four.

At this time, the government was also conducting its investigation of the electrical industry, and these jail sentences encouraged formerly reluctant witnesses to "volunteer" information to the grand jury in hopes of obtaining immunity from criminal prosecution.

As brought out in the electrical case, the conspiracy was remarkably well organized, involving regular meetings of executives in resorts and hotel rooms, coded communications, and complicated formulas for rigging bids on government contracts. With most of the industry represented, the conspiracy directly or indirectly affected almost every dam built, every power generator installed, and every electrical distribution system set up in the United States, and even reached into the new and vital field of atomic energy. The threads wove such a fantastic pattern that Federal District Judge J. Cullen Ganey was prompted to remark:

> This is a shocking indictment of a vast section of our economy, for what is really at stake here is the survival of the kind of economy under which America has grown to greatness, the free enterprise system. The conduct of the corporate and individual defendants alike . . . flagrantly mocked the image of the economic system of free enterprise which we profess to the country and destroyed the model which we offer today as a free world alternative to state control and eventual dictatorship.

Since the electrical equipment case, there have been further indications in other cases that the courts will continue to strike down all types of restrictive agreements with increasing vigor—even to the extent of imposing jail sentences if fines alone seem to be inadequate.

Combination and Monopoly

Concerning monopoly, the state of the law is less certain and the position of the courts less consistent than in cases involving restrictive agreements. There are three aspects of monopoly to be considered: monopoly per se, vertical and horizontal mergers, and conglomerate mergers.

MONOPOLY PER SE

The attitude of the courts has changed fundamentally since 1945. Before then the courts held that the mere size of a corporation, no matter how impressive, is no offense. For a firm to be in violation of the law, "unreasonable" behavior in the form of actual exertion of monopoly power, as shown by

unfair practices, was required. Since the Standard Oil case of 1911, this had been called the *rule of reason* or, what is roughly equivalent, the "good trust versus bad trust" criterion. (See Box 2.)

But the decisions handed down in various antitrust cases since 1945 have reversed this outlook almost completely. In the case against the Aluminum Company of America in 1945, in which Judge Learned Hand turned the trend in judicial thinking on monopoly, it was the court's opinion that:

1. To gain monopolistic power even by growing with the market, i.e., by reinvesting earnings rather than by combining with others, is nevertheless illegal.

2. The mere size of a firm *is* an offense, for the power to abuse and the abuse of power are inextricably intertwined.

3. The company's market share was 90 percent and that "is enough to constitute a monopoly; it is doubtful whether 60 or 64 percent would be enough; and certainly 33 percent is not."

4. The good behavior of the company which, prior to 1945, would have been an acceptable defense to the court, is no longer valid, for "Congress did not condone 'good' trusts and condemn 'bad' ones; it forbade all."

With this decision, Judge Learned Hand greatly tempered the rule of reason criterion. Subsequent court decisions have not repudiated his doctrines, although they have softened them somewhat. At the present time, the judgement of monopoly is based on such factors as the number and strength of the firms in the market, their effective size from the standpoint of technological development and competition with substitutes and with foreign trade, national security interests in maintaining strong productive facilities and maximum scientific research, and the public's interest in lower costs and uninterrupted production.

The Aluminum Company case was a major milestone in the history of antitrust. It suggests that monopoly *may* be held illegal without requiring proof of intent and even if the power were lawfully acquired; and the power may be condemned even if never abused, especially if it tends to limit or bar market access to other firms.

MERGERS

A merger is an amalgamation of two or more firms under one ownership. It may result from one of three types of integration:

The Rule of Reason

The Sherman Act outlawed every contract, combination, and conspiracy in restraint of trade. In both the Standard Oil and the American Tobacco cases of 1911—which were among the most famous in the history of antitrust—the Supreme Court upheld the government. But it went on to write the "rule of reason" into law, contending that a distinction should be made between "good" trusts and "bad" trusts.

1. *Vertical mergers,* which unite under one ownership plants engaged in different stages of production from raw materials to finished products. These mergers may take the form of forward integration into buyer markets or backward integration into supplier markets. They may result in greater economies by combining different production stages and regularizing supplies, thereby increasing profit margins.

2. *Horizontal mergers,* which unite under one ownership plants producing like products. The products may be close substitutes like cement from different plants, or moderate substitutes like tin cans and jars. The objective is to round out a product line which is sold through the same distribution channels, thereby offering joint economies in selling and distribution efforts.

3. *Conglomerate mergers*, which unite under one ownership unlike plants producing unrelated products. These mergers reflect a desire by the acquiring company to spread risks, find outlets for idle capital funds, add products which can be sold with the firm's merchandising knowledge and skills, or simply gain greater economic power on a broader front.

Although the courts have often upheld the government by disapproving of mergers that resulted in a substantial lessening of competition or tendency toward monopoly—regardless of the type of merger involved—the changes in the law on corporate acquisition made in the Celler Antimerger Act of 1950 were given specific meaning in a landmark 1962 decision by the Supreme Court known as the Brown Shoe case.

The Brown Shoe Case

In the Brown Shoe case, which involved both horizontal and vertical merger, the Supreme Court ruled against the defendant. The Brown Shoe Company was the nation's fourth-largest shoe manufacturer, with 4 percent of the industry's total, and it also controlled a number of retail outlets. Seven years earlier, in 1955, it had merged with the G. R. Kinney Corporation, which operated the nation's largest retail shoe chain, accounting for 1.2 percent of national shoe sales and also serving as the nation's twelfth-largest shoe manufacturer. Chief Justice Warren spoke for the Court in upholding a federal district court's decision ordering Brown to divest itself of Kinney. He pointed out that despite the relatively small market shares of the companies:

1. The vertical aspect of the merger of Brown's manufacturing facilities with Kinney's retail outlets would probably "foreclose competition from a substantial share of the markets for men's, women's, and children's shoes, without producing any countervailing competitive, economic, or social advantages."

2. The horizontal aspect of the merger—the marriage of Brown's retailing outlets with those of Kinney—involved a retail market that could be the entire nation or a single metropolitan area. "The fact that two merging firms have competed directly on the horizontal level in but a fraction of the geographic markets in which either has operated does not, in itself, place their merger outside the scope of Section 7" of the Clayton Act. The Court must recognize "Congress' desire to promote competition through

the protection of viable, small, locally owned businesses."

Conclusion: Watch Mergers Closely

On the basis of the Brown Shoe case and other cases, the following conclusion seems plausible:

The government's policy is not to wage an all-out war on mergers in general. Instead, it applies its own judgement to the merits of each situation. However, both vertical and horizontal mergers are likely to be declared illegal unless the companies can clearly demonstrate that the mergers will tend to increase competition (as when a few small or weak firms in an oligopolistic industry merge in order to compete more effectively with the giants in the industry) and thus promote the public interest.

Conglomerate or "circular" mergers, where the merging firms are neither competitors nor have a supplier-customer relationship, have proved to be the most popular form of combination, as shown in Exhibit 2. Some outstanding examples have been Ling-Tempco-Vought (LTV), which acquired airline, computer technology, basic steel, aerospace, electronics, car rental, meat-packing, and sporting-goods firms; and Boise Cascade, which owns lumber, mobile homes, plastics, computer services, and land-development companies. Other well-known conglomerates are International Telephone and Telegraph, Gulf and Western, Litton Industries, and Radio Corporation of America.

Conglomerate mergers raise many difficult antitrust issues, some of which may be settled in the years to come. Until then the most that can be said is that according to the general trend of antitrust attitudes:

☐ Internal growth is preferable to growth by merger.

☐ Any merger in a concentrated or oligopolistic industry like automobiles, chemicals, or steel, will be subjected to an evaluation.

☐ Any industry which has ever been charged with price-fixing will automatically draw attention on a matter of mergers.

☐ Mergers on the part of top companies within industries, as well as between industries, will be scrutinized.

☐ The larger a company, the more carefully it will be watched, especially if it seeks merger in an industry characterized by small companies.

Exhibit 2

The Merger Movement—Recent Trends

Conglomerate mergers outweigh both vertical and horizontal mergers—in number as well as in value of assets. The most recent tidal wave of mergers occurred during the late 1960s. In that period many of today's well-known, diversified corporate giants were born.

Mergers have adverse affects on competition by:

☐ Reducing the number of firms capable of entering concentrated markets

☐ Reducing the number of firms with the capability and incentive for competitive innovation

☐ Increasing the barriers to entry in concentrated markets

☐ Diminishing the vigor of competition by increasing actual and potential customer-supplier relationships among leading firms in concentrated markets

ACQUISITIONS OF MANUFACTURING AND MINING FIRMS WITH ASSETS OF $10 MILLION OR MORE

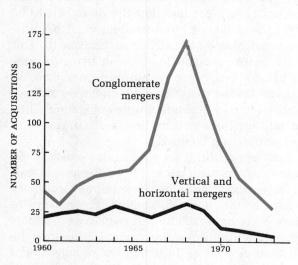

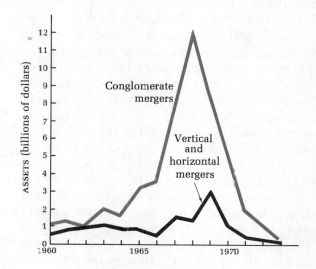

SOURCE: Federal Trade Commission.

Patents

The Constitution of the United States (Art. 1, Sec. 8, Par. 8) empowers Congress "To promote the progress of Science and useful Arts, by securing for limited Times to Authors and Inventors the exclusive Right to their respective Writings and Discoveries. . . ." Though this power was not denied to the states, it came in time to be exercised solely by the federal government, and upon this authority the American patent and copyright system is based.

What are the economic implications of patents?

A *patent* is an exclusive right conferred by government on an inventor, for a limited time. It authorizes the inventor to make, use, transfer, or withhold his invention, which he could do even without a patent, but it also gives him the right to exclude others or to admit them on his own terms, which he can do only with a patent.

Patents thus promote invention by granting temporary monopolies to inventors. But the patent system has also been employed as a means of controlling output, dividing markets, and fixing prices of entire industries. Since these perversions of the patent law have a direct effect on competition, they have been criticized by the antitrusters, and the courts have increasingly limited the scope and abuses of patent monopoly. The trends based on court decisions in each of the following areas may be sketched briefly.

STANDARD OF PATENTABILITY

The chief standard of patentability employed by the courts is the so-called "flash of genius" test. Thus, in the Cuno Engineering Corporation case in 1941, involving the patentability of a wireless lighter, Justice Douglas, speaking for the Supreme Court, said that usefulness and novelty alone do "not necessarily make the device patentable. . . . The device must not only be 'new and useful,' it must also be an 'invention' or 'discovery.' . . . The new device, however useful it may be, must reveal the *flash of creative genius*, not merely the skill of the calling. If it fails, it has not established its right to a private grant on the public domain."

The flash of genius test has been criticized as resting on the subjective judgement of the Court, and as not taking sufficient recognition of inventions that are the product of teams rather than individuals, especially in large corporations. In response to these arguments, Congress passed the Patent Act of 1952 which provides that in order to be patentable, a formula, method, or device, must be "new"—unknown to the public prior to the patent application—or it must be "useful"—demonstrate a substantial degree of technical advance in the object invented or in the process of producing something. But the courts have not found in the Patent Act an adequate definition of "invention" and continue to rely on case law and their own judgement in determining what constitutes an invention. It appears, therefore, that the flash of genius test, tempered perhaps by the political and economic attitudes of the courts with respect to the public interest, will be the chief criterion of patentability.

RIGHT OF NONUSE

The right of a patentee to withhold an invention from use has been upheld by the courts. In numerous cases tried since the turn of the century, the courts have viewed a patent as a form of private property and hence have upheld the patentee's right to refuse putting it to use. In response, it has been argued by some that a patent is a privilege and not a right, that nonuse may retard technological progress and economic development, and hence that the courts should exercise more judgement and discretion in such cases. And even the courts in recent decades have spoken of patents as privileges contingent upon the enhancement of public welfare. But the right of nonuse appears nevertheless to be supported by the law, for as stated by the Supreme Court in the Hartford Empire case in 1945: "A patent owner is not . . . under any obligation to see that the public acquires the free right to use the invention. He has no obligation either to use it or to grant its use to others."

What do you think? Is a patent a privilege or a right? Would society be better off if the law were changed so as to prohibit the right of nonuse?

TYING CONTRACTS

A seller uses a *tying contract* (or tie-in sale) to require the buyer to purchase one or more additional or "tied" products as a condition for purchasing the desired or "tying" product. For the tie-in sale to be effective, the major or tying product must be difficult to substitute, not easily dispensed with, and relatively more inelastic in demand than the subsidiary or tied item. A good example occurs in block-bookings of motion pictures in which movie theaters are required to take a certain number of grade B films as a condition for obtaining grade A films. Many other examples can be cited.

An ideal opportunity for tie-in sales exists when the seller possesses an exclusive and essential patent. A classic example is the United Shoe Machinery Company, which once compelled shoemakers to purchase other materials and intermediate products as a condition for purchasing shoe machinery. In the United case as well as in a number of subsequent cases involving such firms as Radio Corporation of America, International Business Machines, and International Harvester, the courts have struck down tying contracts that were found substantially to lessen competition within the meaning of the Clayton Act. On the whole, the trend of the courts is to disallow a tying contract of any kind, regardless of circumstances, when they believe its effect is to extend the scope of a patent monopoly or cause substantial injury—or even the probability of such injury—to competition.

NOTE: An extreme example was Eastman Kodak prior to 1954. The company sold amateur color film at a price which included the charge for finishing, thereby tying the sale of the film itself to the provision of finishing services. In 1954 the company signed a decree, agreeing to sell the film alone and thus admit competitors to the finishing business.

RESTRICTIVE LICENSING

Under a *restrictive license*, a patentee sells a patented product to a licensee on restricted conditions.

Typically, the restrictions include the patentee's fixing the geographic area of the licensee, his level of output, or the price he may charge in selling the patented good. Usually such licensing is motivated by considerations of reciprocal favor (e.g., the exchange of patents among competitors) or perhaps performed for the purpose of minimizing the incentive of the licensee to develop an alternative process. In any case, three major trends based on various court cases may be noted:

1. The right of a patentee to fix the licensee's prices on patented products has been and still is upheld by the courts.

2. The right of the patentee to fix the prices charged for unpatented products made by patented processes (e.g., a patented machine) has been doubtful since the 1940s.

3. The use of restrictive licensing is illegal when employed for the purpose of eliminating competition among many licensees.

In general, the extent to which a patent owner may license his patent is quite strictly limited. When each of several licensees accepts restrictive terms on condition or with the knowledge that others will do likewise, they are committing a conspiracy in restraint of trade in the opinion of the Court and hence are guilty of violating the law.

CROSS-LICENSING AND PATENT POOLING

"Sharing" devices such as the cross-licensing of patents or the pooling of patents for mutual benefit are not held to be illegal as such, but they generally are declared illegal when, in the eyes of the courts, they are used as a means of eliminating competition among patent owners and licensees. But what constitutes elimination of competition? In the Hartford Empire case, decided in 1945, it was held that Hartford employed the patents in its pool to dominate completely the glass container industry, curtail output, divide markets, and fix prices through restrictive licenses, and therefore this was unlawful conspiracy. In the National Lead case in 1947, a cross-licensing agreement that divided markets and fixed the prices of titanium pigment was also declared illegal. And in the Line Material case of 1948, the Court was most emphatic in its denunciation of a cross-licensing arrangement that fixed the price of fuse cutouts used in electric circuits.

On the whole, it appears that although patent pooling per se is not illegal (the automobile industry being frequently cited as an outstanding example of successful and desirable patent pooling), the courts will declare that abuse exists either when the pool is restricted to certain competitors or available only at excessive royalty payments, or when the pool is used as a device to cross-license competitors for the purpose of fixing prices and allocating markets.

CONCENTRATION OF PATENT OWNERSHIP

Patent concentration within a single firm has been frowned on increasingly since the late 1940s. Prior to that time, the ownership of many patents by a single firm was held to be legal. Since then, the courts have held that the concentration of patents by a dominant firm in an industry—regardless of whether the firm's patents were achieved by research, assignment, or purchase—may constitute monopolization and hence violate the antitrust laws *even if the firm did nothing illegal and did not use the patents to hinder or suppress competition.*

The courts have provided strong remedies in such cases. These include compulsory licensing, sometimes on a royalty-free basis, for a company's existing patents, and on a reasonable royalty basis for future patents; and the provision of necessary know-how in the form of detailed written manuals and even technical consultants, available at nominal charges, to licensees and competitors.

NOTE: Thus Eastman Kodak agreed to provide other color-film finishers with up-to-date manuals on its processing technology and to provide technical representatives to assist competitors in using the methods described. In a number of other cases involving Standard Oil of New Jersey, the Aluminum Company of America, Merck & Co., A. B. Dick, Libbey-Owens-Ford, Owens-Corning Fiberglas, American Can, and General Electric, as well as several dozen other firms, somewhat similar provisions have been arrived at since the 1940s.

Hundreds of patents involving a wide variety of manufacturing areas have thus been freed, and it is to be expected that the courts will continue to move in this direction in future years.

Trademarks

The purpose of a trademark, as originally conceived, was to identify the origin or ownership of a product. In an economic sense, however, managements have come to look upon trademarks as a strategic device for establishing product differentiation and, through advertising, consumer preference. In this way some firms have been able to establish a degree of market entrenchment that has remained substantially unrivaled for as long as several decades. Moreover, by establishing product differentiation through trademarks, firms have exploited this advantage in various ways with the aim of enhancing long-run profits. Five examples may be noted in view of their antitrust significance.

1. *Price discrimination.* This has been implemented by the use of trademarks. Until the court decided against it in 1948, Rohm & Haas sold methyl methacrylate as Lucite and Crystalite to manufacturers at 85 cents per pound, and as Veronite and Crystalex to dentists at $45 per pound. Many firms today sell branded products in one market at higher prices than they sell the same product—unbranded—in other markets.

2. *Output control.* Output control can be accomplished through the use of trademarks. United States Pipe and Foundry licensed companies to produce under its patents at graduated royalty rates on condition that they stamp their products with the trade name "de Lavaud." In 1948, the courts ruled against the company for using a trademark to control output.

3. *Exclusive markets.* These can be attained through the use of trademarks. General Electric was able to persuade procurement agencies to establish specifications requiring the use of Mazda bulbs. It licensed Westinghouse to use the name but denied its other licensees the same right. In 1949 a court ruled that General Electric had used the trademark as a device for excluding competitors from markets.

4. *Market sharing.* Market-sharing cartels have been accomplished through the use of trademarks. A *cartel* (sometimes called an "international monopoly") is an international association of firms in the same industry, established for the purpose of allocating world markets among its members and regulating prices in those markets. Thus a cartel member may be granted the exclusive right to use a trademark in his own territory. If he oversteps his market boundary, he is driven back by an infringement suit. Trade names that have provided examples of such regional monopolies include Mazda, Mimeograph, Merck, and Timken, and the trademarks of General Storage Battery, New Jersey Zinc, American Bosch, and S.K.F. Industries.

Since the 1940s, the courts have found such arrangements to be in violation of the Sherman Act. The courts have sometimes forbidden cartel members to grant their foreign partners exclusive trademark rights abroad, to sell in American markets, and to interfere with American imports.

5. *Resale price maintenance.* This practice, popularly referred to as "fair trade," permits the manufacturer or distributor of a branded product to set the minimum retail price at which that product can be sold, thereby eliminating price competition for the good at the retail level. This practice, though no longer as significant as it was prior to the 1950s, has been implemented by the use of trademarks even where patents and copyrights have failed.

Concentration of Economic Power

We have examined the antitrust laws and their application. Some basic questions that remain to be answered are: (a) To what extent does monopoly power exist in the United States? (b) What should public policy be with respect to competition and monopoly?

HOW MUCH CONCENTRATION IS THERE?

The growth and importance of big business in the United States have resulted in charges, frequently made and widely believed, that: (a) economic power is concentrated in the hands of a few corporate giants, (b) this concentration has grown over the years, and therefore (c) there has been a general "decline of competition." Upon close examination the evidence shows the first of these charges to be only partially true, and the second and third to be highly debatable if not unfounded. Let us see why.

A measure which is extensively used by economists and the antitrust agencies to evaluate the extent of competition in an industry is the *concentration ratio*; this is simply the percentage of an industry's output accounted for by its four leading firms. An illustration of such ratios for a variety of different industries is presented in Exhibit 3.

Since the early 1930s, many studies of this kind have been done by economists working in universities and in research organizations like the Brookings Institution in Washington, D.C., and the Conference Board in New York. Their purpose has been to examine the concentration of assets, employment,

Exhibit 3

**Concentration Ratios: Percentages of Industry Output
Produced by Firms in Ten Selected Low-concentration
and High-concentration Industries**

(latest data)

OUTPUT MEASURED BY VALUE OF SHIPMENTS

Low-concentration industries	Percent of industry output produced by:	
	Four largest firms	Twenty largest firms
Veneer and plywood	26	50
Jewelry, precious metal	23	38
Men's and boy's suits and coats	17	59
Metal furniture	14	40
Upholstered furniture	14	31
Setup paperboard boxes	12	32
Wood furniture	12	29
Millinery	12	27
Women's and misses suits, coats	12	22
Women's and misses dresses	7	14

High-concentration industries	Percent of industry output produced by four largest firms
Primary aluminum	100
Locomotives and parts	97
Motor vehicles	92
Telephone and telegraph equipment	92
Electric lamps	91
Steam engines and turbines	88
Synthetic fibers	86
Cigarettes	81
Sewing machines	81
Gypsum products	80

SOURCE: U.S. Bureau of Census, Census of Manufacturers, 1967.

income, and sales in large firms. The groups studied have included financial corporations, manufacturing as a whole, particular manufacturing industries, and the output of manufactured products.

Has the long-run trend of concentration been increasing, stable, or decreasing? A synthesis of various studies reveals the following indications:

1. Big businesses have grown both in number and in size at a rate proportional to the economy as a whole.

2. The list of the 500 largest corporations in the economy (presented annually by *Fortune* magazine)

is dynamic; many new firms are added each year and many old firms are dropped. However, in the more concentrated industries, the largest firms tend to remain.

3. The overall pattern of concentration ratios for manufacturing as a whole has exhibited two long-run trends: (a) a slight decrease for the period 1900 to 1946; (b) stability or possibly a slight increase from 1947 to 1960, and perhaps a moderate increase since then, although the evidence is extremely murky and is currently being analyzed by many economists in and out of government.

4. Some industries like transportation, communication, and finance have a moderate to high degree of concentration, while the trade and service industries are characterized by a low degree of concentration.

5. Over any long period of time, some concentration figures for individual industries, product groups, and product classes will rise while others fall; hence it is extremely difficult if not impossible to say whether the trend of concentration in the economy as a whole has been increasing, stable, or decreasing.

What can be said about the validity of concentration figures in general? The problem is much more complicated than is readily apparent. The main difficulties are outlined in Exhibit 4.

WHICH FUTURE POLICY FOR ANTITRUST?

What policy should society adopt to encourage competition and discourage monopoly? Three major approaches that have been suggested are: (1) public regulation or ownership of large-scale firms; (2) vigorous enforcement of the antitrust laws; and (3) revision of the antitrust laws to make competition more workable.

Public Regulation and Ownership

Some economic and political reformers have argued that the "engine of monopoly" has overtaken the American economy. As a result, American industry is dominated by large firms with strong monopoly powers, the consequence of which is serious misallocation of society's resources.

Some who take this position—especially those with strong socialist leanings—argue in favor of greater public regulation or even public ownership of large-scale monopolies and oligopolies. (We will

Exhibit 4

What Do Concentration Ratios Really Tell You?

Do concentration ratios measure "monopoly power"? The answer is no, because the results can differ according to the way in which the calculations are made.

CHOICE OF BASE

The degree of concentration will vary depending on the base chosen, such as all businesses, all manufacturing, all corporations, all nonfinancial corporations, or all industries. The concentration figures for all nonbanking corporations include, for instance, railroads and utilities whose monopolistic powers are regulated by public agencies; they also include several firms operating in highly competitive industries (food chains, department stores) as well as other firms that do not necessarily exercise significant control over their output and input markets. The figures, therefore, do not indicate the real degrees of unregulated monopoly.

CHOICE OF UNIT

The degree of concentration will vary depending on the unit of measurement chosen, such as a plant or a firm, or a single-product or multiple-product firm. The figures apply to a heterogeneous conglomeration of industries some of which are highly competitive, some moderately so, and some virtually monopolized. Further, the ratios are obscured because they pertain to the three, four, six,

or eight largest firms in an industry, without revealing the degree of domination by a single firm. The ratios thus disclose little as to the extent of competition or monopoly.

CHOICE OF INDEX

Still another factor affecting the measure of concentration is the index of output itself. In some cases, the concentration ratio is seriously understated because the output figures are national and markets are regional, or because heterogeneous goods are lumped together into a single category. In some cases the ratios are greatly overstated because the figures are limited to domestic production with competition from imports ignored, and because readily substitutable products are listed in unrelated categories. Thus the data on concentration reveal little either as to the structure of markets for particular goods or as to the index of concentrated power.

CONCLUSION

It is apparent, therefore, that measures of economic concentration are not measures of "monopoly power," as is often contended. At best, concentration ratios may reveal the results of monopolistic restriction or collusion, or of innovation, market development, and lower costs and prices. But these ratios may also conceal the influence of potential competition, and the existence—on the other side of the market—of countervailing power.

---

have more to say about this view in a later chapter dealing with the nature of socialism.)

Vigorous Enforcement of Antitrust Laws

Many academic economists and political leaders argue that the growth of monopolies and oligopolies has resulted from inadequate application of the antitrust laws. They believe that much more competition will be encouraged if these laws are vigorously enforced. This requires, of course, that Congress appropriate larger budgets to the antitrust agencies so that they can engage in more extensive and intensive investigations.

Supporters of this view have suggested that vigorous enforcement of the laws can be implemented in at least three ways:

1. The government should be willing to ask for, and the courts should be willing to order, dissolution (the breaking up of large firms into smaller competing firms) on a much broader scale than hitherto, especially if such dissolution would not impair the

efficiency or rate of technological progress of large-scale firms. For example, it has often been suggested that Chevrolet Division should be separated from General Motors and established as an independent corporation.

2. Congress should eliminate all exceptions to the antitrust laws so that labor unions, transport industries, and others are no longer exempt.

3. Congress should consider revising the patent laws and other protective legislation (tariffs) which aid special-interest groups and strengthen their monopolistic position.

Revision of the Laws for More Workable Competition

Finally, some economists and politicians deny that there is a significant absence of competition in big business. They argue that the antitrust laws were written too long ago to reflect the current structure of the economy, and hence the laws may have to be revised to reflect the needs of our time.

Their position may be summarized briefly:

1. Numerous studies indicate that "effective" competition exists in large-scale enterprises and that the traditional assumptions of nineteenth-century (pure) competition are unrealistic and cannot be applied in our twentieth-century economy, characterized by rapid product development, market growth, and vast technological advancement. Firms compete with one another, and for the consumers' dollar, in many ways other than price—through, for example, service, convenience, quality, and style—and so competition is of a "workable" form. It is only in the manufacturing sector of our economy that the problem of unregulated monopoly exists, and even here, as we have seen, the scope is narrowed down to a select group of industries where concentration is high.

2. The tendency of economic reformers to identify the major producers in these fields as monopolies merely because of their size only serves to distort the real nature of the problem. Production in these industries is characterized by a small number of large firms, so that the antitrust problem is one of *oligopoly,* not monopoly. And economic theory does not say that oligopoly is not fiercely competitive; it only states that there may be a stronger tendency to avoid price (as compared to nonprice) competition.

3. Therefore, if the antitrust laws are to preserve or even enhance the workability of competition in our economy, a fundamental revision of these laws is necessary. Moreover, the new or revised laws should be based on the competitive structure of today's oligopolistic economy. Thus, the various forms of nonprice competition should become relevant indicators of competitive behavior, rather than price competition alone, which is too often used by the antitrust agencies and the courts because it happens to be easier to observe and measure.

You may see some elements of truth in all these viewpoints. Of course, problems of enforcement and revision of the antitrust laws are decided in Washington by the administration and Congress. But as educated citizens who are concerned about the relations between business and government, it is our responsibility to be aware of the issues.

SUMMARY OF IMPORTANT IDEAS

1. The antitrust laws are intended to curb monopoly and to maintain competition in the American economy. The chief antitrust laws are the Sherman Act, the Clayton Act, the Federal Trade Commission Act, the Robinson-Patman Act, the Wheeler-Lea Act, and the Celler Antimerger Act. Taken together and in a broad sense, they forbid restraint of trade, monopolization, price discrimination, and unfair competition. Major groups exempt from the antitrust laws are the transport industries and labor unions.

2. The courts have consistently struck down restrictive agreements or conspiracies in restraint of trade. With respect to combination and monopoly, however, the state of the law is less certain and the position of the courts less consistent. Various court decisions suggest that:

  (a) Monopoly may be held illegal, for the power to abuse, even if lawfully acquired and never exercised, is sufficient to rate condemnation.
  (b) Vertical and horizontal mergers will be disallowed unless they increase competition, as when the smaller or weaker firms in an oligopolistic industry merge so as to compete with the giants.
  (c) Conglomerate mergers may be held illegal, but the tests or standards of illegality remain to be established in future court cases.

3. Patent abuse and the power of patent monopoly have been significantly weakened in the past several decades. It appears that the courts will continue to move in the direction of preventing the abuses of the patent grant. Similarly, with respect to trademark abuse, the courts have acted increasingly to prevent the use of trademarks to promote price discrimination, market exclusion, and market sharing in the international sphere (i.e., cartel arrangements) among competitors.

4. Concentration ratios are typically used to evaluate the extent of "monopoly power." According to the available evidence, economic concentration in manufacturing may not be significantly greater today than it was in previous decades. In general, however, concentration ratios do not really measure monopoly power because the results can differ widely according to the way in which the calculations are made. The choice of base unit, and index can all influence the outcome.

5. Three broad alternatives to antitrust policy consist of: (1) public regulation or ownership of large-scale monopolies and oligopolies; (2) more vigorous enforcement of the antitrust laws; (3) fundamental revisions of the antitrust laws to make competition

more workable and to reflect the nature of oligopolistic competition in today's economy.

1. *Terms and concepts to review:*

antitrust laws	consent decree
Sherman Antitrust Act (1890)	restrictive agreement
	conscious parallel
Clayton Antitrust Act (1914)	action
	rule of reason
unfair competition	merger
price discrimination	horizontal merger
interlocking directorate	vertical merger
Federal Trade Commission Act (1914)	conglomerate merger
	patent
Federal Trade Commission	tying contract
Robinson-Patman Act (1936)	restrictive license
	cartel
Wheeler-Lea Act (1938)	resale price
Celler Antimerger Act (1950)	maintenance
	concentration ratio
injunction	

2. "The rationale underlying restrictive agreements among competitors is based on the potential danger arising from the existence of the power of sellers to manipulate prices. Where this power does not exist, the laws pertaining to restrictive agreements are practically meaningless. Thus, there is no point in holding unlawful an agreement among competitors to fix prices, allocate customers, or control production, when the competitors involved are so small that they lack significant power to affect market prices." Evaluate.

3. Suppose that tomorrow morning all grocers in Chicago, without previous public notice, raised their prices for milk by 3 cents per quart. Does this action prove the existence of an agreement or constitute an offense on the part of the grocers? What would your answer be if the automobile manufacturers without notice announced a 5 percent price increase next year on all new model cars? Explain.

4. If all the companies in an oligopolistic industry quote identical prices without prior agreement by following the prices of the industry leader, is this evidence of a combination or conspiracy?

5. In an industry characterized by price leadership without prior arrangement, is there likely to be a charge of combination or conspiracy leveled against that industry if: (a) prevailing prices are announced by the industry's trade association rather than by a leading firm; (b) all firms in the industry report their prices to their industry trade association; (c) all firms in the industry quote prices on a basing point system, i.e., the delivered price is the leader's price plus rail freight from the leader's plant; (d) all firms follow the leader not only in price, but in product and sales policies as well? (These four questions should be answered as a group rather than individually.)

6. In the Columbia Steel case (1948), the Supreme Court said: "We do not undertake to prescribe any set of percentage figures by which to measure the reasonableness of a corporation's enlargement of its activities by the purchase of the assets of a competitor. The relative effect of percentage command of a market varies with the setting in which that factor is placed." Does this conflict with Judge Hand's statement in the ALCOA case? Explain.

7. "Since there are 'good' monopolies and 'bad' monopolies, a company should be judged by its total contribution to society—not by its market behavior alone." Do you agree? Explain.

8. "Many trustbusters and economists forget that *concentration is a function of consumer sovereignty,* and that the same consumers who make big businesses big can make them small or even wipe them out by simply refraining from the purchase of their products. This is a not-so-obvious principle of our free enterprise system which needs to be better understood." Do you agree? Discuss.

9. "To say that the degree of competition depends on the number of sellers in the marketplace is like saying that football is more competitive than tennis." Discuss. (HINT: Can you describe different forms of competition, in addition to price competition, that exist in American industry?)

10. Suppose that General Motors, the largest firm in the automobile industry, were to reduce prices on its automobiles to levels which yield only a "fair" profit for itself, but not for its competitors. As a result, consumer purchases shift to General Motors because of its lower prices, and the other automobile manufacturers subsequently find themselves driven out of business as a result of bankruptcy. In the light of the ALCOA case, would General Motors be guilty of monopolizing the market and hence violating the Sherman Act?

11. It is generally stated that growth, stability, and flexibility are three primary objectives of mergers.

(a) With respect to growth, it has been said that "a firm, like a tree, must either grow or die." Evaluate this statement.

(b) Why may instability be a motive for merger? Instability of what?

(c) What is meant by flexibility as a motive for merger? (HINT: Compare flexibility vs. vulnerability.)

12. Section 7 of the Clayton Act of 1914 and its amendment, the Celler Antimerger Act of 1950, states:

No corporation engaged in commerce shall acquire, directly or indirectly, the whole or any part of the stock or other share capital and no corporation subject to the jurisdiction of the Federal Trade Commission shall acquire the whole or any part of the assets of another corporation engaged also in commerce, where in any line of commerce in any section of the country, the affect of such acquisition may be substantially to lessen competition, or to tend to create a monopoly.

Assume that you are a business economist for a large corporation, and you are asked to prepare a report on why this legislation should be repealed. What main points would you bring out in your argument?

Contemporary Issue

TV: How to Fertilize the Wasteland

In their speeches, politicians proclaim the virtues of competition, free enterprise, and consumer sovereignty. But at other times, most of them do their best—or worst—to ensure that important industries are protected from the discomfort of competition. One of those industries is television, which is dominated by three legally sanctioned nationwide networks. Each of those networks owns TV stations in major cities and also provides programs for so-called affiliate stations. The result: from Portland, Maine, to Portland, Oregon, and from the Mexican to the Canadian borders the lucky viewer can watch the same programs. To be sure, all major cities are enlivened also by local stations not affiliated with any network; these broadcast an intellectual diet that ranges from bland to bloody, but generally includes fourth or fifth reruns of "Lucy" and "This Is Your Life."

Regulating the Air Waves

In theory, the Federal Communications Commission can remove a licence from any broadcasting group that fails to meet the needs and wishes of the community it serves; in practice, the FCC seldom does any such thing, most of its commissioners being remarkably cozy with the industry. Why is the FCC so timid? The answer is, of course, that TV is a multibillion dollar industry with many powerful friends in the administration and in Congress. Upon the FCC's decisions depend the economic well-being of the three networks and of the local stations. Many of those stations are, of course, more local in name than in fact; they are owned by large corporations. Among them: McGraw-Hill, a company that also publishes books and magazines; Whitney Communications, which has publishing interests, including the Paris-based International Herald-Tribune; and the New York Daily News-Chicago Tribune companies.

The FCC is supposed to be a regulatory agency—that is, to regulate the activities of TV and radio stations. But much evidence points to its being regulated by the industry. In a provocative new book, *Economic Aspects of Television Regulation* (Brookings, 1973), economists Roger Noll, Merton Peck, and John McGowan contend that the FCC in particular, and the federal government in general, have retarded innovation and diversification in TV programming. The results:

● TV has failed to exploit its potential for educating, informing, and elevating tastes.

● TV is a "wasteland" that functions as an entertainment medium and fails to offer sufficient variety.

● A very few powerful organizations and individuals control the content of television.

Noll, Peck, and McGowan contend that the FCC has consistently blocked expansion of the television industry. The FCC has rejected authorization of regional rather than local stations; hedged pay-TV with programing restrictions; subjected cable TV to costly constraints and limited the number of channels and programs offered to a community; and generally preserved the *status quo*.

What is the solution? The authors press for a rise in the number of channels, particularly VHF (very high frequency). These should be regional stations; studies show that six VHF regional stations, located in each of the

80 largest cities and affiliated with six national networks, would be profitable.

Those arguments almost certainly do not go far enough. Unlike most other Western nations, the United States still clings to the belief that TV should be financed primarily by advertisers rather than by viewers. The result is that the overwhelming majority of TV stations are forced to broadcast programs that attract the maximum possible number of viewers—for in TV the revenues come from the size of the audience rather than the quality of its programs. This in turn means that programs of high quality but low audience appeal have little or no chance of being screened; and it means that advertisers become the arbiters of what the public shall and shall not see.

The British Approach

What the United States needs is probably some variant of the British television system. In England two television organizations operate side by side and in competition. The elder is the British Broadcasting Corporation (BBC), a public body, financed by licence fees paid by viewers. Although state-owned, the BBC is autonomous of the government and zealously guards its worldwide reputation for independence. The younger TV organization is the Independent Broadcasting Authority (IBA), which licences local and regional stations that obtain their revenues by selling advertising, just as U.S. stations do. However, there is a salient difference between American and British practice. Unlike American stations, British TV broadcasters must "bunch" advertising into "natural breaks" in programs; no advertiser may sponsor a program, and the beginning and end of an advertisement must be clearly labelled as such. When a licence comes up for renewal the IBA hears bids from groups that want to take over certain stations: from time to time the IBA has moved the licence from one group to another, despite screams of financial pain from the losers.

Although the British system probably could not be imported intact into the United States, it does show one way in which American viewers could regain their sovereignty over the air waves—which are a natural resource, not a private prerogative. Further, the British system offers an escape from the timid control of advertisers over what the public shall and shall not see.

QUESTIONS

1. "In television, as in a free market, viewer sovereignty should prevail." What is meant by "viewer sovereignty"?

2. What economic policies would you recommend for improving American television? Evaluate your proposals.

CHAPTER 31

Labor Unions and Industrial Relations

STRIKE THREATENS TO DISRUPT PRODUCTION

UNEMPLOYMENT HIGHER IN THE GHETTOS

UNION WAGE DEMANDS ARE TOP PRIORITY

EXTRA PAY FOR HOLIDAYS A NEW TARGET

These are the kinds of headlines we frequently encounter in the news media. They describe labor problems that involve all of us, not only in our personal capacities as consumers, employees, or employers, but also as citizens concerned with significant economic issues.

We shall find in this chapter that a study of labor problems involves, in a very fundamental way, a study of unions—how they have evolved, how they bargain with management, and how they may affect the general welfare. These concepts are at best only vaguely sensed and, at worst, are generally misunderstood by most people.

We shall also learn that *the primary and continuous objective of all unions is to improve the wages and working conditions of their members by bargaining with employers.* Through a process of negotiation, unions and management work out arrangements for higher wages and salaries, new and better pension plans, holidays and vacations with pay, health and welfare plans, shorter hours, and safer working conditions. This bargaining approach to the solution of labor problems is a characteristic feature of labor economics and industrial relations in the United States and in some other advanced countries.

CHAPTER PREVIEW

How did American labor unions evolve? What sorts of obstacles did they face? What kinds of assistance did they receive in their long and turbulent history?

What is collective bargaining? How does it work?

How do unions seek to raise wages in the labor market? Are unions "good" or "bad"?

History of American Unionism: The Labor Movement

The development of labor unions in the United States during the nineteenth and twentieth centuries is often referred to as the *labor movement*. It is a fascinating story which plays an integral role in the nation's political and economic history.

What is a *union*? It may be defined as an organization of workers which seeks to gain a degree of monopoly power in the sale of its services so that it may be able to secure higher wages, better working conditions, and other economic improvements for its members. The development of unionism spans roughly four periods: (1) the local movement: Revolution to the Civil War, (2) the national movement: post-Civil War to the Depression, (3) the era of rapid growth: Depression to World War II, and (4) the age of maturity: post-World War II to the present.

THE LOCAL MOVEMENT:
REVOLUTION TO THE CIVIL WAR

Although labor organizations were started prior to the Revolutionary War, they were very short-lived and of no significant consequence. Not until the last quarter of the eighteenth century—and particularly in the last decade of that century—did some of the unions have sufficient durability to survive for a number of years. These were localized *craft unions* or "horizontal" unions composed of workers in a particular trade such as bakers, carpenters, longshoremen, printers, shoemakers, and teamsters. Throughout the history of unionism, the crafts have always been the first to organize, largely because their specialized skills or abilities put them in a relatively stronger position to gain monopolistic power in the marketplace.

The efforts of the craft unions did not go unchallenged. Employers organized to meet the threat of unionization, and in major cities union leaders were punished for organizing "labor combinations in restraint of trade" by judges who invoked the conspiracy provisions of English common law.

Not until 1842, in the landmark Massachusetts case of *Commonwealth vs. Hunt*, did a court hold a trade union to be lawful and declare that workers could legally form a union for the purpose of bargaining collectively with employers over wages, hours, and related issues.

This led to some small improvements in working conditions during the two decades preceding the Civil War. The most significant developments were the gradual decline in the length of the average working day from about 13 hours to 10 or 11 hours in most factories, and the passage of 10-hour laws by many states. Laws were also passed to regulate child labor, but these were seldom enforced.

THE NATIONAL MOVEMENT:
POST-CIVIL WAR TO THE GREAT DEPRESSION

After the Civil War, the growth of national craft unions quickened perceptibly with the spread of industrialism across the country and the expansion of the railroads into the West. As the sections of the nation were being welded together, goods produced in different geographic areas began to compete in the same markets, and workers began to find it feasible to move from one part of the country to another to take advantage of better job opportunities.

Unions thus became increasingly "national" as they embraced formerly local unions, which became local branches of their national organization; the movement for an 8-hour working day was begun; and the first signs of the long, bitter, and almost unbelievable hostility toward labor's struggle for union recognition and survival started to take shape.

The following developments mark the highlights of union history from the end of the Civil War to the beginning of the depression of the 1930s.

Knights of Labor

In 1869, seven tailors met in Philadelphia and founded the Noble and Holy Order of the Knights of Labor—or simply the *Knights of Labor*—a national labor organization which attempted to unify all types of workers regardless of their craft, and without regard to race, sex, nationality, or creed. The organization was powerful and influential; it won several strikes against the railroads, and its membership rose rapidly to a peak of 730,000 in 1886. Its growth was so rapid, in fact, that at one point the central office had to suspend organizing to assure that no "lawyers, bankers, gamblers or liquor dealers, and Pinkerton detectives" could gain membership and possibly wreck the union.

The Knights' program called for various improvements and reforms including: establishment of the 8-hour day; equal pay for equal work by women; abolition of child and convict labor; public ownership of utilities; the establishment of cooperatives; and, in general, the peaceful replacement of a competitive society with a socialistic system. Strikes were to be used as weapons only after all other means had failed.

The Knights were a curious group with one foot in the past, the other in the future. They championed the cause of workers in general, but rejected the traditional organizing of workers by crafts, preferring instead the mass unionization of both unskilled and skilled workers. This philosophy ultimately contributed to its decline. After 1886, membership in the Knights fell rapidly for three major reasons:

1. Opposition by craft leaders who saw no reason why the bargaining position of labor's elite—the skilled workers—should be wasted on efforts to secure benefits for the unskilled.

2. Dissension among leading members and groups over whether a more aggressive approach through strikes and collective bargaining should replace the slower evolutionary methods of political and social change.

3. Accusations (which were never proved) that the union was connected with anarchist activities such as the violence and bombing that occurred in Chicago's Haymarket riot in 1886—a famous incident in American political as well as labor history. (See Box 1.)

As a result of these conditions, the Knights of Labor steadily lost ground in the labor movement, and it finally ceased to exist in 1917.

American Federation of Labor

In the early 1880s, representatives of several craft unions became dissatisfied with the philosophy and policies of the Knights and formed their own group, which became known in 1886 as the American Federation of Labor. Under the leadership of Samuel

---

Box 1

The Haymarket Riot: Haymarket Square, Chicago, May 4, 1886

By 1886 the movement for the 8-hour day had gained wide support by striking workers in many cities. In Chicago, about 80,000 workers were demonstrating when a group of anarchists took advantage of the excitement by throwing a bomb into the crowd in front of the McCormick Harvester Works at Haymarket Square. Seven policemen were killed and many people were injured. Although the anarchists bore the wrath of public indignation, organized labor in general, and especially the Knights of Labor, suffered heavily.

Harper's Weekly, May 15, 1886.

Gompers, who served as its president from 1886 until his death in 1924 (except for one year when he was succeeded by William Green), the AFL led and dominated the labor movement. Its philosophy was based on three fundamental principles:

1. Business unionism—a practical policy of seeking short-run "bread and butter" improvements in wages and working conditions and long-run improvements through evolution rather than revolution, without engaging in the class struggles of society.

2. Federalism—an organizational policy of maintaining autonomous national and international craft unions, each controlling its own trade specialty.

3. Voluntarism—a policy of opposition to government interference, either for or against labor, in all matters pertaining to labor organization, labor negotiations with management, and related activities.

The concept of unionism adopted by the AFL was thus largely the opposite of that held by the Knights of Labor. As the Knights declined in importance, the AFL grew, with its membership exceeding 1 million shortly after the turn of the century. By World War I, after decades of extraordinary and often violent public hostility toward unions, the AFL was clearly voicing the views of a majority of organized workers. Union membership exceeded 5 million, and workers had earned substantial gains in wages and working conditions.

But then the growth of unionism started to take a turn for the worse. The government withdrew its limited protection of labor's right to organize, and employers refused to recognize labor unions in their plants. As a result, unions lost members. Lethargy and lack of aggressiveness engulfed American labor as technological changes, unfavorable court decisions, the growth of company unions, and a period of national prosperity all contributed to the dampening of union activity. By the early 1930s, union membership had declined to less than 3 million. (See also Box 2.)

THE ERA OF RAPID GROWTH: DEPRESSION TO WORLD WAR II

The fortunes of organized labor underwent a dramatic reversal during the Depression. The first piece of pro-labor legislation passed by Congress was the *Norris-LaGuardia Act* of 1932 which modified or eliminated the worst abuses against organized labor:

Box 2

Industrial Workers of the World—The "Wobblies"

THE HAND THAT WILL RULE THE WORLD—ONE BIG UNION

Solidarity, June 30, 1917.

The early 1900s saw the formation of the Industrial Workers of the World (IWW), a labor union of immigrants who were mostly unskilled factory workers, miners, lumbermen, and dock workers. Popularly known as the "Wobblies," the organization's members had a militant style with the slogan: "Labor Produces All Wealth. All Wealth Must Go to Labor." Hence their goals were to unite all workers into "One Big Union," tear down capitalism by force, and replace it with socialism. The IWW reached a peak membership of about 100,000 by 1912, but declined thereafter due to internal dissension and the imprisonment of nearly 100 of its leaders on sedition charges.

During the next several decades the IWW faded steadily into obscurity, but it did not become extinct. In the late 1960s there were less than 300 Wobblies, most of them retaining membership in the IWW for philosophical or nostalgic reasons. Since then there has been a renewed interest in the organization—primarily by younger people of the radical left—as a result of which membership has risen considerably. Though still relatively small, the IWW has concentrated mainly on organizing workers in small plants that major unions have skipped as too insignificant. According to its leaders, the Wobblies' bargaining demands today are "basically the normal types of demands for (better) working conditions and rates of pay, but flavored with a different perspective"; violence, they say, is avoided for the most practical of reasons: "The other side has more capacity."

The major publication of the IWW was a weekly magazine called Solidarity. The accompanying song, "Solidarity Forever," composed in 1915 by an IWW member, has long been the anthem of the entire American labor movement, and is by far the best-known union song in the United States.

SOLIDARITY FOREVER!
(Tune: "Battle Hymn of the Republic")

When the Union's inspiration through the workers' blood
   shall run,
There can be no power greater anywhere beneath the sun
Yet what force on earth is weaker than the feeble strength
   of one?
But the Union makes us strong.

   Chorus:
   Solidarity forever!
   Solidarity forever!
   Solidarity forever!
   For the Union makes us strong.

Is there aught we hold in common with the greedy parasite
Who would lash us into serfdom and would crush us with
   his might?
Is there anything left for us but to organize and fight?
For the Union makes us strong.

It is we who plowed the prairies; built the cities where
   they trade;
Dug the mines and built the workshops; endless miles of
   railroad laid.
Now we stand, outcast and starving, mid the wonders we
   have made;
But the Union makes us strong.

All the world that's owned by idle drones, is ours and ours
   alone.
We have laid the wide foundations; built it skyward stone
   by stone.
It is ours, not to slave in, but to master and to own,
While the Union makes us strong.

They have taken untold millions that they never toiled
   to earn.
But without our brain and muscle not a single wheel can
   turn.
We can break their haughty power; gain our freedom when
   we learn
That the Union makes us strong.

In our hands is placed a power greater than their hoarded
   gold;
Greater than the might of armies, magnified a thousand-
   fold.
We can bring to birth the new world from the ashes of the
   old,
For the Union makes us strong.

1. The hated *yellow-dog contract*, which required the employee to promise, as a condition of employment, that he would not belong to a labor union, was declared illegal.

2. The conditions under which court injunctions could be issued against unions were greatly restricted.

The stage was now set. Under President Roosevelt's administration of the 1930s, other favorable labor legislation was passed which set standards for minimum wages, maximum hours, and child labor, and created the U.S. Employment Service and the social security system. But none of these was more important for the union movement than the National Labor Relations Act of 1935, which was hailed as Labor's Magna Carta.

The *National Labor Relations Act* (also known as the *Wagner Act*) of 1935 is the basic labor relations law of the United States. The act has three major provisions:

1. It guarantees the right of workers to organize and to bargain collectively through representatives of their own choosing.

2. It forbids the employer from engaging in "unfair labor practices" such as: (*a*) interfering or discriminating against workers who form unions or engage in union activity; (*b*) establishing a *company union* or organization of workers that is limited to a particular firm; (*c*) refusing to bargain in good faith with a duly recognized union.

3. It established the *National Labor Relations Board* (NLRB) to enforce the act and to supervise free elections among a company's employees to determine which union, if any, is to represent the workers.

With this firm legal umbrella provided by Congress—especially the right of labor to organize and bargain collectively—the labor movement embarked on the fastest and longest upward journey in its history. Thousands of workers went back into their old unions and thousands of others joined new ones. As shown in Exhibit 1, on the next page, union members totaled 10 million by 1940.

Congress of Industrial Organizations

In the mid-1930s, several union leaders in the AFL launched an attack against the craft bias of the Federation. They argued that craft unions were "horizontal" unions which were not well adapted to the

Exhibit 1

Union Membership since 1900

The union movement experienced its most rapid growth during the 1930s. Since the 1950s, union membership has averaged less than 25 percent of the civilian labor force.

THE GROWTH OF UNION MEMBERSHIP

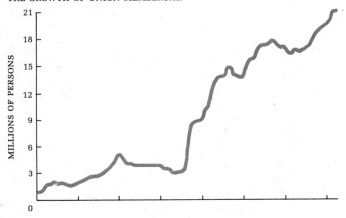

TOTAL UNION MEMBERSHIP AS PERCENTAGE OF CIVILIAN LABOR FORCE

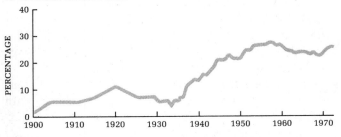

SOURCE: U.S. Department of Labor.

needs of workers in modern mass-production industries. Instead, *industrial unions* or "vertical" unions were needed to organize all workers in a particular industry, for example, automobile manufacturing and coal mining. Although the Federation never refused to recognize industrial unions—indeed, the insurgent leaders were all heads of industrial unions that were affiliated with the AFL—the parent organization had been relatively unsuccessful in organizing workers in mass-production industries.

A controversy thus arose within the AFL leadership that lasted for several years. Finally, in 1938, the insurgent unions were expelled from the Federation. As a result, they banded together to form an independent rival union called the *Congress of Industrial Organizations* (CIO).

The CIO was immediately successful in organizing millions of previously unorganized workers in the automobile, steel, and other mass-production industries. But the AFL also continued to make huge gains. Both the AFL and CIO emerged from World War II stronger than ever before. However, with the termination of wartime economic controls, prices rose faster than wages, and strikes broke out in many major industries during 1945 and 1946. These strikes raised a great wave of antiunion sentiment both in and out of Congress, resulting in the passage of new restrictive labor legislation. Thus came the end of an era in the history of the union movement.

**THE AGE OF MATURITY:
POST-WORLD WAR II TO THE PRESENT**

In June, 1947, after numerous major strikes, a new labor-management relations act was passed. It provided the most detailed and extensive regulation of labor unions and industrial relations in the nation's history.

The *Labor-Management Relations Act (Taft-Hartley Act)* of 1947 amended the 1935 National Labor Relations Act (Wagner Act). The Taft-Hartley Act retains the rights that had been given to labor by the Wagner Act, but it includes the following additional provisions:

1. Outlaws as "unfair labor practices" of unions: (*a*) coercion of workers to join a union; (*b*) failure of a union to bargain with an employer in good faith; and (*c*) *jurisdictional strikes* (or disagreements between two or more unions as to which shall perform a particular job), *secondary boycotts* (or attempts by a union through strikes, picketing, etc., to stop one employer from doing business with another employer), and *featherbedding* (or "make work" rules which are designed to increase the amount of labor or labor time on a particular job).

2. Outlaws the *closed shop*, whereby an employer makes union membership a condition of employment, but permits the *union shop*, which allows a nonunion employee to be hired on condition that he join the union after he is employed.

3. Requires unions to file financial reports with the NLRB, and union officials to sign non-Communist affidavits.

4. Prohibits strikes called before the end of a 60-day notice period prior to the expiration of a collective-bargaining agreement, in order to give conciliation

agencies enough time to try to resolve disputes before a walkout occurs.

5. Enables the President to obtain an 80-day court injunction in order to provide a "cooling-off" period in cases involving strikes which endanger the national health or safety.

The Taft-Hartley Act also permits state legislatures to pass *right-to-work laws*—that is, state laws which make it illegal to require membership in a union as a condition of employment. About 20 states, mostly in the South and Midwest, adopted such laws. Their main effect was to outlaw the union shop. In practice; however, these laws have been relatively weak in many states.

The Taft-Hartley Act was strongly denounced by unions for almost a decade after its passage. In retrospect, however, many economists and labor leaders now agree that the law does not appear to have put the unions at a disadvantage in bargaining, nor is it likely to have been a significant obstacle in the path of union growth.

The AFL–CIO

Most, but not all, labor organizations joined either the AFL or the CIO. Those unions not affiliated with any federation of labor organizations are called *independent unions;* they may be national or international and are not limited to workers in any one firm.

For a number of years during and after World War II, labor leaders in both the AFL and CIO dreamed of merging the two federations into a single and powerful union. Finally, in 1955, a single organization known as the *American Federation of Labor–Congress of Industrial Organizations* (AFL–CIO) was formed. Briefly, the purposes of the organization, as paraphrased from its constitution, are as follows: to improve wages, hours, and working conditions for workers; to realize the benefits of free collective bargaining; and to strengthen America's democratic traditions by protecting the labor movement from Communists, Fascists, and other totalitarians.

The union movement thus entered an age of maturity and power, and with it came a mounting political attack against organized labor. Some union leaders were charged with mismanagement and embezzlement of union funds, and others with extorting money from employers and employees under the threat of invoking "labor trouble." The AFL–CIO dealt with these problems by adopting Codes of

Ethical Practices and by expelling several unions. In 1959, Congress passed a new law: the Labor-Management Reporting and Disclosure Act, which again indicated that the government would discipline labor as a whole in order to protect it from a few of its corrupt leaders.

The *Labor-Management Reporting and Disclosure Act (Landrum-Griffin Act)* of 1959 amended the National Labor Relations Act by: (a) requiring detailed financial reports of all unions and union officers, (b) severely tightening restrictions on secondary boycotting and picketing, (c) requiring periodic secret-ballot elections of union officers, and (d) imposing restrictions on ex-convicts and Communists in holding positions as union officers.

THE FUTURE: STABILIZATION OR EXPANSION?

What will be the future of the American labor movement? Many labor economists believe that union membership will stabilize at about 25 percent of the labor force—somewhat more than the average since the end of World War II. There are several reasons for this belief:

1. *Changing composition of the labor force.* The proportion of blue-collar workers, who are the chief source from which unions draw their membership, has declined steadily from almost 50 percent of the civilian labor force after World War II to less than 30 percent today, while the proportion of white-collar workers has increased correspondingly. Most of the unorganized blue-collar workers are employed in small manufacturing plants and in the trade and service industries, all of which are more difficult to unionize.

2. *Changing attitudes toward unions.* The public as well as some political leaders in Congress have become less sympathetic toward unions as a result of what sometimes appear to be unreasonably prolonged strikes, the discovery of fraudulent practices among union officials, and the growing belief—whether true or not—that union pressures for wage increases are a chief cause of cost-push inflation.

3. *Changing type of union leadership.* Unions have become big businesses with millions of members and hundreds of millions of dollars in welfare funds. As a result, they have come increasingly to seek a new type of leadership—professional *administrators* capable of dealing effectively with Congress, management, the public, and their own rising proportion

of more educated members—rather than men who are merely militant organizers.

Other labor economists, as well as union leaders, contend that union membership will continue to expand since there is still a large pool of unorganized labor in agriculture, government, trade, and the service industries.

Collective Bargaining

The chief objective of unions has been to improve the status of workers. This goal is now achieved for the most part through the method of *collective bargaining*—a process of negotiation between representatives of a company's management and a union for the purpose of arriving at mutually acceptable wages and working conditions for employees.

If a union represents a majority of workers in a firm, it may be "certified" by the government's National Labor Relations Board and recognized by management as the collective-bargaining agent for the employees. Representatives of the union and of management then meet together at the bargaining table to work out a *collective agreement* or contract. The two sides are rarely in accord when they begin, but the bargaining process is one of give and take by both parties until a contract is agreed upon. The union representatives then take the contract back to their members for a vote of acceptance or rejection. If the members reject it, they may send their union representatives back to continue the bargaining process or they may decide to reinforce their demands by going on strike.

When a collective agreement is ratified both by union and management, it becomes a legally binding contract as well as guiding principle of labor-management relations for the period of time specified in the arrangement. More than 95 percent of all such agreements in existence today were successfully negotiated without any strikes or work stoppages.

Collective-bargaining contracts differ greatly in their size and content; some are brief and cover only a few pages, while others are highly detailed and run to several hundred pages. The major issues with which such agreements deal may be divided into four broad groups: (1) wages, (2) industrial relations, (3) multiunit bargaining, and (4) settling labor-management disputes.

WAGES

You may read in a newspaper that a labor-management negotiation has resulted in a 20-cent-per-hour "package," consisting of 12 cents in wages and 8 cents in other benefits. Such packages are composed of two parts:

1. *Basic wages:* payments received by workers for work performed, based on time or output

2. *Supplementary* or *fringe benefits:* compensation to workers other than basic wages, such as bonuses, pension benefits, holiday pay, or vacation pay

The term "wages" is thus a complex one in many collective-bargaining discussions and may give rise to various issues and problems.

Basic Wages: Time or Incentive Payments?

If you were a worker, would you want to be paid on the basis of "time," or would you prefer some sort of incentive system which compensated you according to how much you produced?

About 70 percent of American workers in manufacturing are paid on the basis of time—by the hour, day, week, or month—with extra compensation for work done during nights, weekends, and holidays. The remaining 30 percent of manufacturing workers receive their basic compensation through some type of incentive payment that is related to output or profit. It may be in the form of wages, commissions, bonuses, and so on.

Many employers have criticized the time-payment concept by arguing that it provides no incentive for workers to produce, since it relates earnings received to time worked rather than output. Unions, on the other hand, have usually preferred time pay because it compensates workers on a uniform basis rather than penalizing the slower ones and rewarding the faster ones.

Time-payment systems tend to prevail in industries where an individual's production cannot be precisely measured and where his rate of output is largely controlled by established technology, as in automobiles, chemicals, and machine-tool production. On the other hand, incentive systems have been effective in competitive industries where labor costs are a high proportion of total costs and where workers' outputs are measurable, as in clothing and textile production.

The great majority of unions have not strongly opposed incentive systems as such. However, they have been very much concerned with the operation of such systems and the problems that they pose. For example:

1. How should a worker be compensated if a machine breaks down or if there is a stoppage of material flow due to causes beyond his control?

2. Since it may be possible to measure the outputs of only certain types of workers in a plant (e.g., maintenance personnel or assembly-line operators) can an equitable incentive and time system be established for all workers in the plant?

3. Will management provide an adequate staff of accountants, time-study engineers, and personnel men to see that the incentive system continues to operate effectively and equitably?

Profit Sharing

Many companies have introduced a different type of incentive system known as profit sharing. These firms distribute to their workers a share of the profits after certain costs such as wages, materials, and overhead have been covered. Profit-sharing plans of various types (including bonuses) have existed since the early nineteenth century and are by no means uncommon in American industry. In general, profit sharing is most widespread in firms and industries with the following characteristics:

1. Consistent and relatively large profits, so that profit sharing becomes a worthwhile incentive

2. Year-round stability of the work force (as opposed to high seasonal instability), thus permitting a permanent body of employees to build up an interest and equity in the company

3. High turnover costs among key personnel, for whom profit sharing can have significant holding power

4. Relatively weak or no unionization

The first three characteristics are readily understandable, but why the fourth? The answer is that unions have usually opposed profit sharing for two major reasons. First, it establishes an employer-employee "partnership" in profits and thereby weakens the influence of unions. Second, it makes the employee's compensation dependent on profits, which in turn are due to managerial policies (such

as pricing practices, product design, and technology) over which the worker has no direct control.

For these reasons, unions have argued that workers should be paid for what they do and should not be penalized when a company loses money or be rewarded with a share of the profits when it makes money.

Wage Structure and Job Classification

Should all workers in a particular job classification, such as welders or assemblers, receive a single rate of pay, or should there be a range of wages for each job based on years of experience, merit, length of service, and other factors? Questions of this type are obviously important for many collective-bargaining discussions.

Since World War II most manufacturing firms have adopted formal wage structures. This has been accomplished largely by the process of *job classification*—describing the duties, responsibilities, and characteristics of jobs; point-rating them (perhaps by established formulas based on engineering studies of workers in such jobs); and then grouping the jobs into graduated classifications with corresponding wage rates and wage ranges. Employers prefer job classification since it systematizes the wage structure and facilitates the handling of problems dealing with wage administration.

Some of the chief problems of job-classification plans revolve around the issue of single rates versus rate ranges for each job grouping. Unions have tended to favor the single-rate approach because it reduces friction and dissension among workers in each rank. Employers, on the other hand, have usually preferred the use of rate ranges because it permits them to grant rewards on the basis of merit within each rank.

Supplementary or Fringe Benefits

Wage supplements or fringe benefits such as pensions, insurance, and welfare plans have grown remarkably since the beginning of World War II. This trend is likely to endure as long as union negotiators continue to emphasize the need for worker "security" in their bargaining with employers. Moreover, the various plans are becoming increasingly liberal. Health plans, for example, once included only hospitalization, but now often cover outpatient care, free eyeglasses, psychiatric and dental care, and so on. Similarly, additional benefits such as sick leaves, time off with pay, and vacation allowances, have all expanded substantially.

Supplementary wages or fringe benefits raise at least two fundamental questions:

1. Whereas wages used to be paid exclusively for time worked, there is a significant trend in the payment of some wages for time *not worked*. If this trend continues, with more and more labor costs going into fringe benefits, will payment for time worked decrease in importance and will our traditional mode of payment therefore become outdated?

2. To an employer, total fringe benefit payments vary largely with the number of employees rather than with the hours worked per employee, since a worker receives the same vacations, holidays, group insurance, and so on, whether he puts in 30, 40, or 50 hours per week. It may be cheaper for an employer, therefore, to pay his existing workers at overtime rates than to hire new employees. Does this mean that the growth of fringe benefits in American industry will add so much to employers' costs that it will reduce their propensity to employ?

INDUSTRIAL RELATIONS

A second major area of collective bargaining pertains to *industrial relations*—the rules and regulations governing the relationship between union and management. Since the subject of industrial relations is quite broad, we will focus our attention on a few of the more important topics.

Union Security

"In unity there is strength." This is the fundamental principle upon which unionism is based. It follows that a primary objective of unions is "union security." A union's ability to attain security is determined by two major factors: the type of recognition that it is accorded and its financial arrangement for collecting dues. The more common forms of union recognition are the closed shop and the union shop, and the typical method of dues collection is the "checkoff." Let us see what these concepts involve.

1. *Closed shop.* A plant or business establishment in which the employer agrees that all workers must belong to the union as a condition for employment is known as a *closed shop.* This arrangement may be advantageous to some of the parties and disadvantageous to others. Thus: (*a*) it benefits the union by enabling it to control entry into the job or trade, thereby strengthening the union's bargaining position; (*b*) it harms the employer by depriving him of his right to hire whom he wishes.

The Taft-Hartley Act of 1947 made the closed shop illegal for firms engaged in interstate commerce. The act only drove the closed shop underground, however. The closed shop does not exist in principle in union-management contracts, but does exist in fact in certain skilled trades and industries such as printing, construction, and transportation.

2. *Union shop.* A plant or business establishment in which the employer is free to hire whom he wants, but agrees to require that the employee must join the union within a specified time after hiring (usually 30 days) as a condition for continuing in employment, is called a *union shop.*

The union shop is the most common form of union recognition found in industry today. There are two major reasons for this: (*a*) the Taft-Hartley Act of 1947 made the closed shop illegal; and (*b*) the tendency of various industries to switch to the union shop from other less common types of union recognition arrangements.

Both the closed shop and the union shop have certain obvious disadvantages to employers—the major one being that they give the union greater bargaining strength. Hence management has often argued in favor of the *open shop*—that is, a plant or business establishment in which the employer is free to hire union or nonunion members as he wishes. Unions have always opposed the open shop on the grounds that it often results in a closed nonunion shop because of the antiunion hiring preferences of many employers.

3. *Checkoff.* If a union is to continue to function, it must have an efficient means of collecting dues from its members. In the old days, unions often stationed strongarm men at plant gates on paydays in order to enforce the payment of dues. Those workers who held back their union dues risked a bloody nose or even a fractured skull. But with the growth of unionism and union recognition, the *checkoff* system was introduced. The employer, with the written permission of the workers, withholds union dues and other assessments from paychecks and then transfers the funds to the union, thereby simplifying the dues-collection process and assuring the prompt and regular payment of dues.

Restricting Membership and Output

Many unions seek to obtain higher incomes for their members by restricting membership; this creates a scarcity of their particular kind of labor. Membership may be controlled in several ways: (a) varying apprenticeship requirements; (b) sponsoring state licensing for those in the trade (e.g., barbers, electricians, plumbers); (c) varying initiation fees; and (d) establishing seniority agreements which provide for the order in which workers may be laid off and rehired.

Many unions also seek to restrict their members' output in order to increase the demand for labor and thereby secure higher wages. Output restriction may be accomplished by shortening the working day, limiting the output per worker, and opposing the introduction of labor-saving technology.

Thus, whereas management may seek to increase profits by raising productive efficiency, unions are primarily interested in improving earnings and working conditions for their members. Since these objectives often conflict, the means that are chosen to achieve them must be ironed out around the bargaining table.

MULTIUNIT BARGAINING

Perhaps the most controversial issue in the practice of collective bargaining involves multiunit agreements.

Multiunit bargaining (sometimes inaccurately called "industry-wide bargaining") is a collective-bargaining arrangement covering more than one plant. It may occur between one or more firms in an industry and one or more unions, and it may take place on a national, regional, or local level. Although it can be national in scope and very inclusive, it is rarely completely industry-wide.

A number of examples can be used to illustrate the scope and diversity of multiunit bargaining.

1. In the automobile and steel industries, one employer such as General Motors or United States Steel owns a number of plants and bargains with a single union—the United Automobile Workers or the United Steel Workers.

2. In the construction and retailing industries, two or more employers in an industry may bargain with one or more national unions; the bargaining will usually be subdivided geographically into national, regional, and local areas.

3. In the bituminous coal industry, all employers bargain with one industrial union on a national basis, whereas in the railroad industry employers bargain with several groups and must consider the demands of all groups in arriving at a settlement.

4. In various western cities, bargaining has developed on an area-wide basis between employer associations and unions that cut across industry lines.

5. In the 1960s, a new movement was started called *coalition bargaining*. The AFL–CIO tries to coordinate and establish common termination dates for contracts with firms that deal with a number of unions at plants throughout the United States and Canada, so that the AFL–CIO can strengthen its bargaining position by threatening to close down all plants simultaneously.

Multiunit bargaining in the United States is a widespread and complex process that varies by industry, geography, and even by the nature of the issues involved. This explains why the expression "industry-wide bargaining" is usually not completely accurate. The chief advantages of multiunit bargaining are that it: (a) strengthens the union wage structure within markets and industries by making union-management contracts easier to negotiate and enforce; and (b) increases labor stability by making it more difficult for a rival union to enter an industry. But because of its large-scale and often national nature, multiunit bargaining poses several important problems:

First, it gives unions a strong degree of monopoly power which, coupled with the employer's fear of a widespread strike, often enables unions to extract highly inflationary wage settlements.

Second, it tends to focus on the national settlement of basic economic issues involving wages and working conditions, while leaving important "noneconomic" issues like work standards and working rules for settlement at the local plant level—often at disproportionately higher costs to employers because they lack the funds for counteroffers after national issues have been settled.

Third, it frequently allows matters of local concern to become subjects of national negotiations which might lead to strikes, even though the issues may eventually be referred back and settled at the local level.

Bloody Battles During Labor's Formative Years

Violence and bloodshed often accompanied strikes, especially during the decades of struggle for union recognition.

Since World War II, labor-management differences have almost always been settled by peaceful negotiation.

During the Standard Oil Strike in Bayonne, New Jersey, 1915, private guards were employed by the corporation to act as strikebreakers. Three workers were killed and an unknown number were injured.

United Press International.

National Guardsmen charging strikers in the Electric Auto-Lite Strike in Toledo, Ohio, May 25, 1934. Two died and many were injured.

United Press International.

United Press International.

SETTLING LABOR-MANAGEMENT DISPUTES

The collective-bargaining process can be likened to a game of strategy between opposing players, with each side threatening to employ its own unique weapons in order to defeat the other.

The employer's major weapons include injunctions and lockouts. An *injunction* is a court order forbidding an individual or group of individuals (such as a union) from taking a specified action. Employers' use of this device has been severely restricted since the Norris-LaGuardia Act of 1932. A *lockout* is the closing down of a plant by an employer in order to keep workers out of their jobs.

The union's major weapons include boycotts and strikes. A *boycott* (sometimes called a *primary boycott*) is a campaign by workers to discourage people from dealing with an employer or buying his products. A *strike* is a mutual agreement among workers to stop working, without resigning from their jobs, until their demands are met.

Experience indicates that it is rarely necessary for either side to use its maximum economic strength. Thus:

Although the power to strike is labor's ultimate weapon, it is a major and costly one which unions do not use lightly. An analysis of data since 1935 indicates that on an annual basis, the number of man-days lost due to strikes has never been as high as $1\frac{1}{2}$ percent of total labor-days worked and has averaged less than $\frac{1}{2}$ percent of that amount. This is far less than the proportion of time lost from work due to the common cold. (See Box 3.)

Arbitration and Mediation (Conciliation)

What happens if labor-management negotiations break down? In that case the unsuccessful bargainers may have to resolve their disagreements through processes known as arbitration and mediation.

Arbitration is a method of settling differences between two parties by the use of an impartial third party called an arbitrator who is acceptable to both sides and whose decision is binding and legally enforceable on the contesting parties. The arbitration procedure consists of the company and the union submitting their disagreement to the arbitrator, who, after hearing all of the evidence, issues a decision which is based not on what he thinks is wise and fair, but upon how he understands the language of the contract to apply to the case at hand. Thus, an arbitrator is like a judge: an arbitrator relates the case to the contract, just as a judge relates a case to the law.

This is voluntary arbitration, which is provided for in the great majority of all collective-bargaining agreements in effect today. There is no doubt that the existence and extensive use of this type of arbitration has helped to reduce the number of strikes.

Another plan that has often been proposed as a key to industrial peace, especially in the case of prolonged strikes, is "compulsory arbitration." Obviously, however, this is not a substitute for free collective bargaining, and where it has been tried, for example, in Australia, it has caused more turmoil than peace and has not stopped strikes. (See Box 4.)

Mediation (sometimes called *conciliation*) is a process by which a third party, the mediator, attempts to reconcile the differences between contesting parties. The mediator may try to maintain constructive discussions, search for common areas of agreement, or suggest compromises, but his decisions are not binding and need not be accepted by the contesting parties. The U.S. government provides most mediation services through an independent agency, the Federal Mediation and Con-

---

Box 4

Taking the Grief out of Grievances

Say "arbitration" to most people and they will think of compulsory arbitration, where the government steps into a labor-management contract dispute and names an arbitrator who dictates a settlement. It is a technique generally abhorred by labor and management, and rarely employed in the United States. It has, however, been used in some other countries, including Australia and England.

But say "arbitration" to an industrial relations director, or to a union official, and he will think of something quite different: voluntary—or grievance—arbitration. It's one of the handiest tools in his professional kit—and one of the most effective systems yet developed in the United States for stabilizing labor relations.

This kind of arbitration deals only with the interpretation of an existing contract. Union and management negotiate the provisions; the arbitrator clarifies their meaning when differences of opinion cannot be settled on the lower reaches of the grievance procedure. Meanwhile, work continues on the production line or at the office. That's what a grievance procedure culminating in arbitration is all about—in contrast to the British system, which gives the worker no institutional alternative but a wildcat strike if management shrugs off his grievance.

---

ciliation Service, while most states and some large municipalities provide similar services.

The Economics of Unions

Labor unions have a measurable—though debatable —influence on the economy. Their influence is particularly relevant in the spheres of resource allocation, economic stability, and growth.

HOW UNIONS MAY RAISE WAGES

Chief among the unions' many objectives is the raising of wages. Several interesting theories and models of wage determination can be developed to illustrate different kinds of competitive and monopolistic market situations. Some of these have been formulated in previous chapters that dealt with marginal productivity, income distribution, and the determination of factor prices. In this chapter, we shall focus on some simple competitive models that employ familiar supply and demand diagrams. Three types of situations are illustrated in Exhibit 2, where the supply and demand curves in each diagram relate the price of labor, expressed in wages, and the quantity of labor supplied and demanded.

Featherbedding Model

Exhibit 2, Chart (a), illustrates what happens when the union seeks to increase the demand for labor— that is, shift the demand curve to the right—through the use of *featherbedding* techniques. These are "make-work" rules or practices designed by unions to restrict output by increasing artificially the amount of labor or labor time employed on a particular job. For example, the Painters Union has limited the width of brushes and the sizes of rollers; the Meat Cutters Union has required prewrapped meat to be rewrapped on the job; the Trainmen's Union has demanded that railroads eliminate the use of radio telephones by crewmen and revert back to hand signals and lanterns; and the Railroad Brotherhood was able for years to maintain a "fireman" on diesel locomotives that have no fire.

Most featherbedding practices are imposed under the guise of promoting health or safety, but in reality they are often self-protective devices which reflect the insecurity of workers in a declining industry. There is a fundamental need, therefore, for adequate retraining programs to permit the shifting of workers to new jobs. Otherwise, featherbedding practices, like other restrictive devices whether they are employed by unions or by business firms, must ultimately result in higher prices to consumers as well as a misallocation of society's resources.

Craft Union Model

Chart (b) represents the situation in which a craft union composed of workers in a particular trade, such as carpenters or electricians, seeks to restrict the supply of labor in order to raise wages. The union may do this by imposing high obstacles to entry for those seeking membership—such as long apprenticeship requirements, high initiation fees, or closed membership periods. In the more general sense, unions have often sought to restrict the overall supply of labor in the economy by supporting legislation to: (a) curb immigration, (b) shorten the workweek, (c) reduce child labor, and (d) assure compulsory retirement. The model in Chart (b), therefore, applies to all such policies, since their effect is to shift the supply curve of labor to the left.

Industrial Union Model

The union represented in Chart (c) seeks to organize all workers in an industry and to impose a wage which is above the equilibrium wage. This changes the supply curve as explained in the exhibit. Thus at the union-imposed wage of $0W'$, employers can hire as many as $W'J$ units of labor, and they can hire no labor at less than this wage. The new supply curve $W'JS$ is thus perfectly elastic over the segment $W'J$, signifying that the industry can buy this much labor at the union wage. If it wants more than $W'J$ units of labor, it will have to pay a higher wage. According to the diagram, of course, the industry will demand only $0N'$ units of labor at the wage rate imposed by the union.

ARE UNIONS TOO BIG?

The three models in Exhibit 2 of how unions may seek to raise wages illustrate the following basic criticism often leveled against them:

Unions are monopolies; as such they engage in restrictive practices in order to achieve benefits (wages) above the free-market equilibrium levels that would exist in a competitive system, and thereby cause resource misallocation, unemployment, and inflation.

Exhibit 2

How Unions May Raise Wages in Competitive Markets

Chart (a). Increase the demand for labor. *Through feather-bedding or other restrictive and make-work practices, unions may succeed in shifting the demand for labor to the right from D to D'. This will increase the equilibrium quantity of labor from ON to ON', and the equilibrium wage from OW to OW'.*

Chart (b). Decrease the supply of labor. *If a craft union can restrict the supply of labor by shifting the supply curve from S to S', it will reduce the equilibrium quantity of labor from ON to ON' and raise the equilibrium wage from OW to OW'.*

Chart (c). Organize all workers in an industry. *An industrial union covering an entire industry would seek a wage level such as OW', which is above the equilibrium wage of OW. The supply curve of labor would thus change from its normal shape (which includes the dashed portion) to W'JS, and the equilibrium quantity would therefore change from ON to ON'.*

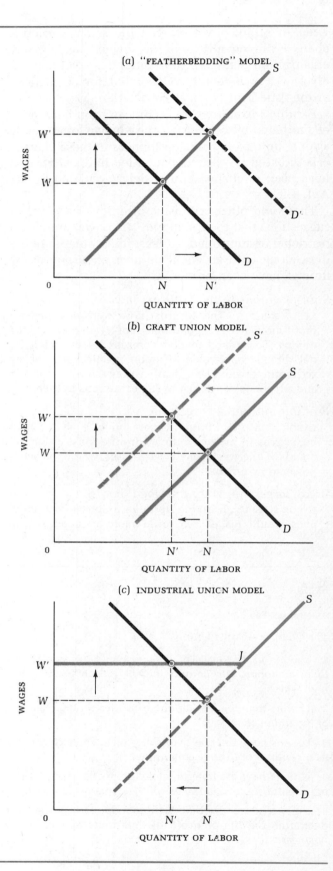

Keep in mind, however, that the same restrictive charges can equally well be leveled against any organization that has a substantial degree of monopoly power—whether it be General Motors, U.S. Steel, or the American Medical Association.

Exhibit 3 examines this criticism from both sides of the fence by comparing the charges often made against unions and their responses to these charges —both based on various pamphlets and leaflets that have been published and widely circulated by the AFL–CIO.

These and other criticisms of unions have led to suggestions that their monopolistic power should be restricted or controlled. At least four common remedies, along with an equal number of responses by unions, have been proposed:

Subject unions to the antitrust laws

LABOR'S REPLY: The antitrust laws were designed for profit-motivated corporations, not welfare-motivated unions. These laws involve complex issues which are not directly applicable to union practices and objectives, and it would be logically wrong as well as socially and economically unjust to subject unions to them.

Prohibit multiunit bargaining

LABOR'S REPLY: Multiunit bargaining enables small businesses to present a united front against union demands. Otherwise, small businesses would be overpowered by unions.

Break large unions up into local bodies

LABOR'S REPLY: Breaking up large unions into smaller ones would make them even more monopolistic in setting the price of labor. There would be several unions in each major industry, with each union monopolizing its own labor supply and seeking the highest possible wage from its employer. The union in General Motors, for example, would press for its own demands without concern with whether Ford, Chrysler, or American Motors could match those demands.

Outlaw the union shop

LABOR'S REPLY: Since workers elect the union that will represent them, the existence of union shops is democracy in action. Besides, eliminating the union shop would not necessarily reduce a union's ability to employ weapons such as boycotts and strikes.

The problem of union monopoly is thus a complex one. Although there is no doubt that unions possess varying degrees of monopoly power, there is no simple solution to the question of what should be done about it. Most observers would probably agree, however, that an attack against specific abuses rather than a sweeping attack against unions in general provides the most realistic and desirable approach.

SUMMARY OF IMPORTANT IDEAS

1. The chief overall objective of unions is to improve the wages and working conditions of their members by bargaining with employers. Much of the history of the union movement in America can be viewed as an attempt to achieve this goal.

2. The period from the Revolution to the Civil War

Exhibit 3

Are Unions Too Big?

The Charges Against Unions

1. *Unions fix the price of labor through the exertion of their monopoly power and thereby extract excessively high wages.*

2. *Unions monopolize job opportunities through the use of the union shop.*

3. *Unions have the power to shut down whole industries as a result of multiunit bargaining.*

4. *Unions have become financial giants because of their tax-exempt status and the use of the dues checkoff system.*

5. *Unions, because of their great monopolistic power, can determine the life or death of thousands of individual businesses.*

How the Unions Reply

1. *Despite the alleged monopoly power of unions, the average worker's take-home pay is still inadequate.*

2. *The union shop is simply an application of the democratic principle of majority rule.*

3. *Multiunit bargaining is necessary in order to stabilize wage rates among competing employers.*

4. *The assets of unions have made possible many significant advances in social welfare, and these assets are minute compared to the assets of giant corporations.*

5. *Unions seek countervailing power against the firms with which they bargain; they try to benefit their workers, not drive firms out of business.*

witnessed the beginnings of the American labor movement. Some craft unions were started despite the opposition of employers and the general unsympathetic attitudes of the courts.

3. From the end of the Civil War to the Depression was the formative period of unionism. The Knights of Labor, followed by the American Federation of Labor, dominated the labor movement.

4. From the depression years of the 1930s until the end of World War II, the labor movement expanded rapidly. Favorable legislation was passed which guaranteed labor's right to organize and bargain collectively with employers. The Congress of Industrial Organizations emerged in this period and was extremely successful in organizing industrial unions.

5. After World War II, unions entered an age of maturity. The following have been among the chief events since then:

    (a) Congress sought to curb some of the power of labor unions by passing the National Labor Relations Act (Taft-Hartley Act) of 1947. This law prohibited the closed shop, outlawed "unfair labor practices" of unions, and imposed other regulations on union practices.

    (b) The AFL and CIO merged in 1955 to form one huge labor organization for the purpose of strengthening the bargaining position of workers.

    (c) The Labor-Management Reporting and Disclosure Act (Landrum-Griffin Act) of 1959 constrained further the power of unions by requiring unions and union officers to submit periodic financial reports, and by imposing other restrictions on various union practices.

6. Unions try to improve the status of workers by bargaining collectively with management. Although there is no "typical" collective-bargaining agreement, the major issues usually involve matters pertaining to wages, industrial relations, multiunit bargaining, and the settlement of labor-management disputes.

7. Supply and demand models may be constructed to illustrate how unions seek to raise the wages of their members. Thus in a featherbedding model, the union tries to shift the demand curve for labor to the right; in a craft union model, the union tries to shift the supply curve of labor to the left; in an industrial union model, the union seeks to impose a wage floor above the market equilibrium level.

8. The basic criticism of unions is that they are monopolies which engage in restrictive practices in order to raise wages above free-market equilibrium levels, and hence cause resource misallocation, unemployment, and inflation. Unions reply that they exert countervailing power against the firms with which they bargain and that they thereby benefit not only workers but also society as a whole.

FOR DISCUSSION

1. *Terms and concepts to review:*

union	closed shop
craft union	Labor-Management
National Labor Rela-	Reporting and Dis-
tions (Wagner) Act	closure Act (1959)
(1935)	collective bargaining
company union	industrial relations
industrial union	open shop
Labor-Management	multiunit bargaining
Relations (Taft–	coalition bargaining
Hartley) Act (1947)	injunction
jurisdictional strike	lockout
featherbedding	boycott
union shop	strike
right-to-work laws	arbitration
AFL–CIO	mediation

2. Outline the highlights of the labor movement from the time of the Revolution to the present.

3. Some pro-labor factions have argued that the Taft-Hartley Act was a major setback to the labor movement and unfair to organized labor. If you were a *defender* of the act, how would you criticize this viewpoint? Give some examples.

4. If you were a union leader bargaining for better wages and working conditions, what criteria would you use to support your arguments? What kinds of issues might you want to negotiate?

5. What would be the probable effects of a law that required all labor-management disputes to be settled by government arbitration?

6. Which has a greater degree of monopoly power— a union's monopoly of a labor market, or a firm's monopoly of a product market? Why?

7. Do unions really raise wages? That is, do wages in unionized industries rise faster than they would if those industries were nonunionized? What are some of the basic considerations to take into account in answering these questions?

Voluntary Overtime—The Backward-bending Supply Curve

If an employee is asked to work overtime, should he have the right to refuse? This was a major issue in the auto negotiations in 1973—and has since drawn widespread attention in other industries.

At the present time, agreements between unions and managements often stipulate that workers must put in extra hours of week-end work—at premium rates—when requested. Management contends that this provision in the labor contract is necessary if a business is to be operated efficiently. When demand is high, companies often have to run their plants six or seven days a week. "It would be impossible," said an executive of a large agricultural implements firm, "to manage a complex system of interrelated manufacturing and assembly lines unless there is assurance of a constant work force. The decision of a few key employees not to work overtime could force the closing of our entire plant."

How do the unions reply? Their answer is simple. "Our members want the right to say 'No thanks,'" said United Automobile Workers president Leonard Woodcock. A number of other union leaders agree. Those representing chemical, rubber, and electrical workers, among others, have declared their intention to make voluntary overtime a bargaining issue in future contract negotiations.

Varied Experiences

Many workers resist overtime because, with large paychecks, they value their leisure more than the additional wages they would get for putting in extra hours—even at premium rates. Some observers believe, however, that this feeling is merely a by-product of prosperity; in recession, workers are faced with the difficulty of getting along on straight-time pay and are anxious to pick up any overtime they can get.

Various companies have settled the overtime question in different ways. In some firms, labor contracts require only a "reasonable amount of overtime." In others, only junior workers are required to accept it; senior employees can reject the extra hours if less-experienced workers can be found to fill the need. In still other firms, outside help is brought in to complete necessary work. But this practice is in disfavor by most companies because it is costly and inflexible.

Actually, the UAW has had more experience with voluntary overtime than any other union. In European auto plants, including those of America's Big Three—General Motors, Ford, and Chrysler—workers, by law, are given a voice on working extra hours. Since 1969, American Motors Corporation has had a voluntary-overtime clause affecting some 9,000 workers at its Kenosha, Wisconsin plant. Company officials are known to be dissatisfied with the provision and would like to scrap it, despite comments made by UAW leaders that American Motors "isn't hurting because of voluntary overtime."

Regardless of what happens in various collective-bargaining negotiations, the problem of voluntary overtime is bound to surface from time to time. It is much too important an issue, both for labor and management, to lie dormant for very long.

QUESTIONS

1. *Should a worker be required to accept available overtime? In answering this question, keep in mind that if he refuses, he may deprive others of the right to work available overtime.*

2. *The refusal of an employee to work overtime means that his supply curve of labor is backward-bending—as shown by the S curve in Chart (a) of Figure 1.*

   (a) Interpret the curve. Why does it have this peculiar shape?

   (b) If OJ is the maximum hourly wage desired, what will be the worker's income at this wage?

3. *In Chart (b), the demand and supply curves of labor for an entire industry are shown. If the equilibrium wage is OR, will this equilibrium be stable or unstable? What if the wage is OP? Explain.* (HINT: *An equilibrium is stable when a small departure from it sets forces into motion which automatically restore the equilibrium.*)

Figure 1

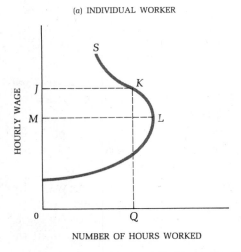

(a) INDIVIDUAL WORKER

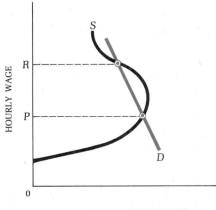

(b) ENTIRE INDUSTRY

CHAPTER 32

Insecurity and Poverty

CHAPTER PREVIEW

What chief social measures exist today to provide protection against the insecurity of old age, unemployment, disability, ill health, and death?

How can we explain the fact that in the richest country on earth, America, more than 10 percent of the families are poor?

What can be done about the problems of poverty and deprivation that confront nearly 25 million Americans? In general, what are the economic effects of proposed programs for social reform?

Security or insecurity? Welfare or illfare?

These are the alternatives that are sometimes posed in discussions of America's social problems—the problems of insecurity and poverty. For there are those who contend that a concern for social reform makes men dependent on their government and is therefore contrary to the American tradition—a tradition based on the Puritan ethic of self-reliance, industry, and thrift.

Anyone who is familiar with the history of social reform in America knows that these contentions are nothing new. From the nineteenth century to the present, we have seen the abolition of slavery, the introduction of free public education, the passage of protective legislation for labor, the provision of public charity for the needy, and the enactment of social security legislation providing some protection against the losses that may result from old age, disability, ill health, and unemployment. And always there were those who cried that such measures of protection were alien to the American tradition. In view of our history, it seems evident that our tradition is not as simple and Puritanical as these stalwart defenders make it out to be.

Thus, we shall find in this chapter that the social reform measures which are proposed today are no different in their underlying philosophy than those which were introduced a century or more ago. The differences that do exist are to be found in the scope of their objectives and in the details of the specific measures.

Insecurity and Social Security

A family is insecure if it stands a chance of suffering economically from a loss of income. Such losses may occur as a result of unemployment, illness, injury, retirement, or death of the breadwinner. Because of the consequent hardships, our present program of social security was instituted during the Great Depression.

The *Social Security Act* of 1935 (with its many subsequent amendments) is the basic comprehensive social security law of the United States. It provides for: (*a*) social insurance programs for old age, survivors, disability, and health insurance (OASDHI), and unemployment payments to insured persons; and (*b*) a public charity program in the form of welfare services, institutional care, food, housing, and other forms of assistance. Some of the provisions of the act are administered and financed by the federal government, some by state and local govern-

ments, and some by all three levels of government. (See Exhibit 1.)

By sketching some of the act's main features, we can gain a better understanding of the underlying logic and philosophy of our social security system.

SOCIAL INSURANCE PROGRAMS

The several insurance programs that are contained in the Social Security Act are diverse in their coverage, benefits, financing, and administration. They can be classified, however, into categories providing protection against: (1) old age, disability, ill health, and death; and (2) unemployment.

Exhibit 1

Social Welfare Expenditures Under Selected Public Programs

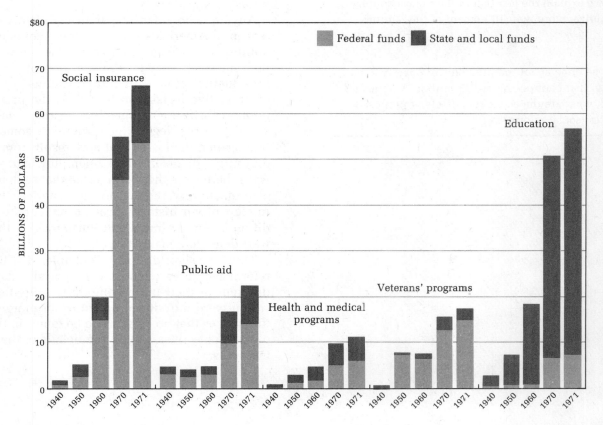

SOURCE: U.S. Bureau of the Census.

Old Age, Survivors, Disability, and Health Insurance (OASDHI)

The OASDHI program embraces what most people commonly refer to as "social security." It is actually an annuity scheme—a special type of compulsory saving program—which provides cash benefits when earnings are cut off by old age, total disability, or death. The benefits vary according to the amount of social security taxes collected from the employer and the employee. These taxes and benefits have increased over the years, presumably to compensate for inflation. More than 90 percent of all employed persons are eligible for benefits, including retirement benefits at age 65, and a similar proportion of mothers and children are eligible to receive survivors' payments if the head of the family dies. Medical and hospital insurance for those over 65, known as Medicare, also exists, providing for the health needs of people with modest incomes.

Unemployment Insurance

The unemployment insurance program is administered by the individual states within a general framework established by the federal government. The program provides for *unemployment benefits*—weekly payments to covered workers who are involuntarily unemployed for a specified number of weeks. In the early 1970s about 53 million workers, or almost two-thirds of the civilian labor force, were eligible for unemployment benefits. The average payment made was $54 per week, and the average period of payment was 14 weeks.

CHARITABLE PROGRAMS—WELFARE

The noninsurance part of the social security system consists of charitable or welfare programs administered by federal, state, and local governments, to which the federal government contributes substantially. These programs are often referred to as special assistance programs because they are intended to help special categories of needy persons. The more important programs are the following:

1. Aid to the aged, the blind, and the totally and permanently disabled

2. Medical assistance to the needy

3. Food distribution through relief programs, food stamp plans, and government subsidization of school lunches

4. Housing subsidies to provide public housing projects and cash rent supplements for low-income groups

5. Welfare services in the form of institutional care (such as free hospitals and orphanages) for needy adults and children; health, rehabilitation, and counseling services; and financial assistance to needy families

In addition to these, there are general assistance programs administered and financed exclusively by various state and local governments.

EVALUATING SOCIAL SECURITY

The social security system—including both federal and state programs—provides a measure of protection against most major forms of insecurity. Nevertheless, it has been the subject of severe criticisms —particularly with respect to financing.

Social security is in no meaningful sense an insurance program for three reasons:

☐ Individual benefits are determined by many factors other than taxes paid, thus creating a disparity between receipts and payments.

☐ Participation and "contributions" are compulsory, and individuals are unable to select and pay for the particular benefits they wish to receive.

☐ The tax used to finance the program is a payroll tax based on a fixed percentage of wages up to a specified minimum-wage level; therefore the burden of the tax is regressive, bearing most heavily on low- and middle-income groups.

In addition, the payroll tax has a destabilizing effect on the national economy. Since it is a tax on wages, increases in the tax rate legislated during recessions delay recovery by reducing income available for spending.

In view of the above shortcomings, a different and fairer way of paying for social security is needed. Three alternative approaches to reform may be considered:

1. *Restructure the payroll tax.* The payroll tax could be revised to permit exemptions and deductions similar to those used for the income tax. This would greatly reduce if not eliminate the tax on families in poverty. Any loss in revenue resulting from the restructuring of the tax could be made up by a small percentage increase in the income tax.

2. *Substitute the income tax.* The payroll tax could be replaced by the income tax as a means of financing social security. This would require a substantial increase in income-tax rates in order to produce larger yields. However, since a major adjustment in the rate schedule of the income tax is not likely to be undertaken at any one time, it would probably be more feasible to restructure it in small steps, thus permitting the full burden of the payroll tax to be transferred gradually in an equitable way.

3. *Finance benefits from general revenues.* The costs of social security could be paid out of the general funds of the U.S. Treasury. Certain benefits are already financed in this way. By extending the procedure to cover all benefits out of general revenues, the financing of social security would be made more equitable because the taxes supplying the general fund are largely progressive.

These reforms are not mutually exclusive. They could be combined in various ways to produce a fairer method of paying for social security. At the very least, if the payroll tax is retained, an equitable system of exemptions for low-income families should be provided and a deliberate effort should be made to avoid worsening recessions by untimely tax increases.

Affluence and Poverty: America's Underdeveloped Nation

America's aggregate wealth and opportunity are unmatched by any nation in history. Its fields and factories generate a superabundance of foods, goods, and gadgets; most of its families possess automobiles and television sets, and the great majority of families own their homes.

The signs of affluence are everywhere—except for 20 to 25 million Americans who live in poverty and deprivation. This group is larger than the population of many countries. It is composed of men, women, and children of all races who live near or below the bare subsistence level. (See Box 1.)

WHAT IS POVERTY?

What constitutes "bare subsistence"? For many years, economists and statisticians have grappled with the problem of defining and measuring poverty. Central to the concept is the so-called *poverty line*—

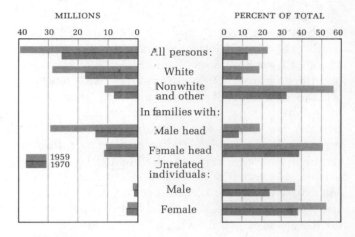

Box 1

Persons in Families and Unrelated Individuals Below Low-income (Poverty) Level

SOURCE: U.S. Bureau of the Census.

a sliding income scale which varies between rural and urban locations according to family size. The level for an urban family of four—which is regarded as fairly typical—was approximately $4,200 in the early 1970s.

Of course, many of the people who fall below the line, such as a married medical school student or an elderly couple on social security who own their home and car, are poor only by definition. Nor does the poverty line distinguish between costs of living in different areas of the country: a low income goes a lot farther in Meridian, Mississippi, than in San Francisco or New York City. Nevertheless, in view of the following facts a simple income measure of poverty seems to understate the real dimensions of the situation:

1. A poverty-line income for a family of four allows for no dental care and practically no medical care; it also permits no movies, newspapers, or books, and very little clothing, meat, fruits, or vegetables.

2. More than 10 percent of the total population is classified as poor. Contrary to a widespread general belief, blacks are not the majority in the group: of 25 million poor Americans, approximately 18 million are white.

3. About 70 percent of the total population live in cities and towns, and so it is not surprising that over 60 percent of the poor are urban dwellers. About half the poor are under 25 years old, and almost a fifth—about 4.7 million of them—are over 65.

As suggested by Exhibit 2, there is no simple and unique definition of poverty—or even "poorness." It is an economic and psychological state of being that varies for different people from time to time and from place to place.

WHAT ARE THE CAUSES AND COSTS OF POVERTY?

We may distinguish among three different types of poverty, according to the economic, social, and personal factors that cause them.

1. *Cyclical poverty.* A fall in aggregate demand for goods and services may cause a depression or a deep recession; the result is mass unemployment and widespread poverty. However, with the growth of modern macroeconomic theory and policy, political leaders have learned how to avoid such severe set-

---

Exhibit 2

The Paradox of Poverty

What constitutes poverty? In some of the poorest counties of the nation, the great majority of homes lack baths and inside toilets, and a large minority have no running water. Their inhabitants, by present-day American standards, would be classified as poverty-stricken.

But let us examine the situation more closely.

In the early 1970s, among households with annual incomes under $5,000:

80 percent have television sets (many of them color)

80 percent have refrigerators

70 percent have one or more cars

62 percent have washing machines

25 percent have freezers

24 percent have clothes dryers

21 percent have air conditioners (including both room and central systems)

4 percent have dishwashers

The poor in America thus have many of the accoutrements of an affluent society. This is the paradox of poverty. The American poor are not the same as the starving poor of India or China, but they are poor nevertheless.

Charles Harbutt.

backs in the economy, and this cause of poverty is no longer considered a serious problem.

2. *Community poverty.* A region may lose its economic base or its major source of income and employment, thereby leaving an entire population in a state of economic deprivation. Among the classic examples of this are the Appalachian coal regions, which have suffered drastically from declining demands for coal and from the introduction of labor-saving technology in coal mining; and many rural areas which have suffered heavy unemployment because technology and machinery have replaced manual labor. This type of poverty can be remedied only through regional economic development programs or outward migration.

3. *Personal poverty.* Poverty has always existed among some individuals and families, in times of prosperity as well as in depression, in high-income regions and in low-income ones. It is due to personal and social factors, some of which are beyond the individual's control. For example, aside from that small proportion of the poor whom sociologists refer to as the "disreputable poor" (the tramps, beggars, derelicts, etc.) there are those families that are poverty-stricken because they are victims of racial prejudice, inadequate training and job opportunities, physical or mental handicaps, desertion of the breadwinner, and other causes.

Poverty levies serious social costs. Sociological studies have concluded that poverty causes ill health and emotional disturbance and helps to spread disease. It also causes delinquency, vice, and crime. All these impose heavy costs on the community, which must maintain more police and fire protection, more courts and jails, more public health and sanitation facilities, and more welfare programs.

Further, there is evidence that poverty breeds poverty—that the children of the poor grow up and marry others who are similarly deprived. They tend to have more children than they can provide with a proper start in life. These children are likewise raised in a poverty environment, and so the cycle perpetuates itself from one generation to the next.

Can We Eliminate Poverty?

Considering the high cost of poverty, what can be done about America's nation of the poor? In order to launch an attack on the problem, Congress passed the *Economic Opportunity Act* of 1964, declaring that a national policy goal will be:

> . . . to eliminate the paradox of poverty in the midst of plenty in this Nation by opening to everyone the opportunity for education and training, the opportunity to work, and the opportunity to live in decency and dignity.

The Economic Opportunity Act opened a door to waging a war on poverty. In addition, a number of specific proposals—beyond those involving improvements in the welfare system itself—have been advanced. These fall loosely into three groups: (1) family allowances or guaranteed annual incomes; (2) negative income taxes; and (3) combinations of both.

FAMILY ALLOWANCES OR GUARANTEED ANNUAL INCOMES

Many sociologists and social workers have suggested the adoption of a *family allowance* system. Under this plan, every family in the country, rich or poor, would receive from the government a certain amount of money based exclusively on the number and age of its children. Those families that are above certain designated income levels would return all or part of the money with their income taxes; those below specified income levels would keep it. More than 60 nations, including Canada and all the European countries, give such family allowances.

A modified version of the family allowance plan is the *guaranteed annual income.* This would award all families under the "poverty line" a straight allowance for each parent plus specified amounts for each child according to the size of the family. As the family's income rose, the payment would be reduced until a break-even level a little higher than the poverty line was reached.

Under both the family allowance and guaranteed annual income plans, families would not be as well or better off by not working. Nevertheless, there is substantial opposition to these proposals in Congress, partly because of the fear that they would be too costly, and partly because many legislators believe that the plans place more emphasis on governmental "big brother" paternalism than on providing jobs.

NEGATIVE INCOME TAXES

A scheme which has received widespread interest and support from liberal and conservative economists, businessmen, and political leaders has been the *negative income tax*. This would guarantee the poor a certain minimum income through a type of reverse income tax: a poor family, depending on its size and private income level, would be paid by the government enough either to reduce or close the gap between what it earned and some explicit minimum level of income which might be equal to or modestly above the government's designated poverty line. The size of payments, of course, would depend on the specific formula adopted. A hypothetical illustration appears in Exhibit 3.

Several major advantages are claimed for this proposal.

1. *Administrative efficiency.* The present governmental administrative machinery—the Internal Revenue Service and the Treasury—would handle records and disburse payments, so that a new government agency would not be needed.

2. *Income criterion.* Income deficiency would be the sole criterion for establishing eligibility for subsidy, instead of the plethora of criteria that have existed in the past. Many more millions of poor families would thus be eligible. With the resulting expanded coverage, many poor families would have an income "floor" under them and they could begin to break the cycle of poverty that has kept some of them on welfare for several generations.

3. *Incentive maintenance.* As the family's income increased, payments from the government would decrease by some proportion. Thus the incentive to work in order to gain more income would not be reduced.

But despite these advantages, there are also difficulties to be recognized:

1. *High cost.* The negative income tax could not be administered, as many of its proponents claim, with only a small addition to the staff of the Internal Revenue Service. Checks would have to be sent out monthly or weekly, and effective controls established. This large task would require substantial changes in the IRS administrative structure.

2. *Opposition by middle-income classes.* Workers in the middle-income groups would receive no benefits from the negative income tax, as they would from a family allowance plan. In addition, they would undoubtedly resent paying taxes to subsidize families whose annual incomes were only a few hundred dollars less than their own.

Exhibit 3

How the Negative Income Tax Might Work

This is how the negative income tax plan might work for a family of six, consisting of two adults and four children:

1. As the family's income increases, the government payments that it receives decrease according to the formula:

Government payments = $2,600 − $\frac{1}{2}$ (earned income)

Thus you can verify with the formula or from the chart that if earned income is zero, the family receives a government payment of $2,600 a year. If earned income rises to $1,000, the family receives a government payment of $2,100, giving it a spendable income of $3,100. Similarly, at an earned income of $2,000, the government payment is $1,600, thus making spendable income $3,600.

2. The break-even point occurs at an earned income of $5,200. At this point government payments are zero, and at higher income levels the family begins to pay income taxes.

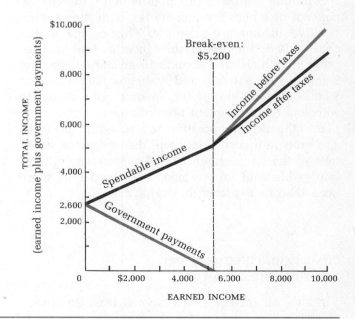

COMBINING THE FAMILY ALLOWANCE AND
THE NEGATIVE INCOME TAX PLANS

Both family allowances and negative income taxes have their advantages and disadvantages. In view of this, can a plan be developed which combines the best features of both? One possibility, which may be called an "income allowance plan," is illustrated for a family of four in Exhibit 4. The same model can be adapted to larger or smaller families.

Look at the table first. The essential feature of the plan is that it grants an annual monetary allowance to each member of a family—regardless of the family's income. (Of course, an upper limit can be set on the total amount granted to any family, and separate allowances can be provided for those covered by OASDHI insurance.) If we assume that the allowance is $500 for every man, woman, and child, and that the tax rate is 30 percent on earned income—income other than the allowance—the way in which the plan would affect a family of four is shown in the table. Note that at any level of earned income before tax, the family's earned income after the 30 percent tax plus its fixed-income allowance of $2,000 equals its disposable income.

These ideas are also conveyed in the chart. The 45-degree line serves as a benchmark. Along this line, the family's earned income would equal its disposable income if there were no taxes or allowances. However, since taxes and allowances exist, their influences on income are shown by the two remaining lines.

A unique feature of this plan is that it merges the concept of a negative income tax with the existing positive income-tax schedule. This occurs in the chart where the disposable income line reaches point A, which corresponds to an earned income before tax of $10,000 and a disposable income of $9,000. Beyond this point, income allowances are zero and the 30 percent tax no longer exists. In its place, the present positive tax schedule prevails. The rates in this schedule will determine the steepness of the line segment AB. A wide range of rates is possible, and no one need end up paying more taxes than he is presently paying.

CONCLUSION: INCOME PLANS
NOT THE WHOLE ANSWER

Virtually all income plans have at least three variables in common:

1. An income "floor"—a minimum level of income to be received by everyone

2. A positive "tax" rate which decreases the government allowance as income increases

3. A break-even level of income at which the government allowance is zero

The problem in setting up an income plan, of course, involves the correct selection of these variables while maintaining proper work incentives. The minimum-income and break-even levels should not be set so high as to subsidize those who do not need assistance.

In general:

All income plans have the same goal—to put money into the hands of the poor. At best, therefore, they can only relieve the symptoms of poverty—not its causes. To cure the disease itself, an income plan must be combined with proper work incentive and job training programs.

Attacking Poverty through the Labor Market

One of the problems encountered in trying to eliminate poverty is that a very large proportion of the poor do not or cannot earn enough money to support their families. Those who fall into this category comprise a mixed bag of "subemployed" human resources. They include not only involuntarily unemployed, but also large numbers of discouraged jobless who have given up looking for work, part-time workers who want but are unable to find full-time employment, and full-time workers who hold jobs at inadequate pay.

In view of this, what measures besides family allowances, negative income taxes, and income allowances can be undertaken to improve the lot of America's poor—and thereby wage the war against poverty on yet another front? There are two approaches which operate directly through the labor market, rather than through income redistribution: (1) minimum-wage adjustments, and (2) manpower programs.

MINIMUM WAGES

Minimum-wage legislation has had a long history, both at home and abroad. The objectives of such legislation are: (a) to prevent firms from paying substandard wages when labor-market conditions en-

Exhibit 4

Income Allowance Plan for a Family of Four
(annual data—hypothetical)

Assumptions: (1) 30% tax on earned income; (2) income allowance = $2,000 (i.e., $500 per person)

Earned income before tax	Income tax at 30%	Earned income after 30% tax		Income allowance		Disposable income
$ 0	$ 0	$ 0	+	$2,000	=	$2,000
1,000	300	700	+	2,000	=	2,700
2,000	600	1,400	+	2,000	=	3,400
3,000	900	2,100	+	2,000	=	4,100
4,000	1,200	2,800	+	2,000	=	4,800
5,000	1,500	3,500	+	2,000	=	5,500
6,000	1,800	4,200	+	2,000	=	6,200
7,000	2,100	4,900	+	2,000	=	6,900
8,000	2,400	5,600	+	2,000	=	7,600
9,000	2,700	6,300	+	2,000	=	8,300
10,000	3,000	7,000	+	2,000	=	9,000

Both the table and chart show that at lower-income levels, the family pays less in taxes than it receives in allowances. At higher-income levels the reverse is true. For example, when earned income before tax is $3,000, the family pays $900 in taxes and receives $2,000 in allowances, so it has a net gain of $1,100. When earned income before tax is $8,000, the family pays $2,400 in taxes and still receives $2,000 in allowances—a net loss of $400.

When the family's earned income before tax exceeds $10,000, the income allowance ceases and the present positive tax schedule goes into effect. The rate structure of the tax schedule determines the slope of the line segment AB.

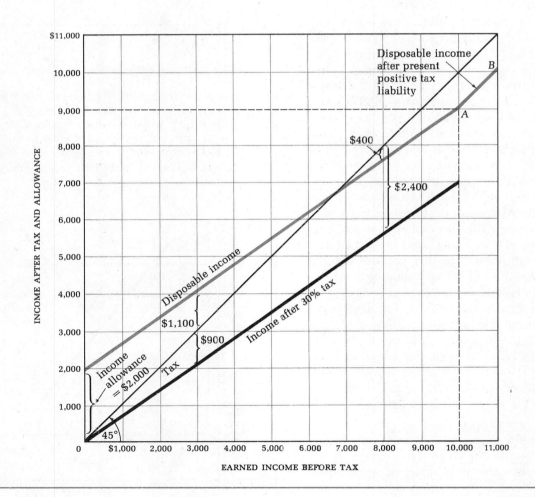

able them to do so; (b) to establish a wage floor representing some minimal level of living; and (c) to increase purchasing power by raising the incomes of low-wage workers. In the United States, the basic minimum-wage law is the *Fair Labor Standards Act of 1938*. Commonly called the Wages and Hours Law, the act has been amended from time to time for the purposes of raising the statutory wage minimum and providing coverage for broader categories of workers. Although the majority of states also have minimum-wage legislation of various forms, most of the state laws are neither well formulated nor properly enforced, as a result of which their desired effects are inadequately realized.

Pros and Cons of Minimum Wages

What are the economic consequences of minimum wages? The answers are not certain. Before examining the issues, you can gain a better appreciation of the problem by analyzing the effects of minimum wages in terms of a supply and demand model.

In Exhibit 5, the curves labeled S and D represent the supply of and demand for workers in a competitive labor market. The upward-sloping supply curve indicates that more units of labor will be supplied at a higher wage than at a lower one, and the downward-sloping demand curve indicates that a larger quantity of labor will be demanded at a lower wage than at a higher one. If no minimum wage is imposed, the equilibrium price at which labor will be bought and sold—the equilibrium wage—will be 0W, and the equilibrium quantity will be 0N.

If society feels that the equilibrium wage is too low, it will support legislation to establish a minimum wage at some higher level. Suppose the legal minimum is set at 0W'. At that wage level the quantity of labor demanded will be W'J, and the quantity supplied will be W'K. There will thus be a surplus of labor equal to the amount JK. This surplus denotes a pool of labor that has become unemployed as a result of government's imposition of a minimum wage. Moreover, the higher the minimum wage, the greater the pool of unemployed. For example, if the minimum wage is raised to the level represented by 0W'', the new labor surplus will be the amount LM as compared to the previous smaller surplus JK.

On the basis of a supply and demand analysis as shown in Exhibit 5, opponents of minimum wages conclude that legally set wage floors cause unemployment. The workers who become unemployed are those whose productivities are not high enough to earn the legal minimum. As a result, they either remain permanently unemployed or seek work in low-wage marginal industries not covered by the minimum-wage law, thereby depressing wages in those industries still further.

How do those who favor wider use of minimum wages as a means of alleviating poverty respond to these conclusions? They offer arguments such as the following:

1. The market for labor is not perfectly competitive, as the supply and demand model assumes. Instead it is imperfectly competitive, with a high degree of employer *monopsony*—monopolistic power—in the hiring of resources. As a result, employers are able to exploit low-skilled workers by paying them less than their productivities warrant. Therefore, by raising minimum wages and by broadening coverage, government can reduce exploitation without causing unemployment.

Exhibit 5

Effect of Minimum Wages in a Competitive Labor Market

In a competitive market the equilibrium wage, 0W, and quantity of labor, 0N, are determined by the intersection of the supply and demand curves for labor. If a minimum wage is imposed, a surplus of labor or unemployment results. Thus at Minimum Wage 1, the surplus is JK; at Minimum Wage 2, it is LM. In general, the higher the minimum wage, the greater the surplus.

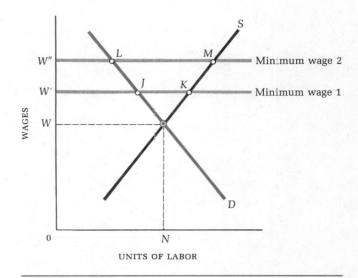

2. Increases in minimum wages raise both consumer purchasing power and production costs. However, low-income workers spend their increased wages quickly, creating multiplier effects on consumption and income. The resulting expansions in aggregate demand, therefore, more than offset the rise in production costs, thereby stimulating a higher rather than lower level of employment.

3. Enforced higher wages encourage employers to develop better ways of utilizing their resources. This leads to improvements in efficiency, resulting in benefits for everyone—business firms, workers, consumers, and society as a whole.

Conclusion: What Does the Evidence Show?

In view of the wide differences between opposing camps, what can be said of the link between minimum wages and poverty? This problem has been the subject of numerous research investigations, both by government and academic economists. Out of the mass of studies done on various national, regional, and industry-wide levels, covering periods of cyclical upswings and downswings, the following conclusion emerges:

The preponderance of evidence indicates that statutory wage minimums do not unqualifiedly aid the poor—as is frequently claimed. Although minimum wages help some workers, they cause unemployment among those who are the least well off in terms of marketable skills or location—the competitively disadvantaged groups of society.

Thus, although minimum-wage legislation may be an effective device for eliminating substandard wages, it is probably not an effective means of reducing poverty. This is because minimum wages attack the effect rather than the cause. Other measures, therefore, are needed if the problem of poverty is to be solved.

MANPOWER POLICIES—THE DUAL LABOR MARKET THEORY

A second approach to attacking poverty via the labor market is through *manpower policies*. These are deliberate efforts undertaken in the private and public sectors to develop and use the capacities of human beings as actual or potential members of the labor force. Many different groups are involved in formulating and implementing such policies. They include government agencies at the national and local levels, employers, unions, colleges, and voluntary organizations. Despite such diversity, however, there is widespread agreement that one of the nation's major manpower problems is to find adequate jobs for its poor.

Most middle-class Americans believe—because they have been taught to believe—that anyone who really wants to work can find a "good job." The facts indicate that this is not so. Evidence suggests that there exists what may appropriately be called a *dual labor market*. This market consists of two submarkets: (1) a primary labor market in which jobs are characterized by relatively high wages, favorable working conditions, and employment stability; and (2) a secondary labor market in which jobs, when they are available, pay relatively low wages, provide poor working conditions, and are highly unstable. Blue-collar workers, many of whom are union members, and white-collar workers comprise most of the participants in the primary market, whereas the competitively "disadvantaged poor"—the unskilled, the undereducated, and the victims of racial prejudice—are confined to the secondary market. In view of this:

Manpower policies for the disadvantaged, at the very least, must provide employment opportunities for individuals who want to work but are unable to find a job. More specifically, such policies must seek to accomplish two goals: (1) provide opportunities for those in the secondary market to qualify for primary employment, and (2) improve the quality of secondary employment.

What can be done to reach these goals? A number of specific measures have existed for many years. Others have been suggested, some of which are in various stages of discussion within the government. Generally speaking, all such policies follow three main avenues of attack:

☐ They seek to break down discriminatory employment practices through government legislation, subsidies, and employer education.

☐ They try to upgrade workers from the secondary to the primary market through training and job-experience programs.

☐ They attempt to qualify people for employment in the secondary market by providing education, counseling, and related services.

Despite these efforts, manpower policies by themselves cannot solve the poverty problem. Such poli-

cies have to be coordinated with other measures
—such as a negative income tax or an income allowance plan—if significant advances are to be made.
But even this may not go far enough in helping to get
people off the welfare roles unless our present
methods of matching workers with jobs can be integrated effectively into a total manpower system.

SUMMARY OF IMPORTANT IDEAS

1. The U.S. social security system is based primarily
on the Social Security Act of 1935 and its many subsequent amendments. Through social insurance, the
system provides a measure of protection against old
age, unemployment, disability, ill health, and death;
through charity, it provides welfare services for the
needy. However, the payroll tax which contributes
to financing the system is regressive, bearing down
most heavily on low- and middle-income groups.

2. Poverty is one of today's most fundamental issues, affecting nearly 25 million Americans. The
basic types of poverty are cyclical poverty, community poverty, and personal poverty. The great
social costs of poverty have resulted in many proposals for reform.

3. Various income schemes and assistance plans
have been proposed to revise and improve our welfare program. Among the most popular are family
allowances, the guaranteed annual income, and the
negative income tax. No matter which approach or
combination of approaches is adopted, it must be
combined with a work incentive and job training
program if it is to remove people from a lifetime on
the dole and make them productive, useful members
of society.

4. The problem of poverty can be attacked through
the labor market. Two approaches which have been
considered are (a) minimum-wage adjustments, and
(b) manpower programs. The preponderance of evidence indicates that the former creates adverse employment effects—particularly among competitively
"disadvantaged groups," while the latter, to be successful, must recognize the existence of a dual labor
market and seek to provide opportunities for those

in the secondary market to qualify for primary employment.

FOR DISCUSSION

1. *Terms and concepts to review:*

Social Security Act (1935)	guaranteed annual income
unemployment benefits	Fair Labor Standards Act (1938)
poverty line	monopsony
family allowance plan	manpower policies
negative income tax	dual labor market

2. What are the main features of our social security
system? Is the system adequate? Explain.

3. Why not solve the problem of poverty by simply
redistributing income equally to everyone?

4. It has been suggested that there is a remarkable
inverse relationship between fecundity and "hot
baths"—the latter representing the reasonable creature comforts of life, such as a basic but adequate
amount of food, clothing, housing, and sanitation
facilities. If such a relationship exists, it might be
better to break the poverty cycle by providing poor
people with these goods. What do you think of this
argument? (NOTE: Do you think the same argument
could apply to underdeveloped, overpopulated
regions like India or China?)

5. In contrast to Question 4, suppose that providing
income allowances to poor families increased their
birth rates. What might this imply about the elasticity relationship between the supply of children
and family income? Explain the various implications of this.

6. Evaluate the various income plans that have been
proposed for attacking the problem of poverty.

7. Two measures have often been advocated by
political leaders as a means of encouraging employers to provide on-the-job training for the disadvantaged: (a) tax incentives, and (b) contract subsidies. Which measure is likely to be more effective?
Discuss.

Racism and Sexism: What Economics Tells Us

Discrimination is a term widely used today. It generally refers to the differential treatment of persons. The most pervasive types of discrimination are racism and sexism. It is interesting to see some of the ways in which these common forms of discrimination can be analyzed in terms of supply and demand. Two practical situations which may be considered are: (1) the effect of neighborhood integration on property values, and (2) discrimination in employment.

Neighborhood Integration and Property Values

You will often hear it said that when blacks move into a white neighborhood, property values decline. Although there is insufficient scientific evidence to confirm or refute this hypothesis, it is instructive to examine conditions under which it may or may not be true.

In Figure 1, the curves S and D represent the normal supply and demand for housing in an unintegrated (white) neighborhood. The equilibrium price of housing is at P and the equilibrium quantity at Q. Now suppose that a black family buys a house in the area. If neither the neighbors nor potential buyers harbor any racial prejudices, the supply and demand curves will be unaffected and the equilibrium price and quantity will remain at their present levels.

Suppose, however, that some of the neighbors discriminate against blacks. If those neighbors do not want to live in an integrated area, they might decide to sell their houses at a price below what they would have accepted earlier. The supply curve of housing will therefore shift to the right from S to S'. As a result, the equilibrium price will decline to the level at P_1, and the equilibrium quantity will increase to the level at Q_1.

Figure 1

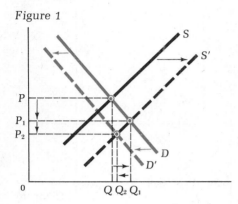

Of course, sellers are not the only ones who can discriminate against blacks; some potential buyers may, too. If buyers discriminate, they will be willing to buy less housing at any given price than they were willing to buy before. The effect of this action is to shift the demand curve to the left—from D to D' in the diagram. The intersection of the new demand curve D' with the new supply curve S' determines a still lower equilibrium price and quantity— namely, P_2 as compared to P_1, and Q_2 as compared to Q_1—than existed when sellers discriminated but buyers did not.

Three important conclusions emerge from this analysis:

1. Property values will be unaffected by neighborhood integration if neither white sellers nor white buyers discriminate against blacks.

2. Property values will be driven down by neighborhood integration if white sellers or white buyers discriminate. The amount by which property values deteriorate will depend on the intensity of discrimination—the extent to which the supply curve is shifted to the right, or the demand curve to the left—as a result of integration.

3. Property values do not decline as a result of integration per se. They decline because whites discriminate against blacks, thereby bringing about

the deterioration in property values that whites fear.

Discrimination in Employment

"There is a great variety of occupations which women have begun to claim as fields for individual effort from which no intelligent, refined man who views things as they really are would seek to exclude them."

This statement appeared in the magazine *Scientific American* in September, 1870. More than 100 years later, evidence exists that women are still a long way from job equality with men. Despite substantial progress, recent studies show that women earn 10 percent to 20 percent less simply because they are women.

Much the same is also true of certain minority groups. Blacks, orientals, homosexuals, and so forth, have long been victims of discrimination in employment. This has had several interesting economic consequences—as the following discussion points out.

Dual-market Model

An opportunity for discrimination exists when a market can be divided into homogeneous submarkets. Price and quantity can then be established in each submarket through the separate interactions of supply and demand. An illustration of this is shown in the dual-labor market model of Figure 2. Chart (a) represents a primary-labor market for males; Chart (b) depicts a secondary-labor market for females. (The same model could be used to analyze discrimination between whites and blacks, skilled and unskilled, or other competing groups.)

In Chart (a), the intersection of the demand curve D for labor in the primary market with the supply curve of males, S_M, results in an equilibrium wage rate for males at W_M and an equilibrium quantity of male employ-

Figure 2

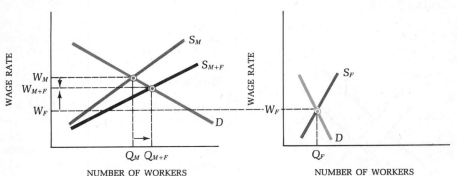

(a) PRIMARY MARKET (b) SECONDARY MARKET

ment, Q_M. Since women are excluded from this market, they must seek employment elsewhere—namely, in the market represented by Chart (b). In this secondary market, occupations are less productive than in the primary market. As a result, Chart (b) shows that the demand for women's services is less, and the supply of females looking for jobs is smaller, than the demand for and supply of men's services in Chart (a). The economic consequence of this is that the equilibrium wage rate for females, W_F, and the equilibrium quantity of female employment, Q_F, are both less than for males.

How can the situation be corrected? The ideal solution would be to eliminate discrimination by permitting women to compete with men in the primary market. If this were done, the supply curve of females S_F in Chart (b) would be added to the S_M curve in Chart (a), yielding a new total market supply curve of males and females, S_{M+F}.

As you can see from Chart (a), the elimination of discrimination would have three major effects:

1. Total employment would be raised from the level at Q_M to the level at Q_{M+F}. This would also lead to increased production because women would be employed in more productive jobs than before. Consequently, society would benefit by receiving a larger volume of output for the same labor input than it receives when markets are segregated.

2. The equilibrium wage of females would increase, and the equilibrium wage of males would decrease, to the level at W_{M+F}. Further, the increase in wages received by women would more than offset the decrease in wages received by men. Society, therefore, would experience a *net monetary gain*.

3. The increased wages received by women would not come at the expense of reduced wages received by men. It would come from the gain in productivity and the additional output that results from the elimination of discrimination.

QUESTIONS

1. *If blacks rather than whites tend to buy in to a newly integrated neighborhood, would property values decline? Illustrate with supply and demand curves.*

2. *"If job discrimination against females were eliminated, the increase in wages received by women would more than offset the decrease in wages received by men. Therefore, society as a whole would be better off because its net satisfactions would be increased." Do you agree?* (HINT: What does "better off" mean?)

CHAPTER 33

City and Suburb

CHAPTER PREVIEW

Education, housing, and transportation are among the critical problems of our cities. What are some of the important principles and concepts that economics can offer as a guide for coping with these problems?

Many of our cities today are faced with a serious fiscal dilemma. What is the nature of this dilemma? How did it arise? What measures can be taken to resolve it in order to improve our urban environment?

The eminent philosopher Alfred North Whitehead once remarked: "The major advances in civilization are processes which all but wreck the societies in which they occur."

According to some observers, American society is already close to being wrecked. Since World War I, the everyday life of Western man has undergone greater changes than it has since the dawn of the Christian era, as a revolution in agricultural technology has shifted a high proportion of the population from the farms to the cities.

In 1918, 50 percent of the nation's population was rural, as shown in Exhibit 1. Today, about 70 percent of the population is urban and living on only 1 percent of the land; by the year 2000, more than 80 percent of the population will be living in urban areas and much of the remaining 20 percent will be at least "semiurbanized."

This trend toward urbanization has created social and economic problems of enormous significance—problems of mass transit, suburban sprawl, medical care, education, crime control, housing, urban renewal, and ghetto unemployment, to mention only a few. As a result, the problems of American cities are among the most seriously debated issues of our time.

The social problems of urbanization are inseparable from the economic ones. To highlight and analyze some of the more important aspects of this extremely complex subject we shall focus most of our attention on the economic issues.

An Overview of Urban Problems

The problems of American cities result from a unique set of pressures. Some of them are deeply rooted in the nation's history; others go back only a few decades. Taken together, they have posed issues

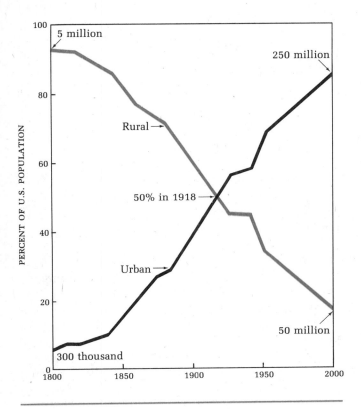

Exhibit 1

Ruralization and Urbanization

and initiated controversies that will be with us for many years to come. Since it is impossible to analyze all the problem areas, we may begin by sketching a few that are of major concern.

1. *Education.* One of the most technologically *unprogressive* segments of the economy is education. It has had to expand its resources to meet the needs of a growing population and to transmit the results of a knowledge explosion. However, it has not expanded efficiently—especially in urban areas where the demands upon it have been relatively greatest. Society has borne the cost in the form of higher taxes and inferior results. New ways must be sought to improve the efficiency and quality of education. Perhaps the most promising possibility is to move the public schools out of the public sector, where they have been dominated by rigid bureaucratic controls, and into the private sector, where they can compete freely for consumers' dollars. Some city governments have already taken steps in this direction, and others are giving it serious consideration.

2. *Housing.* American cities have long had to face the task of assuring an adequate number of decent homes for everyone. Considerable government aid has been given to the middle-income groups, but not enough to the poor. As a result, the cities are still confronted with a mounting demand for low-cost dwellings. Added to this are the problems of discrimination which blacks and other minority groups encounter in the housing market. These are among the more important difficulties that make "the housing problem" a multidimensional issue of great social as well as economic significance.

3. *Transportation.* The ability to move goods and people is basic to the life of a city. Motor vehicles have come to play a dominant role, but cannot alone carry the burden. Hence the cities must now create properly balanced transportation systems, including highways, buses, monorails, subways, and parking spaces. Such systems seek to optimize the use of transportation facilities with minimum congestion and maximum efficiency. At the present time many urban transportation ills are apparent: frequent overcrowding, poor service, inequitable sharing of burdens, and inadequate planning for future needs and costs. With the growth of population and industry, these problems will become progressively worse unless new transportation policies are formulated.

4. *Urban finance.* The most fundamental economic challenge facing the cities is to find ways of raising the money needed to pay for urban improvements. The problems are manifold. Increases in low-income urban populations have brought greater demands for community services such as education, public health, and public safety. Middle- and upper-income groups, as well as businesses, have been moving out of urban areas and into the suburbs, thus depleting the tax base of the cities. Local governments have become fragmented and increasingly inefficient in their efforts to meet new and expanding area-wide needs. What steps can be taken to reduce these difficulties? There are several, but they require the will to do so at all levels of government.

A Free Market in Education

One major problem of all large cities is the public educational system. Critics have accused the public schools of being rigid bureaucracies. Conservatives, liberals, and radicals, regardless of race, have complained that the political mechanisms which are supposed to make public schools accountable to their communities have either failed to work or have worked very clumsily. As a result, only the rich now have a choice—they can either move to other school districts or they can enroll their children in expensive private schools. The average parent, on the other hand, has no alternative but to remain with his local public school. The parent who belongs to one of several religious faiths may be able to send his child to a low-cost church school—but such schools are relatively few.

What can be done to correct the situation? One controversial suggestion is to weaken the monopoly powers of public schools by making them more competitive. The argument can be reduced to three basic propositions:

1. The public schools are monopolies, and monopolies do not offer sufficient quality or diversity of product.

2. If American public schools are to provide variety and excellence, they must be subjected to the competitive pressures of a free market—a market in which parents and children exercise consumer sovereignty by paying their money and taking their choice.

3. If consumers are given this opportunity, they will usually choose the better schools and, in so doing, will force the quality of all schools to improve.

This argument has been advanced by numerous critics from the right and from the left. Like all panaceas, it suffers from oversimplification. Nevertheless, it has considerable merit when viewed as part of a larger, comprehensive effort at school reform. Although there are various means, political and fiscal, of encouraging a free market in education, four proposals in particular have received the greatest attention: (1) decentralization of school systems, (2) creation of publicly financed private schools, (3) performance contracting, and (4) the voucher system. An analysis of each of these approaches will provide an understanding of the role which competition can play in a sorely needed program for school reform.

DECENTRALIZATION OF SCHOOL SYSTEMS

A proposal that is frequently suggested to encourage competition is for school systems to be decentralized so as to make them more responsive to the particular needs of their own communities—whether white or black, rich or poor. Most of the people who favor this approach do not base their beliefs on the benefits of competition per se, but on the conviction that the interests of minority groups in large cities have been totally disregarded by the monopolistic system. In many large cities, community leaders are demanding control over the schools on the grounds that children are not only receiving an inferior education, but also one which is dominated by white middle-class values.

Would total decentralization of large school systems create the beneficial effects of competition that the advocates of this approach seek? Probably not—for several reasons:

1. Each relatively homogeneous community—whether white or black, rich or poor—would be given monopolistic control over its schools. This would fragment the school systems, reduce their efficiency, and return them to the situation that existed in the 1890s. At that time school administrators cried for consolidation rather than decentralization in the hope of bringing about greater economies of scale.

2. The biases and bigotries of each community would be given a disproportionate influence over the education of its children, most of whom are not likely to remain in the same district after their schooling is completed. Further, since teachers are professionals who seek to apply professional standards, they would resent working under local pressures and find it extremely difficult to introduce pedagogical reform.

3. Parents who are dissatisfied with the decentralized school system in one district may in principle be able to move to another, but whether they can do so in fact is doubtful. In New York, Chicago, and other major cities, the better schools would be unable to absorb the large numbers who would want to enroll. And in the suburbs, lower- and middle-income blacks would continue to be effectively restricted from the better schools located in middle-income white communities.

Despite these educational drawbacks, total decentralization may nevertheless be inevitable—for political rather than economic reasons. The black community, too long frustrated, wants to control what its children learn and what its teachers teach. Hence it is not likely to give much weight to the disadvantages of decentralization as a method of achieving its goal.

PUBLICLY FINANCED PRIVATE SCHOOLS

A second proposal for providing free consumer choice in education is the use of public money to create both public schools and private schools—the latter designed to meet the needs of particular minority groups. This means that in a typical large city with a population composed of diverse religions and races, there would be not only public schools run by the city, but also private schools run by different denominations and racial groups for their own constituents. The private schools might receive public financial support based on enrollment, community income levels, or other criteria—somewhat as certain private American universities receive partial financial aid from the federal government.

This proposal is actually another form of decentralization. The difference is that it bases decentralization on religion and race instead of geographic location. This would create competition among schools—but only in terms of ideology rather than educational quality. Even though such schools would be open to all, they would in effect be segregated by race and by religion. Admittedly, segregation has long existed in many school districts, but such a system would tend to perpetuate and perhaps even to encourage it—certainly not reduce it.

PERFORMANCE CONTRACTING

A third competitive scheme proposes that each school district specify the exact educational program it wants and then invite private firms to bid for the opportunity of supplying the desired "package." The firm which offered to deliver the package at the lowest price would be awarded the contract. This scheme would stimulate competition and growth in the educational systems industry, thereby encouraging the development of better teaching machines, learning materials, and other pedagogical aids. Parents, children, and taxpayers would all benefit because they would be getting the program they want at the lowest possible cost, and school districts would be making the most efficient use of the limited funds available to them.

This plan, known as "performance contracting," has had considerable appeal. Its chief difficulty is that it requires a measurable product. Although certain parts of education are well-defined and involve the acquisition of basic skills which are measurable, many other parts are ill-defined and consist of learning how to relate, interpret, and appreciate. These latter parts are not ordinarily susceptible to the type of measurement that would be needed for contractual purposes. As a result, this proposal, which has been tried in some school systems, has had only limited applicability. Its greatest usefulness lies in the role that it might play as part of a more general plan.

THE VOUCHER SYSTEM

A fourth proposal for increasing competition is to give money, or more specifically "vouchers," to families with children and let them choose the school they want—public, parochial, or private. The vouchers would be equivalent in value to the community's expenditures per public school pupil, and the city would reimburse the school to the amount of the voucher. This scheme has long been advocated by various leading educators and economists, among them Professor Milton Friedman of the University of Chicago. In fact, economists have sometimes referred to the proposal as the "Friedman Plan."

According to its supporters, the plan would promote competition in several ways. First, schools would be pressured into stating clearly their objectives and programs—and in living up to them at the risk of being squeezed out of the market. Second, assuming an "open-enrollment" policy, parents would be free to choose the type of school that seemed best to them—traditional or progressive, private or public. Third, if "bonus" vouchers for poor or disadvantaged youngsters were provided, as some supporters of the plan have suggested, schools which have significant numbers of such pupils could better afford to develop programs of wide appeal to all students. And fourth, some of the better suburban schools, faced with mounting educational expenditures, might be encouraged into admitting many poor students from the inner city, thus bringing about a greater degree of class as well as racial integration.

The voucher system, therefore, would provide lower-income families with a range of choice in education that is roughly comparable to that enjoyed by the middle class. This by itself may make it worthy of adoption. Nevertheless, those who support the plan are well aware of its controversial nature and shortcomings. According to them:

1. It might encourage the creation of racially segre-

gated schools—a trend that would run counter to the stated objectives of the government.

2. It would result in the public schools becoming a "last choice" for students not wanted by other schools.

3. It would lead to public support of parochial schools, thereby violating the Constitutional principle of separation of church and state.

4. It would encourage the establishment of weak schools and "diploma mills" by sharp operators seeking to exploit the public's lack of knowledge of educational programs and curricula.

Several suggestions have been made to overcome these objections. For example, racial segregation could be prevented by requiring each school to fill at least half of its openings by lottery among its applicants; administrative controls could be introduced to minimize public subsidization of religious instruction; and, last but not least, state-supervised educational and accreditation standards could be vigorously enforced to prevent the establishment of fly-by-night schools.

The voucher system has been adopted on an experimental basis by some school districts. Unfortunately, it has never been tried on a wide enough scale to permit firm conclusions to be drawn.

NEED FOR COMPREHENSIVE REFORM

There is substantial agreement that increased competition is needed to weaken the monopolistic power of public education. The crisis that exists in public school systems today is due in large measure to their rigid, dull conformity and their failure to respond to new demands. By turning itself into an educational marketplace in which children and their parents could afford to choose the type of school they want, the school system would become more sensitive to the real needs of children and parents.

Competition, however, is not a complete solution. Educational quality should not be decided exclusively in the marketplace, because most parents and children are not capable of evaluating the product they are buying. Nevertheless, they should have some significant influence over it. Therefore, what is needed is a comprehensive program of reform in which some competitive elements represented by all four of the above proposals can play a part. The challenge of developing such a scheme is posed as a problem at the end of this chapter.

Housing in the Inner Cities

The desperate shortage of adequate living space for the poor is one of the major failures of American cities. Large-scale and costly efforts by government to solve the problem have met with only limited success. Nor has entrepreneurial initiative succeeded where government has failed. The provision of low-income housing in the inner cities is one activity in which exclusive reliance on private enterprise has proved to be inadequate.

What are the reasons for this? There are many, including problems of taxation, financing, technology, racial discrimination, law, and politics—to mention only a few. Because of these complexities, it is doubtful that private enterprise can ever solve the problems of low-income urban housing or the closely related problems of urban renewal, without the help of a comprehensive policy by government. Such a policy has been developing since the 1930s, but it has been painfully slow in its evolution and frequently muddled in its administration.

GOVERNMENT HOUSING POLICIES

Although government has failed to develop an effective housing policy, it has not been unconcerned with resolving important issues. Over the years it has: (a) regulated private housing through zoning laws, building codes, and rent controls; (b) promoted private housing construction by making available needed supplies of credit; (c) engaged in the ownership and operation of public housing; and (d) subsidized urban renewal programs by private builders.

Regulation of Private Housing

Government has been directly involved in the regulation of private housing in two major ways: by specifying the conditions under which dwellings can be built, and by limiting the rents that tenants must pay.

All local governments have zoning laws which control the allocation of land for commercial and industrial buildings, and for residential dwellings of the single- and multiple-family type. They also have building and housing codes which specify standards of ventilation, sanitation, and structural safety. Unfortunately, many of these laws are unduly restrictive, and their enforcement has been weakened by political influences. As a result, their economic effect has been to limit the quantity and types of housing that are most needed for large cities, and hence to contribute—along with rising population and income—to the upward pressure on rents in these areas.

To curb such pressures, particularly during war periods, government has sometimes imposed rent controls to keep rents from soaring. Rent ceilings may be necessary during emergencies, but as a permanent policy can be more harmful than beneficial —for several reasons:

1. They cause a malallocation of dwelling space, since families who can afford higher-rent apartments are encouraged to remain where they are instead of moving to make room for lower-income newcomers.

2. They limit the returns to landlords as compared with returns on invested funds in other fields, thereby encouraging them to neglect the maintenance of their buildings and even to abandon them.

3. They curb the supply of rental housing and may even cause it to decline.

Over the long run, all three of these factors tend to injure tenants rather than help them.

The experiences of various cities with rent controls, both in the United States and abroad, strongly confirm these conclusions. New York City, for example, long retained rent controls in one form or another for decades after World War II, largely because of political pressures, and suffered drastically from all of the effects given above. Its apartment buildings in slum areas were often without adequate heat or sanitation, and many were literally abandoned by their owners in favor of a tax loss.

Promotion of Private Housing

Since the 1930s, the federal government has encouraged the construction of private housing and promoted home ownership through various agencies such as the Federal Housing Administration and the Veterans Administration. It has sought to achieve these goals by expanding the supply of housing credit—through federally chartered savings and loan associations, provisions for mortgage insurance, creation of a secondary market for mortgages, and other devices. This program has succeeded in promoting family home ownership, but it has done little to increase the supply of housing for the poor. Its benefits have gone primarily to middle-income rather than to lower-income groups.

Public Housing

Since the 1930s government has been involved in public housing—housing which is privately designed and built, but is owned and operated on a rental basis by public authorities. Under the Housing Act of 1937 and its subsequent amendments, the federal government is authorized to extend financial aid to state and local governments in order to help them provide low-rent housing to low-income families. Municipal governments, through the sale of bonds, contribute 10 percent of the total capital investment for each project, and the federal government pays the remaining 90 percent. The municipal public housing authorities collect the rents and operate the projects—with the objective of breaking even on operating costs. In effect, however, the federal government subsidizes virtually all these projects because interest received by municipal bondholders is exempt from federal income taxes and the projects themselves are exempt from local property taxes. Although on the whole public housing policies have succeeded in expanding the supply of low-rent housing, congressional appropriations have not been sufficient to meet the huge need that exists.

Urban Renewal

During the 1950s, there began a pronounced shift in emphasis from the construction of housing for the poor to the rehabilitation of the cities. Sponsored jointly by federal and municipal governments, and financed primarily by the former, the objective of urban renewal has been to rebuild old or decayed neighborhoods in order to attract industry, stimulate commercial activity, encourage the upper economic classes to return from the suburbs to the cities, and in general to restore property values and tax yields. Although urban renewal programs in the downtown centers of many cities have been impressive, they have also failed on a number of fronts. Reconstruction has been confined to limited areas without relation to an overall plan. Projects have usually been selected for their commercial value and "show appeal" instead of their usefulness to the community as a whole. Tremendous hardships have been imposed on many of the people—most of them blacks—who are evicted from renewal areas with few if any alternative areas to which they can move. Also, the livelihood of small-scale neighborhood businessmen is destroyed because they are unable to relocate at rents they can afford. The overall effects of urban renewal in terms of supply and demand are explained in Exhibit 2.

PROBLEMS OF HOUSING

The enormous need for city housing poses staggering problems of a multidimensional nature. The first and most fundamental problem is the gap between housing costs and what low-income families can pay. With the shortage of land in large cities, the kind of housing that is needed is apartment buildings, either new or rehabilitated. Even if such buildings could be made available in the quantity and density desired, government estimates show that the rental rates (ranging from about $150 to $200 monthly for a one- or two-bedroom apartment) would be beyond the means of most low-income families. In fact, more than two-thirds of such families could not afford to pay even *half* these rents.

A second problem is that government programs to correct this difficulty have been inadequate. Congress has created one program after another since the 1930s, but many have been insufficiently funded and very poorly conceived. As a result, they have often overlapped and even conflicted with earlier programs, creating chaos together with fantastic amounts of red tape, while exerting relatively little impact on urban problems. Nor has urban renewal been of much help because most localities have been concerned with broadening their tax base and have used renewal programs to construct new commercial development or upper-middle-income housing rather than provide low-income housing.

A third problem is that while rehabilitation of slum housing is an alternative to the construction of new housing, it is not an overall solution. There are several reasons. Rehabilitation does not increase the total supply of housing units. It displaces people without successfully relocating them. It is not cheaper than new housing—especially when planning and the costs of rehabilitation are considered. And, it does not reduce the social and cultural barriers which separate the poor from the rest of society.

APPROACHES TO A SOLUTION

There is widespread agreement that ways must be found to broaden the choices available to consumers in the urban housing market. Three general approaches that would lower the price of dwellings are especially noteworthy.

Uniform National Building Code

Local building codes vary widely in the several thousand jurisdictions in the United States. Most set standards far above what is needed for safety and durability, and specify the materials and production methods that must be used. The codes are thus designed to protect special-interest groups such as building-components manufacturers and trade unions, rather than to provide the largest possible supply of housing at the lowest possible prices.

To correct this situation, builders' associations, construction engineers, and governmental advisory groups have long advocated a uniform national building code. Ideally, such a code should specify performance standards rather than materials and methods, thereby encouraging components manufacturers as well as builders to develop new, cost-saving substitutes. Until such a uniform national code is established, there is little hope of improving production efficiency in the home-building industry —an industry which consists mainly of small firms catering to a highly fragmented housing market.

Exhibit 2

Urban Renewal Decreases the Supply of Housing

Given the demand curve D for housing, the destruction of blighted housing by urban renewal decreases the available supply of housing by shifting the supply curve to the left from S to S'. As a result, the equilibrium price rises from P to P' and the equilibrium quantity falls from Q to Q'. In other words, the poor pay more for less housing.

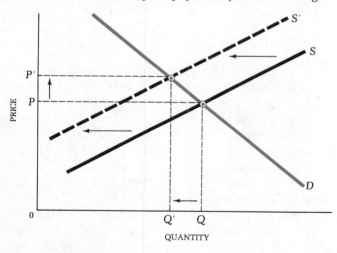

Rent Supplements

A direct approach to widening the housing market for the poor is for the government to supplement a portion of the rental payments of low-income families. This might be done by the government's making up the difference in rents for those families below a specified income level who cannot obtain decent housing at rental rates not exceeding one-fourth of their incomes. (The figure of one-fourth is typically used as a national average by budget counselling services and welfare agencies, but higher or lower figures might be more appropriate in different regions.) Thus the tenant pays one-fourth of his income toward rent, and the government pays the balance up to the "fair market value." As the tenant's income rises, the government's supplement falls until the tenant is paying the full rent himself and the government is paying nothing.

The chief disadvantage of this plan is in its administration: tenants and landlords must be audited periodically to see that the government is not being overcharged. But the plan has several factors in its favor: (a) It gives tenants a wider choice in seeking apartments instead of confining them to public housing projects; (b) it avoids the stigma attached to public housing; and (c) it does not reduce the tenant's incentive to work.

A system of rent supplements somewhat similar to this was established by the government in 1965. Despite its advantages—including the fact that it is less costly to administer than public housing—it has been politically unpopular and has been supported on a limited scale with relatively small budgets.

Interest Subsidies

To encourage home ownership by low-income families, the government could subsidize interest payments on housing—that is, contribute a proportion of the monthly interest which a family must pay on its home mortgage. To help poorer families who would rather rent than buy, an equivalent arrangement could be made in which the government paid the landlord a proportion of his contractual interest and the landlord in turn reduced the tenant's rent. In both instances, the government's interest subsidy varies inversely with the family's income. As the latter rises toward some specified level, the former declines toward zero.

This type of plan was adopted in the Housing and Urban Development Act of 1968. However, it was geared toward helping families whose incomes are just above the poverty line instead of below it. On the whole, the act made a substantial start toward expanding the supply of new dwellings for low- and moderate-income families; but it was only a start. Extensions are needed if decent housing is to be provided for the poorest segments of the population.

An analysis of rent supplements and interest subsidies in terms of supply and demand is presented in Exhibit 3.

CONCLUSION: SUBSIDIES AND A UNIFIED PLAN

Any solution to city housing problems requires some sort of government subsidy. There is a gap between what low-income families can pay for housing and what private enterprise can supply at a reasonable profit. Subsidies are a realistic means of closing this gap.

The most common types of subsidy, in the form of below-market interest rates, rent supplements, and long-term mortgages, can continue, but more extensive plans are also needed. An effective and far-reaching program would be one in which the federal government acquires the land it needs, provides for the construction of dwelling units by private enterprise, and pays no property taxes as long as the buildings are occupied by low-income families. However, since the cities cannot afford to lose the taxes on these properties, the federal government could relieve them of all health, education, and welfare costs, since these services are a national concern. Such a plan would permit business and government to work together in meeting the housing needs of all low-income groups.

Transportation Systems

Any discussion of urban problems must include transportation. The central task is to correct the imbalance that exists between automobiles and other forms of transportation, such as subways and monorails. Why this imbalance? A significant cause is the Federal Highway Act itself; this law allows 90 percent federal funding for expressways, thereby providing cities with virtually free highways, which they have found too tempting to resist. The result has been mounting traffic congestion, a tearing apart of the cities as well as the countryside, and the creation of distorted transportation systems which tend to increase the private and social costs of movement.

Exhibit 3

**Rent Supplements and Interest Subsidies Increase
the Demand for Housing**

Chart (a). *In the short run the stock of housing in existence is fixed; therefore the supply curve S is a vertical line—perfectly inelastic or unresponsive to changes in price. Consequently, factors which tend to increase the demand for housing, such as rent supplements and interest subsidies, cause the demand curve to shift to the right —from D to D'. This brings about a rise in the equilibrium price from P to P' while the equilibrium quantity Q re-*

mains the same. As a result, the entire increase in housing expenditure is absorbed by landlords as increased rents.

Chart (b). *In the long run the supply of housing has been found to be relatively elastic—highly responsive to changes in price. Consequently, an increase in demand from D to D' leads to a higher equilibrium price P' and a larger equilibrium quantity Q'.*

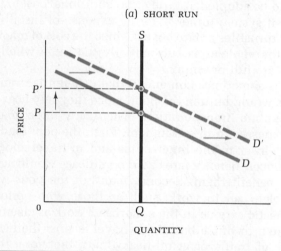

(a) SHORT RUN

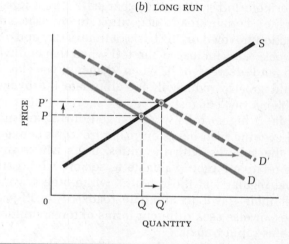

(b) LONG RUN

A city's transportation system consists of all the vehicles and "fixed plant" necessary to move people and goods from one place to another. It may thus include not only automobiles, taxis, buses, and subway trains, but also streets, freeways, stations, parking spaces, and similar facilities. There is no doubt that continued investment in all of these will occur in many large cities during the coming years. Since it is desirable that the growth of urban transportation systems be economically sensible, two classes of policy proposals should be considered: (1) transportation pricing and (2) technological improvements and innovations in transportation systems.

TRANSPORTATION PRICING

We know from the study of supply and demand that a price system rations the use of existing goods among buyers who are willing to pay the market price, and guides the distribution of resources to their most rewarding alternatives. Can a price sys-

tem be used to help correct urban transportation problems?

There is excessive traffic congestion in our cities because of an imbalance between automobiles and other forms of transportation. Most cities have created this imbalance themselves by subsidizing the use of automobiles and discouraging the use of mass transit. They have done this by constructing and maintaining streets and freeways without charging users sufficiently high fees to allow a proper allocation of this resource. Therefore, if the situation is to be corrected, a fundamental principle must be recognized:

At any given time the supply of streets, bridges, and other traffic facilities is fixed. If during some period there is congestion on the roads or shortages of parking spaces, this means that the quantity demanded of the facility at that moment exceeds the quantity supplied, and hence a higher price is needed to bring the two quantities into balance— to "clear" the market.

At the present time the use of most roads is allocated to users on the basis of time delays that they are willing to tolerate. Thus everyone who uses a road at any given moment enjoys the same service; but during rush hours, a person whose time is more valuable pays a higher price in terms of delays than the person whose time is less valuable. This means that the former individual, in effect, "subsidizes" the latter.

Variable Tolls

A *variable toll system* that charged a direct toll to users of certain roads according to mileage and direction traveled on the basis of time of day and day of week—and increased the toll when demand was high and decreased it when demand was low—would greatly reduce if not eliminate the overall problems of "congestion" and "shortage." For example, if higher tolls were charged during morning and evening rush hours on major freeways connecting the suburbs with the cities, users whose time was relatively more valuable to society would still travel regularly at those hours, while others would shift their travel to alternate roads or to off-peak times, or else seek different forms of transportation, such as rapid transit.

Of course, there may be some technical problems in implementing such a proposal, but the solution is well within the grasp of modern technology. In some cases it would be feasible to introduce existing toll systems of the types currently found on various turnpikes and highways, but these could be gradually replaced with modern roadway devices such as magnetic car identifiers and automated computer systems, thus permitting motorists to be billed monthly for the benefits they derive from the use of roads. A considerable amount of research on this has already been done in the United States and other countries, and some of the world's largest cities are experimenting with differential pricing systems in which fares or tolls are based on time, distance, and direction of travel.

Economic analysis thus suggests that with the development of diverse transportation facilities in the cities, the adoption of a variable toll system would correct much of the imbalance that exists between private automobile and public transportation. It would continue to give motorists a free choice as to the alternative streets and the amount of street space they wish to utilize, thereby allocating scarce public streets according to the *benefit principle*, which holds that people should be "taxed" for a service in proportion to the benefit they receive from it.

Public Transit Systems

Variable tolls, as opposed to flat fares, are equally desirable for public transit systems, including subways and buses. Such systems are used at full capacity during the morning and evening peak periods, and usually underutilized the rest of the time. Low or even free off-peak fares would relieve much of the rush-hour congestion. Further, this pricing scheme could be adopted at little or no additional cost to the transit system (other than the expense of installing new turnstiles or fare boxes), since the cost of operating the vehicles is substantially the same whether they are full or empty.

It is sometimes contended that differential transit fares would burden the poor, since they rely heavily on public transportation. There are three major weaknesses in this argument. First, the poor tend to live closer to the inner cities and to travel shorter distances; hence a fare based on mileage would actually benefit them. Second, many of the poor who travel to get to work, such as those who perform domestic service in the suburbs or work as cleaning women in office buildings, travel against the major flow of traffic or at off-peak times; therefore, they too would benefit from a differential fare system. Third, some studies have shown that the poor tend to rely as much or more on public transportation for nonwork trips, so that a lower fare during off-peak hours would be to their advantage.

In general, therefore, although some lower-income families would undoubtedly be hurt by a differential fare structure, it appears that many more would benefit.

TECHNOLOGICAL IMPROVEMENTS AND INNOVATIONS

In addition to establishing an appropriate pricing system for rationing the use of transportation facilities, various technological improvements and supplemental policies are possible. Three independent classes of proposals, none of which would require a massive investment in new facilities, may be considered.

1. Electronic control systems, which regulate access to urban freeways through strategically placed sen-

sors and traffic signals, can be introduced. Such controls have been employed successfully in a number of cities in the United States and Europe. They are likely to gain large-scale adoption in the coming years.

2. Subsidies can be used to reorient bus services in the inner cities. Various studies indicate that present bus systems often do not provide adequate connection and transfer points to meet the needs of the working poor—especially those who must commute by bus to work in the suburbs.

3. Taxicab and jitney services can be expanded. Merely by relaxing somewhat the restrictions which almost all cities exercise on the supply of taxis, their number could be increased and the rates reduced. And by permitting the use of jitneys—that is, cars or station wagons which carry passengers at nominal rates over a regular route (a very common form of public transportation in many foreign and in some American cities)—much of the problem of automobile congestion in the cities would be eliminated.

These proposals suggest that the cities can do much at relatively little cost to relieve the transportation pressures they now face. Experimentation with new and flexible approaches is needed in order to find the "transport mix" that is best suited to the requirements of each city. The money that can be saved from optimum use of a well-designed transportation system might better be spent on education, housing, pollution abatement, and other measures that will make the city a more desirable place to live. (See Box 1.)

Box 1

Urban Transportation

The major transportation problem facing large cities is to get hundreds of thousands—and in some cases millions—of people to and from work in the central business districts with minimum congestion, maximum efficiency, and reasonable comfort. The economic difficulties of accomplishing this include problems of costs, revenues, pricing, and financing.

Costs are a problem because mass-transit systems such as commuter trains and subways suffer from a limited ability to adjust variable costs to fluctuations in passenger

Albert Azarello (*Shostal Associates*).

Photo Researchers, Inc.

volume, and they require large amounts of capital investment to provide for modernization and expansion.

Revenues are inadequate because political pressures have forced regulatory agencies to keep tolls and fares low—too low to meet operating costs, let alone replace obsolete equipment. Pricing policies create other difficulties; distorted fare structures have caused some facilities to be overused while others are relatively idle. Financing is hard to obtain because efforts to support mass-transit operations out of general funds have met with considerable resistance. Many people feel that mass transit benefits only commuters, rather than the public as a whole; and most cities and states are financially hard-pressed.

Clearly, some guidelines for policy are needed. Four in particular may be mentioned:

□ Fast, efficient mass transit is vital to the economic health of our big cities.

□ Public funds must subsidize both capital investment and operating costs of mass transit. Attempts to cover constantly rising operating expenses by increasing fares have diverted commuters to highways.

□ Tolls for the use of highways, bridges, and tunnels should more closely reflect the private and social costs of commuting by private car. The excess revenues should be allocated to mass transit. Such action would help to offset current highway-biased subsidy arrangements.

□ Variable toll systems which charge higher prices during peak periods and lower prices during off-peak periods should be adopted on a more extensive scale, to help to reduce imbalances in the utilization of facilities.

Burk Uzzle.

Burk Uzzle.

Financing Local Government: Our Urban Fiscal Dilemma

Any discussion of urban policies must eventually deal with the difficult problem of balancing local government revenues and expenditures. Why is the problem difficult? Mr. Micawber in *David Copperfield* described a situation that epitomizes the financial squeeze which many of our cities are experiencing today:

> Annual income twenty pounds, annual expenditure nineteen six: result, happiness.
>
> Annual income twenty pounds, annual expenditure twenty pounds ought and six: result, misery.

This is indeed the essence of our urban fiscal dilemma. It is a dilemma which has arisen because of the rapidly changing socioeconomic structures of our cities—their spiraling welfare costs and record budgets in the midst of an affluent and expanding population that leaves many unfortunate people in its wake.

The fundamental economic problem facing an increasing number of American cities—and cities in many other countries as well—is a growing inability to finance public services. The reasons for this can be summarized briefly:

1. As our population expands and our economy grows richer, we not only purchase more goods and services from the private sector, but we also increase our demands from the public sector as well.

2. To meet these demands, urban governments have to increase their expenditures on virtually all types of public services such as sanitation, police and fire protection, education, health, welfare, transportation, recreation, and cultural facilities.

3. While cities have been left to grapple with soaring municipal costs, the groups which pay the heaviest share of taxes—namely, business firms and middle-income families—have for decades been moving to the suburbs and have been replaced by an ever-expanding population of the poor who need but cannot afford the more expensive education, welfare, health services, and other public benefits.

These conditions have forced most cities to face a growing fiscal problem: To raise the revenue needed to pay for public services, they must increase taxes; however, taxes in the cities are already burdensome, and further increases may only hasten the exodus of people and businesses to nearby suburbs where taxes are relatively lower.

Most cities have often had deficits amounting to many millions of dollars—deficits which they covered by dipping into reserves, by borrowing against future budgets, and by selling long-term notes. Not since the days of the Depression, however, has the plight of many city treasuries been as bleak as in the years since the late 1960s.

How should the various levels of government direct their limited resources to combat poverty, crime, pollution, eyesores, and ghetto unemployment, while improving education, housing, mass transit, and the other amenities of a better urban America? The solution rests on finding more effective ways of raising revenues while improving the efficiency of local government. Several proposals for achieving these objectives may be considered: (1) minimize fiscal disparities, (2) utilize revenue sharing, (3) impose user charges, (4) restructure the property tax, and (5) establish metropolitan government. A broad approach to financing urban government should draw on all these proposals.

MINIMIZE FISCAL DISPARITIES

Cities provide many goods and services whose benefits and costs are not appropriately apportioned. People benefit in varying degrees from the expenditures of local governments, and they pay in varying degrees for the values they receive. But the disparities between costs and benefits may be wide because the people who work in the city and the people who visit the city are not always the same people as the taxpayers who own property or live in the city. As a result of these misalignments, there tend to be wide differences not only in the taxable bases and expenditure requirements of the more than 80,000 local governmental units in the United States, but also in the quantity and quality of services provided by these units.

The divergencies of costs and benefits have created extensive "spillover" effects among a wide array of urban government expenditures ranging from health, education, and welfare services to environmental control. Two examples are indicative:

1. The mounting education and welfare budgets of New York, Chicago, Philadelphia, Detroit, and other major cities have been due in large part to our national agricultural policy which, since World War II, has promoted the subsidization and mechanization of the South's cotton and tobacco fields, driving out millions of workers who have streamed into the

cities looking for jobs. Since most of these people are poor, unskilled, and usually illiterate, they have either become public charges or at best have been able to find menial employment at the minimum wage. Meanwhile, many of the "expatriates"—the former residents of the cities—continue to work in the cities and hold the higher-paying jobs while turning over the bulk of their tax bills to the suburban municipalities in which they reside.

2. In the area of environmental control, it was once thought that air and water pollution were strictly local problems peculiar to a few cities. But now it is recognized that geographic boundaries in such matters are largely irrelevant and that the issues are of national or even international concern. Canadian residents, for example, have entered suits in U.S. federal courts against American firms for contaminating the air over Canada.

In these and many other classes of local government expenditures, the disparities between costs and benefits should be minimized. The most effective way to accomplish this is for the federal government to absorb a much larger share of the financial burden. At the present time state and local governments pay almost all the costs of public safety, transportation (except highways), elementary and secondary education, water supply and treatment, parks and recreation, and garbage collection, plus a substantial part of the cost of health, welfare, and social security programs. If a larger portion of the costs of these local activities could be transferred to Washington, many of the spillover effects would be greatly reduced or eliminated and the city governments would be relieved of enormous tax responsibilities.

UTILIZE REVENUE SHARING

An approach for relieving the mounting fiscal pressures facing states and cities is for the federal government to engage in *revenue sharing*. Such a plan requires that the federal government *automatically* turn over a portion of its tax revenues to state and local governments each year.

The concept of revenue sharing makes a great deal of practical sense—not just to many economists but to a large number of businessmen and political leaders as well. They base their justification for it on certain fundamental facts and relationships involving both revenues and expenditures.

First, the federal government collects most of the taxes levied; state and local governments collect a relatively minor proportion. The federal government's chief source of revenue is the income tax, which, because of its progressive rate structure, yields approximately a 1.5 percent increase in revenues for every 1 percent increase in GNP. The state and local governments, on the other hand, receive the great bulk of their revenues from property, sales, and other taxes, and these tend to increase by about 1 percent for every 1 percent increase in GNP.

Second, state and local spending has been increasing at rates of about 7 percent to 10 percent a year—roughly twice as fast as the growth in GNP. At the same time, state and local governments have met growing public resistance to increases in taxes, the imposition of new taxes, and the sale of bonds—these being the only methods available to finance their rising expenditures. Federal government spending, on the other hand (except for extraordinary military needs), tends to rise less than federal revenues when the economy is expanding, thereby leaving a *fiscal dividend*.

According to the revenue-sharing advocates, *the salvation of states and cities lies in sharing the fiscal dividend*. Of course, the federal government has long poured out money to states and localities, but this has been largely in the form of grants-in-aid for specific programs to which Washington attaches many bureaucratic strings and controls. What the governors and mayors want is a kind of philosophical Jeffersonianism—an arrangement whereby the federal government gives out blocks of grants for broad general purposes while allowing all or most of the spending decisions to be made at state and local levels. In this way, by sharing a percentage of its revenues on a fixed basis with hard-pressed states and cities, Washington can encourage much greater local initiative.

Revenue sharing was approved by Washington in 1972, but it has not been consistently implemented on the scale desired by state and local government leaders. As a result, it may be some years before the full effects of revenue sharing can be evaluated.

IMPOSE USER CHARGES

Local governments obtain their revenues from various sources—taxation, license fees, interest earnings, special assessments, sale of property, charges for municipal services, and so on. The last item, often called "user charges," offers promising opportunities for additional revenues. At present, people who receive the benefits of city hospitals, public housing, treated water, mass transit, refuse collection, and public schools help support part of the costs of these locally provided services through special payments, rents, and fees, as well as through taxation. The issue is whether the cities should revise their systems of user charges for these services, and whether they should charge for services which are presently financed out of tax revenues.

The answer to both questions is yes—for several reasons. First, a revision of user charges is based on the recognition that if certain types of services are available too cheaply or at flat rates, their limited supply will be rationed by congestion whenever the quantity demanded exceeds the quantity supplied at the existing price. As mentioned earlier, mass-transit facilities during rush hours serve as striking illustrations. In such cases a *differential* pricing structure rather than a single price would not only provide a better rationing mechanism, but a larger total revenue as well.

Second, by imposing charges on certain services which are currently financed entirely from tax revenues, and by varying the charges according to their use, a more efficient utilization of resources and a greater volume of total revenue can be realized. Public libraries and marinas provide typical examples. The services of these facilities are usually offered free or at little cost to residents of the suburbs as well as the cities. Since the poor make relatively less use of these amenities, the overall effect is for middle-income households to be subsidized in large measure from taxes paid by low-income groups.

User charges have a number of advantages. Among the more important: (a) they enable the municipal government to know the value of its services to its users; (b) they reduce benefit spillovers resulting from geographic differences; and (c) they permit greater efficiency of production, less oversupply of services, and larger total revenues than would occur with tax financing. But user charges also have at least two closely related limitations. First, they are inappropriate for financing "public goods"—goods whose benefits are available to everyone—such as clean streets, traffic lights, and public safety. Second, they are difficult to apply where specific benefits to users are hard to identify and measure.

RESTRUCTURE THE PROPERTY TAX

A fourth approach to improving the finances of local governments is to revise the existing structure of the property tax. This tax, with its diverse rates and bases, is imposed only at the state and local levels, not at the federal level. Although local governments have other sources of revenue such as sales and excise taxes, income taxes, utility revenue, and liquor store revenue, the property tax is nevertheless their largest single source of funds. This tax helps pay the local share of school costs as well as a large part of the expenses incurred for public safety, sanitation, street lighting, and the bulk of other community services.

Despite its widespread use, the property tax suffers from a number of shortcomings. Three are particularly important:

1. It requires tax assessors to "guess" the market value of taxable property, since the true market value cannot be known unless the property is sold. As a result, wide differentials and inequities of assessment exist both within and between districts.

2. The tax is extremely regressive. It bears down much harder on poorer families than richer ones because housing is such a large part of consumer spending for lower-income groups.

3. It causes "fiscal zoning"—that is, the control of land use in order to maximize the tax base. For example, it encourages laws requiring large minimum lot sizes, thereby raising land costs and discouraging the construction of smaller homes for moderate-income families.

These and other factors make the property tax one of the most controversial in the entire tax structure. Nevertheless, it continues to exist, partly because it raises so much revenue and partly because it is the major tax which local governments are permitted by their states to levy.

The Land Value Tax

The many bad economic effects of the property tax have resulted in various proposals for its revision. The most desirable and feasible way to correct its deficiencies would be to restructure it in favor of a land value tax—a tax on bare sites exclusive of buildings that stand on them. This idea was first proposed by the American economist Henry George in his *Progress and Poverty* (1879). But unlike George, who advocated a tax on land as a "single tax" to replace all others, it is suggested here as a partial but substantial substitute for the property tax.

The fundamental idea is to tax the annual unearned gains from land—the so-called economic rent or surplus which accrues to the owners of land not because of improvements they have made upon it but because of community development and population growth which have caused the market value of land to rise. Among the chief arguments advanced in favor of such a tax are that it discourages land from being held out of productive use, it encourages building on property, and it returns to society the increases in the value of land resulting from economic growth. The major criticism of the tax is that it is difficult to administer because it cannot distinguish between increases in the value of land resulting from economic growth and increases due to improvements made on the land.

Even though this criticism is valid, its adverse effects can certainly be mitigated through appropriate tax laws. Experience in other countries which make use of land value taxation, including market-oriented economies such as Canada, Australia, and New Zealand, indicate that such laws are feasible and workable.

At present, the property tax in the United States is relatively light on land and heavy on buildings. Hence the tax favors landowners, who tend to be in the higher-income groups, and speculators who find it more profitable to hold land for future resale than to build upon it. By restructuring the property tax so that it bears down relatively heavier on land than on buildings, these undesirable effects would be greatly reduced without causing revenue losses to local governments. In fact, various studies have concluded that a land value tax which averages about 5 percent nationally would yield the same total revenue that is now produced by property taxes on land and buildings.

ESTABLISH METROPOLITAN GOVERNMENT

A fifth means of coping with the challenges facing local governments is one which realizes the need for regional attacks on pressing urban problems. This approach is as much political as economic. It is based on the recognition that local government authority in most metropolitan areas is too fragmented to provide for overall balanced systems of land use, transportation, public health, and the like. In metropolitan Chicago, for example, there are over 1,100 local government units; many other large urban areas like New York, Philadelphia, and Pittsburgh have considerably more than 500 local units each. The

effects of such proliferation are fiscal duplication, administrative inefficiency, and suburban separatism which hurts minority groups.

To help correct these deficiencies, some form of consolidation is needed. One of the more feasible possibilities is to set up a "two-tier" system of metropolitan government in urban regions. Such a system could consist of an area government and local governments, with functions assigned to each. At the area level, the functions assigned could be those which have broad overlapping interests or which offer advantages of economies of scale, for example, planning, zoning, water supply, sewage disposal, transportation, and public health. At the local levels, community governments could administer their own police departments, fire services, and education. Some functions, of course, could also be shared at both levels where it is advantageous to do so.

There are three major advantages to such a plan: (1) efficiency would be increased by consolidating some of the functions of smaller governmental units; (2) governmental units at all levels would become more responsive to human needs and preferences as a result of decentralizing some of the functions of the larger cities; and (3) the relationship of local governmental units to the states and federal government would be strengthened by a more rational allocation of functions among the various levels.

Metropolitan government has been adopted in varying degrees by some cities in the United States and Canada. But most local officials oppose the idea because they fear the loss of power. Consequently, the majority of states have been reluctant to pass the necessary enabling legislation. Hopefully, if Washington would expand the program of grants which it already provides for some regional activities, it could offer additional incentives to the states and local governments by rewarding them financially if they initiate plans for the establishment of some form of metropolitan government.

SUMMARY OF IMPORTANT IDEAS

1. Critics have accused the public schools—especially those in large cities—of being rigidly controlled educational monopolies. This makes them insensitive to community desires and unresponsive to the need for change. By subjecting them to competition in a free market, it is argued, the quality of all schools will improve. Four proposals have been advanced for increasing competition: decentralization of school systems; creation of publicly financed

private schools; performance contracting; and the voucher system.

2. The inner cities have long been faced with the problem of providing adequate housing for the poor. Government has tried to help but sometimes has done more harm than good. The ultimate solution rests on developing a proper system of federal subsidies to help support low-income housing. The federal government should also absorb the health, education, and welfare costs of the cities so that the latter can afford to exempt all low-income housing from property taxes.

3. The transportation crisis of the cities is due primarily to an imbalance between private automobile and public transportation. This results in congestion, time delays, and a general malallocation of transportation facilities. Two broad steps that can be taken toward developing a balanced transportation system are: (a) the introduction of an appropriate pricing system, in the form of variable tolls, to ration the use of scarce transportation facilities; and (b) technological improvements and innovations such as electronic control systems, mass-transit subsidy schemes, and relaxed restrictions on the use of taxicab and jitney services.

4. The most fundamental problem of the cities is to finance needed urban improvements. This requires that they resolve their present fiscal dilemma. The recommended measures are: minimize fiscal disparities; utilize revenue sharing; impose user charges; restructure the property tax; and establish metropolitan government.

FOR DISCUSSION

1. Terms and concepts to review:
   benefit principle   fiscal dividend
   revenue sharing

2. Can you propose some guidelines for improving public education in the United States by suggesting the kinds of decisions that should be centralized and decentralized at different levels of state and local government?

3. "If the government would stop interfering in the housing market, the price of housing would adjust to the free interaction of supply and demand and there would be no problem." Do you agree? Explain.

4. Various public transit systems have considered raising their fares during morning and evening rush hours and lowering them at other times. Despite the advantages of such schemes, they have rarely been adopted. Why?

5. If the cities need more money to finance urban improvements, why do they not simply raise taxes or borrow?

6. It may be argued that when a city makes available "free" museums, "free" golf courses, "free" tennis courts, "free" marinas etc., it is redistributing income *from the poor to the rich!* How might this happen? What can be done about it?

Case

The Energy Crisis

The first signs of the impending disaster came slowly: increases in the cost of oil and gasoline, reductions in voltage delivered by power companies during peak hours, and occasional dimouts. But then the pace accelerated as the Government began rationing essential fuels and exhorted the public to forsake private cars. The reduced use of automobiles had immediate repercussions in Detroit, where the auto industry began laying off workers by the thousands. Other industries, notably the steel manufacturers, also were severely hit. A "domino effect" of factory shutdowns swept through the U.S. economy.

Eventually shortages of fuel and breakdowns of the transportation system produced growing food shortages as farmers were unable to ship their products to the country's great urban centers. The stock market plummeted. Industrial growth came to a standstill. The Government, attempting to stave off a collapse of the national economy, imposed rigid guidelines for prices, wages and profits. Critics of these policies were severely penalized under new anti-sedition laws that virtually nullified the First Amendment. The U.S., in effect, became a totalitarian state.

This frightening scenario is not out of a science-fiction film, but from a serious book by Professors Lawrence Rocks and Richard Runyon, *The Energy Crisis* (Crown, 1973). The authors, who teach at Long Island's C. W. Post College, conclude that by the 1980s, unless the United States adopts strong measures to cope with the impending shortage of energy, the nation could face massive turmoil of the type described above.

Some evidence of this possibility occurred in England during the winter of 1971. When Britain's coal miners went on strike for almost two months, there was not enough coal to fuel electric power plants. Within a short time, the country was almost totally paralyzed. Lights went off; traffic at major intersections was at a standstill; factories shifted to a four-day, then to a three-day week, laying off 1.6 million workers. Only essential services—hospitals, water, and sewage plants—continued to operate full time, and there were doubts as to how long they could continue.

Since Americans consume nearly twice as much electric power per capita as Britons and six times as much as the world average, two questions demand immediate consideration: (1) How serious is the potential shortage of energy faced by the United States? (2) What positive corrective actions can be taken before the situation becomes critical? The answers to these problems are discussed below. They are adapted from studies done by the Chase Manhattan Bank, Resources for the Future, and the President's Council on International Economic Policy.

Energy Facts

Rising standards of living have caused the per capita use of energy in the United States to double since 1940. And the pace is picking up. Predictably, rising population levels and pressures for improved living standards will continue to swell the demand for energy.

There are five major sources of primary energy—oil, natural gas, coal, water power, and nuclear fission. These will still be the major sources in 1985. Nuclear fusion, geothermal, solar, and other exotic sources will play an increasing role, but not yet one of great significance.

These sources of primary energy serve five basic markets—transportation, industrial, residential, electric

power production, and commercial. The greatest increase in demand for primary energy will come from the electric utilities. By 1985, if not sooner, the production of electricity will account for fully half of the nation's net increase in demand for primary energy. More versatile than any other form of power and completely free of pollution at the place of consumption, electrical energy is becoming the nation's preferred energy form.

A closer look at the primary sources of energy reveals a number of important facts.

1. *Oil* accounts for about 45 percent of total U.S. primary energy consumption. Oil is the only fuel that can serve all facets of the transportation sector—a market that accounts for nearly one-quarter of all domestic primary energy consumption.

2. *Natural gas* has been the fastest growing energy resource in the domestic energy mix. Industry has become its largest customer. However, the Federal Power Commission, in an effort to keep prices low, until recently set the well-head price of natural gas at a level that did not encourage domestic exploration and drilling on a scale adequate to maintain and expand existing reserves.

3. *Coal* supplies are adequate for several hundred years at present consumption rates. Electrical utilities burn a great deal of coal and could burn a lot more. Unfortunately, most of the large low-sulphur coal reserves are located in the western states, far from the big electricity markets. Therefore, large investments would be needed to make the transportation of coal—or electricity derived from that coal—economically feasible. Also costly methods of stripping coal from the ground without devastating the landscape would have to be employed. These

problems, plus increasingly stringent safety and air-pollution regulations, make it unlikely that coal will quickly regain its former position as the major energy source in the United States.

4. *Nuclear (fission) energy* produces only 1 percent of the total output of electricity today. Objections to nuclear power plants on environmental grounds have delayed or cancelled many plant starts and promise to remain a threat in the future.

5. *Water power,* already a relatively small source of energy, will show little growth. Few large undeveloped hydro-electric sites remain. And most of these are jealously guarded by environmentalists.

Conclusion: The Price System

What role can the price system play in bringing about a better balance between energy production and consumption?

In a free market, increasing scarcity of a good or service causes its price to rise. The price increase triggers an adaptive mechanism; demand for the product is reduced, or its growth rate is slowed, as users seek substitute products or seek to use the costlier product more efficiently. In addition, new and unforeseen supplies often come into the market.

However, market forces alone cannot be relied upon to head off a national —and worldwide—energy crisis. Government regulation has kept energy prices too low for too long; exploration and development of new sources have not been developing fast enough. Rising expectations, engendered by increasing incomes, have been pushing energy consumption up too fast. Lead times for construction of even conventional energy producing facilities are too long. And development of fundamentally new energy systems utilizing synthetic and advanced nuclear fuels require technology that may be more than a decade away.

With 6 percent of the world's population, the United States is consuming 33 percent of the world's energy. As the largest consumer, the United States must spearhead a national and global energy policy designed to bring energy production into a safe long-run balance with consumption.

QUESTIONS

1. We hear a great deal these days about the "energy crisis" in the United States. Is this strong term justified? Explain.

2. What are the major reasons for the so-called energy crisis?

3. Some critics have advocated a slowing down of economic growth as a way of reducing energy shortages. Do you agree with this approach?

4. "Balance has not been struck in the energy sector. Part of the reason for this is that one important set of prices is missing—those on environmental products." Explain. How would the attainment of "balance" affect energy consumption?

5. What can government do about the energy crisis? SUGGESTION: Focus attention on (a) government provision of incentives for producers and consumers of energy, and (b) equity problems arising from the rising price of energy. (For example, what can be done about the fact that lower-income families spend a larger portion of their income on electricity than higher income families?)

PART 8

International Economics.
The World's Economies

CHAPTER 34

International Trade: The Commerce of Nations

CHAPTER PREVIEW

What are the chief highlights of world trade? Are there significant regional patterns of trade for the United States?

Why do nations trade? What benefits do they receive? What costs do they incur?

Why do countries impose obstacles to trade? Are their reasons valid?

How does international trade affect income and employment? Is there a relationship between a country's imports, exports, and national income?

The study of international economics is timely because the countries of the world are increasingly interdependent economically. Many of the issues that can either tie nations closer together or drive them apart have their roots in economics.

In general, international economics is concerned with the same fundamental questions as domestic economics. Thus the problems of WHAT to produce, HOW MUCH, and FOR WHOM, are still foremost; the difference is that they are studied for several economies or nations rather than for one.

On the microeconomic side, for example, international economics may show how the price systems of different countries interact to affect resource allocation and income distribution. On the macroeconomic side it may be concerned with the ways in which imports, exports, and investment expenditures among nations affect income, employment, and economic growth. Both microeconomic and macroeconomic principles are often employed simultaneously in the study of international economics.

In this chapter we will concentrate on one broad segment of international economics—trade among nations. The principles of international finance and the results of various commercial and financial policies will be considered in later chapters.

Major Features of World Trade

It is appropriate to begin the study of international trade by asking two questions: (1) Of what relative significance is world trade to nations? (2) What are the distributional patterns of trade between the United States and the major regions of the world?

THE IMPORTANCE OF WORLD TRADE

American students are not as familiar with the importance of international trade as are students in most other countries. This is because in many nations the volume of exports or imports may be as much as 40 percent of GNP. But only about 4 or 5 percent of the GNP of the United States is sold abroad, and approximately the same percentage or slightly less is purchased abroad.

However, neither the dollar volume of U.S. trade nor the U.S. products involved are trivial—as you can see from Exhibit 1. In total dollar volume, the amounts are far larger than the trade carried on by other countries. In terms of relative importance, agricultural goods represent less than 20 percent of what we import and export, whereas nonagricultural goods represent more than 80 percent of these totals.

Since World War II, the major industrial nations' share of world trade has been rising and the underdeveloped nations' share has been falling. As a result there is growing concern over how the poor countries can develop their own manufacturing industries, which would enable them to compete more effectively in world markets. We shall find that this problem is of major interest in international economics.

PATTERNS OF U.S. TRADE

Where do our imports come from? Where do our exports go? Exhibit 1 shows clearly that the least industrialized areas of the world are neither America's biggest suppliers nor its biggest customers. Europe, which includes most of the leading industrial countries of the world, is America's largest market for purchases and sales of goods. Canada and Asia, notably Japan, are the next largest markets.

Of course, changes in the world's economies since the early part of this century have brought changes in our patterns of trade. For example, trade with Asia has grown in relative importance, while trade with Europe, though still large in absolute terms, has declined substantially.

Why Do Countries Trade?

Imagine what would happen if you tried to be completely self-sufficient. You would have to grow your own food, make your own clothing, build your own means of transportation, construct your own shelter, make your own furniture, treat your own illnesses,

Exhibit 1

U.S. Merchandise Exports and Imports, 1972

	Merchandise exports	Merchandise imports
	(billions of dollars)	
Item		
Agricultural products	$ 9.4	$ 6.5
Nonagricultural products*	39.5	49.1
	$48.9	$55.6
Country		
Africa	$ 1.3	$ 1.6
Asia	11.3	15.1
Australia and Oceania	1.0	1.1
Europe	16.1	15.7
Canada	12.4	14.9
Mexico and Central America	3.6	3.5
South America	3.7	3.5

* Minerals, fuels, chemicals, manufactured goods, and machinery.
SOURCE: U.S. Department of Commerce.

and provide for all your needs and desires. Obviously you would not be able to do many things because you lack the necessary material resources, time, and skills. Hence your level of living would be much lower than it is now.

How could you correct the situation? You could *specialize*—that is, concentrate on the things you do best. In that way, you could produce more than enough for yourself and sell or trade your surpluses for the other things you want. That is essentially what we all do. A carpenter, a salesman, a doctor, a teacher, a bricklayer—each "specializes" in the activity that he does best and thereby earns enough to buy the goods and services that he does not produce for himself.

Specialization also exists among nations:

Resources are distributed unevenly throughout the world. Some countries have more or better land, or labor, or capital than others, so it may pay for them to *specialize*. In this way, a larger quantity and greater variety of goods are produced, which nations can exchange with one another. The quantity and variety of goods would be less if each nation tried to be self-sufficient.

These ideas can be understood more clearly by examining the principles and consequences that underlie the exchange of goods between nations and regions.

LAW OF ABSOLUTE ADVANTAGE

The simplest and most obvious reason for trade is provided by what is known as the *law of absolute advantage*. This principle states that a basis for trade between regions exists when each, due to natural or acquired endowments, can provide the other with a good or service for less than it would pay to produce the product at home. Thus, the United States buys coffee from Brazil, and Brazil buys steel from the United States; Libya buys lumber from Sweden, and Sweden buys oil from Libya; Florida buys cars made in Michigan, and Michigan buys oranges grown in Florida. In general, this kind of trading helps both parties. Imagine how costly it would be, for example, if some Florida businessmen tried to acquire the factories and skilled workers needed to make automobiles, or if some Michigan businessmen tried to build the huge hothouses that would be needed for growing orange trees.

NOTE: For convenience, we ordinarily speak of "countries" or "regions" as buyers and sellers of products. But the governments of those areas are not doing all the buying and selling. Most international trade is carried on by private firms; only in communistic or command economies do governments engage significantly in trade.

THE CONCEPT OF COMPARATIVE ADVANTAGE

The reasons for trade are not always as obvious as in the above examples. Trade between individuals or nations can be profitable even if one of the parties can produce *both* products more efficiently than the other. This involves a concept known as "comparative advantage."

For example, a doctor may also be a fast typist. Yet he hires a typist, even though she may not type as well as he does, because the time he spends at his medical practice is more profitable than the time he spends at the typewriter. Thus, suppose the doctor can do all the typing he needs in 1 hour, whereas the typist he hires takes 3 hours to do the same amount of typing. If the doctor earns $30 an hour by practicing medicine, and pays the typist $3 an hour, he gains $21 a day by sticking to his profession. Or, to put the example in a different but equivalent way, he can earn enough money in 18 minutes by practicing medicine to pay for 3 hours of the typist's time.

An Application to Nations

Applying the same principle to nations, let us take the case of England and Portugal, both producing two products—cloth and wine. (This was the kind of example used in 1817 by the great English classical economist David Ricardo, when he first explained the mutual advantages of trade between nations in terms of what is now known as the law of comparative advantage.)

An illustration based on hypothetical data appears in Exhibit 2. It is clear from the table that Portugal is equally as efficient as England in the production of cloth, but three times as efficient as England in the production of wine. Therefore, Portugal has a comparative (or relative) advantage in wine production.

In the charts of Exhibit 2, the data are presented in the form of production-possibilities curves. The "curves," however, are shown here as straight lines, whereas in earlier chapters they appeared as curved lines that were bowed outward. This is because we are assuming for simplicity that production takes place under conditions of constant rather than increasing costs.

Thus in England, the intersection of the production-possibilities curve *DE* with the two axes of the chart tells us that one day's labor can produce either 30 yards of cloth or 10 gallons of wine, or any particular combination in between as determined by any given point along the line. Hence the steepness (slope) of *DE* measures the relative cost of the two products in England and is constant at the ratio 3:1. Similarly in Portugal, the intersection of *D'E'* with the two axes signifies that 1 day's labor can produce either 30 yards of cloth or 30 gallons of wine, or any specific combination in between as determined by any given point along the line. Therefore, the steepness of *D'E'* measures the relative cost of the two products in Portugal and is constant at the ratio 1:1.

How much will each country produce? It is impossible to answer this question without knowing the demands for each product in the two countries. However, if we assume that there is no trade between them, it may be inferred that each will try to be self-sufficient by producing some cloth and some wine as denoted by any given point on each nation's production-possibilities curve. Thus England might choose the point *K* representing *0G* yards of cloth and *0H* gallons of wine; Portugal might choose the point *K'* representing *0'G'* yards of cloth and *0'H'* gallons of wine.

Introducing Trade

What will happen if the two countries decide to engage in free and unrestricted trade? Let us assume for simplicity that for both countries: (*a*) there are no transportation costs between them, (*b*) competitive conditions prevail, and (*c*) labor is the only scarce factor of production and hence prices of the products are equal to their relative labor costs. This means that since the costs, and therefore prices, in both countries are

Price in England: 3 yards cloth = 1 gallon wine
Price in Portugal: 1 yard cloth = 1 gallon wine

it is obvious that *cloth is cheaper in England and wine is cheaper in Portugal.* Therefore, England will import wine from Portugal and Portugal will import cloth from England. As exports of Portuguese wine enter England, the supply of wine in England will increase and its price will fall; likewise, as exports of English cloth enter Portugal, the supply of cloth in Portugal will increase and its price will fall.

THE GAINS FROM TRADE

The price ratios in England and Portugal will thus become equal to one another because, as we have assumed above, there is competition in both nations and there are no trade restrictions or transportation costs between them; hence the two countries will comprise in effect a *single market* with a *single price ratio.* At this new price ratio, it will pay for England to specialize in the production of cloth and for Portugal to specialize in the production of wine, and for both nations to trade a portion of these outputs with one another. In that way the two countries can end up with more wine and more cloth than if each country tried to produce both products by itself.

The point is illustrated graphically in Exhibit 3. Chart (*a*) is constructed by combining the two previous charts from Exhibit 2. Thus the chart for England is in the same relative position as before,

---

Exhibit 2

The Law of Comparative Advantage

The curves DE and D'E' are production-possibilities curves for each country. Without trade between the two nations, England may choose to be self-sufficient in both cloth and wine by producing a combination represented by point K; similarly, Portugal may choose to be self-sufficient by producing a combination represented by point K'.

PRODUCTION FROM 1 DAY'S LABOR AT FULL EMPLOYMENT

	Cloth output (yards per day)	Wine output (gallons per day)	Cost ratio (cloth/wine)
England	30	10	3/1
Portugal	30	30	1/1

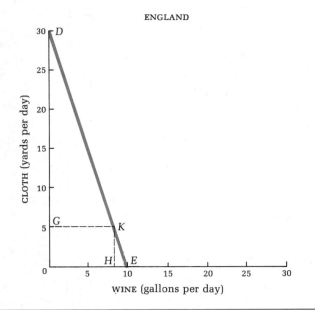

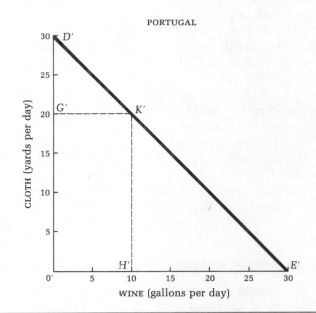

but the chart for Portugal is "flipped over" so that its origin is in the upper right-hand corner at 0'. The construction procedure is shown in Chart (b).

By studying Chart (a), we can observe several interesting features:

1. The dashed line DL defines the trading possibilities for both countries. Since it is a straight line, it has a constant price ratio (or slope) which is somewhere between the price ratios represented by the old production-possibilities curves DE and D'E'.

2. An "exchange point" will tend to be established in the vicinity of P because at a point such as this both England and Portugal can have more cloth and more wine by specializing and trading than by trying to be self-sufficient. For example, suppose

England specializes entirely in cloth and produces OD yards of it. If it consumes OM yards of cloth, it can export the remaining MD yards and acquire ON (= MP) gallons of wine in return. It thus ends up at the point P where it has more cloth than when it was self-sufficient at the point K.

3. Similarly. if Portugal specializes completely in wine, it can produce 0'E' gallons. If it consumes 0'N' of this, it has left over N'E' which it can export to England in return for 0'M' yards of cloth. In this way Portugal also ends up at the point P, where it consumes more of both cloth and wine than when it was self-sufficient at the point K'.

4. Both countries thus benefit from international specialization and exchange. The amount by which a

---

Exhibit 3

The Terms of Trade and the Gains from Trade

Chart (a) combines the two separate charts of Exhibit 2 as shown here in Chart (b).

The lines DE and D'E' are the production-possibilities curves from the previous exhibit. Before trade begins, England is producing at point K and Portugal at point K'. As a result of trade, both countries may extend their production frontiers to the point P, where each country receives more of both goods than before. These increased benefits of trade are called the gains from trade.

The dashed line DL is the new price line representing the trading possibilities of both nations. Its steepness (slope) measures the terms of trade, which is the amount of goods that each nation must give up (or export) for one unit of goods that it receives (or imports). The line must fall somewhere between the two old price lines DE and D'E' in order for trade to occur. If it falls to the left of DE (or to the right of D'E'), it will be cheaper for England (or for Portugal) to produce both products and not trade.

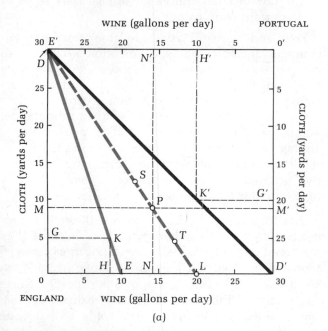

(a)

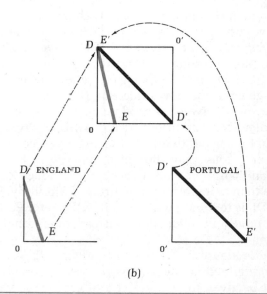

(b)

country benefits from trade is called the *gains from trade*. This concept plays an important role in the trading policies of nations.

It is interesting to note from the chart that only in the vicinity of point *P* along the line *DL* will both countries gain by having more of both wine and cloth. At exchange points which are much higher or lower, one country may gain while the other loses, as compared to when each was self-sufficient without trade. Thus at point *S*, for example, England will gain by having more cloth and more wine than it had at point *K*, but Portugal will lose by having more wine and less cloth than it had at point *K'*. At point *T*, on the other hand, England will have comparatively less cloth and more wine, while Portugal has more of both. Therefore:

Only in the vicinity of point *P* can *both* countries experience the mutual benefits of having more of *both* products. Hence under conditions of competition and unrestricted trade, the exchange point will tend to settle at or near *P*.

THE TERMS OF TRADE

Each country thus gains by specializing in what it can produce with the greatest comparative or relative advantage. The gains will then be divided between them according to the new price ratio which, as we have seen, is simply the slope of the trading-possibilities line *DL* in the chart.

Thus the closer that the line *DL* is to *DE*, the higher will be the price of wine relative to cloth, and hence the greater the gain to Portugal as compared to England. If *DL* should coincide with *DE*, which is unlikely, Portugal will receive all the gains from trade and England will receive none. The converse of these principles, of course, is equally applicable if the line *DL* shifts in the opposite direction toward *D'E'*.

In general, the new price line *DL* must always be somewhere between the old price lines *DE* and *D'E'* in order for trade to occur. For if *DL* is, say, to the left of (or steeper than) *DE*, the trading price of wine will be *greater* than the old price ratio in England. England will then find it cheaper to produce its own wine than to import it from Portugal. Similarly, if the line *DL* is to the right of *D'E'*, it will pay for Portugal to produce its own cloth instead of trading with England.

These ideas involve what is known as the *terms of trade*, defined as the number of units of goods that must be given up for one unit of goods received by each party to a transaction. (Graphically, the terms of trade are measured by the slope of the line *DL* in the chart.) In any transaction, the terms of trade are determined by the relative demands of the trading parties. In general, the terms of trade are said to move *in favor* of the party which gives up less units of goods for one unit of goods received, and *against* the party which gives up more units of goods for one unit of goods received. As we shall see, the terms of trade play a vital and intensely practical role in evaluating exchange relationships between nations.

CONCLUSION: AN IMPORTANT LAW

The foregoing ideas permit us to formulate a principle of fundamental significance in economics, especially in international economics. It is based on the concept of comparative advantage which was developed earlier, but the concept may now be expressed more formally as a law.

The *law of comparative advantage* states that if one nation can produce each of two products more efficiently than another nation, and if the former can produce one of these commodities with comparatively greater efficiency than the other commodity, it should specialize in production of the product in which it is most efficient and leave production of the alternative product to the other country. The two nations will then have more of both goods by engaging in trade. This principle is also applicable to individuals and regions as well as to nations.

The law of comparative advantage thus leads to an important conclusion:

Free and unrestricted trade among nations encourages international specialization according to comparative advantage. It thereby *tends* to bring about: (*a*) the most efficient allocation of world resources as well as a maximization of world production; (*b*) a redistribution of relative product demands, resulting in greater equality of product prices among trading nations; and (*c*) a redistribution of relative resource demands to correspond with relative product demands, resulting in greater equality of resource prices among trading nations.

It is important to emphasize that these outcomes are *tendencies* rather than certainties, because they are based on such idealistic assumptions as the existence of competition and the absence of trade restrictions (including transportation costs). Since these assumptions are not entirely realized in practice, the consequences of free trade will deviate from the above-mentioned tendencies.

Instruments of Protection

Despite the fundamental advantages of free trade—namely, encouragement of the most efficient allocation of world resources and the maximization of world production—nations have not been quick to adopt it. They have often chosen instead to institute various methods of protecting their home industries by imposing barriers to free trade. The reasons usually advanced for such actions will be explained later. But first, the chief forms of protection may be noted briefly.

TARIFFS

Tariffs have played a very significant role in various political and sectional disputes in the United States.

A *tariff* is a customs duty or tax imposed by a government on the importation (or exportation) of a good. Tariffs may be (a) specific, based on a tax per unit of the commodity, or (b) ad valorem, based on the value of the commodity. There are a number of reasons, some of them rather complex, why a government might impose a tariff. For present purposes, however, it will be simplest for us to think of a tariff as a tax on imports exclusively, and to assume that it is imposed for the primary purpose of protecting domestic industry from foreign competition, or for providing the government with more revenue.

Exhibit 4 presents a history of tariff levels in the United States since 1820. Since a tariff is a law which must be approved by Congress, it is often named after the Congressman who sponsored it. As the chart shows, the highest tariffs existed in 1830

Exhibit 4

Average Tariff Rates in the United States

Tariffs have often been a political football in American history. Although rates have fluctuated widely, the trend has been sharply downward since the early 1930s. Since the post-World War II years, America has been a leading low-tariff nation. But the trend may be reversed in the 1970s, due to renewed protectionist efforts in Congress.

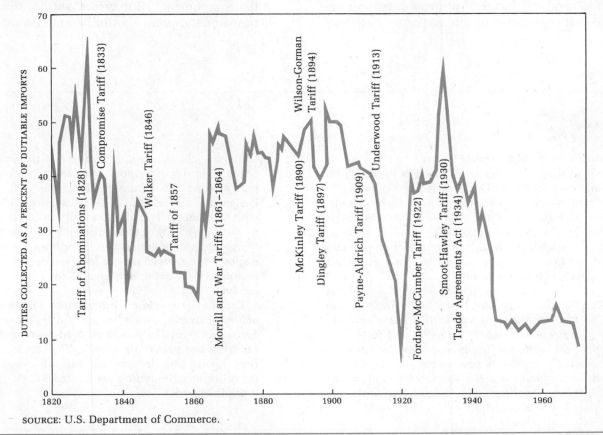

SOURCE: U.S. Department of Commerce.

and in 1930, at rates of about 60 percent. The trend since 1930 has been sharply downward, with average rates of about 12 percent during the 1950s and 1960s. But the decade of the 1970s may see a sharp reversal in the trend, due to renewed protectionist efforts in Congress.

QUOTAS AND OTHER NONTARIFF DEVICES

Tariffs are not the only means that nations employ to protect their home industries. Another common instrument of protection is the *import quota*, which places a precise legal limit on the number of units of a commodity that may be imported during a given period. In addition, countries may impose customs procedures and laws involving import financing, foreign exchange requirements, and regulations involving labeling, health, safety, and shipping, some of which are expressly designed as protectionist devices. Quotas and other nontariff devices have become relatively more significant than tariffs as protective instruments in many countries, including the United States. (See Box 1.)

What are the economic consequences of protection? In general, all forms of protection tend to impede the full advantages of international specialization that are to be gained from free or unrestricted trade. When a nation adopts protective devices such as tariffs or quotas, it (a) causes a shift of resources from more efficient to less efficient uses, and (b) restricts consumers' freedom of choice.

Arguments for Protection

Despite the fact that the law of comparative advantage and the economic benefits of free trade have never been successfully refuted—although there have been many heroic attempts to do so—efforts by special-interest groups to obtain protection are common. American history, for example, is replete with long and eloquent pleas by businessmen, union representatives, and political leaders contending that theirs is a "different" situation requiring special consideration. Most of these arguments for protection can be grouped into one of the following categories: (1) infant-industry argument, (2) national-security argument, (3) diversified-economy argument, (4) wage-protection argument, and (5) employment-protection argument.

We shall see below that there are fallacies in all these arguments. But before we do, the following fundamental point should be understood:

Box 1

A Salami May Sometimes Be Just a Lot of Bologna

When is a sausage not a sausage?

The not-so-simple answer is: When it is exported and bumps into another country's definition of a sausage.

Many countries, mostly European, have their own idea of what a sausage should be—defined by its size, shape, casing, color, the mix of ingredients, and, in some instances, the number per link. Anything that doesn't conform to a particular country's definition of a sausage is ruled a nonsausage and may not be imported.

The restrictions are what are known as nontariff barriers. Broadly, these are any obstacles to international trade other than import duties or tariffs. These obstacles include import quotas, import licensing and foreign exchange controls, state trading monopolies and preferential, nationalistic buying by government agencies. Other, less subtle restrictions range through labeling and packaging requirements, health and industrial standards, and discriminatory taxes and fees.

But the classic nontariff barrier is the provision of a German tariff law of 1902, now obsolete, affecting the import of cows. This granddaddy of nontariff barriers was designed to exclude Dutch and Russian cattle competitive with German types, but allow entry of Swiss cattle. It did so with a definition that gave an extra low duty rate to "large dappled mountain cattle or brown cattle reared at a spot 300 meters above sea level and which have at least one month's grazing at a spot at least 800 meters above sea level."

The old German law, while not mentioning any country, achieved its aim with what amounted to a description of Swiss cattle-raising practices. Modern nontariff barriers, however, are not so diplomatic. The catalog of such barriers seems infinite, and as research develops, almost every country, including the United States, is seen to be a prime offender.

We can sell abroad only if we buy abroad. When the United States imports from foreign countries, those countries earn most of the dollars they need to purchase American exports. In general, *exports are the cost of trade, imports the return from trade,* not the other way around. Over the long run a nation must export in order to import.

As you will see in the following paragraphs, this basic principle is essential for understanding the fallacies that underlie almost all arguments for protection—*including both tariffs and quotas.*

THE INFANT-INDUSTRY ARGUMENT

When George Washington was inaugurated in 1789, he appointed Alexander Hamilton as the first Secretary of the Treasury. In 1791, Hamilton issued his famous *Report on Industry and Commerce* wherein he articulated with remarkable depth and clarity the economic problems of the time and proposed the nation's first protective tariff system. A fundamental justification for this system was the new nation's need to protect its growing infant industries.

An *infant industry* is an underdeveloped industry which may not be able to survive competition from abroad. The infant-industry argument for protection says that such industries should be shielded temporarily with high tariffs or quotas until the industries develop technological efficiency and economies of scale which will enable them to compete with foreign industries.

This type of plea was the basis on which tariffs were established for a number of industries during the nineteenth and twentieth centuries. But economists have come to recognize three major shortcomings of this argument:

1. Tariffs or other protective devices become the vested interests of particular business and political groups and as such are extremely difficult to eliminate.

2. Some protected industries never grow out of the "infant" stage—that is, they never become able to compete effectively with more mature industries in other countries.

3. An increase in tariffs or quotas results in higher prices to domestic consumers; therefore, if an industry must be shielded from foreign competition, a subsidy would be more desirable because it tends to increase output as well as to reduce costs and prices. Above all, a subsidy is visible and must be voted periodically by Congress.

NATIONAL-SECURITY ARGUMENT

From time to time, representatives of various industries have made major efforts, through government and the news media, to gain protection from the onslaught of foreign competition. For example, in one of his many pleas for increased protection, Roger Blough, when he was chairman of the board of the U.S. Steel Corporation, asked a congressional committee in the late 1960s: "Can we be assured of the strong industrial base in steel we need for modern defense if one-quarter or more of the steel we require were imported from countries lying uncomfortably close to the Soviet Union or China?"

This quotation provides a superb illustration of the "national-security argument"—an argument which contends that a nation should be as self-sufficient as possible in the production of goods that it needs for war and defense. On the face of it, this plea for protection seems persuasive, but on closer examination the following criticisms become apparent:

1. It is a political and military argument rather than an economic one, and hence should be decided by the proper authorities in a calm and rational manner without the distortions of parties that have a direct business interest in the outcome. The economist can help by pointing out the costs of protection in terms of resource misallocation and a reduced level of living.

2. Many industries are important for defense or national security and could qualify equally well for increased protection.

3. As in the infant-industry argument, if some form of shielding is necessary, a subsidy is preferable to a tariff or quota.

DIVERSIFIED-ECONOMY ARGUMENT

"Don't put all your eggs in one basket." This maxim is as true for nations as it is for individuals—according to the "diversified-economy" theorists, who contend that increased protection is desirable because it enables a nation to build up a variety of industries for greater economic stability. In that way, they say, a highly specialized economy—like Bolivia's tin economy or Chile's copper economy—will be less susceptible to adverse swings in the world's demand for its exports. This argument contains some elements of truth. A single-crop or single-product economy is highly vulnerable to swings in demand—

which may be permanent. Thus, the introduction of man-made fibers has impoverished or severely damaged economies that concentrated on production of natural fibers. Further, specialized economies are frequently dependent on relatively few purchasers of their goods: the oil-producing nations of the Middle East, for example, sell to a relatively small number of oil companies—the giants in the field. When oil is in short supply, the producing countries can drive hard bargains; when oil is ample, the oil companies have the last word in any bargaining session.

But the diversified-economy argument also contains some shortcomings:

1. It is of little significance to economies that are already diversified and advanced, such as the United States.

2. It assumes that the government is more clairvoyant than private investors, and thus more able to envision the future economic benefits flowing from new and diversified industries.

3. It overlooks the inefficiencies that may result from forced, "unnatural" diversification, and the consequent increase in cost which may more than offset any economic gains.

WAGE-PROTECTION ARGUMENT

Because wages in the United States are higher than they are in other industrialized nations, some economists and business leaders argue that tariffs or quotas are needed to protect American workers from the products of cheap labor abroad.

In essence, advocates of this argument are contending that a high-wage nation cannot compete with a low-wage nation. In reality, however, the contention is false. The products of high-wage U.S. labor compete daily in world markets with the products of low-wage labor. The fact is that for many products high wages do not of themselves prevent or even hinder trade among nations.

Three criticisms and qualifications of the wage-protection argument are particularly important:

1. It assumes that labor is the only resource entering into production. In fact, labor is a resource that is combined in each nation with varying quantities of capital and land; as a result, the products of countries may often be characterized as *labor-intensive,* *capital-intensive,* or *land-intensive,* depending on the relative proportions of resources that are employed in production.

2. Low-wage countries will have an advantage over high-wage countries *only* with products that are labor-intensive—products for which wages are a large proportion of total costs. High-wage countries may be better off not competing with low-wage countries in these products.

3. Even where labor-intensive products are concerned, however, high-wage countries may be able to compete effectively with low-wage countries if labor productivity in the former is high enough to compensate for lower wage levels in the latter. (See Box 2.)

EMPLOYMENT-PROTECTION ARGUMENT

Supporters of trade protection often argue that tariffs or quotas are desirable because they reduce imports relative to exports and thus encourage a favorable balance of trade—that is, a surplus of exports over imports. This in turn stimulates the export industries and helps to bring about a higher level of domestic income, employment, and production.

Is this a valid plea for protection? Like the previous arguments it may seem persuasive, but the following considerations should be kept in mind:

1. Any benefits in the form of higher income and employment, if they occur, are not likely to last long. The history of tariffs and quotas shows that in the long run nations tend to retaliate with their own protective measures, leaving all nations worse off than before.

2. Tariffs and quotas tend to result in higher prices, thus penalizing domestic consumers while benefiting domestic, inefficient producers; in the long run this encourages a movement of resources out of more efficient industries into less efficient (protected) ones, thereby raising costs and reducing comparative advantage.

3. In international trade goods pay for goods, and hence in the long run a nation which exports must also import; protective measures tend to impede the operation of this principle and therefore in the long run limit rather than encourage higher real income and employment.

A fitting conclusion to these arguments for and against protection is presented in Box 3.

Box 2

Labor Fights for Quota Protection

The American labor movement has been actively supporting protectionism since the late 1960s. Liberal trade policy, its leaders contend, is an anachronism; quotas are *needed to protect high-paid American workers from the products of cheap labor abroad.*

Industrial Union Department, AFL–CIO.

The Foreign-trade Multiplier

How does foreign trade affect a nation's income and employment? In order to answer this question, we must think of imports and exports in a special way.

Imports should be regarded as withdrawals from a nation's circular flow of income because they represent money earned at home but not put back into the income stream through consumption expenditures. Thus if students in the United States decide to buy more Hondas and fewer American-made motorcycles, the American motorcycle industry will sell less. As a result, it will reduce its investment expenditures and lay off workers. These unemployed workers will then buy fewer television sets, vacation trips, automobiles, and other goods. Their reduced demands for these products and services will in turn result in a further decline in investment and employment. The initial increase in imports, therefore, will eventually bring about a *multiplied* decrease in national income and output.

Exports should be regarded as injections into a nation's circular flow of income because they represent money received from foreigners who have bought American goods. For example, if Germans decide to buy less of their own goods and more American commodities, some American firms will find the demand for their products increasing. These firms will then expand their investment in plant and equipment and hire more workers, who in turn will

*Box 3

In Defense of Free Trade

Adam Smith defended free trade and condemned protection as long ago as 1776, in this famous passage from the Wealth of Nations:

> . . . It is the highest impertinence of kings and ministers, to pretend to watch over the economy of private people and to restrain their expense, either by sumptuary laws, or by prohibiting the importation of foreign luxuries. They are themselves always, and without any exception, the greatest spend-thrifts in the society. Let them look well after their own expense, and they may safely trust, private people with theirs. If their own extravagance does not ruin the state, that of their subjects never will. . . .
>
> To give the monopoly of the home market to the produce of domestic industry . . . must in almost all cases be either a useless or a hurtful regulation. If the produce of domestic industry can be bought there as cheap as that of foreign industry, the regulation is evidently useless. If it cannot, it must generally be hurtful.
>
> It is the maxim of every prudent master of a family, never to attempt to make at home what it will cost him more to make than to buy. The tailor does not attempt to make his own shoes, but buys them of a shoemaker. The shoemaker does not attempt to make his own clothes, but employs a tailor; the farmer attempts to make neither the one nor the other, but employs those different artificers. All of them find it in their interests to employ their whole industry in a way in which they will have some advantage over their neighbors, and to purchase with a part of its produce, or what is the same thing, with the price of a part of it, whatever else they have occasion for. What is prudence in the conduct of every private family, can scarce be folly in that of a great kingdom. . . .
>
> That it was the spirit of monopoly which originally both invented and propagated this protectionist doctrine cannot be doubted; and they who first taught it were by no means such fools as they who believed it. In every country it always is and must be the interest of the great body of the people to buy whatever they want of those who sell it cheapest. The proposition is so very manifest, that it seems ridiculous to take any pains to prove it; nor could it ever have been called in question had not the interested sophistry of merchants and manufacturers confounded the common sense of mankind.

THE LATE EIGHTEENTH-CENTURY WORLD OF TRADE

Historical Pictures Service, Chicago.

buy more of other products and thereby encourage the expansion of other industries. The initial increase in exports, therefore, eventually brings about a *multiplied* increase in national income and output.

These ideas suggest the existence of a "foreign-trade multiplier"—one of many multiplier concepts in economics. It may be described in the following way:

The *foreign-trade multiplier* is a principle which states that fluctuations in exports or imports may generate magnified variations in national income. This principle is based on the idea that a change in exports relative to imports has the same multiplier effect on national income as a change in autonomous expenditures does; similarly, a change in imports relative to exports has the same multipler effect on national income as a change in withdrawals from the income stream does.

In general, an increase in exports tends to raise domestic income, but the increased income also induces some imports which act as "leakages," tending to reduce the full multiplier effect that would exist if imports remained constant.

SUMMARY OF IMPORTANT IDEAS

1. Trade is important in the world economy. In quantitative terms, merchandise imports or exports range anywhere from about 4 to 40 percent of GNP for many major countries; in qualitative terms, many goods that countries import are virtually impossible to produce domestically.

2. Nations can raise their material standards of living by specializing and trading instead of trying to be self-sufficient. Two basic principles of specialization are the law of absolute advantage and the law of comparative advantage. The latter is more general because it demonstrates that nations can mutually benefit from specialization and trade even if each has only a relative rather than complete advantage over the other in the production of commodities. The *gains* from trade are the benefits that nations receive, whereas the *terms* of trade are the real sacrifices they must make in terms of the goods they give up in return for the goods they receive.

3. Despite the mutual benefits of free and unrestricted trade, nations have instituted various forms of protection. These common instruments of protection consist of tariffs, import quotas, and other protective devices such as unusual types of customs

procedures and laws pertaining to import financing, foreign exchange requirements, and regulations involving labeling, health, safety, and shipping.

4. Many pleas may be advanced in favor of protection. Most can be classified into one of five categories: the infant-industry argument, the national-security argument, the diversified-economy argument, the wage-protection argument, and the employment-protection argument. Each needs qualification and most involve logical fallacies.

5. The foreign-trade multiplier is one of many multiplier concepts in economics. It is a principle which states that fluctuations in a nation's exports or imports may cause magnified changes in its national income.

FOR DISCUSSION

1. *Terms and concepts to review:*

law of absolute advantage	tariff
gains from trade	import quota
terms of trade	infant industry
law of comparative advantage	foreign-trade multiplier

2. Examine the following production-possibilities table based on hypothetical data:

Country	Labor input (days)	Output of	
		Shoes (pairs)	Beef (pounds)
Italy	3	100	75
Argentina	3	50	60

(a) Which country, if any, has an absolute advantage in production? A comparative advantage? Explain.

(b) What is the *range* of possible barter terms—that is, the range within which the two countries may exchange goods? (HINT: What are the *domestic terms of trade* in each country?)

(c) What will determine the actual terms of exchange? Explain carefully.

3. The Constitution of the United States (Article 1, Sec. 10) states: "No State shall, without the consent of the Congress, lay any imposts or duties on imports or exports, except what may be absolutely necessary for executing its inspection laws." Do you

think the Founding Fathers were wise to pass this law? What would happen to the American standard of living if each state was allowed to impose protective barriers to trade?

4. "If you believe in the free movement of goods between nations, you should logically believe in the free movement of people, too. This means that cheap foreign labor should be admitted to the United States, even if it results in the displacement of American labor." Do you agree? Explain your answer.

5. An editorial in the *Washington Inquirer* stated that:

> The United States should develop a large ship-building industry. Such an industry would provide more jobs and higher incomes for workers. Moreover, the ships could be used for passenger and cargo service in peacetime, and could be quickly converted for military purposes in case of war. In view of these advantages, it would be wise for the U.S. government to protect the domestic shipbuilding industry from foreign competition until it can grow to a stronger competitive position.

Do you agree with this editorial? Explain.

6. Abraham Lincoln is reputed to have remarked: "I don't know much about the tariff. But I do know that when I buy a coat from England, I have the coat and England has the money. But when I buy a coat in America, I have the coat and America has the money." Can you show that Lincoln was correct only in the first sentence of his remark?

7. The foreign-trade multiplier is ordinarily smaller than the domestic-investment multipler. Why?

CHAPTER 35

International Finance: The Payments of Nations

CHAPTER PREVIEW

What is the foreign exchange market? What important economic functions does it perform?

How are money flows into and out of a country recorded? Can we analyze the nature and sources of such flows?

What are the economic implications of an imbalance or disequilibrium in a nation's money inflows and outflows?

What are the methods and effects of correcting a disequilibrium in a nation's international money flows?

At one time the study of international economics dealt primarily with the theory and problems of trade between nations. But this has long since ceased to be true. The economic relationships among countries depend as much on financial considerations as on trade. Hence an understanding of international finance is essential in dealing with world economic problems.

What do we mean by international finance? In the most general sense it deals with the monetary side of international trade. It is therefore concerned with the nature of international transactions—their forms of payment, the ways in which they are recorded for purposes of analysis and interpretation, their economic effects on the nations that are involved, and the methods by which their undesirable consequences can be minimized. Since these statements may seem somewhat vague at this point, the questions in the chapter preview will help focus your attention on the more specific issues involved.

International Payments and Foreign Exchange

Each nation has its own unit of currency. This means that when transactions are conducted across national borders one currency must be converted into another.

For example, if a French importer buys machinery from the United States, the American exporter eventually receives payment in dollars, not French francs. Similarly, if an American tourist visits England, he pays for his hotel room, restaurant meals, and other goods and services in British pounds, not dollars. The instruments used to make international payments are called *foreign exchange*. They consist not only of currency, but also to a much larger extent of checks, drafts, or bills of exchange which are simply orders to pay currency.

FUNCTION OF THE FOREIGN EXCHANGE MARKETS

International transactions go on all the time. As a result, some people have dollars which they want to exchange for pounds, and others have pounds which they want to exchange for dollars. How do these people acquire the foreign exchange they desire?

The answer is that foreign exchange is bought and sold in organized markets through dealers, just as stocks, bonds, wheat, and many other commodities are bought and sold. In the United States, the foreign exchange dealers are the large commercial banks located in New York, San Francisco, and other major cities. Overseas, the major foreign exchange centers include London, Zurich, Paris, Brussels, Tokyo, and Hong Kong. If an individual wants to acquire or dispose of foreign exchange, he can easily do so by communicating directly with a dealer or by going through his local commercial bank which will arrange the transaction through one of the large banks dealing in foreign exchange.

The most fundamental function performed by the foreign exchange markets is that they provide a means for transferring purchasing power from one country to another and from one currency to another. Without them, international trade would be virtually limited to barter.

EFFECTS OF INTERNATIONAL TRANSACTIONS

Suppose an American exporter sells a machine to a British importer. The importer might pay for it by purchasing a draft from his bank—that is, an order to pay a specified number of pounds sterling to the American exporter. The exporter then converts the draft into dollars by selling the draft to a foreign exchange dealer. The number of dollars the dealer pays for the draft depends on the rate of exchange between dollars and pounds. (The dealer, like any broker, will also impose a commission charge.)

The American exporter now has his dollars, and the dealer has a draft payable in British pounds. What will each of them do? Since they are businessmen, they are likely to deposit the funds in their own commercial-bank accounts so that they can continue to write the checks they need to carry on their businesses. Thus the American exporter will deposit the dollars in his American bank, and the American foreign exchange dealer will send the draft to England for deposit in his British bank. The dealer, by having such an account, can write a draft or check against it and sell it to an American importer who needs pounds to pay for goods purchased from a British exporter.

What are the results of these activities? In general, international transactions have two economic effects:

1. An export transaction increases the supply of money in the exporting country and reduces it in the importing country. The converse of this, resulting from an import transaction, is also true. (Can you explain why?)

2. By exporting, a nation obtains the foreign monies it needs to acquire imports. In other words, a nation which sells abroad can also buy abroad. (Japan, for example, sells motorcycles, television sets, and other goods to the United States and is thereby able to obtain the dollars it needs to buy American machines, agricultural goods, and other products.)

The Balance of Payments

So far, we have assumed that economic relationships among nations are based solely on international trade. In reality, this is not the whole story. Foreign exchange is demanded and supplied as a result of various other important types of transactions besides importing and exporting. It is necessary, therefore, that we examine the nature of these transactions.

Corporations prepare periodic reports such as balance sheets and income (or profit and loss) statements, summarizing in money terms the results of their business activities. These reports are used by bankers, businessmen, stockholders, creditors, or any other interested parties—even by the government—to evaluate a company's financial position.

Each nation also prepares a somewhat similar periodic report called a "balance of payments." The report summarizes in money terms the results of a nation's international economic activities by showing how some transactions cause an outflow of funds and others an inflow. It should be apparent, therefore, that a nation's balance of payments is of concern not only to economists, but also to businessmen, bankers, government leaders, and anyone interested in world affairs.

AN ILLUSTRATIVE MODEL OF THE BALANCE OF PAYMENTS

What does a balance-of-payments statement actually look like? How is it interpreted? We can best answer these questions by first analyzing the structure of an idealized balance-of-payments form like the one shown in Exhibit 1. This illustration is a generalized model; that is, it clearly emphasizes the major categories and subcategories that should be understood. You will find yourself referring back to this model quite often because, as will be seen later on, most countries do not publish their balance-of-payments statements in such a convenient form.

As was pointed out above, a nation's balance of payments is a financial summary of its international transactions. The first thing to notice is that these money flows are represented in the last two columns of the statement by so-called "debits" and "credits" —two terms that are widely used in discussions involving the balance of payments:

A *debit* is any transaction which results in a money outflow or payment to a foreign country; it may be represented on a balance-of-payments statement by a negative sign. A *credit* is any transaction which results in a money inflow or receipt from a foreign country; it may be represented on a balance-of-payments statement by a positive sign. (NOTE: These definitions are applicable only in international economics; if you take a course in accounting, you will find that the terms "debit" and "credit" are defined in different ways.)

The balance-of-payments model shown in Exhibit 1 is self-explanatory. All you have to do is go down the list and verify for yourself that each item would logically result in either an outflow or inflow of money, and hence would be recorded as either a debit or credit.

The balance of payments is divided into four major categories; these are ranked in what is for most countries the following (decreasing) order of importance: (1) current account; (2) capital account; (3) unilateral transfer account; and (4) gold account. In the first category, the subclassification at the top denoting merchandise trade usually involves the largest debits and credits in balance-of-payments statements. Thus a merchandise import is a debit

Exhibit 1
General Model of the Balance of Payments

	Debit (money outflows or payments) (−)	Credit (money inflows or receipts) (+)
I. Current account:		
A. Merchandise trade:		
1. Merchandise imports	X	
2. Merchandise exports		X
B. Service transactions:		
1. Transportation:		
a. Rendered by foreign vessels, airlines etc.	X	
b. Rendered by domestic vessels, airlines, etc.		X
2. Travel expenditures:		
a. In foreign countries	X	
b. By foreigners in home country		X
3. Interest and dividends:		
a. Paid to foreigners	X	
b. Received from abroad		X
4. Banking and insurance services:		
a. Rendered by foreign institutions	X	
b. Rendered to foreigners by domestic institutions		X
5. Government expenditures:		
a. By home government abroad	X	
b. By foreign government in home country		X
II. Capital account:		
A. Long-term:		
1. Purchase of securities from foreigners	X	
2. Sale of securities to foreigners		X
B. Short-term:*		
1. Increase of bank and brokerage balances abroad	X	
2. Decrease of foreign-held bank and brokerage balances in home country	X	
3. Increase of foreign-held bank and brokerage balances in home country		X
4. Decrease of bank and brokerage balances abroad		X
III. Unilateral transfer account:		
A. Private:		
1. Personal and institutional remittances to nonresidents	X	
2. Remittances received from abroad		X
B. Governmental:		
1. Grants, indemnities, gifts, and reparations made to other countries	X	
2. Grants, indemnities, gifts, and reparations received from other countries		X
IV. Gold Account:		
A. Import of gold and increase of earmarked gold abroad†	X	
B. Export of gold and increase of earmarked gold for foreign account†		X
Errors and omissions		

* Also includes currency holdings, acceptances, and other short-term claims not listed.
† "Earmarked" gold is gold physically held in one country for the account of another.

SOURCE: Adapted with some changes from Delbert Snider, *Introduction to International Economics*, 5th ed., Homewood, Ill., Irwin, 1971.

item because it results in a money outflow or payment to the exporting country; conversely, a merchandise export is a credit item because it results in a money inflow or receipt to the importing country.

The remaining items can be interpreted in a similar way. In the last category, confusion will be avoided by thinking of gold like any other commodity (rather than as money) as far as debits and credits are concerned. Thus, imports of gold are debits; exports of gold are credits.

THE BALANCE OF PAYMENTS ALWAYS BALANCES (IN ACCOUNTING)

If you take a basic course in accounting, you will learn to apply a principle known as *double-entry bookkeeping*. This principle holds that every transaction is of a twofold nature and must be expressed for accounting purposes in the form of *both* debits and credits. In more general terms, for any given debit there must be one or more credits whose total will precisely equal the debit; conversely, for any given credit there must be one or more debits whose total will precisely equal the credit.

This idea can be illustrated with reference to the balance-of-payments model in Exhibit 1. Suppose, for example, that an American firm exports equipment worth $1 million to a foreign country. This part of the transaction is a merchandise export and appears as a credit item on the U.S. balance of payments. The importing country may pay for the goods in any one or combination of several ways, all of which are recorded as debit items on the U.S. balance of payments. For instance, the importing country may pay in dollars by decreasing its foreign-held bank balances in the United States, or it may pay in its own currency, which has the effect of increasing U.S. bank balances held abroad, or it may receive the equipment as a gift under the U.S. foreign-aid program, in which case it is a unilateral transfer similar to a grant.

Double-entry bookkeeping assures in principle that *total debits equal total credits*—or, in other words, that the *balance of payments always balances* in an accounting sense. In practice, however, since a country's balance of payments summarizes millions of individual international transactions, it is rarely accurate down to the last dollar. Hence, total debits will either be less than or greater than total credits. To correct this situation, a balance of payments statement will often show an item called "errors and omissions." This equals the difference between actual total debits and actual total credits, and is added to the smaller of these two totals to bring the total payments into balance.

In a more fundamental sense, however, there is an obvious realistic reason why the balance of payments always balances:

A country, like a household, cannot spend more than its current income unless it draws on its cash reserves, sells some of its assets, borrows, or receives gifts—all of which are credit items; conversely, it cannot spend less than its current income unless it accumulates cash reserves, acquires some assets, lends, or gives gifts—all of which are debit items. Therefore, total debits must always equal total credits.

THE FOUR MAJOR ACCOUNTS

The balance-of-payments model, as we have seen, contains four major accounts. Let us survey briefly the contents of each.

1. *Current account.* This includes all imports and exports of goods and services, and is the most basic account in the balance of payments. It is the "stuff" of which international economic relations are composed. The other three accounts fulfill what are largely auxiliary functions by facilitating the flow of goods and services.

2. *Capital account.* This is composed entirely of paper claims and obligations. The long-term component consists of loans and investments maturing in more than one year. The short-term component consists of claims maturing in less than one year and of foreign exchange and bank balances; these short-term capital movements may flow into or out of a country in order to make up for differences in payments and receipts resulting from a gap between imports and exports or from other transactions.

3. *Unilateral transfer account.* This account is somewhat like the capital account, except that it involves capital movements and gifts for which there are no return commitments or claims. Thus, a personal remittance to a resident of a foreign country involves no commitment for repayment and is classified as a unilateral transfer.

4. *Gold account.* This reflects gold flows and the claims to gold among governments. Gold movements are like short-term capital movements; they

serve primarily to make up the differences in payments and receipts resulting from other international transactions.

Against this background, let us summarize what is meant by "balance of payments":

The _balance of payments_ is a statement of the money value of all transactions that take place between a nation and the rest of the world during a given period. These transactions may consist of imports and exports of goods and services, and movements of short-term and long-term investments, gifts, currency, and gold. The transactions may be classified for convenience into several categories: current account, capital account, unilateral transfer account, and gold account.

THE UNITED STATES BALANCE OF PAYMENTS

The U.S. balance of payments is shown in Exhibit 2 on the next page. Note that the balance of trade is not the same thing as the balance of payments, although many people confuse the two. The _balance of trade_ is that part of a nation's balance of payments dealing with merchandise imports and exports. A "favorable" balance of trade exists when the value of a nation's exports exceeds the value of its imports; an "unfavorable" balance of trade exists when the value of its imports exceeds the value of its exports. The United States long had a favorable balance of trade, but the gap began to narrow in the late 1960s because the rising pressure of inflation made American goods too expensive for foreigners to purchase.

What about the United States balance of payments? The long-run trends have varied. For many years prior to the late 1940s the United States had a surplus or favorable balance of payments because of its strong trade position and its receipt of long-term capital from abroad. As a result, its money inflows exceeded its money outflows. Since 1950, however, the United States has run an almost consistent deficit or unfavorable balance for various reasons: military spending overseas; free-spending American tourists going abroad; surging private foreign investments; and government grants-in-aid to foreign nations. Thus its money outflows have exceeded its money inflows.

Of what significance is this deficit? The theory of balance-of-payments surpluses and deficits is a topic of major importance in international finance; it cannot be overemphasized. Hence, the remainder of this chapter is devoted to an analysis of its causes, nature, and methods of correction.

OFFICIAL SETTLEMENTS BASIS OR LIQUIDITY BASIS?

In a strict accounting sense, of course, the balance of payments always balances because total debits always equal total credits. But a simple accounting balance must not be confused with a meaningful economic balance because the economic behavior underlying some of the transactions may not be sustainable. For this reason, economists and government officials use two different bases for measuring the "balance" in the balance of payments—that is, two different measures of surpluses and deficits: the _official reserve transactions balance_ and the _net-liquidity balance_. Both are shown in Exhibit 2.

Two measures are used because of a disagreement in defining which international transactions _cause_ a deficit in the balance of payments and which _finance_ a deficit. Most of the disagreement hinges on the way in which short-term dollar liabilities of American banks and the U.S. Treasury are treated for balance-of-payments purposes, since some of those liabilities are held by official foreign government agencies such as central banks and some are held by private foreign individuals and organizations. Thus:

☐ Those who favor the official transactions basis as the best measure of the U.S. payments position assume that the only direct claims on the U.S. government's official reserve assets, such as its convertible foreign currencies, are the short-term dollar liabilities held by official foreign agencies. Why? Because the U.S. government will sell these assets only to such agencies, not to private individuals or firms. Therefore, a deficit in the balance of payments is financed by drawing on the government's official reserve assets or by borrowing from foreign government agencies.

☐ Those who favor the net-liquidity basis argue that foreign private holders of short-term dollar liabilities can easily turn them over to an official foreign agency, such as their central bank, so that these, too, represent a significant potential claim on the government's official reserve assets. Therefore, a deficit in the balance of payments is financed not only by borrowing from official agencies, but also by short-term borrowing from private foreign individuals and organizations as well.

Exhibit 2

United States Balance of Payments, 1972

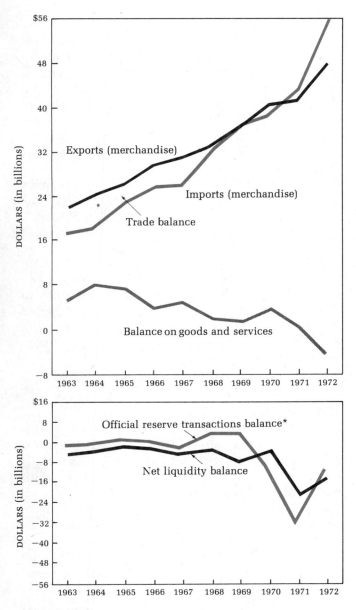

SOURCE: U.S. Department of Commerce.

* Official settlement deficit measured by net decline in United States monetary reserve assets plus net increase in liquid and certain nonliquid United States liabilities to foreign official agencies. Liquidity deficit measured by net decline in United States monetary reserve assets plus net increase in United States liabilities to all foreigners.

SOURCE: U.S. Department of Commerce; Board of Governors of the Federal Reserve System.

Line		Credits +, debits − (millions of dollars)
1	Merchandise trade balance	−$6,816
2	Exports	48,840
3	Imports	−55,656
4	Military transactions, net	− 3,541
5	Travel and transportation, net	− 2,583
6	Investment income, net	7,901
7	U.S. direct investments abroad	10,293
8	Other U.S. investments abroad	3,499
9	Foreign investments in the U.S.	− 5,891
10	Other services, net	819
11	Balance on goods and services	− 4,219
12	Remittances, pensions. and other transfers	− 1,557
13	Balance on goods, services, and remittances	− 5,776
14	U.S. Government grants (excluding military)	− 2,208
15	Balance on current account	− 7,983
16	U.S. government capital flows excluding nonscheduled repayments, net	− 1,708
17	Nonscheduled repayments of U.S. government assets	127
18	U.S. government nonliquid liabilities to other than foreign official reserve agencies	214
19	Long-term private capital flows, net	107
20	U.S. direct investments abroad	− 3,339
21	Foreign direct investments in the U.S.	322
22	Foreign securities	− 619
23	U.S. securities other than Treasury issues	4,502
24	Other, reported by U.S. banks	− 1,102
25	Other, reported by U.S. nonbanking concerns	343
26	Balance on current account and long-term capital	− 9,243
27	Nonliquid short-term private capital flows, net	− 1,634
28	Claims reported by U.S. banks	− 1,530
29	Claims reported by U.S. nonbanking concerns	− 243
30	Liabilities reported by U.S. nonbanking concerns	139
31	Allocations of Special Drawing Rights (SDRs)	710
32	Errors and omissions, net	− 3,806
33	Net-liquidity balance	−13,974
34	Liquid private capital flows, net	3,677
35	Liquid claims	− 1,139
36	Reported by U S. banks	− 733
37	Reported by U.S. nonbanking concerns	− 406
38	Liquid liabilities	4,816
39	To foreign commercial banks	3,905
40	To international and regional organizations	102
41	To other foreigners	809
42	Official reserve transactions balance	−10,297
	Financed by changes in:	
43	Liquid liabilities to foreign official agencies	9,676
44	Other marketable liabilities to foreign official agencies	400
45	Nonliquid liabilities to foreign official agencies	189
46	U.S. official reserve assets, net	32
47	Gold	547
48	Special Drawing Rights (SDRs)	− 703
49	Convertible currencies	35
50	Gold tranche position in IMF	153

Which of these two bases is correct? The question is significant because the two measures may occasionally give conflicting results—one of them showing a surplus and the other a deficit—at the same time. In practice, the net-liquidity balance is more commonly used, but from a theoretical viewpoint the true position is probably somewhere between the official transactions balance and the net-liquidity balance.

Economic Balance and Imbalance

Although a nation's balance of payments always balances in the accounting sense—in the sense that total debits always equal total credits—it need not balance in an economic sense. Among the reasons for economic imbalance are the lack of appropriate relationships between exchange rates, prices, income, and capital movements. In order to comprehend the underlying economic forces that are at work, we must understand two important sets of concepts associated with balance-of-payments analysis: (1) autonomous and compensatory transactions, and (2) equilibrium and disequilibrium.

AUTONOMOUS AND COMPENSATORY TRANSACTIONS

It is useful to think of a nation's balance of payments as a record which reports two distinctly different types of transactions—autonomous and compensatory.

Autonomous transactions are undertaken for reasons that are independent of the balance of payments. Referring back to the general model in Exhibit 1, we see that the main classes of autonomous transactions are merchandise trade and services, long-term capital movements, and unilateral transfers. The reasons for calling these autonomous are not hard to see. Merchandise trade and services are a response to relative differences in prices at home and abroad; long-term capital movements are a response to relative differences in expected rates of return on financial investments at home and abroad; and unilateral transfers are a response to private and governmental decisions based on personal, military, or political considerations. These autonomous transactions are thus unrelated to the balance of payments as such, and may result in total money payments as such, and may result in total money receipts being greater or less than total money payments.

Compensatory transactions, in contrast, are undertaken as a direct response to balance-of-payments considerations. They may be thought of as balancing items which arise in order to accommodate differences in money inflows and outflows resulting from autonomous transactions. Looking back at the general model in Exhibit 1, we see there are two main classes of compensatory transactions: short-term capital movements and shifts in gold holdings. Since these involve primarily changes in bank balances and gold claims at home and abroad, it seems clear that they serve largely as adjustment items to correct for imbalances in autonomous transactions. Thus, in a sense, a man who borrows to pay a debt is financing a deficit in his personal "balance of payments" by means of a compensatory transaction—the money he borrows.

EQUILIBRIUM AND DISEQUILIBRIUM

How do autonomous and compensatory transactions affect the economic position of a nation in relation to other nations? The answer to this question involves the notion of equilibrium and disequilibrium. As we know from earlier chapters in this book, an economic "object" (such as a market price or quantity) is in equilibrium when it is in a state of balance among opposing forces; conversely, it is in disequilibrium when there is an absence of such a state of balance. The same ideas of equilibrium or disequilibrium can be applied to a nation's international economic position as reflected by its balance of payments:

Balance-of-payments disequilibrium exists when, over a given period (usually several years), the sum of autonomous credits does not equal the sum of autonomous debits. A *deficit* disequilibrium occurs when total autonomous debits exceed total autonomous credits; conversely, a *surplus* disequilibrium occurs when total autonomous credits exceed total autonomous debits.

The existence of compensatory transactions is evidence of a nation's balance-of-payments disequilibrium. In practice, of course, we do not always expect the sum of autonomous receipts and payments to match each other exactly—any more than we expect total supply and demand in a competitive market to be precisely equal at all times—because of the numerous decision-making organisms that are involved. But we do expect periodic deficits and surpluses to balance out approximately over a period of a few years. When such a tendency is not apparent there is reason to suspect trouble.

The most common situation is one in which a country suffers from a persistent deficit disequilibrium for a number of years. This means that the nation is spending more than it is earning, and hence must be either drawing on its cash reserves, selling its assets, borrowing, or receiving gifts from other countries.

Adjusting to Equilibrium

How can a nation correct a disequilibrium in its balance of payments? The answer is straightforward: Since disequilibrium is the result of a gap between a country's total autonomous payments and receipts,

the factors that determine these autonomous transactions must undergo a change so that the nation's total money outflows and inflows can be brought into equality. We can best approach the problem by analyzing the adjustment process in terms of four sets of circumstances: (1) freely fluctuating exchange rates, (2) price and income changes, (3) the gold standard, and (4) government controls. Let us see how adjustments in the balance of payments are brought about under each of these conditions.

ADJUSTMENT THROUGH FREELY FLUCTUATING EXCHANGE RATES

The *foreign exchange rate* is the price of one currency in terms of another. If in the wheat market the price of wheat were $1 a bushel, this would mean that anyone could take $1 to the market and exchange it for a bushel of wheat and anyone could take a bushel of wheat to the market and exchange it

---

Leaders in Economics

THOMAS MUN

1571–1641

Mercantilist

At the end of the fifteenth century, a new philosophy of *statism* emerged in Western Europe. Absolute monarchy had replaced the decentralized structure of feudalism; the oceans had been conquered and were no longer considered barriers to trade; and the expansion of world commerce had occurred simultaneously with the development of banking and credit institutions. These factors encouraged dramatic struggles for power by kings and princes, resulting in ultranationalistic policies that tended to make all states enemies, as each sought to achieve world military and economic leadership.

These developments gave rise to what is known as *mercantilism*—a set of doctrines and practices aimed at promoting national prosperity and the power of the state by: (*a*) seeking the accumulation of precious metals (mainly gold and silver) through the maintenance of favorable trade balances or excesses of exports over imports; (*b*) achieving economic self-sufficiency through imperialism; and (*c*) exploiting colonies for the benefit of the mother country by monopolizing the raw materials and precious metals of the colonies while reserving them as exclusive markets for exports. Mercantilism reached its peak in the seventeenth century, serving as a political

and economic ideology in England, France, Spain, and Germany.

The majority of those who wrote on mercantilist theory were businessmen. The most notable was Thomas Mun, a leading English merchant and for many years a director of the famous British East India Company. His book, *England's Treasure by Forraign Trade*, was published posthumously by his son in 1664. This treatise is regarded as the outstanding exposition of mercantilist doctrine. It stressed the importance to England of maintaining a favorable balance of trade—a doctrine of fundamental significance in mercantilism since it was a key means of accumulating bullion—and was the first work to show that it was not the specific balance of trade with any particular nation that was the important consideration, but the total balance with all nations. The former could be unfavorable, according to Mun, as long as the latter was favorable.

In Germany, the chief goal of mercantilism was to increase the revenue of the state; hence it became known as *cameralism* (after *Kammer*, the name of the royal treasury), and its principles were extensively implemented as government policy during the eighteenth century.

for $1. Similarly, if in the foreign exchange market the price of British pounds in terms of dollars were $2 = £1, it would mean that anyone could take $1 to the market and exchange it for the equivalent of £½, or anyone could take £1 to the market and exchange it for $2.

The foreign exchange market is a competitive market which behaves according to the laws of supply and demand. This means that fluctuations in the price of foreign exchange are the result of changes in the demand and supply curves of buyers and sellers. The basic idea is illustrated in Exhibit 3. In this simple model, the "commodity" being bought and sold is British pounds and the price is expressed in terms of dollars. (A similar situation could be depicted in which the commodity is dollars and the price is expressed in terms of British pounds.) For simplicity, we are assuming that there are only two countries, the United States and Britain. The interaction of the demand curve for pounds with the supply curve of pounds thus determines the equilibrium price 0P and the equilibrium quantity 0N.

In the foreign exchange market Americans (such as importers, tourists, etc.) are always looking to

buy pounds; and Britons are always looking to buy dollars. Hence at any given time there are "dollars looking for pounds" and there are "pounds looking for dollars." This makes an active market in foreign exchange.

The Adjustment Process

In order to understand how international adjustments take place under freely fluctuating exchange rates, let us begin by assuming a state of equilibrium in which the exchange rate in Exhibit 3 is at 0P and there is neither a deficit nor a surplus in the American balance of payments. If American imports of British goods should now rise, and if this increase is not offset by long-term capital movements or unilateral transfers from Britain to the United States, the American demand for pounds will also increase; that is, the demand curve will shift to the right from D to D'. As the price rises toward the new equilibrium level 0P', British pounds will become more expensive for Americans to buy, thereby causing the United States to cut down its purchases of British goods. Conversely, American dollars will become cheaper for Britons, thereby causing Britain to expand its purchases of American goods. This slowing down of American imports from Britain and expansion of American exports to Britain will continue until a new equilibrium in the U.S. balance of payments is reached which accords with the equilibrium price in the foreign exchange market. Thus:

Freely fluctuating exchange rates perform at least three important functions: (1) they automatically correct a disequilibrium in the balance of payments through the free play of international market forces; (2) they may make imports cheaper and exports dearer, or vice versa, by altering the price of foreign exchange without *necessarily* affecting domestic or foreign price levels; and (3) to the extent that they operate independently of domestic price and income levels, they bear the burden of balance-of-payments adjustments without imposing constraints on the domestic economy (as will be explained shortly).

Despite these desirable features, freely fluctuating exchange rates involve some disadvantages:

1. They make it difficult and risky for traders to commit themselves for weeks or months in advance to international transactions, since the exchange rate may change between the time that goods are ordered and the time that they are received. This uncertainty may reduce trade between nations.

Exhibit 3

Supply of and Demand for British Pounds

An increase in demand for British pounds will raise the equilibrium price from 0P *to* 0P' *and the equilibrium quantity from* 0N *to* 0N'.

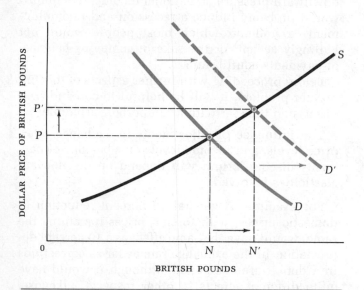

2. Freely fluctuating exchange rates turn the terms of trade against a nation whose currency is depreciated in the foreign exchange market. For example, we saw that an increase in the demand for pounds resulted in a price increase or appreciation in the dollar price of pounds and a price decrease or depreciation in the pound price of dollars. This means that the United States must export more goods to Britain to earn the same total revenue as it earned before.

3. Freely fluctuating exchange rates *may* stimulate or depress a nation's export industries by making its currency either cheaper or dearer in international markets. This could tend to encourage fluctuations in income and employment.

ADJUSTMENT THROUGH PRICE AND INCOME CHANGES

A moment's reflection will make it evident that if exchange-rate adjustments can conceivably bring about an equilibrium in the balance of payments while domestic price and income levels remain stable, the converse principle is also true: Changes in domestic price and income levels can restore equilibrium in a nation's balance of payments while exchange rates remain stable. Let us see why.

Price Changes

In terms of our previous example, if there is a deficit in the U.S. balance of payments due to an excess of imports over exports, a deflation of American prices can have the same effect as a depreciation of the dollar in the foreign exchange market. For if prices in the United States are reduced, it becomes cheaper for Britons to buy American goods. American exports to Britain will therefore increase, and this will tend to eliminate the U.S. balance-of-payments deficit. (Equivalently, an inflation in Britain can have the same effect as an appreciation of the pound in the foreign exchange market. Can you explain why?)

How might a deflation be brought about? There are three possibilities:

1. Some deflationary pressures will be induced automatically through market forces because the excess of American imports over exports will cause a reduction in the United States money supply.

2. Contractionary monetary and fiscal policies may have to be invoked in order to exert a downward push on prices.

3. U.S. manufacturers may try to reduce or stabilize prices so as to compete with foreigners.

We have already learned in earlier chapters that there is likely to be a trade-off between price changes and the level of employment in that reductions in prices will probably increase unemployment and thereby bring about a recession. The question, therefore, is whether such a high cost should be incurred in order to achieve balance-of-payments equilibrium. Most economists believe that it should not and that some other solution should be sought.

Income Changes

A country's balance of payments is also related to its national income. Thus if the domestic level of income increases while exchange rates and domestic prices remain stable, people will tend to import more goods from abroad and to take more trips abroad. (For balance-of-payments purposes, an American tourist visiting a foreign country is equivalent to the United States importing "scenery" from that country.) A deficit in the U.S. balance of payments, therefore, can be corrected through a decrease in the domestic level of income. (Equivalently, it can also be corrected through an increase in other nations' level of income, since American exports will increase if foreign income rises.) The disadvantages of adjustment through domestic income reduction, however, are essentially the same as those of price deflation: Contractionary monetary and fiscal policies would have to be invoked in order to cause a downward pressure on national income; this in turn would probably induce a recession and unemployment—a trade-off which most people would not willingly accept for the sake of achieving balance-of-payments equilibrium.

Before proceeding with further aspects of this important problem, it will be helpful to conclude our discussion thus far with an important principle:

The influence of adjustments in exchange rates, price levels, and income levels on a balance-of-payments disequilibrium will depend on the relevant elasticities involved.

For example: A general 10 percent reduction in domestic prices, with foreign prices remaining the same, would have the same effect as a 10 percent depreciation in the exchange rate as far as corrections in a deficit are concerned, although it would have quite different effects in other respects. Likewise, the influence of income changes on a country's trade depends, among other things, on its income elasticity of demand for imports. What happens if its income elasticity of demand is less than unity? Greater than unity? Factors such as these are of considerable practical significance. Indeed, they have played extremely important roles in the international financial policies of nations, as we shall see later on. (NOTE: You will find it helpful to look up the meaning of *income elasticity of demand* in the Dictionary at the back of this book.)

ADJUSTMENT UNDER THE GOLD STANDARD: THE CLASSICAL MODEL

A very interesting process of adjustment takes place when the trading nations' monetary systems are on a gold standard. This situation existed for several dozen countries during the half century before World War I and for a short time thereafter until the onset of the Depression. From a theoretical standpoint, it can be considered a part of the classical model of income and employment which was studied in earlier chapters. To understand how this adjustment method works, it is necessary to explain both (1) the operation of the gold standard mechanism, and (2) the adjustment process.

The Gold Standard

If a nation were on a gold standard, it would be obliged to: (a) buy and sell gold to the public in exchange for paper money at a *fixed legal rate;* and (b) permit gold to be imported and exported without restrictions. Under these circumstances, the exchange rate would tend to be stable and would never fluctuate beyond very narrow limits.

In 1930, for example, when the United States and England were both on a gold standard, the U.S. Treasury was required by law to buy and sell gold to the public at a price of $20.67 per fine ounce; similarly, the Bank of England was required by law to buy and sell gold at a price of £4.25 per fine ounce. It follows that since an ounce (which is equal to 480 grains) of gold could be exchanged for $20.67 in the United States or for £4.25 in England,

$$\$20.67 = £4.25 \quad (= 1 \text{ ounce gold or } 480 \text{ grains})$$

and hence the par rate of exchange between the two countries was determined by the ratio $20.67 ÷ £4.25, or

$$\$4.86 = £1 \quad (= 0.24 \text{ ounce gold or } 113 \text{ grains})$$

In 1930, the cost (including insurance and freight) of shipping 0.24 ounces or 113 grains of gold between New York and London was about $0.02. As a result, the exchange rate or dollar price of pounds remained within the range of $4.84 and $4.88 for the following reasons:

☐ If the price of pounds in the foreign exchange market rose, say, to $4.89, it would be cheaper for an American importer to acquire 113 grains of gold for his $4.86 and then ship the gold to London at a cost of 2 cents in order to pay the British exporter. The importer would *in effect* be paying $4.88 for a pound instead of $4.89.

☐ If the price in the foreign exchange market fell, say, to $4.83, a British importer would be better off to acquire gold for his £1 (= $4.86) and then ship the gold to New York at a cost of 2 cents in order to pay the American exporter. The importer would *in effect* be getting $4.84 for his pound instead of $4.83.

The upper and lower limits of foreign exchange were thus $4.88 and $4.84, respectively. These were known as the *gold points*—a technical expression which represents the range within which the foreign exchange rates of gold standard currencies will fluctuate. Thus the gold points are equal to the par rate of exchange plus and minus the cost (including insurance) of shipping gold. The upper and lower gold points for a nation are called its *gold export point* and *gold import point*, respectively, because gold will be exported when the foreign exchange rate rises above the upper level and imported when the rate falls below the lower level. One nation's gold export point is thus another nation's gold import point, and vice versa.

We may, therefore, conclude:

Since a gold standard provides free convertibility between paper money and gold, as well as the unrestricted shipment of gold into and out of the country, the exchange rate under such circumstances tends to remain stable within the limits set by the gold points.

The Adjustment Process

How does the existence of a gold standard affect the restoration of equilibrium due to a trade deficit in a nation's balance of payments? This in effect was a question which the classical economists asked—and their answer was that the adjustment is brought about automatically through changes in the price level. Why? Because they assumed that the price level is directly related to the quantity of money in circulation, which in turn is tied to the volume of gold holdings.

Thus if a country experiences a disequilibrium in its balance of payments as a result of a trade deficit, its demand for foreign exchange will rise at least to the gold export point. As gold leaves the country, the quantity of money will decrease, which in turn will reduce prices. With lower prices, the country's exports will rise and its imports fall, thereby correcting the disequilibrium.

What happens if a country experiences a disequilibrium in its balance of payments due to a trade surplus? The process is exactly the opposite: The country's demand for foreign exchange will fall, gold will be imported, prices will increase, and exports will fall while imports rise until equilibrium is again restored.

This explanation of the adjustment process, it should be emphasized, was the classical solution. Logically, it was an integral part of the classical theory of income and employment because it assumed that: (a) there was full employment, and hence an increase in the quantity of money would assure an increase in the general price level; and (b) prices and costs were flexible rather than "sticky," and hence would readily respond to changes in total spending. We have already learned in earlier chapters, of course, that with the development and extensions of Keynesian economics since the 1930s, the first assumption of full employment has been recognized as a special rather than general case, and the second assumption of flexible prices and costs—especially on the downward side—is incorrect in our modern economy, where big businesses and big unions exert monopolistic influences in the marketplace.

We can, therefore, come to a further conclusion:

The gold standard has both desirable and undesirable features: (a) On the one hand it provides for stable exchange rates which tend to reduce risks and encourage international trade, while automatically correcting international disequilibrium. (b) On the other hand, it requires that each nation submit to painful processes of deflation (or inflation) by subordinating its domestic economy to the dictates of external economic relations in order to achieve international equilibrium.

ADJUSTMENT THROUGH GOVERNMENT CONTROLS

The methods of adjustment described thus far rely on market forces to correct a disequilibrium in the balance of payments. Now we turn our attention to a final and radically different method of adjustment—one which suppresses market forces by imposing direct government controls on international transactions. The list of specific controls is almost endless, but for analysis they can be grouped into two categories: (1) exchange controls, and (2) trade controls.

Exchange Controls

One way in which a nation might seek to correct a deficit in its balance of payments is to limit the freedom of its residents to import goods and services and to export funds. To accomplish this objective, the government would impose direct controls over those types of international transactions that are to be curbed, while leaving others relatively uncontrolled or even "free."

Under such a system, all foreign exchange earnings must be sold to the government and all foreign exchange needed to pay for international transactions must be bought from the government. The rates at which the government buys and sells foreign exchange are officially established and need not be equal. The typical method of doing this is by the adoption of a "multiple exchange system." Thus the government may set a relatively high price or rate of exchange on the foreign exchange needed to import unessential luxury goods, and a relatively low rate on the importation of vitally needed raw materials and capital goods. It may also designate some types of transactions as unrestricted and sell portions of its foreign exchange to the highest bidders.

In general, exchange controls require that the government, rather than the free market, decide the order of priority for the importation of goods and services. This decision may then be implemented by allocating the limited supply of foreign exchange among competing uses.

Nations have instituted exchange controls for various reasons and in diverse circumstances: to provide better centralized control over the economy; to reduce wide economic fluctuations; to eliminate persistent deficits in the balance of payments; and to assure essential imports for hastening economic growth and development. The chief advantage of controls is that *some* method of adjustment must be employed to correct a significant balance-of-payments deficit disequilibrium. Exchange controls are usually the least undesirable and least painful of the various choices that have been discussed.

On the other hand, exchange controls also have several disadvantages:

1. By preventing or even limiting the importation of certain goods, controls may shift the demand for these goods to domestic producers, thereby stimulating inflation at home as well as an exodus of resources out of export industries. This will encourage a drop in exports and aggravate rather than cure the deficit disequilibrium.

2. Since exchange controls prevent the free expression of market forces, they encourage the creation of an illegal black market in foreign exchange.

3. By curbing imports, controls help bring on deflation in those countries whose export industries are adversely affected; this may encourage retaliatory measures by the injured nations, thereby reducing trade.

Trade Controls

A government may use another general class of measures, called trade controls, to adjust a balance-of-payments deficit disequilibrium. These may take such forms as tariffs and quotas to curb imports, special taxes on outflows of capital and on tourists going abroad, and subsidies to encourage the export industries. Measures such as these, as we have already learned, prevent the operation of the law of comparative advantage, misallocate world resources, and discourage the flow of trade. As with exchange controls, they may also invite retaliation by other nations.

SUMMARY OF IMPORTANT IDEAS

1. Since nations carry on their business in different currencies, foreign exchange markets exist where currencies and related instruments can be bought and sold, or "converted." The existence of such markets enables nations to engage in international transactions.

2. The international transactions of nations are summarized periodically in a financial statement known as the balance of payments. This records money in-

flows and outflows, classified in categories of accounts.

3. In accounting terms, a nation's balance of payments always balances because the sum of its money inflows must equal the sum of its money outflows—by virtue of the principle of double-entry bookkeeping. But in an economic sense, the balance of payments may not balance because certain transactions may not be sustainable.

4. Balance-of-payments disequilibrium may be corrected by: (a) movements in exchange rates; (b) adjustments in price and income levels; (c) gold flows, with consequent price and income adjustments if nations are on a gold standard; and (d) government controls over foreign exchange and foreign trade. The first three rely on market forces to bring about the needed adjustment; the fourth suppresses market forces by substituting the hand of government.

FOR DISCUSSION

1. *Terms and concepts to review:*

foreign exchange	compensatory
debit	transactions
credit	balance-of-payments
balance of payments	disequilibrium
balance of trade	foreign exchange rate
mercantilism	gold points
cameralism	
autonomous	
transactions	

2. In a free market, if the dollar rate of exchange on French francs rises, what happens to the French rate of exchange on dollars? Explain.

3. How does each of the following transactions affect the supply of money in the United States:
   (a) The United States sells Chevrolets to England.
   (b) France sells perfume to the United States.
   (c) An American tourist visits Japan.
   (d) A Japanese tourist visits the United States.

4. Which of the following transactions results in a debit, and which in a credit, in the United States balance of payments:
   (a) An American student buys a new Honda motorcycle.
   (b) An American tourist flies Air France to Paris.
   (c) General Motors pays a dividend to a British stockholder.

(d) The U.S. Army builds a new military base in Southeast Asia.

(e) An American resident buys shares of stock in a British corporation.

(f) An American resident sends money to his relatives in another country.

5. Can there be a net positive or net negative balance in the balance of payments?

6. Why are autonomous debits and credits not likely to be equal?

7. Compare the processes of adjustment to disequilibrium under (a) freely fluctuating exchange rates, (b) price and income changes, (c) the gold standard, and (d) government controls. (SUGGESTION: Think in terms of what these systems have in common, and develop your answer accordingly.)

CHAPTER 36

International Commercial and Financial Policies

CHAPTER PREVIEW

What economic changes took place during World Wars I and II that led to a weakening and disintegration of the world economy?

How did nations respond to these changes after World War II?

What problems of international economic adjustment have nations come to face? What can be done to solve those problems?

The late Lord Rothschild, a world-famous financier, was once asked by a friend to explain the international financial system. He replied, "My dear chap, there are only two men in the world who understand the international financial system—a young economist in the Treasury and a rather junior man in the Bank of England. Unfortunately, they disagree."

There is no doubt that most people are unfamiliar with the international monetary system, despite the fact that on a number of occasions in recent history the dollar was under attack by foreigners; the Daughters of the American Revolution found our restrictive gold policy a national scandal; and American tourists visiting London, Rome, and various other places were astounded to be told that they could not convert their dollars into foreign currencies.

These are only a few of the events that have occurred in the esoteric world of international finance. But important happenings have also taken place in the area of international trade. In this chapter we shall review the background and consequences of these developments and discuss recommendations for improving the community of soveregin nations held together by economic interdependence.

The Interwar Period: Weakening and Disintegration of the World Economy

In the decades before World War I, most major countries were closely integrated through a well-developed network of trade and finance. The essential features of this complex system may be characterized briefly:

☐ Nations and regions tended to specialize on the basis of their factor endowments, thus making multilateral trade necessary.

☐ Tariffs for the most part affected only moderately the international flow of goods according to the principle of comparative advantage.

☐ London was the center of finance and trade, with its supporting facilities of banks, brokerage houses, insurance companies, shipping firms, and communication lines extending throughout the world.

☐ Almost all major nations and many minor ones—several dozen in all—were on the gold standard, thus permitting the easy convertibility of currencies that is needed for carrying on international transactions smoothly and efficiently.

This was also an era of rapid advances in technology and large migrations of labor and capital. These fundamental changes were assimilated, though not, to be sure, without some major political and economic upheavals. The balances of payments of most trading nations tended to adjust fairly smoothly to gold movements, while exchange rates remained stable.

This, briefly, was the nature of the relatively harmonious international economic setting that prevailed until the eve of World War I. In the next three decades, however, the world economy experienced a series of deep disturbances: (1) structural weakening during the 1920s, (2) disintegration during the 1930s, and (3) disruption during World War II.

STRUCTURAL WEAKENING DURING THE 1920s

World War I destroyed the economic relations between nations that had developed through almost five decades of peace in Europe. International commercial and financial links were broken, markets were disorganized, and the marketing system was shattered. All belligerent nations except the United States abandoned the gold standard; the American government officially discouraged gold withdrawals from banks; and gold exports were subjected to strict legal controls. These steps were necessary to prevent the hoarding of gold and its flight to safer havens in neutral nations—common occurrences in periods of crisis.

After the war there were violent inflations in Continental Europe, and the restoration of the gold standard became a major objective of international policy. Between 1925 and 1929, more than 40 countries returned to gold; only a few continued to operate on the basis of inconvertible paper. But the new gold standard established during this period was based on economic conditions and philosophies different from those that existed before 1914. Some of the more important changes that took place may be noted briefly.

Changes in National Objectives

Governments began to place less emphasis on the automatic operation of an international monetary system provided by the gold standard and more emphasis on domestic economic stability. The war and postwar years brought severe monetary disturbances, inflation, and then depression. With the establishment of the Federal Reserve System in the United States just before the war and the creation of similar institutions in many other countries during the 1920s, government officials became increasingly interested in the possibility of stabilizing prices and economic activity through central bank policy.

With each nation determining its supply of money independently in order to gain greater internal economic control, monetary reserves became a matter of secondary concern. From 1920 to 1924, for example, the United States experienced a substantial net inflow of gold. But in order to maintain stable credit conditions, the Federal Reserve authorities offset the monetary effects of these accumulating gold balances by selling securities in the market. Similarly, in the late 1920s the Bank of England neutralized the effects of gold movements by selling securities when gold flowed into the country and buying securities when gold flowed out. Although these actions may have been justified in terms of domestic economic conditions in both countries, they were clearly contrary to traditional (pre-1914) gold standard policies which dictated that a nation's supply of money vary directly with the supply of gold.

Increased Government Intervention

In the United States, the decade after the war was marked by the beginnings of a retreat from laissez-faire as farmers, labor unions, consumers, and other special-interest groups pressed for greater government protection and reforms. This gave rise to growing nationalism. The Underwood Tariff of 1913, passed by a Democratic Congress, represented important steps toward freer international trade, but in 1922 the Republicans restored the rates to new protective levels in the Fordney-McCumber Tariff. The United States was not alone. Many other nations, including Australia, Great Britain, India, and Japan, enacted new protective legislation during the 1920s.

Conclusion: Increased Importance of the U.S. Economy

The changing national objectives and government policies weakened the international monetary mechanism by making it more rigid. At the same time, the United States gained increasing dominance in the international economy. By 1929, it had become the world's largest exporter, the second largest importer (after Great Britain), and chief creditor. This meant that with other nations heavily dependent on it, the United States would have to maintain a stable, high level of income and employment, and a steady flow of lending to other nations if the well-being of the world economy was to be preserved. Any sudden changes in American economic stability, tariff rates, or credit flows could affect access to markets and produce severe international repercussions. This, as we shall see, is precisely what happened.

DISINTEGRATION DURING THE 1930s

In the United States, prosperity began its rise in 1922 and reached a peak in the first half of 1929. During this period American investment, income, and employment climbed to unprecedented heights. But then the overall decline in economic activity set in—first with a drop in industrial production in July, 1929, and then with a collapse of the stock market three months later.

With this bursting of the bubble of optimism, the economy turned sharply downward, producing severe effects in other countries. In the brief span of only three years—from 1929 to 1932—the total dollars spent or invested abroad by Americans (in the form of imports, service transactions, long-term loans, etc.) fell from $7.4 billion to a mere $2.4 billion—a drop of 68 percent. As would be expected, the foreign-trade multiplier exerted its influence: The export industries of other nations that were closely tied to American markets were adversely affected, thereby pulling down the levels of income and employment.

How did the major trading nations respond to these depressing effects on world commerce? There were several types of reaction, which we shall now examine. As will be seen later, these reactions significantly affected the international economic policies of nations after World War II.

Higher Tariffs

In the United States, Germany, Italy, Russia, Great Britain, and other countries there was a marked tendency to subordinate international trade to national interests. The United States made access to its domestic market difficult by passing the Smoot-Hawley Tariff of 1930. This new law broadened the range of protected commodities to over 25,000, and provided for increases in some 800 rates covering a wide variety of both agricultural and industrial goods. Great Britain, which had been the citadel of free trade for 80 years, abandoned its policy and adopted a protective tariff in 1932. Similarly, other countries attempted to control their foreign trade by establishing tariffs, quotas, special exchange allocations, bilateral trade agreements for the trading of specific products, and monopolistic state-controlled trading systems.

In democratic countries such as the United States and Great Britain, the motivation for increased protection stemmed from the depressed economic conditions of the time; but among the new totalitarian governments in Germany, Italy, and Russia, both economic and military considerations were involved. However, whatever the motives, the actions undertaken during this period more than offset years of effort by the League of Nations to establish freer international trade.

Financial Crises and the Abandonment of Gold

A second major development of international significance occurred in the spring of 1931. The Credit Anstalt, Austria's largest commercial bank, announced it was technically insolvent—its liabilities exceeded its assets. This produced a run on the bank as domestic and foreign creditors rushed to claim their funds. The Austrian government had barely brought the panic under control (through a "freeze" on all obligations to creditors) when the Reichsbank, a major commercial bank in Germany, failed. The fear of further bank failures spread, and the German government instituted a system of exchange controls to prevent a run on the country's gold and foreign exchange reserves.

This action placed Britain in a tenuous position. Germany, as well as other central European countries, had borrowed heavily from British banks; the borrowers now found their credits frozen. Britain, in turn, was in debt to foreigners to the tune of more than half a billion pounds; the British budget was rapidly sliding into a heavy deficit; and Britain's balance of payments was steadily worsening. As foreign confidence in Britain's financial system declined, foreign withdrawals mounted. The situation reached crisis proportions, and both the Bank of France and the U.S. Federal Reserve System extended over $130 million to the Bank of England. But this was not enough to halt the drain of gold and foreign exchange from Britain. Finally, on September 21, 1931, Parliament announced that the Bank of England would no longer be required by law to sell gold. This meant, of course, that Britain had officially gone off the gold standard.

In the months that followed, the international depression deepened and financial panics were repeated in various nations. Waves of domestic and foreign drains on gold reserves were experienced by banking systems throughout the world. By the end of 1932, twenty-four countries had abandoned gold. In the meantime, world trade had disintegrated still further.

Devaluation of the Dollar

The United States, of course, was not immune to the effects of the Depression. The period 1929–1932 was one of severe deflation; wholesale prices fell 32 percent and national income dropped by 50 percent. Banks were especially hard hit as the security behind their loans disappeared with the decline in property values. During these three years more than 5,000 banks—about one-third of the nation's total—were declared insolvent.

Early in 1933, the weakness of the banks became widely recognized, and a wave of currency and gold hoarding ensued. This forced President Roosevelt to declare a bank "holiday," to place an embargo on the export of gold, and to prevent banks and the Treasury from paying out the precious metal. These steps placed the United States on a *gold bullion standard* in which gold was nationalized by the Treasury, taken out of domestic circulation as money, and made available in the form of gold bullion only for industrial uses and international transactions in return for other money.

Meanwhile, despite the fact that the United States was in a strong balance-of-payments position compared to other countries, advisors to President Roosevelt increasingly felt that American exports should be stimulated relative to imports. Hence, the government's attempt at currency stabilization was finalized early in the following year with the devaluation of the dollar.

What is *devaluation*? It may be defined as an official act which makes a domestic currency cheaper in terms of gold or foreign currencies, and is typically undertaken for the purpose of increasing a nation's exports while reducing its imports. Thus on January 31, 1934, the United States devalued the dollar relative to gold by approximately 41 percent, by raising the Treasury's buying and selling price of gold from $20.67 an ounce to $35 an ounce. This act made it cheaper for foreigners to buy dollars, and more expensive for Americans to buy foreign currencies.

Consequences of Devaluation

Other countries responded to the devaluation by imposing higher tariffs and other trade restrictions. But the devalued dollar, which was now stabilized in relation to other depreciated currencies, exerted mounting balance-of-payments pressures on the remaining gold standard countries with their overvalued currencies. During the mid-thirties this, in combination with the growing fear of war in Europe, resulted in a heavy net inflow of capital and gold to the United States for safekeeping. Between 1934 and 1938, the remaining gold standard nations—Belgium, Switzerland, France, and the Netherlands—unable to sustain any further drain, abandoned gold and devalued their currencies. Thus came the end of an era. (See Box 1.)

Conclusion: International Agreements

By the eve of World War II, the leading trading countries of the Western world had learned at least two important lessons:

By releasing their currencies from gold, nations could be free to manage their economies by fiscal and monetary means without the fear of losing reserves and without the need to be regulated by international gold movements. Devaluation, however, is not ordinarily a one-way street; it usually causes opposing reactions by other nations in the form of trade restrictions or retaliatory devaluation.

Box 1

How Did the Gold Standard Come About?

Since the gold standard is always a topic for interesting conversation, it might be worthwhile to see how England came to adopt the gold standard in the first place.

The great English historian Macaulay wrote: "In the autumn of 1695, it could hardly be said that the country [Britain] possessed, for practical purposes, any measure of value of commodities. It was a mere chance [because of "underweighing" of coins] whether what was called a shilling, was really tenpence, sixpence, or a groat."

William and Mary appointed a committee to make recommendations for solving the problems. The membership was quite extraordinary: Sir Isaac Newton, Master of the Mint; John Locke, the great philosopher; and Lord Somers.

Sir Isaac recommended that the Government call in the old coin at face value and issue new full weight coins and that the ratio of silver to gold be established at 16 silver to 1 gold (shades of William Jennings Bryan!). In major countries on the Continent the ratio was $15\frac{1}{2}$ to 1. Sir Thomas Gresham could have predicted the results a century before! Relatively, England overvalued gold and the Continent overvalued silver. Gold was taken to England for exchange into silver, which was taken to the Continent for exchange into gold, which. . . . Newton later recognized his error and recommended that it be corrected, but this latter advice was not followed.*

A century passes and England is once again involved in war with her old enemy, France; this time under Napoleon. She abandons redemption of the currency but decides to resume convertibility after the war. The mint, of course, had very little silver to coin and Lord Liverpool decided to close it to the free coinage of silver because England was "naturally a gold country" and that "gold was the natural currency of England." And, indeed, it was if one admits, as he should, that it is only "natural" for even a Sir Isaac to make a mistake and for this mistake to have "natural" consequences.

It is irrelevant but tempting to speculate what might have happened if Sir Isaac had made a mistake in the other direction, say by adopting a ratio of 15 to 1. England might well have become "naturally a silver country." With the role that sterling acquired on the basis of English leadership in industry and commerce throughout the world, who knows, the world might naturally have been on the silver standard.

Thus it appears that England arrived on the gold standard because of a mistake by Sir Isaac Newton in 1696. The gold standard survived the nineteenth century only because of the miracles of new gold discoveries in the 1840s and 1890s. Finally, when one sees the incredibly small amount of gold frequently held by the Bank of England, he is forced to conclude it was not a self-regulating system but was in fact maintained through management by the Bank of England. Thus, a mistake, miracles, and management describe the system more accurately than does a mystical natural providence.

* This is the story as told by George F. Warren and Frank A. Pearson in their *Prices*, New York, Macmillan, 1933, p. 159.
SOURCE: Adapted from an address by Karl R. Bopp, former president, Federal Reserve Bank of Philadelphia.

The remaining highlights of the immediate pre-World War II years may be summarized briefly.

1. The United States and most Western European countries entered an agreement which, for international purposes, represented a compromise between the rigidities of the gold standard and domestic currency management. Thus:

   (a) Each country established its own government stabilization fund to buy and sell foreign exchange in the open market in quantities necessary to maintain reasonable stability of its own currency in relation to foreign currencies.

   (b) Competitive devaluation for the purpose of expanding exports was renounced.

   (c) The central banks of the participating countries were authorized to buy gold without limit, but gold served largely as an equilibrating device for balance-of-payments purposes.

On the whole, exchange-rate equilibrium was restored among the democratic trading nations, while totalitarian countries like Germany and Russia maintained tightly controlled systems for allocating foreign exchange.

2. In the area of international trade, the United States established a *Reciprocal Trade Agreements program*—a plan for expanding American exports through legislation which authorized the President to negotiate U.S. tariff reductions with other nations in return for parallel concessions. The program con-

sists of the Trade Agreements Act of 1934, with subsequent amendments, and related legislation.

An interesting feature of the Reciprocal Trade Agreements program has been the widespread use of what is known as a *most favored nation clause.* Its inclusion in a trade treaty means that each of the signatories agrees to extend to the other the same preferential tariff and trade concessions that each may in the future extend to nonsignatories, that is, the same treatment that each gives to its "most favored nation." The great majority of trading countries have adhered to this principle since 1948.

DISRUPTION DURING WORLD WAR II (1939–1945)

World War II disrupted world trade. The belligerents as well as the leading neutral nations were largely prevented from engaging in exchange transactions with the United States and the Allies. In order to help the allied nations to buy the goods they needed but could not pay for, the United States instituted a system of Lend Lease in 1941. It provided advances in goods and supplies in return for "reverse" Lend Lease by the recipient countries in the form of care and housing for American troops. In money terms, the value of the grants given by the United States far exceeded the value of the services that it received in return. But as Prime Minister Winston Churchill remarked to Parliament, Lend Lease was not intended to provide for an equal *quid pro quo;* indeed, it was "the most unsordid act in the history of any nation."

Post-World War II International Commerce

In the summer of 1944, few people were concerned about the problems of international trade and finance. Allied troops were engaged in the great battle of the Normandy beachhead; a group of German army officers had tried unsuccessfully to assassinate Adolf Hitler; and a politically obscure man named Harry S Truman was emerging as the potential running mate of President Roosevelt in his bid for a fourth term.

At the same time, an event of less colorful but highly durable significance was taking place in the lovely rural setting of Bretton Woods, New Hampshire. There, in the Mount Washington Hotel, at the foot of New England's highest mountain, the United

Nations Monetary and Financial Conference was holding an international meeting destined to affect the world's economic structure for decades to come. Present at the meeting were representatives from 16 governments, including Lord Keynes in his capacity as advisor to the British treasury.

The primary result of this historic gathering was the formation of a plan for a new and remarkable international financial system. The original agreement was developed largely by the British and American delegations; it was signed by 35 nations, but the membership subsequently increased to more than three times that number. In the remaining sections of this chapter we shall examine the nature of this system and related aspects of world trade.

EUROPEAN ECONOMIC RECOVERY

When the war ended, the European economy was devastated. For five years after the war, Europe's balance of payments on current account suffered from a substantial trade deficit. Among the factors that were responsible for this deficit were (a) the pressure of inflation, (b) the reduction of productive capacity caused by the war, and (c) the loss of overseas export markets.

The immediate task, of course, was to rebuild the European economy while, at the same time, financing its deficit. Most of the responsibility fell to the United States, which extended approximately \$17 billion in foreign aid between 1945 and 1948, about half of which was in the form of outright gifts and half in the form of loans. But it was recognized that these were merely stopgap measures and that more consistent and far-reaching policies were necessary. The result was the formulation of two important types of American aid programs that have had a substantial influence on the economic development of other nations.

European Recovery Program (Marshall Plan)

On June 5, 1947, Secretary of State George C. Marshall delivered a commencement address at Harvard University in which he proposed what came to be known as the *European Recovery Program* (ERP) or *Marshall Plan.* The plan was a comprehensive blueprint for the economic recovery of European countries. Financed by the United States, its purposes were to (a) increase their productive capacity, (b) stabilize their financial systems, (c) promote their mutual economic cooperation, and (d) reduce their dependence on U.S. assistance. Out of this came the Organization for European Economic Cooperation, an association consisting initially of 17 European countries which sought to cooperate in assuring their own economic recovery.

The Marshall Plan ended in 1951, after providing over $10 billion in aid. About 90 percent of this was in outright grants and the rest in loans. There is widespread agreement that the program was a success. It contributed substantially to raising the average level of industrial production among participating nations by more than half their 1947 level and to suppressing a decade of rapid inflation.

Mutual Security Administration

By late 1951, American emphasis had shifted from direct economic aid to containment of communism. The immediate cause of this change in attitude was the outbreak of the Korean War in June, 1950. The ERP was absorbed by the Mutual Security Administration, which provided both military and economic assistance to various nations throughout the world. Since the early 1950s, a substantial part of American economic aid has been directed at the underdeveloped countries in Africa, Asia, and Latin America. A great deal of aid has gone to countries which are regarded as bulwarks against communism. The results have not always been favorable. America has been criticized for propping up repressive regimes and is often regarded by the peoples of such countries as a supporter of dictatorship and even of political terrorism.

TRADE LIBERALIZATION AND REGIONAL INTEGRATION

Even during World War II, it was evident to many political leaders that a new multilateral trading system would be needed after the war—one which provided for liberalization and economic integration of world trade. A significant step in this direction, as we have seen, was the Reciprocal Trade Agreements program adopted by the United States. This program empowered the President to agree on mutual tariff reductions with other countries and to incorporate most favored nation clauses in such agreements. After the war, various trading nations endorsed and adopted additional measures designed to strengthen world commerce. The more important ones are examined briefly.

General Agreement on Tariffs and Trade (GATT)

The first major postwar step toward liberalization of world trade was the General Agreement on Tariffs and Trade (GATT), an international agreement signed in 1947 by 23 countries including the United States, dedicated to four basic principles: (1) nondiscrimination in trade through adherence to unconditional most favored nation treatment; (2) reduction of tariffs by negotiation; (3) elimination of import quotas (with some exceptions permitted); and (4) resolution of differences through consultation. The number of nations participating in GATT has since increased by several dozen, and it has been an important and successful force for the liberalization of world trade.

Regional Integration

Despite the fact that nations have erected trade barriers to shield themselves from one another, the underlying desire for free trade has nevertheless been persistent. Although worldwide free trade may never become a reality, regional free-trade agreements among two or more nations are commonplace. Such agreements have typically taken three forms: free-trade areas, customs unions, and common markets.

1. A free-trade area is an association of trading nations whose participants agree to impose no restrictive devices such as tariffs or quotas on one another, although each is free to impose whatever restrictions it wishes on nonparticipants. The best-known example is the European Free Trade Association (EFTA), established in 1960, consisting of Austria, Great Britain, Sweden, Norway, Denmark, Switzerland, and Portugal. Similar organizations have been established or proposed among Latin American, Asian, and African countries.

2. A customs union is an agreement among two or more trading nations to abolish trade barriers such as tariffs and quotas among themselves, and to adopt a common external policy of trade (such as a common external tariff) with all nonmember nations. The most familiar example is Benelux—Belgium, the Netherlands, and Luxembourg. Similar plans have been adopted or proposed in other geographic areas.

3. A common market is an association of trading nations which agrees to (a) impose no trade restrictions such as tariffs or quotas among participants, (b) establish common external barriers (such as a com-

mon external tariff) to nonparticipants, and (c) impose no national restrictions on the movement of labor and capital among participants. The most significant example has been the European Economic Community (EEC) or European Common Market, established in 1958. Today it consists of Belgium, Denmark, France, Great Britain, West Germany, Ireland, Italy, Luxembourg, and the Netherlands.

A free-trade area, a customs union, and a common market (in that order) represent increasing degrees of economic integration. Of these, the common market is the most significant. What can be said about its economic effects?

On the favorable side:

A common market (a) encourages a more efficient allocation of member nations' resources in accordance with the laws of comparative advantage, and (b) expands the size of the market for member nations, thereby enabling their industries to gain the economies (lower unit costs) of large-scale production.

On the unfavorable side:

A common market places a trade barrier—typically a tariff wall—between the member countries as a whole and all nonmember nations; the result may be a diversion of trade between the two groups, thereby causing an economic loss for all parties concerned.

The Kennedy Round

The United States has long desired to foster greater economic and political unification in Europe and to avoid the diversion of trade that could result from the European Common Market. Therefore, in order to encourage a low common tariff wall against American exports and those of other nonmember nations, the United States passed the Trade Expansion Act of 1962 as part of its Reciprocal Trade Agreements program. This new law greatly broadened the powers of the President; it gave him authority to:

1. Negotiate tariff reductions on broad categories of goods instead of on specific commodities, as had previously been the case

2. Lower or eliminate tariffs on those goods for which the Common Market and the United States together account for at least 80 percent of total world exports

3. Lower tariffs by as much as 50 percent on the basis of reciprocal trade agreements, provided that such agreements include most favored nation clauses so that the benefits of reduced tariffs are extended to other countries.

4. Grant vocational, technical, and financial assistance to American employees and businessmen whose industries are adversely affected by tariff reduction.

This act enabled the United States to embark on the so-called Kennedy Round of tariff negotiations (named after President Kennedy), the purpose of which was to reduce tariffs gradually over a period of 5 years. In all, 37 nations became involved in duty reductions. Most progress was made in lowering the duties on manufactured goods, whereas agricultural products were less affected. Some nations whose industries were injured by tariff reductions have found themselves faced with increased protectionist pressures and have either adopted or are considering adopting various forms of nontariff barriers to trade such as quotas, license requirements, or border taxes.

Post-World War II International Finance

The postwar developments in international trade were paralleled by equally momentous changes in international finance. When the representatives of the allied nations met in Bretton Woods in 1944 to construct an orderly system of international monetary cooperation that would be conducive to global trade, the experiences of the 1930s were still fresh in everyone's mind. It was clear that neither a system of freely fluctuating exchange rates nor one of fixed rates which permitted easy devaluations was the way to strengthen the financial relationships of nations in the postwar world.

INTERNATIONAL MONETARY FUND

One of the most important products of the Bretton Woods conference was the formation of the *International Monetary Fund* (IMF), an organization established by the United Nations in 1944 for the purposes of: (a) eliminating exchange restrictions and providing for worldwide convertibility of currencies so as to encourage multilateral trade based on international specialization; (b) stabilizing exchange rates to reduce or eliminate short-term international fluctuations in a nation's economy due to changes in its imports, exports, or speculative capital movements;

and (c) assuring that changes in a country's exchange rate would occur only with the Fund's approval, and only after the country had experienced a deficit in its balance of payments for a number of years. Today well over 100 nations are members of the Fund.

The IMF has helped many countries to overcome temporary balance-of-payments deficits that might otherwise have resulted in competitive currency devaluations. It has also been a powerful force in helping to maintain stable exchange rates, even though there have been times when member countries altered their exchange rates without the Fund's approval. These and related matters are taken up in further detail later in the chapter.

FROM DOLLAR SHORTAGE TO DOLLAR SURPLUS

The United States emerged from the war as a large creditor to the allied countries. After the war, American lending continued to mount into the billions of dollars as the United States shifted its emphasis from the provision of military goods to the provision of civilian goods to the war-torn nations. The latter, of course, had little if anything to export in return; nor did they have the gold or dollar reserves with which to pay for the American goods that they received. Hence a "dollar shortage" became one of the most talked-about problems of the postwar decade as the United States continued to show a rather persistent deficit in its balance of payments after 1950.

Further, since gold and dollars were the major source of international monetary reserves, the dollar (and to a lesser extent the pound sterling) became known as a *key currency*—in effect, a substitute for gold in meeting international obligations. This meant that during the 1950s, while the United States was accumulating a huge deficit in its balance of payments, other countries—mainly the European nations—were adding to their reserves, primarily in the form of dollar deposits in U.S. banks or of short-term government securities.

By the mid-1950s, the European and Japanese economies were not only rehabilitated, but thriving. The United States, however, was still maintaining heavy troop commitments overseas, providing economic aid to underdeveloped countries, and experiencing a mounting outflow of American tourists going abroad. All this added up to continued deficits, and by the late 1950s it was recognized throughout the world that the dollar shortage had been transformed into a serious and dangerous dollar surplus.

"DEFENDING THE DOLLAR"

How might the deficit be corrected? There were three plausible choices: (1) domestic deflation, (2) devaluation of the dollar, and (3) reductions in foreign outlays. The first two choices would increase international earnings by expanding U.S. exports relative to imports, whereas the third would simply decrease U.S. expenses.

The first choice was ruled out because deflation would lead to an increase in the unemployment rate in the United States, which was already averaging close to 5 percent. The second choice was also ruled out because devaluation by a major trading country such as the United States would undoubtedly have brought on a chain of competitive devaluations by most other countries. This left the third choice—reduction of foreign outlays—as a means of "defending the dollar."

The measures adopted in the early 1960s took several major forms: Families of servicemen stationed overseas were sent back to the United States; the limits on duty-free goods which could be brought back by returning American tourists were cut; European countries were exhorted to carry a larger share of the mutual defense burden and of foreign aid; an "interest equalization tax" and "voluntary restraints" were imposed on the outflow of American capital; nations in debt to the United States were asked to speed up their payments; trading nations were urged to end their remaining restrictions against American imports; and so on.

What were the consequences? At worst, they did not succeed in eliminating the deficit; at best, they may have merely helped to keep the deficit from becoming still larger. But in any case they were more than straws in the wind, for they portended a series of international monetary crises that shook the financial world.

INTERNATIONAL MONETARY CRISES

In terms of what it set out to do, the 1944 conference at Bretton Woods was a smashing success. It stabilized exchange rates and created an international monetary system that was highly productive of world trade and investment. This was accomplished by establishing a modified type of gold exchange standard with two distinctive features:

1. The dollar was tied to gold, and the U.S. Treasury agreed to make gold and dollars mutually convertible

to foreign central banks at the rate of $35 an ounce of gold.

2. Each nation fixed an exchange rate or par value for its currency in relation to the dollar and agreed to maintain that rate within a 1 percent range by buying and selling when others were selling and buying.

This meant that businessmen anywhere in the world could trade with Britain, for example, and be certain that the value of the pound would not vary by more than a few cents above or below its established rate. As before, however, nations still needed monetary reserves to settle their international monetary deficits. Under the pure gold standard, such reserves consisted of gold; however, under the postwar modified gold exchange standard, reserves consisted primarily of gold and dollars, and to a lesser extent of British pounds. The dollars, as we have seen, were derived largely from U.S. deficits and held mainly in the form of bank deposits and short-term government securities. Because of this, the United States became known as the "world's banker," with the dollar serving as the key or reserve currency.

As American and British deficits continued to mount, and as inflationary forces pushed up prices not only in the United States but also in England and various other major trading nations, the accumulation of pressures erupted in large speculative flows of funds that endangered the international payments system. For example, speculative fevers struck the German mark in 1961 and 1968, the Italian lira in 1963, the British pound in 1961, 1964, 1967, and 1968, and the French franc and U.S. dollar in 1968. Both psychological and economic factors were responsible for these crises, but one of the chief causes was a wavering confidence in the dollar—recurring doubts as to whether the United States would be willing and able to maintain convertibility of the dollar into gold at the fixed price of $35 for an ounce of gold. As a result, increasing proportions of dollars were converted into gold during the 1960s by foreign speculators and others who thought it would be safer or more profitable to hold the yellow metal instead of the green paper.

Finally, in the late 1960s, three sets of events capped a decade of international monetary crises.

Special Drawing Rights ("Paper Gold")

After 1958, the European countries began to press the United States to reduce its balance-of-payments deficit. The United States, in return, urged throughout the 1960s that a plan be developed for increasing international liquidity in the absence of dollar outflows. After almost five years of discussion and four years of negotiation, *Special Drawing Rights* (SDRs) —popularly known as "paper gold"—were approved by the International Monetary Fund in 1969. The SDRs are supplementary reserves in the form of account entries on the books of the IMF and are allocated among participating countries in accordance with their relative economic strength as determined by their national income, population, and volume of world trade. SDRs can be drawn upon by governments to help finance balance-of-payments deficits, and it is hoped that the "paper gold" will provide an orderly growth of reserves to meet the expanding needs of world trade. In the opinion of some economists, however, SDRs are a device for postponing what is more fundamentally needed, namely, a better mechanism for international adjustment. The implications of this are considered later in the chapter. Meanwhile, see Exhibit 1.

Devaluation

On November 19, 1967, the twenty-sixth Sunday after Trinity, churchgoers in England heard a somber and particularly apt text from Anglican pulpits. The lesson was from *St. James*, Chapter 5, Verses 1 to 3:

> Go to now, ye rich men, weep and howl for your miseries that shall come upon you.
> Your riches are corrupted, and your garments are moth-eaten.
> Your gold and silver is cankered; and the rust of them shall be a witness against you, and shall eat your flesh as it were fire. Ye have heaped treasure together for the last days.

Why this curious reading from scripture? The answer is that while the creation of SDRs was being discussed among governments, Britain was indulging herself with an easy-money policy that was contributing to inflation, trade deficits, and financial strains. On November 18, 1967, she succumbed to international economic pressures and devalued the pound from $2.80 to $2.40, a decrease of 14.3 percent. This was the third devaluation for Britain in 36 years and was intended to give the country a sharper competitive edge in world markets as well as the breathing time needed to repair its foundering economy and deficit-ridden balance of payments.

What do SDRs mean for the United States? Until 1971, the United States used its gold stock or its "credit line" with the IMF to absorb unwanted dollars that accrued to foreign central banks as the result of the U.S. deficit. With the introduction of SDRs, the United States has, within the rules governing the use of the SDRs by any one country, the additional option of affecting the absorption by exchanging the unwanted dollars for SDRs. This aids conservation of the U.S. gold stock and thus contributes to the viability of the existing international payments mechanism.

In the long run, the introduction of SDRs may be expected to modify the role of the dollar as a reserve currency. The view that the dollar cannot and should not be expected to meet the world's future needs for growth of reserves was the underlying rationale for the introduction of the SDRs. Thus, the relative importance of the dollar as a source of international liquidity should diminish gradually as more SDRs are introduced over time.

At the same time, however, the vital function the dollar has performed as the "international transactions currency" may be strengthened by the introduction of arrangements that hold a promise of a better functioning international payments system.

SOURCE: Adapted from Federal Reserve Bank of Chicago.

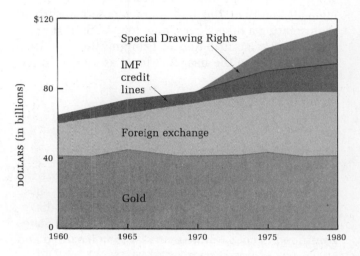

THE CHANGING MIX IN WORLD RESERVES

SOURCE: Data from International Monetary Fund.

Whether or not a devaluation succeeds in eliminating a deficit depends on the various policy measures taken at home to curb inflation. Such measures, which Britain adopted, included heavy new taxes, broad wage controls, and a tight national budget. In the long run, if an austerity policy is sufficiently harsh and if it is combined with an appropriate restrictive monetary policy, it can succeed in curbing an inflation and thereby make a devaluation yield lasting economic benefits.

A Two-tier System for Gold

Following the devaluation of the pound in 1967, confidence in the dollar was further weakened by inflation in the United States and the expectation that the dollar would have to be devalued. Consequently, a rush to buy gold developed late in the year. Most of the buyers were speculators who expected to make a quick profit by reselling the gold at the higher price.

In the meantime, seven countries known as the Gold Pool nations—the United States, Great Britain, West Germany, Belgium, Italy, the Netherlands, and Switzerland—had, since 1961, been holding the free market price of gold in London, Brussels, Zurich, and certain other cities at the American price of $35 an ounce by pooling their gold and standing ready to buy or sell as the need arose. With the onset of the new "gold rush," there was a danger that the gold holdings of these nations would be depleted, thus endangering the entire international monetary system. The speculative fever reached a dramatic climax in March, 1968, with the announcement of a two-tier (or two-price) system for gold by the Gold Pool nations. Henceforth, they said, their central banks would (a) exchange existing gold stocks among themselves at the historic official price of $35 per ounce, and (b) no longer buy or sell gold in private markets, thus leaving the free price of gold to rise or fall like that of any other commodity.

This action further demonetized gold—that is, reduced its influence in the monetary system and thereby removed its threat to the dollar. Thus by the end of the 1960s, the dollar seemed victorious over gold for several reasons: The West German mark had been revalued upward, and the French franc had been devalued, both to more realistic levels; Britain's trade balance had improved; and South Africa, the world's largest producer of gold, was mining the metal faster than the free market could absorb it, thus creating a huge "overhang" of potential supply. These factors contributed to bringing the free price of gold down to the near $35 level as shown in Exhibit 2.

END OF AN ERA

For a brief time it seemed as if the period of recurring international monetary crises was over. But these hopes were short-lived. To the dismay and disapproval of foreign governments, the United States continued to spend more overseas than it earned and refused to take measures that would enable it to pay its own way in the world.

By 1970 the chronic deficit had ballooned to the point of crisis. U.S. imports were rising far faster than exports; banks and corporations were putting billions of dollars annually into investments abroad; and defense spending, swollen by the Vietnam War, was a hemorrhage through which other billions of dollars leaked out.

Moreover, foreigners were holding billions of dollars they did not want. In the summer of 1971 certain countries, headed by France and Switzerland, rushed to convert their dollar holdings into gold. By July only $10 billion was left in Fort Knox. The crunch came on August 15, 1971. On that day, President Nixon announced to the world that the U.S. "gold window" was closed; henceforth, the government would no longer exchange dollars for gold with foreign central banks. Thus the system of fixed exchange rates based on the Bretton Woods agreement with which the free world had lived for twenty-seven years came to an end.

Exhibit 2

Gold Price and the Speculators

WHO ARE THE GOLD SPECULATORS?

In the United States and Britain, it is illegal for private citizens to buy or sell gold. But in many other countries everyone is free to trade in it. Who are the chief purchasers in those countries? By visiting any of the major gold markets of the world—in London, Paris, Brussels, Zurich, or Hong Kong—and conversing with dealers, one can conjecture that there is a mixed bag of gold-buying types: oil-rich sheiks from the Middle East; millionaires from Europe and the Far East; foreign commercial banks, corporations, and businessmen. But the names of these buyers are virtually impossible to obtain, for secrecy is a fetish in gold transactions.

During the week of the mad gold rush in mid-March of 1968, the famous Bourse in Paris was the center of activity. There, according to Newsweek magazine, "a shoving, sweating mob of dealers transacted their business amid shouts of 'Stop pushing, dammit!' and 'Give me room!' The action got so feverish at one point that the gendarmes were called in to make sure that the gold crisis did not claim its first life."

PRICE OF GOLD ON THE FREE MARKET, 1968–1969

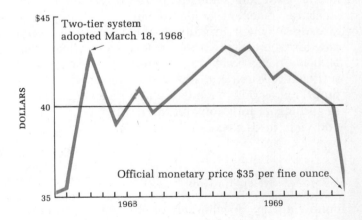

RECENT DEVELOPMENTS

Events since late 1971 have been accompanied by further turmoil in international economic relations. The more important developments may be summarized briefly:

☐ In December, 1971, the United States devalued the dollar against gold by almost 9 percent; at the same time the German mark and Japanese yen were revalued upward, yielding a net dollar devaluation of about 11 percent. Also, Europe, Canada, and Japan —the major markets for American exports—agreed to talk about reducing tariffs and other trade barriers.

☐ In 1972, the United States suffered the worst trade deficit in its history—almost $7 billion. The resulting excess supply of dollars abroad tended to drive the price of the dollar down. In addition, investors around the world became increasingly fearful that the Nixon administration would do little or nothing to stem the outflow of inconvertible dollars. These fears caused the dollar to shrink further in value.

☐ In February, 1973, after several further monetary crises, the dollar was devalued again—this time in terms of SDRs—by 10 percent. For a year or more prior to that time, however, the Japanese yen, the British pound, and some other important currencies had been "floating"—their values determined by the free play of supply and demand. Subsequently, various other nations' currencies were officially swept afloat by the tidal waves of selling that continued to strike the U.S. dollar.

☐ In November, 1973, the two-tier system for gold was abandoned by the Gold Pool nations. This left them free to pursue independently whatever actions they wished with respect to gold.

As a result of these developments, representatives of twenty major trading nations (including the United States) began discussions in 1973 to work out an improved world monetary system. The key question they must answer is whether new rules of the game can be devised which will permit the restoration of stability in international economic relations.

Some further aspects of developments related to these events are described in Box 2 on the next page.

Problems of International Adjustment

Looking back over these historical developments, it is appropriate for us to ask why international monetary crises have occurred. The reasons can be summarized in three steps.

1. The international supply of a nation's currency will tend to exceed the demand for it when that country runs a *deficit* in its balance of payments. This occurs when the nation pays out more money than it takes in, by spending, investing, or giving it away. In order to buy its currency back, the monetary authority must spend its reserves of convertible currencies or gold (by selling the gold to foreign central banks) or borrow from the International Monetary Fund.

2. Conversely, the international demand for a nation's currency will tend to exceed the supply of it when the country runs a *surplus* in its balance of payments. In that case the nation is taking in more money than it is paying out, and to meet foreign demand the central bank must sell its currency in return for foreign exchange. This results in an accumulation of reserves, mostly dollars, which the central bank in the surplus country may not wish to hold.

3. The international monetary system will be threatened whenever major nations continue to run large deficits or surpluses for prolonged periods of time. The problem, therefore, is for each of the leading trading countries to maintain a tendency toward balance between its money inflows and outflows.

What difficulties do nations encounter in achieving international monetary balance? It is to this problem that we now turn our attention.

THE RELUCTANCE TO ADJUST

The heart of any international monetary system is its adjustment mechanism—the process by which nations achieve payments balance.

Under the old gold standard, the adjustment was automatic; a nation with a deficit in its balance of payments tended to lose gold, and the loss of gold brought about a domestic deflation which resulted in increased exports and decreased imports. This meant, however, that the domestic economic goal of full employment through appropriate fiscal and monetary policies had to take second place to international economic adjustment—a situation that all nations found untenable.

Under the Bretton Woods system, exchange rates remained fixed, and so the process of adjustment was left to nations themselves. This meant that coun-

Dollars, Deficits, and Devaluation. Will More Become Less?

Until relatively recent times, only a banana republic would devalue its currency twice within 14 months. But in 1971, and again in 1973, the United States did just that—and found the decision to be not only internationally easy but politically popular.

For 37 years—from 1934 to 1971—the U.S. dollar rode high in the world, preeminent and solid as Fort Knox. During this period the official monetary price of gold was $35 an ounce. But as a result of the devaluation in 1971, the official price was raised to $38; and with the devaluation in 1973, the official price was boosted to $42.22.

In reality, the official monetary price is an accounting measure used by the government and is unrelated to market conditions. The U.S. Treasury need not buy or sell gold if it does not wish to do so, even though the free market price of gold in London, Paris, Hong Kong and elsewhere may be several times higher than the official monetary price.

The cut in the dollar's value was intended to make American products cheaper for foreigners and foreign products more expensive for Americans to buy. Hopefully, this would encourage U.S. exports, discourage imports, and thus work toward preventing future deficits in trade.

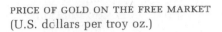

PRICE OF GOLD ON THE FREE MARKET
(U.S. dollars per troy oz.)

Price reached $127 in May, 1973

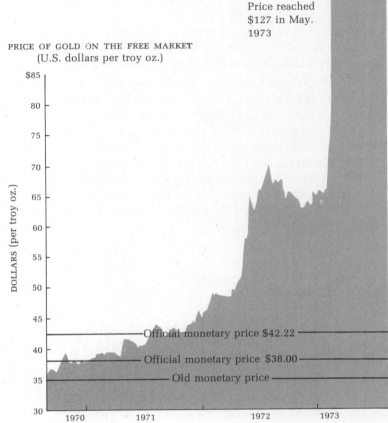

PRICE OF GOLD ON THE FREE MARKET
(U.S. dollars per troy oz.)

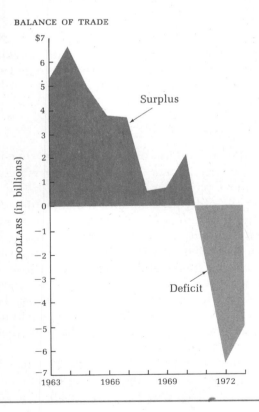

BALANCE OF TRADE

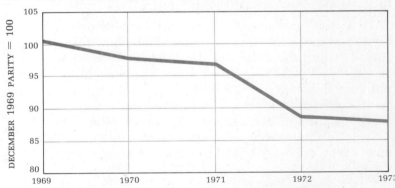

U.S. DOLLAR RELATIVE TO OTHER MAJOR CURRENCIES

SOURCE: Computed from data published by the Board of Governors of the Federal Reserve System and the U.S. Department of Commerce. Data for nine major currencies weighted by share of U.S. trade.

tries had to be willing to adopt either deflationary policies to correct persistent balance-of-payments deficits, or "reflationary" policies to reduce balance-of-payments surpluses. Of course, the pressure on deficit nations to change their domestic policies depends, today as well as then, on how long their reserves hold out or how long they can continue to borrow; surplus nations, on the other hand, tend to gain reserves, and hence may be able to avoid adjustment almost indefinitely.

In general, nations that are committed to the maintenance of full employment do not find it easy to adopt a policy of domestic deflation. The United States and Britain have been prime examples. Both have gone through long periods of deficits, but both were able to delay adjustments because the dollar and the pound are reserve currencies. Eventually, when the United States was forced to adjust in the 1960s because it was losing gold, it took the easier and less effective route of employing indirect forms of exchange controls—such as interest equalization taxes and the imposition of limits on capital exports, corporate overseas investing, and bank lending abroad.

In terms of historical experience, it appears that under a system of fixed exchange rates such as existed in the Bretton Woods era, the most positive approach a government can take to correct an imbalance is to change the par value of its currency. But this is considered to be the most drastic of measures. Thus if a country has been suffering from deficits, a depreciation of its currency in order to restore balance involves a sacrifice of international prestige, for its political leaders are thereby admitting to the world that they have been unable to manage domestic economic affairs properly. On the other hand, if a country has been experiencing surpluses in its balance of payments, an appreciation or upward revaluation of its currency may cause some domestic unemployment, especially in its export industries, and hence is a step which elected political leaders are not easily persuaded to take.

These tendencies are readily apparent. Britain devalued in 1967 after having delayed until it could no longer borrow money to support the pound. France suffered a $3 billion reserve loss in 1968, but deemed it a point of national honor not to devalue the franc, and hence imposed a strict domestic austerity program instead. Finally, however, it had to succumb to the reality of devaluation in August, 1969. And West Germany, after experiencing years of domestic prosperity and surpluses in its balance of payments,

finally yielded to persistent pressure from other deficit nations; in September, 1969, *after* a close election, the mark was permitted to float freely, and its price in the market promptly rose. Since then the mark has been revalued several times.

THE INEVITABILITY OF ADJUSTMENT

Ultimately, of course, nations do adjust, because the forces that create international imbalances—inflation or deflation—also cause domestic economic difficulties which require correction. But the adjustment may take a long time in coming, and in the meantime nations can bump along from one crisis to another.

Was this the world that the men at Bretton Woods envisaged in 1944? The answer is no. They never thought that the dollar would remain the world's key currency for several decades after the war, nor that it would be a currency whose supply might someday exceed the quantity that central banks wished to hold. Likewise, they never foresaw the possibility that there would someday be a huge market for *Eurodollars,* which are dollar deposits in banks outside the United States, mostly in Europe. Eurodollars are held by American or foreign banks, corporations, and individuals, and represent dollar obligations which are constantly crossing national frontiers in search of the highest return; hence they may affect balances of payments and may even turn pressure on a currency into an international monetary crisis. (See Box 3.)

The basic problem, therefore, is for nations to find a suitable method of adjustment; otherwise, the system will continue to stumble along.

Floating, Adjustable, or Crawling Rates?

What can be done to improve the world's monetary system? Central bankers and economists are interested in three types of proposals: (1) floating exchange rates; (2) adjustable pegs; and (3) crawling pegs.

Floating Exchange Rates

Floating exchange rates would leave currencies free to fluctuate according to supply and demand. Thus

Eurodollars—The Expatriate Currency

Eurodollars are dollar accounts held in foreign banks all over the world, but mostly in Europe. As American businessmen and tourists kept spending more money in Europe than Europeans spent in the United States, the difference mounted up in foreign bank accounts.

Since the late 1960s, the total of Eurodollars has far exceeded the amount needed to finance trade. The excess has provided a pool for speculators: banks, oil-producing Arabian sheiks, treasurers of multinational corporations, and others who own the funds and are willing to make them available wherever the returns are highest. As a result, Eurodollars wreak havoc with foreign central bankers who often buy up the funds in order to maintain a desired relation between the U.S. dollar and their own currency.

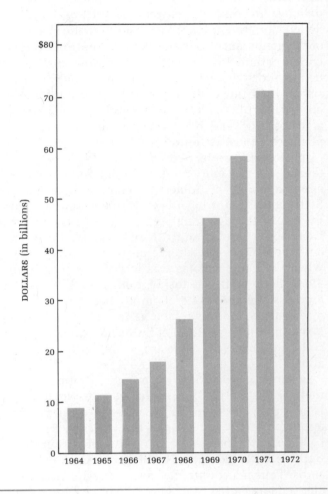

a decrease in the price of a nation's currency in the foreign exchange market would encourage that country's exports and discourage its imports; conversely, an increase in the price of its currency would have the opposite effect. The chief advantages of freely fluctuating exchange rates, therefore, are that: (a) they provide for automatic adjustment in the balance of payments without the intervention of a central authority; and (b) they eliminate the need for stabilization funds and international reserves such as those held by the IMF. The chief disadvantages are that: (a) they may restrict the expansion of world trade by leaving importers, exporters, creditors, and others in a greater state of uncertainty about future exchange rates; and (b) they may encourage speculation in foreign exchange which could accentuate price swings and cause a destabilization of world trade. These undesirable consequences might eventually lead to more rather than fewer trade controls. See, however, Exhibit 3.

Adjustable Pegs

An *adjustable* peg system permits changes in the par rate of exchange after a long-run disequilibrium in the balance of payments; it also allows for short-run variations in the exchange rate within a few percentage points around the par value. (This was essentially the Bretton Woods system.) The most desirable feature of such a system is that it would operate efficiently only if the par rate were consistent with the nation's long-run equilibrium in its balance of payments, so that the adjustment problem is then entirely of a short-term nature. The most undesirable feature is that the threat of speculation and disruption of foreign exchange markets would exist when a change in the basic par rate became necessary.

Crawling Pegs

Under a *crawling peg* system the par value of a nation's exchange rate would change automatically by small increments, downward or upward, if in actual daily trading on the foreign exchange markets the price of its currency persisted on the "floor" or "ceiling" of the established range for a specified period of time. The changes in the par value would be small and gradual (probably about 3 percent annually) so as to discourage speculation, yet sufficient to correct for fundamental imbalances in the balance of payments. The crawling peg system thus represents a compromise between floating exchange rates and the adjustable peg. Although the crawling peg would not eliminate the need for international reserves, it would permit fewer reserves to be needed than with fixed rates. And, since everyone would know how far and in what direction exchange rates were moving, speculation would tend to be minimal while world trade and investment continued to expand. (See Exhibit 4.)

Exhibit 3

Currency Protection in the Forward Exchange Market
(90-day forward spread—hypothetical data)

Forward exchange is bought (or sold) at a given time and at a stipulated current or "spot" price, but is payable at some future date. By buying or selling forward exchange importers and exporters can protect themselves against the risks of fluctuations in the current exchange market.

The spread between spot and future prices can vary considerably, as the chart shows. Currencies that are in strong demand tend to sell at a premium, while those that are in a weaker position sell at a discount. In the more recent months shown, for example, French importers from Germany paid heavily by buying forward marks at a premium, thus restricting their purchases of Volkswagens. But German importers found forward francs so cheap they could afford to buy a lot more French wine.

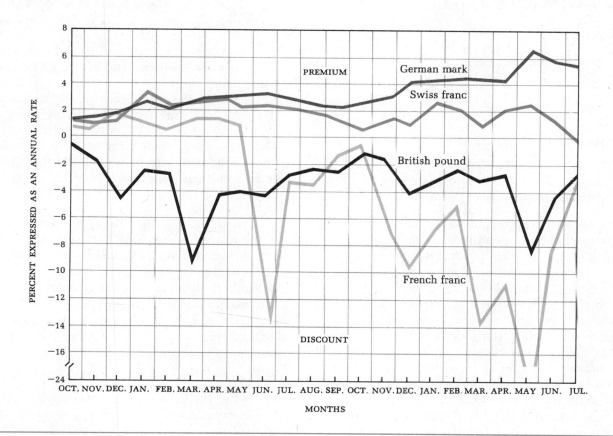

Exhibit 4

How the Crawling Peg Would Work

Under the crawling peg system a deficit nation would find that its exchange rate stays at the lower level of the allowable band of fluctuation. So its exchange rate would move downward in predictable fashion until the impact of a lower exchange rate brought its balance of payments back into equilibrium. On the other side, the exchange rate of a surplus nation would increase in a manner which would gradually reduce its surplus. The merit of the crawling peg is that its movements would be predictable and it would facilitate the adjustment process on the part of both deficit and surplus nations.

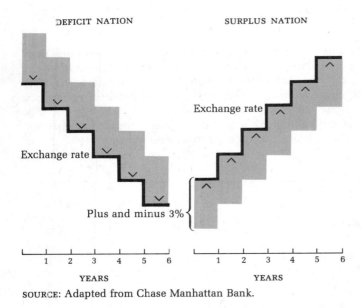

SOURCE: Adapted from Chase Manhattan Bank.

Conclusion: Permanent Agreement Doubtful

The choice between a system of adjustable exchange rates and one that permits either floating or crawling rates has been discussed by bankers, economists, and political leaders for years. Governments tend to believe that an adjustable exchange-rate system is best. Economists, on the other hand, especially those in the academic world, have come increasingly to favor the more flexible systems such as the floating rate or crawling peg described above. Despite international meetings held to discuss the matter, it is doubtful whether any enduring arrangements will ever emerge. In the words of one European central banker: "The system of fixed exchange rates [under Bretton Woods] *succeeded because it was needed.*

It accomplished its objectives—to encourage world trade and to stimulate Europe's economic development. Those achievements were realized by the early 1960s. Since then, the lesson of history has been that it is unrealistic to assume that any government would go along with a permanent policy of exchange rates based on some agreed-upon mechanism that could easily be discarded in a period of adversity."

SUMMARY OF IMPORTANT IDEAS

1. For several decades before World War I, most national economies were closely integrated through a well-developed network of trade and finance. Despite rapid advances in technology and heavy migrations of labor and capital, the international economic setting remained relatively harmonious until the outbreak of the war.

2. World War I disrupted national trading and financial relationships. Although efforts were made at postwar reconstruction, there was a structural weakening of the international economy during the decade of the 1920s as nations shifted their economic goals toward greater internal stability and control at the expense of automatic external adjustment.

3. The world economy, and particularly the interdependence of nations, underwent major deterioration during the Depression of the 1930s. Governments sought to protect themselves from economic crises by imposing higher tariffs, by going off the gold standard, and by devaluing their currencies. Although some significant steps toward international economic reform were made during the late 1930s, the outbreak of World War II prevented further progress.

4. After World War II, most of the war-torn nations of the world became beneficiaries of American economic aid. Major steps were taken toward trade liberalization through GATT and toward economic integration through the development of common markets. In the area of international finance, the Bretton Woods conference of 1944 established the IMF and a world monetary arrangement that was enormously successful in encouraging international trade.

5. By the 1960s, however, it was apparent that economic conditions had changed so much that the world's monetary system was out of date. The vol-

ume of world trade increased faster than reserves, causing international monetary crises that resulted in exchange controls and devaluations. Among the measures taken to alleviate the pressures were the introduction of SDRs and a two-tier (or two-price) system for gold. Finally, in the face of continued adversity, the Bretton Woods system of fixed exchange rates was abandoned in late 1971. Since then, countries have allowed their currencies to float in foreign exchange markets.

6. Three proposals have been suggested to improve the world's monetary system: (1) floating or freely fluctuating exchange rates, (2) an adjustable peg system, and (3) a crawling peg system. Political considerations being what they are, however, it is unlikely that any system of exchange-rate stability will be adhered to by all nations under all circumstances.

FOR DISCUSSION

1. Terms and concepts to review:

gold bullion standard	Trade Expansion Act
devaluation	(1962)
Reciprocal Trade	International Monetary
Agreements program	Fund (IMF)
most favored nation	Special Drawing
clause	Rights (SDRs or
European Recovery	"paper gold")
Program (ERP)	Eurodollars
General Agreements	floating exchange
on Tariffs and	rates
Trade (GATT)	adjustable peg
free-trade area	crawling peg
customs union	forward exchange
common market	

2. What major features would you stress if you were to write a research paper on the history of international commercial and financial policies?

3. If a country's balance of payments is in equilibrium and the nation experiences a decline in exports, does its balance of payments go into disequilibrium? What happens if floating exchange rates prevail?

4. Devaluation stimulates a nation's exports while curbing its imports; upward revaluation has the opposite effects. In view of this, would you recommend the use of devaluation and revaluation as useful countercyclical policies to combat recessions and inflations, similar to the way we currently use fiscal-monetary policies for such purposes? Explain.

5. From the experiences of the 1960s, would you say that the dollar was overvalued or undervalued in world markets? What could have been done to correct the situation?

6. Why do you suppose that many "anti-Keynesians" often propose that the United States go on a gold standard?

7. The economic regions of the United States, that is, the Northeast, Southwest, etc., are somewhat like countries, each with their own particular types of economy. However, unlike countries, they all use the same currency, namely dollars, which puts them in effect on a fixed exchange rate with respect to one another. What happens when some of these regions experience deficits and others surpluses? How do they adjust? How does the regional adjustment process compare with that of nations?

8. Deficits in the U.S. balance of payments were welcomed in the early 1950s but viewed with great concern a decade later. Why?

9. It is often said that the Bretton Woods arrangement resulted in a compromise between fixed and floating exchange rates. Is this true? Explain. What would have been a better compromise?

Multinational Corporations: Has Ricardo's Prophecy Come True?

The great English classical economist, David Ricardo, demonstrated in the early nineteenth century that unrestricted operation of the law of comparative advantage makes everybody better off. Each nation, he said, should be free to specialize in the products in which it is most efficient and leave the production of other things to the countries that can do so most efficiently. The world economy will then have more goods by engaging in trade.

Today the neon signs of American, European, and Japanese multinational corporations light the skylines of most major cities throughout the world. These companies have spawned subsidiaries and branches in order to exploit their own comparative advantages. They have discovered that economies of scale can be enhanced by locating in foreign markets, and that the advantages of such economies outweigh the regulations and financial risks that global operations may entail.

The international economic implications of multinational corporations are examined in the following essay by Professor Kenneth Hammer of the University of Wisconsin at Whitewater.

What Is a Multinational Corporation?

A multinational corporation is a chain of companies conducting similar operations in several nations under separate national charters but under the same top management. More precisely, a multinational corporation is one with sales above $100 million, with operations in at least six nations, and with foreign subsidiaries that account for over 20 percent of its assets. Most major United States corporations meet this qualification.

Companies have long operated across international boundaries. The Virginia Company of London and the Hudson's Bay Company were early ancestors of the modern multinational. The East India Company, based in England, ruled a fifth of the world population for over two centuries. By 1919 there were about 180 multinational corporations based in the United States. The United Fruit Company controlled some 4 million acres of land in Latin America in the 1930s. For years, Liberia was known as the Firestone Republic.

Postwar Boom in Multinationals

The world economy in the 1950s was still in the shadow of the dollar shortage of the earlier years. American decision-makers argued that the outflow of financial capital from the United States was desirable. It would bring American technology to the war-torn nations of Europe. That happened to a far greater degree than was expected. The rapid growth of American multinational corporations, stemming from the immense outflow of investment funds from the United States since World War II, was the inevitable result. Thus between 1950 and 1970 the value of U.S. investments abroad increased from $31 billion to $143 billion—nearly a five-fold growth. About two-thirds was private investment. The direct investment by U.S. multinational corporations in manufacturing facilities alone nearly tripled during the 1960s. Today the financial resources of some multinational corporations are larger than those of some of the nations in which they operate. Further, multinational corporations account for about 15 percent of the entire world's production, with American firms responsible for 44 percent of this amount, or about 6.6 percent of the entire world product. Total sales of the multinationals were $200 billion in 1960 and by 1970 total sales had risen to $450 billion.

The French scholar and critic, Jean-Jacques Servan-Schreiber in his book, *The Challenge of America*, describes the threat to European industry from the rapid growth since World War II of the European operations of United States-based multinational corporations. American firms control 30 percent of the European auto industry, 50 percent of the West German oil industry, and 90 percent of the French computer industry. Only three U.S. companies—Ford, General Motors, and Exxon (formerly Standard Oil of New Jersey) account for 40 percent of the foreign investment in France, England, and West Germany.

Servan-Schreiber failed to mention that the growth of the multinationals was not solely an American phenomenon. In 1972 over half of the multinationals were United States-based. Among the best-known giant corporations based in other nations, in addition to the 15 largest firms shown in Table 1, are Nestlé and Ciba (Switzerland), Necchi and Olivetti (Italy), Massey-Ferguson and Alcan Aluminum (Canada), Volkswagen and Bayer (West Germany), and Volvo and Ericsson (Sweden).

Pros and Cons

The multinationals have greatly altered the process of trade among nations. They have become the vehicle for transferring financial capital, management skill, and technology from one nation to another. Needless to say, they have been subject to various criticisms:

1. Organized labor in the United States argues that multinational corporations export jobs to their foreign subsidiaries. The AFL-CIO estimates that between 1966 and 1971 some 900,000 U.S. job opportunities were lost because of multinationals. Instead of exporting domestically produced goods, the big companies, it is claimed, export their money, management skills, and patents to foreign subsidiaries. The multinationals do so because of lower

Table 1
THE TOP 15 MULTINATIONAL COMPANIES

Company	Total 1971 sales [billions of dollars]	Foreign sales as percentage of total	Number of countries in which subsidiaries are located
General Motors (U.S.)	$28.3	19	21
Exxon (U.S.)	18.7	50	25
Ford (U.S.)	16.4	26	30
Royal Dutch/Shell (Neth.)	12.7	79	43
General Electric (U.S.)	9.4	16	32
IBM (U.S.)	8.3	39	80
Mobil Oil (U.S.)	8.2	45	62
Chrysler (U.S.)	8.0	24	26
Texaco (U.S.)	7.5	40	30
Unilever (U.S.)	7.5	80	31
ITT (U.S.)	7.3	42	40
Gulf Oil (U.S.)	5.9	45	61
British Petroleum (Brit.)	5.2	88	52
Philips Gloeilampenfabrieken (Neth.)	5.2	*	29
Standard Oil of California (U.S.)	5.1	45	26

* Not available.
DATA: United Nations; *Business Week*.

labor costs abroad. The imported products of foreign subsidiaries can be sold at lower prices than goods produced at home. This leads to unemployment in the United States.

2. Another argument against the multinationals is the claim that they enjoy unfair tax advantages over smaller domestic firms. When a U.S. corporation opens a new branch operation abroad, the new branch's initial losses are deducted from corporate taxable income reported in the United States. Once a branch becomes profitable, it can then be converted into a foreign-based subsidiary whose profits are taxed at lower rates than the 48 percent U.S. corporate income tax. The American taxpayer, in effect, subsidizes such a procedure to the tune of several billion dollars annually.

3. A third criticism of the multinationals is that they can make use of "transfer-pricing" techniques to lighten their tax burden. For example, a company will charge an undue percentage of research and development costs to a subsidiary in a country with high taxes. The result is to transfer profits from where the tax is high to where it is low—to the detriment of one national treasury and the benefit of another. National companies do not enjoy this freedom of maneuver.

4. Another attack against multinationals is that they possess excessive economic power: they are able to decide how world markets should be divided, and they can influence tax revenues, foreign exchange earnings, and the rate of capital formation in the nations where their foreign subsidiaries operate. It is also charged that the multinationals are often a main force behind world money crises.

5. Finally, it is argued that the growing economic power of the big companies has been matched by their expanding political power. Multinational operations often defy national regulation, and their political interests do not necessarily coincide with those of any nation.

In contrast, those who favor the growth of multinational corporations argue that these firms break down trade barriers. The multinationals are the prime agents for economic development and world prosperity, and they make significant contributions to the United States balance of payments. In addition, their adherents claim for the multinationals that they: promote cooperation among nations, seek profits by meeting the needs of the great masses of people throughout the world, induce growth among local suppliers, and create new purchasing power and new tax revenues.

Conclusion

It is too early to assess the long-run effects of multinational corporations on the world economy. Many questions remain to be answered. What influences do the multinationals have on world trade and the flow of money? What is their challenge to national governments? Do the operations of multinational corporations disrupt national economies? What are the implications of large investments by corporations in foreign subsidiaries? How much influence do the multinationals exert on a nation's foreign policy?

These and related questions are occupying the attention of many economists and political leaders in the United States and abroad. It seems safe to predict that multinationals are heading into an era of closer scrutiny and regulation, but what the form and effect of that regulation will be is not clear.

QUESTIONS

1. *A multinational company may have operations in—among other countries —the United States and South Africa. In the United States it supports the ideal of equal opportunity regardless of race and religion. In South Africa it goes along with discrimination against blacks. Is the company merely being prudent or is it morally flawed? How should it behave?*

2. *A U.S. company has the choice of serving export markets by building a plant in North Carolina or in Taiwan. In North Carolina it can expect a net profit after taxes equalling 5 percent of sales, and in Taiwan it can expect 15 percent. Where should it locate?*

CHAPTER 37

The Less Developed Countries: Nations in Poverty

What are the chief economic characteristics of less developed countries? How do these countries compare economically with the more advanced nations?

What major forms of assistance have been provided to the less developed countries? Has this assistance been effective? What problems should be understood if foreign aid is to achieve its desired objectives?

Can a set of principles and policies be developed to provide a framework for analyzing the process of development?

In his 1968 Message to Congress, President Johnson said:

> Peace will never be secure as long as:
>
> Seven out of ten people on earth cannot read or write
>
> Tens of millions of people each day—most of them children—are maimed and stunted by malnutrition
>
> Diseases long conquered by science still ravage cities and villages around the world

Conditions have not changed significantly since President Johnson issued his warning.

At home, as we have learned already, a considerable number of Americans do not share either the opportunity or the affluence of our time. Abroad, as we shall see in this chapter, the poor countries contain three-fourths of the world's population. Hence it is the affluent who are in the minority in today's world.

Nations in poverty are part of the larger study of economic growth and development, but with some applications of international economics as well. Although there is no explicit or unified theory of economic development, some of today's most significant insights stem from Adam Smith's *Wealth of Nations* (1776), which was written before the main thrust of the industrial revolutions, but after many important agricultural revolutions.

Some Characteristics of Less Developed Countries

The poor nations are commonly referred to as *less developed countries* (LDCs), or underdeveloped countries, or low-income countries. They are usually characterized by the following conditions:

☐ Poverty levels of income (typically defined as less than $500 per capita annually), and hence little or no saving

☐ High rates of population growth

☐ Substantial majorities of the labor force employed in agriculture

☐ Low proportions of adult literacy

☐ Extensive *disguised unemployment*—a situation in which employed resources are not being used in their most efficient ways (also commonly called *underemployment*)

☐ Heavy reliance on one or a few items for export

☐ Government control by a wealthy elite, which opposes any changes that would harm its economic interests

These characteristics are tendencies rather than certainties among underdeveloped nations; exceptions can be found to all of them.

A question that naturally arises is: How many countries of the world are considered to be "less developed," and which ones are they? From time to time the United Nations has designated dozens of countries as LDCs, with the number ranging between 75 and 100 since the 1960s. These nations are located primarily in Asia, Latin America, and Africa. Among them are Indonesia, Burma, India, Kenya, Pakistan, Nigeria, Syria, Morocco, Taiwan, Paraguay, Ecuador, Honduras, Turkey, and Colombia.

A STUDY IN CONTRASTS

It is necessary to compare the gap, at different points in time, between per capita incomes in the less developed and the advanced countries to see whether the gulf has widened, narrowed, or remained the same. For example, in 1955 average per capita annual income in the half-dozen poorest countries of the world was $97, while in the half-dozen richest countries it was $1,228—more than 12 times higher. Ten years later, in 1965, some of the countries in each group had changed, but average income per capita was still about the same in the six poorest countries, while it had risen to over $2,200 in the six richest. This indicates that the per capita income gap between the richest and the poorest nations has been widening, thus portending serious consequences for the world community.

It is not enough, of course, simply to measure differences in the economic progress of nations; we must see clearly why these differences occur. This requires us to understand the factors determining a nation's economic development—its quantity and quality of human and natural resources; its rate of capital accumulation; its degree of specialization and scale of production; its rate of technological progress; and its environmental factors, including the political, social, cultural, and economic framework within which growth and development take place. Once we comprehend the significance of these factors, it becomes easy to appreciate why the rich nations are getting richer while the poor ones are getting relatively poorer.

This point can be illustrated by comparing the United States with most underdeveloped countries. The United States has a large labor force with a relatively high proportion of skilled workers, and its business leaders are numerous and disciplined. It has a substantial and diversified quantity of natural resources, an extensive system of transportation and power, an efficient and productive technology financed by an adequate supply of savings, a stable and comparatively uncorrupt government, and a culture in which the drive for profit and material gain is generally accepted. These factors in combination have stimulated America's economic development.

In the less developed countries, on the other hand, most of these conditions are absent. Labor is largely unskilled and inefficient, and is often chronically ill and undernourished. Savings are small or even negative, resulting in low rates of investment and capital accumulation. The cultural environment favors the clergy, the military, or government administration, while frowning upon commerce and finance, thus creating a dearth of entrepreneurial talent; and government is often unstable or, if stable, dictatorial, corrupt, and inefficient. Paradoxically, many poor countries are rich in natural resources; but because these are usually controlled by foreigners for their own profit, relatively little of the revenue goes into the local economy. A combination of these factors retards economic development.

WHAT IS ECONOMIC DEVELOPMENT?

The fundamental challenge facing the poor countries is to transform their economies from an underdeveloped to a developed status. This is what economic development means. It is a process that has continued at an accelerating pace in the advanced countries since the birth of capitalism in the late Middle Ages. Today's less developed countries cannot hope, however, to start a similar process without help from the rich nations. Some help has been offered: loans, grants, and technical assistance have enabled certain poor countries to acquire greater quantities of capital and achieve faster rates of economic growth than would otherwise have been possible.

As we shall see later in this chapter, many of the less developed countries are trapped in a vicious circle of poverty from which escape is extremely difficult. Hence the problems which cause this vicious circle must be solved if economic development is to occur. Among those problems are bad government. As many critics point out, one of the world's largest sources of aid, the United States, offers help mainly to governments it wants to keep in power. Foreign aid has thus been a tool of foreign policy; and governments considered desirable by the U.S. State Department are not always those best able to foster economic growth.

Milestones in Foreign Aid

As World War II drew to a close, it became apparent that the richer nations would have to provide substantial aid to countries in need of help. Accordingly, various agencies were established under the auspices of the United Nations. Among the most important was the United Nations Educational, Scientific and Cultural Organization (UNESCO), which today is an association of more than 100 countries that channels a wide range of services to the underdeveloped regions of the world.

The major forms and features of foreign aid since World War II may be sketched within the following framework: (1) the International Bank for Reconstruction and Development (the World Bank), (2) technical cooperation and assistance programs, and (3) problems and dilemmas of foreign aid. Let us see what each involves.

INTERNATIONAL BANK FOR RECONSTRUCTION AND DEVELOPMENT – THE WORLD BANK

When the Bretton Woods conference set up the International Monetary Fund in 1944, plans were also formulated for a special type of bank that would promote the well-being of member nations. The

International Bank for Reconstruction and Development, popularly known as the World Bank, was established by the United Nations in 1945 to provide loans and credit for postwar reconstruction and to promote development of poorer countries. The Bank's chief function today is to finance basic development projects such as dams, communication and transportation facilities, and health programs, by insuring or otherwise guaranteeing private loans or, when private capital is not available, by providing loans itself. In 1956 and 1960, the Bank established two affiliated agencies, the International Finance Corporation (IFC) and the International Development Association (IDA). These help to finance higher-risk investment projects for both private and public enterprises in underdeveloped countries.

The World Bank has been deficient in several respects: (a) It has failed to stimulate sufficient private investment in underdeveloped countries; (b) it has not always made full use of its lending ability; (c) it has often been too restrictive in its lending policies; and (d) it has not always allocated its loans to the neediest nations.

Because of these shortcomings, the Bank has been only moderately successful in fostering economic development. Fundamental changes in policy will be needed if the Bank is to overcome these deficiencies.

TECHNICAL COOPERATION AND ASSISTANCE PROGRAMS

By the late 1940s it became clear that the agencies of the United Nations would be unable to meet all of Europe's postwar reconstruction needs. Accordingly, a plan known as the Point Four Program was launched by President Truman. In his inaugural address of January 20, 1949, he declared: "Fourth, we must embark on a bold new program for making the benefits of our scientific advances and industrial progress available for improvement and growth of underdeveloped areas."

The *Point Four Program* was enacted into law as part of the Foreign Economic Assistance Act of 1950. It seeks to raise living standards in underdeveloped countries by making available to them U.S. technical and financial assistance, largely in the areas of agriculture, public health, and education. Today, this work is carried out partly by specialized agencies of the United Nations.

In subsequent years the United States initiated other forms of technical, financial, and developmental assistance. These have included: (a) the Peace Corps, a group of mostly young people whose objective is to aid in training the masses of the underdeveloped countries; (b) the Alliance for Progress, which helped to finance economic development in Latin American countries that adopted tax and land reform; and (c) several banks that specialize in financing those functions and activities that are beyond the scope of the World Bank. Perhaps the most important organization established by the United States is the *Agency for International Development* (with the appropriate initials AID), a semiautonomous unit of the U.S. State Department. AID's function has been to administer funds voted annually by Congress for the purpose of providing economic, technical, and defense assistance to nations that are identified with the free world.

The United States is not the only source of assistance to underdeveloped countries. Since the early 1950s, the Soviet Union and other nations have played increasingly important roles. Unlike the United States, which has tended to focus on basic capital projects such as irrigation and transportation systems because they appear to be economically "sound," the Soviets have been relatively more willing to finance riskier programs, such as the construction of steel mills and cement plants, in order to encourage a faster rate of industrialization. Although there is no conclusive evidence to show which of these approaches best stimulates development, theoretical considerations outlined later in the chapter provide some useful guides for judgement.

SOME PROBLEMS AND DILEMMAS OF FOREIGN AID

So far we have done little more than sketch the chief forms of economic assistance. It remains for us to identify some of the problems and dilemmas that arise in the provision of such assistance. The basic questions involve the classes, amounts, conditions, and forms of aid that should be given.

1. *Should the United States confine its aid to specific capital projects, or should it provide aid for general programs?* The World Bank, the U.S. Congress, and AID have tended to follow the project approach, because it appears more concrete and less wasteful. Economists, however (including those at AID), tend to prefer the program approach, because

it permits greater flexibility, a more general use of the underdeveloped country's resources, and a recognition of the fact that capital projects which are really needed will probably be undertaken sooner or later anyhow. This latter view seems to make more sense, since in the long run a nation's economic development is not so much dependent on single projects as on a total program whose effectiveness is determined by the way in which it manages its own general resources.

2. *How much aid should the United States give?* Various criteria have been proposed. For example: (a) aid should be provided until income per capita in the recipient country has been raised by a certain percentage; or (b) sufficient aid should be given to make up a deficit in the recipient country's balance of payments; or (c) aid should be provided in proportion to a recipient country's needs as measured by its income per capita. No matter how rational these and other criteria may seem, they ignore the fact that foreign aid is more a tool of foreign policy than an application of economic logic. Demonstrations outside an American embassy, the burning of a U.S. Information Agency library, or the thwarting of a Communist coup can influence congressional appropriations for assistance more than the rational dictates of economic experts. (See also Box 1.)

3. *Should conditions be imposed on foreign aid?* Many political leaders feel that assistance should be provided to any poor country that is trying to improve its economic position. But problems and dilemmas of a political and quasi-political nature tend to obfuscate this simple criterion. For instance, should aid be given to some Communist countries like Poland or Yugoslavia, but not to others like China or Cuba? Should we confine aid only to the non-Communist countries? Should we see to it that the benefits of aid are spread throughout a country rather than being concentrated in a single class? Should aid be given only to countries that accomplish reforms (such as tax, budget, and land reforms), or should it be given without restrictions? These are typical of the problems that face the United States in its foreign-assistance programs. Some people have proposed that aid be given with no strings attached, but this would ordinarily be a foolish course for the United States to follow. With few exceptions, it should at least approve of the goals for which the aid is to be used, and impose conditions that will assure reasonable efficiency in the attainment of these goals.

4. *Should foreign assistance take the form of loans or grants?* The answer to this question involves not only economic, but also moral, ethical, and social considerations. In many Muslim countries, for instance, interest on loans carries an unfavorable religious connotation because it implies that the lender is taking unfair advantage of the distress of the borrower. Nevertheless, some guide for policy decisions is needed. Perhaps the most feasible guide is an "international welfare criterion"—one which provides grants to countries whose per capita incomes are below a specified level and loans to countries above that level. There seems to be no logic in giving grants to advanced Western nations for the purpose

---

Box 1

Trends in Financial Flows to Less Developed Countries

For a great many years the United States has assumed the major burden of economic assistance to less developed countries. Since 1968, however, other developed countries have assumed an increasing share of this responsibility. In 1969 America's share of total aid to the free world dropped below 50 percent for the first time as West European countries and Japan raised the level of their aid contributions.

The U.S. share of private financial flows is similarly declining in comparative terms. These flows, however, made up largely of bank-financed export credits and private direct investments, offer distinct advantages to the capital-exporting nations. Export credits promote foreign sales of U.S. goods and help maintain high levels of domestic employment. Direct investment frequently develops new sources of needed raw materials, stimulates exports of U.S. capital equipment and manufactured goods, and provides financial returns in repatriated earnings, dividends, and royalties. Private financing, as opposed to official economic assistance, avoids budgetary outlays and costs to the U.S. taxpayer.

As the chart shows, most of the increase in nonofficial flows—which have been the principal factor in the growth of total financial movement to the less developed countries—has come from countries other than the United States. Part of the increase stems from large amounts of guaranteed credits and investments other developed countries have been making available. In order to maintain our competitive position in export markets and our ability to obtain new sources of raw materials, the United States is expanding the availability of credits from the Export-Import Bank in Washington.

FREE-WORLD FINANCIAL FLOWS TO LESS DEVELOPED COUNTRIES*

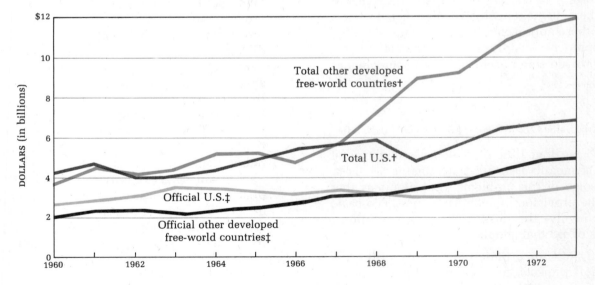

* Excluding repayment of loans.
† All financial flows to less developed countries including private investment.
‡ Government-to-government and to multilateral organizations.
SOURCE: *International Economic Report of the President 1973: OECD.*

of raising their relatively high per capita consumption levels, while providing loans to underdeveloped nations for the purpose of raising their per capita incomes.

Economic Growth in the Less Developed Countries

What has been the less developed countries' record of growth? The United Nations designated as a target for them in the 1960s an average annual growth of 5 percent in real GNP. At the time this goal was thought too high. Before the end of the decade, however, it was clear that the target would be realized. The growth of GNP in real terms for the less developed countries averaged 5.4 percent during the period 1960–1970, or approximately 2.7 percent per capita.

This is indeed an extraordinary achievement when it is considered that (a) long-run growth rates for most of Asia and Africa have been close to zero on a per capita basis, and (b) for the period 1870–1964, no country in the Western world attained overall growth rates exceeding 3.8 percent, or per capita growth rates higher than 2.0 percent. It is possible, therefore, that the less developed world after centuries of stagnation may be in the early stages of a vast transformation or developmental process. (See Exhibit 1.)

DISPARITY IN GROWTH RATES

We must be careful of averages. Although the average growth rate is impressive, there is a wide disparity among the underdeveloped nations and regions of the world. Since 1960, for instance, the most rapid growth has taken place in certain countries of the Middle East and East Asia, while the poorest growth rates have been registered in parts of Africa, Latin America, and South Asia. Thus, countries like Israel, Taiwan, Korea, and Pakistan have shown

---

Exhibit 1

Real Growth of Free World GNP
(latest data)

Economic growth among the less developed countries has been very impressive by recent historical standards. Their percentage growth has even rivaled the developed countries. And although unemployment and equitable distribution of the benefits of growth remain serious problems, major gains have been made in furthering education, health, and other social services.

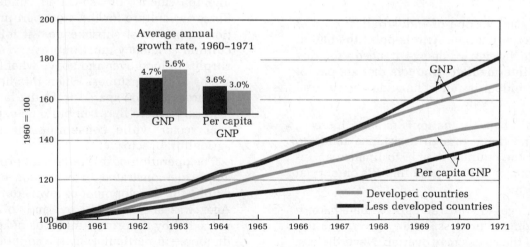

SOURCE: *International Economic Report of the President, 1973;* Agency for International Development.

better than average per capita growth rates, while Burma, India, and the Philippines have been below average.

Does this mean that the lagging countries are doomed to remain within the vicious circle of poverty and stagnation? Not necessarily. As will be seen later, certain policies can lead to higher rates of economic growth. Nations such as Pakistan and Guatemala, for example, were regarded in 1958 as among the poorest prospects for successful economic development, but within 10 years they made a dramatic turnaround.

ECONOMIC ASSISTANCE AND THE STAGES OF DEVELOPMENT

Countries differ in size, resource endowments, state of technology, extent of specialization, social and political environment—most of the factors that determine economic development. Since each country is unique, no single course of development is best for all. However, there appears to be a relationship between the stage of development already achieved and the form of assistance that is needed:

1. In the earliest stage there is a lack of basic skills; hence, technical assistance is needed to establish a political, social, and economic framework for development.

2. The next stage requires development of an essential infrastructure in the form of roads, harbors, communication and transportation facilities, power plants, and so on. Since domestic saving is insufficient to pay for these requirements, external financing is needed.

3. The third stage is one of industrialization and agricultural modernization. At this point the nation is short of the foreign exchange it needs for raw materials and intermediate products that are part of its expanding industrial and changing agricultural sector.

4. In the final stage the nation's exports increase rapidly. The need for foreign assistance tends to diminish, and the country is able to finance an increasing proportion of its capital imports on normal commercial terms.

These four stages are only an approximate pattern of the development process; in any given country two or more of the stages may overlap. Nevertheless, the pattern tends to be typical, and it emphasizes the role of foreign assistance in conjunction with private investment as the means of helping less developed countries make the most effective use of their human and material resources.

Some Principles, Policies, and Problems of Development

Although there is no single or unified theory of development, various principles and policies would undoubtedly serve as ingredients if such a theory should ever evolve. Moreover, a modern theory would have to embrace *several* social sciences rather than economics alone. This will become evident as we discuss some of the more important concepts and issues of development theory: (1) the need for an agricultural revolution, (2) escaping from the "population trap," (3) investing in physical capital, (4) investing in human capital, (5) labor-intensive versus capital-intensive projects, (6) small versus large projects, and (7) private versus community profitability.

NEEDED: AN AGRICULTURAL REVOLUTION

One of the most important propositions of economic development is that in an underdeveloped economy the growth of the industrial sector depends directly on technical progress in the agricultural sector. The reason is not hard to see. In underdeveloped countries the great bulk of human resources is devoted to agriculture, and, because these resources are inefficiently employed, there is a great deal of disguised unemployment or so-called underemployment. Since agriculture for the most part produces the nation's "means of subsistence," it follows that agricultural efficiency must improve so as to produce a surplus of food over and above what the agricultural sector itself consumes. When this happens, human resources can be spared from the farms to work in factories, where they can build an expanding industrial sector while consuming the surplus of the agricultural sector.

The operation of this important principle has been amply demonstrated in economic history. For example, the development of towns during the Middle Ages was accompanied by, and to a larger extent preceded by, improved methods of agricultural production—in particular, by the adoption of the three-field system. And the industrial revolution of the eighteenth and nineteenth centuries in Europe and the United States was the result of an agricultural revolution. This was marked by a number of major innovations, including the introduction of root crops, horse-hoeing husbandry, four-course rotation, and scientific animal breeding. The implications of developments such as these are described in the quotation in Exhibit 2.

An agricultural revolution seldom occurs without land reform. In many underdeveloped countries, agricultural land is owned by a few rich people but is farmed by large numbers of poor families. Proponents of land reform have almost always advocated the division of the land among the families working it, on the grounds that the broadening of land ownership would yield important psychologi-

---

Exhibit 2

The Necessity of an Agricultural Revolution

It is an instructive exercise in the interpretation of economic history to consider how far the discovery of root crops (e.g., the turnip) is responsible for the development of the past three centuries.

Root crops did two main things: they eliminated the "fallow field" and made possible scientific animal breeding. The fallow field was necessary to eliminate weeds, and the practice of planting roots in rows between which horses could hoe the ground made the fallow field unnecessary. Also the roots enabled the farmer to feed his stock through the winter and thereby prevented the monstrous slaughter at Christmas. This made selective breeding possible, with astounding results. The increased production of food probably was the principal cause of the amazing fall in mortality, and especially in infant mortality, in the middle years of the eighteenth century, to which most of the rise in population of the western world is due. The extra food enabled more babies to live and thus provided the inhabitants for the industrial cities. The new techniques enabled agriculture to produce a large surplus and thus made it possible to feed the hungry mouths of the new towns. Even if there had been no startling changes in industrial techniques, therefore, it is probable that the agricultural revolution itself would have produced many of the phenomena which we usually associate with the industrial revolution. It is possible that the vast developments in agricultural techniques which are now proceeding may foreshadow a new revolution in economic life as great as that of the last century.

SOURCE: Kenneth E. Boulding, *Economic Analysis*, 3rd ed., New York, Harper & Row, 1955, p. 719n.

---

cal and political values as well as possible economic benefits. But various studies of land reform have found that: (a) The economic effects of fragmenting land ownership have often been to reduce farm productivity rather than raise it; (b) in order to achieve increases in productivity, it is likely that land reform must be accompanied (as in Taiwan and Mexico, for example) by agricultural reform such as improvements in plant strains, irrigation systems, and fertilization programs; and (c) nominal ownership of land is less of a determinant of agricultural productivity than the availability of financial resources and skills.

ESCAPING FROM THE "POPULATION TRAP"

To solve their economic problems the less developed countries must either avoid or extricate themselves from the "population trap"—that is, their real GNP must continue to increase faster than their population.

Although not all underdeveloped countries are "overpopulated," most of them are. In poor regions in Asia, parts of Latin America, and Africa, population presses heavily on physical resources, and accumulation or saving is difficult because the level of production is low and resources are committed primarily to agriculture in order to produce the bare necessities of consumption. As long as the pressure on food supplies continues, large numbers of people must subsist at the barest survival level, making it extremely difficult if not impossible for the nation to extricate itself from the population trap. One solution to the problem, of course, would be for people to emigrate from overpopulated to underpopulated regions, but legal, social, and economic obstacles prevent this adjustment from taking place.

The most practical solution is to meet the population problem head-on. Various studies have demonstrated quite conclusively that (a) it is cheaper to increase real incomes per capita by slowing population growth than by investing in new factories, irrigation, infrastructure, and so on, and (b) it is not so much the absolute *size* of the population as the population growth *rate* that lessens improvements in real income per capita. Because of this, a number of countries, including Japan, Korea, Taiwan, India, and Pakistan, have instituted family-planning programs. These have ranged from simple counseling services to large-scale voluntary sterilization schemes (usually vasectomies). A chief difficulty is that any population-control scheme may interfere with local religious traditions, thereby impeding if not preventing the development of effective programs.

An interesting *economic* approach to the problem is proposed in Exhibit 3. Although it is not likely that such a plan would ever be adopted, it provides a thought-provoking exercise for discussion.

INVESTING IN PHYSICAL CAPITAL

Until around 1960, many economists and government officials believed that massive infusions of "capital" were alone sufficient to induce economic development. "Capital is (virtually) everything" was the motto until that time; increases in real output, it was contended, were attributable almost entirely to expansions in the stock of capital rather than to increases in labor employment or improvements in technology.

Why this unusual assumption? The answer is based on the economic concept of *marginal productivity*—that is, the increase in output resulting from a unit change in a variable input while all other inputs are held fixed. This concept, it will be recalled, is associated with the familiar law of diminishing returns. Thus, since most underdeveloped countries have a shortage of capital and a surplus of labor, the marginal productivity of capital in such countries is high while the marginal productivity of labor is low or close to zero (or perhaps even negative). Therefore, the infusion of large doses of capital appears to be the most effective means of raising real GNP per capita.

This conclusion, though largely correct, has been greatly modified since about 1960. Research studies

---

Exhibit 3

Can Population Be Controlled Through the Price System?

Can the price system be used to help plan the size of a nation's population?

Population control might be exercised through the sale of "birth rights." The government, for example, might decide that each married couple should be entitled to two "free births." Beyond that, a couple would have to pay a price if they wanted to have more children. How much would they have to pay? The answer depends on the current market price of "birth rights" or certificates, each certificate permitting a woman to have one completed pregnancy.

The government would issue a fixed amount of these certificates for a period of time. Hence the supply curve S would be a vertical line, but the demand curve D would be normal or downward-sloping. Through the free interaction of supply and demand, the equilibrium price would settle at P and the corresponding equilibrium quantity at Q.

Over a period of time income (and perhaps population) would grow, and therefore the demand curve would shift rightward to D'. The government might then decide to issue additional certificates as shown by the new supply curve S'. This would result in a different equilibrium price at P' and equilibrium quantity at Q'. The additional certificates the government decided to issue would depend on the degree of control it wished to exercise over the market price and the size of the population.

SUPPLY OF, AND DEMAND FOR, "BIRTH RIGHTS"

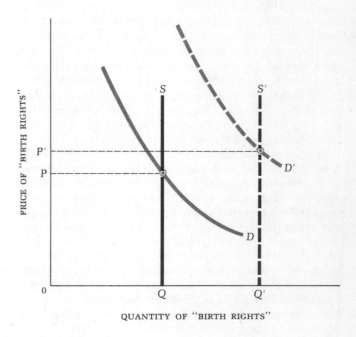

QUANTITY OF "BIRTH RIGHTS"

QUESTION. *What are some of the social and economic difficulties in implementing such a system?*

---

and experiences in less developed countries have revealed several interesting findings:

1. There are limits to the amount of new capital that LDCs can "absorb" or utilize effectively in any given period. These limits are set by such factors as the availability of related skilled labor and the level of effective demand for the output of the new capital. It does little good, obviously, to build a railroad if there is not enough skilled labor to operate and maintain it, and enough demand to support it.

2. Both extra capital and extra but related labor are needed to obtain extra output. The notion that in the LDCs the marginal productivity of capital is high while that of labor is low is undoubtedly correct, but only in a general sense. When used in proper combinations, the marginal productivities of *related* classes of labor and capital may be quite high.

3. The marginal productivity of farm labor may be low because it is employed in densely populated areas where arable land is relatively scarce. Yet in most LDCs large sections of fairly fertile lands are underpopulated for cultural, political, or locational reasons. Injections of capital may help; but increases in output would be greater if the infusions of capital were accompanied by shifts of farm labor from over-populated to underpopulated areas.

INVESTING IN HUMAN CAPITAL

Investments in physical capital must be accompanied by investments in human capital if increased productivity is to accelerate economic development. The "quality" of a people, as measured by its skills, education, and health, is more important than its quantity in influencing a nation's cultural and economic progress. It is no accident that the populations of advanced countries have higher average levels of education and greater longevity than those of underdeveloped countries.

Three main areas call for particular attention:

1. *Emphasize basic technical training.* Underdeveloped countries usually suffer from a glut of unskilled workers and a shortage of skilled workers. These nations should place more emphasis on vocational instruction and less on academic training. For example, primary and secondary school curricula should be oriented toward technical education and on-the-job training in such fields as agriculture, commerce, industry, and construction rather than concentrating on preparing students for passing entrance examinations at universities in London and Paris.

2. *Develop middle-level skills.* Similarly, most LDCs suffer from a relative shortage of people with middle-level as compared to high-level skills—for example, draftsmen rather than engineers, technicians rather than scientists. Universities and educational institutes should therefore focus on the development of these middle-level skills in order to enhance productivity.

3. *Utilize foreign experts.* The LDCs have long suffered from a serious "brain drain" that results from their most talented younger people going to universities in the advanced nations and then remaining there instead of returning to their home countries where they are desperately needed. Although underdeveloped nations may not always be able to eliminate this form of emigration, they can minimize it by making greater use of foreign experts in domestic education and training programs.

In addition to education, there is the need for investment in health. For the most part this takes the form of public health programs to reduce mortality rates. But reductions in mortality rates result in greater population growth, thereby adding to the burden of people pressing against limited resources. The solution is not to reduce public health, but to supplement it with voluntary birth control programs. Only when men and women gain some degree of control over their lives does investment in human capital become a force for cultural as well as economic change.

LABOR-INTENSIVE VERSUS CAPITAL-INTENSIVE PROJECTS

Should an underdeveloped country that is trying to industrialize concentrate on labor-using or capital-using investment projects? Consulting economists have often had to face this issue when advising their own as well as recipient governments on the problems of administering foreign assistance.

The fundamental issue can be expressed in terms of what may conveniently be called a "labor-intensity" versus a "capital-intensity" criterion. The labor-intensity criterion states that where labor is excessive relative to capital, emphasis should be placed on projects that make maximum use of the redundant factor of production, that is, labor, and minimum use of the scarce factor, that is, capital. Such an approach will tend to reduce the degree of disguised unemployment while increasing industrial output.

The capital-intensity criterion, which has received much less attention than the labor-intensity argument, holds that capital-using projects should be favored even if labor is excessive, because the potential gains in productivity which are achieved by maximizing the amount of capital per worker will more than offset the loss of output resulting from unemployment. This is particularly true, it is argued, when the developing country must face competition for its manufactured products from more advanced industrial economies. Thus, in viewing the economic history of Europe during the nineteenth century, the impression is very strong that only when industrial development and modern technology took root on a large scale did a rapid "takeoff" phase of economic development really commence.

To a considerable extent, the controversy over labor-intensive versus capital-intensive investments is academic and shows a lack of understanding of the real nature of manufacturing processes. In most industries there is little room for substitution between capital and labor because production processes within plants are *predetermined* by technology. Combinations of labor and capital are established by engineering rather than economic requirements. A given plant is designed with a predetermined capacity to be operated by a certain number of workers. Although some variations in output may be made within a single-shift operation, multiple shifts are the only way in which large changes in output can be realized.

It is a fact of life, and one which often comes as a great shock to American economists serving as first-time consultants to LDCs, that the governments of these countries usually want the most modern factories and equipment—regardless of how well these investments mesh with their total economic needs and resources. Hence, the labor-intensity versus capital-intensity criterion is usually of little practical value in implementing investment decisions *within* a particular industry. On the other hand, it assumes greater realism when it is used to compare *interindustry* investments for the purpose of noting which projects will tend to be more labor-using (or capital-saving) and which more capital-using (or labor-saving). Such comparisons can help in deciding the types of industries that should be promoted by a developing country.

SMALL VERSUS LARGE PROJECTS

Should LDCs try to develop large and complex production operations, or should they concentrate first on small-scale industries?

Practical considerations favor the latter approach. In most underdeveloped countries it is highly probable that one or more of the necessary ingredients of industrialization, such as adequate capital, transportation facilities, suitable marketing channels, modern technical knowledge, and effective managerial skills, is lacking. Small projects demand fewer of the scarce ingredients; at the same time they develop needed entrepreneurship, can be instituted more rapidly, and can begin to impart their beneficial economic effects to the community more quickly. Large industrial projects, on the other hand, have a smaller chance of succeeding under these conditions, and their payoffs in terms of economic benefits to the nation are likely to lie far in the future.

The limitations of this conclusion must be recognized, however. The distinction between "small" and "large" projects is not always clear-cut. Moreover, such projects are often complementary rather than competitive; a large manufacturing plant, for instance, will frequently stimulate the development of many small plants to provide parts and services. Hence, it cannot be stated as a firm rule that one size or scale of manufacturing is always preferable to another. The alternatives must be identified and measured in each case. For certain types of manufacturing, a large, integrated production process may be necessary in order to gain economies that will permit internationally competitive pricing. For other types of manufacturing, differences in scale may hinge on other factors besides productive efficiency, for example, size of market or availability of the right type of labor supply. In many LDCs, modern manufacturing plants and paved roads have been provided by foreign aid, while ox-drawn wagons are used to transport the goods. Therefore, cost is not the only factor to be considered when deciding on the size of plant to be constructed.

PRIVATE VERSUS COMMUNITY PROFITABILITY

Every real investment yields two kinds of returns: One may be called the "private" rate of return; the other can be referred to as the "community" or "social" rate of return. Under certain theoretical conditions they may be identical. In reality, however, they usually differ, sometimes by a wide margin. Therefore an explanation of the nature of these rates of return and their role as guides for promoting the best type of real investment for a particular nation or community is warranted.

The *private rate of return* on an investment is the financial rate—the rate which businessmen try to anticipate prior to investing their funds—and is the expected net profit after taxes and all costs, including depreciation. It may typically be expressed as a percentage annual return upon either the total cost of the project or upon the net worth of the stock-holder-owners. From the viewpoint of investors, this rate is the most important criterion, since it measures the profitability of the investment.

The *community* or *social rate of return* (the term "community" may refer to a town, city, state, or country) is the net value of the project to the economy. The community rate is estimated on the basis of the net increase in output which a project such as a new industry may be expected to bring, directly or indirectly, to the area being developed. The industry's contribution is measured by subtracting from the value of what it produces the cost of the resources it uses. Therefore the concept of a community rate of return is that of a net return.

A divergence usually exists between the private and community rates of return because: (a) the costs of various inputs to the private owner may be different from the cost to the economy; and (b) the value of the sales receipts to the private owner may be different from the value to the economy of having the goods produced.

Consider the case of a factory in a certain area. This investment may yield a high private rate of return to its owners. If the factory employs a significant segment of the area's labor force, it may also seem to be yielding a high community rate of return. However, before the latter can be ascertained, it would be necessary to consider such offsetting factors as the pattern of resource utilization by the factory, the alternative uses of those resources, the social "disproduct" created in the area, and so on.

After these considerations are taken into account, the difference between the private and community rates may be quite substantial. Indeed, a project may have a high private rate of return and a low—possibly even negative—community rate, as in the case of an industry that pollutes its environment. Alternatively, a high community rate and a low private rate may also be encountered, usually with certain types of public works projects. Between these extremes is a range of projects which are suitable for a particular

community in accordance with its stock of human and material resources. This is the range which must be sought out, identified, and developed by the government agencies and organizations that are encouraging industrialization.

SUMMARY OF IMPORTANT IDEAS

1. The per capita income gap between the richest nations and the poorest nations appears to be widening over the long run. This is due to differences in the factors that account for economic development—for example, the quantity and quality of human and natural resources, the rate of capital accumulation, the degree of specialization and scale of production, the rate of technological progress, and the environmental (political, social, cultural, and economic) framework.

2. The International Bank for Reconstruction and Development (World Bank), with its affiliates, helps to finance loans for investment projects in underdeveloped countries. The United States, through its technical cooperation and assistance programs, has also been a major source of foreign aid, along with several other countries including the Soviet Union.

3. A number of problems and dilemmas of foreign aid are of continuous concern to government officials. They involve such questions as (a) the purposes for which aid should be given, (b) the amount of aid to be provided, (c) the conditions under which aid may be extended, and (d) the forms which aid may take. Since political and foreign-policy considerations play a significant role in foreign aid, it is probably impossible to establish a firm set of guidelines that will be applicable in all situations.

4. Average growth rates of many underdeveloped countries have been extremely impressive for the years since 1960. But averages can be deceptive; actually, there is still a wide disparity in performance among the underdeveloped nations and regions of the world. A study of the development process indicates that foreign assistance in conjunction with private investment is necessary if the LDCs are to make the most effective use of their human and material resources.

5. The economic process of development can be analyzed within a framework of certain fundamental ideas. Some of the more important are (a) the need

for an agricultural revolution to release underemployed resources for industrialization; (b) the need to reduce birth rates so as to relieve the pressure of population against resources; (c) the recognition that investment in physical capital alone is not the most effective way of stimulating development; (d) the realization that investment in human capital, as well as physical capital, is important; (e) the distinction between labor-intensive and capital-intensive projects; (f) the difference between small-scale and large-scale projects, which is often more relevant for inter-industry than for intraindustry investment planning; and (g) the distinction between private and community profitability, which is a useful guide for judging the desirability of an investment project.

FOR DISCUSSION

1. *Terms and concepts to review:*

    less developed (under-developed) country

    disguised unemployment (underemployment)

    International Bank for Reconstruction and Development (World Bank)

    Point Four Program

    Agency for International Development

    marginal productivity

    private rate of return

    community or social rate of return

2. It is sometimes suggested that underdeveloped nations which are seeking to industrialize should simply follow the historical paths taken by the more advanced nations. After all, why not benefit from the experiences of others? Evaluate this argument.

3. In the early years of the Point Four Program, it was argued by many critics that the provision of health and sanitation facilities to LDCs would worsen their situation rather than better it because it would *reduce* their death rate. Can you explain the logic of this argument?

4. Among the first investments usually undertaken by LDCs are (a) an international airline and (b) a steel mill. Does this make sense? Explain.

5. Rapid economic development requires that a nation save and invest a substantial proportion of its income. What would you advise for the many LDCs whose savings rates are low or virtually zero because the great majority of their population is close to starvation?

6. "Rapid population growth is by far the single most serious obstacle to overcome as far as most LDCs are concerned." Can you suggest some *economic* approaches to the solution of this problem?

7. Evaluate the proposals made in Box 2.

Box 2

A Gloomy Dissent on South Asia

To Gunnar Myrdal, the 74-year-old Swedish economist who wrote the classic study of race relations in the U.S., An American Dilemma, prospects for real growth in at least one part of the underdeveloped world—South Asia—are gloomy indeed. That is the clear implication of Asian Drama, a three-volume, 2,221-page inquiry into development in eight countries. Reporting on 10 years of study and observation, Myrdal concluded that growth in South Asia is hamstrung by hostile social, cultural, and political institutions. Thus, development plans that seek to manipulate strictly economic factors are doomed to failure.

Instead, says Myrdal, countries have to massively reform their institutions before any real growth will take place. Among his proposals:

☐ *Governments must be strengthened—for better policy-making and greater immunity from ethnic, social, and geographic divisions.*

☐ *Patterns of land ownership must be changed—to give the men who work the land an incentive to improve it.*

☐ *Population growth must be slowed—because, says Myrdal, it "holds the threat of economic stagnation or deterioration."*

☐ *Education must be modernized—to make it an instrument of development policy.*

Up to now, says Myrdal, governments have always depended on aid from the West—partly because that is what economic theories dictated, partly because the reforms needed to produce economic growth would have antagonized the ruling classes. "The population explosion has been the only major economic and social change in these countries," says Myrdal. He hopes that his book will redirect the Western point of view on development, which he says is "corrupt and biased."

CHAPTER 38

Understanding Socialism and Communism

CHAPTER PREVIEW

What major types of radical philosophy have grown up as reactions to capitalism?

Who was Karl Marx? What radical theories did he propose that virtually shook the world?

What are the strengths and weaknesses of Marx's theories? What can we gain from understanding them?

How do socialism and communism today differ from the concepts of socialism and communism that were developed by Marx in the third quarter of the nineteenth century?

The history of socialism is a history of social protest. Protest against what? All of the economic, social, political, and cultural ailments of capitalism.

Social protest is by no means new, of course. It can be found in writings dating back at least as far as the Old Testament. But two characteristics distinguish socialism from most earlier rebellions against established orders.

First, it is avowedly economic in nature. Second, it is international in scope and appeal. Socialism as we know it today has roots less than two centuries old. But in that time—brief as history goes—the movement has split into two factions. The first, and older, seeks to right wrongs primarily through democratic procedures. The second, communism, regards parliamentary democracy as a tool of capitalism.

Each of these broad factions has, in turn, split into further groups. But despite the many different types of socialistic theory that flourish in various parts of the world, all have this much in common: *They seek to change the structure of capitalistic institutions and to establish new institutions for the purpose of building a better world.*

Reactions to Capitalism: Four Radical Philosophies

Modern socialism, like capitalism, grew out of the industrial revolution. While such early British classical economists as Adam Smith, Thomas Malthus, and David Ricardo were seeking to explain and justify the economic transformation that was taking place in England during the late eighteenth and early nineteenth centuries and were advocating policies of economic liberalism such as laissez-faire and free or unrestricted international trade, other scholars both in Britain and on the Continent were challenging the classicists with ideas of their own.

In England, for example, the factory system had already taken hold. Critics of the new order saw frightful working conditions (including cases of horrible cruelty toward very young children in the factories and mines), crowded and filthy cities, and mobs of angry workers displaced by the introduction of new machines. In France, years of wars and waste had brought crushing taxes for the support of a corrupt government, resulting in the Revolution of 1789, one of the greatest social upheavals in world history. And in Germany manufacturers were seeking to build up industrial establishments that could compete with those of Britain.

Against this setting arose several major reactions to capitalism. They took the form of four great radical philosophies: (1) utopian socialism, (2) Marxian socialism and communism, (3) syndicalism, and (4) Christian socialism. We sketch briefly the historical backgrounds of these movements before proceeding to a closer examination of the second and most important one, Marxian socialism and communism.

UTOPIAN SOCIALISM

Men have always dreamed of a better world—Moses, Buddha, Plato, Jesus, Mohammed, Aquinas, and Maimonides, to mention only a few. It is correct, therefore, to refer to such people as "socialists"—that is, as social reformers.

In this sense, the first and perhaps the best book in socialist literature was written by Sir Thomas More (1478–1535), the famous English statesman under Henry VIII, as well as saint and martyr in the Roman Catholic Church. More's great satirical classic, *Utopia* (which is often required reading in English literature courses), was an attack on the evils of poverty, waste, idleness, and the institution of private property—the last, of course, being a pillar of capitalism. More was critical of conditions in England and certain other European states during the early sixteenth century. As a solution, he proposed the creation of a "utopia"—an ideal city-state (somewhat similar to Plato's *Republic*) in which everyone was happily employed, there was ample opportunity for cultural enrichment, and democracy prevailed with all citizens working for the good of society. (The name Utopia, incidentally, which was invented by More, is Greek for *no place*.)

More's book stimulated a flood of publications advocating social reform—a flood which has lasted until the present day. First among these reformist writers were the so-called *utopian socialists*—a group of English and French theorists of the early nineteenth century who proposed the creation of model communities, largely self-contained, where the instruments of production were collectively owned, and government was primarily on a voluntary and wholly democratic basis. The chief propagators of such plans were, in England, Robert Owen (1771–1858) and, in France, Charles Fourier (1772–1837).

Robert Owen was by far the best known of the utopian socialists. In the gloomy squalor of factory life in Britain, this young Horatio Alger rose from an apprentice to co-proprietor and manager, in his twenties, of a huge cotton mill at New Lanark in Scotland.

Here, in the first quarter of the nineteenth century, he built a model community of neat houses and free schools for his workers and their families—a community which attracted many thousands of visitors, including political dignitaries, social reformers, writers, and businessmen from around the world. He shortened the workday, improved working conditions, and rewarded each employee in proportion to his actual hours of labor. Later he constructed similar model communities—one of them in the United States, in New Harmony, Indiana—but they turned out to be financial failures.

Owen's place as a social reformer is significant. He played a key role in giving England its first effective factory laws for the protection of workers—the Factory Act of 1844. In retrospect, of course, it is now evident that he was a prophet of improvements he never lived to see, for his ideas profoundly influenced the betterment of industrial life both in Britain and the United States.

In 1884, a movement known as *Fabian socialism* was founded in England. An outgrowth of utopian socialism, it advocated gradual or evolutionary reform within a democratic framework. The movement has attracted many prominent people over the years. Some of its most active supporters were economists Beatrice and Sydney Webb, who helped to build the British Labour Party; the distinguished Anglo-Irish dramatist George Bernard Shaw; and the noted economist and historian G. D. H. Cole.

MARXIAN SOCIALISM AND COMMUNISM

Toward the middle of the nineteenth century, a series of events began to unfold in Europe that strongly influenced the future course of the world.

In December, 1847, on one of London's typically damp and cold winter days, a small but clamorous group of labor leaders met at a convention of the newly formed Communist League. There were strong currents of anxiety and trepidation in the air, for although England was relatively calm at the time, the Continent was on the verge of an upheaval. Through an almost continuous belt stretching from France to Russia there was seething discontent over the long prevailing miseries of poverty, injustice, and political and social intolerance. No one doubted that a series of revolutions would sweep Europe in the coming months.

Among those who attended this historic meeting were two relatively young and unknown intellectual radicals: one was Karl Marx, aged twenty-nine; the other was his close friend and associate, Friedrich Engels, aged twenty-seven. They had been commissioned by the League to prepare a statement of principles and a program for action that would help incite the masses and foment revolt against the existing order of society. Their tract opened with the following inflammatory, dramatic, and ominous words:

A spectre is haunting Europe—the spectre of Communism. All the powers of old Europe have entered into a Holy Alliance to exorcise this spectre; Pope and Czar, Metternich and Guizot, French radicals and German police-spies.

After pages of historical analyses and predictions, their treatise ended with the following exhortation:

The Communists disdain to conceal their views and aims. They openly declare that their ends can be attained only by the forcible overthrow of all existing social conditions. Let the ruling classes tremble at a Communist revolution. The proletarians have nothing to lose but their chains. They have a world to win.
Working men of all countries, unite!

In the following month, January, 1848, this statement of principles and objectives was published as a pamphlet under the title of the *Communist Manifesto*. It is significant not for its economic content, for it had practically none. Its importance lies in the manner in which it presented Marx as a brilliant and forceful revolutionary.

But there is another side to Marx—that of a ponderous scholar and deep philosophical economist—which is of much greater significance. In most of the three decades that followed publication of the *Manifesto*, Marx devoted almost all his working time to developing an extensive and extraordinary "scientific" theory, which was eventually published as a mammoth treatise entitled *Das Kapital* (1867). This was the so-called "Doomsday Book of Capitalism"— a powerfully written work in which Marx predicted the revolutionary overthrow of the capitalistic system and its ultimate replacement by a *classless* society composed only of workers, or proletariats, who would own and operate the means of production for the benefit of all.

Marx called this ultimate state "communism" in order to distinguish it from various "unscientific" forms of socialism, such as utopian socialism which existed during his time. Much of the spirit of his ideas was incorporated in the Russian and Chinese revolutionary systems of communism that were established in the twentieth century. In contrast, in some Western nations various evolutionary or moderate Marxian systems were also founded, represented largely by social-democratic types of political parties. These groups have preferred to retain the title of socialism in order to help bridge the gap between certain features of Marxian theory and the rest of the socialist movement. In general, Marxism is by far the most significant of the radical philosophies to have emerged as a reaction to capitalism.

SYNDICALISM

The third great radical philosophy spawned by the industrial revolution was syndicalism. This movement, which was both a strategy of revolution and a plan for social reorganization, was influenced by the wave of anarchism that spread through parts of Europe during the late nineteenth and early twentieth centuries.

The advocates of *syndicalism* demanded the abolition of both capitalism and the state, which they viewed as instruments of oppression, and the reorganization of society into industry-wide associations or syndicates of workers. Thus, there would be a syndicate of all the steel mills, which would be owned and operated by the workers in the steel industry; a syndicate of all the coal mines made up of workers in the coal industry; and so on. In this way, the syndicates, which were fundamentally trade unions, would replace the state, each syndicate governing its own members in their activities as producers, but leaving them free from interference in all other matters. The chief exponent of syndicalism was the French social philosopher Georges Sorel (1847–1922); ironically, his views later influenced the growth of fascism.

In the United States, the syndicalists organized a revolutionary industrial union in 1905 called the Industrial Workers of the World (IWW). The union was founded in Chicago by Eugene V. Debs, William D. Haywood, and Daniel De Leon—all of them well-known names in the history of radicalism. The group's avowed aim was to overthrow capitalism and to establish socialism by calling a general strike throughout industry, locking out employers, and seizing the nation's factories. Despite the organization's success in gathering a peak membership of 100,000 before World War I and in leading over 150 strikes, it suffered from growing internal dissension and almost fell apart after the war. However, it continued to survive. Today, with its distinctly moderate philosophy, it is a small but vigorous union.

CHRISTIAN SOCIALISM

The late nineteenth century also saw the rise of the Christian socialists, whose ideas were the most moderate of the four great radical philosophies. The movement was started in France by a Catholic priest; it then spread to England, where it caught on among a number of Protestant intellectuals and clerics, and subsequently reached the United States. Variations of it still exist in these and other countries.

In general, *Christian socialism* is a movement of various church groups to preach the "social gospel" —a type of social legislation and reform that is grounded in theology. It seeks to improve the well-being of industrial workers by advocating the formation of labor unions, the passage of legislation, and above all by appealing to employers to respect the dignity of workers as men and as Christians, rather than as so much muscle or physical power. It also repudiates the Marxian doctrine of the class war or revolution. Among the leading forces in this movement have been Pope Leo XIII, the "workingman's Pope," whose famous encyclical *Rerum Novarum* (1891) enunciated these principles; Pope Pius XI, whose encyclical *Quadragesimo Anno* (1931) reaffirmed them; and Protestant theologians like Reinhold Niebuhr and Paul Tillich.

The Economic Theories of Karl Marx

None among the various radical philosophies that emerged as reactions to capitalism during the nineteenth century has had deeper or more widespread effects than that of Karl Marx. Indeed, his views, in one form or another, are the basic beliefs of more than one-third of the inhabited globe.

Marx, a "philosophical economist," was deeply influenced by the writings of the eminent early nineteenth-century German philosopher Georg Hegel, and in particular by the Hegelian *dialectic*. This technical term denotes a method of logic or reasoning in Hegelian philosophy. It holds that any concept, which may be called a *thesis*, can have meaning only when it is related to its opposite or contradictory concept called an *antithesis*; the interaction of the two then forms a new concept of understanding called a *synthesis*. Thus the concept of "high" (thesis) evokes the opposite concept of "low" (antithesis), and the two then interact to form the new concept of "height" (synthesis). Similarly, contradictory concepts like "light" and "dark," "truth" and "falsity," "being" and "not being," interact to form new concepts, each of which brings us a step closer to understanding the ever-changing nature of the real world.

In Hegelian philosophy, the dialectic process, through its reconciliation of opposites, becomes a method of interpreting history. Thus in the evolution of cultures we observe a process in which the higher form of culture triumphs over the lower form; in the development of art, one "period" is succeeded by another; in the history of religion, primitive and simplistic types of worship give way to more sophisticated forms and concepts. In general, history is a record of progress from lower to higher manifestations of the dialectic principle.

How did these Hegelian ideas influence Marx's thinking? We can seek to answer this question by sketching briefly the fundamental doctrines that appear in his enormous work *Das Kapital* (translated *Capital*), Volume 1 of which was published in 1867: (1) economic interpretation of history, (2) theory of value and wages, (3) theory of surplus value and capital accumulation, (4) the class struggle, and (5) theory of socialistic and communistic evolution.

These doctrines constitute the framework of Marxian theory. Although they are attributed to Marx, they were formulated during his many years of association with his close friend and intellectual collaborator, Friedrich Engels. Each man had a profound influence on the other.

ECONOMIC INTERPRETATION OF HISTORY

Marx sought to discover the basic principles of history. His method was to construct what he regarded as a completely logical system in which he presented in scientific fashion the laws of historical development, the sources of economic and social power, and a prediction of the inevitable future.

In order to predict the future course of events, Marx had to understand the causal forces that were at work. This, he believed, could only be done by studying the past. Hence he looked for the fundamental causes of historical events, and he found them in the economic environments in which societies develop.

According to Marx, all great political, social, intellectual, and ethical movements of history are determined by the ways in which societies organize their social institutions to carry on the basic economic activities of production, exchange, distribution, and consumption of goods. Although economic motives may not always be the sole cause of human behavior, every fundamental historical development is basically the result of changes in the way in which one or more of these economic activities is carried out. This, in essence, is the *economic interpretation of history*.

Thus in the Marxian system, economic forces are the prime cause of change—the alpha and omega of history—which operate with the inevitability of natural laws to determine the development of a society. Even the Protestant Reformation of the sixteenth century, which for all intents and purposes was a major religious movement in world history, was cloaked in ideological veils according to Marx, thereby serving to conceal its true causes, which were fundamentally economic.

Dialectical Materialism

This philosophy became known as *dialectical materialism*—a logical method of historical analysis used by Marx which employed the philosopher Hegel's idea that historical change is the result of conflicting forces and that these forces are basically economic or materialistic. In the Marxian view of history, every economic system, based on a set of established production, exchange, distribution, and consumption relationships, grows to a state of maximum efficiency and then develops internal contradictions or weaknesses which cause it to decay. By this time the roots of an opposing system have already begun to take hold; eventually this new system displaces the old while absorbing its most useful features. This dynamic process continues, with society being propelled from one historical stage to another as each new system triumphs over the old.

THEORY OF VALUE AND WAGES

The second major doctrine in Marxian economics is the theory of value and wages. This, of course, was also a fundamental area of concern to the classical economists who preceded Marx—including Smith, Ricardo, and others. But Marx, unlike the other classical economists, used these concepts to a different end in explaining the historical development and future course of capitalism.

To Marx, the term "value" had the same meaning as it had to other orthodox economists both before and after: *value* is the power of a commodity to command other commodities in exchange for itself; this power is measured by the proportional quantities in which a commodity exchanges with all other commodities. Likewise, to Marx and other economists, the *price* of a commodity is its power to command money in exchange for itself; price is simply the "money name" of the value of a commodity.

But what determines the value of a commodity? The answer, according to Marx, is labor. In his words:

> That which determines the magnitude of the value of any article is the amount of . . . labor time socially necessary for its production. . . . Commodities, therefore, in which equal quantities of labor are embodied, or which can be produced in the same time, have the same value. The value of one commodity is to the value of another, as the labor-time necessary for the production of one is to that necessary for the production of the other. As values, all commodities are only definite masses of congealed labor-time.

In general terms, therefore, if it takes twice as much labor-time to produce coats as hats, the price of coats will be twice the price of hats. Note from the last sentence of the quotation that Marx did not restrict his concept of labor-time to direct labor spent on the production of commodities; he included indirect labor as well, such as the labor-time necessary to construct the factories and machines which are then used to produce other goods. Therefore:

Since capital and all other commodities are congealed labor, they are all reducible to the common denominator of labor-time, and will exchange for one another at prices that are proportional to the amount of labor-time they contain.

From this theory of value, it was a short step for Marx to develop his theory of wages. In his view, a mature capitalistic society consists of only two classes—a capitalist class which owns and controls the means of production, and a working class which owns and controls nothing and is subservient to the capitalist class. (The land-owning class, at this relatively advanced stage of capitalism's development, has declined to a position of minor importance.) This leads to the following theory of wages:

The capitalist class finds, in its competitive struggle to earn profits, that it must pay the lowest possible level of wages to the working class. The wages it will pay, therefore, will be at a subsistence level— a wage level which is just high enough for the working population to maintain itself, based primarily on its physical or biological needs and to a lesser extent on its social and customary needs.

This theory of wages, it may be noted, did not originate with Marx. It was the familiar *subsistence theory of wages* which Marx adopted from the classical economists who preceded him.

THEORY OF SURPLUS VALUE AND CAPITAL ACCUMULATION

When Marx combined his theories of value and wages, the logical outcome was the third feature of his theoretical system: the doctrine of surplus value. From this, there emerged the natural process of capital accumulation.

In Marx's model, surplus value arises in the following way. When a worker is employed in the production of a commodity, it is the capitalist who sets the length of the working day. Thus on the one hand, the value of what the worker produces is determined by the labor-time embodied in the commodity; on the other hand, the wage that the worker receives is determined by the "subsistence level" of living. The worker does not stop producing when the value of what he creates is equal to his subsistence wage; instead, he continues to produce, and the value that he creates over and above his subsistence wage represents "surplus value," which goes to the capitalist. In numerical terms, the capitalist may set the

working day at 12 hours, but the worker may produce a value equal to his subsistence wage in 7 hours; the remaining 5 hours of his labor-time is, therefore, surplus value which is literally appropriated or stolen by the capitalist.

To Marx, surplus value is the driving force of the capitalistic system—the key incentive that prompts capitalists to carry on production. Efforts on the part of capitalists to increase surplus value may take the form of (a) increasing the length of the working day, (b) intensifying or speeding up the worker's production (by offering "piece rates" or other incentives), and (c) introducing labor-saving machinery, thereby permitting some workers to be released while those who remain are made to work longer hours or more intensively.

Capital Accumulation

What does the capitalist do with the surplus value which, according to Marx, has been literally stolen from the labor of workers? Marx's answer is that the capitalist uses part of the surplus for his personal consumption and part to acquire more labor and machines. He acquires these, of course, because he expects to get back more money than he lays out. His inflow of surpluses, over and above his money outlays, continues in an unending series from one production operation to the next, thereby generating a sequence of capital accumulations. Thus, whereas other economists contended that capitalists were engaging in "abstinence" or "saving" when they acquired funds to hire more labor for production, Marx argued that the funds which capitalists "saved" were stolen from workers in the form of surplus value.

These ideas, which lie at the heart of the Marxian model of capitalism, may be summarized briefly:

Surplus value is the difference between the value that a worker creates as determined by the labor-time embodied in a commodity that he produces, and the value that he receives as determined by the subsistence level of wages. Surplus value is not created by the capitalist, but is appropriated by him through his exploitation of the worker; hence the capitalist is a robber who steals the fruits of the laborer's toil. The accumulation of capital comes from surplus value and is the key to, as well as the incentive for, the development of a capitalistic system.

It is interesting to note that Marx harbored no particular animosity toward the capitalist as such, even though he characterized him as a greedy robber baron. In Marx's view it was the competitive capitalistic system itself that was evil. The capitalist was merely a participant in the great race; he had to exploit and accumulate or else he himself would be exploited and accumulated.

THE CLASS STRUGGLE

What are the consequences of capitalistic production? In order to answer this question, Marx turned to an examination of the past, and again used the method of dialectical analysis—thesis and antithesis—to interpret the historical process.

All history, he said, is composed of struggles between classes. In ancient Rome it was a struggle between patricians and plebeians and between masters and slaves; in the Middle Ages it was a conflict between guildmasters and journeymen and between lords and serfs; and in the modern society that has sprouted from the ruins of feudal society, class antagonisms have narrowed down to a struggle between two opposing groups—the oppressing capitalist or bourgeois class and the oppressed proletariat or working class. The former derive their income from *owning* the means of production and from exploiting the labor of workers; the latter own nothing but their labor power and, since they are dependent for a living upon the receipt of a wage, must sell their labor power in order to exist.

What is the role of the state in this two-class society? Marx's answer was precise: "The state," he said, "is nothing but the organized collective power of the possessing classes." It is an agency controlled by the bourgeoisie to advance its own interests, and its power "grows stronger in proportion as the class antagonisms within the state grow sharper." The state, in short, is an agency of oppression.

The Consequences of Capitalist Production

The class struggle might go on indefinitely, according to Marx, were it not for certain "contradictions" that automatically and inevitably develop within the capitalistic system. Among the more important ones are these:

1. *Increasing unemployment.* The capitalists' drive to increase their surplus value and to accumulate capital results in the displacement of labor (i.e., in modern terminology, technological unemployment), and in ever-increasing misery as a "reserve army of the unemployed" builds up.

2. *Declining rate of profits.* As capital accumulates, a growing proportion of it goes into physical capital such as labor-saving machinery, which yields no surplus value, while a declining proportion of it goes into human capital or labor, which is the sole producer of surplus value. Hence the capitalist's rate of profit—or the surplus value that he appropriates from labor—tends to be a declining percentage of the total capital that is accumulated.

3. *Business cycles.* With increasing unemployment, a declining rate of profit, and the tendency for wages to remain at the subsistence level, uncertainty and instability are inevitable; depressions recur "each time more threateningly" as capitalists find themselves under continual competitive pressure to acquire more physical capital and to displace workers.

4. *Concentration and monopolization of capital.* Competition among capitalists thus becomes increasingly intense. A dog-eat-dog situation develops as small capitalists are either fatally weakened or absorbed by a few larger ones. In this way capital becomes concentrated in large-scale industrial units or monopolies. As Marx put it, "hand in hand with this centralization" of capital goes the "expropriation of many capitalists by the few."

5. *Finance capitalism and imperialism.* Marx implied that a fifth "contradiction" would emerge from the monopoly stage of capitalistic development. The nature of this contradiction was amplified in the early twentieth century by V. I. Lenin, the founder of Soviet Russia. Lenin argued that the growing tendency toward concentration and monopolization of capital would produce an economy dominated by "finance capital"—a situation in which huge business trusts or monopolies, in conjunction with a handful of large banks, control and manipulate the masses. Those who manage finance capital would then reach out beyond their own national boundaries, forming cartels and international combines to dominate and control the markets and resources of other nations. When this happens, the economy has reached the stage of "capitalistic imperialism"—the highest stage of capitalism.

Summary

Marx concluded that these conditions, especially the first, imposed miseries and hardships on workers which they would not tolerate indefinitely. The working class, he said, would eventually revolt against the capitalist class and bring about a system in which economic justice prevails. Before we examine the nature of this change, let us summarize the foregoing Marxian ideas briefly.

The *class struggle* represents an irreconcilable clash of interests between the bourgeoisie or capitalist class and the proletariat or working class. The source of this clash is the surplus value which capitalists steal from workers, resulting over the long run in increasing unemployment, a declining rate of profit, business cycles, concentration of capital, and finance capitalism and imperialism.

According to Marx, the class struggle will eventually be resolved when the proletariat overthrows the bourgeoisie and establishes a new and equitable economic order.

THEORY OF SOCIALIST AND COMMUNIST EVOLUTION

Marx held that capitalism must someday receive its death blow at the hands of the workers. When this happens, capitalism will be succeeded by socialism, which Marx regarded as a *transitory stage* on the road to communism. This stage will have two major characteristics:

1. *"Dictatorship of the proletariat"*—a state of affairs in Marxian socialism in which the bourgeoisie have been toppled from power and are subject to the control of the working class; in other words, the "expropriators have been expropriated," and capitalists' properties are under the management of the proletariat who are also in control of the state.

2. *Payment in accordance with work performed*—laborers will earn wages, each worker receiving "for an equal quantity of labor an equal quantity of products," and "he who does not work, shall not eat."

Socialism, in Marxian ideology, may thus be defined as a transitory stage between capitalism and full communism—a stage in which the means of production are owned by the state, the state in turn is controlled by the workers ("dictatorship of the proletariat"), and the economy's social output is distributed by the formula: from each according to his ability, to each according to his labor.

Communism, in Marxian ideology, is the final, perfect goal of historical development. It means: (a) a classless society in which all men live by earning and no man lives by owning; (b) the state is nonexistent, having been relegated to the museum of antiquities "along with the bronze ax and the spinning wheel"; and (c) the wage system is completely abolished and all citizens live and work according to the motto: *"from each according to his ability, to each according to his needs."*

This last quotation, it may be noted, represents the essence of pure communism and is one of the most famous phrases in all of literature.

Evaluation of Marxian Theory

Now that we have sketched the main features of Marxian theory, it is appropriate for us to discuss its achievements and failures. It is evident that Marx sought to reach three major objectives:

1. To develop a *theory of history* which would explain the fundamental causes of capitalistic development

2. To formulate *theories of value, wages, and surplus value* which would describe the basic processes at work in the capitalistic economy

3. To establish a foundation for *revolutionary socialism and communism*

We may evaluate Marx's theories in terms of these objectives.

THEORY OF HISTORY

As you recall, Marx's interpretation of history was based on *economic* thesis and antithesis. Although he recognized that political, social, and other factors influenced historical development, he regarded them as distinctly subordinate. To him, the basic or causal forces were fundamentally economic, centering around the activities and institutions relating to production, exchange, distribution, and consumption of goods.

Critics have pointed out that this is a one-sided, oversimplified interpretation because it leaves out or fails to give sufficient weight to the many non-economic forces and institutions in history. Despite this criticism, many distinguished historians have long believed that Marx's interpretation of history provided the first deep awareness of the importance of economic forces in the historical process.

In the past several decades modern historians have increasingly incorporated economic causation in their historical studies. Although it cannot be said that Marx was solely responsible for this trend, there is general agreement that his approach to the study of history played a significant role.

THEORIES OF VALUE, WAGES, AND SURPLUS VALUE

Marx's theory of value, we have seen, was a *labor* theory of value. In essence, his argument can be stated in the form of a syllogism—a type of reasoning in logic consisting of two premises or assumptions, and a logical conclusion which follows directly from the premises. Thus, according to Marx:

Labor creates all value

Labor does not receive all of the value it has created

Therefore, labor is being cheated

It should be remembered, of course, that according to Marx the first premise is true because capital and all other commodities are nothing more than congealed labor; the second premise is true because labor receives a subsistence wage which is less than the value it creates; and the conclusion is true because capitalists literally appropriate or steal the surplus value of labor for themselves.

Was Marx correct? We can answer this question by offering the following criticisms of his ideas, based on economic principles and concepts learned in previous chapters.

Neglect of Entrepreneurial Functions

By attributing all value to labor alone, Marx neglected the functions performed by the entrepreneur as a risk taker and organizer of the factors of production. Without the entrepreneur, labor would be an amorphous mass. It is the entrepreneur who gives "shape and form" to labor by bringing workers together, providing them with capital, and giving them a purpose for working. In a socialistic or communistic society, these functions might be performed by the government or by a committee of workers, but they are functions that must be performed by somebody.

Failure to Recognize Demand

Marx's theory of value, based as it was on the labor-time embodied in a commodity, failed to recognize that the normal value of a good is as much a result of demand as of supply. As we know already, in a competitive capitalistic system the concept of long-run normal value is that of an equilibrium value which reflects diverse consumer demands bidding for the services and products of scarce factors of production. This means that consumers must be willing and able to buy and to express their preferences through the price system if prices are to serve the function of inducing both human and nonhuman resources into production. Marx did not fully understand this role of the price system, and hence his theory of value provided an inaccurate and unrealistic measure of the real values at which commodities are exchanged.

Inadequate Theoretical Support of Surplus Value

Surplus value, according to Marx, arises because workers are paid a subsistence wage which is less than the value of the commodities that they create. The question we must now ask is whether this theory of surplus value is plausible. The answer appears to be no, for the following reasons:

1. *Definition of subsistence is vague.* Marx did not use the concept of subsistence in a consistent manner, nor did he define it as a determinate quantity. At certain times he employed the term in a biological sense to refer to the goods needed for physical well-being, and at other times he used it to mean the "conventional" goods to which people become "socially accustomed."

2. *Competition among capitalists will eliminate the surplus.* Marx placed strong emphasis on the competitive forces that exist in a capitalistic society—and in particular the highly competitive relationships among capitalists themselves. This means that if wages are sufficiently flexible to adjust to the "socially accustomed" level of living, there is every reason to believe that the surplus itself will be eliminated as capitalist employers bid higher and higher wages for the services of employees. For if an employee yields a surplus to *his* capitalist employer, it will pay for *some other* capitalist employer to hire him away at a higher wage. Competition among capitalists will thus bid wages up to a level at which the surplus no longer exists.

These are among the chief reasons to conclude that Marx's theory of surplus value lacks theoretical support. Further, there is no evidence to indicate that there exists in the capitalistic system a fund of

Leaders in Economics

KARL HEINRICH MARX

1818–1883

If it is true that a man is ultimately judged by the influence of his ideas, then Karl Marx surely ranks as one of the most important individuals who ever lived. For his thoughts have shaped the policies of nations and have affected the lives of millions of people.

Who was Karl Marx? He was born in Treves, Germany, the son of a successful lawyer with liberal philosophical leanings. The young Marx was educated at the Universities of Bonn and Berlin, and received his doctorate in philosophy from the University of Jena in 1841 at the age of twenty-three.

In Marx's undergraduate years his radical ideas began to flourish when he fell in with an extremist student group called the Young Hegelians—disciples of the German philosopher Georg Hegel. During the 1840s while Marx was still in his twenties, he spent short periods in Germany, France, and Britain, always one step ahead of the police who continually sought to expel him because of his incendiary articles in newspapers and other periodicals extolling communism and revolution, and his attacks against religion and utopian socialism. "Religion," he once wrote in a quotation that has since become famous, ". . . is the sigh of the oppressed creature, . . . the opium of the people." As for utopian socialism, it was "unscientific" because it lacked an understanding of the role of history and of the certainty of the class struggle.

It was also during the 1840s that Marx became involved with the two most important people of his life: one of them was named Jenny von Westphalen, daughter of an aristocrat who was a privy councilor of Treves; the other was a gallant named Friedrich Engels, son of a wealthy industrialist.

Marx married Jenny whom he had known since childhood; she was literally "the girl next door." The match itself was a study in opposites: she was slender, beautiful, and genteel; he was short, stocky, and caustic. But they loved each other deeply, and she gave up her refined and prestigious life in Treves in return for his unstinting devotion to her and to their children. Their life together was one of great hardship and extreme poverty as they moved from one slum to another while Marx struggled to earn a living—a task which, as a writer, he never mastered.

Marx met Engels during a brief stay in Paris in 1843. The two men struck up an immediate intellectual rapport—a fact which was especially surprising because Engels' father was a rich businessman who owned factories in Germany and England, and the young Engels never exhibited any aversion to the social and pecuniary advantages which this background afforded him. Engels became Marx's lifelong friend, collaborator, and alter ego, as well as his benefactor. Indeed, there is no evidence that Marx ever had any other close friends.

In 1849, after being hounded by police and expelled from three countries, Marx moved to London, where he lived, except for brief intervals, until the time of his death. Here he existed in the depths of poverty, depending for bare survival on small and irregular remunerations of $5 to $10 that he received for articles submitted to the *New*

value of the type that Marx conceived in his concept of surplus value.

REVOLUTIONARY SOCIALISM AND COMMUNISM

Marx predicted that the increasing misery of workers would prompt the proletariat class to overthrow capitalism and to replace it first by socialism and then by communism. This, he said, would be the inevitable result of the "internal contradictions" that were inherent in capitalism and that would eventually destroy it.

Was Marx's prediction correct? For the most part no—at least not in the sense that he meant. For despite the mistakes that exist in the Marxian model, the views of its author have long been accepted by hundreds of millions of people in many nations. In some totalitarian countries his theory was adopted intact; in many nontotalitarian nations a brand of "modified" or "revised" Marxism developed. We may refer to the latter as *post-Marxism*—a type of socialism which is not necessarily antagonistic to capitalism, but which seeks to achieve socialistic goals through a much greater degree of government regulation and control than exists in market-oriented capitalistic systems. More will be said about this later.

CONCLUSIONS

We may conclude this evaluation of Marxian theory by answering briefly three fundamental questions that are often asked.

Historical Pictures Services.

Friedrich Engels (*left*) with Karl Marx and his family.

York *Tribune*, and on the benevolence of Engels who, for some unexplained reason, led a double life: he was fully in accord with Marx's anticapitalistic views, yet he also managed his father's factory in Manchester and even held a seat on the Manchester Stock Exchange.

Marx sacrificed everything for his research, an activity which engaged his full time and effort from morning until night in the great library of the British Museum. The result, after many years of painstaking work, was the publication of his enormous treatise, *Das Kapital* (vol. I, 1867). But his health was never too good; in 1881, after the death of two of his five children, his devoted and tired wife Jenny also passed away, and Marx followed her two years later. His eulogy was delivered by Engels and the funeral was attended by eight persons.

Engels labored on Marx's notes for the next several years, thereby making possible the publication of volumes II and III of *Das Kapital* (1885, 1894). Four additional volumes titled *Theorien uber den Mehrwert* (*Theories of Surplus Value*) were published from still other notes in the period 1905–1910. On the basis of these and many other writings, Marx has come to be regarded as an economist of major significance. But note this important point: It was Lenin, not Marx, who fashioned the content of communism; Marx predicted its eventual occurrence, while it remained for Lenin to design the final structure. This he did in his writings and speeches during the first two decades of the present century, and in his founding of Soviet Russia after the Revolution of 1917.

Have Marx's Deductions Been Borne Out?

Some of Marx's deductions of the so-called "economic consequences of capitalist production" have evidently not been realized. Thus: (*a*) The proletariat, far from experiencing increasing misery, has in fact experienced a long-run growth of real wages and a rising standard of living. (*b*) The rate of profits has not declined, nor have business cycles been entirely an overproduction phenomenon as Marx claimed. (*c*) The proletariat and the capitalists, at least in the United States, have not congealed into two distinct and opposing classes; indeed, they often overlap to the extent that the great majority of corporation stockholders are also workers.

There is thus no question that some of Marx's most important theoretical deductions have turned out to be fallacious.

Are There Elements of Truth in Marx's Predictions?

Despite his incorrect predictions of economic events, we cannot conclude that Marx was totally wrong. Some of his prophecies contained important truths. For example: (*c*) It would be foolish to deny that technological, cyclical, and structural unemployment have continued to plague the capitalistic system. (*b*) There has certainly been a growth in the concentration of capital and monopoly power since the time of Marx's writings during the third quarter of the nineteenth century (although there is considerable disagreement among economists as to the direction of monopoly trends during most of the present century). (c) Although capitalism has not ended in final collapse, it was certainly dealt a serious blow in 1930 with the emergence of a prolonged and desperate depression that eventually ushered in many new measures of social reform.

On this score, therefore, some of Marx's prophecies were disturbingly meaningful.

What is the Value of Marxian Theory?

We are thus led to conclude that Marx put his finger on some of the most important economic problems of our society—problems of unemployment, business cycles, and industrial concentration and monopoly, to mention a few. Most of our efforts in previous chapters were devoted to the development of methods for curing these ills within a framework of democratic capitalism. It is appropriate, therefore, that in the following chapter we focus our attention on the ways in which Marxian theory has been adapted and modified by socialist nations in *their* efforts to solve some of these and other basic economic problems.

The Meaning of Socialism and Communism

When the nineteenth century drew to a close, Marxism had already become an international movement of considerable significance. But it was a movement whose members had divergent viewpoints. As a result, the followers of Marx began to divide into two factions: One of these consisted of a large and heterogeneous majority called "revisionists"; the other was composed of a smaller but more homogeneous minority known as "strict Marxists."

The basic philosophies of these two groups are implied by their names. The revisionists believed that the theories of Marx must be *revised* in order to accord with conditions of the times, and that socialism should be achieved by peaceful and gradual means through a process of evolution rather than revolution. The strict Marxists, on the other hand, adhered to a literal interpretation of their master's teachings, contending that the workers of the world formed one great brotherhood which must revolt in order to overthrow the capitalistic system and establish a dictatorship of the proletariat.

Since the early part of this century, the revision-

ists have been in control of most of the socialist parties of Western nations—the Socialist party in France, the Social Democratic party in Germany, and the Socialist party in the United States—to mention only a few. In Britain, mass support for socialism has come from the Labour party, whose leaders are primarily Fabian socialists, and in Scandinavia from large-scale consumer cooperative movements. Christian Socialist parties have also exercised influence in some countries.

By the end of World War I, all ties between the moderate revisionists and the strict Marxists were severed. The latter group withdrew completely from the socialist parties and became known as Communists. Although modern socialism and communism have evolved as branches of the same Marxian tree, they are vastly different both politically and economically, as we shall see below. In general, since the first third of this century, socialistic governments have been in power at one time or another in a number of democratic countries, including England, France, Sweden, Norway, Denmark, Australia, and New Zealand. In most of these and various other nations, socialist leaders were placed in office—and subsequently voted out of office—through free elections. This suggests that when we talk about socialism we are referring to *democratic* socialism of the liberal reformist type, as distinguished from authoritarian socialism or communism such as exists in the Soviet Union, Eastern Europe, Cuba, and China.

SOCIALISM BETWEEN WORLD WARS I AND II

In order to appreciate the meaning of modern democratic socialism, it is desirable that we sketch briefly the historical development of socialist thought and practice in the period between the two world wars.

During the 1920s and 1930s, socialists of peaceful Marxian persuasion both in Europe and America launched a renewed and vigorous attack against the shortcomings of capitalism. Expressions like "economic inequality," "chronic unemployment," "private wealth and public poverty," and "degeneration of social and cultural values" become familiar shibboleths. In Europe, social democratic parties were strongly committed to revisionist Marxism, the solidarity of the working class, and the ultimate establishment of socialism by democratic means as a way of correcting the deficiencies of the capitalistic system. This was an era of great ferment in socialist activity.

The Theoretical Model

At the same time, some economists at European and American universities began to grapple with a question that eventually evolved into one of the most interesting controversies in the history of economics. The essence of the problem may be summarized by recalling that in the theoretical or pure model of capitalism there are at least three important features: (1) the means of production are privately owned, (2) product and resource prices are freely determined in competitive markets, and (3) resources are allocated efficiently in accordance with consumer and occupational choice. Now, if we adopt the classical definition of socialism as an economy in which the means of production are owned by society, the question we ask is this:

Can a socialistic economic system, seeking to be democratic rather than authoritarian, and lacking the prices that are freely established in competitive markets, achieve the same degree of efficiency in resource allocation as the pure model of capitalism, without destroying the basic economic freedoms of consumer and occupational choice?

This question, it may be noted, is the fundamental theoretical problem of democratic socialism.

Notice that the issue is complicated by the fact that the system must remain democratic. It might be easier to achieve greater efficiencies in resource use by *telling* consumers what they can have and by *ordering* workers to their jobs, but such actions would be completely contrary to the basic philosophy of democratic socialism.

This problem became the subject of widespread discussion in the 1930s and was finally resolved in 1938 with the publication of a remarkable theoretical model of a socialist economy. The chief architect of the model was a well-known Polish economist, Professor Oskar Lange.

According to this theoretical model, a democratic socialist economy could be administered by a Central Planning Board which would set prices "*as if*" the competitive market had set them. The Board would, for example, manipulate prices in the product and resource markets with the objective of equating supplies and demands, thereby assuring that equilibrium was maintained without surpluses or shortages. In this way the Board, through *trial-and-error*, would guide the factors of production into their most efficient uses in accordance with the wishes expressed by households—*all through the operation of a price system which permits freedom of consumer and occupational choice.*

This type of economy, the socialist theorists contended, would yield a double benefit; it would achieve efficient resource utilization as in the theoretical competitive model of capitalism, while at the same time overcoming the major disadvantages of real-world capitalism by bringing about: (a) a more equitable distribution of income resulting from the elimination of private ownership, (b) an adjustment of production according to consumer demands, and (c) a continuous high level of employment assured by stable investment policies by government.

DEVELOPMENTS SINCE WORLD WAR II: A NEW CONCEPT OF SOCIALISM

The outbreak of World War II prevented these ideas from being pursued further. Nor were they taken up again after the war, because of three major developments which reduced much of the enthusiasm for "traditional" socialism:

1. Mixed capitalist-socialist economies like Austria, Belgium, England, France, Italy, the Scandinavian nations, and West Germany went through a rapid postwar recovery in the late 1940s and then experienced moderate to high rates of economic growth during the 1950s. This alone was sufficient to prove that capitalism was not an anachronistic economic system, as many socialists had contended.

2. Various conservative governments in Western Europe adopted far-reaching social welfare measures which even transcended the liberal policies instituted by President Roosevelt during the 1930s. So significant were these new changes that by 1960, socialist leaders throughout the Western world were pointing proudly to policies which their parties had long advocated that were now laws.

3. A number of nationalization policies (involving government ownership of the means of production) that had been adopted in varying degrees by some West European nations turned out to yield disappointing results. Many socialist leaders agreed that such nationalization policies created problems of excessive bureaucratization and inefficiency which were even greater than the problems they were originally designed to solve. Further, among the more sophisticated socialists there was a growing realization during the 1950s, that by carefully constructed legislation, tax policies, and other devices,

a government could control its important industries without necessarily owning them.

These events led to a substantial change in the mainstream of socialist thinking. By the early 1960s, many of the European social democratic parties severed completely whatever remaining ideological ties they had with Marx, abandoned their traditional opposition to private property and their goal of total social ownership, and turned their attention instead toward "improving the mix" in already mixed economies. As a result, the distinction between socialism and the modern "welfare state" has now come to be recognized as only a difference in degree. In general terms, the following definition of modern socialism sums up the present position of most social democratic parties in the Western world:

Socialism of the modern democratic form is a movement which seeks to improve society's well-being by: (a) permitting predominantly private ownership of the means of production; (b) instituting public ownership only where it appears necessary in the interests of society; and (c) placing maximum reliance on the market economy while supplementing it with government direction and planning in order to achieve desired social and economic objectives.

NOTE: This definition represents a fundamental change in socialist thought since about 1960. Prior to that time it was the primary objective of socialism to replace private property with public ownership of the means of production and distribution.

As C.A.R. Crosland, a distinguished socialist and British Labour party leader, stated in the late 1950s, there is now considerable doubt about the compatibility of state monopoly and the freedoms that socialists cherish; further, we are ". . . less concerned about who owns a factory, and more concerned about who manages it and how, and whether it is working according to socialist plans."

These views, it may be noted, have subsequently been echoed by many other democratic socialist leaders throughout the Western world.

WHAT IS COMMUNISM?

The modern concept of socialism, of course, does not even remotely resemble the type which Marxists envision as the stage through which society must pass in its evolution from capitalism to full communism. How does Marxian ideology differ from this view? We can perhaps best answer this question by expressing three operating principles of modern communism.

Social Ownership of Property

Communist countries have developed the Marxian theory that private property is not only the means by which capitalists can exploit workers in order to gain an unearned share of the social product; it is also the basis for dividing society into two great classes. Accordingly, state ownership of the means of production is fostered in communist nations, with some concession to small-scale private ownership in the production or distribution of consumer goods. These concessions, however, are only temporary; they exist during the transitional stage of Marxian socialism and are expected to disappear when full communism is achieved and all property is in the generalized possession of everyone.

Government Planning and Control

A second keynote of communism today is extensive government planning and control of the economic system. The method of *command* largely replaces the method of the free market. Capital investment, innovation, technological change, income distribution, resource allocation—all these strategic economic activities and functions are part of a centralized decision-making process rather than the result of free-market interactions between buyers and sellers. Market mechanisms—such as price increases or decreases to balance supplies and demands— are used only to fulfill the objectives of the plan or to regulate certain segments of the economy which the leaders do not wish to regulate themselves.

System of Rewards and Punishments

In accordance with Marxian ideology, communist nations today do not claim to have arrived at the stage of full communism in which the state is nonexistent and workers live by the motto: "From each according to his ability, to each according to his *needs.*" Instead, they claim to be in the preparatory or transitory stage of socialism where income is distributed by the formula: "From each according to his ability, to each according to his *labor.*" Payments to workers in communist countries today, therefore, are based on skill, rate of output, and type of work performed—or, in other words, on the kinds of incentives that are used in capitalistic and in democratic socialistic countries. This system of rewards has been supplemented by a system of punishments, including various types of penalties and even forced labor for those found guilty of excessive absenteeism, tardiness, and other poor work habits. But rewards and punishments are expected to vanish when full communism is achieved, since people will then work cheerfully and efficiently for the common good.

Finally, from a noneconomic standpoint, communism as we know it today is also a political system involving one-party rule and the indoctrination of the population to full participation in the communist movement.

We can summarize the foregoing ideas with the following definition:

Communism today, as an economic system, is based on: (a) social ownership of property including most of the means of production and distribution; (b) government planning and control of the economy; and (c) a scheme of rewards and punishments to achieve maximum productive effort. According to communist leaders, the system that exists in communist nations today is not true communism; instead, it is socialism of the type which Marxian ideology holds as being preparatory for the attainment of full communism.

SUMMARY OF IMPORTANT IDEAS

1. The major reactions to capitalism have been utopian socialism, Marxian socialism and communism, syndicalism, and Christian socialism. Of these, the Marxian reaction has had the most significant impact on the political and economic relationships of nations.

2. Karl Marx was strongly influenced by the early-nineteenth-century German philosopher Georg Hegel, and particularly by the latter's use of the dialectic—the reconciliation of opposites—as a method of interpreting history. This approach provided much of the basis for Marx's (and Engels' theories. There are five major features of the Marxian system which are the pillars of his model: (a) economic interpretation of history, (b) theory of value and wages, (c) theory of surplus value and capital accumulation, (d) the class struggle, and (e) theory of socialist and communist evolution.

3. Critics of Marx have pointed out that: (a) his economic interpretation of history is oversimplified and one-sided, although there has indeed been a growing emphasis on economic causation in modern historical studies; and (b) his theories of value, wages, and surplus value neglected the entrepreneurial functions, failed to recognize the role of demand in the determination of value, and rested on inadequate theoretical foundations. Despite these criticisms, there are elements of truth in Marx's predictions, and much is to be gained from a knowledge of Marxian theory in understanding some of the pronouncements and policies of communist nations today.

4. Socialism in the Western world is conceived as a democratic process. Since about 1960, the mainstream of socialist thinking has been disassociated completely from Marxism and has come increasingly closer to matching the concept of a "welfare state."

5. Communism today is not the pure communism that Marx envisioned; instead, according to communist leaders, it is the transitory stage of socialism which Marx predicted, and it is merely a preparatory state for the eventual attainment of full communism. The future date of this millennium is not known, however, and its prediction is not ventured by the leaders of the communist movement.

FOR DISCUSSION

1. _Terms and concepts to review:_

utopian socialism	price
Fabian socialism	surplus value
syndicalism	subsistence theory of
Christian socialism	wages
dialectical materialism	socialism
economic interpreta-	"dictatorship of the
tion of history	proletariat"
value	communism

2. Why should a student of today be familiar with the nature and origins of radical ideas, some of which are well over a century old?

3. What is meant by an "interpretation of history"? Can you suggest several different types of interpretations? In your previous history courses in high school or college, which interpretations were stressed?

4. Marx was aware of the fact that direct labor is only one of several inputs used in production, and that raw materials, machines, and other resources were also necessary. How, then, could he argue that labor alone was the basis of value?

5. According to Marx, would there be such a thing as surplus value if capitalists paid workers "what they were worth"? Explain.

6. Do you believe that there is such a thing as a "class struggle" in the Marxian sense? Why or why not? (HINT: Can we divide a complex social structure into dichotomous or opposed subclasses?)

7. If we prove that Marx's theory of surplus value is logically incorrect, does this mean that workers *in fact* are not exploited in our capitalistic system? Explain by defining what you mean by "exploitation." (NOTE: If you were a profit-maximizing employer, would you hire someone to work for you if the added value he created were less than the wages you paid him?)

8. What major shortcoming do you find in the Marxian model of capitalism?

9. Marxism, it has been said, is like religion: "For those who believe, no explanation is necessary; for those who do not believe, no explanation is possible. Logical arguments, therefore, are not the grounds for acceptance or rejection. It is emotion, not logic, that is the influencing factor. This is why Marxism remains as the basic ideology of several nations and many millions of people throughout the world." Do you agree? Can you add anything to the proposition?

10. How did socialist ideology compare with communist ideology prior to about 1960? What have been the major changes in these ideologies since 1960?

11. Is it possible to have political and social freedom in a command economy? Is it possible to have a market economy without political and social freedom? Explain.

Contemporary Issue

Land Reform in Chile: An Aborted Experiment in Socialism

The following report by Professor Barry L. Duman of West Texas State University highlights some of the results of his study of Chile's efforts toward land reform.

Only about 38 percent of Chile's land area is suitable for agricultural pursuits. By 1965, land ownership in Chile had become so concentrated that only 6.9 percent of the organized farms contained 81.3 percent of the land area under cultivation. These facts helped to bring about chronic food shortages and a persistent and disruptive inflation. Of the major Latin American countries, only Peru showed an equally distorted distribution of land ownership.

Several Chilean presidents had attempted to initiate agrarian reforms. In 1962, President Jorge Alessandri, eager to placate the emerging peasant class and those promoting the Alliance for Progress, signed legislation establishing an Agrarian Reform Corporation (CORA). This agency was charged with the responsibility of buying land at market prices, subdividing it, and selling the plots to those who wanted to develop them. Due to a lack of real commitment, the legislation was largely a failure. Understandably, Alessandri was not disposed to undermine the economic base that had given him and his conservative followers considerable political power.

By 1967, three years after the election of Eduardo Frei and his Christian Democratic Party, the mood in Chile had changed: an effective land-reform program had become an absolute necessity. The result was the passage of Law 16,640 which made CORA autonomous and with substantial economic, political, and judicial power. The law provided that the state, acting through CORA, could expropriate land for a variety of reasons, each phrased in such a way as to permit CORA's directors enormous latitude. Beyond that, the law provided for an *asenta-*

miento (farm cooperative) stage designed to inject stability into the program by training farmers for a three- to five-year period before giving them title to the land.

When Salvador Allende was elected president of Chile on September 4, 1970, he became the first Marxist in the Western Hemisphere to achieve that position through a free election. Quite understandably, Allende and his followers interpreted the election results to be a reflection of widespread discontent with existing agrarian conditions. Intent on redistributing land and breaking up the power base of the landed classes, Allende's government intensified the application of Law 16,640 and in one and a half years acquired nearly twice the number of plots expropriated in the preceding five years. However, Allende's government was only able to organize about 16 percent of the seized land, leaving roughly seven million acres abandoned. When the government did organize the land, it established farmer-controlled Agrarian Reform Centers (CERAS) instead of the stabilizing *asentamientos* of the Frei regime which had not satisfied the peasant's impatient demands for land ownership.

On the basis of almost two years of Allende's accelerated implementation of Agrarian Reform Law 16,640, certain preliminary observations may be drawn:

1. As a result of landowner resistance, insufficient technological know-how, and under-utilization of expropriated land, the output of key crops—especially wheat, sugar beets, and potatoes—decreased dramatically.

2. Due to insufficient planning, the government was not able to organize and utilize the expropriated land efficiently.

3. Because of widespread economic insecurity, small entrepreneurs were uncooperative in providing fertilizers, seeds, and distributive services.

The evidence thus indicates that while Chile is in desperate need of effective land reform, any such program can only be undertaken where there has been sufficient prior planning. As became apparent in Chile by September, 1973, when Allende's government was overthrown by a military coup, to do otherwise is potentially disastrous.

QUESTIONS

1. *Political and social activists in some countries, especially the less-advanced ones, often advocate agrarian reforms. Why? What are the major goals of such reform?*

2. *What conditions are likely to prompt a country to seek agrarian reforms?*

3. *Can you suggest specific types of plans that are needed prior to undertaking a program of agrarian reform?*

4. *What groups and sectors of the economy are affected by agrarian reforms? In what way are they affected?*

5. *How does one measure the success of agrarian reform?*

CHAPTER 39

The Command Economies of Russia and China

CHAPTER PREVIEW

What is the nature of the Soviet economy—its methods of operation, its accomplishments, and its failures?

How has the economy of China progressed since the Communist takeover in 1949, and what would be an optimum economic policy for that country today?

Is a gradual convergence taking place between communism and capitalism—an eventual meeting of East and West?

Russia and China remain mysterious to most Americans. Though they are constantly in the news, their economic policies and performance are widely misunderstood. Indeed public opinion surveys made in the United States have found that of those people who believe they know something about the Soviet Union and China a surprisingly large proportion think they have puny economies, simply because their levels of living have not caught up with that of America. Such beliefs can lead to serious misconceptions.

Why should we study the Soviet Union and China? The answer is that they are the major examples of what are known as *planned economies*—economic systems in which the government directs resources for the purpose of deciding what to produce, how much, and possibly for whom. These are fundamental problems in every economy—capitalistic, socialistic, and communistic. What distinguishes communist economies from all others is their virtually total reliance on government mandate rather than market forces for solutions to these problems.

The Soviet Economy

In November, 1917, the revolutionary Bolshevik (later known as Communist) party of Russia, under the leadership of V. I. Lenin, overthrew the government and, five years later, established the Union of Soviet Socialist Republics. The ultimate objective of the party, which identified itself with the "dictatorship of the proletariat," was to establish Marxian socialism and eventually full communism in Russia and throughout the world, thereby ending what it referred to as the "want, misery, and injustice of capitalist society."

When the Communists took over, Russia was poor, predominantly agricultural, but with the fifth largest industrial complex in the world (after the United States, England, Germany, and France). To revive the war-ravaged economy, Lenin inaugurated the moderately capitalistic New Economic Policy of 1921 which restored temporarily a limited system of private enterprise. Lenin died in 1924 and was succeeded by the general secretary of the Communist party, Joseph Stalin, who ruled the country as an absolute dictator until his death in 1953.

Under Stalin, the Soviet system became a command economy with the primary objective of raising itself to the status of a major industrial and military power. It eventually attained these goals with little outside help, largely through a series of so-called Five-Year Plans—the first in 1928—which aimed at rapid industrialization and centralization of the economy's resources. By the time World War II broke out, Russia had achieved, among other things: (a) a planned economy which could operate without unemployment; (b) a major expansion of industrialization with all factories, mines, railroads, and public utilities owned by the state; (c) a virtual elimination of private manufacturing and private trade; and (d) a practically complete socialization of all stores and farms, either by outright government ownership or by collective ownership on a cooperative basis. Social and cultural achievements included the opening of educational opportunities to the common people, a substantial reduction in the illiteracy rate, government assistance for working mothers and their children, and free medical and hospital care for most citizens.

But these accomplishments were not realized without heavy costs. Industrialization and defense were pushed at maximum speed with almost no concern for the severe privations imposed on the public, and a ruthless reign of police terror liquidated hundreds of Stalin's political opponents while sending more than 9 million other persons to prison or Siberia.

This brief historical sketch is useful only as a background, for the Soviet economic system has undergone many significant changes since World War II. We can best understand the Soviet economy of today by surveying it in terms of the following distinguishing features: (1) Soviet economic institutions and organization, (2) Soviet economic planning, (3) the challenge of economic growth, and (4) reorganization and changes in the Soviet economy.

In discussing these aspects of the Soviet system, we shall often find it meaningful to provide comparisons with the United States.

SOVIET ECONOMIC INSTITUTIONS AND ORGANIZATION

Every society is characterized by certain institutions —established ways of doing things based on customs, practices, or laws, which in combination affect its organizational structure. We examine here the more important ones in the Soviet economy.

Social Ownership of Industry

The Soviet Union defines its economic system as socialist, not communist. Socialism, according to Marxian doctrine, is a preparatory stage in the attainment of full communism. Unlike the United States, therefore, all means of industrial production in the U.S.S.R. which require the use of hired labor are owned by "society," represented by the government. Although individuals such as professionals and handicraftsmen can work for themselves, they must do so without the help of hired labor; except for a few special cases (e.g., domestic servants) no individual may employ another for a wage or for private gain. In general, the publicly owned enterprises in the U.S.S.R. are not significantly different in form from similar types of American publicly owned firms such as the Tennessee Valley Authority, the U.S. Postal Service, and municipally owned public utilities.

Public ownership, however, does not apply to consumer goods. In the Soviet Union, virtually all consumer goods are privately owned. And, as in the United States, people may own automobiles, houses, furniture, clothing, government bonds, savings deposits, and so on.

Social Ownership of Agriculture

Agriculture in the U.S.S.R. is organized along somewhat more complex lines. Two types of farms are in operation, both socially owned:

1. *State farms* are agricultural lands owned and operated as state enterprises under government-appointed managing directors. Workers and administrators are hired to run the farms and are usually paid set wages as well as bonuses if their work exceeds basic norms of output.

2. *Collective farms* are agricultural cooperatives, consisting of communities of farmers who pool their resources, lease land from the government on a long-term basis, and divide the profits among the members according to the amount and kind of work done by each. Collective farms, which are subject to detailed government regulation, are the dominant form of agriculture in the Soviet Union.

Collective farms were introduced in the late 1920s as a compromise between socialistic principles and political expediency. They were meant to reduce the hostile resistance of the agrarian class (at that time about 80 percent of the Russian population) to total centralization and control of agriculture. Under the collectivization laws, the farms must sell the bulk of their output to the government at low preset prices, and can dispose of the rest as they wish—usually through farmers' markets or bazaars. These are free markets where prices and quality are invariably higher than in government stores.

The agricultural sector has lagged far behind the industrial sector in terms of efficiency. There are several reasons for this: (*a*) much of the fertile land is located too far north, where growing seasons are short and dry; (*b*) economic incentives have usually been inadequate to stimulate sufficient productivity; (*c*) continued heavy emphasis on industrialization and defense has drained able-bodied men from the rural areas, leaving a disproportionate number of women, older men, and children in the agricultural labor force; and (*d*) government investment programs have typically given greater weight to capital expansion in industry than in agriculture, leaving the farms with inadequate power and mechanical facilities. Despite the government's efforts to correct these shortcomings through various agricultural reform measures, it is evident that the Soviets have not yet solved the problem of farm inefficiency.

Economic Incentives

A fundamental feature of the Soviet economy is its widespread use of monetary rewards to induce people to exert the efforts needed for accomplishing specific tasks. Two major forms of economic incentive exist:

First, differential rewards are paid to persons in occupations requiring different skills. For example, within the high-income groups are academic research scientists, ballet and opera stars, and university professors of science; in the middle-income groups are engineers, physicians, teachers, and skilled workers; in the lower-income groups are technicians, semiskilled workers, and unskilled workers.

Second, productivity incentives are provided for workers and managers. Thus basic pay rates for workers in industry and on state farms are usually calculated not in relation to hours of work, but in terms of units produced, with special graduated rates paid to those who exceed the norm. (It is interesting to note that in the United States and other noncommunistic countries piecework payments of this type have long been bitterly criticized by labor unions as exploitative.) Managerial incentives, on the other hand, consist of bonuses and various types of fringe benefits including housing, free meals at the plant, and so forth.

Are economic incentives of this type contrary to Marxian thinking? The Soviets think not. In a *socialistic* society, they say, people have not yet been prepared for full communism, and therefore incentives may be needed to persuade individuals to produce at their full potential.

Freedom of Consumer and Occupational Choice

In the competitive model of capitalism, there is both consumer sovereignty and freedom of consumer choice. That is, consumers register their demands for goods through the price system, and producers compete with one another to fulfill those demands. In such a system the consumer is theoretically king; he not only decides *what* is produced, but also is free to choose *how much* he wants from the supplies that are available.

In the Soviet economy the state decides which and how many consumer goods will be produced (except for the free market portion of goods produced by collective farms). It then places these goods in government stores—under normal conditions without rationing—and at equilibrium prices that it believes will clear the market in a given period. Consumers are then free to purchase the products or not, as they see fit, at the established prices. Hence it is correct to say that generally speaking there is freedom of consumer choice in the Soviet Union, but there is not consumer sovereignty.

Under normal conditions there is also freedom of occupational choice. As was suggested above, the state sets differential wage and salary structures according to types of occupation, skill, geographic location, and other conditions and workers are largely free to choose the kinds of jobs for which they can qualify.

Broadly speaking, therefore, Soviet households have much the same freedoms of consumer and occupational choice as do households in the United States and most other countries. Although there are exceptions, the Soviet leaders have found through hard experience that the preservation of such freedoms provides for more orderly markets and much greater administrative efficiency.

Money and Taxes

The monetary unit in the Soviet Union is the ruble, but in effect two kinds of money circulate: (1) currency, which is used for transactions within the household sector and between households and the state; and (2) bank money, which is used in the government sector among state enterprises. These currencies are convertible into one another for business purposes (e.g., to pay wages), but such conversion is under strict government control. The dual monetary system is designed to prevent the excessive issue of currency in the household sector and to facilitate budgetary control over state enterprises.

Taxes in the Soviet Union, as a percentage of national income, are much higher than in the United States, and probably higher than in most other countries. The reason is the Soviet government's greater proportion of total expenditures: its military outlays; its welfare spending on socialized medicine, free education, and numerous other benefits; its complete operation of state enterprises; and its financing of most new investment in industry, trade, communication, and transport. What are the chief sources of the revenue that pays for these expenditures? In the United States it would be primarily a graduated personal income tax and to a lesser extent a corporation income tax—the latter averaging roughly 50 percent of corporate profits. But in the Soviet Union the bulk of the government's revenue comes from a profits tax on state enterprises and a sales tax—called a "turnover" tax—on goods sold to the public. Although the rates vary, the profits tax has tended to bring in about 40 percent of the state's annual revenue and the sales tax about 30 percent.

SOVIET ECONOMIC PLANNING

The Soviet Union has been a planned economy since the 1920s, but its economic plans have varied from time to time. What do we mean by an *economic plan?* It may be defined as a detailed design for the achievement of specific objectives by governing the activities and interrelationships of those economic organisms (e.g., firms and households) that have an influence on the desired outcome.

In the Soviet Union, economic plans have taken the form of enormous comprehensive blueprints for coordinating the parts of most or all of the economy. Beginning in 1928, the state embarked on a series of Five-Year Plans (with occasional shorter or longer ones at different times), each with the purpose of achieving certain objectives. There is no need for us to explore the details of each of these plans; however, it will be useful to examine their general features.

The Problems of Balance and Flexibility

Some of the difficulties that arise very early in the planning process involve the problems of achieving appropriate balance and flexibility among the interrelated parts of the economy.

In formulating a five-year plan, for example, production targets are established not only for enterprises and industries but also for geographic regions of the economy. If the plan is to be ideal, it must utilize fully all resources in the most efficient way. Therefore, the quantities of inputs to be produced, such as iron, steel, and glass, must be balanced by the quantities of outputs such as houses, automobiles, and agricultural machinery which utilize these inputs. Otherwise, there will be excess production of some of these commodities relative to others with the result that certain resources will be used inefficiently.

These difficulties are further complicated by the fact that the planned balances must be dynamic rather than static—that is, they must allow for growth in the quantities of outputs and inputs to be produced over a period of time. This requires that the plan be sufficiently flexible to permit readjustment of any of its parts at any point during the life of the plan in the event that the desired targets are not being met as originally intended.

How is this needed flexibility achieved in Soviet planning? One major device is the formulation of plans which sketch the intended goals of the economy for the coming year—its volume of consumption, its level and distribution of investment, its national product, and so forth. Thus a five-year plan (or any other plan of several years duration) may be regarded as a series of consecutive one-year plans, each of which picks up where the various segments of the economy left off at the end of the preceding year's plan.

The Formulation of Objectives

The various five-year plans that have guided the Soviet Union since 1928 have emphasized different objectives based on economic, social, political, and military considerations. For the most part, the biggest problem has been deciding on the proportion of the nation's limited resources to be devoted to the production of consumer goods, capital goods, and military goods. In general, the major objectives of the plans, stated in qualitative rather than quantitative terms, have been to:

☐ Attain the highest standard of living in the world by overtaking the advanced capitalistic countries in output per capita as rapidly as possible

☐ Build a major military complex with the most modern nuclear capabilities

☐ Provide for universal health and education so as to further the nation's growth and scientific progress

☐ Achieve a substantial degree of economic independence from the outside world

On the whole, the effort to attain these goals has made it necessary for the Soviet planners to follow a threefold strategy: (1) place major reliance on agriculture to supply the food and raw materials needed for rapid industrialization; (2) give high priority to the use of the country's limited resources for the development of heavy industry such as steel, machine-building, fuel, and power; and (3) give low priority to the production of consumer goods. The consequences of these policies on the Soviet Union have been painful. Standards of living have remained low compared to the United States, and agriculture has experienced repeated failures and setbacks which have been the cause of serious concern to government leaders.

The Details of Planning

A comprehensive economic plan of the type prepared in the Soviet Union is extraordinarily detailed. It includes a number of "subplans," such as an output plan, a capital budget or expenditures plan, a financial plan, a labor utilization plan, and various regional plans. A few words may be said about the problems of preparing the first two of these plans: the output plan and the capital budget.

1. *Output plan.* In the preparation of the output plan, the government leaders must be concerned both with (a) consumer preferences, and (b) sacrifices in production.

The Soviets recognize that, on the one hand, it would be irrational to produce goods that consumers desire if the production of such goods interfered with the overall objectives of the plan. On the other hand, it would be equally irrational to produce goods that consumers do not desire—that is, would not purchase in sufficient quantities at specified prices. This helps to explain why advertising exists in the Soviet Union, although on a much smaller scale than in the United States: it not only seeks to influence the marketing of new products, but also helps to clear the market of unsold goods.

Soviet planners must take relative production costs into account when they set output targets. Labor costs are relatively easy to measure because they are reflected by wage rates which serve as an indication of the "real costs" of labor—the sacrifices in production that must be made in order to attract labor out of alternative employments. But the means by which the Soviet leaders measure nonlabor costs of production are not always so clear. For example, some experts in the field believe that the Soviet authorities do not attempt to include in their estimates of money costs all the real sacrifices in production resulting from the use of natural resources, capital funds, and land. Nor do they include the value of distributing goods (e.g., warehousing, transportation, etc.) in their calculation of national income, because they regard distribution activities as unproductive.

These Soviet attitudes are due partly to the difficulties of measurement, partly to the influence of Marxian ideology, and partly to the belief that certain types of price and cost calculations are "capitalistic economics." As a result, there is no doubt that the Soviet planners must often sacrifice economic efficiency in order to attain desired objectives.

2. *Capital budget.* How do the Soviet authorities determine the output of specific types of producers' goods—for example, a bulldozer versus a power shovel, or a truck versus a railroad flat car? Such decisions are governed by the capital budget. This is a list of specific investment projects arranged in decreasing order of priority according to each project's *coefficient of relative effectiveness* (CRE)—a technical term used in the Soviet Union to mean the expected payoff or percent rate of return on a capital

investment; it is akin to the concept of "marginal efficiency of investment" encountered in Western economics. A particular investment project is thus either accepted or rejected by the planning authorities according to whether its CRE is above or below the prescribed minimum. In this sense, the CRE is seen as a device for rationing the scarce supply of capital among alternative uses, and its method of calculation is quite similar to procedures used by business economists and financial managers in the United States. The factors that enter into its calculation include economic costs, interest rates, and the returns and expenses expected on the project over its estimated life.

Adoption and Supervision of the Plan

When the Soviet planners complete their plan, it is reviewed by the government, by the representatives of labor and management, and by the Communist party. The advice and suggestions of these groups may then be incorporated by the planners before they submit it to the Politbureau—the highest organ of the Communist party—for the resolution of disputes and final approval. Supervision of the plan is then entrusted to various agencies whose responsibility is to see it through to fulfillment. In the process of supervision, however, the plan is revised periodically to correct for unforeseen developments and errors. As stated earlier, therefore, the "plan" is actually a series of plans rather than a rigid once-and-for-all arrangement.

THE CHALLENGE OF ECONOMIC GROWTH

The major challenge to the Soviet Union, of course, is to achieve rapid economic growth. All its other goals can be subsumed under this.

How successful have the Soviets been in attaining a high rate of economic growth? The answer is difficult because various problems of definition and measurement are encountered in dealing with Soviet data, and this makes comparisons with the United States that much harder. Nevertheless, the available data suggest the following growth patterns:

1. During the 1950s and 1960s, the growth of real GNP in the Soviet Union averaged approximately 6 percent a year, compared with about 4 percent for the United States.

2. Within the two decades of the 1950s and 1960s, the growth of the Soviet economy slowed down, but its annual percentage increases in output nevertheless exceeded those of the United States. Hence, real GNP in the Soviet Union continued to increase relative to the United States, but at a slower rate in the 1960s than in the 1950s.

3. In 1950, real GNP in the Soviet Union was about one-third that of the United States; in 1970 it was approximately one-half. However, almost the entire gain was made during the 1950s; the ratio of Soviet to United States GNP was fairly constant at about 45 percent during the 1960s. (See Exhibit 1.)

Exhibit 1

Economic Growth—U.S.S.R. and U.S.A.

Since 1960, Russia has grown somewhat faster than the United States—but still lags far behind in total output. At present, the Russian economy is roughly half as big as that of the United States.

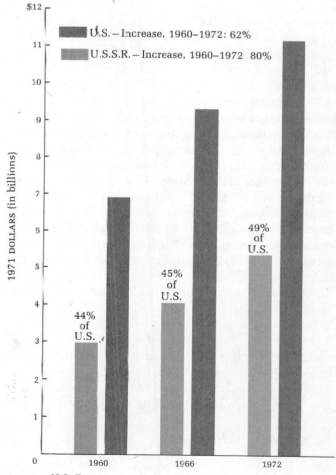

SOURCE: U.S. Department of State.

How can we explain this substantial growth record? Is Soviet success based on some magic formula? The answer is no. It is simply due to a consistent economic policy which has stressed several underlying factors: (a) the maintenance of a high proportion (between $\frac{1}{4}$ and $\frac{1}{3}$) of gross investment to GNP; (b) the granting of major priority to the development of heavy industries such as steel, machine-building, and power, all of which have high multiplier effects on income and output; (c) the construction and importation of vast quantities of modern equipment; and (d) the training of hundreds of thousands of technicians to operate and maintain the physical plant. These factors have been combined with a rapid increase in the nonagricultural labor force, thereby helping to provide the supply of labor needed in the industrial sector.

REORGANIZATION AND CHANGES IN THE SOVIET ECONOMY

In the early 1960s, the Soviet economy experienced an alarming slowdown in growth rates. At the same time, several studies published in the United States and abroad came up with a number of interesting conclusions. Some of the more important ones were that Soviet labor productivity is lower than U.S. labor productivity, but Soviet capital productivity is at least equal to if not greater than that of the United States; Soviet labor-and-capital productivity combined is substantially lower than the level prevailing in the United States; the concentration on output goals by Soviet planners has resulted in a neglect of cost, efficiency, and quality considerations; and Soviet ideology has brought about unrealistic policies which tend to prevent the development of adequate measures of economic efficiency. (For example, Soviet planners long refused to follow the "capitalistic" practice of calculating interest on capital investment.)

To repeat: These were among the typical criticisms that were hurled at the Soviet economy prior to the mid-1960s—and some of them, of course, are still heard from reliable sources today. Moreover, they were criticisms leveled not only by outsiders, but also by some economists inside the Soviet Union.

The Failure of "Libermanism"

Among the insiders was Professor Yevsei Liberman, a spokesman for the reformers who led the way to certain significant reorganizational changes that began taking place in the Soviet economy during the years 1965–1966. Western observers have dubbed these changes "Libermanism." Fundamentally, they took three major forms:

1. Production targets and delivery dates should still be established by a central authority, but enterprise managers should be free to make decisions on all other matters, including hiring workers, setting wages, varying product mixes, contracting with suppliers, and making small investments in new equipment. This would enable managers to exercise greater control over their production efficiency and the salability of their products.

2. A system of incentives should be introduced in which workers receive bonuses, welfare benefits, and so on, according to the efficiency of the enterprise. Efficiency should be measured by the ratio of the firm's profit to its total capital investment (that is, by its "return on assets," primarily fixed assets). In order to encourage improvements in quality and the production of commodities that consumers want, the profits of enterprises should be linked to goods sold rather than to goods produced.

3. Pricing methods should be revised to reflect production costs more accurately, and interest should be charged (in the form of a tax) on all fixed and working capital made available to enterprises.

Liberman's proposals thus placed greater reliance on economic indicators and incentives and less on administrative fiat as a basis for Soviet economic planning. However, by the early 1970s it was clear that the reforms in large part had not succeeded—for political as well as economic reasons:

1. The central planning agency was unwilling to surrender the real power needed to make decentralization work. As a result, managers who tried to go along with the reforms found themselves faced with too many frustrations.

2. The economic system itself did not undergo any fundamental changes in organization and administration. This made it impossible to introduce the new methods of production and distribution that were needed.

3. Soviet workers lost interest in money incentives when they discovered there was little they could buy in the way of more or better consumer goods with their higher incomes. As a consequence, total personal savings rose rapidly in the late 1960s, the incentive to improve productivity declined, and

increased pressure was put on the Kremlin to provide a larger quantity and better quality of consumer goods.

CONCLUSION: BETTER PLANNING

Since about 1970, therefore, the Russians have given up on broad reform. They have undertaken instead to improve central planning and management systems in order to reduce inefficiencies and improve productivity. Emphasis has been shifted from more planning to better planning—through the application of modern economic and management principles. Imports from the West, ranging from agricultural goods to advanced equipment and systems, will show a rising trend as a result of these efforts. The ultimate goal is to meet the needs of restive consumers—whose living standards are far below those in other industrial nations. (See Box 1.)

Box 1

Russia's Latest Five-year Plan

For the first time ever, a Soviet five-year plan calls for a larger increase in production of consumer goods than of heavy industrial products. By 1975, according to the current Russian plan, output of consumer goods will rise by 49 percent above the 1970 level—and of industrial items by 45 percent. The production targets for consumer products are shown in the tables and charts.

Consumer durables	Output, 1970	Target, 1975
Vacuum cleaners	1,500,000	4,000,000
Tape recorders	1,200,000	2,700,000
Refrigerators	4,100,000	6,900,000
Motorcycles	800,000	1,200,000
Radios	7,800,000	11,100,000

Consumer services (millions of dollars)	Value, 1970	Target, 1975
Auto repair	$53	$400
Rental stores	$44	$155
Dry cleaning	$114	$344
Home repairs	$479	$1,279
Repair of household goods	$478	$1,012

Food products (pounds consumed per person)	1970	1975
Fish products	34	48
Vegetables, melons	180	240
Meat products	106	130
Eggs (number)	159	192
Sugar	85	95

SOURCE: Official Soviet data.

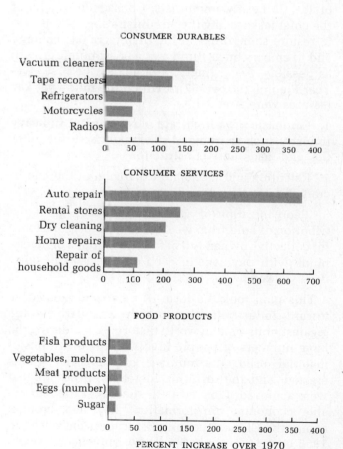

PERCENT INCREASE OVER 1970

SOURCE: Official Soviet data.

The Economic Policies of Communist China

In 1949, the Communist People's Liberation Army swept victoriously into Peking, the ancient capital of China. Under the leadership of Mao Tse-tung it took control of a largely underdeveloped economy containing one-quarter of the world's population in an area one-third larger than the continental United States.

What was the nature of the Chinese economy when the Communists came into power? First of all, the country had been devastated by many years of war with Japan. Foreign trade was negligible, labor productivity was extremely low, currency was wildly inflated, there was virtually no saving or capital formation, and farming was primitive. The Chinese people were in the deepest conceivable state of poverty, and the economy was battered and disordered.

This, in bare essence, was the economic heritage of the Chinese Communists. Consequently, one of the chief tasks facing the administration in 1949 was to restore some order to the disintegrated economy and to embark on as rapid a rate of economic growth as possible. Accordingly, it launched the first Five-Year Plan of 1952–1957 in which the following key features were stressed:

1. Emphasis on a high rate of investment in heavy industry such as iron and steel manufacturing, mining, and machinery construction

2. Retention and moderate expansion of the handicraft and small-scale industries

3. Reorganization of agriculture through (a) redistribution of land from wealthy to poor peasants, and (b) collective ownership of farms by groups of households with payment to each on the basis of labor days worked

This plan took the form of a concentrated drive toward industrialization which was perhaps the greatest of its type in world history—considering the large numbers of people involved, the quantities of material used, the number of industrial plants erected, and the resulting increases in output that were achieved. Flushed with success at the remarkable economic transformation they had brought about, the Chinese communist leaders embarked in 1958 on a second phase of development. However, this new policy for economic growth failed almost completely and left the economy near collapse. We may outline the main features of this and other as-

pects of Chinese economic development within a framework of four major areas: (1) the Great Leap Forward, (2) consequences of the Great Leap, (3) shift in priority from industry to agriculture, and (4) an optimum economic policy.

THE GREAT LEAP FORWARD

The plan launched in 1958 was called the Great Leap Forward and was a topic of discussion throughout the world. Its objective was to accelerate enormously the rate of China's economic growth. The plan had three essentials:

1. Individual output was to be increased by at least 25 percent per annum. This represented a substantial increase over the extraordinary gains that had already been made in the first Five-Year Plan of 1952–1957.

2. A dual economy consisting of producer goods and consumer goods was to be encouraged. The producer goods sector was to place an even heavier emphasis on rapid development of heavy industry than before, but with greater use of labor-intensive rather than capital-intensive processes in order to reduce the unemployment that resulted from a rapid rate of modernization. The consumer goods sector was to be dominated by small-scale enterprises using a very high proportion of labor-intensive techniques in order to provide new employment opportunities.

3. The supervision of all enterprises, except for the large heavy industrial plants, was to be transferred from central government to local appointees. The purpose of this decentralization was to encourage greater initiative at the local level.

What was the economic rationale behind this strategy? China was faced at the time with a fundamental problem of *underemployment*—a situation in which employed resources are not being used in their most efficient ways. In such circumstances there is a tendency, especially among the self-employed, to spread the work thinly by sharing it among members of the family or group. It was plausible for the Chinese planners to assume, therefore, that if jobs could be found for the underemployed—even jobs involving the lowliest tasks—the result would be a gain in the nation's net product. Further, since the underemployed were already living at a subsistence level, the additional costs of putting them to work would consist primarily of the extra food that would be required for sustenance plus the minimum equipment needed for performing the simplest tasks.

CONSEQUENCES OF THE GREAT LEAP

How successful was the plan? One way of answering this question is to compare China's economic development with that of Russia's during the first 10 years of each nation's communist regime. On this score, as shown in Exhibit 2, the Chinese appear to have advanced much more than the Russians. But such a chart may be deceiving because it says nothing about the means that were used, the differences

Exhibit 2

China's and Russia's Economic Development:
The First Ten Years

These charts compare China's and Russia's economic development in the pre-communist peak production years (bars at left in each chart) and during the first 10 years of each country's communist regime.

The more rapid growth of China compared to the Soviet Union can be attributed to such factors as (a) help from

other communist countries, (b) a tighter degree of discipline, (c) a larger work force, and (d) opportunities to take advantage of more advanced technology. It should be remembered, too, that economic planning in Russia did not start until 1928, whereas it began in China in 1952. This makes a true comparison more difficult.

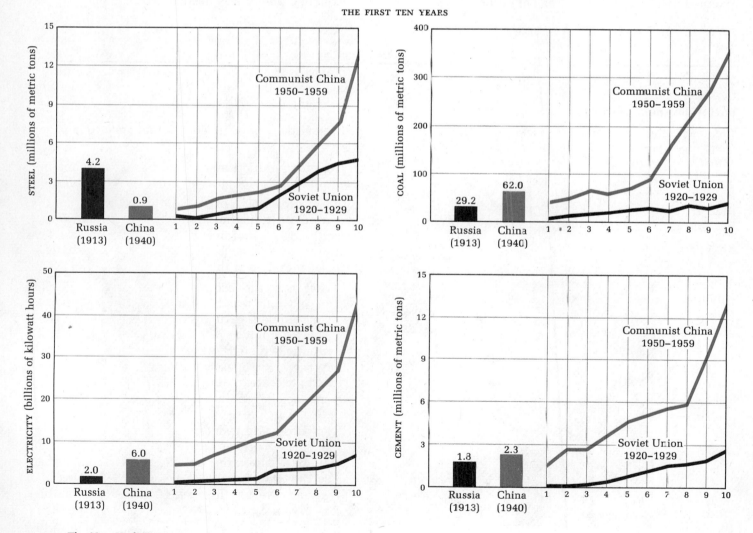

THE FIRST TEN YEARS

SOURCE: *The New York Times,* January 31, 1960.

in the timing of plans, or the *real costs* of China's advances.

In order to accelerate industrialization, the Chinese authorities should have relied more on better machines and technology, and on the training of personnel and the granting of material rewards, than on propaganda-inspired speeches and slogans. For as subsequent events indicated, to say that the Great Leap Forward was a failure is a gross understatement; it was a disaster which brought a near-collapse of the Chinese economy.

The fundamental difficulty was that the program was unrealistic. Many millions of workers were engaged in producing products that were of little or no value. Females of all ages were employed to replace the men on the farms, who in turn were assigned to the construction of large-scale and frequently misplanned irrigation projects. Tens of millions of men, women, and children were ordered to make steel, using primitive, unsafe, backyard furnaces which produced iron of inferior and often unusable quality. Farm and city workers alike put in 12- to 14-hour days which for the most part turned out to be wasted and even destructive because of poor planning and inefficiencies. And, to hasten industrialization, there was an excessive transfer of labor from the agricultural to the industrial sector which resulted in a serious food shortage. (See Box 2.)

By 1960, the consequences of the Great Leap Forward were a bitter reality. Urban unemployment was high, morale had largely collapsed, and the nation was in a major economic crisis. Most of what had been gained from a decade of hard work and deprivation had been wiped out. It was clear to the Chinese authorities that a new and different type of economic policy was needed.

Box 2

Steel Manufacturing in Backyard Furnaces

Chinese peasants were employed making steel during the Great Leap Forward, 1958–1960. Manufacturing methods, which involved the use of backyard furnaces, were primi- *tive and dangerous, resulting in the production of very poor quality steel.*

Henri Cartier-Bresson.

SHIFT IN PRIORITY FROM INDUSTRY TO AGRICULTURE

In 1961, the Chinese Communist party announced a fundamental change in development planning. A new national policy was instituted which consisted of three major features:

1. Agriculture was to become the foundation of the national economy, with assistance provided to it by all other sectors.

2. The light industries were to overcome the problem of raw-material shortages by exploring new sources of raw material while doing their best to increase production and to guarantee the supply of necessities of living.

3. The heavy industries were to undergo a readjustment in their rate of development, with greater emphasis to be placed on improvements in efficiency, cost reduction, labor productivity, and product quality.

The Chinese planners thus shifted the nation's priority from industry to agriculture. The test of whether new industrial investment should be undertaken became a question of what the effects would be on agriculture. A new investment project such as a chemical fertilizer plant or a farm machinery factory, for example, would directly benefit agriculture, and hence would receive priority over investment projects that were aimed at producing capital goods for nonagricultural purposes. Emphasis also came to be placed on the modernization of existing plants rather than on the construction of new ones. And in the consumer goods industries priorities were given over heavy industries to those firms that produced goods for peasant consumption.

One might expect that with the higher priority given to agriculture, this sector of the economy would experience a rapid recovery. But such was not the case. Agriculture had been too long neglected and had suffered too much damage during the Great Leap period to undergo rapid growth. Although there were some significant improvements such as the greater use of chemical fertilizers and the development of new irrigation systems, the gains in farm output were relatively moderate. Indeed, by the mid-1960s the cultivated area and the level of crop production per capita were less than they had been 10 years earlier.

On the whole, however, Chinese economic development during these early years of planning was not unimpressive. For the 15-year period 1950–1965, the average annual rate of growth was about 4 percent. But the pattern of growth was distorted rather than "balanced." By the end of the 1960s, China had developed an industrial base that was economically capable of producing a variety of important manufactured goods as well as supporting a thermonuclear capability. However, its agriculture was still inefficient, underemployment was still prevalent, and there was no indication that the Malthusian specter of an expanding population pressing on a limited food supply was any less serious than it had been when the Communists took over in 1949.

CONCLUSION: AN OPTIMUM ECONOMIC POLICY

The Communist regime has had a profound influence on Chinese society and culture. Never before in the country's long history had so many people been changed in such a short time. Legal equality was established between the sexes; medical and sanitation facilities were greatly expanded in the cities and villages; education was revised and extended by establishing full-time day schools, part-time evening and correspondence schools, and combined work-study programs; and language reform was undertaken to promote unification and simplification—with the eventual goal of replacing the characters with more easily learned phonetic symbols. While China is still poor in comparison with Western nations, there is no doubt that most of her people have acquired more material necessities under communism than they ever had in previous centuries. The growth of China's GNP, based on the most recent data available, is shown in Exhibit 3.

Against this background, what steps should the Chinese leadership take to assure a steady and self-sustaining rate of growth for the economy as a whole? Three proposals may be regarded as essential ingredients of an optimum economic policy.

Population

China's rate of population growth should be reduced. In 1970 the country had a population of close to 750 million which was increasing at an annual rate of 2 percent, thus portending a rise to 1 billion in little more than a decade. Although the Chinese leadership at first derided Malthusian theories and hailed the growth in population as an indication of a new-found robustness brought about by socialism,

Exhibit 3

China in 2001: Where Will It Be?

Will China, with one-fourth of the world's population, become a superpower by the turn of the century? The answer depends on whether it can maintain the rising trend of expansion it has experienced since the early 1960s. Politics as well as economics will play a decisive role. China must not only become politically stable; it must also resolve the contradictions that arise from a need to mechanize agriculture, curb population growth, and improve productivity in manufacturing.

SOURCE: Alexander Eckstein, "Economic Development Prospects and Problems in China," *The Annals*, July, 1972; U.S. Congress; author's estimates.

it has since had second thoughts about the matter and has played an increasing role in encouraging the practice of birth control.

Agriculture

China's agricultural productivity should be increased. The nation needs a dramatic expansion in farm output so that a significant portion of its human resources can be moved out of agriculture into the production of industrial goods and of services. The required gain in farm production cannot be achieved merely by intensifying the use of labor or by cultivating additional land. These traditional methods have already been employed to their limit. What is needed instead is the adoption of new technology and new practices through the use of improved seeds, fertilizers, pesticides, and farm equipment.

Foreign Trade

China should expand its foreign trade so that it may become an integral part of the world economy. In this way it could specialize in the production of labor-intensive commodities embracing a wide array of agricultural and handicraft products, along the lines dictated by the law of comparative advantage. In view of China's factor endowments, the development of large capital-intensive plants producing automobiles, steel, ships, and heavy machinery should be deemphasized in favor of small labor-intensive plants producing clothing, textiles, toys, electronics, and optical goods. The latter types of products have played an important part in Japan's economic growth and could be increasingly used by China in her path toward further development.

The Convergence Hypothesis: A Meeting of East and West?

> *The only choice is either bourgeois or socialist ideology. There is no middle course.*
>
> V. I. Lenin

Is this view of Lenin's really true? Some scholars in both the East and West think not. They believe in a so-called *convergence hypothesis*—a theory which proposes that capitalism and communism, driven by the process of industrialization, will eventually merge to form a new kind of society in which the personal freedoms and profit motive of Western capitalistic democracies blend with the government controls that exist in a communistic (especially in the Soviet) economy.

Perhaps the most dramatic statement of this rapprochement between East and West was made by the distinguished Soviet physicist Andrei Sakharov. In a 10,000-word essay that was smuggled to the West in 1968, he wrote (according to a translation appearing in *The New York Times*, July 22, 1968):

> The continuing economic progress being achieved under capitalism should be a fact of great theoretical significance for any dogmatic Marxist. It is precisely

this fact that lies at the basis of peaceful coexistence and it suggests, in principle, that if capitalism ever runs into an economic blind alley it will not necessarily have to leap into a desperate military adventure. Both capitalism and socialism are capable of long-term development, borrowing positive elements from each other and actually coming closer to each other in a number of essential aspects.

The only hope for world peace, Sakharov concluded, was a coalescence of socialistic and capitalistic systems. Otherwise we stand on the brink of disaster.

THREE BASIC ASSUMPTIONS

The convergence hypothesis, of course, is an adaptation of the familiar Marxian doctrine that economic forces determine a nation's political and social development. But it departs from orthodox Marxism by challenging the conviction that communism is the only route to attaining the highest form of social evolution. Thus in the simplest sense, the key factor is the ongoing process of industrialization. As Harvard economist John Kenneth Galbraith put it in his *New Industrial State*, advancing technology has different implications for the United States and for the Soviet Union. In the United States it must lead to increased intellectual curiosity and freedom; in the Soviet Union, to much greater government planning and control.

The convergence hypothesis rests on three basic assumptions:

1. Industrialization leads to urbanization and to many common challenges of effective resource organization and management. The skills, training, and desires of a steel worker in Pittsburgh are not significantly different from one in Magnitogorsk. Hence they tend to evolve toward a similar way of life.

2. Industrialization inevitably produces a more complex society with problems of specialization and exchange that are common to all advanced economies.

3. Industrialization raises living standards and improves economic well-being. This in turn leads to intellectual independence and probably to ideological nonconformity.

CONCLUSION: MANY GAPS REMAIN

On the basis of these assumptions, there appear to be more surface similarities today between the United States and the Soviet Union than there were several decades ago. Thus in order to make its economy work better, the United States has accepted a degree of "socialism" and welfare statism which in the more distant past would have been unthinkable; the Soviet Union, on the other hand, has followed a policy of greater freedom and decentralization since the mid-1960s.

Are we to conclude from this that the convergence hypothesis is becoming a reality? The answer is no. For even if communism is capable of achieving its economic goals, the evidence does not show that the political and social objectives of the United States are anywhere present in communist countries. Indeed, there is at least as much evidence to suggest that social and political inequalities are widening, thus bringing into question some of the underlying implications of the above assumptions. We are led to the conclusion, therefore, that even if the Soviet Union and the United States actually do come closer in the economic sphere, there are still major if not unbridgeable gaps over the traditions, value systems, and goals of the two societies.

SUMMARY OF IMPORTANT IDEAS

1. Since the late 1920s, the Soviet system has been a command economy. Its primary objective has been to raise itself to the status of a major industrial and military power. Through state ownership of industry and extensive planning, it has succeeded in achieving these fundamental goals. But its citizens have paid a heavy cost in terms of deprivation of consumer goods and lack of political and economic freedoms.

2. The major challenge to the Soviet Union is to achieve rapid economic growth. It has sought to accomplish this goal through various reorganizations and changes within the economy. Although Russia's rate of economic growth has been faster than that of the United States, Russia still lags far behind in total output of goods and services.

3. The Chinese economy, like other command systems, has also sought vigorous growth. In its formal planning since 1952, it has emphasized a high rate of investment in heavy industry, reorganization of agriculture to achieve greater efficiency in food and raw materials production, and expansion of handicraft and small-scale industries. Despite some serious setbacks, the long-run growth of China's GNP under communist leadership has been reasonably

satisfactory—averaging 4 to 5 percent annually. Its ability to sustain this rate of expansion will depend on whether it can maintain political stability, curb population growth, improve agricultural productivity, and expand exports in those commodities in which it has comparative advantages—such as agricultural and handicraft products.

4. Some observers contend that the process of industrialization must lead eventually to a convergence of communism and capitalism—a meeting of East and West. Even if this hypothesis were valid on economic grounds, which is doubtful, it overlooks the traditions and goals which make the Soviet Union and the United States vastly different in their institutions and value systems.

FOR DISCUSSION

1. *Terms and concepts to review:*

planned economy	Great Leap Forward
state farms	underemployment
collective farms	(disguised
economic plan	unemployment)
coefficient of relative	convergence hypothesis
effectiveness (CRE)	

2. Since the Soviet Union is a centrally directed and collectivist economy, there is no competition as in American capitalism. True or false? Explain.

3. Why would a socialist economy such as that of the Soviet Union want to employ the capitalistic device of providing economic incentives? What types of incentives do they use?

4. Is there freedom of consumer choice in the Soviet Union? Is there consumer sovereignty? Explain.

5. Which would you suggest as a better guide for judging the efficiency of firms in the United States and in the Soviet Union: profits or sales? What are some of the assumptions underlying your answer?

6. What criteria would you use in judging whether one nation's economy is better than another's? Are there noneconomic criteria too?

7. Why do the Soviet authorities want to engage in the complex and difficult task of planning? Why do they not simply let a free-market system allocate the resources and distribute the income for them?

8. What are some of the "capitalistic" practices that the Soviet Union has adopted over the years? Do the Soviets view these as a step toward capitalism? Explain.

9. Was China's Great Leap Forward a success or a failure? Discuss.

10. What steps should China take to improve its rate of economic development and to achieve balanced growth?

Petroleum and Poverty in the Middle East: Can You Buy Development with Oil?*

In the Middle East there are two countries whose sharply contrasting paths of economic growth dramatize a crucial question facing every developing society. Turkey is a poor country which has had to pay its way with a hodgepodge of exports: raisins, hazelnuts, and tobacco. Nevertheless, along with sweeping reforms of her society has come slow, steady economic growth, so that after Israel, Turkey now has the most advanced economy in the region. Her neighbor Iran, on the other hand, appears to float on oil. She is now the world's second largest petroleum exporter, but paradoxically her economy remained stagnant until the mid-1960s. Social reform has been slower and far less vigorous than in Turkey. Thus Turkey with little oil and early social reform, and Iran with $2 billion annual petroleum revenues and little social reform, pose a fundamental question: If a society is loaded down with archaic and/or corrupt institutions, will the application of massive doses of capital (foreign aid or oil revenues) be able to cut through the social stagnation and produce growth? Or, will the society, unable to absorb the capital, produce only luxuries for the few and armaments for the state, but provide little true modernization of the economy and no change in the lives of the vast bulk of the population?

Oil—Revolution and Growth in Iran

Since 1960 Iran has been riding the crest of an oil boom. Has this produced growth? It would seem to have, because Iran is now one of the fastest growing countries in the world and is generating such rapid increases in per

*I am grateful to George E. Wright, Jr., of the Center for Research on Economic Development, University of Michigan, for providing this case.

capita income that she may achieve present British levels by the end of this century.

Such a cursory conclusion, however, hides much of the real dynamics of oil. Iran had been receiving massive increases in oil revenue since 1954, but her rate of growth between 1959 and 1965 was not that much higher than Turkey's. (See Tables 1 and 2.) Turkey, possessing no magic pot of liquid gold, has been forced to plod steadily along and until very recently lived from day to day in an almost continuous foreign-exchange crisis. At times her industrial plants have shut down simply because there was no international credit left to purchase necessary raw materials. In addition, in 1960 she suffered through a *coup* which brought the economy to a virtual standstill. Given Turkey's disadvantages, Iranian growth before 1965 seems hardly spectacular by comparison.

This point is clearly emphasized if we consider oil as totally foreign to the real domestic economy of Iran—as a sector controlled by a foreign corporation for a foreign market. If we subtract out this "foreign enclave" from GNP, how has the rest of the economy,

that is, non-oil GNP, been performing? The adjusted GNP given in Table 1 provides the answer. Quite clearly, prior to 1965 the difference between the two nations narrows. If oil is the drive engine of Iran, providing the resources which generate growth in the domestic economy, then it was an inefficient and poorly tuned engine for growth. From 1959 to 1965 every 10 percent increase in the oil sector generated only a 4.7 percent increase in the rest of the economy (rate of growth of adjusted GNP ÷ rate of growth of oil sector = 5.7 ÷ 12.2 = .47).

This sluggish performance, leading to increasing inequities and discontent, finally forced the Shah of Iran to take action. Disbanding the landlord-dominated parliament, he announced a new program of reform. The key was a comprehensive land-reform program to which was added an extensive rural cooperative system and a Literacy Corps, Health Corps, and Development Corps, paramilitary cadres of urban-educated people to bring development to the villages. Profit-sharing by large industrial concerns was required, all forests and water resources were nationalized, and exten-

Table 1

ANNUAL RATES OF GROWTH OF GNP
(at constant prices in percent)

	1959–1965		1965–1970	
	Turkey (percent)	Iran (percent)	Turkey (percent)	Iran (percent)
Agriculture	1.3	2.6	4.9	3.6
Industry	5.9	9.9	10.3	14.7
Oil and mining	5.6	12.2	4.9	15.2
Public services and utilities	6.7	11.9	7.1	17.2
Other services	6.7	4.4	7.7	12.1
GNP	4.5	6.5	7.3	11.6
Adjusted GNP	4.4	5.7	6.9	11.0

Table 2

COMPOSITION OF GNP
(at constant prices in percent)

| | 1959 | | 1971 | |
	Turkey (percent)	Iran (percent)	Turkey (percent)	Iran (percent)
Agriculture	44.0	30.4	30.4	14.8
Industry and mines	15.2	10.5	20.1	14.2
Oil		16.8		26.5
Construction	6.3	3.9	6.6	3.7
Water and power	4.8	0.4	1.4	2.3
Transportation/ communication	6.7	7.7	6.9	6.1
Public services	8.3	8.2	11.0	12.5
Other services	19.0	22.1	23.5	19.8

sive administrative reforms were promised. This comprehensive program was instantly tagged the "White Revolution," the road to the future between "black reaction" and "red destruction."

Explaining Iran's Boom: Too Many Causes

The implementation of this reform plan has come at a steady, if sometimes sluggish, pace. Though there is debate over actually how much has been accomplished, land reform has reached every corner of the country and has been effective enough to diminish the political power of the landed aristocracy and cause considerable dislocation of some rural poor. The striking fact, however, is that immediately following the implementation of the White Revolution, the economy began a sustained and accelerating boom as sum-marized in the 1965–1971 portion of Table 1. The regime is convinced that the Shah's White Revolution loosened the bonds which fettered the society, vastly increasing the capital-absorbing capacity of the economy and allowing Iran to make use of her oil revenues. The critics of the government hold that this is nonsense and view the so-called boom in GNP as reflecting only mammoth oil revenues feeding overblown bureaucratic salaries and overseas-arms purchases. They see no real structural change; only economic growth, but no real development.

Other observers point to structural changes not associated with the White Revolution. In the late 1950s Iran started creating institutions to control her economy: a large private banking network, a central bank to manage the money supply, a centralized Ministry of Water and Power, and a large state Plan Organization with a competent staff. These basic changes, it is argued, plus the pursuit of highly expansionary monetary and fiscal policies have played a key role in generating growth.

Finally we come to the basic problem: In the case of Iran, has the application of massive amounts of capital overridden the institutional rigidities and created a development boom? Or is the boom really a Middle Eastern mirage, the façade of growth without any real change? Or is the boom real, but caused by rapid social change allowing the economy to use the flood of capital?

QUESTIONS

1. *Is there a difference between economic growth and economic development? Using Tables 1 and 2, can we argue that Iran has simply been enjoying more foreign income while experiencing little development?*

2. *The Shah's White Revolution was basically concerned with restructuring agriculture. Land was redistributed and the credit and development programs extensively implemented. Can the White Revolution explain the boom? Does the experience of Iran and Turkey confirm the hypothesis often advanced that an agricultural revolution must precede an industrial revolution?*

3. *Has the ability of the oil sector to transmit growth to the rest of the economy changed between 1959–1965 and 1965–1970? What can account for the change? How much of Iranian growth is due to these changes?*

References and
Reading Suggestions

PART 1: THE PROBLEM AND ITS SETTING

BJORK, GORDON C., *Private Enterprise and Public Interest*, Prentice-Hall, 1969.

BOULDING, KENNETH E., *Economic Analysis: Microeconomics*, 4th ed., Harper & Row, 1966, vol. 2. A classic exposition of supply and demand, the market system, and related topics.

———, *Principles of Economic Policy*, Prentice-Hall, 1958. Discusses a variety of economic issues, many of which are as timely today as when they were first written.

DILLARD, DUDLEY, "Capitalism," *Encyclopaedia Britannica*, 1968. Analyzes the changing nature of capitalism and some of today's important problems.

EBENSTEIN, WILLIAM, *Today's Isms*, 6th ed., Prentice-Hall, 1970. Emphasizes the politics and political economy of capitalism.

ECKSTEIN, OTTO, *Public Finance*, 3rd ed., Prentice-Hall, 1973. A concise and lucid discussion of public goods, taxation, and other topics in public finance.

FRIEDMAN, MILTON, *Capitalism and Freedom*, University of Chicago Press, 1962. A survey of many timely, interesting and controversial issues, by a leading economist and libertarian.

GALBRAITH, JOHN KENNETH, *Economics and the Public Purpose*, Houghton Mifflin, 1973. Synthesizes the author's views on American capitalism today.

GURLEY, JOHN G., "The State of Political Economy," *American Economic Review*, May, 1971. A radical critique of mainstream economics.

HAVEMAN, ROBERT HENRY, *The Economics of the Public Sector*, Wiley, 1970. Especially recommended for its analyses of public goods.

HUMPHREY, THOMAS, M., "Income Distribution and Its Measurement," *Monthly Review*, Federal Reserve Bank of Richmond, August and October, 1971.

KRISTOL, IRVING, "When Virtue Loses All Her Loveliness—Some Reflections on Capitalism and 'The Free Society,'" *The Public Interest*, Fall, 1970, pp. 3–15. A thoughtful and stimulating essay, by a prominent conservative social philosopher.

LOUCKS, WILLIAM N., and WILLIAM G. WHITNEY, *Comparative Economic Systems*, 9th ed., Harper & Row, 1973. Surveys of capitalism and alternative economic systems. A classic textbook.

MERRILL LYNCH, PIERCE, FENNER & SMITH, INC., *How To Read a Financial Report*, rev. ed., 1968. A free booklet explaining accounting statements, written for the individual investor.

MUSGRAVE, RICHARD A., and PEGGY B. MUSGRAVE, *Public Finance in Theory and Practice*, McGraw-Hill, 1973. Presents many applications and uses of public finance.

PECHMAN, JOSEPH A., *Federal Tax Policy*, rev. ed., Norton, 1972. Provides critical evaluations of tax policy.

ROSE, SANFORD, "The Truth About Income Inequality in the U.S.," *Fortune*, Dec., 1972.

SCHUMPETER, JOSEPH A., *Capitalism, Socialism, and Democracy*, 3rd ed., Harper & Row, 1950. A profound treatise, much of it within the grasp of beginning students.

STIGLER, GEORGE J., *The Theory of Price*, Macmillan, 1949. (See also 3rd ed., 1966, chap. 1.) A classic discussion of the scope and method of economics.

UPTON, LETITIA, and NANCY LYONS, *Basic Facts: Distribution of Personal Income and Wealth in the United States*, Cambridge Institute, 1972.

PART 2: NATIONAL INCOME, EMPLOYMENT, AND FISCAL POLICY

ABRAHAM, WILLIAM I., *National Income and Economic Accounting*, Prentice-Hall, 1969.

DAVIS, J. RONNIE, *The New Economics and the Old Economists*, Iowa State University Press, 1971. A provocative study, pointing out that some leading American economists of the early 1930s, including traditionally conservative University of Chicago economists, were more Keynesian than Keynes.

DILLARD, DUDLEY, *The Economics of John Maynard Keynes*, Prentice-Hall, 1948. A classic elementary exposition of Keynesian ideas.

Economic Report of the President, annual.

GORDON, R. A., "How Obsolete Is the Business Cycle?" *The Public Interest*, Fall, 1970, pp. 127–139.

GORDON, ROBERT J., "Steady Anticipated Inflation: Mirage or Oasis?" *Brookings Papers on Economic Activity*, The Brookings Institution, 1971, vol. 2, pp. 499–510.

HEILBRONER, ROBERT L., and PETER L. BERNSTEIN, *A Primer on Government Spending*, 2nd ed., Random House, 1971.

HOSKINS, W. LEE, "Inflation: Gainers and Losers," *Business Review*, Federal Reserve Bank of Philadelphia, February, 1970. Illustrates the calculations of gains and losses from inflation.

MCKENNA, JOSEPH R., *Aggregate Economic Analysis*, 4th ed., Dryden, 1972.

OKUN, ARTHUR M., "Should GNP Measure Social Welfare?" *Survey of Current Business*, July, 1971, part 2; and *Brookings Bulletin*, Summer, 1971.

———(ed.), *The Battle Against Unemployment*, rev. ed., Norton, 1972, part II.

———, *The Political Economy of Prosperity*, Norton, 1970.

ROSEN, SAM, *National Income and Other Social Accounts*, Holt, Rinehart and Winston, 1972.

SCHULTZE, CHARLES L., *National Income Analysis*, 3rd ed., Prentice-Hall, 1971.

SHAPIRO, EDWARD, *Macroeconomic Analysis*, 3rd ed., Harcourt Brace Jovanovich, 1973. An excellent undergraduate text, perhaps the clearest at the intermediate level.

SIRKIN, GERALD, *Introduction to Macroeconomic Theory*, 3rd ed., Irwin, 1970.

U.S. DEPARTMENT OF COMMERCE, "The Economic Accounts of the United States: Retrospect & Prospect," *Survey of Current Business*, Anniversary Issue, July, 1971.

Brief essays by 43 well-known economists on various matters pertaining to national-income accounting.

PART 3: MONEY, BANKING, AND MONETARY POLICY: THE FISCAL-MONETARY MIX

ANGELL, N., *The Story of Money*, Stokes, 1929. A classic history of money.

BACH, GEORGE L., "Price Stability and Full Employment Too?" *Harvard Business Review*, Sept.–Oct., 1971, pp. 68–78.

BERNSTEIN, PETER L., *A Primer on Money, Banking, and Gold*, 2nd. ed., Random House, 1967, part 3.

BRIET, WILLIAM, and ROGER L. RANSOM, *The Academic Scribblers*, Holt, Rinehart and Winston, 1971. Includes a delightful essay on Milton Friedman's ideas and contributions.

CHANDLER, LESTER V., *The Economics of Money and Banking*, 6th ed., Harper & Row, 1973.

COCHRAN, JOHN A., *Money, Banking, and the Economy*, 2nd ed., Macmillan, 1971.

COX, WILLIAM N., III, "The Money Supply Controversy," *Monthly Review*, Federal Reserve Bank of Atlanta, June, 1969. An excellent survey of fiscal-monetary issues. Much of it served as the basis for portions of the discussion on stabilization policy.

DILLARD, DUDLEY, *The Economics of John Maynard Keynes*, Prentice-Hall, 1948. A lucid, elementary exposition of Keynesian monetary theory.

DOUGALL, HERBERT E., *Capital Markets and Institutions*, 2nd ed., Prentice-Hall, 1970.

DUESENBERRY, JAMES S., *Money and Credit: Impact and Control*, 3rd ed., Prentice-Hall, 1972.

ECKSTEIN, OTTO, and ROGER BRINNER, *The Inflation Process in the United States*, Joint Economic Committee, Congress of the United States, Washington, D.C., 1972.

FAND, DAVID I., "Some Issues in Monetary Economics," *Review*, Federal Reserve Bank of St. Louis, January, 1970, pp. 10–27.

FEDERAL RESERVE BANK OF CLEVELAND, *Money Market Instruments*, 3rd ed., 1970.

FEDERAL RESERVE BANK OF RICHMOND, *Instruments of the Money Market*, 2nd ed., 1970.

———, *The Federal Reserve at Work*, 5th ed., 1971.

FRIEDMAN, MILTON, "The Role of Monetary Policy," *The American Economic Review*, March, 1968, pp. 1–17. A highly readable article by the leading monetarist economist.

GOLDSMITH, RAYMOND W., *Financial Institutions*, Random House, 1968.

HABERLER, GOTTFRIED, "Incomes Policy and Inflation: Some Further Reflections," *The American Economic Review*, May, 1972, pp. 234–41. Very readable discussion for beginning students.

HOUTHAKKER, HENDRIK, "Are Controls the Answer?" *Review of Economics and Statistics*, Aug., 1972, pp. 231–34. A concise and lucid discussion.

HUMPHREY, THOMAS M., "The Economics of Incomes Policies," *Monthly Review*, Federal Reserve Bank of Richmond, Oct., 1972, pp. 3–11. Discussion of wage and price controls as a means of curbing inflation.

KLISE, EUGENE, S., *Money and Banking*, 5th ed., South-Western, 1972, parts 3, 8.

LYON, ROGER A., *Investment Portfolio Management in the Commercial Bank*, Rutgers University Press, 1960.

MEIGS, JAMES A., *Money Matters*, Harper & Row, 1972. A monetarist's explanation of the role of monetarism.

NICHOLS, DOROTHY M., *Modern Money Mechanics*, rev. ed., Federal Reserve Bank of Chicago, 1971.

OKUN, ARTHUR M., "The Mirage of Steady Inflation," *Brookings Papers on Economic Activity*, The Brookings Institution, 1971, pp. 485–97.

OSER, JACOB, *The Evolution of Economic Thought*, 2nd ed., Harcourt Brace Jovanovich, 1970. Brief and lucid survey of the monetary theories of Wicksell, Fisher, and Hawtrey.

ROBOCK, STEFAN H., "We Can Live with Inflation," *Harvard Business Review*, Nov.–Dec., 1972. Suggests what the United States can learn from Brazil's record of high inflation and economic growth.

ROUSSEAS, STEPHEN W., *Monetary Theory*, Knopf, 1972.

SPRINKEL, BERYL WAYNE, *Money and Markets: A Monetarist View*, Irwin, 1971.

WEIDENBAUM, MURRAY L., "New Initiatives in National Wage and Price Policy," *Review of Economics and Statistics*, Aug., 1972, pp. 213–34. Well within the grasp of beginning students.

WHITTLESAY, CHARLES R., ARTHUR M. FREEDMAN, and EDWARD S. HERMAN, *Money and Banking: Analysis and Policy*, 2nd ed., Macmillan, 1968.

WRIGHTSMAN, DWAYNE, *An Introduction to Monetary Theory and Policy*, The Free Press, 1971.

PART 4: ECONOMIC GROWTH AND ECOLOGY

BALDWIN, ROBERT E., *Economic Development and Growth*, 2nd ed., Wiley, 1972.

BARKLEY, PAUL W., and DAVID W. SECKLER, *Economic Growth and Environmental Decay*, Harcourt Brace Jovanovich, 1972.

BORTS, GEORGE, and JEROME STEIN, *Economic Growth in a Free Market*, Columbia University Press, 1964.

BOULDING, KENNETH E., "Economics and Ecology," in F. F. Darling and J. P. Milton (eds.), *Future Environments of North America*, Natural History Press, 1966.

CHAMBER OF COMMERCE OF THE UNITED STATES, *The Promise of Economic Growth*, Washington, D.C., 1963.

CROCKER, THOMAS D., and A. J. ROGERS III, *Environmental Economics*, Dryden, 1971.

DALE, EDWIN L., JR., "The Economics of Pollution," *New York Times Magazine*, April 19, 1970.

DOLAN, EDWIN G., *TANSTAAFL* (There ain't no such thing as a free lunch), Holt, Rinehart and Winston, 1971.

GALBRAITH, JOHN KENNETH, *Economic Development*, Houghton Mifflin, 1964. A short provocative collection of essays.

GILL, RICHARD T., *Economic Development: Past and Present*, 3rd ed., Prentice-Hall, 1972.

HACKER, LOUIS M., *The Course of American Economic Growth and Development*, Wiley, 1970.

HALL, GUS, *Ecology: Can We Survive Under Capitalism?* International Publishers, 1972. A short paperback by a leading American communist.

HEILBRONER, ROBERT H., *The Worldly Philosophers*, 4th ed., Simon & Schuster, 1972. Includes a warm and informative essay on John Stuart Mill.

HESSION, CHARLES H., and HYMAN SARDY, *Ascent to Affluence*, Allyn & Bacon, 1969. Emphasizes the "new economic history"—an analytical view in the light of econometric findings.

HICKS, JOHN R., *A Theory of Economic History*, Oxford University Press, 1969. Contains many profound philosophical insights by a leading economic theorist.

HITE, JAMES C., and others, *The Economics of Environmental Quality*, American Enterprise Institute for Public Policy Research, 1972.

JARRET, HENRY (ed.), *Environmental Quality in a Growing Economy*, Johns Hopkins University Press, 1966.

JOHNSON, WARREN A., and JOHN HARDESTY (eds.), *Economic Growth vs. Environment*, Wadsworth, 1971.

KNEESE, ALLEN V., *Economics and the Quality of the Environment*, Resources for the Future, Washington, D.C., Reprint No. 71, April, 1968.

MANSFIELD, EDWIN, *The Economics of Technological Change*, Norton, 1968.

MILLS, EDWIN A., *Urban Economics*, Scott, Foresman, 1972.

MORRIS, BRUCE R., *Economic Growth and Development*, Pitman, 1967.

PERLOFF, HARVEY, *The Quality of the Urban Environment*, Johns Hopkins University Press, 1969.

REUFF, LARRY E., "The Economic Common Sense of Pollution," *The Public Interest*, Spring, 1970.

ROBERTSON, ROSS M., *History of the American Economy*, 3rd ed., Harcourt Brace Jovanovich, 1973.

ROSTOW, W. W., *The Stages of Economic Growth*, 2nd ed., Cambridge University Press, 1971.

"The Environment: A National Mission for the Seventies," *Fortune*, February, 1970. See especially the article by Sanford Rose.

TUTTLE, FRANK W., and JOSEPH M. PERRY, *An Economic History of the United States*, South-Western, 1970. Treats both the chronological-institutional as well as the national-income approaches to economic growth and development.

PART 5: USING SUPPLY AND DEMAND. THE LAWS OF PRODUCTION AND COST

BOULDING, KENNETH E., *Economic Analysis: Microeconomics*, 4th ed., Harper & Row, 1966, vol. 1.

CLARKSON, KENNETH W., and COURTENAY C. STONE, *Microeconomics in Action*, Prentice-Hall, 1971. Reproduces newspaper articles, some of which lend themselves to analysis by supply and demand.

CLOWER, ROBERT W., and JOHN F. DUE, *Microeconomics*, Irwin, 1972. Emphasizes "stock" and "flow" concepts in supply and demand analysis.

DOOLEY, PETER C. *Elementary Price Theory*, 2nd ed., Appleton-Century-Crofts, 1973.

DUE, JOHN F., and ROBERT W. CLOWER, *Intermediate Economic Analysis*, 5th ed., Irwin, 1966.

FERGUSON, C. E., and S. CHARLES MAURICE, *Economic Analysis*, Irwin, 1970.

HAVEMAN, ROBERT H., and KENYON A. KNOPF, *The Market System*, 2nd ed., Wiley, 1970.

SPENCER, MILTON H., *Managerial Economics*, 3rd ed., Irwin, 1968.

STIGLER, GEORGE, *The Theory of Price*, 3rd ed., Macmillan, 1966.

WARD, BENJAMIN, *Elementary Price Theory*, The Free Press, 1967.

WATSON, DONALD S., *Price Theory and Its Uses*, 3rd ed., Houghton Mifflin, 1972.

PART 6: THE ECONOMICS OF THE FIRM: HOW ARE PRICES AND OUTPUTS DETERMINED?

ALLEN, CLARK LEE, *The Framework of Price Theory*, Wadsworth, 1967. Contains many algebraic exercises.

BAIN, JOE S., "Survival-Ability as a Test of Efficiency," *The American Economic Review, Papers and Proceedings*, May, 1969, pp. 99–104. Discusses the reasons firms survive in imperfect competition, based on empirical research.

BAUMOL, WILLIAM J., *Economic Theory and Operations Analysis*, 3rd ed., Prentice-Hall, 1972. A somewhat advanced but stimulating discussion of welfare economics.

BOBER, M. M., *Intermediate Price and Income Theory*, rev. ed., Norton, 1962.

BREIT, WILLIAM, and ROGER L. RANSOM, *The Academic Scribblers*, Holt, Rinehart and Winston, 1971. Includes an excellent essay on Paul Samuelson's contributions to scientific economics.

BRENNAN, MICHAEL J., *Theory of Economic Statics*, 2nd ed., Prentice-Hall, 1970.

BURCK, GILBERT, "The Myths and Realities of Corporate Pricing," *Fortune*, April, 1972. Summarizes the results of research on corporate pricing and points out some inconsistencies between "theory and practice."

COLE, CHARLES L., *Microeconomics*, Harcourt Brace Jovanovich, 1973.

FERGUSON, C. E., and S. CHARLES MAURICE, *Economic Analysis*, Irwin, 1970. An excellent, concise text. Discussions of general equilibrium and welfare economics are especially recommended.

KESSEL, REUBIN L., "Price Discrimination in Medicine," *Journal of Law and Economics*, October, 1958, pp. 20–53. A famous article, reprinted in some readings books.

KOPLIN, H. T., *Microeconomic Analysis*, Harper & Row, 1971. Emphasizes a welfare approach.

MANSFIELD, EDWIN, *Microeconomics*, Norton, 1970.

MCKENNA, JOSEPH, *The Logic of Price*, Dryden, 1973.

MEANS, GARDINER C., "The Administered-Price Thesis Reconfirmed," *The American Economic Review*, June,

1972, pp. 292–306. Compares administered-dominated prices with market-dominated prices and shows how they vary during business cycles.

SCHERER, FREDERIC M., *Industrial Market Structure and Economic Performance*, Rand McNally, 1970. Very readable exposition of price discrimination.

SIMON, JULIAN A., *Issues in the Economics of Advertising*, University of Illinois Press, 1970. Surveys various aspects of advertising from a business-economic as well as a socioeconomic viewpoint.

PART 7: DOMESTIC ECONOMIC PROBLEMS

ADELMAN, M. A., "The Two Faces of Economic Concentration," *The Public Interest*, Fall, 1970, pp. 117–26.

BEAL, EDWIN F., EDWARD D. WICKERSHAM, and PHILIP KIENAST, *The Practice of Collective Bargaining*, 4th ed., Irwin, 1972.

BERNSTEIN, IRVING, *The Turbulent Years*, Houghton Mifflin, 1970. A history of the American worker during the gut era of the labor movement, 1933–1941. The same author's *The Lean Years*, the first book in the two-volume series, covers the period 1920–1933.

BLOOM, GORDON F., and HERBERT R. NORTHRUP, *Economics of Labor Relations*, 6th ed., Irwin, 1969.

BROWN, J. DOUGLAS, *An American Philosophy of Social Security*, Princeton University Press, 1972.

BUDD, EDWARD C. (ed.), *Inequality and Poverty*, Norton, 1967.

CARTTER, ALLAN M., and F. RAY MARSHALL, *Labor Economics*, rev. ed., Irwin, 1972.

CAVES, RICHARD, *American Industry: Structure, Conduct, Performance*, 3rd ed., Prentice-Hall, 1972.

CHAMBERLIN, NEIL W. (ed.), *Business and the Cities*, Basic Books, 1970.

"Education in the Ghetto, A Search for Solutions," *Saturday Review*, January 11, 1969. Contains several articles on educational problems, but see especially the one by Theodore R. Sizer, Dean of the Graduate School of Education at Harvard University.

EINHORN, HENRY ADLER, and WILLIAM PAUL SMITH, *Economic Aspects of Antitrust: Readings and Cases*, Random House, 1968.

FISHMAN, LEO (ed.), *Poverty and Affluence*, Yale University Press, 1966.

FRIEDMAN, MILTON, *Capitalism and Freedom*, University of Chicago Press, 1962.

GREEN, CHRISTOPHER, *Negative Taxes and the Poverty Problem*, The Brookings Institution, 1967.

HECHINGER, FRED M., "School Vouchers: Can the Plan Work?" *The New York Times*, June 7, 1970, sec. E–11.

HENDERSON, WILLIAM L., and LARRY C. LEDEBUR, *Urban Economics*, Wiley, 1972.

MARKHAM, JESSE, *Conglomerate Mergers and Public Policy*, Division of Research, Harvard Business School, 1973.

MILLS, EDWIN S., *Urban Economics*, Scott, Foresman, 1972.

MUND, VERNON, *Government and Business*, 4th ed., Harper & Row, 1965.

NETZER, DICK, *Economics and Urban Problems*, Basic Books, 1970.

NEVITT, ADELA ADAM (ed.), *The Economic Problems of Urban Housing*, St. Martin's Press, 1967.

RASMUSSEN, DAVID W., *Urban Economics*, Harper & Row, 1973.

ROWAN, RICHARD L., and HERBERT R. NORTHRUP (eds.), *Readings in Labor Economics and Labor Relations*, Irwin, 1968.

SCHILLER, BRADLEY, R., *The Economics of Poverty and Discrimination*, Prentice-Hall, 1972.

SICHEL, WERNER (ed.), *Industrial Organization and Public Policy: Selected Readings*, Houghton Mifflin, 1967.

STELZER, IRWIN M., *Selected Antitrust Cases*, 4th ed., Irwin, 1972.

THEOBALD, ROBERT (ed.), *The Guaranteed Income*, Doubleday, 1966.

THOMPSON, WILBUR R., *A Preface to Urban Economics*, Johns Hopkins University Press, 1968.

U.S. DEPARTMENT OF LABOR, *A Brief History of the American Labor Movement*, Bulletin 1000, Washington, D.C., 1970.

WILCOX, CLAIR, *Toward Social Welfare*, Irwin, 1969.

PART 8: INTERNATIONAL ECONOMICS. THE WORLD'S ECONOMIES

BALDWIN, ROBERT E., *Economic Development and Growth*, Wiley, 1960.

BALINKY, ALEXANDER, *Marx's Economics, Origin and Development*, Heath, 1970.

BAUER, F. T., *Dissent on Development*, Harvard, 1973. A scholarly challenge to the dominant view that grants and loans are indispensable to the economic progress of less developed countries.

BELL, JOHN FRED, *A History of Economic Thought*, 2nd ed., Ronald, 1967. Includes a comprehensive analysis of Marxian economics.

CAMPBELL, ROBERT W., *Soviet Economic Power*, 2nd ed., Houghton Mifflin, 1966.

EBENSTEIN, WILLIAM, *Today's Isms*, 6th ed., Prentice-Hall, 1970.

ELLSWORTH, PAUL T., *The International Economy*, 4th ed., Macmillan, 1969.

FRIEDMAN, MILTON, and ROBERT V. ROOSA, *The Balance of Payments: Free Versus Fixed Exchange Rates*, Washington, D.C., American Enterprise Association, 1967.

GALENSON, WALTER, and NAI-RUENN CHEN, *The Chinese Economy Under Communism*, Aldine, 1969.

GROSSMAN, GREGORY, *Economic Systems*, Prentice-Hall, 1967.

HABERLER, GOTTFRIED, *U.S. Balance of Payments Policy and the International Monetary System*, Washington, D.C., American Enterprise Institute, 1973.

HAGEN, EVERETT E., *The Economics of Development*, Irwin, 1968.

HEILBRONER, ROBERT L., *The Worldly Philosophers*, 4th ed., Simon and Schuster, 1971. Includes stimulating essays on Utopian socialism and on Marx.

HIGGINS, BENJAMIN, *Economic Development*, rev. ed., Norton, 1968.

International Economic Report of the President, annual.

KENEN, PETER B., and RAYMOND LUBITZ, *International Economics*, 3rd ed., Prentice-Hall, 1971.

KINDLEBERGER, CHARLES P., *International Economics*, 5th ed., Irwin, 1973.

KOHLER, HEINZ, *Welfare and Planning*, Wiley, 1966.

KREININ, MORDECHAI E., *International Economics, A Policy Approach*, Harcourt Brace Jovanovich, 1971.

LINDBECK, ASSAR, *The Political Economy of the New Left, An Outsider's View*, Harper & Row, 1971.

LOUCKS, WILLIAM N., and WILLIAM G. WHITNEY, *Comparative Economic Systems*, 9th ed., Harper & Row, 1973. The classic text in its field. Excellent surveys on socialism, Marxism, and related topics.

MANDEL, ERNEST, *An Introduction to Marxist Economic Theory*, Pathfinder Press, 1970.

MARCUS, EDWARD, and MILDRED RENDL MARCUS, *Economic Progress and the Developing World*, Scott, Foresman, 1971.

NEWMAN, CHARLES P., ARTHUR D. GAYER, and MILTON H. SPENCER, *Source Readings in Economic Thought*, Norton, 1954, pp. 240–86. Includes selections from Marx.

NOVACK, GEORGE, *An Introduction to the Logic of Marxism*, 5th ed., Pathfinder Press, 1971.

PEN, JAN, *A Primer on International Trade*, Random House, 1967.

PRESTON, NATHANIEL STONE, *Politics, Economics, and Power*, Macmillan, 1967.

RAFFAELE, JOSEPH A., *The Economic Development of Nations*, Random House, 1971.

ROOT, FRANKLIN R., *International Trade and Investment*, 3rd ed., South-Western, 1973.

SCHNITZER, MARTIN C., and JAMES W. NORDYKE, *Comparative Economic Systems*, South-Western, 1971.

SCHWARTZ, HARRY, *An Introduction to the Soviet Economy*, Merrill, 1968.

SHERMAN, HOWARD J., *The Soviet Economy*, Little, Brown, 1969.

SNIDER, DELBERT A., *Introduction to International Economics*, 5th ed., Irwin, 1971. An excellent undergraduate text, perhaps the clearest in the field.

WEXLER, IMMANUEL, *Fundamentals of International Economics*, 2nd ed., Random House, 1972.

Index

Dictionary of Economic Terms and Concepts

This dictionary catalogs the definitions of every technical word, phrase, and concept given in the text, plus definitions of many other terms as well. It also presents brief examples and cross references that explain the significance of important terms. Hence it will be a convenient and permanent source of reference—not only for this course, but for future courses you may take in economics, business administration, and other social sciences.

ability-to-pay principle: Theory of taxation which holds that the fairest tax is based on the financial ability of the taxpayer—regardless of any benefit he may receive from the tax. Financial ability may be determined by either wealth or income. The U.S. personal income tax is founded on this principle.

absolute advantage, law of: Principle which states that a basis for trade exists between nations or regions when each of them, due to natural or acquired advantages, can provide a good or service that the other wants at a lower cost than if each were to provide it for itself. This law accounts for much of the world's trade.

accelerator principle: Proposition that small changes in the demand for consumer goods can generate magnified changes in the demand for investment goods (including inventory holdings) needed for consumer goods production. The accelerator coefficient is measured by the formula:

$$\text{Accelerator} = \frac{\text{change in net investment}}{\text{change in consumption from preceding period}}$$

The principle can also be used to show that a mere slowing down of the percentage rate of growth in consumption is capable of producing an actual decline in net investment, and hence an adverse effect on income.

accounts payable: A company's debts to suppliers of goods or services.

accounts receivable: Amounts due to a firm from customers.

accrued expenses payable: Obligations such as wages and salaries, interest on borrowed funds, and pensions.

adjustable peg: System which permits changes in the par rate of foreign exchange after a nation has had long-run disequilibrium in its balance of payments. It allows also for short-run variations within a narrow range of a few percent around the par value.

ad valorem subsidy: Fixed percentage subsidy based on the price or value of a commodity.

ad valorem tax: Fixed percentage tax on the price or value of a commodity. *Examples:* sales taxes, property taxes, and most import duties.

Agency for International Development: Semiautonomous unit of the State Department. It administers funds voted by Congress for economic, technical, and defense assistance to nations identified with the "free world."

aggregate demand: Total value of output that all sectors of the economy are willing to purchase at any given time or level of income.

aggregate supply: Total value of output produced or available for purchase by the economy at any given time or level of income.

Agricultural Adjustment Act (1938): Basic farm law (with subsequent amendments) of the United States. It provides for (1) price supports of selected farm products at specified levels, to be implemented by purchases and nonrecourse loans by the Commodity Credit Corporation; (2) production control through acreage allotments of certain crops; (3) marketing agreements and quotas between the Department of Agriculture and producers in order to control the distribution of selected commodities; (4) payments to farmers and others who follow approved soil conservation practices; and (5) parity payments to farmers for selected agricultural staples.

American Federation of Labor–Congress of Industrial Organizations (AFL–CIO): Federation of labor unions formed in 1955 by a merger of the AFL and CIO. Its purposes are to improve the wages, hours, and conditions of workers, and to realize the benefits of free collective bargaining. It exercises no authority or control over member unions other than requiring them to abide by its constitution and code of ethical practices.

annually balanced budget: Philosophy which holds that total revenues and expenditures in the government's budget should be balanced or brought into equality every year.

antitrust laws: Acts passed by Congress since 1890 to prevent monopoly and to maintain competition. The chief ones are: (1) the Sherman Antitrust Act (1890); (2) the Clayton Antitrust Act (1914); (3) the Federal Trade Commission Act (1914); (4) the Robinson-Patman Act (1936); (5) the Wheeler-Lea Act (1938); and (6) the Celler Antimerger Act (1950).

arbitrage: Act of buying a commodity in one market and simultaneously selling it in a dearer market at a higher price. Arbitrage tends to equalize prices of a commodity in different markets, except for differences in the costs of transportation, risk, etc.

arbitration: Settlement of differences between parties (such as a union and management) by the use of an impartial third party called an arbitrator who is acceptable to both sides and whose decision is binding and legally enforceable on the contesting parties. The arbitrator issues a decision based not on what he thinks is wise and fair, but on how he thinks the language of the contract applies to the case.

assets: Resources or things of value owned by an economic entity, such as an individual, household, or firm. *Examples:* cash, property, and the rights to property.

automatic fiscal stabilizers: Nondiscretionary or "built-in" features that automatically cushion recession by helping to create a budget deficit and curb inflation by helping to create a budget surplus. *Examples:* (1) income tax receipts; (2) unemployment taxes and benefits; (3) agricultural price supports; and (4) corporate dividend policies.

autonomous consumption: Consumption independent of income. It is that part of total consumption which is unrelated to income. (Contrast with **induced consumption.**)

autonomous investment: Investment independent of income, output, and general economic activity. (Contrast with **induced investment.**)

autonomous transactions: Transactions among nations that arise from factors unrelated to the balance of payments as such. The main classes are merchandise trade and services, long-term capital movements, and unilateral transfers.

average cost price: *See* **full cost price.**

average fixed cost: Ratio of a firm's total fixed cost to the quantity it produces. Also, the difference between average total cost and average variable cost. Thus:

$$\text{Average fixed cost} = \frac{\text{total fixed cost}}{\text{quantity of output}}$$

Also:

$$\text{Average fixed cost} = \text{average total cost} - \text{average variable cost}$$

average marginal relationship: Relationship between all corresponding average and marginal curves such that: when an average curve is rising, its corresponding marginal curve is above it; when an average curve is falling, its corresponding marginal curve is below it; and when an average curve is neither rising nor falling, i.e., it is either at a maximum or at a minimum, its corresponding marginal curve intersects (is equal to) it.

average product: Ratio of total product to the amount of variable input needed to produce that product. Thus:

$$\text{Average product} = \frac{\text{total product}}{\text{variable input}}$$

average propensity to consume: Ratio of consumption to income:

$$\text{Average propensity to consume} = \frac{\text{consumption}}{\text{income}}$$

It thus reveals the proportion of income that is spent on consumption.

average propensity to save: Ratio of saving to income:

$$\text{Average propensity to save} = \frac{\text{saving}}{\text{income}}$$

It thus reveals the proportion of income that is saved (i.e., not spent on consumption).

average revenue: Ratio of a firm's total revenue to its quantity of output sold—or equivalently, its price per unit of quantity sold. Thus:

$$\text{Average revenue} = \frac{\text{total revenue}}{\text{quantity}} = \frac{(\text{price})(\text{quantity})}{\text{quantity}} = \text{price}$$

average revenue product: Ratio of total revenue to the quantity of an input employed. Thus:

$$\text{Average revenue product} = \frac{\text{total revenue}}{\text{quantity of input employed}}$$

average tax rate: Ratio or percentage of a total tax to the base on which it is imposed. *Example:*

$$\text{Average personal income tax rate} = \frac{\text{total personal income tax}}{\text{total taxable income}}$$

average total cost: Ratio of a firm's total cost to the quantity it produces. Also, the sum of average fixed cost and average variable cost. Thus:

$$\text{Average total cost} = \frac{\text{total cost}}{\text{quantity of output}}$$

Also:

$$\text{Average total cost} = \text{average fixed cost} + \text{average variable cost}$$

average variable cost: Ratio of a firm's total variable cost to the quantity it produces. Also, the difference between a firm's average total cost and average fixed cost. Thus:

$$\text{Average variable cost} = \frac{\text{total variable cost}}{\text{quantity of output}}$$

Also:

Average variable cost = average total cost − average fixed cost

balanced budget: Budget with total revenues and total expenditures that are equal.

balanced-budget multiplier: Principle which asserts that if government spending and taxes are increased or decreased simultaneously by a balanced or equal amount, NNP will be increased or decreased by the same amount. *Example:* A balanced increase in government spending and taxes of $1 will raise NNP by $1, and a balanced decrease of $1 will lower NNP by $1. The reason for this is that the effects of balanced increases in government spending and taxes are equal but opposite, and hence the two multiplier processes cancel each other out—except on the first round when the full amount of government spending is added to NNP.

balance of payments: Statement of the money value of all transactions between a nation and the rest of the world during a given period. These transactions may consist of imports and exports of goods and services, and movements of short-term and long-term investments, gifts, currency, and gold; they may be classified as current account, capital account, unilateral transfer account, and gold account.

balance-of-payments disequilibrium: Circumstance which exists when, over an unspecified period lasting several years, a nation's autonomous credits do not equal its autonomous debits. A deficit disequilibrium exists when total autonomous debits exceed total autonomous credits; a surplus disequilibrium occurs when total autonomous credits exceed total autonomous debits.

balance of trade: That part of a nation's balance of payments dealing with merchandise imports and exports. A "favorable" balance of trade exists when the value of exports exceeds the value of imports; an "unfavorable" balance exists when the value of imports exceeds the value of exports.

balance sheet: Statement of a firm's financial position on a given date. It shows what the firm owns (its assets), what it owes (its liabilities), and the residual or equity of the owners (the net worth).

banker's acceptance: Bill of exchange drawn on or accepted by a bank instead of an individual or firm. It is a promise by a bank to pay specific bills for one of its customers when the bills become due. (*See* **bill of exchange; draft.**)

barter: Simple exchange of one good for another without the use of money.

basic wages: Payments received by workers for work performed, based on time or output.

benefit-cost analysis: Technique of evaluating alternative programs by comparing for each the (discounted) present value of all expected benefits with all expected costs. The discount factor is a percentage representing the "opportunity cost" of capital—that is, what the funds would have earned in their best alternative use at equal risk. The chief weakness of benefit-cost analysis is that some benefits and costs cannot always be defined and measured. Hence the use of relative benefits and costs for setting priorities among different programs may result in conflicting choices.

benefit principle: Theory of taxation which holds that a fair tax is one which is levied on people according to the benefits they receive from government. The chief difficulties are that: (1) for many goods, benefits cannot be readily determined (e.g., national defense, public education, police and fire protection); and (2) those who receive the benefits are not always able to pay for them (e.g., recipients of welfare or unemployment compensation).

bilateral monopoly: Market structure in which a monopsonist buyer faces a monopolist seller. The equilibrium quantity may be determinate. However, the price level for that quantity is logically indeterminate. That is, the price will end up somewhere between the minimum price preferred by the monopsonist and the maximum price preferred by the monopolist.

bill of exchange: Draft (or type of "check") used between countries. (*See* **draft.**)

bimetallic standard: Monetary standard which defines the national unit of currency (such as the dollar) in terms of a fixed weight of two metals, usually gold and silver. The U.S. was on this standard during the nineteenth century, but it usually worked unsatisfactorily due to the operation of Gresham's Law. (*See* **Gresham's Law; mint ratio.**)

black market: Illegal market in which a good is sold for more than the legal ceiling price.

Board of Governors: Group of seven people that supervises the Federal Reserve System. Members are appointed by the President and confirmed by the Senate for terms of 14 years each, one term expiring every two years.

bond: Agreement to pay a specified sum (called the "principal") either at a future date or periodically over the course of a loan, during which time a fixed rate of interest may be paid on certain dates. Bonds are issued by corporations, and by the federal, state, and local governments. They are typically used for long-term financing.

boycott: Campaign to discourage people from dealing with a particular firm. (Sometimes called a "primary boycott.")

Brannan Plan: Proposal made by Secretary of Agriculture, Charles F. Brannan, in 1949. It would eliminate parity payments to farmers and give them direct payments instead. Under the plan, agricultural prices would be determined in a free market by supply and demand; farmers would then be compensated by a subsidy from the government for the difference between the market price they receive and some higher target price established according to a selected base period in the past.

break-even point: Level of output at which a firm's total revenue equals its total cost (or its average revenue equals its average total cost) so that its net revenue is zero. At a break-even point as defined in economics, a firm is normally profitable since total cost in economics includes normal profit.

budget: Itemized estimate of expected revenues and expenditures for a given period in the future.

budget deficit: Budget in which total expenditures exceed total revenues.

budget surplus: Budget in which total revenues exceed total expenditures.

business cycles: Recurrent but nonperiodic fluctuations in general business and economic activity that take place over a period of years. They occur in aggregate variables like income, output, employment, and prices, most of which may move at approximately the same time in the same direction, but at *different rates*.

Business cycles are thus accelerations and retardations in the rates of growth of important economic variables.

cameralism: Form of mercantilism extensively implemented by German governments during the eighteenth century. Its chief objective was to increase the revenue of the state. (The word comes from *Kammer*, the name of the royal treasury.)

capital: 1. As a factor of production, capital is a produced means of further production (such as capital goods or investment goods in the form of raw materials, machines, or equipment) for the ultimate purpose of manufacturing consumer goods. Hence human resources are also part of an economy's capital. **2.** As money, capital represents the funds which businessmen use to purchase capital goods. **3.** In accounting, capital may sometimes represent net worth or the stockholders' equity in a business.

capital consumption allowance: Expression used in national-income accounting to represent the difference between "gross" and "net" private domestic investment. It consists almost entirely of depreciation and is often used synonymously with it.

capital deepening: Increases in an economy's stock of capital at a faster rate than the growth of its labor force, thus expanding the volume of capital per worker and raising average output per worker.

capitalism: Economic organization characterized by private ownership of the means of production and distribution (such as land, factories, railroads) and their operation for profit under predominantly competitive conditions.

capital market: Center where long-term credit and equity instruments such as bonds, stocks, and mortgages are bought and sold.

capital/output ratio: Concept sometimes used in a "total" sense, and sometimes in a "marginal" sense. Thus: **1.** The "total" capital/output ratio is the ratio of an economy's total stock of real capital to the level of its income or output. **2.** The "marginal" capital/output ratio is the change in an economy's income or output resulting from a unit change in its stock of real capital. Thus a ratio of 3/1 means that three units of additional capital produce one unit of additional output.

capital stock: Unit of ownership in a corporation. It represents the stockholder's proprietary interest. Two major classes are common stock and preferred stock.

capital widening: Increases in an economy's stock of capital at the same rate as the growth of its labor force, thus maintaining the same volume of capital per worker and hence the same average output per worker.

cartel: International association of firms in the same industry, established to allocate world markets among its members and to regulate prices. Sometimes called an "international monopoly."

Celler Antimerger Act (1950): Major antitrust law. An extension of Section 7 of the Clayton Antitrust Act, it prohibits a corporation from acquiring the stock *or assets* of another corporation if the effect would be a substantial lessening of competition or tendency toward monopoly. *Note:* Prior to this law, only the acquisition of *stock* by competing corporations was illegal under the Clayton Act.

certificate of deposit (CD): Special type of time deposit which a purchaser agrees to keep in a bank for a specified period, usually three months or more. Many CDs are negotiable, and hence can be sold in a secondary market because they offer both liquidity and a yield. Banks began to offer CDs in the early 1960s at rates competitive with other money market instruments, in order to discourage corporations from withdrawing money for the purpose of investing in securities.

change in amount consumed: Increase or decrease in the amount of consumption expenditure due to a change in income. It may be represented by a movement along a consumption-function curve.

change in consumption: Increase or decrease in consumption, represented by a shift of the consumption-function curve to a new position. The shift results from a change in any of the factors that were assumed to remain constant when the curve was drawn. These may include (1) the volume of liquid assets owned by households, (2) expectations of future prices and incomes, (3) anticipations of product shortages, and (4) credit conditions.

change in demand: Increase or decrease in demand, represented by a shift of the demand curve to a new position. The shift results from a change in any of the factors that were assumed to remain constant when the curve was drawn. These may include (1) buyers' money incomes, (2) the prices of related goods, (3) buyers' tastes or preferences, (4) the number of buyers in the market, and (5) buyers' expectations about future prices and incomes.

change in quantity demanded: Increase or decrease in the quantity demanded of a good due to a change in its price. It may be represented by a movement along a demand curve.

change in quantity supplied: Increase or decrease in the quantity supplied of a good due to a change in its price. It may be represented by a movement along a supply curve.

change in supply: Increase or decrease in supply represented by a shift of the supply curve to a new position. The shift results from a change in any of the factors that were assumed to remain constant when the curve was drawn. These may include (1) the state of technology, (2) resource prices or the costs of the factors of production, (3) the prices of other goods, (4) the number of sellers in the market, and (5) sellers' expectations regarding future prices.

checkoff: Procedure by which an employer, with the written permission of the worker, withholds union dues and other assessments from paychecks and then transfers the funds to the union. This provides an efficient means by which the union can collect dues from its members.

Christian socialism: Movement, since the late nineteenth century, by various church groups to preach the "social gospel"—a type of social legislation and reform that seeks to improve the well-being of the working classes by appealing to Christian ethical and humanitarian principles.

circular flow of economic activity: Model demonstrating the movement of goods, resources, payments, and expenditures among sectors of the economy. A simple model may include the household and business sectors, and the product and resource markets—but other models may be constructed which are more complex.

classical economics: Body of economic thought dominant in the Western world from the late eighteenth century until the 1930s. Among its chief proponents were Adam Smith (1723–1790), Jean Baptiste Say (1767–1832), Jeremy Bentham (1748–1832), Thomas Robert Malthus (1766–1834), David Ricardo (1772–1823), Nassau William Senior (1790–1864), and John Stuart Mill (1806–1873). It emphasized man's self-interest, and the operation of universal economic laws which tend automatically to guide the economy toward full-employment equilibrium if the government adheres to a policy of laissez-faire or noninterventionism.

class struggle: In the theories of Karl Marx, an irreconcilable clash between the bourgeoisie or capitalist class and the proletariat or working class, arising out of the surplus value which capitalists appropriate from workers. The class struggle will eventually be resolved when the proletariat overthrows the bourgeoisie and establishes a new and equitable economic order.

Clayton Antitrust Act (1914): A major antitrust law aimed at preventing unfair, deceptive, dishonest, or injurious methods of competition. It declares as illegal, where the effect is a substantial lessening of competition or tendency toward monopoly: (1) price discrimination, except where there are differences in grade, quality, or quantity sold, or where the lower prices make due allowances for cost differences in selling or transportation, or where the lower prices are offered in good faith to meet competition; (2) tying contracts between sellers and purchasers; and (3) intercorporate stockholdings among competing corporations. It also makes illegal, regardless of the effect on competition: (4) interlocking directorates if the corporations involved are competitive and if any one of them has capital, surplus, and undivided profits in excess of $1 million.

closed shop: A firm which agrees that an employee must be a union member before he is employed, and must remain a union member after he is employed. Outlawed by the Labor-Management Relations (Taft-Hartley) Act of 1947.

coalition bargaining: Method of bargaining by which a federation of unions (such as the AFL–CIO) tries to coordinate and establish common termination dates for contracts with firms that deal with a number of unions at their plants throughout the economy. Its purpose is to enable the federation to strengthen union bargaining positions by threatening to close down all plants simultaneously.

cobweb theorem: Generic name for a theory of cyclical fluctuations in the prices and quantities of various agricultural commodities—fluctuations which arise because for certain agricultural products: (1) the quantity demanded of the commodity at any given time depends on its price at that time, whereas (2) the quantity supplied at any given time depends on its price at a previous time when production plans were initially formulated. Hogs and beef cattle have been notable examples.

coefficient of relative effectiveness (CRE): Term used in the Soviet Union to mean the expected payoff or percent rate of return on a capital investment; akin to the concept of marginal efficiency of investment in Western economics.

coincident indicators: Time series that tend to move approximately "in phase" with the aggregate economy, and hence are measures of current economic activity.

collective agreement: A collective-bargaining contract worked out between union and management, describing wages, working conditions, and related matters.

collective bargaining: Negotiation between a company's management and a union for the purpose of agreeing on mutually acceptable wages and working conditions for employees.

collective farms: Agricultural cooperatives in the Soviet Union, consisting of communities of farmers who pool their resources, lease land from the government, and divide the profits among the members according to the amount and kind of work done by each. This type of farming, which is subject to detailed government regulation, dominates agriculture in the Soviet Union.

collective good: See **public good.**

command economy: Economic system in which an authoritarian government exercises primary control over decisions concerning what and how much to produce; it may also, but does not necessarily, decide for whom to produce. (Contrast with **planned economy.**)

commercial bank: Financial institution, chartered by federal or state governments, primarily engaged in making short-term industrial and commercial loans by creating demand or checking deposits, and retiring loans by canceling demand deposits. It may also perform other financial functions such as holding time or savings deposits and making long-term mortgage loans.

common market: Association of trading nations which agrees to: (1) impose no trade restrictions such as tariffs or quotas among participants; (2) establish common external barriers (such as a common external tariff) to nonparticipants; and (3) impose no national restrictions on the movement of labor and capital among participants. *Example:* European Economic Community (EEC).

common stock: Shares that have no fixed rate of dividends, and hence may receive higher dividends than the fixed rate on preferred stock if the corporation's earnings are sufficiently high.

Commonwealth (Mass.) vs. Hunt (1842): The first case in which a (Massachusetts) court held a trade union to be a lawful organization. It declared that workers could form a union to bargain collectively with employers.

communism: 1. In the theories of Karl Marx, the final and perfect goal of historical development, characterized by: (a) a classless society in which all men live by earning and no man lives by owning; (b) a nonexistent state; and (c) a wage system which is completely abolished and all citizens live and work according to the motto: "from each according to his ability, to each according to his needs." **2.** In most communist countries today, an economic system based on (a) social ownership of property including most of the means of production and distribution; (b) government planning and control of the economy; and (c) a scheme of rewards and penalties to achieve maximum productive effort. *Note:* Communist leaders claim that the system which exists in communist countries today is socialism of the type which Marxian ideology holds as being preparatory to the attainment of full communism.

community (social) rate of return: Net value of a project to an economy (i.e., a town, city, state, or country). It is estimated on the basis of the net increase in output which a project such as a new industry may be expected to bring, directly or indirectly, to the area being developed. The industry's contribution is determined by subtracting from the value of what it produces the cost of the resources it uses. Hence the measure is intended to reflect all economic and social benefits as well as costs. (Contrast with **private rate of return.**)

company union: A labor union limited to a particular firm. It is usually unaffiliated with any other union.

comparative advantage, law of: Principle which states that if one nation can produce each of two products more efficiently than another nation and can produce one of these commodities more efficiently than the other, it should specialize in the product in which it is most efficient and leave production of the alternative product to the other country. The two nations will then have more of both goods by engaging in trade. This principle is applicable to individuals and regions as well as to nations.

comparative statics: Method of analysis in which the effects of a change in one or more of the determining conditions in a static model are evaluated by comparing the results after the change with those before the change. *Example:* Comparing the effects on equilibrium prices and quantities (in a supply-and-demand model) resulting from a shift in supply or demand curves. It is like comparing two "snapshots" of a phenomenon—one taken before the change and one after.

compensatory transactions: Transactions among nations that are a direct response to balance-of-payments considerations. They may be thought of as balancing items which arise to accommodate differences in money inflows and outflows resulting from so-called autonomous transactions. The two main classes are short-term capital movements and shifts in gold holdings.

competition: Rivalry among buyers and sellers of goods or resources. Competition tends to be directly related to the degree of diffusion (as opposed to the concentration) of market power, and the freedom with which buyers and sellers can enter or leave particular markets. It is sometimes used to mean perfect (pure) competition, depending on whether it is employed in that context.

complementary goods: Commodities which are related such that at a given level of buyers' incomes, an increase in the price of one good leads to a decrease in the demand for the other, and a decrease in the price of one good leads to an increase in the demand for the other. *Examples:* ham and eggs; hamburgers and buns. (Contrast with **substitute goods.**)

compound interest: Interest computed on a principal sum and also on all the interest earned by that principal sum as of a given date.

concentration ratio: Percentage of an industry's output accounted for by its four leading firms.

conglomerate merger: Amalgamation under one ownership of unlike plants producing unrelated products. It reflects a desire by the acquiring company to spread risks, find outlets for idle capital funds, add products which can be sold with the firm's merchandising knowledge and skills, or simply gain economic power on a broader front.

conscious parallel action: Identical price behavior among competing firms. It may or may not be the result of collusion or prior agreement, but has nevertheless been held illegal by the courts in various antitrust cases.

consent decree: A means of settling cases in equity among the parties involved (such as a defendant firm and the Department of Justice). The defendant does not declare himself guilty, but agrees nevertheless to cease and desist from certain practices and abide by the rules of behavior set down in the decree. This is the chief instrument employed by the Justice Department and by the Federal Trade Commission in the enforcement of the Sherman and Clayton Acts. The majority of antitrust violations are settled in this manner.

conspicuous consumption: Expression originated by Thorstein Veblen (1857–1929) to mean that those above the subsistence level, i.e., the so-called "leisure class," are mainly concerned with impressing others through their standard of living, taste, and dress—that is, through what he called "pecuniary emulation." ("Keeping up with the Joneses" is a popular expression of this concept.)

constant-cost industry: Industry which experiences no increases in resource prices or in costs of production as it expands, despite new firms entering it. This will happen only when the industry's demand for the resources it employs is an insignificant proportion of the total demand for those resources.

constant dollars: Expression reflecting the actual prices of a previous year or the average of actual prices of a previous period of years. Hence economic data are often quoted in constant dollars. (Contrast with **current dollars.**)

consumer sovereignty: Concept of the consumer as "king"—in the sense that the consumer registers his preferences for goods by his "dollar votes" in the marketplace. In a highly competitive economy competition among producers will cause them to adjust their production to the changing patterns of consumer demands. In less competitive economies, where monopolistic forces and other imperfections exist, resources will not be allocated in accordance with consumer wishes.

consumer's surplus: Payment made by a buyer that is less than the maximum amount he would have been willing to pay for the quantity of the commodity that he purchases.

consumption: Expenditures on consumer goods and services.

consumption function: Relationship between consumption expenditures and income such that as income increases, consumption increases, but not as fast as income. The expression **propensity to consume** is often used synonymously. (*Note:* Since the word "function" is employed here in its mathematical sense to mean a variable whose value depends on the value of another variable, the expression "consumption function" can also be used to designate *any* type of relationship between consumption and income—not necessarily the type defined above. However, the above type is the most common one.)

convergence hypothesis: Conjecture that capitalism and communism, driven by the process of industrialization, will eventually merge to form a new kind of society in which the personal freedoms and profit motive of Western capitalistic democracies blend with the government controls that exist in a communistic (especially Soviet) economy.

corporation: Association of stockholders created under law, but regarded by the courts as an artificial person existing only in the contemplation of the law. The chief characteristics of a corporation are: (1) limited liability of its stockholders; (2) stability and permanence; and (3) ability to accumulate large sums of capital for expansion through the sale of stocks and bonds.

cost: Sacrifice that must be made to do or to acquire something. What is sacrificed may be money, goods, leisure time, security, prestige, power, or pleasure.

cost-effectiveness analysis: Technique of selecting from alternative programs the one that attains a given objective at the lowest cost. It is a type of analysis most useful when benefits cannot be measured in money.

cost-push inflation: Condition of generally rising prices caused by factor payments to one or more groups of resource owners increasing faster than productivity or efficiency. It is usually attributed to monopolistic market power possessed by some resource owners, unions, or business firms. Thus "wage-push" and "profit-push" are the most common forms of cost-push inflation.

countervailing power: Proposition that in the U.S. the growth of market power by one group may tend to stimulate the growth of a counterreaction and somewhat offsetting influence by another group. *Examples:* Big labor unions face big corporations at the bargaining table; chain stores deal with large processing and manufacturing firms; and big government faces big business and big unions.

craft union: Labor union composed of workers in a particular trade such as bakers, carpenters, and teamsters. It is thus a "horizontally" organized union.

crawling peg: System of foreign exchange rates which permits the par value of a nation's currency to change automatically by small increments, downward or upward, if in actual daily trading on the foreign exchange markets the price in terms of other currencies persists on the "floor" or "ceiling" of the established range for a specified period.

credit: In international economics, any transaction which results in a money inflow or receipt from a foreign country. It may be represented on a balance-of-payments statement by a plus sign.

credit instrument: Written or printed financial document serving as either a promise or order to transfer funds from one person to another.

creeping inflation: Slow but persistent upward movement in the general level of prices over a long period of years, typically at an average annual rate of up to 3 percent.

currency: Paper money. (Coins are not part of currency.)

current assets: Cash and other assets that can be turned quickly into cash.

current dollars: An expression reflecting actual prices of each year. Hence economic data are often quoted in current dollars. (Contrast with **constant dollars.**)

current liabilities: Debts that fall due within a year.

customs union: Agreement among two or more trading nations to abolish trade barriers such as tariffs and quotas among themselves, and to adopt a common external policy of trade (such as a common external tariff with all nonmember nations). *Example:* Benelux (i.e., Belgium, Luxembourg, and the Netherlands).

cyclically balanced budget: Philosophy which holds that total revenues and expenditures in the government's budget should be balanced or brought into equality over the course of a business cycle.

cyclical unemployment: Unemployment which results from business recessions or depressions because aggregate demand falls too far below the full-employment level of aggregate output and income.

death taxes: Taxes imposed on the transfer of property after death. They consist of estate and inheritance taxes, and are imposed by federal and state governments at progressive rates.

debit: In international economics, any transaction which results in a money outflow or payment to a foreign country. It may be represented on a balance-of-payments statement by a minus sign.

decreasing-cost industry: Industry which experiences decreases in resource prices or in its costs of production as it expands because of new firms entering it. This situation might arise for a while as a result of substantial external economies of scale.

deduction: In logical thinking, a process of reasoning from premises to conclusions. The premises are more general than the conclusions, so deduction is often defined as reasoning from the general to the particular. (Opposite of **induction.**)

deflation: **1.** Statistical adjustment of data by which an economic time series expressed in current dollars is converted into a series expressed in constant dollars of a previous period. The purpose of the adjustment is to compensate for the distorting effects of inflation—i.e., the long-run upward trend of prices—through a reverse process of "deflation." **2.** Decline in the general price level

of all goods and services—or equivalently, a rise in the purchasing power of a unit of money. (Contrast with **inflation.**)

deflationary gap: Amount by which aggregate demand falls short of full-employment aggregate supply, thereby pulling down the real value of a nation's output.

demand: Relation expressing the various amounts of a commodity that buyers would be willing and able to purchase at possible alternative prices during a given period of time, all other things remaining the same. This relation may be expressed as a table (called a **demand schedule**), as a graph (called a **demand curve**), or as a mathematical equation.

demand curve: Graph of a demand schedule, showing the number of units of a commodity that buyers would be able and willing to purchase at various possible prices during a given period of time, all other things remaining the same.

demand deposit: Promise by a bank to pay immediately an amount of money specified by the customer who owns the deposit. It is thus "checkbook money" because it permits transactions to be paid for by check rather than with currency.

demand, law of: Principle which states that the quantity demanded of a commodity varies inversely with its price, assuming that all other things which may affect demand remain the same. These "all other" things include: (1) buyers' money incomes; (2) the prices of related goods in consumption; and (3) tastes and other nonmonetary determinants such as consumer preferences, number of buyers in the market, or composition of buyers.

demand price: Highest price a buyer is willing to pay for a given quantity of a commodity.

demand-pull inflation: Condition of generally rising prices caused by increases in aggregate demand at a time when available supplies of goods are becoming more limited. Goods may go into short supply because resources are fully utilized or because production cannot be increased rapidly enough to meet growing demand.

demand schedule: Table showing the number of units of a commodity that buyers would be able and willing to purchase at various possible prices during a given period of time, all other things remaining the same.

deposit-expansion multiplier: Proposition which states that an increase in excess reserves of the banking system can cause a magnified increase in total deposits; similarly, a decrease in the banking system's legal reserves may cause a magnified decrease in total deposits. The total cumulative expansion (or contraction) will at most be some multiple of the required reserve ratio. The deposit-expansion multiplier can be expressed by the formula:

$$\text{Deposit-expansion multiplier} = \frac{1}{\text{required reserve ratio}} = \frac{1}{R}$$

Therefore, if we let D represent the change in demand deposits for the banking system as a whole, and E the amount of excess reserves, then

$$D = E \times \text{deposit-expansion multiplier}$$

or

$$D = E \times \frac{1}{R}$$

Example: If $E = \$1,000$ and $R = 10$ percent, then $D = \$1,000 \times \frac{1}{0.10} = \$10,000$. Thus, excess reserves of $\$1,000$ can result in as much as a $10,000 increase in demand deposits.

There are "leakages," however, which prevent this multiplier from exerting its full impact. They include: (1) the leakage of cash into circulation, since some deposits will be withdrawn in cash and some checks will be "cashed" instead of deposited; (2) a margin of excess reserves which banks for one reason or another may not lend out; and (3) the failure of businessmen to borrow all that the banks want to lend.

depreciation: Decline in the value of a fixed asset, such as plant or equipment, due to wear and tear, destruction, or obsolescence resulting from the development of new and better techniques.

depression: Lower phase of a business cycle in which the economy is operating with substantial unemployment of its resources, and a sluggish rate of capital investment and consumption resulting from little business and consumer optimism.

derived demand: Demand for a product or resource based on its contribution to the product for which it is used. *Examples:* The separate demands for bricks, lumber, etc., are derived partly from the demand for construction; the demand for steel is derived partly from the demand for automobiles.

devaluation: Official act which makes a domestic currency cheaper in terms of gold or foreign currencies. It is typically designed to increase a nation's exports while reducing its imports.

dialectical materialism: Logical method of historical analysis. In particular, it was used by Karl Marx, who employed the philosopher Hegel's idea that historical change is the result of inherently conflicting or opposing forces in society, and that the forces are basically economic or materialistic.

"dictatorship of the proletariat": Expression used by Karl Marx to describe a stage of Marxian socialism in which the bourgeoisie or capitalist class has been toppled from power and, along with its properties, is under the management of the proletariat or working class, which is also in control of the state.

diminishing marginal utility, law of: In a given period of time, the consumption of a product while tastes remain constant may at first result in increasing marginal utilities per unit of the product consumed, but a point will be reached beyond which further units of consumption of the product will result in decreasing marginal utilities per unit of the product consumed. This is the point of diminishing marginal utility. *Note:* Even though marginal utility may rise at first, it *must eventually fall*. It is the diminishing phase of marginal utility that is relevant and serves as the basis for the law.

diminishing returns (variable proportions), law of: In a given state of technology, the addition of a variable factor of production to other fixed factors of production may at first yield increasing marginal returns per unit of the variable factor added, but a point will be reached beyond which further additions of the variable factor will yield diminishing marginal returns per unit of the variable factor added. This is the point of diminishing marginal returns. *Note:* Even though marginal returns may rise at first, they *must eventually fall*. It is the diminishing phase of marginal returns that is relevant and serves as the basis for the law.

direct tax: Tax that is not shifted—that is, its burden is borne by the persons or firms originally taxed. *Examples:* personal income taxes, social security taxes paid by employees, and death taxes.

discount rate: Interest rate charged to member banks on their loans from the Federal Reserve Banks. It is called a "discount rate" because the interest on a loan is discounted when the loan is made, rather than collected when the loan is repaid.

disequilibrium: State of nonequilibrium. *Example:* A situation in which the quantities supplied and demanded of a commodity at a given price are unequal, so that there is a tendency for market prices and/or quantities to change. Any economic organism or system such as a household, a firm, a market, or an economy which is not in equilibrium is said to be in disequilibrium.

disguised unemployment (underemployment): Situation in which employed resources are not being used in their most efficient ways.

disinvestment: Reduction in the total stock of capital goods caused by failure to replace it as it wears out. *Example:* The consumption or using up of factories, machines, etc., at a faster rate than they are being replaced so that the productive base is diminishing.

disposable personal income: Income remaining after payment of personal taxes.

dissaving: Expenditure on consumption in excess of income. This may be accomplished by drawing on past savings, borrowing, or receiving help from others.

dividend: Earnings which a corporation pays to its stockholders. Payments are usually in cash, but may also be in property, securities, or other forms.

division of labor: Specialization in productive activities among workers, resulting in increased production because it: (1) permits development and refinement of skills; (2) avoids the time that is wasted in going from one job to another; and (3) simplifies human tasks, thus permitting the introduction of labor-saving machines.

double coincidence of wants: Situation which is necessary in a barter exchange, because each party must have what the other wants and must be willing to trade at the exact quantities and terms suitable to both.

double taxation: Taxation of the same base in two different forms. A typical example is the corporate income tax: the corporation pays an income tax on its profits, and the stockholder pays an income tax on the dividends he receives from those profits.

draft: Unconditional written order by one party (the creditor or drawer) on a second party (the debtor or drawee) directing him to pay a third party (the bearer or payee) a specified sum of money. An ordinary check, therefore, is an example of a draft.

dual labor market: Labor market consisting of two submarkets: (1) a primary labor market in which jobs are characterized by relatively high wages, favorable working conditions, and employment stability; and (2) a secondary labor market in which jobs, when they are available, pay relatively low wages, provide poor working conditions, and are highly unstable. Blue-collar workers, many of whom are union members, comprise most of the participants in the primary market, whereas the competitively "disadvantaged poor"—the unskilled, the undereducated, and the victims of racial prejudice—are confined to the secondary market.

dumping: Sale of the same product in different markets at different prices. *Example:* A monopolist might restrict his output in the domestic market and charge a higher price because demand is relatively inelastic, and "dump" the rest of his output in a foreign market at a lower price because demand there is relatively elastic. He thereby gains the benefit of lower average total costs on his entire output (domestic plus foreign) and earns a larger net profit than if he sold the entire output in the domestic market—which he could do only by charging a lower price per unit on all units sold.

duopoly: Oligopoly consisting of two sellers. Hence it may be either a perfect duopoly or an imperfect one, depending on whether the product is standardized or differentiated.

dynamic model: One in which economic phenomena are studied by relating them to preceding or succeeding events. The influence of time is therefore taken explicitly into account. A dynamic model is thus like a "motion picture" as distinguished from a "snapshot." (Contrast with **static model.**)

econometrics: Integration of economic theory, mathematics, and statistics. It consists of expressing economic relationships in the form of mathematical equations and verifying the resulting models by statistical methods.

economic costs: Payments made to the owners of the factors of production to persuade them to supply their resources in a particular activity.

economic good: Scarce good—that is, any good for which the market price is greater than zero at a particular time and place. (Opposite of **free good.**)

economic growth: Rate of increase in an economy's real output or income over time—that is, the rise in its full-employment output in constant prices. Economic growth may be expressed in terms of either real GNP or real NNP, on either a total or per capita basis over a period of time. The "total" measure is employed to describe the expansion of a nation's economic output or potential, whereas the "per capita" measure is used to express its material standard of living and to compare it with other countries.

economic indicators: Time series of economic data, classified as either leading, lagging, or coincident indicators. They are used in business cycle analysis and forecasting.

economic interpretation of history: Proposition advanced by Karl Marx (and others) that the great political, social, intellectual, and ethical movements of history are determined by the ways in which societies organize their social institutions to carry on the basic economic activities of production, exchange, distribution, and consumption of goods. Thus, economic forces are the prime cause of fundamental historical change.

economic man: The notion that each individual in a capitalistic society, whether he be a worker, businessman, consumer, investor, etc., is motivated by economic forces, and hence will always act to obtain the greatest satisfaction for the least sacrifice or cost. Satisfaction may take the form of profits to a businessman, wages or leisure hours to a worker, pleasure to a consumer from the goods that he purchases, and so on.

economic plan: Detailed method, formulated beforehand, for achieving specific economic objectives by governing the activities and interrelationships of those economic organisms, namely firms, households, and governments, that have an influence on the desired outcome.

economic (pure) profit: Payment to a firm in excess of its economic costs, including normal profit. It is the same as **net revenue.**

economic rent: Payment to an owner of a factor of production, in an industry in equilibrium, in excess of the factor's supply price or opportunity cost—that is, in excess of the minimum amount necessary to keep that factor in its present occupation. It is thus a surplus to the recipient.

economics: Social science concerned chiefly with the way society chooses to employ its limited resources, which have alternative uses, to produce goods and services for present and future consumption.

economic system: Relationships between the organisms or components of an economy (such as its households, firms, and government) and the institutional framework of laws and customs within which these organisms operate.

economies (diseconomies) of scale: The decreases (increases) in a firm's long-run average costs as the size of its plant is increased. Those factors that give rise to economies of scale or decreasing long-run average costs of production as the plant size increases are: (1) greater specialization of resources; (2) more efficient utilization of equipment; (3) reduced unit costs of inputs; (4) opportunities for economical utilization of by-products; and (5) growth of auxiliary facilities. Diseconomies of scale may eventually set in, however, due to: (1) limitations of (or "diminishing returns" to) management in its decision-making function; and (2) competition among firms in bidding up the prices of limited resources.

elasticity: Percentage change in quantity demanded or supplied resulting from a 1 percent change in price. Mathematically, it is the ratio of the percentage change in quantity (demanded or supplied) to the percentage change in price:

$$\text{Elasticity, } E = \frac{\text{percentage change in quantity}}{\text{percentage change in price}}$$

$$= \frac{(Q_2 - Q_1)/(Q_2 + Q_1)}{(P_2 - P_1)/(P_2 + P_1)}$$

where Q_1 and Q_2, and P_1 and P_2, denote the corresponding quantities and prices before and after the change. This coefficient of elasticity is usually stated numerically without regard to algebraic sign, and may range from zero to infinity. It may take any of five forms:

perfectly elastic	$(E = \infty)$
relatively elastic	$(E > 1)$
unit elastic	$(E = 1)$
relatively inelastic	$(E < 1)$
perfectly inelastic	$(E = 0)$

The above definition refers to what is known as *price elasticity* of demand or supply. It is one of several types of elasticities that exist in economics and is the one that is commonly understood unless otherwise specified. In general, elasticity may be thought of as the responsiveness of changes in one variable to changes in another, where responsiveness is measured in terms of percentage changes.

Employment Act of 1946: Act of Congress which requires the government to maintain high levels of employment, production, and purchasing power. To assist the President in this task, the act authorizes him to appoint a panel of experts known as the Council of Economic Advisors.

Engel's Laws: Set of relationships between consumer expenditures and income, derived by a nineteenth-century German statistician, Ernst Engel, based on research into workingmen's purchases in Western Europe during the 1850s. The relationships state that as a family's income increases: (1) the percentage it spends on food decreases; (2) the percentage it spends on housing and household operations remains about constant (except for fuel, light, and refrigeration, which decreases); and (3) the percentage it spends on all other categories and the amount it saves increase, except for medical care and personal care items, which remain fairly constant). In general, the *total* amount spent increases as a family's income increases. *Note:* Strictly speaking, only the first relationship above is attributed to Engel; the other two are modernized versions of his early findings, based on more recent research.

entrepreneurship: Factor of production which designates the function performed by those who assemble the other factors of production, raise the necessary money, organize the management, make the basic business policy decisions, and reap the gains of success or the losses of failure. The entrepreneur is the innovator and the catalyst in a capitalistic system. He need not be exclusively an owner or a manager; the entrepreneurial function may be performed by both, depending on the size and complexity of the firm.

equal advantage, law of: In a market economy, owners of resources will always transfer them from less advantageous to more advantageous uses. As this happens, the occupations *out* of which resources are transferred often tend to become more advantageous while the occupations *into* which resources are transferred tend to become less advantageous. This transfer process continues until all occupations are equally advantageous. At this point there is no gain to be made by further transfer of resources. Hence the economy is in equilibrium. *Note:* The term "advantageous" includes both monetary and nonmonetary considerations. The latter helps explain why permanent differences in monetary rewards may exist between various occupations.

equation of exchange: Expression of the relation between the quantity of money (M), its velocity of circulation (V), the average price (P) of final goods and services, and the physical quantity (Q) of those goods and services, thus:

$$MV = PQ$$

The equation is actually an identity which states that the total amount of money spent on goods and services (MV) is equal to the total amount of money received for goods and services (PQ). (*See* **quantity theory of money.**)

equilibrium: State of balance between opposing forces. An object in equilibrium is in a state of rest and has no tendency to change.

equilibrium conditions: Set of relationships that defines the equilibrium properties of an economic organism such as a household, a firm, or an entire economy.

equilibrium price: 1. Price of a commodity determined in the market by the intersection of a supply and demand curve. (Also called **normal price.**) **2.** Price (and corresponding equilibrium quantity) that maximizes a firm's profit.

equilibrium quantity: 1. Quantity of a commodity determined in the market by the intersection of a supply and demand curve. **2.** Quantity (and corresponding equilibrium price) that maximizes a firm's profit.

escalator clause: Provision in a contract whereby payments such as wages, insurance or pension benefits, or loan repayments, over a stated period are tied to a comprehensive measure of living costs or price-level changes. The consumer price index and the implicit price index (GNP deflator) are the most common measures used.

estate tax: Progressive (graduated) tax imposed by the federal government and by most state governments on the transfer of all property owned by a decedent at the time of death. Exemptions, deductions, and rates vary widely among the states.

Eurodollars: Dollar deposits in banks outside the United States, mostly in Europe. They are held by American and foreign banks, corporations, and individuals, and represent dollar obligations which are constantly being shifted from one country to another in search of the highest return; hence they may affect balances of payments and may even turn pressure on a currency into an international monetary crisis.

European Recovery Program (ERP): Commonly known as the "Marshall Plan" (after Secretary of State, George C. Marshall, who proposed it in 1947), this was a comprehensive recovery blueprint for European countries, financed by the United States, for the purposes of: (1) increasing their productive capacity; (2) stabilizing their financial systems; (3) promoting their mutual economic cooperation; and (4) reducing their dependence on U.S. assistance. The ERP was terminated in 1951 after considerable success, and its functions were absorbed by other government agencies and programs.

excess reserves: Quantity of a bank's legal reserves over and above its required reserves. Thus:

Excess reserves = legal reserves − required reserves

Excess reserves are the key to a bank's lending power.

excise tax: Tax imposed on the manufacture, sale, or consumption of various commodities such as liquor, tobacco, and gasoline.

exclusion principle: Basis for distinguishing between nonpublic and public goods. A good is nonpublic if anyone who does not pay can be excluded from its use; otherwise, it is a public good.

explicit costs: Money outlays of a firm recorded in its books of account. (Contrast with **implicit costs.**)

external economies and diseconomies of scale: Conditions that bring about decreases or increases in a firm's long-run average costs as a result of factors that are entirely outside of the firm as a producing unit. They depend on adjustments of the industry and are related to the firm only to the extent that the firm is a part of the industry. *Example:* External economies may result from improvements in public transportation and marketing facilities as an industry develops in a particular geographic area; however, diseconomies may eventually set in as firms bid up the prices of limited resources in the area.

externalities: External benefits or costs of activities for which no compensation is made. (Externalities are also called **spillovers.**)

Fabian socialism: Form of socialism founded in England in 1884. It emerged as an outgrowth of utopian socialism by advocating gradual and evolutionary reform within a democratic framework.

factors of production: Human and nonhuman productive resources of an economy, usually classified into four groups: land, labor, capital, and entrepreneurship.

Fair Labor Standards Act (Wages and Hours Law) 1938: An act, with subsequent amendments, which specifies minimum hourly wages, overtime rates, and prohibitions against child labor for workers producing goods in interstate commerce.

family allowance plan: Plan that provides every family, rich or poor, with a certain amount of money based exclusively on the number and age of its children. Families above certain designated income levels return all or a portion of the money with their income taxes, but those below specified income levels keep it. More than 60 countries have family allowance plans.

featherbedding: Labor union "make work" rules designed to increase the labor or labor time on a particular job. Outlawed by the Labor-Management Relations (Taft-Hartley) Act of 1947.

Federal Advisory Council: Committee within the Federal Reserve System that advises the Board of Governors on important current developments.

Federal Open Market Committee: The most important policy-making body of the Federal Reserve System. Its chief function is to establish policy for the System's purchase and sale of government and other securities in the open market.

Federal Reserve Bank: One of the 12 banks (and branches) which make up the Federal Reserve System. Each serves as a "banker's bank" for the member banks in its district by acting as a source of credit and a depository of resources, and by performing other useful functions.

Federal Reserve System: Central banking system created by Congress in 1913. It consists of: (1) 12 Federal Reserve Banks—one located in each of 12 districts in the country; (2) a Board of Governors; (3) a Federal Open Market Committee and various other committees; and (4) several thousand member banks which hold the great majority of all commercial bank deposits in the nation.

Federal Trade Commission: Government agency created in 1914. It is charged with preventing unfair business practices by enforcing the Federal Trade Commission Act, and exercising concurrently with the Justice Department the enforcement of prohibitive provisions of the Clayton Antitrust Act as amended by the Robinson-Patman Act.

Federal Trade Commission Act (1914): A major antitrust law of the U.S. Its chief purpose is to prevent unfair (i.e., deceptive, dishonest, or injurious) methods of competition and, as amended by the Wheeler-Lea Act (1938), to safeguard the public by preventing the dissemination of false and misleading advertising of food, drugs, cosmetics, and therapeutic devices.

financial intermediaries: Business firms that serve as middlemen between lenders and borrowers by creating and issuing financial obligations or claims against themselves in order to acquire profitable financial claims against others. Examples of such firms are commercial banks, mutual savings banks, savings and loan associations, credit unions, insurance companies, and all other financial institutions. In general, they are wholesalers and retailers of funds.

financial markets: The money and capital markets of the economy. In the former, short-term credit instruments are bought and sold; in the latter, long-term credit and equity instruments are dealt in.

firm: Business organization which owns and directs the activities of one or more of its plants or offices.

fiscal drag: Tendency of a high-employment economy to be held back from its full growth potential because it is incurring budgetary surpluses. Such surpluses may arise because, other things being equal, a progressive tax system tends to generate increases in revenues relative to expenditures during periods of high employment.

fiscal policy: Deliberate exercise of the government's power to tax and spend in order to achieve price stability, help dampen the swings of business cycles, and bring the nation's output and employment to desired levels.

Fisher equation: See **equation of exchange.**

fixed assets: Durable assets of an enterprise used to carry on its business, such as land, buildings, machinery, equipment, office furniture, automobiles, and trucks.

fixed costs: Costs that do not vary with a firm's output. *Examples:* rental payments, interest on debt, property taxes.

floating exchange rates: Foreign exchange rates determined in a free market by supply and demand.

"forced" saving: Situation in which consumers are prevented from spending part of their income on consumption. Some examples include: (1) prices rising faster than money wages, causing a decrease in real consumption and hence an increase in real (forced) saving; (2) a corporation which plows back some of its profit instead of distributing it as dividend income to stockholders; and (3) a government which taxes its citizens and uses the funds for investment, thereby preventing the public from utilizing a portion of its income for the purchase of consumer goods.

foreign exchange: Instruments used for international payments. Such instruments consist not only of currency, but also of checks, drafts, and bills of exchange (which are orders to pay currency).

foreign exchange rate: Price of one currency in terms of another.

foreign-trade multiplier: Principle which states that fluctuations in exports or imports may generate magnified variations in national income. It is based on the idea that a change in exports relative to imports has the same multiplier effect on national income as a change in autonomous expenditures; similarly, a change in imports relative to exports has the same multiplier effect on national income as a change in withdrawals from the income stream. In general, an increase in exports tends to raise domestic income, but the increased income also induces some imports which act as "leakages," tending to reduce the full multiplier effect that would exist if imports remained constant.

forward exchange: Foreign exchange bought (or sold) at a given time and at a stipulated current or "spot" price, but payable at some future date. By buying or selling forward exchange, importers and exporters can protect themselves against the risks of fluctuations in the current exchange market.

forward prices: Proposed plan for reducing price uncertainty and encouraging greater stability in agriculture through the use of the price system as an adjustment mechanism. Under the plan, a government-appointed board would predict in advance of breeding or seeding time the equilibrium prices of commodities, based on expected supply and demand. The government would then guarantee those predicted or forward prices in two ways: by storage programs and direct payments to farmers if actual prices should fall below forward prices, and by a direct tax on farmers if actual prices should rise above forward prices.

free good: Good for which the market price is zero at a particular time and place.

free-trade area: Association of trading nations whose participants agree to impose no restrictive devices such as tariffs or quotas on one another, but are free to impose whatever restrictive devices they wish on nonparticipants. *Example:* The European Free Trade Association (EFTA).

frictional unemployment: Unemployment due to frictions in the economic system resulting from imperfect labor mobility, imperfect knowledge of job opportunities, and a general inability of the economy to match people with jobs instantly and smoothly. A common form of frictional unemployment consists of people who are temporarily out of work because they are between jobs.

full cost (average cost) price: Price for a given volume of output which is at least high enough to cover all of a firm's costs of production—that is, its average total cost for that volume of output. If demand is great enough to enable the firm to sell its entire output at that price, then the firm will earn a normal profit. If it can sell its output at a still higher price, it will earn an economic or pure profit.

full employment: Condition in which the economy's resources available for employment are being utilized with maximum efficiency. In terms of society's human resources, this means that the entire civilian labor force is working, except for those who are temporarily out of work or who are changing jobs.

full-employment budget: Estimate of annual government expenditures and revenues that would occur if the economy were operating at full employment. Any resulting surplus (or deficit) is called a full-employment surplus (or deficit).

"functional finance": Philosophy which holds that the government should pursue whatever fiscal measures are needed to achieve noninflationary full employment and economic growth—without regard to budget balancing per se. The federal budget is thus viewed functionally as a flexible fiscal tool for achieving economic objectives, rather than as an accounting statement to be balanced periodically.

functional income distribution: Payments in the form of wages, rents, interest, and profits made to the owners of the factors of production in return for supplying their labor, land, capital, and entrepreneurial ability.

gains from trade: Net benefits or increases in goods which a country receives as a result of trade.

General Agreements on Tariffs and Trade (GATT): International commercial agreement signed in 1947 by the U.S. and many other countries for the purpose of achieving four basic long-run objectives: (1) nondiscrimination in trade through adherence to unconditional most-favored nation treatment; (2) reduction of tariffs by negotiation; (3) elimination of import quotas (with some exceptions); and (4) resolution of differences through consultation.

general equilibrium theory: Theory or model of the interrelations between prices and outputs of goods and resources in different markets, and the possibility of simultaneous equilibrium among all of them. It is primarily of theoretical interest, but focuses attention on the fact that in the real world markets are often interdependent.

general price level: Expression representing the "average" level of prices in the economy. It is often represented by the **Implicit Price Index,** although no index can accurately reflect all prices.

gift tax: Progressive (graduated) tax imposed by the federal and by some state governments. It is paid by the donor or person who makes the gift, not the donee or recipient of it. Exemptions, deductions, and rates vary widely among the states.

Gini coefficient of inequality: A measure of the degree of inequality in distribution. On a Lorenz diagram, it equals the numerical value of the area between the Lorenz curve and the diagonal line, divided by the entire area beneath the diagonal line. The ratio may vary between 0 (no inequality) and 1 (complete inequality).

GNP deflator: *See* **implicit price index.**

gold bullion standard: Monetary standard under which: (1) the national unit of currency (such as the dollar, pound, mark, etc.) is defined in terms of a fixed weight of gold; (2) gold is held by the government in the form of bars rather than coin; (3) there is no circulation of gold in any form within the economy; and (4) gold is available solely to meet the needs of industry (e.g., jewelry, dentistry) and settle international transactions among central banks or treasuries. This is the standard that the U.S. and most advanced nations adopted when they went off the gold coin standard in the early 1930s.

gold (coin) standard: Monetary standard under which: (1) the national unit of currency (such as the dollar, pound, franc) is defined by law in terms of a fixed weight of gold; (2) there is a free and unrestricted flow of the metal in any form into and out of the country; (3) gold coins are full legal tender for all debts; (4) there is free convertibility between the national currency and gold coins at the defined rate; and (5) there are no restrictions on the coinage of gold. Nearly 50 countries of the world were on this standard in the late nineteenth and early twentieth centuries.

gold exchange standard: Monetary standard under which a nation's unit of currency is defined in terms of another nation's unit of currency which in turn is defined in terms of, and convertible into, gold. This standard prevailed in the noncommunist world from 1944 to 1971 and is primarily of international economic significance. Thus in this period, the U.S. dollar was defined as equal to 1/35 of an ounce of gold and was convertible to foreign central banks at this rate. Each foreign central bank, in turn, defined the par value of its own currency in terms of the U.S. dollar and maintained it at that level. The entire system operated by international agreement (under the **International Monetary Fund**).

gold points: Range within which the foreign exchange rates of gold standard countries will fluctuate. Thus, the gold points are equal to the par rate of exchange plus and minus the cost (including insurance) of shipping gold. The upper and lower gold points for a nation are called its "gold export point" and "gold import point," respectively, because gold will be exported when the foreign exchange rate rises above the upper level and will be imported when the rate falls below the lower level. One nation's gold export point is thus another nation's gold import point, and vice versa.

goldsmiths' principle: Principle discovered centuries ago by the English goldsmiths. In modern terms, it enables banks to maintain a fractional—rather than 100 percent—reserve against deposits, because customers will not ordinarily withdraw their funds at the same time. Hence the banks can earn interest by lending out unused or excess reserves.

goodwill: One of the "intangible" assets of a firm (like patents and trademarks), the value of which is arbitrarily established on a company's balance sheet.

government monopoly: Monopoly both owned and operated by either a federal or local government. *Examples:* the U.S. Postal Service, many water and sewer systems, and the central banks of most countries.

grants-in-aid: Financial aid at the intergovernmental level which consists of: (1) revenues received by local governments from their states and from the federal government; and (2) revenues received by state governments from the federal government. These revenues are used mainly to help pay for public welfare assistance, highways, and education.

Great Leap Forward: Ambitious economic plan undertaken by Mainland China during 1958–1960 to accelerate enormously its rate of economic growth. The plan was unrealistic and forced the country into a major economic crisis.

Gresham's Law: Principle which asserts that cheap money tends to drive dear money out of circulation. Thus, if two kinds of metals such as gold and silver circulate with equal legal tender powers (as happened in the U.S. under the bimetallic standard during the nineteenth century), the cheaper metal will become the chief circulating medium while the dearer metal will be hoarded, melted down, or exported, thereby disappearing from circulation. The law is named after Sir Thomas Gresham, Master of the Mint under Queen Elizabeth I during the sixteenth century. (See **bimetallic standard; mint ratio.**)

gross national disproduct: Sum of all social costs or reductions in benefits to society that result from producing the gross national product. *Example:* Pollution of air and water is part of gross national disproduct, to the extent that it is caused by production of the gross national product.

gross national expenditure: Total amount spent by the four sector accounts of the economy (i.e., household, government, business, and foreign) on the nation's output of goods and services. It is equal, by definition, to gross national product.

gross national income: The equivalent of gross national product from the "income" viewpoint. It consists of national income at factor cost (i.e., the sum of wages, rent, interest, and profit) plus two nonincome or business expense items: indirect business taxes and capital consumption allowance.

gross national product: Total market value of all final goods and services produced by an economy during a year.

guaranteed annual income: Plan that awards all families under a certain "poverty line" level a straight allowance for each parent plus specified amounts for each child according to the size of the family. No family receives less than a designated amount, and as a family's income rises the payment from the government is reduced until a break-even level, which is a little higher than the poverty line, is reached.

hard-core unemployed: People who are unemployed because they lack the education and skills for today's complex economy. (Discrimination may also be a contributing factor.) They consist mainly of certain minority groups such as Negroes, Mexicans, the "too-old," the "too-young," the high-school dropouts, and the permanently displaced who are victims of technological change.

hog-corn price ratio: Number of bushels of corn required to buy 100 pounds of live pork, thus:

$$\text{Hog-corn price ratio} = \frac{\text{price of live hogs per 100 pounds}}{\text{price of corn per bushel}}$$

When the ratio is relatively low, hog production decreases because farmers find it more profitable to sell their corn in the market than to use it for feeding hogs; conversely, when the ratio is relatively high, hog production increases because farmers use the corn to feed more hogs, and to market them at heavier weights.

horizontal merger: Amalgamation under one ownership of plants engaged in producing similar products. The products might be close substitutes like cement, or moderate substitutes like tin cans and jars. The objective is to round out a product line which is sold through the same distribution channels, thereby offering joint economies in selling and distribution efforts.

human resources: Productive physical and mental talents of the people who comprise an economy.

hyperinflation: Situation in which prices are rising with little or no increases in output; hence it is also sometimes called "runaway" or "galloping" inflation.

hypothesis: A working guess about the behavior of things, or an expression about the relationship between variables in the real world. In economics, the "things" may include consumers, workers, business firms, investors, etc., and the variables may include prices, wages, consumption, production, or other economic quantities.

imperfect competition: A classification of market structures that falls between the two extremes of perfect competition and monopoly. It consists of monopolistic competition and oligopoly.

implicit costs: Costs of self-owned or self-employed resources that are not entered in a company's book of account. *Example:* the alternative interest return, rental receipts, and wages that a self-employed proprietor forgoes by owning and operating his own business.

Implicit Price Index (GNP deflator): Weighted average of the price indexes used to deflate the components of GNP. Thus for any given year:

$$\text{GNP in constant prices} = \frac{\text{GNP in current prices}}{\text{Implicit Price Index (= IPI)}}$$

Therefore:

$$\text{IPI} = \frac{\text{GNP in current prices}}{\text{GNP in constant prices}}$$

Because of its comprehensiveness, the IPI is the best single measure of broad price movements in the economy.

import quota: Law that limits the number of units of a commodity that may be imported during a given period.

incidence: Range of occurrence or influence of an economic act. It is a term used primarily in the study of taxation and refers to the economic organism such as a household or a firm that bears the ultimate burden of a tax.

income: Gain derived from the use of human or material resources. A flow of dollars per unit of time. (Contrast with **wealth.**)

income-consumption curve: In indifference-curve analysis, a line showing the amounts of two commodities that a consumer will purchase when his income changes while the prices of the commodities remain the same. Geometrically, it is a line connecting the tangency points of price lines and indifference curves as income changes while prices remain constant.

income effect: Change in quantity of a good demanded by a buyer due to a change in his real income resulting from a change in the price of a commodity. It assumes that the buyer's money income, tastes, and the prices of all other goods remain the same. (Contrast with **substitution effect.**)

income elasticity of demand: Percentage change in the demand for a good resulting from a one percent change in income. Thus:

Income elasticity of demand

$$= \frac{\text{percentage change in demand}}{\text{percentage change in income}}$$

$$= \frac{(Q_2 - Q_1)/(Q_2 + Q_1)}{(Y_2 - Y_1)/(Y_2 + Y_1)}$$

where Q_1 and Q_2 represent the quantities purchased before and after the change in income, and Y_1 and Y_2 represent the corresponding levels of income before and after the change. Thus it denotes the responsiveness of changes in purchases to changes in income, where responsiveness is measured in terms of percentage changes.

income statement: Financial statement of a firm showing its revenues, costs, and profit during a period. Also known as a profit-and-loss statement.

income tax: Tax on the net income or residual that remains after certain items are subtracted from gross income. The two types of income taxes are the personal income tax and the corporation income tax.

income velocity of money: Average number of times per year that a dollar is spent on purchasing the economy's annual flow of final goods and services—its GNP. It equals the ratio of GNP to the quantity of money. (See **equation of exchange.**)

inconvertible paper standard: Monetary standard under which the nation's unit of currency may or may not be defined in terms of any metal or other precious substance; however, there is no free convertibility into these other forms. Historically, this standard has existed on a domestic basis in all countries since the world-wide abandonment of gold in the 1930s.

increasing-cost industry: Industry which experiences increases in resource prices or in its costs of production as it expands because of new firms entering it. This will happen when the industry's demand for the resources it employs is a significant proportion of the total demand for those resources.

increasing costs, law of: Principle which states that on an economy's production-possibilities curve relating two kinds of goods, the real cost of acquiring either good is not the money that must be spent for it, but the increasing amount of the alternative good that the society must sacrifice or "give up" because it cannot have all it wants of both goods.

independent union: Labor union not affiliated with any federation of labor organizations. It may be national or international, and is not limited to workers in any one firm.

index numbers: Figures which disclose the relative changes in a series of numbers, such as prices or production, from a base period. The base period is usually defined as being equal to an index number of 100, and all other numbers in the series both before or after that period are expressed as percentages of that period. Index numbers are widely used in reporting business and economic data.

indifference curve: Graph of an indifference schedule. Every point along the curve represents a different combination of two commodities, and each combination is equally satisfactory to a recipient because each one yields the same total utility.

indifference schedule: Table showing the various combinations of two commodities that would be equally satisfactory or yield the same total utility to a recipient at a given time.

indirect tax: Tax that can be shifted either partially or entirely to someone other than the individual or firm originally taxed. *Examples:* sales taxes, excise taxes, taxes on business and rental properties.

induced consumption: That part of total consumption which is related to income.

induced investment: Tendency of rising income, output, and economic activity to stimulate higher levels of investment. That part of total investment which is related to aggregate income or output. It may also be directly related to induced consumption, which in turn is related to income. (Contrast with **autonomous investment.**)

induction: Process of reasoning from particular observations or cases to general laws or principles. Most human knowledge is inductive or empirical since it is based on the experiences of our senses. (Opposite of **deduction.**)

industrial relations: Rules and regulations governing the relationship between union and management. It often deals with such matters as union security (e.g., the type of recognition that the union is accorded, or its financial arrangement for collecting dues) and methods of controlling the quantity and kind of union membership through apprenticeship requirements, licensing provisions, initiation fees, and seniority rules.

industrial union: Labor union consisting of all members from a particular industry, such as a union of coal miners or a union of steel workers. It is thus a "vertically" organized union.

industry: Group of firms producing similar or identical products.

infant industry: Underdeveloped industry which, in the face of competition from abroad, may not be able to survive the early years of struggle before reaching maturity.

inferior good: A good whose consumption varies inversely with money income (prices remaining constant) over a certain range of income. *Examples:* potatoes, used clothing, and other "cheap" commodities bought by poor families. The consumption of these commodities declines in favor of more nutritious foods, new clothing, etc., as the incomes of low-income families rise.

inflation: Rise in the general price level (or average level of prices) of all goods and services—or equivalently, a decline in the purchasing power of a unit of money (such as the dollar). The general price level thus varies inversely with the purchasing power of a unit of money. For example, if prices double, purchasing power decreases by one-half; if prices halve, purchasing power doubles.

inflationary gap: Amount by which aggregate demand exceeds aggregate supply at full employment, thereby causing inflationary pressures.

inheritance tax: Tax imposed by most state governments on property received from the dead. It is primarily progressive (graduated) in rate structure, but exemptions, deductions, and rates vary widely among the states.

injunction: Court order requiring that a defendant refrain from certain practices, or that he take a particular action.

innovation: Adoption of a new or different product, or of a new or different method of production, marketing, financing, etc. It thus establishes a new relation between the output and the various kinds of inputs (capital, land, labor, etc.) in a production process. In a more formal sense, it is the setting up of a new production function.

innovation theory: Theory originated by Joseph Schumpeter (1883–1950) which attributes business cycles and economic development to innovations that forward-looking businessmen adopt in order to reduce costs and increase profits. Once an innovation proves successful, other businessmen follow with the same or with similar techniques, and these innovations cause fluctuations in investment which result in business cycles. The innovation theory has also been used as a partial explanation of how profits arise in a competitive capitalistic system.

interest: 1. Return to those who supply the factor of production known as "capital," i.e., the payment for supplying the funds with which businessmen buy capital goods. **2.** Price paid for the use of money or loanable funds over a period. It is stated as a rate—that is, as a percentage of the amount of money borrowed. Thus an interest rate of 5% means that the borrower pays 5¢ per $1 borrowed per year, or $5 per $100 borrowed per year, and so on.

interlocking directorate: Situation in which an individual serves on two or more boards of directors of competing corporations.

internal economies and diseconomies of scale: Conditions that bring about decreases or increases in a firm's long-run average costs or scale of operations as a result of size adjustments within the firm as a producing unit; they occur irrespective of adjustments within the industry and are due mainly to physical economies or diseconomies. *Example:* Internal economies may result from greater specialization and more efficient utilization of the firm's resources as its scale of operations increases, but internal diseconomies may eventually set in because of the limited decision-making abilities of the top management group.

International Bank for Reconstruction and Development (World Bank): Established by the United Nations in 1945 to provide loans for postwar reconstruction and to promote development of less developed countries. The Bank's chief function is to aid the financing of basic development projects such as dams, communication and transportation facilities, and health programs by insuring or otherwise guaranteeing private loans or, when private capital is not available, by providing loans from its own resources and credit. Affiliated agencies also exist to help finance higher-risk investment projects in underdeveloped countries.

International Monetary Fund (IMF): Established by the United Nations in 1944 for the purpose of: (1) eliminating exchange restrictions and providing for worldwide convertibility of currencies so as to encourage multilateral trade based on international specialization; (2) stabilizing exchange rates to reduce or eliminate short-term fluctuations in a nation's economy due to changes in its imports, exports, or speculative capital movements; and (3) assuring that changes in a country's exchange rate occur only with the Fund's approval, and only after the country has experienced a prolonged deficit or surplus in its balance of payments. Over 100 nations are in the Fund.

inventory: Stocks of goods which business firms have on hand, including raw materials, supplies, and finished goods.

investment: Spending by business firms on new job-creating and income-producing goods. It consists of replacements of or additions to the nation's stock of capital including its plant, equipment, and inventories, i.e., its nonhuman productive assets.

"invisible hand": Expression coined by Adam Smith in *The Wealth of Nations* to convey the idea that each individual, if left to pursue his self-interest without interference by government, would be led as if by an invisible hand to achieve the best good for society.

involuntary unemployment: Situation in which people who want work are unable to find jobs at going wage rates for the related skills and experiences they have to offer.

job classification: Process of describing the duties, responsibilities, and characteristics of jobs, point-rating them (perhaps by established formulas based on engineering time-studies of workers in such jobs), and then grouping the jobs into graduated classifications with corresponding wage rates and wage ranges.

jurisdictional strike: Strike caused by a dispute between two or more craft unions over which shall perform a particular job. Outlawed by the Taft-Hartley Act, 1947.

kinked demand curve: A "bent" demand curve, and a corresponding discontinuous marginal revenue curve, facing an oligopolistic seller. It signifies that if the seller raises his price above the kink, his sales will fall off rapidly because other sellers are not likely to follow his price upward; if he drops his price below the kink, he will expand his sales relatively little because other sellers are likely to follow his price downward. The market price, therefore, tends to stabilize at the kink.

Knights of Labor: National labor organization founded in 1869. It rejected the traditional organizing of workers by crafts, preferring instead the mass unionization of both unskilled and skilled workers. The Knights championed the cause of workers and achieved many liberal improvements and reforms, but began to decline in the late 1880s due to several factors: (1) opposition by craft leaders who preferred organization along craft lines; (2) internal dissension among leading members and groups; and (3) suspicion—unproved—of its involvement in Chicago's Haymarket riot and bombing of 1886. By 1917 it ceased to exist.

labor: 1. Factor of production which represents those hired workers whose human efforts or activities are directed toward production. **2.** All personal services including the activities of wageworkers, professional people, and independent businessmen. "Laborers" may thus receive compensation not only in the form of wages, but also as salaries, bonuses, commissions, etc.

labor force: The employable population, defined for measurement purposes as all people 16 years of age or older who are employed, plus all those who are unemployed but actively seeking work.

Labor-Management Relations (Taft-Hartley) Act (1947): An amendment to the National Labor Relations (Wagner) Act of 1935. It retains the rights given to labor by the 1935 Act, but also: (1) outlaws "unfair labor practices" of unions, such as coercion of workers to join unions, failure to bargain in good faith, jurisdictional strikes, secondary boycotts, and featherbedding; (2) outlaws the closed shop but permits the union shop; (3) requires unions to file financial reports with the NLRB, and union officials to sign non-Communist affidavits; (4) prohibits strikes called before the end of a 60-day notice period prior to the expiration of a collective-bargaining agreement; and (5) enables the President to obtain an 80-day court injunction against strikes which endanger national health or safety.

Labor-Management Reporting and Disclosure (Landrum-Griffin) Act (1959): Act which amended the National Labor Relations Act of 1935 by: (1) requiring detailed financial reports of all unions and union officers; (2) severely tightening restrictions on secondary boycotting and picketing; (3) requiring periodic secret-ballot elections of union officers; and (4) imposing restrictions on ex-convicts and Communists in holding positions as union officers.

lagging indicators: Time series that tend to follow or trail aggregate economic activity.

laissez-faire: "Leave us alone"—an expression coined in France during the late seventeenth century, but which today is interpreted to mean freedom from government intervention in all economic affairs.

land: Factor of production which includes land itself in the form of real estate as well as mineral deposits, timber, water, and other nonhuman or "natural" resources.

law: Expression of a relationship between variables, based on a high degree of unvarying uniformity under the same conditions. (Often used synonymously with **principle.**)

leading indicators: Time series that tend to move ahead of aggregate economic activity, thus reaching peaks and troughs before the economy as a whole.

legal monopoly: Privately owned firm which is granted an exclusive right by government to operate in a particular market, in return for which government may impose standards and requirements pertaining to the quantity and quality of output, geographic areas of operation, and the prices or rates that are charged. The justification of legal monopoly is that unrestricted competition in the industry is socially undesirable. Public utilities are typical examples of legal monopolies.

legal reserves: Assets that a bank may lawfully use as reserves against its deposit liabilities. For a member bank of the Federal Reserve System, legal reserves consist of deposits held with the district Federal Reserve Bank plus cash in the vaults of the member bank—called "vault cash." For a nonmember bank, legal reserves vary by state law, but they commonly include vault cash, demand deposits with other banks, and in some cases state and federal securities.

less developed (underdeveloped) country: A nation which, in comparison with the more advanced countries, tends to exhibit such characteristics as: (1) poverty level of income and hence little or no saving; (2) high rate of population growth; (3) substantial majority of its labor force employed in agriculture; (4) low proportion of adult literacy; (5) extensive disguised unemployment; and (6) heavy reliance on a few items for export.

liabilities: Monetary debts or things of value owed by an economic entity (such as an individual, household, or business firm) to creditors.

limited liability: Restriction of the liability of an investor, such as a stockholder in a corporation, to the amount of his investment.

liquidity: Ease with which an asset can be converted into cash quickly without loss of value in terms of money. Liquidity is thus a matter of degree. Money is perfectly liquid, whereas any other asset possesses a lower degree of liquidity—depending on the above condition.

liquidity preference (theory of interest): Theory formulated by J. M. Keynes (1883–1946) contending that households and businesses would rather hold their assets in the most liquid form, namely cash or checking accounts, in order to satisfy three motives: (1) the "transactions motive" to carry out everyday purchasing needs; (2) the "precautionary motive" to meet possible unforeseen conditions; and (3) the "speculative motive" to take advantage of a change in interest rates. These motives determine the demand for money, whereas the monetary authority determines its supply. The demand for, and supply of, money together determine the equilibrium rate of interest.

liquidity trap: Condition in which an increase in the supply of money will not reduce further the rate of interest, because the total demand for money at that relatively low interest rate (expressed in terms of a liquidity-preference curve) is infinite. This means that at the low rate of interest, everyone would rather hold money in idle balances than risk the loss of holding long-term securities offering poor yields. (In geometric terms, the liquidity trap exists at that rate of interest where the liquidity-preference curve becomes perfectly horizontal.)

loanable funds theory of interest: Theory which holds that the interest rate is determined by the demand for, and supply of, loanable funds only, as distinguished from *all* money. The sources of demand for loanable funds are businesses that want to invest, households that want to finance consumer purchases, and government agencies that want to finance deficits. The sources of supply of loanable funds are the central banking system, which influences the supply of money (and hence loanable funds) in the economy, and households and businesses that make loanable funds available out of their past or present savings.

lockout: Closing down of a plant by an employer in order to keep workers out of their jobs.

long run: Period that is long enough for a firm to enter or leave an industry, and to vary its output by varying all of its factors of production including its plant scale.

long-run average cost curve (planning curve): Curve that is tangent to, or envelops, the various short-run average total cost curves of a firm over a range of output representing different scales or sizes of plant. Thus it shows what the level of average costs would be for alternative outputs of different-sized plants.

long-run industry supply curve: Locus or "path" of a competitive industry's long-run equilibrium points. That is, the long-run industry supply curve connects the stable equilibrium points of the industry's supply and demand curves over a period of time, both before and after these curves have adjusted completely to changed market conditions. The long-run industry supply curve may be either upward sloping, horizontal, or downward sloping, depending on whether the industry is an increasing-, constant-, or decreasing-cost industry.

Lorenz curve: Graphic device for comparing cumulative percentage relationships between two variables. It is often used to compare a society's actual distribution of income with an equal distribution. For example, each axis of the chart is scaled from 0 to 100 percent, and the cumulative percentage relationships between two variables such as "percent of income" and "percent of families" are plotted against each other. The resulting curve of actual income distribution is then compared to a 45° diagonal line representing equal income distribution. The degree of departure between the two curves indicates the extent of income inequality. Similar curves may be constructed to show other types of distributions (e.g., distribution of wealth, distribution of wages in a factory).

macroeconomics: That part of economics which studies and theorizes about the economy as a whole, or about large subdivisions of it. It analyzes the economic "forest" as distinct from its "trees."

Malthusian theory of population: First published by Thomas Malthus in 1798 and then revised in 1803, this theory states that population tends to increase as a geometric progression (1, 2, 4, 8, 16, 32, etc.) while the means of subsistence increase at most only as an arithmetic progression (1, 2, 3, 4, 5, 6, etc.). This is because a growing population applied to a fixed amount of land results in eventually diminishing returns to workers. Human beings are therefore destined to misery and poverty unless the rate of population growth is retarded. This may be accomplished either by (1) preventive checks such as moral restraint, late marriages, and celibacy, or if these fail then by (2) positive checks such as wars, famines, and disease.

manpower policies: Deliberate efforts undertaken in the private and public sectors to develop and use the capacities of human beings as actual or potential members of the labor force.

marginal cost: Change in total cost resulting from a unit change in quantity. It is measured by the ratio:

$$\text{Marginal cost} = \frac{\text{change in total cost}}{\text{change in quantity}}$$

le–ma

Marginal cost is also the change in total variable cost resulting from a unit change in quantity, since total cost changes because total variable cost changes, whereas total fixed cost remains constant. In general, marginal cost measures the gain in total cost from an additional unit of quantity produced.

marginal cost price: Price (or production) of output as determined by the point at which a firm's marginal cost equals its average revenue (demand). This is an optimum price for society, because the value of the last unit to the marginal user (measured by the price he pays for the last unit, which is equal to the price he pays for any other unit) is equivalent to the value of the resources used to produce that unit. However, this so-called marginal cost price will leave the firm suffering a loss if it results in a price below the firm's average total cost.

marginal efficiency of investment: Expected rate of return on an addition to investment. More precisely, it is the expected rate of return over the cost of an additional unit of a capital good. It is determined by such factors as: (1) the demand for the product which the investment will produce; (2) the level of production costs in the economy; (3) technology and innovation; and (4) the stock of capital available to meet existing and future market demands.

marginal product: Change in total product resulting from a unit change in the quantity of a variable input employed. It is measured by the ratio:

$$\text{Marginal product} = \frac{\text{change in total product}}{\text{change in a variable input}}$$

Marginal product thus measures the gain (or loss) in total product from adding an additional unit of a variable factor of production.

marginal productivity theory of income distribution: Principle which states that when there is perfect competition for inputs, a firm will purchase factors of production up to the point where the price or marginal cost of the factor is equal to its marginal revenue productivity. Therefore, in real terms, each factor of production will be paid a value equal to what it contributes to total output—that is, it will be paid what it is "worth."

marginal propensity to consume: Change in consumption resulting from a unit change in income. It is measured by the ratio:

$$\text{Marginal propensity to consume} = \frac{\text{change in consumption}}{\text{change in income}}$$

It thus reveals the fraction of each extra dollar of income that is spent on consumption.

marginal propensity to invest: Change in investment resulting from a unit change in aggregate output. It is measured by the ratio:

$$\text{Marginal propensity to invest} = \frac{\text{change in investment}}{\text{change in aggregate output}}$$

marginal propensity to save: Change in saving resulting from a unit change in income. It is measured by the ratio:

$$\text{Marginal propensity to save} = \frac{\text{change in saving}}{\text{change in income}}$$

It thus reveals the fraction of each extra dollar of income that is saved.

marginal propensity to spend: Change in total spending on consumption and investment resulting from a unit change in aggregate output or income. The marginal propensity to spend, MPE, consists of the marginal propensity to consume, MPC, and the marginal propensity to invest, MPI. Thus out of any change in aggregate output or income:

$$MPE = MPC + MPI$$

marginal rate of substitution: In demand theory, the rate at which a consumer is willing to substitute one commodity for another along an indifference curve. It is the amount of change in the holdings of one commodity that will just offset a unit change in the holdings of another commodity, so that the consumer's total utility remains the same. Thus, along an indifference curve:

$$\text{Marginal rate of substitution} = \frac{\text{change in commodity } Y}{\text{change in commodity } X}$$

The marginal rate of substitution is always negative because one commodity must be decreased when the other is increased in order to keep total utility the same, i.e., to remain on a given indifference curve. (A parallel concept involving factor substitution exists in production theory.)

marginal revenue: Change in total revenue resulting from a unit change in quantity. It is measured by the ratio:

$$\text{Marginal revenue} = \frac{\text{change in total revenue}}{\text{change in quantity}}$$

Marginal revenue thus measures the gain (or loss) in total revenue that results from producing and selling an additional unit.

marginal revenue product: Change in total revenue resulting from a unit change in the quantity of a variable input employed. It is measured by the ratio:

$$\text{Marginal revenue product} = \frac{\text{change in total revenue}}{\text{change in a variable input}}$$

Marginal revenue product thus measures the gain (or loss) in total revenue from adding an additional unit of a variable factor of production.

marginal tax rate: Ratio, expressed as a percentage, of the change in a total tax resulting from a unit change in the base on which it is imposed. *Example:*

Marginal personal income tax rate

$$= \frac{\text{change in total personal income tax}}{\text{change in total taxable income}}$$

marginal utility: Change in total utility resulting from a unit change in the quantity of a commodity consumed. It is given by the ratio:

$$\text{Marginal utility} = \frac{\text{change in total utility}}{\text{change in quantity consumed}}$$

Marginal utility thus measures the gain (or loss) in satisfaction from an additional unit of a good.

margin requirements: Percentage down payment required of a borrower to finance purchase of stock. This rate is set by the Federal Reserve System's Board of Governors. An increase in margin requirements is designed to dampen security purchases; a decrease to encourage it.

market economy: Economic system in which the questions of what to produce, how much to produce, and for whom to produce are decided in an open market through the free operation of supply and demand. There are no "pure" market economies, but several specialized markets (such as the organized commodity exchanges) closely approximate some of the properties of a pure market system.

market price: Actual price that prevails in a market at any particular moment.

market rate of interest: Actual or money rate of interest which prevails in the market at any given time. (Contrast with **real rate of interest**.)

median: Special type of average that divides a distribution of numbers into two equal parts—one-half of all cases being equal to or greater than the median value, and one-half being equal to or less.

mediation: Method of settling differences between two parties (such as a union and management) by the use of an impartial third party, called a mediator, who is acceptable to both sides but makes no binding decisions. The mediator tries to maintain constructive discussions, search for common areas of agreement, and suggest compromises. Federal, state, and most large local governments provide mediation services for labor-management disputes. Mediation is also sometimes called "conciliation."

member bank: Bank which belongs to the Federal Reserve System. All national banks (chartered by the federal government) must be members. State banks may join if they meet certain requirements.

mercantilism: Set of doctrines and practices aimed at promoting national prosperity and the power of the state by: (1) accumulating precious metals (mainly gold and silver) through the maintenance of favorable trade balances; (2) achieving economic self-sufficiency through imperialism; and (3) exploiting colonies by monopolizing their raw materials and precious metals while reserving them as exclusive markets for exports. Mercantilism reached its peak in the seventeenth century, serving as a political and economic ideology in England, France, Spain, and Germany.

merger: Amalgamation of two or more firms under one ownership. The three common forms are: (1) *horizontal*, uniting similar plants and products; (2) *vertical*, uniting dissimilar plants in various stages of production; and (3) *conglomerate*, uniting dissimilar plants and products.

microeconomics: That part of economics which studies and theorizes about the specific economic units or parts of an economic system, such as its firms, industries, and households, and the relationships between these parts. It analyzes the "trees" of the economy as distinct from the "forest."

mint ratio: Under a bimetallic standard, the ratio of the weight of one metal to the other, and their equivalent in terms of the national unit of currency (such as the dollar) as defined by the government. For example, during the nineteenth century when the United States was on a bimetallic standard, the government defined the mint ratio for many years as:

15 grains silver = 1 grain gold = $1

The mint ratio was therefore 15 to 1. Since it remained fixed by law, it resulted in either gold or silver being driven out of circulation, depending on the relative market values of the two metals. (See **Gresham's Law; bimetallic standard**.)

mixed economy: Economic system in which the questions of what to produce, how much to produce, and for whom to produce, are decided partially by the free market and partially by a central government authority. There are varying forms and degrees of mixed economies.

model: Representation of the essential features of a theory or of a real-world situation, expressed in the form of words, diagrams, graphs, mathematical equations, or combinations of these.

monetary asset: Claim against a fixed quantity of money, the amount of which is unaffected by inflation or deflation. Examples: bonds, accounts receivable, savings deposits, promissory notes, and cash. For every monetary asset, there is an equal monetary liability. (See **monetary liability**.)

monetary liability: Promise to pay a claim against a fixed quantity of money, the amount of which is unaffected by inflation or deflation. For every monetary liability, there is an equal monetary asset. (See **monetary asset**.)

monetary policy: Deliberate exercise of the monetary authority's (i.e., Federal Reserve's) power to induce expansions or contractions in the money supply in order to help dampen the swings of business cycles and bring the nation's output and employment to desired levels.

monetary standard: Laws and practices which determine the quantity and quality of a nation's money, and establish the conditions, if any, under which its currency is ultimately redeemable.

monetary theory of business cycles: Theory which attributes business cycles to monetary factors, such as changes in the quantity of money and credit, or to changes in interest rates. Upswings occur when credit and borrowing conditions become favorable enough for businessmen to borrow; downswings occur when the banking system begins to restrict its expansion of money and credit.

money: Anything which has at least these four functions: (1) a medium of exchange for conducting transactions; (2) a measure of value for expressing the prices of current and future transactions; (3) a standard of deferred payments which permits borrowing or lending for future repayment with interest; and (4) a store of value which permits saving for future as well as current spending.

money illusion: Situation in which a rise in all prices and incomes by the same proportion leads to an increase in consumption, even though real incomes remain unchanged.

money income: Amount of money received for work done. (Contrast with **real income**.)

money market: Center where short-term credit instruments such as U.S. Treasury bills and certificates, short-term promissory notes, and bankers' acceptances are bought and sold.

Money Supply Rule: Guide for economic expansion advanced by some economists, especially by Professor Milton Friedman. The "Rule" states that the Federal Reserve should expand the nation's money supply at a steady rate in accordance with the economy's growth and capacity to produce, such as 3 to 5 percent a year for the United States. More than this would lead to strong inflationary pressures; less would tend to be stagnating if not deflationary.

money wages: Wages received in cash. (Contrast with **real wages**.)

monopolistic competition: Industry or market structure characterized by a large number of firms of different sizes producing heterogeneous (similar but not identical) products, with relatively easy entry into the industry.

monopoly: Industry or market structure characterized by a single firm producing a product for which there are no close substitutes. The firm thus constitutes the entire industry and is a "pure" monopoly.

monopoly price: Price (and production) of output as determined by the equality of marginal cost and marginal revenue—but with marginal revenue less than average revenue (demand). It is the profit-maximizing price for an imperfect competitor. At this price, the value of the last unit to the marginal user (measured by the price he pays for the last unit, which is equal to the price he pays for any other unit) is greater than the value of the resources used to produce that unit.

monopsony: Market structure consisting of a single buyer of a good or service. It may be thought of as a "buyer's monopoly."

moral suasion: Oral or written appeals by the Federal Reserve Board to member banks, urging them to expand or restrict credit but without requiring them to comply.

most-favored nation clause: Clause in a trade treaty by which each signatory nation agrees to extend to the other the same preferential tariff and trade concessions that it may in the future extend to nonsignatories, i.e., the same treatment that each gives to its "most favored nation." Most trading countries have adhered to this principle since 1948.

multiple expansion of bank deposits: Process by which a loan made by one bank is used to finance business transactions, and ends up as a deposit in another bank. Part of this may be used by the second bank as a required reserve, and the rest lent out for business use so that it is eventually deposited in a third bank, etc. The total amount of credit granted by the banking system as a whole will thus be a multiple of the initial deposit. (See **deposit-expansion multiplier.**)

multiplier: Principle which states that changes in investment bring about magnified changes in income, as expressed by the equation: multiplier × change in investment = change in income. The multiplier coefficient is given by the formula:

$$\text{Multiplier} = \frac{\text{change in income}}{\text{change in investment}} = \frac{1}{MPS} = \frac{1}{1 - MPC}$$

where MPS stands for the marginal propensity to save, and MPC the marginal propensity to consume. (*Note:* This multiplier is sometimes called the "simple multiplier" and the "investment multiplier" in order to distinguish it from other types of multipliers in economics.)

multiunit bargaining: Collective-bargaining arrangement covering more than one plant. It may occur between one or more firms in an industry and one or more unions, and it may take place on a national, regional, or local level. It is sometimes inaccurately called "industry-wide bargaining," although it is rarely completely industrywide.

municipals: Marketable financial obligations—mostly bonds—issued by state and local governmental authorities (the latter including cities, towns, school districts, etc.). Interest income paid to their owners is exempt from federal income taxes, and usually from state income taxes of the state in which they are issued.

national income (at factor cost): 1. Total of all net incomes earned by or ascribed to the factors of production—that is, the sum of wages, rent, interest, and profit which accrues to the suppliers of labor, land, capital, and entrepreneurship. (*Note:* It should not be confused with the total income received by people from all sources, i.e., personal income. The difference between the two is based on various accounting considerations.) **2.** In general terms and in theoretical discussions, the expression "national income"

is often used in a simple generic sense to represent the income or output of an economy.

National Labor Relations (Wagner) Act (1935): Basic labor relations law of the United States. It: (1) guarantees the right of workers to organize and bargain collectively through representatives of their own choosing; (2) forbids employers to engage in "unfair labor practices" such as discrimination or interference; and (3) authorizes the National Labor Relations Board to enforce the act and supervise free elections among a company's employees.

National Labor Relations Board: Government agency established under the National Labor Relations Act of 1935 to enforce that act; investigate violations of it; and supervise free elections among a company's employees so as to determine which union, if any, is to represent them in collective bargaining.

natural monopoly: Firm which experiences increasing economies of scale—i.e., long-run decreasing average costs of production—over a sufficiently wide range of output, enabling it to supply an entire market at a lower unit cost than two or more firms. Electric companies, gas companies, and railroads are classic examples.

near-monies: Assets which are almost, but not quite, money. They can easily be converted into money because their monetary values are known. *Examples:* time or savings deposits, U.S. government bonds, and cash values of insurance policies.

negative income tax: Plan for guaranteeing the poor a minimum income through a type of reverse income tax. A poor family, depending on its size and other income, would be paid by the government enough either to reduce or close the gap between what it earns and some explicit minimum level of income. That level might be equal to or above the government's designated "poverty line." As the family's income increases, the government's payment declines to zero.

neoclassical economics: Approach to economics which flourished in Europe and the United States between 1870 and World War I. Among its leaders were William Stanley Jevons in England; Carl Menger in Austria; Leon Walras in Switzerland; Vilfredo Pareto in Switzerland; Alfred Marshall in England; and John Bates Clark and Irving Fisher in the United States. The neoclassicists were primarily concerned with refining the principles of price and allocation theory, "marginalism," the theory of capital, and related aspects of economics. They made early and extensive use of mathematics, especially differential and integral calculus, in the development of their analyses and models. Much of the structure of modern economic science is built on their pioneering work.

net national product: Total sales value of goods and services available for society's consumption and for adding to its stock of capital equipment. It represents society's net output for the year and may be obtained by deducting a capital consumption allowance from gross national product.

net profit ratio: Ratio of a firm's net profit after taxes to its net sales. It is one of several general measures of a company's performance.

net revenue: A firm's "pure" or net profit—equal to its total revenue minus its total cost.

net worth: Difference between the total assets or things of value owned by a firm or individual, and the liabilities or debts that are owed.

New Economics: Body of economic thought which originated with the British economist John Maynard Keynes (1883–1946) in the 1930s. It has since been extended and modified to the point where its basic analytical tools and methods are now used by practically all economists. In contrast to classical economics, which emphasized the automatic tendency of the economy to achieve full-employment equilibrium under a government policy of laissez-faire, the New Economics demonstrates that an economy may be in equilibrium at any level of employment. It therefore concludes that appropriate government fiscal and monetary policies are needed in order to maintain full employment and steady economic growth with a minimum rate of inflation.

nonprice competition: Methods of competition that do not involve changes in selling price. *Examples:* advertising, product differentiation, customer service, etc.

normal good: A good whose consumption varies directly with money income, prices remaining constant. Most consumer goods are normal goods. (Same as **superior good.**)

normal price: The dynamic equilibrium price toward which the market price is always tending but may never reach.

normal profit: Least payment that the owner of an enterprise will accept as compensation for his entrepreneurial function, including risk-taking, management, etc. Normal profit is part of a firm's total economic costs, since it is a payment which the owner must receive in order to keep him from withdrawing his capital and managerial effort and putting them into some other alternative.

normative economics: Approach to economics which deals with what "ought to be" as compared to what "is." It involves statements which are value judgements, and hence much of it cannot be empirically verified. (Contrast with **positive economics.**)

Norris-La Guardia Act (1932): Act of Congress which outlawed the yellow-dog contract and greatly restricted the conditions under which court injunctions against labor unions could be issued.

notes payable: Promises to pay the holder, such as a bank, a sum of money within the year at a stated rate of interest.

oligopoly: Industry or market structure composed of a few firms selling either: (1) a homogeneous or undifferentiated product—the industry is then called a "perfect" or "pure" oligopoly; or (2) heterogeneous or differentiated products—the industry is then called an "imperfect" oligopoly. Some examples of perfect oligopoly are the copper, steel, and cement industries; some examples of imperfect oligopoly are the automobile, soap, detergent and household appliance industries.

open-market operations: Purchases and sales of government securities by the Federal Reserve System. Purchases of securities are expansionary because they add to commercial banks' reserves; sales of securities are contractionary because they reduce commercial banks' reserves.

open shop: Business firm in which the employer is free to hire either union or nonunion members.

operating profit ratio: Ratio of a firm's operating profit to its net sales.

opportunity cost: Value of the benefit that is forgone by choosing one alternative rather than another. Also called "alternative cost" since it represents the implicit cost of the forgone alternative to the individual, household, firm, or other decision-making organism. Opportunity costs are not entered in a firm's public accounting records. (Contrast with **outlay costs.**)

outlay costs: Money expended to carry on a particular activity. They are the explicit costs which are entered in a firm's public

accounting records, such as its income statement, to arrive at a measure of profit. *Examples:* wages and salaries, rent, and other money expenditures of a firm.

overinvestment theory: Theory of business cycles which holds that economic fluctuations are caused by too much investment in the economy as businessmen try to anticipate rising demands during an upswing, and from sharp cutbacks in investment during a downswing when businessmen realize they expanded too much in the previous prosperity.

paradox of thrift: Proposition which demonstrates that if people as a group try to increase their saving they will end up by saving less. The conclusion of the paradox is that an increase in saving may be desirable for an individual or family, but for an entire economy will lead to a reduction in income, employment, and output if it is not offset by an increase in investment. The concept was first introduced by Bernard Mandeville in *The Fable of the Bees* (1714) and was later recognized in the writings of the classical economists.

Pareto optimum: Condition which exists in a social organization when no change can be made which will make at least one person better off (in his own estimation) without making someone else worse off. (*Note:* When an economic system has attained a Pareto optimum, it is said to be *efficient.*)

parity price: Price which yields an equivalence to some defined standard. *Examples:* (1) In agriculture, a price of an agricultural commodity which gives the commodity a purchasing power, in terms of the goods that farmers buy, equivalent to that which it had in a previous base period. (2) In international economics, the price or exchange rate between the currencies of two countries that makes the purchasing power of one currency substantially equivalent to the purchasing power of the other.

parity ratio: In agriculture, an index of the prices farmers receive divided by an index of the prices they pay. It is used to measure the economic well-being of agriculture.

partial equilibrium theory: Theory or model of a particular market that assumes other markets are in balance. It thus ignores the interrelationships of prices and quantities that may exist between markets. *Example:* Ordinary supply and demand analysis is normally of a partial equilibrium nature since it usually focuses on a single market while neglecting others.

partnership: Association of two or more individuals to carry on, as co-owners, a business for profit. The partners are solely responsible for the activities and liabilities of the business.

patent: Exclusive right conferred by government on an inventor, for a limited time. It authorizes the inventor to make, use, transfer, or withhold his invention, which he might do even without a patent, but it also gives him the right to exclude others or to admit them on his own terms, which he can only do with a patent. Patents are thus a method of promoting invention by granting temporary monopolies to inventors.

patent monopoly: Firm which exercises a monopoly because the government has conferred upon it the exclusive right—through issuance of a patent—to make, use, or vend its own invention or discovery.

perfect competition: Name given to an industry or market structure characterized by a large number of buyers and sellers all engaged in the purchase and sale of a homogeneous commodity, with perfect knowledge of market prices and quantities, no discrimination in buying or selling, and perfect mobility of resources.

ne-pe

(*Note:* The term is usually employed synonymously with *pure competition*, although there is a technical distinction: pure competition does not require perfect knowledge or perfect resource mobility, and hence does not produce as smooth or rapid an adjustment to equilibrium as does perfect competition. However, both types of competition lead to essentially the same results in economic theory.)

personal income: In national-income accounting, the total income received by persons from all sources.

personal income distribution: The way in which income is distributed within the economy—often expressed in terms of percentages of aggregate income received by each fifth of all families, or in terms of the percentage of families falling within specific income classes.

Phillips curve: Curve which represents a tradeoff between unemployment and inflation. Every point along the curve denotes a different combination of unemployment and inflation, and a movement along the curve measures the reduction in one of these at the expense of a gain in the other.

planned economy: Economic system in which the government, according to a preconceived plan, plays a primary role in directing economic resources for the purpose of deciding what to produce, how much, and possibly for whom. A planned economy may or may not be a command economy, depending on whether the government operates within a substantially authoritarian or democratic framework. (*See* **command economy.**)

plant: Establishment that produces or distributes goods and services. In economics, a "plant" is usually thought of as a firm, but it may also be one of several plants owned by a firm.

Point Four Program: Part of the Foreign Economic Assistance Act of 1950. The Program seeks to raise living standards in the underdeveloped countries by making available to them U.S. technical and financial assistance, largely in the areas of agriculture, public health, and education. Much of this work is now carried out by agencies of the United Nations and by the U.S. Agency for International Development.

positive economics: An approach to economics which deals with what "is" as compared with what "ought to be." Much of positive economics involves the use of statements that can be verified by empirical research, i.e., by an appeal to the facts. (Contrast with **normative economics.**)

poverty line: Measure of poverty among families, defined in terms of a sliding income scale which varies between rural and urban locations according to family size.

precautionary motive: Desire on the part of households and businesses to hold part of their assets in liquid form so that they can be prepared for unexpected contingencies. This motive is influenced primarily by income levels rather than by changes in the interest rate and is one of the chief sources of demand for loanable funds in the modern theory of interest.

preferred stock: Shares of stock that receive preference over common stock at a fixed rate in the distribution of dividends, or in the distribution of assets if the company is liquidated.

prepayments: Business expenditures made in advance for items that will yield portions of their benefits in the present and in future years. *Examples:* advance premiums on a fire insurance policy; expenses incurred in marketing a new product.

price: Power of a commodity to command money in exchange for itself; hence, price is the "money name" of the value of a commodity.

price-consumption curve: In indifference curve analysis, a line which connects the tangency points of price lines and indifference curves by showing the amounts of two commodities that a consumer will purchase when his income and the price of one commodity remain constant while the price of the other commodity varies.

price discrimination: Practice by a seller of charging different prices to the same or to different buyers for the same good.

price leadership: Adherence by firms in an oligopolistic industry, often tacitly and without formal agreement, to the pricing policies of one of its members. Frequently but not always, the price leader will be the largest firm in the industry, and other firms will simply go along with the leader, charging the same price as he charges.

price line (budget line): In indifference curve analysis, a line representing all of the possible combinations of two commodities that a consumer can purchase at a particular time, given the market prices of the commodities and the consumer's money budget or income.

price system: Mechanism that allocates scarce goods or resources by rationing them among those buyers and sellers in the marketplace who are willing and able to deal at the going prices. The term is often used to express the way prices are established through the free play of supply and demand in competitive markets composed of many buyers and sellers. In reality, of course, there may be "noncompetitive" price systems in markets where buyers or sellers are relatively few in number.

primary reserves: A bank's legal reserves (consisting of vault cash and demand deposits with the Federal Reserve Bank) and demand deposits with other banks.

prime rate: Interest rate charged by banks on loans to their most credit-worthy customers.

principle: Fundamental law or general truth. It is often stated as an expression of a relationship between two or more variables. (*See* **law.**)

private benefit: Reward that accrues to an individual, household, or firm as a result of a particular act. (Contrast with **social benefit.**)

private cost: Economic cost that accrues to an individual, household, or firm as a result of a particular act. (Contrast with **social cost.**)

private property: Basic institution of capitalism which gives each individual the right to acquire economic goods and resources by legitimate means, and use or dispose of them as he wishes. This right may be modified by society to the extent that it affects public health, safety, or welfare.

private rate of return: The business or financial rate of return on an investment—that is, the rate which businessmen try to anticipate before investing their funds. In financial terms, it is the expected net profit after taxes and all costs, including depreciation, and may typically be expressed as a percentage annual return upon either the total cost of a project, or upon the net worth of the stockholder owners. (*Contrast with* **community rate of return.**)

private sector: That segment of the total economy consisting of households and businesses, but excluding government.

"process of creative destruction": An expression coined by the economist Joseph Schumpeter (1883–1950) to describe the growth of a capitalistic economy as a process of replacing the old with the new—that is, old methods of production, old sources of supply, and old skills and resources with new ones.

production function: Relationship between the number of units of inputs that a firm employs and the corresponding units of output that result.

production-possibilities curve: Curve which depicts all possible combinations of total output for an economy, assuming that there is: (1) a choice between producing either one or both of two kinds of goods; (2) full and efficient employment of all resources (i.e., no underemployment); and (3) a fixed supply of resources and a given state of technological knowledge.

product markets: Markets in which businesses sell the outputs that they produce (in contrast with resource markets in which they buy the inputs they need in order to produce).

profit: 1. Return to those who perform the entrepreneurial function. The residual (if any) after the payment of wages, rent, and interest to the owners of labor, land, and capital. **2.** Difference between total revenue and total cost. It is the same as net revenue, a residual or surplus over and above normal profit that accrues to the entrepreneur-owner after all economic costs including explicit (outlay) costs and implicit (opportunity) costs have been deducted from total revenue.

progressive tax: Tax whose percentage rate increases as the tax base increases. The U.S. personal income tax is an example. The tax is graduated so that, other things being equal and assuming no loopholes, a man with a higher income pays a greater percentage of his income and a larger amount of tax than a man with a lower income.

promissory note: Promise by one person to pay another a specified sum of money by a given date, usually within a year.

propensity to consume: Relationship between consumption expenditures and income such that as income increases, consumption increases, but not as fast as income. The expression **consumption function** is often used synonymously.

propensity to save: Relationship between saving and income such that as income increases, saving increases, but faster than income.

property resources: Nonhuman productive resources of an economy, including its natural resources, raw materials, machinery and equipment, transportation and communication facilities, etc.

property tax: Tax on any kind of property, such as real property in the form of land and buildings, or personal property like stocks, bonds, and home furnishings.

proportional tax: Tax whose percentage rate remains constant as the tax base increases; hence the amount of the tax paid is proportional to the tax base. The property tax is an example. Thus if the tax rate remains constant at 10 percent, a taxpayer who owns $10,000 worth of property pays $1,000 in taxes; a taxpayer who owns $100,000 worth of property pays $10,000 in taxes.

proprietorship: Simplest form of business organization in which the owner or proprietor is solely responsible for the activities and liabilities of the business.

prosperity: Upper phase of a business cycle in which the economy is operating at or near full employment, and a high degree of business and consumer optimism is reflected by a vigorous rate of capital investment and consumption.

psychological theory (of business cycles): Theory which holds that business cycles arise from people's responses to political,

social, and economic events. These responses become cumulative waves of optimism and pessimism, setting off cycles in economic activity.

public good: Commodity not subject to the exclusion principle—that is, its benefits are indivisible and hence no one can be excluded from its consumption whether he pays or not. Therefore most public goods, but not all, are produced by the public sector because the private sector is usually unable or unwilling to provide them. Other characteristics of a public good are (a) zero incremental or marginal costs, and (b) spillover costs or benefits. *Examples:* National defense, fire protection, air traffic control, radio broadcasting, most television transmission, and fireworks displays.

public sector: That segment of the total economy consisting of all levels of government. It is thus exclusive of the household and business segments which comprise the private sector.

public works: Government-sponsored construction, defense, or development projects which usually (but not always) entail public investment expenditures that would not ordinarily be undertaken by the private sector of the economy.

pure competition: See **perfect competition** for similarities and differences.

pure interest rate: Theoretical interest rate on a long-term, riskless loan, where the interest payments are made solely for the use of someone else's money. In practice, this rate is often approximated by the interest rate on long-term negotiable government bonds.

pure market economy: Competitive economic system composed of many buyers and sellers, so that prices are determined by the free interaction of supply and demand.

quantity theory of money: Classical theory of the relationship between the price level and the money supply. It holds that the level of prices in the economy is directly proportional to the quantity of money in circulation, such that a given percentage change in the stock of money will cause an equal percentage change in the price level in the same direction. The theory assumes that the income velocity of circulation of money remains fairly stable, and that the quantity of goods and services is constant because the economy always tends toward full employment. (See **equation of exchange.**)

ratio (logarithmic) scale: Scale on a chart such that equal distances are represented by equal percentage changes. (It is equivalent to plotting the *logarithms* of the same data on an ordinary arithmetic scale.)

rationing: Any method of restricting the purchases or usage of a good when the quantity demanded of the good exceeds the quantity supplied at a given price.

real asset: Claim against a fixed amount of a commodity or the right to a commodity, the money value of which is affected by inflation or deflation. *Examples:* house, car, and most other goods and services. (See **real liability.**)

real income: Purchasing power of money income or the quantity of goods and services that can be bought with money income. (Contrast with **money income.**)

realized investment: Actual investment out of any realized level of income. Equal to the sum of planned and unplanned (inventory) investment.

real liability: Promise to pay a fixed amount of a commodity, or right to a commodity, the money value of which is affected by inflation or deflation. (See **real asset.**)

pr–re

real output: Value of physical output unaffected by price changes.

real rate of interest: In classical theory, the interest rate measured in terms of goods. It is the rate which would prevail in the market if the general price level remained stable. Factors determining it are "real demand" for funds by businesses and "real supply" of funds by households. The former in turn is determined by the productivity of borrowed capital, and the latter by the willingness of consumers to abstain from present consumption.

real wages: Quantity of goods that can be bought with money wages. Real wages thus depend on the prices of the goods bought with money wages.

recession: Downward phase of a business cycle in which the economy's income, output, and employment are decreasing, and a falling off of business and consumer optimism is reflected by a declining rate of capital investment and consumption.

Reciprocal Trade Agreements program: Plan for expanding American exports through legislation which authorizes the President to negotiate U.S. tariff reductions with other nations in return for parallel concessions. The program consists of the Trade Agreements Act of 1934, with subsequent amendments, and related legislation.

recovery: Upward phase of a business cycle in which the economy's income, output, and employment are rising, and a growing degree of business and consumer optimism is reflected by an expanding rate of capital investment and consumption.

refunding: Replacement or repayment of outstanding bonds by the issue of new bonds. It is thus a method of prolonging a debt by paying off old obligations with new obligations.

regressive tax: Tax whose percentage rate decreases as the tax base increases. In this strict sense there is no regressive tax in the U.S. However, if we compare the rate structure of the tax with the taxpayer's net income rather than with its actual base, the term "regressive" applies to any tax which takes a larger share of income from low-income taxpayers than from high-income taxpayers. Most proportional taxes are thus seen to have regressive effects. A sales tax, for instance, is the same for rich people as for poor people, but the latter spend a larger percentage of their incomes on consumer goods and hence the sales taxes they pay — assuming that there are few if any exemptions — are a greater proportion of their incomes.

rent: Return to those who supply the factor of production known as "land."

required reserves: Minimum amount of legal reserves that a bank is required by law to keep behind its deposit liabilities. Thus if the reserve requirement is 10 percent, a bank with demand deposits of $1 million must hold at least $100,000 of required legal reserves.

resale price maintenance: Practice whereby a manufacturer or distributor of a branded product sets the minimum retail price at which that product can be sold, thereby eliminating price competition at the retail level.

resource markets: Markets in which businesses buy the inputs or factors of production they need to carry on their operations.

restrictive agreement: Conspiracy of firms that restrains trade among separate companies. It may involve a direct or indirect form of price fixing, output control, market sharing, coercion, exclusion of competitors, etc., and is illegal under the antitrust laws.

restrictive license: Agreement whereby a patentee permits a licensee to sell a patented product under restricted conditions. The restrictions may include the patentee's fixing the geographic area of the licensee, his level of output, or the price he may charge in selling the patented good.

return on net worth: Ratio of a firm's net profit after taxes to its net worth. It provides a measure of the rate of return on stockholders' investment.

return on total assets: Ratio of a firm's net profit after taxes to its total assets. It measures the rate of return on, or productivity of, total assets.

revenue sharing: Plan by which the federal government turns over a portion of its tax revenues to state and local governments each year.

right-to-work laws: State laws which make it illegal to require membership in a union as a condition of employment. These laws exist mostly in southern and midwestern states; their main effect is to outlaw the union shop, but in practice they have been relatively ineffective.

risk: Quantitative measurement of an outcome, such as a gain or a loss, in a manner such that the mathematical probability (or "odds") of the outcome can be predicted. Since risk is predictable, losses that arise from risk can be estimated in advance and can be "insured" against — either by the firm itself or by an insurance company. *Examples:* The losses resulting from rejects on an assembly line can be "self-insured" by being built into the firm's cost structure; the possibility of fire damage can be externally insured by an insurance company.

Robinson-Patman Act (1936): A major antitrust law of the United States, and an amendment to Section 2 of the Clayton Antitrust Act dealing with price discrimination. Commonly referred to as the "Chain Store Act," it was passed to protect independent retailers and wholesalers from "unfair discriminations" by large sellers who enjoy "tremendous purchasing power." The act declared the following illegal: (1) payment of brokerage fees where no independent broker is employed; (2) granting of discounts and other concessions by sellers such as manufacturers to buyers such as wholesalers and retailers, unless such concessions are made to all buyers on proportionately equal terms; (3) price discrimination, except where the price differences make "due allowances" for differences in cost or are offered "in good faith to meet an equally low price of a competitor"; and (4) charging lower prices in one locality than in another, or selling at "unreasonably low prices," where either of these practices is aimed at "destroying competition or eliminating a competitor."

rule of reason: Interpretation of the courts (first announced in the Standard Oil case of 1911) that the mere size of a corporation, no matter how impressive, is no offense, and that it requires "unreasonable" behavior in the form of actual exertion of monopoly power, as shown by unfair practices, for a firm to be held in violation of the antitrust laws. This interpretation, also known as the "good-trust-versus-bad-trust" criterion, was largely reversed in the Aluminum Company of America case in 1945, as well as in subsequent cases.

rule of 72: Approximate formula for expressing the relationship between the number of years Y required for a quantity to double if it grows at an annual rate of compound interest R. Thus:

$$YR = 72$$

therefore:

$$Y = \frac{72}{R} \quad \text{and} \quad R = \frac{72}{Y}$$

Example: At 6% interest compounded annually, a quantity will double in $Y = \frac{72}{6} = 12$ years. Conversely, if a quantity doubles in 12 years, the compounded annual rate of growth is $R = \frac{72}{12} = 6\%$.

sales tax: A flat percentage levy imposed on retail prices of items.

"satisfice": A concept to convey the idea that in reality firms do not seek to maximize profit, but rather to achieve certain levels of satiation. For example, firms try to attain a particular target level or rate of profit, and they try to achieve a specific share of the market or a certain level of sales.

saving: That part of income not spent on the consumption of goods and services.

Say's Law: An assertion that "supply creates its own demand." That is, the total supply of goods produced must always equal the total demand for them, since goods fundamentally exchange for goods while money serves only as a convenient medium of exchange. Therefore, any general overproduction is impossible. This assertion, named after the French economist Jean Baptiste Say (1767–1832), was fundamental in classical economic thought, for it led to the conclusion that the economy would automatically tend toward full-employment equilibrium if the government followed a policy of laissez-faire.

scarcity, law of: Principle which states that at any given time and place economic goods, including resources and finished goods, are scarce in the sense that there are not enough to provide all that people want; these scarce goods can be increased, if at all, only through sacrifice.

scientific method: A disciplined mode of inquiry represented by the processes of induction, deduction, and verification. The essential steps of the scientific method consist of: (1) recognition and definition of a problem; (2) observation and collection of relevant data; (3) organization and classification of data; (4) formulation of hypotheses; (5) deductions from the hypotheses; and (6) testing and verification of the hypotheses. All scientific laws may be modified or challenged by alternative theoretical formulations, and hence the entire cycle consisting of these six steps is a self-corrective process.

seasonal fluctuations: Short-term fluctuations in business and economic activity within the year, due to weather and custom. *Examples:* upswings in retail sales during holiday periods such as Christmas and Easter; changes between winter and summer buying patterns.

secondary boycott: Attempts by a union through strikes, picketing, or other methods to stop one employer from doing business with another employer. Outlawed by the Labor-Management Relations (Taft-Hartley) Act of 1947.

secondary reserves: A bank's earning assets that are near-liquid, i.e., readily convertible into cash on short notice without substantial loss. *Examples:* short-term financial obligations like U.S. Treasury bills, high-grade commercial paper, bankers acceptances, and call loans.

selling costs: Marketing expenditures aimed at adapting the buyer to the product. *Examples:* advertising, sales promotion, merchandising, etc.

separation of ownership and control: The notion that in a modern large corporation there is a distinction between those who own the business (the stockholders) and those who control it (the hired managers). If stock ownership is widely dispersed, the managers may be able to keep themselves in power for their own benefit rather than for the primary benefit of the corporation and its stockholders.

Sherman Antitrust Act (1890): A major antitrust law of the United States. It prohibits contracts, combinations, and conspiracies in restraint of trade, as well as monopolization or attempts to monopolize in interstate trade or foreign commerce. Violations are punishable by fines and/or imprisonment.

shortage: Any type of deficiency. For example: the amount by which the quantity demanded of a commodity exceeds the quantity supplied at a given price, as when the given price is below the free-market equilibrium price. (Contrast with **surplus.**)

short run: Period in which a firm can vary its output through a more or less intensive use of its resources, but cannot vary production capacity because it has a fixed plant scale.

simple multiplier: See **multiplier.**

single tax: Proposal advanced by the American economist Henry George (1839–1897) that the only tax a society should impose is a tax on land, because all rent on land is unearned surplus which increases as a result of natural progress and economic growth. Three major shortcomings leveled against this thesis are that the single tax would: (1) not yield enough revenues to meet government's spending needs; (2) be unjust, because surpluses may accrue to other resource owners besides landlords if the owners can gain some monopolistic control over the sale of their resources in the marketplace; and (3) be difficult to administer because it does not distinguish between land and capital—that is, between the proportion of rent that represents a surplus and the proportion that results from improvements made on the land.

slope: Rate of change or steepness of a line as measured by the change (increase or decrease) in its vertical distance per unit of change in its horizontal distance. It may be measured by the ratio:

$$\text{Slope} = \frac{\text{change in vertical distance}}{\text{change in horizontal distance}}$$

Hence a horizontal line has a zero slope; a vertical line has an "infinite" slope. All straight lines which are upward or positively inclined have a slope greater than zero. (Analogously, all straight lines which are downward or negatively inclined have a slope less than zero.) Parallel lines have equal slopes. The slope of a straight line is the same at every point, but the slope of a curved line differs at every point. Geometrically, the slope of a curve at a particular point can be found by drawing a straight-line tangent to the curve at that point. The slope of the tangent will then be equal to the slope of the curve at the point of tangency. In economics, all "marginals" are slopes or rates of change of their corresponding "totals." *Examples:* The marginal propensity to consume represents the rate of change or slope of its corresponding total propensity to consume; a marginal cost curve is the slope of its corresponding total cost curve; a marginal revenue curve is the slope of its corresponding total revenue curve; and so on. The concept of slope or rate of change (i.e., "marginal") is unquestionably the most powerful and important analytical tool of economics.

social balance: Existence of an optimum distribution of society's resources between the private and public sectors—the former represented by the production of private goods such as cars, clothing, and television sets, and the latter by the production of certain types of social goods like libraries, public health, and education.

social benefit: Benefit that accrues to society as a result of a par-

sa–so

ticular act, such as production or consumption of a commodity. (Contrast with **private benefit.**)

social cost: Cost that accrues to society as a result of a particular act, such as production or consumption of a commodity. It includes real costs, the costs of sacrificed alternatives, and reductions in incomes or benefits caused by the act. It thus includes noneconomic as well as economic costs. (Contrast with **private cost.**)

socialism: 1. In the theories of Karl Marx, a transitory stage between capitalism and full communism, in which the means of production are owned by the state, the state in turn is controlled by the workers (i.e., "dictatorship of the proletariat"), and the economy's social output is distributed by the formula: From each according to his ability, to each according to his labor. **2.** In its non-Marxist form, a movement which seeks to improve society's well-being by: (1) permitting predominantly private ownership of the means of production; (2) instituting public ownership only where it appears necessary in the interests of society; and (3) placing maximum reliance on the market economy while supplementing it with government direction and planning in order to achieve desired social and economic objectives. (*Note:* This definition represents a fundamental change in socialist thought since about 1960. Before then, Western socialism emphasized the replacement of private property with public ownership of the means of production and distribution. Today it is more of a "welfare state" concept.)

Social Security Act (1935): A basic comprehensive social security law of the United States. It provides for two types of social security: (1) social insurance programs for old age, survivors, disability, and health insurance (OASDHI), and for unemployment, both of which yield payments to insured persons or their survivors; and (2) a public charity program in the form of welfare services, institutional care, food, housing, and other forms of assistance. Some of the provisions of the act (with its many subsequent amendments) are administered and financed by the federal government, some by state and local governments, and some by all three levels of government.

social security tax: Payroll tax which finances the U.S. compulsory social insurance program covering old-age and unemployment benefits. The taxes are paid by both employees and employers, based on the incomes of the former.

Special Drawing Rights (SDRs or "paper gold"): Supplementary reserves (established in 1969) in the form of account entries on the books of the International Monetary Fund. They are allocated among participating countries in accordance with their quotas, and can be drawn upon by governments to help finance balance-of-payments deficits. They are meant to promote an orderly growth of reserves that will help the long-run expanding needs of world trade.

specialization: Division of productive activities among individuals and regions so that no one person or area is self-sufficient. Total production is increased by specialization, thus permitting all participants to share in a greater volume of output through the process of exchange or trade.

specific subsidy: Per unit subsidy on a commodity. (See **subsidy.**)

specific tax: Per unit tax on a commodity. (See **tax.**)

speculation: Act of buying or selling goods or securities in the hope of making a profit on price movements.

speculative motive: Desire on the part of households and businesses to hold part of their assets in liquid form so that they can take advantage of changes in the interest rate. This motive is thus tied specifically to the interest rate and is one of the chief sources of demand for loanable funds in the modern theory of interest.

spillovers: External benefits or costs of activities for which no compensation is made. (Spillovers are also called **externalities.**)

stable equilibrium: Condition in which an object or system (such as a price, firm, industry, or market) in equilibrium, when subjected to a shock sufficient to disturb its position, returns toward its initial equilibrium as a result of self-restoring forces. (In contrast, an equilibrium which is not stable may be either unstable or neutral.)

state farms: Lands in the Soviet Union that are owned and operated as state enterprises under elected or governmentally appointed managing directors. Workers and technicians are hired to run the farms, and are usually paid set wages as well as bonuses if their work exceeds basic norms of output.

static model: One in which economic phenomena are studied without reference to time—i.e., without relating them to preceding or succeeding events. Time, in other words, is not permitted to enter the analysis in any matter that will affect the results. A static model is thus like a "snapshot" as distinguished from a "motion picture." (Contrast with **dynamic model.**)

static multiplier: The multiplier without regard to the time required to realize its full effect. (Contrast with **truncated multiplier.**)

stock: Units of ownership interest in a corporation. The kinds of stock include common stock, preferred stock, and capital stock.

strategic-resource monopoly: Firm which has a monopoly because it controls an essential input to a production process. *Example:* DeBeers of South Africa owns most of the world's diamond mines.

strike: Agreement among workers to stop working, without resigning from their jobs, until their demands are met.

structural inflation: Condition of generally rising prices caused by uneven upward demand or cost pressures in some key industries such as automobiles, construction, or steel, even if aggregate demand is in balance with aggregate supply for the economy as a whole.

structural unemployment: Type of unemployment, usually prolonged, resulting from fundamental alterations or "structural" variations in the economy, such as changes in technology, markets, or national priorities. Most types of workers—unskilled, skilled, or professional—are subject to structural unemployment as a result of any of these factors.

subsidy: Payment (usually by government) to businesses or households that enables them to produce or consume a product in larger quantities or at lower prices than they would otherwise.

subsistence theory of wages: Theory developed by some classical economists of the late eighteenth and early nineteenth centuries. It held that wages per worker tend to equal what the worker needs to "subsist"—that is, to maintain himself and to rear children. If wages per worker rose above the subsistence level, people would tend to have more children and the population would increase, thereby lowering per capita real incomes; conversely, if wages per worker fell below the subsistence level, people would tend to have fewer children and the population would decline, thereby increasing per capita real incomes. Wages per worker would thus tend to remain at the subsistence level over the long run. This theory is also known as the "brazen" or "iron law of wages."

substitute goods: Commodities which are related such that at a given level of buyers' incomes, an increase in the price of one good leads to an increase in the demand for the other, and a decrease in the price of one good leads to a decrease in the demand for the other. *Examples:* gin and vodka; beef and pork. (Contrast with **complementary goods.**)

substitution effect: Change in quantity of a good demanded by a buyer resulting from a change in the good's price while the buyer's real income, tastes, and the prices of other goods remain the same. (Contrast with **income effect.**)

sunspot theory: Theory of business cycles proposed in England during the late nineteenth century. It held that sunspot cycles (disturbances on the surface of the sun) exhibited an extremely high correlation with agricultural cycles for a number of years; therefore, sunspots must affect the weather, the weather influences agricultural crops, and the crops affect business conditions. This theory received worldwide popularity when it was first introduced, but then fell into disrepute because the high correlation between sunspots and agricultural cycles did not endure; it was the result of accidental rather than causal factors.

superior good: A good whose consumption varies directly with money income, prices remaining constant. Most consumer goods are superior goods. (A superior good is also called a **normal good** because it represents the "normal" situation.)

super-multiplier: An enlargement of the simple multiplier, reflecting the inclusion of the marginal propensity to invest, *MPI*. It may be expressed by the formula:

$$\text{Super-multiplier} = \frac{1}{1 - (MPC + MPI)} = \frac{1}{1 - MPE}$$

where *MPE* denotes the marginal propensity to spend.

supplementary (fringe) benefits: Forms of compensation to workers other than basic wages, such as bonuses, pension benefits, and holiday and vacation pay.

supply: A relation expressing the various amounts of a commodity that sellers would be willing and able to make available for sale at possible alternative prices during a given period of time, all other things remaining the same. This relation may be expressed as a table (called a supply schedule), as a graph (called a supply curve), or as a mathematical equation.

supply curve: Graph of a supply schedule, showing the number of units of a commodity that sellers would be able and willing to sell at various possible prices during a given period of time, all other things remaining the same.

supply, law of: Principle which states that the quantity supplied of a commodity usually varies directly with its price, assuming that all other things which may affect supply remain the same. These "all other" things include: (1) resource prices, (2) prices of related goods in production, and (3) the state of technology and other nonmonetary determinants such as the number of sellers in the market.

supply price: Least price necessary to bring forth a given output. Hence it is the lowest price a seller is willing to accept in order to persuade him to supply a given quantity of a commodity.

supply schedule: Table showing the number of units of a commodity that sellers would be able and willing to sell at various possible prices during a given period of time, all other things remaining the same.

surplus: Any type of excess. For example: the amount by which the quantity supplied of a commodity exceeds the quantity demanded at a given price, as when the given price is above the free-market equilibrium price. (Contrast with **shortage.**)

surplus value: In the theories of Karl Marx, the difference between the value that a worker creates as determined by the labor-time embodied in the commodity that he produces and the value that he receives as determined by the subsistence level of wages. This surplus, according to Marx, is appropriated by the capitalist, and is the incentive for the development of a capitalistic system.

surtax: Tax imposed on a tax base in addition to a so-called normal tax. *Example:* a surtax on income in addition to the normal income tax. Note that a surtax is imposed on an existing tax base; it is not a "tax on a tax" as is popularly believed.

syndicalism: Economic system which demands the abolition of both capitalism and the state as instruments of oppression, and in their place the reorganization of society into industry-wide associations or syndicates of workers. The syndicates, fundamentally trade unions, would replace the state. Each syndicate would then govern its own members in their activities as producers, but leave them free from interference in all other matters. The chief exponent of syndicalism was the French social philosopher, Georges Sorel (1847–1922), some of whose views later influenced the growth of fascism.

tariff: Customs duty or tax imposed by a government on the importation (or exportation) of a good. Tariffs may be: (1) specific, based on a tax per unit of the commodity; or (2) ad valorem, based on the value of the commodity.

tax: A compulsory payment to government. Its purposes may be to influence (1) resource allocation (so as to produce more of some commodities and less of others), (2) income and wealth distribution, and (3) economic stabilization.

tax avoidance: Legal methods or "loopholes" used by taxpayers to reduce their taxes. (Contrast with **tax evasion.**)

tax base: An object that is being taxed, such as income in the case of an income tax, or the value of property in the case of a property tax, or the value of goods sold in the case of a sales tax.

tax evasion: Illegal methods of escaping taxes, such as lying or cheating about income or expenses. (Contrast with **tax avoidance.**)

tax incidence: Burden of a tax—that is, the economic organisms such as households, consumers, or sellers that ultimately bear the tax.

tax rate: Amount of tax applied per unit of tax base—expressed as a percentage. *Example:* A tax of $10 on a base of $100 represents a tax rate of 10 percent.

tax shifting: Changing of the burden or incidence of a tax from the economic organism upon which it is initially imposed to some other economic organism. *Example:* Sales and excise taxes are imposed on the products of sellers, but these taxes are shifted in whole or in part through higher prices to buyers of the goods.

terms of trade: Number of units of goods that must be given up for one unit of goods received, by each party (e.g., nation) to a transaction. In general, the terms of trade are said to move in favor of the party that gives up fewer units of goods for one unit of goods received, and against the party that gives up more units of goods for one unit of goods received. In international economics, the concept of "terms of trade" plays an important role in evaluating exchange relationships between nations.

theory: Set of definitions, assumptions, and hypotheses put together in a manner that expresses apparent relationships or underlying principles of certain observed phenomena in a meaningful way.

time deposit: Money held in a bank account of an individual or firm for which the bank can require advance notice of withdrawal.

time series: A set of data ordered chronologically. Most of the published data of business and economics are expressed in the form of time series.

token money: Any object (usually coins) whose value as money is greater than the market value of the materials of which it is composed. *Example:* pennies, nickels, etc.

total cost: Sum of a firm's total fixed costs and total variable costs.

total fixed costs: Costs that do not vary with a firm's output. *Examples:* rental payments, interest on debt, property taxes.

total-marginal relationship: Relationship between all corresponding total and marginal curves such that when a total curve is increasing at an increasing rate, its corresponding marginal curve is rising; when a total curve is increasing at a decreasing rate, its corresponding marginal curve is falling; and when a total curve is increasing at a zero rate, as occurs when it is at a maximum, its corresponding marginal curve is zero. (*Note:* The case of decreasing total curves gives rise to negative marginal curves, but these situations need not be included in the definition because they are not ordinarily relevant or realistic in an economic sense.)

total revenue: A firm's total receipts; equal to price per unit times the number of units sold.

total variable costs: Costs that vary directly with a firm's output, rising as output increases over the full range of production. *Examples:* costs of raw materials, fuel, labor, etc.

Trade Expansion Act (1962): Part of the U.S. Reciprocal Trade agreements program, this act broadened the powers of the President to: (1) negotiate further tariff reductions on broad categories of goods; (2) lower or eliminate tariffs on those goods for which the European Common Market and the United States together account for at least 80 percent of total world exports; (3) lower tariffs by as much as 50 percent on the basis of reciprocal trade agreements, provided that such agreements include most-favored-nation clauses so that the benefits of reduced tariffs are extended to other countries; and (4) grant vocational, technical, and financial assistance to American employees and businessmen whose industries are adversely affected by tariff reduction.

transactions motive: Desire on the part of households and businesses to hold some of their assets in liquid form so that they can engage in day-to-day spending activities. This motive is influenced primarily by the level of income rather than by changes in the interest rate and is one of the chief sources of demand for loanable funds in the modern theory of interest.

transfer payments: Expenditures within or between sectors of the economy for which there are no corresponding contributions to current production. *Examples:* social security payments, unemployment compensation, relief payments, veterans' bonuses, net interest paid on government bonds and on consumer loans, and

business transfers (such as charitable contributions, and losses resulting from theft and debt defaults).

Treasury bills: Marketable financial obligations of the U.S. Treasury, maturing in up to 1 year from date of issue.

Treasury bonds: Marketable financial obligations of the U.S. Treasury, maturing in more than 7 years from date of issue. (These are not the Savings Bonds most people are familiar with.)

Treasury notes: Marketable financial obligations of the U.S. Treasury, maturing in 1 to 7 years from date of issue.

trend: Long-run growth or decline of an economic time series over a long period of years.

truncated multiplier: The multiplier applicable to a finite number of time periods. Its size approaches that of the static multiplier as the number of periods increases. However, it always realizes more than half the effect of the static multiplier within the first few periods. Thus the truncated multiplier for, say, four periods is measured by the formula:

Truncated multiplier for four periods =
$$1 + MPC + (MPC)^2 + (MPC)^3$$

tying contract (tie-in sale): Practice whereby a seller requires the buyer to purchase one or more additional or "tied" products as a condition for purchasing the desired or "tying" product. *Examples:* block bookings of motion pictures in which movie theaters are required to take Grade B films as a condition for obtaining Grade A films; the United Shoe Machinery Co., which once required shoemakers to purchase other materials as a condition for purchasing shoe machinery.

uncertainty: State of knowledge in which the probabilities of outcomes resulting from specific actions are not known and cannot be predicted because they are subjective rather than objective phenomena. Uncertainties, therefore, are not insurable, and cannot be integrated into the firm's cost structure.

underconsumption theory: Theory of business cycles which holds that recessions result from consumer expenditures lagging behind output because too large a proportion of society's income is not spent on consumption. According to the theory, society distributes income too inequitably to enable people to purchase all the goods produced.

underemployment (disguised unemployment): State of affairs in which employed resources are not being used in their most efficient ways.

unemployment: Situation which exists whenever resources are out of work or are not being used efficiently. There are various types of unemployment such as technological, frictional, structural, disguised, involuntary, and cyclical.

unemployment benefits: Weekly payments to "covered" workers who are involuntarily unemployed.

unfair competition: Competition that involves deceptive, dishonest, or injurious methods. Such practices are illegal under the antitrust laws.

union: Organization of workers which seeks to gain a degree of monopoly power in the sale of its services so that it may be able to secure higher wages, better working conditions, and other economic improvements for its members.

union shop: Business firm whose owner allows a nonunion member to be hired on condition that he join the union after he is employed.

utility: Ability or power of a good to satisfy a want as determined by the satisfaction that one receives from consuming something.

utopian socialism: Philosophy advanced by a group of English and French writers in the early nineteenth century which advocated the creation of model communities, largely self-contained, where the instruments of production were collectively owned and government was primarily on a voluntary and wholly democratic basis. The leading propagators were Robert Owen (1771–1858) in England and Charles Fourier (1772–1837) in France.

value: Power of a commodity to command other commodities in exchange for itself, as measured by the proportional quantities in which a commodity exchanges with all other commodities.

value added: Increment in value at each stage in the production of a good. The sum of the increments for all stages of production gives the total income—the aggregate of wages, rent, interest, and profit—derived from the production of the good.

value added tax: Type of national sales tax paid by manufacturers and merchants on the value contributed to a product at each stage of its production and distribution.

variable costs: Costs that vary directly with a firm's output, rising as output increases over the full range of production. *Examples:* costs of raw materials, fuel, labor, etc.

variable proportions, law of: *See* **diminishing returns, law of.**

verification: Testing of alternative hypotheses or conclusions by means of actual observation or experimentation—that is, by reference to the facts.

vertical merger: Amalgamation under one ownership of plants engaged in different stages of production from raw materials to finished products. It may take the form of forward integration into buyer markets or backward integration into supplier markets. The chief objective is to achieve greater economies by combining different production stages and by regularizing supplies, thereby increasing profit margins.

wages: 1. Payment to those owners of resources who supply the factor of production known as "labor." This payment includes wages, salaries, commissions, etc. **2.** The price paid for the use of labor. It is usually expressed as time rates such as so much per hour, day, or week, or less frequently as rates of so much per unit of work performed.

wages-fund theory: Classical theory of wages best articulated by John Stuart Mill in 1848. It held that producers set aside a portion of their capital funds for the purpose of hiring workers needed for production. The amount of the fund depends on the stock of capital relative to the number of workers. In the long run, however, the accumulation of capital is itself limited or determined by the tendency toward a minimum "subsistence rate" of profits; hence the only effective way to raise real wages is to reduce the number of workers or size of the population. (*Note:* This theory was a reformulation of the **subsistence theory of wages.**)

"wastes" of monopolistic competition: Expression used to denote overcrowded "sick" industries of monopolistic competition; the wastes are characterized by chronic excess capacity and inefficient operations. *Examples:* retail trades; textile manufacturing.

wealth: Anything which has value because it is capable of producing income. A "stock" of value as compared to a "flow" of income. (Contrast with **income.**)

welfare economics: Branch of economic theory concerned with the development of principles for maximizing social welfare.

Wheeler-Lea Act (1938): Amendment to the Federal Trade Commission Act. It was passed primarily to protect consumers, rather than just business competitors, from unfair (deceptive, dishonest, or injurious) methods of competition. Thus, injured consumers are given equal protection before the law with injured merchants. The act also prohibits false or misleading advertisements for food, drugs, cosmetics, and therapeutic devices.

yellow-dog contract: Contract which requires an employee to promise as a condition of employment that he will not belong to a labor union. Declared illegal in the Norris-La Guardia Act of 1932.

yield: Effective or going market rate of interest on a security. In a broader sense, it is the effective rate of return on any type of investment.

yield to maturity: Percentage figure reflecting the effective yield on a bond, based on the difference between its purchase and redemption price, and any returns received by the bondholder in the interim.